PRINCIPLES OF
EVIDENCE
Sixth Edition

LexisNexis Law School Publishing Advisory Board

PRINCIPLES OF EVIDENCE

SIXTH EDITION

IRVING YOUNGER
1932–1988

MICHAEL GOLDSMITH
1951–2009

DAVID A. SONENSHEIN
Jack E. Feinberg Professor of Litigation
Temple University Beasley School of Law

ANTHONY J. BOCCHINO
Professor of Law
Temple University Beasley School of Law

ISBN: 978-0-7698-8193-5
Looseleaf ISBN: 978-0-7698-8194-2
eBook ISBN: 978-0-7698-8195-9

Library of Congress Cataloging-in-Publication Data
Younger, Irving, author.
Principles of evidence / Irving Younger, 1932-1988; Michael Goldsmith, 1951-2009; David A. Sonenshei, Jack
E. Feinberg Professor of Litigation, Temple University Beasley School of Law; Anthony J. Bocchino, Professor
of Law, Temple University Beasley School of Law. -- Sixth edition.
pages cm
Includes index.
ISBN 978-0-7698-8193-5 (hard cover)
1. Evidence (Law)--United States. I. Goldsmith, Michael, 1951-2009, author. II. Sonenshein, David A., author.
III. Bocchino, Anthony J., author. IV. Title.
    KF8935.Y68 2014
    347.73'6--dc23
 2014018126

This publication is designed to provide authoritative information in regard to the subject matter covered. It is sold with the understanding that the publisher is not engaged in rendering legal, accounting, or other professional services. If legal advice or other expert assistance is required, the services of a competent professional should be sought.

NOTE TO USERS

To ensure that you are using the latest materials available in this area, please be sure to periodically check the LexisNexis Law School web site for downloadable updates and supplements at www.lexisnexis.com/lawschool.

Editorial Offices
121 Chanlon Rd., New Providence, NJ 07974 (908) 464-6800
201 Mission St., San Francisco, CA 94105-1831 (415) 908-3200
www.lexisnexis.com

MATTHEW◊BENDER

Dedication

IRVING YOUNGER
1932–1988

Preface

This casebook has its origins in one conceived by Irving Younger and published in 1980 as *Materials for the Basic Course in Evidence*.

Younger was already famous when his book came out. Indeed, he was about the closest thing to a rock star the legal profession has seen, having served as professor, prosecutor, judge, trial lawyer, and author. He had a unique ability to take the most difficult material and present it in an entertaining and understandable way. He appealed alike to law students and members of the profession. Younger's presentations, whether in class, in court, or in the lecture hall, were always crowded. They were exquisitely crafted, eloquent, and memorable. To his audiences they seemed effortless. They were, in fact, the result of very hard work. Younger's love of the law and his excitement about it came through to those he taught. He still teaches via his judicial opinions, many of which have been incorporated into evidence casebooks. His recordings are still best-sellers.[1]

Throughout his career and despite his celebrity Younger thought of himself as just another hard-working trial lawyer striving to do his best. That was the novelty and essential theme of his casebook. On the need for another casebook, Younger said:

> There being no dearth of evidence casebooks, the appearance of yet another requires explanation.
>
> Years of struggling with the course have left me with certain settled preferences. Since it is the basic course, the only course in evidence most students ever take, I prefer to present the subject matter as the doctrinal foundation for what trial lawyers do in court.

Thirty years after Younger's initial publication, this new edition of Principles of Evidence remains true to Younger's original. The authors have built on and enhanced it. They have added their own love of, and excitement about, the law to Younger's. The result is a casebook that not only updates cases and evidentiary rules but prepares students for the conduct of litigation in court.

---

[1] The complete and classic collections of Professor Irving Younger's lectures and speeches have been digitally re-mastered. They are available as DVDs, CDs, and MP3s exclusively from THE PROFESSIONAL EDUCATION GROUP (www.proedgroup.com 800.229.2531).

Acknowledgments

The authors acknowledge and express their appreciation for outstanding research support provided by the following students: Blake Bertagna, Rob Delong, Sophie Hayes, Trevor Hickey, Holly Hinckley, Lindy Langston, Brant Lillywhite, Charlene Martin, Pam Mazahari, Andrew Platt, Tyler Waltham, and Keith Willis. In addition, Professor Goldsmith thanks Carolyn Goldsmith for meticulously working overtime to proofread portions of the manuscript.

Evidence Challenge

Get courtroom experience with Evidence Challenge!

Want a higher score on your evidence exam? Throughout this publication, you will see notations at the end of chapters for further case challenges related to the evidence topic. To prepare you for exams and challenge your comprehension, go to www. EvidenceChallenge.com to purchase access to the website. This interactive problem- and role-based exam preparation tool is available as a companion study aid for this publication. The interface was developed by an education expert partnering with LexisNexis® product development teams. Evidence Challenge case problems give students the opportunity to repeatedly practice application of chapter-relevant rules and concepts while preparing for exams.

Here's how it works:

- Launch a problem, and enter a virtual courtroom where you are one of the attorneys.

- Uncover all the information you need for the questions posed by clicking on the characters and exhibit icons in the courtroom.

- You may be prompted to review further resources including documents, images, audio or video.

- Each problem offers a variety of possible responses and a feedback loop that tells you where you need to focus your studies.

- Links to applicable case problems will appear at the end of chapters in this publication:

 EVIDENCE CHALLENGE: Challenge yourself to learn more about this topic. Enter the following address into your browser to access Evidence Challenge and apply these concepts to realistic problems set in a virtual courtroom.
http://www.EvidenceChallenge.com. Additional purchase required.

- Each problem will take 5 – 10 minutes to complete as you work through various decision points in the realistic courtroom scenario: read instructions, review testimony or other evidence, link to the Problem Study Resources on Lexis Advance® and choose how to proceed.

- At the conclusion of the problem, review your detailed results page, see how well you answered each question within the problem, and see your performance relative to how others scored.

- Depending on your score, you may be granted an achievement!

- Retry problems when recommended, or just play them again for practice and to improve your score.

Evidence Challenge: www.EvidenceChallenge.com Included with specially marked ***enhanced*** LexisNexis® law school eBooks or purchase access separately directly at the Evidence Challenge website.

TABLE OF EVIDENTIARY FOUNDATIONS

Summary Table of Contents

Table of Contents

Table of Contents

Table of Contents

Table of Contents

Table of Contents

Table of Contents

Table of Contents

Table of Contents

Table of Contents

Table of Contents

Table of Contents

Table of Contents

Table of Contents

Table of Contents

Chapter I

INTRODUCTION: THE CONCEPT OF EVIDENCE

"Shall we let it in?"

— John Chipman Gray[1]

"To refuse evidence is to refuse to hear the cause."

— Edmund Burke, Report on the Lord's Journal (1794)

JOHN H. WIGMORE, 1 EVIDENCE § 1
(3d ed. 1940)[2]

Definition of Evidence. It is of little practical consequence to construct a formula defining what is to be understood as Evidence. Nevertheless, its content is capable of being stated. What we are concerned with is the process of presenting evidence for the purpose of demonstrating an asserted fact. In this process, then, the term Evidence represents:

> Any knowable fact or group of facts, not a legal or a logical principle, considered with a view to its being offered before a legal tribunal for the purpose of producing a persuasion, positive or negative, on the part of the tribunal, as to the truth of a proposition, not of law or of logic, on which the determination of the tribunal is to be asked.

Of the definitions of judicial evidence that have been proposed from time to time, some have been framed merely in view of emphasizing partial aspects of the subject, others have been intended to embody some theory or classification or the relation between certain parts of the law of Evidence; and a comparison of them can hardly be made upon a common basis. Nevertheless, a collation of the classical definitions is interesting, if only for the singular variety of phrasing exhibited upon a subject apparently so simple and so exempt from practical controversy.

---

[1] Quoted in J. MAGUIRE, EVIDENCE: COMMON SENSE AND COMMON LAW 2 (1947).

[2] Reprinted by permission of Little, Brown and Company, Boston, 1940.

James B. Thayer, A Preliminary Treatise on Evidence at the Common Law
263–64 (1898)

What is our Law of Evidence? It is a set of rules and principles affecting judicial investigations into questions of fact; for the most part, controverted questions. . . . [I]t does not undertake to regulate the processes of reasoning or argument, except as helping to discriminate and select the material of fact upon which these are to operate; these processes themselves go on, after their own methods, even when all the "evidence" is in, or when there is none and all the facts are admitted. . . . But when one offers "evidence," in the sense of the word which is now under consideration, he offers . . . to prove a matter of fact which is to be used as a basis of inference to another matter of fact. He offers, perhaps, to present to the senses of the tribunal a visible object which may furnish a ground of inference; or he offers testimony, oral or written, to prove a fact; for even direct testimony, to be believed or disbelieved, according as we trust the witness, is really but a basis of inference. . . .

It must be noticed, then, that "evidence," in the sense used when we speak of the law of evidence, has not the large meaning imputed to it in ordinary discourse. It is a term of forensic procedure; and imports something put forward in a court of justice. When men speak of historical evidence and scientific evidence, and the evidences of Christianity, they are talking about a different sort of thing. The law of evidence has to do with the furnishing to a court a matter of fact, for use in a judicial investigation. . . . (1) It prescribes the manner of presenting evidence, as by requiring that it shall be given in open court, by one who personally knows the thing, appearing in person, subject to cross-examination, or by allowing it to be given by deposition, taken in such and such a way; and the like. (2) It fixes the qualifications and the privilege of witnesses, and the mode of examining them. (3) And chiefly, it determines, as among probative matters, matters in their nature evidential, — what classes of things shall not be received. This excluding function is the characteristic one in our law of evidence.

Sir William Blackstone, Commentaries on the Laws of England
367 (1C 768)

Evidence signifies that which demonstrates, makes clear, or ascertains the truth of the very fact or point in issue, either on one side or on the other. . . .

Jerome Michael & Mortimer J. Adler, *Real Proof*
5 Vand. L. Rev. 344, 350–51 (1952)[3]

As we use the word "evidence" only a thing or an event can be evidence, but all things and events which a jury can know directly in any respect can become evidence. However, a particular thing or event which is in this sense potentially an item of evidence may never become so actually. It may never be offered as evidence

---

[3] Copyright, Vanderbilt Law Review, 1952.

or, if offered, may be excluded by the judge. To become evidence, a thing or event must satisfy three conditions: first, it must exist or occur in the presence of the jury; second, it must be sensible in some respect, that is, capable of being sensed or perceived in that respect by the jury; and, third, it must be made sensibly apparent to the jury. In our usage, therefore, evidence consists of things and events and only of things and events which judges permit to be exhibited to juries so that the latter can observe them.

NOTES AND QUESTIONS

1. How do Wigmore, Thayer, Blackstone, and Michael & Adler differ in the use of the term evidence in the same sense? Consider the following statement suggesting three different meanings for the term evidence: Evidence is admissible into evidence if it complies with the rules of evidence.

2. "They [rules of evidence] are founded in the charities of religion, in the philosophy of nature, in the truths of history, and in the experience of common life. . . ." Thomas Erskine, arguendo, *Trial of Thomas Hardy*, 24 How. St. Tr. 966 (1794).

3. "It is for ordinary minds, and not for psychoanalysts, that our rules of evidence are framed. They have their source very often in considerations of administrative convenience, of practical expediency, and not in rules of logic." *Shepard v. United States*, 290 U.S. 96, 104 (1933) (Cardozo, J.).

Chapter II

PRELIMINARY MATTERS

A. ALTERNATIVES TO FORMAL PROOF

1. Judicial Notice

a. Introduction

JAMES B. THAYER, A PRELIMINARY TREATISE ON
EVIDENCE AT THE COMMON LAW
277, 279–80 (1898)

We have observed that not all the matter of fact which courts and juries rest upon, in deciding cases, needs to be communicated to them by the parties. Much, in every case, is known already, and much is common to all cases; such things are assumed, stated and reasoned upon without discussion. Often, also, much of which there might, in point of mere theory, be a doubt, will, as a matter of established practice, be allowed by the court, in the first instance, without formal proof. And there is much which belongs in a dubious and arguable region, as to which a court may or may not proceed in this manner.

* * *

. . . The subject of judicial notice, then, belongs to the general topic of legal or judicial reasoning. It is, indeed, woven into the very texture of the judicial function. In conducting a process of judicial reasoning, . . . not a step can be taken without assuming something which has not been proved; and the capacity to do this, with competent judgment and efficiency, is imputed to judges and juries as part of their necessary mental outfit.

b. Adjudicative Facts

VARCOE v. LEE
181 P. 223 (Cal. 1919)

OLNEY, J.

This is an action by a father to recover damages suffered through the death of his child, resulting from her being run over by an automobile of the defendant Lee, driven at the time by the other defendant, Nichols, the chauffeur of Lee. The

5

automobile was going south on Mission Street in San Francisco, and was approaching the crossing of Twenty-first Street, when the child, in an endeavor to cross the street, was run over and killed. The cause was tried before a jury, which returned a verdict of $5,000 for the plaintiff. From the judgment upon this verdict, the defendants appeal.

In appellant's reply brief a . . . question is raised for the first time. As we have stated, the claim of negligence is based upon the speed at which the machine was going. On this point the testimony was sharply conflicting. . . . When he came to charge the jury, the trial judge instructed them that if they found that the defendant Nichols was running the automobile along Mission Street at the time of the accident at a greater speed than fifteen miles an hour, he was violating the city ordinance and also the State Motor Vehicle Act and that such speed was negligence in itself. The trial judge then read to the jury the portion of subdivision B of section 22 of the Motor Vehicle Act, which provides that it shall be unlawful to operate a motor "in the business district" of any incorporated city or town at a greater speed than fifteen miles an hour, and defines a business district as "territory . . . contiguous to a public highway, which is at that point mainly built up with structures devoted to business." Having read this definition, the court proceeded with its charge as follows: "That is the situation on Mission Street between Twentieth and Twenty-second Streets where this accident happened, so that is a business district and the maximum legal rate of speed on that street at the time of the happening of this accident was fifteen miles an hour."

In connection with . . . the giving of the foregoing instructions, it is contended by appellant . . . that the instruction that Mission Street at the point in question was a business district, and therefore the maximum legal speed there was fifteen miles an hour was a charge as to a question of fact and an invasion of the province of the jury.

*　　*　　*

So far as the record goes, there is little to show what the character of Mission Street between Twentieth and Twenty-second Streets is. The defendant Nichols himself refers to it in his testimony as part of the "downtown district," undoubtedly meaning thereby part of the business district of the city. The evidence shows incidentally that at the scene of the accident there was a drug store, a barber shop, a haberdashery, and a saloon. If there had been any issue or question as to the character of the district, the record in this meagre condition would not justify the taking of the question from the jury, as was undoubtedly done by the instruction complained of.

The actual fact of the matter is, however, that Mission Street, between Twentieth and Twenty-second Streets, is a business district, within the definition of the Motor Vehicle Act, beyond any possibility of question. It has been such for years. Not only this, but its character is known as a matter of common knowledge by any one at all familiar with San Francisco. Mission Street from its downtown beginning at the waterfront to and beyond the district of the city known as the Mission, is second in importance and prominence as a business street only to Market Street. The probabilities are that every person in the courtroom at the trial, including judge, jury, counsel, witnesses, parties, and officers of the court, knew perfectly well what the character of the location was. It was not a matter about which there could be any dispute or question. If the court had left the matter to the determination of the jury, and they for some inconceivable reason had found that it was not a business district, it would have been the duty of the court to set aside the verdict. We are asked now to reverse the judgment because the court assumed, without submitting to the jury, what could not be disputed, and what he and practically every resident in the county for which the court was sitting knew to be a fact. If error there was, it is clear that, upon the actual fact, there was no prejudice to the defendants.

It would have been much better if counsel for the plaintiff or the trial judge himself had inquired of defendants' counsel, before the case went to the jury, whether there was any dispute as to the locality being a business district within the meaning of the state law. There could have been but one reasonable answer, and, if any other were given, the matter could have been easily settled beyond any possibility of question. But this was not done, and we are now confronted by the question whether either this court or the trial court can take judicial notice of the real fact.

An appellate court can properly take judicial notice of any matter of which the court of original jurisdiction may properly take notice. . . .

In fact a particularly salutary use of the principle of judicial notice is to sustain on appeal a judgment clearly in favor of the right party, but as to which there is in the evidence an omission of some necessary fact which is yet indisputable and a matter of common knowledge, and was probably assumed without strict proof for that very reason. . . .

The question, therefore, is: Was the superior court for the city and county of San Francisco, whose judge and talesman were necessarily residents of the city, entitled to take judicial notice of the character of one of the most important and best-known streets in the city? If it were, the court was authorized to charge the jury as it did. . . .

It should perhaps be noted that the fact that the trial judge knew what the actual fact was, and that it was indisputable, would not of itself justify him in recognizing it. Nor would the fact that the character of the street was a matter of common knowledge and notoriety justify him in taking the question from the jury if there were any possibility of dispute as to whether or not that character was such as to constitute it a business district within the definition of the statute applicable. If such question could exist, the fact involved — whether the well-known character of the street was sufficient to make it a business district — was one for determination by the jury. But we have in this case a combination of the two circumstances. In the first place, the fact is indisputable and beyond question. In the second place, it is a matter of common knowledge throughout the jurisdiction in and for which the court is sitting.

A consideration of the reasons underlying the matter of judicial notice and its fundamental principles leaves, we believe, but little doubt as to its applicability here. Judicial notice is a judicial short-cut, a doing away with the formal necessity for evidence because there is no real necessity for it. So far as matters of common knowledge are concerned, it is saying there is no need of formally offering evidence of those things because practically everyone knows them in advance and there can be no question about them. The rule in this respect is well stated in 15 R.C.L. 1057, as follows:

It may be stated generally with regard to the question as to what matters are properly of judicial cognizance that, while the power of judicial notice is to be exercised with caution, courts should take notice of whatever is or ought to be generally known, within the limits of their jurisdiction, for justice does not require that courts profess to be more ignorant than the rest of mankind. This rule enumerates three material requisites:

1. The matter of which a court will take judicial notice must be a matter of common and general knowledge. The fact that the belief is not universal, however, is not controlling, for there is scarcely any belief that is accepted by everyone. Courts take judicial notice of those things which are common knowledge to the majority of mankind, or to those persons familiar with the particular matter in question. But matters of which courts have judicial knowledge are uniform and fixed, and do not depend upon uncertain testimony; as soon as a circumstance becomes disputable, it ceases to fall under the head of common knowledge, and so will not be judicially recognized.

2. A matter properly a subject of judicial notice must be "known," that is, well established and authoritatively settled, not doubtful or uncertain. In every instance the test is whether sufficient notoriety attaches to the fact involved as to make it safe and proper to assume its existence without proof. In harmony with that view it has been said that courts must "judicially recognize whatever has the requisite certainty and notoriety in every field of knowledge, in every walk of practical life."

3. A matter to be within judicial cognizance must be known "within the limits of the jurisdiction of the court."

The three requirements so mentioned — that the matter be one of common and general knowledge; that it be well established and authoritatively settled, be practically indisputable; and that this common, general, and certain knowledge exist in the particular jurisdiction — all are requirements dictated by the reason and purpose of the rule, which is to obviate the formal necessity for proof when the matter does not require proof.

It is truly said that the power of judicial notice is, as to matters claimed to be matters of general knowledge, one to be used with caution. If there is any doubt whatever, either as to the fact itself or as to its being a matter of common knowledge, evidence should be required. But, if the court is of the certain opinion that these requirements exist, there can properly be no hesitation. In such a case there is, on the one hand, no danger of a wrong conclusion as to the fact — and such danger is the reason for the caution in dispensing with the evidence — and, on the other hand, purely formal and useless proceedings will be avoided.

*   *   *

Applying this [analysis] to the facts of the case the matter is not in doubt. The character of Mission Street is as well known to San Franciscans as the character of . . . Forty-second Street to residents of New York, or of F Street to residents of Washington. It is a matter of every-day common information and experience, and one about which there can be no dispute.

The conclusion follows that the charge of the trial court that Mission Street between Twentieth and Twenty-second Streets was a business district was not error. The judgment is therefore affirmed.

Edmund M. Morgan, *Judicial Notice*
57 HARV. L. REV. 269, 273–74 (1944)[1]

In any system designed to adjust relations between members of a society, the applicable law ought not to be allowed to vary with the diligence and skill of counsel, and a decision contrary to what is accepted as indisputable fact in that society cannot be justified. In an adversary system such as ours, where the court is bound to know the law and the parties to make known the facts, it is particularly important that the court prevent a party from presenting a moot issue or inducing a false result by disputing what in the existing state of society is demonstrably indisputable among reasonable men. Just as the court cannot function unless the judge knows the law and unless the judge and jury have the fund of information common to all intelligent men in the community as well as the capacity to use the ordinary processes of reasoning, so it cannot adjust legal relations among members of society and thus fulfill the sole purpose of its creation if it permits the parties to take issue on, and thus secure results contrary to, what is so notoriously true as not to be the subject of reasonable dispute, or what is capable of immediate and accurate demonstration by resort to sources of indisputable accuracy easily accessible to men in the situation of members of the court. This, it is submitted, is the rock of reason and policy upon which judicial notice of facts is built. It is true that its liberal application greatly expedites trials. . . . It is true also that this desire for expedition may be an important factor in causing an extension of the field of application of the doctrine. But it is important to observe that these facts do not alter the nature of judicial notice and should not be allowed to confuse consideration of the subject. That there is *a priori* a high degree of probability of the truth of a particular proposition may be a good reason for putting upon the party asserting its untruth the burden of producing credible evidence, or of persuading the trier, of its untruth, but it cannot justify a tribunal in taking judicial notice of its truth. To warrant such judicial notice the probability must be so great as to make the truth of the proposition notoriously indisputable among reasonable men.

NOTES AND QUESTIONS

1. Examples of judicial notice of adjudicative fact abound: *DeTore v. Local No. 245*, 511 F. Supp. 171 (D.N.J. 1981) (judicial notice that Jersey City is a municipality of New Jersey); *EEOC v. Delta Airlines, Inc.*, 485 F. Supp. 1004 (N.D. Ga. 1980) (judicial notice that only women can become pregnant); *Record Museum v. Lawrence Township*, 481 F. Supp. 768, 771 (D.N.J. 1979) ("judicial notice of the phenomenon known as the Counterculture of the Seventies wherein untraditional attire such as spoons and hand-crafted pipes adorn both home and person"); *Kircher v. Atchison, T. & S.F. Ry.*, 195 P.2d 427 (Cal. 1948) (judicial notice that purchasing power of dollar has declined); *LeMoine v. Spicer*, 1 So. 2d 730 (Fla. 1941) (judicial notice that the "drinking of intoxicating liquor is probably as prevalent among women as it is among men and that great numbers of men and women, young and old, indulge in drinking parties, commonly known as cocktail parties, promiscuously and without segregation of the sexes"); *Shaw v. Tague*, 177 N.E. 417 (N.Y. 1931) (judicial notice that hair may turn white after shock of an accident); *Rau v. People*, 1875 N.Y. LEXIS 41 (Nov. 30, 1875) (judicial notice of whiskey being intoxicating); *Matter of Holthausen*, 175 Misc. 1022 (N.Y. Sup. Ct. 1941) (judicial notice of 9-month gestation period). Do each of these present cases equally plausible examples of indisputable common knowledge in the relevant jurisdiction?

2. May a judge take judicial notice of a fact merely because it is personally known by him to be true? *See, e.g., Fox v. City of West Palm Beach*, 383 F.2d 189, 194–95 (5th Cir. 1967). For an example of how even the finest of judges may err in this respect, *see Pina v. Henderson*, 752 F.2d 47 (2d Cir. 1985) (former evidence professor turned trial judge reversed); *see also United States v. Lewis*, 833 F.2d 1380 (9th Cir. 1987) (trial judge erred in relying upon personal experience as basis for taking judicial notice that, after receiving general anesthetic, a person is not responsible for statements made within a few hours of coming out of surgery).

3. May a court take judicial notice of the widespread availability of pornography in a particular community? *See United States v. Various Articles of Obscene Merchandise*, 709 F.2d 132 (2d Cir. 1983). What about judicial notice that a neighborhood is a high crime area? *See United States v. Evans*, 994 F.2d 317 (7th Cir. 1993). May a court take judicial notice that Miami has become a center for drug smuggling and money laundering? *See United States v. $4,255,000*, 762 F.2d 895 (11th Cir.), *cert. denied*, 474 U.S. 1056 (1985).

JOHN H. WIGMORE, 9 EVIDENCE § 2579
(3d ed. 1940) (Court Records)

The proceedings in a Court are constituted by the record, and this record originally took its name from the judicial memory ("recordari") which could be invoked for recalling those prior proceedings. Nevertheless, it seems today unreasonable, having regard to the general principle of judicial notice . . . , to predicate an actual judicial knowledge of the proceedings in specific prior litigations (for they are commonly neither notorious, nor within the judge's duty of knowledge), or to expect the Court to make its own researches into the mass of the records for the purpose of informing itself. Accordingly, it may be said generally that a Court is not by any rule bound to take notice of the tenor of any legal proceedings (other than those transacting at the moment in its presence).

However, for reasons of convenience, where controversy is unlikely . . . Courts are often found taking notice of the tenor or effect of some part of a judicial proceeding, without requiring formal evidence. Since this dispensation is not obligatory on the part of the Court, and since it must depend more or less on the practical notoriety and certainty of the fact under the circumstances of each case, little uniformity can be seen in the instances. It is often done for a part of the record in the same proceeding, or in a prior stage of the same controversy; less often for the record of a distinct litigation, especially when in another Court.

NOTES AND QUESTIONS

1.   Suppose that the Court's file contains an affidavit, executed by the Astronomer Royal of England, stating that it rained in London on November 30, 1932. Counsel asks the Court to take judicial notice of this affidavit. If the Court grants this request, will the facts set forth in the affidavit be taken as true? In this respect, consider the following observation:

> **Caveat:** *Limitations on judicial notice of court records.* What is meant by taking judicial notice of court records? There exists a mistaken notion that this means taking judicial notice of the existence of facts asserted in *every document* of a court file, including pleadings and affidavits. However, a court *cannot* take judicial notice of *hearsay allegations* as being true, just because they are part of a court record or file. A court may take judicial notice of the *existence* of each document in a court file, but can only take judicial notice of the truth of facts asserted in documents such as orders, findings of fact and conclusions of law, and judgments.

> The trial judge should always be careful to *specify exactly* the document or portion of a document contained in a court file of which he is taking judicial notice. Also, counsel should be required to state, with *like specificity*, the exact document or portion of a document from a court file or record, when requesting the court to take judicial notice of a court record.

B. Jefferson, California Evidence Benchbook § 47.3 at 840 (1972); *see Kramer v. Time Warner*, 937 F.2d 767 (2d Cir. 1991) ("courts routinely take judicial notice of documents filed in other courts, . . . not for the truth of the matters asserted in the other litigation, but rather to establish the fact of such litigation and related filings."); *United States v. Walters*, 510 F.2d 887 (3d Cir. 1975) (taking judicial notice of briefs and documents filed in state court "to determine whether petitioner had exhausted state remedies").

2.   In *Shuttlesworth v. City of Birmingham*, 394 U.S. 147, 157 (1969), the Supreme Court took judicial notice of facts established in related litigation involving the same parties; the Court found that the record established many of the "surrounding relevant circumstances" of a Good Friday protest march. Did this constitute a proper exercise of judicial notice?

3.   May a district court, based on previous litigation involving numerous other defendants, take judicial notice at a sentencing proceeding that highjacking gangs

have been preying on Kennedy Airport? *See United States v. Fatico*, 441 F. Supp. 1285, 1288 (E.D.N.Y. 1977).

CHARLES T. McCORMICK,
HANDBOOK OF THE LAW OF EVIDENCE § 330
(4th ed. 1992)[2]

(Otherwise readily verifiable facts)

The earlier and probably still the most familiar basis for judicial notice is "common knowledge," but a second and distinct principle has come to be recognized as an even more significant ground for the invocation of the doctrine. This extension of judicial notice was first disguised by a polite fiction so that when asked to notice a fact not generally known, but which obviously could easily be ascertained by consulting materials in common use, such as the day of the week on which January 1 fell ten years ago, the judges resorted to calendars but purported to be "refreshing memory" as to a matter of common knowledge. Eventually it was recognized that involved here was an important extension of judicial notice to the new field of facts "capable of accurate and ready demonstration," "capable of such instant and unquestionable demonstration, if desired, that no party would think of imposing a falsity on the tribunal in the face of an intelligent adversary," or "capable of immediate and accurate demonstration by resort to easily accessible sources of indisputable accuracy."

Evidentiary Foundation:
The Trial of William "Duff" Armstrong

[The following is reconstructed from accounts of the trial in A. WOLDMAN, LAWYER LINCOLN 111–16 (1936), and E. HERTZ, LINCOLN TALKS 23–25 (1929):]

William "Duff" Armstrong was charged with murdering James Metzker on the night of August 29, 1857. The State's star witness was Charles Allen, who had earlier testified in the trial of James Norris, accused of participating in the murder with Armstrong. Norris had been found guilty of manslaughter. On direct examination Allen testified that he had seen Norris hit Metzker on the back of the head with a club and Armstrong strike him in the right eye with a slingshot.

Lincoln, according to one young lawyer present in the courtroom, "sat with his head thrown back, his steady gaze apparently fixed upon one spot of the blank ceiling, entirely oblivious to what was happening around him, and without a single variation of feature or noticeable movement of any muscle of his face." Finally, Lincoln arose and cross-examined:

Q.   Did you actually see the fight?

A.   Yes.

Q.   And you stood very near to them?

---

[2] Reprinted with permission from McCORMICK'S HANDBOOK OF THE LAW OF EVIDENCE, Fourth Edition, Copyright © 1992 by West Publishing Co.

A.	No, it was one hundred and fifty feet or more.
Q.	In the open field?
A.	No, in the timber.
Q.	What kind of timber?
A.	Beech timber.
Q.	Leaves on it are rather thick in August?
A.	It looks like it.
Q.	What time did this all occur?
A.	Eleven o'clock at night.
Q.	Did you have a candle there?
A.	No, what would I want a candle for?
Q.	How could you see from a distance of one hundred and fifty feet or more, without a candle, at eleven o'clock at night?
A.	The moon was shining real bright.
Q.	Full moon?
A.	Yes, a full moon.

At this point, Lincoln drew out of his back pocket a blue-covered almanac, opened it slowly, and offered it in evidence. It was received. Showing it to the witness, Lincoln asked:

Q.	Does not the almanac say that on August 29 the moon was barely past the first quarter instead of being full?
A.	(No answer.)
Q.	Does not the almanac also say that the moon had disappeared by eleven o'clock?
A.	(No answer.)
Q.	Is it not a fact that it was too dark to see anything from fifty feet, let alone one hundred and fifty feet?
A.	(No answer.)

Armstrong was acquitted.

NOTES AND QUESTIONS

1.   Although Lincoln did not formally ask the Court to take judicial notice of the moon on August 29th he could have done so. What is the basis for judicial notice of almanac type facts? Consider the following observation:

Sometimes the ultimate fact that is sought to be proved is noticed, and sometimes the thing noticed is the trustworthiness of a certain medium of proof, and not the thing itself which this tends to prove. . . . The doctrine that almanacs may be referred to in order to ascertain upon what day of the week a given day of a month fell in any year, to learn the time of sunrise or sunset, and the like, and that, in order to prove facts of general history, approved books of history may be consulted, may also be regarded as illustrating the taking notice of the authenticity of evidential matters, — of certain media of proof. But in such cases the truth often is that the court takes notice of the fact itself which these books authenticate; and wherever that is so, a court may refer to whatever source of information it pleases, — the statement that it may consult an almanac or a general history being only an unnecessary and misleading specification of a particular sort of document that may be examined.

Thayer, *Judicial Notice and the Law of Evidence*, 3 HARV. L. REV. 285, 308–09 (1890).

2.   What type of foundation, if any, must counsel establish before a court may take judicial notice of the kind of facts contained on almanac?

3.   Reconsider whether judicial notice may properly be taken of the facts asserted in the Astronomer Royal's affidavit in Note 1 following the excerpt from WIGMORE, EVIDENCE, *supra*.

c.   Law

JOHN MAGUIRE,
EVIDENCE: COMMON SENSE AND COMMON LAW
168–69 (1947)[3]

To a large extent the subjects of judicial notice are, as already indicated, rudimentary commonplaces — propositions of generalized knowledge and specific fact so notorious as not to be either ignored or disputed. But judicial notice goes a great deal further than this. Judges of first instance and of appeal judicially notice the common law and public statutes, State or Federal, and of course all constitutional provisions, which are in force in their jurisdiction. The reason is obvious. This is their main judicial apparatus, and they are responsible for its proper recognition and application.

At common law judges usually have not been authorized to notice in this fashion private acts or resolves of local legislatures or Congress, or ordinances or regulations of subdivisions of their State governments. Likewise the decisions and statutes of other States or nations have not been subjects of notice at common law — but this limitation will be misunderstood unless it is remembered that so far as Federal courts act under their original jurisdiction conferred by the national constitution and laws, the law of every State is domestic to these tribunals. . . . Why the distinctions between foreign law and the law of the home State, between public and private legislation, and between the law of that State as a whole and the law of its municipal subdivisions? As to foreign law, two highly practical reasons at once suggest themselves: first, it might be very difficult for the judge of the District Court of Siwash to lay his hands on a reliable version of the decisions or statutes of

---

[3] Copyright Foundation Press, Inc., 1947.

Zanzibar; and, second, even if he could get the books, all their presuppositions might be so strange that he could not by solitary perusal assure himself of the true legal meaning. The second of these reasons will not apply to domestic private acts or county, city, and town law, but the first will. American municipalities have often fallen woefully short of presenting, in form upon which legal experts can rely, proper collations of their ordinances, regulations, and so on; nor have private acts and resolves always been reliably accessible.

The legal profession is coming to believe that under modern conditions important parts of the old rule about judicial notice of foreign law ought to be changed. A Uniform State Law carrying this view into effect has had numerous legislative adoptions. Other related legislation has gone through. Quite likely, before many years pass, we shall find the common practice in the United States to be that each State's courts notice the decisions and public statutes of sister States; that courts notice domestic ordinances, private acts, etc.; possibly even that within reasonable limits courts notice the law of foreign countries.

d.　Legislative Facts

MULLER v. OREGON
208 U.S. 412 (1908)

[The Supreme Court held constitutional an Oregon statute limiting the hours a female might work in certain establishments to no more than 10 per day. In the course of his opinion, JUSTICE BREWER remarked as follows:]

In patent cases counsel are apt to open the argument with a discussion of the state of the art. It may not be amiss, in the present case, before examining the constitutional question, to notice the course of legislation as well as expressions of opinion from other than judicial sources. In the brief filed by Mr. Louis D. Brandeis, for the defendant in error, is a very copious collection of all these matters, an epitome of which is found in the margin.[4] While there have been but few decisions

---

[4] [1] The following legislation of the States imposes restrictions in some form or another upon the hours of labor that may be required of women: Massachusetts: chap. 221, 1874, Rev. Laws 1902 chap. 106 § 24; Rhode Island: 1885, Acts and Resolves 1902, chap. 994, p. 73; Louisiana: § 4, Act 43, p. 55, Laws of 1886, Rev. Laws 1904, vol. 1, p. 989; Connecticut: 1887, Gen. Stat. revision 1902, § 4691; Maine: chap. 139, 1887, Rev. Stat. 1903, chap. 40, § 48, p. 401; New Hampshire: 1887, Laws 1907, chap. 94, p. 95; Maryland: chap. 455, 1888, Pub. Gen. Laws 1903, art. 100, § 1; Virginia: p. 150, 1889–1890, Code 1904, tit. 51A, chap. 178A, § 3675b; Pennsylvania: No. 26, p. 30, 1897, Laws 1905, No. 226, p. 352; New York: Laws 1899, § 1, chap. 560, p. 752, Laws 1907, chap. 507, § 77, subdiv. 3, p. 1078; Nebraska: 1899, Comp. Stat. 1905, § 7955, p. 1986; Washington: Stat. 1901, chap. 68, § 1, p. 118; Colorado: Acts 1903, chap. 138, § 3, p. 310; New Jersey: 1892, Gen. Stat. 1895, p. 2350, §§ 66, 67; Oklahoma: 1890, Rev. Stat. 1903, chap. 25, art. 58, § 729; North Dakota: 1877, Rev. Code 1905, § 9440; South Dakota 1877, Rev. Code (Penal Code, § 764), p. 1885; Wisconsin: § 1, chap. 83, Laws of 1867, Code 1898, § 1728; South Carolina: Acts 1907, No. 233, p. 487.

In foreign legislation Mr. Brandeis calls attention to these statutes: Great Britain Factories Act of 1844, chap. 15, pp. 161, 171; Factory and Workshop Act of 1901, chap. 22, pp. 60, 71; and see 1 Edw. VII, chap. 22, France, 1848; Acts Nov. 2, 1892, and March 30, 1900. Switzerland, Canton of Glarus, 1848; Federal Law 1877, art. 2, § 1. Austria, 1855; Acts 1897, art. 96a, §§ 1–3. Holland, 1889; art. 5, § 1. Italy, June 19, 1902, art. 7. Germany, Laws 1891.

Then follow extracts from over ninety reports of committees, bureaus of statistics, commissioners of

bearing directly upon the question, the following sustain the constitutionality of such legislation: *Commonwealth v. Hamilton Mfg. Co.*, 120 Massachusetts 383; *Wenham v. State*, 65 Nebraska 394, 400, 406; *State v. Buchanan*, 29 Washington 602; *Commonwealth v. Beatty*, 15 Pa. Sup. Ct. 5, 17; against them is the case of *Ritchie v. People*, 155 Illinois 98.

The legislation and opinions referred to in the margin may not be, technically speaking, authorities, and in them is little or no discussion of the constitutional question presented to us for determination, yet they are significant of a widespread belief that woman's physical structure, and the functions she performs in consequence thereof, justify special legislation restricting or qualifying the conditions under which she should be permitted to toil. Constitutional questions, it is true, are not settled by even a consensus of present public opinion, for it is the peculiar value of a written constitution that it places in unchanging form limitations upon legislative action, and thus gives a permanence and stability to popular government which otherwise would be lacking. At the same time, when a question of fact is debated and debatable, and the extent to which a special constitutional limitation goes is affected by the truth in respect to that fact, a widespread and long continued belief concerning it is worthy of consideration. We take judicial cognizance of all matters of general knowledge.

ROE v. WADE
410 U.S. 113, 207–08 (1973)

[In declaring unconstitutional a state statute unduly limiting the availability of abortions, the Supreme Court's majority opinion made frequent references to extra-record scientific and historical facts. In response, the Chief Justice filed the following caveat:]

Mr. Chief Justice Burger, concurring.

I agree that, under the Fourteenth Amendment to the Constitution, the abortion statutes of Georgia and Texas impermissibly limit the performance of abortions necessary to protect the health of pregnant women, using the term health in its broadest medical context. I am somewhat troubled that the Court has taken notice of various scientific and medical data in reaching its conclusion; however, I do not believe that the Court has exceeded the scope of judicial notice accepted in other contexts.

---

hygiene, inspectors of factories, both in this country and in Europe, to the effect that long hours of labor are dangerous for women, primarily because of their special physical organization. The matter is discussed in these reports in different aspects, but all agree as to the danger. It would of course take too much space to give these reports in detail. Following them are extracts from similar reports discussing the general benefits of short hours from an economic aspect of the question. In many of these reports individual instances are given tending to support the general conclusion. Perhaps the general scope and character of all these reports may be summed up in what an inspector for Hanover says:

The reasons for the reduction of the working day to ten hours — (a) the physical organization of women, (b) her maternal functions, (c) the rearing and educating of the children, (d) the maintenance of the home — are all so important and so far reaching that the need for such reduction need hardly be discussed.

Dean Alfange, Jr., *The Relevance of Legislative Facts in Constitutional Law*
114 U. Pa. L. Rev. 637, 639–40, 667–69 (1966)[5]

The examination of existing factual reality is a task for courts as well as legislatures. Certain objections, however, are traditionally raised to judicial consideration of facts. These objections are based on either or both of two assumptions — that courts cannot, or else should not, venture deeply into this area.

They cannot, it is sometimes said, because "the factual determinations involved are enormously difficult and time-consuming, and quite unsuitable for the judicial process." Yet making factual determinations has always been an integral part of judicial decision making. In those cases in which the law is settled beyond dispute, the courts must determine whether, as a matter of fact, the actions of the parties fall within the scope of the law; and such a determination cannot be avoided because it would be "enormously difficult and time-consuming." However, there is a recognized distinction between the determination of such adjudicative facts, which deal with particular circumstances, relating the actions of the parties to the law, and legislative facts, which deal with general problems and demonstrate a need for legislation; while consideration of the former is normally conceded to be within the province of the judiciary, consideration of the latter is usually said to be the task of the legislature. But, as Professor Paul Freund has noted, this distinction, "like most categorizations, will have to give a little at the seams." To the extent that the legislature, in most instances quite properly, specifies the particular acts that are to be proscribed or required in order to carry out the general policy, it is making decisions of an adjudicative nature. Similarly, when courts examine the public need underlying a piece of legislation or attempt to discern the policy which it embodies, they are considering legislative facts, again in most instances quite properly.

Conscious consideration of legislative facts is often nothing less than essential to the proper accomplishment of judicial tasks. In cases involving questions of statutory interpretation, courts should understand the nature of the evil that the legislature was seeking to correct and the manner in which it was seeking to correct it. Furthermore, to the extent that the legislature employs vague language in its enactments, achievement of the public purpose would seem to require judicial familiarity with legislative facts.

*   *   *

The problem faced by challengers and defenders of legislation in a constitutional case is to be allowed to bring sufficient facts before the courts to persuade them of the soundness of their contentions, for when the question of constitutionality is not obvious, "the validity of the legislation depends on the conclusions reached by the court with reference to . . . question[s] of fact." The sole purpose of the Brandeis brief filed by Louis Brandeis as counsel for the state of Oregon in the *Muller* case, and which was successful in persuading a majority of the Court of the reasonableness of state legislation regulating the maximum hours of employment of women in industry, was to focus judicial consciousness on present facts rather than previous

---

[5] Reprinted by permission of University of Pennsylvania Law Review.

precedents. And, although the doctrine of freedom of contract that the Brandeis brief was originally designed to combat has long since been discarded, the importance of questions of fact in the adjudication of constitutional claims has not been the least diminished. Thus the Brandeis brief has not lost its usefulness in constitutional law, for it remains a device by which a large amount of data can be assembled, organized and presented for judicial consideration in digestable form. Although two basic difficulties have been seen as arising from the use of the legal brief for the presentation of constitutionally relevant factual data, neither seems serious. First, the form of the brief and reply brief is not always the best means of making data available for accurate appraisal by the courts.

But the use of the brief surely ought not to preclude a trial of the legislative facts, if only because fuller examination would be preferable. The important factor is that courts be as fully apprised as possible of pertinent legislative fact; the ingenuity of advocates and the stimulation of advocacy may well be able to overcome technical difficulties. Where an adequate trial of the facts is not held, however, and the appellate courts find it necessary to be more fully informed on factual questions, a remand to the lower court for a more thorough trial would be entirely in order.

Second, and considerably more significant, is Professor Paul Freund's observation that the Brandeis brief "is designed to support legislation rather than to undermine it — to vindicate an experiment, not to veto it." For implicit in the original concept of the brief was the understanding that it was not necessary to prove the validity of the conclusions drawn by the legislature from the data it contained, but simply to show that the legislature had a reasonable basis for arriving at its conclusion — to show that a reasonable relationship existed between the provisions of the challenged statute and a proper legislative objective. Thus any material presented in a reply brief for the purpose of demonstrating the invalidity of the legislative conclusions would be entirely irrelevant, for once it had been shown that the legislature had a reasonable basis for its belief, the presumption of constitutionality would sustain the statute. But this maximum reliance on the presumption of constitutionality would be appropriate only when the presumption is at its strongest — when the challenge to the constitutionality of the statute is based solely on a claim that the law, if federal, is outside the scope of the delegated powers of Congress, or else that it is not related to a proper public purpose, which was, incidentally, the primary claim in the liberty of contract cases. When the presumption is balanced, either partially or completely, by virtue of the law's potential abridgment of a constitutionally protected right, factual data tending to undermine the statute by showing that the abridgment is unnecessary to the accomplishment of the public purpose, or that it is unjustifiably severe in light of the magnitude of the public purpose to be served, would become quite relevant. In such cases, it would not be enough to show that there was a reasonable basis for the legislative belief in the propriety of the law; it would have to be shown that there was an adequate basis for the belief that the law, both as enacted and as applied, was sufficiently *necessary* in the public interest to warrant the degree of abridgment of constitutional rights that it would bring about. And degree of necessity, if not reasonableness of belief, is open to rebuttal by counter demonstrations of fact in a Brandeis brief or by testimony at a trial.

NOTES AND QUESTIONS

1. Determination of legislative facts often requires arduous judicial research. *See, e.g., Turner v. United States*, 396 U.S. 398 (1970) (concerning importation of heroin and cocaine).

2. To what extent, if any, is judicial notice of legislative fact inconsistent with the right of cross-examination? *See* Karst, *Legislative Facts in Constitutional Litigation*, 1960 SUP. CT. REV. 75, 101–02.

3. Judicial notice of legislative fact is often taken despite conflicting authority on the point in issue. *See, e.g., Brown v. Board of Education*, 347 U.S. 483, 494 (1954); Kaplan, *Segregation Litigation and the Schools Part II: The General Northern Problem*, 58 Nw. U. L. REV. 157, 172–73 (1963). What standard, if any, must counsel satisfy before a court may take judicial notice of legislative fact? Does the Fed. R. Evid. 201 address this issue?

4. Consider the following observation:

Among commentators, there has been controversy as to how high a degree of certainty a proposition of fact must possess before it would be consonant with fair procedure to dispense with proof. One school, led by Professor Morgan, has insisted that judicial be limited . . . to those facts which cannot reasonably be disputed. This means not only that the fact be true but also that reasonable men would not dispute it. The other view, supported by Wigmore and Thayer in the past, and now most avidly supported by Professor Davis, argues that the convenient system is to assume all facts that are unlikely to be challenged, as well as those considered to be absolutely indisputable. According to this approach, judicial notice operates in the way of a presumption — a fact is considered indisputable until such time as it is disputed.

Under the Morgan view fairness to the parties is the prime concern; under the Wigmore-Thayer view convenience is the principal goal, which is to give way only when considerations of fairness rise to constitutional proportions.

WEINSTEIN'S EVIDENCE § 201[03] (1982). Which view does Fed. R. Evid. 201 adopt? To what extent, if any, might the standard for judicial notice more appropriately reflect the nature of the proceeding at hand (*e.g.*, civil versus criminal trial, jury versus non-jury trial)?

5. Why does Rule 201(g) distinguish between the impact of judicial notice in civil and criminal cases? Suppose that a criminal prosecutor neglects to prove an essential fact. One would expect the court to direct a judgment of acquittal. But should this necessarily occur if the missing item of proof is a matter of common knowledge. Under what circumstances, if any, may the court take judicial notice of that fact, thereby completing the prosecution's prima facie case? *See State v. Main*, 180 A.2d 814 (R.I. 1962); *State v. Lawrence*, 234 P.2d 600 (Utah 1951). *Compare Ross v. United States*, 374 F.2d 97 (8th Cir. 1967); *People v. Mayes*, 45 P. 860 (Cal. 1896). *See also Garner v. Louisiana*, 368 U.S. 157 (1961) (addressing, the propriety of taking judicial notice in a criminal case on appeal).

6. The Federal Rules of Evidence do not treat judicial notice of legislative fact. Why not? Consider the following:

> My opinion is that judge-made law would stop growing if judges, in thinking about questions of law and policy, were forbidden to take into account the facts they believe, as distinguished from facts which are "clearly . . . within the domain of the indisputable." Facts most needed in thinking about difficult problems of law and policy have a way of being outside the domain of the clearly indisputable.

Davis, *A System of Judicial Notice Based on Fairness and Convenience, in* PERSPECTIVES OF LAW 69, 82 (1964).

7. Not all facts, however, are clearly adjudicative or clearly legislative:

> Of course the facts concerning the parties before the court — the "adjudicative facts" as recent fashion would have it — may [also] be important as demonstrations of the general effects of the governmental action. Thus many adjudicative facts are also legislative facts in that they bear on the legislative question of the reasonableness, or constitutionality, of governmental action. The adjudicative facts may even carry a disproportionately heavy weight as legislative facts just because a court is more at home in dealing with facts concerning the immediate parties.

Karst, *Legislative Facts in Constitutional Litigation*, 1960 SUP. CT. REV. 75, 77. The Court's perspective on what type of fact is at issue may determine whether judicial notice will be taken. *See* D. LOUISELL & C. MUELLER, FEDERAL EVIDENCE § 56 (1977); *Garner v. Louisiana*, 368 U.S. 157 (1961); *Goodman v. Stalfort, Inc.*, 411 F. Supp. 889 (D.N.J. 1976). Some jurisdictions have declined to distinguish between adjudicative and legislative facts. *See, e.g.*, Alaska Rules of Evidence, Rule 201 (1980); Mont. Code Ann. § 23-10-201 (1981). For an interesting attempt at distinguishing between adjudicative and legislative facts, *see Korematsu v. United States*, 584 F. Supp. 1406 (N.D. Cal. 1984).

8. Judicial notice of legislative facts may change over time. *Compare Hawkins v. United States*, 358 U.S. 74 (1958) (adverse spousal testimony is likely to destroy almost any marriage), *with Trammel v. United States*, 445 U.S. 40 (1980) (foundations of spousal "privilege have long since disappeared"; willingness of spouse to testify indicates that "relationship is almost certainly in disrepair.").

2. Other Options

Federal Rule of Civil Procedure 16
Pretrial Conferences; Scheduling; Management

(c) Attendance and Matters for Consideration at a Pretrial Conference.

(1) Attendance. A represented party must authorize at least one of its attorneys to make stipulations and admissions about all matters that can reasonably be anticipated for discussion at a pretrial conference. If appropriate, the court may require that a party or its representative be present or reasonably available by other means to consider possible settlement.

(2) Matters for Consideration. At any pretrial conference, the court may consider and take appropriate action on the following matters:

(A) formulating and simplifying the issues, and eliminating frivolous claims or defenses;

(B) amending the pleadings if necessary or desirable;

(C) obtaining admissions and stipulations about facts and documents to avoid unnecessary proof, and ruling in advance on the admissibility of evidence;

(D) avoiding unnecessary proof and cumulative evidence, and limiting the use of testimony under Federal Rule of Evidence 702;

(E) determining the appropriateness and timing of summary adjudication under Rule 56;

(F) controlling and scheduling discovery, including orders affecting disclosures and discovery under Rule 26 and Rules 29 through 37;

(G) identifying witnesses and documents, scheduling the filing and exchange of any pretrial briefs, and setting dates for further conferences and for trial;

(H) referring matters to a magistrate judge or a master;

(I) settling the case and using special procedures to assist in resolving the dispute when authorized by statute or local rule;

(J) determining the form and content of the pretrial order;

(K) disposing of pending motions;

(L) adopting special procedures for managing potentially difficult or protracted actions that may involve complex issues, multiple parties, difficult legal questions, or unusual proof problems;

(M) ordering a separate trial under Rule 42(b) of a claim, counterclaim, crossclaim, third-party claim, or particular issue;

(N) ordering the presentation of evidence early in the trial on a manageable issue that might, on the evidence, be the basis for a judgment as a matter of law under Rule 50(a) or a judgment on partial findings under Rule 52(c);

(O) establishing a reasonable limit on the time allowed to present evidence; and

(P) facilitating in other ways the just, speedy, and inexpensive disposition of the action.

NOTES AND QUESTIONS

1.   This stipulation is also a common mechanism for expediting proof. In essence, a stipulation is an agreement between the parties concerning how any particular matter should be handled at trial. Thus, for example, the parties may agree to stipulate to the existence of a specified fact or set of facts. The operative

scope of the stipulation is determined by its own terms. Accordingly, caution should be exercised in negotiating any such agreement. For example, a stipulation concerning how a certain witness, if called, would have testified, does not bind the jury to accept that testimony as true. *See, e.g., Koenig v. Frank's Plastering Co.*, 227 F. Supp. 849 (D. Neb. 1964), *aff'd*, 341 F.2d 257 (8th Cir. 1965).

2.   Presumptions are also a way to expedite (or, indeed, substitute for) formal proof. *See* Chapter VII, *infra.*

3.   When one party offers to stipulate as to a fact, must the other necessarily accept? *See Old Chief v. United States*, 519 U.S. 172 (1997), *infra.*

B.   TYPES OF FORMAL PROOF

1.   Real Evidence

JOHN H. WIGMORE, 1 EVIDENCE § 24
(3d ed. 1940)[6]

There are two possible modes of proceeding for the purpose of producing persuasion on the part of the tribunal as to the Proposition at issue.

The first is by the presentation of the *thing itself* as to which persuasion is desired.

The second is the presentation of some *independent* fact by inference from which the persuasion is to be produced. Instances of the first are the production of a blood-stained knife; the exhibition of an injured limb; the viewing of premises by the jury; the production of a document.

NOTES AND QUESTIONS

1.   Consider the following:

> [I]n an unreported Texas case, the defendant being indicted for aggravated assault by biting off a piece of the complainant's ear, the complainant was permitted to exhibit the maimed ear to the jury. In exhibiting such a "gaping wound of Caesar" or photographs of such a wound, how far can the proponent go in emphasizing the character of the wound?

Cady, *Objections to Demonstrative Evidence*, 32 MO. L. REV. 333, 341–42 (1967). Should gruesomeness, alone, automatically preclude admissibility? If not, under what circumstances, if any, should gruesomeness be a basis for exclusion? *See Sheker v. State*, 644 P.2d 560 (Okla. Crim. App. 1982) (admissibility of skull in homicide prosecution). This issue often arises in connection with Fed. R. Evid. 403.

2.   Aside from considerations of possible undue prejudice, the admissibility of real evidence primarily turns on a showing that the evidence is what it purports to be (*i.e.*, that *it* actually *is* the real thing).

---

[6] Reprinted by permission of Little, Brown and Company, 1940.

2. Demonstrative Evidence

USS v. TOWN OF OYSTER BAY
339 N.E.2d 147 (N.Y. 1975)

JONES, J.

We are asked to set aside a jury verdict for defendants on the ground that the trial court erroneously permitted defense counsel to conduct an in-court demonstration employ[ing] a physical exhibit introduced by plaintiffs and a model introduced by defendants.

While walking home from a high school double date, infant plaintiff was injured when a dual street sign at an intersection fell on his head. It was his claim that the street sign had been dislodged from atop its supporting metal pole when his companion struck the pole with his hand.

On trial, the street sign in question (which had been promptly recovered by the infant plaintiff's father and there[after] remained in counsel's custody) was introduced and received as part of plaintiff's case. In its turn defendant town offered a model metal pole similar to that on which the sign had been mounted. The model pole was some four feet shorter than the original pole and was imbedded in a movable concrete block rather than in stationary blacktop as at the sidewalk intersection. Plaintiffs objected to any courtroom demonstration making use of the model pole. After inviting the jury's attention to differences between the model and the original, the court received the model pole as an exhibit and the dual street sign was placed on the pole.

During his direct examination of the Superintendent of the Town's Sign Bureau, counsel for defendant town struck the model pole sharply with his hand. The sign was not unseated. Plaintiff's objection to the particular demonstration was overruled, and without restriction plaintiff's counsel proceeded to cross-examination with reference to the installation of the street sign, the physical details of its assembly and the possibilities of its being dislodged when struck by a "human blow." Without objection the street sign and the model pole were later taken into the jury room.

In the circumstances of this case we cannot say as a matter of law that there was an abuse of discretion by the trial court. The thrust of plaintiffs' objection is directed at the subsequent demonstration by defendants' counsel rather than at the admission of the model pole in evidence. In matters of this sort a broad but sound discretion is properly vested in the trial court. The court here might have been justified in forbidding a demonstration since it can be argued that the conditions in the courtroom were not substantially similar to those at the scene of the accident. On the other hand it was not error as a matter of law for the court, after the demonstration had taken place, to determine that plaintiffs' legitimate interests could be sufficiently protected by affording plaintiffs' counsel unrestricted opportunity for cross examination. By effective exploitation of the dissimilarities between the model and the original it was thus open to counsel to minimize the significance to be attached to the demonstration.

The physical features of the sign assembly as well as the principles of mechanics involved in this demonstration were well within the experience and comprehension of an average juror. Thus its probative worth could be independently weighed by the jurors themselves. Nor was the demonstration deceptive, sensational, disruptive of the trial, or purely conjectural.

The order of the Appellate Division should be affirmed.

COOKE, J. (dissenting).

Demonstrations are permitted in court to show that an object behaves in a certain way provided the conditions under which they are performed are identical or substantially the same as those existing at the time of the event to which they relate. . . . Since there were substantial dissimilarities regarding the actual pole and the model employed, both as to height and embedment, and in the absence of proof that the severity of the force applied in the courtroom even approximated that expended at the time in question, the demonstration was not relevant to the issue and should have been excluded as a matter of law. . . . In the frame of this case, the demonstration was sufficiently prejudicial to plaintiffs so as to warrant a reversal and new trial.

NOTES AND QUESTIONS

1.   Although definitions vary, in simple terms demonstrative evidence may be viewed as evidence that illustrates or "demonstrates" the real thing. Examples include the following: maps, models, duplicates, diagrams, photographs, movies, courtroom demonstrations, and experiments.

2.   Given this definition, what requirements should be imposed as prerequisites to admitting any demonstrative exhibits into evidence? *See* Cady, *Objections to Demonstrative Evidence*, 32 MO. L. REV. 333 (1967); Spangenburg, *The Use of Demonstrative Evidence*, 21 OHIO ST. L.J. 178 (1960).

3.   Most courts would have resolved *Uss* by applying the substantial similarity test urged by the dissent. Would the outcome, however, necessarily have been any different? Consider the following:

> The rule of substantial similarity does not require an identity of conditions but only that degree of similarity which will insure that the results of the experiment are probative. In some cases a high degree of similarity may not be attainable, yet the evidence nevertheless may be enlightening to the jury.

American National Watermattress Corp. v. Manville, 642 P.2d 1330, 1337 (Alaska 1982).

4.   At times, a particular item of evidence may not be readily classifiable as either real evidence or demonstrative evidence. For example, how should the following evidence be characterized: (1) the movie film, taken by Abraham Zapruder, depicting the assassination of President John F. Kennedy; (2) x-rays; (3) a bank surveillance film showing a robbery in progress; and (4) the tape recording

of a conversation? Does classification as real or demonstrative evidence have legal significance? *See* Comment, *Photographic Evidence — Is There a Recognized Basis for Admissibility?*, 8 HASTINGS L.J. 310 (1957); MCCORMICK, HANDBOOK OF THE LAW OF EVIDENCE § 214 (4th ed. 1999); *Cf. Bosco v. United States*, 164 Fed. Appx. 226, 2006 U.S. App. LEXIS 1948 (3d Cir. Jan. 24, 2006); *McEachron v. Glans*, 1999 U.S. Dist. LEXIS 21926 (N.D.N.Y. Aug. 23, 1999) (reviewing foundational requirements).

3. Testimonial Evidence

Testimonial evidence is the most common mode of proof. Professor Wigmore defined this concept rather formally as "the assertions of human beings [that are] regarded as the basis of inference to the propositions asserted by them." 1 WIGMORE EVIDENCE § 25, at 398 (3d ed. 1940). In less eloquent terms, however, testimonial evidence is any oral proof that is presented to the factfinder by a duly sworn witness. Such proof has been characterized as *viva voce* evidence — the living voice — and is obviously the basic ingredient of every trial. Moreover, testimonial evidence is normally required before a foundation can be established for the introduction of any real or demonstrative evidence.

C. BASIC CONDITIONS OF ADMISSIBILITY

1. Introduction

JAMES B. THAYER, A PRELIMINARY TREATISE ON
EVIDENCE AT THE COMMON LAW
264–65 (1898)

Observe, at this point, one or two fundamental conceptions. There is a principle — not so much a rule of evidence as a presupposition involved in the very conception of a rational system of evidence, as contrasted with the old formal and mechanical systems — which forbids receiving anything irrelevant, not logically probative. How are we to know what these forbidden things are? Not by any rule of law. The law furnishes no test of relevancy. For this, it tacitly refers to logic and general experience, — assuming that the principles of reasoning are known to its judges . . . , just as a vast multitude of other things are assumed as already sufficiently known to them.

There is another precept which should be laid down as preliminary, in stating the law of evidence; namely, that unless excluded by some rule or principle of law, all that is logically probative is admissible. This general admissibility, however, of what is logically probative is not, like the former principle, a necessary presupposition in a rational system of evidence; there are many exceptions to it. Yet, in order to have a clear conception of the law, it is important to notice this also as being a fundamental proposition. In an historical sense it has not been the fundamental thing, to which the different exclusions were exceptions. What has taken place, in fact, is the shutting out by the judges of one and another thing from time to time; and so, gradually, the recognition of this exclusion under a rule. These rules of exclusion have had their exceptions; and so the law has come into the shape of a set of primary rules of exclusion; and then a set of exceptions to these rules.

NOTE

Evidence is admissible if it is relevant, material, and competent. Scholars have often differed in defining these concepts, *see* E. MORGAN, BASIC PROBLEMS OF EVIDENCE 183 (1961), but agree that the terms are analytically distinct. As such, they should not be blurred when objecting to the introduction or exclusion of evidence. Historically, however, counsels have frequently relied upon the boilerplate objection — "incompetent, irrelevant, and immaterial" — made famous by the forlorn Hamilton Burger in the old Perry Mason television series. Does Hamilton Burger's objection style comply with the requirements of Fed. R. Evid. 103 set forth below?

NOTES AND QUESTIONS

1.   According to Rule 103, who has primary responsibility for contesting the admissibility of evidence?

2.   What purpose is served by requiring objections to be specific rather than general? *See* Ladd, *Objections, Motions and Foundation Testimony*, 43 CORNELL L.Q. 543 (1958); Note, *Raising New Issues on Appeal*, 64 HARV. L. REV. 652 (1951).

3.   For some good examples of the consequences of failure to abide by Rule 103, *see Chicago College of Osteopathic Medicine v. George A. Fuller Co.*, 719 F.2d 1335 (7th Cir. 1983); *James v. Bell Helicopter*, 715 F.2d 166 (5th Cir. 1983); *MCI Communications v. AT&T*, 708 F.2d 1081 (7th Cir. 1983).

"Oh, I object now and then, but, as lawyers go, I'm pretty laid back."

Drawing by M. Twohy; © 1983

The New Yorker Magazine, Inc.

2. Legal Relevance and Materiality

George F. James, *Relevancy, Probability and the Law*
29 CAL. L. REV. 689, 690–91 (1941)[7]

Relevancy . . . , is not an inherent characteristic of any item of evidence but exists as a relation between an item of evidence and a proposition sought to be proved. If an item of evidence tends to prove or to disprove any proposition, it is relevant to that proposition. If the proposition itself is one provable in the case at bar, or if it in turn forms a further link in a chain of proof the final proposition of which is provable in the case at bar, then the offered item of evidence has probative value in the case. Whether the immediate or ultimate proposition sought to be proved is provable in the case at bar is determined by the pleadings, by the procedural rules applicable thereto, and by the substantive law governing the case. Whether the offered item of evidence tends to prove the proposition at which it is ultimately aimed depends upon other factors, shortly to be considered. But because relevancy as used by Thayer and in the Code, means tendency to prove a proposition properly provable in the case, an offered item of evidence may be excluded as "irrelevant" for either of these two quite distinct reasons: because it is not probative of the proposition at which it is directed, or because that proposition is not provable in the case. The distinction between these two senses of irrelevance seems not to have been observed by the early authors.

---

[7] Copyright © 1941, California Law Review, Inc. Reprinted from California Law Review, Vol. 29, No. 6 pp. 689–691, by permission.

BARNETT v. STATE
135 N.E. 647 (Ohio 1922)

But, what is relevant evidence? What do we mean by the term, as used in due process of law? Let us get back to some first principles. Jeremy Bentham's old definition can hardly be improved on today:

> Any matter of fact, the effect, tendency, or design of which, when presented to the mind, is to produce a persuasion concerning the existence of some other matter of fact — a persuasion either affirmative or disaffirmative of its existence.

Relevant

LYNCH v. ROSENBERGER
249 P. 682 (Kan. 1926)

. . . Evidence offered in a cause, or a question propounded, is "material" when it is relevant and goes to the substantial matters in dispute, or has a legitimate and effective influence or bearing on the decision of the case.

Material

QUESTIONS

1. In a murder prosecution in which the victim's identity is not in issue, may the prosecution introduce posed photographs of the victim taken before the homicide occurred? *See Smith v. State*, 650 P.2d 904 (Okla. Crim. App. 1982).

2. In a prosecution for passing counterfeit money, may the defendant introduce evidence of his motive to demonstrate the illegality of the United States monetary system? *See United States v. Snow*, 670 F.2d 749 (7th Cir. 1982).

Federal Rule of Evidence 401
Test for Relevant Evidence

Evidence is relevant if:

(a) it has any tendency to make a fact more or less probable than it would be without the evidence; and

(b) the fact is of consequence in determining the action.

UNITED STATES v. CURTIS
568 F.2d 643 (9th Cir. 1978)

WALLACE, CIRCUIT JUDGE:

Curtis appeals from his conviction of first degree murder pursuant to 18 U.S.C. § 1111. He raises questions concerning the admissibility of certain testimony and the sufficiency of the evidence. We affirm.

I

On April 27, 1976 the body of Barbara Bently was discovered in Ahwanee Meadow of Yosemite National Park. During an interview with the victim's room-mate, police officers learned that the victim had been with Curtis on the evening prior to the discovery of her body. The agents interviewed Curtis and learned that on the night of April 26, he and Bently had gone out to dinner and then returned to Curtis' room. He told them that the victim thereafter physically rejected Curtis' sexual advances which resulted in her scratching his face as she pushed him away.

In addition, a significant amount of physical evidence was admitted which suggested that Curtis had killed Bently during the course of a rape or attempted rape. For example, maroon fibers taken from the victim's thigh, buttocks, and head were microscopically identical to the fibers of a maroon blanket found in Curtis' room. This same blanket also contained hair which had been forcefully removed and which was microscopically similar to the victim's. Additionally, green fibers found in the victim's buttocks were microscopically identical to the fibers of a green blanket found in Curtis' closet. Samples of pubic hair microscopically identical to that of the victim were found on a brown handkerchief which was discovered in a car used by Curtis; the brown handkerchief matched a handkerchief found in Curtis' room. The victim's pocketbook, a man's sweater, a sheet, a pillow case, and mattress cover, each stained with blood matching that of the victim, were also found in the car. Finally, semen was found in the victim's underpants. The semen was found to have been deposited by an individual having the same blood type as Curtis.

In his statement to the investigating officers, Curtis claimed that prior to the argument, the victim did not remove any of her clothing and that she departed immediately after the disagreement. If this were true, it would foreclose the possibility that the physical evidence was generated by consensual sexual activity between Curtis and the victim.

At trial, the prosecutor elicited the following testimony from an acquaintance of Curtis.

Q.   Referring you to about the last week in March, and the early part of April, can you state whether or not you had a conversation with this Allen?

A.   Yeah.

*   *   *

Q.   Can you tell us, the Court and the Jury, what conversation took place between the both of you?

A.   We was talking about ladies in general.

Q.   Talking about ladies?

A.   Uh-huh.

Q.   Did Mr. Curtis say anything about ladies?

A.   Uh, yeah.

Q.   What did he say?

A.   Uh, well, we was talking about, you know, getting down with certain ladies, and he said if he ever took a lady out and she didn't give him what he wanted, he'd kick their [expletive deleted] and take it.

Timely objection was made to this testimony as being unduly prejudicial and irrelevant. Curtis renews these contentions on appeal.

* * *

Curtis' second attack on the admissibility of this testimony centers around its relevance. The core of this argument is that because the challenged statement was made approximately a month prior to the murder, and was a vague bravado statement not referring to the victim or any other particular person, the statement is not relevant to this specific crime and, therefore, should have been excluded. We cannot agree.

Rule 401 of the Federal Rules of Evidence contains a very expansive definition of relevant evidence. In addition, Rule 402 provides that all relevant evidence is ordinarily admissible.[8] Applying these rules to the facts of this case, we believe the district judge correctly admitted the challenged testimony over the relevancy objection. Curtis stated that on the night of the murder the victim rejected his sexual advances. Thus, his prior statement as to what he would do in such circumstances is plainly relevant. Although relevant evidence may be excluded in certain cases under Rule 403, the district judge did not abuse his discretion in declining to do so.

* * *

AFFIRMED.

QUESTION

May *Curtis* be reconciled with *State v. Rowe*, 479 A.2d 1296 (Me. 1984)?

In *Roe*, a trial judge was sustained in rejecting defense evidence showing that, six weeks before an alleged homicide, defendant tried to dissuade the victim from committing suicide?

Evidentiary Foundation:
The Trial of Sirhan Sirhan

[The following testimony was elicited by the prosecution during Sirhan Sirhan's trial for the 1968 assassination of Senator Robert F. Kennedy. The witness, Jesse Unruh, had been Kennedy's campaign chairman.]

---

[8] [3] Fed. R. Evid. 402 provides:

All relevant evidence is admissible, except as otherwise provided by the constitution of the United States by Act of Congress, by these rules, or by other rules prescribed by the Supreme Court pursuant to statutory authority. Evidence which is not relevant is not admissible.

DIRECT EXAMINATION

BY MR. FITTS:

Q.   Mr. Unruh, did you participate in the campaign of Senator Robert F. Kennedy of New York, for the Presidential nomination in California, the primaries of last June?

A.   Yes, I did. I was chairman of the Kennedy Presidential Campaign and chairman of the Kennedy Delegation to the National Committee. [Mr. Unruh goes through the process of telling how he witnessed the assassination of Robert F. Kennedy.] . . .

Q.   Could you see people actually restraining the assailant, sir.

A.   Yes, I could. But there were only two or three of them that really stick in my memory.

Q.   Do you remember who they were?

A.   Yes. I can remember Roosevelt Grier, and I remember him in a rather strange circumstances, because it was so hot when we were out on the podium and here Rosie was standing behind and I think you will admit he was a little overweight at that point. He is sitting right behind you, sir. It was so hot in there, I remember the perspiration streaming down his face, and I can remember when we finally got the crowd somewhat peeled off from the defendant, the tears coming from Rosie's eyes, and I remember thinking, even at that moment . . . .

MR. COOPER: Pardon the interruption, but I think we are going afield.

THE COURT: Yes. Mr. Unruh, I want to caution you about voluntary statements. You understand that this jury has to be protected from hearing too much, and I will ask you if you will be good enough not to make voluntary statements.

THE WITNESS: Judge, I am sorry you have to admonish me. I remember seeing Mr. Grier, Mr. Frank Burns, and I think Mr. George Plimpton.

Q.   They all had something to do with laying their hands on the defendant, is that right?

A.   Right.

Q.   Did you proceed north along the corridor?

A.   Through the corridor and then . . . . We went out the main door; there were a great many people following us, screaming and shouting and all that.

MR. COOPER: I move to strike that last one, as a conclusion of the witness and immaterial.

THE COURT: It may go out, the remark relative to the shouting, etc. The jury is to disregard it, as though they never heard it.

Q.   Did you hear the defendant say anything else?

A.   I think I did during the course of the ride to the police station.

Q.   Either at the police car or during the course of the ride did you hear him say anything . . . Mr. Unruh?

A.   Yes, I did. I asked him, "Why him? Why him?" and, Your Honor, may I explain why I asked him this?

MR. COOPER: To which I would object as immaterial.

QUESTIONS

1.   How should the trial judge have ruled on Mr. Cooper's materiality objection?

2.   In view of the difference between relevancy and materiality as set forth in the excerpts from Professor James and the *Barnett* and *Lynch* cases, which portions of the preceding testimony constitute relevant but immaterial evidence?

3.   Reconsider Fed. R. Evid. 401. How does it redefine the concept of relevancy as explained by the excerpts from Professor James and the *Barnett* and *Lynch* cases?

3.   Competence

CHARLES E. TORCIA, 1 WHARTON'S CRIMINAL EVIDENCE § 154
(13th ed. 1972)[9]

Competence is applied both to evidence and to witnesses. As applied to evidence, it means that the evidence has been obtained in such a way, from such a source, and is in such a form that it is deemed proper to admit it.

Evidence must be competent to be admissible. Thus, a confession obtained as a result of coercion is not admissible because it would represent evidence which was obtained in an improper way; a statement by a witness of what a third person had told him is generally not admissible because the source of such evidence would be hearsay; and a carbon copy of a writing would represent an improper form of evidence which would not be admissible unless a satisfactory explanation has been given for the failure to produce the original. In such cases, exclusion is based on the belief that the evidence would not be reliable. Hence, the law categorically rejects such evidence as incompetent.

*   *   *

Competence . . . is distinct from the requirement of relevance of evidence. The evidence offered may be relevant, but still would be excluded if it or the witness were not competent. Thus, evidence that the defendant shot the victim is relevant in a prosecution for the victim's murder, but such evidence would nevertheless be excluded if it were offered by an incompetent person who claims to have witnessed

---

[9] Reprinted with permission.

the event, or by a competent person who states that he did not see the event but that he is repeating what the people in the neighborhood had said. In such cases, the exclusion is based, not on irrelevance, but on the incompetence of the witness or the evidence.

4. Legal Relevance

"Unquestionably, though, the presence of jurors has somewhat complicated probative methods. . . ."

— Professor John MacArthur Maguire[10]

Herman L. Trautman, *Logical or Legal Relevance — A Conflict in Theory*
5 VAND. L. REV. 385, 389–90 (1952)[11]

Assuming that the trial judge believes that there is logical relevance between the item of evidence offered (Fact A), and an ultimate probandum in the case (Fact B), is it necessary for the trial judge to weigh such evidence for the purpose of determining a legal minimum quantity of probative value? Thayer's answer was "that everything which is thus probative, should come in, unless a clear ground of policy or law excludes it." The American Law Institute's Model Code of Evidence, Rule 9(f), states that "all relevant evidence is admissible"; but this rule is made subject to Rule 303 which provides that the trial judge may in his discretion exclude evidence if he finds that its probative value "is out-weighed" by certain policy considerations, namely, that the risk of its admission will (a) necessitate undue consumption of time, or (b) create substantial danger of undue prejudice or of confusing the issues or of misleading the jury, or (c) unfairly surprise a party who has not had reasonable ground to anticipate that such evidence could be offered. While the Introductory Note to Rules 303 to 313 states that "It would be as futile as it would be unwise to attempt to prescribe measurements of logical value," Rule 303 expressly provides that the judge may exclude the offered evidence if he finds that its probative value is "out-weighed" by the above policy considerations. Wigmore champions a concept called "legal relevance" of which "the effect is to require a generally higher degree of probative value for all evidence to be submitted to a jury" and that "legal relevancy denotes, first of all, something more than a minimum of probative value. Each single piece of evidence must have a plus value."

NOTES AND QUESTIONS

1.   Under the doctrine of legal relevance, logical relevance becomes a necessary but not always sufficient condition for admissibility.

2.   Despite its title, is "legal relevance" more appropriately characterized as a competency-based principle?

3.   The term legal relevance has been criticized by scholars as being too prone

---

[10] EVIDENCE: COMMON SENSE AND COMMON LAW 166 (1947).

[11] Copyright Vanderbilt Law Review, 1952. Reprinted with permission.

to confusion. For this reason, Professor McCormick apparently chose to refer to it as a "counterweight" to logical relevance. MᴄCᴏʀᴍɪᴄᴋ's Hᴀɴᴅʙᴏᴏᴋ ᴏғ ᴛʜᴇ Lᴀᴡ ᴏғ Eᴠɪᴅᴇɴᴄᴇ § 184 (2d ed. 1972). How else might this principle be characterized? In this regard, consider the following commentary by Professor James.

George F. James, *Relevancy, Probability and the Law*
29 Cᴀʟ. L. Rᴇᴠ. 689, 701–04 (1941)[12]

Probably the greatest part of judicial rulings excluding evidence as irrelevant go primarily on the first principle — that the evidence is relevant, but its probative value is so slight as not to justify the time and expense involved in receiving it and the confusion of issues which might result in the mind of the trier of fact. Does this sound practical policy justify creation of the concept of "legal relevancy" — higher and more strict than logical relevancy, to which offers of proof must be referred? On the contrary, the concept can only be a nuisance. In the first place, it defies definition. No statement of a standard of probative value higher than logical relevancy can be made precise enough for use without excluding much evidence which is used daily, without argument and to good effect. And there is a definite reason for this. When a judge must decide whether a particular item of evidence, logically relevant, is of sufficient force to justify the time and expense necessary to establish it, he should not confine his attention to the effect of the offered evidence alone. He should consider how difficult it will be to establish the evidentiary fact — whether there is any real contest about it and whether confusing side issues must be explored. He should consider how the offered evidence may fit in with other evidence. It may form a small but useful part of a pattern of proof. It may stand alone, lending it negligible aid to unconnected lines of proof. It may be merely cumulative, so that the trouble of establishing it will result in little of practical value. He may even want to consider the importance to the parties of the issues being tried, in the light of mounting trial expense. Such considerations cannot usefully be reduced to a simple formula for relevancy of particular items of evidence.

The method suggested by Chief Justice Cushing, that of building up a body of rulings on the bearing of particular facts upon particular issues, is no better — for the same reason. The ruling in each case will seldom if ever be that the offered fact has *no* bearing upon the issue. It will be that it has no sufficient bearing to justify its use in view of all the circumstances of the case in which it is offered. Such a precedent, rightly understood, is of no value save in another case substantially identical in all of its particulars. Treated more broadly, its tendency will be to mislead subsequent judges.

Take, as an example, *State v. LaPage* (1876 NH) where Chief Justice Cushing enunciated his theories on legal relevancy. The state, in a prosecution for murder of one Josie L. in which there was some evidence of murder during an attempted rape, was permitted to show that the defendant had raped one Julienne R. The evidence was offered not to show that the defendant had killed Josie, but to show that if he had done so it was in the course of an attempted rape and therefore first degree murder

---

under the New Hampshire statute. A conviction was reversed, the court holding that evidence of another crime, not relevant *save as showing the character or disposition of the accused*, could not be presented by the prosecution when the accused had not "put his character in issue." The reasons for this ruling are clear on principle and from the opinion itself. First, the offered evidence, while it had some probative value, was not particularly cogent. Second, by attacking the character of the accused, it raised the danger that he might be "overwhelmed by prejudice, instead of being convicted on that affirmative evidence which the law of this country requires." Third, by using specific instances of misconduct to demonstrate bad character, it confronted the accused with a dangerous issue which he might have been entirely unprepared to meet. These are substantial arguments for exclusion, which are in no way aided by saying that the defendant's bad character is not "legally relevant," or that specific instances of misconduct are not "legally relevant" to prove bad character.

On the contrary, there is real danger that talk of legal relevancy in such cases may mislead other judges. Thus in a prosecution for murder the character of the decedent as quarrelsome and violent should be admissible in aid of a plea of self-defense. Most courts admit it, but those who do not often seem confused by the inadmissibility of the violent character of the accused. If the ruling excluding the bad character of criminal defendants were always expressly made on the ground that such evidence is relevant but inadmissible because unduly prejudicial, without reference to "legal irrelevancy," such confusion would be unlikely.

Similarly the argument of undue surprise is less likely to lead courts into error if stated as such. Specific immoral acts clearly are not irrelevant as evidence of lack of the corresponding virtue. If not actually conclusive they are certainly much more cogent than reputation. If they are really excluded because of the danger of surprise, it would be better to say so. Then courts might in time discover in pre-trial practice a method of obviating unfair surprise in the use of the specific instance whenever its value is sufficiently great to justify the time and expense of trying a collateral issue.

Such considerations, whether taken singly or together, afford most unsuitable materials for the construction of a body of case law. Like the simpler problem of time and expense, all involve a balance of competing considerations — the value of the evidence, the importance of the point sought to be established, the availability of other evidence, the precise degree of inconvenience or prejudice — never likely to be duplicated in different cases. "The evidence of particular facts as bearing on particular issues" does not repeat its pattern closely enough to permit its petrifaction into rules having "the authority of law" without over simplification. The history of evidence has been in the development of sound principles into arbitrary and unworkable rubrics, a development not to be encouraged in case law or by code.

QUESTION

Does Rule 403 adequately address the concerns raised by Professor James?

OLD CHIEF v. UNITED STATES
519 U.S. 172 (1997)

JUSTICE SOUTER delivered the opinion of the Court.

Subject to certain limitations, 18 U.S.C. § 922(g)(1) prohibits possession of a firearm by anyone with a prior felony conviction, which the government can prove by introducing a record of judgment or similar evidence identifying the previous offense. Fearing prejudice if the jury learns the nature of the earlier crime, defendants sometimes seek to avoid such an informative disclosure by offering to concede the fact of the prior conviction.[13] The issue here is whether a district court abuses its discretion if it spurns such an offer and admits the full record of a prior judgment, when the name or nature of the prior offense raises the risk of a verdict tainted by improper considerations, and when the purpose of the evidence is solely to prove the element of prior conviction. We hold that it does.

I

In 1993, petitioner, Old Chief, was arrested after a fracas involving at least one gunshot. The ensuing federal charges included not only assault with a dangerous weapon and using a firearm in relation to a crime of violence but violation of 18 U.S.C. § 922(g)(1). This statute makes it unlawful for anyone "who has been convicted in any court of, a crime punishable by imprisonment for a term exceeding one year" to "possess in or affecting commerce, any firearm. . . ."

> "[A] crime punishable by imprisonment for a term exceeding one year" is defined to exclude "any Federal or State offenses pertaining to antitrust violations, unfair trade practices, restraints of trade, or other similar offenses relating to the regulation of business practices" and "any State offense classified by the laws of the State as a misdemeanor and punishable by a term of imprisonment of two years or less." 18 U.S.C. § 921(a)(20).

The earlier crime charged in the indictment against Old Chief was assault causing serious bodily injury. Before trial, he moved for an order requiring the government" to refrain from mentioning — by reading the Indictment, during jury selection, in opening statement, or closing argument — and to refrain from offering into evidence or soliciting any testimony from any witness regarding the prior criminal convictions of the Defendant, except to state that the Defendant has been convicted of a crime punishable by imprisonment exceeding one (1) year." He said that revealing the name and nature of his prior assault conviction would unfairly tax the jury's capacity to hold the Government to its burden of proof beyond a reasonable doubt on current charges of assault, possession, and violence with a firearm, and he offered to "solve the problem here by stipulating, agreeing and requesting the Court to instruct the jury that he has been convicted of a crime punishable by imprisonment exceeding one (1) year[]." He argued that the offer to stipulate to the fact of the prior conviction rendered evidence of the name and

---

[13] [1] The standard of review applicable to the evidentiary rulings of the district court is abuse of discretion. *United States v. Abel*, 469 U.S. 45, 54–55 (1984).

nature of the offense inadmissible under Rule 403 of the Federal Rules of Evidence, the danger being that unfair prejudice from that evidence would substantially outweigh its probative value. . . .

* * *

The Assistant United States Attorney refused to join in a stipulation, insisting on his right to prove his case his own way, and the District Court agreed, ruling orally that, "If he doesn't want to stipulate, he doesn't have to." At trial, over renewed objection, the Government introduced the order of judgment and commitment for Old Chief's prior conviction. This document disclosed that on December 18, 1988, he "did knowingly and unlawfully assault Rory Dean Fenner, said assault resulting in serious bodily injury," for which Old Chief was sentenced to five years' imprisonment. The jury found Old Chief guilty on all counts, and he appealed.

* * *

We granted Old Chief's petition for writ of certiorari because the Courts of Appeals have divided sharply in their treatment of defendants' efforts to exclude evidence of the names and natures of prior offenses in cases like this. . . . We now reverse the judgment of the Ninth Circuit.

II

A

As a threshold matter, there is Old Chief's erroneous argument that the name of his prior offense as contained in the record of conviction is irrelevant to the prior-conviction element, and for that reason inadmissible under Rule 402 of the Federal Rules of Evidence. Rule 401 defines relevant evidence as having "any tendency to make the existence of any fact that is of consequence to the determination of the action more probable or less probable than it would be without the evidence." Fed. Rule Evid. 401. To be sure, the fact that Old Chief's prior conviction was for assault resulting in serious bodily injury rather than, say, for theft was not itself an ultimate fact, as if the statute had specifically required proof of injurious assault. But its demonstration was a step on one evidentiary route to the ultimate fact, since it served to place Old Chief within a particular sub-class of offenders for whom firearms possession is outlawed by § 922(g)(1). A documentary record of the conviction for that named offense was thus relevant evidence in making Old Chief's § 922(g)(1) status more probable than it would have been without the evidence.

Nor was its evidentiary relevance under Rule 401 affected by the availability of alternative proofs of the element to which it went, such as an admission by Old Chief that he had been convicted of a crime "punishable by imprisonment for a term exceeding one year" within the meaning of the statute. The 1972 Advisory Committee Notes to Rule 401 make this point directly:

The fact to which the evidence is directed need not be in dispute. While situations will arise which call for the exclusion of evidence offered to prove a point conceded by the opponent, the ruling should be made on the basis of such considerations as waste of time and undue prejudice (*see* Rule 403), rather than under any general requirement that evidence is admissible only if directed to matters in dispute.

Advisory Committee's Notes on Fed. Rule Evid. 401, 28 U.S.C. App., p. 859.

*   *   *

B

The principal issue is the scope of a trial judge's discretion under Rule 403, which authorizes exclusion of relevant evidence when its "probative value is substantially outweighed by the danger of unfair prejudice, confusion of the issues, or misleading the jury, or by considerations of undue delay, waste of time, or needless presentation of cumulative evidence." Fed. Rule Evid. 403. Old Chief relies on the danger of unfair prejudice.

1

The term "unfair prejudice," as to a criminal defendant, speaks to the capacity of some concededly relevant evidence to lure the factfinder into declaring guilt on a ground different from proof specific to the offense charged. So, the Committee Notes to Rule 403 explain, " 'Unfair prejudice' within its context means an undue tendency to suggest decision on an improper basis, commonly, though not necessarily, an emotional one." Advisory Committee's Notes on Fed. Rule Evid. 403, 28 U.S.C. App., p. 860.

Such improper grounds certainly include the one that Old Chief points to here: generalizing a defendant's earlier bad act into bad character and taking that as raising the odds that he did the later bad act now charged . . . . As then-Judge Breyer put it, "Although . . . 'propensity evidence' is relevant, the risk that a jury will convict for crimes other than those charged — or that, uncertain of guilt, it will convict anyway because a bad person deserves punishment — creates a prejudicial effect that outweighs ordinary relevance." . . .

*   *   *

As for the analytical method to be used in Rule 403 balancing, two basic possibilities present themselves. An item of evidence might be viewed as an island, with estimates of its own probative value and unfairly prejudicial risk the sole reference points in deciding whether the danger substantially outweighs the value and whether the evidence ought to be excluded. Or the question of admissibility might be seen as inviting further comparisons to take account of the full evidentiary context of the case as the court understands it when the ruling must be made. This second approach would start out like the first but be ready to go further. On objection, the court would decide whether a particular item of evidence raised a danger of unfair prejudice. If it did, the judge would go on to evaluate the degrees of probative value and unfair prejudice not only for the item in question but for any actually available substitutes as well. If an alternative were found to have substantially the same or greater probative value but a lower danger of unfair prejudice, sound judicial discretion would discount the value of the item first offered and exclude it if its discounted probative value were substantially outweighed by unfairly prejudicial risk. As we will explain later on, the judge would have to make these calculations with an appreciation of the offering party's need for evidentiary richness and narrative integrity in presenting a case, and the mere fact that two pieces of evidence might go to the same point would not, of course, necessarily mean that only one of them might come in. It would only mean that a judge applying Rule 403 could reasonably apply some discount to the probative value of an item of evidence when faced with less risky alternative proof going to the same point. Even under this second approach, as we explain below, a defendant's Rule 403 objection offering to concede a point generally cannot prevail over the Government's choice to offer evidence showing guilt and all the circumstances surrounding the offense.

The first understanding of the rule is open to a very telling objection. That reading would leave the party offering evidence with the option to structure a trial in whatever way would produce the maximum unfair prejudice consistent with relevance. He could choose the available alternative carrying the greatest threat of improper influence, despite the availability of less prejudicial but equally probative evidence. The worst he would have to fear would be a ruling sustaining a Rule 403 objection, and if that occurred, he could simply fall back to offering substitute evidence. This would be a strange rule. It would be very odd for the law of evidence to recognize the danger of unfair prejudice only to confer such a degree of autonomy on the party subject to temptation, and the Rules of Evidence are not so odd.

Rather, a reading of the companions to Rule 403, and of the commentaries that went with them to Congress, makes it clear that what counts as the Rule 403 "probative value" of an item of evidence, as distinct from its Rule 401 "relevance," may be calculated by comparing evidentiary alternatives. The Committee Notes to Rule 401 explicitly say that a party's concession is pertinent to the court's discretion to exclude evidence on the point conceded. Such a concession, according to the Notes, will sometimes "call for the exclusion of evidence offered to prove [the] point conceded by the opponent . . . ." The Notes to Rule 403 then take up the point by stating that when a court considers "whether to exclude on grounds of unfair prejudice," the "availability of other means of proof may . . . be an appropriate factor." . . . Thus the notes leave no question that when Rule 403 confers discretion by providing that evidence "may" be excluded, the discretionary judgment may be informed not only by assessing an evidentiary item's twin tendencies, but by placing the result of that assessment alongside similar assessments of evidentiary alternatives. *See* 1 MCCORMICK 782, and n. 41 (suggesting that Rule 403's "probative value" signifies the "marginal probative value" of the evidence relative to the other evidence in the case); 22 C. WRIGHT & K. GRAHAM, FEDERAL PRACTICE AND PROCEDURE § 5250, pp. 546–47 (1978) ("The probative worth of any particular bit of evidence is obviously affected by the scarcity or abundance of other evidence on the same point").

2

In dealing with the specific problem raised by § 922(g)(1) and its prior-conviction element, there can be no question that evidence of the name or nature of the prior offense generally carries a risk of unfair prejudice to the defendant. . . . Where a prior conviction was for a gun crime or one similar to other charges in a pending case the risk of unfair prejudice would be especially obvious, and Old Chief sensibly worried that the prejudicial effect of his prior assault conviction, significant enough with respect to the current gun charges alone, would take on added weight from the related assault charge against him.

The District Court was also presented with alternative, relevant, admissible evidence of the prior conviction by Old Chief's offer to stipulate . . . .

Old Chief's proffered admission would, in fact, have been not merely relevant but seemingly conclusive evidence of the element. The statutory language in which the prior-conviction requirement is couched shows no congressional concern with the specific name or nature of the prior offense beyond what is necessary to place it within the broad category of qualifying felonies, and Old Chief clearly meant to admit that his felony did qualify, by stipulating "that the Government has proven one of the essential elements of the offense." As a consequence, although the name of the prior offense may have been technically relevant, it addressed no detail in the definition of the prior-conviction element that would not have been covered by the stipulation or admission. Logic, then, seems to side with Old Chief.

3

There is, however, one more question to be considered before deciding whether Old Chief's offer was to supply evidentiary value at least equivalent to what the Government's own evidence carried. In arguing that the stipulation or admission would not have carried equivalent value, the Government invokes the familiar, standard rule that the prosecution is entitled to prove its case by evidence of its own choice, or, more exactly, that a criminal defendant may not stipulate or admit his way out of the full evidentiary force of the case as the government chooses to present it. The authority usually cited for this rule is *Parr v. United States*, 255 F.2d 86 (5th Cir.), *cert. denied*, 358 U.S. 824 (1958), in which the Fifth Circuit explained that the "reason for the rule is to permit a party 'to present to the jury a picture of the events relied upon. To substitute for such a picture a naked admission might have the effect to rob the evidence of much of its fair and legitimate weight.'"

This is unquestionably true as a general matter. The "fair and legitimate weight" of conventional evidence showing individual thoughts and acts amounting to a crime reflects the fact that making a case with testimony and tangible things not only satisfies the formal definition of an offense, but tells a colorful story with descriptive richness. Unlike an abstract premise, whose force depends on going precisely to a particular step in a course of reasoning, a piece of evidence may address any number of separate elements, striking hard just because it shows so much at once; the account of a shooting that establishes capacity and causation may tell just as much about the triggerman's motive and intent. Evidence thus has force beyond any linear scheme of reasoning, and as its pieces come together a narrative gains momentum, with power not only to support conclusions but to sustain the willingness of jurors to draw the inferences, whatever they may be, necessary to reach an honest verdict. This persuasive power of the concrete and particular is often essential to the capacity of jurors to satisfy the obligations that the law places on them. Jury duty is usually unsought and sometimes resisted, and it may be as difficult for one juror suddenly to face the findings that can send another human being to prison, as it is for another to hold out conscientiously for acquittal. When a juror's duty does seem hard, the evidentiary account of what a defendant has thought and done can accomplish what no set of abstract statements ever could, not just to prove a fact but to establish its human significance, and so to implicate the law's moral underpinnings and a juror's obligation to sit in judgment. Thus, the prosecution may fairly seek to place its evidence before the jurors, as much to tell a story of guiltiness as to support an inference of guilt, to convince the jurors that a guilty verdict would be morally reasonable as much as to point to the discrete elements of a defendant's legal fault.

But there is something even more to the prosecution's interest in resisting efforts to replace the evidence of its choice with admissions and stipulations, for beyond the power of conventional evidence to support allegations and give life to the moral underpinnings of law's claims, there lies the need for evidence in all its particularity to satisfy the jurors' expectations about what proper proof should be. Some such demands they bring with them to the courthouse, assuming, for example, that a charge of using a firearm to commit an offense will be proven by introducing a gun in evidence. A prosecutor who fails to produce one, or some good reason for his failure, has something to be concerned about. "If [jurors'] expectations are not satisfied, triers of fact may penalize the party who disappoints them by drawing a negative inference against that party." Saltzburg, *A Special Aspect of Relevance: Countering Negative Inferences Associated with the Absence of Evidence*, 66 CAL. L. REV. 1011, 1019 (1978) (footnotes omitted).[14]

Expectations may also arise in jurors' minds simply from the experience of a trial itself. The use of witnesses to describe a train of events naturally related can raise the prospect of learning about every ingredient of that natural sequence the same way. If suddenly the prosecution presents some occurrence in the series differently, as by announcing a stipulation or admission, the effect may be like saying, "never mind what's behind the door," and jurors may well wonder what they are being kept from knowing. A party seemingly responsible for cloaking something has reason for apprehension, and the prosecution with its burden of proof may prudently demur at

---

[14] [9] *Cf.* Green, *"The Whole Truth?": How Rules of Evidence Make Lawyers Deceitful*, 25 LOYOLA (LA) L. REV. 699, 703 (1992) ("[E]videntiary rules . . . predicated in large measure on the law's distrust of juries [can] have the unintended, and perhaps ironic, result of encouraging the jury's distrust of lawyers. The rules do so by fostering the perception that lawyers are deliberately withholding evidence" (footnote omitted)). The fact that juries have expectations as to what evidence ought to be presented by a party, and may well hold the absence of that evidence against the party, is also recognized in the case law of the Fifth Amendment, which explicitly supposes that, despite the venerable history of the privilege against self-incrimination, jurors may not recall that someone accused of crime need not explain the evidence or avow innocence beyond making his plea. The assumption that jurors may have contrary expectations and be moved to draw adverse inferences against the party who disappoints them undergirds the rule that a defendant can demand an instruction forbidding the jury from drawing such an inference.

a defense request to interrupt the flow of evidence telling the story in the usual way.

In sum, the accepted rule that the prosecution is entitled to prove its case free from any defendant's option to stipulate the evidence away rests on good sense. . . .

4

This recognition that the prosecution with its burden of persuasion needs evidentiary depth to tell a continuous story has, however, virtually no application when the point at issue is a defendant's legal status, dependent on some judgment rendered wholly independently of the concrete events of later criminal behavior charged against him. As in this case, the choice of evidence for such an element is usually not between eventful narrative and abstract proposition, but between propositions of slightly varying abstraction, either a record saying that conviction for some crime occurred at a certain time or a statement admitting the same thing without naming the particular offense. The issue of substituting one statement for the other normally arises only when the record of conviction would not be admissible for any purpose beyond proving status, so that excluding it would not deprive the prosecution of evidence with multiple utility. . . . Nor can it be argued that the events behind the prior conviction are proper nourishment for the jurors' sense of obligation to vindicate the public interest. The issue is not whether concrete details of the prior crime should come to the jurors' attention but whether the name or general character of that crime is to be disclosed. Congress, however, has made it plain that distinctions among generic felonies do not count for this purpose; the fact of the qualifying conviction is alone what matters under the statute. "A defendant falls within the category simply by virtue of past conviction for any [qualifying] crime ranging from possession of short lobsters to the most aggravated murder." The most the jury needs to know is that the conviction admitted by the defendant falls within the class of crimes that Congress thought should bar a convict from possessing a gun, and this point may be made readily in a defendant's admission and underscored in the court's jury instructions. Finally, the most obvious reason that the general presumption that the prosecution may choose its evidence is so remote from application here is that proof of the defendant's status goes to an element entirely outside the natural sequence of what the defendant is charged with thinking and doing to commit the current offense. Proving status without telling exactly why that status was imposed leaves no gap in the story of a defendant's subsequent criminality, and its demonstration by stipulation or admission neither displaces a chapter from a continuous sequence of conventional evidence nor comes across as an officious substitution, to confuse or offend or provoke reproach.

Given these peculiarities of the element of felony-convict status and of admissions and the like when used to prove it, there is no cognizable difference between the evidentiary significance of an admission and of the legitimately probative component of the official record the prosecution would prefer to place in evidence. For purposes of the Rule 403 weighing of the probative against the prejudicial, the functions of the competing evidence are distinguishable only by the risk inherent in the one and wholly absent from the other. In this case, as in any other in which the prior conviction is for an offense likely to support conviction on some improper ground, the only reasonable conclusion was that the risk of unfair prejudice did substantially outweigh the discounted probative value of the record of conviction, and it was an abuse of discretion to admit the record when an admission was available. What we have said shows why this will be the general rule when proof of convict status is at issue, just as the prosecutor's choice will generally survive a Rule 403 analysis when a defendant seeks to force the substitution of an admission for evidence creating a coherent narrative of his thoughts and actions in perpetrating the offense for which he is being tried.

[handwritten margin note: general rule for proof of convict]

The judgment is reversed, and the case is remanded to the Ninth Circuit for further proceedings consistent with this opinion.

It is so ordered.

UNITED STATES v. McVEIGH
153 F.3d 1166 (10th Cir. 1998)

EBEL, CIRCUIT JUDGE.

Defendant-appellant Timothy J. McVeigh ("McVeigh") was tried, convicted, and sentenced to death on eleven counts stemming from the bombing of the Alfred P. Murrah Federal Building ("Murrah Building") in Oklahoma City, Oklahoma, that resulted in the deaths of 168 people. McVeigh appeals his conviction . . . [on numerous grounds including] that . . . (C) the district court erred by excluding evidence that someone else may have been guilty, . . . [and] (E) the district court erred by admitting victim impact testimony during the guilt phase of trial. . . . We affirm.

BACKGROUND

At 9:02 in the morning of April 19, 1995, a massive explosion tore apart the Murrah Building in Oklahoma City, Oklahoma, killing a total of 168 people and injuring hundreds more. On August 10, 1995, a federal grand jury returned an eleven-count indictment against McVeigh and Terry Lynn Nichols ("Nichols") charging: one count of conspiracy to use a weapon of mass destruction in violation of 18 U.S.C. § 2332a and 18 U.S.C. § 2(a) & (b); one count of use of a weapon of mass destruction in violation of 18 U.S.C. § 2332a and 18 U.S.C. § 2(a) & (b); one count of destruction by explosives in violation of and 18 U.S.C. § 2(a) & (b); and eight counts of first-degree murder in violation of 18 U.S.C. § 1111 & 1114 and 18 U.S.C. § 2(a) & (b). . . .

* * *

At the guilt phase of trial, which encompassed twenty-three days of testimony, the government proved the following set of facts.[15] Fifteen children in the Murrah Building day care center, visible from the front of the building, and four children visiting the building were included among the victims. Eight federal law enforcement officials also lost their lives. The explosion, felt and heard six miles away, tore

---

[15] [1] The destruction of the Murrah Building killed 163 people in the building and five people outside.

a gaping hole into the front of the Murrah Building and covered the streets with glass, debris, rocks, and chunks of concrete. Emergency workers who reported to the scene made heroic efforts to rescue people still trapped in the building.

The Murrah Building was destroyed by a 3,000–6,000 pound bomb comprised of an ammonium nitrate-based explosive carried inside a rented Ryder truck. In the fall of 1994, McVeigh and Nichols sought, bought, and stole all the materials needed to construct the bomb. First, on September 30, 1994, and October 18, 1994, McVeigh purchased a total of 4,000 pounds of ammonium nitrate from the McPherson branch of the Mid-Kansas Cooperative using the alias "Mike Havens." Second, in October of 1994, McVeigh and Nichols stole seven cases of Tovex explosives and a box of Primadet non-electric blasting caps from the Martin Marietta rock quarry near Marion, Kansas. Third, on October 21, 1994, McVeigh purchased three drums of nitromethane at a race track outside of Dallas, Texas. Prior to the nitromethane purchase, McVeigh had sought bomb ingredients, including nitromethane, both in person and through the use of a prepaid telephone calling card under the name "Daryl Bridges." Using various aliases, McVeigh and Nichols rented a number of storage lockers in Kansas where they stored the bomb components. In order to fund their conspiracy, McVeigh and Nichols robbed a gun dealer in Arkansas in November of 1994.

In a letter to Michael and Lori Fortier written around September of 1994, McVeigh disclosed that he and Terry Nichols had decided to take some type of positive offensive action against the federal government in response to the government's siege of the Branch Davidians in Waco, Texas in 1993. On a subsequent visit to their home, McVeigh told the Fortiers that he planned to blow up a federal building. McVeigh later informed the Fortiers that he wanted to cause a general uprising in America and that the bombing would occur on the anniversary of the end of the Waco siege. McVeigh rationalized the inevitable loss of life by concluding that anyone who worked in the federal building was guilty by association with those responsible for Waco.

McVeigh stated that he had figured out how to make a truck into a bomb using fifty-five-gallon drums filled with ammonium nitrate combined with explosives stolen from the quarry. McVeigh demonstrated the shaped charge he intended to use for the bomb by arranging soup cans on the floor in the same triangle shape in which he was going to place fifty-five-gallon barrels filled with ammonium nitrate combined with nitromethane in the truck. McVeigh also diagramed the truck, barrels, and fusing system on a piece of paper, and stated that he intended to use a Ryder truck. McVeigh told the Fortiers that he chose the Murrah Building as the target because he believed that (1) the orders for the attack at Waco emanated from the building, (2) the building housed people involved in the Waco raid, and (3) the building's U-shape and glass front made it an easy target. On a later trip through Oklahoma City, McVeigh showed Michael Fortier the Murrah Building, asking Fortier whether he thought a twenty-foot rental truck would fit in front of the building.

Also, towards the end of 1994, McVeigh typed a number of letters discussing the justified use of violence against federal agents as retaliation for the events in Waco. McVeigh told his sister and one of his friends that he had moved from the propaganda stage to the action stage in his dispute with the federal government. McVeigh then warned his sister that "something big" was going to happen in April, and asked her to extend her April 1995 Florida vacation. He also instructed her not to write to him any more lest she incriminate herself. The manner in which the bombing was carried out closely tracked several books bought by McVeigh, which he often encouraged his friends to read, describing how to make a powerful bomb mixing ammonium nitrate with nitromethane and romanticizing self-declared patriots who blow up federal buildings. McVeigh was familiar with explosives and had detonated a pipe bomb prior to the attack on the Murrah Building.

From April 14 to 18, 1995, McVeigh stayed at the Dreamland Motel located in Junction City, Kansas. On April 14, 1995, McVeigh purchased a 1977 yellow Mercury Marquis from Junction City Firestone in Junction City, Kansas. While waiting to take possession of the car from the dealer, McVeigh made a phone call using the Bridges calling card to Elliott's Body Shop ("Elliott's") in Junction City, Kansas, seeking a twenty-foot Ryder truck for a one-way rental to Omaha. McVeigh also called Nichols.

During the search of the blast site, the FBI located the rear axle of the Ryder truck used to carry the bomb. The vehicle identification number from the axle matched that of the Ryder truck rented to McVeigh by Elliott's on April 15, 1995, and picked up by McVeigh two days prior to the blast. McVeigh rented the truck under the name "Robert Kling" using a phony South Dakota driver's license that Lori Fortier had helped McVeigh create.

McVeigh drove to Oklahoma City in the rented Ryder truck, which he had made into a bomb, parking the vehicle in front of the Murrah Building and running to the yellow Mercury that he and Nichols had stashed as a getaway car in a nearby alley a couple of days before the bombing. A Ford key fitting the Ryder truck was found in an alley near where McVeigh had told Michael Fortier that the getaway car would be parked. McVeigh hand-printed a sign inside the yellow Mercury, "Not Abandoned; Please do not tow; will move by April 23 (Needs Battery & Cable)." McVeigh deliberately parked the car so that a building would stand between the car and the blast, shielding McVeigh from the explosion. The bomb then exploded.

Just 77 minutes after the blast, Oklahoma State Trooper Charles Hanger ("Hanger") stopped the yellow Mercury driven by McVeigh because the car had no license tags. . . .

Hanger arrested McVeigh upon discovering that he was carrying a concealed, loaded gun. . . . An FBI test performed later found that McVeigh's clothing and the earplugs contained explosives residue, including PETN, EGDN, and nitroglycerine — chemicals associated with the materials used in the construction of the bomb.

A subsequent inventory search of the yellow Mercury uncovered a sealed envelope containing documents arguing that the federal government had commenced open warfare on the liberty of the American people and justifying the killing of government officials in the defense of liberty. Finally, three days after the arrest, Hanger found a Paulsen's Military Supply business card on the floor of his cruiser bearing McVeigh's fingerprints. McVeigh had written on the back of the card, "TNT at $ 5/stick Need more" and "Call After 01, May, See if I can get some more."

Closing arguments were made on May 29, 1997, and the district court charged the jury on May 30, 1997. On June 2, 1997, after four days of deliberations, the jury returned guilty verdicts on all eleven counts charged in the Indictment. The penalty phase of trial commenced on June 4, 1997, and concluded with summations and jury instructions on June 12, 1997. The jury deliberated for two days before returning special findings recommending that McVeigh be sentenced to death. After denying McVeigh's motion for a new trial, the district court accepted the jury recommendation on August 14, 1997, sentencing McVeigh to death on all eleven counts. . . .

* * *

C. EVIDENCE OF ALLEGED ALTERNATIVE PERPETRATORS

McVeigh challenges the district court's decision to exclude two lines of evidence that McVeigh argues would suggest that persons connected with a white-supremacist, anti-government organization in Stillwell, Oklahoma, known as "Elohim City," were involved in the conspiracy to destroy the Murrah Building. McVeigh contends that the district court abused its discretion when it excluded as "not sufficiently relevant" both the proffered testimony from Carol Howe ("Howe"), an undercover government informant at Elohim City, and other proffered evidence that McVeigh argues would have shown the government suspended its independent investigation of Elohim City in the wake of McVeigh's arrest.

McVeigh argues that this ruling was based solely on the relevance standard of Rule 401. The government, however, argues that the court's ruling incorporates both the relevance standard of Rule 401 and the balancing required in Rule 403. The text of the court's ruling appears to favor the government's position, indicating that the court found some "relevance" under Rule 401, but not enough to be "sufficient" under Rule 403.

1. Standard of review

Generally, we review a district court's ruling on the relevance and potential prejudice of proffered evidence under the abuse-of-discretion standard. . . . Furthermore, this circuit has never found a per se abuse of discretion simply because a trial court failed to make explicit, on-the-record findings for a decision under Federal other than when the disputed evidence is offered pursuant to one of the specialized character evidence rules. *See generally Navarro de Cosme v. Hospital Pavia,* 922 F.2d 926, 931 (1st Cir. 1991) (explaining that "it is understood that in Rule 403 decisions explicit findings need not always be made") (quotation omitted); 22 Charles Alan Wright & Kenneth W. Graham, Jr., Federal Practice & Procedure § 5224, at 321 (1978) (noting that on-the-record findings are not required by Rule 403, but encouraged by commentators). . . .

Although the trial court should, of course, always make explicit findings to support its Rule 403 rulings, there may be occasions when the record is such that we can do our own de novo balancing of the Rule 403 factors without requiring a remand of that issue to the district court. Here, the district court failed to make an explicit record of its balancing of the Rule 403 factors. However, we may conduct a de novo balancing because the record contains a colloquy between the court and counsel that sheds considerable light on how the district court viewed the evidence. We conclude that even if there was probative value to McVeigh's proffered evidence, it was "substantially outweighed by the danger of unfair prejudice, confusion of the issues, or misleading the jury. . . ." *See* Fed. R. Evid. 403. Thus, there was no error in excluding such evidence.

2. Background

Near the end of the trial's guilt phase, McVeigh's defense counsel made an oral proffer . . . concerning the defense's evidence of alternative perpetrators. This proffer focused on Howe's expected testimony concerning her various visits to Elohim City in 1994–1995.

Howe allegedly would have testified that during her trips to Elohim City, she met Dennis Mahon ("Mahon"), one of Elohim City's leaders, and that Mahon was a violent opponent of the federal government. Howe would have testified that Mahon instructed her in the preparation of napalm and had shown her various bomb components at Elohim City, including a tap, green fuse, black powder, bolts, a funnel, and a grenade shell. Mahon also discussed the availability and cost of the explosive Semtex, as well as his experience in building and exploding a 500-pound ammonium nitrate bomb under a truck in Michigan.

Howe's proffered testimony also promised to discuss Andreas Strassmeir ("Strassmeir"), another leader at Elohim City, who allegedly discussed acquiring bomb components for Elohim City. Howe was to testify that Mahon and Strassmeir had discussed targeting a federal building in either Oklahoma City or Tulsa, or an IRS building. Howe also was to testify about the appearance at Elohim City in the spring of 1995 of James Ellison, who had developed plans to bomb the Murrah Building in 1983 before he was imprisoned on unrelated charges. Furthermore, Howe would have testified about the affinity of the Elohim City members for the people killed in the government's siege of the Branch Davidian compound in Waco, Texas. Finally, two days after the bombing, Howe told federal agents that she allegedly had seen two brothers at Elohim City before the bombing who resembled the composite drawings of "John Doe 1" and "John Doe 2," the suspects originally sought by the government in the immediate aftermath of the bombing.[16]

*   *   *

McVeigh contends that this proffered evidence was relevant to . . . [prove] that there were other perpetrators of the bombing . . . .

After hearing the proffer, the district court ruled, "Well, we've had a number of disclosures concerning Mahon, Strassmeir, Elohim City and now some additional

---

[16] [11] The government responded that it had followed up Howe's report of seeing the "John Doe" suspects, and its investigators concluded that these brothers were not involved in the Oklahoma City bombing.

information from Carol Howe. But my ruling is that it's excluded, not sufficiently relevant to be admissible."

3. Analysis

a. Relevance under Rule 401

Under the Federal Rules of Evidence, "all relevant evidence is admissible," subject to the limitations provided by the Federal Rules and other laws; any evidence "which is not relevant is not admissible." *See* Fed. R. Evid. 402. Thus, the threshold to admissibility is relevance. The scope of relevancy is bounded only by the liberal standard of Rule 401, which provides that evidence is relevant if it has "any tendency to make the existence of any fact that is of consequence to the determination of the action more probable or less probable than it would be without the evidence." *See* Fed. R. Evid. 401. As commentators have noted, Rule 401's definition of relevancy incorporates notions of both materiality and probativity. *See* 1 Kenneth S. Broun, et al., *McCormick on Evidence* § 185, at 774–75 (John William Strong ed., 4th ed. 1992); Wright & Graham, *supra*, §§ 5164, 5165, at 37–38, 48–50.

As for materiality, under Rule 401 a fact is "of consequence" when its existence would provide the fact-finder with a basis for making some inference, or chain of inferences, about an issue that is necessary to a verdict. *See* Wright & Graham, *supra*, § 5164, at 42–43. As for the degree of probative value required under Rule 401, the rule sets the bar very low. . . . The rule establishes that even a minimal degree of probability — *i.e.*, "any tendency" — that the asserted fact exists is sufficient to find the proffered evidence relevant. *See* Fed. R. Evid. 401. The Advisory Committee explained that the "any tendency" language establishes that the "standard of probability under the rule is 'more . . . probable than it would be without the evidence.'" *See id.* Adv. Comm. Notes (1972 Proposed Rules) (quoting Fed. R. Evid. 401).

b. Balancing under Rule 403

Even though evidence may meet the relevancy standard of Rule 401, a trial court still may exclude it on the grounds that its probative value — the evidence's probability of establishing a fact of consequence — is "substantially outweighed" by certain negative factors. *See* Fed. R. Evid. 403. Those factors include "unfair prejudice," "confusion of the issues," and "misleading the jury." *See id.*

The danger of "unfair prejudice" under Rule 403 is not simply the tendency of evidence to undermine a party's position. Rather, the prejudice that is "unfair" is prejudice arising from the tendency of proffered evidence to suggest to the jury that it should render its findings "on an improper basis, commonly, though not necessarily, an emotional one." *See* Fed. R. Evid. 403, Adv. Comm. Notes (1972 Proposed Rules).

The danger of "confusion of the issues" and "misleading the jury" arises when circumstantial evidence would tend to sidetrack the jury into consideration of factual disputes only tangentially related to the facts at issue in the current case.

. . . The classic explanation of this danger comes from Dean Wigmore: "The notion here is that, in attempting to dispute or explain away the evidence thus offered, new issues will arise as to the occurrence of the instances and the similarity of conditions, [and] new witnesses will be needed whose cross examination and impeachment may lead to further issues." 2 JOHN HENRY WIGMORE, EVIDENCE § 443, at 528–29 (James H. Chadbourn rev., 1979).

In the course of weighing probative value and adverse dangers, courts must be sensitive to the special problems presented by "alternative perpetrator" evidence. Although there is no doubt that a defendant has a right to attempt to establish his innocence by showing that someone else did the crime, a defendant still must show that his proffered evidence on the alleged alternative perpetrator is sufficient, on its own or in combination with other evidence in the record, to show a nexus between the crime charged and the asserted "alternative perpetrator." *See Matthews v. Price*, 83 F.3d 328, 332 (10th Cir. 1996). It is not sufficient for a defendant merely to offer up unsupported speculation that another person may have done the crime. Such speculative blaming intensifies the grave risk of jury confusion, and it invites the jury to render its findings based on emotion or prejudice.

Finally, after identifying the degree of probative value and adverse danger, courts exclude relevant evidence if the adverse dangers "substantially outweigh" the probative value. *See* Fed. R. Evid. 403.

c. Admissibility of Carol Howe's proffered testimony

Even if we assume that the proffered evidence had some marginal relevance, the Howe testimony cannot survive the balancing under Rule 403. First, we conclude that the probative value of such proffered testimony was slight because of its highly generalized and speculative nature. The fact that another group held similar anti-government views as did McVeigh and that some of its members expressed vague threats to bomb a variety of potential targets in Oklahoma, possibly including a federal building in Oklahoma City, says very little about whether this group actually bombed the Murrah Building. That others shared McVeigh's political views is a slender reed upon which to vault the dangers of unfair prejudice and jury confusion. Howe's alleged identification of "John Doe 1" and "John Doe 2" arguably increases the probative value of her other testimony. However, the composite sketches included no particular identifying features that would strengthen the significance of Howe's allegation of two matches. In fact, there are undoubtedly thousands of men across America who resembled the government's composite sketches. Finally, there was no evidence in this proffer, or in the record, that would establish a probative nexus between the alleged Elohim City conspiracy and the bombing of the Murrah Building.

In the face of the speculative probative value of Howe's testimony, we must confront the very real dangers of unfair prejudice and confusion of the issues. The Howe testimony presented a great threat of "confusion of the issues" because it would have forced the government to attempt to disprove the nebulous allegation that Elohim City was involved in the bombing. This side trial would have led the jury astray, turning the focus away from whether McVeigh — the only person whose actions were on trial — bombed the Murrah Building. It also presented a threat of "unfair prejudice" as it would invite the jury to blame absent, unrepresented individuals and groups for whom there often may be strong underlying emotional responses.

Thus, the district court did not err in excluding this testimony.

E. GUILT PHASE VICTIM TESTIMONY

The government presented a number of witnesses during the guilt phase of the trial who identified deceased victims of the blast and described the impact of the explosion, including the carnage and destruction caused by the bombing. McVeigh divides this testimony into four categories: (a) detailed personal and professional histories of the witnesses; (b) accounts of witness activities prior to the explosion; (c) accounts of the explosion and its immediate aftermath as experienced or observed by the witnesses; and (d) long-term impacts of the bombing. McVeigh argues that the district court erred by admitting this testimony under Federal Rule of Evidence 403 and that the introduction of the testimony unconstitutionally allowed passion to overwhelm reason in the jury's determination of guilt.

1. Standard of Review

a. Rule 403

The admission of evidence under Federal Rules of Evidence 401 and 403 generally is reviewed for an abuse of discretion. . . . McVeigh argues that we should adopt a more exacting standard of review because of the heightened concern for reliability in death penalty cases . . . . We reject this contention.

. . . Appeals courts . . . have . . . appl[ied] a traditional abuse of discretion standard of review to discretionary rulings by a trial judge in a capital case. . . .

b. Continuing Objections and Plain Error Review

McVeigh first challenged the victim evidence at issue during a lunch break midway through the testimony of Hunt, the fifth victim witness, by objecting to "extensive conversations and things not related to what the witness saw, heard, experienced during the relevant time period." The district court granted McVeigh a "continuing objection" to testimony dealing with the "long-range effects" of the bombing that went beyond the "immediate effects" of the blast.[17]

---

[17] [23] The objection was made in the following manner:

    THE COURT: Mr. Nigh [counsel for McVeigh], did you have something before the jury returns?

    MR. NIGH: I did, your Honor. I wanted to interpose an objection to testimony in the nature of victim impact evidence during the first stage. It's my understanding that two of the witnesses coming up are also witnesses in the second stage; and rather than interrupt during the examination, I wanted to impose — or interpose the objection now.

    THE COURT: What are you characterizing as victim impact? The type of testimony we've had from this witness and also from Mr. Norfleet?

Because McVeigh made no objections to the testimony of the first four witnesses (Lou Klaver, Michael Norfleet, Phil Monahan, and Richard Williams), we review the admission of that testimony for plain error. *See United States v. McDonald*, 933 F.2d 1519, 1524 (10th Cir. 1991). Similarly, we review for plain error that portion of Susan Hunt's testimony presented before McVeigh lodged his continuing objection.

We have serious doubts as to whether McVeigh's continuing objection was a proper form of objection for the victim testimony that followed. In certain circumstances, a continuing objection has been allowed as a specific, timely objection under Federal Rule of Evidence 103. . . .

However, continuing objections generally are considered inappropriate for preserving error on appeal under Rule 403. In *United States v. Mangiameli*, 668 F.2d 1172, 1177 (10th Cir. 1982), this court cautioned that "in our view, the considerations bearing upon a decision whether to admit or exclude evidence under Rules 404(b) and 403 are sufficiently complex that ordinarily neither counsel nor the trial court should rely on a standing objection with respect to evidence coming within the purview of these rules." *See also People v. Smith*, 155 Cal. App. 3d 1103, 203 Cal. Rptr. 196, 231 (Cal. Ct. App. 1984). *But see United States v. Gomez-Norena*, 908 F.2d 497, 500 n.2 (9th Cir. 1990) (allowing continuing objection under Rule 404(b)); *Ladd*, 885 F.2d at 958 (allowing continuing objection under Rule 403).

We believe that the question of whether a continuing objection under Rule 403 was effective to preserve the objection for later testimony should be reviewed under the same standards used for determining whether a pretrial motion in limine to exclude evidence preserved an objection to later-admitted evidence. A motion in limine will not preserve an objection if it is not renewed at the time the evidence is introduced unless "the issue (1) is fairly presented to the district court, (2) is the type of issue that can be finally decided in a pretrial hearing, and (3) is ruled upon without equivocation by the trial judge. . . . Most objections will prove to be dependent on trial context and will be determined to be waived if not renewed at trial." *United States v. Mejia-Alarcon*, 995 F.2d 982, 986–88 (10th Cir. 1993) (citations omitted). McVeigh never identified specific statements that he believed were unduly prejudicial. Given the sheer number of witnesses involved and the variety of factual contexts presented, the admissibility of victim testimony would not ordinarily be an issue that could be decided in a pretrial hearing or by means of a continuing objection.[18]

MR. NIGH: Yes, your honor. Some of the previous witnesses, in terms of extensive conversations and things not related to what the witness saw, heard, experienced during the relevant time period.

THE COURT: Well, I haven't considered that we've gone beyond the bounds of what the immediate effects were; so as long as we're staying with the immediate effects and not the long-range effects, I think it's permissible; and you can have a continuing objection to it.

[18] [24] Before trial, McVeigh offered to stipulate to the identity of all the persons killed in the bombing, that all died as a result of the bombing, and that the eight federal law enforcement officers who were the subject of the individual murder counts in the indictment were killed while engaged in the performance of their duties. Relying on *Old Chief v. United States*, 519 U.S. 172, 117 S. Ct. 644, 136 L. Ed. 2d 574 (1997), McVeigh filed a pretrial motion in limine to compel acceptance of the proposed stipulation and to exclude evidence offered by the government to prove the facts included in the

Nevertheless, in this case the district court explicitly granted a continuing objection to McVeigh on this issue. Thus, we feel it would be unfair to hold that McVeigh could not rely on his continuing objection. As a result, we review for abuse of discretion the district court's decision to admit testimony covered by McVeigh's continuing objection. However, "a standing objection should not be given broader scope than is found in its establishing statement." . . . A party may not rely on a continuing objection lodged on one evidentiary ground to argue a different ground for exclusion on appeal. . . . Thus, our abuse-of-discretion review is restricted to evidence within the scope of McVeigh's objection, as ruled on by the district court. The court's ruling allowed testimony regarding the "immediate effects" but "not the long-range effects" of the bombing. The continuing objection does not fairly cover witness histories, pre-explosion witness activities, or descriptions of the bombing and its immediate aftermath, and thus we review claims of error pertaining to those categories of testimony only under a plain error standard. We also review for abuse of discretion the decision by the district court overruling a specific objection lodged by McVeigh to Garrett's testimony describing the activities of the children present at the Murrah Building day care center before the explosion.

2. Relevance Versus Prejudice

McVeigh concedes in his brief on appeal that the challenged testimony was relevant, although he argues that it was only minimally so. He also concedes that ascertaining the line between factual and emotional descriptions of the bombing "is not always an easy task, and Mr. McVeigh's counsel were faced with the very difficult task of discerning when the testimony crossed the line sufficiently to object." However, McVeigh focuses his argument on the claim that the challenged victim testimony was so laden with emotionally prejudicial content that its admission violated Rule 403 and created a significant risk that the jury reached its verdict based on emotion rather than reason. Having reviewed the record, we find no plain error in the introduction of any of the guilt phase victim testimony challenged by McVeigh on appeal. Even if the district court abused its discretion in allowing the introduction of certain long-range-impact testimony during the guilt phase, we hold such error would be harmless.

a. Personal Histories

McVeigh identifies the following personal history testimony as objectionable: Norfleet's description of his career as a Marine Corps pilot in Desert Storm and various drug interdiction missions and the irony of his decision to accept a recruiting job in Oklahoma in order to placate his wife's desire that he avoid

---

stipulation as overly prejudicial under Federal Rule of Evidence 403. The district court denied McVeigh's motion.

McVeigh argues that his motion in limine preserved a Rule 403 objection to the challenged testimony. We disagree. "Fact-bound determinations dependent upon the character of the evidence introduced at trial" are inappropriate for final disposition through motions in limine. *Mejia-Alarcon*, 995 F.2d at 987. In addition, McVeigh's motion in limine only objected to testimony identifying the victims and the cause of death — the very testimony McVeigh concedes on appeal was "appropriately admitted" — and did not seek to exclude other evidence under Rule 403.

dangerous combat duty; Hunt's pre-continuing objection testimony about her educational and employment history and her reference to her "grandchild and beautiful daughter-in-law and an almost second daughter-in-law"; Helena Garrett's explanation for the reason that her son was in the day care center; Donna Weaver's description of her deceased husband's involvement in their sons' sports teams and her regular lunches and meetings with him downtown; and Dr. Brian Espe's, Capt. Lawrence Martin's, and Mike Shannon's detailed highlights of their personal and professional histories. McVeigh complains that this testimony "allowed the jury to get to know [the witnesses] as individuals and to be more receptive to the stories that followed." However, reasonable background information about a witness is always admissible, precisely because it allows the jury to make better informed judgments about the credibility of a witness and the reliability of that witness' observations. *See* 2 JACK B. WEINSTEIN & MARGARET A. BERGER, WEINSTEIN'S FEDERAL EVIDENCE ¶ 401.04[4][a], at 401–37 (Joseph M. McLaughlin, ed., 1997). The evidence McVeigh challenges served this proper purpose. The defense asked similar personal history questions during direct examination of its witnesses. The personalization of witnesses through descriptions of their individual histories is inevitable. Although personalizing a witness can be overdone, the question of whether the district court erred in this case is not even close. We find no error by the district court under either an abuse of discretion or plain error review.

b. Pre-Explosion Activities

McVeigh challenges the following pre-explosion activity testimony: Norfleet's attendance at a "leadership prayer breakfast" the morning of the blast; Hunt's pre-continuing objection description of her encounters with various co-workers who died in the explosion, including one ordering the flowers for her wedding, one who offered her candy, and one who diligently made coffee; Garrett's recollection of her son Tevin's endearing interactions with his sister and of Tevin's tears when Garrett dropped him off at the day care center and the efforts of other children to console him; Martin's notation that Sergeant Bill Titsworth was killed because he chose the day of the blast as his first day of work even though he could have reported for work any other day over the next two weeks; and Regina Bonny's account of her reaction to ultrasound pictures brought in by Carrie Lenz, a pregnant co-worker who died in the blast.

. . . [T]his testimony was proper. This evidence places the witnesses at the scene of the crime, demonstrates how they knew the deceased victims, and sets a foundation for their testimony describing the explosion, identifying the specific location of deceased victims in the building before the explosion, and explaining why individual victims were present in the building. . . . The testimony allowed the jury to evaluate the accuracy of each witness' memory and determine whether the related details formed a consistent whole. For example, Norfleet's testimony about his attendance at a prayer breakfast explains why he came to the Murrah Building the day of the explosion (he generally did not work at the building) and why he took a specific route to the building that allowed him to notice the Ryder truck parked out front. The evidence also formed part of the res gestae of the crime, providing proof that the bomb interfered with interstate commerce and with government officials performing government business. . . .

In only one case do we find any potential prejudice: Bonny's testimony about the ultrasound pictures shown by Carrie Lenz. Nevertheless, the testimony was in response to a single question, and Bonny's answer comprised less than four lines out of fourteen pages of testimony. The prejudicial effect of the evidence did not substantially outweigh its relevance. Thus, we find no plain error. Even if we were to review the admission of the testimony under an abuse-of-discretion standard, we still would find no error.

c. Immediate Impacts

McVeigh challenges almost all of the testimony presented on this subject by the various witnesses,[19] including, for example: Norfleet's loss of his eye, fractured skull, and near-death experience, and his description of following a trail of blood out of the building; Hunt's post-continuing objection account of assisting a survivor who had lost an eye but who had not yet realized it and helping hold parents back as rescue workers brought out dead children from the day care center; Garrett's frantic search to find her son and her description of the dead children lined up on the street covered with glass combined with her pleas to "please don't lay our babies on this glass" because she did not realize that the babies were "already dead"; Weaver's search for her husband and her intuitions that he was dead; John Avera's rescue efforts, including finding a baby he heard choking, comforting a woman trapped in the rubble, and collapsing from his efforts; Luke Franey's remembrance of "running down the stairwell holding on the handrail and it being covered in blood"; Martin's substantial injuries and hearing wailing sounds from two female co-workers; Priscilla Salyers' panic while trapped under the rubble for four and a half hours; and Shannon's account of the rescue effort.

In order to prove the elements of the various offenses charged, the government had to prove, inter alia, that the bomb was a weapon of mass destruction used against persons and property, that the explosion substantially interfered with interstate commerce, which could be established by showing disruption of government operations, that the bomb foreseeably would result in death, and that use of the bomb evidenced a malicious intent to kill. The bulk of the contested testimony showed either the magnitude of the destruction or identified the victims and the cause of death.

The description of the destruction and carnage following the explosion is the most emotionally powerful of the evidence presented during the guilt phase. Hunt's and Garrett's descriptions of the dead children from the day care center are particularly powerful. Nevertheless, even "graphic depictions" of a murder are relevant to support "other evidence about how the crime occurred . . . even when the element is uncontested — indeed, even when the defendant offers to admit to the element . . . ." *Gonzalez v. DeTella*, 127 F.3d 619, 621 (7th Cir. 1997), *cert. denied*, 118 S. Ct. 1325, 140 L. Ed. 2d 487 (1998).

---

[19] [25] At one point in his brief, McVeigh complains that the government did not present this evidence in a way to minimize its emotional impact. However, the government has no obligation to minimize the emotional impact of testimony. Rule 403 is designed to insure only that the prejudicial effects of emotional testimony do not overwhelm the jury.

* * *

d. Long-Term Effects

McVeigh identifies portions of the testimony of eight witnesses that he claims amounted to overly prejudicial discussions of the long-term impacts of the bombings, including: Norfleet's loss of his pilot status and of his "pride and joy" gold aviator wings on his license plate and his explanation that Sergeant Benjamin Davis died without learning about his acceptance into a Marine Corps officer training program; Hunt's testimony that she attended twenty-two funerals; Garrett's inability to kiss the body of her son above his waist because of his "severe head injury"; Weaver's testimony that her husband was "buried two years ago today" and that she felt fortunate to be able to identify the body; Martin's medical discharge from the Army as a result of his injuries just as he was slated for a possible promotion; and Cooper's attendance at two funerals and his description of the deceased men.

Most of this evidence was not particularly relevant to the issues presented during the guilt phase. In addition, some of it had emotional content. . . . However, even if the district court abused its discretion by admitting some of this evidence,[20] we believe such error was harmless. As for the admission of Norfleet's pre-continuing objection testimony, we find no plain error given the fine line between appropriate and inappropriate evidence under Rule 403.

A trial court's admission of inadmissible evidence will disturb a defendant's conviction only if the error is not harmless. The erroneous admission of evidence . . . is harmless unless it had a substantial influence on the outcome or leaves one in grave doubt as to whether it had such an effect . . . . Further, cautionary instructions are ordinarily sufficient to cure any alleged prejudice to the defendant. Given the strength of the prosecution's case as a whole, and the cautionary instruction, we find the error harmless. . . .

CONCLUSION

For the foregoing reasons, Timothy McVeigh's conviction and sentence are AFFIRMED.

NOTES

1.   The prosecution of Timothy McVeigh was one of the most high profile trials in history, and he was represented by very able lawyers. Yet even they failed to preserve issues properly for appeal. Never take such points for granted and always think in terms of preserving your record for appeal.

2.   For an example of a case in which the trial court used Rule 403 to exclude

---

[20] [28] We again caution that we accept the efficacy of McVeigh's continuing objection. McVeigh did not object specifically to the testimony of the eight witnesses challenged on appeal. Had McVeigh objected to this evidence, the district court may well have been alerted to exclude portions of it. This illustrates the danger of granting a continuing objection in an area as nebulous as this.

some photographs of murder victim while admitting others, see *United States v. Sampson*, 335 F. Supp. 2d 166 (D. Mass. 2004).

5. Evidentiary Foundations

Evidentiary Foundation:
People v. Chambers

[The State of New York submitted the following memorandum in the case of *People v. Chambers*, the so-called "yuppie-murder" or "rough sex" case. The defendant, Robert Chambers, admitted killing Jennifer Levin, but claimed that her death occurred accidentally in the course of "rough sex." The State, over defense objections, offered post-mortem photographs of the victim's body taken at the crime scene to negate the defendant's claim of accident.]

MEMORANDUM OF LAW

Jennifer Levin's body was discovered in Central Park by a bicyclist on the morning of August 26, 1986. Police and medical personnel arrived shortly thereafter. These individuals observed the condition and position of Jennifer Levin's body at the crime scene. They also observed various injuries to her body. Photographs were taken to preserve the evidence.

Later the body was removed to the New York City Medical Examiner's Office. An autopsy was performed where more injuries were observed, including severe abrasions to Jennifer Levin's neck. Findings were made about the manner and cause of Jennifer Levin's death. In the course of the autopsy many photos were taken to preserve the evidence which supported the autopsy findings.[21]

After Jennifer Levin's body was discovered but before the autopsy was performed, this defendant was located. The defendant told the police various lies. After a long period of lying, the defendant told a story which he offered as the truth. That story was preserved on a videotape which will be part of the People's direct case at trial. The defendant claimed that he accidentally caused Jennifer Levin's death by grabbing her around the neck in a single motion.

At the trial of this case the People intend to offer into evidence the crime scene and autopsy photographs. This memorandum is submitted now in support of that offer.

The main issue in this case, as is clear from the videotaped statement and as defense counsel observed in his bail application of September 24, 1987, is whether or not the defendant's story of accidentally causing Jennifer Levin's death is consistent with the physical evidence in the case. The observations made at the crime scene and at the autopsy have been preserved by the photographs which we seek to introduce. Therefore, they are directly relevant to the central issue in the case.

---

[21] A copy of one such photograph is included at the end of the memorandum.

The law is clear that photographs of a murder victim are admissible *even* though they portray a gruesome spectacle as long as they are relevant to a disputed element or material issue, or if they serve to illustrate or elucidate other relevant evidence. *People v. Fish*, 125 N.Y. 136 (1891); *People v. Pobliner*, 32 N.Y.2d 356 (1973), *cert. den.*, 449 U.S. 905 (1974).

It is our contention that these photographs contradict and repudiate the defendant's explanation of how he accidentally caused Jennifer Levin's death. Every bruise, every contusion and every abrasion present all over her body, and depicted in these photographs, demonstrates the implausibility of the defendant's story. Indeed, when viewed together, these photographs tell their own story. They depict injuries which are the best evidence of a struggle which the defendant would have the jury believe never occurred. That is why the jury must see every one of these photos. They are *the* most probative evidence that this defendant intentionally strangled and asphyxiated Jennifer Levin.

The photographs of Jennifer Levin's body at the crime scene and at the autopsy are relevant to prove the key disputed issue in the case: the defendant's intent. They disprove the defendant's story that he had no criminal intent. They disprove the defendant's claim that Jennifer Levin's death was an accident. They show the nature and extent of her injures and thereby prove that a violent struggle took place after which Jennifer Levin's body was dragged. They show that the defendant applied pressure to Jennifer Levin's neck in a manner evincing a depraved indifference to human life. They illustrate and elucidate the testimony of those witnesses who observed Jennifer Levin's body at the crime scene and at the autopsy. They serve as part of the basis for the opinions of outside experts as to the cause and manner of Jennifer Levin's death.

Since the photographs are crucially relevant to disputed elements and material issues in this case, they are clearly admissible. The probative value of each and every photograph is enormous. It is clear that they are not offered to arouse the jury's emotions. Indeed, any reasonable juror will surely accept these photographs for what they are: highly probative evidence on the key issues in this case.

Further they are not a particularly gruesome spectacle. They *do* show a young woman who was beaten, who struggled with her attacker, who was dragged and who was ultimately strangled and asphyxiated to death. However, photographs decidedly more gruesome than these have often been admitted into evidence where relevant. In *People v. Medina*, 120 A.D. 749 (2d Dept. 1986), photographs of the charred remains of a child were properly admitted to disprove the defendant's account and to corroborate expert testimony. In *People v. Winchell*, 93 A.D. 2d 838 (3rd Dept. 1983), photographs of the badly decomposed body of a 16 year old girl which were "admittedly gruesome" were properly admitted because they showed how the victim was killed and because they demonstrated an inconsistency in the defendant's testimony. *See also People v. Millson*, 93 A.D. 2d 899 (3rd Dept. 1983) (photograph of child's scalp peeled back to the skull was properly admitted to show nature and extent of injuries, implausibility of accident defense and that defendant acted with depraved indifference to human life); *People v. Arca*, 72 A.D. 2d 205 (4th Dept. 1980) (photographs of various injuries to dead child properly admitted and shown to jury as relevant to the extent of the injuries and to prove that defendant acted in depraved manner).

The photographs which we seek to introduce here are more relevant to the key elements and disputed issues of this case than were the photographs introduced in the cases cited. Furthermore, the photographs here are not gruesome.

Therefore, the New York case law clearly supports the admission into evidence of every one of the photographs of Jennifer Levin's body at the crime scene and at the autopsy.

Mason Ladd, *Objections, Motions and Foundation Testimony*
43 Cornell L.Q. 543, 543 (1958)[22]

The rules of admission and exclusion of evidence are not self-operative in our adversary system of trial. As important as the rules are, counsel for litigants must be alert to obtain their benefits and to employ with nicety recognized methods both to exclude improper evidence and to secure the admission of acceptable evidence.

. . . [P]aving the way for admissibility of evidence requires the use of foundation testimony which in a larger sense is basic to the admission of all evidence. Some foundation testimony is not formally designated as such but the foundation aspect is so interrelated with the rules of evidence that it goes to the very heart of admissibility.

The broader conception of foundation testimony includes any preliminary inquiries which help the expected testimony to escape from the rules of exclusion or to be more highly evaluated when admitted. Thayer's observation that all relevant evidence is admissible unless barred by one of the rules of exclusion presupposes the necessity of laying proper foundation or making such preliminary inquiries as are required to avoid, or to show the inapplicability of, the rules of exclusion. As the anticipation of pertinent objections prescribes the course of foundation testimony, the methods to exclude and the process to gain admission of evidence may profitably be considered together. Objections, motions and the methods of laying foundation testimony are a part of the law of evidence but are so often absorbed in the study of the principles of admissibility that their independent significance is obscured.

James W. McElhaney, Trial Notebook
304, 298–303 (3d ed. 1981)[23]

The trouble with foundations is that they lurk everywhere, waiting for a chance to trip you up. Usually, it seems, the gods of litigation save the most complex and arcane foundations for times when your client is at your side and your opponent makes an obscure objection that is sustained by a trial judge whose dual determination is to force you to turn some square corner and to refuse to tell you what it is.

Part of the problem is due to the usual law school courses in evidence, which are organized around abstract conceptual progressions rather than proof of facts at trial. Even if you check as helpful a book as *McCormick on Evidence* (2d ed. 1972) and look under "Foundations" in the index on p. 930, you will be referred to "Preliminary questions and particular topics." If you then turn to "Preliminary questions of fact" on p. 935, you will find only eight entries.

Why?

Probably because nearly everywhere you look in the law of evidence there is something you have to introduce first before you can prove what you are really after. In other words, you can, if you like, view the whole law of evidence from the question: What do I have to prove first?

The results are worth the effort. Evidence will begin to fall in place. Instead of a disjointed collection of rules, a pattern will emerge that will help change evidence from a troublesome hurdle to a commanding strength in the courtroom. A reputation for knowing evidence is beyond price.

*   *   *

It is essential that the trial lawyer be thoroughly acquainted with the necessary procedural steps for introducing exhibits into evidence. Yet this routine trial procedure is for many litigators — particularly those with less experience — a troublesome task. The result is often confusion and delay, preventing some lawyers from taking full advantage of the effective use of demonstrative evidence. The procedural checklist set forth below is suggested as a guide for avoiding confusion and delay.

1. *Request that the exhibit be marked for identification.* Counsel should make the request as follows: "I request that this be marked as (plaintiff's) (prosecution's) (defendant's) exhibit for identification." Technically, identifying the object or document in more than very general terms violates the rule against unsworn testimony. While you may or may not be challenged by the opposition, it is improper to identify the exhibit as, for example, "a picture of the plaintiff's car taken after the collision." Further, you should permit the reporter or clerk to assign the appropriate exhibit number or letter. That is his domain, and he may well resent any intrusion on it. Of course, if he makes a mistake, it should be called to his attention. Typically reporters or clerks keep a list of the numbers or letters used, and are less likely to make a mistake than you are.

When the case is one with a large number of exhibits, especially where they are similar in nature, it is often wise, as part of the pre-trial order, to agree to the numbering and lettering of exhibits in advance, and even to stipulate to their admissibility. There are many situations, to be sure, when you do not want your adversary to know you have a particular document or exhibit, particularly if its chief value is for impeachment. It is essential, therefore, to know the entire process well for use at trial.

2. *Lay the foundation for the exhibit.* Failing to lay a complete foundation for an exhibit (or for other testimony, for that matter) is a typical failing of even experienced trial lawyers. Unless one is blessed or cursed with total recall, the best

method is to have a foundation checklist in the trial notebook for each type of exhibit you plan to use. While the subject of foundations justifies an entire volume, a few of the more typical problems are covered here.

For a photograph of a scene, all that is required is the statement of a witness that the picture is a true and accurate representation of the scene, and testimony that the scene is relevant to the case. The simplest way to lay such a foundation is through an ordinary fact witness. There are instances, however, when one is not available for this purpose. Then the photographer can establish at least part of the foundation, describing the technical details of his photographic process to help show that the picture is a true and accurate representation of the scene it portrays. Laying this foundation does not guarantee the admissibility of the picture, however, because its probative value may be outweighed by some prejudicial aspect of it. But the foundation is an essential step to its admissibility.

Models and charts are somewhat simpler. For example, in a head injury case, a plastic model of a skull and brain might make a neurologist's testimony more understandable. The proper foundation for the use of such an exhibit is that the object is an accurate reproduction of the human skull and brain for the purpose of illustrating the testimony of the witness. Absolute accuracy is not the test, and the model or chart need only be as detailed and accurate as required by the function it is to serve. Some courts take a relaxed approach to such exhibits and do not even require a foundation to be laid to permit their use. Others, however, insist on their being marked, a foundation laid, and formal introduction into evidence. This is an important step to have a complete record and to allow the exhibit to be taken to the jury room. Thus, it is often the better practice to take the trouble to make a formal introduction. With the court's permission, a description or picture can be substituted for the exhibit for inclusion in the record at the close of trial.

When something is used to refresh a witness's recollection, it is not itself introduced into evidence. Nevertheless, some courts require such items — typically documents — to be marked for identification, and it often is best to do so. This is especially true since the foundation for the admissibility of past recollection recorded includes the inability of the witness to have his recollection refreshed by the document. Stated briefly, the requirements for the admissibility of past recollection recorded are: (a) a writing, (b) made at or near the event by the witness or someone acting under his direction and control, (c) no present recollection by the witness as to the matters recorded and sought to be introduced and (d) a "voucher of correctness" or statement that the witness is certain that the information recorded was accurate at the time made.

real evidence

With real evidence — such as murder weapons, defective machinery in a products liability case and other such exhibits which are the things themselves — the foundation is complicated by the necessity to show a chain of custody. The requirement is to show from whose custody the object is produced, who had custody in a continuous chain from the relevant time, and that the object is in the same condition as when originally received. The trial court has discretion, when the object is readily identifiable and not subject to easy tampering, to admit the object on merely a foundation that it is in substantially the same condition as at the relevant time. The court, however, can require a meticulous chain of custody when the object is subject to change, is not easily identifiable, or may easily have been tampered with.

When one cannot establish a chain of custody, all is not necessarily lost. The trial court may exercise its discretion to admit a "model" or "duplicate" for the purpose of illustrating testimony. The object which fails to pass the chain of custody test *may* qualify for these purposes. For a short but adequate discussion of the chain of custody problem, *see McCormick on Evidence* 527–30 (2d ed. 1972).

3. *Let opposing counsel examine the exhibit.* Professor Keeton suggests that the exhibit be offered into evidence before it is shown to opposing counsel. R. Keeton, *Trial Tactics and Methods* 63 (2d ed. 1973). However, waiting until that time is an invitation to a pointed request from the other side to see the document which can be embarrassing.

4. *Offer the exhibit into evidence.* Too often this step is overlooked, with the result that the jury cannot take the exhibit to the jury room with them, or they do so improperly. It can be a fatal omission.

The offer should be as follows: "Defense exhibit 14 for identification is offered into evidence (as defense exhibit 14)." Some courts prefer all exhibits to be offered into evidence at once, usually near the time the party rests. This practice saves time and makes an accidental omission less likely. Such a procedure, however, keeps the exhibit from the jury until admission or blinks at the prohibition against testimony concerning an exhibit — as opposed to testimony authenticating it — until it is formally admitted in evidence. Arguably, therefore, it is the better practice to offer the exhibit directly after authentication and examination by opposing counsel whenever you want the jury to view the exhibit right away or when there is to be additional testimony concerning it.

5. *Give the exhibit to the trial judge for his inspection.* If the judge does not already have a copy of the exhibit, the right time to show it to him is simultaneously with the formal offer into evidence.

6. *Voir dire examination of the witness, objection and argument by opposing counsel.* Because it is possible to have laid a prima facie foundation for the admissibility of an exhibit which is nonetheless inadmissible, opposing counsel can conduct a preliminary examination of the witness on the apparent foundation. Whether such an examination will be permitted usually lies within the discretion of the trial court.

When done properly, this form of examination is not preliminary cross examination of the witness generally, but only as to those matters which relate to the apparent foundation which is being tested. Moreover, it is usually better not to ask for a *voir dire* examination unless you feel there is a good chance that the exhibit will be excluded as a result. Should the court rule that the objection goes to the weight rather than to the admissibility of the exhibit, there is the danger that the jury will interpret the ruling as a statement that your attack was legally without force and should be ignored. Therefore, unless you feel you can exclude the exhibit, it is better to save your attack for cross-examination.

While some trial lawyers feel to the contrary — that two cross-examinations of a witness are better than one — use of the *voir dire* examination of a witness for that purpose is impermissible. And while some judges have never heard of a *voir dire* examination of a witness, others know the procedure well and are quick to cut off examination which goes beyond its appropriate scope.

7. *Ruling from the court.*

8. *The testimony concerning the exhibit.* Any testimony about the exhibit not necessary as a foundation to its introduction should only come after it has been admitted into evidence.

9. *Give the jury the exhibit or copies of it.* Trial courts usually permit copies of pictures and documents to be distributed to the jury. When you want the jury to look at something during the testimony concerning it, it is useful to have a copy for each juror or an exhibit large enough for all jurors to see at once. Giving the jury exhibits is important, since they are permitted to take them into the jury room for use during their deliberations — a procedure which heightens the impact of demonstrative evidence considerably. However, testimonial exhibits, such as depositions, are usually not permitted in the jury room, on the theory that the jury will give disproportionate weight to that testimony.

If only a portion of an exhibit is relevant, such as one entry in an entire log or record, it is customary to request the court's permission to read from the exhibit, identifying what excerpt is being called to the jury's attention. The rule of completeness, the antidote to unfair selectivity, permits the opposition to present explanatory or modifying materials from the same exhibit.

QUESTION

In *United States v. Curtis, supra,* the prosecution sought to introduce into evidence various items of real evidence taken from the scene of a crime. What foundation must counsel establish to admit such items? What special problems arise for blood samples or DNA scrapings? *See DeLaTorre v. Minnesota Life,* 2005 U.S. Dist. LEXIS 20938 (N.D. Ill. Sept. 16, 2005); *Hulmes v. Honda Motor Co.,* 936 F. Supp. 195, 206 (D.N.J. 1996); *In re Swine Flu Immunization Products Liability Litigation,* 533 F. Supp. 567 (D. Colo. 1980). Consider generally Federal Rule of Evidence 901.

Federal Rule of Evidence 901
Authenticating or Identifying Evidence

(a) In General. To satisfy the requirement of authenticating or identifying an item of evidence, the proponent must produce evidence sufficient to support a finding that the item is what the proponent claims it is.

(b) Examples. The following are examples only — not a complete list — of evidence that satisfies the requirement:

(1) Testimony of a Witness with Knowledge. Testimony that an item is what it is claimed to be.

(2) Nonexpert Opinion About Handwriting. A nonexpert's opinion that hand-

writing is genuine, based on a familiarity with it that was not acquired for the current litigation.

(3) Comparison by an Expert Witness or the Trier of Fact. A comparison with an authenticated specimen by an expert witness or the trier of fact.

(4) Distinctive Characteristics and the Like. The appearance, contents, substance, internal patterns, or other distinctive characteristics of the item, taken together with all the circumstances.

(5) Opinion About a Voice. An opinion identifying a person's voice — whether heard firsthand or through mechanical or electronic transmission or recording — based on hearing the voice at any time under circumstances that connect it with the alleged speaker.

(6) Evidence About a Telephone Conversation. For a telephone conversation, evidence that a call was made to the number assigned at the time to:

(A) a particular person, if circumstances, including self-identification, show that the person answering was the one called; or

(B) a particular business, if the call was made to a business and the call related to business reasonably transacted over the telephone.

(7) Evidence About Public Records. Evidence that:

(A) a document was recorded or filed in a public office as authorized by law; or

(B) a purported public record or statement is from the office where items of this kind are kept.

(8) Evidence About Ancient Documents or Data Compilations. For a document or data compilation, evidence that it:

(A) is in a condition that creates no suspicion about its authenticity;

(B) was in a place where, if authentic, it would likely be; and

(C) is at least 20 years old when offered.

(9) Evidence About a Process or System. Evidence describing a process or system and showing that it produces an accurate result.

(10) Methods Provided by a Statute or Rule. Any method of authentication or identification allowed by a federal statute or a rule prescribed by the Supreme Court.

UNITED STATES v. REILLY
33 F.3d 1396 (3d Cir. 1994)

GREENBERG, CIRCUIT JUDGE.

Fed. R. Evid. 901(b) provides examples of appropriate methods of authentication. These examples include "[t]estimony that a matter is what it is claimed to be,"

Rule 901(b)(1), and "[a]ppearance, contents, substance, internal patterns, or other distinctive characteristics, taken in conjunction with circumstances," Rule 901(b)(4). Thus, "[i]t is clear that the connection between a message (either oral or written) and its source may be established by circumstantial evidence." *United States v. Addonizio*, 451 F.2d 49, 71 (3d Cir. 1971), *cert. denied*, 405 U.S. 936 (1972). Moreover, "[a]ny combination of items of evidence illustrated by Rule 901(b) . . . will suffice so long as Rule 901(a) is satisfied." 5 WEINSTEIN'S EVIDENCE ¶ 901(b)(1)[01] at 901–32. Finally, "[t]he burden of proof for authentication is slight." *Link v. Mercedes-Benz of North America, Inc.*, 788 F.2d 918, 927 (3d Cir. 1986). . . . We have explained that "the showing of authenticity is not on a par with more technical evidentiary rules, such as hearsay exceptions, governing admissibility. Rather, there need be only a prima facie showing, to the court, of authenticity, not a full argument on admissibility. Once a prima facie case is made, the evidence goes to the jury and it is the jury who will ultimately determine the authenticity of the evidence, not the court. The only requirement is that there has been substantial evidence from which they could infer that the document was authentic." . . . *[S]ee also* MICHAEL H. GRAHAM, FEDERAL PRACTICE AND PROCEDURE: EVIDENCE § 6821 at 849 (Interim Edition 1992) ("Satisfaction of the requirement of authentication or identification is a matter to be approached in accordance with Rule 104(b). Accordingly once the court finds that evidence has been introduced sufficient to permit a reasonable juror to find that the matter in question is what its proponent claims, a sufficient foundation for introduction in evidence has been laid, Rule 104(b).") (citations omitted).

UNITED STATES v. DUMEISI
424 F.3d 566 (7th Cir. 2005)

OPINION: KANNE, CIRCUIT JUDGE.

In the years leading up to the 2003 invasion of Iraq, Palestinian Khaled Abdel-Latif Dumeisi was in close contact with the Iraqi Mission to the United Nations ("IMUN"). Dumeisi's relationship with the IMUN (as well as his 1999 trip to Baghdad) was ostensibly related to the publication of his Arabic language newspaper in a Chicago suburb. Certain evidence obtained by the FBI, however, suggested that Dumeisi was actually acting as an agent of Saddam Hussein's Iraqi regime. He was ultimately tried by a jury and convicted for acting in the United States as an agent of a foreign government without prior notification to the Attorney General, conspiracy to do so, and perjury. Dumeisi appeals, illeging a number of evidentiary and other errors by both the trial court and the Foreign Intelligence surveillance Act ("FISA") court. For the reasons stated herein, we affirm.

I. History

Dumeisi was born in Palestine in 1946. In 1948, he moved to Jordan, then to Kuwait in 1970. Finally, in March 1993, Dumeisi emigrated to the United States. Thereafter, he began publishing an Arabic language newspaper out of Burbank, Illinois. The paper was initially called "Palestine," but was more recently titled

"*Al-Mahjar*," which translates to "place of immigration." Dumeisi received revenue from advertisers and distributed new issues of the free paper every three or four weeks. *Al-Mahjar* primarily contained articles about Middle Eastern politics. Dumeisi published a number of articles in support of Saddam Hussein and against the Iraqi Opposition; Dumeisi felt that the former leader of Iraq was the only Arab leader who had unwaveringly supported the Palestinian cause. Dumeisi sometimes received threats and harassment from Opposition sympathizers.

A. Contact with Iraqi Mission to the United Nations

In 1996, Dumeisi hired Kawther Al-Khatib to assist with the newspaper. Although Al-Khatib was a Palestinian, she spoke the Iraqi Arabic dialect fluently. Dumeisi directed Al-Khatib to contact the IMUN in New York City and to notify the personnel there that *Al-Mahjar* was "at their disposal" and would be interested in publishing materials or articles supplied by the IMUN.

After Al-Khatib's initial contact, Dumeisi developed a close relationship with the IMUN and was a guest there on several occasions. On one of his IMUN-sponsored visits to New York, Dumeisi met and interviewed the Foreign Minister of Iraq. In 1999, at the invitation of the Foreign Minister, Dumeisi traveled to Baghdad for Saddam Hussein's birthday party. After this visit, Dumeisi spoke with Shifiq El-Khalil, an acquaintance since 1992 with whom he shared office space. According to El-Khalil, Dumeisi said that he had been in Iraq to garner support for his newspaper and that the people he met were interested in having him monitor and report on the activities of the Iraqi Opposition in the United States. Shortly after he returned from Baghdad, Dumeisi took another trip to the IMUN in New York. He returned with $ 3000, which he told El-Khalil he had received from the IMUN. Dumeisi also stated that the IMUN would be calling him at 1:00 P.M. every Thursday to give him "instructions." El-Khalil saw Dumeisi on his cell phone Thursday afternoons, and Dumeisi once told El-Khalil that his IMUN contact placed calls from a restaurant rather than from the IMUN because "it was private and secret conversation."

Dumeisi also discussed his trip to Baghdad with Al-Khatib. He explained that his visit was facilitated by the Iraqi Embassy in Amman, Jordan, so that his passport would not be stamped with an Iraqi entry visa. Dumeisi also told her that he had been met by two members of the *Mukhabbarat*, the Iraqi Intelligence Service ("IIS"), who had preset a full schedule of activities for him while he was in Baghdad. Some time after his return to Illinois, Dumeisi and Al-Khatib were watching an Arab film in which an intelligence officer was putting a microphone in the handset of a telephone. Dumeisi remarked that the technique was quite primitive and proceeded to show Al-Khatib a silver pen that could be used as a camera and a tape recorder. Dumeisi said that he had received the pen in Baghdad and that he had used it in an Illinois meeting with a member of the Iraqi Opposition. Al-Khatib also observed Dumeisi on his Thursday afternoon phone calls. On one occasion when she tried to overhear Dumeisi's end of the conversation, she managed only to hear him say, "Lunch is ready. Let the group come." When she asked him about lunch, Dumeisi responded that it was none of her business.

In July 2000, Dumeisi made the acquaintance of former ISS officer Hazim

El-Dilemi at the residence of the Iraqi Ambassador to the U.N. in New York. El-Dilemi's cousin, Kassim Mohammed, was an IIS officer stationed at the IMUN. Mohammed introduced Dumeisi and El-Dilemi. Dumeisi described *Al-Mahjar* as a "newspaper for Iraq" and asked Mohammed for financial help for the paper.

In April 2001, at the IMUN celebration of Saddam Hussein's birthday, Dumeisi gave a speech praising Saddam Hussein. After the speech, Dumeisi repaired to the basement of the IMUN with El-Dilemi, Mohammed, and several IMUN personnel. Dumeisi again asked Mohammed for financial assistance. Dumeisi indicated that he had been approached by other groups offering him more money to write articles for them but that he had refused, telling the group, "I want to stay with you guys." Dumeisi was given a computer, a fax machine, and some articles to be printed in the next issue of *Al-Mahjar*. At Mohammed's request, Dumeisi provided press identification cards for himself, El-Dilemi, and IIS officer Saleh Ahman. These identification cards purported that Dumeisi, El-Dilemi, and Ahman were employees of *Al-Mahjar*, and would allow them to gain entry to meetings inaccessible to a diplomat.

*   *   *

B. The Baghdad File

One of the most important pieces of evidence in Dumeisi's trial has an interesting history all its own. It begins with Dumeisi's female part-time employee, named Wafa Zaitawi, who delivered newspapers for him. Zaitawi also sold longdistance telephone service for FoneTel.

Fawzi Al-Shammari was a member of the Iraqi Opposition in the United States. He had been a general in Saddam's military, but defected to the United States in 1986 and created an organization, called the Iraqi Officers' Movement to Save Iraq, dedicated to overthrowing Saddam Hussein. Al-Shammari was recognized as a possible successor to Saddam Hussein in the event of a regime change, and he had received publicity in numerous newspapers, magazines, and television programs in the United States.

In early 2002, Al-Shammari received a phone call from a friend of his, who also happened to be a friend of Zaitawi, suggesting that he call Zaitawi to get a good deal on long-distance telephone service. This mutual friend also hinted that Al-Shammari might form a more personal relationship with Zaitawi. AlShammari purchased long-distance service from Zaitawi, and the two did, in fact, "hit it off" on a personal level. They exchanged photographs and went so far as to discuss the possibility of marriage.

In March 2002, Al-Shammari traveled to Chicago, using the trip as an opportunity to meet Zaitawi in person and to make two public speeches against Saddam Hussein's regime in Iraq. The speeches went well, but the matchmaking did not. Al-Shammari was "shocked" at Zaitawi's appearance — apparently quite different from her photo — and abandoned all thoughts of marriage when she picked him up at the airport. Nevertheless, to be diplomatic, he gave her a necklace, went home with her to meet her daughters, and took her to his hotel cafeteria for some snacks. Al-Shammari did not call Zaitawi again after he left Chicago.

As a FoneTel employee, Zaitawi had access to the records of customers' calling activity. IIS records recovered in Iraq after the fall of Baghdad in 2003 contained listings of telephone numbers called from Al-Shammari's telephone in Zaitawi's handwriting. These documents were part of a larger collection of IIS records which came to be known as "the Baghdad File." The file also contained a report in Dumeisi's handwriting on one of Al-Shammari's anti-Saddam speeches in Chicago. This report identified Al-Shammari as the leader of a possible successor government in Iraq, and contained photographs of Al-Shammari and the names of two of Al-Shammari's associates who had accompanied him to Chicago.

The Baghdad File contained correspondence between IMUN personnel in New York and IIS headquarters in Baghdad. This correspondence referred to Dumeisi as "Symbol Sirhan"; symbols were considered IIS "sources" as opposed to fully vetted "agents." The IMUN communicated with the IIS regarding Dumeisi's relationship with Zaitawi and Zaitawi's relationship with "the Criminal Fawzi Al Shammari." This communication also reported on the plan prepared for Dumeisi to "start moving on hostile organizations in Chicago and Detroit, and to monitor the activities of group leaders for the so-called opposition in The United States of America." Among other things, Dumeisi was to "exploit his friend [Zaitawi], who works for a communication company" in achieving that goal. This correspondence preceded a summary of Al-Shammari's activities in Chicago, Al-Shammari's telephone numbers and records, and Dumeisi's handwritten report. On May 22, 2002, the IIS directed the IMUN to continue to provide information on Al-Shammari. The IMUN did so in June and August 2002, with further reports and an indication that Dumeisi was paid $ 877.65 for expenses.

John Andrews was the American counterintelligence officer who obtained the Baghdad File in Iraq. Andrews was assigned to Baghdad in late May 2003. He was part of the Iraq Survey Group, an interagency organization created for the purpose of exploiting documents and locating weapons of mass destruction following the invasion of Iraq. Andrews met weekly with Aras Kareem, a member of the Opposition group known as the Iraqi National Congress ("INC"). Kareem gave Andrews a number of documents that the INC had found. Andrews would typically have the documents translated and, if they did not appear to have a nexus to the Department of Defense, turn them over to the FBI office in Baghdad. Andrews testified at trial that Kareem gave him the Baghdad File, contained in a blue and clear plastic folder, sometime in June 2003. Having determined that it contained some U.S. telephone numbers, Andrews turned it over to the FBI about two days later.

*   *   *

E. Trial

On July 16, 2003, Dumeisi was indicted for acting in the United States as an agent of a foreign government without prior notification to the Attorney General (in violation of 18 U.S.C. 951(a)); conspiracy to do so (in violation of 18 U.S.C. 371); perjury in an immigration proceeding (in violation of 18 U.S.C. 1621); and perjury before a federal grand jury (in violation of 18 U.S.C. 1623). A jury trial commenced on January 5, 2004, and a week later Dumeisi was found guilty on all four counts.

He was sentenced to 46 months' imprisonment.

II. Analysis

Dumeisi appeals his conviction on . . . [various] different grounds. First, he argues that the Baghdad File was erroneously admitted in evidence. . . .

A. *Admission of the Baghdad File*

Dumeisi filed a motion *in limine* objecting to the admission of the Baghdad File. He described the Baghdad File as "the single most important piece of government evidence," but asserted that it was unauthenticated hearsay. The government responded that the Baghdad File was admissible under Federal Rule of Evidence 807, the residual exception to the hearsay rule, as well as under Rule 803(6) (business records), Rule 803(8) (public records), and Rule 801(d)(2)(E) (co-conspirators' statements). The district court postponed ruling on this matter until trial was underway, ultimately admitting the evidence under Rule 807.

* * *

We first tackle the question of whether the Baghdad File was properly authenticated. Federal Rule of Evidence 901(a) requires, as a condition precedent to admissibility, "evidence sufficient to support a finding that the matter in question is what its proponent claims." Authentication can be established in a variety of ways, including by "testimony of [a] witness with knowledge . . . that a matter is what it is claimed to be[,]" Rule 901(b)(1), and by distinctive characteristics such as "appearance, contents, substance, [or] internal patterns . . . taken in conjunction with circumstances[,]". Dumeisi challenges authentication under both methods.

The government presented "Mr. Sargon"[24] as a "witness with knowledge" who could identify the Baghdad File as genuine IIS records. Indeed, Sargon had worked for the IIS from 1979 to 2003 and had advanced in rank to a high position not spoken on the record but made known to the jury. He had been assigned to posts outside of Iraq, including the United States, and had knowledge of the IIS missions as well as the organizational structure of the IIS. Sargon worked in Directorate M4, the group concerned with external intelligence, from 1999 to 2003. In that role, he had regular contact and information exchange with the M40 Directorate, which was responsible for "hostile activities," or opposition groups within and outside of Iraq. Sargon unequivocally testified that he could "positively identify [documents making up the Baghdad File] as Iraqi Intelligence cables, as well as correspondence between the New York Station and M40." (Tr. at 406–07.) Sargon was also the primary witness for the second method of authentication used by the government; he identified distinctive characteristics including the style and form of the documents ("in line with the way that the Iraqi Intelligence service will prefer to produce a document"), symbols, codes, abbreviations, and signatures of some fellow IIS officers. (Tr. at 406.) The one thing Sargon did not identify as a typical trait of

---

[24] [1] Sargon is not the true name of the witness; he testified under an assumed name pursuant to agreement.

IIS documents was the blue and clear plastic folder in which the Baghdad File was found.

The "circumstances" which we must consider in conjunction with the physical characteristics discussed above include circumstances surrounding discovery. *See United States v. Harvey* (approving introduction of written materials as sufficiently authenticated because they were found in an isolated campsite occupied only by the defendant); *United States v. Arce* (finding the fact that drug ledgers were discovered in known drug trafficker's home to be evidence of authenticity). In this case, classified information surrounding the initial discovery of the Baghdad File bolsters the contention that the file is what the government purports it to be.

We find this authentication evidence taken together to be at least as reliable as that relied upon in *United States v. Elkins*. In that case, the defendant was convicted of conspiracy and engaging in illegal exporting activity involving the sale of two aircraft to Libya. *Id.* The defendant challenged the use of circumstantial evidence to authenticate two documents used to show that the aircraft were purchased by the Libyan military. *Id.* The Eleventh Circuit held that Rule 901 "requires only some competent evidence in the record to support authentication"; the circumstantial evidence of where the documents were found (in West Germany, in the briefcase of a Libyan arms dealer) was sufficient to authenticate the documents in the absence of any evidence of adulteration or forgery. *Id.* Here, in addition to the circumstantial evidence regarding the discovery of the file alluded to above, we have Sargon's testimony that the file contained genuine IIS documents. The district court did not abuse its discretion in determining that the Baghdad File was properly authenticated . . . .

NOTES AND QUESTIONS

1.   Which principle of admissibility does the authentication requirement represent: relevancy, materiality, or competency?

2.   Was a specific rule of evidence necessary to implement that principle? *See* Fed. R. Evid. 401 and 104(b).

3.   What effect, if any, would a post-incident change in the condition of the proffered item have on its admissibility? *See generally,* Gianelli, *Chain of Custody and the Handling of Real Evidence,* 20 Am. Crim. L. Rev. 527 (1980).

4.   Once an evidentiary item has been authenticated, is it automatically admissible?

5.   Certain types of evidence are said to be self-authenticating. *See* Fed. R. Evid. 902. Does this mean that no evidentiary foundation must be established in connection with such proof?

Evidentiary Foundation:
The Trial of Sacco and Vanzetti[25]

[On August 23, 1927, Nicola Sacco and Bartolomeo Vanzetti, two Italian anarchists, were executed after conviction for a 1920 payroll robbery in which two men were killed. Their trial in 1921 had been one of the most controversial in American history. Given the anti-immigrant climate then prevailing, many doubted that two Italians could receive a fair trial. Critics also maintained that, at best, the evidence against them was contradictory and, at worst, it established their innocence. A vast literature on the case has developed. *See, e.g.*, EHRMANN, THE CASE THAT WILL NOT DIE (1969); FRANKFURTER, THE CASE OF SACCO AND VANZETTI (1927); FRANKEL, THE SACCO-VANZETTI CASE (1931); MORGAN & JOUGHLAN, THE LEGACY OF SACCO AND VANZETTI (1964). The following transcript excerpt concerns the admissibility of a revolver and bullet cartridges. These items, found on Sacco at the time of his arrest, linked him to the robbery murders. Consider whether the following witness testimony provided an adequate foundation to admit these items.]

Dedham, Mass.

Thursday, June 21, 1921.

Afternoon session

*   *   *

Merle A. Spear, *Sworn.*

Q.   [By Mr. Williams.] What is your name?

A.   Merle A. Spear.

Q.   Where do you live, Mr. Spear?

A.   Brockton.

Q.   You are a police officer?

A.   I am.

Q.   Of the city of Brockton?

A.   The city of Brockton.

Q.   And have been for how long?

A.   Eighteen years.

Q.   Were you on duty, or, strike that out. Do you remember the evening of May 5, 1920?

A.   I do.

Q.   Were you on duty that night?

---

[25] Excerpted from: The Sacco-Vanzetti Case: Transcript of the Record of the Trial of Nicola Sacco and Bartolomeo Vanzetti in the Court of Massachusetts and Subsequent Proceedings with a Supplemental Volume on the Bridgewater Case (Holt Record, 1929).

A.   I was.

Q.   And where were you on duty?

A.   In the police station.

*   *   *

Q.   Did you see the defendants that night?

A.   I did.

Q.   Now, will you tell the jury when you saw the defendants, where, what you did in respect to them, and what you observed regarding them?

A.   I saw the defendants in the cross seat on the right-hand side of an electric car, just as they got up to come forward, coming out of the car.

Q.   What police officers, if any were with them at that time?

A.   Officers Connolly and Vaughn.

*   *   *

Q.   Now, I take it you got to the police station?

A.   I did.

Q.   What time did you arrive there?

A.   Somewhere around quarter past ten.

Q.   Now, what was done in respect to searching the defendant at that time, if anything?

A.   I helped to search Sacco.

Q.   Will you describe to the jury what you did in respect to Sacco, where you did it and what you found, if anything, upon him?

A.   At the desk in the central police station they were brought and searched, and I first, — we took a number of automatic cartridges from his right hip pocket. I took an automatic revolver.

THE COURT.   How many, did you say?

THE WITNESS.   Later counted twenty-three. From in his waist I took an automatic .32 Colt revolver.

Q.   What?

A.   A Colt revolver, automatic revolver.

Q.   Are you sure?

A.   I am.

Q.   A revolver?

A.   Yes.

Q.   Where did you take it from?

A.   From inside his waist, in here, to this side [indicating].

Q.   Now, just where was it? I want to be sure of this.

A.   Inside of his waist, to the button, to the right.

Q.   And what line? You showed your belt line to the jury. Where, in respect to your belt line, was the revolver placed?

A.   In here [indicating].

Q.   What does that "in here" mean, to the right or left of the centre line of your body?

A.   To the right.

Q.   Did you find anything else on him?

A.   Nothing that I found.

Q.   In what condition was the gun which you took from him?

A.   Fully loaded.

Q.   What?

A.   Fully loaded.

Q.   How many shots were in it?

A.   There was eight in the clip, and one in the barrel.

Q.   You now say it was a revolver?

A.   A Colt automatic revolver.

Q.   Did you make any mark on that gun when you took it?

A.   Not when I took it.

Q.   Did you while it was in your possession?

A.   I did.

Q.   Whereabouts?

A.   On the stock I put the initials "M.S.", I think.

Q.   Now, will you look at the gun I show you and see if you find any mark on there by which you can identify it?

A.   [Witness examines gun.] I do.

Q.   Will you tell the jury what gun that is?

A.   The gun I took from Sacco.

Q.   Now, will you look at it and see if it is a revolver?

A.   I do call it a revolver.

Q.   What? Is that what you call a revolver?

A.   Yes.

Q.   That is what you meant when you told me it was a revolver?

A.   Yes.

Q.   As a matter of fact, it is a pistol, is it not?

A.   Well, I call it a revolver. There [indicating] is the initial I put on it.

THE COURT.   That has been examined, so there is no question about that it is unloaded?

MR. WILLIAMS.   I don't know enough about these things to find out whether there is anything in it or not, Judge.

THE SHERIFF.   There is nothing in it.

MR. WILLIAMS.   Nothing in it.

Q.   How many bullets does that hold, do you know?

A.   I took eight from the clip and one from the barrel.

Q.   What did you do with them, Mr. Spear?

A.   I turned them over to the state police, the next evening, the evening of May 6th.

Q.   Do you know which member of the state police you turned it over to?

A.   Scott, I think.

Q.   Was anybody present when you turned it over to Scott?

A.   Proctor was there.

Q.   Captain Proctor?

A.   Yes.

MR. WILLIAMS.   I offer this gun, if you please. I will put a tag on it after I show it to the jury.

THE COURT.   I understand you object to the competency?

MR. MOORE.   To the same.

THE COURT.   On any ground, on every ground?

MR. MOORE.   Yes, if your Honor please, we make an objection.

THE COURT.   You object.

MR. MOORE.   Yes.

THE COURT.   And on the ground it is not competent for any purpose whatever?

MR. MOORE.   Yes, your Honor.

THE COURT.   All right. Your objection is overruled and exception noted.

MR. JEREMIAH McANARNEY.   To both.

THE COURT.   Certainly.

            [The pistol found on Defendant Sacco is admitted in evidence and marked "Exhibit 28."]

            [Mr. Williams shows Exhibit 28 to the jury.]

Q.   While the jury are looking at it, I will ask you what you did with the bullets you took from his right hip pocket?

A.   I turned them over to the state police at the time with the revolver.

Q.   At the same time the revolver was turned over?

A.   Yes.

Q.   What kind of bullets were those, Mr. Spear?

A.   Automatic revolver bullets. Steel jacketed.

Q.   When you keep saying "revolver" you mean the same kind of a weapon that is being examined by the jury at the present time?

A.   I meant that weapon there, yes.

Q.   I don't want any misunderstanding about it, that is why I am pressing it. Do you know what make those bullets were you found in the hip pockets?

A.   Four different makes.

Q.   Do you have in mind what they were?

A.   There were sixteen of Peters make.

Q.   Sixteen of Peters?

A.   Yes.

Q.   Yes.

A.   Seven of U.S., — United States make.

Q.   Sixteen Peters and seven U.S.?

A.   There were six of Winchester, and there were three of the Remington.

Q.   Three Remington, — Peters, U.S., and Winchester?

A.   Yes.

*   *   *

Q.   Did you put any marks on them?

A.   No.

Q.   Well, will you just examine these cartridges which I now show you and tell the jury what they are? I mean, what the calibre is, and what the makes of them are [handing bullets to the witness]?

A.   [Witness examines bullets.] .32 calibre.

Q.   Just put, if there are any of that same kind, just put them aside, if you will, and we will group them.

MR. WILLIAMS.   [To the jury.] To see the mark, I suggest, gentlemen, you hold the barrel, looking at the left.

Q.   I won't bother you to go through that whole bunch of bullets. Have
            you grouped them into, — have you separated them into roughly
            different groups, those you have already looked at?

A.   These are Peters, these United States, Winchester and Remington.

Q.   Are those bullets of the same type of bullet you took from that gun?

A.   Yes.

Q.   From his pocket and pistol?

A.   Pocket and gun.

Q.   No identifying marks on them, as I understand?

A.   No.

            [Mr. Williams shows bullets to defendant's counsel.]

MR. WILLIAMS.   [To the jury.] I am just going to show you, gentlemen, the four
                 types of bullets which the witness says he described. The
                 pistol becomes Exhibit 28.

                                *   *   *

Q.   I notice in reply to my question, Mr. Spear, you simply said all of the
            bullets found there, there was a certain number of a certain kind,
            and so forth. Can you tell the jury what makes of bullet or what
            make of bullets were in the pistol itself?

A.   I cannot.

Q.   You simply grouped all together those that were in the pistol and
            those that were loose in the pocket?

A.   I did.

Q.   Were the bullets loose in the pocket or were they in some receptacle?

A.   They were loose in the pocket.

            [Mr. Williams returns bullets to sheriff.]

Q.   Was there anything else found by you on the defendant Sacco?

A.   There was not.

Evidentiary Foundation:
The Trial of John W. Jenrette, Jr.[26]

[John W. Jenrette, Jr., a Congressman from South Carolina, was successfully
prosecuted for a bribery scheme that the FBI's ABSCAM investigation uncovered.
At trial, the government proffered videotapes of Rep. Jenrette's meetings with
Anthony Amoroso, an FBI undercover agent, and Melvin Weinberg, an FBI
informant. Does the following transcript establish an adequate foundation for
admitting this videotape?]

---

[26] This transcript was prepared for the Committee on Standards of Official Conduct, House of
Representatives, 96th Congress, 2nd Sess. (1981).

* * *

Counsel, are we ready to proceed?

MR. KOTELLY: Yes, Your Honor. The Government's next witness is R. David
                Burch.

                Whereupon,

                R. DAVID BURCH, JR., was called as a witness by and on behalf of
                the Government, and having been first duly sworn was examined and
                testified as follows:

THE COURT: Mr. Kotelly?

DIRECT EXAMINATION

BY MR. KOTELLY:

Q.   Would you please state your full name for the record?

A.   R. David Burch, Jr.

Q.   Mr. Burch, what is your present employment?

A.   I'm a special agent with the Federal Bureau of Investigation.

Q.   How long have you been employed with the FBI?

A.   Approximately eight years.

Q.   Where is your present duty assignment?

A.   Washington field office in Washington, D.C.

Q.   How long have you been assigned there?

A.   Three and one half years.

Q.   What are your general duties with the FBI?

A.   Basically an investigator and in addition to being an investigator I
          am a sound-trained agent.

Q.   Would you explain very briefly what you mean by a sound-trained
          agent?

A.   I mean by a sound-trained agent I have technical training involving
          closed circuit television sets, microphones, other types of recording
          devices that are used by the FBI.

Q.   When did you receive such training?

A.   In March of 1978.

Q.   Now, Agent Burch, are you familiar with a residence at 4407 W
          Street, N.W., Washington?

A.   Yes, I am.

Q.   How are you familiar with that residence?

A.   This was a residence that was used by the FBI in an undercover operation.

Q.   Was this residence to your knowledge owned or leased by the FBI?

A.   It was leased.

Q.   When did you first have contact with the house on W Street?

A.   It would have been some time in the latter part November or December of 1978.

Q.   What was the nature of that contact with the house?

A.   I was responsible for coordinating the technical equipment setup in the house for surveillance purposes.

Q.   What type of technical equipment was installed in that house under your supervision?

A.   We utilized hidden microphones and hidden cameras.

Q.   How long did the installation of this monitoring equipment take?

A.   Approximately three months.

Q.   Was this on a full-time basis on your part?

A.   No, it was not, not this location alone.

Q.   At the time that this equipment was installed, the end of 1978, was this part of the ABSCAM operation?

A.   No, it was not.

Q.   What was the purpose then of the installation of this surveillance equipment?

A.   It was another undercover operation ongoing in Washington, D.C., at that time.

Q.   Now, you have indicated that there were various cameras and microphones installed in the house. Could you tell the jury the locations of these cameras and listening devices?

A.   Yes. We had a hidden camera and microphone in the library or study area. We had a hidden camera and microphone in the living room, a hidden camera and microphone in the dining room and a hidden camera and microphone in the basement recreation area.

Q.   Would you briefly describe the physical layout of the house on W Street?

A.   It's a two-story home with a full basement underneath.

Q.   Would you describe the types of rooms on each of those floors?

A.   The basement area is a recreation area, a laundry room, a bathroom down there and the main floor is a living room, a dining room, a kitchen area and a library or study. On the upstairs are bedrooms.

Q.   And were there any surveillance equipment in the upstairs floor in the bedroom areas?

A.   There was none.

Q.   Now, Agent Burch, regarding these cameras, were you able to monitor what was going on during any undercover meetings at that house on W Street?

A.   Yes, I was.

Q.   Where would you be during the monitoring of these meetings?

A.   I was in a room in the basement directly off from the recreation room there.

Q.   Could you describe to the jury the type of monitoring equipment that you had in the basement?

A.   Yes. I had a cassette recorder, a Betamax, Sony Cassette Recorder — video recorder and a monitor set up down there to monitor as anything was occurring in that particular room.

Q.   How many rooms did you have the capability of recording at the same time?

A.   Only three rooms at the same time.

Q.   Could you describe to the jury which three rooms you could monitor at the same time?

A.   I could monitor the library and the recreation room at the same time but then I had to decide between the dining room and then the living room because there was only one recorder and monitor for that. I had a switcher for me to select which room to record in.

Q.   The living room and the dining room, where were they physically located in relation to each other?

A.   They were adjoining each other, just a common archway between the two.

Q.   Were there any difficulties in the microphone positions regarding meetings that were taking place in more than one room at a time?

A.   We had a problem with microphone recordings between the library and living room because the concealed microphone was in an adjoining wall and you would pick up conversations happening in both rooms.

Q.   If you were in the living room could you actually hear conversations going on in the library?

A.   No, you could not.

Q.   Now, Agent Burch, did you have occasion to have photographs taken of the house on W Street?

A.   Yes, I did.

Q.   Were you present when those photographs were taken?

A.   Yes, I was.

MR. ROBINSON: No Objection.

MR. KOTELLY: Your Honor, for the record these four photographs have already
              been shown to defense counsel.

BY MR. KOTELLY:

Q.   Agent Burch, I first show you Government's Exhibit 1A for identi-
              fication and ask you if you can identify that exhibit?

A.   Yes. This is a photograph of the house located at 4407 W Street,
              N.W., Washington, D.C.

Q.   Does that photograph accurately depict the way the house appeared
              in December of 1979 and January of 1980?

A.   Yes, it does.

Q.   I next show you Government's Exhibits 1B and 1C for identification
              and ask you first to look at Government's Exhibit 1B and ask you if
              you can identify that exhibit?

A.   This is a photograph of the library located in 4407 W Street, N.W.,
              Washington, D.C., that depicts the area, the wall area as you
              immediately enter the doorway.

Q.   Is that doorway into the room?

A.   That is correct, the doorway into the room there.

Q.   How many doors were there into the library at W Street?

A.   Only one door.

Q.   I next ask you to look at Government's 1C for identification and ask
              you if you can identify that photograph?

A.   Yes. This is a photograph of the library again at 4407 W Street and
              the area shown here is the wall and other side of the room opposite
              the doorway as you enter into the room.

Q.   Photographs, Government's 1B and 1C for identification, do they
              accurately depict the way the library appeared in December 1979
              and January 1980?

A.   Yes, they do.

Q.   Finally I show you Government's Exhibit 1D and ask you if you can
              identify that exhibit?

A.   Yes. This is a photograph of the technical equipment, monitoring
              equipment that was set up in the basement area at 4407 W Street.

Q.   Does that photograph accurately depict the way that the monitoring
              equipment was in December of 1979 and January of 1980?

A.   Yes, it does.

Q.   Now, Agent Burch, regarding those four photographs, Government's 1A through 1D, specifically as to the second and third which you have identified as showing the den of the W Street house, do either of those photographs depict what the television or what the camera rather in the library would show when you were monitoring any meeting in that room?

A.   Yes. This is the library as opposed to the den and photograph 1B depicts the area that would be covered by the hidden camera in this particular room.

Q.   And if Mr. Amoroso and Mr. Weinberg were present during any meetings do either of those photographs, 1B or 1C for identification, reflect where Mr. Amoroso and Mr. Weinberg would normally sit?

A.   Yes. Government's Exhibit 1C would show the area that Mr. Amoroso and Mr. Weinberg would be seated during this time.

Q.   Agent Burch, directing your attention to September 4th of 1979 were you on duty on that date?

A.   Yes, I was.

Q.   Were you present at the townhouse on W Street on that date at a time in which you monitored and recorded a meeting with anyone that's here today in Court?

A.   Yes, I was.

Q.   Who was that that is here today in Court that was present at the meeting on December 4th?

A.   John Stowe and John Jenrette.

Q.   Would you point those individuals out and describe what clothing they are wearing right now so they can be identified on the record?

MR. ROBINSON: No objection on behalf of Mr. Jenrette. MR. DOHNAL: Likewise on behalf of Mr. Stowe. THE COURT: All right.

BY MR. KOTELLY:

Q.   On December 4th what type of monitoring did you do at that meeting of Mr. Jenrette and Mr. Stowe?

A.   On December the 4th I had video monitoring and audio in the library, in the living room and in the recreation room downstairs.

Q.   During this meeting when Mr. Jenrette and Mr. Stowe were there, was any one from the FBI present at the meeting?

A.   Yes, there was.

Q.   Who was that?

A.   It was Special Agent Anthony Amoroso.

Q.   Was there anyone else who was paid by the FBI who was present during the meeting?

A.   Yes, there was. It was Mel Weinberg.

Q.   What rooms did you actually monitor and record on during that meeting on December 4th?

A.   In the library, the living room and the basement recreation room.

Q.   Now, after the meeting had ended, Agent Burch, what, if anything, did you do with the video cassettes?

A.   These video cassettes were removed from the recording machines. They were initialed by myself and turned over to Special Agent John Good of the Federal Bureau of Investigation.

Q.   Who is Special Agent John Good?

A.   He's the supervisory senior resident agent at the Hauppauge [office] located in New York.

* * *

Q.   Now, Agent Burch, does the FBI have set procedures in the manner in which videotapes of meetings are maintained by the bureau?

A.   Yes, they do.

Q.   Could you specifically describe to the jury the procedures that are used?

A.   In a video recording the tapes are removed from the recording machines, initialed by the technician or individual that is doing the recording and turned over to another special agent of the FBI and then they're put into an envelope which we refer to as a chain of custody envelope. Thereafter they are transported to a special designated area within each field office.

Q.   Who would have access to those videos after they are made and placed into the special vault?

A.   Special Agents or employees of the FBI and if anyone were to retrieve these particular recordings they would have to show initial receipt and purpose of the tape being removed.

Q.   Did you have occasion to retrieve from the FBI evidence room the tape recordings that you made on December the 4th, 1979?

A.   Yes, I did.

Q.   Since the time that you retrieved them have they been in your custody since that time?

A.   Yes, they have.

MR. KOTELLY: For the record, Your Honor, I have shown defense counsel the envelopes 2A and 3A.

BY MR. KOTELLY:

Q.   Agent Burch, I first show you Government's Exhibit 2A for identification and ask you if you can identify that document?

A.   Yes. Government's Exhibit 2A is what I refer to as a chain of custody envelope that indicates a recording on December 4th, 1979.

Q.   Does your name appear on that document as receiving custody of that exhibit, that envelope?

A.   Yes, it does.

Q.   What does that envelope contain?

A.   This envelope contains a videotape of the meeting on December 4th, 1979.

Q.   Now, would you take the contents of that out of the envelope, sir.

        I would ask you what government Exhibit number has that been given, premarked?

A.   This has Government's Exhibit Number 2B.

Q.   Can you identify that cassette, sir?

A.   Yes. This is a video cassette of a meeting that took place on December 4th, 1979, at W Street, and it has my initials etched on it.

Q.   Is that the original video cassette that you recorded on that night?

A.   Yes, it is.

Q.   What room would that video cassette have been in?

A.   This was in the library.

Q.   I next show you Government's Exhibit 3A for identification and ask you if you can identify that envelope?

A.   Yes. Again, this is a chain of custody envelope that has the date of December 4th, 1979.

Q.   Does your name appear on it as having received custody of that envelope?

A.   Yes, it does.

Q.   What are the contents of 3A for identification?

A.   This is a videotape recording of the meeting that took place on December 4, 1979.

Q.   Is that marked 3B for identification?

A.   Yes, it is marked 3B.

Q.   Can you identify that cassette recording?

A.   Yes, I can by my initials that are placed on this tape.

Q.   When were your initials placed on that tape?

A.   On December 4th.

Q.   What room would that recording have been in?

A.   This would have been in the library also.

Q.   Agent Burch, since December the 4th of 1979 have you had an opportunity to review those tape recordings since you have received custody of them prior to trial?

A.   Yes, I have.

Q.   That would be 2B for identification and 3B for identification, correct?

A.   Correct.

Q.   Do those videotapes accurately reflect what you monitored and observed on the evening of December 4th in the library at W Street?

A.   Yes, they do.

D. PRELIMINARY QUESTIONS OF FACT: THE ROLE OF JUDGE AND JURY

Edmund M. Morgan, *Functions of Judge and Jury in the Determination of Preliminary Questions of Fact*
43 HARV. L. REV. 165, 165–69 (1929)[27]

Whenever an objection is interposed to evidence proffered in a jury trial, the judge must rule upon it. He alone must determine whether the jury shall hear or see the challenged item. If it has no probative value, he will, of course, reject it. Irrelevant evidence obviously cannot be considered in any system in which disputes are to be rationally resolved.[28] On the other hand relevant evidence may be declared incompetent[29] and be withheld from the jury upon one or more of several grounds. Its probative value may be so slight as to be negligible. Or it may be of such character as to be incapable of reasonably accurate evaluation and therefore likely to mislead the jury. Or it may have less intrinsic accuracy than other evidence to the same point available to the proponent. Or the social value of the interests which will be protected by its exclusion may be deemed to exceed the social value of the contribution toward the ascertainment of truth which its reception would make.

When the relevancy or competency of the questioned matter does not depend upon the existence . . . of another disputed fact, no serious problem of division of function between judge and jury arises. It is universally agreed that the judge is to decide whether the jury shall get the evidence, and is to direct the jury as to the purposes for which it may be properly considered; the jury is to weigh it in accordance with the instructions of the judge. It often happens, however, that a fact, irrelevant in itself, will have great probative value in conjunction with another fact. For example, if the issue is whether P is responsible to T for an injury caused by P's automobile striking T, the fact that A drove the automobile into T is entirely irrelevant in and of itself. If, however, it is accompanied with the fact that A was

---

[27] Copyright © 1929 by the Harvard Law Review Association.

[28] [1] Relevancy will be determined by the applicable rules of pleading and of substantive law. [Ed. — This author defines relevancy in terms of common law materiality.]

[29] [2] The courts do not use the word "incompetent" to denote any particular kind of inadmissibility. In this article, it is used to designate evidence which is relevant but which is nevertheless excluded.

acting in the course of his employment as *P's* servant, it becomes of controlling importance. Likewise, a fact incompetent in itself may, when conjoined with another, lose its incompetency. Thus the dying declaration of a wounded man accusing *D* of having inflicted the fatal wound will not, without more, be received against *D* upon *D's* trial for the homicide. It is incompetent as hearsay. If, however, it is shown that the declarant when making the statement realized that death was immediately impending, it becomes competent under a well-recognized exception to the rule against hearsay. To put it generally, it frequently occurs that the relevancy or competency of fact *A* depends upon the existence of fact *B*. Under such circumstances, who is to determine whether *B* exists, the judge or the jury?

To say that the relevancy of *A* depends upon the existence of *B is* only to say that it requires a combination of *A* and *B* to produce a relevant factor in the case. No argument can be framed for taking from the jury the question as to *A* which will not be equally applicable to the question as to *B*. If when evidence upon *A* is offered, an objection of irrelevancy puts the determination of *B* into the province of the judge, by the same token when *B* is offered, an objection of the same sort will produce a similar result as to *A*. If both *A* and *B* are not thus to be taken from the jury, at least the proponent can at his pleasure determine which shall be decided by the judge by first tendering evidence of the other. In no case, it is believed, where the analysis can be so baldly made, has any court held that, under the guise of ruling upon the admissibility of evidence, a judge may exclude the jury from determining an issue otherwise properly within its field. But such an analysis is not always so obvious.

Where the competency of *A* depends upon the existence of *B*, it is not a whit more difficult for the jury to determine the existence of *B*. It can as easily determine the state of mind of the dying declarant as the intent or motive of the defendant. The same is true of any fact upon the existence of which the admissibility of otherwise incompetent evidence depends, as, for example, the circumstances under which a confession was made, the availability or unavailability of an original document, the status of marriage or non-marriage between a witness and a party, or the relationship of client and attorney between a witness and another. Consequently, if such questions are to be taken from the jury, it must be on some other ground than the incapacity of the jury to determine the facts.

On the other hand, if these preliminary questions are to be left to the jury, and if at the same time the objects designed to be accomplished by the exclusionary rules are to be attained, it will be necessary sharply to distinguish and separate the preliminary question upon which the admissibility of the challenged evidence depends from the evidence itself. In many cases, this could be done by making a special issue of the preliminary question, confining the tes- timony strictly thereto, and taking a special interlocutory verdict. If the verdict found the preliminary basis, *B*, the jury would then get the evidence as to *A*; otherwise not. It needs no argument to show that the time, already too great, which a jury trial consumes, would under such a procedure be substantially increased. Moreover, in many cases, it would be a practical impossibility so to divorce the evidence of the preliminary fact from the challenged testimony as not to indicate the tenor or content of the latter to the jury.

If evidence as to both *A* and *B* is submitted to the jury, and the jurors are instructed to cast out that as to *A* unless they find *B*, several very practical objections at once obtrude themselves. Such a procedure will enormously compli-cate the work of the jury. It will not do to disregard realities. The jury is a casual group taken from the body of the citizenry. Jurors are compelled to perform their duties in rooms in which vile ventilation, inadequate acoustics, and limited light make keen, accurate work especially difficult. They are usually required to rely upon their memories unaided by memoranda. A trial may occupy days or weeks or even months. It takes great faith to expect jurors to distinguish between bare assertions, argument, and objections of counsel, on the one hand, and evidence on the other, and to rely only on the evidence as a basis for their verdict. To require them at the outset of their deliberations to separate the questions of admissibility from the ultimate questions, to apply to the former the testimony touching their foundations, and to reach rulings thereon prior to a consideration of the merits, is to demand the practically impossible. Furthermore, the only method of ascertaining whether the jury really went through the form of complying with such instructions would be the submission of special questions. Even assuming that the answers to these questions were made final, such a process would add enormously to the opportunities to assign errors on appeal or motion for new trial.

But a more fundamental objection exists. If the jury be credited with the capacity to perform the task of ruling intelligently upon such a mass of testimony — a capacity which every judge and trial lawyer knows that it does not possess — can it be credited with the capacity to wipe its mind clean of the objectionable testimony which it has heard or seen, and rest its decision upon the admissible evidence only? It is a familiar fiction that the trial judge in equity cases regularly performs this psychological feat. But there is no trial lawyer who does not rejoice when he gets such a judge to admit *de bene* a piece of evidence which is emotionally potent in his favor, even though it may later be formally stricken, and no trial lawyer against whom it is received who is not convinced that the trial judge is purporting to strain out the water of prejudice from the milk of legitimate evidence through a totally ineffective mental sieve. A mind trained to sift evidence may substantially accom-plish even so difficult a task; but to expect the unskilled minds of jurors to do so is little short of ridiculous.

In many instances, moreover, the chief objective of the exclusionary rule would be destroyed. Where the exclusion is based on a policy of protection of an interest, nothing could be more absurd than to violate the interest and then to instruct the jury to repair the damage by disregarding the wrongfully extracted evidence. If a lawyer is compelled to repeat in open court the confidential communications of his alleged client, and the jury is told to disregard them in case they find the relationship exists, the harm of disclosure is beyond remedy. In this respect certainly the only sensible option must be between a decision of the preliminary questions by the judge, and an interlocutory verdict thereon by the jury.

On theory, then, where the relevancy of *A* depends upon the existence of *B*, the existence of *B* should normally be for the jury; where the competency of *A* depends upon the existence of *B*, the existence of *B* should always be for the judge.

[margin handwritten note: doctrine of conditional relevance]

NOTES AND QUESTIONS

1.   What standard of proof is to be employed in resolving preliminary questions of fact? *See* Saltzburg, *Standards of Proof and Preliminary Questions of Fact*, 27 STAN. L. REV. 271 (1975). In *Bourjaily v. United States*, 483 U.S. 171 (1987), the Supreme Court held that Rule 104(a) determinations are governed by a preponderance of the evidence standard. The appropriate standard for conditional relevancy questions under Rule 104(b) was addressed in *Huddleston v. United States*, 485 U.S. 681 (1988), in which the Court ruled "in determining whether the Government has introduced sufficient evidence to meet Rule 104(b), the trial court . . . examines all the evidence in the case and decides whether the jury could reasonably find the conditional fact . . . by a preponderance of the evidence."

2.   Professor Morgan's characterization of the situation in which the relevance of a proffered fact depend upon the occurrence of another fact is usually referred to as the doctrine of conditional relevance. To what extent, if any, does Rule 104 follow the traditional distinction between questions of competence and those of conditional relevance?

3.   Is the concept of conditional relevance fundamentally inconsistent with Federal Rule of Evidence 401, which defines relevant evidence as "evidence having any tendency to make the existence of any fact that is of consequence to the determination of the action more or less probable than it would be without the evidence." For example, using Professor Morgan's illustration, if the ultimate issue is whether plaintiff was negligently injured by defendant's agent, doesn't proof of A's negligence enhance the overall probability that plaintiff was, in fact, so injured? *See* Ball, *The Myth of Conditional Relevancy*, 14 GA. L. REV. 435 (1980). Professor Ball further maintains that strict application of the conditional relevancy principle would wreak havoc in the courtroom:

> This wholesale incorporation of the technique for resolving problems of materiality would mean that no fact could be relevant unless all the other necessary facts were already known to "exist." Proof of one element of a claim would be "entirely irrelevant" unless all the remaining elements had already been established. The resemblance between this notion and the presentation of a jigsaw puzzle with instructions that no piece could be put into place "unless it is the last one" is especially clear in the automobile injury example. No reason is given for failing to say that the fact of A's driving into T is irrelevant and inadmissible unless (a) it was negligent and (b) caused (c) injury to T, and (d) was done in the course of A's employment as D's servant.

*   *   *

> The far greater danger, already realized in these new codifications of evidence, is that once codifiers go off on this false trail, they will find a problem of "conditional relevancy" behind every tree and bring in their rescue apparatus in a way which will confuse the jury and muddle the administration of the evidence rules far more than letting matters alone would have done.

> From the statements in the Note to Rule 104(b) that conditional relevancy arises "in some situations"; that it is to be distinguished from "logical relevancy," and a sentence in the Note to Rule 401 defining "relevant evidence," which begins "Passing mention should be made of so-called 'conditional relevancy,'" the impression might be given that the doctrine is a small and relatively minor pigeon-hole in the Rules, with few occasions for application.
>
> Quite the contrary is the case.

Id. at 439–40, 454. Thus, Professor Ball suggests that every fact is potentially conditionally relevant upon some other fact. If this is true, what kind of instruction should be fashioned for the jury? Consider the following:

> [I]t is clear that upon request a party is entitled to instructions to the jury about it. . . . Since either A or B "is irrelevant without the other," the instruction must run along the following lines: The jury are to disregard the evidence of fact A unless they find fact B, and to disregard the evidence of B unless they find fact A. This is in addition to the usual instruction defining C and instructing that they can find it only if they find that A and B occurred. The serious effort to put a jury through these gymnastics as to every witness's testimony, everything admitted as an exhibit, and nearly all inferences from circumstances seems . . . staggering in its possibilities for misunderstanding, mistake, and mistrial.

Id. at 458. Must the jury also reach a unanimous decision as to each conditionally relevant fact?

4. Consider the following question:

> [H]ow should a trial judge operating along traditional lines handle a case of objections for *both* incompetency *and* irrelevancy? An anonymous memorandum: "I killed Cock Robin," is offered in the trial for murder of that notorious victim. The assertion is incompetent hearsay, and also irrelevant, unless authorship by defendant makes it his admission. Should the trial judge admit the memorandum if there is enough evidence of such authorship to warrant a favorable finding to this effect, or should he exclude it unless he himself finds such authorship?

J. MAGUIRE, EVIDENCE: COMMON SENSE AND COMMON LAW 224 (1947).

5. Conditional relevance continues to trouble many students because it is often difficult to illustrate this doctrine at work. *Lataille v. Ponte*, 754 F.2d 33, 37 (1st Cir. 1985), provides some assistance. *Lataille* was a civil rights action brought by a prisoner whom corrections officers had beaten. Over objection, the defense introduced into evidence Plaintiff's disciplinary record, which contained numerous instances of assaults on guards and escape attempts. On appeal, this ruling was reversed *inter alia* because of the absence of evidence indicating that guards knew about his record at the time of the beating. Thus, the guards could not rely upon these prior incidents in support of claims that they acted in self-defense and to prevent another escape attempt. Similarly, courts have excluded evidence of a murder victim's drug usage in support of a defense of self-defense, absent evidence

that the defendant knew the victim was under the influence of a dangerous drug. *See, e.g., Edds v. State*, 2002 Ark. App. LEXIS 529 (Sept. 25, 2002).

E. AUTHENTICATION OF DOCUMENTS — ELECTRONIC EVIDENCE

UNITED STATES v. SAFAVIAN
435 F. Supp. 2d 36 (D.D.C. 2006)

OPINION AND ORDER

PAUL L. FRIEDMAN, DISTRICT JUDGE.

This matter is before the Court on: (1) defendant's motion in limine to deny the government's Rule 902(11) certifications; (2) the government's motion in limine for pretrial determination of admissibility of certain evidence and the supplement to that motion; and (3) defendant's motion in limine to exclude hearsay and irrelevant evidence. These motions all make arguments regarding the admissibility of approximately 260 e-mails that the government seeks to admit in its case against the defendant.

A. Authentication of E-mails

Authentication is an aspect of relevancy. Advisory Committee Note, Fed. R. Evid. 901(a) (citations omitted); 31 WRIGHT & GOLD, FEDERAL PRACTICE AND PROCEDURE: EVIDENCE § 7102 at 13 (2000). "The requirement of authentication or identification as a condition precedent to admissibility is satisfied by evidence sufficient to support a finding that the matter in question is what its proponent claims." Fed. R. Evid. 901(a). *See* 5 SALTZBURG, MARTIN & CAPRA, FEDERAL RULES OF EVIDENCE MANUAL § 901.02[1] at 901-5 (8th ed. 2002). The threshold for the Court's determination of authenticity is not high. *See, e.g., United States v. Reilly*, 33 F.3d 1396, 1404 (3d Cir. 1994) ("the burden of proof for authentication is slight"); *United States v. Holmquist*, 36 F.3d 154, 168 (1st Cir. 1994) ("the standard for authentication, and hence for admissibility, is one of reasonable likelihood"); *United States v. Coohey*, 11 F.3d 97, 99 (8th Cir. 1993) ("the proponent need only demonstrate a rational basis for its claim that the evidence is what the proponent asserts it to be"). The question for the Court under Rule 901 is whether the proponent of the evidence has "offered a foundation from which the jury could reasonably find that the evidence is what the proponent says it is." 5 FEDERAL RULES OF EVIDENCE MANUAL § 901.02[1] at 901-5–901-6. The Court need not find that the evidence is necessarily what the proponent claims, but only that there is sufficient evidence that the *jury* ultimately might do so. *See* 31 FEDERAL PRACTICE AND PROCEDURE: EVIDENCE § 7102 at 16.

1. Rule 902(11)

Rule 902 of the Federal Rules of Evidence lists those documents that are self-authenticating — that is, those that do not require extrinsic evidence of authenticity as a condition precedent to admissibility. Rule 902(11) is intended to set forth "a procedure by which parties can authenticate certain records of regularly conducted activity, other than through the testimony of a foundation witness." Advisory Committee Note, Fed. R. Evid. 902. Similarly, the Advisory Committee Notes to Rule 803 state that Rule 902(11) "provides that the foundation requirements of Rule 803(6) can be satisfied under certain circumstances without the expense and inconvenience of producing time-consuming foundation witnesses." Advisory Committee Note, Fed. R. Evid. 803. These comments to each Rule make clear that they were intended to go "hand in hand." *Rambus, Inc. v. Infineon Technologies AG*, 348 F. Supp. 2d 698, 701 (E.D. Va. 2004) ("Rule 902(11) is . . . the functional equivalent of testimony offered to authenticate a business record tendered under Rule 803(6)").

Pursuant to Rule 902(11), the government submitted a certification from Jay Nogle, the official custodian of records for Greenberg Traurig, LLP, the law firm that once employed Jack Abramoff. Mr. Nogle stated that in his capacity as official custodian he could certify that 467,747 e-mails had been produced by Greenberg Traurig to the United States and that those e-mails comport with the requirements of Rule 902(11), in part because the e-mails "would be admissible under Fed. R. Evid. 803(6) if accompanied by a written declaration of [their] custodian or other qualified person." The government does not, however, seek to admit these e-mails pursuant to the business records exception to the hearsay rule in Rule 803(6), but offers other hearsay exceptions and non-hearsay arguments (discussed later in this Opinion) as bases for admission. The defendant objects to the authentication of the Greenberg Traurig e-mails pursuant to Mr. Nogle's Rule 902(11) certification.[30] Because Rule 902(11) was intended as a means of authenticating *only* that evidence which is being offered under the business records exception to the hearsay rule, the Court will not accept the proffered Rule 902(11) certification of Mr. Nogle with reference to the Greenberg Traurig e-mail exhibits.

2. Rule 901

Because it is not appropriate for these e-mails to be admitted as self-authenticating under Rule 902 of the Federal Rules of Evidence, the Court turns to the authentication requirements set forth in Rule 901. The question under Rule 901 is whether there is sufficient evidence "to support a finding that the matter in question is what its proponent claims," Fed. R. Evid. 901(a) — in this case, e-mails between Mr. Safavian, Mr. Abramoff, and other individuals. As noted, the Court need not find that the e-mails are necessarily what the proponent claims, only that there is evidence sufficient for the jury to make such a finding. *See* 5 Federal Rules of Evidence Manual § 901.02[1] at 901-5–901-6 (8th ed. 2002); *id.* at 901-14

---

[30] [1] The government has submitted 902(11) certifications for other documents, but the defendant at a hearing before the Court on the motions conceded that the other ones were appropriate, leaving its only remaining objection to Mr. Nogle's certification of the Greenberg Traurig e-mails.

("Evidence is sufficient for authentication purposes if the foundation for particular evidence warrants the trier of fact in finding that it is what the proponent claims."). Rule 901(b) sets forth illustrations of how evidence may be authenticated or identified; it emphasizes, however, that these are "illustration(s) only" and are not intended to be the only methods by which the Court may determine that the e-mails are what the government says they are. *See United States v. Dean*, 989 F.2d 1205, 1210 n. 7 (D.C. Cir. 1993) ("The rule contains an illustrative, but not exhaustive, list of suggested methods of identification.").[31] For the reasons that follow, the Court finds that there is ample evidence for the jury to find that these exhibits are, in fact, e-mail exchanges between Mr. Safavian, Mr. Abramoff, and other individuals.

One method of authentication identified under Rule 901 is to examine the evidence's "distinctive characteristics and the like," including "[a]ppearance, contents, substance, internal patterns, or other distinctive characteristics, taken in conjunction with circumstances." Fed. R. Evid. 901(b)(4). Most of the proffered exhibits can be authenticated in this manner. The e-mails in question have many distinctive characteristics, including the actual e-mail addresses containing the "@" symbol, widely known to be part of an e-mail address, and certainly a distinctive mark that identifies the document in question as an e-mail. *See United States v. Siddiqui*, 235 F.3d 1318, 1322 (11th Cir. 2000). In addition, most of the e-mail addresses themselves contain the name of the person connected to the address, such as "abramoffj@gtlaw.com," "David.Safavian@mail.house.gov," or "david.safavian@gsa.gov." *See, e.g.*, Exhibits 101, 105, 106. Frequently these e-mails contain the name of the sender or recipient in the bodies of the e-mail, in the signature blocks at the end of the e-mail, in the "To:" and "From:" headings, and by signature of the sender. The contents of the e-mails also authenticate them as being from the purported sender and to the purported recipient, containing as they do discussions of various identifiable matters, such as Mr. Safavian's work at the General Services Administration ("GSA"), Mr. Abramoff's work as a lobbyist, Mr. Abramoff's restaurant, Signatures, and various other personal and professional matters.[32]

Those e-mails that are not clearly identifiable on their own can be authenticated under Rule 901(b)(3), which states that such evidence may be authenticated by comparison by the trier of fact (the jury) with "specimens which have been [otherwise] authenticated" — in this case, those e-mails that already have been independently authenticated under Rule 901(b)(4). For instance, certain e-mails contain the address "MerrittDC@aol.com" with no further indication of what person uses that e-mail address either through the contents or in the e-mail heading itself. *See, e.g.*, Exhibit 134. This e-mail address on its own does not clearly demonstrate who was the sender or receiver using that address. When these e-mails are examined alongside Exhibit 100 (which the Court finds is authenticated under Rule 901(b)(4) by its distinctive characteristics), however, it becomes clear that

---

[31] [2] The first method identified by the Rule is testimony of a witness with knowledge that the matter is what it is claimed to be. Fed. R. Evid. 901(b)(1). Apparently, however, the government has decided not to call the one witness who could authenticate almost every one of the proffered e-mails, Jack Abramoff.

[32] [3] Presumably, a person with personal knowledge will testify that Mr. Safavian worked at GSA, and that Mr. Abramoff worked as a lobbyist and owned a restaurant named Signatures.

MerrittDC@aol.com was an address used by the defendant. Exhibit 100 is also an e-mail sent from that address, but the signature within the e-mail gives the defendant's name and the name of his business, Janus-Merritt Strategies, L.L.C., located in Washington, D.C. (as well as other information, such as the business' address, telephone and fax numbers), thereby connecting the defendant to that e-mail address and clarifying the meaning of both "Merritt" and "DC" in it. The comparison of those e-mails containing MerrittDC@aol.com with Exhibit 100 thereby can provide the jury with a sufficient basis to find that these two exhibits are what they purport to be — that is, e-mails to or from Mr. Safavian. The Court will not perform this exercise with respect to each exhibit. Suffice it to say that the Court has examined each of these e-mails and found that all those that the Court is admitting in whole or in part meet the requirements for authentication under Rule 901.

The defendant argues that the trustworthiness of these e-mails cannot be demonstrated, particularly those e-mails that are embedded within e-mails as having been forwarded to or by others or as the previous e-mail to which a reply was sent. The Court rejects this as an argument against authentication of the e-mails. The defendant's argument is more appropriately directed to the weight the jury should give the evidence, not to its authenticity. While the defendant is correct that earlier e-mails that are included in a chain — either as ones that have been forwarded or to which another has replied — may be altered, this trait is not specific to e-mail evidence. It can be true of any piece of documentary evidence, such as a letter, a contract or an invoice. Indeed, fraud trials frequently center on altered paper documentation, which, through the use of techniques such as photocopies, white-out, or wholesale forgery, easily can be altered. The *possibility* of alteration does not and cannot be the basis for excluding e-mails as unidentified or unauthenticated as a matter of course, any more than it can be the rationale for excluding paper documents (and copies of those documents). We live in an age of technology and computer use where e-mail communication now is a normal and frequent fact for the majority of this nation's population, and is of particular importance in the professional world. The defendant is free to raise this issue with the jury and put on evidence that e-mails are capable of being altered before they are passed on. Absent specific evidence showing alteration, however, the Court will not exclude any embedded e-mails because of the mere possibility that it can be done.

STATE v. THOMPSON
777 N.W.2d 617 (N.D. 2010)

[The court construes North Dakota Rule of Evidence 901(a), which is identical to Federal Rule of Evidence 901(a), in an assault prosecution.]

At trial, the complainant testified on direct examination about several text messages sent to him on October 31, 2008. He testified he knew the text messages were from Thompson because the messages said "Fr: Jen" at the beginning, which was the way he stored her phone number in his cell phone, and the end of the message included her phone number and her signature, "cuzImJenIcan," which he was familiar with. . . . The complainant . . . testified . . . that during the course of several text messages that day, Thompson made threats toward him, including one specific profane threat.

During Thompson's case, she testified she sent several text messages to the complainant on October 31, 2008. On cross-examination, she testified about the text messages, including that she could have sent the complainant one specific profane and threatening text message . . . . [T]he court . . . admonished the jury that evidence about the text messages was allowed for a limited purpose to show Thompson's state of mind. During further cross-examination of Thompson, the State offered into evidence a picture of one specific text message sent at 8:20 a.m., which included profane and threatening language. . . .

Thompson thereafter testified the complainant may have used her phone to send that message to himself, and the court allowed the State to introduce the picture of the text message with further "appropriate evidentiary foundation." The State elicited further foundational testimony from Thompson about her cell phone number and her signature for text messages, which were both depicted on the picture of the text message. The State again offered the picture of the text message into evidence, and the court allowed the jury to see the picture . . . .

Rule 901(a), N.D.R.Ev., deals with the procedure for authenticating evidence and provides that the "requirement of authentication or identification as a condition precedent to admissibility is satisfied by evidence sufficient to support a finding that the matter in question is what its proponent claims." Rule 901(a), N.D.R.Ev., is identical to F.R.Ev. 901(a), and we may consider persuasive federal authority in construing our rule. . . .

Although this Court has not previously considered an issue about the foundational requirements for the admissibility of text messages, other courts have held that similar electronic messages were authenticated by circumstantial evidence establishing the evidence was what the proponent claimed it to be. *See United States v. Siddiqui*, 235 F.3d 1318, 1322–23 (11th Cir. 2000) (e-mails properly authenticated when they included defendant's e-mail address, the reply function automatically dialed defendant's e-mail address as sender, messages contained factual details known to defendant, messages included defendant's nickname, and messages were followed with phone conversations on same topic); *United States v. Tank*, 200 F.3d 627, 630–31 (9th Cir. 2000) (foundational requirement for chat room conversation established when defendant admitted he used screen name "Cessna" when he participated in recorded conversations, several co-conspirators testified he used that name, and defendant showed up at meeting arranged with person using screen name "Cessna"); *United States v. Simpson*, 152 F.3d 1241, 1249–50 (10th Cir. 1998) (authentication established when chat room printout showed individual using name "Stavron" gave officer defendant's name and address and subsequent e-mail exchanges indicated e-mail address belonged to defendant); *United States v. Safavian*, 435 F. Supp. 2d 36, 40 (D.D.C. Cir. 2006) (e-mail messages held properly authenticated when the e-mail addresses contain distinctive characteristics including the e-mail addresses and a name of the person connected to the address, the bodies of the messages contain a name of the sender or recipient, and the contents of the e-mails also authenticate them as being from the purported sender to the purported recipient); *Dickens v. State*, 175 Md. App. 231, 927 A.2d 32, 36–38 (Md. Ct. Spec. App. 2007) (threatening text messages received by victim on cell phone were properly authenticated when circumstantial evidence provided adequate proof message was sent by defendant); *Kearley v. Mississippi*, 843 So.2d 66, 70 (Miss. Ct.

App. 2002) (e-mails adequately authenticated when witness vouched for accuracy of e-mail printouts and police officer testified defendant admitted sending e-mails); *State v. Taylor*, 178 N.C. App. 395, 632 S.E.2d 218, 230–31 (N.C. Ct. App. 2006) (text messages properly authenticated when telephone employees testified about logistics for text messages and about how particular text messages were stored and received and messages contained sufficient circumstantial evidence the victim was the person who sent and received the messages); *In re F.P.*, 2005 PA Super 220, 878 A.2d 91, 93–95 (Pa. Super. Ct. 2005) (instant messages properly authenticated through circumstantial evidence including screen names and context of messages and surrounding circumstances); *Massimo v. State*, 144 S.W.3d 210, 215–17 (Tex. App. 2004) (e-mails admissible when victim recognized defendant's e-mail address, e-mails discussed things only the victim, defendant, and few others knew, e-mails written in way defendant would communicate, and third-party witnessed defendant sending similar threatening e-mail); *see generally* 5 Jack B. Weinstein & Margaret A. Berger, *Weinstein's Federal Evidence*, at § 901.08[3] and [4]; 5 Christopher B. Mueller & Laird C. Kirkpatrick, *Federal Evidence*, at § 9:9; 5 Stephen A. Saltzburg, Michael M. Martin, & Daniel J. Capra, *Federal Rules of Evidence Manual*, at § 901.02[12].

In *F.P.*, 878 A.2d at 95 (citation and footnote omitted), the Pennsylvania Superior Court aptly rejected an argument that electronic messages are inherently unreliable because of the messages' relative anonymity:

Essentially, appellant would have us create a whole new body of law just to deal with e-mails or instant messages. The argument is that e-mails or text messages are inherently unreliable because of their relative anonymity and the fact that while an electronic message can be traced to a particular computer, it can rarely be connected to a specific author with any certainty. Unless the purported author is actually witnessed sending the e-mail, there is always the possibility it is not from whom it claims. As appellant correctly points out, anybody with the right password can gain access to another's e-mail account and send a message ostensibly from that person. However, the same uncertainties exist with traditional written documents. A signature can be forged; a letter can be typed on another's typewriter; distinct letterhead stationary can be copied or stolen. We believe that e-mail messages and similar forms of electronic communication can be properly authenticated within the existing framework of Pa. R.E. 901 and Pennsylvania case law. We see no justification for constructing unique rules for admissibility of electronic communications such as instant messages; they are to be evaluated on a case-by-case basis as any other document to determine whether or not there has been an adequate foundational showing of their relevance and authenticity.

Here, the district court heard sufficient evidence from the complainant, including the circumstances of that day and his knowledge of Thompson's cell phone number and signature on text messages, to authenticate the complainant's testimony about the text messages he received on October 31, 2008. That evidence was sufficient to authenticate the complainant's testimony under N.D.R.Ev. 901(b)(1) and (4).

EVIDENCE CHALLENGE: Challenge yourself to learn more about this topic. Enter the following address into your browser to access Evidence Challenge and apply these concepts to realistic problems set in a virtual courtroom.
http://www.EvidenceChallenge.com. Additional purchase required.

Chapter III

THE EXAMINATION OF WITNESSES

A. TESTIMONIAL COMPETENCE

1. Introduction

3 THE COLLECTED WORKS OF AMBROSE BIERCE 415 (1910)[1]

In "The Difficulty of Crossing A Field," Ambrose Bierce tells of the disappearance into thin air of a man named Williamson while walking across his lawn in Selma, Alabama, in July, 1854, in full view of his wife and house servants. The probate court concluded that he was dead of unknown causes. Summarizing the evidence, Bierce notes that "Mrs. Williamson had lost her reason and the servants were, of course, not competent to testify." *Id.* at 418.

Scott Rowley, *The Competency of Witnesses*
24 Iowa L. Rev. 482, 485–90 (1939)[2] (reprinted with permission)

The Norman Conquest . . . brought into the law of England little, if any, conception of the modern idea of fact witnesses. It was still an age of feudalism, pageantry and superstition. God was still supposed to indicate his judgment between man and man or between man and the State by means of burned feet and drownings, by the unhorseing or injury of hired champions or by the prearranged formal oath of the *secta*. Formalism had become so strongly entrenched that form was the all-in-all, the *ne plus ultra*. Apparently, it did not often occur to the medieval legal mind that a direct approach to the merits of a controversy, through a narration, a true narration, of the facts involved therein, had any part or place in the determination of the merits of the point in dispute.

* * *

It is perhaps fair to assume that the modern fact witness idea was developed by and through the ancient jury, more than through any other one influence. The early jury, unlike our modern jury, was selected from men who had, or were supposed to have had, fact information regarding the matters in issue. They were selected from the neighborhood in question, a certain number from the particular hundred, who were supposed to give particular information to the others. . . .

In early records there are instances where the witness to a deed and the jury

---

[1] Copyright New York, Neale Publishing Company.
[2] Copyright © 1939. Reprinted with permission.

determining its genuineness were combined. In all these instances the witnesses seem to have been a part of the jury; and the jury itself, in the earliest stages, seems to have had the aspect of being a group of witnesses as well as of being a determining body. Later, however, the functions of the two groups drifted apart and became sharply defined. This development is clearly observed in the fourteenth century, but even then the witness and the jury occupied, from our modern viewpoint, a singular relation. As expressed in 1349, "If the witnesses and the jury cannot agree upon one verdict, that of the jury shall be taken."

*   *   *

Holdsworth assumes, and probably rightly so, that, regardless of the ancestry of the modern witness concept, the Act of 1562–1563 which created the statutory offenses of perjury and provided for compulsory attendance of witnesses, initiated a new epoch in the law of evidence, and brought forth new questions regarding the competency of witnesses. Dean Wigmore places the advent of the modern witness, as a main source of evidence to the jury in the1600's.

Under the old theory, the competency of the witness, plus a stilted formality, satisfied the mind and terminated the controversy.

*   *   *

As early as the twelfth century certain rules . . . developed, in canon law regarding the designation of certain persons as incompetent to act as witnesses. Some of these crept into the English common law, in an indirect way; but, on the whole, in the sixteenth and seventeenth centuries . . . , many of the rules of the canon law were discarded, and the English law of competency developed along somewhat more liberal lines.

Holdsworth groups these rules of incompetency under two main heads, natural and artificial incompetencies. Jones classifies witnesses, under the common-law rules of incompetency in four groups, insofar as total incompetencies are concerned: (1) those insensible to the obligations of an oath; (2) those wanting in capacity or understanding; (3) those having a pecuniary interest in the issue; (4) parties to the issue. The last group was sometimes included among those interested in the result. This author also lists types of partial incompetencies, where the witness was held incompetent to testify only as to certain matters, on the ground of public policy. The simplicity of Holdsworth's grouping has much to commend it, although it is subject to an extended breakdown into various particular bases of incompetency. Perhaps, after all, there is not much difference in the two classifications except as to the degree of breakdown.

In discussing the canon law, Holdsworth states that:

> the canon law rejected the testimony of all males under fourteen and females under twelve, of the blind and the deaf and dumb, of slaves, infamous persons, and those convicted of crime, of excommunicated persons, of poor persons and women in criminal cases, of persons connected with either party by consanguinity and affinity, or belonging to the household of either party, of the enemies of either party, and of Jews, heretics and pagans.

* * *

This idea of exclusion of witnesses in trials may seem strange to us, in as much as the common practice of mankind is to adjust domestic and business disputes outside legal tribunals, in many cases, by a consideration of the transactions involved, these facts being established by oral or written declarations, or by conversations, of persons having knowledge thereof, without disqualifications and in most informal manner, or by any formal or informal aids. However, as stiff and stilted as some of the common-law rules of evidence may seem to be, from our viewpoint, we have been fortunate, perhaps, that they were not worse. We have excellent authority that "It is not forgotten that an exclusion of witnesses is ancient and universal. In this respect the peculiarity of the English law lay in shutting out fewer classes of persons than other systems."

2.   Incompetence by Reason of Status: Traditional Limitations

a.   Spousal Incompetence

Robert M. Hutchins & Donald Slesinger, *Some Observations on the Law of Evidence: Family Relations*
13 Minn. L. Rev. 675, 675 (1929)[3]

Except in cases of necessity the wife was incompetent to testify for or against her husband at common law. Coke suggests that the reason for the rule lay in the fact that husband and wife were one, and naturally could not be divided for the purposes of testimony. Although the courts soon got beyond this doctrine, they insisted on the value of the rule. They argued that spouses, though perhaps not physically identical, were identical in interest. When disqualification by interest was removed, the judges had to take other ground, and did so . . . [reasoning] that the true basis for the rule was the necessity of marital harmony and confidence.

But even this philosophy has been unable to sustain the notion that one spouse cannot appear for or against the other. The disqualification has gradually been reduced to a disqualification in criminal cases alone.

NOTES AND QUESTIONS

1.   Most jurisdictions now allow spouses to testify for or against each other in civil cases. At common law, a "necessity" exception was developed for cases involving misconduct by the defendant spouse against the witness spouse. In modern criminal cases, jurisdictions have taken differing approaches. As of 1995, federal courts and a majority of states recognized a privilege against adverse spousal testimony. All jurisdictions, however established exceptions for cases in which one spouse is accused of committing a crime or tort against the other. In federal court and 21 states, the witness spouse held the privilege and could decide

---

[3] Copyright © 1929, University of Minnesota.

whether to testify. The remaining 13 states which recognized the privilege required both spouses to consent to spousal testimony; in effect, this gave one spouse a veto even if the other volunteered to testify. *See* Milton C. Regan, *Spousal Privilege and the Meaning of Marriage*, 81 VA. L. REV. 2045 (1995); Comment, *The Husband and Wife Privilege of Testimonial Non-Disclosure*, 56 NW. L. REV. 208, 209 (1961). *See also* MILTON C. REGAN, JR., ALONE TOGETHER: LAW AND THE MEANINGS OF MARRIAGE 89–135 (1999).

2.   In any jurisdiction recognizing the concept of spousal incompetence, the spouses must, in fact, be married. *See Lutwak v. United States*, 344 U.S. 604 (1953) (sham marriage). Moreover, spousal incompetence lasts only so long as the marriage exists. Upon dissolution of the marriage, spouses become competent to testify; however, their confidential marital communications remain privileged. Thus, competent spouses are often restricted to testifying about actions rather than words.

3.   The validity of any marriage is a matter of state law. *See, e.g., United States v. Jarvison*, 409 F.3d 1221 (10th Cir. 2005) (spousal testimonial privilege applied to valid common law marriage according to Navajo custom); *People v. Schmidt*, 579 N.W.2d 431 (Mich. Ct. App. 1998) (spousal communications privileges are extended to common law marriages recognized by other states).

4.   May a bachelor defendant, who fears adverse testimony from his lover, marry her and subsequently rely upon spousal incompetence? What steps, if any, could a prosecutor take to prevent this occurrence? *See In re Grand Jury Subpoena of Witness*, 884 F. Supp. 188 (D. Md. 1995); *Vance v. Rice*, 524 F. Supp. 1297 (S.D. Iowa 1981); *State v. Williams*, 650 P.2d 1202 (Ariz. 1982); *see generally United States v. Clark*, 712 F.2d 299 (7th Cir. 1983). Under such circumstances, some courts have restricted spousal incompetency to events and communications that occurred after the marriage. *But see A.B. v. United States*, 24 F. Supp. 2d 488, 490–92 (D. Md. 1998) (collecting cases and applying testimonial incompetence to acts that occurred pre-marriage).

5.   The concept of spousal incompetence has been held to extend to the grand jury context. Nevertheless, consider the following: suppose a spouse has been called to testify before a grand jury under circumstances in which the prosecutor has represented that none of her testimony would be used against her husband; the testimony would instead be used exclusively to help convict target *X*. May the witness spouse successfully assert spousal incompetence on the theory that, as a result of her testimony, target *X* might later choose to cooperate with the government by testifying against her husband — thereby constituting derivative use of spousal testimony? *See* Purdy, *The Marital Privilege: A Prosecutor's Perspective*, 18 CRIM. L. BULL. 309 (1982).

6.   Because spousal incompetence serves as a shield against adverse testimony, it is often considered an evidentiary privilege. Although this characterization is accurate in terms of operative effect, the doctrine stems from different roots than the marital communications privilege. In *Trammel v. United States*, the Supreme Court reviewed the doctrine's historical basis and underlying policy concerns during the course of defining the modern scope of spousal incompetence in the federal courts. This case is set forth in the privileges section of this book, *infra* Chapter

VI(D), so that it can be studied in a context in which the distinction between spousal incompetence and the marital communications privilege can be better understood.

STATE v. LEE
54 So. 356 (La. 1911)

PROVOSTY, J.

The accused was convicted of murder and sentenced to be hanged, and has appealed.

On December 1, 1901, one James Williams, a white man, was murdered by a negro named Mack Lee, in the parish of Avoyelles. Mack Lee escaped, leaving, as we understand, his wife behind him; and was no further heard from. In April, 1910, a negro by the name of Guy Fenner was arrested in San Antonio, Tex., for the crime. It was thought he was Mack Lee. Accordingly, he was brought to Avoyelles to be tried for the crime of 1901. On the way, when the train stopped at Opelousas, some persons came on board, and one of them said he identified him as Mack Lee. At Whiteville, ten miles before reaching Eola, a Mr. O'Quinn, came on board and again identified him, and told him he ought to be hanged. The prisoner was manacled and fettered; and all this put him in great fear. The sheriff, who had him in charge, told O'Quinn not to scare the man anymore than he was already.

*   *   *

The fact of there having been a homicide and of its having been murder not being disputed, and the sole question before the jury being as to the identity of the prisoner with Mack Lee, the wife of Mack Lee was put upon the stand by the defense, and asked whether the prisoner was her husband. Objection was made that the wife could not testify for or against her husband, and was sustained. The reason assigned by the learned trial judge was that he was satisfied that the prisoner was Mack Lee. The rule is that it is for the judge to pass upon the competency of witnesses . . . and therefore it would seem that it was for the judge to decide whether the woman was . . . the prisoner's wife, and to exclude her testimony if she was. But the rule is also that the identification of the accused as the person who committed the crime is a question for the jury . . . ; and also that the judge is forbidden to express an opinion on the facts of the case. Now, by excluding the witness as being the wife of the prisoner, the judge would be identifying the prisoner as Mack Lee, thereby expressing an opinion upon the facts of the case; in fact, expressly adjudging the prisoner guilty, since the very and sole question before the jury was as to the identity of the prisoner with Mack Lee. We find here, therefore, a conflict of rules. And the situation is further complicated by the fact that, by allowing the woman to testify, the judge would be virtually deciding that the prisoner was not Mack Lee, and thus expressing an opinion upon the facts adverse to the state. The situation was, no doubt, peculiar, but, nevertheless, offered no reason, we think, for departing from the rule that the competency of witnesses is a matter for the court, and not for the jury, to pass upon.

NOTES AND QUESTIONS

1. To what extent, if any, does the holding in *State v. Lee* pose the potential for contradictory findings between the judge and jury?

2. The issues raised by *State v. Lee* and similar cases are analyzed in Maguire & Epstein, *Preliminary Questions of Fact in Determining the Admissibility of Evidence*, 40 HARV. L. REV. 392 (1927), and Morgan, *Function of Judge and Jury in the Determination of Preliminary Questions of Fact*, 43 HARV. L. REV. 165 (1929).

b. Dead Person's Statutes

Roy R. Ray, *Dead Man's Statutes*
24 OHIO ST. L.J. 89, 89–108 (1963)[4]

At common law in England and the United States, parties to a lawsuit and all other persons having a direct pecuniary or proprietary interest in the outcome of the action were excluded from testifying in the case. A party could not testify in his own behalf nor could he be required to testify if called by his adversary. The rule was thus a combination of disqualification and privilege. The theory of the disqualification was that self-interest would probably cause such persons to perjure themselves. . . . Defenders of the rule of exclusion realized, of course, that perjury would not always result from self-interest and that by silencing truthful persons the rule threatened honest litigants with injustice, but they argued that the rule did more good than harm. . . . Jeremy Bentham, the great English Reformer, made a determined attack upon the rule in his TREATISE ON EVIDENCE published in 1827 and, in the words of Wigmore, "first furnished the arsenal of arguments for transforming public opinion." The unanswerable arguments that pecuniary interest did not make it probable that parties and witnesses would commit perjury, that the rule underestimated the ability of the judge and jurors to detect perjury, and that it created intolerable injustice, were taken up by such reformers as Denman and Brougham who led the assault on the disqualification. Through their efforts and those of others, professional opinion was gradually brought to the realization that the disqualification created more injustice than it prevented. In 1843 a statute was enacted by Parliament abolishing the disqualification of interested persons. And in 1851 another statute swept away the disqualification of parties and those on whose behalf a suit was brought or defended. These reforms spread to the United States, and the English statutes served as models for legislation here. As in England the change was brought about in two steps: the first qualifying interested nonparties and the second qualifying parties. Unfortunately most of the states which enacted similar statutes departed from the English model in a most significant respect. They retained a portion of the old disqualification as an exception to the new rule of qualification. At the time when the first statutes abolishing the interest disqualification were offered to the state legislatures in this country, the objection was made that if parties and interested persons were allowed to testify in cases involving contracts and transactions where one party had died and the other survived, this

---

[4] Reprinted by permission of Roy Ray, Emeritus Professor of Law, Southern Methodist University, and of The Ohio State Law Journal.

would work a hardship on the estate of the deceased. Since the lips of one party to the transaction were sealed by death, the suggestion was that the living party's lips should be sealed by excluding his testimony. This compromise was accepted in most of the early statutes and became the pattern of legislation in this country. Today in most jurisdictions the statutes contain a general statement to the effect that no person shall be disqualified because he is a party to a suit or proceeding or interested in the issue to be tried. But they add a provision to the effect that in suits brought or defended by an executor or administrator, such persons shall remain incompetent to testify concerning a communication with the testator or intestate. While this is the most common type of statute, there are many which vary substantially from this in certain respects. . . . The statutes usually provide that the surviving party or interested person may testify if called by the opposite party. . . . These statutes which retain the common law interest disqualification of parties and interested persons with respect to testimony as to transactions with decedents are popularly known as "Dead Man's Statutes."

*   *   *

They vary greatly in their wording and coverage, and the attitudes of the courts differ as to their interpretation, even where similar provisions are involved. . . .

As a background for the subsequent discussion, it seems worthwhile to set forth the text of a few statutes to illustrate variation in phraseology and the extent of the disqualification which the legislatures sought to retain.

Alabama:

In civil suits and proceedings, . . . no person having a pecuniary interest in the result of the suit or proceeding shall be allowed to testify against the party to whom his interest is opposed, as to any transaction with, or statement by the deceased person whose estate is interested in the result of the suit or proceeding, or when such deceased person, at the time of such transaction or statement, acted in any representative or fiduciary relation whatsoever to the party against whom such testimony is sought to be introduced, unless called to testify thereto by the party to whom such interest is opposed, or unless the testimony of such deceased person in relation to such transaction or statement is introduced in evidence by the party whose interest is opposed to that of the witness, or has been taken and is on file in the cause. No person who is an incompetent witness under this section shall make himself competent by transferring his interest to another. Code of Alabama (1960) Title 7, § 433.

California:

Persons incompetent to be witnesses — Parties or assignors of parties to a suit or proceeding, or persons in whose behalf an action or proceeding is prosecuted, against an executor or administrator upon a claim or demand against the estate of a deceased person, as to any matter or fact occurring before the death of such deceased person. California Code of Civil Procedure § 1880 (1959).

New York:

Personal transaction or communication between witness and decedent or lunatic. Upon the trial of an action or the hearing upon the merits of a special proceeding, a party or a person interested in the event, or a person from, through or under whom such a party or interested person derives his interest or title by assignment or otherwise, shall not be examined as witness in his own behalf or interest, or in behalf of the party succeeding to his title or interest against the executor, administrator or survivor of a deceased person or the committee of a lunatic, or a person deriving his title or interest from, through or under a deceased person, or lunatic, by assignment or otherwise, concerning a personal transaction or communication between the witness and the deceased person or lunatic, except where the executor, administrator, survivor, committee or person so deriving title or interest is examined in his own behalf, or the testimony of a lunatic or deceased person is given in evidence, concerning the same transaction or communication. A person shall not be deemed interested for the purposes of this section by reason of being a stockholder or officer of any banking corporation which is a party to the action or proceeding, or interested in the event thereof.

No party or person interested in the event, who is otherwise competent to testify, shall be disqualified from testifying by the possible imposition of costs against him or the award of costs to him. A party or person interested in the event or a person from, through, or under whom such a party or interested person derives his interest or title by assignment or otherwise, shall not be qualified for the purposes of this section, to testify in his own behalf or interest, or in behalf of the party succeeding to his title or interest, to personal transactions or communications with the donee of a power of appointment in an action or proceeding for the probate of a will, which exercises or attempts to exercise a power of appointment granted by the will of a donor of such power, or in an action or proceeding involving the construction of the will of the donee after its admission to probate.

Nothing contained in this section, however, shall render a person incompetent to testify as to the facts of an accident or the results therefrom where the proceeding, hearing, defense or cause of action involves a claim of negligence or contributory negligence in an action wherein one or more parties is the representative of a deceased or incompetent person based upon, or by reason of, the operation or ownership of a motor vehicle being operated upon the highways of the state, or the operation or ownership of aircraft being operated in the air space over the state, or the operation or ownership of a vessel on any of the lakes, rivers, streams, canals or other waters of this state, but this provision shall not be construed as permitting testimony as to conversations with the deceased. N.Y. Civil Practice Act (1961) § 347.

*   *   *

The case against the statutes may be summarized on the following points:

(1) The statutes are based upon a fallacious philosophy, *i.e.*, that the number of dishonest men is greater than the number of honest ones; and that self interest makes it probable that men will commit perjury. These assumptions run contrary to all human experience.

(2) The statutes create an intolerable injustice by preventing proof of honest claims and defenses. In seeking to avoid the *possibility* of injustice to one side, they work a *certain* injustice to the other. It is difficult to understand why all the concern is for the possibility of unfounded claims against the estate. Why is there no concern for loss by the survivor who finds himself unable to prove his valid claim against decedent's estate? Surely a litigant should not be deprived of his claim merely because his adversary dies. It cannot be more important to save dead men's estates from false claims than it is to save living men's estates from loss by lack of proof.

(3) The statutes are psychologically unsound. They do not disqualify many persons who are vitally interested in the outcome of the suit but who have no direct pecuniary interest such as spouses of parties, close relatives, or officials of corporate parties. On the other hand, they often disqualify certain totally disinterested persons or persons with only a slight pecuniary interest. The pecuniary interest limitation is unsound.

(4) The statutes fail to accomplish their purported purpose since they suppress only a small part of the opportunities for perjured testimony. They block the testimony of the witness only as to certain subjects, leaving him free to testify falsely as to other matters if he sees fit to do so. Furthermore, a witness who will not stick at perjury will not hesitate to suborn perjury by getting a third person to testify as to those matters as to which his own testimony is barred.

(5) The statutes impede the search for truth. The real hazard in shaping any exclusionary rule is that the jury cannot be expected to make sensible findings when it is deprived of substantial parts of available evidence bearing on the issue in dispute. The great danger thus lies in the suppression of truth.

(6) The statutes underestimate the efficacy of cross-examination in exposing falsehood, and the abilities of the judge and jury to separate the false from the true. These safeguards have proved adequate in other situations involving the testimony of parties and interested persons. Why not here?

(7) The statutes burden the parties with uncertainties and appeals. For a hundred years or more, our courts have been struggling with the interpretation of these statutes. The result is a labyrinth of decisions which have often brought confusion rather than clarity. The statutes continue to mystify able judges and lawyers in endless complexities of interpretation and application.

(8) There is no Dead Person's Statute in federal law.

c. Infamous Crimes

42 Pa. Cons. Stat. Ann. § 5922 (2005)

§ 5922. Disqualification by perjury.

In a civil matter, a person who has been convicted in a court of this Commonwealth of perjury, which term is hereby declared to include subornation of or solicitation to commit perjury, shall not be a competent witness for any purpose, although his sentence may have been fully complied with, unless the judgment of conviction be judicially set aside or reversed, or unless the matter is one to redress or prevent injury or violence attempted, done or threatened to his person or property, in which cases he shall be permitted to testify.

Vt. Stat. Ann., Title 12, § 1608 (2006)

§ 1608. Conviction of crime

A person shall not be incompetent as a witness in any court, matter or proceeding by reason of his conviction of a crime other than perjury, subornation of perjury, or endeavoring to incite or procure another to commit the crime of perjury. The conviction of a crime involving moral turpitude within fifteen years shall be the only crime admissible in evidence given to affect the credibility of a witness.

NOTES AND QUESTIONS

1.   Statutes of this kind are all that remain of the common law doctrine which deemed convicted felons incompetent to testify. The liberalization of this traditional restriction received widespread support from prosecutors. Why did prosecutors take this position?

2.   At one time, some state statutes precluded defendants or their accomplices in the charged crime from testifying in each other's behalf. This restriction, however, was eventually held to violate the Sixth Amendment's Compulsory Process Clause. *See Washington v. Texas*, 388 U.S. 14 (1967).

d. Jurors

HOFFMAN v. CITY OF ST. PAUL
245 N.W. 373 (Minn. 1932)

DIBELL, J.

Action to recover damages for personal injuries sustained by . . . plaintiff while a passenger in an automobile. There was a verdict for the plaintiff. The defendants appeal from an order denying their motion for a new trial.

* * *

5. It is a contention of the defendants that the verdict was a quotient verdict and

therefore invalid.

A quotient verdict, that is, one reached through an agreement that each juror put down the amount which he would award, and that the quotient resulting upon a division of the total by 12 shall be the verdict, is invalid. It is not supposed that jurors usually are at once in agreement upon the amount which is proper compensation for injury. They consider and discuss and finally come to a conclusion of what is fair and compensatory. They compare and may compromise their views. If in the process of reaching their award they set down the sums representing their individual views, add them, divide by 12, and upon further consideration and deliberation all agree upon the quotient as the fair amount of the award, nothing else appearing, the verdict is valid. . . .

6. Affidavits or the testimony of jurors as to what transpired in the jury room are not admissible to impeach their verdict. This is the long settled doctrine of Minnesota. In 5 WIGMORE, Ev. (2d ed.) §§ 2353, 2354, the history of the doctrine is traced and a critical discussion is had of the cases and the basis of their decision. It is stated that there are but five or six jurisdictions holding to the contrary. The injustice of the application of the doctrine in a particular case is recognized; but the thought is that on the whole greater wrong would be done by the application of a different rule and that good policy sustains the one adopted. A typical statement is found in *McDonald & U.S.F. & G. Co. v. Pless*, 238 U.S. 264, 267, where Mr. Justice Lamar, in referring to the rule against the reception of the affidavit of a juror to impeach the verdict in which he joined, said:

> The rule is based upon controlling considerations of a public policy which in these cases chooses the lesser of two evils. When the affidavit of a juror, as to the misconduct of himself or the other members of the jury, is made the basis of a motion for a new trial the court must choose between redressing the injury of the private litigant and inflicting the public injury which would result if jurors were permitted to testify as to what had happened in the jury room. . . . And, of course, the argument in favor of receiving such evidence is not only very strong but unanswerable — when looked at solely from the standpoint of the private party who has been wronged by such misconduct. The argument however, has not been sufficiently convincing to induce legislatures generally to repeal or to modify the rule. For, while it may often exclude the only possible evidence of misconduct, a change in the rule would open the door to the most pernicious arts [sic] and tampering with jurors.

*   *   *

The court in the case at bar correctly ruled in refusing an inquiry on the polling of the jury into the question of whether the verdict had been reached by a quotient process. Doing so would be a clear evasion of the rule that jurors will not be permitted by affidavit or testimony to impeach their verdict.

Order affirmed.

NOTES AND QUESTIONS

1. Why are quotient verdicts improper?

2. Other examples of jury irregularities include the following:

intoxication, exposure to threats, acceptance of bribes, or possession of knowledge relevant to the facts in issue obtained not through the introduction of evidence but acquired prior to trial, or during trial through unauthorized views, experiments, investigations, news media, books or documents, or through consultation with parties, witnesses . . . or through other extra-record channels, regardless of whether the jury misconduct occurred within or without the jury room.

3 WEINSTEIN'S EVIDENCE § 606[04] at 32–39.

3. Some of the above irregularities Judge Weinstein cites are obvious abuses, but others are not. What is wrong, for example, with jurors independently viewing the scene of a crime, conducting experiments in the jury room, or using information acquired from books? *See People v. Crimmins*, 258 N.E.2d 708 (N.Y. 1970) (unauthorized jury view); *People v. Stanley*, 665 N.E.2d 190 (N.Y. 1996) (unauthorized experiment at crime scene). How can information acquired in this manner be distinguished from generalized information concerning the outside world that the jurors bring with them when the trial begins?

4. Not all questions of juror competence necessarily involve jury misconduct. For example, should a juror be permitted to impeach a verdict with evidence that, during the course of deliberations, the court reporter mistakenly read back a portion of the transcript out of context? *See People v. Johnson*, 79 Misc. 2d 880 (N.Y. County Ct. 1974). Suppose the proffered juror's testimony is that the jury did not return the verdict they agreed upon during their deliberations. *Martin v. State*, 732 So. 2d 847 (Miss. 1998).

UNITED STATES v. STEWART
433 F.3d 273 (2d Cir. 2006)

OPINION: PETER W. HALL, CIRCUIT JUDGE:

Defendants Martha Stewart and Peter Bacanovic appeal from the final judgments of conviction entered July 20, 2004 in the United States District Court for the Southern District of New York. Following trial before the Honorable Miriam Goldman Cedarbaum, the jury found Stewart and Bacanovic guilty of conspiracy, concealing material information from and making false statements to government officials, and obstructing an agency proceeding. . . . For the reasons set forth below, we conclude that none of the numerous grounds upon which Defendants challenge their convictions provides a basis to disturb the jury's verdict and, therefore, we affirm the judgments of the District Court . . . .

BACKGROUND

A. Procedural history

Defendants Martha Stewart and Peter Bacanovic were charged in Superseding Indictment S1 03 Cr. 717 with offenses that arose from their communications to government investigators who were probing trading activity of ImClone Systems, Inc. ("ImClone") stock on December 27, 2001, just ahead of the company's public announcement that its lead pharmaceutical product would not receive government approval. . . .

The trial lasted five weeks. At the close of evidence, pursuant to Fed. R. Crim. P. 29, the District Court granted Stewart's motion for judgment of acquittal as to Count Nine. The jury deliberated for three days and returned a verdict convicting Stewart on specifications in Counts One, Three, Four and Eight and convicting Bacanovic on specifications in Counts One, Two, Six and Seven. The jury acquitted Stewart of one specification in Count Three and one specification in Count Four

. . . .

*   *   *

B. The trial

At trial, the Government sought to prove that Stewart and Bacanovic conspired and acted to mislead the ImClone investigation in order to deflect attention from the fact that, on December 27, 2001, Stewart sold shares of ImClone from her personal account at Merrill Lynch & Co. ("Merrill Lynch") after she learned from Bacanovic, her broker, that ImClone's CEO, Samuel Waksal, was attempting to sell all of his own shares in the company. In connection with the investigation, Stewart was interviewed twice, on February 4, 2002 and April 10, 2002, by the Securities and Exchange Commission ("SEC"), the Federal Bureau of Investigation ("FBI") and members of the United States Attorney's Office for the Southern District of New York (the "U.S. Attorney"). Those agencies interviewed Bacanovic on January 7, 2002, and he testified before the SEC on February 13, 2002.

At trial, the Government offered the testimony of SEC attorney Helene Glotzer and FBI agent Catherine Farmer, who attended each of the Defendants' interviews, to inform the jury of what Stewart and Bacanovic said — and did not say — about Stewart's ImClone investment, its liquidation, and the Defendants' communications regarding those matters on and after December 27,2001. In addition, the jury heard a tape recording of Bacanovic's SEC testimony.

To demonstrate that the story Defendants told to investigators was a cover-up of the events of December 27th, the Government called a number of witnesses to testify about their recollections of what happened that day and in the following months. Various portions of the testimony of those witnesses were corroborated by phone records, copies of emails and phone message logs. . . .

*   *   *

DISCUSSION

Stewart and Bacanovic both argue that we must reverse their convictions . . . because the trial was tainted by . . . extraneous influences on the jury . . . .

*   *   *

B. Jury bias and extraneous influence

Defendants charge that the District Court erred by denying . . . relief without holding an evidentiary hearing on alleged juror misconduct. Bacanovic makes the . . . argument that a new trial, or at least an evidentiary hearing, is warranted because post-verdict public statements by Hartridge and other jurors demonstrate that matters outside of the record improperly influenced the verdict of conviction.

1. Standard of review

Post-trial jury scrutiny is disfavored because of its potential to undermine "full and frank discussion in the jury room, jurors' willingness to return an unpopular verdict, and the community's trust in a system that relies on the decisions of laypeople." *Tanner v. United States*, 483 U.S. 107, 120–21, 107 S. Ct. 2739, 97 L. Ed. 2d 90 (1987). Accordingly, probing jurors for "potential instances of bias, misconduct or extraneous influences" after they have reached a verdict is justified "only when reasonable grounds for investigation exist," in other words, where there is "clear, strong, substantial and incontrovertible evidence that a specific, nonspeculative impropriety has occurred which could have prejudiced the trial." *United States v. Moon*, 718 F.2d 1210, 1234 (2d Cir. 1983) . . . . The inquiry should end whenever it becomes apparent to the trial judge that "reasonable grounds to suspect prejudicial jury impropriety do not exist." *Id.*

We review for abuse of discretion the District Court's . . . decision regarding the effect on the jury of "potentially prejudicial occurrences." . . .

2. Analysis

a. false *voir dire* responses

District Court's decision was an abuse of discretion. *See Moon*, 718 F.2d at1235.

*   *   *

b. consideration of extra-record evidence

During the course of a televised interview shortly after the verdict was returned, jurors were asked what they thought about the testimony of Stewart's friend, Mariana Pasternak. Their responses give rise to Bacanovic's argument that the jury impermissibly considered matters outside the record in reaching the verdict as to him.

During direct examination by the Government, Pasternak testified that while vacationing with Stewart at the end of December 2001, she "recalled Martha saying that [Sam Waksal's] stock is going down, or went down, and I sold mine." When asked whether she recollected speaking with Stewart about brokers during the vacation, Pasternak replied, "I remember one brief statement, which was: 'Isn't it nice to have brokers who tell you those things.' " Pasternak was then asked if she knew who Stewart's broker was and she replied "I know that Peter Bacanovic was Martha's broker." The District Court instructed the jury that the testimony could be considered only in connection with the charges against Stewart. On cross-examination, Pasternak stated that she could not remember with certainty whether the statements she attributed to Stewart were actually made by Stewart or whether they were Pasternak's own thoughts. Bacanovic's motion for a mistrial was denied, and prior to cross-examination of Pasternak, the District Court instructed the jury as follows:

> Testimony about what Martha Stewart told Ms. Pasternak is received in evidence only with respect to Martha Stewart. None of the statements of Martha Stewart to Ms. Pasternak that you heard yesterday afternoon are received in evidence against Peter Bacanovic, and it is not evidence against Peter Bacanovic. So that remember I told you at the beginning of the trial that guilt is personal, that you must separately consider each defendant and each charge. In considering the charges against Peter Bacanovic, you may not consider the testimony about those statements of Martha Stewart to Ms. Pasternak in any respect. They have no bearing as to Peter Bacanovic.

The jury received similar limiting instructions in the jury charge at the close of evidence.

Bacanovic now contends that certain public remarks by Hartridge and other jurors reveal that the jury did consider Pasternak's testimony in connection with the charges against him. In the interview, jurors were asked the following questions about the portion of Pasternak's testimony quoted above: "What did you think when she said that?" and "But you found that pretty incriminating?" Hartridge replied, "Oh, very. Yeah. It took down two people with one shot because she mentioned Peter's name. 'It's good to have a broker to tell you things.' " Other jurors seemed to agree. Bacanovic asserts that these remarks indicate that his conviction was improperly influenced by extra-record prejudicial material, and that the District Court erred by denying his motion for a new trial and his request for an evidentiary hearing in holding, in part, that Hartridge's statement was inadmissible under Fed. R. Evid. 606(b). . . .

Fed. R. Evid. 606(b) precludes a juror from testifying about deliberations and jurors' mental processes in the course thereof, but allows testimony regarding extraneous prejudicial information that came to the jury's attention. Bacanovic argues that the juror's statement regarding Pasternak's testimony falls within the exception to Rule 606(b) because (i) it was outside the record, as the record pertained to him and (ii) was highly prejudicial because it was the only evidence corroborating Faneuil's testimony that Bacanovic was involved with telling Stewart that Waksal was attempting to sell his stock.

According to Bacanovic, a ruling against him on this point would have the effect of barring, under, testimony that the jury improperly considered evidence extraneous to one defendant in a multi-defendant trial, where Rule 606(b) would permit such testimony from a juror regarding the same extraneous evidence if the defendant was tried alone. We do not agree with that articulation of the issue. In fact, a ruling in Bacanovic's favor would enable an end-run around the well-settled proposition that jurors are presumed to follow instructions . . . by permitting inquiry into a matter at the core of jury deliberations protected by Rule 606(b) . . . .

In so deciding, we agree with the Eighth Circuit's decision to reject an argument, similar to Bacanovic's, that did not prohibit the trial court from inquiring about jurors' alleged discussion of the defendant's failure to testify. *See United States v. Rodriquez*, 116 F.3d 1225 (8th Cir. 1997). Like Bacanovic, the *Rodriguez* defendant argued that his failure to testify "was not evidence and should not have been considered, it should be considered an 'outside influence' about which the jurors should be allowed to testify." *Id.* The Eighth Circuit responded,

> "That [defendant] did not testify is not a fact the jurors learned through outside contact, communication, or publicity. It did not enter the jury room through an external, prohibited route. It was part of the trial, and was part of the information each juror collected. It should not have been discussed by the jury, and indeed was the subject of a jury instruction to that effect. But it was not "extraneous information,"[5] and therefore does not fall within the exception outlined in Rule 606(b).

Id. We reach the same conclusion, for the same reasons.

. . . [T]he alleged impermissible influence was not the result of information "the jurors learned through outside contact, communication, or publicity" or that "entered the jury room through an external, prohibited route." . . . Rather, Pasternak's testimony came " 'from the witness stand in a public courtroom where there is full judicial protection of the defendant's right of confrontation, of cross-examination, and of counsel.' " . . . As such, the testimony cannot be considered extraneous information. Accordingly, . . . the District Court did not abuse its discretion by refusing to order a new trial or an evidentiary hearing that was clearly proscribed by Rule 606(b).

*   *   *

CONCLUSION

We have considered Defendants' remaining arguments and find them to be without merit. For the reasons set forth above, we affirm the judgments of conviction of Stewart and Bacanovic . . . .

---

[5] By contrast, each of the cases cited by Bacanovic involved a jury's consideration of information that was not admitted into evidence at all, as opposed to information properly admitted into evidence but used for an improper purpose. *See United States v. Hall; Benjamin v. Fischer; United States v. Pinto; see also United States v. Schwarz* (district court admitted evidence of police officer's guilty plea, but did not admit details of his allocution, which constituted off-the-record evidence that the jury subsequently discovered).

NOTES AND QUESTIONS

1.   What qualifies as "extraneous prejudicial information" or improper "outside influence?" The Sixth Circuit has explained as follows:

> Historically, a limited exception to the common law rule applied in cases where it was alleged that an "extraneous influence" affected the jury. In *Mattox [v. United States*, 146 U.S. 140 (1892),] for example, while emphasizing that jurors were prohibited from impeaching or supporting their verdict by testifying as to the motives and influences affecting that verdict, the Court explained that a juror could nonetheless testify as "to any facts bearing upon the question of the existence of any extraneous influence, although not as to how far that influence operated upon his mind." *Mattox*, 146 U.S. at 149 (holding admissible the testimony of jurors about the introduction of a prejudicial newspaper account into the jury room). Federal courts applied the "extraneous influence" exception to allow juror testimony regarding (1) statements made to the jury by a bailiff, *Parker v. Gladden*, 385 U.S. 363, 87 S. Ct. 468, 17 L. Ed. 2d 420 (1966); (2) a juror's contact with a party during trial, *Washington Gas Light Co. v. Connolly*, 214 F.2d 254, 94 U.S. App. D.C. 156 (D.C. Cir. 1954); and (3) a juror's contact with someone who suggested that the juror could profit by bringing in a verdict for the defendant. *Remmer v. United States*, 347 U.S. 227, 74 S. Ct. 450, 98 L. Ed. 654 (1954). Absent evidence that fell into the narrow "extraneous influence" exception, federal courts adhered to the common-law rule against admitting juror testimony to impeach a verdict.

United States v. Gonzales, 227 F.3d 520, 524 (6th Cir. 2000).

2.   How would Rule 606 operate in the case of a juror who provides an affidavit alleging that the jury completely misunderstood the trial judge's instructions? *Williams v. State*, 564 S.E.2d 759 (Ga. Ct. App. 2002); *State v. Boyles*, 567 N.W.2d 856 (S.D. 1997); *See United States v. Jelsma*, 630 F.2d 778 (10th Cir. 1980). Suppose the affidavit alleged an intentional misapplication of the law? *See United States v. D'Angelo*, 598 F.2d 1002 (5th Cir. 1979). What result in the case of an affidavit claiming that the jury had improperly considered a criminal defendant's failure to take the stand? *See United States v. Rutherford*, 371 F.3d 634, 640 (9th Cir. 2004) (jury allegedly disregarded instruction concerning defendant's privilege against self-incrimination).

3.   Assuming that a juror's allegation is deemed admissible under Fed. R. Evid. 606(b), may he likewise testify about its impact on jury deliberations or should the Court apply an objective test that considers the likely impact on a reasonable juror? *See United States v. Lloyd*, 269 F.3d 228, 237–240 (3d Cir. 2001).

4.   For a rare example of judicial incompetence (at least in terms of the judge as a witness), *see Cline v. Franklin Pork, Inc.*, 313 N.W.2d 667 (Neb. 1981). *See also* Fed. R. Evid. 605.

5.   Does a federal district court err when it refuses to admit, at a post-verdict hearing, juror testimony as to alleged juror drug and alcohol intoxication during the trial? The Supreme Court ruled in *Tanner v. United States*, 483 U.S. 107 (1987), that juror intoxication or drug use does not amount to an outside influence about which

jurors may testify to impeach their verdict pursuant to Fed. R. Evid. 606(b).

3. The Elements of Modern Competence

Robert M. Hutchins & Donald Slesinger, *Some Observations on the Law of Evidence — The Competency of Witnesses*
37 YALE L.J. 1017, 1017–18 (1928)[6]

Courts of last resort now seldom reverse a ruling on the competency of witnesses. Convinced, and rightly so, that they cannot learn from the record all the circumstances which influenced the decision below, they usually let it stand, even when the transcript alone might suggest another conclusion. Trial courts, in their turn, to a greater extent than formerly prefer to admit the evidence of infants, insane people, and mental defectives, and leave the jury to estimate its value. Perhaps this is because exclusion has heretofore worked particular hardship in prosecutions for crimes against children and the insane, where the only evidence available was that of the victim. Now these aggrieved individuals may testify even when the gist of the action, as in statutory rape, or the title of the action, as where a "lunatic" sues by his next friend, indicates their infirmity. The infirmity alone does not render them incompetent.

In all jurisdictions witnesses must show that they possess intelligence enough to observe what went on, recollect it, and tell a comprehensible story. In a few no additional requirements must be met. In others the witness must appear able to tell right from wrong, truth from falsehood, and to appreciate the duty to tell the truth on the stand. In most courts, however, that is not enough. The witness must understand the nature and obligation of the oath. It will not suffice that he knows enough to testify; he must understand that divine punishment will follow false swearing. These are apparently the only items the trial court need consider. If these requirements are satisfied, the witness will not be incompetent because he was hysterical at the time of the event, or an insane epileptic at time of the trial.

NOTE

Courts no longer require recitation of a formal oath, much less that the witness "understand that divine punishment will follow false swearing." Affirmation of the obligation to testify truthfully is sufficient. *See* Note, *A Reconsideration of the Sworn Testimony Requirement: Securing Trust in the Twentieth Century*, 75 MICH. L. REV. 1681 (1975). What is the modern-day substitute for divine retribution? *See Rethinking the Constitutionality of Ceremonial Deism*, 96 COLUM. L. REV. 2083 (1996).

---

[6] Reprinted by permission of the Yale Law Journal Company and Fred B. Rothman & Company from The Yale Law Journal Vol. 37, pages 1017–1028.

SCHNEIDERMAN v. INTERSTATE TRANSIT LINES
69 N.E.2d 293 (Ill. 1946)

MR. JUSTICE MURPHY delivered the opinion of the court:

Jack Schneiderman started this suit in the superior court of Cook county against Interstate Transit Lines, Inc., to recover damages for personal injuries sustained when the automobile he was driving collided with one of defendant's buses. A jury trial resulted in a verdict for plaintiff for $100,000. . . . On appeal the Appellate Court reversed the judgment without remanding the cause. We granted plaintiff's petition for leave to appeal.

*   *   *

Plaintiff's injuries affected his power to speak coherently and intelligently at all times and he could not make answer to any but simple questions. The Appellate Court held that plaintiff's mental condition was such as to render him incompetent to testify and that, therefore, none of his evidence should be considered. On the remainder of the evidence it was held that no cause of action was proved and that defendant's motion for a directed verdict, made at the close of the evidence, . . . should have been allowed. The questions presented here are as to plaintiff's competency to testify and whether the evidence was such as to require the allowance of defendant's motion for judgment *non obstante veredicto.*

The facts pertinent to the inquiry on plaintiff's competency are as follows: Plaintiff received chest and head injuries and two medical experts were called as witnesses to prove the nature and extent of such injuries. After the doctors testified, plaintiff was called as a witness by his counsel and in response to the questions propounded he gave a few, short, simple answers. He gave his name, residence, age, the day of the month and year on which the accident occurred. He was unable to state the month, but he fixed the location of the accident at the particular street intersection. He stated that there were traffic lights at the intersection, and the following questions and answers concluded his direct examination:

Q.   What street were you driving in when the accident happened?

A.   Oak Park and Madison Street.

Q.   Were there any traffic lights at Oak Park and Madison Street?

A.   Yes.

Q.   What direction were you going?

A.   South.

Q.   Now what was the color of the light as you approached and reached the intersection?

A.   Green.

Q.   What happened as you were going over? Tell the jury what happened?

A.   Green and amber, amber and bus struck.

Q.   What happened as you were going over the crossing?

A.   I get hit.

Q.   You got hit?

A.   Yes.

Q.   By what?

A.   A bus.

Q.   What do you next remember after that?

A.   I don't remember.

At no time during the trial did defendant object to plaintiff's competency. It is for the court to decide upon the competency of the witness and for the jury to determine what credit shall be given to his testimony under the various tests recognized by the law. . . . Except for the possible future course that this case may take, the question of the competency of plaintiff might well be disposed of on the ground that the question was not raised by defendant in the trial court.

The cross-examination covers twenty pages of the record. It will be impossible to detail all the answers which reflect plaintiff's mental condition. A summary of it is that his answers to the questions that were first asked on cross-examination fixed the time when he left his home on the morning of the accident, that he went some place to eat but could not tell where, that he drove on to Oak Park Avenue at Washington Boulevard. Plaintiff stated that this intersection was one block north of the intersection where the collision occurred and that answer was correct. His testimony shows that there were traffic control lights at the Washington Boulevard intersection, that he drove onto Oak Park Avenue on the flash of the green light, that he turned south on the avenue, that he was driving 20 or 25 miles per hour. In reference to seeing the light at Madison Street intersection as covered by his direct examination, it is as follows:

Q.   Now, you saw an amber light, did you?

A.   Yes.

Q.   And where did you see the amber light?

A.   Green.

Q.   No, I say, where were you when you saw the amber light?

A.   About half a block.

Q.   You were half a block north of the corner when you saw the amber light, were you?

A.   Yes.

Q.   Now, was there any other light on besides the amber light when you saw it? Wasn't there a green and amber light on together when you saw it?

A.   Amber.

Q.   But was there more than one color light on when you saw it? Wasn't there both green and amber lights when you saw it?

A.   No.

Q.   Did the green light go off when the amber light came on?

A.   Yes.

Q.   At the time the amber light came on you were about in the middle of the block between Washington and Madison, were you?

A.   Yes.

Q.   And you were going about twenty or twenty-five miles an hour then?

A.   Yes.

He further stated that the brakes on his automobile were good and when going at 20 to 25 miles per hour, he could stop his automobile in 3 or 4 feet. At first he stated he did not apply his brakes and when interrogated further he said, he put them on "right away." At times his answers lack consistency; that is, he would testify differently to the same question. At times his answers were incoherent and meaningless. A fair sample of such incoherent and meaningless testimony is set forth in the Appellate Court opinion (326 Ill. App. 1.).[7] On the other hand, some of his answers are corroborated by other credible evidence.

Prior to the accident plaintiff was a strong, healthy, active individual, 37 years of age and had served six years on the police force of the city of Chicago. One of the

---

[7] [Ed. — The Appellate Court opinion made the following observation:

The nature of plaintiff's testimony and the degree of his incompetency may be judged from the following excerpts from his cross-examination:

Q. When did you go to the Cook County Hospital?

Ans. Right arm and brain.

Q. Do you remember when you went to the County Hospital?

Ans. One day.

And later:

Q. Then after you were in the Cook County Hospital, where did you go?

Ans. Five weeks, Cook County, five weeks.

Q. Well, from Cook County Hospital, where did you go?

Ans. Oak Park Hospital, thirteen days, and County Hospital five weeks.

Q. Where did you go from County Hospital?

Ans. I was going to take light, doctor, Light.

Q. You went to Doctor Light?

Ans. Yes. Green.

Q. Green light?

Ans. Light.

Q. Was that the name of your doctor at Cook County Hospital?

Ans. No, no. Six days, Light.

Q. Light for six days?

Ans. Kalamazoo.

326 Ill. App. at 7; 60 N.E.2d at 910.]

physicians who cared for him immediately after the accident testified to a head injury but stated there was no skull fracture. Plaintiff was taken from the scene of the accident to an Oak Park hospital in an unconscious condition. The doctor stated that when the plaintiff arrived at the hospital he had lost his power of reason and speech and that physical restraint was necessary. He improved, and in about two weeks the doctors consented that he be removed from the hospital to his home. On being taken to his home he suffered an embolus, which the doctor testified was due to a traumatic injury of the chest, the left side of the brain became involved and there was a complete paralysis of his right limbs and side. He was taken to the Cook County Hospital, placed under the care of a neurologist and in about five weeks he was removed to the University Hospital where he remained under the care of the same specialist for more than a year. The neurologist testified that for a period of two years following the accident there was slow but continuous improvement, but since then there had been no change in his mental condition. He stated that immediately after the accident he could not enunciate clearly, that he spoke in a jargon, but that after a lapse of time he had improved, and that it was apparent he understood the questions asked. The medical experts said that his speech was involved, his mental condition disturbed, he could not repeat simple phrases, his judgment was poor, he could not recall events or names correctly. At times he was confused on directions. He testified plaintiff could answer single word questions correctly but that on repeated questioning, he tired easily and became confused. This he said was typical of this class of cases known in the medical profession as aphasia, or the inability to coordinate thoughts and use words to express them.

The question of the competency of a witness and the credit to be attached to his testimony are closely related and should not be confused. The question of competency is for the court, and the weight to be accorded the testimony is for the jury. On the question of competency it is said in WIGMORE ON EVIDENCE, 2d ed. sec. 501:

> The tendency of modern times is to abandon all attempts to distinguish between incapacity which affects only the degree of credibility and incapacity which excludes the witness entirely. The whole question is one of degree only, and the attempt to measure degrees and to define that point at which total incredibility ceases and credibility begins is an attempt to discover the intangible. The subject is not one which deserves to be brought within the realm of legal principle, and it is profitless to pretend to make it so. Here is a person on the stand; perhaps he is a total imbecile, in manner, but perhaps, also, there will be a gleam of sense here and there in his story. The jury had better be given the opportunity of disregarding the evident nonsense and of accepting such sense as may appear. There is usually abundant evidence ready at hand to discredit him when he is truly an imbecile or suffers under a dangerous delusion. It is simpler and safer to let the jury perform the process of measuring the impeached testimony and of sifting out whatever traces of truth may seem to be contained in it.

In *Truttmann v. Truttmann*, 328 Ill. 338, it was noted that there was a time when an idiot could not be sworn as a witness but that the test now is whether the derangement or feeble-mindedness is such as to make the person untrustworthy as a witness. The standard by which the competency of the witness may be ascertained is to determine whether the witness has the capacity to observe, recollect and communicate. If he has, he is competent and his mental deficiency is considered only insofar as it affects the weight to be given his testimony. . . .

We have referred to the record to study the exact language employed by plaintiff in making his answers and, in view of such answers and in the light of evidence of medical experts as to the character of his mental ailment and the effect it has had on his powers of speech, we conclude that he was competent to testify and that the Appellate Court erred in rejecting his testimony *in toto*. The discrepancies in answers given to the same or similar questions to a great measure indicate lack of control of the power of speech and under the circumstances shown it was for the jury to determine which answers would be given greater weight.

QUESTIONS

1.   What difficulty may be encountered under Federal Rule of Evidence 601 in federal question cases involving pendant state claims? Suppose a witness called to testify on matters relevant to both the federal and state claims, is incompetent under state law. How should Rule 601 be interpreted in this situation? *See generally* Wellborn, *The Federal Rules of Evidence and the Application of State Law in the Federal Courts*, 55 TEX. L. REV. 371, 442–51 (1977); *McDowell v. Brown*, 392 F.3d 1283 (11th Cir. 2004).

2.   Notwithstanding Federal Rule of Evidence 601, may some persons be deemed incompetent by virtue of being inherently unworthy of belief? *See generally Gillars v. United States*, 182 F.2d 962, 970 (D.C. Cir. 1950) (treason trial; testimony of government witness who was member of the Nazi party). Suppose a psychiatric report indicates that the potential witness has "a long history of apparent severe psychological abnormalities," thereby arguably rendering him "totally unworthy of belief." Should the witness be held to be incompetent? *See United States v. Roach*, 590 F.2d 181 (5th Cir. 1979); *United States v. Boffa*, 89 F.R.D. 523 (D. Del. 1981).

3.   Suppose a witness has used narcotics on the day his testimony is to be given. Should he automatically be deemed incompetent? *See United States v. Van Meerbeke*, 548 F.2d 415 (2d Cir. 1976), *cert. denied*, 430 U.S. 974 (1977) (trial judge observed witness ingesting some of the prosecution's opium evidence); *United States v. Bevans*, 728 F. Supp. 340, 346 (E.D. Pa.), *aff'd*, 914 F.2d 244 (3d Cir. 1990). Suppose a witness testifies while medicated by pain killers. Under what circumstances should his testimony be deemed incompetent? Do the rules even provide for "mental incompetence"? This issue arose when the Reverend Jerry Falwell sued "Hustler" magazine publisher Larry Flynt for emotional distress. *See Falwell v. Flynt*, 797 F.2d 1270 (4th Cir. 1986).

4.   May a judge circumvent Rule 601 by relying upon Rule 403 as a basis for holding a witness incompetent? Consider the following situation that arose in *United States v. Thompson*, 615 F.2d 329 (5th Cir. 1980):

> When trial began, the United States Attorney called Brown and several other witnesses who had previously told the grand jury that [defendant] Thompson's campaign workers had tried, with varying measures of success, to buy their votes. To the prosecutor's chagrin, however, one witness

deviated from her grand jury testimony, omitting any reference to cash offers for her vote. To refresh her memory, the prosecutor read parts of her recorded prior statements to her, outside the jury's presence. Eventually she acknowledged having admitted to the grand jury that she took $5.00 for her vote. When the jury returned, however, the witness denied ever having taken money for her vote. Confronted with this contradiction, the trial judge interrupted the prosecutor's questioning and initiated the following exchange:

THE COURT: This Court finds this witness unworthy of belief. I direct the jury not to consider anything she has said as having any bearing on the case and direct the United States Attorney to hold her for perjury. The witness is dismissed from this proceeding.

MR. TEAGUE [United States Attorney]:   Your Honor, may I ask her one further question?

THE COURT: No, sir, she is not worthy of belief.

MR. TEAGUE: Okay, thank you, Your Honor.

THE COURT: You may come down. You are in the custody of the marshal.

Let me make it very plain to this jury that nothing this witness has said should be considered either in favor of or against either party. Just disregard her testimony and all of the questions that have been asked her. Do not consider any part of it.

Id. at 331.

5.   If a judge believes a witness to be insane, on what basis, if any, may he deem the witness incompetent? *See United States v. Gutman*, 725 F.2d 417 (7th Cir. 1984). Should a competency hearing be held? *See id.*

Evidentiary Foundation: State v. Ramsey

[Robin Ramsey was convicted in Utah of sexually abusing his children Chris and Crystal during periods when he exercised his parental visitation rights. After the children testified, defense counsel moved to strike their testimony as incompetent witnesses.]

MR. YENGICH: Moreover, your honor, at this time I would most respectfully move that the court strike all testimony of Crystal and Chris based on the wide ranging variations in the stories that have been told, and declare them not competent at this time to testify, and that all of that testimony be stricken.

THE COURT: [What] do you say about the motion to strike the testimony of Chris and Crystal?

MR. GUNNARSON: That is a fact for the jury to decide, inconsistency or enough consistency and enough reliability and indicia of reliability. That is a question that should go to the jury.

I suggest that the court cannot take — that would be, in effect, granting a summary judgment at this time, based upon the court's decision that they're not competent.

*   *   *

THE COURT: I agree that a child could be a competent witness. Some children are, but not all children.

MR. GUNNARSON: If they don't understand the difference between right and wrong, they are not competent. I don't argue with that. It's for the trier of the facts, the jury to decide the weight and credibility to be given to the testimony.

THE COURT: That is true of any witness.

MR. GUNNARSON: I think it would be improper for the court to determine that question. Now, that's a question of fact and I don't think it would be proper —

THE COURT: Well, we're not talking about the same thing. You're talking about evaluating credibility and whether or not the witness is telling the truth. Mr. Yengich is suggesting, as I understand his motion, that the witness' testimony does not rise to the level of being a competent witness to testify.

MR. YENGICH: The Court has adequately stated my argument.

MR. GUNNARSON: Could I respond?

THE COURT: Go ahead.

MR. GUNNARSON: Both said they understand the difference between the truth and a lie. They have been adequately able to relate facts within their — they describe the circumstances, have shown that they are mentally alert, communicative. They are articulate, both of them, that they understand the significance of the oath and they have told their story, and merely to strike it because of age or because of some discrepancies in their testimony, I think, would be improper. I think they abundantly qualify to testify as any other witness.

THE COURT: Anything further?

MR. YENGICH: I just ask the court to harken back to my cross-examination of both witnesses, particularly Crystal and my asking her about wearing a red suit with stripes that run horizontally and going to get ice cream cones, none of which ever happened. I never met the little girl before. I ask the court to harken to Chris' testimony and the testimony which I asked him: What is right and wrong? What is truth? He maintains what has been in effect stipulated to that Crystal hit her father in the eye with a rock is, in fact, a truthful point up to that point and that when telling a lie what happens is that you are punished, and he is here to please other people. That is the problem and that is why I don't believe that they are competent witnesses.

*   *   *

MR. GUNNARSON: . . . After the incident Mr. Yengich, who wears a beard just like Mr. Metos, met the child, and if she's confused as to the meeting, fine; . . . and her colors were confused, but the only thing he can show is that she said it was a red suit and it was a ridiculous suit, which meant nothing to the statement, was relative to her consciousness or story. No way was the fact of what happened — even though questions were asked by both sides — ever changed or deviated. She said this is what happened. She was articulate. After that a peripheral matter that meant nothing to her, Mr. Yengich or the color of the suit — I think that is within the court's discretion, to look at the child and say this child is going to be evaluated as a child. The truthfulness of the statement should be the heart of the issue and because the child says something that is obviously ridiculous, . . . I think now to grant a summary disposition would be improper.

THE COURT: I don't know that it comes to summary motion, but in any event the question is moot because I think the children do have sufficient basis to testify in this court. The jury will weigh and evaluate their credibility and their understanding, the difference that the children perceive between right and wrong and what is truth and a lie. I think there has been sufficient foundation, at least based on the state of the evidence as it is right now, for this court to find that they do meet the minimum requirements for testifying in a court. Whether or not anybody wants to believe what they said will be up to the jury. That is a question of credibility and not a question of competency, and they are distinctly different.

So, the motion to strike the testimony at this state of the proceedings will be denied.

NOTES AND QUESTIONS

1. What is meant by the term personal knowledge? Suppose a witness was exposed to the event at issue, but is now only able to testify that he "believes" or "thinks" it occurred. Is this witness competent to testify? What follow-up questions might counsel ask to make a favorable competency finding more likely? *See United States v. Cantu*, 167 F.3d 198 (5th Cir. 1999); *United States v. Neal*, 36 F.3d 1190, 1206 (1st Cir. 1994) ("Personal knowledge can include 'inferences and opinions so long as they are grounded in personal observation and experience.' "); *Folio Impressions, Inc. v. Byer Cal.*, 937 F.2d 759 (2d Cir. 1991).

2. Consider the following situation: A government agent overhears an incriminating conversation conducted in a foreign language of which he has a rudimentary understanding. Should he be deemed incompetent? *See United States v. Villalta*, 662 F.2d 1205 (5th Cir. 1981), *cert. denied*, 456 U.S. 916 (1982).

3.   Suppose a witness has no present recollection of an event, but is apparently able to describe it with clarity while under the influence of hypnosis or sodium pentathol (a so-called truth serum). Should his testimony be admissible?

4.   What about a witness who claims to have a present recollection of a past event, but whose memory was stimulated by the assistance of hypnosis or sodium pentathol? Should his testimony be admitted? In this respect, consider the following commentary by a prominent professor of law and clinical psychiatry:

> I believe that once a potential witness has been hypnotized for the purpose of enhancing memory his recollections have been so contaminated that he is rendered effectively incompetent to testify. Hypnotized persons, being extremely suggestible, graft onto their memories fantasies or suggestions deliberately or unwittingly communicated by the hypnotist. After hypnosis the subject cannot differentiate between a true recollection and a fantasy or a suggested detail. Neither can any expert or the trier of fact. This risk is so great, in my view, that the use of hypnosis by police on a potential witness is tantamount to the destruction or fabrication of evidence.

Diamond, *Inherent Problems in the Use of Pretrial Hypnosis on a Prospective Witness*, 68 CAL. L. REV. 313, 314 (1980). Should this question be considered under the balancing rubric provided by Federal Rule of Evidence 403 rather than automatically deeming the witness incompetent? *See*, Note, *Are the Courts in a Trance? Approaches to Admissability of Hypnotically Enhanced Witness Testimony in Light of Empirical Evidence*, 40 AM. CRIM. L. REV. 1301 (2003).

ROCK v. ARKANSAS
483 U.S. 44 (1987)

[Ed. — In *Rock v. Arkansas*, the Supreme Court sustained the admissibility of hypnotically refreshed testimony. The decision overturned a state ruling which had held such testimony per se inadmissible. Because the issue arose in the context of a defendant's constitutional right to testify in her own behalf, the 5-4 decision did not resolve the question of whether hypnosis might otherwise make a witness incompetent. *Rock*, however, began to lay the foundation for subsequent analysis. The excerpt below summarizes the current state of the law.]

JUSTICE BLACKMUN delivered the opinion of the Court.

*   *   *

Although the Arkansas court concluded that any testimony that cannot be proved to be the product of prehypnosis memory is unreliable, many courts have eschewed a *per se* rule and permit the admission of hypnotically refreshed testimony.[8] Hypnosis by trained physicians or psychologists has been recognized as a valid

---

[8] [16] Some jurisdictions have adopted a rule that hypnosis affects the credibility, but not the admissibility, of testimony. . . . Other courts conduct an individualized inquiry in each case. . . .

therapeutic technique since 1958, although there is no generally accepted theory to explain the phenomenon, or even a consensus on a single definition of hypnosis. *See* Council on Scientific Affairs, *Scientific Status of Refreshing Recollection by the Use of Hypnosis*, 253 J.A.M.A. 1918, 1918–19 (1985) (Council Report).[9] The use of hypnosis in criminal investigations, however, is controversial, and the current medical and legal view of its appropriate role is unsettled.

Responses of individuals to hypnosis vary greatly. The popular belief that hypnosis guarantees the accuracy of recall is as yet without established foundation and, in fact, hypnosis often has no effect at all on memory. The most common response to hypnosis, however, appears to be an increase in both correct and incorrect recollections.[10] Three general characteristics of hypnosis may lead to the introduction of inaccurate memories: . . . the subject becomes "suggestible" and may try to please the hypnotist with answers the subject thinks will be met with approval; the subject is likely to "confabulate," that is, to fill in details from the imagination in order to make an answer more coherent and complete; and, the subject experiences "memory hardening," which gives him great confidence in both true and false memories, making effective cross-examination more difficult. *See generally* M. ORNE, ET AL., HYPNOTICALLY INDUCED TESTIMONY, IN EYEWITNESS TESTIMONY: PSYCHOLOGICAL PERSPECTIVES 171 (G. Wells and E. Loftus, eds., 1985); Diamond, *Inherent Problems in the Use of Pretrial Hypnosis on a Prospective Witness*, 68 CAL. L. REV. 313, 333–42 (1980). Despite the unreliability that hypnosis concededly may introduce, however, the procedure has been credited as instrumental in obtaining investigative leads or identifications that were later confirmed by independent evidence. . . .

The inaccuracies the process introduces can be reduced, although perhaps not eliminated, by the use of procedural safeguards. One set of suggested guidelines calls for hypnosis to be performed only by a psychologist or psychiatrist with special training in its use and who is independent of the investigation. *See* Orne, *The Use and Misuse of Hypnosis in Court*, 27 INT'L J. CLINICAL & EXPERIMENTAL HYPNOSIS 311, 335–36 (1979). These procedures reduce the possibility that biases will be communicated to the hyper suggestive subject by the hypnotist. Suggestion will be less likely also if the hypnosis is conducted in a neutral setting with no one present but the hypnotist and the subject. Tape or video recording of all interrogations, before, during, and after hypnosis, can help reveal if leading questions were asked.

In some jurisdictions, courts have established procedural prerequisites for admissibility in order to reduce the risks associated with hypnosis. . . .

[9] [17] Hypnosis has been described as "[involving] the focusing of attention; increased responsiveness to suggestions; suspension of disbelief with a lowering of critical judgment; potential for altering perception, motor control, or memory in response to suggestions; and the subjective experience of responding involuntarily." *Council Report*, 253 J.A.M.A., at 1919.

[10] [18] "When hypnosis is used to refresh recollection, one of the following outcomes occurs: (1) hypnosis produces recollections that are not substantially different from nonhypnotic recollections; (2) it yields recollections that are more inaccurate than nonhypnotic memory; or, most frequently, (3) it results in more information being reported, but these recollections contain both accurate and inaccurate details. . . . There are no data to support a fourth alternative, namely, that hypnosis increases remembering of only accurate information." *Id.* at 1921.

Id., at 336.[11] Such guidelines do not guarantee the accuracy of the testimony, because they cannot control the subject's own motivations or any tendency to confabulate, but they do provide a means of controlling overt suggestions.

The more traditional means of assessing accuracy of testimony also remain applicable in the case of a previously hypnotized defendant. Certain information recalled as a result of hypnosis may be verified as highly accurate by corroborating evidence. Cross-examination, even in the face of a confident defendant, is an effective tool for revealing inconsistencies. Moreover, a jury can be educated to the risks of hypnosis through expert testimony and cautionary instructions. Indeed, it is probably to a defendant's advantage to establish carefully the extent of his memory prior to hypnosis, in order to minimize the decrease in credibility the procedure might introduce.

We are not now prepared to endorse without qualifications the use of hypnosis as an investigative tool; scientific understanding of the phenomenon and of the means to control the effects of hypnosis is still in its infancy. Arkansas, however, has not justified the exclusion of all of a defendant's testimony that the defendant is unable to prove to be the product of prehypnosis memory. A State's legitimate interest in barring unreliable evidence does not extend to per se exclusions that may be reliable in an individual case. Wholesale inadmissibility of a defendant's testimony is an arbitrary restriction on the right to testify in the absence of clear evidence by the State repudiating the validity of all post hypnosis recollections. The State would be well within its powers if it established guidelines to aid trial courts in the evaluation of posthypnosis testimony and it may be able to show that testimony in a particular case is so unreliable that exclusion is justified. But it has not shown that hypnotically enhanced testimony is always so untrustworthy and so immune to the traditional means of evaluating credibility that it should disable a defendant from presenting her version of the events for which she is on trial.

KAELIN v. STATE
410 So. 2d 1355 (Fla. Dist. Ct. App. 1982)

Dell, Judge.

Appellant appeals his conviction on five counts of sexual battery. We affirm.

The victim, Claire, is a thirty-two year old mentally retarded woman. She is afflicted with cerebral palsy and a severe hearing deficiency. She has an IQ of fifty-four and the sign language ability of a six to eight year old child. Her ability to speak is also extremely limited.

Prior to trial, a hearing was conducted on defendant's motion to exclude Claire as a witness. The trial court found that she was capable of communicating but determined that her language deficiencies precluded effective cross-examination. The court deferred ruling on the motion so that she would have an opportunity to enhance her communicative ability. To this end, appellant's expert, Dr. Dunstall, recommended that Bill Cohn assist Claire in improving her language skills. Mr.

---

[11] [19] Courts have adopted varying versions of these safeguards. . . .

Cohn spent approximately fourteen hours over the course of several weeks working with Claire. Thereafter, based upon such improvement, the motion to exclude Claire as a witness was denied. Mr. Cohn thereafter served as her interpreter during trial.

Three points are raised on appeal. First, appellant asserts that the court erred in finding Claire competent to testify.

* * *

We have carefully reviewed the transcript of the proceedings below. Both parties have requested that we review video tapes of Claire's testimony. We decline to do so. The record more than adequately depicts the evidence considered by the jury. Moreover, it is the function of the trial judge, whose observations are firsthand, to determine the competency of a witness to testify. The prerequisites of competency have been universally recognized. A witness must have sufficient intelligence to understand the nature and obligations of the oath and the ability to perceive, remember and narrate the incident. . . .

* * *

We now turn to the issue of Claire's competency to testify. This question is by no means clear. Undeniably, Claire has a very low intelligence quotient, and intelligence is a primary component of witness competency. . . . Additionally, we recognize that Claire's other handicaps severely strain opportunity for effective cross-examination. However, we cannot conclude, on the record before us, that allowing Claire to testify was an abuse of discretion. As limited as she was, Claire was nevertheless able to relate the circumstances of the assaults upon her with sufficient clarity and decisiveness so that her testimony was properly submitted to the jury. Claire was firm in her identification of appellant as her assailant. She was likewise consistent in her description of the assaults. We have no doubt that the defense of appellant was made more difficult by the limitations of Claire's communicative ability. Yet the record is clear that "a comprehensible narrative does emerge from the sum of her testimony." . . .

Competency to testify is established when a witness has sufficient understanding to comprehend the obligations of the oath and is capable of giving a correct account of the matters which the witness has seen or heard relative to the question at issue. A case similar to that *sub judice* is *People v. Parks*, 41 N.Y.2d 36, 390 N.Y.S.2d 848, 359 N.E.2d 358 (1976). In that case, a sixteen year old, mentally retarded girl was sexually assaulted three times during a four month period by her school bus driver. The victim had an IQ of seventy-three and mental development similar to that of a twelve or thirteen year old girl. The appellant alleged that she was incompetent to testify. The Court responded:

> The test is whether the prospective witness has sufficient intelligence to understand the nature of an oath and to give a reasonable, accurate account of what he has seen and heard, vis-a-vis the subject about which he is interrogated. . . . The resolution of the issue of witness competency is exclusively the responsibility of the trial court, subject to limited appellate review. It is the trial judge who has the opportunity to view the witness, to observe manner, demeanor and presence of mind, and to undertake such

inquiries as are effective to disclose the witness's capacity and intelligence. . . . Impressions that may be validly drawn only from close hand personal observation cannot be *"photographed into the record"* for later study by appellate courts. (Emphasis added).

The record amply demonstrates that the trial judge closely observed Claire's interrogation and was satisfied that she was competent to testify.

We do not find that Claire was so deficient because of her afflictions and mental infirmity that the admission of her testimony was a clear abuse of discretion. Accordingly, the judgment and sentence of the trial court is affirmed.

AFFIRMED.

BERANEK AND HERSEY, JJ., concur.

Evidentiary Foundation:
U.S. v. Spotted War Bonnet[12]

The three year old victim in a sexual abuse testified as set forth below. Did she satisfy minimal competency requirements under the Federal Rules of Evidence?

Q. Last night when you talked to me did we tell you to say anything here today?

A. Yeah.

Q. What did we tell you to say?

A. [No response.]

Q. Can you remember?

A. No.

Q. You don't remember anything about last night?

A. No.

Q. Do you know what it is to tell a lie?

A. No.

* * *

Q. Do you ever make up stories?

A. [No response.]

Q. Can you answer that one?

A. [No response.]

Q. Can you answer me, Annie?

A. No.

Q. Can you answer me?

A. Yes.

---

[12] 1282 F.2d 1360 (8th Cir. 1989).

Q.   Do you ever make up stories?

A.   No.

Q.   Are you going to make one up today?

A.   No.

Q.   Do you promise not to make up any stories today?

A.   No.

NOTES AND QUESTIONS

1.   In *People v. Parks*, cited by the *Kaelin* Court, the prosecution called the complainant's teacher as its first witness. The teacher testified that complainant was mentally retarded, tended to be quiet, and kept to herself in class. On appeal, receipt of this testimony was sustained on two grounds: (1) any pertinent testimony may be received in order to evaluate the competence of a witness; and (2) so long as the teacher's testimony was confined to "objective" facts, such evidence may be admissible to assist the jury in evaluating the witness' credibility (by explaining the nature of the witness' infirmity). The *Kaelin* decision represents the way most courts handle this issue. *See, e.g., United States v. Allen J.* 127 F.3d. 1292 (10th Cir. 1997).

2.   Even as summarized above, was the testimony really confined to "objective" facts?

3.   What results if a defendant-witness in a criminal trial refuses "either to swear or affirm that he would tell the truth"? *Mercer v. United States*, 864 A.2d 110, 115 (D.C. 2004).

4.   Suppose that a witness is willing to take the oath, but personally believes that a "higher duty" may excuse him from the obligation of testifying truthfully. *See generally* Report of the Select Committee on Assassinations, H.R. Rep. No. 95-1868, 95th Cong., 2d Sess. 248 (1979) (concerning impact of CIA secrecy oath on testimony of CIA employees); *Helms Makes a Deal*, TIME, Nov. 14, 1977, at 18.

PEOPLE v. WALKER
69 Cal. App. 475 (1924)

WORKS, J.

Defendant was convicted of the crime of obtaining money by false pretenses. The information charges that one Elgin and his wife paid to defendant $1,500 for a partnership interest in a business conducted by her as a divine healer, and that the payment was made because of false representations which defendant made to the Elgins. . . .

*   *   *

The next point to be considered is of a most unusual character. The prosecution called one Graham as a witness. . . . A colloquy then occurred between the court and respective counsel, during which the following appears:

Mr. Kelly:	. . . I want at this time the record to show that this witness was brought in here by the assistant district attorney, Mr. Johnson, and by the wife of the witness in a crippled condition, almost impossible for him to walk, and impossible for him to speak; so that his wife makes the answer for him; and I assign it as misconduct . . . on the part of the district attorney on the ground that the witness' testimony is immaterial, incompetent, irrelevant and . . . that he was brought in here solely to prejudice this defendant before the jury. . . .
The Court:	Go ahead, Mr. Kempley.

Several questions, some of which met with objections, were then put to the witness and the record shows answers to them. Then the following transpired:

Mr. Kelly:	I wish the record to show that all of these answers are made by the wife of the witness, and that it is impossible for anyone, including the reporter—
The Court:	The record is not going to be made just the way you recite it, Mr. Kelly. You cannot say "Let the record show," and then recite a lot of things when the answers are made by the witness and repeated by the wife to the jury.
Mr. Kelly:	Then I will ask that the Court . . . make the record show that this witness cannot speak loud enough to be heard even by those in his immediate vicinity. . . . Standing right along beside of him I cannot even hear him whisper.

The judge made no statement into the record pursuant to this request. After a colloquy a question was put. The record then shows:

A.	He said "No."
Mr. Kelly:	Did your honor hear that?
The Court:	No, I did not hear that.
A.	Did you see his mouth?
The Court:	No. It has got to be a little more distinct than that, I fear. . . . Well, it is not audible enough . . . .
Mr. Kelly:	. . . There is no means by which we can say it is [the testimony of this witness]. I stood here and I tried to hear a whisper . . .
The Court:	You can start all over again if you want to, but . . . there should be some reply [from the witness himself].
Mr. Kempley:	She is the wife of the witness and she undoubtedly can see things that we cannot.

Various questions were then propounded to the witness, after which this appears:

Mr. Kelly:	. . . There are no answers given by the witness so far as I can see.

This is all that is shown by the record as to the appearance of the witness on the stand. Up to the point at which the trial judge stated that the district attorney might recommence his examination of the witness, his wife had conveyed his answers to the jury, if answers there were, under a stipulation which was stated to have been made before the trial, but it transpired that the stipulation was not broad enough to cover the situation which arose as above outlined, and appellant was by the court relieved from it. In addition to directing that the examination be begun again the court struck out the testimony of the witness shown by the record up to that point. The district attorney then commenced the examination anew after this statement by the judge:

> There must be some testimony from the witness himself. . . . Now you can try it again if you want to, with a few questions.

After several preliminary questions, to which answers were stated into the record by the wife of the witness, the following occurred:

Mr. Kempley: Now do you want Mrs. Graham sworn that she will repeat his answers?

Mr. Kelly: I submit . . . it is not a case where an interpreter can act. It is not apparent here that Mrs. Graham can understand his answers. There are no answers given by the witness so far as I can see [this being a statement already quoted]. It is not the testimony of the witness, but the testimony of the interpreter.

The Court: You can swear her to repeat them correctly.

Mr. Kelly: How can she be sworn? She is not an interpreter from Spanish into English, or vice versa. What can she swear to do?

The Court: You can swear her to repeat correctly the answers.

              (Ella Graham is sworn to correctly repeat the statements made by the witness Fred Graham.)

The examination then proceeded in the manner directed by the judge and was concluded. It is now contended that error was committed by the court in swearing Mrs. Graham to repeat the statements of the witness and in permitting her to recite answers to the jury. No response is made to this contention in the brief of respondent, but we cannot but regard it as both important and serious.

Before we proceed to a discussion of the questions of law presented by the point thus suggested by appellant it will conduce to clarity if we make some further remark as to the state of the record before us. While the showing is not as clear as it might be, because of the failure of the trial judge, pursuant to a minute survey of the appearance of the witness Graham and following the urgent request of counsel for defendant, to state into the record what that appearance was, we shall endeavor to outline what, to our minds, the record does show. It appears certainly and conclusively that the witness could give forth no sound, not even a whisper, by means of the organs of speech. It sufficiently appears that, if it cannot be said that there was no movement of his lips whatever, there was none which conveyed to any person but his wife the impression that he attempted to put forth articulate speech in response to the questions which were propounded to him. . . .

In addition to this state of facts it is to be observed that there was no attempt to show, either by way of preliminary or in response to the objection made by Mr. Kelly, by what means Mrs. Graham possessed or assumed an ability to understand what her husband said, or, in fact, that he actually said anything. She was not only left a free hand to repeat what he said, if he really spoke, but to decide whether he spoke. No one else could determine, we think the record shows, that he even attempted to speak. Certainly, if he made answers, they were interpreted to the jury through no system which anyone but the wife could understand. Such is not the case in the ordinary instances in which interpreters are employed in courts of justice, those in which a translation from one language into another is essayed, or in which the testimony of a deaf-mute, given in the common language of such unfortunates, is conveyed to a jury by adepts in it. The errors or perjuries of the usual interpreter are subject to detection and correction. The same thing may not be said of the efforts of Mrs. Graham. She could "interpret," she could answer, with complete immunity from fear of contradiction, impeachment, or punishment. She might commit errors or she might commit the crime of perjury and go scot-free.

*   *   *

. . . On the whole, we are convinced that the trial court erred in permitting the use of Mrs. Graham as an "interpreter" for the reason that, by the very circumstances surrounding the condition of her husband, appellant was denied the right to impeach or to ascertain the correctness of the "interpretation" or "translation" rendered by her, even admitting that she heard or saw something which was susceptible of interpretation or translation.

*   *   *

Judgment and order reversed.

FINLAYSON, P.J., and CRAIG, J., concurred.

B. INTERROGATION OF WITNESSES

CHARLES A. WRIGHT & KENNETH W. GRAHAM
21 FEDERAL PRACTICE & PROCEDURE, EVIDENCE § 5036 (1977)[13]

With the exception of leading questions, the law of evidence has little to say about the proper form of interrogation. Yet despite what the books may say, every court has a collection of stock objections to the form of the question that will be honored in that court, if no place else. Indeed, in some courts most of the objections made are of this variety. "Asked and answered," "argumentative," "compound," "assumes a fact not in evidence" are just a few examples; one judge even sustained an objection to a line of questioning on the grounds it wastedious! (It was.)

Federal Rule 611(a) leaves the method of interrogation to the discretion of the judge and nowhere does it authorize these old objections to the form of the question.

---

[13] Reprinted with permission from Charles Alan Wright and Kenneth W. Graham. Copyright © 1977 by West Publishing Co.

Obviously a mere statute passed by Congress and signed by the President is not going to change the way lawyers try their cases. And so long as everyone recognizes that the judge is exercising a discretion, these time honored "objections" are a harmless verbal shorthand, however startling they may be to the lawyer encountering one of them for the first time.

Federal Rule of Evidence 611(a)

(a) **Control by the Court; Purposes.** The court should exercise reasonable control over the mode and order of examining witnesses and presenting evidence so as to:

(1) make those procedures effective for determining the truth;

(2) avoid wasting time; and

(3) protect witnesses from harassment or undue embarrassment.

NOTES AND QUESTIONS

1. For a detailed review of the types of objections that are often made to the form of interrogation, *see* Denbeaux & Risinger, *Questioning Questions: Objections to Form in the Interrogation of Witnesses*, 33 ARK. L. REV. 439 (1979).

2. Is there anything objectionable to the following line of inquiry described by Edward Abbott Parry in his 1924 work entitled THE SEVEN LAMPS OF ADVOCACY:

> In a state trial in the days of Queen Anne, the name of the lady is announced in the oath, and then counsel approaches her. . . . "Pray, madam, will you be pleased to acquaint my lord and the jury what you know concerning the matter, and what passed between your brother, Mr. Colepper and Mr. Denew at his first coming to him?"

Quoted in Denbeaux & Risinger, *supra*, at 471. *See* 3 WIGMORE, EVIDENCE § 767 (3d ed. 1940). There is no *per se* prohibition against narrative type questions. Typically, this matter is one of judicial discretion. C. McCORMICK, HANDBOOK OF THE LAW OF EVIDENCE § 5 (2d ed. 1972).

1. The Rule Against Leading Questions

BARON BRAMPTON,
1 THE REMINISCENCES OF SIR HENRY HAWKINS 30
(R. Harris ed. 1904)

Let me illustrate it by a trial which I heard: Jones was the name of the prisoner. His offense was that of picking pockets, entailing of course, a punishment corresponding in severity with the barbarity of the times. . . . The accused having "held up his hand," and the jury having solemnly sworn to hearken to the evidence, and "to well and truly try, and true deliverance make," etc., the witness for the prosecution climbs into the box, which was like a pulpit, and before he has time to look around and see where the voice comes from he is examined as follows by the prosecuting counsel:

"I think you were walking up Ludgate Hill on Thursday, 25th, about half past two in the afternoon and suddenly felt a tug at your pocket and missed your handkerchief, which the constable now produces. Is that it?" "Yes Sir." "I suppose you have nothing to ask him?" says the judge. "Next witness." Constable stands up. "Were you following the prosecutor on the occasion when he was robbed on Ludgate Hill, and did you see the prisoner put his hand into the prosecutor's pocket and take this handkerchief out of it?" "Yes Sir." Judge to prisoner: "Nothing to say, I suppose?" Then to the jury: "Gentlemen, I suppose you have no doubt. I have none." Jury: "Guilty, my lord," as though to oblige his lordship. Judge to prisoner: "Jones, we have met before — we shall not meet again for some time — seven years' transportation — next case." Time: Two minutes, fifty-three seconds.

Copyright, 1980, G. B. Trudeau

NOTES AND QUESTIONS

1. What is the principal vice of the so-called leading question? To what extent, however, is concern with this type of question somewhat naive? Consider the following observation:

> The witness is protected against suggestion only while on the stand, seemingly on the assumption either that intervening influences are unimportant or that he comes untouched from event to court. The former is directly contrary to the theory upon which leading questions are prohibited. The latter simply is not so. . . . Under the system of party responsibility for the production of witnesses, no competent attorney dreams of calling witnesses who have not previously been interviewed. The preliminary interview affords full play to suggestion and context and evokes in advance of trial a complete verbalization, the importance of which cannot be overlooked. When the witness testifies, are his verbalizations at that time based upon his recall of the event or upon his recall of his former verbalizations? In any event it seems inevitable that he will attempt to be consistent with his earlier statement. The trial assumes the character of a play, and the witness proceeds to "tell his own story" under a type of questioning which is required by the rules of evidence, even if the good sense of counsel fails to suggest such a technique, to produce an almost

wholly false impression of spontaneity. The essential naivete of this procedure must afford some amusement to any experimental scientist.

Cleary, *Evidence as a Problem in Communicating*, 5 Vand. L. Rev. 277, 287 (1952) (footnotes omitted).

2. How can an improper leading question be identified? Does the vice merely lie in the form of the question?

3. What form of question might best avoid the leading question objection?

4. Why are leading questions permitted on cross-examination and for direct examination of hostile witnesses?

5. Despite its broad prohibition against leading questions, Rule 611(c), generally allows leading questions for handling preliminary, transitional, and corrective matters. Waltz& Kaplan, Evidence: Making the Record 15–16 (1982).

STAHL v. SUN MICROSYSTEMS, INC.
775 F. Supp. 1397 (D. Colo. 1991)

ORDER

Sherman G. Finesilver, Chief Judge.

This matter comes before the Court on Defendant's objection to Plaintiff's use of leading questions on direct examination of witness Teresa Cox during trial. This case involves breach of contract claims and Title VII cause of action arising out of Stephanie Stahl's employment as a Sales Representative for Defendant Sun Microsystems. Trial began on June 10, 1991. On June 18, 1991, the jury returned a verdict for Plaintiff in the amount of $500,000.00 on the breach of contract claims. The Court held for the Defendant on the Title VII claim on June 27, 1991. *Stahl v. Sun Microsystems, Inc.*, No. 90-1203, slip op. (D. Colo. June 27, 1991). Both parties have filed notices of appeal.

During the course of the trial, Plaintiff called Teresa Cox as an adverse witness and requested leave to propound leading questions to Ms. Cox. Ms. Cox is a former employee of Sun Microsystems. She served as a district administrative secretary under Darrell Waters, Ms. Stahl's District Manager, between 1988 and1990. Defendant objected to the use of leading questions on direct examination principally on the grounds that Ms. Cox is no longer affiliated with Sun. The court overruled the objection and allowed counsel to propound leading questions on both direct and cross-examination. We now expand on that ruling.

Rule 611(c) of the Federal Rules of Evidence permits leading questions on direct examination when a party calls a hostile witness, an adverse party, or a witness identified with an adverse party. Fed. R. Evid. 611(c). Although Ms. Coxis no longer employed by Sun, she is clearly identified with Defendant, both through her previous employment and her ongoing relationship with Mr. Waters, a key witness who attended the trial on behalf of Sun. . . . Use of leading questions on direct examination of Ms. Cox is therefore appropriate.

Defense counsel may also propound leading questions of Ms. Cox on cross-examination. While leading questions should generally not be used by counsel in examining his or her own client, the scope and method of cross-examination is within the discretion of the trial judge. It is well recognized that the Court may allow counsel to propound leading questions to his or her own witness when such witness has been called as an adverse witness by opposing counsel. *See* Advisory Committee Notes, 56 F.R.D. 183, 276 (1972); *Shultz v. Rice*, 809 F.2d 643, 654–55 (10th Cir. 1986); *Ardoin v. J. Ray McDermott & Co.*, 684 F.2d 335, 336 (5th Cir. 1982); *Oberlin v. Marlin American Corp.*, 596 F.2d 1322, 1328 (7th Cir. 1979); Annotation, *Cross-examination by leading questions of witness friendly to or biased in favor of cross-examiner*, 38 A.L.R. 2d 952 (1954 and Supp. 1989 and 1991).

ACCORDINGLY, it is hereby ordered that Defendant's objection is OVER-RULED. Counsel's utilization of leading questions on . . . direct examination . . . of Ms. Cox was appropriate.

2. Assisting the Forgetful Witness

UNITED STATES v. RICCARDI
174 F.2d 883 (3d Cir. 1949)

KALODNER, CIRCUIT JUDGE.

The defendant was indicted under 18 U.S.C. (1940 ed.) Sections 415 and 417 in four counts charging him with willfully, unlawfully and feloniously having transported or having caused to be transported in interstate commerce certain chattels of the value of $5,000 or more. The first and third counts were dismissed, and the defendant was convicted on the second and fourth counts, from which conviction he appeals.

We are not here primarily concerned with the particular fraudulent representations which the defendant made. Rather we are called upon to decide the propriety of the method utilized at the trial to prove what chattels the defendant obtained and transported, and their value. In short, the principal question is whether the witnesses who testified to these essentials were properly permitted to refresh their memory. . . .

The chattels involved are numerous items of bric-a-brac, linens, silverware, and other household articles of quality and distinction. They were the property of Doris Farid es Sultaneh, and were kept in her home at Morristown, New Jersey, from which the defendant is alleged to have transported them to Arizona in a truck and station wagon. The defendant did not deny receiving some of the lady's chattels, but did deny both the quantity and quality alleged. Moreover, it does not appear open to doubt that the truck made but one trip, and the station wagon three, carrying the goods in controversy.

To prove the specific chattels involved, the government relied on the testimony of Doris Farid; to prove their value, it relied on the testimony of an expert, one Leo Berlow.

Farid testified that as the chattels were being moved from the house, she made longhand notes, and that later she copied these notes on her typewriter. Only one of the original notes was produced, and became part of the evidence of the case, a search by Farid having failed to disclose the others. The government sought to have Farid testify with respect to the chattels by using the typewritten notes for the purpose of refreshing her recollection.[14] Although the defendant's objection was overruled, the government, on the next day of the trial, submitted to Farid lists of chattels taken out of a copy of the indictment, but from which had been deleted such information as dates and values.[15] With the aid of these lists, the witness testified that her recollection was refreshed[16] and that she presently recognized and could identify each item. She was then permitted to read the lists aloud, and testified that she knew that the items were loaded on the truck or station wagon, as the case was. The lists were neither offered nor received in evidence.

The expert, Berlow, testified that he had visited Doris Farid's home on numerous occasions in his professional capacity as dealer in antiques, bric-a-brac, etc.; that he was very familiar with the furnishings therein, having examined the household for the purpose of buying items from Farid or selling them for heron commission. He was shown the same lists which Farid had used to refresh her recollection, and with their aid testified that he could recall the items individually, with some exceptions; that he remembered them to the extent that he could not only describe the items,

---

[14] [2] At pages 114a–115a of Appellant's Appendix, the following appears:

The Court: That isn't the question. When you look at that typewritten sheet, does that refresh your recollection as to the items therein mentioned?

The Witness: It does.

The Court: In what way?

The Witness: Well, every item here — for instance: "2 Chinese vases octagonal shape Satsuma, light for mantel" I remember.

The Court: You remember those items individually as packed?

The Witness: Individually, each one.

The Court: I will allow her to refresh her recollection. . . .

[15] [3] At page 136a of Appellant's Appendix it appears that government counsel began by showing to Farid a list which did not have values. At page 137a, the following appears:

The Court: Well, I think with these evaluations cut off it is all right. This is the same paper that was shown to the witness yesterday?

Mr. Pearse (defendant's counsel): No, sir, this is the indictment.

Mr. Tyne (U. S. Attorney): No, sir, this is the indictment.

Following this, at the suggestion of the trial judge, the dates on the lists, to which defendant had previously objected, were cut off. The lists were then shown to the witness.

[16] [4] For example at page 140a of Appellant's Appendix:

The Court: Well, Madam, as you look at that list does it refresh your recollection?

The Witness: I lived with these things, your Honor, I know them.

The Court: You lived with them yourself?

The Witness: I did.

The Court: So when you look at that paper, it does refresh your recollection?

The Witness: Absolutely.

but in many instances could state where in the house he had seen them; and that he could give an opinion as to their value. This he was permitted to do.

In denying the acceptability of the evidence related, the defendant rests primarily on *Putnam v. United States*, 1896, 162 U.S. 687, and refers to this Court's decision in *Delaney v. United States*, 3 Cir., 1935, 77 F.2d 916. It is his position that the lists should not have been used because they were not made by the witnesses at or shortly after the time of the transaction while the facts were fresh in memory. It is further contended that the witnesses were not hostile to the government, and what Farid did, in fact, was to read off the lists as proof of the actual articles loaded on the vehicles.

The government, on the other hand, asserts that the witnesses gave their independent recollection, which is admissible, albeit refreshed, because it is the recollection and not the writing which is the evidence. It goes further, and urges that where the witness has an independent recollection, anything may be used to stimulate and vitalize that recollection without regard to source or origin.[17]

Refreshing the recollection of a witness is not an uncommon trial practice, but as a theory of evidentiary law its content and application are far from clear. The large collection of cases found in 125 A.L.R. 19-250 illustrates the point. An analysis as good and trustworthy as presently exists appears in Chapter XXVIII, 3 WIGMORE ON EVIDENCE (3rd ed. 1940). Professor Wigmore separated, broadly, what he called "past recollection recorded" from "present recollection revived,"[18] attributing much of the confusion in the cases to a failure to make this distinction and to the use of the phrase "refreshing the recollection" for both classes of testimony. The primary difference between the two classifications is the ability of the witness to testify from present knowledge: where the witness' memory is revived, and he presently recollects the facts and swears to them, he is obviously in a different position from the witness who cannot directly state the facts from present memory, and who must

---

17 [5] This is in paraphrase of Lord Ellenborough's statement in *Henry v. Lee*, 2 Chitty 124: "If upon looking at any document he can so far refresh his memory as to recollect a circumstance, it is sufficient; and it makes no difference that the memorandum is not written by himself, for it is not the memorandum that is the evidence but the recollection of the witness."

18 [7] Morgan, *The Relation between Hearsay and Preserved Memory*, 40 HARV. L. REV. 712, 717–719 (1927), makes the following classification:

(1) where the witness, by some stimulus, be it memorandum or other device, has his recollection so revived as to be able to testify entirely from present memory; (2) where by a memorandum his mind is so moved that he has a present recollection of making or verifying the memorandum and of a part only of the facts therein recorded; (3) where by the aid of the memorandum he can recall only that some event occurred and that he made or verified the memorandum as a record of it; (4) where the memorandum has no effect whatever upon his present memory; it does not enable him to recollect the making or verifying of the memorandum or any of the facts set forth in it. In the first situation the memory of the witness is actually refreshed. . . . He is not asking the tribunal to believe it because he stated it on a former occasion, but because he is now relating it under oath and subject to cross-examination. . . . If in any of the last three situations the memorandum is to be received as evidence of the unremembered matter contained in it, because, for reasons satisfactory to himself and to the court, the witness swears that its contents are true, it cannot be on the ground of refreshment of recollection. If accepted at all, it must be as a substitute for present memory. This means, in short, the reception in evidence of an extrajudicial statement as probative of the matter asserted in it.

ask the court to accept a writing for the truth of its contents because he is willing to swear, for one reason or another, that its contents are true.

Recognition of the basic difference between the two categories of evidence referred to is explicit in the federal cases, although in some the distinction is obscured by the lack of necessity for it. In *Cohen v. United States*, 3 Cir., 1929, 36 F.2d 461, 462, this Court noted that the witness "testified not from her present recollection . . . but rather from her past recollection recorded." And in *Delaney v. United States*, 3 Cir., 1935, 77 F.2d 917, we referred with approval to *Jewett v. United States*, 9 Cir., 1926, 15 F.2d 955, 956, wherein the Court said:

> "It is one thing to awaken a slumbering recollection of an event, but quite another to use a memorandum of a recollection, fresh when it was correctly recorded, but presently beyond the power of the witness so to restore that it will exist apart from the record."

The difference between present recollection revived and past recollection recorded has a demonstrable effect upon the method of proof. In the instance of past recollection recorded, the witness, by hypothesis, has no present recollection of the matter contained in the writing. Whether the record is directly admitted into evidence, or indirectly by the permissible parroting of the witness, it is nevertheless a substitute for his memory and is offered for the truth of its contents. It assumes a distinct significance as an independent probative force, and is therefore ordinarily required to meet certain standards. These requirements are the more understandable in consideration of the fact that the court is at once desirous of determining whether the writing may be safely received as a substitute for the witness' memory and for the truth of the matter therein asserted, and of affording to the trier of fact information upon which it can forma reliable judgment as to its worth for the purposes offered.

In the case of present recollection revived, the witness, by hypothesis, relates his present recollection, and under oath and subject to cross-examination asserts that it is true; his capacities for memory and perception may be attacked and tested; his determination to tell the truth investigated and revealed; protestations of lack of memory, which escape criticism and indeed constitute a refuge in the situation of past recollection recorded, merely undermine the probative worth of his testimony. It is in recognition of these factors that we find:

> The law of contemporary writing or entry qualifying it as primary evidence has no application. The primary evidence here is not the writing. It was not introduced in evidence. It was not offered. The primary evidence is the oral statement of the hostile witness. It is not so important when the statement was made or by whom if it serves the purpose to refresh the mind and unfold the truth. . . .
>
> When a party uses an earlier statement of his own witness to refresh the witness' memory, the only evidence recognized as such is the testimony so refreshed. . . . Anything may in fact revive a memory: a song, a scent, a photograph, an allusion, even a past statement known to be false. When a witness declares that any of these has evoked a memory, the opposite party may show, either that it has not evoked what appears to the witness as a

memory, or that, although it may so appear to him, the memory is a phantom and not a reliable record of its content. When the evoking stimulus is not itself an account of the relevant occasion, no question of its truth can arise; but when it is an account of that occasion, its falsity, if raised by the opposing party, will become a relevant issue if the witness has declared that the evoked memory accords with it.

It is important to note that *Putnam v. United States, supra,* on which the defendant relies, does not distinguish between past recollection recorded and present recollection revived. Insofar as the condition of contemporaneity is concerned, that decision is no longer construed as stating an unyielding rule.

Since the purpose of the writing is to activate the memory of the witness, there is always the possibility, if not probability, that the writing will exert a strong influence upon the direction of the memory, that is, the nearer the writing to the truth, the lesser the deviation of the witness' memory from the truth. But this is not a binding reason for insistence upon establishing the reliability of the writing previous to permitting the witness to state whether his memory is refreshed. The reception of a witness' testimony does not depend upon whether it is true; truth is a matter for the trier of fact unless, of course, the evidence is so improbable that reasonable men would not differ upon it. When the witness testifies that he has a present recollection, that is the evidence in the case, and not the writing which stimulates it. If his recollection agrees with the writing, it is pointless to require proof of the accuracy of the writing, for such proof can only amount to corroborative evidence. The testimony is received for what it is worth. . . . And the testimony should be received if it is capable of a reasonably satisfactory evaluation. Undoubtedly, the nature of the writing which the witness says is effective to stimulate his memory plays a part in that evaluation, and the dangers from deficiencies in the witness' testimonial qualifications are not less susceptible of evaluation by the trier of fact than in the case of past perception recorded; indeed, they are more readily subject to test, for the witness, as already noted, asserts a present memory and cannot gain protection from a denial of the very memory which he claims to have.

Of course, the categories, present recollection revived and past recollection recorded, are clearest in their extremes, but they are, in practice, converging rather than parallel lines; the difference is frequently one of degree. Moreover, it is in complication thereof that a cooperative witness, yielding to suggestion, deceives himself, that a hostile witness seizes an opportunity, or that a writing is used to convey an improper suggestion. Circumstances, or the nature of the testimony, may belie an assertion of present memory; more often the credibility of the witness generally, and the cross-examiner's attack upon the reliability of his memory, will decide the claim to an independent recollection.

Properly, the burden to ascertain the state of affairs, as near as may be, devolves upon the trial judge, who should in the first instance satisfy himself as to whether the witness testifies upon a record or from his own recollection. It is upon this satisfaction that the reception of the evidence depends, for if it appears to the court that the witness is wholly dependent for the fact upon the memorandum he holds in his hand, the memorandum acquires a significance which, as stated, brings into operation certain guiding rules. Similarly, the trial judge must determine whether the device of refreshing recollection is merely a subterfuge to improperly suggest to the witness the testimony expected of him. It is axiomatic, particularly with respect to the reception of evidence, that much depends upon the discretion of the trial judge. . . .

In the instant case, the learned trial judge determined that both Farid and the expert, Berlow, testified from present recollection. On the record, we cannot say that it was plainly not so. Both witnesses stated that they knew the chattels and could identify them. Farid, who testified that she was present and helped to pack them, said she could remember which were transported; Berlow said he could give an opinion of their value. On a number of occasions the trial judge investigated the foundations of their claim to present recollection and satisfied himself as to its bona fides. The case is, therefore, distinguishable from *Jewett v. United States, supra,* wherein it was held that the witness had no independent recollection, and from *Delaney v. United States, supra,* where the Court concluded that the witness did no more than read from a photostatic copy. While the defendant asserts that neither Farid nor Berlow did more, the trial judge immediately recognized that the items of property involved were so numerous that in the ordinary course of events no one would be expected to recite them without having learned a list by rote memory. On the other hand, the items were such that a person familiar with them reasonably could be expected to recognize them and tell what he knows. Under these circumstances, the District Judge might well have permitted the government, in lieu of the procedure followed, to ask Farid leading questions, directing her attention to specific items, and asking her whether she knew what happened to them. This is especially true of Berlow, who did not purport to have any knowledge of the movement of the articles. Clearly, it would have been pointless to ask him to give the value of every article he had ever seen in Farid's home. The same result could have been achieved legitimately without the use of the lists by orally directing his attention to any specific article previously identified by Farid and asking him whether he had seen it, presently remembered it, and could give an opinion as to its value. By the use of lists, nothing more or different was accomplished.

Moreover, we think the procedure followed lay within the discretion of the trial court, and that no prejudicial error ensued. The evidence was capable of a reasonably satisfactory evaluation and was receivable for what it was worth. In the long run, the primary issue of the case was that of credibility, and it is sufficient that the jury had as sound a basis of weighing the testimony as it would in any other instance. The defense had at its disposal the customary opportunities and all the necessary material to test the witnesses' recollection and other testimonial qualifications, including the single original longhand list which Farid located, the typewritten lists which she said were made at the time of the events involved, and the lists the prosecution used. It might very well have put Farid through severe cross-examination with respect to each chattels he identified on direct examination, but chose instead to attack the reliability of her memory by other means.

Accordingly, it is our conclusion that the learned trial judge did not abuse his discretion, either in determining that the witnesses testified from present recollection, or in permitting the use of the lists described herein.

* * *

For the reasons stated, the judgment of the District Court will be affirmed.

NOTES AND QUESTIONS

1.   Since the concept of past recollection recorded involves offering a memorandum into evidence "for the truth of the matter therein asserted," it triggers the rule against hearsay. *See* Morgan, *The Relation Between Hearsay and Preserved Memory*, 40 Harv. L. Rev. 712 (1927). Accordingly, an exception to the hearsay rule has been developed for such situations. *See* Fed. R. Evid. 803(5). The rule against hearsay is discussed in Chapter V.

2.   *Riccardi* represents the majority view regarding the use of evidence to stimulate a witness' recollection. A minority of jurisdictions apply a "limited rule[that] permits the examiner to refresh a witness' memory only with a writing prepared by the witness at or near the time of the event, when it was fresh in his mind." Kalo, *Refreshing Recollections: Problems with Laying a Foundation*, 10 Rut.-Cam. L.J. 233, 234 (1979). The latter approach "apparently [combines]the concepts of refreshing and recorded recollection . . . and imposed recorded recollection requirements upon the refreshing recollection process." *Id.* at 235, n.13.

3.   May writing prepared primarily for litigation be used to refresh recollection? *See Bankers Trust Co. v. Publicker Industries, Inc.*, 641 F.2d 1361 (2d Cir. 1981).

4.   Does Rule 612, by analogy, suggest a possible solution for dealing with the witness whose recollection has been stimulated through hypnosis? *See, e.g., State v. Beachum*, 643 P.2d 246, 254 (N.M. Ct. App. 1981).

SPORCK v. PEIL
759 F.2d 312 (3d Cir. 1985)

James Hunter, III, Circuit Judge.

This case arises on a Petition for Writ of Mandamus involving a discovery dispute between the parties to a securities fraud class action suit. The underlying action involves an allegation by plaintiff-respondent Raymond K. Peil that defendant National Semiconductor Corporation ("NSC"), defendant-petitioner Charles F. Sporck, NSC's president, and defendant Peter J. Sprague, NSC's chairman, conspired to inflate artificially the value of NSC stock, in order to enable Sporck and Sprague to sell their own shares at the inflated level. The wrongful conduct alleged includes various misrepresentations and nondisclosures of material facts during an eight-month period continuing from July 1, 1976, until March 1, 1977. . . .

During pretrial discovery, attorneys for Peil served numerous sets of combined interrogatory and document requests on defendants. In response, defendants produced hundreds of thousands of documents, from which Peil's attorneys selected more than 100,000 for copying. There is no allegation in this case that defendants have improperly concealed or refused to produce requested documents.

The issue presently before this court arose on May 16, 1983, at the deposition of defendant-petitioner Sporck. Prior to the deposition, counsel for defendants had prepared Sporck for his expected week-long deposition by showing him an unknown quantity of the numerous documents produced by defendants in response to plaintiff's discovery requests. Defense counsel selected and compiled these documents in a folder in Philadelphia, and transported them to California solely for the deposition. According to defense counsel, the selected documents represented, as a group, counsel's legal opinion as to the evidence relevant both to the allegations in the case and the possible legal defenses. It is conceded that none of the individual documents, in their redacted form, contained work product of defense counsel.

At the inception of the Sporck deposition, Peil's attorney asked: "Mr. Sporck, in preparation for this deposition, did you have occasion to examine any documents?" . . . Sporck answered affirmatively, and Peil's attorney first orally, and then by written motion pursuant to Federal Rule of Civil Procedure 34, requested identification and production of "[a]ll documents examined, reviewed or referred to by Charles E. Sporck in preparation for the session of his deposition commencing May 16, 1983." . . . Defense counsel refused to identify the documents, arguing first that all the documents had previously been produced, and second, that the select grouping of the documents was attorney work product protected from discovery by Federal Rule of Civil Procedure 26(b)(3). Defense counsel agreed, however, to allow Peil's counsel to ask Sporck about his reliance on individual documents in the context of specific factual questions, and Sporck's deposition continued on this basis.

Peil filed a motion to compel identification and production of the selected documents, on the ground that all documents used in preparing a witness for a deposition are properly discoverable under Federal Rule of Evidence 612. (Petition, Exhibit D). By order of August 22, 1984, Judge John B. Hannum granted Peil's motion, and ordered that defendant produce or identify all documents reviewed by Sporck in preparation for his deposition. (Petition, Exhibit E). Upon petitioner's motion for reconsideration, Judge Hannum reaffirmed his order, holding that although the select grouping of documents constituted attorney work product, it was not "opinion" work product entitled to absolute protection, and that the principles behind Federal Rule of Evidence 612 supported Peil's claim to identification of the documents. . . . Sporck now asks this court to issue a writ of mandamus directing the trial court to vacate both orders.

I.

The remedy of mandamus is properly invoked only in extraordinary situations and where "necessary or appropriate in aid of [appellate] jurisdiction." 28 U.S.C. § 1651(a) (1982); *see, e.g., Allied Chemical Corp. v. Daiflon, Inc.*, 449 U.S. 33, 34 (1980). In order to ensure that a writ of mandamus will issue only in limited circumstances, the Supreme Court has required that "a party seeking issuance have no other adequate means to attain the relief he desires," *id.* at 35, and that the petitioner satisfy the "burden of showing that [his] right to issuance of the writ is 'clear and indisputable.' " *Bankers Life & Casualty Co. v. Holland*, 346 U.S. 379, 384 (1953). Further, because "[w]here a matter is committed to discretion, it cannot be said that a litigant's right to a particular result is 'clear and indisputable,' " a writ of mandamus will only be granted for clear error of law. *Allied Chemical Corp. v. Daiflon, Inc.*, 449 U.S. 33, 36 (1980).

The question remains, however, whether petitioner's right to immediate relief by writ of mandamus is "clear and indisputable" because of clear error of the law by the trial court. Although discovery orders are normally committed to the discretion of the trial court, *see, e.g., DeMasi v. Weiss*, 669 F.2d 114, 122 (3d Cir. 1982), petitioner argues that the trial court's failure to protect defense counsel's work product from discovery as mandated by Federal Rule of Civil Procedure 26(b)(3) constituted clear error of law. Respondent argues, however, that the trial court correctly ordered the identification of the documents used to prepare petitioner for his deposition, either under a theory of waiver of work product immunity, or through a balance of the respective policies of Federal Rule of Evidence 612 and Federal Rule of Civil Procedure 26(b)(3). Because we find neither a waiver of work product immunity nor a correct application of Federal Rule of Evidence 612 apply to this case, we agree with petitioner that the trial court should not have ordered the identification of the documents selected by counsel.

II.

The threshold issue in this case is whether the selection process of defense counsel in grouping certain documents together out of the thousands produced in this litigation is work product entitled to protection under Federal Rule of Civil Procedure 26(b)(3) and the principles of *Hickman v. Taylor*, 329 U.S. 495 (1947). Petitioner concedes that the individual documents that comprise the grouping are not attorney work product, but argues that the selection process itself represents defense counsel's mental impressions and legal opinions as to how the evidence in the documents relates to the issues and defenses in the litigation. Because identification of the documents as a group will reveal defense counsel's selection process, and thus his mental impressions, petitioner argues that identification of the documents as a group must be prevented to protect defense counsel's work product. We agree.

The work product doctrine had its modern genesis in the seminal opinion in *Hickman v. Taylor*, 329 U.S. 495 (1947). In *Hickman*, the Court rejected "an attempt, without purported necessity or justification, to secure written statements, private memoranda and personal recollections prepared or formed by an adverse party's counsel in the course of his legal duties." 329 U.S. at 510. Preserving the privacy of preparation that is essential to the attorney's adversary role is the central justification for the work product doctrine. Without this zone of privacy: Much of what is now put down in writing would remain unwritten. An attorney's thoughts, heretofore inviolate, would not be his own. Inefficiency, unfairness and sharp practices would inevitably develop in the giving of legal advice and in the preparation of cases for trial. The effect on the legal profession would be demoralizing. And the interests of the clients and the cause of justice would be poorly served. *Hickman*, 329 U.S. at 511.

The work product doctrine as articulated in *Hickman* has been partially codified in Federal Rule of Civil Procedure 26(b)(3). That rule conditions the production of "documents and tangible things" prepared in anticipation of litigation by or for an opposing party on the moving party's showing of substantial need and undue hardship. Even where such a showing is made, however, the trial court, in ordering the production of such materials, "shall protect against disclosure of the mental impressions, conclusions, opinions, or legal theories of an attorney or other representative of a party concerning the litigation." Fed. R. Civ. P. 26(b)(3). Thus, Rule 26(b)(3) recognizes the distinction between "ordinary" and "opinion" work product first articulated by the Supreme Court in *Hickman v. Taylor*, 329 U.S. 495 (1947).

Opinion work product includes such items as an attorney's legal strategy, his intended lines of proof, his evaluation of the strengths and weaknesses of his case, and the inferences he draws from interviews of witnesses. . . . Such material is accorded an almost absolute protection from discovery because any slight factual content that such items may have is generally outweighed by the adversary system's interest in maintaining the privacy of an attorney's thought processes and in ensuring that each side relies on its own wit in preparing their respective cases. . . .

We believe that the selection and compilation of documents by counsel in this case in preparation for pretrial discovery falls within the highly-protected category of opinion work product. As the court succinctly stated in *James Julian, Inc. v. Raytheon Co.*, 93 F.R.D. 138, 144 (D. Del. 1982): In selecting and ordering a few documents out of thousands counsel could not help but reveal important aspects of his understanding of the case. Indeed, in a case such as this, involving extensive document discovery, the process of selection and distillation is often more critical than pure legal research. There can be no doubt that at least in the first instance the binders were entitled to protection as work product. *See also Berkey Photo, Inc. v. Eastman Kodak Co.*, 74 F.R.D. 613, 616 (S.D.N.Y. 1977) (notebooks representing "counsel's ordering of 'facts,' referring to the prospective proofs, organizing, aligning, and marshalling empirical data with the view to combative employment that is the hallmark of the adversary enterprise" categorized as work product). Further, in selecting the documents that he thought relevant to Sporck's deposition, defense counsel engaged in proper and necessary preparation of his client's case. As the Supreme Court noted in *Hickman*: Proper preparation of a client's case demands that he assemble information, sift what he considers to be the relevant from the irrelevant facts, prepare his legal theories and plan his strategy without undue and needless interference. That is the historical and the necessary way in which lawyers act within the framework of our system of jurisprudence to promote justice and to protect their client's interest. . . . In the instant case, without the protection that the work product doctrine accords his preparation, defense counsel may have foregone a sifting of the documents, or at the very least chosen not to show the documents to petitioner. As a result, petitioner may not have been as well-prepared for his deposition, and neither plaintiff nor defendant would have realized the full benefit of a well-prepared deponent's testimony. For these reasons, Rule 26(b)(3) placed an obligation on the trial court to protect against unjustified disclosure of defense counsel's selection process.

This conclusion, however, does not end the issue. Respondent argues, and the trial court agreed, that operation of Federal Rule of Evidence 612 removed any protection that defense counsel's selection process would ordinarily enjoy. Because we find that Federal Rule of Evidence 612 does not apply to the facts of this case, we disagree.

III.

Federal Rule of Evidence 612 provides in relevant part:

> [I]f a witness uses a writing to refresh his memory for the purpose of testifying, . . . (2) before testifying, if the court in its discretion determines it is necessary in the interest of justice, an adverse party is entitled to have the writing produced at the hearing, to inspect it, to cross-examine the witness thereon, and to introduce in evidence those portions which relate to the testimony of the witness.

This rule is applicable to depositions and deposition testimony by operation of Federal Rule of Civil Procedure 30(c) ("Examination and cross-examination of witnesses may proceed as permitted at the trial under the provisions of the Federal Rules of Evidence."). . . . Although applicable to depositions, Rule 612 is a rule of evidence, and not a rule of discovery. Its sole purpose is evidentiary in function "to promote the search of credibility and memory." Fed. R. Evid. 612 advisory committee note.

By its very language, Rule 612 requires that a party meet three conditions before it may obtain documents used by a witness prior to testifying: 1) the witness must use the writing to refresh his memory; 2) the witness must use the writing for the purpose of testifying; and 3) the court must determine that production is necessary in the interests of justice. Fed. R. Evid. 612. The first requirement is consistent with the purposes of the rule, for if the witness is not using the document to refresh his memory, that document has no relevance to any attempt to test the credibility and memory of the witness. *See, e.g., United States v. Wright*, 489 F.2d 1181, 1188–89 (D.C. Cir. 1973) (party must lay foundation for document production request by establishing first that witness used document prior to testifying to refresh his memory).

The second requirement — that the witness use the document for the purpose of testifying — was designed "to safeguard against using the rule as a pretext for wholesale exploration of an opposing party's files and to insure that access is limited only to those writings which may fairly be said in part to have an impact upon the testimony of the witness." Fed. R. Evid. 612 advisory committee note. As with the first requirement, the second requirement recognizes that the document is of little utility for impeachment and cross-examination without a showing that the document actually influenced the witness' testimony. . . . Finally, the third requirement codifies the Supreme Court's holding in *Goldman v. United States*, 316 U.S. 129, 132 (1942), that even though a witness may review notes prior to testifying, a trial court should exercise discretion to guard against "fishing expeditions among a multitude of papers which a witness may have used in preparing for trial." H.R. Rep. No. 93-650, 93d Cong. 1st Sess. (1973).

In the case before us, the apparent conflict between the protected status of defense counsel's document selection process under Rule 26(b)(3) and the asserted need, for cross-examination purposes, of the identification of the documents actually selected resulted from the failure to establish the first two requirements under Rule 612. In seeking identification of all documents reviewed by petitioner prior to asking petitioner any questions concerning the subject matter of the deposition, respondent's counsel failed to establish either that petitioner relied on any documents in giving his testimony, or that those documents influenced his testimony. Without first eliciting the testimony, there existed no basis for asking petitioner the source of that testimony. . . . We conclude, therefore, that deposing counsel failed to lay a proper foundation under Rule 612 for production of the documents selected by counsel.

Indeed, if respondent's counsel had first elicited specific testimony from petitioner, and then questioned petitioner as to which, if any, documents informed that testimony, the work product petitioner seeks to protect — counsel's opinion of the strengths and weaknesses of the case as represented by the group identification of documents selected by counsel — would not have been implicated. Rather, because identification of such documents would relate to specific substantive areas raised by respondent's counsel, respondent would receive only those documents which deposing counsel, through his own work product, was incisive enough to recognize and question petitioner on. The fear that counsel for petitioner's work product would be revealed would thus become groundless.

Rule 612, therefore, when properly applied, does not conflict with the protection of attorney work product of the type involved in this case. Because the trial court did not properly condition its application of Rule 612 on a showing that petitioner relied upon the requested documents for his testimony and that those documents impacted on his testimony, the court committed legal error. . . . Proper application of Rule 612 should never implicate an attorney's selection, in preparation for a witness' deposition, of a group of documents that he believes critical to a case. Instead, identification of such documents under Rule 612 should only result from opposing counsel's own selection of relevant areas of questioning, and from the witness' subsequent admission that his answers to those specific areas of questioning were informed by documents he had reviewed. In such a case, deposing counsel would discover the documents through his own wit, and not through the wit of his adversary.

IV.

We conclude, therefore, that the trial court committed clear error of law in ordering the identification of the documents selected by counsel. Because we are confident that the district court will proceed in accordance with our opinion without formal issuance of the writ, we will remand to the district court. *See, e.g., Bogosian v. Gulf Oil Corp.*, 738 F.2d 587, 596 (3d Cir. 1984); *United States v. RMI Co.*, 599 F.2d 1183, 1190 (3d Cir. 1979); *Rapp v. Van Dusen*, 350 F.2d 806, 814 (3d Cir. 1965) (*en banc*).

Evidentiary Foundation:
The Trial of Roland Burnham Molineux[19]

[During the Christmas season of 1898, Harry Cornish found in his mailbox at New York City's exclusive Knickerbocker Athletic Club a pleasantly wrapped little box that apparently contained a vial of Bromo Seltzer. The package sender was anonymous. Cornish took the box home, but the next day, when an acquaintance took some of the medication to treat a headache, she died almost instantly. Only six weeks earlier, one Harry C. Barnett, also a club member, had similarly succumbed to poison delivered by mail.

The investigation of these crimes eventually focused on Roland Burnham Molineux, a third club member, who apparently had the motive to eliminate both Barnett and Cornish. In the following excerpt, the prosecution seeks to establish the defendant's connection to a private mailbox service that allegedly was instrumental to the homicides. Was a proper foundation established for refreshing recollection?]

JOSEPH J. KOCH, a witness called on behalf of the People, being duly sworn, testified as follows:

DIRECT EXAMINATION.

By Mr. Osborne:

What is your business? — I am the manager at No. 1620 Broadway; I have been in business there five years; I am now . . . the publisher and editor of an article called the "Studio"; I was for some years the manager of the "Studio"; in 1897 I was manager.

I show you People's Exhibit 41, prime, in evidence, and I ask you if you received that? — That was received at our place of business.

It was? — Yes, sir; 1898, in the early part of 1898. The early part of 1898? — Yes, sir.

I show you an envelope, which is postmarked January 3, I believe, 1.30 p.m., 1898, addressed to the "Studio" Publishing Company, No. 1620 Broadway, with the stamp Morris Herrmann & Co. in the corner, and I ask you whether or not that is the envelope which in closed People's Exhibit 41 prime? — It is.

Now did you receive that about the date mentioned on the back of that envelope? — I received it on the 4th of January, 1898.

It was mailed the 3d of January, 1898, at Newark, New Jersey? — Yes, sir.

Now, Mr. Koch, what did you do in reference to this letter, or in answer to it; it says, "Kindly send me a sample copy of your paper to the above address, and oblige, yours, respectfully, Roland B. Molineux, per C. D. A."? Is there anything on the face of this paper which will tend to refresh your recollection as whether or not anything was done in answer to that letter? — Yes, sir.

---

[19] Excerpted from S. KLAUS (ED.), THE MOLINEUX CASE 286–87 (Alfred A. Knopf, 1929).

What is it on that paper that refreshes your recollection? — The stamp we have in our office.

By the Court:

Was this stamp in use in your business? — Yes, sir; we used it continually. It was placed upon the letter at the date of its receipt. It was our custom that all letters that came in we always stamped; it is a custom in every publishing office to stamp letters; it was the habit in our office to place a stamp upon these letters.

Go right on and tell what you did, if you ever did anything else in reference to this paper beside what you have stated; did you send anything through the mail to this address or not — did you or did you not? — Yes, sir.

What did you mail? — We mailed a copy of the paper in reply to the letter. Naturally having charge of the office, all these things came under my direction.

3. The Original Document Rule

JOHN MAGUIRE,
EVIDENCE: COMMON SENSE AND COMMON LAW
31–32 (1947)[20]

One more tool of the trade which must be given a brief working description is called the best evidence rule. This title misleads. Despite some loose talk by judicial Pollyannas, there is no effective general doctrine that the best available evidence is always admissible. Neither is there any general doctrine that a litigant trying to establish a fact must always adduce the best evidence he can scrape up. However, the best evidence rule which really exists and about which we are talking, does amount to a limited application of the principles suggested in both the preceding sentences. It has to do only with proof of the contents of writings and may be put in this simple form of words: For the purpose of proving the content of a writing, secondary evidence — that is, any evidence other than the writing itself — is inadmissible unless failure to offer the original writing is satisfactorily explained. The good sense of this rule is entirely clear. Words are slippery things. Details of phraseology may get lost or twisted in memory or in efforts to make exact copies. Furthermore, the very phrasing of the rule indicates reasonable flexibility. It is not a blank unyielding wall of exclusion, but rather a doctrine of priority or preference. But — there always seems to be a but as to any rule of evidence — there has been trouble, minor and major, in its application. The nature of some of this trouble will come out hereafter.

ANTHONY J. BOCCHINO & DAVID A. SONENSHEIN,
A PRACTICAL GUIDE TO FEDERAL EVIDENCE
(2013)[21]

The original document rule requires the proponent to offer the original of a document, photograph, or recording in evidence where the proponent seeks to prove its contents and the contents are directly in issue, unless production is excused under the terms of the rule.

The key to understanding the original document rule is the following. The rule applies where the facts contained in the document are directly in issue in the case and the facts do not exist independent of the document. For example, the bequests in a will are clearly in issue in a will contest and such bequests only exist because they are contained in the will. In other words, the facts are embodied in the writing, and have no existence independent of the writing. If the writing, the will, does not exist, then the operative facts, the bequests, do not exist. Contrarily, where a proponent seeks to prove the fact of payment for which she has a receipt, the proponent need not offer the original receipt (or any receipt). This is because the fact of payment exists irrespective of whether a writing, a receipt, has been created to evidence it. In other words, the fact of payment exists, whether or not a receipt was made to memorialize payment. Therefore, secondary evidence of payment, including oral testimony, would be admissible.

Thus, in deciding whether the original document rule applies to a particular proffer, the ultimate question is whether the writing is more like a will or a receipt, *i.e.* whether the facts to be proved have an existence independent from the writing. Note that if the proponent chooses to use a writing as the sole method of proof of its terms, *e.g.*, chooses to prove payment solely by way of a receipt, then the proponent must normally offer the original of the writing unless excused.

CHARLES T. MCCORMICK,
HANDBOOK OF THE LAW OF EVIDENCE §§ 231, 233
(4th ed. 1992)[22]

§ 231. The Reasons for the Rule.

Since its inception in the early 18th century, various rationales have been asserted to underlie the "best evidence rule." Many older writers have asserted that the rule is essentially directed to the prevention of fraud. Wigmore, however, vigorously attacked this thesis on the analytical ground that it does not square with certain recognized applications and non-applications of the rule. Most modern commentators follow his lead in asserting that the basic premise justifying the rule is the central position which the written word occupies in the law. Because of this centrality, presenting to a court the exact words of a writing is of more than average importance, particularly in the case of operative or dispositive instruments such as

---

[21] Copyright, National Institute for Trial Advocacy (1988).

[22] Reprinted with permission from MCCORMICK'S HANDBOOK OF THE LAW OF EVIDENCE, Fourth Edition, Copyright © 1992 by West Publishing Co.

deeds, wills or contracts, where a slight variation of words may mean a great difference in rights. In addition, it is to be considered (1) that there has been substantial hazard of inaccuracy in some of the commonly utilized methods of making copies of writings, and (2) oral testimony purporting to give from memory the terms of a writing is probably subject to a greater risk of error than oral testimony concerning other situations generally. The danger of mistransmitting critical facts which accompanies the use of written copies or recollection, but which is largely avoided when an original writing is presented to prove its terms, justifies preference for original documents.

§ 233. What Constitutes Proving the Terms

It is apparent that this danger of mistransmission of the contents of the writing, which is the principal reason for the rule, is only important when evidence other than the writing itself is offered for the purpose of proving its terms. Consequently, evidence that a certain document is in existence or as to its execution or delivery is not within the rule and may be given without producing the document.

In what instances, then, can it be said that the terms of a writing are sought to be proved, rather than merely its identity, or existence? First, there are certain writings which the substantive law, *e.g.*, the Statute of Frauds, the parol evidence rule, endow with a degree of either indispensability or primacy. Transactions to which substantive rules of this character apply tend naturally to be viewed as written transactions, and writings embodying such transactions, *e.g.*, deeds, contracts, judgments, etc., are universally considered to be within the present rule when actually involved in the litigation. Contrasted with the above described types of writings are those, essentially unlimited in variety, which the substantive law does not regard as essential or primary repositories of the facts recorded. Writings of this latter sort may be said merely, to happen to record the facts of essentially nonwritten transactions. Testimony descriptive of nonwritten transactions is not generally considered to be within the scope of the present rule and may be given without producing or explaining the absence of a writing recording the facts. Thus evidence of a payment may be given without production of the receipt, or evidence of a marriage without production of the marriage certificate.

While, however, many facts may be proved without resort to writings which record them, the party attempting to prove a fact may choose to show the contents of a writing for the purpose. Thus, for example, a writing may contain a recital of fact which is admissible under an exception to the hearsay rule. Here the recited fact might possibly be established without the writing, but if the contents are relied upon for that purpose the present rule applies and oral testimony as to its contents will be rejected unless the original writing is shown to be unavailable.

SIRICO v. COTTO ET AL.

67 Misc. 2d 636 (N.Y. Civ. Ct. 1971)

OPINION BY: Irving Younger, Judge

In the course of trying this personal injury action, there arose a problem in evidence the solution of which seemed to elude plaintiff's attorney. For whatever assistance it will be to him, and because others may find it useful, I am filing this memorandum.

To support her case on damages, plaintiff called as a witness Dr. Stanley Wolfson, a specialist in radiology. Dr. Wolfson testified that plaintiff had been sent to him by the treating physician and that, in due course, Dr. Wolfson had taken a number of X-ray photographs of plaintiff's spine. After studying them, he wrote a report setting forth his conclusions and sent it, together with the X-ray plates, directly to the treating physician. All that Dr. Wolfson had with him as he sat on the witness stand was a copy of his report. Having refreshed his recollection from it, he was asked to describe what he had found in the X rays and to state his opinion with respect to plaintiff's physical condition. At this point, defense counsel objected. In order to afford plaintiff an opportunity to make her record, the jury was excused, and Dr. Wolfson completed his testimony in its absence. He said that the X rays showed a flattening of plaintiff's lumbar lordosis and a scoliosis of her mid-lumbar spine with convexity towards the left, from which he would conclude that plaintiff was suffering from the consequences of a lumbar-sacral sprain. As to the whereabouts of the X-ray plates, Dr. Wolfson knew only that he had sent them to the treating physician. That gentleman did not testify. Plaintiff's counsel did not have the plates in his possession, nor did he explain his failure to produce them. I sustained defendants' objection and, upon the jury's return to the courtroom, excused Dr. Wolfson.

The problem, then, is whether Dr. Wolfson, without the X-ray plates, might describe what he had seen in them and state the significance he ascribed to his observations. Two lines of analysis are available, each of which leads to the same conclusion — that Dr. Wolfson's testimony is inadmissible.

First, the best evidence rule. This oft-mentioned and much misunderstood rule merely requires a party who seeks to prove the contents of a document to offer in evidence the original copy of that document. (*Taft v. Little*, 178 N.Y. 127,133 [1904]; *Mahaney v. Carr*, 175 N.Y. 454, 462 [1903]; *Butler v. Mail & Express Pub. Co.*, 171 N.Y. 208, 211 [1902]; Thayer, Preliminary Treatise on Evidence, p. 503 [1898].) If he does not, but rather offers secondary evidence (such as a photostat, a carbon, or a witness' *viva voce* description of the document), the adversary's objection must be sustained. But if the proponent explains his failure to offer the original copy of the document, he may then proceed to prove its contents by whatever secondary evidence is available to him. (4 Wigmore, Evidence, § 1192 *et seq.* [3d ed., 1940].) A "document", within the meaning of the best evidence rule, is any physical embodiment of information or ideas — a letter, a contract, a receipt, a book of account, a blueprint, or an X-ray plate. . . .)

So much for basics. Here, plaintiff asked Dr. Wolfson to describe what he saw when he looked at the X-ray plates. This was secondary evidence of their contents. The best evidence rule, we see, requires plaintiff to offer the originals, which, in the instance of X rays, would be the familiar negative plates one "reads" by affixing to a shadow box. Plaintiff's failure to offer these original plates would have been excused had counsel explained his failure (by proof competent for that purpose, needless to say). This he did not do, and hence I sustained defendants' objection.

* * *

Turning to the case at bar, we observe that Dr. Wolfson's opinion to the effect that plaintiff was suffering from the consequences of a lumbar-sacral sprain was based upon information not in evidence. It was based wholly upon the X-ray plates, and those plates, as discussed above, were strangers to the record of this trial. I therefore sustained defendants' objection.

* * *

Here, the consequence of my sustaining defendants' objection to Dr. Wolfson's testimony was a rather complicated excision from the jury's ken of part of another physician's opinion based upon Dr. Wolfson's. That, however, is a matter of interest only to counsel in this case, and so I leave it in the obscurity of the stenographer's minutes.

NOTE

Although Judge Younger's ruling correctly applied the best evidence rule, the Federal Rules of Evidence sometimes authorize experts to refer to extra-record facts that constitute the basis for their opinion. Even under such circumstances, however, the extra-record facts are admissible only insofar as they enable the jury to evaluate the expert's opinion; such facts are not admissible substantively.

MEYERS v. UNITED STATES
171 F.2d 800 (D.C. Cir. 1948)

[In this prosecution for subornation of perjury, the government sought to prove the testimony of a witness named Lamarre before a United States Senate Committee. Although a transcript of the testimony was available, the government called the counsel for the committee to recount orally the substance of Lamarre's testimony.]

WILBUR K. MILLER, J.

. . . Three of the indictment's counts charged that Lamarre: (1) knowingly and willfully testified falsely that Meyers "was not financially interested in or connected with the Aviation Electric Corporation of Dayton and Vandalia, Ohio," during the years 1940 to 1947, inclusive; (2) knowingly and willfully testified falsely that a Cadillac automobile purchased in Washington by Meyers, and paid for by Aviation Electric Corporation, was purchased for the corporation and for its use; (3) knowingly and willfully testified falsely that the sum of $10,000, paid by means of Aviation Electric's checks, for decorating and furnishing Meyers' Washington apartment "was a gift from himself, Bleriot H. Lamarre." . . .

At the opening of the dissent it is said, "The testimony given by Lamarre before the Senate Committee was presented to the jury upon the trial in so unfair and prejudicial a fashion as to constitute reversible error."

The reference is to the fact that William P. Rogers, chief counsel to the senatorial committee, who had examined Lamarre before the subcommittee, and consequently had heard all the testimony given by him before that body, was permitted to testify as to what Lamarre had sworn to the subcommittee. Later in the trial the government introduced in evidence a stenographic transcript of Lamarre's testimony at the senatorial hearing.

In his brief here the appellant characterizes this as a "bizarre procedure" but does not assign as error the reception of Rogers' testimony. The dissenting opinion, however, asserts it was reversible error to allow Rogers to testify at all as to what Lamarre had said to the subcommittee, on the theory that the transcript itself was the best evidence of Lamarre's testimony before the subcommittee.

That theory is, in our view, based upon a misconception of the best evidence rule. As applied generally in federal courts, the rule is limited to cases where the contents of a writing are to be proved. Here there was no attempt to prove the contents of a writing; the issue was what Lamarre had said, not what the transcript contained. The transcript made from shorthand notes of his testimony was, to be sure, evidence of what he said, but it was not the only admissible evidence concerning it. Rogers' testimony was equally competent, and was admissible whether given before or after the transcript was received in evidence. Statements alleged to be perjurious may be proved by any person who heard them, as well as by a reporter who recorded them in shorthand. . . .

The Court of Appeals for the Third Circuit held, *In re Ko-Ed Tavern*, 1942, 129 F.2d 806, 810, the best evidence rule does not have the application which the dissent here seeks to give it:

> As to Light's half ownership of the bankrupt corporation, William Kochansky, president of the company, testified at the hearing before the referee that he and Light each owned fifty percent of the capital stock of the corporation but that no stock certificates had ever been issued to either of them. The appellant objected to this testimony on the ground that the books of the bankrupt corporation were the best evidence of the matter under inquiry and that the parol evidence offered was inadmissible because the nonproduction of the books had not been satisfactorily explained. It is quite apparent that the appellant misconceives the scope of the "best evidence" rule. That rule is applicable when the purpose of proffered evidence is to establish the terms of a writing. In this case there was no attempt to prove by parol either book entries or the terms of written instruments. . . .

As we have pointed out, there was no issue as to the contents of the transcript, and the government was not attempting to prove what it contained; the issue was what Lamarre actually had said. Rogers was not asked what the transcript contained but what Lamarre's testimony had been.

After remarking, ". . . there is a line of cases which holds that a stenographic transcript is not the best evidence of what was said. There is also a legal cliche that the best evidence rule applies only to documentary evidence," the dissenting opinion asserts that the rule is outmoded and that "the courts ought to establish a new and correct rule." We regard the principle set forth in the cases which we have cited as being, not a legal cliche, but an established and sound doctrine which we are not prepared to renounce.

With the best evidence rule shown to be inapplicable, it is clearly seen that it was neither "preposterously unfair," as the appellant asserts, nor unfair at all, to permit the transcript of Lamarre's evidence to be introduced after Rogers had testified. Since both methods of proving the perjury were permissible, the prosecution could present its proof in any order it chose.

There is no substance in the criticism, voiced by the appellant and in the dissent, of the fact that Rogers testified early in the unduly protracted trial and the transcript was introduced near its close. Appellant's counsel had a copy of the transcript from the second day of the trial, and had full opportunity to study it and to cross-examine Rogers in the light of that study. The mistaken notion that, had the transcript been first put in evidence, Rogers' testimony would have been incompetent is, of course, based on the erroneous idea that the best evidence rule had application.

It is quite clear that Meyers was in no way prejudiced by the order in which the evidence against him was introduced, nor does it appear that his position before the jury would have been more favorable had the transcript been offered on an earlier day of the trial. . . .

Since we perceive no prejudicial error in appellant's trial, the judgment entered pursuant to the jury's verdict will not be disturbed.

Affirmed.

PRETTYMAN, J. (dissenting).

I am of strong opinion that the judgment in this case should be reversed.

The testimony given by Lamarre before the Senate Committee was presented to the jury upon the trial in so unfair and prejudicial a fashion as to constitute reversible error.

Lamarre testified before the Committee in executive session, only Senators, Mr. William P. Rogers, who was counsel to the Committee, the clerk, the reporter, and the witness being present. An official stenographic record was made of the proceedings. The testimony continued for two days, and the transcript is 315 typewritten pages. When Meyers was indicted, he moved for a copy of the transcript. The United States Attorney opposed, on the ground that the executive proceedings of a Senate Committee are confidential. The court denied Meyers' motion.

When the trial began, the principal witness called by the Government was Mr. Rogers. He was asked by the United States Attorney, "Now, will you tell the Court and the jury in substance what the testimony was that the defendant Lamarre gave before the Committee concerning the Cadillac automobile?" Two counts of the indictment related to this automobile.

The court at once called counsel to the bench and said to the prosecutor:

> Of course, technically, you have the right to proceed the way you are doing. . . . I do not think that is hearsay under the hearsay rule, but it seems to me . . . that, after all, when you have a prosecution based on perjury, and you have a transcript of particular testimony on which the indictment is based, that you ought to lay a foundation for it or ought to put the transcript in evidence, instead of proving what the testimony was by someone who happens to be present, who has to depend on his memory as to what was said.

Counsel for the defense, objecting, insisted that the procedure was "preposterously unfair." The trial judge said that it seemed to him that the transcript ought to be made available to defense counsel. That was then done, but the prosecutor insisted upon proceeding as he had planned with the witness.

Mr. Rogers then testified: "I will try to give the substance of the testimony . . . . I am sure your Honor appreciates that I do not remember exactly the substance of the testimony. The substance of testimony was this. . . ." And then he gave "in substance" the testimony in respect to the Cadillac car. The same process was followed in respect of the matters covered by the other counts of the indictment, *i.e.*, the redecoration of Meyers' apartment and Meyers' interest in the Aviation Electric Corporation. Defense counsel reserved part of his cross-examination until he could read the transcript.

The notable characteristics of this testimony of Rogers are important. In each instance, the "substance" was a short summation, about half a printed page in length. The witness did not purport to be absolute in his reproduction but merely recited his unrefreshed recollection, and his recollection on each of the three matters bears a striking resemblance to the succinct summations of the indictment. . . .

From the theoretical viewpoint, I realize that there is a line of authority that (absent or incompetent the original witness) a bystander who hears testimony or other conversation may testify as to what was said, even though there be a stenographic report. And there is a line of cases which holds that a stenographic transcript is not the best evidence of what was said. There is also a legal cliche that the best evidence rule applies only to documentary evidence. The trial judge in this case was confronted with that authority, and a trial court is probably not the place to inaugurate a new line of authority. But I don't know why an appellate court should perpetuate a rule clearly outmoded by scientific development. I know the courts are reluctant to do so. I recognize the view that such matters should be left to Congress. But rules of evidence were originally judge made and are an essential part of the judicial function. I know of no reason why the judicial branch of Government should abdicate to the legislative branch so important a part of its responsibility.

I am of opinion, and quite ready to hold, that the rules of evidence . . . are outmoded and at variance with known fact, and that the courts ought to establish a new and correct rule. The rationale of the so-called "best evidence rule" requires that a party having available evidence which is relatively certain may not submit evidence which is far less certain. The law is concerned with the true fact, and with that alone. It should permit no procedure the sole use of which is to obscure and confuse that which is otherwise plain and certain. . . .

The doctrine that stenographic notes are not the best evidence of testimony was established when stenography was not an accurate science. The basis for the decisions is succinctly stated in the 1892 case quoted as leading by Professor Wigmore: "Stenographers are no more infallible than any other human beings, and while as a rule they may be accurate, intelligent, and honest, they are not always so; and therefore it will not do to lay down as a rule that the stenographer's notes when translated by him are the best evidence of what a witness has said, in such a sense as to exclude the testimony of an intelligent bystander who has heard and paid particular attention to the testimony of the witness." [4 WIGMORE, EVIDENCE, § 1330 (3d ed. 1940), quoting McIver, C.J., in *Brice v. Miller*, 1892, 35 S.C. 537, 549, 15 S.E. 272.]

But we have before us no such situation. Stenographic reporting has become highly developed, and official stenographic reports are relied upon in many of the most important affairs of life. . . . In the present instance, at least, no one has disputed the correctness of the transcript.

From the theoretical point of view, the case poses this question: Given both (1) an accurate stenographic transcription of a witness' testimony during a two-day hearing and (2) the recollection of one of the complainants as to the substance of that testimony, is the latter admissible as evidence in a trial of the witness for perjury? I think not. To say that it is, is to apply a meaningless formula and ignore crystal-clear actualities. The transcript is, as a matter of simple, indisputable fact, the best evidence. The principle and not the rote of the law ought to be applied. . . .

UNITED STATES v. GONZALES-BENITEZ
537 F.2d 1051 (9th Cir. 1976)

KENNEDY, CIRCUIT JUDGE:

Aida Gonzales-Benitez and Ambrosio Hernandez-Coronel were convicted for importing and distributing heroin in violation of 21 U.S.C. §§ 952(a), 960(a)(1), 841(a)(1). On appeal they argue that the trial court gave incorrect jury instructions on the defense of entrapment and that the court erred in various other respects. We consider these contentions below, after stating the facts.[23]

*   *   *

Ana Maria Gutierrez, a paid informer who had worked on prior occasions with the Drug Enforcement Administration, initiated a series of telephone conversations

---

[23] [3] In stating the facts we are of course bound to read the record in a manner consistent with the jury's verdict, resolving all conflicts in the evidence in favor of the prosecution.

with appellant Gonzales, who was staying in Culiacan, Mexico. Gonzales indicated she could obtain good quality heroin for the informant. Gonzales asked if Gutierrez would distribute the narcotic to reliable persons, and Gutierrez responded that her buyers could be trusted. In June Mrs. Gutierrez and her daughter traveled to Culiacan, where they spent all day with Gonzales and also met with appellant Hernandez. Together they discussed delivery and transportation of heroin in further detail. Gonzales offered to sell 16 ounces to Gutierrez and allow Hernandez to travel to the border with Gutierrez for protection, but the informer refused to make a purchase at that time.

There followed other telephone conversations and another meeting in which Mrs. Gutierrez introduced Gonzales to a purported buyer, Hector Berrellez. Berrellez was an agent for the Drug Enforcement Administration.

Thereafter a sale was arranged. It was agreed that Berrellez would take delivery of the drugs within the United States. On the day of the border crossing Mrs. Gutierrez and her daughter met with Gonzales and Hernandez in a hotel room in Nogales, Mexico. Appellants produced 13 ounces of heroin and Hernandez stated he would bring two additional kilograms of heroin the next day. He demonstrated certain belts with pouches which he used to transport heroin on his person.

. . . The three met Gonzales on the Arizona side and together they drove to the motel to meet Berrellez, the ostensible buyer. After Berrellez took possession of the heroin, a signal was given and appellants were arrested.

The Best Evidence Argument

Appellants contend the trial court erred in permitting testimony that related their conversations with the informers during a certain meeting in a motel room in Arizona. They claim that since the conversations were recorded on tapes, the tapes themselves, and not testimony of one of the participants, were the "best evidence" of the conversations. We are puzzled that this argument should be advanced so seriously and would not consider it if attorneys for both appellants had not argued the point so strenuously both in their briefs and in the court below. Certainly the trial court was correct in dismissing the objection out of hand.

The appellants simply misconstrue the purpose and effect of the best evidence rule. The rule does not set up an order of preferred admissibility, which must be followed to prove any fact. It is, rather, a rule applicable only when one seeks to prove the contents of documents or recordings. Fed. R. Evid. 1002. Thus, if the ultimate inquiry had been to discover what sounds were embodied on the tapes in question, the tapes themselves would have been the "best evidence."

However, the content of the tapes was not in itself a factual issue relevant to the case. The inquiry concerned the content of the conversations. The tape recordings, if intelligible,[24] would have been admissible as evidence of those conversations. But testimony by the participants was equally admissible and was sufficient to establish what was said.

---

[24] [4] We note that the reason the tapes were not introduced here was that the recording quality was so poor that the court translator was unable to understand and translate them.

NOTES AND QUESTIONS

1. If the original document is legitimately unavailable, is the admissibility of secondary evidence governed by any prioritization requirement (*i.e.*, so that the proponent must then introduce the "next best" evidence)? *Compare* Comment, *Evidence — Degrees of Secondary Evidence — Problems in Application of the So-Called "American" Rule*, 38 MICH. L. REV. 864 (1940), *and* Comment, *Authentication and the Best Evidence Rule Under the Federal Rules of Evidence*, 16 WAYNE L. REV. 195, 233 (1969), *with* Levin, *Authentication and Content of Writings*, 10 RUTGERS L. REV. 632, 643 (1956).

2. Under what circumstances, if any, might a duplicate document properly be considered an original for purposes of the best evidence rule? *See Railroad Management Company v. CFS Louisiana Midstream Co.*, 428 F.3d 214 (5th Cir. 2005); *United States v. Johnson*, 362 F. Supp. 2d 1043, 1067 (N.D. Iowa 2005); *Lorch v. Page*, 115 A. 681 (Conn. 1921) (recognizing duplicate may have the "force of" original).

3. After recovering stolen property, the police photograph the evidence. At trial, does the Original Document rule require introduction of the actual chattels or may the prosecution simply introduce the photographs? *See Wegman-Fakunle v. State*, 626 S.E.2d 170 (Ga. Ct. App. 2006); *Hill v. State*, 142 S.E.2d 909 (Ga. 1965). Does your answer depend on whether any of the recovered contained inscriptions? *See* 4 WIGMORE, EVIDENCE § 1182 (Chadbourn Rev. 1972).

4. In the case of a Photograph, when does counsel seek to prove its content within the meaning of the best evidence rule? Consider the fundamental difference between real and demonstrative evidence. For example, is the content of a photograph really being proven when counsel offers for demonstrative purposes? How might such use compare with the evidentiary value of a photograph in pornography prosecutions, copyright infringement actions, or other situations in which the photograph constitutes real evidence (which arguably speaks for itself rather than merely demonstrates)? *See Sisk v. State*, 204 A.2d 684 (Md. 1964) (bank surveillance photograph had independent probative value); *see generally Milton H. Greene Archives, Inc. v. BPI Communs., Inc.*, 378 F. Supp. 2d 1189, 1196 (D. Cal. 2005) (copyright); *United States v. Levine*, 546 F.2d 658 (5th Cir. 1977) (pornography prosecution).

5. Does the Original Document rule present any special problem in cases involving computer printouts? *See* Roberts, *A Practioner's Primer on Computer-Generated Evidence*, 4 U. CHI. L. REV. 254 (1974); Riccio, *Securities Litigation and Computer-Generated Evidence*, 46 RI BAR JNL. 17 (1998); *United States v. Bennett*, 363 F.3d 947, 953 (9th Cir. 2004); *Guillermety v. Sec'y of Education*, 341 F. Supp. 2d 682, 689 (E.D. Mich. 2003) *King v. State ex rel. Murdock Acceptance Corp.*, 222 So. 2d 393 (Miss. 1969) (recognizing that printouts are only tangible indicators of tape data).

6. What is the rationale underlying Rule 1008? Why might it be appropriate to leave certain preliminary factual determinations to the jury? How does this question relate to the rationale underlying Rule 104(b)?

Evidentiary Foundation:
The Trial of Jeffrey Weissberg et al.

[In 1985, the New York State Organized Crime Task Force indicted Jeffrey Weissberg and several co-conspirators for narcotics trafficking. The defense moved to suppress crucial evidence on grounds of alleged prosecutorial misconduct by Assistant Attorney General Karel Keuker. During the suppression hearing, the government attempted to introduce an important memorandum that had been telefaxed from Keuker's office in Buffalo to Task Force headquarters in White Plains. The defense objected on best evidence grounds.]

MR. GOLDSMITH: I, at this time, move for the introduction of the — the exhibits, the items that have been marked for identification previously . . .

In addition to that, we offered into evidence yesterday Mr. Keuker's May 9th, 1984 memorandum.

* * *

THE COURT: Okay. That's People's number 4 for identification. At the time that People's 4 for identification was offered there was a request made for the original. The original—

THE COURT: Do you gentlemen agree to the copy?

MR. CAMBRIA: No.

MR. GOLDSMITH: We have contacted the White Plains office for the copy that was sent to them. In fact, all that was sent to them was a faxed copy of that document which it is my position constitutes a duplicate original since that is the only one which they received. I can represent to the Court that Mr. Keuker spoke to Marty Marcus who conducted a search for the document and Marty . . . advised Keuker that what they had in their file was a faxed copy and that that faxed copy was, in fact, in correct chronological order within that file. So I have the — this fax copy available for the court and beyond that there is no other original as such. It is my position first that this fax copy does constitute a duplicate original. Beyond that it is also my position that a duplicate is every bit as admissible as — as an original and that this is not an appropriate case for the application of the best evidence rule.

* * *

MR. CAMBRIA: . . . As far as the May 9th '84 memo, some — there had to be some original someplace. You have to put something on a machine to telefax or whatever other way they did it. I still would like to see an original or have somebody explain where it is. Yesterday Mr. Keuker said it's in White Plains and so now we're told it's not in White Plains, it was in Buffalo, apparently, because somebody had to put it on a telefax machine. So I — I just, — we've had one set of papers not show up in this case, . . . and I would — they think this is such an important report then we should have the original.

* * *

MR. GOLDSMITH: Your Honor, may I respond to that?

THE COURT: Yes, sir.

MR. GOLDSMITH: I'd like to indicate that it's fundamental Hornbook principle that when a document is issued and a copy happens to be sent to a recipient, for example, if I send you a telegram and by virtue of the process that the telegram company employs you get a copy of it, that copy, in fact, constitutes an original. In this case the fax version sent to White Plains does constitute the original. It is absolutely possible that we will have two original documents. If someone comes to you with a wire tap application you may sign one original document. You may sign a duplicate. Both of them constitute original documents. There's nothing unusual about that.

THE COURT: Do you admit that there's an original?

MR. GOLDSMITH: I admit that there was at some time some other document prepared which was also an original.

THE COURT: You're not — you're not singing the same tune. Is there an original?

MR. GOLDSMITH: I have brought into court a fax document and a copy of an original. Where that original is, has not been determined.

THE COURT: Then it's not going into evidence.

MR. GOLDSMITH: Your Honor—

* * *

THE COURT: I want the original. Period.

MR. GOLDSMITH: Since when does the best evidence rule apply in this context?

THE COURT: That is the best evidence rule because you haven't adequately explained why you're submitting a copy.

* * *

MR. GOLDSMITH: Your Honor, I'm not submitting a copy. That constitutes a duplicate original.

THE COURT: Oh, I know you wrote a book on evidence, and that's the evidence according to Goldsmith. It isn't the rule in New York.

MR. GOLDSMITH: I don't cite the evidence according to Goldsmith. . . . [W]hat we have here is the Court becoming a rubber stamp for the defense.

* * *

[Although the trial court eventually suppressed the evidence at issue, this ruling was reversed on appeal.]

4. Rules Limiting Opinion Testimony

a. The Non-Opinion Rule

CARTER v. BOEHM
3 Burr. 1905, 97 ENG. REP. 1162 (K.B. 1796)

LORD MANSFIELD now delivered the resolution of the Court.

* * *

. . . [W]e all think the jury ought not to pay the least regard to it. It is mere opinion; which is not evidence. It is opinion after an event. It is opinion without the least foundation from any previous precedent or usage. It is an opinion which, if rightly formed, could only be drawn from the same premises from which the Court and jury were to determine the cause: and therefore it is improper and irrelevant in the mouth of a witness.

Mason Ladd, *Expert Testimony*
5 VAND. L. REV. 414, 414–16 (1952)[25]

. . . Coincident with the transition and ultimate change from the inquisitorial to the adversary system of trial the opinion rule emerged. Under the new system of the independent jury, knowledge about the controversy disqualified prospective jurors. The testimony of witnesses and real evidence became the sole source of factual data upon which a verdict could be rendered. It was natural that witnesses were required to have personal knowledge of the matters of which they spoke, since the jury no longer had any knowledge. As stated by Lord Coke in 1622, "It is not satisfactory for a witness to say, that he thinks or persuadeth himself." From this and similar expressions, the opinion rule later developed, but it is questionable whether the earlier declarations meant more than that a witness must have personally perceived what he is to speak about. It is doubtful that the object of the rule was to attempt to control the language through which witnesses expressed facts. It could more reasonably be regarded as a requirement that the witness have personal knowledge thus prohibiting him from merely repeating the statements of others who had perceived or expressing his opinion when it was based on conjecture of the mind rather than personal observation. In this sense the opinion rule and the hearsay rule arose from the same source. Both are based upon the conception of the function of a witness in an adversary proceeding, namely, to state what he knows and not what he thinks or has heard others say. Thus, the earlier law upon this subject involved fundamental considerations but out of it arose the opinion rule of

---

[25] Reprinted with permission.

exclusion which became directed as much to the form of expression of a witness in relating what he had perceived as to excluding the testimony of a witness who attempted to testify without having perceived the matter which he attempted to report. A different expression of the same idea became common, that it is the province of the jury to exercise opinions and reach conclusions in determining its verdict and the function of a witness is to state the facts only.

The opinion rule would be reasonable enough if there were always a sharp line between a statement of fact and an expression of opinion. The rule has accomplished some good in requiring a witness to communicate his perceptions in language other than inferences where the subject matter is plainly susceptible to factual statement. Indeed, the examiner of a witness may gain much more from his testimony if the questions require and the witness narrates the facts rather than his conclusions from them. If a witness answers in terms of opinion rather than facts or if the question calls for such an answer, a wise opponent may choose not to urge the opinion objection because if sustained, a new question would be asked which would cause the witness to speak factually with much more telling effect than the expression of an opinion. Except when the opinion objection is used because of want of perception of the witness or faulty perception which has caused him to speak in terms of inference, it is doubtful if much is gained from use of the rule. If inferences stated by a witness are not warranted by the facts, cross-examination is an effective weapon to expose their weakness. It would thus appear that the dangers of admitting testimony in terms of opinion have been greatly magnified. Nevertheless, perhaps no objection is more commonly used than that "the question calls for the opinion or conclusion of the witness." Furthermore, few rules have caused the courts more trouble than their legalistic struggle to determine whether the testimony in question is fact or opinion, with the penalty of reversal in the event of an erroneous ruling.

b. The Lay Witness Exception

UNITED STATES v. LEROY
944 F.2d 787 (10th Cir. 1991)

McWilliams, Circuit Judge.

Reggie LeRoy and five others were charged with conspiring with each other, and others, from August 1, 1988, to July 20, 1989, in Tulsa, Oklahoma, in violation of 21 U.S.C. § 846 as follows: (1) to knowingly and intentionally distribute a mixture or substance which contained cocaine base, . . . and (2) to knowingly and intentionally possess with an intent to distribute cocaine in an amount in excess of five hundred grams in violation of 21 U.S.C. §§ 841(a)(1)and 841(b)(1)(B)(ii).

LeRoy was tried jointly with four of the other five defendants and the jury convicted LeRoy of conspiring to knowingly and intentionally distribute in excess of fifty grams of a mixture or substance which contained cocaine base, a Schedule II controlled substance, in violation of 21 U.S.C. §§ 841(a)(1) and 841(b)(1)(A)(iii). LeRoy was sentenced under the Sentencing Guidelines to imprisonment for 320 months. LeRoy appeals.

On May 4, 1989, officers of the Tulsa, Oklahoma police department searched the apartment of one Willie Junior Louis with the latter's consent. The search disclosed various drug paraphernalia, a quantity of ammunition and a Molotov cocktail. Louis explained to the police that in March, 1989, he was in Oklahoma City, Oklahoma, for several days and had left a girlfriend in charge of his apartment. During this absence, according to Louis, LeRoy and the others had simply "moved" into his apartment and thereafter conducted a "crack" cocaine business out of his apartment. He told the police that he did not report the matter because he was fearful for his life. He also explained in detail, and later so testified at trial, how LeRoy and the others brought rock cocaine to the apartment, cut large pieces into smaller pieces with a razor blade and sold it to persons who came to the apartment. Louis also described the use of runners, often juveniles, who would come to the apartment, obtain crack cocaine, and then go into the street near his apartment and make sales to persons driving by in automobiles. Louis described how the runners would return with the money obtained from street sales.

Louis testified at trial as a government witness. Since no cocaine was found in his apartment, his testimony concerning the use of his apartment by LeRoy and the others in the drug operation from March, 1989, to the date the police searched his apartment on May 4, 1989, was quite critical. On direct examination, Louis admitted that he had suffered two prior felony convictions and was on probation from a state conviction at the time of the search of his apartment.

In an effort to further attack Louis' credibility, counsel for certain defendants, including LeRoy, called as a defense witness one Ronny Goins, who was Louis' probation officer at the time of the May 4 search. Goins testified, interalia, that he had visited Louis at his apartment on two occasions during March and April, 1989, and that he had seen no evidence of any drug operation, nor did Louis tell him that any drug operation was being conducted out of his apartment by others.

Goins brought with him Louis' probation file. On the file was a handwritten notation "mentally unbalanced." This notation was not made by Goins, but was apparently made by another probation officer who had previously handled Louis' case. The notation was ostensibly made on or about February 9, 1989, when Louis reported to his probation officer that someone had shot at him. In any event, counsel sought to introduce into evidence this two-word notation "mentally unbalanced" through witness Goins. Objection was made and sustained.

On appeal, LeRoy argues that exclusion of this evidentiary matter requires reversal. In moving for the admission of this two-word notation, defense counsel agreed that it was hearsay but sought admission on the grounds that it came under the business record exception and/or the state record exception to hearsay. In rejecting this proffer, the district court spoke as follows: "[I]t is hearsay and while it may be a report, I don't think that they [probation officers]regularly assess mental competency through many of these records and what they do is report stories, tales, all sorts of things and you've got to know who made the report and what the backup is and the data is, before you ever evaluate what they said and, there's no indication of competency or what the basis of the statement was nor purport for what purpose."

The notation on Louis' probation file was supposedly made by a Mr. Hughes, who was unavailable to testify at LeRoy's trial. Presumably, Hughes was not an expert in the field of mental health. However, Fed. R. Evid. 701 permits a lay witness to express an opinion if, inter alia, it is "rationally based on the perception of the witness." So, if Hughes himself had been present at the trial of this matter, he would not have been permitted to express any opinion that Louis was "mentally unbalanced" unless it was first shown that his opinion was "rationally based on the perceptions of the witness." Lay opinion of a witness as to a person's sanity is admissible if the witness is sufficiently acquainted with the person involved and has observed his conduct. . . . A lay witness should be required to testify regarding the person's unusual, abnormal or bizarre conduct before being permitted to express an opinion as to sanity. *Id.* In other words, just what Hughes was basing his opinion on would have to first be shown, and in the absence of such, his opinion would not be admitted in evidence.

Because Probation Officer Hughes was not present at trial, his notation expressing his opinion of Louis' mental competency should not be admitted into evidence without any showing as to the basis for his opinion. Neither the business record exception to the hearsay rule, nor the official state record exception, would justify admission of evidence which is itself inadmissible on grounds other than hearsay.

UNITED STATES v. COX
633 F.2d 871 (9th Cir. 1980)

EDWARD C. REED, JR., DISTRICT JUDGE:[26]

Appellant, Gregory Waldo Thomas Cox, seeks appellate review of his convictions, following a jury trial held December 5-17, 1979, on three counts of an indictment charging him with possession of unregistered firearms in violation of Title 26, United States Code Section 5861(d). . . .

The charges resulting in the convictions which the appellant now contests came about as a consequence of three bombing incidents in the Phoenix, Arizona, area in the first half of 1979. Each incident involved the use of a "pipebomb" strapped to the gas tank of an unoccupied motor vehicle. The bombs were exploded by a time delay device. All of the bombs consisted of a length of galvanized pipe with threaded nipples on each end, filled with a double base smokeless gun powder, and sealed at both ends with pipe caps. Each bomb used a Baby Ben alarm clock and two batteries as its detonating device. All the pipes used were scored for fragmentation. All used masking tape in some manner.

Defendant presents four questions on appeal:

---

[26] [*] HONORABLE EDWARD C. REED, JR., UNITED STATES DISTRICT JUDGE FOR THE DISTRICT OF NEVADA, sitting by designation.

III

Did the district court commit reversible error by allowing a witness to state her impression and understanding of a conversation with the appellant?

*   *   *

Witness Jeanette Carter testified in response to the Government's question that appellant told her:

"A: He never actually said that, you know, he had blown it up but it was my understanding, or by his mentioning that he had a friend and that when he showed me the article that it was my impression when we were done talking that he was involved in having it blown up."

Carter's testimony as to her impression of what the appellant meant by his statements and contemporaneous conduct goes beyond the literal meaning of appellant's words and actions themselves. Lay witnesses are normally not permitted to testify about their subjective interpretations or conclusions as to what has been said. . . . Under Rule 701 of the Federal Rules of Evidence, some lay expressions of opinion or inference may be permitted but only if rationally based on perception of a witness and helpful either to an understanding of the testimony of the witness on the stand or to the determination of a fact in issue.

Carter's conclusions derived from the fact that on two occasions the appellant had told her he knew someone who would blow up cars for fifty dollars, and that on one of these occasions he had also shown her a newspaper article concerning the second bombing incident. While her statement does go to the determination of a fact in issue, *i.e.*, whether or not appellant was involved in the second bombing, the facts underlying her impression do not rationally lead to the conclusion made. Her "understanding" did not aid the triers of fact in their understanding of what the appellant had said and done. The jury could draw its own conclusions from what Carter had already testified. Her additional analysis was irrelevant and should not have been admitted.

A trial court's ruling to allow lay opinion testimony should not be disturbed absent a clear abuse of discretion. . . . The type of error involved in this case does not rise to a level of constitutional dimension especially where, as here, found in the midst of overwhelming evidence of appellant's guilt. . . . Any error committed by the trial court in admitting the witness' testimony is harmless.

*   *   *

The judgment of the lower court is affirmed.

NOTE

Photographic identifications provide another example of a situation in which courts frequently find that lay witness testimony would not assist the jury. Reasoning that a jury is ordinarily fully capable of examining a surveillance photograph, some courts will not permit a lay witness who knows the defendant to opine that the defendant is the person shown in that photograph. *See United States v. Dixon*, 413 F.3d 540 (6th Cir. 2005). In such cases, admissibility depends on whether lay witness' testimony will really be helpful. This, in turn, depend upon factors such as whether the defendant disguised himself at the time of the crime, whether the defendant altered his appearance prior to trial, the clarity of the photograph, and whether the photograph only displays an incomplete image of the defendant. *Id. See also Current Circuit Splits: Criminal Matters*, 2 Seton Hall Cir. Rev. 261 (2005).

Evidentiary Foundation:
The Trial of Julius and Ethel Rosenberg[27]

[The facts of this case are set forth *supra* p. 183. The first witness for the government was Max Elitcher, whom Julius Rosenberg had asked to participate in espionage affairs related to his employment for the Navy Department. Elitcher acknowledged having cooperated with Rosenberg in significant respects. At one point, the prosecution asked Elitcher about a conversation he had had with Morton Sobell, a co-defendant, concerning a proposed meeting with Julius Rosenberg:]

MAX ELITCHER, called as a witness on behalf of the Government, being first duly sworn, testified as follows:

Mr. Saypol: May I proceed, if the Court please.

The Court: Yes.

                Direct examination.

                             *   *   *

Q.   Did he state to you the purpose for which you should see him?

A.   Well, he said, I don't know in what words, or implied that it had to do with this espionage business, but I don't recall the exact nature of the words.

Mr. Phillips: I move to strike out the answer as a conclusion of the witness. He spoke of something being implied.

The Court: Well, I want to say this right now so that we have no further difficulty on this business of conclusions. I suggest that you read the most recent holding by the Court of Appeals for this circuit in *United States v. Petrone*, decided November 20, 1950. I don't know what the official citation is. You will find that the latest pronouncement by the Court of Appeals on this business of conclusions. In effect they tell the district court not to adhere to the old form of law book teaching on the matter of taking of evidence, that a conclusion should necessarily be excluded, the important thing, the important function of the district court is to attempt to elicit the truth from the witness and whatever form, in effect they say, the district court determines would best elicit the truth, with the exception of the old hearsay

---

[27] Excerpted from Transcript of the Record, *supra* p. 183, at 248–250.

doctrine which is still adhered to, that is the form which the testimony should take.

Now, I will, in my good judgment, at times sustain objection to exclusions, and at other times I will overrule them, in my good judgment.

Mr. Phillips: The point of my objection is to the use of the words "the conversation implied something." That is certainly objectionable.

The Court: That means an impression that he got. That is what a conclusion is, a man gets an impression of something.

Mr. Phillips: And the latest ruling is that a witness' impressions may be stated in that form?

The Court: Under certain circumstances, for the purpose of eliciting the truth.

Am I stating the law correctly as you understand it, Mr. Saypol and Mr. Cohn?

Mr. Cohn: No doubt about it.

Mr. Saypol: Mr. Cohn tried the case; he argued the case.

Mr. Cohn: No doubt about it. The Court of Appeals specifically held that an impression of a witness is competent, and in fact suggested it was error on the part of the District Court—

The Court: So to exclude an impression.

Mr. Cohn: The specific question, very briefly, in that case was, an FBI agent was asked his impression of whether or not a counterfeiter knew that counterfeit money was in his house and was under his control, and the Court of Appeals held it was error not to permit the FBI agent to give his impression of whether the defendant knew at the time.

The Court: That is correct.

Mr. Phillips: I don't think it is quite analogous for a man saying something was implied.

The Court: The doctrine which they enunciate there is that the District Court should not be rigid in repeating and adhering to the old law school type of teaching, that all conclusions are not admissible, and I happen to think the Court of Appeals is absolutely right, for whatever that is worth.

Evidentiary Foundation:
The Trial of Dr. Carl Coppolino[28]

[Marjorie Farber, a former lover of Dr. Carl Coppolino, accused him of killing her husband, Bill Farber. Based on that accusation, the state of New Jersey indicted Dr. Coppolino, who then hired F. Lee Bailey as defense counsel. During the trial, Mrs.

[28] Excerpted from J. MACDONALD. NO DEADLY DRUG 286 (Doubleday & Co., 1968). Dr. Coppolino was

Farber testified that Dr. Coppolino hypnotized her and then caused her to inject a deadly drug into her husband. Mrs. Farber claimed that the injection was not enough to kill her husband and that Dr. Coppolino had to finish the job by smothering Mr. Farber. The following is a portion Mrs. Farber's testimony concerning how Dr. Cappolino killed her husband. Did her testimony constitute an impermissible lay opinion?]

Bailey: Will you tell the jury and the Court where his (Dr. Coppolino's) hands were placed?

Mrs. Farber: He put the pillow over my husband's head, and face, and chest. . . . He was standing at the head of the bed. The bed was like — this is where my husband's head was. I was standing over there at the door. And he pulled the pillow out, and my husband's head sort of turned over that way. He was completely relaxed. My husband was unconscious at that point from this drug. He was—

Bailey: I object!

Court: Sustained. You may say that he wasn't conscious, but whether or not he was unconscious from the drug is inadmissible.

c. The Expert Witness Exception to the Non-Opinion Rule

Mason Ladd, *Expert Testimony*
5 Vand. L. Rev. 414, 417–19 (1952)[29]

* * *

WHEN MAY EXPERT TESTIMONY BE USED?

The use of expert opinion has expanded with the continuous and rapid progress of science which has opened up new areas of scientific proof. New developments involved new sources of litigation, the solution of which requires the knowledge of experts. Also, scientific methods of proof upon ordinary issues have opened a broader field of expert testimony. Illustrative of the advances of scientific proof is the analysis of blood to determine paternity or to determine intoxication. In the criminal law area, crime detection laboratories have immeasurably widened the use of scientific methods of proof. Expert comparative analyses of handwriting, fingerprints, ballistic tests and many other matters involving identity, are a regular procedure in criminal investigations. Experts have been permitted to testify that an important witness in a criminal case was a pathological liar. The unfair trade practice cases and the rise of pollsters to get the low-down on everything have resulted in a new area of expert testimony to provide a method of proof, or perhaps lessen the degree of guess work where the issue is whether the public has been misled. The courts have even resorted to experts in literature or art to give their

---

acquitted in New Jersey, but later convicted in Florida for the murder of his wife. *See Coppolino v. State,* 223 So. 2d 68 (Fla. Dist. Ct. App. 1968), *appeal dismissed,* 239 So. 2d 120, *cert. denied,* 399 U.S. 927 (1969).

[29] Reprinted with permission.

opinion as to whether a writing is literature or a painting is art, so as to escape the legal ban on the obscene. Property valuations, accounting problems and matters involving engineering science require much reliance upon experts. Medical testimony is perhaps the most common type of expert testimony because of the wide variety of litigation in which the physical or mental condition of persons is a major issue. The prospect for the future is more, rather than less, expert testimony, as a part of the growth of a scientific society in a complicated age. There is no more certain test for determining when experts may be used than the common sense inquiry whether the untrained layman would be qualified to determine intelligently and to the best possible degree the particular issue without enlightenment from those having a specialized understanding of the subject involved in the dispute. Whenever the triers of fact are confronted with issues which cannot be determined intelligently on the basis of ordinary judgment and practical experience gained through the usual affairs of life, the benefit of scientific or specialized knowledge or experience may be provided by use of expert testimony. Stated in the negative, expert testimony is not admissible to prove or disprove matters within common knowledge as to which facts may be so described that the triers of fact may form a reasonable opinion themselves. Furthermore, the issue must be such that the expert may answer by giving an opinion that is a reasonable probability rather than conjecture or speculation.

EEN v. CONSOLIDATED FREIGHTWAYS, INC.
120 F. Supp. 289 (D.N.D. 1954)

VOGEL, DISTRICT JUDGE.

This is an action for damages for personal injuries arising out of a collision between a car driven by the plaintiff Clarence O. Een, now an incompetent, and a truck driven by the defendant Dulski and owned by the defendant Consolidated Freightways. The jury returned a verdict for the defendants. The Court is now presented with plaintiffs' motion for a new trial. Such motion is based principally upon the grounds that the Court erred in allowing a defendants' witness, one John Holcomb, to testify, over objection, that from his observations he believed the collision had occurred on the west (defendants') side of the highway.

Holcomb was a deputy sheriff and former city policeman with over 17 years' experience investigating accidents as a law enforcement officer. He arrived at the scene of the accident approximately an hour and twenty minutes after its occurrence but before the damaged vehicles had been moved from the positions in which they had come to rest after the impact, and before the highway had been opened to other traffic. . . .

After establishing Holcomb's qualifications and having him describe what he found and what he did, defendants' counsel asked him if, from his observations, he had formed an opinion as to where the impact occurred. Upon receiving an affirmative answer, he was asked to state the opinion. Plaintiffs' counsel objected on the grounds that it was incompetent, irrelevant and immaterial, calling for speculation, guess and conjecture, invading the province of the jury and called for a conclusion. The objections were overruled and the witness was allowed to state that in his opinion the impact occurred in the west lane of traffic. There was no objection to the qualifications of the witness and plaintiffs make no point of this in the motion for a new trial. . . . The issue, then, seems to be whether the matter was a proper subject for opinion testimony.

*   *   *

In the case at hand, contrary inferences as to which side of the road the accident occurred on were earnestly argued by opposing counsel from the physical facts existing immediately after the accident. It would seem, therefore, that this is not a case where the conclusion as to where the collision occurred is so obvious that any reasonable person, trained or not, could easily draw the inference. Rather, it would seem to be a case where trained experts in the field would be of considerable assistance to the jurors in arriving at their conclusions.

Modern legal thinking indicates quite clearly that the rule excluding opinion evidence is to be applied sparingly, if at all, so that the jury may have all evidence that may aid them in their determination of the facts. Thus, Wigmore states that, rightfully understood, the true test of the rule is whether opinion testimony upon this subject matter from this particular witness may appreciably assist the jury. 7 WIG., EV'D., 3d Ed., sec. 1923. He even suggests that the rule should be that all opinion testimony is admissible subject only to the trial court's discretion to exclude it upon considerations of trial convenience. 7 WIG., EV'D., 3d Ed. sec. 1929.

*   *   *

This court is of the opinion that under the circumstances as they existed and in considering the evidence introduced at the trial, the opinion of the witness Holcomb was properly admitted. It was the view of this Court at the time the ruling was made during the trial that the subject was a proper one for the admission of an opinion of a concededly qualified expert. The physical facts and circumstances found immediately after the accident prompted contrary inferences to be argued with equal earnestness by able and experienced counsel. The witness had personally observed the physical facts and circumstances soon after the accident occurred, before the damaged vehicles had been moved, and before the highway had been opened to the other traffic, and the witness was qualified through long years of experience in the investigation of automobile accidents. Where the inference or conclusion to be drawn is not so obvious that it can be said that the jurors were as equally competent to reach it as one skilled through long experience, then the opinion of one who is so skilled is not only admissible but may be of aid to the jurors. The witness was subject to cross-examination concerning the basis for his opinion but plaintiffs' counsel did not see fit to inquire into it and refused to permit the witness to state his reasons when he offered to do so. In the instructions of the Court to the jurors, they were told specifically that they were not bound by the opinions of expert witnesses, that the testimony of expert witnesses was purely advisory and that they should give such weight and value to such opinions as they thought right and proper under the circumstances. If this Court had been sitting as the trier of the facts, then under the peculiar circumstances here existing it would have felt that the opinion of the witness Holcomb would have been of assistance in determining the ultimate facts.

The motion for a new trial must be denied.

STAFFORD v. MUSSERS POTATO CHIPS, INC.
39 A.D.2d 831 (N.Y. App. Div. 1972)

On April 17, 1966 at about 8:20 p.m. decedent's pickup truck was proceeding northerly on a two-lane macadam highway when it collided with defendant's southbound tractor-trailer at a point where there was a slight incline proceeding south. Decedent and his passenger were killed. There was no eyewitness to the accident. It was dark at the time. Skid marks from the southbound vehicle veered across into the northbound lane and debris was scattered all around. Photographs showing the conditions immediately after the accident were received in evidence. Although parts of the defendant's examination before trial were read into evidence, no explanation for the accident was offered by defendant. At the close of plaintiff's proof the court granted defendant's motion for a nonsuit. . . . In our opinion upon all the proof a prima facie case was made out sufficient to go to the jury to determine liability in plaintiff's action. . . .

The trial court based its dismissal on the testimony of the State Trooper who investigated the accident. He was permitted upon cross-examination to fix the point of impact in the southbound or defendant's lane of travel. We have previously held that the receipt into evidence of such testimony is error, since the Trooper was not qualified as an expert, and, even had he been, the conclusion he drew as to the point of impact was within the competence of the jury. . . .

NOTES AND QUESTIONS

1.   Which case — *Een* or *Stafford* — did the original version of Rule 702 follow? Does the amendment to Rule 702 take a different approach or merely reinforce the original version?

2.   In a suit against an insurance company for "alleged bad faith in failing to settle [a] personal injury action within the policy limits," should an attorney experienced in personal injury action be permitted to testify as an expert regarding the factors typically considered in evaluating both whether settlement should be effected and the "viability" of the defenses which were available in the personal injury case? *See Johnson v. Am. Family Mut. Ins. Co.*, 674 N.W.2d 88 (Iowa 2004) (testimony of experienced personal injury attorney proffered as expert witness on behalf of insurer to refute claim that settlement offer was rejected in bad faith); *Cotton States Mut. Ins. Co. v. Brightman*, 580 S.E.2d 519 (Ga. 2003)

3.   Under Rule 702, may a witness lacking in formal education or training qualify as an expert witness merely on the basis of experience? Consider, for example, *United States v. Johnson*, 575 F.2d 1347 (5th Cir. 1978), in which the government tried to prove that marijuana had been imported from Colombia through the testimony of a witness with the following qualifications:

> [The witness] admitted that he had smoked marijuana over a thousand
> times and that he had dealt in marijuana as many as twenty times. He also
> said that he had been asked to identify marijuana over a hundred times and

had done so without making a mistake. He based his identification upon the plant's appearance, its leaf, buds, stems, and other physical characteristics, as well as upon the smell and the effect of smoking it. . . . [H]e stated that he had been called upon to identify the source of various types of marijuana. He explained that characteristics such as the packaging, the physical appearance, the smell, the taste, and the effect could all be used in identifying the source of the marijuana. It was stipulated that he had no special training or education for such identification. Instead, his qualifications came entirely from "the experience of being around a great deal and smoking it." He also said that he had compared Colombian marijuana with marijuana from other places as many as twenty times. Moreover, he had seen Colombian marijuana that had been grown in the United States and had found that it was different from marijuana grown in Colombia.

Id. at 1360. *See also* "My Cousin Vinny" (1992 Twentieth Century Fox).

DAUBERT v. MERRELL DOW PHARMACEUTICALS, INC.
509 U.S. 579 (1993)

JUSTICE BLACKMUN delivered the opinion of the Court.

In this case we are called upon to determine the standard for admitting expert scientific testimony in a federal trial.

I

Petitioners Jason Daubert and Eric Schuller are minor children born with serious birth defects. They and their parents sued respondent in California state court, alleging that the birth defects had been caused by the mothers' ingestion of Bendectin, a prescription anti-nausea drug marketed by respondent. Respondent removed the suits to federal court on diversity grounds.

After extensive discovery, respondent moved for summary judgment, contending that Bendectin does not cause birth defects in humans and that petitioners would be unable to come forward with any admissible evidence that it does. In support of its motion, respondent submitted an affidavit of Steven H. Lamm, physician and epidemiologist, who is a well-credentialed expert on the risks from exposure to various chemical substances.[30] Doctor Lamm stated that he had reviewed all the literature on Bendectin and human birth defects — more than 30 published studies involving over 130,000 patients. No study had found Bendectin to be a human teratogen (*i.e.*, a substance capable of causing malformations in fetuses). On the basis of this review, Doctor Lamm concluded that maternal use of Bendectin during the first trimester of pregnancy has not been shown to be a risk factor for human birth defects.

---

[30] [1] Doctor Lamm received his master's and doctor of medicine degrees from the University of Southern California. He has served as a consultant in birth-defect epidemiology for the National Center for Health Statistics and has published numerous articles on the magnitude of risk from exposure to various chemical and biological substances. App. 34–44.

Petitioners did not (and do not) contest this characterization of the published record regarding Bendectin. Instead, they responded to respondent's motion with the testimony of eight experts of their own, each of whom also possessed impressive credentials.[31] These experts had concluded that Bendectin can cause birth defects. Their conclusions were based upon "in vitro" (test tube) and "in vivo" (live) animal studies that found a link between Bendectin and malformations; pharmacological studies of the chemical structure of Bendectin that purported to show similarities between the structure of the drug and that of other substances known to cause birth defects; and the "reanalysis" of previously published epidemiological (human statistical) studies.

The District Court granted respondent's motion for summary judgment. The court stated that scientific evidence is admissible only if the principle upon which it is based is "sufficiently established to have general acceptance in the field to which it belongs." 727 F. Supp. 570, 572 (S.D. Cal. 1989), quoting *United States v. Kilgus*, 571 F.2d 508, 510 (9th Cir. 1978). The court concluded that petitioners' evidence did not meet this standard. Given the vast body of epidemiological data concerning Bendectin, the court held, expert opinion which is not based on epidemiological evidence is not admissible to establish causation. 727 F. Supp. at 575. Thus, the animal-cell studies, live-animal studies, and chemical-structure analyses on which petitioners had relied could not raise by themselves a reasonably disputable jury issue regarding causation. *Ibid.* Petitioners' epidemiological analyses, based as they were on recalculations of data in previously published studies that had found no causal link between the drug and birth defects, were ruled to be inadmissible because they had not been published or subjected to peer review. *Ibid.*

The United States Court of Appeals for the Ninth Circuit affirmed. 951 F.2d 1128 (1991). Citing *Frye v. United States*, 293 F. 1013, 1014 (1923), the court stated that expert opinion based on a scientific technique is inadmissible unless the technique is "generally accepted" as reliable in the relevant scientific community. 951 F.2d at 1129-1130. The court declared that expert opinion based on a methodology that diverges "significantly from the procedures accepted by recognized authorities in the field . . . cannot be shown to be generally accepted as a reliable technique." *Id.* at 1130, quoting *United States v. Solomon*, 753 F.2d 1522, 1526 (9th Cir. 1985).

The court emphasized that other Courts of Appeals considering the risks of Bendectin had refused to admit reanalyses of epidemiological studies that had been neither published nor subjected to peer review. 951 F.2d at 1130–1131. Those courts had found unpublished reanalyses "particularly problematic in light of the massive weight of the original published studies supporting [respondent's] position, all of

---

[31] [2] For example, Shanna Helen Swan, who received a master's degree in biostatics from Columbia University and a doctorate in statistics from the University of California at Berkeley, is chief of the section of the California Department of Health and Services that determines causes of birth defects, and has served as a consultant to the World Health Organization, the Food and Drug Administration, and the National Institutes of Health. App. 113–114, 131–132. Stewart A. Newman, who received his master's and a doctorate in chemistry from Columbia University and the University of Chicago, respectively, is a professor at New York Medical College and has spent over a decade studying the effect of chemicals on limb development. App. 54–56. The credentials of the others are similarly impressive. *See* App. 61–66, 73–80, 148–153, 187–192, and Attachment to Petitioners' Opposition to Summary Judgment, Tabs 12, 20, 21, 26, 31, 32.

which had undergone full scrutiny from the scientific community." *Id.* at 1130. Contending that reanalysis is generally accepted by the scientific community only when it is subjected to verification and scrutiny by others in the field, the Court of Appeals rejected petitioners' reanalyses as "unpublished, not subjected to the normal peer review process and generated solely for use in litigation." *Id.* at 1131. The court concluded that petitioners' evidence provided an insufficient foundation to allow admission of expert testimony that Bendectin caused their injuries and, accordingly, that petitioners could not satisfy their burden of proving causation at trial.

We granted *certiorari*, . . . in light of sharp divisions among the courts regarding the proper standard for the admission of expert testimony. *Compare, e.g., United States v. Shorter*, 809 F.2d 54, 59–60 (applying the "general acceptance" standard), *cert. denied*, 484 U.S. 817 (1987), *with DeLuca v. Merrell Dow Pharmaceuticals, Inc.*, 911 F.2d 941, 955 (3d Cir. 1990) (rejecting the "general acceptance" standard).

II

A

In the 70 years since its formulation in the Frye case, the "general acceptance" test has been the dominant standard for determining the admissibility of novel scientific evidence at trial. . . . Although under increasing attack of late, the rule continues to be followed by a majority of courts, including the Ninth Circuit.[32]

The *Frye* test has its origin in a short and citation-free 1923 decision concerning the admissibility of evidence derived from a systolic blood pressure deception test, a crude precursor to the polygraph machine. In what has become a famous (perhaps infamous) passage, the then Court of Appeals for the District of Columbia described the device and its operation and declared:

> Just when a scientific principle or discovery crosses the line between the experimental and demonstrable stages is difficult to define. Somewhere in this twilight zone the evidential force of the principle must be recognized, and while courts will go a long way in admitting expert testimony deduced from a well-recognized scientific principle or discovery, *the thing from which the deduction is made must be sufficiently established to have gained general acceptance in the particular field in which it belongs.*

54 App. D.C., at 47, 293 F., at 1014 (emphasis added).

Because the deception test had "not yet gained such standing and scientific recognition among physiological and psychological authorities as would justify the courts in admitting expert testimony deduced from the discovery, development, and experiments thus far made," evidence of its results was ruled inadmissible. *Ibid.*

The merits of the *Frye* test have been much debated, and scholarship on its

---

[32] [3] For a catalogue of the many cases on either side of this controversy, *see* P. GIANELLI & E. IMWINKELRIED, SCIENTIFIC EVIDENCE § 1–5, pp. 10–14 (1986 & Supp. 1991)

proper scope and application is legion.[33] Petitioners' primary attack, however, is not on the content but on the continuing authority of the rule. They contend that the *Frye* test was superseded by the adoption of the Federal Rules of Evidence.[34] We agree.

We interpret the legislatively-enacted Federal Rules of Evidence as we would any statute. . . . Rule 402 provides the baseline:

> All relevant evidence is admissible, except as otherwise provided by the Constitution of the United States, by Act of Congress, by these rules, or by other rules prescribed by the Supreme Court pursuant to statutory authority. Evidence which is not relevant is not admissible.

"Relevant evidence" is defined as that which has "any tendency to make the existence of any fact that is of consequence to the determination of the action more probable or less probable than it would be without the evidence." Rule 401. The Rule's basic standard of relevance thus is a liberal one.

Frye, of course, predated the Rules by half a century. In *United States v. Abel*, 469 U.S. 45 (1984), we considered the pertinence of background common law in interpreting the Rules of Evidence. We noted that the Rules occupy the field, *id.* at 49, but, quoting Professor Cleary, the Reporter, explained that the common law nevertheless could serve as an aid to their application:

> In principle, under the Federal Rules no common law of evidence remains. "All relevant evidence is admissible, except as otherwise provided. . . ." In reality, of course, the body of common law knowledge continues to exist, though in the somewhat altered form of a source of guidance in the exercise of delegated powers.

---

[33] [4] *See, e.g.*, Green, *Expert Witnesses and Sufficiency of Evidence in Toxic Substances Litigation: The Legacy of Agent Orange and Bendectin Litigation*, 86 Nw. U. L. Rev. 643 (1992) (hereinafter Green); Becker & Orenstein, *The Federal Rules of Evidence After Sixteen Years — the Effect of "Plain Meaning" Jurisprudence, the Need for an Advisory Committee on the Rules of Evidence, and Suggestions for Selective Revision of the Rules*, 60 Geo. Wash. L. Rev. 857, 876–885 (1992); Hanson, *James Alphonso Frye is Sixty-Five Years Old; Should He Retire?*, 16 W. St. U.L. Rev. 357 (1989); Black, *A Unified Theory of Scientific Evidence*, 56 Fordham L. Rev. 595 (1988); Imwinkelried, *The "Bases" of Expert Testimony: The Syllogistic Structure of Scientific Testimony*, 67 N.C. L. Rev. 1 (1988); *Proposals for a Model Rule on the Admissibility of Scientific Evidence*, 26 Jurimetrics J. 235 (1986); Gianelli, *The Admissibility of Novel Scientific Evidence:* Frye v. United States, *A Half-Century Later*, 80 Colum. L. Rev. 1197 (1980); *The Supreme Court, 1986 Term*, 101 Harv. L. Rev. 7, 119, 125–127 (1987). Indeed, the debates over *Frye* are such a well-established part of the academic landscape that a distinct term — *"Frye*-ologist" — has been advanced to describe those who take part. *See* Behringer, *Introduction, Proposals for a Model Rule on the Admissibility of Scientific Evidence*, 26 Jurimetrics J., at 239, quoting Lacey, *Scientific Evidence*, 24 Jurimetrics J. 254, 264 (1984).

[34] [5] Like the question of *Frye*'s merit, the dispute over its survival has divided courts and commentators. *Compare, e.g., United States v. Williams*, 583 F.2d 1194 (2d Cir. 1978), *cert. denied*, 439 U.S. 1117 (1979) (*Frye* is superseded by the Rules of Evidence), *with Christophersen v. Allied-Signal Corp.*, 939 F.2d 1106, 1111, 1115–1116 (5th Cir. 1991) (*en banc*) (*Frye* and the Rules coexist), *cert. denied*, 503 U.S. 912, 112 S. Ct. 1280, 117 L. Ed. 2d 506 (1992), 3 J. Weinstein& M. Berger, Weinstein's Evidence ¶ 702[03], pp. 702–36 to 702–37 (1988) (hereinafter Weinstein& Berger) (*Frye* is dead), and M. Graham, Handbook of Federal Evidence § 703.2 (2d ed. 1991) (*Frye* lives). *See generally* P. Gianelli& E. Imwinkelried, Scientific Evidence § 1–5, pp. 28–29 (1986 & Supp. 1991) (citing authorities).

Id. at 51–52.

We found the common-law precept at issue in the *Abel* case entirely consistent with Rule 402's general requirement of admissibility, and considered it unlikely that the drafters had intended to change the rule. *Id.* at 50–51. In *Bourjaily v. United States*, 483 U.S. 171 (1987), on the other hand, the Court was unable to find a particular common-law doctrine in the Rules, and so held it superseded.

Here there is a specific Rule that speaks to the contested issue. Rule 702, governing expert testimony, provides:

> If scientific, technical, or other specialized knowledge will assist the trier of fact to understand the evidence or to determine a fact in issue, a witness qualified as an expert by knowledge, skill, experience, training, or education, may testify thereto in the form of an opinion or otherwise.

Nothing in the text of this Rule establishes "general acceptance" as an absolute prerequisite to admissibility. Nor does respondent present any clear indication that Rule 702 or the Rules as a whole were intended to incorporate a "general acceptance" standard. The drafting history makes no mention of *Frye*, and a rigid "general acceptance" requirement would be at odds with the "liberal thrust" of the Federal Rules and their "general approach of relaxing the traditional barriers to 'opinion' testimony." *Beech Aircraft Corp. v. Rainey*, 488 U.S., at 169 (citing Rules 701 to 705). *See also* Weinstein, *Rule 702 of the Federal Rules of Evidence is Sound; It Should Not Be Amended*, 138 F.R.D. 631, 631 (1991) ("The Rules were designed to depend primarily upon lawyer-adversaries and sensible triers of fact to evaluate conflicts."). Given the Rules' permissive backdrop and their inclusion of a specific rule on expert testimony that does not mention "general acceptance," the assertion that the Rules somehow assimilated *Frye* is unconvincing. *Frye* made "general acceptance" the exclusive test for admitting expert scientific testimony. That austere standard, absent from and incompatible with the Federal Rules of Evidence, should not be applied in federal trials.[35]

B

That the *Frye* test was displaced by the Rules of Evidence does not mean, however, that the Rules themselves place no limits on the admissibility of purportedly scientific evidence.[36] Nor is the trial judge disabled from screening such evidence. To the contrary, under the Rules the trial judge must ensure that any and all scientific testimony or evidence admitted is not only relevant, but reliable.

The primary locus of this obligation is Rule 702, which clearly contemplates some

---

[35] [6] Because we hold that *Frye* has been superseded and base the discussion that follows on the content of the congressionally-enacted Federal Rules of Evidence, we do not address petitioners' argument that application of the *Frye* rule in this diversity case, as the application of a judge-made rule affecting substantive rights, would violate the doctrine of *Erie R. Co. v. Tompkins*, 304 U.S. 64, 58 S. Ct. 817, 82 L. Ed. 1188 (1938).

[36] [7] THE CHIEF JUSTICE "do[es] not doubt that Rule 702 confides to the judge some gatekeeping responsibility," *post*, but would neither say how it does so, nor explain what that role entails. We believe the better course is to note the nature and source of the duty.

degree of regulation of the subjects and theories about which an expert may testify. "If scientific, technical, or other specialized knowledge will assist the trier of fact to understand the evidence or to determine a fact in issue" an expert "may testify thereto." The subject of an expert's testimony must be "scientific . . . knowledge."[37] The adjective "scientific" implies a grounding in the methods and procedures of science. Similarly, the word "knowledge" connotes more than subjective belief or unsupported speculation. The term "applies to anybody of known facts or to any body of ideas inferred from such facts or accepted as truths on good grounds." WEBSTER'S THIRD NEW INTERNATIONAL DICTIONARY 1252 (1986). Of course, it would be unreasonable to conclude that the subject of scientific testimony must be "known" to a certainty; arguably, there are no certainties in science. *See, e.g.*, Brief for Nicolaas Bloembergen et al. as *Amici Curiae* 9 ("Indeed, scientists do not assert that they know what is immutably 'true' — they are committed to searching for new, temporary theories to explain, as best they can, phenomena."); Brief for American Association for the Advancement of Science and the National Academy of Sciences as *Amici Curiae* 7–8 ("Science is not an encyclopedic body of knowledge about the universe. Instead, it represents a *process* for proposing and refining theoretical explanations about the world that are subject to further testing and refinement.") (emphasis in original). But, in order to qualify as "scientific knowledge," an inference or assertion must be derived by the scientific method. Proposed testimony must be supported by appropriate validation — *i.e.*, "good grounds," based on what is known. In short, the requirement that an expert's testimony pertain to "scientific knowledge" establishes a standard of evidentiary reliability.[38]

Rule 702 further requires that the evidence or testimony "assist the trier of fact to understand the evidence or to determine a fact in issue." This condition goes primarily to relevance. "Expert testimony which does not relate to any issue in the case is not relevant and, ergo, non-helpful." 3 WEINSTEIN & BERGER ¶ 702[02], p. 702–18. *See also United States v. Downing*, 753 F.2d 1224, 1242 (3d Cir. 1985) ("An additional consideration under Rule 702 — and another aspect of relevancy — is whether expert testimony proffered in the case is sufficiently tied to the facts of the case that it will aid the jury in resolving a factual dispute."). The consideration has been aptly described by Judge Becker as one of "fit." *Ibid.* "Fit" is not always obvious, and scientific validity for one purpose is not necessarily scientific validity for other, unrelated purposes. *See* Starrs, Frye v. United States *Restructured and*

---

[37] [8] Rule 702 also applies to "technical, or other specialized knowledge." Our discussion is limited to the scientific context because that is the nature of the expertise offered here.

[38] [9] We note that scientists typically distinguish between "validity" (does the principle support what it purports to show?) and "reliability" (does application of the principle produce consistent results?). *See* Black, *A Unified Theory of Scientific Evidence*, 56 FORDHAM L. REV. 595, 599 (1988). Although "the difference between accuracy, validity, and reliability may be such that each is distinct from the other by no more than a hen's kick," Starrs, Frye v. United States *Restructured and Revitalized: A Proposal to Amend Federal Evidence Rule 702*, 26 JURIMETRICS J. 249, 256 (1986), our reference here is to evidentiary reliability — that is, trustworthiness. *Cf., e.g.*, Advisory Committee's Notes on Fed. Rule Evid. 602 ("[T]he rule requiring that a witness who testifies to a fact which can be perceived by the senses must have had an opportunity to observe, and must have actually observed the fact" is a "most pervasive manifestation" of the common law insistence upon "the most reliable sources of information." (citation omitted)); Advisory Committee's Notes on Art. VIII of the Rules of Evidence (hearsay exceptions will be recognized only "under circumstances supposed to furnish guarantees of trustworthiness"). In a case involving scientific evidence, evidentiary reliability will be based upon scientific validity.

Revitalized: A Proposal to Amend Federal Evidence Rule 702, 26 JURIMETRICS J. 249, 258 (1986). The study of the phases of the moon, for example, may provide valid scientific "knowledge" about whether a certain night was dark, and if darkness is a fact in issue, the knowledge will assist the trier of fact. However (absent creditable grounds supporting such a link), evidence that the moon was full on a certain night will not assist the trier of fact in determining whether an individual was unusually likely to have behaved irrationally on that night. Rule 702's "helpfulness" standard requires a valid scientific connection to the pertinent inquiry as a precondition to admissibility.

That these requirements are embodied in Rule 702 is not surprising. Unlike an ordinary witness, *see* Rule 701, an expert is permitted wide latitude to offer opinions, including those that are not based on first-hand knowledge or observation. *See* Rules 702 and 703. Presumably, this relaxation of the usual requirement of first-hand knowledge — a rule which represents a "most pervasive manifestation" of the common law insistence upon "the most reliable sources of information," Advisory Committee's Notes on Fed. Rule Evid. 602 (citation omitted) — is premised on an assumption that the expert's opinion will have a reliable basis in the knowledge and experience of his discipline.

C

Faced with a proffer of expert scientific testimony, then, the trial judge must determine at the outset, pursuant to Rule 104(a),[39] whether the expert is proposing to testify to (1) scientific knowledge that (2) will assist the trier of fact to understand or determine a fact in issue.[40] This entails a preliminary assessment of whether the reasoning or methodology underlying the testimony is scientifically valid and of whether that reasoning or methodology properly can be applied to the facts in issue. We are confident that federal judges possess the capacity to undertake this review. Many factors will bear on the inquiry, and we do not presume to set out a definitive checklist or test. But some general observations are appropriate.

Ordinarily, a key question to be answered in determining whether a theory or technique is scientific knowledge that will assist the trier of fact will be whether it can be (and has been) tested. "Scientific methodology today is based on generating hypotheses and testing them to see if they can be falsified; indeed, this methodology is what distinguishes science from other fields of human inquiry." Green, at 645. *See also* C. HEMPEL, PHILOSOPHY OF NATURAL SCIENCE 49 (1966).("[T]he statements

[39] [10] Rule 104(a) provides: "Preliminary questions concerning the qualification of a person to be a witness, the existence of a privilege, or the admissibility of evidence shall be determined by the court, subject to the provisions of subdivision (b) [pertaining to conditional admissions]. In making its determination it is not bound by the rules of evidence except those with respect to privileges." These matters should be established by a preponderance of proof. *See Bourjaily v. United States*, 483 U.S. 171, 175–176 (1987).

[40] [11] Although the *Frye* decision itself focused exclusively on "novel" scientific techniques, we do not read the requirements of Rule 702 to apply specially or exclusively to unconventional evidence. Of course, well-established propositions are less likely to be challenged than those that are novel, and they are more handily defended. Indeed, theories that are so firmly established as to have attained the status of scientific law, such as the laws of thermodynamics, properly are subject to judicial notice under Fed. Rule Evid. 201.

constituting a scientific explanation must be capable of empirical test."); K. POPPER, CONJECTURES AND REFUTATIONS: THE GROWTH OF SCIENTIFIC KNOWLEDGE 37 (5th ed. 1989) ("[T]he criterion of the scientific status of a theory is its falsifiability, or refutability, or testability.").

Another pertinent consideration is whether the theory or technique has been subjected to peer review and publication. Publication (which is but one element of peer review) is not a sine qua non of admissibility; it does not necessarily correlate with reliability, *see* S. JASANOFF, THE FIFTH BRANCH: SCIENCE ADVISORS AS POLICYMAKERS 61–76 (1990), and in some instances well-grounded but innovative theories will not have been published, *see* Horrobin, *The Philosophical Basis of Peer Review and the Suppression of Innovation*, 263 J. AM.MED. ASS'N. 1438 (1990). Some propositions, moreover, are too particular, too new, or of too limited interest to be published. But submission to the scrutiny of the scientific community is a component of "good science," in part because it increases the likelihood that substantive flaws in methodology will be detected. *See* J. ZIMAN, RELIABLE KNOWLEDGE: AN EXPLORATION OF THE GROUNDS FOR BELIEF IN SCIENCE 130–133 (1978); Relman and Angell, *How Good Is Peer Review?*, 321 NEW ENG. J. MED. 827 (1989). The fact of publication (or lack thereof) in a peer-reviewed journal thus will be a relevant, though not dispositive, consideration in assessing the scientific validity of a particular technique or methodology on which an opinion is premised.

[handwritten margin note: Not dispositive either way]

Additionally, in the case of a particular scientific technique, the court ordinarily should consider the known or potential rate of error, *see, e.g., United States v. Smith*, 869 F.2d 348, 353–354 (7th Cir. 1989) (surveying studies of the error rate of spectrographic voice identification technique), and the existence and maintenance of standards controlling the technique's operation. *See United States v. Williams*, 583 F.2d 1194, 1198 (2d Cir. 1978) (noting professional organization's standard governing spectrographic analysis), *cert. denied*, 439 U.S. 1117 (1979).

Finally, "general acceptance" can yet have a bearing on the inquiry. A "reliability assessment does not require, although it does permit, explicit identification of a relevant scientific community and an express determination of a particular degree of acceptance within that community." *United States v. Downing*, 753 F.2d at 1238. *See also* 3 WEINSTEIN & BERGER ¶ 702[03], pp. 702–41 to 702–42. Widespread acceptance can be an important factor in ruling particular evidence admissible, and "a known technique that has been able to attract only minimal support within the community," *Downing, supra*, may properly be viewed with skepticism.

[handwritten margin note: also]

The inquiry envisioned by Rule 702 is, we emphasize, a flexible one.[41] Its overarching subject is the scientific validity — and thus the evidentiary relevance and reliability — of the principles that underlie a proposed submission. The focus,

---

[41] [12] A number of authorities have presented variations on the reliability approach, each with its own slightly different set of factors. *See, e.g., Downing*, 753 F.2d at 1238–1239 (on which our discussion draws in part); 3 WEINSTEIN& BERGER ¶ 702[03], pp. 702–41 to 702–42 (on which the *Downing* court in turn partially relied); McCormick, *Scientific Evidence: Defining a New Approach to Admissibility*, 67 IOWA L. REV. 879, 911–912 (1982); and *Symposium on Science and the Rules of Evidence*, 99 F.R.D. 187, 231 (1983) (statement by Margaret Berger). To the extent that they focus on the reliability of evidence as ensured by the scientific validity of its underlying principles, all these versions may well have merit, although we express no opinion regarding any of their particular details.

of course, must be solely on principles and methodology, not on the conclusions that they generate.

Throughout, a judge assessing a proffer of expert scientific testimony under Rule 702 should also be mindful of other applicable rules. Rule 703 provides that expert opinions based on otherwise inadmissible hearsay are to be admitted only if the facts or data are "of a type reasonably relied upon by experts in the particular field in forming opinions or inferences upon the subject." Rule 706 allows the court at its discretion to procure the assistance of an expert of its own choosing. Finally, Rule 403 permits the exclusion of relevant evidence "if its probative value is substantially outweighed by the danger of unfair prejudice, confusion of the issues, or misleading the jury. . . ." Judge Weinstein has explained:

> "Expert evidence can be both powerful and quite misleading because of the difficulty in evaluating it. Because of this risk, the judge in weighing possible prejudice against probative force under Rule 403 of the present rules exercises more control over experts than over lay witnesses." Weinstein, 138 F.R.D., at 632.

III

We conclude by briefly addressing what appear to be two underlying concerns of the parties and *amici* in this case. Respondent expresses apprehension that abandonment of "general acceptance" as the exclusive requirement for admission will result in a "free-for-all" in which befuddled juries are confounded by absurd and irrational pseudoscientific assertions. In this regard respondent seems to us to be overly pessimistic about the capabilities of the jury, and of the adversary system generally. Vigorous cross-examination, presentation of contrary evidence, and careful instruction on the burden of proof are the traditional and appropriate means of attacking shaky but admissible evidence. *See Rock v. Arkansas*, 483 U.S. 44, 61 (1987). Additionally, in the event the trial court concludes that the scintilla of evidence presented supporting a position is insufficient to allow a reasonable juror to conclude that the position more likely than not is true, the court remains free to direct a judgment, Fed. Rule Civ. Proc. 50(a), and likewise to grant summary judgment, Fed. Rule Civ. Proc. 56. *Cf., e.g., Turpin v. Merrell Dow Pharmaceuticals, Inc.*, 959 F.2d 1349 (6th Cir.) (holding that scientific evidence that provided foundation for expert testimony, viewed in the light most favorable to plaintiffs, was not sufficient to allow a jury to find it more probable than not that defendant caused plaintiff's injury), *cert. denied*, 506 U.S. 826, 113 S. Ct. 84, 121 L. Ed. 2d 47 (1992); *Brock v. Merrell Dow Pharmaceuticals, Inc.*, 874 F.2d 307 (5th Cir. 1989) (reversing judgment entered on jury verdict for plaintiffs because evidence regarding causation was insufficient), ... These conventional devices, rather than wholesale exclusion under an uncompromising "general acceptance" test, are the appropriate safeguards where the basis of scientific testimony meets the standards of Rule 702.

Petitioners and, to a greater extent, their *amici* exhibit a different concern. They suggest that recognition of a screening role for the judge that allows for the exclusion of "invalid" evidence will sanction a stifling and repressive scientific orthodoxy and will be inimical to the search for truth. . . . It is true that open debate is an essential part of both legal and scientific analyses. Yet there are important differences between the quest for truth in the courtroom and the quest for truth in the laboratory. Scientific conclusions are subject to perpetual revision. Law, on the other hand, must resolve disputes finally and quickly. The scientific project is advanced by broad and wide-ranging consideration of a multitude of hypotheses, for those that are incorrect will eventually be shown to be so, and that in itself is an advance. Conjectures that are probably wrong are of little use, however, in the project of reaching a quick, final, and binding legal judgment — often of great consequence — about a particular set of events in the past. We recognize that in practice, a gatekeeping role for the judge, no matter how flexible, inevitably on occasion will prevent the jury from learning of authentic insights and innovations. That, nevertheless, is the balance that is struck by Rules of Evidence designed not for the exhaustive search for cosmic understanding but for the particularized resolution of legal disputes.[42]

IV

To summarize: "general acceptance" is not a necessary precondition to the admissibility of scientific evidence under the Federal Rules of Evidence, but the Rules of Evidence — especially Rule 702 — do assign to the trial judge the task of ensuring that an expert's testimony both rests on a reliable foundation and is relevant to the task at hand. Pertinent evidence based on scientifically valid principles will satisfy those demands.

The inquiries of the District Court and the Court of Appeals focused almost exclusively on "general acceptance," as gauged by publication and the decisions of other courts. Accordingly, the judgment of the Court of Appeals is vacated and the case is remanded for further proceedings consistent with this opinion.

It is so ordered.

QUESTION

Does *Daubert*, in effect, render polygraph test results admissible? *See United States v. Lee*, 315 F.3d 206 (3rd Cir. 2003) (collecting cases); *United States v. Canter*, 338 F. Supp. 2d 460 (S.D.N.Y. 2004).

KUMHO TIRE CO., LTD. v. CARMICHAEL
526 U.S. 137 (1999)

JUSTICE BREYER delivered the opinion of the Court.

In *Daubert v. Merrell Dow Pharmaceuticals, Inc.*, 509 U.S. 579 (1993), this Court focused upon the admissibility of scientific expert testimony. It pointed out that

---

[42] [13] This is not to say that judicial interpretation, as opposed to adjudicative factfinding, does not share basic characteristics of the scientific endeavor: "The work of a judge is in one sense enduring and in another ephemeral. . . . In the endless process of testing and retesting, there is a constant rejection of the dross and a constant retention of whatever is pure and sound and fine." B. CARDOZO, THE NATURE OF THE JUDICIAL PROCESS 178, 179 (1921).

such testimony is admissible only if it is both relevant and reliable. And it held that the Federal Rules of Evidence "assign to the trial judge the task of ensuring that an expert's testimony both rests on a reliable foundation and is relevant to the task at hand." . . . The Court also discussed certain more specific factors, such as testing, peer review, error rates, and "acceptability" in the relevant scientific community, some or all of which might prove helpful in determining the reliability of a particular scientific "theory or technique." . . .

This case requires us to decide how *Daubert* applies to the testimony of engineers and other experts who are not scientists. . . .

I

On July 6, 1993, the right rear tire of a minivan driven by Patrick Carmichael blew out. In the accident that followed, one of the passengers died, and others were severely injured. In October 1993, the Carmichaels brought this diversity suit against the tire's maker and its distributor, whom we refer to collectively as Kumho Tire, claiming that the tire was defective. The plaintiffs rested their case in significant part upon deposition testimony provided by an expert in tire failure analysis, Dennis Carlson, Jr., who intended to testify in support of their conclusion.

Carlson's depositions relied upon certain features of tire technology that are not in dispute. A steel-belted radial tire like the Carmichaels' is made up of a "carcass" containing many layers of flexible cords, called "plies," along which (between the cords and the outer tread) are laid steel strips called "belts." Steelwire loops, called "beads," hold the cords together at the plies' bottom edges. An outer layer, called the "tread," encases the carcass, and the entire tire is bound together in rubber, through the application of heat and various chemicals. *See generally, e.g.,* J. DIXON, TIRES, SUSPENSION AND HANDLING 68–72 (2d ed. 1996). The bead of the tire sits upon a "bead seat," which is part of the wheel assembly. That assembly contains a "rim flange," which extends over the bead and rests against the side of the tire. *See* M. MAVRIGIAN, PERFORMANCE WHEELS & TIRES 81, 83 (1998) (illustrations).

Carlson's testimony also accepted certain background facts about the tire in question. He assumed that before the blowout the tire had traveled far. (The tire was made in 1988 and had been installed some time before the Carmichaels bought the used minivan in March 1993; the Carmichaels had driven the van approximately 7,000 additional miles in the two months they had owned it.) Carlson noted that the tire's tread depth, which was 11/32 of an inch when new, App. 242, had been worn down to depths that ranged from 3/32 of an inch along some parts of the tire, to nothing at all along others. . . . He conceded that the tire tread had at least two punctures which had been inadequately repaired. . . .

Despite the tire's age and history, Carlson concluded that a defect in its manufacture or design caused the blow-out. He rested this conclusion in part upon three premises which, for present purposes, we must assume are not in dispute. . . .

Carlson's conclusion that a defect caused the separation, however, rested upon certain other propositions, several of which the defendants strongly dispute. First, Carlson said that if a separation is *not* caused by a certain kind of tire misuse called "over deflection" (which consists of underinflating the tire or causing it to carry too much weight, thereby generating heat that can undo the chemical tread/carcass bond), then, ordinarily, its cause is a tire defect. Second, he said that if a tire has been subject to sufficient over deflection to cause a separation, it should reveal certain physical symptoms. These symptoms include (a) tread wear on the tire's shoulder that is greater than the tread wear along the tire's center; (b) signs of a "bead groove," where the beads have been pushed too hard against the bead seat on the inside of the tire's rim; (c) sidewalls of the tire with physical signs of deterioration, such as discoloration; and/or (d) marks on the tire's rim flange. Third, Carlson said that where he does not find *at least two* of the four physical signs just mentioned (and presumably where there is no reason to suspect a less common cause of separation), he concludes that a manufacturing or design defect caused the separation.

Carlson added that he had inspected the tire in question. He conceded that the tire to a limited degree showed greater wear on the shoulder than in the center, some signs of "bead groove," some discoloration, a few marks on the rimflange, and inadequately filled puncture holes (which can also cause heat that might lead to separation). But, in each instance, he testified that the symptoms were not significant, and he explained why he believed that they did not reveal over deflection. . . . Carlson concluded that the tire did not bear at least two of the four overdeflection symptoms, nor was there any less obvious cause of separation; and since neither overdeflection nor the punctures caused the blowout, a defect must have done so.

Kumho Tire moved the District Court to exclude Carlson's testimony on the ground that his methodology failed Rule 702's reliability requirement. The court agreed with Kumho that it should act as a *Daubert*-type reliability "gatekeeper," even though one might consider Carlson's testimony as "technical," rather than "scientific." The court then examined Carlson's methodology in light of the reliability-related factors that *Daubert* mentioned, such as a theory's testability, whether it "has been a subject of peer review or publication," the "known or potential rate of error," and the "degree of acceptance . . . within the relevant scientific community." . . . The District Court found that all those factors argued against the reliability of Carlson's methods, and it granted the motion to exclude the testimony (as well as the defendants' accompanying motion for summary judgment).

* * *

The Eleventh Circuit reversed. . . . It "review[ed] . . . *de novo*" the "district court's legal decision to apply *Daubert*." . . . It noted that "the Supreme Court in *Daubert* explicitly limited its holding to cover only the 'scientific context,'" "adding that "a *Daubert* analysis" applies only where an expert relies "on the application of scientific principles," rather than "on skill- or experience-based observation." . . . It concluded that Carlson's testimony, which it viewed as relying on experience, "falls outside the scope of *Daubert*," that "the district court erred as a matter of law by applying *Daubert* in this case," and that the case must be remanded for further (non-*Daubert*-type) consideration under Rule 702. . . .

Kumho Tire petitioned for *certiorari*, asking us to determine whether a trial court "may" consider *Daubert*'s specific "factors" when determining the "admissibility of an engineering expert's testimony." . . . We granted *certiorari* in light of uncertainty among the lower courts about whether, or how, *Daubert* applies to expert testimony that might be characterized as based not upon "scientific" knowledge, but rather upon "technical" or "other specialized" knowledge.

II

A

In *Daubert*, this Court held that Federal Rule of Evidence 702 imposes a special obligation upon a trial judge to "ensure that any and all scientific testimony . . . is not only relevant, but reliable." . . . The initial question before us is whether this basic gatekeeping obligation applies only to "scientific" testimony or to all expert testimony. . . .

For one thing, Rule 702 itself says:

> If scientific, technical, or other specialized knowledge will assist the trier of fact to understand the evidence or to determine a fact in issue, a witness qualified as an expert by knowledge, skill, experience, training, or education, may testify thereto in the form of an opinion or otherwise.

This language makes no relevant distinction between "scientific" knowledge and "technical" or "other specialized" knowledge. It makes clear that any such knowledge might become the subject of expert testimony. In *Daubert*, the Court specified that it is the Rule's word "knowledge," not the words (like "scientific") that modify that word, that "establishes a standard of evidentiary reliability." . . . Hence, as a matter of language, the Rule applies its reliability standard to all "scientific," "technical," or "other specialized" matters within its scope. . . .

Neither is the evidentiary rationale that underlay the Court's basic *Daubert* "gatekeeping" determination limited to "scientific" knowledge. *Daubert* pointed out that Federal Rules 702 and 703 grant expert witnesses testimonial latitude unavailable to other witnesses on the "assumption that the expert's opinion will have a reliable basis in the knowledge and experience of his discipline." . . . The Rules grant that latitude to all experts, not just to "scientific" ones.

Finally, it would prove difficult, if not impossible, for judges to administer evidentiary rules under which a gatekeeping obligation depended upon a distinction between "scientific" knowledge and "technical" or "other specialized" knowledge. There is no clear line that divides the one from the others. Disciplines such as engineering rest upon scientific knowledge. Pure scientific theory itself may depend for its development upon observation and properly engineered machinery. And conceptual efforts to distinguish the two are unlikely to produce clear legal lines capable of application in particular cases. . . .

Neither is there a convincing need to make such distinctions. Experts of all kinds tie observations to conclusions through the use of what Judge Learned Hand called "general truths derived from . . . specialized experience." Hand, *Historical and Practical Considerations Regarding Expert Testimony*, 15 Harv. L. Rev. 40, 54 (1901). And whether the specific expert testimony focuses upon specialized observations, the specialized translation of those observations into theory, a specialized theory itself, or the application of such a theory in a particular case, the expert's testimony often will rest "upon an experience confessedly foreign in kind to [the jury's] own." . . . The trial judge's effort to assure that the specialized testimony is reliable and relevant can help the jury evaluate that foreign experience, whether the testimony reflects scientific, technical, or other specialized knowledge.

We conclude that *Daubert's* general principles apply to the expert matters described in Rule 702. The Rule, in respect to all such matters, "establishes a standard of evidentiary reliability." . . . It "requires a valid . . . connection to the pertinent inquiry as a precondition to admissibility." . . . And where such testimony's factual basis, data, principles, methods, or their application are called sufficiently into question, *see* Part III, *infra*, the trial judge must determine whether the testimony has "a reliable basis in the knowledge and experience of [the relevant] discipline." . . .

B

The petitioners ask more specifically whether a trial judge determining the "admissibility of an engineering expert's testimony" *may* consider several more specific factors that *Daubert* said might "bear on" a judge's gate-keeping determination. These factors include:

— Whether a "theory or technique . . . can be (and has been) tested"; — Whether it "has been subjected to peer review and publication";

— Whether, in respect to a particular technique, there is a high "known or potential rate of error" and whether there are "standards controlling the technique's operation"; and

— Whether the theory or technique enjoys "general acceptance" within a "relevant scientific community."

Optional additional factors

Emphasizing the word "may" in the question, we answer that question yes.

Engineering testimony rests upon scientific foundations, the reliability of which will be at issue in some cases. . . . In other cases, the relevant reliability concerns may focus upon personal knowledge or experience. As the Solicitor General points out, there are many different kinds of experts, and many different kinds of expertise. *See* Brief for United States as *Amicus Curiae* 18–19, and n.5 (citing cases involving experts in drug terms, handwriting analysis, criminal *modus operandi*, land valuation, agricultural practices, railroad procedures, attorney's fee valuation, and others). Our emphasis on the word "may" thus reflects *Daubert's* description of the Rule 702 inquiry as "a flexible one." *Daubert* makes clear that the factors it mentions do *not* constitute a "definitive checklist or test." And *Daubert* adds that the gatekeeping inquiry must be " 'tied to the facts' " of a particular "case." We agree with the Solicitor General that "[t]he factors identified in *Daubert* may or may not be pertinent in assessing reliability, depending on the nature of the issue, the expert's particular expertise, and the subject of his testimony." The conclusion, in our view, is that we can neither rule out, nor rule in, for all cases and for all time the applicability of the factors mentioned in *Daubert*, nor can we now do so for subsets of cases categorized by category of expert or by kind of evidence. Too much depends upon the particular circumstances of the particular case at issue.

Daubert itself is not to the contrary. It made clear that its list of factors was meant to be helpful, not definitive. Indeed, those factors do not all necessarily apply even in every instance in which the reliability of scientific testimony is challenged. It might not be surprising in a particular case, for example, that a claim made by a scientific witness has never been the subject of peer review, for the particular application at issue may never previously have interested any scientist. Nor, on the other hand, does the presence of *Daubert*'s general acceptance factor help show that an expert's testimony is reliable where the discipline itself lacks reliability, as, for example, do theories grounded in any so-called generally accepted principles of astrology or necromancy.

At the same time, . . . some of *Daubert*'s questions can help to evaluate the reliability even of experience-based testimony. In certain cases, it will be appropriate for the trial judge to ask, for example, how often an engineering expert's experience-based methodology has produced erroneous results, or whether such a method is generally accepted in the relevant engineering community. Likewise, it will at times be useful to ask even of a witness whose expertise is based purely on experience, say, a perfume tester able to distinguish among 140 odors at a sniff, whether his preparation is of a kind that others in the field would recognize as acceptable.

We must therefore disagree with the Eleventh Circuit's holding that a trial judge may ask questions of the sort *Daubert* mentioned only where an expert "relies on the application of scientific principles," but not where an expert relies "on skill- or experience-based observation." . . . We do not believe that Rule 702 creates a schematism that segregates expertise by type while mapping certain kinds of questions to certain kinds of experts. Life and the legal cases that it generates are too complex to warrant so definitive a match.

To say this is not to deny the importance of *Daubert*'s gatekeeping requirement. The objective of that requirement is to ensure the reliability and relevancy of expert testimony. It is to make certain that an expert, whether basing testimony upon professional studies or personal experience, employs in the courtroom the same level of intellectual rigor that characterizes the practice of an expert in the relevant field. Nor do we deny that, as stated in *Daubert*, the particular questions that it mentioned will often be appropriate for use in determining the reliability of challenged expert testimony. Rather, we conclude that the trial judge must have considerable leeway in deciding in a particular case how to go about determining whether particular expert testimony is reliable. That is to say, a trial court should consider the specific factors identified in *Daubert* where they are reasonable measures of the reliability of expert testimony.

*   *   *

III

We further explain the way in which a trial judge "may" consider *Daubert*'s factors by applying these considerations to the case at hand, a matter that has been briefed exhaustively by the parties and their 19 *amici*. The District Court did not doubt Carlson's qualifications, which included a masters degree in mechanical engineering, 10 years' work at Michelin America, Inc., and testimony as a tire failure consultant in other tort cases. Rather, it excluded the testimony because, despite those qualifications, it initially doubted, and then found unreliable, "the methodology employed by the expert in analyzing the data obtained in the visual inspection, and the scientific basis, if any, for such an analysis." After examining the transcript in "some detail," and after considering respondents' defense of Carlson's methodology, the District Court determined that Carlson's testimony was not reliable. It fell outside the range where experts might reasonably differ, and where the jury must decide among the conflicting views of different experts, even though the evidence is "shaky." In our view, the doubts that triggered the District Court's initial inquiry here were reasonable, as was the court's ultimate conclusion.

*　*　*

The particular issue in this case concerned the use of Carlson's two-factor test and his related use of visual/tactile inspection to draw conclusions on the basis of what seemed small observational differences. We have found no indication in the record that other experts in the industry use Carlson's two-factor test or that tire experts such as Carlson normally make the very fine distinctions about, say, the symmetry of comparatively greater shoulder tread wear that were necessary, on Carlson's own theory, to support his conclusions. Nor, despite the prevalence of tire testing, does anyone refer to any articles or papers that validate Carlson's approach. *Compare* BOBO, TIRE FLAWS AND SEPARATIONS, IN MECHANICS OF PNEUMATIC TIRES 636–637 (S. Clark ed. 1981); C. Schnuth et al., *Compression Grooving and Rim Flange Abrasion as Indicators of Over-Deflected Operating Conditions in Tires*, presented to Rubber Division of the American Chemical Society, Oct. 21–24, 1997; J. Walter & R. Kiminecz, *Bead Contact Pressure Measurements at the Tire-Rim Interface*, presented to Society of Automotive Engineers, Feb. 24–28, 1975. Indeed, no one has argued that Carlson himself, were he still working for Michelin, would have concluded in a report to his employer that a similar tire was similarly defective on grounds identical to those upon which he rested his conclusion here. Of course, Carlson himself claimed that his method was accurate, but, as we pointed out in *Joiner*, "nothing in either *Daubert* or the Federal Rules of Evidence requires a district court to admit opinion evidence that is connected to existing data only by the *ipse dixit* of the expert."

*　*　*

In sum, Rule 702 grants the district judge the discretionary authority, reviewable for its abuse, to determine reliability in light of the particular facts and circumstances of the particular case. The District Court did not abuse its discretionary authority in this case. Hence, the judgment of the Court of Appeals is

Reversed.

JUSTICE SCALIA, with whom JUSTICE O'CONNOR and JUSTICE THOMAS join, concurring.

I join the opinion of the Court, which makes clear that the discretion it endorses — trial-court discretion in choosing the manner of testing expert reliability — is not discretion to abandon the gatekeeping function. I think it worth adding that it is not discretion to perform the function inadequately. Rather, it is discretion to choose among *reasonable* means of excluding expertise that is *fausse* and science that is junky. Though, as the Court makes clear today, the *Daubert* factors are not holy writ, in a particular case the failure to apply one or another of them may be unreasonable, and hence an abuse of discretion.

JUSTICE STEVENS, concurring in part and dissenting in part [omitted].

UNITED STATES v. LOCASCIO
6 F.3d 924 (2d Cir. 1993)

ALTIMARI, CIRCUIT JUDGE:

Defendants-appellants John Gotti and Frank Locascio appeal from judgments of conviction entered on June 23, 1992 in the United States District Court for the Eastern District of New York. . . .

Gotti and Locascio were convicted after a jury trial of . . . violations of the Racketeer Influenced Corrupt Organizations Act, 18 U.S.C. § 1962(c) and (d) (1988), and various predicate acts charged as separate counts. They were each principally sentenced to life imprisonment. The charges stemmed from their involvement with the Gambino Crime Family of La Cosa Nostra, an extensive criminal organization.

On appeal, Gotti and Locascio raise numerous challenges to their convictions and the subsequent denial of their motion for a new trial. For the reasons stated below, we affirm the judgments of the district court.

*   *   *

II. Admission of Expert Testimony

Gotti and Locascio both contend that the district court committed reversible error in admitting the testimony of government experts to assist the jury in understanding the structure of organized crime families. More specifically, they principally challenge various facets of FBI Agent Lewis Schiliro's testimony, arguing that: (1) Schiliro's testimony was too broad and went beyond the scope of expert testimony; (2) he was not properly qualified as an expert; (3) his use of hearsay and un-introduced evidence to substantiate his opinions violated Fed. R. Evid. 703, as well as the Confrontation Clause; and (4) the availability of similar testimony by an accomplice witness rendered his testimony unnecessary.

A. Background

At trial, Special Agent Schiliro testified at great length on the nature and function of organized crime families, imparting the structure of such families and disclosing the "rules" of the La Cosa Nostra. For example, Schiliro testified that a "boss" must approve all illegal activity and especially all murders, and that the functions of the "consigliere" and "underboss" are only "advisory" to the "boss." In addition, as part of his testimony, he interpreted the numerous surreptitiously taped conversations introduced into evidence, and identified the individuals speaking by their voices. Schiliro specifically named John Gotti as the boss of the alleged Gambino Family and Gravano as the consigliere. Additionally, he identified, together with their titles, ranks, and functions, numerous members and associates of the Gambino Family and other criminal organizations. When pressed about his sources for individuals' titles, ranks, and functions, Schiliro admitted that his sources of information were not necessarily before the court.

B. Discussion

Under the Federal Rules of Evidence, an expert is permitted to testify in the form of an opinion or otherwise when that testimony would "assist the trier of fact to understand the evidence or to determine a fact in issue." Fed. R. Evid. 702. In determining whether such evidence will assist the jury, the district court must make a "common sense inquiry" into "whether the untrained layman would be qualified to determine intelligently and to the best possible degree the particular issue without enlightenment from those having a specialized understanding of the subject involved in the dispute." Fed. R. Evid. 702, advisory committee note, (quoting Ladd, *Expert Testimony*, 5 VAND. L. REV. 414, 418 (1952)), ... In applying this standard, the district court has broad discretion regarding the admission of expert testimony, and this Court will sustain the admission unless "manifestly erroneous." *United States v. DiDomenico*, 985 F.2d 1159, 1163 (2dCir. 1993); *United States v. Rivera*, 971 F.2d 876, 887 (2d Cir. 1992).

Gotti and Locascio contend that the district court erred in admitting Schiliro's testimony for several reasons. The thrust of their argument is that Schiliro did not actually testify as an expert, but rather was simply a conduit allowing inadmissible evidence and arguments to flow into the court. They assert that Schiliro's testimony was too broad, sweeping, and unsubstantiated to be admissible. We will consider their specific points in turn.

1. Challenge to Scope of Expert Testimony

The defendants-appellants challenge the admission of expert testimony on the inner workings of the Gambino Family as being outside the scope of expert testimony. We have, however, previously upheld the use of expert testimony to help explain the operation, structure, membership, and terminology of organized crime families. *See United States v. Daly*, 842 F.2d 1380, 1388 (2d Cir.), *cert. denied*, 488 U.S. 821 (1988); *see also United States v. Skowronski*, 968 F.2d 242, 246 (2d Cir. 1992) (upholding expert testimony of government agents explaining organized crime jargon); . . . .

In *Daly*, this Court confronted a similar claim that a district court committed reversible error in admitting expert testimony on the structure of organized crime families. There, the government agent who testified "identified the five organized crime families that operate in the New York area; he described their requirements for membership, their rules of conduct and code of silence, and the meaning of certain jargon, . . . and he described how, in general, organized crime has infiltrated labor unions." . . . Additionally, the expert identified voices on surveillance tapes. In sustaining the admission of such testimony, we explained that such expert testimony "was relevant to provide the jury with an understanding of the nature and structure of organized crime families." *Id.* We further added that there was "no question that there was much that was outside the expectable realm of knowledge of the average juror." *Id.*

We continue to believe that despite the unfortunate fact that our society has become increasingly familiar with organized crime and its activities from such sources as newspapers, movies, television, and books, it is still a reasonable assumption that jurors are not well versed in the structure and methods of organized crime families. Moreover, much of the information gleaned from such sources may be inaccurate. Consequently, the subject matter of Agent Schiliro's testimony, namely the structure and operations of organized crime families, was properly admitted.

2. Schiliro's Qualifications as an Expert

The defendants-appellants argue that Schiliro was not properly qualified as an expert, since his testimony required knowledge of linguistics, the sociology of crime, tape recording technology, and voice analysis. Gotti and Locascio contend that because he was not an expert in any of those areas, he was not qualified to interpret tapes or give his opinion on the Gambino Family structure.

This argument ignores the fact that Schiliro had been an FBI agent for seventeen years, and for five years had been on the FBI's Organized Crime Program, a squad that investigated only organized crime cases. For more than two years, he was the supervisor of the Organized Crime Program. Rule 702 only requires that an expert witness have "scientific, technical, or other specialized knowledge" gained through "knowledge, skill, experience, training, or education." Fed. R. Evid. 702. Because Schiliro's background qualifies as "specialized knowledge," the district court did not err in qualifying him as an expert. *See United States v. Simmons*, 923 F.2d 934, 946 (2d Cir.) (holding that a veteran DEA agent was "well-suited" to offer expert testimony about coded narcotics terminology), *cert. denied*, [500] U.S. [919], 111 S. Ct. 2018, 114 L. Ed. 2d 104 (1991); *United States v. Roldan-Zapata*, 916 F.2d 795, 804–05 (2d Cir. 1990) (holding that a narcotics investigator was properly qualified to testify about "the narcotics-related nature" of items found in a defendant's apartment and about "drug trafficking techniques generally"), *cert. denied*, 499 U.S. 940 (1991). Schiliro did not need to be a voice analysis expert to be able to recognize the defendants-appellants' voices on the tapes, nor did he need a linguistics degree to understand what was being said. Schiliro testified as an expert on organized crime, and he was sufficiently qualified on that basis. Although he had never before been qualified as an expert witness, even the most qualified expert must have his first day in court.

3. Sources of Information

Defendants-appellants next argue that because Schiliro relied upon "countless nameless informers and countless tapes not in evidence," his testimony violated Fed. R. Evid. 703 and the Confrontation Clause of the Sixth Amendment. The government responds that, although Schiliro relied upon information that was not before the court, this reliance is permitted under the rules of evidence.

According to Rule 703, the facts that form the basis for an expert's opinions or inferences need not be admissible in evidence "[i]f of a type reasonably relied upon by experts in the particular field." Fed. R. Evid. 703 (emphasis added).Thus, expert witnesses can testify to opinions based on hearsay or other inadmissible evidence if experts in the field reasonably rely on such evidence in forming their opinions. *See Daly*, 842 F.2d at 1387 (holding that organized crime expert can rely on otherwise inadmissible hearsay in forming his opinion); *cf. Reardon v. Manson*, 806 F.2d 39, 42 (2d Cir. 1986) (holding that reliance by experts on information provided by others does not violate Sixth Amendment rights if expert is available for cross examination), *cert. denied*, 481 U.S. 1020 (1987). Therefore, Schiliro was entitled to rely upon hearsay as to such matters as the structure and operating rules of organized crime families and the identification of specific voices heard on tape in forming his opinion, since there is little question that law enforcement agents routinely and reasonably rely upon such hearsay in the course of their duties. An expert who meets the test of Rule 702, as Schiliro does, is assumed "to have the skill to properly evaluate the hearsay, giving it probative force appropriate to the circumstances." *In re "Agent Orange" Product Liability Litigation*, 611 F. Supp. 1223, 1245 (E.D.N.Y. 1985), *aff'd*, 818 F.2d 187 (2d Cir. 1987), *cert. denied*, 487 U.S. 1234 (1988). The fact that Schiliro relied upon inadmissible evidence is therefore less an issue of admissibility for the court than an issue of credibility for the jury. *See United States v. Young*, 745 F.2d 733, 761 (2d Cir. 1984) (pointing out that the defendants were free to expose the weaknesses in the prosecution's widespread use of expert testimony through cross examination), ...

Gotti and Locascio do not seriously contest the point that hearsay and other inadmissible evidence are often reasonably relied upon by law enforcement agents in the field, and that this reliance is anticipated by Rule 703. Rather, they argue that a district court admitting expert testimony based on inadmissible evidence must make an explicit finding that the underlying sources of information used by the expert are trustworthy. *See Barrel of Fun, Inc. v. State Farm Fire & Casualty Co.*, 739 F.2d 1028, 1033 (5th Cir. 1984) (holding that an expert's testimony was inadmissible because the factual premises underlying the opinion were "inherently suspect"). We agree that a district court is not bound to accept expert testimony based on questionable data simply because other experts use such data in the field. The Supreme Court's recent decision of *Daubert v. Merrell Dow Pharmaceuticals, Inc.*, 509 U.S. 579, 113 S. Ct. 2786, 125 L. Ed. 2d 469 (1993), makes this clear. In *Daubert* the Court abandoned the traditional rule of *Frye v. United States*, 293 F. 1013, 1014 (D.C. Cir. 1923), which required "general acceptance" in the particular field before novel scientific evidence or techniques could be admitted in court. The Court in *Daubert* asserted that such a rigid standard for admitting expert scientific testimony was inconsistent with the liberal thrust of the federal rules, . . . holding that district courts have the authority and discretion to determine whether novel scientific evidence is trustworthy. . . . Although *Daubert* involved Rule 702 and scientific evidence, the flexibility of the federal rules also applies to Rule 703 and the determination of the trustworthiness of the sources of expert testimony. The district court has broad discretion to decide the admissibility of expert testimony based on inadmissible evidence.

We decline, however, to shackle the district court with a mandatory and explicit trustworthiness analysis. The district judge, who has the ideal vantage point to evaluate an expert's testimony during trial, already has the authority under Fed. R. Evid. 703 to conduct an explicit trustworthiness analysis should she deem one necessary. *See Shatkin v. McDonnell Douglas Corp.*, 727 F.2d 202, 208 (2d Cir. 1984) (noting that the district court has the "discretionary right under Rule 703 to determine whether the expert acted reasonably in making assumptions of fact upon which he would base his testimony"). In fact, we assume that the district court consistently and continually performed a trustworthiness analysis sub silentio of all evidence introduced at trial. We will not, however, circumscribe this discretion by burdening the court with the necessity of making an explicit determination for all expert testimony. This is especially true in this case, because the sources relied upon by Schiliro are no different from those previously allowed by this Court. . . .

4. Availability of Alternative Methods of Proof

Finally, the defendants-appellants argue that because an accomplice witness was available to provide similar testimony concerning the operations of organized crime families, the government was not permitted to introduce expert testimony on the subject. Rule 702, however, requires only that an expert have "some specialized knowledge that will assist the trier of fact." There is no requirement that prohibits a government agent from testifying as an expert merely because an accomplice witness is also available.

NOTES AND QUESTIONS

1.   When *Locascio* was decided, Federal Rule of Evidence 702 provided: "If scientific, technical, or other specialized knowledge will assist the trier of fact to understand the evidence or to determine a fact in issue, a witness qualified as an expert by knowledge, skill, experience, training, or education, may testify thereto in the form of an opinion or otherwise." In 2000, Congress amended Rule 702, *supra*, p. 203, to impose additional requirements in compliance with the Supreme Court's decision in *Kumho Tire*, *supra*. Would the outcome in *Locascio* remain the same under Rule 702 as amended?

2.   When the expert testimony is admitted despite its failure to meet the helpfulness standard of Rule 702, can the error ever be grounds for reversal on appeal? At worst, is such evidence merely cumulative? *See United States v. Arenal*, 768 F.2d 263 (8th Cir. 1985).

Mason Ladd, *Expert Testimony*
5 Vand. L. Rev. 414, 421–22 (1952)[43]

QUALIFICATION AND FOUNDATION TESTIMONY

There are two general classes of experts and some attempt has been made to divide them into skilled witnesses and expert witnesses. In the first class are grouped those who have personal knowledge about the subject in inquiry and provide both factual information and opinions or conclusions upon it. In the second class are the super-experts or specialists who may have no knowledge at all about the facts of the case but are highly trained or educated in their field so that their opinions upon the subject in inquiry should have special value. This class will be referred to as super-experts and their testimony is confined to answering hypothetical questions. Both classes are regarded as expert witnesses or they would not be permitted to express opinions. An expert who is personally familiar with the facts, as the physician or surgeon who attends a patient, may express his opinions based upon personal observation and also answer hypothetical questions involving his specialized knowledge upon the subject. The qualifications of experts and right to use them are interrelated. The expert must be shown to be informed upon the matters in issue upon which the ordinary person is not informed. Wide discretion is given to the trial judge in determining the qualifications and his decision is final except in the case of a clear and flagrant abuse. The qualification of the expert is not perfunctory, although its significance and its ultimate effect upon evaluation of the testimony is sometimes overlooked. . . . If the expert is permitted to testify because of his experience through which he has gained special knowledge, that experience is as important to the weight of his testimony as it is to its admissibility. It is equally important to show the detailed educational background of an expert whose qualification is his special training. A wide range of witnesses with varying degrees of expertness are permitted to express their opinions and the respect for their testimony rests in the qualification process and the foundation testimony.

QUESTION

Suppose counsel is unable to qualify a witness as an expert. To what extent, if any, may counsel elicit lay opinion testimony from this witness? Rule 701, as originally enacted, did not address this issue. As the following case illustrates, some courts imposed their own limitations instead.

---

[43] Reprinted with permission.

Skilled
Witness w/ personal Knowledge

UNITED STATES v. FIGUEROA-LOPEZ
125 F.3d 1241 (9th Cir. 1997)

OPINION: Trott, Circuit Judge:

OVERVIEW

Raul Figueroa-Lopez ("Lopez") appeals his jury conviction and sentence for possession of cocaine with intent to distribute, in violation of 21 U.S.C. 841(a)(1). Lopez contends that the district court erred by: 1) admitting damaging opinion testimony from law-enforcement officers, who the Government did not qualify as experts. . . .

*   *   *

BACKGROUND

I. The Underlying Offense

At the end of May 1994, federal agents arrested Darryl Storm. Storm and others were charged with conspiracy to distribute cocaine and marijuana, and with money laundering.

Storm agreed to cooperate with the government and provided agents with a list of names of narcotics traffickers known to him. This list included Lopez, although at that time Storm only knew him as "Raul." At the instruction of DEA Agent Sam Larsen, Storm contacted Lopez to explore whether Lopez would sell him some narcotics. Storm met with Lopez on February 1, 1995. Agents attempted to record this meeting, but the audiotape malfunctioned. According to Storm, Storm told Lopez that he wanted to buy 5–10 kilograms of cocaine.

On March 24, 1995, Storm taped a telephone conversation with Lopez, during which Lopez offered to sell Storm ten kilograms of cocaine for $170,000. Lopez and Storm used oblique terminology borrowed from the construction industry to refer to the type, quantity, and price of the drugs.

On March 27, 1995, Storm again met with Lopez. This meeting was not recorded because the recording device malfunctioned again. Lopez gave Storm a sample of cocaine.

During the next month, Storm and Lopez spoke by telephone several times about the impending cocaine deal. These conversations were recorded. On May 25, 1995, Storm called Lopez and arranged to meet later that day to complete the cocaine transaction. Before meeting with Storm, Lopez drove in circles around the parking lot in a Monte Carlo. Storm and Lopez then met in the parking lot. Lopez drove away from Storm and parked next to a silver Nissan Sentra. Lopez entered the Nissan, bent down for several minutes, and then returned to the Monte Carlo.

Lopez returned to Storm's location and showed Storm a kilogram package of cocaine. Storm gave the arrest signal, and agents arrested Lopez. In the Monte

Carlo, the agents found the keys to the Nissan and one kilogram of cocaine on the floor below the front seat. In the Nissan, the agents found nine kilograms of cocaine concealed in the car's door panels.

II. The Trial

A. *Opinion Testimony*

Throughout the trial, the Government presented opinion testimony by law-enforcement witnesses as to how Lopez's conduct, as observed by the agents, conformed to the methods and techniques of experienced drug dealers. Lopez objected to this testimony, claiming that it was "improper opinion testimony," hearsay, lacking foundation, and speculative. He also argued that it was improper expert testimony because the Government had not given prior notice as required by Federal Rule of Criminal Procedure 16(a)(1)(E). The district court overruled all of Lopez's objections and admitted the testimony as *lay* opinion testimony, presumably pursuant to Federal Rule of Evidence 701. The court ruled that the testimony regarding the way Lopez was driving — from which the agent inferred that Lopez was behaving as an "experienced narcotics trafficker" — was admissible notwithstanding Lopez's objections because the officer was a "percipient witness."

The court also overruled without explanation Lopez's objections to Agent Larsen's testimony that: 1) Lopez's actions were "counter surveillance" and "a common practice for narcotics dealers"; and 2) the use of a rental car was "indicative of an experienced narcotics trafficker." In response to Lopez's objection to an agent's opinion as to the street value of the cocaine found in the Nissan, the district court stated that "the Court has repeated over and over that the witness is giving testimony relating to matters in which he has participated and which he personally observed, and his testimony may incorporate his knowledge and his observations, so on that basis, it will be admitted." Agents repeatedly referred to Lopez's actions as consistent with an "experienced narcotics trafficker." The prosecution relied on this testimony in its closing arguments.

*   *   *

DISCUSSION

I. The Law-Enforcement Opinion Testimony

A. *The Error*

Lopez contends that the district court abused its discretion by admitting without a proper foundation opinion testimony of law-enforcement officers that Lopez's actions were consistent with those of an experienced drug trafficker. Specifically, Lopez contends that the testimony improperly "profiled" him as a drug trafficker and was not the proper subject of lay opinion testimony.

As detailed above, at numerous points throughout Lopez's trial, law-enforcement officers testified:

- that Lopez was engaging in counter surveillance driving;

- that certain terms used by Lopez and informant Storm were code words for a drug deal, a common practice of narcotics dealers;

- that Lopez's use of a rental car was consistent with the practices of an experienced drug trafficker;

- that the manner of hiding the cocaine was consistent with the practices of experienced drug traffickers; and

- that the large quantity and high purity of the cocaine indicated that Lopez was close to the source of the cocaine.

Lopez vigorously objected throughout this testimony.

* * *

If "specialized knowledge will assist the trier of fact to understand the evidence or to determine a fact in issue," a qualified expert witness may provide opinion testimony on the issue in question. Fed. R. Evid. 702. The rule recognizes that an intelligent evaluation of the facts by a trier of fact is "often difficult or impossible without the application of some . . . specialized knowledge." Fed. R. Evid. 702 (advisory comm. n.). In this light, we have held that "drug enforcement *experts* may testify that a defendant's activities were consistent with a common criminal modus operandi." *United States v. Webb*, 115 F.3d 711, 713–14 (9th Cir. 1997) (emphasis added) (citing cases). This testimony "helps the jury to understand complex criminal activities, and alerts it to the possibility that combinations of seemingly innocuous events may indicate criminal behavior." *United States v. Johnson*, 735 F.2d 1200, 1202 (9th Cir. 1994), "Further, we even allow modus operandi expert testimony in cases that are not complex." *Webb*, 115 F.3d at 714 (internal quotation and citation omitted).

The testimony in the instant case is similar to *expert* testimony properly admitted in other drug cases. *See, e.g., United States v. Cordoba*, 104 F.3d 225, 229–30, *amended*, 1997 WL 54578 (9th Cir. 1997) (allowing expert testimony that a sophisticated drug dealer would not entrust large quantities of cocaine to an unknowing dupe); *United States v. Espinosa*, 827 F.2d 604, 611–12 (9th Cir. 1987), (allowing expert testimony regarding the use of apartments as "stash pads" for drugs and money); *United States v. Patterson*, 819 F.2d 1495, 1507 (9th Cir. 1987), (allowing expert testimony on how criminal narcotics conspiracies operate); *United States v. Maher*, 645 F.2d 780, 783 (9th Cir. 1981) (per curiam) (permitting expert testimony that defendant's actions were consistent with the modus operandi of persons transporting drugs and engaging in counter surveillance).

In the above cases, the testimony was necessary to inform the jury of the techniques employed by drug dealers in their illegal trade, techniques with which an ordinary juror would most probably be unfamiliar. Thus, the testimony in the instant case could have been admitted as *expert opinion* testimony to inform the jury about the methods and techniques used by experienced drug dealers, *if* the law-enforcement agents had been called as experts and properly qualified as such pursuant to Rule 104 of the Federal Rules of Evidence. In fact, Special Agent

Larsen began his testimony with a recitation of his extensive training and experience with the DEA. It appears virtually certain that had the Government opted to do so, Larsen could have been formally qualified as an expert witness on the dispositive issue of whether Lopez's behavior suggested that he was an "experienced" — as contrasted with a fledgling — drug trafficker. However, this routine process did not occur. The testimony was neither offered nor admitted as *expert* testimony, but rather as *lay opinion* testimony. The Government concedes that it made no effort properly to qualify the witnesses as having the knowledge, experience, training, or education to render their testimony admissible under Rule 702.

. . . [P]art of the testimony in this case . . . provide[s] . . . a clear example of when a witness may give his lay opinion as to the implications of his observations. INS Special Agent Rapp testified that the movements of the Monte Carlo were "suspicious." . . . [S]uch testimony related to matters "common enough" to qualify as lay opinion testimony.

The Government's argument simply blurs the distinction between Federal Rules of Evidence 701 and 702. Lay witness testimony is governed by Rule701, which limits opinions to those "rationally based on the perception of the witness."[44] Rule 702, on the other hand, governs admission of *expert* opinion testimony concerning "*specialized* knowledge." The testimony in this case is precisely the type of "specialized knowledge" governed by Rule 702. A holding to the contrary would encourage the Government to offer all kinds of specialized opinions without pausing first properly to establish the required qualifications of their witnesses. The mere percipience of a witness to the facts on which he wishes to tender an opinion does not trump Rule 702. Otherwise, a lay person witnessing the removal of a bullet from a heart during an autopsy could opine as to the cause of the decedent's death. Surely a civilian bystander, or for that matter a raw DEA recruit would not be allowed to interpret for the jury Lopez's behavior in the parking lot on May 25, 1995 as that of an "experienced" trafficker merely because that person was an eyewitness to the same.

In addition, the Government's argument subverts the requirements of Federal Rule of Criminal Procedure 16(a)(1)(E). Rule 16 requires the Government to "disclose to the defendant a written summary of [expert] testimony the government intends to use . . . during its case in chief." The Rule "is intended to minimize surprise that often results from unexpected testimony, reduce the need for

---

[44] Editor: In 1997, Federal Rule of Evidence 701 provided as follows: "If a "witness is not testifying as an expert, his testimony in the form of opinions or inferences is limited to those opinions or inferences which are (a) rationally based on the perception of the witness and (b) helpful to a clear understanding of his testimony or the determination of a fact in issue."

As originally enacted, Rule 609(a) provided as follows: Impeachment by Evidence of Conviction of Crime

    (a) General rule. — For the purpose of attacking the credibility of a witness, evidence that he has been convicted of a crime shall be admitted if elicited from him or established by public record during cross-examination but only if the crime (1) was punishable by death or imprisonment in excess of one year under the law under which he was convicted, and the court determines that the probative value of admitting this evidence outweighs its prejudicial effect to the defendant, or (2) involved dishonesty or false statement, regardless of the punishment.

continuances, and to provide the opponent with a fair opportunity to test the merit of the expert's testimony through focused cross-examination." Fed. R. Evid. 16(a)(1)(E) (advisory committee's note).

In sum, rather than testimony "based on the perceptions of the witness" — as the district court described it when overruling Lopez's objections — the bulk of the above opinion testimony is properly characterized as testimony based on the perceptions, education, training, and experience of the witness. It requires precisely the type of "specialized knowledge" of law enforcement governed by Rule 702. Trial courts must ensure that experts are qualified to render their opinions and that the opinions will assist the trier of fact. This careful analysis was absent in this case . . .

NOTE

In response to *Figueroa-Lopez* and its civil counterpart, *Asplundh Mfg. Div. v. Benton Harbor Engineering*, 57 F.3d 1190 (3rd Cir. 1995), Congress added subsection (c) to Fed. R. of Evid. 701. In addition to existing restrictions on lay opinion testimony, the amendment limited lay "opinions or inferences to those "which are . . . (c) not based on scientific, technical, or other specialized knowledge within the scope of Rule 702." In effect, this amendment codified the holding in *Figueroa-Lopez*. The Advisory Committee explained that "Rule 701 has been amended to eliminate the risk that the reliability requirements set forth in Rule 702 will be evaded through the simple expedient of proffering an expert in lay witness clothing." Adv. Comm. Note to Amended Rule 701 (2000). *See United States v. Dulcio*, 441 F.3d 1269 (11th Cir. 2006).

Evidentiary Foundation:
The Trial of Wayne Williams

[Twenty-eight black youths were abducted and killed in Atlanta during a two-year period commencing in July, 1979. As new killings occurred, public outcry led to the establishment of a joint federal-state task force to investigate the deaths. On April 21, 1981, the body of Jimmy Ray Payne, age 21, was found in the Chattahoochee River. On May 21, 1981, Nathaniel Cater disappeared. A few days later, members of a stake-out team from the Atlanta Police Department heard a loud splash near the James Jackson Parkway Bridge, and saw a white station wagon driven by Wayne Williams, a self-styled music talent scout, driving slowly across the bridge. Cater's body surfaced two days later in the river. The FBI questioned Williams, and on June 17, 1981, he was indicted for the murders of Payne and Cater. The trial began on December 28, 1981.]

[On February 27, 1982, a jury found Williams guilty of two counts of first degree murder. He received two life sentences. Especially damaging to his case had been evidence of carpet fibers found on the bodies which matched fibers in Williams' home and car. Consider whether the following fiber specialist, Dr. Harold Deadman, was properly qualified as an expert.]

Direct Examination

By Mr. Miller:

Q.   Would you tell us your name, sir?

A.   My name is Harold A. Deadman, Jr.

Q.   And what is your occupation, sir?

A.   I'm a special agent with the Federal Bureau of Investigation, presently assigned to the FBI laboratory in Washington, D.C.

Q.   And how long have you been employed by the FBI, sir?

A.   I've been an agent since November of 1970.

Q.   Has all that time been in the FBI lab in Washington?

A.   No, it has not.

Q.   All right, sir. Could you tell us where else you have served in the FBI and in what capacity, sir?

A.   Upon entering on duty in the FBI, I attended a training school for approximately three months.

In February of 1971, I was assigned to the Jacksonville Field Office. I was involved in general criminal investigations for approximately seven to eight months. I was transferred to the Washington office of the FBI in November of 1971. I was then transferred to the FBI laboratory in February of 1972.

Q.   Since being assigned to the FBI lab in 1972, have you undergone any additional training at the lab?

A.   My first year in the laboratory was spent in a training program.

Q.   Could you tell us, please, something about your educational background?

A.   I attended DePauw University in Greencastle, Indiana, for undergraduate school. I obtained a Bachelor of Arts Degree with a major in Chemistry and a minor in Mathematics.

I attended graduate school at Southern Illinois University in Carbondale, Illinois. I obtained a Ph.D. My major field was organic chemistry. My minor field was inorganic chemistry.

Q.   Prior to being employed by the FBI, did you have occasion to use your training in industry anywhere?

A.   I worked for the Dupont Company for approximately two years. I was assigned to the organic chemicals department outside of Kenton, Delaware.

At Dupont, I was involved in the preparation and testing of various textile additives. These would be such things as flame retardants and dyes, items that would be used to affect the properties of different types of textiles.

Q.   Could you tell us, please, what the nature of your work at the FBI laboratory is?

A.   In the FBI laboratory, I'm presently assigned to the microscopic analysis unit. In this unit, I'm concerned primarily with the examination of several types of trace evidence. This is evidence that is extremely small. Because of its size, it necessitates the use of microscopes to examine it.

The types of trace evidence that I'm primarily concerned with are hairs and textile fibers. My major job, then, is the examination and comparison of hairs, both human and animal, and textile fibers.

I also am involved from time to time with the examination of other types of fibrous materials. These would be such things as fabric, rope, and tape.

I am also involved in teaching a number of courses dealing with the examination and comparison of hairs and textile fibers.

The FBI has an academy at Quantico, Virginia. It's called the FBI Academy. We're concerned there primarily with training, both our own people and people from state and local agencies.

The courses I teach are specialized courses, as I said, dealing with the examination of hairs and textile fibers.

I've taught approximately 16 to 17 courses to approximately 150 people. These are scientists from forensic science laboratories throughout the United States.

I would estimate I have taught students from approximately 100 laboratories throughout the United States.

Q.   Is your time at the FBI devoted specifically to this kind of work?

A.   It is, except when I'm testifying in court as I am today.

Q.   Can you tell us, please, just approximately how many times you have testified in court?

A.   I've testified approximately 90 times.

Q.   And could you tell us, was that both in state and federal courts.

A.   The majority of time I've testified in state court, but I have testified in federal court on a number of occasions.

Q.   Could you estimate for us [in] how many different states in the union you have testified.

A.   I would estimate approximately 25.

Q.   Have you ever had occasion to testify as an expert witness for the defense?

A.   I have on several occasions.

Q.	Could you estimate for us, please, how many fiber examinations you have conducted in your approximately 10 years in the FBI laboratory?
A.	It would be hard to say, but I would estimate in the hundreds of thousands.
Q.	Are you a member of any professional associations.
A.	I am.
Q.	Could you tell us about that, sir?
A.	I'm presently a member of the American Chemical Society. I was a former member of the American Association of Textile Chemists and Colorists. I'm a member of the Midatlantic Association of Forensic Scientists.
Q.	Doctor Deadman, have you had occasion to deliver technical and scientific papers at scientific meetings?
A.	I have.
Q.	All right, sir. Could you tell us about that, sir?
A.	I have participated in programs that have been put on by the Canadian Society of Forensic Scientists. I have given papers at the meetings held by the Midatlantic Association of Forensic Scientists.
	I have also presented a paper in New York to the New York Microscopic Society.
Q.	And have you had occasion to serve as a consultant to the National Science Foundation?
A.	I have on one occasion.
Mr. Miller:	Your Honor, we submit Doctor Deadman as an expert.
Mr. Biner:	No objection.
The Court:	Let the record so reflect.

UNITED STATES v. LEESON
453 F.3d 631 (4th Cir. 2006)

HAMILTON, SENIOR CIRCUIT JUDGE:

Larry Leeson (Leeson) appeals his conviction and sentence on one count of being a felon in possession of a firearm, 18 U.S.C. §§ 922(g)(1), 924(a)(2). For reasons that follow, we affirm.

*   *   *

On September 4, 2003, a federal grand jury sitting in the Northern District of West Virginia indicted Leeson on one count of being a convicted felon in possession of a firearm. 18 U.S.C. §§ 922(g)(1), 924(a)(2). Following Leeson's arraignment, he was remanded to custody to await his trial. Leeson then filed a notice of insanity defense and moved for a psychiatric examination.[45]

Leeson's motion for a psychiatric examination was granted by a United States Magistrate Judge and, as a consequence, Leeson was transported to the Metropolitan Correctional Center (MCC Chicago), Federal Bureau of Prisons, Chicago, Illinois, for psychiatric examination.

Once at MCC Chicago, Dr. Jason Dana (Dr. Dana), holder of a doctorate in clinical psychology, examined and evaluated Leeson's mental health. On April 6, 2004, Dr. Dana prepared a forensic psychological report detailing his findings and diagnosis regarding Leeson. With regard to Leeson's sanity at the time of the instant offense, Dr. Dana's report opined: "there is no indication that he was suffering from any form of cognitive impairment or mental illness impacting his ability to understand the nature and quality, or wrongfulness of his actions at the time of the instant offense." (J.A. 867). Rather, Dr. Dana's report diagnosed Leeson as being a malingerer and of having opiate dependence by history.[46]

Leeson's trial commenced on September 16, 2004, wherein he continued to assert an insanity defense. Leeson called Dr. Jonathan Himmelhoch (Dr. Himmelhoch), a psychiatrist, to render an expert opinion in support of his insanity defense. The district court ruled that Dr. Himmelhoch was qualified to render such an expert opinion. At trial, Dr. Himmelhoch testified that he diagnosed Leeson with Post Traumatic Stress Disorder, partial lobe epilepsy, depression, and migraine headaches. He then testified that, on the day of Leeson's charged offense, August 6, 2003, these illnesses worked together to make Leeson severely mentally ill such that Leeson did not understand the nature and quality or the wrongfulness of his conduct.

The government called Dr. Dana in rebuttal. The district court ruled that Dr. Dana was qualified to render an expert opinion regarding the presence or absence of severe mental illness or defect in connection with Leeson's insanity defense. Consistent with his expert witness report, Dr. Dana testified at trial that, in his opinion, Leeson was not suffering from any form of cognitive impairment or mental illness which impacted his ability to understand the nature and quality of or the wrongfulness of his actions on August 6, 2003. Also consistent with his expert witness report, Dr. Dana testified that his diagnostic workup of Leeson indicated malingering and opiate dependence. At issue on appeal is the following portion of Dr. Dana's direct testimony at trial in rebuttal to Leeson's offered testimony of Dr. Himmelhoch:

---

[45] [1] Title 18, United States Code § 17 sets forth the federal standard for an insanity defense:

　　(a) Affirmative defense. — It is an affirmative defense to a prosecution under any Federal statute that, at the time of the commission of the acts constituting the offense, the defendant, as a result of a severe mental disease or defect, was unable to appreciate the nature and quality or the wrongfulness of his acts. Mental disease or defect does not otherwise constitute a defense.

　　(b) Burden of proof. — The defendant has the burden of proving the defense of insanity by clear and convincing evidence. 18 U.S.C. § 17.

[46] [2] At trial, Dr. Dana testified that "malingering is specifically the reporting of symptoms of mental illness for the purposes of obtaining a secondary gain." (J.A. 544).

Q.   Now regarding your — your diagnosis of malingering, what specific
            action or criteria did you utilize in reaching that conclusion?

A.   Going through the different information that he provided to me,
            cross-referencing it with records and other information that was
            available to me in order to identify the validity of the claims, the
            assessment of malingering, it was done with the services that we
            mentioned before and behavioral observations, providing him with
            opportunities to speak to other members of the psychology services
            department. Generally the more times a person is asked to explain
            their problems and concerns, the more opportunity they have to be
            inconsistent, so it gets into all of those things.

Q.   And you said, of course, he was observed in the — in the depart-
            ment?

A.   Yes.

Q.   And so you relied upon information from other members, of course?

A.   Not only other members of the department but information regard-
            ing observed behaviors from people who were not in our department
            as well.

Q.   Give us some examples of information that you utilized that came
            from people not within the department but still up there at the BOP
            Institution in Chicago.

A.   The Correctional Officers that are responsible for supervising the
            units, often times when they see information that is not in the realm
            of mainstream, not what is usually identified, they will leave
            messages for us, contact us of course personally about information.

Q.   What about other inmates, do you ever receive information from
            other inmates or people incarcerated at the BOP?

A.   Yeah. Occasionally. Though you have to be careful about that
            information but in this case there were two separate inmates during
            the time that Mr. Leeson was there that approached the other
            forensic psychologist. They did not talk to me directly.

MR. WALKER

[(counsel for Leeson)]:   Your Honor, I object to this. I think this is inappropriate
                          and it is not something that is considered a basis for his
                          medical or psychological evaluation and it's hearsay.

THE COURT: Overruled.

MR. WALKER: I'd like to cross-examine those individuals.

THE COURT: I said overruled.

A.   It is actually a standard in order to gather information about a
            person from sources and information. Again, you have to weigh the
            validity of all circumstances. In a situation where this was the only
            piece of information that I had, [I] would not generally rely on it. In

situations where it's one of several pieces of information, it then becomes more reliable.

Q.   And, of course, you're speaking of the information provided by the inmates at the institution?

A.   Yes.

Q.   And — and what information did they provide? You said there were two separate ones.

A.   Yeah. They — they essentially indicated that Mr. Leeson had approached them to recruit them in assisting him in looking crazy while he was on the unit.

Q.   I — I'm sorry?

A.   And, that — that — that he had approached them and asked them to assist him in looking crazy on the unit. And one — one of the inmates said that he was asked by Mr. Leeson to go to the officer and tell him that an inmate in the back was acting crazy.

(J.A. 545–47). On appeal, Leeson contends the district court abused its discretion in allowing Dr. Dana to testify regarding the statements of Leeson's fellow inmates at MCC Chicago.

The district court ultimately sentenced Leeson to 230 months' imprisonment. This timely appeal followed.

III.

Leeson's second assignment of error pertains to Dr. Dana's testimony to the effect that, in forming his expert opinion that Leeson did not suffer from a severe mental illness which prevented him from appreciating the nature and quality or the wrongfulness of possessing a firearm as a convicted felon on August 6, 2003, he (Dr. Dana) relied, *inter alia*, upon statements by two different prison inmates that Leeson "had approached them to recruit them in assisting him in looking crazy while he was on the unit," and upon a statement by one of those inmates that "he was asked by Mr. Leeson to go to the officer and tell him that an inmate in the back was acting crazy." (J.A. 547). According to Leeson, the district court abused its discretion in admitting this testimony because it was hearsay, *see* Fed. R. Evid. 801, which did not otherwise qualify for admission under Federal Rule of Evidence 703 (Rule 703).

Rule 703 provides:

The facts or data in the particular case upon which an expert bases an opinion or inference may be those perceived by or made known to the expert at or before the hearing. If of a type reasonably relied upon by experts in the particular field in forming opinions or inferences upon the subject, the facts or data need not be admissible in evidence in order for the opinion or inference to be admitted. Facts or data that are otherwise inadmissible shall not be disclosed to the jury by the proponent of the opinion or inference unless the court determines that their probative value in assisting the jury to evaluate the expert's opinion substantially outweighs their prejudicial effect.

Fed. R. Evid. 703.

Leeson argues that the challenged testimony did not qualify for admission under Rule 703 for three reasons. First, he claims that Dr. Dana did not sufficiently establish that inmates in a federal mental health facility, in general, are reasonably relied upon by experts in his field. Second, he claims that Dr. Dana was not in a position to determine whether the two fellow inmates were trustworthy sources of information, and therefore, Dr. Dana could not have reasonably relied upon their statements. Finally, he claims the district court failed to make a finding that the probative value of the inmates' statements substantially outweighed their prejudicial effect.

As previously stated, we review a district court's ruling on the admissibility of evidence for abuse of discretion. *Brooks*, 111 F.3d at 371. Here, we hold the district court did not abuse its discretion in admitting Dr. Dana's testimony regarding the inmates' out-of-court statements.

Assuming *arguendo* the challenged testimony constitutes hearsay as defined by Federal Rule of Evidence 801,[47] we hold the challenged testimony otherwise qualifies for admission under Rule 703. First, contrary to Leeson's position, during Dr. Dana's testimony, Dr. Dana sufficiently established that inmates in a federal mental health facility, in general, are reasonably relied upon by experts in his field. Critically, we read the following portion of Dr. Dana's trial testimony to state that the inmates' statements were of a type reasonably, but admittedly cautiously, relied upon by experts in the mental health field in forming opinions regarding whether a particular inmate is a malingerer:

Q.   And so you relied upon information from other members, of course?

A.   Not only other members of the department but information regarding observed behaviors from people who were not in our department as well.

Q.   What about other inmates, do you ever receive information from other inmates or people incarcerated at the BOP?

A.   Yeah. Occasionally. Though you have to be careful about that information but in this case there were two separate inmates during the time that Mr. Leeson was there that approached the other forensic psychologist. They did not talk to me directly.

A.   *It is actually a standard in order to gather information about a person from sources and information. Again, you have to weigh the validity of all circumstances. In a situation where this was the only*

---

[47] [3] Federal Rule of Evidence 801(c) defines the term "hearsay" as "a statement, other than one made by the declarant while testifying at the trial or hearing, offered in evidence to prove the truth of the matter asserted." Fed. R. Evid. 801(c).

piece of information that I had, [I] would not generally rely on it.
. . .

Q.   *And, of course, you're speaking of the information provided by the inmates at the institution?*

A.   *Yes.*

(J.A. 545–47) (emphasis added). As for Leeson's argument that Dr. Dana was not in a position to determine whether the two fellow inmates were trustworthy sources of information, and therefore Dr. Dana could not have reasonably relied upon their statements in forming his expert opinion, Leeson's argument is a nonstarter given that Leeson had full opportunity at trial to cross-examine Dr. Dana on this point and to make such an argument to the jury in closing argument. Finally, on the issue of whether the district court made a determination that the probative value of the inmates' out-of-court statements substantially outweighed their prejudicial effect, we conclude from our reading of the trial transcript that the district court implicitly made such a finding. We also conclude the district court properly determined that the probative value of the inmates' out-of-court statements outweighed their prejudicial effect. The information that Dr. Dana relied upon in formulating his expert opinion was highly and directly relevant to the jury's task of evaluating that opinion. The district court did not abuse its discretion in finding that such probative value substantially outweighed any prejudicial effect of the statements, especially given that Leeson had the opportunity to cross-examine Dr. Dana regarding the reasonableness of his reliance on the statements and the opportunity during closing argument to downgrade the credibility of such out-of-court statements in the eyes of the jury.

In conclusion, we uphold the district court's admission of Dr. Dana's testimony regarding the challenged out-of-court statements by two of Leeson's fellow inmates at MCC Chicago.

Mason Ladd, *Expert Testimony*
5 Vand. L. Rev. 414, 423–24 (1952)[48]

ULTIMATE FACT

Some courts still struggle with the propriety of asking an opinion question calling for the ultimate fact which the jury is to decide. Reversals are predicated upon this assumed error alone, even though these courts would have approved a series of questions which hedged about the problem but from the answers to which the view of the experts on the ultimate issue was as plain as the sun on a bright day. The tricky process of wording the questions, disguising the opinion so that it appears to be a secondary rather than a primary inference with the subtle distinctions of phraseology, is necessary under the views of these courts to preclude the jury from stealing their final conclusion directly from the opinion expressed. The fact that a jury is no more required to accept a questionable opinion of an expert than it is required to accept a false statement of fact, does not alter the position taken. Nor

---

[48] Reprinted with permission.

does it make a difference that the experts for each side express exactly opposite opinions and that it is for the jury to select the opinions which correspond to their own thinking upon the problem. The wrong has been done if the form in which the opinion is asked calls for the ultimate issue submitted to the jury for a decision.

A great deal has been said about the province of the jury to draw conclusions, and this helps to clutter up the reasoning upon the point. Fortunately in this day of more realistic law, many courts are making the break and are treating this problem in a more sensible fashion. The Iowa court overthrew many sins of the past and got on the right road in the case of *Grismore v. Consolidated Products Company* [232 Iowa 328, 5 N.W.2d 646 (1942)]. A turkey raiser wanted to make his turkeys grow faster and he yielded to the sales talk of the salesman of a food products company. The magic food was called "E-emulsion" and the turkey raiser contracted for quantities of it which he fed to great numbers of healthy poults. Although assisted by the salesman so as to feed it properly, the turkeys died in great numbers long prior to their normal execution date. As a result, a lawsuit was instituted. There was no question that the turkeys were dead. The sole issue for the jury to decide was what caused the death of the turkeys. The trial court permitted counsel for the turkey raiser to ask of an expert on turkey raising, in substance, what in his opinion, caused the death of the turkeys? To this question vigorous and learned objections were urged. The court, a practical-minded judge, thought the jury ought to know what the expert did think about it, overruled the objections and permitted the answer. The expert then placed the entire blame on "E-emulsion." On appeal it took a very able supreme court judge 34 solidly printed pages to prove that the trial court was right. Six leading cases of the jurisdiction were overruled by name and an endless number of decisions were overruled by implications.

UNITED STATES v. SCAVO
593 F.2d 837 (8th Cir. 1979)

HENLEY, CIRCUIT JUDGE.

Frank Scavo appeals from his conviction of being engaged in the business of betting or wagering and knowingly using wire communication facilities for the transmission in interstate commerce of information assisting in the placing of bets or wagers, in violation of 18 U.S.C. § 1084 (a). We affirm.

*   *   *

At trial the government's evidence consisted principally of playing recordings of telephone conversations obtained from the court-authorized wiretaps on the telephones of Dwight Mezo. In addition, F.B.I. Special Agent William Holmes was qualified as an expert in gambling and testified about the nature of gambling operations, gambling terminology, and his opinion as to appellant's role in Mezo's bookmaking operation. He testified that appellant, then a resident of Las Vegas, provided Mezo with much-needed "line" information — *i.e.*, the odds or point spread established to equalize or induce betting on sporting events.

*   *   *

D. *Expert Testimony.*

Appellant next contends that the district court erred in allowing Special Agent Holmes to give certain opinion testimony. Appellant does not contest Agent Holmes' qualifications as an expert in the field of gambling; rather, he contends that Agent Holmes' testimony "invaded the province of the jury." Specifically, he objects to Holmes' testimony about his role in Mezo's bookmaking operation and his knowledge of, and assistance to, Mezo's operation.

We reject appellant's contention of error. Rule 704 of the Federal Rules of Evidence provides:

> Testimony in the form of an opinion or inference otherwise admissible is not objectionable because it embraces an ultimate issue to be decided by the trier of fact.

One purpose of the Federal Rules of Evidence was to make opinion evidence admissible if it would be of assistance to the trier of fact. Rule 704 is consistent with this purpose by doing away with the "ultimate issue" rule, a rule which Professor Wigmore aptly characterized as "empty rhetoric." 7 J. WIGMORE, EVIDENCE § 1920 at 17 (3d ed. 1940).

Rule 704 does not, of course, render all expert testimony admissible. Expert testimony must still meet the criterion of helpfulness expressed in Rule 702 and is also subject to exclusion under Rule 403 if its probative value is substantially outweighed by the risks of unfair prejudice, confusion or waste of time. 3 J. WEINSTEIN & M. BERGER, WEINSTEIN'S EVIDENCE ¶ 704 [01] at 704–9 (1978).

Judged under these standards, Agent Holmes' testimony was properly admitted. The structure of a gambling enterprise is not something with which most jurors are familiar. In addition, the business employs a jargon foreign to all those who are not connected with the business. The latter consideration assumes particular importance in a case, such as this one, where the prosecution's evidence consists largely of tape recorded conversations. These conversations, which are at times virtually incomprehensible to the layman, are fraught with meaning to a person familiar with gambling enterprises.

Accordingly, we conclude that Agent Holmes' concededly relevant expert opinion would be helpful to the jury and was thus admissible under Rule 702. Any possibility of undue prejudice was removed by the trial court's careful instructions regarding the juror's role in deciding the facts and weighing the credibility of witnesses, including expert witnesses.

BERRY v. CITY OF DETROIT
25 F.3d 1342 (6th Cir. 1994)

RALPH B. GUY, JR., CIRCUIT JUDGE.

A jury awarded Doris Berry (plaintiff), six million dollars for the death of her son, Lee Berry, Jr., who was shot by a Detroit police officer. On appeal, the City of Detroit (City) raises three arguments. First, the City asserts that plaintiff failed to offer any evidence that the City's policymakers had adopted a policy or ratified a custom of unconstitutional use of deadly force. Second, the City argues that plaintiff's evidence of the City's alleged failure to train and discipline its officers failed to show any custom or policy of the City that amounted to deliberate indifference to the rights of citizens or, alternatively, that there was no evidence that any alleged failure on the City's part was a proximate cause of Lee Berry's death. Finally, the City takes issue with the jury instructions. We conclude that plaintiff's evidence was insufficient to prove deliberate indifference on the part of the City such as to give rise to municipal liability under 42 U.S.C. Sec. 1983. Therefore, we reverse the judgment against the City.

I.

On June 23, 1987, Lee Berry, Jr. (Lee), who was employed in a family moving business, was driving the company van in rush-hour traffic to the family residence in Detroit. According to the testimony of Lee's sixteen-year-old brother, Dwayne Berry, and his eight-year-old nephew, David Askew, both of whom were in the van, Lee committed several misdemeanor traffic violations during this journey. The infractions consisted of running a red light, driving on the wrong side of the road, and passing three cars that were stopped for a red light.

These traffic offenses attracted the attention of Officer Joseph Hall, a 17-year veteran of the Detroit Police Department. Exactly what happened immediately thereafter, however, is a matter of some dispute. On the witness stand, Hall testified — in contrast to the testimony of the surviving occupants of the van and in partial contradiction of his earlier deposition testimony — that the violations prompted a dangerous, high-speed chase involving the police. Dwayne and David, on the other hand, offered a markedly different account of what transpired. They testified that Lee had not been speeding, had not attempted to flee from arrest, and had not committed any traffic violations other than those described above.

Moments after the van arrived at the Berry family home, Hall arrived on the scene. Hall confronted Lee Berry and a struggle then ensued, during which Hall shot Lee in the back from a distance estimated as being between three and ten feet. Although no eyewitnesses observed the shooting, David, Dwayne, and several bystanders stated that Hall, upon his arrival at the Berry home, used profanity, threats, and physical force in attempting to effect an arrest. Hall, however, claimed that Lee attacked him; that the gun fired accidently when Lee, during their struggle, attempted to wrestle the pistol away from him; and that he continued to fire at Lee while Lee was fleeing because the firearm was set on "automatic" and because his (Hall's) vision had been impaired by blood. Plaintiff's expert witnesses opined that Lee had not touched Hall's revolver because Lee was several feet away from the gun when it fired, that Hall had not been blinded by blood, and that Hall's service revolver lacked any type of "automatic" firing mechanism.

Shortly after the incident, the police department conducted an investigation that exonerated Hall. No criminal charges were brought against him and no sanctions were imposed upon him. At the time of trial, Hall remained a member of the Detroit Police Department on disability retirement with full pension benefits.

Plaintiff initiated this suit against Hall and the City under 42 U.S.C. Sec. 1983. Plaintiff's complaint also listed several state law causes of action. Plaintiff claimed that the City pursued a deliberate policy of failing to train or discipline adequately its police officers in the proper use of deadly force, which failures caused the violation of Lee's constitutional rights under the Fourth and Fourteenth Amendments. At the conclusion of the trial, the jury returned verdicts against both Hall and the City in the amount of six million dollars.

*   *   *

Moreover, although the touchstone of the Sec. 1983 action against a government body is an allegation that official policy is responsible for a deprivation of rights protected by the Constitution, local governments, like every other Sec. 1983 "person," by the very terms of the statute, may be sued for constitutional deprivations visited pursuant to governmental "custom" even though such a custom has not received formal approval through the body's official decision making channels.

[*Monell v. Department of Social Services*, 436 U.S. 658] 690–01 [(1978)].

More recently, the Court addressed the issue of municipal liability under Sec. 1983 when the plaintiff has alleged that his or her rights were violated as a result of a municipality's failure to train its police officers adequately. In *City of Canton v. Harris*, 489 U.S. 378 (1989), the plaintiff had been arrested and brought to the police station, whereupon she slumped to the floor on two separate occasions and was left lying there. The plaintiff brought a Sec. 1983 action against the city for failure to train its officers to recognize when a person in custody is in need of medical assistance. The Court held that the inadequacy of police training may serve as the basis for Sec. 1983 liability only where the failure to train amounts to deliberate indifference to the rights of persons with whom the police come into contact. This rule is most consistent with our admonition in *Monell*, 436 U.S., at 694, and *Polk County v. Dodson*, 454 U.S. 312, 326 (1981), that a municipality can be liable under Sec. 1983 only where its policies are the "moving force [behind] the constitutional violation." Only where a municipality's failure to train its employees in a relevant respect evidences a "deliberate indifference" to the rights of its inhabitants can such a shortcoming be properly thought of as a city "policy or custom" that is actionable under Sec. 1983.

*   *   *

Postill . . . testified that 277 of the 636 incidents included shootings at burglary suspects. Postill then testified that even prior to the Supreme Court's decision in *Tennessee v. Garner*, 471 U.S. 1 (1985), the Detroit Police Department had a policy requiring officers to exhaust all reasonable means before shooting at a burglar. Again, it should be emphasized that Postill's statistics were taken from the one-page summary sheet of shooting incidents for each year. Postill did not review the underlying facts in these cases to determine, among other things, whether the suspect was armed. Pursuant to Garner, fatal force may be used when an officer has reason to believe that a felon poses a danger to himself or to others.

Postill also testified concerning his review of the actual records of 161 of the 636 incidents. In his opinion, 78 of these incidents were "unjustifiable" on the basis of "existing law and Detroit City policy." Postill concluded that out of these 161 incidents only 15 officers were disciplined and, in seven of these cases, the disciplinary action was held in abeyance. Postill then described 13 incidents in which he thought police officers should have been disciplined. In one of these incidents, the officer fired his weapon, accidently hitting a bystander, only after the officer already had been shot twice. Postill still felt that the officer should have been disciplined. The fact that the officer fired only after having been shot twice was not volunteered by Postill and was only revealed upon cross-examination.

After describing these 13 specific cases, Postill concluded that "the department tolerates this kind of reckless use of firearms. They either get no discipline or a slap on the wrist." It was his "opinion that their failure to direct and discipline and train their officers not to use improper deadly force constitute a pattern of gross negligence." Postill equated "gross negligence" with "deliberate indifference" and defined it as "conscious knowledge of something and not doing anything about it."

This latter testimony was particularly suspect. It was carefully couched in the precise language used in case law, either indicating a keen awareness by Postill of the direction in which he had to head, or else careful coaching prior to his testimony. "Gross negligence" is not enough to ground liability according to the Supreme Court, so Postill testified that gross negligence equates to "deliberate indifference." We apparently now have an etymology expert testifying.

We also believe this testimony was received in violation of the Federal Rules of Evidence. Although an expert's opinion may "embrace[] an ultimate issue to be decided by the trier of fact[,]" Fed. R. Evid. 704(a), the issue embraced must be a factual one. The expert can testify, if a proper foundation is laid, that the discipline in the Detroit Police Department was lax. He also could testify regarding what he believed to be the consequences of lax discipline. He may not testify, however, that the lax discipline policies of the Detroit Police Department indicated that the City was deliberately indifferent to the welfare of its citizens.

It would have been easy enough for the drafters of the Federal Rules of Evidence to have said that a properly qualified expert may opine on the ultimate question of liability. They did not do so. When the rules speak of an expert's testimony embracing the ultimate issue, the reference must be to stating opinions that suggest the answer to the ultimate issue or that give the jury all the information from which it can draw inferences as to the ultimate issue. We would not allow a fingerprint expert in a criminal case to opine that a defendant was guilty (a legal conclusion), even though we would allow him to opine that the defendant's fingerprint was the only one on the murder weapon (a fact). The distinction, although subtle, is nonetheless important.

Furthermore, "deliberate indifference" is a legal term, as the questioning of Postill indicated. It is the responsibility of the court, not testifying witnesses, to define legal terms. The expert's testimony in this regard invaded the province of the court. The courts have addressed this issue, and typical of their holdings is that reached in *Hygh v. Jacobs*, 961 F.2d 359 (2d Cir. 1992). *Jacobs* was an excessive police force case. The expert was allowed to testify that "in his opinion, the use of a baton or flashlight to strike a person in the head would constitute 'deadly physical force' that would not be 'justified under the circumstances.'" *Id.* at 361–62.

In condemning this line of testimony, the court stated: "This circuit is in accord with other circuits in requiring exclusion of expert testimony that expresses a legal conclusion." *Id.* at 363. In concluding on this issue, the court held:

> Even if a jury were not misled into adopting outright a legal conclusion proffered by an expert witness, the testimony would remain objectionable by communicating a legal standard — explicit or implicit — to the jury. Whereas an expert may be uniquely qualified by experience to assist the trier of fact, he is not qualified to compete with the judge in the function of instructing the jury . . . .
>
> . . . .
>
> Far more troubling, [the expert] testified that Jacobs' conduct was not "justified under the circumstances," not "warranted under the circumstances," and "totally improper." We have held that an expert's testimony that a defendant was "negligent" should not have been allowed. We see no significant distinction in [the expert's] conclusory condemnations of Jacobs' actions here, which, in the language of the advisory committee, "merely [told] the jury what result to reach."

961 F.2d at 364 (citations omitted). If the rule were other than as indicated by the Second Circuit, we would soon breed a whole new category of "liability experts" whose function would be to tell the jury what result to reach — exactly what the expert did here.

NOTES AND QUESTIONS

1.   May counsel simply ask an expert "which side should win this case?" What about the question, "Did *T* have capacity to make a will?" *See* Advisory Committee Note, Federal Rule of Evidence 704.

2.   Expert testimony has been offered in some courts to establish "battered woman syndrome" as a defense to murder charges. In essence, this syndrome purports to explain that a woman's fear of her spouse may be such that she feels compelled to defend herself violently against him even absent imminent danger to her. Should such testimony be permitted? *See* John W. Roberts, *Between the Heat of Passion and Cold Blood: Battered Woman's Syndrome as an Excuse for Self-Defense in Non-Confrontational Homicides*, 27 Law & Psychol. Rev. 135 (2003).

3.   Expert testimony has been offered in rape cases to establish that the alleged victim suffered from so-called rape trauma syndrome commonly experienced by victims of such sexual assaults. Based upon the presence of this syndrome, one expert testified that the complainant had been the victim of "a frightening assault, an attack." Does such testimony impermissibly invade the jury's province? *See People v. Baenziger*, 97 P.3d 271 (Colo. Ct. App. 2004); *People v. Nelson*, 22 A.D.3d 769 (N.Y. App. Div. 2005).

4.   In 1984, Rule 704(b) was added to the original text. The new language was part of the reform of the insanity defense under Federal law:

> The purpose of this amendment is to eliminate the confusing spectacle of competing expert witnesses testifying to directly contradictory conclusions as to the ultimate legal issue to be found by the trier of fact. Under this proposal, expert psychiatric testimony would be limited to presenting and explaining their diagnoses, such as whether the defendant had a severe mental disease or defect and what the characteristics of such a disease or defect, if any, may have been.

H. Rep. No. 98-1030, 98th Cong., 2d Sess. 224, 232 (1984), *reprinted in* 1984 U.S.C.C.A.N. 1.

In *United States v. Frisbee*, 623 F. Supp. 1217, 1224 (D.C. Cal. 1985), the court ruled:

> The legislative history of [R]ule 704(b) states that the rule is intended to limit experts to presenting and explaining their diagnoses, such as whether the defendant had a severe mental disease or defect and what the characteristics of such a disease or defect, if any, may have been. . . . No testimony directly or indirectly opening on the issue of specific intent will be allowed. (Citations omitted)

According to the district court in *United States v. Gold*, 661 F. Supp. 1127, 1132 (D.D.C. 1987):

> [While] the expert proffered by [the] defendant will be allowed to testify as to the facts of defendant's mental state or condition, he cannot offer "the jury a conclusion as to whether said condition rendered the defendant unable to appreciate the nature and quality or the wrongfulness of his acts. The "ultimate issues" about which experts are not now allowed to testify include insanity, the capacity to distinguish right from wrong, and the capacity to conform behavior to the requirement of the law. (Citations omitted)

In *United States v. Dubray*, 854 F.2d 1099, 1102 (8th Cir. 1988), the court ruled:

> The present version of Rule 704(b) was not intended to prevent psychiatric experts from "testify[ing] fully about the defendant's diagnosis, mental state and motivation . . . at the time of the alleged act so as to permit the jury or judge to reach the ultimate conclusion about which they and only they are expert." It is true that Dr. Kennelly's diagnosis that Dubray was not psychotic has definite <u>implications</u> for the determination of Dubray's legal sanity, but this is true of all expert testimony in trials with an insanity defense. Diagnoses of "psychosis," "schizophrenia," or other mental disorders must be made using the methodology and assumptions of psychiatric medicine, which are not necessarily the same as those of criminal law. . . . In this case, Dr. Kennelly's testimony was limited to the medical question of psychosis, and did not state an opinion whether Dubray was able to appreciate the wrongfulness of his actions. (Citation omitted)

5. To what extent does Rule 704(b) go beyond insanity defense situations? For example, may an expert witness give an opinion concerning defendant's ability to form the specific intent necessary for second degree murder? *See United States v. Hillsberg*, 812 F.2d 328 (7th Cir. 1987).

6. In the bank robbery trial of Patty Hearst, heir to the Hearst fortune who allegedly assisted a terrorist group known as the SLA after the SLA kidnapped her, the government negated her defense of duress through expert psychiatric testimony. One government expert, Dr. Fort, opined that Ms. Hearst "did not perform the bank robbery because she was in fear of her life. She did it as a voluntary member of the SLA." The other expert, Dr. Kozol, stated: "I think she entered that bank voluntarily in order to participate in the robbing of that bank. This was an act of her own free will." What result under Rule 704 as originally enacted? *See United States v. Hearst*, 563 F.2d 1331, 1351 (9th Cir. 1977), *cert. denied*, 435 U.S. 1000 (1978). What result under Rule 704 as amended?

Charles T. McCormick, *Some Observations upon the Opinion Rule and Expert Testimony*
23 TEX. L. REV. 109, 122–26 (1945)[49]

HYPOTHETICAL QUESTIONS

If an expert witness has first-hand knowledge of material facts, as when a physician has examined an injured plaintiff, naturally he may describe what he has seen, and give his expert inferences therefrom, such as his opinion as to the cause or the probable duration of the condition. In these circumstances, it is unnecessary to couch the question in hypothetical form and it would certainly weaken the effect of the testimony to do so. We have assumed that the expert witness has first specified the data gleaned from observation on which he found his inferences. Is this required? Some courts insist that this be done, so that the jury may know the premises before they hear the conclusions. Others say that it is not essential since the opponent is free to elicit the grounds on cross-examination. The wisest view, it seems, is to leave to the trial court's discretion whether this shall be required.

When the expert has no first-hand knowledge of the situation at issue, and has made no investigation of the facts for himself, then the most convenient way of securing the benefit of his scientific skill is to ask him to assume certain facts and then to give his opinions or inferences in view of such assumptions. These are known as hypothetical questions, and the rules regulating the form and content of such questions have been evolved with perhaps more of logical rigor than of practicality.

In many jurisdictions, it seems customary to have the expert witnesses in court during the taking of testimony, and then when the expert is himself called as a witness, to simplify the hypothetical question by asking the expert to assume the truth of the previous testimony, or some specified part of it. This practice has some advantages, and some limitations. Two obvious requirements are that the facts that

[49] Published originally in 23 TEXAS LAW REVIEW 109 (1945). Copyright 1945 by the Texas Law Review Association. Reprinted by permission.

the witness is assuming must be clear to the jury, and that the data assumed must not be conflicting. A question which asks the witness to assume the truth of one previous witness' testimony will usually meet these requirements, but as the range of assumption is widened to cover the testimony of several witnesses, or all the testimony for one side the risk of infraction is increased, and when it covers all the testimony in the case, the question would manifestly be approved only when the testimony on the issue is not conflicting and is brief and simple enough for the jury to recall its outlines without having them recited. . . .

The type of hypothetical questions just discussed, namely those based on other testimony in the case, have the advantage of satisfying the requirement imposed upon all hypothetical questions that the facts assumed must be supported by evidence in the case. This requirement is based on the notion that if the answer is founded on premises of fact which the jury, for want of evidence, cannot find to be true, then they are equally disabled from using the answer as the basis for a finding. Direct testimony supporting the fact assumed is not required. It is sufficient if it is fairly inferable from circumstances proved. Moreover, the supporting evidence need not have been already adduced if the interrogating counsel gives assurance that it will be. And of course, it is no objection that the supporting evidence is controverted. The proponent is entitled to put his side of the case to the witness for his opinion.

In doing this, however, there is danger that by omitting some of the facts, he may present an unfair and inadequate picture to the expert, and that the jury may give undue weight to the answer, without considering its faulty basis. What safeguards should be supplied?

Some courts have required that all facts material to the question should be embraced in the hypothesis, but this seems undesirable as likely to multiply disputes as to the sufficiency of the hypothesis, and as tending to cause counsel, out of abundance of caution, to propound questions so lengthy as to be wearisome and almost meaningless to the jury. The more expedient and more widely prevailing view is that there is no rule requiring that all material facts be included. The safeguards are that the adversary may on cross-examination supply omitted facts and ask the expert if his opinion would be modified by them, and further that the trial judge if he deems the original question unfair may in his discretion require that the hypothesis be reframed to supply an adequate basis for a helpful answer.

John H. Wigmore, 2 Evidence § 686
(3d ed. 1940)[50]

Abolition of the [Hypothetical] Question as a Requirement. What is to be the future of the hypothetical question? *Must the hypothetical question go*, as a requirement?

Its abuses have become so obstructive and nauseous that no remedy short of extirpation will suffice. It is a logical necessity, but a practical incubus; and logic must here be sacrificed. After all, Law (in Mr. Justice Holmes' phrase) is much more than Logic. It is a strange irony that the hypothetical question, which is one of the

---

[50] Reprinted by permission of Little, Brown and Company, Boston, 1940.

few truly scientific features of the rules of Evidence, should have become that feature which does most to disgust men of science with the law of Evidence.

The hypothetical question, misused by the clumsy and abused by the clever, has in practice led to intolerable obstruction of truth. In the first place, it has artificially clamped the mouth of the expert witness, so that his answer to a complex question may not express his actual opinion on the actual case. This is because the question may be so built up and contrived by counsel as to represent only a partisan conclusion. In the second place, it has tended to mislead the jury as to the purport of actual expert opinion. This is due to the same reason. In the third place, it has tended to confuse the jury, so that its employment becomes a mere waste of time and a futile obstruction.

No partial limitation of its use seems feasible, by specific rules. Logically there is no place to stop short: practically, any specific limitations would be more or less arbitrary, and would thus tend to become mere quibbles.

How can the extirpating operation be performed? By exempting the offering party from the *requirement* of using the hypothetical form; by according him the *option* of using it, — both of these to be left to the trial Court's discretion; and by permitting the opposing party, *on cross-examination*, to call for a hypothetical specification of the data which the witness has used as the basis of the opinion. The last rule will give sufficient protection against a misunderstanding of the opinion, when any actual doubt exists.

The foregoing proposals, be it understood, represent a mere practical rule of thumb. They do violence to theoretical logic. But in practice they would produce less actual misleading of the jury than the present complex preciosities. After all, the only theoretical object of the hypothetical question . . . is to avoid misunderstanding; and "if the salt has lost its savor, wherewith shall it be salted? It is thenceforth good for nothing but to be cast out and trodden under foot of men." The present proposal does not tread under foot the hypothetical question, but merely transfers its function to the hand of the cross examiner.

NOTES AND QUESTIONS

1.   Would the following line of inquiry be permissible in federal court?

Q.   *Doctor, do you have an opinion based upon a reasonable degree of medical certainty as to the extent of permanent disability suffered by the plaintiff as a result of this automobile accident?*

A.   Yes.

Q.   *What is your opinion?*

A.   She is totally permanently disabled.

Q.   *Thank you, doctor, that is all.*

See Rules of Evidence (Supplement), Hearings Before the Subcommittee on Criminal Justice of the Committee on the Judiciary, House of Representatives, 93rd Cong., 1st Sess., on Proposed Rules of Evidence, Serial No. 2, 355–56 (Supp. 1973) (emphasis in original).

2.   Is there any drawback to leaving the development of underlying facts to cross-examination? What difficulties might cross-examining counsel encounter by virtue of this procedure?

3.   How might Rule 705 be used to curtail the potential impact of the expert's newly acquired right to testify on the ultimate issue?

4.   Compare the following Ohio rule of evidence:

> The expert may testify in terms of opinion or inference and give his reasons therefor after disclosure of the underlying facts or data. The disclosure may be in response to a hypothetical question or otherwise.

Ohio Rule of Evidence 705. *See* Note, *The Roads Not Taken: Expert and Opinion Testimony Under the Ohio Rules of Evidence*, 50 U. Cin. L. Rev. 82 (1981). *In re Lauren P.*, 2004 Ohio 1656, P27 (Ohio Ct. App. 2004) (applying Ohio disclosure requirement).

C.   RELIANCE ON INADMISSIBLE DATA

McCLELLAN v. MORRISON
434 A.2d 28 (Me. 1981)

McKusick, Chief Justice.

In this automobile negligence action, tried to a jury in Lincoln County, plaintiff Donna McClellan appeals from a Superior Court judgment in favor of defendant Dean P. Morrison, Jr., Plaintiff's two claims of error on appeal relate to the admission of a physician's opinion on causation and to the jury's special verdict that, even though defendant's negligence was the proximate cause of the automobile collision, plaintiff suffered no damages therefrom. We deny her appeal.

On Friday evening, June 16, 1978, plaintiff was a passenger in a car driven by her brother, Durwood Lewis, on Route 27 in Boothbay. The accident giving rise to this litigation occurred when a vehicle driven by defendant and approaching the Lewis car from the opposite direction crossed the highway's center line and struck the Lewis car. At the trial of her suit for damages on account of alleged personal injuries, plaintiff testified that she was aware immediately after the accident of having sustained a sizable lump on the left side of her head, a bruised right knee, and a cut on the left elbow. She did not, however, go to a hospital because she believed the injuries were not serious. Over the weekend she suffered severe headaches that caused her to sleep most of the time. After trying unsuccessfully to work Monday morning, she visited her personal physician, Dr. Carl R. Griffin, that afternoon. On examining her, he found tiny abrasions on her left elbow and right knee and a subsiding lump on the side of her head. He prescribed medication for the head injury. Plaintiff testified that her headaches persisted for a couple of weeks and then went away.

Following the accident, plaintiff testified, she also experienced a minor ache in her left elbow. In about November 1978 the ache became worse and plaintiff began also to feel a tingling sensation in her left hand. In January 1979, at plaintiff's regular medical checkup, Dr. Griffin determined that her symptoms were caused by her ulnar nerve's lying too loosely in the ulnar groove of the elbow. To correct that condition, Dr. Griffin operated on plaintiff's left arm in February 1979, moving the ulnar nerve out of the ulnar cavity and repositioning it next to the skin. Following that procedure, plaintiff continued to experience numbness in the fourth and fifth fingers of her left hand; she could use her arm but not as extensively as previously. At trial, plaintiff could recall no injury to her elbow other than the one that occurred at the time of the automobile accident.

The jury returned a special verdict concluding that defendant's negligence caused the collision, but that plaintiff was entitled to recover no damages. Plaintiff then moved in the alternative for a judgment notwithstanding the verdict or for a new trial, asserting that the evidence was insufficient to warrant the verdict. The presiding justice denied both motions[51] and plaintiff now appeals.

I.

At trial, defendant offered the testimony of plaintiffs personal physician, Dr. Griffin. The doctor testified that in his opinion there was no causal connection between the June 1978 accident and the injury to plaintiffs ulnar nerve. Plaintiff asserts that Dr. Griffin had based his opinion in part on a telephone conversation he had with a Portland neurosurgeon after the surgery and that, since the contents of the conversation would not themselves have been admissible, the doctor's opinion should not have been admitted either. We disagree.

M.R. Evid. 703, entitled "Basis of Opinion Testimony by Experts," reads in full as follows:

> The facts or data in the particular case upon which an expert bases an opinion or inference may be those perceived by or made known to him at or before the hearing. If of a type reasonably relied upon by experts in the particular field in forming opinions or inferences upon the subject, the facts or data need not be admissible in evidence.

Where an expert has relied on inadmissible material in forming his opinion and that material would not be used by experts other than for the purpose of preparing to testify at trial, his opinion testimony will not be admitted. *See State v. Rolls*, 389 A.2d 824, 829–30 (Me. 1978), citing and quoting FIELD & MURRAY, MAINE EVIDENCE § 7C3.2 at 175 (Me. 1976). However, the purpose of Rule 703 is not to exclude testimony, but rather "to bring judicial practice into line with the practice of experts themselves when not in court." Advisers' Note to M. R. Evid. 703; *State v. Rolls, supra* at 829. Thus, if the proponent of expert opinion testimony based on underlying matter that is itself inadmissible is able to show that experts in the field ordinarily rely on similar facts or data in forming their conclusions, the opinion testimony will be admitted. *Id.* The admissibility of such opinion testimony is to be determined by the presiding justice, whose ruling will not be overturned unless

---

[51] [1] The presiding justice correctly denied the motion for judgment n.o.v. because plaintiff had made no motion for a directed verdict at the close of the evidence. M.R. Civ. P. 50(b).

clearly erroneous. *See State v. Bridges*, 413 A.2d 937, 942 (Me. 1980).

On this record, the presiding justice's ruling admitting Dr. Griffin's testimony was not clearly erroneous. Prior to going on the stand and testifying to his opinion as to the lack of causal relationship between the June 1978 accident and plaintiff's ulnar nerve condition, Dr. Griffin had consulted by telephone with a Portland neurosurgeon concerning the matter; exactly what the Portland physician told Dr. Griffin was, however, never revealed. In addition, Dr. Griffin had himself had training and experience qualifying him to give that opinion as to causation. He had performed the same ulnar nerve surgery on others and had twice undergone the procedure as a patient himself. He testified that during the surgery on plaintiff he had observed no scar tissue in her elbow and that he would normally have expected to see scar tissue had the ulnar nerve been injured at the time of the automobile accident some eight months earlier.

Based on his own training, experience, and observations, Dr. Griffin was fully qualified to give his expert medical opinion that plaintiffs ulnar nerve condition was not related to the June 1978 automobile accident. His telephone consultation with a Portland neurosurgeon was but one of the deliberative steps he took in forming his opinion as to the cause of plaintiff's particular elbow problem. In conferring with another medical expert, Dr. Griffin was merely following a procedure similar to consulting a medical textbook to obtain a confirmation of his own tentative conclusion. His expert medical opinion was no less his own by reason of having been backed up by his consultation with another expert. There was no error in the Superior Court's admission of that opinion testimony.

Judgment affirmed.

NOTES AND QUESTIONS

1.   As originally enacted, Rule 703 was criticized for creating, in effect, abroad exception to the rule against hearsay. *See* Blakely, *An Introduction to the Oklahoma Evidence Code: The Thirty-Fourth Hearsay Exception: Information Relied upon as a Basis for Admissible Expert Opinion*, 16 TULSA L.J. 1 (1980). In response, Congress amended the Rule by adding the last sentence of the current version. Does this amendment cure the problem? Under what circumstances should the trial judge allow an expert to state the basis for his opinion when it reflects otherwise inadmissible information? If the judge does not permit the expert to state the basis for his opinion,, the impact of his testimony might be diminished, but disclosure of basis risks exposing the jury to prejudicial evidence that is not ordinarily admissible. Can a suitable jury instruction be framed to resolve this problem? *Cf. Brennan v. Reinhart Institutional Foods*, 211 F.3d 449, 450–451 (8th Cir. 2000).

2.   Compare the following Ohio rule of evidence: "The facts or data in the particular case upon which an expert bases an opinion or inference may be those perceived by him or admitted in evidence at the hearing." Ohio Rule of Evidence 703.

3.   May a judge disregard an expert's assertion that the facts or data at issue are of a type reasonably relied upon by experts in the particular field, if the judge

considers the facts or data unreliable? *See In re Japanese Electronics Products Antitrust Litigation*, 723 F.2d 238 (3d Cir. 1983). Courts are divided over whether inadmissible data may be used by experts if it is merely of a type reasonably relied upon by experts in the field or whether an additional finding must be made that the data is sufficiently reliable. Is there necessarily a difference between these two approaches? *See United States v. Corey*, 207 F.3d 84, 88 (1st Cir. 2000); *In re "Agent Orange" Product Liability Litigation*, 611 F. Supp. 1223 (E.D.N.Y. 1985).

Evidentiary Foundation: The Trial of Richard Herrin[52]

[Richard Herrin, a Mexican-American from a Los Angeles barrio, was a Yale undergraduate who bludgeoned to death his girlfriend, Bonnie Garland (also a Yale student), on July 6, 1977. Herrin's actions allegedly occurred because he was distraught over Ms. Garland's decision to terminate their relationship. At his trial, Herrin relied principally upon the insanity defense. Although he was convicted of manslaughter, the trial has been criticized for exemplifying the courts' tendency to concern themselves with the plight of the defendant rather than the victim.]

[The following testimony by prosecution witness Dr. A. Leonard Abrams sought to establish Herrin's sanity. Was this testimony within the permissible bounds of expert testimony?]

Q. In this case, when you spoke with the Defendant, Richard Herrin, sir, what were you looking for?

A. I was looking for psychotic manifestations. I found none.

Q. Now, Doctor, we've heard some testimony in this Court — we've heard the word "psychosis." Could you tell us what that means, sir?

A. Yes. A psychosis is a major mental illness, which includes the inability to think, the inability to communicate, usually manifested by delusions, by hallucinations, disorientation.

Q. All right. Now, in relation to this Defendant, Richard Herrin, sir, do you have an opinion as to whether or not he, in the early morning hours of July 7, 1977, was suffering from a psychosis, sir?

A. It is my opinion that he was not.

Q. Did you find any indications of psychosis in the materials you've reviewed, sir?

A. I found no indication of psychosis. Absolutely not.

Q. All right. Now, Doctor, do you have an opinion as to whether or not this Defendant, Richard Herrin, again in the early morning hours of July 7, 1977, as a result of a mental disease or defect, lacked substantial capacity to know or appreciate the nature and consequences of his conduct, or that such conduct was wrong?

[52] Excerpted from W. GAYLIN, THE KILLING OF BONNIE GARLAND 187–91. Copyright © 1982 by Pip Enterprises, Inc. Reprinted by permission of Simon & Schuster, Inc.

A.   My opinion is that he was not psychotic, that he did not lack substantial ability to understand what was going on, or that it was wrong.

Q.   All right. Now, Doctor, as a result of, again, your examination and the documents that you've reviewed, sir, did you find any indication that this Defendant suffered from a mental disease or defect?

A.   He did not suffer from a mental disease or defect. There was absolutely no indication anywhere in all that I've reviewed — that there was such a situation.

Q.   Just with particularity, referring to the early morning hours of July 7, 1977, when he struck Bonnie Garland in the head with a hammer?

A.   That is my opinion.

Q.   Now, do you have an opinion, Doctor, as to whether or not in the early morning hours of July 7, 1977, this Defendant suffered from an extreme, unusual, or overwhelming environmental stress?

A.   It was my opinion that he did not. He did suffer from stress, in a sense of that there was a romance that he was having a problem with. But there was not an overwhelming stress.

Q.   Okay. Now, Doctor, assume that this Defendant — and again, this is a hypothetical, Doctor — assume that this Defendant, sometime before hitting Bonnie in the head with the hammer — when I say, "sometime," I'm referring to thirty to ninety minutes prior to hitting her in the head with a hammer — made a decision that he would kill Bonnie and kill himself, and that after making that decision, Doctor, he considered the use of several weapons to carry out his intent to kill — that is he considered the use of a beer mug, stockings, and eventually settled on and used a hammer in this case, sir — does that tell you anything medically, sir?

A.   Yes. It tells me that his thinking processes were going on, that he was intact. The very fact that he remembers this is of interest, too, because it indicates, for example, there is no impairment of memory, and that he was aware of what was happening or what was going on.

Q.   What is the significance, Doctor, medically speaking, of no impairment of memory?

A.   Well, if someone has impaired memory, that would indicate a psychosis, a form of psychosis.

Q.   Now, assume further, Doctor, that after picking up the hammer, he went from the area of the kitchen, where he got the hammer, to a room on the first floor of the Garland residence, where he took the hammer and wrapped it in a towel, and while doing that, he noticed a two-page note written by Mrs. Garland, on legal paper, that he picked up the note, read it, put the note back on the bed, went upstairs to the bedroom in which Bonnie Garland was sleeping, laid the hammer down in the towel outside of Bonnie Garland's bedroom

A.

Q.

A.

Q.

A.

Q.

A.

Q.

A.

Q.

door, went into the bedroom, made sure that Bonnie was still asleep, came back out to the hallway, retrieved the towel with the hammer in it, went back into Bonnie's room, placed the towel with the hammer in it under Bonnie's bed, made sure she was still asleep, then took the hammer, and hit her in the head with it, Doctor. What does that tell you medically, sir, about the state of the man's mind at that time on the morning of July 7, 1977.

A. That he absolutely was not psychotic.

Q. And what are your reasons for that, Doctor?

A. Because somebody that would be psychotic might — would not behave in a way as not to be detected. After all, this is what he was doing. He didn't want to be detected, and this is what the activity indicated. So, he was protecting himself. Psychotic people do not protect themselves.

Q. Assume further, Doctor, that after leaving Bonnie Garland's bedroom, he took the keys — withdrawn. While in Bonnie Garland's bedroom, he took the keys to a family car, left the Garland house, began to drive this car around Westchester County, with the intent of avoiding detection by the Police. What does that indicate to you, if anything, medically speaking, sir?

A. It indicated the individual was not psychotic.

Q. And for what reasons do you say that, sir?

A. Because he is thinking things through. He does not want to be detected.

Q. All right. Now, assume that the — assume, Doctor, that the Defendant, in thinking about suicide, thought about crashing this 1974 Impala automobile into an abutment of some type, but thought that he might not die because the hood of the car was too large, sir. Does that indicate anything to you medically?

A. Yes. That he is thinking things through. He is making decisions. Psychotic people don't think things through. They spontaneously respond. They don't know why they respond.

But here there is mentation going on, there is thinking, ideation going on. He differentiates in his mind which way to commit suicide. This is not a psychotic way of functioning.

Q. When you spoke with the Defendant, sir, in January of 1978, in the presence of his attorney, did you discuss with him, sir, the various methodologies that he claims he thought about committing suicide with?

A. Mentioned them.

Q. Doctor, in examining this Defendant and in examining the various data which you already testified to, sir, do you find any history of previous psychiatric treatment, sir?

A.   There was absolutely no indication from my examination or from the examinations of the other doctors that there was any previous psychiatric help or hospitalization.

Q.   What does that indicate to you medically speaking, sir?

A.   That the individual is not psychotic. There was no basis to make a determination that he was psychotic.

Q.   All right. Now, you mentioned earlier that you had occasion to review the Report of a gentleman by the name of Lawrence Abt; is that correct, sir?

A.   Yes. He is a psychologist.

Q.   Did you read his report, sir?

A.   I certainly did.

Q.   And what did that Report indicate to you?

A.   Indicated to me that this individual had a high I.Q. and that there was absolutely no indication of psychoses in the psychological testing. Absolutely no indication.

And it is interesting, because psychological tests — very often where there is psychosis in an individual who then becomes well or goes into remission, very often you find a residual of psychotic manifestations in the psychological testing. In this case, there was absolutely no indication of any kind of psychotic manifestation.

Q.   Doctor, you also mentioned to us that you had occasion to review a Report of the Forensic Unit at the County Jail; is that correct, sir?

A.   Yes.

Q.   All right. What, if anything, sir, did that Report indicate to you?

A.   Well, I think that is a very, very significant Report. That Report was made on July 8th, the day after the incident. It revealed that there was no psychos is present. This was done by a Dr. Harvey Lothringer at the Jail, who indicated that there was no psychotic manifestations of psychosis at that time. This is the next day.

Q.   And what does that mean, the closeness in time, Doctor?

A.   Well, I think that is as close as you possibly can get to the situation, to know what the situation was at the time of the incident.

Q.   Doctor, you're aware, sir, are you not, that the Defendant struck Bonnie several times in the head with a hammer.

A.   Yes.

Q.   Could you tell us, Doctor, based upon everything that you've studied in this case — that is, the interview with the Defendant and the other documents that you've outlined for us — what was, in your opinion, sir, based on a reasonable degree of medical certainty —

what is the state of the Defendant's mind at the time he struck Bonnie?

A.   Well, the very fact that he remembers in detail what happened at the particular time indicates that he was intact and that there was no psychosis. That is what it means. If an individual was psychotic and was responding and doing this in a psychotic state, they wouldn't remember the details, the completeness; the gurgling, the eyes falling back. They wouldn't remember this. This doesn't indicate a psychotic individual.

Q.   Doctor, what about the memory for details in a person who — if a person suffered an extreme reaction to an overwhelming environmental stress, sir?

A.   I don't quite understand what you're saying.

Q.   Yes. In a person — if a person suffered an extreme emotional reaction to an overwhelming environmental stress, would they be able to recall the details of their actions while under this stress, sir?

A.   Not if they were psychotic.

Q.   Did you, sir, find, in any of your interviews with the Defendant, or any of the other documents, any indication of mental disease or defect in Richard Herrin, sir?

A.   Absolutely none.

D. IMPEACHMENT, CROSS-EXAMINATION, AND RELATED PROBLEMS

1. Impeachment by Cross-Examination

JOHN H. WIGMORE, A POCKET CODE OF THE RULES OF EVIDENCE IN TRIALS AT LAW 137 (1910)[53]

General Principle of Impeachment. The process of introducing evidence tending to diminish the trustworthiness of a person whose testimonial statement has been already admitted as evidence is termed Impeachment.

JOHN H. WIGMORE, 5 EVIDENCE § 1367 (3d ed. 1940)[54]

Cross-examination as a distinctive and vital feature of our law. For two centuries past, the policy of the Anglo-American system of evidence has been to regard the necessity of testing by cross-examination as a vital feature of the law. The belief that no safeguard for testing the value of human statements is

---

[53] Reprinted by permission of Little, Brown and Company, Boston, 1910.

[54] Reprinted by permission of Little, Brown and Company, Boston, 1940.

comparable to that furnished by cross-examination, and the conviction that no statement (unless by special exception) should be used as testimony until it has been probed and sublimated by that test, has found increasing strength in lengthening experience.

Not even the abuses, the mishandlings, and the puerilities which are so often associated with cross-examination have availed to nullify its value. It may be that in more than one sense it takes the place in our system which torture occupied in the mediaeval system of the civilians. Nevertheless, it is beyond any doubt the greatest legal engine ever invented for the discovery of truth. However difficult it may be for the layman, the scientist, or the foreign jurist to appreciate this its wonderful power, there has probably never been a moment's doubt upon this point in the mind of a lawyer of experience. "You can do anything," said Wendell Phillips, "with a bayonet — except sit upon it." A lawyer can do anything with a cross-examination — if he is skillful enough not to impale his own cause upon it. He may, it is true, do more than he ought to do; he may "make the worse appear the better reason, to perplex and dash maturest counsels" — may make the truth appear like falsehood. But this abuse of its power is able to be remedied by proper control. The fact of this unique and irresistible power remains, and is the reason for our faith in its merits. If we omit political considerations of broader range, then cross examination, not trial by jury, is the great and permanent contribution of the Anglo-American system of law to improved methods of trial procedure.

Striking illustrations of its power to expose inaccuracies and falsehoods are plentiful in our records; and it is apparent enough, in some of the great Continental trials, that the failures of justice could hardly have occurred under the practice of effective cross-examination . . .

NOTES AND QUESTIONS

1.   Impeachment can be effected either by cross-examination or via contradiction testimony of another witness. Impeachment by contradiction rests on the inference that if the witness made a mistake on one fact, he may be mistaken on other facts, and, therefore, all of his testimony may be untrustworthy. 3 WEINSTEIN'S EVIDENCE § 607.06 (1997). The admissibility of such contradiction testimony, however, has traditionally been dependent upon the significance of the point in issue. In general, if the point in issue is relatively minor, the matter is deemed "collateral" and thereby inadmissible. But courts have experienced difficulty in determining when proffered contradiction testimony is merely collateral. *See* 3 WEINSTEIN'S EVIDENCE § 607.06[03] (1997). While the principal focus of this chapter will be on impeachment by cross-examination, the matter of contradiction impeachment will nevertheless be a recurring theme.

2.   Given the importance of impeachment by cross-examination, what result is appropriate when intervening circumstances prevent a witness from being cross-examined? *See* Note, *Evidence — Admissibility of Direct Examination Where No Opportunity to Finish Cross Examination Is Given*, 9 ARK. L. REV. 170 (1954). *See generally People v. Rogers*, 650 N.W.2d 338 (Mich. Ct. App. 2001).

2.   Impeaching Your Own Witness: The Vouching Rule

COLLEDGE'S TRIAL
8 How. St. Tr. 549, 636 (1681)

[Remarks of Lord Chief Justice North to the defendant:]

Look you, Mr. Colledge, I will tell you something for law, and to set you right; whatsoever witnesses you call, you call them as witnesses to testify the truth for you; and if you ask them any questions, you must take what they have said for truth: . . . Let him answer if you will; but you must not afterwards go to disprove him.

[Colledge was executed.]

Note, *Impeaching One's Own Witness*
49 VA. L. REV. 996 (1963)[55]

The rule of evidence which prohibits impeachment of a witness by the party calling him is one of the most ancient of the common-law principles, and it is also, to some minds, one of the most anachronistic. Although the exact origin of the rule is unknown, scholars have advanced three major theories concerning its genesis. One theory traces the rule to . . . Roman law, whereas a second school of thought finds its origin in the development of trial by compurgation during the Middle Ages in England and on the continent. Dean Ladd, however, advances the hypothesis that "a more probable origin of the rule can be found in the transition from the inquisitorial method of trial as it gradually emerged into an adversary system."

In spite of the disagreement as to the exact derivation of the rule, the authorities are agreed that it was formulated at a time when issue was joined at trial on the basis of testimony given by "oath helpers," usually relatives or close friends brought along by the parties to testify to their veracity rather than to the occurrence of facts. Understandably, it was thought just to hold the litigants to the testimony their "witnesses" produced. Modern methods of litigation, however, demand a different service of the witness. Under present-day conditions most witnesses

---

[55] Reprinted with permission.

testify to facts relevant to the dispute rather than to the veracity of the parties. These considerations, among others, have moved many commentators to question the utility of the principle prohibiting impeachment of one's own witness.

JOHNSON v. BALTIMORE & O.R. CO.
208 F.2d 633 (3d Cir. 1952)

GOODRICH, Circuit Judge.

This is an action brought by the administratrix of a decedent under the Pennsylvania Fiduciaries Act of 1917 to recover damages for an alleged wrongful death. The acts complained of, the injury and the death all occurred in Pennsylvania. The only basis for federal jurisdiction is diversity and the substantive law rules which govern are those of Pennsylvania. It may be said at the outset that the case presents no problem with regard to substantive rules of tort law. The plaintiff won in the district court and defendant appeals.

The factual background is one of bizarre and unusual circumstances. The decedent was a man named George Johnson, age approximately 35. That he was shot and killed by a railroad policeman named Clyde Hall is clear from all the testimony and not denied by the defendant. The defense is that Hall was working in the course of his duty as a railroad policeman, had a reasonable belief that Johnson had committed the felony of "angle-cocking"[56] and while attempting to take him into custody was forced to shoot Johnson to save his own life. Hall's story was that as he attempted to put handcuffs on Johnson he received a blow in the face from the latter which knocked him down and temporarily dazed him. As Hall recovered consciousness, he says, he was aware that Johnson was astride his thighs brandishing a knife with apparent intent to deal a fatal blow. Testimony from several witnesses, in addition to Hall, corroborated the fact that Hall was, on the occasion in question, rather badly cutup.

As above stated the case did seem to present a fairly simple fact question: Did Hall kill Johnson in the reasonable belief that such killing was necessary to save his own life? If he did, the killing was justified and there is no civil or criminal liability involved. *See* RESTATEMENT, TORTS § 65 (1934).

The description of the brief but tragic encounter came from the testimony of Hall. The other participant, Johnson, died within a short time after the affray. There were other witnesses on subordinate points. The trier of the facts did not believe Hall's story. The main question in the case is whether there is some rule of law which says his story must stand for the purpose of this litigation as a true account of the transaction whether the jury believed it or not.

To the above statement it should be added that Hall was called as a witness by the plaintiff upon the judge's suggestion that up to the time he was called there was not a sufficient case made out on which the plaintiff could recover. We agree with the trial judge on that. Without Hall's story or part of it there was not a sufficiently clear

---

[56] [2] "Angle-cocking" is the illegal halting of a train by application of an air valve. *See* Pa. Stat. Ann. tit. 18, § 4919.

outline of the facts and circumstances to give a jury anything to pass upon.

The plaintiff having called Hall, is he necessarily bound by everything Hall said? We could probably dispose of this case and be technically sound in doing so by saying that, whatever the rule may be with regard to the question framed, the defendant has lost his chance to raise the point. After the testimony was closed, counsel for the defense made a motion for directed verdict. The court asked him if he had the authorities he was going to give the court "that the plaintiff is bound by the testimony of Hall whom he called as his witness." Counsel apologized for not having been able to look up the authorities, due to the press of other business, and after a short colloquy with the court said: "I will say that I abandon my position in that regard, because I don't have what your Honor asked me to get." If counsel had, in the pressing business of trying a case and having to look after other matters at the same time, inadvertently conceded the determining point of law, we should hesitate to hold him to that concession. But here we do not think that he gave away anything by abandoning the point he had raised.

During the argument Rule 43(b) Fed. R. Civ. P., 28 U.S.C., was talked about. That rule permits a party to interrogate an unwilling or hostile witness by leading questions and it makes provision for calling an adverse party for something comparable to cross-examination.

That rule is not in this case. The plaintiff did not call Hall as an adverse party or an unwilling witness. We are not saying that he would be compelled to designate him by that label if he wanted to take advantage of Rule 43(b). The point is that counsel for the plaintiff simply called Hall as a witness and asked him questions in the same way as he did the other witnesses. He asked for no special privileges with regard to the examination. We think, therefore, that Rule 43(b) has nothing to do with this case.

Then there is the further question whether, when one calls a witness, everything which that witness says, so far as the party calling him is concerned, must be taken as gospel truth. . . . [Previously, we have not been] called upon to repudiate the old rule that a party is bound by the testimony of his witness.

When witnesses were called by a party from among his friends to act as compurgators it was completely rational that the party calling them would have to stand by what they said. After all he chose his friends. But when witnesses a recalled, in some stranger's lawsuit, to tell about things they saw, heard, or did, there is no reason in logic or common sense or fairness why the party who calls them should have to vouch for everything they say. All this has been said vigorously and strikingly by Dean Wigmore, who stated: "There is no substantial reason for preserving this rule, — the remnant of a primitive notion." It is onlynecessary to cite Wigmore for full discussion of the matter.[57]

All the modern writers in the law of evidence speak to the same effect. Thus, Edmund M. Morgan, in a forthcoming book,[58] says:

---

[57] [4] 3 WIGMORE ON EVIDENCE 383, 389 (3d ed. 1940).

[58] [5] MORGAN, BASIC PROBLEMS OF EVIDENCE (to be published by the Committee on Continuing Legal Education of the American Law Institute).

The fact is that the general prohibition, if it ever had any basis in reason, has no place in any rational system of investigation in modern society. And all attempts to modify it or qualify it so as to reach sensible results serve only to demonstrate its irrationality and to increase the uncertainties of litigation.

John M. Maguire also has attacked the rule:

According to the best professional thought, sweeping prohibition of impeachment by a party of his own witnesses is nonsense — most regretably not simple nonsense, but very complex nonsense. . . .[59]

Likewise, see John E. Tracy: "The reasons given for this rule . . . are none of them very sound."[60] In an exhaustive article, Mason Ladd advocates "complete abolition of the rule" and proposes as a statutory substitute: "No party shall be precluded from impeaching a witness because the witness is his Own."[61] Finally, the Model Code of Evidence framed by the American Law Institute abolishes the prohibition: ". . . for the purpose of impairing or supporting the credibility of a witness, any party including the party calling him may examine him and introduce extrinsic evidence concerning any conduct by him and any other matter relevant upon the issue of his credibility as a witness."

*   *   *

Nothing could make the rule look more foolish than its application in a case like this. Only two people were present when this affray occurred and one of them died immediately after. The employer of the survivor is being sued. What could be more human than that Hall would make his story show the propriety of his own conduct and the wrongfulness of that of his opponent in the fight. And what would be sillier than to insist that the jury is compelled to believe all that testimony which the witness offered in explanation of an intentional killing on his part?

There were some points at which the witness, Hall, could well not have been believed. His identification of Johnson at night, seen through the opening between two cars of a freight train, is one. A quick shifting of a gun from left to right hand in the course of exchange of blows that could have lasted but a few seconds is another. But most of all is the background of the interest of this witness in establishing an impression favorable to himself.

The judge, in a very thorough charge, left the critical questions in the case clearly to the jury. They must have known just exactly what they were doing, as well as one can tell from seeing the way the case was left to them. The trial judge said that he would not have come to the conclusion which the jury did. Perhaps we would not either, were we to judge the facts. But this case has been submitted to two juries. (A third jury passed on the question of damages only.) One disagreed; the other brought in a verdict for the plaintiff. Trial by jury is no litmus test for finding what

---

[59] [6] MAGUIRE, EVIDENCE — COMMON SENSE AND COMMON LAW 43 (1947).

[60] [7] TRACY, HANDBOOK OF THE LAW OF EVIDENCE 193 (1952).

[61] [8] Ladd, *Impeachment of One's Own Witness — New Developments*, 4 U. OF CHI. L. REV. 69, 96 (1936).

is true or false but it is the system which we have. Twelve responsible citizens, under oath sworn to give their verdict on the law and evidence, have decided the fact issues. The judge has put the law accurately to them. Whether he or we agree with their conclusion is not the determining factor.

*   *   *

The judgment of the district court will be affirmed.

3. The Scope of Cross-Examination

CHARLES T. McCORMICK,
HANDBOOK OF THE LAW OF EVIDENCE § 21
(4th ed. 1992)[62]

The practice varies widely in the different jurisdictions on the question whether the cross-examiner is confined in his questions to the subjects testified about in the direct examination, and if so to what extent.

The traditional rule of wide-open cross-examination. In England and in about one-fifth of the states, the simplest and freest practice prevails. In these jurisdictions, the cross-examiner is not limited to the topics which the direct examiner has chosen to open, but is free to cross-examine about any subject relevant to any of the issues in the entire case, including facts relating solely to the cross-examiner's own case or affirmative defence.

The "restrictive" rule, in various forms, limiting cross-examination to the scope of the direct. The majority of states have agreed in the view that the cross-examination must be limited to the matters testified to on the direct examination. This general rule was adopted by Federal Rule of Evidence 611(b).This doctrine can be employed narrowly to restrict the cross-questions to those relating only to the same acts or facts, and, perhaps, those occurring or appearing at the same time and place. The doctrine has often been formulated in a way to suggest this meaning. Thus, the cross-examination has been said to be limited to "the same points" brought out on direct, to the "matters testified to," to the "subjects mentioned," and the like. Slightly more expansive is the extension to "facts and circumstances connected with" the matters stated on direct, but this still suggests the requirement of identity of transaction, and proximity in time and space. Seemingly a much wider extension is accomplished by another variation of the formula. This is the statement that the cross-examination is limited to the matters opened in direct and to facts tending "to explain, contradict, or discredit the testimony given in chief," and even more widely, facts tending to rebut any "inference or deduction" from the matters testified on direct. There is little consistency in the expression and the use of formulas, even in the same jurisdiction. All express criteria are too vague to be employed with precision. Assuming that cross-examination is somehow to be limited to the subject matter of the direct examination, the subject matter of questions on direct examination can always be defined in particular instances with greater or

---

[62] Reprinted with permission from McCORMICK'S HANDBOOK OF THE LAW OF EVIDENCE, Fourth Edition. Copyright © 1992 by West Publishing Co.

lesser generality regardless of the general formulas.

All these limiting formulas have a common escape valve, namely, the notion that where part of a transaction, "res gestae," contract, or conversation has been revealed on direct, the remainder may be brought out on cross examination. The fact that this is substantially a mere statement of the converse of the limiting rule itself does not detract from its usefulness as an added tool for argument. This particular rule of completeness is unaffected by Federal Rule of Evidence 106, which does not apply to cross-examination after testimony upon direct. Another escape valve for appeal purposes is the notion that the trial judge has a certain amount of discretion in ruling upon the scope of cross-examination.

David W. Louisell & Christopher B. Mueller, 3 Federal Evidence § 332 (1979)[63]

Subdivision (b): Scope of cross-examination. The first sentence of this subdivision endorses pre-Rules federal tradition, by limiting cross-examination to the subject matter of the direct examination and matters affecting witness credibility. The second sentence authorizes the trial judge to permit inquiry into additional matters, "as if on direct examination."

The endorsement of the traditional scope-of-direct limit was highly controversial. Although the Advisory Committee's original draft of Rule 611(b) proposed substantially the language which Congress ultimately enacted, the Committee's intervening two drafts, which included the language endorsed by the Court and transmitted to Congress, would have done away with the scope-of-direct limit in favor of wide open cross-examination, in the following terms:

> A witness may be cross-examined on any matter relevant to any issue in the case, including credibility. In the interests of justice, the judge may limit cross examination with respect to matters not testified to on direct examination.

During the House hearings, the Chairman of the Advisory Committee, Albert

E. Jenner, Esq., described the difficulties which attended the Committee's resolution of the scope-of-direct problem:

Mr. JENNER.   The committee went up the mountain and down the mountain on the question of the scope of cross-examination. The rule in the Federal court today is and has been that the scope of cross-examination is limited to the scope of the direct examination.

There are very strong views around the country that the scope of cross-examination should not be limited, [and] even under the present law the scope of cross-examination is not limited where a party is a witness.

You may ask a party any questions. He tenders the whole issue when he is on the stand. Well, the committee took many votes on this

---

subject. It was either one way or the other by 1 vote. It was 8 to 7 one way or the other and [in] the final vote, virtually within the last few weeks of the meetings of the committee, the committee opted for the present proposed rule 611 that the scope of cross examination be limited to the direct.

Now, there is an area in which the Congress . . . may very well [differ] — it is a close question. Litigators are of the view that the scope of cross should be limited to the direct. The scholars in their great wisdom feel that should be wide open as it is now [in the version of Rule 611(b) endorsed by the Court].

Mr. CLEARY.   I think we could probably a line [sic] the judges on our side, Mr. Chairman.

Mr. JENNER.   Align those judges who had not been litigators before they assumed the bench.

Mr. HUNGATE.   They will have to qualify as scholars then, won't they?

Mr. SMITH.   On your final option was it still a one vote decision?

Mr. JENNER.   Yes, it was, one vote.

Judge MARIS.   It was one vote in the Advisory Committee. It was by one vote in the Standing Committee [of the Judicial Conference on Rules of Practice and Procedure]. We [on the Standing Committee]approved the draft that the majority of that [Advisory] [C]ommittee had presented.

The House Judiciary Committee reinstated the Advisory Committee's original language, thus endorsing the scope-of-direct standard. In its accompanying Report, the Committee noted that it was returning to the practice which "prevails in the federal courts and thirty-nine state jurisdictions"; it also noted that the traditional rule "facilitates orderly presentation by each party" and observed that "in light of existing discovery procedures, there appears to be no need to abandon the traditional rule." The Senate Judiciary Committee concurred, noting that the need for "an orderly and predictable development of the evidence" weighs in favor of the traditional rule, and adding that the Committee approves the grant of discretionary authority of the trial judge to permit additional inquiry on cross-examination "whenever appropriate."

NOTES AND QUESTIONS

1.   The unrestricted rule originally proposed by the Supreme Court, has served as the basis for legislation in several states. For example, in Maine, the state evidentiary rule provides "A witness may be cross-examined on any matter relevant to any issue in the case, including credibility. In the interests of justice, the court may limit cross-examination with respect to matters not testified to on direct examination." Maine Rule of Evidence 611(b) (2006); *see also* Michigan Rule of Evidence 611 (2006).

2.   Three reasons have traditionally been advanced in support of the restrictive rule: a) a party vouches for the credibility of his witness only to the extent of direct examination; b) a party may not ask, in effect, his own witness leading questions; and c) the restrictive practice preserves the orderly presentation of proof. *See* Notes of Advisory Committee on Proposed Rules, Fed. R. Evid. 611. To what extent are these reasons still valid today?

3.   What special problem concerning the scope of cross-examination is raised when a defendant wants to testify in a criminal case? *See generally*, Nesson & Leota, *The Fifth Amendment Privilege Against Cross-Examination*, 85 GEO. L.J. 1627 (1997); Carlson, *Cross Examination of the Accused*, 52 CORNELL L.Q. 705 (1967).

4.   Impeachment Modes

a.   Pursuing the Competence Factors

IRVING YOUNGER,
THE ART OF CROSS-EXAMINATION
2–7 (1976)[64]

. . . What are the first four modes of impeachment? Although he may not think about them in these terms, every trial lawyer uses the first four modes of impeachment every single time he is in court. He learned about these first four modes of impeachment, perhaps abstractly and imperfectly, in an evidence course in law school. They are based on the elements of competence — the eligibility of a human being to take the witness stand. Now, what does it take for a human being to be eligible to take the witness stand today? We put aside incompetence by reason of status, the dead man's statutes, spousal incompetence, the incompetence of a judge or a juror to testify in that very trial; we need to consider the great mass of proposed witnesses, ordinary persons. What is it that must be present before the ordinary person is eligible to take the witness stand as a competent witness?

Four elements must be present. What is the first thing that happens when you call someone to the stand? Think back to last week or ahead to next week. You are in your home courtroom. The judge says, "Call your next witness." You look around and realize that you do not have a next witness; the doctor has not yet arrived. What do you do? You know what to do. You turn to the audience, and you say, "You. Take the stand." It does not matter who it is. Waste a lot of time. Meanwhile, maybe the doctor will arrive. Is the person eligible to be a witness? Not yet. The first requirement of competence is that the person take the oath or some substitute for the oath. "I swear to tell the truth," or "I affirm to tell the truth," or "I promise to tell the truth," or "As one grandfather to another, Your Honor, I will tell the truth," or something like that. If he says that he will not take the oath or some substitute for the oath, he is not competent. He may go to jail for contempt, but he may not take the stand to testify. The first requirement of competence is that he take the oath.

---

[64] Copyright, American Bar Association, 1976. Reprinted by permission.

What is the second requirement? He has taken the oath. Now what? You ask, "What did you see or hear or smell or touch or taste?" The witness must have perceived — through one or more of his five senses — something which relates to the transaction that forms the subject matter of the lawsuit. The second requirement is perception. We call the witness to the stand. He takes the oath. No problem. "Sir, did you see the accident?" "No, I did not." "Where were you?" "I was in Europe." What happens now? "Well," the judge says, "thank you for your assistance; you may go home, sir." He is an incompetent witness; he perceived nothing.

The third element of competence requires that we move from time past — when the transaction that forms the subject matter of this lawsuit occurred — to time present in the courtroom. In other words, we must establish memory, recollection or remembrance; we must bridge the temporal gap. The witness must remember something of what he perceived concerning the transaction that is the subject matter of the lawsuit. "Take the oath." "Yes, sir." "Did you see the accident?" "Yes, sir." We have satisfied the first two requirements. "What do you remember seeing?" "Nothing." "Go home. You are incompetent." He has failed to satisfy the third requirement.

Finally, the witness must satisfy a fourth requirement. The witness must be able to get across to the jury or the judge the substance of what he perceived and presently remembers about the transaction in question. The witness must be able to communicate in some rational fashion what he remembers perceiving — typically, in the English language, or in a foreign language if that is necessary. He can write it out if he is unable to speak, or he can use the international sign language. The only requirement is that the mode of communication be rational.

Oath

At trial, the most frequently raised question of competence concerns the capacity of a witness to take the oath. Almost every trial lawyer has been involved in a trial in which a child has been called to the witness stand — an eight-year-old, a nine-year-old, a ten-year-old. What does the lawyer do? If tactically appropriate, he raises a question concerning the competence of the witness. Mechanically, the child can raise his or her right hand and say, "Yes, I swear." To judge the witness's competence, however, we must look more deeply into the question; it is necessary to determine whether the witness has sufficient maturity to understand the nature and significance of the oath. The judge must make this determination because competence is a question of law. How will he decide? Generally, the judge will conduct a voir dire, usually in the robing room. Sometimes, he will voir dire the witness in open court, but probably not in the presence of the jury, if there is a jury. And what will the judge do? He will say: "Sonny, how old are you?" "Eight, sir." "Do you go to Sunday School?" "Yes, sir." "You know what happens when you tell a lie?" The judge then decides whether this witness has sufficient maturity to understand the nature and significance of the oath. And that is an either/or proposition. The witness knowingly can take the oath or he cannot. If the former, he is competent, with respect to that first element; if the latter, he is incompetent.

The competence of a witness is rarely challenged on grounds of perception, recollection, or communication. If a witness's competence were challenged on these grounds, however, the trial judge would decide the question of competence by the same procedures that he uses to test a witness's capacity to take the oath.

As green-thumb psychologists, we all know that no human being perceives everything, that no human being remembers everything and that no human being is supremely eloquent. We all fail to measure up in some respect or another to those three faculties. If a question is raised concerning the competence of a witness, the judge will take out his handy judicial thermometer, calibrated from zero to one hundred, and he will take the witness's temperature with respect to perception, recollection, or communication. No one will score one hundred. Occasionally, a witness will score zero. If a witness scores zero, the judge will say, "You are incompetent; you perceived nothing, you remembered nothing, or you can communicate nothing. Go home." That is very rare.

Usually, when there is a bona fide question of competence, the thermometer reading will be low, but more than zero. Of course, we are quantifying what cannot be quantified. To make it easy, we will assume that the question raised concerns the degree to which the witness remembers, the degree to which the proposed witness satisfies the third requirement of competence. The judge uses his handy thermometer and gets a reading of five on a scale of one hundred. If the witness gets any perceptible reading on the thermometer, anything more than zero, no matter how low, the court will usually conclude that the witness is competent. The witness may testify; the court will leave it to the cross-examiner to bring out the extent to which the witness did not perceive, does not remember, or cannot communicate.

When the judge rules that the witness may testify, the subject of the inquiry changes from competence, a question of law, to credibility, which is a question of fact for the jury to decide. The judge may rule that a reading of five on the recollection thermometer is sufficient to render the witness competent. Although the judge has ruled that the witness is competent, the jury is free to conclude that a witness who remembers only five out of one hundred should not be believed and that his testimony is not worth crediting. The jury is perfectly free to reject that testimony in its entirety. In doing so, the jury is not overruling the judge; it is simply deciding a different question. Competence, on the one hand, is for the judge to decide; credibility, on the other hand, falls within the province of the jury.

We have now established the basis for the first four categories of impeachment. We take the four elements of competence, turn them around, and use them destructively. Tactically, of course, we may not want to use some, or all, of them. We are working out a checklist of all the possibilities; these are the first four. Take the oath, for instance, and turn it around. Cross-examination: "Sir, you just took an oath to tell the truth?" "Yes." "When was the last time you went to church or synagogue?" Is that the kind of cross-examination that you need to know about and will want to use? Well, yes and no. It is included because it is the first item on the checklist. Will you ever use such a question on cross-examination? Not if you are in your right mind, because it is greasy kid stuff. You may have used it when you were a youngster at the bar. But nowadays you never would; it is embarrassing. If that is the only kind of question you have to ask on cross-examination, you will not ask it. As a matter of fact, Rule 610 of the Federal Rules of Evidence prohibits you from impeaching a witness by asking questions about religious belief or practice. This first pigeonhole is not available in the federal courts. It is available in most other courts, but not in the federal courts. The draftsmen of the Federal Rules excluded it in federal courts because it is greasy kid stuff. You should not do it, so they put it right in the rule. At this stage, however, we are developing a checklist. We are not talking now about how to do it or what, tactically, makes sense. We are talking only about what is, theoretically, available.

Perception

Perception is the second requirement of competence and it provides the second pigeonhole of impeachment. A witness's competence could be challenged when he is sworn, but the judge will find the witness competent if the question is raised at that stage. Consequently, we wait for cross-examination. Assume that the witness has testified on direct examination that he saw the automobile accident and that it took place in front of the Cloisters in Triumph Park in Upper Manhattan. On cross-examination: "Mr. Witness, where were you when the accident occurred?" "I was at Thirty-Second Street and Fifth Avenue."

What should the cross-examiner do now? Of course, he should stop and sit down. It may be difficult for a trial lawyer of any age to overcome his congenital inability to stop, sit down and be quiet, but he must attempt to do so. The witness has testified that he saw an accident at the northern tip of the Island when he was standing at Fifth Avenue and Thirty-Second Street, three miles to the South.

The cross-examiner should stop, of course, and argue in summation that the witness was three miles away. Of course he did not see the accident. What will the average trial lawyer do? He will be unable to overcome the temptation; he will go on to the next question: "Then how come you could see the accident if you were three miles away?" And every time he fails and succumbs to the temptation, the answer to the question will be: "Well, I was on top of the Empire State Building with high-powered binoculars and I saw it through the binoculars."

Recollection

The third requirement of competence is recollection or memory. This element of competence provides a very useful mode of impeachment. Every experienced trial lawyer will have used it, but perhaps without knowing the right label for what he was doing with memory or recollection. An example from the criminal field will demonstrate the use of recollection impeachment. In my days in the U.S. Attorney's Office, conspiracy was still conspiracy. Perhaps it is beginning to change now, but conspiracy cases have been a kind of joke. Recently, a conspiracy has consisted of a baby doctor, two nuns, and a priest. In my day, however, in the cops and robbers business, conspiracy was really conspiracy — thirteen guys whose last names ended with a vowel, plus a stoolpigeon.

We will assume that you are a defense lawyer in a great conspiracy case, the *Rosenberg* case. It does not fit the definition, but is just the exception that proves the rule: a conspiracy to steal the secret of the atom bomb and send it behind the Kremlin wall. One of the overt acts charged in the Rosenberg indictment was that one of the conspirators registered at the Waldorf-Astoria Hotelin New York City on a particular day. The prosecutor calls a witness for direct examination. "Who are you, sir?" "I'm the desk clerk at the Waldorf-Astoria." "Were you on duty on January 1, 1949?" "Yes." And now we start to play the game. What does the prosecutor say? He says: "Mr. Witness, look around this court room and tell us, yes or no, whether you see in court somebody who registered on that day." And now, how do we play it? You know.

First the witness takes off his glasses and spends thirty seconds polishing them up. The tension builds to the point where the jury is no longer continent. Now the witness starts. He begins with the judge. No, it is not the judge. Then he starts with the people in the jury box, runs right down the line, and surveys all twelve of them. No, it is none of the jurors. He starts working across those chairs in the well of the court. Now, I can only describe the Federal Court where I used to practice. There was a special chair, and on that chair there was a big sign that said: "This is where the defendant sits. Make no mistake about it." Finally, the witness gets up to that chair, and he says, "Ah ha, that's the person I registered that day." The prosecutor sits down; he has proved that devastating overt act.

You are the defense lawyer. You may cross-examine. You may use the three modes of impeachment we have developed. Will you impeach by asking him when he last went to church? Of course not. Are you going to impeach by asking him whether he really saw the person register? No, he is not lying. Finally, how can he remember? So, how might we cross-examine? "The Waldorf-Astoria is a big hotel, isn't it?" "Yes." "How long had you been a desk clerk before the day in question?" "Nine years." "How many days a week do you work?" "Five." "How many weeks a year?" "Forty-eight." "And how many people a day do you register?" "About two hundred and fifty." "So, in the nine years before this date, by my arithmetic, you had registered one million, two hundred twelve thousand, nine hundred and seventeen people? Correct?" "Correct." "Now, have you been working since then?" "Yes." "Right up until today?" "Yes." "So in the time since, you have registered another two million, four hundred twelve thousand, eight hundred and thirteen, correct?" "Correct." And now what do you do? Stop. Sit down. And what will you argue in summation? He cannot possibly remember one person out of four million.

Will you stop? No. Will you sit down? No. Instead, you will ask the next question: "Then, how come, Mr. Bigshot, you can remember this person out of four million?" And every time you ask that question, you will get the answer: "Well, he walked up to me, and he put a gun to my head, and he said to me, 'If you don't register me, I'll kill you.' So I remembered."

Communication

The fourth element of competence is communication. This mode of impeachment is not used very frequently. In my own career at the bar, such as it was, I remember using it only once. But when you are able to impeach through communication, the impeachment is devastating.

Assume that you are in court. Your opponent calls a witness. You will have to cross-examine that witness. You watch the witness. Every meter is on. Your tentacles are out; you are picking up the radar, the emanations, the impressions; you are operating for those few minutes or few hours at a degree of concentration and sensitivity unknown to practitioners in other branches of the profession or other professions. At once, you size up the witness. He has the intelligence of an earthworm and the morals of a scorpion. He talks. You listen to the direct examination. Suddenly, in the middle of his testimony on direct examination, there comes the word that clinks. He says, "antidisestablishmentarianism." On cross-examination, you use the fourth mode of impeachment: communication. "Mr. Witness, you used the word, "antidisestablishmentarianism'?" "Yes." "What does it mean?" "I don't know." "Here is a yellow pad. Write it down." "I can't." "You mean, you don't know how to spell it?" "No." "When is the first time in your life you ever heard that word?" "When the District Attorney told me what to say on the witness stand."

You sit down. What will you argue in summation? "That's no witness, that's a human tape recorder, just repeating what the District Attorney programmed into him before this trial started."

We have outlined the first four modes of impeachment. They are really quite easy.

UNITED STATES v. SAMPOL
636 F.2d 621 (D.C. Cir. 1980)

PER CURIAM:

On September 21, 1976, in Washington, D.C., Orlando Letelier, former Chilean Ambassador to the United States, and Ronni Moffitt, an American associate, were mortally wounded by the remote control detonation of a bomb attached to the undercarriage of the automobile in which they were riding.

On August 1, 1978, Guillermo Novo Sampol (Guillermo Novo) [and six others were indicted for these murders]. . . .

Trial by jury commenced January 8, 1979 on the charges against Guillermo Novo, Alvin Ross and Ignacio Novo only. At the close of trial on February 14, 1979 each was found guilty of all charges lodged against him. This appeal followed.

*   *   *

VII

CROSS-EXAMINATION OF RICARDO CANETE

Ricardo Canete, a government witness, testified that appellant Ross had admitted his complicity in the assassination of Letelier and that Canete had provided Ross with false identification papers. Appellants challenge the trial court's refusal to permit counsel for Ignacio Novo to cross-examine Canete about his religious beliefs and his alleged addiction to narcotics.

A. CANETE'S RELIGION

Counsel for Ignacio Novo proffered to the trial court that Canete had discussed with his client his devotion to the Luceme religion. On voir dire, Canete testified that he faithfully adhered to the teachings of that sect and consulted with spirits of his religion before taking certain actions. He had no religious beliefs which would cause him to violate his oath to testify truthfully. The trial judge cut off further inquiry into Canete's religious practices at that point.

The government correctly points out that the court's exclusion of this evidence was not only justified but required by the Federal Rules of Evidence. Rule 610 bars the admission of evidence of the religious beliefs of a witness for the purpose of showing that his credibility is impaired as a result of those beliefs. The purpose of the rule is to guard against the prejudice which may result from disclosure of a witness's faith. The scope of the prohibition includes unconventional or unusual religions. *See Government of Virgin Islands v. Petersen*, 553 F.2d 324 (3rd Cir. 1977) (defense counsel could not elicit testimony that alibi witness was a member of the Rastafarian sect). The fact that Canete professed adherence to a religion which is not commonly shared does not prevent the application of the rule. The trial judge committed no abuse of discretion.

B. CANETE'S ALLEGED DRUG ADDICTION

Counsel for Ignacio Novo informed the trial court that Canete's father had said that the witness was addicted to drugs. Counsel had previously told the court that Canete's father considered his son to be mentally incompetent and that Canete had alienated his entire family by his persistent involvement in legal troubles. Without conducting a hearing, the judge barred all inquiry into Canete's drug use.

We have recognized that it is proper to explore the drug addiction of a witness in order to attack his credibility and capacity to observe the events in question. . . . In *United States v. Fowler*, [465 F.2d 664 (D.C. Cir. 1972)], this court held that defense counsel had a right to cross-examine the government's principal witness, a former undercover narcotics agent, where the agent had taken a urine test showing signs of possible narcotics use and had been dismissed by the Police Department shortly thereafter. And in *Wilson v. United States*, 232 U.S. 563 (1914), the Supreme Court ruled that the trial court had improperly denied cross-examination of an admitted drug user to determine whether her powers of recollection had been impaired.

Although the narcotics addiction of a witness is relevant to his capacity to observe, a trial judge must deal with an allegation of drug use with some sensitivity because of the highly inflammatory nature of such a charge. The possibility that exploration of a witness's addiction will generate unwarranted prejudice demands that the judge exercise discretion to keep the scope of such examination within proper bounds. Accordingly, before the court will permit a witness to be questioned before the jury about his use of narcotics, counsel must establish a foundation showing either that the witness was using drugs at the time he observed the events in dispute, . . . or that he is under the influence of narcotics while testifying. . . .

Applying these principles to the facts in this case, we discern no error in the trial court's ruling. To justify exploration of this particularly sensitive area, defense counsel proffered only that the witness's father, who openly disapproved of his son, had informed counsel of Canete's addiction to drugs. No offer was made to prove that Canete was influenced by narcotics during his testimony or at the time of the events which were the subject of his testimony. Counsel had previously attempted without success to show that Canete was mentally incompetent and immoral, and his effort to present the witness's unusual religious beliefs to the jury had also failed. Furthermore, the fact that Canete was not the government's principal witness weakens the argument of the appellants. . . .

Appellants stress that the judge prohibited any questioning of the witness even outside the presence of the jury, where there would have been no danger of prejudice. It is true that normally the better practice in this situation is to permit counsel to establish a foundation by examining the witness outside the hearing of the jurors. . . . On the other hand, we by no means favor, and do not intend to establish, a general rule requiring a factual proffer as a precondition for cross-examination into uncharted areas. Defense counsel often cannot foresee what new information a particular line of questioning will divulge, and inquiry is usually permissible when counsel has merely a reasonable basis for suspecting that a circumstance is true.

In this case, however, given the dubious basis of counsel's proffer, the fact that Canete was not the key witness for the government, and the sensitive nature of the subject matter, we cannot say that the trial judge exceeded the boundaries of his discretion. . . .

Evidentiary Foundation:
The Trial of Julius and Ethel Rosenberg[65]

[This facts of this case are set forth *supra* p. 183. After his direct examination, prosecution witness Max Elitcher was cross-examined as follows:]

Q.	Let me ask you: Did you ever sign a loyalty oath for the Federal Government?

A.	I did.

Q.	When?

A.	I think it was sometime in 1947. I don't remember the time or the time of year.

Q.	Do you know what that oath provided?

A.	What do you mean, as a penalty or as just—

Q.	No, do you know the contents of the oath you signed and swore to?

A.	Not completely, not right now, no.

Q.	Did you know it at the time?

---

[65] Excerpted from Transcript of the Record, *supra* p. 183, at 276–78.

A.   I know generally what it referred to, but I don't know the specific wording.

Q.   In substance?

A.   In substance, I know.

Q.   What do you think you signed?

A.   I signed a statement, saying that I was not or had not been a member of an organization that was dedicated to overthrow of the Government by force and violence. I don't remember whether the statement specifically mentioned the Communist Party or not, but at least it said I was not a member of an organization that believed in the overthrow of the Government by force and violence.

Q.   At the time you verified that oath, did you believe that you were lying when you concealed your membership in the Communist Party?

A.   Yes, I did.

Q.   So you have lied under oath?

A.   Yes.

Q.   Were you worried about it?

A.   Yes.

Q.   Were you worried about it in 1946?

A.   I think I was always worried about it.

Q.   And you were worried about it in 1947?

A.   Yes.

Q.   And were you worried about it in 1948?

A.   Yes.

b.   Pursuing the Credibility Factors

1)   Bias, Interest, Prejudice, and Corruption

William G. Hale, *Bias as Affecting Credibility*
1 HASTINGS L.J. 1 (1949)[66]

It is accepted doctrine that the bias of a witness will affect his credibility. The existence of bias does not necessarily imply conscious falsehood. It is quite likely however to shade at least, though unwittingly, a witness' testimony; the bias may be in favor of one side or against the other. Granted its existence it may be appropriately taken into consideration in weighing the testimony.

---

[66] Copyright © 1949 by University of California, Hastings College of the Law. Reprinted from HASTINGS LAW JOURNAL, Vol. 1, No. 1, by permission.

Since bias is a state of mind, its existence can be determined only circumstantially. These circumstances may consist of relationships (*e.g.*, that witness is the father of the plaintiff) or dealings or encounters calculated to develop a prejudice (*e.g.*, a fight with the party against whom the testimony is given) or conduct, or utterances. These designations are only by way of illustration. As Mr. Wigmore (Sec. 949) has well said, "The range of external circumstances from which probable bias may be inferred is infinite." Experience tells us for all practical purposes what those circumstances are in individual situations. Evidence of bias is considered of such value that the existence of facts, implicit of it, may be ascertained either by cross-examination or by extrinsic testimony. Considerations of auxiliary policy, such as surprise or collateral issue, have not been deemed relatively sufficient to limit the method of proof.

Evidentiary Foundation:
The Trial of Bernhard Goetz

[James Ramseur was one of the four victims of "Subway Gunman" Bernhard Goetz. Ramseur was called as a government witness at Goetz's trial for attempted murder and other charges. Prior to the criminal trial, Ramseur had filed a civil action for damages against Goetz. On cross-examination at the Goetz criminal trial, Barry Slotnick, Goetz' attorney, pursued the following cross-examination.]

Q: [Y]ou knew that in order to get Mr. Goetz' money you would have to be able to show you weren't part of a robbery.

A: Is that why you all set me up?

Q: Did you know that in order for you to get Mr. Goetz' money you have to prove you weren't part of a robbery?

A: Of course, I never was until this — until after this Goetz case.

Q: And, as a matter of fact, you knew quite clearly that in order for you to prevail you would have to maintain a story that you were innocent of attempting to rob Mr. Goetz?

A: Yes, and that's exactly why I got set up, right? You, Goetz, are in on it.

Q: As a matter of fact, Mr. Ramseur, you knew, did you not, as far as Mr. Goetz went, that if in any way whatsoever he were to be found not guilty of shooting you, you wouldn't get any money, is that correct?

A: He's going to be found not guilty anyway, I know what time it is.

NOTES AND QUESTIONS

1.   For classic examples of impeachment involving witness corruption, *see Commonwealth v. Min Sing*, 88 N.E. 918 (Mass. 1909) (attempted subornation of another witness); *Schmertz v. Hammond*, 35 S.E. 945 (W. Va. 1900) (agreement to share in proceeds of litigation).

2.   If a witness denies allegations of bias or prejudice, what recourse is left to opposing counsel?

UNITED STATES v. ABEL
469 U.S. 45 (1984)

JUSTICE REHNQUIST delivered the opinion of the Court.

Respondent John Abel and two cohorts were indicted for robbing a savings and loan. . . . The cohorts elected to plead guilty, but respondent went to trial. One of the cohorts, Kurt Ehle, agreed to testify against respondent and identify him as a participant in the robbery.

Respondent informed the District Court at a pretrial conference that he would seek to counter Ehle's testimony with that of Robert Mills. Mills was not a participant in the robbery but was friendly with respondent and with Ehle, and had spent time with both in prison. Mills planned to testify that after the robbery Ehle had admitted to Mills that Ehle intended to implicate respondent falsely, in order to receive favorable treatment from the Government. The prosecutor in turn disclosed that he intended to discredit Mills' testimony by calling Ehle back to the stand and eliciting from Ehle the fact that respondent, Mills, and Ehle were all members of the "Aryan Brotherhood," a secret prison gang that required its members always to deny the existence of the organization and to commit perjury, theft, and murder on each member's behalf.

Defense counsel objected to Ehle's proffered rebuttal testimony as too prejudicial to respondent. After a lengthy discussion in chambers the District Court decided to permit the prosecutor to cross-examine Mills about the gang, and if Mills denied knowledge of the gang, to introduce Ehle's rebuttal testimony concerning the tenets of the gang and Mills' and respondent's membership in it. . . .

At trial Ehle implicated respondent as a participant in the robbery. Mills, called by respondent, testified that Ehle told him in prison that Ehle planned to implicate respondent falsely. When the prosecutor sought to cross-examine Mills concerning membership in the prison gang, the District Court conferred again with counsel outside of the jury's presence, and ordered the prosecutor not to use the term "Aryan Brotherhood" because it was unduly prejudicial. Accordingly, the prosecutor asked Mills if he and respondent were members of a "secret type of prison organization" which had a creed requiring members to deny its existence and lie for each other. When Mills denied knowledge of such an organization the prosecutor recalled Ehle.

Ehle testified that respondent, Mills, and he were indeed members of a secret prison organization whose tenets required its members to deny its existence and "lie, cheat, steal [and] kill" to protect each other. The District Court sustained a defense objection to a question concerning the punishment for violating the organization's rules. Ehle then further described the organization and testified that "in view of the fact of how close Abel and Mills were" it would have been "suicide" for Ehle to have told Mills what Mills attributed to him. Respondent's counsel did not request a limiting instruction and none was given.

The jury convicted respondent. On his appeal a divided panel of the Court of Appeals reversed. 707 F.2d 1013 (1983). The Court of Appeals held that Ehle's rebuttal testimony was admitted not just to show that respondent's and Mills' membership in the same group might cause Mills to color his testimony; the court held that the contested evidence was also admitted to show that because Mills belonged to a perjurious organization, he must be lying on the stand. This suggestion of perjury, based upon a group tenet, was impermissible. . . . The court [also] concluded that Ehle's testimony implicated respondent as a member of the gang; but since respondent did not take the stand, the testimony could not have been offered to impeach him and it prejudiced him "by mere association." . . .

We hold that the evidence showing Mills' and respondent's membership in the prison gang was sufficiently probative of Mills' possible bias towards respondent to warrant its admission into evidence. . . .

Both parties correctly assume, as did the District Court and the Court of Appeals, that the question is governed by the Federal Rules of Evidence. But the Rules do not by their terms deal with impeachment for "bias," although they do expressly treat impeachment by character evidence and conduct, Rule 608, by evidence of conviction of a crime, Rule 609, and by showing of religious beliefs or opinion, Rule 610. . . .

Before the present Rules were promulgated, the admissibility of evidence in the federal courts was governed in part by statutes or Rules, and in part by case law. . . . This Court had held in *Alford v. United States*, 282 U.S. 687 (1931), that a trial court must allow some cross-examination of a witness to show bias. This holding was in accord with the overwhelming weight of authority in the state courts as reflected in Wigmore's classic treatise on the law of evidence. . . . Our decision in *Davis v. Alaska*, 415 U.S. 308 (1974), holds that the Confrontation Clause of the Sixth Amendment requires a defendant to have some opportunity to show bias on the part of a prosecution witness.

With this state of unanimity confronting the drafters of the Federal Rules of Evidence, we think it unlikely that they intended to scuttle entirely the evidentiary availability of cross-examination for bias. One commentator, recognizing the omission of any express treatment of impeachment for bias, prejudice, or corruption, observes that the Rules "clearly contemplate the use of the above-mentioned grounds of impeachment." E. CLEARY, McCORMICK ON EVIDENCE § 40, p. 85 (3d ed. 1984). Other commentators, without mentioning the omission, treat bias as a permissible and established basis of impeachment under the Rules. 3 D. LOUISELL & C. MUELLER, FEDERAL EVIDENCE § 341, p. 470 (1979); 3 J. WEINSTEIN& M. BERGER, WEINSTEIN'S EVIDENCE ¶ 607[03] (1981).

We think this conclusion is obviously correct. Rule 401 defines as "relevant evidence" evidence having any tendency to make the existence of any fact that is of consequence to the determination of the action more probable or less probable than it would be without the evidence. Rule 402 provides that all relevant evidence is admissible, except as otherwise provided by the United States Constitution, Act of Congress, or by applicable rule. A successful showing of bias on the part of a witness would have a tendency to make the facts to which he testified less probable in the eyes of the jury than it would be without such testimony.

The correctness of the conclusion that the Rules contemplate impeachment by showing of bias is confirmed by the references to bias in the Advisory Committee Notes to Rules 608 and 610, and by the provisions allowing any party to attack credibility in Rule 607, and allowing cross-examination on "matters affecting the credibility of the witness" in Rule 611(b). . . .

We think the lesson to be drawn from all of this is that it is permissible to impeach a witness by showing his bias under the Federal Rules of Evidence just as it was permissible to do so before their adoption. In this connection, the comment of the Reporter for the Advisory Committee which drafted the Rules is apropos:

> "In principle, under the Federal Rules no common law of evidence remains. 'All relevant evidence is admissible, except as otherwise provided.' In reality, of course, the body of common law knowledge continues to exist, though in the somewhat altered form of a source of guidance in the exercise of delegated powers." Cleary, *Preliminary Notes on Reading the Rules of Evidence*, 57 NEB. L. REV. 908, 915 (1978) (footnote omitted).

Ehle's testimony about the prison gang certainly made the existence of Mills' bias towards respondent more probable. Thus it was relevant to support that inference. Bias is a term used in the "common law of evidence" to describe the relationship between a party and a witness which might lead the witness to slant, unconsciously or otherwise, his testimony in favor of or against a party. Bias may be induced by a witness' like, dislike, or fear of a party, or by the witness' self-interest. Proof of bias is almost always relevant because the jury, as finder of fact and weigher of credibility, has historically been enticed to assess all evidence which might bear on the accuracy and truth of a witness' testimony. The "common law of evidence" allowed the showing of bias by extrinsic evidence, while requiring the cross-examiner to "take the answer of the witness" with respect to less favored forms of impeachment. . . .

Mills' and respondent's membership in the Aryan Brotherhood supported the inference that Mills' testimony was slanted or perhaps fabricated in respondent's favor. A witness' and a party's common membership in an organization, even without proof that the witness or party has personally adopted its tenets, is certainly probative of bias. . . . Mills' and respondent's membership in the Aryan Brotherhood was not offered to convict either of a crime, but to impeach Mills' testimony. Mills was subject to no sanction other than that he might be disbelieved. . . . For purposes of the law of evidence the jury may be permitted to draw an inference of subscription to the tenets of the organization from membership alone, . . . though such an inference would not be sufficient to convict beyond a reasonable doubt in a criminal prosecution. . . .

Respondent argues that even if the evidence of membership in the prison gang were relevant to show bias, the District Court erred in permitting a full description of the gang and its odious tenets. Respondent contends that the District Court abused its discretion under Federal Rule of Evidence 403, because the prejudicial effect of the contested evidence outweighed its probative value. In other words, testimony about the gang inflamed the jury against respondent, and the chance that he would be convicted by his mere association with the organization outweighed any probative value the testimony may have had on Mills' bias.

Respondent specifically contends that the District Court should not have permitted Ehle's precise description of the gang as a lying and murderous group. Respondent suggests that the District Court should have cut off the testimony after the prosecutor had elicited that Mills knew respondent and both may have belonged to an organization together. This argument ignores the fact that the *type* of organization in which a witness and a party share membership may be relevant to show bias. If the organization is a loosely knit group having nothing to do with the subject matter of the litigation, the inference of bias arising from common membership may be small or nonexistent. If the prosecutor had elicited that both respondent and Mills belonged to the Book of the Month Club, the jury probably would not have inferred bias even if the District Court had admitted the testimony. The attributes of the Aryan Brotherhood — a secret prison sect sworn to perjury and self-protection — bore directly not only on the fact of bias but also on the *source* and *strength* of Mills' bias. The tenets of this group showed that Mills had a powerful motive to slant his testimony towards respondent, or even commit perjury outright.

A district court is accorded a wide discretion in determining the admissibility of evidence under the Federal Rules. . . .

Before admitting Ehle's rebuttal testimony, the District Court gave heed to the extensive arguments of counsel, both in chambers and at the bench. In an attempt to avoid undue prejudice to respondent the court ordered that the name "Aryan Brotherhood" not be used. The court also offered to give a limiting instruction concerning the testimony, and it sustained defense objections to the prosecutor's questions concerning the punishment meted out to unfaithful members. These precautions did not prevent *all* prejudice to respondent from Ehle's testimony, but they did, in our opinion, ensure that the admission of this highly probative evidence did not *unduly* prejudice respondent. We hold there was no abuse of discretion under Rule 403 in admitting Ehle's testimony as to membership and tenets.

Respondent makes an additional argument based on Rule 608(b). That Rule allows a cross-examiner to impeach a witness by asking him about specific instances of past conduct, other than crimes covered by Rule 609, which are probative of his veracity or "character for truthfulness or untruthfulness." The Rule limits the inquiry to cross-examination of the witness, however, and prohibits the cross-examiner from introducing extrinsic evidence of the witness' past conduct.

Respondent claims that the prosecutor cross-examined Mills about the gang not to show bias but to offer Mills' membership in the gang as past conduct bearing on his veracity. This was error under Rule 608(b), respondent contends, because the mere fact of Mills' membership, without more, was not sufficiently probative of Mills' character for truthfulness. Respondent cites a second error under the same Rule, contending that Ehle's rebuttal testimony concerning the gang was extrinsic evidence offered to impugn Mills' veracity, and extrinsic evidence is barred by Rule 608(b).

*   *   *

It seems clear to us that the proffered testimony with respect to Mills' membership in the Aryan Brotherhood sufficed to show potential bias in favor of respondent; because of the tenets of the organization described, it might also impeach his veracity directly. But there is no rule of evidence which provides that testimony admissible for one purpose and inadmissible for another purpose is thereby rendered inadmissible; quite the contrary is the case. It would be a strange rule of law which held that relevant, competent evidence which tended to show bias on the part of a witness was nonetheless inadmissible because it also tended to show that the witness was a liar.

* * *

The judgment of the Court of Appeals is Reversed.

NOTES AND QUESTIONS

1.   *Abel* clarified the status of bias impeachment under the Federal Rules of Evidence. However does the Court ever explain why the Federal Rules of Evidence chose not treat bias impeachment explicitly? What, if anything, would a specific provision for bias impeachment have achieved?

2.   Although a witness' common membership with the defendant in a secret prison organization certainly establishes his potential bias, was it proper to permit testimony that the organization's tenets included murder? Is it surprising that no one dissented on this question? At what point does such evidence become unduly prejudicial?

3.   Under *Abel*, is it permissible to cross-examine a criminal defendant, charged with heroin trafficking, as follows:

Evidentiary Foundation:
The Trial of Bruno Richard Hauptmann[67]

[The background to this case is set forth *supra* 234. Bessie Gow, who had been baby Lindbergh's nurse, and the last person to see him in the family residence, returned from her home in Scotland to testify for the prosecution. She was cross-examined, in relevant part, as follows:]

Q.   By the way, how did you come back to this trial — who paid your expenses?

A.   I came back here to aid justice.

MR. REILLY: I move to strike that out as not responsive.

MR. WILENTZ: If your honor please, I think it is a partial answer.

MR. REILLY: It is a voluntary explanation on the part of the witness.

THE COURT: Well, you see it is a matter that is volunteered and not responsive to counsel's question, and I suppose that technically he has a right to have it stricken out, and that will be the order.

Q.   Who paid your expenses?

A.   The state of New Jersey paid my expenses.

---

[67] Excerpted from S. WHIPPLER, *supra* p. 211, at 167.

Q. 　　　Amounting to how much?

A. 　　　Altogether $650.

Q. 　　　When did you determine that your visit to this country and your return and your services here would be worth $650?

A. 　　　I decided that when it was decided that I would get that amount — that that amount—

Q. 　　　Who decided it?

A. 　　　I did.

Q. 　　　After corresponding with the attorney general's office?

A. 　　　After corresponding with Colonel Schwarzkopf.

Q. 　　　Had he written to you and asked you what your price would be to come to this country and testify and go home?

A. 　　　He did not.

2)　　Prior Crimes

Mason Ladd, *Credibility Tests — Current Trends*
89 U. Pa. L. Rev. 166, 174–76 (1940)[68]

PREVIOUS CONVICTION OF A CRIME AS A TEST OF VERACITY

At the common law the conviction of a person for an infamous crime rendered him thereafter incompetent as a witness. This doctrine was established by the sixteenth century and persisted well into the nineteenth century. It rested upon the theory that one who had engaged in such reprehensible conduct was a person without honor and wholly unworthy of belief. The incompetency also was regarded as a part of the punishment. Blackstone in his commentaries states that "Infamous persons are such as may be challenged as jurors, *propter delictum*, and thereafter never shall be admitted to give evidence to inform the jury, with whom they were too scandalous to associate." This strict rule of law included not only those crimes pertaining to dishonesty but to all infamous crimes under the laws of England, generally enumerated as treason, felony, and the crimen falsi. The reason, apparently unsurmountable (sic) at that time, was stated by Greenleaf that since "almost all felonies were punishable with death, it was very natural that crimes, deemed of so grave a character as to render the offender unworthy to live, should be considered as rendering him unworthy of belief in a court of justice." In America likewise in the earlier period of our history persons convicted of felonious crimes were held thereafter incompetent to testify in court. Both in England and in this country the incompetency has been removed by statute, with but few exceptions, but usually by the same act it is provided that the conviction of a crime shall thereafter be admissible as a test of the credibility of witnesses. The statutes widely vary in their provisions as to what crimes afford the basis of testimonial impeach-

---

[68] Reprinted by permission of University of Pennsylvania Law Review.

ment; none of them being drafted upon the basis of the specific relationship of the crime to the character of the witness for truthfulness. It is quite generally provided that convictions of a felony may be so used. This limits the use of previous convictions to crimes serious enough to carry a penitentiary sentence but does not distinguish between the various grades of crimes carrying such penalties, as for example operating a motor vehicle while intoxicated, murder and perjury, all of which might provide a penitentiary sentence. Conviction of a felony, crimes of infamous nature, crimes involving moral turpitude, and crimes without further designation thus inclusive of misdemeanors are representative of the statutory provisions permitting proof of a crime to be used to impeach the veracity of a witness.

The theory of the use of previous convictions to test credibility is well stated in the case of *Gertz v. Fitchburg Railroad Company,* in which the plaintiff sought to recover damages for personal injuries received by him while in the defendant's employ. The plaintiff had testified as a witness and the defendant put in evidence the record of his conviction for impersonating a United States revenue officer several years before the trial. . . . On appeal, exceptions to the trial court's ruling were sustained, Justice Holmes saying:

> . . . when it is proved that a witness has been convicted of a crime, the only ground for disbelieving him which such proof affords is the general readiness to do evil which the conviction may be supposed to show. It is from that general disposition alone that the jury is asked to infer a readiness to lie in the particular case, and thence that he has lied in fact. The evidence has no tendency to prove that he was mistaken, but only that he has perjured himself and it reaches that conclusion solely through the general proposition that he is of bad character and unworthy of credit.

This statement by Justice Holmes pointedly presents the whole of the theory upon which previous convictions are now admitted. The reason for disbelieving the witness is his supposed readiness to lie inferred from his general readiness to do evil which is predicated upon his former conviction of a crime. It is not the specific tendency of the witness to falsify but the general bad character of the witness as evidenced by the single act of which he was convicted that creates the basis of admissibility. By the common law such a witness was not permitted to testify at all because of this strong inference of unworthiness. Today the theory is retained but its application is changed, permitting the conviction to brand the witness with the stigma of distrust. . . .

QUESTION

1.   Does this impeachment mode unfairly place criminal defendants in an intractable dilemma? Consider the following article by a distinguished jurist:

Federal Rule of Evidence 609
Impeachment by Evidence of Conviction of Crime

(a) In General. The following rules apply to attacking a witness's character for truthfulness by evidence of a criminal conviction:

(1) for à crime that, in the convicting jurisdiction, was punishable by death or by imprisonment for more than one year, the evidence:

(A) must be admitted, subject to Rule 403, in a civil case or in a criminal case in which the witness is not a defendant; and

(B) must be admitted in a criminal case in which the witness is a defendant, if the probative value of the evidence outweighs its prejudicial effect to that defendant; and

(2) for any crime regardless of the punishment, the evidence must be admitted if the court can readily determine that establishing the elements of the crime required proving — or the witness's admitting — a dishonest act or false statement.

(b) Limit on Using the Evidence After 10 Years. This subdivision (b) applies if more than 10 years have passed since the witness's conviction or release from confinement for it, whichever is later. Evidence of the conviction is admissible only if:

(1) its probative value, supported by specific facts and circumstances, substantially outweighs its prejudicial effect; and

(2) the proponent gives an adverse party reasonable written notice of the intent to use it so that the party has a fair opportunity to contest its use.

(c) Effect of a Pardon, Annulment, or Certificate of Rehabilitation. Evidence of a conviction is not admissible if:

(1) the conviction has been the subject of a pardon, annulment, certificate of rehabilitation, or other equivalent procedure based on a finding that the person has been rehabilitated, and the person has not been convicted of a later crime punishable by death or by imprisonment for more than one year; or

(2) the conviction has been the subject of a pardon, annulment, or other equivalent procedure based on a finding of innocence.

(d) Juvenile Adjudications. Evidence of a juvenile adjudication is admissible under this rule only if:

(1) it is offered in a criminal case;

(2) the adjudication was of a witness other than the defendant;

(3) an adult's conviction for that offense would be admissible to attack the adult's credibility; and

(4) admitting the evidence is necessary to fairly determine guilt or innocence.

(e) Pendency of an Appeal. A conviction that satisfies this rule is admissible even if an appeal is pending. Evidence of the pendency is also admissible.

NOTES AND QUESTIONS

1.   Would Judge McGowan, author of the article that precedes Rule 609 above, have been pleased with this enactment (as amended in 1990)?

2.   What factors should a judge consider in balancing prejudice against probative value? In this respect, *U.S. v. Mahone*, below, may prove helpful.

UNITED STATES v. MAHONE
537 F.2d 922 (7th Cir. 1976)

BAUER, CIRCUIT JUDGE.

Appellant challenges his conviction under 26 U.S.C. 5861(d) and (i) for possessing a sawed-off shotgun not registered to him and not identified by a serial number. The principal question[] . . . concern[s] . . . the procedure to be followed by the trial judge in admitting evidence of the defendant's prior conviction for impeachment purposes under Federal Rule of Evidence 609. We affirm the conviction.

I.

In the early morning of March 26, 1975, four East Chicago, Indiana, police officers in an unmarked car responded to a radio call reporting an armed robbery at the Soul Snack Shop at the corner of 150th and Alexander Streets in East Chicago. At the scene, a witness told the officers that he had observed "three carloads of subjects" armed with weapons and that one of the cars was a black over blue Plymouth. The officers then left the shop and patrolled the area.

About fifteen minutes later they saw a black over blue Plymouth pull to the side of the road behind a parked car about one block from the snack shop. The policemen pulled behind the Plymouth, preventing it from moving. The officers then left their car with their weapons drawn, two officers going to either side of the Plymouth. As they approached the right side of the Plymouth, one of the policemen, Officer Belzeski, saw the passenger in the front seat holding a weapon. While ordering the front seat passenger to drop the weapon, Officer Belzeski saw the passenger in the right rear seat, the defendant, place a weapon on the floor of the car. After the suspects left the Plymouth, Officer Belzeski retrieved a sawed-off shotgun from the rear seat floor of the car. The defendant was convicted of possessing the shotgun.

*   *   *

IV.

Petitioner's next point of error is that the trial judge failed to make the determination required by Federal Rule of Evidence 609(a) . . . before admitting evidence of the defendant's prior robbery conviction for impeachment purposes.

The relevant portion of Rule 609 reads:

> "(a) General Rule. For the purpose of attacking the credibility of a witness, evidence that he has been convicted of a crime shall be admitted if elicited from him or established by public record during cross-examination but only if the crime (1) was punishable by death or imprisonment in excess of one year under the law under which he was convicted, and the court determines

that the probative value of admitting this evidence outweighs its prejudicial effect to the defendant. . . ."

The trial judge allowed the admission of the prior conviction, *in limine*, prior to trial, after hearing argument by the attorneys regarding the nature of the prior conviction, the possible prejudice to the defendant if it was admitted, and the proper procedure to be followed for its admission under Rule 609. The judge ruled on the record:

"If the defendant takes the stand and testifies, the Court will permit, on the basis of the record now before it, impeachment of this defendant in the normal manner by the robbery conviction" (Tr. at 10).

The appellant claims that the court erred by not making an explicit determination on the record that the probative value of the evidence outweighed its prejudicial effect to the defendant. The government argues that such a determination is one within the discretion of the trial judge and that the appellant has not shown that this discretion was abused.

On the basis of the record we cannot say that the trial judge failed to meaningfully exercise the discretion given him by Rule 609. His ruling permitting the admission of the evidence "on the basis of the record now before it" indicates implicitly that, in line with the rule, he weighed the prejudicial effect against the probative value of the evidence. The record before the judge, upon which he explicitly relied in his ruling, consisted of argument by the parties over those very matters.

In the future, to avoid the unnecessary raising of the issue of whether the judge has meaningfully invoked his discretion under Rule 609, we urge trial judges to make such determinations after a hearing on the record, as the trial judge did in the instant case, and to explicitly find that the prejudicial effect of the evidence to the defendant will be outweighed by its probative value. When such a hearing on the record is held and such an explicit finding is made, the appellate court easily will be able to determine whether the judge followed the strictures of Rule 609 in reaching his decision. . . .

The hearing need not be extensive. Bearing in mind that Rule 609 places the burden of proof on the government, Cong. Rec. 12254, 12257 (daily ed., December 18, 1974) (remarks of House conferees); . . . the judge should require a brief recital by the government of the circumstances surrounding the admission of the evidence, and a statement of the date, nature and place of the conviction. The defendant should be permitted to rebut the government's presentation, pointing out to the court the possible prejudicial effect to the defendant if the evidence is admitted.

Some of the factors which the judge should take into account in making his determination were articulated by then Judge Burger in *Gordon v. United States*, 383 F.2d 936, 940, 127 U.S. App. D.C. 343 (1967):

(1) The impeachment value of the prior crime.

(2) The point in time of the conviction and the witness' subsequent history.

(3) The similarity between the past crime and the charged crime.

(4) The importance of the defendant's testimony.

(5) The centrality of the credibility issue.

*   *   *

AFFIRMED.

NOTES AND QUESTIONS

1.   What advantage does the defendant gain by raising this issue via a motion in limine? Suppose a defendant, in fact, has no intention of taking the stand. May he file a motion in limine in the hope of creating an appealable issue? *See Luce v. United States*, 469 U.S. 38 (1984), *infra*.

2.   Fed. R. Evid. 609(a) restricts extrinsic proof of a prior conviction to situations in which it may be established by public record. Moreover, the prosecution is not permitted to delve into the underlying facts of the conviction.

Why? *See United States v. White*, 222 F.3d 363, 370 (7th Cir. 2000).

3.   In applying the Rule 609(a)(1) balancing test, may the judge consider the underlying facts of the conviction or is the court restricted to the statutory elements of the crime? *See United States v. Estrada*, 430 F.3d 606 (2d Cir. 2005); *United States v. Alexander*, 2005 U.S. Dist. LEXIS 19687 (D. Me. 2005); *United States v. Lipscomb*, 702 F.2d 1049 (D.C. Cir. 1983).

4.   Assuming a prior conviction is admitted to impeach an accused, what type of limiting instruction might defense counsel be expected to request?

5.   Which of the following convictions are admissible against a testifying defendant: Under Fed. Rule 609:

a) a rape conviction in a trial for arson and second-degree murder?

b) a murder conviction in a trial for murder?

c) an attempted armed robbery conviction in a trial for attempted larceny by false pretenses?

d) a perjury conviction in a trial for perjury?

6.   May defense counsel ask a government witness about a prior conviction for cruelty to animals? *See United States v. Cunningham*, 638 F.2d 696 (4th Cir. 1981). In the *Cunningham* case, the following colloquy also occurred:

Q.   And how many counts of worthless checks have you had?
ASST. U. S.

ATTY. BENDER: Objection.

THE COURT: Counsel, I believe that under state law none of those are felonies, are they?

MR. MYERS: I don't believe they are if they are North Carolina charges.

THE COURT: Well.

MR. MYERS: Oklahoma has a felony, felonious check charges. I don't know if
                         there —

THE COURT: Well, is there any indication that there's any Oklahoma violation
                         here?

MR. MYERS: I don't know.

THE COURT: Let's don't proceed that way, Counselor. That's not the way to do
                         it.

Id. at 698.

What was objectionable about defense counsel's cross-examination?

Even if the prior conviction was merely a misdemeanor, does Fed. R. Evid. 609 necessarily render it inadmissible to impeach?

LUCE v. UNITED STATES
469 U.S. 38 (1984)

CHIEF JUSTICE BURGER delivered the opinion of the Court.

I

Petitioner was indicted on charges of conspiracy, and possession of cocaine with intent to distribute, in violation of 21 U.S.C. §§ 846 and 841(a)(1). During his trial in the United States District Court for the Western District of Tennessee, petitioner moved for a ruling to preclude the Government from using a 1974 state conviction to impeach him if he testified. There was no commitment by petitioner that he would testify if the motion were granted, nor did he make a proffer to the court as to what his testimony would be. In opposing the motion, the Government represented that the conviction was for a serious crime — possession of a controlled substance.

The District Court ruled that the prior conviction fell within the category of permissible impeachment evidence under Federal Rule of Evidence 609(a). The District Court noted, however, that the nature and scope of petitioner's trial testimony could affect the court's specific evidentiary rulings; for example, the court was prepared to hold that the prior conviction would be excluded if petitioner limited his testimony to explaining his attempt to flee from the arresting officers. However, if petitioner took the stand and denied any prior involvement with drugs, he could then be impeached by the 1974 conviction. Petitioner did not testify, and the jury returned guilty verdicts.

II

. . . The Court of Appeals held that when the defendant does not testify, the court will not review the District Court's *in limine* ruling.

III

It is clear, of course, that had petitioner testified and been impeached by evidence of a prior conviction, the District Court's decision to admit the impeachment evidence would have been reviewable on appeal along with any other claims of error. The Court of Appeals would then have had a complete record detailing the nature of petitioner's testimony, the scope of the cross- examination, and the possible impact of the impeachment on the jury's verdict.

A reviewing court is handicapped in any effort to rule on subtle evidentiary questions outside a factual context. This is particularly true under Rule 609(a)(1), which directs the court to weigh the probative value of a prior conviction against the prejudicial effect to the defendant. To perform this balancing, the court must know the precise nature of the defendant's testimony, which is unknowable when, as here, the defendant does not testify.

Any possible harm flowing from a district court's *in limine* ruling permitting impeachment by a prior conviction is wholly speculative. The ruling is subject to change when the case unfolds, particularly if the actual testimony differs from what was contained in the defendant's proffer. Indeed even if nothing unexpected happens at trial, the district judge is free, in the exercise of sound judicial discretion, to alter a previous *in limine* ruling. On record such as here, it would be a matter of conjecture whether the District Court would have allowed the Government to attack petitioner's credibility at trial by means of the prior conviction.

When the defendant does not testify, the reviewing court also has no way of knowing whether the Government would have sought to impeach with the prior conviction. If, for example, the Government's case is strong, and the defendant is subject to impeachment by other means, a prosecutor might elect not to use an arguably inadmissible prior conviction.

Because an accused's decision whether to testify "seldom turns on the resolution of one factor," *New Jersey v. Portash*, 440 U.S. 450, 467 (1979) (Blackmun, J., dissenting), a reviewing court cannot assume that the adverse ruling motivated a defendant's decision not to testify. In support of his motion a defendant might make a commitment to testify if his motion is granted; but such a commitment is virtually risk free because of the difficulty of enforcing it.

Even if these difficulties could be surmounted, the reviewing court would still face the question of harmless error. . . . Were *in limine* rulings under Rule 609(a) reviewable on appeal, almost any error would result in the windfall of automatic reversal; the appellate court could not logically term "harmless" an error that presumptively kept the defendant from testifying. Requiring that a defendant testify in order to preserve Rule 609(a) claims, will enable the reviewing court to determine the impact any erroneous impeachment may have had in light of the record as a whole; it will also tend to discourage making such motions solely to "plant" reversible error in the event of conviction.

* * *

Affirmed.

JUSTICE STEVENS took no part in the consideration or decision of this case.

JUSTICE BRENNAN, with whom JUSTICE MARSHALL joins, concurring.

I join the opinion of the Court because I understand it to hold only that a defendant who does not testify at trial may not challenge on appeal an *in limine* ruling respecting admission of a prior conviction for purposes of impeachment under Rule 609(a) of the Federal Rules of Evidence. . . .

I do not understand the Court to be deciding broader questions of appealability *vel non* of *in limine* rulings that do not involve Rule 609(a). . . . In . . . case[s] . . . in which the determinative question turns on legal and not factual considerations, a requirement that the defendant actually testify at trial to preserve the admissibility issue for appeal might not necessarily be appropriate.

NOTES AND QUESTIONS

1. Some state courts interpreting their own rules of evidence have disavowed *Luce.* In *State v. McClure*, 692 P.2d 579 (Or. 1984), for example, the court suggested that appellate rights may be preserved if the defendant commits himself to testifying if the trial judge excludes the prior conviction. Is this viewpoint realistic? *See also State v. Swanson*, 707 N.W.2d 645 (Minn. 2006); *Warren v. State*, 124 P.3d 522, 526 (Nev. 2005).

2. Did Justice Brennan's concurring opinion succeed in limiting *Luce* to Fed. R. Evid. 609(a)(1) determinations? *See United States v. Fallon*, 348 F.3d 248, 254 (7th Cir. 2003); *United States v. Weichert*, 783 F.2d 23 (2d Cir. 1986); *United States v. Johnson*, 767 F.2d 1259 (8th Cir. 1985).

3. If the trial court rules against the defendant *in limine*, may the defendant still preserve the issue for appeal if he "draws the sting" himself by preemptively bringing out his prior conviction on direct examination? *See Ohler v. United States*, 529 U.S. 753 (2000)? The outcome may depend on whether you are in state or federal court. *See also Pineda v. State*, 88 P.3d 827, 831 (Nev. 2004) (collecting state cases).

UNITED STATES v. SMITH
551 F.2d 348 (D.C. Cir. 1976)

McGOWAN, CIRCUIT JUDGE:

On November 11, 1974, the Seventh Street branch of the National Bank of Washington was robbed by two armed men who wore hats completely covering their hair, but employed no other form of disguise. The bandits disarmed the bank's private security guard immediately upon entering the bank lobby. While one stood watch, the other proceeded through the bank manager's office into the teller's cage area, where he filled a brown paper bag with bills of various denominations. The entire incident consumed less than five minutes. A subsequent audit revealed that the robbers fled with $13,214 in cash, as well as the bank guard's revolver.

Under an indictment filed in the District Court on February 12, 1975, appellants were convicted by a jury of armed bank robbery (18 U.S.C. § 2113(a) (1970) and armed robbery (of the gun; 22 D.C. Code §§ 2901, 3202 (1973)). On appeal both appellants claim to have been denied effective assistance of counsel. Appellant Gartrell asserts further that his conviction should be overturned because the trial judge ruled that a prior attempted robbery conviction could be used to impeach him if he chose to testify. We find appellants' contentions unpersuasive with respect to ineffective assistance of counsel, but we think that the trial court must reexamine the ruling challenged by Gartrell. Accordingly, the conviction of Smith is affirmed, and the case is remanded as to Gartrell for further proceedings of the nature hereinafter described.

*   *   *

II

Appellant Gartrell seeks reversal of his conviction on the ground that the district judge erred in ruling that a prior conviction would be admissible for impeachment purposes if Gartrell chose to testify in his own defense. The trial in this case was held on July 17, 18, and 21, 1975. The new Federal Rules of Evidence became effective on July 1, 1975. The impeachment by prior conviction issue, therefore, was and is governed by Fed. R. Evid. 609(a)[69] Gartrell's claim in this regard presents difficulty, because the controlling relevance of Rule 609 was unrecognized at trial. In the colloquy of record about admissibility, the Rule was never mentioned by the prosecution, the defense, or the court. The district judge seems to have decided to permit use of Gartrell's prior conviction by reference to earlier law in this Circuit. *See Luck v. United States*, 348 F.2d 763 (1965); *Gordon v. United States*, 383 F.2d 936 (1967), *cert. denied*, 390 U.S.1029 (1968). This was error.

Despite substantial surface similarity, the inquiry to be conducted by the trial court under Rule 609(a) differs significantly from that mandated by *Luck* and its progeny. Adherence to the proper standard by the District Court might have produced a different ruling on the impeachment question. Had evidence of his prior conviction been excluded, appellant Gartrell in all likelihood would have taken the stand and the jury presumably would have heard him deny participation in the bank robbery. As explained further below, we cannot say, on the facts of this case, that failure to apply Rule 609 constituted harmless error. Therefore, we remand the case to the District Court for a determination of whether, within the meaning of Rule 609(a), the probative value of Gartrell's prior conviction outweighs its prejudicial effect.[70] If it decides that the prior conviction was admissible, the conviction stands,

---

[69] Ed. As originally enacted, Rule 609(a) provided as follows:

Impeachment by Evidence of Conviction of Crime

a. General rule. — For the purpose of attacking the credibility of a witness, evidence that he has been convicted of a crime shall be admitted if elicited from him or established by public record during cross-examination but only if the crime (1) was punishable by death or imprisonment in excess of one year under the law under which he was convicted, and the court determines that the probative value of admitting this evidence outweighs its prejudicial effect to the defendant, or (2) involved dishonesty or false statement, regardless of the punishment.

[70] [17] Since we are persuaded that the District Court did not operate within the proper framework

subject to further review on appeal; if it decides that it should have been excluded, the conviction is reversed and a new trial ordered.

Judicial construction of the provisions of Rule 609 has thus far been rather sparse, especially when contrasted with the veritable flood of decisions treating problems of impeachment by prior conviction under the *Luck* norms. Our review of the available materials persuades us that Rule 609 has been designed to work at least three important changes in the approach of federal courts to the problems of impeachment by prior conviction:

(i) Evidence of *some* prior convictions (*i.e.*, convictions for crimes involving dishonesty or false statement) is now *automatically* admissible for the purpose of attacking the credibility of a witness. With respect to these convictions, trial courts are no longer free to exercise the discretion they enjoyed under *Luck.*[71]

---

in evaluating the admissibility of Gartrell's prior conviction, we need not assess the independent significance of the lack of an explicit finding that probative value outweighs prejudicial effect to the defendant. In particular, we need not decide whether the lack of such a finding inevitably implies a failure to exercise meaningfully the discretion conferred upon the trial court by Rule 609. Likewise we do not reach the question of whether a trial judge must provide an on-the- record explanation of his Rule 609 findings. However, it must be obvious to any careful trial judge that an explicit finding in the terms of the Rule can be of great utility, if indeed not required, on appellate review, . . . and some indication of the reasons for the finding can be very helpful.

[71] [20] *But see* Fed. R. Evid. 403 . . . . The potential interaction between Rule 403 and Rule 609(a) elicited comment at legislative hearings on the Proposed Federal Rules of Evidence. Although it offers no solutions, the following colloquy between Congressmen Dennis and Hungate and Judge Friendly is instructive:

Judge FRIENDLY.   [D]o you really think if you were on a jury, you would not like to know if the witness had committed a murder. I think I would like to know.

Mr. DENNIS.   I think I would like to know it, but I think it is very unfair to ask a man who is on trial for some irrelevant or unrelated offense, whether he committed murder or manslaughter 5 years ago. All it does is prejudice the case. It has nothing to do with his credibility in my judgment, especially murder. That is the primary example. Those are usually one time offenses.

Judge FRIENDLY.   Perhaps in taking murder I chose an unfortunate case. But, of course, there is the overriding rule that the judge can always exclude testimony where probative value he thinks is outweighed by its prejudicial effect and perhaps in the case we are discussing he should do that.

Mr. HUNGATE.   Would that be true with or without the rules?

Judge FRIENDLY.   That is true today.

Mr. HUNGATE.   Would it remain true if these rules became effective?

Judge FRIENDLY.   I assume they have such a rule in here. I could easily check.

Mr. DENNIS.   It seems to me if he has to follow this rule [*i.e.*, Rule 609(a)] he does not have much discretion. Maybe he still could rule something out. I am not sure.

Mr. HUNGATE.   I apologize for interrupting. Go ahead.

Mr. [sic] FRIENDLY.   I want to check whether there was such a general rule. I thought there was.

Mr. HUNGATE.   I believe section 403 is the rule to which you are referring. [Quotes the rule.]

Judge FRIENDLY.   I think the Congressman's point is a good one. You have the problem: Does that apply when there is a specific rule on the subject? This just says relevant evidence may be excluded if it has this effect. But then somebody is going to argue, this other rule dealt very specifically with the question and rule 403 is out. I don't know what the answer would be.

Rules of Evidence, Hearings on S. 583, H.R. 4958, and H.R. 5463 before the Special Subcomm. on Reform of Federal Criminal Laws of the House Comm. on the Judiciary, 93d Cong., 1st Sess., ser. 2, at

Congress has substituted its judgment that evidence of such crimes is always sufficiently related to credibility to justify its admission, regardless of possible prejudice to the defendant. . . .

(ii) The addition of the phrase "to the defendant" at the end of Rule 609(a)(1) reflects a deliberate choice to regulate impeachment by prior conviction *only* where the *defendant's* interests might be damaged by admission of evidence of past crimes, and *not* where the prosecution might suffer, or where a non-defendant witness complains of possible loss of reputation in the community.[72] This procedure

---

251–52 (1973). (In connection with Congressman Dennis's remark about the limited discretion available to a trial judge under Rule 609(a), at the time of the above exchange the version of the rule under consideration mandated that all felony convictions, as well as all convictions for crimes involving dishonesty or false statement, be automatically admissible for impeachment purposes.)

As Judge Friendly observed, the language of Rule 609(a)(2) is absolute in nature, suggesting that the subsection's command, authorizing use of prior convictions for crimes involving dishonesty or false statement, may not be abrogated by reference to Rule 403. Partial support for this proposition can be derived from the original Advisory Committee Note to Rule 403, a rule whose text remained unchanged throughout Congressional consideration. The Advisory Committee said that Rule 403 was "designed as a guide for the handling of situations for which no specific rules have been formulated." Since Gartrell's prior crime, attempted robbery, did not involve dishonesty or false statement as those terms are used in Rule 609(a)(2) (see text accompanying notes 26–30 infra), we express no opinion on the issue of whether evidence admissible under Rule 609(a)(2) may nevertheless be excluded by a trial judge in the exercise of his discretion under Rule 403.

[72] [21] The Conference Committee Report states:

The danger of prejudice to a witness other than the defendant . . . was considered and rejected by the Conference as an element to be weighed in determining admissibility. It was the judgment of the Conference that the danger of prejudice to a nondefendant witness is outweighed by the need for the trier of fact to have as much relevant evidence on the issue of credibility as possible. Such evidence should only be excluded where it presents a danger of improperly influencing the outcome of the trial by persuading the trier of fact to convict the defendant on the basis of his prior criminal record.

H.R. Conf. Rep. No. 93-1597, 93d Cong., 2d Sess. 9–10. . . . In explaining the Conference Report and urging adoption of the new Federal Rules, Representative Hungate, the leading Conference Committee Manager, announced flatly that Rule 609(a) "means that in a criminal case the prior felony conviction of a prosecution witness may always be used." 120 Cong. Rec. H. 12,254 (daily ed. Dec. 18, 1974). Similarly, Representative Dennis, another Conference Committee member, told the House that "now a defendant can cross examine a government witness about any of his previous felony convictions; he can always do it, because that will not prejudice him in anyway [sic]. . . . Only the Government is going to be limited. . . ." *Id.* at H. 12,257.

In his treatise on the Federal Rules of Evidence, Judge Weinstein recognizes the accuracy of the above descriptions of the effect of Rule 609(a). Prosecution witnesses may be impeached by their prior felony convictions, subject only to Rule 611(a)(3)'s instruction that the court exercise control over interrogation so as to "protect witnesses from harassment or undue embarrassment." *See* 3 WEINSTEIN'S EVIDENCE 1609[03], at 609–66 n. 11 and accompanying text (1975). However, in *United States v. Jackson*, 405 F. Supp. 938 (E.D.N.Y. 1975), Judge Weinstein fashioned a significant modification of the rule that prior felony convictions may always be used to impeach prosecution witnesses.

Defendant in *Jackson* was charged with armed bank robbery. His record revealed a recent state felony conviction for assault. One or more government witnesses apparently also had prior assault convictions. Judge Weinstein excluded evidence of defendant's prior conviction, but conditioned the exclusion upon defense counsel's agreement to refrain from using prior assault convictions to impeach prosecution witnesses, absent the court's express advance approval of such tactics. Imposition of this condition was justified by a pretrial finding that if government witnesses were so impeached, then the probative value of defendant's assault conviction would outweigh the risk of prejudice under Rule 609(a). Judge

may be contrasted with earlier possibilities under *Luck*.

Although in practice *Luck* hearings were most frequently conducted to determine whether a criminal defendant who wished to testify could be impeached with evidence of his prior convictions, in theory the *Luck* discretionary standard was equally applicable to all witnesses and parties. In order to avoid undue prejudice to *any* individual, the trial court could exclude prior conviction evidence which it concluded had only limited probative value with respect to credibility.

(iii) Crucial for present purposes, the language of Rule 609(a)(1), as enacted, manifests an intent to shift the burden of persuasion with respect to admission of prior conviction evidence for impeachment. *Luck* held that such evidence could be excluded "where the trial judge believes the prejudicial effect of impeachment *far* outweighs the probative relevance of the prior conviction to the issue of credibility." 348 F.2d at 768 (emphasis added). *Gordon* reiterated this test, and emphasized that "[t]he burden of persuasion in this regard is on the accused. . . . The underlying assumption [of *Luck*] was that prior convictions would ordinarily be admissible unless this burden is met." 383 F.2d at 939. Presumably, the House Subcommittee version of Rule 609(a)(1) would have preserved the approach already developed by the case law in this Circuit. As amended by the Subcommittee, the rule provided that previous felony convictions could be used to impeach a witness *"unless* the court determines that the danger of unfair prejudice outweighs the probative value of the evidence of the conviction[s]." H.R. Rep. No. 93-650, 93d Cong., 1st Sess. . . . (emphasis added). Rejecting this option, the version of Rule 609 which ultimately emerged from the Conference Committee and became law allows impeachment by prior felony conviction (for a crime not involving dishonesty or false statement) *"only* if . . . the court determines that the probative value of admitting this evidence outweighs its prejudicial effect to the defendant." Fed. R. Evid. 609(a)(1) (emphasis added). This modest variation in language is not purely semantic. The prosecution now must bear the burden of establishing that prior conviction evidence should be admitted. Our grammatical interpretation of the bare wording of Rule 609 is reinforced by the remarks of two leading conferees during debate on the floor of the House. Defending the Conference Committee product, Congressman Dennis said:

> What the present compromise does is to say that you can inquire on cross examination about these [sic] type of prior convictions which really bear on credibility, and you can ask about all other felonies on cross examination, only if you can convince the court, and the burden is on the government, which is an important change in the law, that the probative value of the question is greater than the damage to the defendant. . . .

120 Cong. Rec. H. 12,257 (daily ed. Dec. 18, 1974). Representative Hungate declared, "[T]he rule puts the burden on the proponent of [prior conviction]evidence to show that it should be used — to show that the probative value of the evidence outweighs its prejudicial effect to the defendant." *Id.* at 12,254. . . .

Weinstein asserted that, under the general purpose formulation of Rule 102, district judges are obliged to "interpret the [Federal] Rules [of Evidence] creatively." 405 F. Supp. at 943 (Rule 102 directs that the rules "be construed to secure fairness in administration, . . . and promotion of growth and development of the law of evidence to the end that the truth may be ascertained and proceedings justly determined.").

The labyrinthine history of Rule 609 has been authoritatively canvassed elsewhere. We mention only those aspects of the Rule's background which bear on the present controversy. Rule 609 was one of the most hotly contested provisions in the Federal Rules of Evidence. The current language of the Rule is unquestionably the product of careful deliberation and compromise. The House of Representatives and the Senate Judiciary Committee agreed that *criminal defendants* should not be impeached by evidence of prior convictions unless the earlier offenses involved dishonesty or false statement. Adoption of this position by the full Senate was blocked only at the last moment, only by a bare majority, and only after Senator McClellan had succeeded in forcing a second vote on the matter.

Faced with the task of forging a consensus between views both strongly held and widely divergent, the Conference Committee was aware of the substantial sentiment in both chambers for limiting impeachment by prior conviction, especially in the criminal defendant-as-witness context. The House debate almost ten months earlier was particularly revealing. As reported by the Judiciary Committee, Rule 609 banned impeachment by prior conviction, regardless of the identity of the witness, except where the crime in question had involved dishonesty or false statement. Representative Hogan vigorously pressed for amendment of the proposal to authorize impeachment by any prior felony conviction. Resurrecting the suggestion previously advanced by a Special House Subcommittee, Representative Smith countered with a compromise amendment along the line of *Luck.* Sitting as a Committee of the Whole, the House first replaced the Hogan amendment with the Smith amendment, and then rejected the latter in favor of the Judiciary Committee version by a vote of 48-10. 120 Cong. Rec. H. 551–57 (daily ed. Feb. 6, 1974). The small minority of members voting overwhelmingly favored the "dishonesty or false statement" approach. The Conference Committee sought a formula which would improve upon *Luck* in providing at least the appearance of more definite restrictions on the use of prior convictions for impeachment purposes. At the same time, the Conference could not avoid the fact that a narrow majority of the Senate wished to permit impeachment with any prior felony conviction. Rule 609, as currently effective, resolves these opposing tensions by retaining the trial court's discretion to allow impeachment with any prior felony, but shifting to the prosecution the burden of demonstrating that probative value on the issue of credibility outweighs prejudicial effect to the defendant.

The Government has contended, both in its brief and on oral argument, that Gartrell's earlier crime, attempted robbery, involved "dishonesty or false statement," as that phrase is used in the Federal Rules of Evidence. If this contention were accurate, the Government would be correct in its conclusion that Rule 609(a)(2) provides for the *automatic* admissibility of evidence of Gartrell's prior conviction. The District Court's decision could be upheld, even though rendered without reference to the newly-applicable Rules. However, the Government has misconstrued the language in question, partially through a misplaced reliance on comments of this court in cases decided under *Luck.* Attempted robbery is not a crime involving "dishonesty or false statement" within the meaning of Rule 609(a)(2). If Gartrell's prior conviction is to be admitted at all, it must be admitted only after the court makes the determination prescribed in Rule 609(a)(1).

The Conference Committee Report fully supports this position:

By the phrase "dishonesty and false statement" the Conference means crimes such as perjury or subornation of perjury, false statement, criminal fraud, embezzlement, or false pretense, or any other offense in the nature of crimen falsi, the commission of which involves some element of deceit, untruthfulness, or falsification bearing on the accused's propensity to testify truthfully.

H.R. Conf. Rep. No. 93-1597, 93d Cong., 2d Sess. 9. . . . Numerous remarks made in the course of floor debate, set forth in the Appendix to this opinion, substantiate the interpretation that robbery may not be classified legitimately as an "offense in the nature of crimen falsi." Congress clearly intended the phrase to denote a fairly narrow subset of criminal activity. Moreover, research into the derivation of the term "crimen falsi" indicates that Congress's restrictive construction comports with historical practice. While commentators have uncovered some divergence between civil and common law usage, the expression has never been thought to comprehend robbery or other crimes involving force. Even in its broadest sense, the term "crimen falsi" has encompassed only those crimes characterized by an element of deceit or deliberate interference with a court's ascertainment of truth. As graphically observed by Senator McClellan, robbery is not such a crime:

> There is no deceit in armed robbery. You take a gun, walk out, and put it in a man's face and say, "Give me your money," or walk up to the counter of the cashier and say, "this is a holdup; give me your money." There is no deceit in that. They are not lying. They mean business. They will murder you if you do not do it.

120 Cong. Rec. S. 19913 (daily ed. Nov. 22, 1974).

Our interpretation of the words "dishonesty or false statement" is consistent with that adopted by the majority of courts which have had occasion to apply Rule 609(a)(2) in the period since July 1, 1975. In *United States v. Millings*, . . . this court held that "dishonesty or false statement" did not comprehend either of appellant's two prior convictions, one for unlawful possession of narcotics, the other for carrying a pistol without a license. Judge Robb explained:

> An intent to deceive or defraud is not an element of either offense. . . . Certainly we cannot say that either offense, in the language of the Conference Committee, is "peculiarly probative of credibility". Although it may be argued that any willful violation of law . . . evinces a lack of character and a disregard for all legal duties, including the obligations of an oath, Congress has not accepted that expansive theory.

*   *   *

The Government has invoked *Gordon v. United States*, . . . and *United States v. Simpson*, . . . in aid of the proposition that stealing, and in particular the crime of robbery, involves dishonesty or false statement under Rule 609(a)(2). *Gordon* and *Simpson* are not unique. Other cases decided by this court pursuant to the *Luck* standard might also have been cited. . . . The simple answer to the Government's argument is that none of these cases involved Rule 609. *Luck* had held that, under the then applicable version of D.C. Code§ 14-305, trial courts should exercise discretion in determining whether to permit impeachment by prior conviction. . . .

Gordon represented the effort of this tribunal to be helpful to the District Court in its exercise of that discretion. The nature of the prior crime was one factor identified in both the *Luck* and *Gordon* opinions as relevant to the impeachment issue. When Judge (now Chief Justice) Burger, writing in *Gordon*, characterized stealing as "conduct which reflects adversely on a man's honesty and integrity," he was not holding that all prior convictions for theft and related crimes were automatically admissible for impeachment purposes. He said merely that such offenses had some bearing on an individual's credibility, a bearing which the trial court should consider in exercising its discretion. By contrast, the *Gordon* opinion noted, acts of violence "generally have little or no direct bearing on honesty and veracity," thus implying that virtually any showing of prejudicial effect should be sufficient to exclude evidence of such prior convictions. . . .

The issue under Rule 609(a)(2) is entirely different from that confronted by this court in *Gordon, Simpson*, and other cases descendant from *Luck*. The new Rule provides that a prior conviction for a crime involving dishonesty or false statement is *automatically* admissible for impeachment purposes. With respect to such evidence, the trial court enjoys no discretion. . . . In its Conference Committee Report, Congress has spelled out the meaning of the phrase "dishonesty or false statement" as it is used in Rule 609(a)(2). . . . The Report plainly shows that the set of crimes involving dishonesty or false statement under the Rule is not coterminous with the set of crimes bearing on credibility in the *Luck-Gordon* analysis. The *Gordon* and *Simpson* precedents are not controlling in this case, and indeed are essentially irrelevant.

NOTES AND QUESTIONS

1.   Most federal courts have held both robbery and larceny not to qualify as crimes of dishonesty under Rule 609. *See Walker v. Horn*, 385 F.3d 321 (3d Cir. 2005) (robbery is not a crime of dishonesty); *United States v. Foster*, 227 F.3d 1096 (9th Cir. 2000) (robbery/shoplifting not crimes of dishonesty); *United States v. Johnson*, 388 F.3d 96 (3rd Cir. 2004) (purse snatching not crime of dishonesty). *But see United States v. Smith*, 2006 U.S. Dist. LEXIS 9692 (E.D. Pa. Mar. 13, 2006) (robbery/larceny are crimes of dishonesty); *United States v. Carden*, 529 F.2d 443 (5th Cir.), *cert. denied*, 429 U.S. 848 (1976) (petit larceny is crime of dishonesty).

2.   Which of the following involves a crime of dishonesty under Rule 609(a)(2): food stamp violations (*United States v. Mejia-Alarcon*, 995 F.2d 982 (10th Cir. 1993)), failure to file income tax returns (*United States v. Wilson*, 985 F.2d 348 (7th Cir. 1993)), embezzlement (*Elcock v. Kmart*, 233 F.3d 734 (3rd Cir. 2000)). See Stuart P. Green, *Deceit and Classification of Crimes: Federal Rule of Evidence 609(a)(2) and the Origin of Crimen Falsi*, 90 J. Crim. L. & Criminology 1087 (2000)?

3.   Before amendment of Rule 609(a)(2) in 2006, courts differed in evaluating the question of "dishonesty or false statement." Some courts considered only the statutory elements of the prior crime while others took into account the underlying facts of the conviction? *See United States v. Lewis*, 626 F.2d 940 (D.C. Cir. 1980); *Tussel v. Witco Chemical Corp.*, 555 F. Supp. 979 (W.D. Pa. 1983); *State v. Eugene*, 340 N.W.2d 18 (N.D. 1983). The 2006 amendment "mandates the admission of evidence of a conviction only when the conviction required proof (or in the case of

guilty plea, the admission of) an act of dishonesty or false statement." Advisory Committee Note to 2006 Amendment.

4.   Hawaii takes a totally different approach to the impeachment use of prior convictions (based on the English model discussed in Judge McGowan's article):

> (a) General rule. For the purpose of attacking the credibility of a witness, evidence that he has been convicted of a crime is inadmissible except when the crime is involving dishonesty. However, in a criminal case where the defendant takes the stand, the defendant shall not be questioned or evidence introduced as to whether he has been convicted of a crime, for the sole purpose of attacking credibility, unless the defendant has himself introduced testimony for the purpose of establishing his credibility as a witness, in which case he shall be treated as any other witness as provided in this rule.

Hawaii Rule of Evidence 609 (2006).

5.   The *Smith* case reviews the complicated legislative history of Rule 609, and notes that the Rule 403 balancing test may not apply when a prior conviction involves dishonesty under Fed. R. Evid. 609(a)(2). In 1990, Congress amended Rule 609 to make plain that Rule 403 carries no force for crimes involving dishonesty or false statement. As for other crimes, the following case addresses the role of Rule 403 under Rule 609(a)(1) as amended in 1990.

UNITED STATES v. TSE
375 F.3d 148 (1st Cir. 2004)

LIPEZ, CIRCUIT JUDGE.

Defendant Clyde Tse was convicted of distributing cocaine in violation of 21 U.S.C. 841(a)(1). In evaluating one of his claims on appeal relating to a limitation on the cross-examination of the government's principal witness, we must address the important differences in analysis between admitting a prior conviction to impeach a defendant's testimony and admitting such a conviction to impeach the testimony of a government witness. . . .

I.

On November 24, 1998, agents of the Drug Enforcement Agency (DEA) attempted to record a drug transaction between Tse and a cooperating witness, Stephen Williams. The DEA agents outfitted Williams with an audio transmitter called a "kel." The device allowed the agents to listen to and record Williams's conversations, but did not allow them to communicate with Williams. After searching Williams and his car to ensure that he did not have any drugs or cash, the agents gave him $ 450 and instructed him to purchase crack cocaine from Tse.

At approximately 6:30 P.M., Williams drove to Tse's residence in Mattapan, Massachusetts. The DEA recorded the ensuing conversation in which Williams told Tse that he had only $ 450 and that he wanted to buy a half ounce of crack cocaine for that amount. Tse told Williams to return in ten minutes. Williams left Tse's residence and again met with the DEA agents. They instructed him to return to Tse's house to make the drug purchase. At approximately 7:10 P.M. Williams returned to Tse's house where Tse was on the phone, apparently receiving directions to a nearby location. After the phone call, Tse told Williams "we're on," and said that they needed to travel "just around the corner." Tse and Williams left the house and entered Williams's car.

* * *

At trial, Williams testified that he and Tse drove to a house only a few minutes away. Williams remained in the car while Tse spoke with a man in the doorway and entered the building. According to Williams, Tse returned several minutes later and gave a bag of crack cocaine to Williams. Williams and Tse then drove back to Tse's house, where Tse gave Williams a scrap of paper with Tse's pager number written on it.

After Williams dropped Tse off at his residence, he met with the DEA agents and handed over the drugs and the scrap of paper on which Tse had written his pager number. DEA laboratory tests confirmed that the drugs that Tse had allegedly supplied to Williams included 11.2 grams of crack cocaine.

* * *

On September 27, 2000, a grand jury charged Tse with . . . distributing a controlled substance in violation of 21 U.S.C. 841(a)(1). . . .

Because the DEA agents had been unable to record the November 24 transaction, the government relied heavily on Williams's testimony to describe the events of that evening. Williams was not an ideal witness, and Tse's primary strategy was to discredit Williams's testimony. Through both direct and cross- examination, the jury heard, inter alia, that Williams had used and sold drugs in the past, had been convicted of at least one crime, had made inaccurate statements to the grand jury about his prior involvement with drugs,[73] had received substantial compensation for his work as a DEA informant, and had purchased a new car shortly after receiving payments from the DEA.

The trial lasted four days, ending on December 15, 2000. Despite Tse's aggressive impeachment of Williams's testimony, the jury found Tse guilty of distributing a controlled substance. . . .

On appeal, Tse claims that the district court made a number of errors. . . . Tse argues . . . that the district court erred in limiting his cross-examination of Williams by preventing him from (1) impeaching Williams's credibility by introducing evidence that Williams had been convicted of assault and battery against a police officer . . .

* * *

---

[73] [1] Before the grand jury, Williams testified that he had never sold crack cocaine and that he had used marijuana only once. On cross-examination Williams admitted that those statements were not correct and that he had sold crack cocaine and had used marijuana on several occasions.

IV.

Tse argues that the district court impermissibly limited his cross-examination of Williams . . . [because] the court did not allow Tse to impeach Williams with Williams' previous conviction for assault and battery against a police officer. . . .

A. Conviction for Assault and Battery Against a Police Officer

Tse attempted to impeach Williams's credibility by introducing evidence of Williams's prior conviction for assault and battery against a police officer (ABPO). At first, the district court agreed that the evidence was admissible pursuant to Federal Rule of Evidence 609(a)(1).[74] However, at a sidebar conference, the court addressed a related matter: Tse's motion to exclude Tse's own convictions, one of which was for ABPO, if Tse should choose to testify. The court viewed the admissibility of Williams's conviction as closely related to the admissibility of Tse's conviction, stating that "although it's not an identical analysis, it's close enough that it may be that . . . if it's allowed in this case, it would be allowed in the other as well." The court later reiterated:

> And if a particular offense is admitted as impeachment for the witness under [Rule 609](a)(1), then that may — consistency may result in a similar ruling with respect to the defendant, although I note there is a distinction in (a)(1) between an accused and someone who is not an accused. . . .

After hearing counsel's arguments about whether any of Tse's convictions should be admitted if he were to testify, the court again compared Williams's ABPO conviction to Tse's ABPO conviction, stating that "if it's probative enough in one case, it has to be probative enough in the other, it seems to me . . . There is a difference [in standards of admissibility], but I'm not sure it's a pertinent difference with respect to this." The court added: "I don't know that there's, in fact, a different standard, except that maybe it's a caution to make sure that it has probative value ." Finally, the court determined that it would "keep them both out," ruling that neither Williams's ABPO conviction nor Tse's ABPO conviction was admissible. Tse objected and now argues on appeal that the court improperly excluded Williams's ABPO conviction provides different standards for admitting prior convictions to impeach the accused and to impeach witnesses other than the accused. When the witness is the accused, evidence of a prior conviction "shall be admitted if the court determines that the probative value of admitting this evidence outweighs its prejudicial effect to the accused." Fed. R. Evid. 609. When the witness is other than the accused, such evidence "shall be admitted, subject to Rule 403." Id. Rule 403 in turn states that "evidence may be excluded if its probative value is substantially outweighed by the danger of unfair prejudice, confusion of the issues, or misleading the jury, or by considerations of undue delay, waste of time or needless presentation of cumulative evidence." Fed. R. Evid. 403

This dual approach is the result of a 1990 amendment to Rule 609. Prior to that

---

[74] [9] . . . In Massachusetts, ABPO is punishable by up to two and one half years in prison. Mass. Gen. Laws ch. 265, 13D. Thus, it qualifies for admission under Rule 609 as a "crime punishable by . . . imprisonment in excess of one year under the law under which the witness was convicted."

D. IMPEACHMENT, CROSS-EXAMINATION, AND RELATED PROBLEMS 265

amendment, the rule did not explicitly distinguish between the accused and witnesses other than the accused. Rather, a district court could admit prior convictions against any witness if it determined that "the probative value of admitting this evidence outweighed its prejudicial effect to the defendant." *See* 4 JACK B. WEINSTEIN & MARGARET A. BERGER, WEINSTEIN'S FEDERAL EVIDENCE, § 609 App.03[1] (Joseph M. McLaughlin, ed., Matthew Bender 2d ed. 2004) (stating the language of Rule 609 prior to the 1990 amendment). The language of the rule, explicitly protecting only against prejudice to the defendant in a criminal case, seemingly provided no protection to litigants in civil cases or to prosecution witnesses in criminal cases. *See Green v. Bock Laundry Mach. Co.*, 490 U.S. 504, 509, 527, 109 S. Ct. 1981, 104 L. Ed. 2d 557 (1989) (holding that the pre-1990 version of Rule 609 required courts to admit prior convictions against civil litigants regardless of prejudice, and noting that "impeaching evidence detrimental to the prosecution in a criminal case 'shall be admitted' without any such balancing [of probative value against prejudice]").

The 1990 amendment "[did] not disturb the special balancing test for the criminal defendant who chooses to testify." Fed. R. Evid. 609 advisory committee's notes on 1990 amendment. Rather, the amendment made prior convictions of witnesses other than the accused explicitly subject to the Rule 403 analysis. *See id.* ("The ordinary balancing test of Rule 403 . . . is appropriate for assessing the admissibility of prior convictions for impeachment of any witness other than a criminal defendant.").

This change may not have been aimed explicitly at providing protection for witnesses other than the accused in a criminal trial. *See* H. Richard Uviller, *Essay: Credence, Character, and the Rules of Evidence: Seeing Through the Liar's Tale*, 42 DUKE L.J. 776, 798 (1993) ("A solid argument might be made that the entire purpose to the amendment to Rule 609(a) was to clarify its application to civil cases. . . ."). Nevertheless, "whether intended or not, . . . the amendment of Rule 609(a) has had a dramatic impact on the impeachment of prosecution witnesses in criminal cases." *Id.* at 798. "Prosecution witnesses should be shielded from impeachment by prior conviction if revealing the prior conviction would result in prejudice to the prosecution." *Id.* at 801 (emphasis in original). Indeed, the Advisory Committee Notes indicate that the drafters were aware of the amendment's impact on government witnesses:

> Some courts have read Rule 609(a) as giving the government no protection for its witnesses. This approach is . . . rejected by the amendment. There are cases in which impeachment of government witnesses with prior convictions that have little, if anything, to do with credibility may result in unfair prejudice to the government's interest in a fair trial and unnecessary embarrassment to a witness.

Fed. R. Evid. 609 advisory committee's notes on 1990 amendment (citations omitted). Thus, there is no doubt that we must apply a Rule 403 analysis to prior convictions of government witnesses in a criminal prosecution.

Although Rule 609 sets out two different evidentiary standards for admitting prior convictions for impeachment, it does not make clear whether the court's application of each standard requires a substantively different analysis. Some commentators have suggested that Rule 609 provides greater protection to the accused than it does to other witnesses in the use of prior convictions for impeachment. *See* Weinstein, *supra*, § 609.02 ("If the witness to be impeached is the accused in a criminal case, the rule establishes a more stringent discretionary standard [for admissibility]."). Others are skeptical that the difference between the two balancing tests is sufficiently different to draw a practical distinction in the evidentiary showing required for admission of a prior conviction. *See* Uviller, *supra*, at 800 (suggesting that "the practical possibility of such fine calibration of the danger of prejudice is dubious."). Although "the nature of the distinction is elusive," Uviller, *supra*, at 799, the drafting of the rule suggests that the distinction is intentional. If the drafters had wanted to apply the same evidentiary test to all prior convictions, they could easily have stated a universal rule instead of differentiating between the accused and all other witnesses. We therefore examine closely the two standards to determine the precise nature of their differences.

To describe accurately the distinctions in Rule 609(a)(1), however, we must first unravel a linguistic oddity in its language. With respect to a witness other than the accused, the rule provides that a conviction "shall be admitted, subject to Rule 403." The instruction that convictions "shall be admitted" indicates that Rule 609 is a rule of inclusion; any conviction meeting Rule 609's requirements will be admitted. However, the reference to Rule 403 complicates the analysis. That rule, applicable when a party objects to otherwise relevant evidence, provides that evidence "may be excluded if its probative value is substantially outweighed by the danger of unfair prejudice." Thus, by its language, Rule 403 is a rule of exclusion. These conflicting formulations of inclusion in rule 609 and exclusion in Rule 403 raise some uncertainty about whether the impeaching party (here Tse, who sought to impeach Williams with his prior conviction) bears the burden of demonstrating the superior probative value of the prior convictions to justify admission of the evidence, or whether the impeached party (here the government, which sought to avoid the impeachment of Williams with his prior conviction) bears the burden of demonstrating the danger of unfair prejudice to justify exclusion of the evidence. *See* Uviller, *supra*, at 799–800 (noting this distinction).

The advisory committee notes offer some clarification regarding the use of a prior conviction to impeach government witnesses. The notes state that the "[Rule 403] balancing test protects . . . the government in criminal cases" and that "only when the government is able to point to a real danger of prejudice that is sufficient to outweigh substantially the probative value of the conviction for impeachment purposes will the conviction be excluded." Fed. R. Evid. 609 advisory committee's notes on 1990 amendment. Therefore, although the proponent of the admission of the evidence of a prior conviction is the accused who seeks to impeach the government witness, the government bears the burden of protecting its witnesses from such impeachment by demonstrating to the court, pursuant to Rule 403's exclusionary rule, that the probative value of the conviction at issue is substantially outweighed by the danger of unfair prejudice, or the other grounds for exclusion noted in Rule 403.

This standard of prejudice differs from the standard of prejudice applicable to the court's consideration of requests by the government to impeach a defendant with prior convictions. The court may exclude a prior conviction of the accused, offered for the purpose of impeachment, if the prejudicial effect of the conviction merely outweighs its probative value; the court may exclude a conviction of a government witness, offered by the accused for the purpose of impeachment, only if the danger of unfair prejudice from the conviction substantially outweighs its probative value.

In addition, Rule 403 protects government witnesses only against the danger of "unfair prejudice," while Rule 609 protects the accused against any "prejudicial effect."

"Usually, courts use the term 'unfair prejudice' for evidence that invites the jury to render a verdict on an improper emotional basis." Thus, while a court must weigh all potential "prejudicial effect" to the defendant when deciding whether to admit a prior conviction of the accused, it must weigh only the kind of prejudice that can be deemed "unfair" when deciding whether to admit the prior conviction of a government witness.

These distinctions — "substantially outweighs" versus "outweighs," and "unfair prejudice" versus "prejudicial effect" — support the assertion of the Weinstein treatise that the standard for the admission of prior convictions of the accused is stricter than the standard for the admission of prior convictions of a government witness. These distinctions also recognize that the potential prejudice to the defendant from the admission of prior convictions is simply not the same as the potential prejudice to a government witness. In particular, there is a heightened risk that a jury will use evidence of a prior conviction of the accused to draw an impermissible propensity inference:

In virtually every case in which prior convictions are used to impeach the testifying defendant, the defendant faces a unique risk of prejudice — *i.e.*, the danger that convictions that would be excluded under Fed. R. Evid. 404 will be misused by a jury as propensity evidence despite their introduction solely for impeachment purposes. Fed. R. Evid. 609 advisory committee's notes on 1990 amendment. *See also* Uviller, *supra*, at 802–803 ("The outstanding difference between harm to a defendant and harm to other witnesses is undeniable: A jury might conclude from the testifying defendant's criminal career (despite vociferous instructions from the court to the contrary) that he committed the crime charged because of a demonstrated propensity to engage in criminal conduct. That kind and degree of damage cannot be suffered by the prosecution or its witnesses. . . .").

In contrast, the prior convictions of a government witness are unlikely to inflame the jury or invite a propensity inference:

The probability that prior convictions of an ordinary government witness will be unduly prejudicial is low in most criminal cases. Since the behavior of the witness is not the issue in dispute in most cases, there is little chance that the trier of fact will misuse the convictions offered as impeachment evidence as propensity evidence. Fed. R. Evid. 609 advisory committee's notes on 1990 amendment. Rather, the prior convictions of government witnesses are more likely to cause "unfair prejudice to the government's interest in a fair trial and unnecessary embarrassment to [the] witness." *Id.* While these are important concerns, . . . "trial courts will be skeptical when the government objects to impeachment of its witnesses with prior convictions." Fed. R. Evid. 609 advisory committee's notes on 1990 amendment.

We summarize. With respect to the use of prior convictions for impeachment, Rule 609 distinguishes between the accused and mere witnesses. A court may admit a conviction of the accused only if the probative value "outweighs its prejudicial effect to the accused." By contrast, a court shall admit a conviction of a government witness unless that conviction should be excluded under Rule 403. The burden under is on the party opposing admission, who must show that the probative value "is substantially outweighed by the danger of unfair prejudice." In this case, in considering the admission of a prior conviction of Tse and a prior conviction of Williams, the government's principal witness, the district court appeared to apply a uniform standard of exclusion. If so, the failure to apply the different standards for exclusion was an error of law. [The Court proceeded to rule the error harmless.]

Evidentiary Foundation:
The Trial of Mumia Abu-Jamal

Mumia Abu-Jamal, a Philadelphia journalist and former Black Panther, was convicted for the 1982 murder of police officer Daniel Faulkner. Abu-Jamal has always maintained his innocence. During his trial, however, a witness named Robert Chobert testified that he saw Abu-Jamal shoot Faulkner. The following issue arose during cross-examination:

MR. MCGILL

(prosecutor):   Cross-examine. May we see you at sidebar, Your Honor?

THE COURT: Yes.

(The following transpired at sidebar out of the hearing of the jury:)

MR. MCGILL: Your Honor . . . — he is on probation for arson, five years probation. There is no criminal conviction of crimen falsi. Do you—

MR. JACKSON

(defense counsel):   . . . I'm not so sure that arson isn't crimen falsi.

MR. MCGILL: Arson is definitely not crimen falsi.

MR. JACKSON: If it's done for personal gain, if it's done for hire, it's crimen falsi. You can't say just because he is convicted of setting a fire—

THE COURT: I don't think arson is crimen falsi. Burglary would be, robbery would be.

MR. JACKSON: Anything that shows dishonesty generally.

THE COURT: Arson doesn't necessarily show—

MR. JACKSON: That's what I'm saying. If it's done for personal gain or for profit, then it would be.

THE COURT: Well, we'll have to do that out of the hearing of the jury.

MR. JACKSON: I would like to find that out, Judge.

THE COURT: Take a five-minute recess with the jury please.

(The jury is excused for a five-minute recess, and the following transpired at sidebar:)

THE COURT: What he wants to do is out of the hearing of the jury go into that arson to see if it was done for monetary gain.

MR. MCGILL: Wait a minute, Judge.

THE COURT: I don't know that—

MR. MCGILL: Wait a minute, Judge. This is not — the answer is no. There is no way this is crimen falsi.

THE COURT: Do you have any law to support what you're saying?

MR. MCGILL: All right, Arson for personal gain, but it's not theft. It's not theft.

MR. JACKSON: It would be if he did it for hire, if he did it for insurance. It would be the same thing, what's the difference? It's fraud. That's what it is. It constitutes fraud and to say that he just lit a match and burned something — what I'm saying is if he did it for money, for personal gain of some sort, it's crimen falsi. You have to look beyond the conviction. You just can't go to arson. Do you have anything in your records? What does it show, just arson? What happened in the case?

MR. MCGILL: The case — it's not the case, Judge, it's the charge that's relevant. It's not the case, it's the charge.

MR. JACKSON: I would disagree.

MR. MCGILL: There's just no way that arson is crimen falsi. Here it is, here's his record.

        (Pause.)

THE COURT: See, we don't know whether he was convicted of the arson or criminal mischief or what. You don't have the complete record?

MR. MCGILL: We can — you mean the computer? I don't have the computer sheet, but he tells me arson. Judge, if you want to bring him over here out of the hearing of the jury, if you want to bring him over and ask him; I just don't feel that it's fair to him in public with this press around him, Judge. That's what would bother me very much.

THE DEFENDANT: Judge, I got to go to the bathroom.

THE COURT: Go ahead. Take him to the bathroom.

THE COURT: Come over here, Mr. Chobert.

        (The witness complies with the court's request and comes to sidebar.)

MR. MCGILL: Mr. Chobert, we're trying to determine in terms of background your criminal history. You are presently under probation for, what is the conviction?

THE WITNESS: Arsonist.

MR. MCGILL: Arson?

THE WITNESS: Yes.

MR. MCGILL: And were you also convicted of burglary, or was it just arson?

THE WITNESS: It was just arsonist. [sic]

MR. MCGILL: All right. There are other charges on there. What is there?

THE COURT: Causing a catastrophe and criminal mischief. What happened on those, do you know?

MR. MCGILL: Criminal mischief, that's not crimen falsi.

* * *

MR. MCGILL: What were you found guilty of?

The Judge wants to know what you were found guilty of.

THE WITNESS: I threw a bomb into a school.

THE COURT: You threw a bomb into a school?

THE WITNESS: Yes.

THE COURT: What kind of a bomb?

THE WITNESS: A Molotov.

THE COURT: A Molotov cocktail?

THE WITNESS: Yes.

THE COURT: You just threw it into a school building?

THE WITNESS: Yes.

THE COURT: Where was this, what school building?

THE WITNESS: John Bartram.

THE COURT: And how old were you when you did that?

THE WITNESS: Eighteen.

THE COURT: You were eighteen?

THE WITNESS: Yes.

THE COURT: Did you go to that school?

THE WITNESS: Yes.

THE COURT: And that's why you threw it in there?

THE WITNESS: No, that ain't why. I got paid for doing it.

MR. JACKSON: I'm sorry, I didn't hear that.

THE WITNESS: I said I got paid for doing it.

MR. MCGILL: What do you mean—

MR. JACKSON: That's the reason, that's crimen falsi.

THE COURT: That's not crimen falsi.

MR. JACKSON: If you've got—

MR. MCGILL: That is not crimen falsi. He got paid for doing it—

MR. JACKSON: He got paid for doing it, that is crimen falsi.

MR. MCGILL: Even first degree murder is not crimen falsi if you get paid on a contract basis. That's not crimen falsi, and that's not theft by deception. That's definitely wrong. A murder is not crimen falsi when you have a contract.

THE WITNESS: Your Honor, can I say something?

THE COURT: Yes.

THE WITNESS: How come you bring this up, my background?

THE COURT: Well, he is raising the issue and that's why I want to hear this while the jury is not here.

THE WITNESS: It doesn't matter about nobody else, it's my background.

THE COURT: I know that, but the only time it would be is if it was in the nature of crimen falsi. I guess I have to make a decision, and I don't think that arson is crimen falsi.

MR. MCGILL: It is not?

THE COURT: I will make that decision.

MR. JACKSON: If that's your ruling, sir.

THE COURT: Okay.

QUESTION

If Rule 609 had applied to the above prosecution, would Chobert's arson conviction have been admissible for impeachment?

3)   Prior Bad Acts

William G. Hale, *Specific Acts and Related Matters as Affecting Credibility*
1 HASTINGS L.J. 89, 89–91 (1949)[75]

It is important to observe whether the attack is upon the character of the witness as affecting his credibility, or whether it goes to a matter of bias or motive to falsify. First let us consider the *character* phase of the problem.

Let us take a concrete case. It is claimed that *W* when a witness in another case committed perjury.

If *W* had been convicted of this act of perjury all courts would agree that the record of this conviction would be admitted. Even in such case the evil of surprise is present but only to a minor degree. The essence of such evil is that one is not

---

[75] Copyright © 1949 by University of California, Hastings College of the Law. Reprinted from HASTINGS LAW JOURNAL, Vol. 1, No, 1, pp. 89, 89–91, by permission.

advised in advance that the issue will arise and, therefore, that he will not be prepared in advance to meet it with countervailing evidence. But in the instance supposed only two issues are involved, one whether there was a conviction (and this is limited to the record — a simple matter — and the record speaking for itself), and the other the identity of W as the one thus convicted. The latter could be a more difficult issue and evidence opposing the identity might not be readily available. Such evil might be somewhat obviated by requiring that W first be asked on cross-examination as to such conviction. This would serve as a warning and thus make possible some time to prepare to meet the issue by other witnesses. As a practical matter such inquiry is usually made. In any event the collateral issue involved is simple and hence weighs but little against admissibility.

But suppose W had not been convicted of the perjury, *i.e.*, had never been called to answer for it. The issue of logic is the same as where there has been a conviction. But considerations of auxiliary policy, looking to exclusion, become more pronounced. If it is sought to prove W's guilt of the offense by other witnesses the evils of surprise and collateral issue are significant enough, as compared with the evidential value of the fact, to justify the uniform rule of exclusion. The determination of W's guilt could easily loom as large as the main issue in the case and there would be no opportunity in advance to prepare to defend W against such an accusation. Extrinsic testimony to particular acts, except where there has been conviction, is universally conceded to be inadmissible, because of consideration of auxiliary policy. . . . These considerations of auxiliary policy are: (1) confusion of issues; (2) undue consumption of time; (3)unfair surprise since such collateral issue cannot be anticipated and, hence, no preparation can be made to meet it. . . . If, however, the method of securing evidence of W's guilt of the offense were restricted to admissions that might be secured from him on cross-examination, these adverse auxiliary considerations would be eliminated. And thus it is that England and a substantial number of American jurisdictions, within the court's discretion, permit this mode of attacking the veracity-character of a witness, the evils of both surprise and collateral issue being avoided by holding that the cross-examiner is bound by the answer of the witness. . . .

The contrary view, which precludes even resort by cross-examination to particular acts, where there is no record of conviction, is based in part upon a misconception of the evils of surprise and collateral issue. If the attack upon the witness does not go beyond cross-examination, none of the considerations of policy embraced in confusion of issues, waste of time and unfair surprise would be present. But, in support of the rule of complete exclusion, there are other considerations of auxiliary policy, the force of which cannot be lightly pushed aside. It is true, as even the courts which allow such cross examination concede, that an unfair, if not to say unethical, attorney may subvert the whole process evidentially, by insinuating a baseless course of misconduct to the witness by the mere asking of questions relative thereto. It is also urged that any procedure so calculated as this, even at its best, to convert the witness stand into a chamber of horrors will tend to deter persons from appearing as witnesses.

* * *

In answer to these arguments it may be urged (1) that rules should not be predicated on factors that can enter only through unethical practices; (2) that the witness is afforded some protection by exercising his privilege against incrimination and in some jurisdictions against disgracing himself (though as a practical matter this protection is quite inadequate for the reason that the harm is done when the question is asked and the privilege is asserted); (3) that the court, by discretionary power of interceding, may prevent the more, obvious abuses, and finally (4) that the urge to do justice in the pending case outweighs the possible evils that inhere in the method, especially the evil of embarrassment to the witness.

UNITED STATES v. PROVOO
215 F.2d 531 (2d Cir. 1954)

SWAN, CIRCUIT JUDGE.

After a long jury trial the defendant was convicted of treason. . . . He was a staff sergeant in the United States Army who was captured by the Japanese upon the surrender of Corregidor, Philippine Islands. The indictment charged twelve separate overt acts of treason alleged to have been committed by him between May 6, 1942 and August 14, 1945 while he was a prisoner of war. Only seven of the overt acts charged were submitted to the jury, the others having been dismissed by the trial judge. The jury found him guilty of four of the seven submitted, and as to three reached no agreement. Of the four acts of which the defendant was found guilty one was an offer of services to the Japanese on Corregidor; another was reporting that Captain Thomson, who was also a prisoner of war on Corregidor, was anti-Japanese and uncooperative, with the result that Thomson was put to death by the Japanese; and the other two were radio broadcasts from Tokyo during the spring of 1944. The main defense was duress and lack of treasonable intent. On March 12, 1953 Provoo was sentenced to life imprisonment and the statutory mandatory fine of $10,000 was imposed. . . .

* * *

On the main appeal the appellant has alleged numerous errors; they relate to the charge to the jury, the sufficiency of the evidence to support the verdict, the admission of certain exhibits, and alleged unfairness in the conduct of the trial, particularly in respect to cross-examination of the defendant which, it is urged, was intended to, and did, bring home to the jury collateral matters so prejudicial and inflammatory as to require a reversal for this reason alone, regardless of other errors. We shall at once address consideration to this contention.

The defendant took the stand in his own defense. His direct examination dealt with four periods of his life: (1) his birth in San Francisco in 1917 and the years prior to his capture by the Japanese in 1942; (2) his experiences and conduct while he was a prisoner of war; (3) his experiences in Japan after liberation by the American forces; (4) his return to the United States in April 1946 and his experiences in the Army from the date of his return up to September 2, 1949. The challenged cross-examination is concerned only with the fourth period. Provoo's direct examination on this period brought out that he had received an honorable discharge at Fort Dix, New Jersey on August 17, 1946; that he reenlisted at Camp Beale,

California, on September 5, 1946, and thereafter was ordered to various Army posts and hospitals. At Fort Bragg, North Carolina, in 1948 and Fort Meade, Maryland, in 1949, he was imprisoned in the stockade, and on two other occasions he was under physical restraint during hospitalization at Walter Reed Hospital, Washington, D. C. While he was in the Walter Reed Hospital and in the stockade at Fort Meade he was interrogated by representatives of the Department of Justice concerning his prisoner of war days and gave signed statements. On September 2, 1949 he was brought under guard from Fort Meade to Fort Jay, Governors Island, N.Y., was ordered to accept an "undesirable discharge" from the Army, and was thereupon turned over to F.B.I. agents who forthwith arrested him on the charges of treason for which he was later indicted and tried.

The direct examination of Provoo on the subject of his experiences after reenlistment occupies less than ten pages of the record. It contains no intimation as to the reason for his imprisonment at Fort Bragg and Fort Meade or for his confinement at the Walter Reed Hospital. Almost at once the cross examiner put the question, "What were the circumstances, please, that caused your arrest and confinement," at Fort Bragg. An objection to this line of inquiry was overruled, and the cross-examination as to the reasons for his imprisonments and hospitalizations was continued over repeated objections for more than 200 pages of the record. It was designed to draw from the witness an admission that he had been charged with, or suspected of, being a homosexualist, and it culminated in the direct question: "Now, Mr. Provoo, isn't it a fact that in November 1946 you were hospitalized at Camp Lee, Virginia, because of homosexual aberrations?" A motion for a mistrial was promptly made and overruled, the court telling the jury that "this question and any similar questions and the answer to these questions is being permitted solely in connection with the question of the credibility and the weight to be given to the witness' testimony." The defendant answered that he was hospitalized at Camp Lee "because I was sick, and I haven't any idea what diagnosis was made at that time or what the doctor may or may not have put in his report at that time. But I am not a homosexual." The prosecutor then showed the defendant certain pages of Government's Exhibit 2 for identification (his army record) and asked if that refreshed his recollection as to the reason he was at the hospital at Camp Lee. The answer was that it did not refresh his recollection. He was then shown another page of Exhibit 2 for identification and asked if that refreshed his recollection as to the reason for his confinement in Fort Sill, Oklahoma in 1947. The defendant answered it did not but added "It does state I was a suspect." The next question was: "Now Mr. Provoo, isn't it a fact that you were sent from Fort Sill, Oklahoma to Brook General Hospital at Fort Sam Houston because you were a homosexual suspect?" The answer was "No, Sir. That is a lie." Similar questions were then asked as to the defendant's confinement at Fort Bragg, at the Walter Reed Hospital and at Fort Meade.

It is obvious that the cross-examination informed the jury that on several occasions after reenlistment the defendant had been charged with being, or suspected by military authorities or hospital doctors of being, a homosexualist. Neither by court martial nor by a civil court was he ever brought to trial and convicted on any charge of sodomy. Obviously such a charge was utterly irrelevant to the issue whether he had committed treason while a prisoner of war. But these highly inflammatory and prejudicial collateral and irrelevant charges were brought to the jury's attention. Nor was it done by accident or unintentionally. In colloquy between court and counsel in argument as to their admissibility, the prosecutor stated: "I also said I was going to bring it out through the defendant . . . and I made the declaration that if the defendant took the stand, he was laying himself open to that kind of cross-examination." That the facts so developed were so prejudicial as to constitute reversible error, if they were improperly admitted, is too plain for debate. They had no relevancy to charges on which he was being tried and were certain to degrade him in the eyes of the jury. . . .

Two theories are advanced by government counsel in attempted justification for bringing such prejudicial matter to the knowledge of the jury. It is urged, first, that the direct examination "opened the door" to inquiry on cross-examination as to the true nature of defendant's incarceration and hospitalization; and, secondly, that in any event a defendant who takes the stand in a criminal trial may be questioned as to any criminal or immoral act of his life since such information is relevant to his credibility as a witness.

This court had occasion to discuss the doctrine of "opening the door" in *United States v. Corrigan*. . . . As there explained, with the citation of authorities, "The doctrine . . . is an application of the principle of 'completeness'; that is, if one party to litigation puts in evidence part of a document, or a correspondence or a conversation, which is detrimental to the opposing party, the latter may introduce the balance of the document, correspondence or conversation in order to explain or rebut the adverse inferences which might arise from the fragmentary or incomplete character of the evidence introduced by his adversary." At page 3961 of the Record, in colloquy with counsel, the trial judge expressed the view that "a fair inference from that testimony [Provoo's testimony on direct examination that he had been confined in various stockades and hospitals in the United States after his reenlistment] would be that those incarcerations were a result, directly or indirectly of an investigation by either the Army or the F.B.I. of his conduct during his prisoner of war days." We do not think such an inference was permissible. The Army lacked jurisdiction to court-martial him for conduct preceding his honorable discharge in August 1946 . . . hence it is not to be inferred that he was imprisoned by the Army for what occurred in Japan. Provoo's direct testimony was entirely neutral as to the cause of his confinements after reenlistment. Moreover, even on the assumption that the jury might infer that these confinements were related to his conduct as a prisoner of war, it is difficult to see how such an inference could be deemed *adverse* to the prosecution. The direct testimony contains no suggestion that the confinements were illegal or that the defendant was a victim of prolonged persecution. If sympathy could have been created by the fact of his frequent hospitalizations, we think it would have been far outweighed by the inference of guilt which the jury would be likely to attach to the fact of imprisonment. . . .

We pass now to the alternative contention that even if the door was not opened to inquiry as to the true reasons for defendant's incarceration and hospitalization, the prosecution could lawfully cross-examine him as to immoral or vicious acts, since such information has a bearing upon the defendant's credibility as a witness in his own behalf. It is true that a defendant who takes the stand subjects himself to cross-examination, within the limits of the appropriate rules of evidence, like any other witness, and may be cross-examined for the purpose of impeaching his credibility. In *People v. Sorge*, . . . it is stated that a defendant, like any other witness, may be interrogated upon cross-examination in regard to any vicious or criminal act of his life that has a bearing on his credibility. Whether this is a correct statement of the New York law we need not stop to consider. Concededly local rules of evidence are not controlling in criminal trials in the United States courts. . . . In the Federal courts there has been an impressive unanimity of view on the point before us. As generally held, specific acts of misconduct not resulting in conviction of a felony or crime of moral turpitude are not the proper subject of cross-examination for impeachment purposes. In this circuit, apparently under the influence of the broader New York rule, we have at times allowed impeaching questions as to misdemeanors, . . . and even criminal acts which were not established by a judgment of conviction. . . . Of these last, however, one may be explained as tending to show the necessary criminal intent . . . and two as proceeding on the theory that the door had been opened. . . . On the strength of this meager authority we cannot say that we are committed to a position so radically at variance with that of the other circuits as to allow this examination.

Even if the course of our precedents was clearer, we would have difficulty espousing the Government's position. Under F.R. Cr. P. 26 we are governed "by the principles of the common law as they may be interpreted by the courts of the United States in the light of reason and experience." In proposing the rule, the Notes of the Advisory Committee remark that: "Since all federal crimes are statutory and all criminal prosecutions in the federal courts are based on acts of Congress, uniform rules of evidence appear desirable if not essential in criminal cases, as otherwise the same facts under differing rules of evidence may lead to a conviction in one district and to an acquittal in another." We have set forth above the interpretation of the common law adopted by the overwhelming majority of federal courts. As for experience, WIGMORE, EVIDENCE (3d ed.) §§ 980(a)–983 presents numerous examples of the abuses resulting from unrestrained inquiry into a witness's history, suggests that the inquiry be confined to the trait of veracity, § 982 (1), and offers the suggestion that a defendant-witness is entitled to even greater protection, in order to prevent unfair prejudice.§§ 891(3), 983(4), 2277(4). As for reason, we do not conceive that inquiry into every accusation of criminal or vicious conduct will further the search for truth. Where, as here, the defendant's general character has not been put in issue, it is difficult to justify any examination other than into the trait of veracity. No authority has been cited which suggests that homosexuality indicates a propensity to disregard the obligation of an oath. The sole purpose and effect of this examination was to humiliate and degrade the defendant, and increase the probability that he would be convicted, not for the crime charged, but for his general unsavory character. Permitting it was error.

The error was plainly prejudicial. Indeed we can conceive of no accusation which could have been more degrading in the eyes of the jury nor more irrelevant to the issue of treason on which he was being tried. On the main appeal the judgment must be reversed and the cause remanded for a new trial. This disposition makes unnecessary consideration of the other alleged errors in the course of the trial.

Evidentiary Foundation:
The O.J. Simpson Civil Trial

Rufo, et al., v. Simpson

After O.J. Simpson's acquittal for the murder of his wife and her companion, the victims' families filed a wrongful death civil suit against Mr. Simpson. The following excerpt involved former Playboy Playmate India Allen. On direct examination, Ms. Allen testified that she worked at a veterinary hospital in Beverly Hills when Nicole Brown took her two Chows in for a bath. Ms. Allen testified that, on one occasion, Mr. Simpson drove up, got out of his car appearing to be very upset, and yelled at his wife for having an affair; Mr. Simpson then struck his wife. This testimony refuted Mr. Simpson's happy-marriage/no-motive-to-kill defense. Ms. Allen was cross-examined as follows:

CROSS-EXAMINATION BY MR. BAKER:

Q.   Good morning.

A.   Good morning.

Q.   Do you have an agent?

A.   Do I have an agent?

Q.   Yes.

A.   No, I don't.

Q.   Did you have an agent?

A.   Yes, I used to.

Q.   Did you ever appear in Playboy magazine?

A.   Yes, I did.

MR. KELLY: Objection, relevance.

THE COURT: Sustained.

Q. (BY MR. BAKER)   Do you have a web page presently?

MR. KELLY: Objection, relevance.

THE COURT: Sustained.

Q. (BY MR. BAKER)   In the web page did you have — do you appear without clothes?

MR. KELLY: Objection, relevance, Your Honor.

THE COURT: Sustained.

MR. BAKER: Your Honor, this goes to the issue of bias.

NOTES AND QUESTIONS

1.   Does the above testimony "go to the issue of bias"? If not, is it still admissible as bad act impeachment?

2. In *People v. Sorge*, 93 N.E.2d 637 (N.Y. 1950),[76] the following cross-examination, based upon previous abortions allegedly performed by defendant, was sustained in defendant's trial for yet another abortion:[77]

Q.   During the month of January, 1947 did you perform an abortion in your home at 64 Eleanor Street on Mrs. John Peeler, of Willow Springs, North Carolina, also known as "Sandy"?

A.   No.

* * *

Q.   I ask you . . . [d]id you on April 12, 1948, at approximately 8:30, P.M. perform an abortion on Ruth Schultz, of Jersey City?

A.   No.

Q.   I show you this copy of a statement and ask you if it refreshes your recollection.

A.   Yes, it does.

Q.   Having seen that, will you now tell us whether or not you performed an abortion on Ruth Schultz?

A.   No.

Q.   And on November 12, 1948 did you tell Loraine Schymanski that you wouldn't perform an abortion for her, but that you had a friend by the name of Margaret in New Jersey, who would do it for $150?

A.   No.

Q.   On November 12, 1948, at nine o'clock in the morning did you, in your automobile bearing license number R-U-88, pick up Loraine Schymanski in front of the lunch wagon at Meyers Corners?

A.   No.

Q.   Did you a few minutes after that, on the same day, pick up Mae Florentine at the corner of Bradley Avenue and Victory Boulevard?

A.   I did not, no.

Q.   Did you drive Loraine Schymanski, Mae Florentine, and another girl, to the home of Henrietta Forster, at 15 Fourth Place, South Beach, on November 12th?

A.   No, I did not.

Q.   Were you present in the living room of Henrietta Forster at 15 Fourth Place about nine o'clock in the morning of November 12th, 1948 when Mrs. Florentine performed an abortion on Loraine Schymanski in the kitchen of Mrs. Forster's home?

---

[76] This excerpt is reproduced from J. WEINSTEIN, J. MANSFIELD, N. ABRAMS & M. BERGER, CASES AND MATERIALS ON EVIDENCE (7th ed. 1983).

[77] This excerpt is reproduced from J. WEINSTEIN, J. MANSFIELD, N. ABRAMS & M. BERGER, CASES AND MATERIALS ON EVIDENCE (7th ed. 1983).

A.   No.

Q.   You told this jury that on August 20, 1948 you pleaded guilty to the practice of — to the unlawful practice of medicine, is that correct?

A.   That's right.

Q.   And you did that in this court?

A.   That's right.

Q.   And do you remember Judge Walsh reading to you exactly what you pleaded guilty to on that day?

A.   I don't recall the words right now.

Q.   Do you remember Judge Walsh sitting up in the same place where he is sitting now and asking you if you, Louise Sorge, pleaded guilty to the crime of unlawful practice of medicine, in that on April 12, 1948, in premises situate 64 Eleanor Street, Egbertville, you administered and used upon one Ruth Schultz a certain instrument, to wit, a rubber tube known as a catheter with intent thereby to procure the miscarriage of the said Ruth Schultz, the same not being necessary to preserve the life of the aforesaid Ruth Schultz or the life of the child with which she was then and there pregnant, against the form of the statute in such case made and provided, and against the peace of the People of the State of New York and their dignity?

Judge Tiernan

[defense counsel]:   I object to that on the ground it is incompetent, irrelevant and immaterial and that the question is framed purposely for the purpose of inflaming the minds of the jury against the defendant, and I now move for the withdrawal of a juror and the direction of a mistrial.

The Court: Objection overruled. Motion to withdraw and for the declaration of a mistrial denied.

Judge Tiernan: Exception.

The Court: She may say, "Yes, I remember," or "No, I don't."

A.   No, I don't remember those words.

3.   In what way, if any, does a witness' participation in a prior illegal abortion bear upon credibility?

4.   Why did the witness in *Sorge* face a special risk of prejudice from inquiry about her participation in a prior abortion?

5.   Fed. R. Evid. 608(b)(1) restricts counsel to asking about prior bad acts that bear upon the witness' "character for truthfulness. Crimes involving perjury, fraud, or deception obviously relate to character for truthfulness. What about immigration violations (*United States v. Thiongo*, 344 F.3d 55 (1st Cir. 2003)), failure to register a gun (*United States v. Miles*, 207 F.3d 988 (7th Cir. 2000)), failure to file tax returns (*Chnapkova v. Koh*, 985 F.2d 79 (2d Cir. 1993)), and bribery (*United States v. Wilson*, 985 F.2d 348 (7th Cir. 1993))?

6. Note that Fed. R. Evid. 608(b)(1) prohibits counsel from refuting a witness' denial through extrinsic evidence. In *Simmons, Inc. v. Pinkerton*, 762 F.2d 591, 605 (7th Cir. 1985), the Court explained this prohibition as follows:

> Fed. R. Evid. 608(b) . . . is exactly tailored to strike the balance that the collateral evidence rule was designed to achieve with respect to impeachment by contradiction. Rule 608(b) allows cross examination of a witness about specific instances of her past conduct, if probative of truthfulness or untruthfulness, but prohibits the proof of such conduct by extrinsic evidence. Thus, as with the collateral evidence rule, a relevant fact bearing on the witness' credibility — in this case, that he has lied in the past or acted in some other manner that casts doubt on veracity — may, in the discretion of the trial judge, be considered sufficiently important and probative to be elicited on cross-examination; yet, because of the dangers of confusion, prejudice, waste of time, and so on, that would be inherent if a "mini-trial" on the existence of that fact were allowed, extrinsic evidence of the matter is prohibited.

7. In theory, the absence of a conviction renders bad act impeachment less prejudicial than prior conviction impeachment. However, does Fed. R. of Evid. 608(b) provide protections comparable to those contained in Fed. R. Evid. 609? If not, does Rule 608(b) actually contain more potential for prejudice? For example, compare how Rules 608 and 609 treat misconduct that occurred when the defendant was a juvenile.

8. Despite the absence of limiting language in Rule 608 similar to Rule 609(a)(1), may the court rely upon Rule 403 to preclude evidence that, on balance, is considered prejudicial or extraneous? *See United States v. Turning Bear*, 357 F.3d 730, 734 (8th Cir. 2004).

9. Courts routinely restrict impeachment under Rule 609 to the crime, date, and court of conviction; counsel may not inquire about the underlying facts of a conviction. *United States v. White*, 222 F.3d 363, 370 (7th Cir. 2000). May this prohibition be circumvented by framing the question in terms of the witness' prior bad acts? *Compare United States v. Wilkerson*, 251 F.3d 273, 280 (1st Cir. 2001) *with United States v. Pickard*, 236 F. Supp. 2d 1204, 1213 (D. Kan. 2002)

10. May acquitted conduct serve as the basis for bad act impeachment? *See United States v. Johnson*, 1996 U.S. App. LEXIS 29029 (9th Cir.); *cf. United States v. Radabaugh*, 840 F.2d 18 (6th Cir. 1988).

11. Under Rule 608(b), may the cross-examiner refer to a witness' prior arrests? *See United States v. Johnson*, 75 Fed. Appx. 296 (5th Cir. 2003); *United States v. Ling*, 581 F.2d 1118 (4th Cir. 1978); *United States v. Domingo*, 2006 U.S. Dist. LEXIS 17890 (D. Ariz. 2006).

If it goes to truthfulness

Evidentiary Foundation:
The Trial of Henry Lazarus

[Henry E. Lazarus, a prominent merchant, was indicted for bribery of a United States officer and violation of the Sabotage Act. The jury acquitted him after deliberating just 30 minutes. Defense cross examination of, Charles L. Fuller, Supervising Inspector, probably accounted for this outcome. On direct examination, Fuller testified that Lazarus gave money to him to influence performance of his general duties as an inspector and to overlook the fact that Lazarus was manufacturing defective coats, thereby violating the Sabotage Act. Cross-examination focused on an application for government employment that Fuller had completed years earlier.]

[After Fuller testified on direct, he was cross-examined by Lazarus' attorney regarding an application for government employment Fuller completed years earlier.]

Q.	"Did you sign such an application?"
A.	"I did, sir."
Q.	"Did you swear to it?"
A.	"No, I did not swear to it."
Q.	"I show you your name signed on the bottom of this blank, and ask you if you signed that?"
A.	"Yes, sir."
Q.	"Do you see it is sworn to?"
A.	"I had forgotten it."
Q.	"You see there is a seal on it?"
A.	"I had forgotten that also."
Q.	"This application appears to be subscribed on the 24th of May, 1918, by Charles Lawrence Fuller."
A.	"It must be right if I have sworn to it on that date."
Q.	"Do you remember in May, 1918, that you signed and swore to this application?"
A.	"That is so, I must have sworn to it, sir."
Q.	"Do you remember it?"
A.	"Let me look at it and I can probably refresh my memory." (Paper handed to witness)
Q.	"Look at the signature. Does that help you?"
A.	"That is my signature."
Q.	"You said that. Do you remember in May, 1918, you signed and swore to this?"
A.	"Well, the date is there."

Q.   "Do you know that?"

A.   "Yes, sir, I must have sworn to it. I don't remember the date."

Q.   "Don't you remember you signed your name, Charles Lawrence Fuller, there?"

A.   "I did, sir."

Q.   "And you swore to this paper and signed it?"

A.   "That date is correct there, yes, sir."

Q.   "Don't you remember you swore to it the date you signed it?"

A.   "I swore to it."

Q.   "Was your name Fuller?"

A.   "Yes, sir."

Q.   "Has your name always been Fuller?"

A.   "No, sir."

Q.   "What was your name?"

[The witness protested against any further inquiry along that line, but counsel was permitted to show that his name at one time was Finkler and that he changed his name, back and forth, from Finkler to Fuller. Counsel then proceeded to bring the witness down to the actual oath he had taken in his application.]

Q.   "Now, Mr. Fuller, in your application you made to the Government, on which I showed you your signature and affidavit, you attached your picture, did you not?"

A.   "Yes, sir."

Q.   "And you stated in your application you were born in Atlanta, Georgia, did you not?"

A.   "Yes, sir."

Q.   "You were asked, when you sought this position, these questions: 'When employed, the years and the months,' and you wrote it, 'February, 1897 to August 1917, number of years 20; Where employed — Brooklyn; Name of Employer — Vulcan Proofing Company; Amount of salary, — $37.50 a week; also superintendent in the rubber and compound room.'"

Q.   "You wrote that, didn't you?"

A.   "Yes, sir."

Q.   "And swore to that, didn't you?"

A.   "Yes, sir."

Q.   "Now, were you employed from February, 1897 to August 1917, twenty years, with the Vulcan Proofing Company?"

A.   "No, sir."

Q.   "That was not true, was it?"

A.   "No, sir."

Q.   "And had you been assistant superintendent of the rubber and compound room?"

A.   "No, sir."

Q.   "That was false, wasn't it?"

A.   "Yes, sir."

Q.   " 'And through my experience as chief inspector of the rubber and slicker division,' that was false, wasn't it?"

A.   "Yes, sir."

Q.   "And you knew you were swearing a falsehood when you swore to it?"

A.   "Yes, sir."

Q.   "And you knew you were committing perjury when you swore to it?"

A.   "I did not look at it in that light."

Q.   "Didn't you know you were committing perjury by swearing and pretending you had been twenty years in this business?"

A.   "Yes, sir."

Q.   "And you are swearing now, aren't you?"

A.   "Yes, sir."

Q.   "In a matter in which a man's liberty is involved?"

A.   "Yes, sir."

Q.   "And you know that the jury is to be called upon to consider whether you are worthy of belief or not, don't you?"

A.   "Yes, sir."

Q.   "When you swore to this falsehood deliberately, and wrote it in your handwriting, and knew it was false, you swore to it intentionally, and you knew that you were committing perjury, didn't you?"

A.   "I did not look at it in that light."

Q.   "Well, now when you know you are possibly swearing away the liberty of a citizen of this community, do you look at it in the same light?"

A.   "Yes, sir, I do."

Evidentiary Foundation:
The Trial of Jesse R. Davis[78]

The Bellevue Hospital Case

On December 15, 1900, there appeared in the *New York World* an article written by Thomas J. Minnock, a newspaper reporter, in which he claimed to have been an eyewitness to the shocking brutality of certain nurses in attendance at the Insane Pavilion of Bellevue Hospital, which resulted in the death, by strangulation, of one of its inmates, a Frenchman named Hilliard. This Frenchman had arrived at the hospital at about four o'clock in the afternoon of Tuesday, December 11. He was suffering from alcoholic mania, but was apparently otherwise in normal physical condition. Twenty-six hours later, or on Wednesday, December 12, he died. An autopsy was performed which disclosed several bruises on his forehead, arm, hand, and shoulder, three broken ribs and a broken hyoid bone in the neck (which supports the tongue), and a suffusion of blood or hemorrhage on both sides of the windpipe. The coroner's physician reported the cause of death, as shown by the autopsy, to be strangulation. The newspaper reporter, Minnock, claimed to have been in Bellevue at the time, feigning insanity for newspaper purposes; and upon his discharge from the hospital he stated that he had seen the Frenchman strangled to death by the nurses in charge of the Pavilion by the use of a sheet tightly twisted around the insane man's neck.

*   *   *

The other local papers immediately took up the story, and it is easy to imagine the pitch to which the public excitement and indignation were aroused. The three nurses in charge of the pavilion at the time of Hilliard's death were immediately indicted for manslaughter, and the head nurse, Jesse R. Davis, was promptly put on trial in the Court of General Sessions, before Mr. Justice Cowing and a "special jury." The trial lasted three weeks, and after deliberating five hours upon their verdict the jury acquitted the prisoner.

*   *   *

The first fifteen minutes of the cross-examination were devoted to showing that the witness was a thoroughly educated man, twenty-five years of age, a graduate of St. John's College, Fordham, New York, the Sacred Heart Academy, St. Francis Xavier's and the De La Salle Institute, and had traveled extensively in Europe and America. The cross-examination then proceeded:—

Counsel

(amiably).   "Mr. Minnock, I believe you have written the story of your life and published it in the *Bridgeport Sunday Herald* as recently as last December? I hold the original article in my hand."

Witness.   "It was not the story of my life."

---

[78] The account of this case has been excerpted from trial attorney Francis Wellman's classic work, THE ART OF CROSS EXAMINATION 414–16, 418–24 (4th ed. 1962).

Counsel.	"The article is signed by you and purports to be a history of your life."
Witness.	"It is an imaginary story dealing with hypnotism. Fiction, partly, but it dealt with facts."
Counsel.	"That is, you mean to say you mixed fiction and fact in the history of your life?"
Witness.	"Precisely."
Counsel.	"When in this article you wrote that at the age of twelve you ran away with a circus, was that dressed up?"
Witness.	"Yes, sir."
Counsel.	"It was not true?"
Witness.	"No, sir."
Counsel.	"When you said that you continued with this circus for over a year, and went with it to Belgium, there was a particle of truth in that because you did, as a matter of fact, go to Belgium, but not with the circus as a public clown; is that the idea?"
Witness.	"Yes, sir."
	Counsel. "So there was some little truth mixed in at this point with the other matter?"
Witness.	"Yes, sir."
Counsel.	"When you wrote that you were introduced in Belgium, at the Hospital General, to Charcot, the celebrated Parisian hypnotist, was there some truth in that?"
Witness.	"No, sir."
Counsel.	"You knew that Charcot was one of the originators of hypnotism in France, didn't you?"
Witness.	"I knew that he was one of the original hypnotists."
Counsel.	"How did you come to state in the newspaper history of your life that you were introduced to Charcot at the Hospital General if that was not true?"
Witness.	"While there I met Charcot."
Counsel.	"Oh, I see."
Witness.	"But not the original Charcot."
Counsel.	"Which Charcot did you meet?"
Witness.	"A woman. She was a lady assuming the name of Charcot, claiming to be Madame Charcot."
Counsel.	"So that when you write in this article that you met Charcot, you intended people to understand that it was the celebrated Professor Charcot, and it was partly true, because there was a woman by the name of Charcot whom you had really met?"

Witness.	"Precisely."
Counsel (quietly).	"That is to say, there was some truth in it?"
Witness.	"Yes, sir."
Counsel.	"When in that article you said that Charcot taught you to stand pain, was there any truth in that?"
Witness.	"No."
Counsel.	"Did you as a matter of fact learn to stand pain?"
Witness.	"No."
Counsel.	"When you said in this article that Charcot began by sticking pins and knives into you little by little, so as to accustom you to standing pain, was that all fiction?"
Witness.	"Yes, Sir."
Counsel.	"When you wrote that Charcot taught you to reduce your respirations to two a minute, so as to make your body insensible to pain, was that fiction?"
Witness.	"Purely imagination."
Court (interrupting).	"Counselor, I will not allow you to go further in this line of inquiry. The witness himself says his article was almost entirely fiction, some of it founded upon fact. I will allow you the greatest latitude in a proper way, but not in this direction."
Counsel.	"Your Honor does not catch the point."
Court.	"I do not think I do."
Counsel.	"This prosecution was started by a newspaper article written by the witness, and published in the morning *Journal.* It is the claim of the defence that the newspaper article was a mixture of fact and fiction, mostly fiction. The witness has already admitted that the history of his life, published but a few months ago, and written and signed by himself and sold as a history of his life, was a mixture of fact and fiction, mostly fiction. Would it not be instructive to the jury to learn from the lips of the witness himself how far he dressed up the pretended history of his own life, that they may draw from it some inference as to how far he has likewise dressed up the article which was the origin of this prosecution?"
Court.	"I shall grant you the greatest latitude in examination of the witness in regard to the newspaper article which he published in regard to this case, but I exclude all questions relating to the witness's newspaper history of his own life."
Counsel.	"Did you not have yourself photographed and published in the newspapers in connection with the history of your life, with your

mouth and lips and ears sewed up, while you were insensible to pain?"

Court. "Question excluded."

Counsel. "Did you not publish a picture of yourself in connection with the pretended history of your life, representing yourself upon a cross, spiked hand and foot, but insensible to pain, in consequence of the instruction you had received from Professor Charcot?"

Court. "Question excluded."

Counsel. "I offer these pictures and articles in evidence."

Court

(roughly). "Excluded."

Counsel. "In the article you published in the *New York Journal*, wherein you described the occurrences in the present case, which you have just now related upon the witness stand, did you there have yourself represented as in the position of the insane patient, with a sheet twisted around your neck, and held by the hands of the hospital nurse who was strangling you to death?"

Witness. "I wrote the article, but I did not pose for the picture. The picture was posed for by some one else who looked like me."

Counsel (stepping up to the witness and handing him the newspaper article).

"Are not these words under your picture, 'This is how I saw it done, Thomas J. Minnock,' a facsimile of your handwriting?"

Witness. "Yes, sir, it is my handwriting."

Counsel. "Referring to the history of your life again how many imaginary articles on the subject have you written for the newspapers throughout the country?"

Witness. "One."

Counsel. "You have put several articles in New York papers, have you not?"

Witness. "It was only the original story. It has since been redressed, that's all."

Counsel. "Each time you signed the article and sold it to the newspaper for money, did you not?"

Court. "Excluded."

Counsel (with a sudden change of manner, and in a loud voice, turning to the audience). "Is the chief of police of Bridgeport, Connecticut, in the court room? (turning to the witness.) Mr. Minnock, do you know this gentleman?"

Witness. "I do."

Counsel. "Tell the jury when you first made his acquaintance."

Witness.   "It was when I was arrested in the Atlantic Hotel, in Bridgeport, Connecticut, with my wife."

Counsel.   "Was she your wife at the time?"

Witness.   "Yes, sir."

Counsel.   "She was but sixteen years old?"

Witness.   "Seventeen, I guess."

Counsel.   "You were arrested on the ground that you were trying to drug this sixteen-year-old girl and kidnap her to New York. Do you deny it?"

Witness

(doggedly).   "I was arrested."

Counsel

(sharply).   "You know the cause of the arrest to be as I have stated? Answer yes or no!"

Witness

(hesitating).   "Yes, sir."

Counsel.   "You were permitted by the prosecuting attorney, F. A. Bartlett, to be discharged without trial on your promise to leave the state, were you not?"

Witness.   "I don't remember anything of that."

Counsel.   "Do you deny it?"

Witness.   "I do."

Counsel.   "Did you have another young man with you upon that occasion?"

Witness.   "I did. A college chum."

Counsel.   "Was he also married to this sixteen-year-old girl?"

Witness   (no answer).

Counsel

(pointedly at witness).   "Was he married to this girl also?"

Witness.   "Why, no."

Counsel.   "You say you were married to her. Give me the date of your marriage."

Witness.   (hesitating). "I don't remember the date."

Counsel.   "How many years ago was it?"

Witness.   "I don't remember."

Counsel.   "What is your best memory as to how many years ago it was?"

Witness.   "I can't recollect."

Counsel.   "Try to recollect about when you were married."

Witness.   "I was married twice, civil marriage and church marriage."

Counsel.	"I am talking about Miss Sadie Cook. When were you married to Sadie Cook, and where is the marriage recorded?"
Witness.	"I tell you I don't remember."
Counsel.	"Try."
Witness.	"It might be five or six or seven or ten years ago."
Counsel.	"Then you cannot tell within five years of the time when you were married, and you are now only twenty-five years old?"
Witness.	"I cannot."
Counsel.	"Were you married at fifteen years of age?"
Witness.	"I don't think I was."
Counsel.	"You know, do you not, that your marriage was several years after this arrest in Bridgeport that I have been speaking to you about?"
Witness.	"I know nothing of the kind."
Counsel (resolutely).	"Do you deny it?"
Witness (hesitating).	"Well, no, I do not deny it."
Counsel.	"I hand you now what purports to be the certificate of your marriage, three years ago. Is the date correct?"
Witness.	"I never saw it before."
Counsel.	"Does the certificate correctly state the time and place and circumstances of your marriage?"
Witness.	"I refuse to answer the question on the ground that it would incriminate my wife."

4)   Prior Inconsistent Statements

CHARLES T. McCORMICK,
HANDBOOK OF THE LAW OF EVIDENCE § 28
(4th ed. 1992)[79]

A fatal weakness of liars is letter writing. Betraying letters are often inspired by mere boastfulness, sometimes by greed or other reasons. Properly used they have destroyed many a fraudulent witness. An eminent trial lawyer makes these suggestions to the attacking cross-examiner:

. . . There is an art in introducing the letter contradicting the witness' testimony. The novice will rush in. He will obtain the false statement and then quickly hurl the letter in the face of the witness. The witness, faced

---

[79] Reprinted with permission from MCCORMICK'S HANDBOOK OF THE LAW OF EVIDENCE, Fourth Edition, Copyright © 1992 by West Publishing Co.

with it, very likely will seek to retrace his steps, and sometimes do it skillfully, and the effect is lost.

The mature trial counsel will utilize the letter for all it is worth. Having obtained the denial which he wishes, he will, perhaps, pretend that he is disappointed. He will ask that same question a few moments later, and again get a denial. And he will then phrase — and this requires preparation — he will then phrase a whole series of questions not directed at that particular point, but in which is incorporated the very fact which he is ready to contradict — each time getting closer and closer to the language in the written document which he possesses, until he has induced the witness to assert not once, but many times, the very fact from which ordinarily he might withdraw by saying it was a slip of the tongue. Each time he draws closer to the precise language which will contradict the witness, without making the witness aware of it, until finally, when the letter is sprung, the effect as compared with the other method is that, let us say, of atomic energy against a firecracker.

Citing Nizer, *The Art of Jury Trial*, 32 Cornell Law Quarterly 59, 68 (1946).

However, there may be an obstacle in the way of this effective method. This is the rule in *Queen Caroline's Case*, pronounced by English judges in an advisory opinion in 1820. The significant part of the opinion for present purposes is the pronouncement that the cross-examiner cannot ask the witness about any statements made by the witness in writing, or ask whether the witness has ever written a letter of a given purport, without *first* producing the writing or letter and exhibiting it to the witness, and permitting the witness to read the writing or such part of it as the cross-examiner seeks to ask him about. Thus, in vain is the potential trap laid before the eyes of the bird. While reading the letter the witness will be warned by what he sees not to deny it and can quickly weave anew web of explanation.

The rule that the writing must first be shown to the witness before he can be questioned about it was thought by the judges to be an application of the established practice requiring the production of the original document *when its contents are sought to be proved.* This notion was a misconception in at least two respects. First, the cross-examiner is not seeking to prove *at this stage* the contents of the writing by the answers of the witness. On the contrary, his zealous hope is that the witness will deny the existence of the letter. Second, the original documents rule is a rule requiring the production of the document as proof of its contents to the judge and jury, not to the witness. So obstructive did the powerful Victorian cross-examining barristers find the rule in the *Queen's Case* that they secured its abrogation by Parliament in 1854.

When urged upon them, this practice requiring exhibition to the witness has been usually accepted without question by American courts and occasionally by legislators. It is believed, however, that its actual invocation in trials is relatively infrequent in most states, and that the generality of judges and practitioners are unaware of this possible hidden rock in the path of the cross-examiner.

NOTES AND QUESTIONS

1. At common law, prior inconsistent statements were admitted for the limited purpose of attacking a witness' credibility. This meant that the fact finder could not consider such statements for the truth of the matter asserted (which would improperly touch upon hearsay considerations); the fact finder could consider a prior statement for the narrow proposition that inconsistency demonstrates that the witness' courtroom testimony should not be believed. Consequently, this mode of impeachment required inconsistency in fact.

2. Under what circumstances, if any, might prior silence be regarded as inconsistent with present testimony? To what extent does this issue bear upon constitutional, as well as evidentiary, considerations? *See Fletcher v. Weir*, 455 U.S. 603 (1982); *California v. Green*, 399 U.S. 149 (1970).

3. Suppose a witness has previously asserted his privilege against self-incrimination. May such an assertion be deemed inconsistent with subsequent courtroom testimony? Consider the following cross-examination of a defense witness in a federal racketeering case:

Q. Mr. Wells, I notice that Mr. Flax asked you your occupation.

A. Yes, sir.

Q. Have you ever given a different response on a previous occasion?

A. Not that I know of as far as my occupation. No, I don't.

* * *

BY MR. STEINBERG:

Q. Did you ever give a different response on a previous occasion, Mr. Wells?

A. Not that I know of, sir.

Q. Did you testify in the Federal Grand Jury on April 29, 1975, sir?

A. This year?

Q. That's correct.

A. No, sir, I didn't.

Q. You did not?

A. I came before the Federal Grand Jury.

Q. Were you asked this question? "Q. What is your occupation?"

A. I was asked that question.

Q. Did you give the same response that you gave to Mr. Flax?

A. I gave my address at that time, sir, 836 West Drive.

Q. After you gave your address, were you asked your occupation?

A. Yes.

Q. Did you give the same response that you gave Mr. Flax?

A.   No, sir. I took the Fifth Amendment.

MR. FLAX: May we approach the bench, Your Honor?

THE COURT: Come right up.

(Side-bar conference:)

MR. ROSENFIELD: Your Honor, I would suggest that because the man answered the question before the grand jury that he refused to answer on the ground that it might tend to incriminate him, this would be improper and highly prejudicial. There is nothing inconsistent about a witness' trying to invoke the Fifth Amendment in front of a grand jury and testifying here. There is nothing inconsistent about that at all. This kind of questioning is improper . . .

THE COURT: . . . You can certainly bring out that he refused to testify before the grand jury. I think that is proper cross examination.

*   *   *

BY MR. STEINBERG:

Q.   Mr. Wells, were you called to testify before the Federal Grand Jury on two occasions, October 29, 1974, and April 29, 1975?

A.   Sir, I could not possibly swear to that because I don't have anything at all to tell me what time that I went up there. You could ask me a question of that nature and I can't tell you exactly what date or when those specifics took place.

Q.   Without respect to the exact date, sir, did you appear twice before the Federal Grand Jury?

A.   Yes, sir.

Q.   Were you asked questions concerning your labor-union activities and Mr. Rubin?

A.   Yes, sir.

Q.   Did you refuse to testify on both of those occasions?

A.   Yes, sir, I did.

*   *   *

United States v. Rubin, 559 F.2d 975, 980, n.1 (5th Cir. 1977), *vacated,* 439 U.S. 810 (1978), *reinstated,* 591 F.2d 278 (5th Cir.), *cert. denied,* 444 U.S. 864 (1979). *See Farace v. Independent Fire Ins.,* 699 F.2d 204 (5th Cir. 1983).

5)   The Character Witness for Veracity

Mason Ladd, *Credibility Tests — Current Trends*
89 U. Pa. L. Rev. 165, 171–74 (1940)[80]

CHARACTER AS A TEST OF VERACITY — METHODS OF PROOF

The character of an individual is important in the business world. It is a significant factor in the extension of credit, the selection of employees, the formation of various business associations, the determination of qualifications of those admitted to the professions and in almost every relationship of social living. As intangible as the source of the estimation of character may be, and although indefinite as a basis of the prediction of future conduct, it is nevertheless commonly relied upon in the affairs of everyday life. It is, therefore, not surprising that the courts have made use of character testimony . . . as a test of credibility of witnesses. While truth is true whether it comes from a polluted or a pure source, when facts are in dispute the source of the conflicting testimony may cast light in determining what the truth is. In judging credibility the courts in the past have permitted use of character evidence and in the future may be expected to use this proof in appropriate cases. The means, however, of testing character and applying it are in need of revision.

The courts are in conflict on the question as to whether in proving character the inquiry is limited to the witness's character for truthfulness, or whether his general moral character may be shown. While the totality of the personality of an individual is undoubtedly significant in predicting many types of things which he may be expected to do, including the making of false statements, general qualities of character are regarded by the majority of courts as too broad to afford a reliable credibility test. What is good and what is bad generally in a person's make-up would depend in a large measure upon the environment and attitudes of the particular person judging character, whereas all persons are responsive in singling out qualities related to truthfulness. Consequently as a practical measure, it is believed desirable to limit testimony upon the character of a witness to test his credibility to the specific traits of honesty and veracity. The test as usually applied has been to truth and veracity, but the broader expression of honesty and veracity would seem to encompass more nearly the traits of an individual which would show his regard for the truth or his propensity to falsify when it would be to his advantage. Therefore, the future of the law of evidence in its trend toward realism may be expected to permit impeachment of a witness only by proof of his character for honesty or veracity.

An equally vital problem concerns the method by which character may be proved. Because of the fear of founding character proof upon some limited personal experience or prejudice and through a misunderstanding of the earlier cases, the rule has developed in many jurisdictions that when character is the subject of inquiry, the method of proof must be by reputation alone. A substantial body of law has been built up in defining what is meant by reputation and the extent to which

---

[80] Reprinted by permission of University of Pennsylvania Law Review.

reputation must have expanded in order to be admissible. In a pioneer period where communities were small, there was some justification in requiring that the reputation be community wide or at least that it not be limited to a specific group. With our modern urban society and more scattered activities of people even in smaller localities, the community-wide reputation as a requisite for proof of character is difficult to secure. More consistent with conditions today is the rule fast gaining recognition that reputation as a means of proving character should be sufficiently established if it exists among the people with whom the person habitually associates in his work or business or otherwise.

The distinction between reputation and character is sound, the latter being what a party is in fact, the former being the composite hearsay opinion of people generally in regard to what a person is or what particular traits he possesses. When a trait of character has demonstrated itself sufficiently through external manifestations so that persons with whom an individual habitually associates speaks of him generally concerning these traits, a reputation in respect to them is acquired. This reputation becomes the means of proof of character.

New developments in the law have not tended to exclude reputation as a means of proof where character is involved but have tended to supplement it by personal opinion of a character witness. This represents the orthodox view in the opinion of Professor Wigmore and is consistent with the modern notion that the best evidence of a fact should supplant the use of indirect fictions. If a witness testifies that another's general reputation for honesty and veracity is bad, it undoubtedly expresses his personal opinion as well. Most courts are willing to admit in evidence a statement by the character witness that from his knowledge of that reputation he would not believe the person in question on oath. It is going but little further to permit the character witness to express his personal opinion directly based upon his perception of that person's behavior. In reshaping the rules of evidence for the future, personal opinion as well as reputation ought to be available as a means of proving character. Cross-examination of the character witness would provide an equal safeguard against personal prejudice under both methods of proof.

QUESTIONS

1.   Under Rule 608(a), would it be permissible to call a psychiatrist and ask for his opinion concerning a witness's character for veracity? *See generally United States v. Hiss*, 88 F. Supp. 559 (E.D.N.Y. 1949), *aff'd*, 185 F.2d 822 (2d Cir. 1950), *cert. denied*, 340 U.S. 948 (1951); Slovenko, *Witnesses, Psychiatry and the Credibility of Testimony*, 19 U. FLA. L. REV. 1 (1966).

2.   Alternatively, would it be permissible to send a pollster into the community to discern a witness's reputation for veracity?

3.   Expert testimony has been offered with increasing frequency in the context of so-called "syndrome" evidence. *See State v. Myles*, 887 So. 2d 118 (La. Ct. App. 2004). Under such circumstances, experts generally testify that victims of alleged assaults (child abuse, rape, battered wives) display characteristics consistent with established patterns for the incidents in question. May the expert also testify that the victim's testimony is credible? *See Earls v. McCaughtry*, 379 F.3d 489 (7th Cir.

2004); *United States v. Azure*, 801 F.2d 336 (8th Cir. 1986); *State v. Moran*, 728 P.2d 248 (Ariz. 1986); *State v. Brodniak*, 718 P.2d 322 (Mont. 1986).

UNITED STATES v. MANDEL
591 F.2d 1347 (4th Cir. 1979)

WIDENER, CIRCUIT JUDGE:

Marvin Mandel, governor of the State of Maryland, W. Dale Hess, Harry W. Rodgers, William A. Rodgers (brother of Harry Rodgers), Irvin Kovens, Maryland businessmen, and Ernest N. Cory, a Maryland attorney (hereinafter "Appellants"), appeal from their convictions for mail fraud and racketeering violations under 18 U.S.C. § 1341 and 18 U.S.C. § 1961 et seq. (The Organized Crime Control Act), respectively. . . .

* * *

V

Defendant Cory argues that the trial court committed error by restricting the impeachment of Katherine O'Toole, a former secretary in his office and a key government witness against him. Cory had called a former co-worker of O'Toole's to testify as to her opinion of O'Toole's character with respect to truth and veracity.

While the record is not exactly clear as to the exact reason for the restriction of the impeaching testimony, whether for an insufficiently detailed foundation being laid, or because the limitation to the community in which O'Toole lived, we think a broader scope should have been allowed.

Rule 608(a) changed the common law rule which would admit only knowledge of reputation for truth and veracity as impeaching evidence under the circumstances present here. The rule now permits either knowledge of reputation for truth and veracity or opinion thereof, which the rule calls "character for truthfulness or untruthfulness."

This is made clear by the Senate amendment, adding "opinion or," which was adopted by the conference committee. . . . So the inquiry under the new rules is not limited as heretofore to knowledge of reputation for truth and veracity, but also may include opinion of character for truthfulness or untruthfulness.

We also think there should be no restriction necessarily limited to the community in which the witness sought to be impeached lives, and that the realities of our modern, mobile, impersonal society should also recognize that a witness may have a reputation for truth and veracity in the community in which he works and may have impressed on others in that community his character for truthfulness or untruthfulness. Therefore, we believe the community in which the witness worked, the law office of Cory in this instance, was a proper locality in which to prove O'Toole's reputation or character for truthfulness or untruthfulness. . . .

Finally, we think the trial court should have considerable discretion in determining whether the impeaching witness is qualified to speak on the subject; for example, how well the impeaching witness knows the witness sought to be impeached, under what circumstances, etc. We do not think the district court abused its discretion in that respect.

Mason Ladd, *Techniques and Theory of Character Testimony*
24 Iowa L. Rev. 498, 518–26 (1939) (reprinted with permission)[81]

Techniques in Using Character Testimony

Whether the devices employed by the law to prove character are good or bad, whether they are but formalistic ceremonies or create a realistic approach, whether they accomplish their purpose as effectively as they might, it is important that they be known and the art of their use be mastered. From the great number of appellate court decisions involving character testimony continuously repeating themselves in pointing out errors, as well as from the observations of almost any trial court on the process of introducing character evidence, it is apparent that the techniques of its introduction present many difficulties, indeed more than there should be if the theory of proof of character by reputation were more carefully interpreted in relation to its practical application in trial. Furthermore, if the techniques of the prevailing methods of proof are well enough known so that they may be used with understanding and ease, without stumbling through the examination of the character witness in a trial and error fashion, about as much can be accomplished under the present methods of proof as by any other.

For the sake of simplicity the methods will be illustrated first by treating their use in a situation involving proof of moral character. Let it be assumed that the trial is between X, the plaintiff, and Y, the defendant, and that X desires to prove that the witness, A, who was called and testified for Y was unreliable and that A's testimony was false. The character witness called by X will be referred to as W. It will be assumed that all persons live in the town of Z and that the case is being tried in a jurisdiction where the witness A may be impeached by proof of bad moral character.

(1) General questions identifying W, the character witness, should be first asked. It is important to show who W is, how long he has lived in the community, whether he is married or single, whether he has a family, his occupation, and such additional facts as apply to the particular W that will show that W is a man whose word is reliable and who is competent to evaluate the statements which he may have heard concerning A.

(2) General questions should be asked also to show that W personally knew A, and to show the length of time and the place where he knew him. The purpose of these questions is to show that W has properly identified A as the individual to whom the statements made by others referred, and also to identify A as living in a particular place during a specified period of time. The questions should create a foundation for the following questions which will establish A's reputation among people generally in a particular place at the time of and preceding the trial. . . . It

---

may be conceivable that *W* knew the reputation of a person whom he did not personally know, but for the purpose of identifying that reputation to the particular individual, *W* ought to show that he knew who *A* was. This is an important connecting link in the character testimony. It also has the indirect effect of causing the jury to realize that the reputation of *A* expressed by *W* undoubtedly represents *W's* own views as well. The legal basis, however, of this identification is purely to connect the reputation to this particular individual, *A*, who has testified in the court room and whose veracity is questioned.

Questions bringing out the facts suggested under (1) and (2) involve no particular art in phraseology. The subject matter mentioned, however, is very important foundation testimony both from the standpoint of creating a basis for the admission of subsequent testimony and of establishing the witness so that the evidence upon the issue of character involved, when given, will carry weight with the triers of fact. These same preliminary facts need to be brought out insubstantially the same way whether the character issue relates to the credibility of a witness or to the issue of probability in a criminal case. In bringing out this foundation testimony the questions, although preliminary in nature, should not be asked by the examiner in a perfunctory manner, but rather in such a way as to impress upon the jury their significance in respect to the testimony to be offered upon the particular issue. The examiner may then proceed in the examination of the witness as follows:

(3) *Question:* Mr. *W*, have you heard remarks or comments concerning *A* made by people generally in and about the community of *Z* town?

Answer: Yes, I have.

Comment: A person's reputation must always be established in some place. It was necessary that *A* be in and about the community of *Z* town for a long period of time to acquire a reputation. The hearsay comments, talk, gossip and remarks by people generally in the place where *A* lives is the basis upon which reputation testimony is admissible. This question interrogates *W* upon the fact as to whether comments have been made about *A*. It also shows that the comments were made by people generally. The whole course of questioning must emphasize the generality of the talk about *A*. It is to be noted that the exact substance of those comments cannot be gone into by *X* in his examination of *W*.

Question (3) is designed to prove that *A* had been talked about by people generally in the community or vicinity in which he lives.

(4) *Question:* Have these remarks and comments been many or few in number?

Answer: I have heard a large number of people talk about *A* on many occasions.

Comment: This question is asked to bring out the fact that there was a substantial amount of comment about *A* and that the remarks were frequent. Again, what the remarks were cannot be asked as they might bring up specific instances of misconduct, which would be inadmissible both on grounds of hearsay and irrelevancy. The character of these remarks is known only when *W* states whether *A's* reputation is good or bad. The question is not believed objectionable as leading because it does not suggest the answer although it is disjunctive in form.

(5) *Question:* Were these persons members of some particular group of people?

Answer: No. The remarks which I have heard came from various individuals in different occupations in the community.

Comment: There is a danger that the witness, *W*, may be considering the statements made by a limited group of people such as the members of his church, lodge or club. If *W* is a peace officer it may be that the talk from which *W* plans to testify as to reputation came from police officers only. To preclude this possibility and to forestall cross-examination prior to the completion of the direct examination, this question should be asked so as to establish the fact that the comments do not emanate from a limited source. If the witness should answer that he had heard comments in certain designated groups, the further question should be asked, "Have you heard comments generally in the community by others than those in this group (naming the group)?" If the witness is likely to experience difficulty in answering question (5) in the form suggested, a better question may be: "Were these remarks and comments made by persons having various occupations and different associations among the people in the community of *Z* town?" The question in the form first asked is preferred because of the desire to get away from the constant affirmative answer of the witness.

(6) *Question:* Over how long a period of time have you heard comment and talk about *A* by people generally in and about *Z* town?

Answer: For the last several years and quite recently.

Comment: This question is designed to bring out the period of time over which comments have been made about *A*. A reputation is not ordinarily gained in a day but is gradually acquired through a slow process, the length of time depending on how seriously the individual departs from the norm of human conduct and how much this departure comes before the public eye. It is important that the reputation be shown to exist at the time of the trial because that is the time in which *A's* testimonial reliability is to be judged. If the witness is shown to have been the subject of comment recently and for a long period of time preceding, the value of the character testimony is proportionately enhanced. The reputation must be during a period from which character may be inferred at the time in question.

(7) *Question:* Does *A* have a *general* reputation for *general* moral character in and about the community of *Z* town?

Answer: Yes, he does.

Comment: This is the first of the series of questions which ought to be asked substantially as stated. The placement of the word "general" before "reputation" and before "moral character" is significant. This adjective as applied to reputation again precludes the idea that the reputation is among the members of a particular class. It represents reputation in its broader aspects as being inclusive of the estimate of many people from various walks of life. The adjective "general" before "moral character" excludes the idea of specific defects in the personality of *A* and eliminates the association of character with any specific kind of misdoings. The use of the word "general" in both places will eliminate many of the objections which might otherwise be urged. The peculiar thing is that sometimes the word "general" is omitted altogether and most courts regard its omission as error if the question is properly objected to. Sometimes this adjective is placed before "moral character" but not before "reputation," which would leave open the possibility that the reputation was from a limited group rather than the community generally. Sometimes it is placed before the word "reputation" but omitted before "moral character" and again a critical court might sustain an objection to the question as being improper in form and substance. It is so easy and so simple to include the word "general" both before "reputation" and before "moral character" that it is believed such course should always be followed . . .

(8) *Question:* Do you know the *general* reputation of A for *general* moral character in and about the community of Z town at the present time?

Answer: Yes, I do.

Comment: All that is said under question (7) applies to question (8). . . . It is noted that the question includes the place of the reputation and specifies the time as being the present, thus including the time of the trial when the veracity of A is questioned. The law also recognizes that both reputation and character may change and even be different in different places. Therefore, time and place as set out in the suggested question are important.

(9) *Question:* Will you please tell the jury whether it is good or bad?

Answer: It is bad.

Comment: The point raised by this question should be presented in substantially the form indicated. Marginal degrees of good or bad are not proper subjects of inquiry on character testimony. The general moral character in the estimate of the community to be admitted to establish the character of a witness or party must be either good or bad. The individual's conduct in the aggregate as established by the general reputation in the community must be such that it is subject to a definite classification. However, the answer of the witness might be that it is very good or very bad. Increasing a statement of the quality of the individual one way or another would not be objectionable, while limiting it would be. A general discussion by the character witness of the good or the bad of the person in question is not permissible. The answer must be brief and to the point. Possible statements other than good or bad, meaning the same thing, would not be objectionable, but there is something gained through the short, pointed method raised in the suggested question and answer.

(10) *Question:* From your knowledge of that reputation would you believe statements made by A under oath?

Answer: I would not.

Comment: This question has been the subject of criticism by a few courts, but by better authority it is considered proper. This is particularly true where general moral character is being used to prove veracity, because it ties the method of proof to its function. But even where the general reputation is directed to the specific trait of truth and veracity the question is also believed proper. It would, however, be improper to ask W if from that reputation he believed the testimony of the witness in a particular trial. This would be invading the province of the jury who are to make the final deduction on credibility. In the form in which question (10) is asked it may be claimed that it is asking for the opinion of W which most courts regard objectionable. However, inasmuch as that opinion is founded upon *W*'s knowledge of *A*'s reputation, an objection to the question should not be sustained.

*   *   *

If instead of using general moral character to discredit the witness, *A*, the more common method of impeachment by proof of *A*'s character as it relates to truth and veracity were employed, the foregoing examination would be the same, with the exception of question (7) and (8). The questions as to the truth and veracity of *A* would be substituted as follows:

(7) *Question:* Have these comments and remarks which you have heard about *A* related to his truth and veracity?

Answer: Yes, they have.

Comment: This question should be asked to disclose the fact that the community observations of *A* commonly spoken of have been directed to the specific trait in inquiry, namely, his credibility. The question is important particularly in the jurisdictions in which reputation testimony is admissible only when it relates to the specific trait. A question of this type should always be asked whenever a particular trait of character is involved.

(7a) *Question:* Does *A* have a *general* reputation for truth and veracity in and about the community of *Z* town?

Answer: Yes, he does.

Comment: It will be noted that in this question the adjective "general" precedes the word "reputation" but it does not precede "truth and veracity." The comment under question (8) expressed the view that this is necessary if moral character were involved. The word "general" before "moral character" performs a specific function in emphasizing the aggregate of *A*'s personal qualities. But where the specific trait of truth and veracity is the issue, it is specifically intended to exclude other general elements of character. The addition of this word would serve no other function than to exclude specific falsifications. As the expression "truth and veracity" is itself the statement of a general quality, the additional expression is not needed nor is it commonly used. However, for emphasis the question might be asked as to the *general* reputation for truth and veracity *generally* if the examiner desired to frame his question in that manner.

(8) *Question:* Do you know the *general* reputation of *A* for truth and veracity in and about the community of *Z* town at the present time?

Answer: Yes, I do.

This question is then followed by questions (9) and (10), which disclose what that reputation is. The comments previously made under these numbers apply equally to impeachment for truth and veracity.

6)   Special Procedures for Experts

RUTH v. FENCHEL
121 A.2d 373 (N.J. 1956)

WILLIAM J. BRENNAN, JR., J.

In this automobile accident case Mrs. Ruth had a verdict of $2,000 for personal injuries. She was allowed a new trial as to damages only at which a verdict of $10,000 was returned in her favor. Defendant appealed to the Appellate Division, . . . asserting error at the new trial in permitting cross examination of defendant's medical experts, Dr. Solk and Dr. Reilly, based upon medical treatises which were not relied upon by them in forming their expert opinions. The Appellate Division affirmed . . . and we granted certification upon defendant's petition, 118 A.2d 559 (N.J. 1955).

*   *   *

The attack grounded in the cross-examination of defendant's medical experts relates to Mrs. Ruth's claim that she suffered a "whiplash" injury of the neck from the accident. The neck pains did not manifest themselves until some four months after the mishap. Defendant's medical testimony was in substance that the onset of pain symptomatic of "whiplash" must appear within a few hours. Mrs. Ruth's medical experts, on the other hand, testified that a "whiplash" could first manifest itself up to a year or even two years after the accident.

When Dr. Solk [defendant's expert] was cross-examined at the new trial the cross-examiner produced a copy of the medical treatise by Key and Conwell, Fractures, Dislocations and Sprains, published in 1946. Dr. Solk identified the authors as "orthopedic surgeons," and to the question, "Do you recognize Key and Conwell?", answered, "Yes, they are very, very capable." He said that he had read "these authors" but not "that volume." (There is more than one edition of the treatise.) Over objection by defendant's counsel, the cross-examiner was permitted to require Dr. Solk to read excerpts from the treatise. Then Dr. Solk summarized what he had read as saying "that you can have a whiplashing injury to the cord, to the cervical spine and the symptoms complained of in some future date . . . up to a two year period. They said that." . . . Dr. Solk said that he did "not fully" agree with this opinion.

Dr. Reilly characterized the Key and Conwell treatise as "an excellent textbook," "one of the textbooks I have in my library." (. . . At the first trial, although not at the second, Dr. Reilly testified that Key and Conwell was one of the authorities upon which he based his opinion.) Dr. Reilly acknowledged that he had read the book and that it contained the statement that a good many times the symptoms of whiplash do not show up for years after the injury. He said that he agreed with that statement "but not in its entirety," "I agree in general with the conclusions, but not the whole statement."

*   *   *

The trial judge permitted the cross-examiner's action over defendant's objection because, as the judge stated during one colloquy, each medical expert "recognized these gentlemen as an authority" and because, as he several times admonished the jury during the examinations, the cross-examiner was utilizing the treatise for the purpose of "questioning his [the witness's] judgment and his credibility": "May I say to the jury that any matter that has been read from this authority, from the book, has no probative force as a proven statement of the statements that are made in the book. They are only used for the purpose of cross-examination of this witness by counsel for the plaintiff insofar as it may or may not affect the credibility in your minds as to his opinion; that is the only purpose of the reading from the volume. It is not proof as to the facts of this case, or his opinion." And, again, "I will instruct the jury now, as I did heretofore. Any expression of opinion or statement in these articles is not to be taken by you as proof of those conditions. It is merely given as to what may or may not affect the witness's credibility." And, finally, during the examination of Dr. Reilly, "My first instructions go to the same discussion of these different authorities. They are merely for the purpose, insofar as they may, to affect the credibility of the witness, as an expert witness. Only for that purpose and that purpose alone is it offered and considered."

The question to be decided is thus one of very narrow compass and may be phrased as follows: May the attention of an expert witness be called in the course of cross-examination to statements in conflict with his testimony contained in relevant scientific works not relied upon by him to support his opinion but which he recognizes as authoritative?

Where the contents of a treatise is offered as substantive evidence in the case, the general rule has been to deny admission principally upon the ground that the offer of the contents in evidence purports to employ testimonially a statement out of court by a person not subjected to cross-examination. The decisions of our former Court of Errors and Appeals in *Kingsley v. Delaware, L. & W.R. Co.*, 80 A. 327, (N.J. 1911), and *New Jersey Zinc & Iron Co. v. Lehigh Zinc & Iron Co.*, 35 A. 915 (N.J. 1896), instance the general rule against admission of learned treatises as a substantive medium of proof of the facts they set forth. In both cases texts were offered in evidence to buttress the opinion of an expert witness testifying in behalf of the party making the offer.

But where, as in the instant case, the cross-examiner directs the attention of the expert witness to the contents of treatises expressing an opinion at variance with the opinion of the witness, and does so, not to prove the contrary opinion but merely to call into question the weight to be attached by the fact finder to the opinion of the witness, the law of this State allows such use of the treatise even if not relied upon by the witness in arriving at his opinion, provided the witness admits that the treatise is a recognized and standard authority on the subject. This was decided in *New Jersey Zinc & Iron Co. v. Lehigh Zinc & Iron Co., supra.* That case was tried before Justice Magie, later Chief Justice and chancellor. The plaintiff offered several witnesses to testify as experts as to what minerals were available or useful for the production of zinc. Two of the experts were a Mr. Cook and a Professor Williams. Upon Williams' cross-examination he was asked whether he knew WHITNEY'S METALLIC WEALTH OF THE UNITED STATES and objection was made that the witness had not said he relied upon that work for his opinion. The following colloquy appears at pages 563 to 566 of the trial record printed in volume 208 of Records of the Court of Errors and Appeals (1896):

The cross-examiner:

Q.   Do you remember Whitney's Metallic Wealth of the United States?

A.   Yes Sir. I know that well.

Q.   Is it considered a standard book and referred to as such generally?

A.   Yes Sir, it is a standard work.

Q.   And referred to as such by scientific men?

A.   Yes, sir.

Plaintiff's counsel: I object, it has not been spoken of or referred to by this witness at all.

Justice Magie: If it is a standard work, and he is acquainted with it, and it contains something that ought to have modified his opinion, I think it can be shown.

Plaintiff's counsel: [The treatise is] not under oath, and it is entirely incompetent — He did not give Whitney as one of the grounds of his opinion. Whitney is still living and can be called.

Justice Magie: The evidence will not be available for any purpose except to affect the opinion of this witness. I shall tell the jury that what is read to them must not be considered by them as proving the facts stated therein, or anything of the sort, because it cannot be proved in that way.

Plaintiff's counsel: That is the reason we object to it; it is not competent.

Justice Magie: *It is competent to affect the expression of opinion by the witness. If he admits this is a standard work, and he ought to have read something in it which will affect his opinion, I shall have to admit it in that way.* (Emphasis supplied.)

The cross-examiner then confronted Professor Williams with statements read from Whitney which expressed an opinion contrary to the opinion which the professor gave on his direct examination.

The same procedure was followed, with the same result, during the cross-examination of plaintiff's witness Cook, who also was asked to say what authorities he had relied upon. During his re-direct examination plaintiff's counsel sought to put in evidence excerpts from the treatises upon which Cook had said he relied. Justice Magie refused to allow this to be done.

Both rulings of Justice Magie were assigned as error upon the appeal to the former Court of Errors and Appeals. . . .

The high court affirmed the judgment for the defendant and found no merit in either assignment of error. The rule quoted from 7 Am. & Eng. Encyc. L. 513 was approved and adopted, vis., "Books of science are inadmissible in evidence to prove the opinion contained in them; but, if a witness refers to them as an authority, they may be received for the purpose of contradicting him." It was expressly held that "the course adopted at the trial was right" within this principle. The exclusion of the books on which Cook relied was proper since offered by the party producing him not to contradict but to buttress his testimony. And the ruling as to the cross-examination of Professor Williams based upon Whitney's work not relied upon by the witness was also correct. "The rule covers also the admission of WHITNEY'S METALLIC WEALTH OF THE UNITED STATES on the cross-examination of Mr. Williams," . . . because having been acknowledged by the witness to be a standard authority it was within the language of the principle "if a witness *refers to them as an authority* they may be received for the purpose of contradicting him."

Thus the law settled by the former high court in the *New Jersey Zinc & Iron Co.* case was this: Experts may state what books they relied on in forming their opinions but may not give the contents unless these are asked for in cross-examination (in which case "the treatise may be read to show that it does not contain . . . corroboration, on the principle of discrediting a witness by showing misstatements on a material point," 6 WIGMORE, EVIDENCE (3d ed.) sec. 1700, p.19), and the witness may also be cross-examined as to whether he admits other books to be recognized and standard authorities, and upon such admission maybe confronted with statements in those books. The statements from such books and documents may be thus admitted on the cross-examination of the witness either when the authorities have been cited by him or are admitted by him to be recognized and standard authorities on the subject. Even then the work itself is not to be admitted in evidence, but the statements only may be read by the cross-examiner so far as they are material and have first been brought to the attention of the witness. It is plain then that what was done in the instant case was within the cover of this principle.

NOTES AND QUESTIONS

1.   To avoid potential hearsay dangers, the court in *Fenchel* stressed that the treatise material would be admitted only insofar as it pertained to the expert's credibility; the jury may not give the statements any substantive probative weight. How effective is a limiting instruction likely to be under such circumstances?

2.   To what extent are the court's concerns regarding hearsay dangers obviated today by Fed. R. Evid. 703? Note also that a hearsay exception has been established for situations of this kind. *See* Fed. R. Evid. 803(17). Thus, such statements are now admissible substantively as well as to attack the expert's credibility.

Evidentiary Foundation:
The Trial of Herman Marion Sweatt[82]

[When Herman Marion Sweatt was denied admission to the University of Texas Law School because of racial reasons, he filed suit in federal court to compel his admission. Although he lost his case on the trial level, the Supreme Court later

---

[82] Excerpted from R. KLUGER, SIMPLE JUSTICE — THE HISTORY OF BROWN V. BOARD OF EDUCATION AND BLACK AMERICA'S STRUGGLE FOR EQUALITY 265 (Alfred A. Knopf, 1976).

reversed because he could not receive an equivalent education in a separate law school for blacks. *Sweatt v. Painter*, 339 U.S. 629 (1950). At his trial, the NAACP, representing Sweatt, put on the stand Robert Redfield, chairman of the department of anthropology at the University of Chicago, who testified that segregation "prevents the student from the full, effective, and economical coming to understand the nature and capacity of the group from which he is segregated."* He was cross-examined, in relevant part, as follows:]

Q.   Doctor, are you acquainted with the Encyclopaedia Britannica, the publication by that name?

A.   I have a set. I don't look at it very often.

Q.   You are from the University of Chicago?

A.   Yes.

Q.   Is that publication now published under the auspices of that university?

A.   Yes.

Q.   Have you read the article therein on education and segregation of the races in American schools?

A.   If I have, I don't remember it.

Q.   You don't remember it. Have you written any articles for the Encyclopaedia Britannica?

A.   No, we are just beginning a revision of anthropological articles, and it seems there has to be a very drastic change.

Q.   Do you know who wrote the articles in the Encyclopaedia Brittanica on the subject of higher education for Negroes and segregation?

A.   I don't remember such articles.

Q.   Do you recognize the Encyclopaedia Britannica and the articles on such subjects as an authority in the field?

A.   No, I do not.

Q.   You do not?

A.   No, sir.

Evidentiary Foundation:
The Trial of Dr. Sam Sheppard[83]

[In 1954, Sam Sheppard, a Cleveland osteopathic surgeon, was successfully prosecuted for the murder of his wife. Although Dr. Sheppard always maintained his innocence, he spent ten years in prison until F. Lee Bailey won him the right to a new trial. *Sheppard v. Maxwell*, 384 U.S. 333 (1966). At his second trial, Sheppard was acquitted. His experience ultimately served as the predicate for the popular television show entitled *The Fugitive.*]

---

[83] Excerpted from F. LEE BAILEY, THE DEFENSE NEVER RESTS 89–90 (Stein & Day, 1971).

[One of the major issues in Dr. Sheppard's trial concerned blood spots found on the wall of the bedroom in which his wife was murdered. During the second trial, F. Lee Bailey called blood pattern expert Dr. Paul Leland Kirk, who testified that one of the blood spots on the wall had been left by someone other than the Sheppards. The prosecution then called a rebuttal witness, Dr. Roger Marsters, who refuted Dr. Kirk's contention. On cross-examination F. Lee Bailey attempted to impeach Dr. Marsters' credibility in the following manner:]

Bailey: You have some substantial experience with grouping whole blood, Dr. Marsters, have you not?

Marsters: Yes, I do.

Bailey: And prior to your participation in this case in 1955 had you ever tried to group dried blood, doctor?

Marsters: As a matter of fact, no.

Bailey: Dr. Marsters, there has been evidence that the blood spots that Dr. Kirk grouped were at one time dusted with fingerprint powder. Do you have an opinion as to whether or not this might interfere with later attempts to group the blood?

Marsters: Oh yes, I think it might substantially interfere with or contaminate the blood.

Bailey: You are firm in this opinion, Dr. Marsters?

Marsters: Oh yes, definitely.

Bailey: Did you, Dr. Marsters, by chance write an article about the deterioration of dried blood?

Marsters: Yes.

Bailey: And did you, Dr. Marsters, report in that writing some tests which you made, in depth, in order to determine whether the presence of fingerprint powder would contaminate dried blood?

Marsters: Yes, I think I did make tests like that.

Bailey: And did you not report that fingerprint powder does not contaminate dried blood?

Marsters: Yes, I did.

7)   Rehabilitation After Impeachment

PEOPLE v. SINGER
89 N.E.2d 710 (N.Y. 1949)

DESMOND, J.

Defendant, convicted of manslaughter . . . and abortion, . . . argues in this court . . . fourth, that it was error to receive into evidence proof of a prior extra-judicial "consistent statement" made by the accomplice-witness Schneidewind. . . .

Schneidewind, at the trial, gave testimony most damaging to defendant. When cross-examined, he admitted that when he (Schneidewind) had first appeared before the grand jury as a witness, on November 12, 1947, four weeks after the abortion, he had made statements utterly at variance with his trial testimony, and not inculpating defendant at all. Previously, when giving his evidence in chief at the trial, he had told the jury that he, with defendant and another accomplice had, just after the abortion, gotten together and concocted the false story. Later, during Schneidewind's cross-examination, it was brought out that after his first (November 12, 1947) grand jury appearance, he was taken into custody and that he then went again before the grand jury on November 14, 1947, and that on that second occasion he recanted, and gave the grand jury the same version of the occurrence that he related in his direct testimony on this trial. During this cross-examination of Schneidewind, defense counsel brought out the fact that Schneidewind, although guilty on his own story, had not been indicted. By those and other questions, the defense at least suggested to the jury that Schneidewind hoped for clemency for himself, and that his trial testimony was a fabrication, as a reward for which he hoped to go unwhipped of justice.

The prosecutor then called as a rebuttal witness the father of the victim of the abortion. Over objection, the father was permitted to tell the jury that, on the day following the abortion (thirteen months before the trial), Schneidewind had told the father the same things that he told the jury on this trial, as to his (Schneidewind's) and defendant's complicity in the abortion.

Defendant argues to us that this rebuttal testimony of the father was an illegal buttressing of Schneidewind's sworn trial testimony by a showing of previous extrajudicial, unsworn statements of like import. The contention is that this rebuttal did not come within the exception to the hearsay rule, stated by this court . . . [previously] as follows: "where the testimony of a witness is assailed as a recent fabrication, it may be confirmed by proof of declarations of the same tenor before the motive to falsify existed." Defendant says that two essential bases for the application of that exception are missing here: first, in that Schneidewind's trial testimony was not claimed by the defense to have been a *recent* fabrication, since it was the same story he had told before the grand jury a year earlier, and also at an earlier trial of this very case; and, second, in that, according to defendant, there was no sufficient accusation or showing here of any motive to falsify, arising after the disclosure to the father and before the first telling of Schneidewind's present version of the facts. We think both conditions necessary for the use of the exception, were fairly present here.

Of course, if the word "recent" in this court's formulation of the exception, in the cases above cited, means that the witness' statements at the trial must have been assailed as having been fabricated at some point just before the trial, this was no case for applying the exception. But we think that "recent" as soused, has a relative, not an absolute meaning. It means, we think, that the defense is charging the witness not with mistake or confusion, but with making up a false story well after the event. . . . "Recently fabricated" means the same thing as fabricated to meet the exigencies of the case. . . . JUDGE HAND, *in DiCarlo v. United States* (6 F.2d 364, 366), after careful examination of authorities and reasons, stated the exception thus: "that, when the veracity of a witness is subject to challenge because of motive to fabricate, it is competent to put in evidence statements made by him consistent with what he says on the stand, made before the motive arose." We think that well describes the situation in this case, and that the father's evidence was properly received, to refute the inference urged by the defense, that Schneidewind was testifying at the trial under the influence of a motive which prompted him to falsify. Defense counsel was obviously trying to get the jury to conclude that Schneidewind was motivated by a hope, still strong at the time of trial, that he would be favorably treated because of his cooperation with the prosecutor. Of course, in this instance, Schneidewind, before the girl's father was called to the witness stand, had told the exculpating story at least twice and the damaging story at least three times, but nonetheless, it was the defense's position that he had made up the latter to save his own skin, and so the exception came into play, and it was for the jury to choose between the two versions, after a full disclosure of all the times and occasions on which each had been put forward by Schneidewind.

* * *

Judgment affirmed.

NOTES AND QUESTIONS

1. By contrast, prior consistent statements made *after* the event triggering the alleged motive to falsify constitute improper "bolstering" of a witness' credibility *See, e.g., People v. Jordan*, 59 A.D.2d 746 (N.Y. App. Div. 1977). A witness' credibility ordinarily may not be accredited until he has been subject to impeachment. *See United States v. Drury*, 396 F.3d 1303 (11th Cir. 2005). What policy concern supports this restriction? *See Cox v. Brookings International Life Ins. Co.*, 331 N.W.2d 299 (S.D. 1983).

2. Because of the rule against hearsay, the common law courts admitted prior consistent statements *only* for their rehabilitative value rather than for their substantive truth. *See* Note, *Evidence: Prior Consistent Statements Admissible for Rehabilitation When Witness's Testimony Assailed as Recent Fabrication*, 45 CAL. L. REV. 202 (1957). *Compare* Federal Rule of Evidence 801(d)(1)(B) discussed in Chapter V.

Evidentiary Foundation:
The Trial of Harrison A. Williams, Jr.[84]

[Among the high government officials ensnared by the FBI's ABSCAM investigation was Harrison A. Williams, Jr., a United States senator from New Jersey. Williams was charged with conspiracy, bribery, receipt of unlawful gratuities, and conflict of interest. In large part, the prosecution's case relied upon the testimony of Melvin Weinberg, a convicted swindler who had decided to cooperate with federal officials in order to obtain a lighter sentence. Weinberg served as the government's primary front man in dealing with ABSCAM targets.]

[At one point in the proceedings, FBI informant Melvin Weinberg was cross-

---

[84] Excerpted from trial transcript, supra p. 342, at 810, 820–21, 873–74.

examined concerning his use of the word "bullshit" in a conversation with the defendant. That cross-examination and the government's subsequent efforts to rehabilitate him, in relevant part, follow:]

CROSS-EXAMINATION BY MR. KOELZER: (Continues.)

The Court: All right, Mr. Koelzer, you may proceed.

Q.   You used an eight-letter word in a certain tape or in a number of tapes. Would you agree with me, sir, that when you used the words, quoting you, "bullshit," that it means something to you that isn't true or giving a story; would you agree with that?

A.   No.

Q.   Do you recall testifying in this courthouse on November 18, 1980, before Judge Pratt?

A.   Yes.

Q.   Were you asked certain questions?

A.   Yes, that's correct.

Q.   Did you give answers?

A.   That's correct.

Q.   Were those answers truthful?

A.   That's correct.

Q.   Were they under oath?

A.   That's correct.

Q.   Were they recorded just as they are being recorded here by a court reporter?

A.   That's correct.

Q.   Were you asked this question and did you give this answer, Page 1482, Line 16:

What does bullshit mean to you, sir, something that isn't true?

Answer: Could mean that or give them a story.

Do you recall being asked that question and giving that answer?

A.   I don't recall giving that answer, but that's what I said.

BY MR. MCDONALD:

Q.   Mr. Koelzer asked you about your understanding of the term "bullshit"; do you recall that?

A.   Yes.

Q.   Do you recall using the term "bullshit" in a conversation with Senator Williams at the Mariott Hotel in Virginia?

A.   Yes.

Q.   In the context you used the word "bullshit," in that conversation with Senator Williams, what were you referring to?

MR. KOELZER: I object. His state of mind, your Honor. The same reason why your Honor sustained the objection earlier.

THE COURT: Overruled in this context.

A.   I was saying to him that we went through this, we know that he said he was going to get the contracts, he was going to do it, all he had to do is say it to the Sheik; that it was bullshit that he had to say it over again.

Q.   What do you mean "over again"?

A.   He had told us already he was going to do it. We already knew he was going to do it.

Q.   When was that?

A.   At different meetings, he said it at the Pierre Hotel, later on we were told he was going to do it by Alex Feinberg, by George Katz, he said he was going to do it and the meeting he had — I forgot the meeting, but he said he was going to do it.

 EVIDENCE CHALLENGE: Challenge yourself to learn more about this topic. Enter the following address into your browser to access Evidence Challenge and apply these concepts to realistic problems set in a virtual courtroom.
http://www.EvidenceChallenge.com. Additional purchase required.

Chapter IV

RELEVANCY REFINED

A. MATHEMATICAL PROOF

Laurence H. Tribe, *Trial by Mathematics: Precision and Ritual in the Legal Process*
84 Harv. L. Rev. 1329, 1332–38 (1971)[1]

I. FACTFINDING WITH MATHEMATICAL PROBABILITIES

A. *Mysteries of Expertise*

The infamous trial in 1899 of Alfred Dreyfus, Captain in the French General Staff, furnishes one of the earliest reported instances of proof by mathematical probabilities. In attempting to establish that the author of a certain document that allegedly fell into German hands was none other than Captain Dreyfus . . . . To identify the writing in the document as that of Dreyfus, the prosecution's witnesses reported a number of close matches between the lengths of certain words and letters in the document and the lengths of certain words and letters in correspondence taken from Dreyfus' home. Obscure lexicographical and graphological "coincidences" within the document itself were said by the witnesses to indicate the high probability of its disguised character and of its use to convey coded information.[2] To establish the validity of the hypothesis that the document had been traced over the handwriting of Dreyfus' brother, the prosecution's witnesses computed the "amazing" frequency with which certain letters in the document appeared over the same letters of the word chain constructed by repeating *intérêt* a number of times, once a variety of complex adjustments had been made.[3]

---

[1] Copyright © 1971 by the Harvard Law Review Association.

[2] [8] For example, one witness stressed the presence of four coincidences out of the 26 initial and final letters of the 13 repeated polysyllabic words in the document. He evaluated at .2 the probability of an isolated coincidence and calculated a probability of $(0.2)4 = .0016$ that four such coincidences would occur in normal writing. But $(0.2)4$ is the probability of four coincidences out of four; that of four or more out of 13 is some 400 times greater, or approximately .7. *See* Rappord de Mm. Les Experts Darboux, Appell, et Poincaré, in Les Documents Judicliares DeL'affaire Dreyfus, *in* La Revision du Proces Rennies (1909) [hereinafter cited as Rappord]. . . .

[3] [9] Two witnesses observed that, when the word chain "intérêt/intérêt/intérêt/intérêt . . . ." was compared with the document itself, allowing one letter of slipping-back for each space between words and aligning the word chain with the actual or the ideal left-hand margin as convenient, the letter I appeared with particular frequency over the word-chain letter i; the letters n and p appeared frequently

The very opacity of these demonstrations protected them to some degree from effective spontaneous criticism, but the "mathematics" on which they were based was in fact utter nonsense. As the panel of experts appointed several years later to review the evidence in the Dreyfus case easily showed, there was nothing statistically remarkable about the existence of close matches in some word lengths between the disputed document and Dreyfus' correspondence, given the many word pairs from which the prosecution was free to choose those that displayed such similarities. Moreover, the supposed coincidences within the document itself reflected no significant deviation from what one would expect in normal French prose. Finally, the frequency with which various letters in the document could be "localized" over the letters of intérêt was likewise statistically insignificant.

Armand Charpentier, a prominent student of the Dreyfus affair, reports that counsel for Dreyfus and the Government Commissioner alike declared that they had understood not a word of the witness' mathematical demonstrations. Charpentier adds that, although the judges who convicted Dreyfus were in all likelihood equally mystified, they nonetheless "allowed themselves to be impressed by the scientific phraseology of the system." It would be difficult to verify that proposition in the particular case, but the general point it makes is a crucial one: the very mystery that surrounds mathematical arguments — there lative obscurity that makes them at once impenetrable by the layman and impressive to him — creates a continuing risk that he will give such arguments a credence they may not deserve and a weight they cannot logically claim.

The California Supreme Court recently perceived this danger when it warned that "[m]athematics, a veritable sorcerer in our computerized society, while assisting the trier of fact in the search for truth, must not [be allowed to] cast a spell over him."[4] The court ruled improper a prosecutor's misconceived attempt to link an accused interracial couple with a robbery by using probability theory. The victim of the robbery, an elderly woman, had testified that she saw her assailant, a young woman with blond hair, run from the scene. One of the victim's neighbors had testified that he saw a Caucasian woman, with her hair in a dark blond ponytail, run from the scene of the crime and enter a yellow automobile driven by a male negro wearing a mustache and beard. Several days later, officers arrested a couple that seemed to match these descriptions. At the week-long trial of this couple, the victim was unable to identify either defendant, and her neighbor's trial identification of the male defendant was effectively impeached. Moreover, the defense introduced evidence that the female defendant had worn light-colored clothing on the day of the robbery, although both witnesses testified that the girl they observed had worn dark clothing. Finally, both defendants took the stand to deny any participation in the crime, providing an alibi that was at least consistent with the testimony of another defense witness.

In an effort to bolster the identification of the defendants as the perpetrators of the crime, the prosecutor called a college mathematics instructor to establish that, if the robbery was indeed committed by a Caucasian woman with a blond ponytail

---

over the word-chain letter n; and so on. Far from being in any way remarkable, however, the probability that some pattern can be discerned in any document is nearly certain. *See Rapport* 534.

[4] [14] *People v. Collins*, 68 Cal. 2d 319, 320, 66 Cal. Rptr. 497, 438 P.2d 33 (1968).

accompanied by a Negro with a beard and mustache and driving a yellow car, there was an overwhelming probability that the accused couple were guilty because they matched this detailed description.

The witness first testified to the "product rule" of probability theory, according to which the probability of the joint occurrence of a number of mutually independent events equals the product of the individual probabilities of each of the events. Without presenting any supporting statistical evidence, the prosecutor had the witness assume specific probability factors for each of the six characteristics allegedly shared by the defendants and the guilty couple.[5] Applying the product rule to the assumed factors, the prosecutor concluded that there was but one chance in twelve million that any couple chosen at random would possess the characteristics in question, and asked the jury to infer that there was therefore but one chance in twelve million of the defendants' innocence.

The jury convicted but the California Supreme Court reversed, holding the mathematical testimony and the prosecutor's associated argument inadmissible on four separate grounds. First, the record was devoid of any empirical evidence to support the individual probabilities assumed by the prosecutor.

Second, even if the assumed probabilities were themselves correct, their multiplication under the product rule presupposed the independence of the factors they measured — a presupposition for which no proof was presented, and which was plainly false. If two or more events tend to occur together, the chances of their separate occurrence obviously cannot be multiplied to yield the chance of their joint occurrence. For example, if every tenth man is black and bearded, and if every fourth man wears a mustache, it may nonetheless be true that most bearded black men wear mustaches, so that nearly one man in ten — not one in forty — will be a black man with a beard and a mustache.

Third, even if the product rule could properly be applied to conclude that there was but one chance in twelve million that a randomly chosen couple would possess the six features in question, there would remain a substantial possibility that the guilty couple did not in fact possess all of those characteristics — either because the prosecution's witnesses were mistaken or lying, or because the guilty couple was somehow disguised. "Traditionally," the court reasoned, "the jury weighs such risks in evaluating the credibility and probative value of trial testimony," but — finding itself unable to quantify these possibilities of error or falsification — the jury would be forced to exclude such risks from any effort to assign a number to the probability

---

[5] [18]

Characteristic	Assumed Probability of its Occurrence
1. Partly yellow automobile	1/10
2. Man with mustache	1/4
3. Girl with ponytail	1/10
4. Girl with blond hair	1/3
5. Negro man with beard	1/10
6. Interracial couple in car	1/1000

of guilt or innocence and would be tempted to accord disproportionate weight to the prosecution's computations.

Fourth, and entirely apart from the first three objections, the prosecutor erroneously equated the probability that a randomly chosen couple would possess the incriminating characteristics, with the probability that any given couple possessing those characteristics would be innocent. After all, if the suspect population contained, for example, twenty-four million couples, and if there were a probability of one in twelve million that a couple chosen at random from the suspect population would possess the six characteristics in question, then one could well expect to find two such couples in the suspect population, and there would be a probability of approximately one in two — not one in twelve million — that any given couple possessing the six characteristics would be innocent. The court quite reasonably thought that few defense attorneys, and fewer jurors, could be expected to comprehend these basic flaws in the prosecution's analysis. Under the circumstances, the court concluded, this "trial by mathematics" so distorted the jury's role and so disadvantaged defense counsel as to constitute a miscarriage of justice.

But the California Supreme Court discerned "no inherent incompatibility between the disciplines of law and mathematics and intend[ed] no general disapproval . . . of the latter as an auxiliary in the fact-finding processes of the former." Thus expressed, the court's position seems reasonable enough. Any highly specialized category of knowledge or technique of analysis is likely to share in some degree the divergence between impressiveness and understandability that characterizes mathematical proof; surely, adjudication should not for that reason be deprived of the benefits of all expertise. On the contrary, the drawing of unwarranted inferences from expert testimony has long been viewed as rectifiable by cross-examination, coupled with the opportunity to rebut. Particularly if these devices are linked to judicial power to give cautionary jury instructions and to exclude evidence altogether on a case-by-case basis if prejudicial impact is found to outweigh probative force, and if these techniques are then supplemented by a requirement of advance notice of intent to use a particular item of technical proof, and by some provision for publicly financed expert assistance to the indigent accused confronted with an expert adversary, there might seem to be no valid remaining objection to probabilistic proof.

But can such proof simply be equated with expert evidence generally, or does it in fact pose problems of a more pervasive and fundamental character? A consideration of that question requires the more careful development of just what" mathematical proof" should be taken to mean, and what major forms it can assume.

STATE v. GARRISON
585 P.2d 563 (Ariz. 1978)

STRUCKMEYER, VICE CHIEF JUSTICE.

Bobby Joe Garrison was convicted by jury of the crime of first degree murder and sentenced to life imprisonment. He appeals.

On the morning of October 24, 1976, the body of Verna Marie Martin was found on the desert near Tucson, Arizona. Her death was caused by strangulation and her body was mutilated by bite marks . . .

* * *

Appellant complains of the testimony of an expert witness, Homer Richardson Campbell, Jr., a dentist, that there is an eight in one million probability that the teeth marks found on the deceased's breasts were not made by appellant. The witness, Campbell, is a board certified specialist in forensic dentistry and a member of the American Society of Orthodontology. His testimony is that the wounds in the deceased's breasts had ten points of similarity with appellant's teeth. He testified: "My conclusion was that the bite marks on the deceased, and the bite marks produced by the model that I received, were consistent, the marks were consistent with those being made by the teeth that I received."

He further testified:

. . . the probability factor of two sets of teeth being identical in a case similar to this is, approximately, eight in one million, or [two] in two hundred and fifty — one in one hundred and twenty-five thousand people.

Appellant points to *People v. Collins*, 68 Cal. 2d 319, 66 Cal. Rptr. 497, 438 P.2d 33 (1968), which he asserts "is exactly on point with the situation in the present case." We, however, do not think so. . . .

In the instant case, Dr. Campbell obtained the figure of eight in one million not from personal mathematical calculations, but from "articles written in the journals of the American Academy of Forensic Sciences" and two books, and "there are articles written throughout the literature that do mention the possibility or the numerical values of finding two [sets of teeth] of the same."

Arizona's Rules of Evidence, 17A A.R.S., effective September 1, 1977, provides by Rule 803(18) that statements contained in published treatises, periodicals, or pamphlets on the subject of medicine are not excluded by the hearsay rule. Although the Arizona Rules of Evidence were not in effect at the time of the trial of this case, we do not think the admission of the eight in a million statement is reversible error. Were we to reverse on this ground, it would only result in are trial at which the same evidence would be admitted since Dr. Campbell's testimony, obtained from published treatises and periodicals, would be admissible under Rule 803(18). Courts should not engage in such futile practices.

* * *

Judgment affirmed.

HAYS and HOLOHAN, JJ., concur.

GORDON, JUSTICE (concurring in part, dissenting in part):

* * *

I agree with the majority that "[a]n expert is one whose opinions depend upon special knowledge with which he can assist the jury." In fact, it is precisely because the value of an expert's opinion lies in his mastery of a field that will aid the jury that I am unable to agree with the majority's conclusion on the admissibility of the evidence probability presented by Dr. Campbell.

A reading of Dr. Campbell's testimony reveals that, not only did he not perform any of his own mathematical calculations in reaching the eight in one million figure, but also that he was unaware of the formula utilized to arrive at that figure other than it was "computerized," and that he was ignorant of the statistical weight assigned to each variable used in the equation. (See discussion below.) In short, it is obvious that while Dr. Campbell may have a great deal of expertise in the actual comparison techniques of bite mark identification, he is totally out of his field when the discussion turns to probability theory.

Since Dr. Campbell was able to testify that the figure was obtained from articles and books in the field, the majority presses into service the newly adopted hearsay exception for "learned treatises" to justify admission of the testimony, in spite of Dr. Campbell's lack of expertise. The majority's theory is apparently that so long as probability studies have been performed and published in the past by experts in the practical application of probability theory, it is not necessary that the expert on the witness stand be capable of independently generating the results reached by the published study. I cannot agree.

Preliminarily, I have serious reservations as to the applicability of Rule 803(18) 17A A.R.S. After discussing the circumstances in which statements contained in learned treatises are admissible, the last sentence of Rule 803(18) reads as follows, "If admitted, the statements may be read into evidence but may not be received as exhibits." It seems to me that this sentence qualifies the exception with a requirement that the articles and books within which the relevant statements are contained be physically present in the courtroom and that the witness read the statement directly from the book. Of course, this construction of the sentence does nothing more than affirm the well-established requirement that the contents of a writing be proven by production of the original writing. Arizona Rules of Evidence, Rule 1002 17A A.R.S. *See also* Rule 1001(3) 17A A.R.S. for the definition of "original."

Dr. Campbell's testimony provides a classic example of why a witness' memory of the contents of a writing is not a preferred method of proving those contents. As indicated in the majority opinion, Dr. Campbell was unsure as to precisely where he obtained the figure "eight in one million." My independent research reveals that of the two treatises which he could name as containing statistical information, only WARREN AND HARVEY, DENTAL IDENTIFICATION AND FORENSIC ODONTOLOGY (1976) lists any figures on the uniqueness of a bite- mark. Rather than the eight in one million figure vouched for by Dr. Campbell, though, that treatise, at page 139, contains the figure eight in one hundred thousand.[6]

---

[6] [1] Moreover, the applicability of even an eight in one hundred thousand figure to the defendant is dubious. Warren and Harvey are referring to the probability of a specific combination of distinctive tooth characteristics occurring in Scotland where "not more than sixty percent of the adult population over sixteen have some natural teeth." Dr. Campbell never suggests that any of these same specific characteristics were present in the bite-marks that he studied.

Assuming that the jury took seriously Dr. Campbell's "eight in one million" apparently erroneous probability figure, and further assuming that the members of the jury tried it out on the estimated population of Pima County at the time of trial (approximately 465,000) it would come to the conclusion that only 3.72 people in Pima County could make teeth marks similar to those found on the victim's body. If, however, the figure eight in one hundred thousand is the correct figure, there would be thirty-seven people in Pima County whose teeth could make similar marks. This example graphically illustrates just one of the reasons I am so concerned about allowing such unfounded probability figures into evidence — a little error can paint a drastically distorted picture. The other reason is that the stunning impact of dramatic figures makes the picture indelible in the minds of the jurors, especially when the posture of Dr. Campbell's testimony left counsel unable to dispute the figure.

I would hold that when, as in this case, an expert offers a statement that is represented as being a direct quote from a book, the testimony is admissible only if the source material is present in the court room and available for inspection by opposing counsel.

Even if the statistical testimony qualifies for treatment as a hearsay exception, I nevertheless feel that there was an inadequate foundation laid for its admission in this case. Because of the overwhelming impact on a jury of statistical evidence that indicates an almost insurmountably conclusive probability of an accurate identification, and because of the ever present danger that the presumptions on which such calculations are based might be flawed, evidence of mathematical probabilities should be admitted only if there is a thorough foundation articulated by the expert supporting the legitimacy of the conclusion reached. . . . To permit an expert to offer a probability figure without a complete explanation of how the number was calculated would not only intensify the mystery surrounding pronouncements of such huge probability figures but also," foreclose(s) the possibility of an effective defense by an attorney apparently unschooled in mathematical refinements." *People v. Collins*, 66 Cal. Rptr. at 502, 438 P.2d at 38. In this case, the defense attorney's difficulty in attempting to defuse the impact of the large numbers was compounded by the fact that Dr. Campbell had not performed his own calculations and could not cite the source of the general formula. Because of his ignorance of not only the method by which the figure was calculated, but also the treatise where it could be verified or disputed, his testimony was essentially immune from the test of cross-examination.

The science of comparing bite-marks begins with the assumption that any individual's bite-mark is unique. In attempting to identify a bite-mark by comparing it with the known mark of an accused, the forensic orthodontologist selects several distinct features or characteristics of a bite-mark such as the individual shape of the teeth (as evidenced by the mark), the spacing between the teeth, and the size of the arch. The expert then conducts a methodical comparison of each aspect of the two bite-marks, determining whether there is similarity with respect to any or all of the features. As in fingerprint analysis, as the incidence of the finding of similarity among the "points of comparison" increases, so does the assurance that any overall identification is "positive." *See* WARREN AND HARVEY, DENTAL IDENTIFICATION AND FORENSIC ODONTOLOGY (1976).

While Dr. Campbell's testimony on the matter is of little assistance, it appears that the probability figure, "eight in one million" is reached by application of the so called "product rule" to the comparison technique described above. In simple form, the rule is that if two or more events are mutually independent, the probability of their co-occurrence is equal to the product of their individual probabilities. *See* McCormick on Evidence, § 204 (2d ed. 1972). In bite-mark analysis, the underlying events used as the basis for calculating a product are the individual probabilities that there will be similarity in two bite-marks with respect to any one of the isolated characteristics described above.

The California Supreme Court's primary objection to the testimony offered in *People v. Collins, supra,* was that there was no empirical evidence offered to justify the probability figure assigned to each "event" used to calculate the figure "one in twelve million." The difficulty with the testimony of this case is just as serious. There was no evidence offered to justify the statistical weight assigned to each identification factor. Moreover, the absence of an explanatory foundation disguised the fact that the eight in one million figure taken from the literature was completely misleading when applied to the comparison study actually performed in this case.

Assume, for ease of calculation, that the probability of finding similarity in two bite-marks with respect to each discrete aspect is one in four. Assuming the independence of each variable, the probability of finding similarity with respect to two features is one in sixteen; with respect to three features, one in sixty-four. It should be apparent that as the number of findings of similarity increases, the denominator of the probability fraction rises exponentially. Far more significant jumps occur, for instance, when the findings of similarity increase from seven to ten.

The problem with Dr. Campbell's having utilized the figure "eight in one million" in this case is that while he was able to testify that that figure represents the product of the probabilities that there will be similarity in ten major points of comparison, he also testified that because of "inconsistency," he did not employ all of the ten major factors in making his identification. It is clear that the discrepancy between the comparative assumptions underlying the figure announced by Dr. Campbell and the actual comparison study performed by him in this case render the eight in one million figure totally irrelevant. However, because of his unfamiliarity with the statistical weight assigned to each comparison factor, Dr. Campbell would have been completely unable to explain to the jury the degree to which his figure was exaggerated when applied to this pair of bite-marks.

As an illustration, assume that Dr. Campbell failed to consider three of the ten major factors in making his comparison. Assume further that the variables not considered are independent and that each has a statistical weight of one in four. It would seem then that considering only the remaining seven points of comparison, the probability of the bite-marks being identical would be reduced to below one in two thousand.[7]

When this failure of Dr. Campbell to perform his own calculations is compounded by the fact that the figure in the literature for a study based on all ten factors is

---

[7] [3] This figure is reached by calculating the product of the hypothetical probabilities of the excluded factors, and dividing the figure eight in one million by that product.

eight in one hundred thousand, it is obvious that a proper application of the product rule would have yielded a substantially less imposing figure than eight in one million.

In conclusion this case highlights the numerous pitfalls that can be encountered by permitting probability evidence without a demonstration of the validity of the figure announced by the expert. I would hold that such testimony is admissible only if the witness is thoroughly familiar with the relevant probability formula and can justify the statistical weight assigned to each variable in that formula. I would further require that the expert be able to fully explain to the court the calculations he performed in arriving at his ultimate conclusion.

NOTES AND QUESTIONS

1.   Other courts have been more critical of statistical evidence in the context of bite mark analysis. *See Ege v. Yukins*, 380 F. Supp. 2d 852 (E.D. Mich. 2005). For an interesting analysis of the admissibility of statistical evidence in DNA "cold hit" cases, *see United States v. Jenkins*, 887 A.2d 1013 (D.C. 2005).

2.   In a case charging the defendant with arson and insurance fraud, the evidence showed that four homes occupied by the defendant burned during 10 years. May the prosecution introduce evidence from an actuary that the probability of four residential fires occurring over a period of 10 years or so was one in 1.773 trillion? *See United States v. Veysey*, 334 F.3d 600 (7th Cir. 2003).

3.   Consider the following situation: Toxic Shock Syndrome (TSS) is a severe illness characterized by a sudden onset of high fever, vomiting, diarrhea, and, in severe cases, shock. As of January 30, 1981, 941 confirmed cases of TSS had been reported to the U.S. Center for Disease Control, including 73 cases that resulted in death. TSS is clearly related in some way to tampon use in menstruating women. Studies by the U.S. Center for Disease Control have demonstrated that the brand of tampon a woman uses is likely to affect her risk of developing TSS: "[W]hile cases of TSS have occurred with tampons produced by all five of the major U.S. tampon manufacturers, a substantially greater proportion of cases than controls in the present study used Rely Tampons." Morbidity and Mortality Weekly Report 444 (U.S. Center for Disease Control, Sept. 19, 1980). *See also* Fischer, *Products Liability — An Analysis of Market Share Liability*, 34 VAND. L. REV. 1623, 1625–26 (1981).

More support for the proposition that Rely tampons have some significant relationships to TSS can be found in statistics compiled by the Center on Disease Control indicating that the incidence of TSS decreased after the manufacturer of Rely tampons, Procter and Gamble Company, removed the product from the market in September, 1980. If a plaintiff wanted to prove that Rely tampons caused her to develop TSS, she would almost certainly have to introduce this statistical data. Would such proof be admissible? To what extent is mathematical evidence being used differently in this context than in *Collins* and *Garrison. See generally Wolf v. Procter & Gamble Co.*, 555 F. Supp. 613 (D.N.J. 1982).

4.   May the prosecution introduce statistical data concerning a defendant's blood type? This issue initially generated considerable controversy. *Compare, e.g.,*

People v. Thorin, 336 N.W.2d 913 (Mich. Ct. App. 1983), *with People v. McMillen*, 336 N.W.2d 895 (Mich. Ct. App. 1983). *See* Jonakait, *When Blood Is Their Argument: Probabilities in Criminal Cases, Genetic Markers, and, Once Again, Bayes' Theorem*, 1983 U. ILL. L. REV. 369. Eventually, courts became more accepting of such evidence. *See United States v. Peters*, 1995 U.S. Dist. LEXIS 20950 (D.N.M. Sept. 7, 1995) *aff'd*, 1998 U.S. App. LEXIS 773 (10th Cir. Jan. 20, 1998) (admitting statistical analysis of DNA evidence); *People v. Axell*, 235 Cal. App. 3d 836 (1991) (same).

5.   For further analysis of mathematical proof, see, e.g., Callen, *Adjudication and the Appearance of Statistical Evidence*, 65 Tul. L. Rev. 457 (1991); Finkelstein & Fairley, *A Bayesian Approach to Identification Evidence*, 83 HARV. L. REV. 489 (1970); Kaye, *The Laws of Probability and the Law of the Land*, 47 U. CHI. L. REV. 34 (1979); Koehler & Shaviro, *Veridical Verdicts: Increasing Verdict Accuracy Through the Use of Overtly Probabilistic Evidence and Methods*, 75 CORNELL L. REV. 247 (1990); Shaviro, *Statistical-Probability Evidence and the Appearance of Justice*, 103 HARV. L. REV. 530 (1989).

SMITH v. RAPID TRANSIT
58 N.E.2d 754 (Mass. 1945)

SPALDING, JUSTICE.

The decisive question in this case is whether there was evidence for the jury that the plaintiff was injured by a bus of the defendant that was operated by one of its employees in the course of his employment. If there was, the defendant concedes that the evidence warranted the submission to the jury of the question of the operator's negligence in the management of the bus. The case is here on the plaintiff's exception to the direction of a verdict for the defendant.

These facts could have been found: While the plaintiff at about 1:00 A.M. on February 6, 1941, was driving an automobile on Main Street, Winthrop, in an easterly direction toward Winthrop Highlands, she observed a bus coming toward her which she described as a "great big, long, wide affair." The bus, which was proceeding at about forty miles an hour, "forced her to turn to the right," and her automobile collided with a "parked car." The plaintiff was coming from Dorchester. The department of public utilities had issued a certificate of public convenience or necessity to the defendant for three routes in Winthrop, one of which included Main Street, and this was in effect in February, 1941."There was another bus line in operation in Winthrop at that time but not on Main Street." According to the defendant's time-table, buses were scheduled to leave Winthrop Highlands for Maverick Square via Main Street at 12:10 A.M.,12:45 A.M., 1:15 A.M., and 2:15 A.M. The running time for this trip at that time of night was thirty minutes.

The direction of a verdict for the defendant was right. The ownership of the bus was a matter of conjecture. While the defendant had the sole franchise for operating a bus line on Main Street, Winthrop, this did not preclude private or chartered buses from using this street; the bus in question could very well have been one operated by someone other than the defendant. It was said in *Sargent v. Massachusetts*

Accident Co., 307 Mass. 246, at page 250, 29 N.E.2d 825, at page 827, that it is "not enough that mathematically the chances somewhat favor a proposition to be proved; for example, the fact that colored automobiles made in the current year outnumber black ones would not warrant a finding that an undescribed automobile of the current year is colored and not black, nor would the fact that only a minority of men die of cancer warrant a finding that a particular man did not die of cancer." The most that can be said of the evidence in the instant case is that perhaps the mathematical chances somewhat favor the proposition that a bus of the defendant caused the accident. This was not enough. A "proposition is proved by a preponderance of the evidence if it is made to appear more likely or probable in the sense that actual belief in its truth, derived from the evidence, exists in the mind or minds of the tribunal notwithstanding any doubts that may still linger there." Sargent v. Massachusetts Accident Co., 307 Mass. 246, at page 250, 29 N.E.2d 825 at page 827.

In cases where it has been held that a vehicle was sufficiently identified so as to warrant a finding that it was owned by the defendant, the evidence was considerably stronger than that in the case at bar. . . .

Exceptions overruled.

NOTES AND QUESTIONS

1. *Rapid Transit* is considered the classic case. It has evolved into a famous hypothetical:

> Plaintiff is negligently run down by a blue bus. The question is whether the bus belonged to the defendant. Plaintiff is prepared to prove that defendant operates four-fifths of all the blue buses in town. What effect, if any, should such proof be given? Tribe, *supra*, at 1340–41.

In evaluating this hypothetical, the following analysis may be helpful.

> Consider a case in which it is common ground that 499 people paid for admission to a rodeo, and that 1,000 are counted on the seats, of whom *A* is one. Suppose no tickets were issued and there can be no testimony as to whether *A* paid for admission or climbed over the fence. So there is a .501 probability, on the admitted facts, that he did not pay. The conventionally accepted theory of probability would apparently imply that in such circumstances the rodeo organizers are entitled to judgment against *A* for the admission money, since the balance of the probability would lie in their favor. But it seems manifestly unjust that *A* should lose when there is an agreed probability of as high as .499 that he in fact paid for admission.
>
> Indeed, if the organizers were really entitled to judgment against *A*, they would be entitled to judgment against each person in the same position as *A*. So they might conceivably be entitled to recover 1,000 admission prices when it was admitted that 499 had actually been paid. The absurdity of this suffices to show that there is something wrong somewhere. Where?

Kaye, *The Paradox of the Gatecrasher and Other Stories*, 1979 ARIZ. ST. L.J. 101, 101.

2. *Rapid Transit* indicates that pure mathematical evidence may be insufficient to withstand a motion for a directed verdict. Does it likewise follow, however, that such evidence should also be deemed irrelevant? In this respect, consider Professor Tribe's comments:

> But the fact that mathematical evidence *taken alone* can rarely, if ever, establish the crucial proposition with sufficient certitude to meet the applicable standard of proof does not imply that such evidence — when properly combined with other, more conventional, evidence in the same case — cannot supply a useful link in the process of proof. Few categories of evidence indeed could ever be ruled admissible if each category had to stand on its own, unaided by the process of cumulating information that characterizes the way any rational person uses evidence to reach conclusions. The real issue is whether there is any acceptable way of combining mathematical with non-mathematical evidence.

Tribe, supra, at 1350.

B. SUBSTANTIVE CHARACTER EVIDENCE

1. A Critical Distinction

You have already been introduced to the concept of character evidence. In an impeachment context counsel may call a character witness to establish that a prior witness had a poor character for truthfulness. In the federal courts, impeachment of this kind is governed by Federal Rule of Evidence 608. In addition, other modes of impeachment (*i.e.,* those pursuing the credibility factors) may also seek to establish that a witness had a poor character for veracity. Under such circumstances, character pertains solely to a witness' credibility; it "does not [otherwise] directly touch upon the issues in the case. It serves only as a means of persuading the jury to disregard testimony of the impeached witness as it might bear on the issues."[8]

In the present context, however, character evidence is being used for *substantive* purposes. Specifically, we are now concerned with issues arising when evidence of character is used to prove "substantive facts which are in issue."[9] Such use of character evidence is controlled in federal court by Federal Rules of Evidence 404 and 405. Consequently, since the rules governing character evidence depend upon the particular purpose for which it is being applied, a distinction must be drawn between substantive and credibility concerns. Nevertheless, while easy to articulate, this distinction occasionally becomes difficult for students (and, indeed, for many judges) to retain. Thus, for example, lines of analysis mistakenly tend to blur when the substantive character witness' credibility is impeached. In all likelihood, your mastery of character evidence will reflect the extent to which you are able to keep its substantive and credibility components analytically distinct.

---

[8] Udall, *Character Proof in the Law of Evidence — A Summary*, 18 U. Cin. L. Rev. 283, 285 (1949).
[9] *Id.*

NOTE

For a good example of a case reversing because the prosecutor failed to distinguish between substantive and credibility applications of character evidence, see People v. Haines, 306 N.W.2d 455 (Mich. Ct. App. 1981).

2. Types of Substantive Character Evidence

Graham C. Lilly,
An Introduction to the Law of Evidence
103–05 (1978)[10]

§ 35. Character Evidence: Character An Essential Element of a Claim, Charge or Defense

The substantive law sometimes makes character a dispositive issue at trial: the existence or nonexistence of a character trait is itself an issue that directly determines the outcome of the case. In these instances, it is not necessary to utilize character as the basis for inferences about particular conduct — that is, to use character circumstantially. Such a case is a libel or slander suit where character is defamed and the defense is truth. The defendant, for example, states that the plaintiff is "corrupt and dishonest"; in the resulting suit for defamation, the defendant bases his defense upon the truth of his statement. Plaintiff's character for dishonesty and corruption is directly in issue, and the inferential chain stops with the establishment of these traits: further inferences about particular conduct are not required. Likewise, where an employer is sued for negligently engaging an employee of uncontrollable temper or intemperance, the character of the employee is placed directly in issue.

The distinguishing characteristics of these cases, or of any action in which character is said to be "directly in issue," is that character constitutes an essential "element of a charge, claim or defense." In these cases, of course, there exists no question as to the relevance of character evidence. Because character is itself a dispositive issue in the case, evidence intended to establish (or refute)the character trait in issue is always received. Furthermore, many jurisdictions admit any form of character evidence that has probative value including testimony of (1) specific past acts; (2) opinions held by qualified observers; and (3) reputation in the community. This generous receptivity stands in marked contrast to the begrudging approach that has traditionally prevailed when character is used circumstantially. In the latter instance, . . . not only are the restrict limitations as to when character may be shown, but there are additional restrictions upon the type of evidence that may be used to establish character.

---

[10] Reprinted from Lilly, An Introduction to the Law of Evidence 103–05 (1978) with permission of the West Group.

§ 36. Character Evidence: Character Used Circumstantially

The circumstantial use of character involves not only the establishment of the relevant character trait, but also the inference that the conduct in question was consistent with the actor's character. If, for example, the issue in a prosecution for criminal assault is who attacked first, the defendant or the victim, the defense may wish to offer evidence that the victim has an aggressive and violent character; the desired inference is that his actions were commensurate with his character and, hence, that he attacked first. Specifically, the inferential chain is this: from the evidence presented, the fact finder infers a particular character trait, from which it further infers relevant actions that are manifestations of this trait. Used circumstantially, character serves only the subsidiary function of helping the trier reach an ultimate proposition about conduct.

3.   Character Evidence in a Civil Context

MUTUAL LIFE INS. CO. OF BALTIMORE v. KELLY
197 N.E. 235 (Ohio Ct. App. 1934)

SHERICK, PRESIDING JUDGE.

The Mutual Life Insurance Company of Baltimore, defendant in the trial court, here seeks reversal of a judgment entered against it and in favor of Blanche Kelly, the beneficiary named in a life policy upon the life of one Harold Farson; and also an additional sum upon an accidental death provision thereof.

The petition avers that the insured was accidentally shot on the 19th of April, 1933, by a trap gun which had been placed on the inside of a cottage located on the banks of the Muskingum river, and that the insured died as a result thereof.

To this petition the insurer interposed three defenses, the first being a general denial; the second averred a condition of the policy of non-liability in the event that "insured dies in consequence of his or her own criminal action," and that insured did die in consequence of his own criminal act; the third defense pleaded a further contractual provision, in that "no accidental death benefit will be paid if the death of the insured resulted . . . from violation of law by the insured," and that he, the insured, did die as a result of violating the law. The reply filed is a general denial.

The facts disclose that the insured and another had purchased a pair of pliers, and had thereafter proceeded to hunt mushrooms, and on their return home entered an enclosed lot belonging to one Brown. It is in evidence that four or five "keep out" notices were posted in conspicuous places about the premises which notices the companion of the insured says he did not see. There is evidence of the fact that the cottage had a screened-in porch; that a few days prior to the happening the screen door was intact, closed, and hooked in two places with nails bent over the hooks; that after the happening this door was found open, the nails bent and broken, and the screen torn in two places convenient to the hooks. It further appears that the insured called his associate to the porch window to see a canoe that was inside the cottage, and that while he stood there admiring the canoe, he heard a shot and saw the deceased run off the porch; further than this he knows little or nothing of the transaction.

It is affirmatively in evidence as a part of the company's case that a readable sign was glued on the inside of the glass in the door through which the insured was shot. It read "Friendly warning, Keep out." This fact is negatively denied by several of the plaintiff's witnesses who were called in rebuttal. It is further proved and not denied that the gun set upon a tripod near the door had an iron rod attached to the trigger of the gun, which rod extended to within three or four inches from the lower part of the door, and that the door was bolted at the top. The almost conclusive inference is that the insured must have pushed in the door sufficiently at the bottom to spring the door, and thereby caused the gun to be discharged. The further evidence is, from one of the first arrivals on the scene, that the door "burst at the top" when he applied pressure, and that he then entered thereby. There is some evidence pro and con concerning a strip nailed to the floor at the bottom of the door, but whatever the fact may be as to that seems to us to be immaterial. It is further in evidence that a box of fishing tackle that had belonged to Brown, which had reposed on the window ledge inside the porch, was afterwards found in the insured's pocket, along with the recently purchased pliers, which showed jaw marks like those on the nails found broken off at the screen door.

In view of this chain of circumstances we are unable to conceive how the jury could have arrived at the conclusion that the insured's trespass was but a technical trespass, and not a criminal trespass; unless it be that the jury was influenced by certain testimony which we feel was improperly admitted in evidence over objection.

We have painstakingly read every word of the evidence in this case to discover whether the company introduced any evidence which would place in issue the character of the insured. Such was not done by the pleading; nor was it done by the proof offered. No attempt was made to show that the insured had ever done a prior similar act, and the truth is that only facts and circumstances pertaining to this affair were placed in evidence.

In rebuttal the beneficiary was permitted to call a number of character witnesses, who testified that the deceased bore a good reputation and was a peaceable and law-abiding citizen. In this we think the court erred to the prejudice of the plaintiff in error.

The defendant in error asserts that this evidence was admissible and competent because of the fact that the second and third defenses in effect charge that the insured had committed a crime, that thereby his character was questioned and placed in issue, where for the rule applicable in criminal cases applied, to wit, that reputation evidence is admissible for the reason that a man with a good reputation is not as likely to commit a criminal act as one with a bad reputation. But the fact is overlooked that this is a civil action based upon a contract, wherein the insured's general character was not involved.

It is the generally accepted rule that in civil actions, even where fraud is imputed or dishonesty is charged, evidence of a party's good or bad character is incompetent in evidence unless it be made an issue by the pleadings or the proof, as in actions for libel and slander, malicious prosecution, or cases of seduction. In these exceptions to the rule, character is generally involved, and the amount of the damages recoverable may be affected thereby.

Jones in his COMMENTARIES ON THE LAW OF EVIDENCE (2d Ed.) vol. 2, pp. 1190 to 1193, inclusive, §§ 639 and 640, adopts the reasoning of *Heileg v. Dumas*, 65 N.C. 214, and *Quinalty v. Temple*, 176 F. 67, in discussing the general rule:

> If such evidence is proper, then a person may screen himself from the punishment due to fraudulent conduct till his character becomes bad. . . . Every man must be answerable for every improper act, and the character of every transaction must be ascertained by its own circumstances, and not by the character of the parties.

> At best, such evidence is a mere matter of opinion, and, in matters of opinion, witnesses are apt to be influenced by prejudice or partisanship, of which they may be unconscious, or by the opinions of those who first approach them on the subject. The introduction of such evidence, in civil cases, to bolster the character of parties and witnesses who have not been impeached, would make trials intolerably tedious and greatly increase the expense and delay of litigation.

The author further points out that in the ordinary case character evidence has but a remote bearing as proof as to whether or not the act in question has or has not been committed, for, as said in *Thompson v. Church*, 1 Root (Conn.) 312," The general character is not in issue. The business of the court is to try the case and not the man; and a very bad man may have a very righteous cause."

* * *

The reason for the rule is obvious. It is twofold. Administrative policy requires that litigation be kept within bounds, and in order that the real issue of a cause may be tried and not be confused with or beclouded by an irrelevant matter having but a remote bearing on the proof of the act or fact in issue.

* * *

Judgment reversed, and cause remanded.

QUESTION

Should character evidence be allowed in civil cases involving alleged criminal misconduct (*i.e.*, such as wrongful death)? *See Perrin v. Anderson*, 784 F.2d 1040 (10th Cir. 1986). *Compare Taylor v. Hudson*, 2003 U.S. Dist. LEXIS 26738 (D.N.M. July 16, 2003) *with SEC v. Towers Fin. Corp.*, 966 F. Supp. 203, 205–06 (S.D.N.Y. 1997).

4. Character Evidence in a Criminal Context

Evidentiary Foundation:
The Trial of Alger Hiss[11]

[In 1948, noted diplomat Alger Hiss was indicted for having committed perjury before a federal grand jury investigating allegations that he had been a Communist sympathizer. On December 15, 1948, Hiss had sworn to the grand jury that "he had never, nor had his wife in his presence, turned over any documents of the State Department . . . to one Whittaker Chambers or any other unauthorized person." *United States v. Hiss*, 18[5] F.2d 822, 824 (2d Cir. 1950).

At his trial, Alger Hiss testified in his own behalf. A vast array of prominent citizens testified for Mr. Hiss as character witnesses. Among them was CALVERT MAGRUDER, CHIEF JUDGE of the First Circuit Court of Appeals.]

New York, December 19, 1949, 11:30 o'clock a.m. Trial resumed.

CALVERT MAGRUDER, called as a witness on behalf of the defendant, being duly sworn, testified as follows:

Direct examination by Mr. Cross:

Q.   Judge Magruder, you are the Chief Judge of the United States Circuit Court of Appeals for the First Circuit, are you not?

A.   Yes, sir.

Q.   And that Circuit has its headquarters where?

A.   Boston.

Q.   How long have you been on that court?

A.   Over ten years.

Q.   Prior to being appointed to that court what official positions had you held, say from 1920 on?

A.   I was professor at the Harvard Law School from 1920 to 1939. I had leave of absence from that school two years and I was serving in Washington in various capacities; in 1934–35 I was general counsel of the old National Labor Relations Board, and 1938–39 I was general counsel of the Wage and Hour Division of the Department of Labor.

Q.   Do you know Alger Hiss?

A.   I do.

Q.   When did you first meet him?

A.   I met him when he was a student at the Harvard Law School, perhaps 1928 or thereabouts.

Q.   Before going to Harvard Law School had you lived in Maryland?

---

[11] Excerpted from The Record on Appeal, Vol. 1, Transcript of Record, pp. 347–52.

A.   That was my home.

Q.   Will you tell his Honor and the jury the occasions when you met him, if you can, from the time you first met him on, Judge Magruder?

A.   I don't recall my first meeting with him but he was prominent as a student at the Law School. I do not believe he ever took a course with me but he came from my home state and I got to know him quite well socially and saw a good deal of him and had him in my home and I have since then remained a friend of his.

Q.   When you were in Washington did you see him?

A.   I did.

Q.   Have you been in his home in Washington?

A.   I have.

Q.   Do you know other people who know Alger Hiss?

A.   Yes.

Q.   What is his reputation for integrity, loyalty and veracity?

A.   Excellent.

MR. CROSS: You may inquire.

QUESTIONS

1. What is the pertinent substantive character trait that the defense was seeking to establish?

2. Why does Judge Magruder's testimony serve as a good example of character evidence used both substantively and for credibility purposes?

3. How would you have cross-examined this witness?

MICHELSON v. UNITED STATES
335 U.S. 469 (1948)

Mr. Justice Jackson delivered the opinion of the Court.

In 1947 petitioner Michelson was convicted of bribing a federal revenue agent. The Government proved a large payment by accused to the agent for the purpose of influencing his official action. The defendant, as a witness on his own behalf, admitted passing the money but claimed it was done in response to the agent's demands, threats, solicitations, and inducements that amounted to entrapment. It is enough for our purposes to say that determination of the issue turned on whether the jury should believe the agent or the accused.

*   *   *

Defendant called five witnesses to prove that he enjoyed a good reputation. Two of them testified that their acquaintance with him extended over a period of about thirty years and the others said they had known him at least half that long. A typical examination in chief was as follows:

Q.   Do you know the defendant Michelson?

A.   Yes.

Q.   How long do you know Mr. Michelson?

A.   About 30 years.

Q.   Do you know other people who know him?

A.   Yes.

Q.   Have you had occasion to discuss his reputation for honesty and truthfulness and for being a law-abiding citizen?

A.   It is very good.

Q.   You have talked to others?

A.   Yes.

Q.   And what is his reputation?

A.   Very good.

*   *   *

To four of these witnesses the prosecution . . . addressed the question the allowance of which, over defendant's objection, is claimed to be reversible error: "Did you ever hear that on October 11, 1920, the defendant, Solomon Michelson, was arrested for receiving stolen goods?"

None of the witnesses appears to have heard of this.

The trial court asked counsel for the prosecution, out of presence of the jury, "Is it a fact according to the best information in your possession, that Michelson was arrested for receiving stolen goods?" Counsel replied that it was, and to support his good faith exhibited a paper record which defendant's counsel did not challenge.

The judge also on three occasions warned the jury, in terms that are not criticized, of the limited purpose for which this evidence was received.[12]

Defendant-petitioner challenges the right of the prosecution so to cross- examine his character witnesses. The Court of Appeals held that it was permissible. The opinion, however, points out that the practice has been severely criticized and invites us, in one respect, to change the rule.[13] Serious and responsible criticism has

---

[12] [3] In ruling on the objection when the question was first asked, the Court said:

. . . I instruct the jury that what is happening now is this: the defendant has called character witnesses, and the basis for the evidence given by those character witnesses is the reputation of the defendant in the community, and since the defendant tenders the issue of his reputation the prosecution may ask the witness if she has heard of various incidents in his career. I say to you that regardless of her answer you are not to assume that the incidents asked about actually took place. All that is happening is that this witness' standard of opinion of the reputation of the defendant is being tested. Is that clear?

[13] [4] Footnote 8 to that court's opinion reads as follows:

been aimed, however, not alone at the detail now questioned by the Court of Appeals but at common-law doctrine on the whole subject of proof of reputation or character.[14] It would not be possible to appraise the usefulness and propriety of this cross-examination without consideration of the unique practice concerning character testimony, of which such cross-examination is a minor part.

Courts that follow the common-law tradition almost unanimously have come to disallow resort by the prosecution to any kind of evidence of a defendant's evil character to establish a probability of his guilt. Not that the law invests the defendant with a presumption of good character, . . . but it simply closes the whole matter of character, disposition and reputation on the prosecution's case- in-chief. The state may not show defendant's prior trouble with the law, specific criminal acts, or ill name among his neighbors, even though such facts might logically be persuasive that he is by propensity a probable perpetrator of the crime. The inquiry is not rejected because character is irrelevant; on the contrary, it is said to weigh too much with the jury and to so over persuade them as to prejudge one with a bad general record and deny him a fair opportunity to defend against a particular charge. The overriding policy of excluding such evidence, despite its admitted probative value, is the practical experience that its disallowance tends to prevent confusion of issues, unfair surprise and undue prejudice.

But this line of inquiry firmly denied to the State is opened to the defendant because character is relevant in resolving probabilities of guilt. He may introduce affirmative testimony that the general estimate of his character is so favorable that

---

WIGMORE, EVIDENCE (3d ed. 1940) § 988, after noting that "such inquiries are almost universally admitted," not as "impeachment by extrinsic testimony of particular acts of misconduct," but as means of testing the character "witness' grounds of knowledge," continues with these comments: "But the serious objection to them is that practically the above distinction — between rumors of such conduct, as affecting reputation, and the fact of it as violating the rule against particular facts — cannot be maintained in the mind of the jury. The rumor of the misconduct, when admitted, goes far in spite of all theory and of the judge's charge, toward fixing the misconduct as a fact upon the other person, and thus does three improper things, — (1) it violates the fundamental rule of fairness that prohibits the use of such facts, (2) it gets at them by hearsay only, and not by trustworthy testimony, and (3) it leaves the other person no means of defending himself by denial or explanation, such as he would otherwise have had if the rule had allowed that conduct to be made the subject of an issue. Moreover, these are not occurrences of possibility, but of daily practice. This method of inquiry or cross-examination is frequently resorted to by counsel for the very purpose of injuring by indirection a character which they are forbidden directly to attack in that way; they rely upon the mere putting of the question (not caring that it is answered negatively) to convey their covert insinuation. The value of the inquiry for testing purposes is often so small and the opportunities of its abuse by underhand ways are so great that the practice may amount to little more than a mere subterfuge, and should be strictly supervised by forbidding it to counsel who do not use it in good faith."

[14] [5] A judge of long trial and appellate experience has uttered a warning which, in the opinion of the writer, we might well have heeded in determining whether to grant certiorari here:

. . . evidence of good character is to be used like any other, once it gets before the jury, and the less they are told about the grounds for its admission, or what they shall do with it, the more likely they are to use it sensibly. The subject seems to gather mist which discussion serves only to thicken, and which we can scarcely hope to dissipate by anything further we can add.

L. Hand in *Nash v. United States*, 54 F.2d 1006, 1007.

the jury may infer that he would not be likely to commit the offense charged. This privilege is sometimes valuable to a defendant for this Court has held that such testimony alone, in some circumstances, may be enough to raise a reasonable doubt of guilt and that in the federal courts a jury in a proper case should be so instructed.

When the defendant elects to initiate a character inquiry, another anomalous rule comes into play. Not only is he permitted to call witnesses to testify from hearsay, but indeed such a witness is not allowed to base his testimony on anything but hearsay. What commonly is called "character evidence" is only such when "character" is employed as a synonym for "reputation." The witness may not testify about defendant's specific acts or courses of conduct or his possession of a particular disposition or of benign mental and moral traits; nor can he testify that his own acquaintance, observation, and knowledge of defendant leads to his own independent opinion that defendant possessed a good general or specific character, inconsistent with commission of acts charged. The witness is, however, allowed to summarize what he has heard in the community, although much of it may have been said by persons less qualified to judge than himself. The evidence which the law permits is not as to the personality of defendant but only as to the shadow his daily life has cast in his neighborhood. . . .

While courts have recognized logical grounds for criticism of this type of opinion-based-on-hearsay testimony, it is said to be justified by "overwhelming considerations of practical convenience" in avoiding innumerable collateral issues which, if it were attempted to prove character by direct testimony, would complicate and confuse the trial, distract the minds of jurymen and befog the chief issues in the litigation.

*   *   *

Thus the law extends helpful but illogical options to a defendant. Experience taught a necessity that they be counterweighted with equally illogical conditions to keep the advantage from becoming an unfair and unreasonable one. The price a defendant must pay for attempting to prove his good name is to throw open the entire subject which the law has kept closed for his benefit and to make himself vulnerable where the law otherwise shields him. The prosecution may pursue the inquiry with contradictory witnesses to show that damaging rumors, whether or not well-grounded, were afloat — for it is not the man that he is, but the name that he has which is put in issue. Another hazard is that his own witness is subject to cross-examination as to the contents and extent of the hearsay on which he bases his conclusions, and he may be required to disclose rumors and reports that are current even if they do not affect his own conclusion.[15] It may test the sufficiency of his knowledge by asking what stories were circulating concerning events, such as one's arrest, about which people normally comment and speculate. Thus, while the law

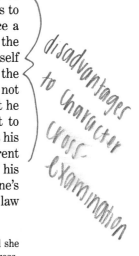

disadvantages to character cross-examination

---

[15] [16] A classic example in the books is a character witness in a trial for murder. She testified she grew up with defendant, knew his reputation for peace and quiet, and that it was good. On cross-examination she was asked if she had heard that the defendant had shot anybody and, if so, how many. She answered, "three or four," and gave the names of two but could not recall the names of the others. She still insisted, however, that he was of "good character." The jury seems to have valued her information more highly than her judgment, and on appeal from conviction the cross examination was held proper. . . .

gives defendant the option to show as a fact that his reputation reflects a life and habit incompatible with commission of the offense charged, it subjects his proof to tests of credibility designed to prevent him from profiting by a mere parade of partisans.

. . . Both propriety and abuse of hearsay reputation testimony, on both sides, depend on numerous and subtle considerations difficult to detect or appraise from a cold record, and therefore rarely and only on clear showing of prejudicial abuse of discretion will Courts of Appeals disturb rulings of trial courts on this subject.

Wide discretion is accompanied by heavy responsibility on trial courts to protect the practice from any misuse. The trial judge was scrupulous to so guard it in the case before us. He took pains to ascertain, out of presence of the jury, that the target of the question was an actual event, which would probably result in some comment among acquaintances if not injury to defendant's reputation. He satisfied himself that counsel was not merely taking a random shot at a reputation imprudently exposed or asking a groundless question to waft an unwarranted innuendo into the jury box.[16]

The question permitted by the trial court, however, involves several features that may be worthy of comment. Its form invited hearsay; it asked about an arrest, not a conviction, and for an offense not closely similar to the one on trial; and it concerned an occurrence many years past.

Since the whole inquiry, as we have pointed out, is calculated to ascertain the general talk of people about defendant, rather than the witness' own knowledge of him, the form of inquiry, "Have you heard?" has general approval, and "Do you know?" is not allowed.

A character witness may be cross-examined as to an arrest whether or not it culminated in a conviction, according to the overwhelming weight of authority. This rule is sometimes confused with that which prohibits cross-examination as to credibility by asking a witness whether he himself has been arrested.

Arrest without more does not, in law any more than in reason, impeach the integrity or impair the credibility of a witness. It happens to the innocent as well as the guilty. Only a conviction, therefore, may be inquired about to undermine the trustworthiness of a witness.

---

[16] [18] This procedure was recommended by Wigmore. But analysis of his innovation emphasizes the way in which law on this subject has evolved from pragmatic considerations rather than from theoretical consistency. The relevant information that it is permissible to lay before the jury is talk or conversation about the defendant's being arrested. That is admissible whether or not an actual arrest had taken place; it might even be more significant of repute if his neighbors were ready to arrest him in rumor when the authorities were not in fact. But before this relevant and proper inquiry can be made, counsel must demonstrate privately to the court an irrelevant and possibly unprovable fact — the reality of arrest. From this permissible inquiry about reports of arrest, the jury is pretty certain to infer that defendant had in fact been arrested and to draw its own conclusions as to character from that fact. The Wigmore suggestion thus limits legally relevant inquiries to those based on legally irrelevant facts in order that the legally irrelevant conclusion which the jury probably will draw from the relevant questions will not be based on unsupported or untrue innuendo. It illustrates Judge Hand's suggestion that the system may work best when explained least. Yet, despite its theoretical paradoxes and deficiencies, we approve the procedure as calculated in practice to hold the inquiry within decent bounds.

Arrest without more may nevertheless impair or cloud one's reputation. False arrest may do that. Even to be acquitted may damage one's good name if the community receives the verdict with a wink and chooses to remember defendant as one who ought to have been convicted. A conviction, on the other hand, maybe accepted as a misfortune or an injustice, and even enhance the standing of one who mends his ways and lives it down. Reputation is the net balance of so many debits and credits that the law does not attach the finality to a conviction, when the issue is reputation, that is given to it when the issue is the credibility of the convict.

The inquiry as to an arrest is permissible also because the prosecution has a right to test the qualifications of the witness to bespeak the community opinion. If one never heard the speculations and rumors in which even one's friends indulge upon his arrest, the jury may doubt whether he is capable of giving any very reliable conclusions as to his reputation.

In this case the crime inquired about was receiving stolen goods; the trial was for bribery. The Court of Appeals thought this dissimilarity of offenses too great to sustain the inquiry in logic, though conceding that it is authorized by preponderance of authority. It asks us to substitute the Illinois rule which allows inquiry about arrest, but only for very closely similar if not identical charges, in place of the rule more generally adhered to in this country and in England. We think the facts of this case show the proposal to be inexpedient.

The good character which the defendant had sought to establish was broader than the crime charged and included the traits of "honesty and truthfulness" and "being a law-abiding citizen." Possession of these characteristics would seem as incompatible with offering a bribe to a revenue agent as with receiving stolen goods. The crimes may be unlike, but both alike proceed from the same defects of character which the witnesses said this defendant was reputed not to exhibit. It is not only by comparison with the crime on trial but by comparison with the reputation asserted that a court may judge whether the prior arrest should be made subject of inquiry. By this test the inquiry was permissible. It was proper cross-examination because reports of his arrest for receiving stolen goods, if admitted, would tend to weaken the assertion that he was known as an honest and law-abiding citizen. The cross-examination may take in as much ground as the testimony it is designed to verify. To hold otherwise would give defendant the benefit of testimony that he was honest and law-abiding in reputation when such might not be the fact; the refutation was founded on convictions equally persuasive though not for crimes exactly repeated in the present charge.

The inquiry here concerned an arrest twenty-seven years before the trial. Events a generation old are likely to be lived down and dropped from the present thought and talk of the community and to be absent from the knowledge of younger or more recent acquaintances. The court in its discretion may well exclude inquiry about rumors of an event so remote, unless recent misconduct revived them. But two of these witnesses dated their acquaintance with defendant as commencing thirty years before the trial. Defendant, on direct examination, voluntarily called attention to his conviction twenty years before the trial. While the jury might conclude that a matter so old and indecisive as a 1920 arrest would shed little light on the present reputation and hence propensities of the defendant, we cannot say that, in the context of this evidence and in the absence of objection on this specific ground, its admission was an abuse of discretion.

We do not overlook or minimize the consideration that "the jury almost surely cannot comprehend the judge's limiting instruction," which disturbed the Court of Appeals. The refinements of the evidentiary rules on this subject are such that even lawyers and judges, after study and reflection, often are confused, and surely jurors in the hurried and unfamiliar movement of a trial must find them almost unintelligible. However, limiting instructions on this subject are no more difficult to comprehend or apply than those upon various other subjects.

[I]n cases such as the one before us, the law foreclosed this whole confounding line of inquiry, unless defendant thought the net advantage from opening it up would be with him. Given this option, we think, defendants in general and this defendant in particular have no valid complaint at the latitude which existing law allows to the prosecution to meet by cross-examination an issue voluntarily tendered by the defense.

*   *   *

We concur in the general opinion of courts, text writers and the profession that much of this law is archaic, paradoxical and full of compromises and compensations by which an irrational advantage to one side is offset by a poorly reasoned counter privilege to the other. But somehow it has proved a workable even if clumsy system when moderated by discretionary controls in the hands of a wise and strong trial court. To pull one misshapen stone out of the grotesque structure is more likely simply to upset its present balance between adverse interests than to establish a rational edifice.

*   *   *

The judgment is *affirmed*

Mr. Justice Rutledge, with whom Mr. Justice Murphy joins, dissenting.

The Court's opinion candidly and interestingly points out the anomalous features characterizing the exclusion and admission of so-called character evidence in criminal cases. It also for the first time puts the stamp of the Court's approval upon the most anomalous and, what is more important, the most unfair stage in this evidentiary sequence.

There are three stages. The first denies the prosecution the right to attack the defendant's reputation as part of its case in chief, either by proof of bad general reputation or by proof of specific derogatory incidents disconnected from the one charged as the crime. The second permits the defendant, at his option, to prove by qualified witnesses that he bears a good general reputation or at least one not tarnished by ill-repute. The witness is forbidden, however, to go into particular incidents or details of the defendant's life and conduct. The witness, once qualified, can state only the general conclusion of the community concerning the defendant's character as the witness knows that reputation. The third stage comprehends the prosecution's rebuttal, and particularly the latitude of cross- examination to be allowed.

I do not agree that this whole body of law is anomalous, unless indeed all the law of evidence with its numerous rules of exclusion and exceptions to them is to be so regarded. Anomalies there are, no doubt with much room for improvement. But here, if anywhere, the law is more largely the result of experience, of considerations of fairness and practicability developed through the centuries, than of any effort to construct a nicely logical, wholly consistent pattern of things. Imperfect and variable as the scheme has become in the application of specific rules, on the whole it represents the result of centuries of common-law growth in the seeking of English-speaking peoples for fair play in the trial of crime and other causes.

Moreover, I cannot agree that, in the sequence of the three stages relating to character evidence, the anomalous quality is equally present in each. In my judgment there is a vast difference in this respect between the rulings summarizing our experience in the first two stages and those affecting the third.

Regardless of all considerations of mere logical consistency, I should suppose there would be few now, whether lawyers or laymen, who would advocate change in the prevailing rules governing the first two stages of the sequence. In criminal causes especially, there are sound reasons basic to our system of criminal justice which justify initially excluding the Government from showing the defendant's bad general character or reputation.

* * *

The rule which allows the defendant to prove his good standing by general reputation is, of course, a kind of exception to the hearsay rule of exclusion, though one may inquire how else could reputation be proved than by hearsay if it is to be proved at all. This indeed presents the substantial question. Apart from its long acceptance, . . . the rule allowing the evidence to come in rests on very different considerations from the one which forbids the Government to bring in proof of bad public character as part of its case in chief. The defendant's proof comes as rebuttal. It is subject to none of the dangers involving the possibility of conviction for generally bad conduct or general repute for it which would characterize permitting the prosecution initially to show bad general reputation. The basic reason for excluding the latter does not apply to the defendant's tender of proof.

On the positive side the rule is justified by the ancient law which pronounces that a good name is rather to be chosen than riches. True, men of good general repute may not deserve it. Or they may slip and fall in particular situations. But by common experience this is more often the exception than the rule. Moreover, most often in close cases, where the proof leaves one in doubt, the evidence of general regard by one's fellows may be the weight which turns the scales of justice. It may indeed be sufficient to create a clear conviction of innocence or to sow that reasonable doubt which our law requires to be overcome in all criminal cases before the verdict of guilty can be returned.

* * *

But, for a variety of reasons, the law allows the defendant to prove no more than his general reputation, by witnesses qualified to report concerning it. He cannot show particular acts of virtue to offset the proof of his specific criminality on any theory that "By their fruits ye shall know them." Whether this be because such proof is irrelevant, is too distracting and time-consuming, is summarized in the general report of good character, or perhaps for all of these reasons, the rule is settled, and I think rightly, which restricts the proof to general repute.

Thus far, whatever the differences in logic, differences which as usual in here in the premises from which thinking starts, there is no general disagreement or dissatisfaction in the results. All of the states and the federal judicial system as well, approve them. No one would open the doors initially to the prosecution. No one would close them to the defense.

But the situation is different when we come to the third stage, that of the prosecution's rebuttal. Obviously rebuttal there should be, when the defendant has opened a line of inquiry closed to the prosecution and has sought to gain advantage by proof which it has had no chance to counteract. But the question of how the rebuttal shall be made presents the difficult problem.

There can be no sound objection, of course, to calling witnesses who will qualify as the witnesses for the defense are required to do, but who also will contradict their testimony. And the prosecution may inquire concerning the qualifications of the witnesses for the defense to speak concerning the defendant's general reputation. Thus far there is nothing to exceed the bounds of rebuttal or take the case out of the issues as made.

But these have not been the limits of proof and cross-examination. For, in the guise of "testing the standards of the witness" when he speaks to reputation, the door has been thrown wide open to trying the defendant's whole life, both in general reputation and in specific incident. What is worse, this is without opportunity for the defendant to rebut either the fact or the innuendo for which the evidence is tendered more generally than otherwise. Hardly any incident, however remote or derogatory . . . can be drawn out by asking the witness who testifies to the defendant's good character, "Have you heard this" or "Have you heard that." And many incidents, wholly innocent in quality, can be turned by the prosecutor, through an inflection or tone, to cast aspersion upon the defendant by the mere asking of the question, without hope of affirmative response from the witness. The dangers, the potential damage and prejudice to the defendant and his cause, have not been more clearly summarized than in the excerpt from Wigmore's classic treatise, quoted in note 4 of the Court's opinion, ante. . . .

These consequences are not denied. But it is said two modes of protection are available to the accused. One is to refrain from opening the inquiry into his reputation. That answer would have weight if the rebuttal were limited to inquiry concerning the witness' opportunity for knowing the accused and his reputation and to producing contrary evidence by other witnesses of the same general sort as that which is refuted. But if the rule is sound which allows the accused to show his good repute and restricts him to that showing, it not only is anomalous, it is highly unjust, to exact, as the price for his doing so, throwing open to the prosecution the opportunity not only to rebut his proof but to call in question almost any specific act of his life or to insinuate without proving that he has committed other acts, leaving him no chance to reply. A fair rule either would afford this chance or would restrict the prosecution's counter proof in the same way his own is limited. The prevailing rule changes the whole character of the case, in a manner the rules applying to the two earlier stages seek to avoid.

* * *

Moreover, I do not think the mere question of knowledge of a prior arrest is one proper to be asked, even if inquiry as to clearly derogatory acts is to be permitted. Of course men take such an inquiry as reflecting upon the person arrested. But, for use in a criminal prosecution, I do not think they should be allowed to do so. The mere fact of a single arrest twenty-seven years before trial, without further showing of criminal proceedings or their outcome, whether acquittal or conviction, seldom could have substantial bearing upon one's present general reputation; indeed it is not per se a derogatory fact. But it is put in generally, and I think was put in evidence in this case, not to call in question the witness' standard of opinion but, by the very question, to give room for play of the jury's unguarded conjecture and prejudice. This is neither fair play nor due process. It is a perversion of the criminal process as we know it. For it permits what the rule applied in the first stage forbids, trial of the accused not only for general bad conduct or reputation but also for conjecture, gossip, innuendo and insinuation.

Accordingly, I think this judgment should be reversed.

Evidentiary Foundation:
The Trial of Pete Seeger

[On March 27, 1961, the popular folksinger Pete Seeger went on trial to defend against an indictment charging him with 10 counts of contempt of Congress. These charges stemmed from Seeger's refusal to answer 10 questions that the House Un-American Activities Committee asked him in 1955. After a 3-day trial, Seeger was convicted on all counts.

During his trial, Seeger chose not to testify in his own behalf. He did, however, call numerous character witnesses. Helen Parkhurst, a prominent educator and editor, was one of those witnesses. Did counsel establish an adequate foundation for her testimony? Did counsel's questions of the witness properly encompass the character pertinent to the alleged crime? Did cross-examination fall within the permissible scope of Michelson?]

HELEN PARKHURST, called as a witness on behalf of the defendant, being duly sworn, testified as follows:

DIRECT EXAMINATION BY MR. ROSS:

* * *

Q.   What is your occupation?

A.   Editor, author and broadcaster.

Q.   And what has been the nature of your associations as an editor? What schools have you been associated with?

A.   I founded the Dalton School and I was head of it from 1916 to 1942, at which time I went to Yale to be a part of the department of education.

Q.   And what have been your activities in connection with writing in the field of education?

A.   I have written four books: EDUCATION ON THE DALTON PLAN, which is in sixteen languages; WORKS RHYTHMS IN EDUCATION; EXPLORING THE CHILD'S WORLD, which is just recently in its seventh edition and was published by the Department of Information — the Agency of Information, in German, for dissemination abroad to show the American way of life; EDUCATION ON THE DALTON PLAN, was the first one. I am currently engaged in writing two more which will be out this fall.

Q.   Now, do you know Peter Seeger?

A.   I know Peter Seeger—

Q.   Do you? Do you?

A.   I know Peter Seeger.

Q.   How long have you know him?

A.   All his years, really. He was about one or two when I first knew him.

Q.   And did he at any time attend the Dalton School?

A.   Yes, he did.

Q.   Are you familiar with his education?

A.   Yes.

Q.   Tell us about it.

MR. YOUNGER: Objection, your Honor.

THE COURT: Sustained.

Q.   Do you know his family?

A.   I know his — I knew his grandparents, I knew his father, I knew his mother, I knew his brothers. I knew the whole family.

Q.   Do you know other people who know him?

A.   Yes, many people.

Q.   Now, do you know what his profession is?

A.   Yes.

Q.   Tell us.

A.   I know of him as a musician and a singer.

Q.   Now, are you familiar with his general reputation? Are you familiar with his general reputation?

A.   Yes. Yes, I am.

Q.   Now, I would like to ask you some questions and indicate to you that the answers may be either excellent, good, fair or bad.

MR. YOUNGER: Your Honor, I object. I don't think this witness's qualifications have been established.

THE COURT: Did you understand the District Attorney?

MR. ROSS: I beg your pardon?

THE COURT: Did you understand the District Attorney?

MR. ROSS: I did not, sir.

THE COURT: He said that the qualifications of the witness have not been established as yet.

Q.   Well, are you familiar with the general reputation in the community in which he lives?

A.   Yes.

Q.   Are you familiar with his general reputation in the professional circles in which he moves?

A.   Yes.

Q.   Now, will you tell us what his general reputation is?

MR. YOUNGER: Your Honor—

THE COURT: Excuse me, there is an objection.

MR. YOUNGER: Your Honor, at the very least my request is that I be permitted to examine this witness on the voir dire as to her qualifications.

THE COURT: Well, she has said that she knows the man's reputation in the community in which he lives and his reputation in his profession.

MR. YOUNGER: That is why I ask that I be permitted to examine her at this time.

THE COURT: Yes, all right.

PRELIMINARY CROSS EXAMINATION BY MR. YOUNGER:

Q.   Do you know where Mr. Seeger lives?

A.   Yes.

Q.   Where does he live?

A.   In Beacon, New York.

Q.   Where do you live?

A.   I have lived in New York since 1915 and currently I am living partly in Connecticut, where I have a studio.

Q.   And the rest of the time? You said partly in Connecticut. The rest of the time where do you live?

A.   I have an office, a resident office in New York and I have a residence in Connecticut.

Q.   When you say New York, do you mean New York City?

A.   New York City.

Q.   And when you said you have been in New York since 1915, did you mean New York City?

A.   Yes, I did.

Q.   I see. You have known Peter Seeger since his early years, you say?

A.   Yes. He went to the Dalton School — the Children's University School, which became the Dalton School.

Q.   I see. Do you know any other folk singers?

A.   Well, by name only.

Q.   Not as personal — as friends?

A.   Only that you hear. Well, not intimately.

MR. YOUNGER: Your Honor, I think this witness is not qualified to testify as a character witness.

THE COURT: Oh, I think it is a question of fact for the jury. I will permit it.

DIRECT EXAMINATION CONTINUED BY MR. ROSS:

Q.   Now, will you tell us what his general reputation is as to character and integrity?

A.   Excellent.

MR. YOUNGER: Objection your Honor. I don't think that is an element in this case.

THE COURT: Well, as I said, I have some misgivings about the whole relevancy, but I am permitting it, though.

           You said it was excellent, madam?

THE WITNESS: Yes, your Honor.

Q.   Will you tell us what his general reputation is for conducting himself as a law-abiding citizen?

A.   As far as I know, excellent.

THE COURT: No. You see, they are not asking — what the lawyer wants is the sum total of the gossip in the community that you heard, not your personal opinion. Is the sum total of the gossip in the community that his reputation for acting as an upright and good citizen one that is excellent?

THE WITNESS: In the community that I traveled in.

THE COURT: Yes.

THE WITNESS: Excellent.

THE REPORTER: I didn't hear.

THE WITNESS: In the community that I traveled in, excellent.

* * *

A.   I have known him intimately for a long, long time.

THE COURT: Yes, but unfortunately only his reputation is involved, and reputation is the sum total of the gossip we hear from people.

THE WITNESS: Your Honor, maybe I don't hear much gossip—

THE COURT: But unfortunately that is what reputation is. We all have it. In fact, you said it is excellent.

MR. ROSS: Will you tell us what his general reputation is for frankness, honesty, forthrightness and sincerity?

MR. YOUNGER: Objection, your Honor.

THE COURT: Sustained.

* * *

Q.   Will you tell us what his general reputation is for truth and veracity?

MR. YOUNGER: I will object to that.

THE COURT: I don't think that one is relevant, counsel. You may have an exception.

* * *

Q.   Will you tell us what his reputation is for loyalty and adherence to the principles of our constitution?

MR. YOUNGER: Objection.

THE COURT: No. I will allow that.

                What is his reputation for loyalty and adherence to the Constitution?

THE WITNESS: Your Honor, I have asked many, many people in different parts of the country and it is excellent.

MR. ROSS: The answer can only be as the Court has indicated to you.

THE COURT: You have to say what his reputation is, if you know it, without giving the reason for knowing it.

THE WITNESS: It is excellent.

MR. ROSS: No further questions.

MR. YOUNGER: Mr. Ross, will you approach the bench with me? (Discussion at the bench.)

MR. YOUNGER: Your Honor, I would have only one question on cross, but I will present it at the bench first rather than in the jury's hearing.

                I would ask this witness whether she ever heard that Peter Seeger was a member of the Communist Party. I think it is proper cross considering the last question which was allowed.

MR. ROSS: I would object to that question.

THE COURT: I have to ask you whether you have information which has a basis for asking that.

MR. YOUNGER: I will make that representation in detail.

*   *   *

(In open court.)

THE COURT: We are going to take a short recess and we will be back in five minutes.

(In the robing room.)

THE COURT: Would you repeat, again, your statement?

MR. YOUNGER: Your Honor, what I am proposing to ask this witness on cross-examination is the following question: Have you heard whether or not Peter Seeger is a member of the Communist Party or was a member in the period between 1948 and 1955.

The basis of this question is as follows: Your Honor, Herman Thomas, an F.B.I. informant, who testified for the government in a Smith Act case in the Eastern District of Pennsylvania called United States against Kuzma, this Mr. Thomas having been a member of the Communist Party as an undercover agent, on September 12, 1949, and identifying Seeger as a member of the Communist Party.

In addition, John Lautner, a former chairman of the New York State Review Commission of the Communist Party, who was expelled from the party in January 1950, has informed the F.B.I. that he knew Seeger as a Communist Party member in the period 1947 to 1949.

In addition, Lewis F. Budenz, formerly the managing editor of the Daily Worker and former Communist Party member, in 1949 identified Seeger as a member of the Communist Party.

MR. ROSS: None of these people whom he mentioned were referred to in any of the testimony, in any of the questions which Mr. Tavenner asked Mr. Seeger at the hearing. As a matter of fact, as I recall, in the hearing before Tavenner he once said to Mr. Seeger that he had [not] been identified as a member of the Communist Party by anybody.

THE COURT: You miss the point. The Supreme Court has said that the Court has to satisfy itself that the question isn't asked frivolously or without some foundation, and the duty on the Court is to inquire of the United States Attorney what the basis is for the question, and that is what you have to address yourself to, as to whether the basis that Mr. Younger has said is a sufficient basis for me to permit the cross-examination. As I understand the *Michelson* case, that is the rule.

MR. ROSS: Of course, I object to the question. The Kuzma case, for instance, was reversed on appeal. And Lautner's testimony has been subjected to very severe question as to the credibility of some of his assertions.

Now, the third man, Budenz, of course, in many of the hearings at which he has testified, has been a pretty substantially discredited man. I have particularly in mind his testimony in the Lattimore case, where he said that he knew Lattimore to be a Communist.

It seems to me, in the light of this kind of experience with these witnesses, that there doesn't seem to be a rational foundation based on fact.

THE COURT: Well, you miss the point. The government doesn't have to prove as a fact that the man is or was a member of the Communist Party. All he has to do is satisfy me that there is a rational basis for asking the question.

MR. ROSS: I am addressing myself to that.

THE COURT: I will permit it and you may have an exception to it.

MR. ROSS: The question, as I understand it is, did you hear?

THE COURT: Have you ever heard.

MR. YOUNGER: Have you ever heard, right.

*   *   *

(Witness Parkhurst resumed the stand.)

CROSS-EXAMINATION BY MR. YOUNGER:

Q.   Dr. Parkhurst, you have testified that Peter Seeger's reputation for loyalty and adherence to the Constitution is excellent; is that correct?

A.   Yes.

Q.   Now, Dr. Parkhurst, I ask you this: Have you ever heard that Peter Seeger, sometime after 1947 and before 1956, was a member of the Communist Party?

A.   Recently.

Q.   You have recently heard this?

A.   Only recently I heard it. That he was accused; I didn't hear that he was.

MR. YOUNGER: I have no further questions.

MR. ROSS: That is all of this witness.

NOTES AND QUESTIONS

1.   For a state decision rejecting the *Michelson* approach, see *Commonwealth v. Morgan*, 739 A.2d 1033 (Pa. 1999).

2.   To what extent, if any, is *Michelson* reflected in the Federal Rules?

3. In a prosecution for narcotics trafficking, may the defendant introduce character testimony to the effect that he is a "law abiding" and "truthful" person? *See United States v. Angelini*, 678 F.2d 380 (1st Cir. 1982). No unless (b)(2)

4. Defendant is on trial for "conspiracy to commit offenses against the United States" involving the bombings of military recruitment centers. During his direct examination, he referred to 18 books and articles that he claimed were indicative of his revolutionary, but nonviolent, political philosophy. These books were later introduced into evidence. Has the defendant thereby "opened the door" to the introduction of character evidence by the prosecution? May he be cross-examined about the contents of another of his books, entitled "FROM THE MOVEMENT TOWARD REVOLUTION," which endorsed violence as a means to effect political change? *See United States v. Giese*, 597 F.2d 1170 (9th Cir.), *cert. denied*, 444 U.S. 979 (1979).

5. What are the consequences of the following cross-examination conducted by a pro se murder defendant?

Q: I take it you know me personally?

A: Yes.

Q: Have I ever presented myself to you as a mad man? Do I just run around wanting to kill everybody?

A: No, no.

Q: Have I presented myself to you as being basically fair and just towards everyone in a general way?

A: Yeah, I would say you have as far as I know.

Q: Isn't it a fact, Mr. Van Buskirk, that of your own personal knowledge, you have known me to stop more things, a tremendous amount of things, go out of my way to keep things in order to keep people from getting hurt?

A: I don't understand what you are talking about.

Q: Anytime there has been a misunderstanding that you have been aware of and I have become aware of it, have I tried to be basically fair and get to the root of it?

A: Between us?

Q: Between us, dealing with you and I on a personal level.

A: We haven't had any problems when we were together that I know of, that I can remember.

United States v. Mills, 704 F.2d 1553, 1562–63 (11th Cir. 1983).

6. Under Rules 404(a) and 405(a), may a defendant present expert testimony concerning a victim's psychological profile to establish the victim's propensity towards violence? *Cf.* Note: *Hard Cases Make Bad Law:* Commonwealth v. Adjutant *and Evidence of the Deceased's Propensity for Violence in Self-Defense Cases in Massachusetts*, 86 B.U.L. REV. 793 (2006). Note, *Diagnosing the Dead: The Admissibility of the Psychiatric Autopsy*, 18 AM. CR. L. REV. 617 (1981); Note, *Psychological Autopsy: A New Tool for Criminal Defense Attorneys?*, 24 ARIZ. L.

REV. 421 (1981). *Cf. United States v. Emeron Taken Alive*, 262 F.3d 711, 714–15 (8th Cir. 2001) ("trial court should not have excluded defendant's evidence of arresting officer's character for violence offered in support of self-defense claim to charges of resisting arrest and assaulting arresting officer").

5. Special Rules for Evidence of Other Wrongs

REX v. SMITH
[1914–15] All E.R. 262 (Crim. App. 1915)

LORD READING, C.J. — The appellant was convicted of the murder of Bessie Munday. His appeal to this court is based on points of law relating to the admission of evidence. . . . On the charge of murder preferred against the appellant, evidence was admitted showing that he murdered two other women at a later date. The first question raised by the appeal is whether the judge acted rightly in admitting evidence of the deaths of the two other women, Alice Burnham and Margaret Lofty. The principles of law governing the admission of evidence of this nature have been often under the consideration of this court and depend chiefly on the statement of the law in *Makin v. A. G. for New South Wales* (2), where LORD HERSCHELL says ([1894] A.C. at p. 65): It is undoubtedly not competent for the prosecution to adduce evidence tending to show that the accused has been guilty of criminal acts other than those covered by the indictment, for the purpose of leading to the conclusion that the accused is a person likely from his criminal conduct or character to have committed the offence for which he is being tried. On the other hand, the mere fact that the evidence adduced tends to show the commission of other crimes does not render it inadmissible if it be relevant to an issue before the jury, and it may be so relevant if it bears upon the question whether the acts alleged to constitute the crime charged in his indictment were designed or accidental, or to rebut a defence which would otherwise be open to the accused. In the present case the prosecution tendered evidence relating to the other two women, and it was admitted by the judge as tending to show that the act charged was committed with design. It is sufficient to say that it is not disputed, and cannot be disputed, that if as a matter of law there was prima facie evidence that the appellant committed the act charged, evidence of similar acts becomes admissible. We have come to the conclusion that undoubtedly there was as a matter of law prima facie evidence that the appellant committed the act charged. The point, therefore, taken by the defence under this head fails.

* * *

Appeal dismissed.

UNITED STATES v. BEECHUM $(404(b)(2)$ — Intent
582 F.2d 898 (5th Cir. 1978) (en banc)

TJOFLAT, CIRCUIT JUDGE:

This case comes before the court en banc for reconsideration of this circuit's doctrine on the admissibility of offenses extrinsic to a defendant's indictment to

↓
prior/similar

can occur before or after

prove his criminal intent.[17] That doctrine, deriving in part from the case of *United States v. Broadway*, 477 F.2d 991 (5th Cir. 1973), requires that the essential physical elements of the extrinsic offense include those of the offense charged and that each of these elements be proved by plain, clear, and convincing evidence. We are here called upon to determine the effect of the recently enacted Federal Rules of Evidence on this doctrine, an issue expressly reserved in a number of our cases decided prior to the panel opinion in this case.[18] The panel hearing this case was of the opinion, Judge Gee dissenting, that *Broadway* and its progeny survived intact the enactment of the rules. *United States v. Beechum*, 555 F.2d 487, 504–08 (5th Cir. 1977). With deference to the panel, we must disagree.

A jury convicted Orange Jell Beechum, a substitute letter carrier for the United States Postal Service, of unlawfully possessing an 1890 silver dollar that he knew to be stolen from the mails, in violation of 18 U.S.C. § 1708 (1976). To establish that Beechum intentionally and unlawfully possessed the silver dollar, the Government introduced into evidence two Sears, Roebuck & Co. credit cards found in Beechum's wallet when he was arrested. Neither card was issued to Beechum, and neither was signed. The Government also introduced evidence indicating that the cards had been mailed some ten months prior to Beechum's arrest to two different addresses on routes he had serviced. The propriety of the admission of this evidence is the primary issue in this appeal. Before we reach this issue, however, we must round out the facts and note several additional issues.

---

[17] [1] We shall use the term "extrinsic offense" to denote an "offense," *see infra* this note, for which the defendant is not charged in the indictment that is the subject of the case sub judice. Commentators and cases have referred to such offenses as "prior" or "similar" offenses. We choose to avoid the connotations carried by these more commonly used terms for the following reasons.

The principles governing extrinsic offense evidence are the same whether that offense occurs before or after the offense charged. *See United States v. Pollard*, 509 F.2d 601 (5th Cir.), *cert. denied*, 421 U.S. 1013, 95 S. Ct. 2419, 44 L. Ed. 2d 681 (1975). The term "prior offense" is therefore unnecessarily restrictive and misleading.

"Similar offense" is a phrase that assumes the conclusion that extrinsic offenses are admissible only if similar to the offense charged. Although in a technical sense this is true, the common connotations of the word are misleading. The meaning and significance of similarity depends on the issue to which the extrinsic offense evidence is addressed. Stone, *The Rule of Exclusion of Similar Fact Evidence: England*, 46 Harv. L. Rev. 954, 955 (1933); *See* note 15 *infra*. Therefore, to avoid an ambiguous application of the term, we shall speak of similarity only when its meaning is clear in the context.

We use the term "offense" to include "other crimes, wrongs, or acts," as set forth in Fed. R. Evid. 404(b). *See* Part III. C. *infra*. Our analysis applies whenever the extrinsic activity reflects adversely on the character of the defendant, regardless whether that activity might give rise to criminal liability.

[18] [2] *United States v. Brunson*, 549 F.2d 348, 360 n. 17 (5th Cir.), *cert. denied*, 434 U.S. 842 (1977); *United States v. Brown*, 548 F.2d 1194, 1206 (5th Cir. 1977); *United States v. Maestas*, 546 F.2d 1177, 1180–81 (5th Cir. 1977). Several cases decided since oral argument at the rehearing en banc have also reserved the issue. *United States v. Wilson*, 578 F.2d 67, 73 n. 3 (5th Cir. 1978); *United States v. Evans*, 572 F.2d 455, 484 n. 38 (5th Cir. 1978); *United States v. Bradford*, 571 F.2d 1351, 1353 n. 1 (5th Cir. 1978).

Although language in the panel opinion in *United States v. Bloom*, 538 F.2d 704, 708 (5th Cir. 1976), *cert. denied*, 429 U.S. 1074 (1977), seems to indicate that Broadway and the cases following it are consistent with the Federal Rules of Evidence, that language is clearly dictum. *Bloom* held the extrinsic offense evidence admissible under the strict *Broadway* test. A fortiori, that evidence satisfies the less stringent requirements of the Federal Rules. *See* Part III. C. *infra*. Therefore, the court was not presented with a case, such as the one at hand, in which *Broadway* would exclude evidence that the rules would allow.

I. Facts

Orange Jell Beechum had been a substitute letter carrier in South Dallas, Texas for approximately two and one-half years prior to his arrest on September 16, 1975. Because Beechum had been suspected of rifling the mail on several occasions, postal inspectors planted in a mailbox on Beechum's route a letter containing the silver dollar, a greeting card, and sixteen dollars in currency. According to the testimony of one of the inspectors, the currency had been dusted with a powder visible only under ultraviolet light. A postal inspector observed Beechum retrieving the mail from the mailbox in which the letter had been planted and noted that Beechum stopped at a record shop for approximately one hour before returning to the South Dallas Postal Station. At the station, Beechum turned in the raw mail containing the test letter, and it was discovered that the letter had been opened and resealed. The silver dollar and the currency were missing.

Approximately thirty minutes after having arrived at the station, Beechum was apprehended as he walked toward his automobile, whose engine was running. The arresting inspector informed Beechum that a letter had been planted in the mailbox Beechum had emptied earlier and that the letter had been opened and its contents were missing. Before any questioning, the inspector read Beechum the warnings required by *Miranda v. Arizona*, 384 U.S. 436 (1966), and Beechum indicated that he understood his rights. The inspector then asked Beechum to empty his pockets. Standing with his front pockets everted, Beechum professed to have relinquished all, but a frisk revealed the silver dollar in his hip pocket. At this time, the inspector discovered in Beechum's wallet the two Sears credit cards, which, as we have noted, were not issued to Beechum and had not been signed.

The arresting inspector questioned Beechum about the credit cards, and Beechum responded first that the only credit cards he possessed were his own. Later, when confronted with the Sears cards, he stated that he had never used them. The inspector testified that in response to further questioning concerning the cards, Beechum said, "Since you have all the answers, you tell me." Record, vol. 2, at 31, 201. The inspector inquired no further.

The Government indicted Beechum on one count for unlawfully possessing the silver dollar. Argument at the preliminary hearing indicated that the primary issue in the case would be whether Beechum harbored the requisite intent to possess the silver dollar unlawfully. Defense counsel, by motion in limine heard in the absence of the jury, sought to exclude the credit cards as irrelevant and prejudicial. The court overruled the motion, in part on the basis that the cards were relevant to the issue of intent.[19] *Id.* at 36–37.

In its case in chief, the Government introduced the credit cards and explained the circumstances surrounding their obtention. By stipulation, the Government introduced Sears documents indicating that the two cards had been issued to the parties named on those cards. It was also stipulated that the regular business practice of Sears was to mail such cards within ten days after their issuance. The Government also elicited testimony that the addresses to which the credit cards had been mailed

---

[19] [3] The court also ruled that the cards were admissible as part of the res gestae of the crime for which Beechum was indicted. Record, vol. 2, at 36. *See* note 15 *infra*.

were on routes that Beechum had serviced during the ten month period between the date the cards were issued and the date of Beechum's arrest.

In anticipation that Beechum would claim that he sought to turn in the silver dollar, the Government called to the stand Beechum's supervisor, Mr. Cox. Cox testified that he was in the view of Beechum on several occasions, and, indeed, that he had taken mail directly from Beechum. *Id.* at 101–09.

At the close of the Government's case in chief, the defense moved for a directed verdict of acquittal, alleging that the Government had failed to come forward with sufficient evidence "to establish that Mr. Bonner (Sic) possessed the silver dollar with a requisite specific intent that the government is required to establish in this case." *Id.* at 138. The defense argued that the Government had failed to demonstrate that the credit cards were unlawfully taken from the mail or that Beechum possessed the cards without authorization. The motion was overruled.

At this time defense counsel indicated to the court that Beechum would take the stand and would testify "as to matters concerning the offense for which he is charged," but that he would invoke the fifth amendment as to any questions concerning the credit cards. *Id.* at 140–41. The defense sought a ruling that the Government be precluded from asking Beechum any question about the cards; the rationale was that the defendant should not be required to invoke his fifth amendment privilege in the presence of the jury. The court declined so to limit the prosecution and indicated that Beechum would have to invoke the amendment in response to the questions he did not wish to answer.

On direct examination Beechum testified that the silver dollar fell out of the mailbox as he was raking out the mail and that he picked it up and placed it first in his shirt pocket, and later (after it had fallen out) in his hip pocket, where he claimed to keep his change. Beechum also testified that, upon return to the postal station, he intended to turn in the silver dollar to Cox but that he could not find Cox.[20] Beechum also stated that he was not leaving the station when he was arrested.[21] No mention was made of the credit cards.

On cross-examination the Government asked Beechum if the credit cards were in his wallet when he was arrested. Defense counsel objected on the basis that inquiry about the cards was outside the scope of cross-examination, and the court overruled the objection. On reassertion of the question, Beechum invoked his fifth amendment rights, but the prosecutor continued questioning on the subject of the cards. This occasioned repeated invocation of the fifth amendment by Beechum and vehement objection by defense counsel. Eventually, Beechum did admit to stating shortly after his arrest that the inspector could "answer his own questions" when the inspector quizzed him about the cards and that the only credit cards he had were his own. *Id.* at 201.

---

[20] [4] Two postal employees, friends of Beechum, testified that Beechum had asked if they had seen Cox.

[21] [5] Whether Beechum intended to leave was a much contested issue. Beechum claimed to have been waiting for a friend whom he was to drive to a service station.

II. Issues

As we have noted, the central issue in this case is whether the district court properly allowed the credit cards to be admitted as extrinsic offense evidence going to the issue of Beechum's intent to possess the silver dollar unlawfully. We hold that the credit cards were properly admissible. The case, however, presents several additional and substantial issues that we must address.

* * *

C. The Extrinsic Offense

At the time of his arrest, Beechum possessed a silver dollar and two credit cards, none of which belonged to him. The only contested issue concerning the silver dollar was whether Beechum intended to turn it in, as he claimed, or to keep it for himself. Apparently, he had possessed the credit cards for some time, perhaps ten months, prior to his arrest. The obvious question is why would Beechum give up the silver dollar if he kept the credit cards. In this case, the Government was entitled to an answer.

It is derogative of the search for truth to allow a defendant to tell his story of innocence without facing him with evidence impeaching that story. A basic premise of our adversary system of justice is that the truth is best attained by requiring a witness to explain contrary evidence if he can. As we have seen, for this reason the defendant who chooses to testify waives his fifth amendment privilege with respect to relevant cross-examination. This is not to say that merely by taking the stand a defendant opens himself to the introduction of evidence that is relevant solely to his propensity to commit bad acts or crimes. But where the defendant testifies to controvert an element of the Government's case, such as intent, to which the extrinsic offense is highly relevant, the integrity of the judicial process commands that the defendant be faced with that offense.

In this case, the jury was entitled to assess the credibility of Beechum's explanation but was deprived of the most effective vehicle for determining the veracity of Beechum's story when the judge erroneously allowed Beechum to invoke the fifth amendment and avoid the critical question on cross-examination. The Government was relegated to the inferences the jury might draw from the credit cards themselves and the additional evidence relating to them. The panel held that the cards and this evidence were insufficient to satisfy the strict standards for admissibility of extrinsic offense evidence established by *United States v. Broadway*, 477 F.2d 991 (5th Cir. 1973). We agree that Broadway dictates that the credit cards should not have been admitted; because this is so, we must reject the Broadway standards.

Broadway established two prerequisites to the admissibility of extrinsic offense evidence. First, it required that the physical elements of the extrinsic offense include the essential physical elements of the offense for which the defendant was indicted. Second, the case mandated that each of the physical elements of the extrinsic offense be established by plain, clear, and convincing evidence.[22] The elements of the offense for which Beechum was convicted, violation of 18 U.S.C. § 1708 (1976), include the following: (1) that the defendant possessed the item, (2) that the item was stolen from the mail, (3) that the defendant knew that the item was stolen, and (4) that the defendant specifically intended to possess the item unlawfully. *See United States v. Ellison*, 494 F.2d 43 (5th Cir. 1974); *United States v. Kimbrell*, 487 F.2d 219 (5th Cir. 1973); *United States v. Martinez*, 466 F.2d 679 (5th Cir. 1972), *cert. denied*, 414 U.S. 1065 (1973). The first three elements were not disputed, except to the extent that a denial of the fourth renders the item not stolen for the purposes of the second and third elements. The physical elements of the crime are the first two. The panel held that the Government's proof as to the credit cards failed to establish the second element, that the cards were stolen from the mail, by the plain, clear, and convincing evidence required by the second prong of the Broadway test. For the purposes of the following analysis, we accept this conclusion as valid.

We must overrule *Broadway* because a straightforward application of the Federal Rules of Evidence calls for admission of the cards. The directly applicable rule is Fed. R. Evid. 404(b), which provides as follows:

> Other crimes, wrongs, or acts. Evidence of other crimes, wrongs, or acts is not admissible to prove the character of a person in order to show that he acted in conformity therewith. It may, however, be admissible for other purposes, such as proof of motive, opportunity, intent, preparation, plan, knowledge, identity, or absence of mistake or accident.

The rule follows the venerable principle that evidence of extrinsic offenses should not be admitted solely to demonstrate the defendant's bad character. Even though such evidence is relevant, because a man of bad character is more likely to commit a crime than one not, the principle prohibits such evidence because it is inherently prejudicial. *See, e.g., Michelson v. United States*, 335 U.S. 469 (1948). Without an issue other than mere character to which the extrinsic offenses are relevant, the probative value of those offenses is deemed insufficient in all cases to outweigh the inherent prejudice. Where, however, the extrinsic offense evidence is relevant to an issue such as intent, it may well be that the evidence has probative force that is not substantially outweighed by its inherent prejudice. If this is so, the evidence may be admissible.[23]

---

[22] [12] This standard of proof was termed "plain, clear, and *conclusive*" in the *Broadway* opinion. 477 F.2d at 995 (emphasis supplied). Later cases substituted "convincing" for "conclusive." *E.g. United States v. San Martin*, 505 F.2d 918, 921 (5th Cir. 1974).

[23] [13] We think it significant that Congress acted to amend rule 404(b) to place greater emphasis on admissibility of extrinsic offense evidence than had the Supreme Court's version. The House Committee Report states,

> The second sentence of Rule 404(b) as submitted to the Congress began with the words "This subdivision does not exclude the evidence when offered". The Committee amended this language to read "It may, however, be admissible", the words used in the 1971 Advisory Committee draft, on the ground that this formulation properly placed greater emphasis on admissibility than did the final Court version.

H.R. Rep. No. 93-650, 93rd Cong., 1st Sess. 7, *reprinted in* (1974) U.S. Code Cong. & Admin. News 1974, pp. 7075, 7081. The Department of Justice had recommended this amendment to bring the rule in line

What the rule calls for is essentially a two-step test. First, it must be determined that the extrinsic offense evidence is relevant to an issue other than the defendant's character. Second, the evidence must possess probative value that is not substantially outweighed by its undue prejudice and must meet the other requirements of rule 403.[24] *See Rule 404(b) Other Crimes Evidence: The Need for a Two-Step Analysis*, 71 Nw. U. L. Rev. 636 (1976). The test for relevancy under the first step is identical to the one we have already encountered. The standards are established by rule 401, which deems evidence relevant when it has "any tendency to make the existence of any fact that is of consequence to the determination of the action more probable or less probable than it would be without the evidence." Where the evidence sought to be introduced is an extrinsic offense, its relevance is a function of its similarity to the offense charged. In this regard, however, similarity means more than that the extrinsic and charged offense have a common characteristic. For the purposes of determining relevancy, "a fact is similar to another only when the common characteristic is the significant one for the purpose of the inquiry at hand." Stone, *The Rule of Exclusion of Similar Fact Evidence: England*, 46 Harv. L. Rev. 954, 955 (1933). Therefore, similarity, and hence relevancy, is determined by the inquiry or issue to which the extrinsic offense is addressed.

Where the issue addressed is the defendant's intent to commit the offense charged, the relevancy of the extrinsic offense derives from the defendant's indulging himself in the same state of mind in the perpetration of both the extrinsic and charged offenses. The reasoning is that because the defendant had unlawful

---

with rule 402, which establishes the presumption that relevant evidence is admissible. Proposed Rules of Evidence: Hearings on H.R. 5463 Before the Special Subcomm. on Criminal Justice of the House Comm. on the Judiciary, 93rd Cong., 1st Sess. 344 (1973).

The legislative history indicates that Congress intended the admissibility of extrinsic offense evidence to be determined by the same standards as any other evidence, once the preliminary determination that the extrinsic offense is relevant to an issue other than the defendant's character has been made. Indeed, the Senate Committee Report evidences an intent carefully to delimit the trial judge's discretion to exclude extrinsic offense evidence. It states as follows:

> [T]he use of the discretionary word "may" with respect to the admissibility of evidence of crimes, wrongs, or acts is not intended to confer any arbitrary discretion on the trial judge. Rather, it is anticipated that with respect to permissible uses for such evidence, the trial judge may exclude it only on the basis of those considerations set forth in Rule 403, i. e. prejudice, confusion or waste of time.

S. Rep. No. 93-1277, 93rd Cong., 2d Sess. 24–25, *reprinted in* (1974) U.S. Code Cong. & Admin. News 1974, pp. 7051, 7071.

[24] [14] The Advisory Committee Notes to rule 404(b) indicate that this is the analysis contemplated by the rule:

> No mechanical solution (to the issue of admissibility of extrinsic offense evidence) is offered. The determination must be made whether the danger of undue prejudice outweighs the probative value of the evidence in view of the availability of other means of proof and other facts appropriate for making decision of this kind under Rule 403.

28 U.S.C.A. Rules of Evidence at 109 (1975).

The Advisory Committee Note's directive is reinforced by the Senate Committee Report, which states, "with respect to permissible uses for (extrinsic offense) evidence, the trial judge may exclude it only on the basis of those considerations set forth in Rule 403, i.e. prejudice, confusion or waste of time." S. Rep. No. 93-1277, 93rd Cong., 2d Sess. 24–25, *reprinted in* (1974) U.S. Code Cong. & Admin. News, 1974, pp. 7051, 7071. *See* note 13 *supra*.

intent in the extrinsic offense, it is less likely that he had lawful intent in the present offense.[25] *See Weiss v. United States*, 122 F.2d 675, 683 (5th Cir.), *cert. denied*, 314 U.S. 687 (1941); 2 WIGMORE, EVIDENCE § 302 (3d ed. 1940). Under *Broadway*, that the defendant had unlawful intent in the commission of the extrinsic offense is established by requiring the Government to prove each physical element of that

---

[25] [15] It is crucial to distinguish the use of extrinsic offense evidence to prove issues other than intent. In other contexts different standards apply because the inference to be drawn from the extrinsic offense is not based upon the reasoning applicable here. To illustrate this proposition and to place our discussion in the proper context, we digress briefly and examine the use of extrinsic offense evidence in other settings.

Evidence of extrinsic offenses may be admissible to show motive, which has been defined as "the reason that nudges the will and prods the mind to indulge the criminal intent." Slough & Knightly, *Other Vices, Other Crimes*, 41 IOWA L. REV. 325, 328 (1956) (footnote omitted). For example, the prosecution may establish impecuniousness as a motive for robbery by showing that the defendant had been threatened for nonpayment of a debt incurred in a drug transaction. *United States v. Johnson*, 525 F.2d 999, 1006 (2d Cir. 1975), *cert. denied*, 424 U.S. 920 (1976). The only point of similarity between the charged and extrinsic offenses in this instance is that the same individual committed both. Therefore, overall similarity is not required when the offense is introduced to show motive.

Such evidence is admissible to indicate knowledge. Thus, the Government may prove that the defendant knew that he was passing counterfeit securities by eliciting testimony that the defendant knowingly had purchased counterfeit currency on a prior occasion. *Peters v. United States*, 376 F.2d 839 (5th Cir. 1967). Again, similarity of the physical elements of the crime need not be established. The extrinsic offense need merely be of such a nature that its commission involved the same knowledge required for the offense charged.

The identity of the defendant may be established by evidence of offenses extrinsic to the indictment. In this instance, the likeness of the offenses is the crucial consideration. The physical similarity must be such that it marks the offenses as the handiwork of the accused. In other words, the evidence must demonstrate a modus operandi. *United States v. Goodwin*, 492 F.2d 1141, 1154 (5th Cir. 1974). Thus, "[a] much greater degree of similarity between the charged crime and the uncharged crime is required when the evidence of the other crime is introduced to prove identity than when it is introduced to prove a state of mind." *United States v. Myers*, 550 F.2d 1036, 1045 (5th Cir. 1977). As an example, a prior conviction for possession of heroin may not in itself establish that in an unrelated prosecution a defendant possessed heroin with intent to distribute. If, however, that conviction and the charged offense involved white heroin, an extremely rare type in the region, a distinctiveness may be established that is sufficient to allow admission of the prior offense to show identity. *United States v. Baldarrama*, 566 F.2d 560 (5th Cir. 1978).

Extrinsic offenses may be admitted if part of a common plan, scheme, or design. Although this category encompasses a variety of circumstances, *See* 2 WEINSTEIN & BERGER, WEINSTEIN'S EVIDENCE ¶ 404(09) (1976), we shall address only one. If the uncharged offense is "so linked together in point of time and circumstances with the crime charged that one cannot be fully shown without proving the other, the general rule of exclusion does not apply." Slough & Knightly, *supra*, at 331. Evidence admitted under this test is termed part of the res gestae of the crime charged. *E.g.*, *United States v. McDaniel*, 574 F.2d 1224, 1227 (5th Cir. 1978). Physical similarity is not a requisite here. Illustrative is the case of *United States v. Hughes*, 441 F.2d 12 (5th Cir.), *cert. denied*, 404 U.S. 849 (1971). This was an appeal from convictions for printing counterfeit obligations, possessing counterfeit plates and negatives, and possessing counterfeit federal reserve notes. We held that it was not prejudicial error for the trial court to have admitted several sawed-off shotguns found at the premises of the operation. "The record of entry and use of [the premises] for their counterfeiting operation would be grossly incomplete without the account of their guns, intimidations, beatings, and violence. . . . [T]he guns in question were pertinent evidence because they were so closely blended and inextricably bound up with the history of the crime itself as to constitute a part of the plan or system of criminal action involved in this case." *Id.* at 20.

We have taken this opportunity to digress to point out that the meaning and nature of the "similarity" requirement in extrinsic offense doctrine are not fixed quantities. Each case must be decided in its own context, with the issue to which the offense is directed firmly in mind.

offense by plain, clear, and convincing evidence. And the extrinsic offense is deemed admissible only if its physical elements include those of the offense charged. We think that *Broadway* runs afoul of the Federal Rules of Evidence by imposing on the Government too strict a standard of proof and by requiring too close an identity of elements.

Obviously, the line of reasoning that deems an extrinsic offense relevant to the issue of intent is valid only if an offense was in fact committed and the defendant in fact committed it. Therefore, as a predicate to a determination that the extrinsic offense is relevant, the Government must offer proof demonstrating that the defendant committed the offense. If the proof is insufficient, the judge must exclude the evidence because it is irrelevant. The issue we must decide is by what standard the trial court is to determine whether the Government has come forward with sufficient proof.

The standard of proof for ruling upon factual conditions to relevancy is supplied by Fed. R. Evid. 104(b), which states as follows:

> Relevancy conditioned on fact. When the relevancy of evidence depends upon the fulfillment of a condition of fact, the court shall admit it upon, or subject to, the introduction of evidence sufficient to support a finding of the fulfillment of the condition.

As the rule provides, the task for the trial judge is to determine whether there is sufficient evidence for the jury to find that the defendant in fact committed the extrinsic offense. *See* Morgan, *Functions of Judge and Jury in the Determination of Preliminary Questions of Fact*, 43 HARV. L. REV. 165 (1927). The judge need not be convinced beyond a reasonable doubt that the defendant committed the extrinsic offense, nor need he require the Government to come forward with clear and convincing proof.[26] The standard for the admissibility of extrinsic offense evidence is that of rule 104(b): "the preliminary fact can be decided by the judge against the proponent only where the jury could not reasonably find the preliminary fact to exist." 21 WRIGHT & GRAHAM, FEDERAL PRACTICE AND PROCEDURE: EVIDENCE § 5054, at 269 (1977).

[handwritten margin note: Impossible for D to have done it]

Once it is determined that the extrinsic offense requires the same intent as the charged offense and that the jury could find that the defendant committed the extrinsic offense, the evidence satisfies the first step under rule 404(b). The extrinsic offense is relevant (assuming the jury finds the defendant to have committed it) to an issue other than propensity because it lessens the likelihood that the defendant committed the charged offense with innocent intent. See text accompanying note 15 *supra*. It is not necessary that the physical elements of the charged and extrinsic

---

26 [16] It is not true that every fact or issue in a criminal case need be proved beyond a reasonable doubt. Indeed, the admissibility of highly prejudicial, and perhaps even dispositive, evidence is governed by lesser standards. For instance, findings at suppression hearings are made by a preponderance of the evidence. *United States v. Matlock*, 415 U.S. 164, 177 n. 14 (1974); *Lego v. Twomey*, 404 U.S. 477 (1972). Of course, each of the essential elements of the offense for which the defendant is being tried must be proved beyond a reasonable doubt. *In re Winship*, 397 U.S. 358, 361–63 (1970). *Winship*, however, "was not concerned with standards for determining the admissibility of evidence or with the prosecution's burden of proof at a suppression hearing when evidence is challenged on constitutional grounds." *Lego v. Twomey*, 404 U.S. at 486.

offenses concur for this inference to be drawn and relevancy established. If the elements do match, the extrinsic offense may have greater probative value, but this is not an issue of relevancy. Evidence is relevant once it appears "to alter the probabilities of a consequential fact." WEINSTEIN & BERGER, WEINSTEIN'S EVIDENCE ¶ 401(06), at 401–18 (1976). The probative value of the evidence is a matter to be weighed against its potential for undue prejudice, and the similarity of the physical elements of the charged and extrinsic offenses figures in at this stage. Therefore, we turn to the second step of the analysis required by rule 404(b), whether the evidence satisfies rule 403.

As we have stated, the central concern of rule 403 is whether the probative value of the evidence sought to be introduced is "substantially outweighed by the danger of unfair prejudice." *Broadway* would reverse this standard by requiring a high degree of similarity between the extrinsic and charged offenses and a stringent standard of proof. In effect, the case attempts to establish a threshold requirement that the evidence possess great probative value before it can be admitted. This requirement not only contravenes rule 403 but also fails to meet its own declared ends. Demanding that the Government prove by excessive evidence each physical element of the extrinsic offense does not necessarily enhance its probative value and may in fact increase its unfair prejudice. One of the dangers inherent in the admission of extrinsic offense evidence is that the jury may convict the defendant not for the offense charged but for the extrinsic offense.[27] *See* Note, *Other Crimes Evidence at Trial: Of Balancing and Other Matters*, 70 YALE L. REV. 763, 773 (1961). This danger is particularly great where, as here, the extrinsic activity was not the subject of a conviction; the jury may feel that the defendant should be punished for that activity even if he is not guilty of the offense charged. Moreover, "[e]ven if the jury is no more disposed to punish the accused for his unpunished past crimes, 'over-persuasion' may lead them to conclude that, having committed a crime of the type charged, he is likely to repeat it." *Id.* It is for fear that the jury would draw just this inference that extrinsic offense evidence is excluded when it is relevant solely to the issue of the defendant's character. The touchstone of the trial judge's analysis in this context should be whether the Government has proved the extrinsic offense sufficiently to allow the jury to determine that the defendant possessed the same state of mind at the time he committed the extrinsic offense as he allegedly possessed when he committed the charged offense. Forcing the Government to "over persuade" the jury that the defendant committed an offense of substantial similarity engenders excessive and unnecessary prejudice.

The task for the court in its ascertainment of probative value and unfair prejudice under rule 403 calls for a commonsense assessment of all the circumstances surrounding the extrinsic offense. As the Advisory Committee Notes to rule 404(b) state: "No mechanical solution is offered. The determination must be made whether the danger of undue prejudice outweighs the probative value of the evidence in view of the availability of other means of proof and other facts

---

[27] [17] The reader should recall that we use the term "offense" to include noncriminal activity that impugns the defendant's character. *See* note 1 *supra*. The danger of a jury's reprisal for unpunished extrinsic activity is likely to be less when that activity is not of a criminal nature but merely "bad." The trial judge should recognize, however, that the conscience of a jury does not always coincide with the perimeters of criminality.

appropriate for making decision of this kind under Rule 403." 28 U.S.C.A. Rules of Evidence at 109 (1975).

Probity in this context is not an absolute; its value must be determined with regard to the extent to which the defendant's unlawful intent is established by other evidence, stipulation, or inference.[28] It is the incremental probity of the evidence that is to be balanced against its potential for undue prejudice. Dolan, *Rule 403: The Prejudice Rule in Evidence*, 49 S. CAL. L. REV. 220, 234–35 & n. 52 (1976); *see United States v. Baldarrama*, 566 F.2d 560, 568 (5th Cir. 1978). Thus, if the Government has a strong case on the intent issue, the extrinsic offense may add little and consequently will be excluded more readily. *See, e.g., United States v. Lawrance*, 480 F.2d 688, 691–92 n. 6 (5th Cir. 1973). If the defendant's intent is not contested, then the incremental probative value of the extrinsic offense is inconsequential when compared to its prejudice; therefore, in this circumstance the evidence is uniformly excluded.[29] *E.g., United States v. Kirk*, 528 F.2d 1057, 1060–61 (5th Cir. 1976); *United States v. Goodwin*, 492 F.2d 1141, 1151 (5th Cir. 1974). In measuring the probative value of the evidence, the judge should consider the overall similarity of the extrinsic and charged offenses. If they are dissimilar except for the common element of intent, the extrinsic offense may have little probative value to counterbalance the inherent prejudice of this type of evidence. Of course, equivalence of the elements of the charged and extrinsic offenses is not required. But the probative value of the extrinsic offense correlates positively with its likeness to the offense charged.[30] Whether the extrinsic offense is sufficiently similar in its physical

---

[28] [18] Cases and commentators have discussed this notion of probative value in reference to the "necessity" for the extrinsic crime evidence. *E.g., United States v. Baldarrama*, 566 F.2d 560, 568 (5th Cir. 1978); Note, *Other Crimes Evidence at Trial: Of Balancing and Other Matters*, 70 YALE L.J. 763, 771 (1961). As the Note cited above indicates, "in determining probative worth, the court should evaluate the prosecution's other admitted and admissible evidence to determine whether the offered other crimes evidence is necessary to prove the issue beyond a reasonable doubt." *Id.* at 772 (footnote omitted).

[29] [19]

> Although it would seem that the extrinsic offense would be irrelevant if the issue of intent were not contested, the rules apparently deem evidence that has probative force with regard to an uncontested issue to be relevant. The fact to which the evidence is directed need not be in dispute. While situations will arise which call for the exclusion of evidence offered to prove a point conceded by the opponent, the ruling should be made on the basis of such considerations as waste of time and undue prejudice (*see* Rule 403), rather than under any general requirement that evidence is admissible only if directed to matters in dispute.

Advisory Committee Notes to Rule 401, 28 U.S.C.A. Rules of Evidence at 85 (1975). Where, however, intent is not an element of the crime charged, extrinsic offense evidence directed to that issue would be irrelevant and therefore subject to exclusion under rule 402. *United States v. Lawrance*, 480 F.2d 688, 690 (5th Cir. 1973).

[30] [20] It is true as well that the more closely the extrinsic offense resembles the charged offense, the greater the prejudice to the defendant. The likelihood that the jury will convict the defendant because he is the kind of person who commits this particular type of crime or because he was not punished for the extrinsic offense increases with the increasing likeness of the offenses. Of course, it is also true that this prejudice is likely to be less when the extrinsic activity is not of a criminal nature. *See* notes 1 & 17 *supra.*

In any event, the judge must consider the danger of undue prejudice of this type when he determines whether to admit the extrinsic offense evidence. The judge should be mindful that the test under rule 403 is whether the probative value of the evidence is Substantially outweighed by its unfair prejudice. As one commentator has put it, "the discretionary policy against undue prejudice would seem to require

elements so that its probative value is not substantially outweighed by its undue prejudice is a matter within the sound discretion of the trial judge. The judge should also consider how much time separates the extrinsic and charged offenses: temporal remoteness depreciates the probity of the extrinsic offense. *E.g., United States v. Carter*, 516 F.2d 431, 434–35 (5th Cir. 1975).

As this case demonstrates, a significant consideration in determining the probative value of extrinsic offense evidence is the posture of the case. If at the commencement of trial it is not certain that the defendant will contest the issue of intent, the judge is in a poor position to weigh the probative value against the prejudice of the evidence because he cannot foresee the nature or extent of either the Government's case or the defendant's response. Whether a mere plea of not guilty justifies the Government in introducing extrinsic offense evidence in its case in chief is an open question in this circuit. *United States v. Adderly*, 529 F.2d 1178, 1181–82 (5th Cir. 1976); *United States v. Urdiales*, 523 F.2d 1245, 1247 (5th Cir. 1975), *cert. denied*, 426 U.S. 920 (1976); *cf. United States v. Ring*, 513 F.2d 1001 (6th Cir. 1975) (holding extrinsic offense evidence inadmissible in case in chief where innocent intent not pleaded). We need not now answer it. Although the credit cards in this case were introduced by the Government in its case in chief, it was clear before the case went to trial that the crucial issue would be Beechum's intent. In effect all the other elements of the crime for which Beechum was indicted were conceded. *See* text following note 12 *supra*. Where it is evident that intent will be an issue at trial, we have held the admission of the extrinsic offense as part of the Government's case in chief not to be grounds for reversal. *United States v. Adderly*, 529 F.2d at 1182. In any event, Beechum waived any objection he might have had to the Government's order of proof when he took the stand and professed the innocence of his intent.

We shall now apply the precepts we have set forth to the facts of this case. As we have demonstrated above, the credit card evidence is relevant to Beechum's intent with respect to the silver dollar. That Beechum possessed the credit cards with illicit intent diminishes the likelihood that at the same moment he intended to turn in the silver dollar. If there is sufficient evidence to establish that Beechum wrongfully possessed the credit cards, the requirement of the first step under rule 404(b), that the evidence be relevant to an issue other than propensity, is met. This is so even if the evidence were insufficient for a finding that the cards were stolen from the mail. As we have said, relevancy is established once the identity of the significant state of mind is established. The similarity of the physical elements of the extrinsic and charged offenses is a measure of probity.

The standard for determining whether the evidence is sufficient for a finding that Beechum wrongfully possessed the credit cards is provided by rule 104(b): whether the evidence would support such a finding by the jury. We think the evidence in the record clearly supports a finding that Beechum possessed the credit cards with the intent not to relinquish them to their rightful owners. Beechum possessed the credit

---

exclusion only in those instances where the trial judge believes that there is a genuine risk that the emotions of the jury will be excited to irrational behavior, and that this risk is disproportionate to the probative value of the offered evidence." Trautman, *Logical or Legal Relevancy a Conflict in Theory*, 5 VAND. L. REV. 385, 410 (1952).

cards of two different individuals. Neither card had been signed by the person to whom it was issued. When asked about the cards, Beechum answered first that the only cards he had were his own. When confronted with the credit cards, which were obviously not his own, Beechum responded that they had never been used. He refused to respond further because the inspector "had all the answers." The logical inference from this statement is that Beechum was attempting to mitigate his culpability, having been caught red-handed. The undisputed evidence indicated that he could have possessed the cards for some ten months. The jury would have been wholly justified in finding that Beechum possessed these cards with the intent permanently to deprive the owners of them. This is all the rules require the court to determine to establish the relevancy of the extrinsic offense evidence.

We move now to the second step of the rule 404(b) analysis, the application of rule 403. The incremental probity of the extrinsic offense evidence in this case approaches its intrinsic value. Indeed, the posture of this case and the nature of the Government's proof with respect to the intent issue present perhaps the most compelling circumstance for the admission of extrinsic offense evidence. From the very inception of trial, it was clear that the crucial issue in the case would be Beechum's intent in possessing the silver dollar. He took the stand to proclaim that he intended to surrender the coin to his supervisor. The issue of intent was therefore clearly drawn, and the policies of justice that require a defendant to explain evidence that impugns his exculpatory testimony were in full force. As we have seen, these policies dictate that a defendant waive his fifth amendment privilege against self-incrimination as to cross-examination relevant to his testimony. Where a privilege so central to our notions of fairness and justice yields to the search for truth, we should not lightly obstruct that quest. The credit card evidence bore directly on the plausibility of Beechum's story; justice called for its admission.[31]

'That the posture of this case demanded the admission of the credit card evidence is reinforced by the nature of the Government's proof on the issue of intent apart from that evidence. This proof consisted of the following. The Government called Cox, Beechum's supervisor, who testified that Beechum had had several opportunities to surrender the coin to him. Beechum denied this, and called two fellow employees who testified that Beechum had asked them if they had seen Cox. Absent the credit card evidence, the issue would have been decided wholly by the jury's assessment of the credibility of these witnesses. The Government, therefore, did not make out such a strong case of criminal intent that the credit card evidence would have been of little incremental probity. In fact, the credit card evidence may have been determinative.

The overall similarity of the extrinsic and charged offenses in this case generates

---

[31] [22] A consideration peculiar to the unique setting of this case weakens considerably Beechum's objection to the admission of the credit card evidence. The court below improperly allowed Beechum to invoke the fifth amendment in response to the Government's cross-examination concerning the credit cards. Had the Government been allowed to elicit the responses to which it was entitled, it is highly likely that the Government would have established from Beechum's own mouth facts sufficient to satisfy even the Broadway standards. The court's error cut short this line of proof, to Beechum's undeserved benefit. We think the argument that the credit cards should not have been admitted for failure of sufficient proof that Beechum took them from the mails somewhat disingenuous under these circumstances.

sufficient probity to meet the rule 403 test that the probative value of the evidence not be substantially outweighed by its unfair prejudice. We think this to be true even if it could not be established that the credit cards were stolen from the mail. At the least, there was sufficient evidence for the jury to find that Beechum possessed property belonging to others, with the specific intent to deprive the owners of their rightful possession permanently. That Beechum entertained such intent with respect to the credit cards renders less believable the story that he intended to turn in the coin in this instance. The force of this inference is not appreciably diminished by the failure of the Government to prove that the cards actually were stolen from the mail.

The probity of the credit card evidence in this case is augmented by the lack of temporal remoteness. Although Beechum may have obtained the cards as much as ten months prior to his arrest for the possession of the silver dollar, he kept the cards in his wallet where they would constantly remind him of the wrongfulness of their possession. In effect, Beechum's state of mind with respect to the credit cards continued through his arrest. He maintained contemporaneously the wrongful intent with respect to the cards and the intent as regards the coin. The force of the probity of this circumstance is illustrated by what Beechum would have had to convince the jury in order to avoid it. He would have been forced to argue that his state of mind was schizoid that he intended at the same time to relinquish the coin but to keep the cards. This situation does not differ significantly from one in which a thief is caught with a bag of loot, is charged with the larceny as to one of the items, but claims that he intended to return that item. Would any reasonable jury believe this story when it is established that he had stolen the rest of the loot?

The remaining considerations under rule 403 do not alter our conclusion as to the admissibility of the extrinsic offense evidence in this case. The extrinsic offense here is not of a heinous nature; it would hardly incite the jury to irrational decision by its force on human emotion. The credit card evidence was no more likely to confuse the issues, mislead the jury, cause undue delay, or waste time than any other type of extrinsic offense evidence. Since the need for the evidence in this case was great, it can hardly be said that the admission of the cards constituted "needless presentation of cumulative evidence."

It is significant that the court was careful to allay, as much as limiting instructions can, the undue prejudice engendered by the credit card evidence. It gave extensive instructions to the jury on the limited use of extrinsic offense evidence employed to prove unlawful intent.[32]

---

[32] [23] The Advisory Committee Notes to rule 403 require the judge to consider the effectiveness of a limiting instruction in reducing the prejudicial impact of evidence. "In reaching a decision whether to exclude on grounds of unfair prejudice, consideration should be given to the probable effectiveness or lack of effectiveness of a limiting instruction." 28 U.S.C.A. Rules of Evidence at 102–03 (1977). *See also* Fed. R. Evid. 105.

This is a context in which limiting instructions are of substantial efficacy, *United States v. Evans*, 572 F.2d 455, 484–85 (5th Cir. 1978), and we think the judge adequately admonished the jury to consider the credit card evidence solely on the issue of Beechum's intent. We reproduce below the instructions he gave.

During the course of this trial certain evidence has been presented concerning an alleged

Having examined at length the circumstances of this case, we conclude that the credit card evidence meets the requirements of rule 403. Therefore, the conditions imposed by the second step of the analysis under rule 404(b) have been met, and the extrinsic offense evidence in this case was properly admitted at trial.

IV. Conclusion

For the reasons stated above, we AFFIRM Beechum's conviction. The opinion of the panel in this case, reported at 555 F.2d 487, is hereby VACATED.

AFFIRMED.

GOLDBERG, CIRCUIT JUDGE, with whom GODBOLD, SIMPSON, MORGAN and RONEY, CIRCUIT JUDGES, join, dissenting:

As the lights are being extinguished on Broadway, I feel impelled to light a few candles in requiem.

The majority has gone well out of its way[33] to overrule *Broadway*. In the panel

---

transaction similar to that charged in the indictment, to wit, the possession by the Defendant of the two Sears credit cards, admitted in evidence as Government Exhibits 6 and 7.

This evidence, if you choose to accept it, is admitted for the limited purpose of assisting you in determining the intent with which a defendant may have acted. In this regard, you are instructed that evidence of an alleged similar transaction may not be considered by the jury in determining whether an accused committed the acts or participated in the activity alleged in the indictment.

Nor may evidence of such an alleged similar transaction of a like nature be considered for any other purpose whatever unless the jury first finds that the other evidence in the case, standing alone, establishes beyond a reasonable doubt that the accused participated in the activity alleged in the indictment.

If the jury should find beyond a reasonable doubt from other evidence in the case that the accused participated in the activity alleged in the indictment, then the jury may consider evidence as to transactions of a like nature, in determining the state of mind or intent with which the accused did the act charged in the indictment.

I want to instruct you very explicitly and unequivocally as to the very limited extent to which you may consider this evidence as to a similar offense.

As I just instructed you, you may consider such evidence of another transaction of a like nature in determining the state of mind or intent with which the accused may have done the act charged in the indictment, but only if you first find that the other evidence standing alone establishes beyond a reasonable doubt that the defendant committed the act alleged in the indictment.

Record, vol. 1, at 23–24.

[33] [1] There are numerous reasons why an overruling of *United States v. Broadway*, 477 F.2d 991 (5th Cir. 1973) was unnecessary and inappropriate in this case. In some ways, the court's overruling of *Broadway* might even be viewed as a form of dictum.

The most obvious reason is that the majority seems to view the facts of this case in such a way that the *Broadway* test is actually satisfied. In order to overrule *Broadway* it mistakenly defines the *Broadway* test as stricter than it really is. The majority is of the opinion that the "physical elements" part of the *Broadway* test would require that both offenses involve thefts from the mails. But of course the panel opinion left this an open question under *Broadway*. 555 F.2d 487, 499–500.

The panel opinion said the credit card evidence flunked the *Broadway* test because there was an

opinion, 555 F.2d 487 (5th Cir. 1977), the panel majority explained why the policies and doctrines of *Broadway* are sound. I affirm those views here. But I must add a few comments because the opinion of the en banc majority leaves the law in this area in such a confused state. In this dissent I make two broad arguments. First I show how the majority misinterpreted Rule 404(b) of the Federal Rules of Evidence. Basically the majority's reading of the rule fails because it reads so broadly the second sentence in Rule 404(b), which makes certain evidence admissible, that it allows the second sentence to swallow up the first sentence of Rule 404(b), which explicitly bars the admissibility of certain evidence. In addition, this too broad reading of Rule 404(b)'s second sentence conflicts with explicit language in other related federal evidence rules, such as Rules 609 and 608. Finally I note that no other circuit or legal commentator has seen in Rule 404(b) the same destructive and revolutionary intent that the majority apparently sees. On the contrary, many circuits calmly preserved doctrines similar to *Broadway* in the wake of Rule 404(b)'s passage, often even terming the rule a codification of their law. My second broad argument concerns the test with which the majority replaces *Broadway*. I argue that not only is this test little more than a subjective, difficult to apply version of *Broadway*, but that it is even *more* hostile to extrinsic offense evidence than *Broadway* in some respects.

---

insufficient showing that the cards were stolen or wrongfully possessed at all, not whether they were stolen from the mails. *Id.* at 499. The panel majority felt the evidence showed neither unlawful nor illicit possession of the cards, just "unexplained possession." *Id.* It is not illegal or illicit to possess credit cards loaned to one by friends, or even perhaps to carry and not use cards found in the street. In any case, the physical elements and intents of these acts are quite different from the elements and intent of keeping a coin one knows is stolen from the mails. The majority does not dispute this. Instead the majority asserts that it is convinced the evidence Did prove wrongful possession. At one point it states, "we think the evidence in the record *clearly* supports a finding that Beechum possessed the credit cards with the intent not to relinquish them to their rightful owners." (emphasis added.) p. 916. *See also* p. 917. If so, then the majority should change the result under Broadway, not the underlying law itself. To reach the extreme position of overruling *Broadway* in this case, instead of just disputing the result of its application to the facts in this particular case, as Judge Gee did in his panel dissent, 555 F.2d at 510, the majority had to define *Broadway*'s test too strictly and to break down doors left open by the panel.

In addition, the majority replaced the "clear and convincing" proof part of the *Broadway* test with a loose Rule 104 test. But then the majority goes on to state that in this particular case the evidence "clearly" supports incriminating findings. (*Id.* at p. 916.)

Second, the majority itself writes of the "peculiar" and "unique" aspects of the case insofar as it is colored by the 5th amendment waiver and scope of cross-examination issues. (*See, e.g.,* p. 916 n. 21) It is easy to see how such collateral issues could preempt the *Broadway* test. For example, consider a case where a defendant took the stand and testified that he knew he intended to return the silver dollar because he recently found two Sears credit cards and returned those immediately. Clearly this might open the door to evidence of the cards that *Broadway* otherwise would keep out. But in such a case *Broadway* would be pre-empted, not overruled. And yet the majority repeatedly states that *Broadway* must be overruled here because justice demands that the defendant's testimony be rebutted. *See, e.g.,* p. 909 ("But where the defendant testifies to controvert an element of the Government's case, such as intent, to which the extrinsic offense is highly relevant, the integrity of the judicial process commands that the defendant be faced with that offense.") The problem with this sort of logic is that in the next case when the defendant does not so testify, *Broadway* is no longer pre-empted by a conflicting policy, but it is also no longer law, because it was overruled in an earlier "peculiar" and "unique" case. We suggest to the majority that *Harris v. New York*, 401 U.S. 222 (1971), restricted *Miranda v. Arizona*, 384 U.S. 436 (1966), it did not presume to overrule it.

I. The Majority Misinterprets Rule 404(b).

A. The Majority's Too Broad Reading of the Second Sentence in Rule 404(b) Allows it to Swallow Up the First Sentence.

Rule 404(b) provides:

> (b) Other crimes, wrongs, or acts. Evidence of other crimes, wrongs, or acts is not admissible to prove the character of a person in order to show that he acted in conformity therewith. It may, however, be admissible for other purposes, such as proof of motive, opportunity, intent, preparation, plan, knowledge, identity, or absence of mistake or accident.

Rule 404(b) seems to me to identify two conflicting policies and to require the courts to reconcile them. One policy is that extrinsic acts evidence is sometimes probative of material facts. For that reason, the second sentence authorized us to reason from unrelated past acts and states of mind to current states of mind. But at the same time the drafters of the rule were wary of such reasoning. Thus they wrote the first sentence. Its purpose is to caution us that extrinsic acts evidence is fraught with dangers of prejudice extraordinary dangers not presented by other types of evidence. Had the drafters not thought the dangers were extraordinary, they would never have given us the first sentence; they would have written only the second sentence and the general balancing test of Rule 403. Broadway and similar doctrines were designed precisely to deal with such extraordinary dangers.

The majority reads this rule differently. It thinks that so long as the probative value of extrinsic acts evidence is not "substantially outweighed" by its prejudicial effect, Rule 403, the evidence is to be admitted. (Majority opinion, p. 911.) How does the majority dispose of the first sentence, then? Here is where, to my mind, it seriously misapprehends the rule. The majority reads the rule to establish two watertight compartments: extrinsic acts evidence which relates "solely to . . . the defendant's character", *ante* at 914; *see also ante* at 910, 911, 913, 914 in n. 19, and that which is relevant for other purposes, including state of mind. Thus the majority thinks the rule unequivocally allows us to reason that because a defendant displayed an improper intent in the past, he is more likely to have had an evil intent in the act for which he is tried. *See* p. 913. How this differs from reasoning that the defendant has a "propensity" to act with evil intent, *id.* is beyond reason; but the majority says the rule prohibits references based on propensity. There simply are no such watertight compartments to be found, unless we engage in subtle and sophisticated metaphysical analysis.

Even the majority implies at one point that extrinsic offense evidence submitted allegedly to show intent is really just bad character evidence in sheep's clothing. The majority writes:

> "Our analysis applies whenever the extrinsic activity reflects adversely on the *character* of the defendant, regardless whether that activity might give rise to criminal liability." (emphasis added.) Majority opinion p. 903 n. 1.

And in footnote 17 the majority adds: "The reader should recall that we use the term 'offense' to include noncriminal activity that impugns the defendant's *charac-*

ter." (emphasis added.) Majority opinion p. 914 n. 17. These comments don't nibble at the first sentence in Rule 404(b) they consume it altogether.

Moreover, the majority's "watertight compartment" view of Rule 404(b) leads to a conclusion that the first sentence of Rule 404(b) is superfluous. Simply, evidence which is probative "solely" of bad character and not of any fact related to the elements of the crime, such as intent, identity, etc., is inadmissible in any event, under Rule 401, because it is irrelevant. As Rule 401 provides:

> "Relevant evidence" means evidence having any tendency to make the existence of any fact that is of consequence to the determination of the action more probable or less probable than it would be without the evidence.

To be sure, I find it nearly impossible to imagine any "extrinsic offense" which would make a jury think that the defendant had a bad character or a criminal propensity, but which did not also have at least *some tendency* to make it less probable than it would be without the evidence that he had a purely innocent, law-abiding intent in the charged offense. But, more importantly, if such "extrinsic offense" evidence were so purely irrelevant to intent and to the other elements of the charged crime, I can not see how it could pass the Rule 401 relevancy test even to necessitate the application of the Rule 404(b) bar to its admission.

The "watertight compartment" view of Rule 404(b) could lead to other peculiarities as well. Constrained by the explicit words of Rule 404(b), the majority concedes that extrinsic offense evidence which relates "solely" to a defendant's propensity to commit the charged crime is barred by the first sentence of Rule 404(b), no matter how much its probative value outweighs its prejudicial effect.[34] But when a judge thinks the extrinsic offense also relates to the defendant's propensity to intend to commit the charged crime, then the question leaps over to the second watertight compartment, where the presumption is heavily in favor of admitting the evidence, unless its probative value is substantially outweighed by prejudice. The alchemy of the majority opinion would radically change the rule from a total bar of the evidence regardless of the probative-prejudice balance to a balancing test substantially weighted in favor of admissibility, simply because a judge metaphysically classifies the question as propensity to intend rather than as propensity to commit. Since propensity is largely a concept of a person's psychological bent or frame of mind, it seems extreme to have so much turn on so little, if any, of a distinction. I respectfully refuse to adopt the majority's Dr. Jekyll-Mr. Hyde interpretation of Rule 404(b). It is a horror fantasy that should pass by the boards of *Broadway*.[35]

---

[34] [4] On page 910 of its opinion the majority "deems" that the probative value of this evidence could never outweigh its prejudicial impact, but deeming is not believing. Of course some scale-tipping probative evidence is kept out by this sentence, or else it is made superfluous by Rule 403 and the second sentence in Rule 404(b).

[35] [5] At worst, of course, the extreme result of the majority position might even be that the first sentence in Rule 404(b) effectively applies only to crimes in which criminal intent is not an element.

Even where intent is not disputed by the defendant, the majority notes at p. 914 n. 18, extrinsic offense evidence would still be relevant and admissible. Thus, it might be that once intent is an element of the crime as it is with almost all crimes then the defendant is left only with the minimal protection afforded by the "substantial prejudice" test in Rule 403. Such a lop-sided reading of Rule 404(b) is sheer illogic.

* * *

Conclusion

The concepts in this case are not simplistic. But our task is made especially difficult here by the language we use to solve it. We are all guilty to some extent (mea culpa) of indulging in jurisprudential jargon. But the analysis of the majority too often bogs down by trying to solve problems with a few key words, phrases and clauses, such as "substantially outweighed," "relevance," "probative," "similarity," "prejudicial effect," and the like. To make matters worse, the majority debases these words by trading their established meanings for its own language of semantic subjectivity, such as its "psychological indulgence" test.

At the heart of the majority's error in this case is its mistaken placement of the spotlight on the Federal Rules of Evidence, instead of where it rightfully belongs on the criminal trial of a human being. The majority places the vague and uninformed stage hands of the drama the Federal Rules of Evidence in the center of the stage, and pushes the principles of a fair criminal trial into weak, whispered supporting roles off to the edge of the proscenium wall. This means the death of *Broadway*, the majority admits. But it is also an assault on the legitimacy of our criminal system. The majority has, and is, misdirected. The Federal Rules can be supporting actors, at most. They must be directed one way in a civil trial and another way altogether in a criminal trial where human freedom is at stake. Rule 404(b), and most of the other federal rules as well, were designed to be broadly applicable to both criminal and civil trials. But evidence is allowed into a civil trial under a much more flexible, utilitarian standard than in a criminal trial. Due process requires extreme vigilance against the contamination of a criminal trial with cheap and mean character slander, and against the conviction of a citizen for improper reasons. The majority cannot possibly think that Rule 404(b) overrules this central principle of justice, or that it collapses the criminal trial into the utilitarianism of civil litigation.

Broadway may not be stylish, it may not be chic, but its old-fashioned virtues should command our reverence. Broadway was one more last bastion of judging a man by the specifics of the charged crime, rather than by a vague, undocumented, unauthenticated record of misbehavior. The protective mantle of presumed innocence is under severe attack in some modern-day jurisprudence, but the majority's Cain marks become almost ineradicable. The majority's opinion goes far in making one slip a noose.

At the heart of this dissent is a concern about the proper level of hostility or hospitality to extrinsic offense evidence. But in this dissent I am even more concerned about the practicality and integrity of the analysis this circuit will employ in making these judgments. In this case the majority has obliterated a venerable, well-reasoned body of law for no good reason at all, and has replaced it with a Freudian, difficult to apply subjective test that, outside this and a few other similar

---

More importantly, it invites a flagrant abuse of the rights of accused citizens.

To escape this unthinkable result, the majority reads into Rule 401 a "same intent" requirement that is little more than a subjective version of Broadway, and in some ways is even stricter than *Broadway*. This aspect of the majority opinion is discussed in Part II *infra*.

cases, will not even accomplish what the majority wants. It is especially ironic that the majority should justify its evisceration of *Broadway* by declaring that the "revolutionary" drafters of Rule 404(b) wanted the old standards cleared from the stage to make room for the free form, uncontrolled balancing-test discretion of the new Theatre of the Absurd. For no sooner were the objective flats and screens of the legitimate *Broadway* stage pulled aside, than the majority brought in the psychological psychedelics of the Theatre of Indulgence. I can only hope that the majority will soon see the error of its ways and return to the Great White Way of *Broadway* with the appreciation and respect that the grand old boulevard deserves.

I would reverse the judgment of the district court and remand the case for a new trial.

UNITED STATES v. WOODS
484 F.2d 127 (4th Cir. 1973)

WINTER, CIRCUIT JUDGE:

Martha L. Woods was found guilty by a jury of murder in the first degree and seven other charges of assault with intent to murder, attempt to murder, and mistreatment of her eight-month-old pre-adoptive foster son, Paul David Woods.

* * *

In this appeal, Mrs. Woods contends first that the government failed to prove beyond a reasonable doubt the corpus delicti of murder, both because the evidence concerning the death of Paul Woods failed to supply that proof and because evidence about her nine other children was not admissible for that purpose; second, that even if such evidence of prior acts was admissible to prove corpus delicti, the evidence in this case was inadmissible because it was too insubstantial to prove that defendant caused the prior incidents. . . . We find no merit in any of these contentions, and we affirm.

I.

The issues before us arise from the manner in which the government, by necessity, undertook to prove its case. The government showed that Paul was born February 9, 1969, and that he spent the first five months of his life in a foster home. During that time his physical health was uneventful and he never suffered from any breathing problems or cyanosis (a blue color, principally around the lips, due to a lack of oxygen). At the time he was placed in Mrs. Woods' home, he was a normal, healthy baby. Beginning August 4, 1969, a bizarre series of events occurred. Twice on that date, and once again on August 8, August 13, and August 20, Paul suffered instances of gasping for breath and turning blue from lack of oxygen. Each time he responded to mouth-to-mouth resuscitation, except on August 20, when he went into a coma which persisted until September 21, when he died at an age of slightly more than seven months. On each of these occasions the evidence indicated that Paul had been in Mrs. Woods' custody, and only Mrs. Woods had had access to him. On each occasion prior to August 20, Paul was taken to the hospital.

On the first occasion, he was immediately released because an examination disclosed that he was apparently well. On the other occasions, even after several days' observation, no reason for his cyanosis or respiratory difficulties could be discovered. To prove that Paul's death was neither accidental nor the result of natural causes, the government presented the testimony of a forensic pathologist, Dr. DiMaio, who, based upon Paul's medical history, the records of his various hospitalizations, and the results of an autopsy which the pathologist had performed after Paul's death stated that Paul's death was not suicide or accident and that he found no evidence of natural death. Dr. DiMaio expressed his opinion as one of seventy-five percent certainty that Paul's death was homicide caused by smothering. Dr. DiMaio explained his twenty-five percent degree of doubt as being the possibility that Paul died naturally from a disease currently unknown to medical science, and he agreed that his doubt was a "reasonable doubt" within the standard definition given by the court. Next, the government showed that beginning in 1945 Mrs. Woods had had custody of, or access to, nine children who suffered a minimum of twenty episodes of cyanosis. Seven children died, while five had multiple episodes of cyanosis. Three of the children were her own natural born children; two were children she had adopted; one was a niece; one was a nephew; and two were children of friends.

* * *

II.

Defendant's contention that the government failed to prove the corpus delicti beyond a reasonable doubt rests upon the three propositions that (a) proof of the corpus delicti for culpable homicide requires proof of death of the alleged victim and proof that that death occurred by means other than suicide, accident or natural causes, in short, that death occurred by a criminal act, (b) evidence of other crimes is not admissible to show that the death of the alleged victim occurred by homicide, but (c) even if admissible, the proof of other crimes presented by the government in the instant case was not so clear and convincing as to permit the jury to find that Paul's death was homicide.

The government counters by asserting that (a) for culpable homicide, the corpus delicti is established by proof of the fact of death alone, i.e., a dead body; a guilty verdict would still require proof that the death was caused by the criminal agency of this defendant, (b) in any event, evidence of these prior acts was admissible to establish both the corpus delicti and the accused's criminality, and (c) the government evidence of defendant's prior acts, combined with the evidence concerning the death of Paul Woods, was sufficient to permit the jury to find beyond a reasonable doubt that Paul's death was a culpable homicide perpetrated by defendant. . . . Most jurisdictions require proof of (a) death and (b) death by foul means to establish the corpus delicti of homicide.

The parties agree that in order to sustain defendant's convictions the government must have proved beyond a reasonable doubt that Paul's death was caused by culpable homicide and that defendant was the perpetrator of the crime. . . . [E]vidence of incidents concerning the other children was admissible generally and was admissible specifically to prove corpus delicti, so that at the end of the government's case, it had fully met the burden which defendant contends was placed on it. Thus, we proceed directly to discuss whether proof of the prior events concerning the other children was legally admissible to prove that (a) Paul's death was the result of culpable homicide and not of natural causes, and (b) defendant was the perpetrator of the crime.

* * *

We state, at the outset, that if otherwise legally admissible, we have no doubt about the relevance of the proof and its probative effect to establish both propositions. The evidence of what happened to the other children was not, strictly speaking, evidence of other crimes. There was no evidence that defendant was an accused with respect to the deaths or respiratory difficulties of the other children except for Judy. Simultaneously with her trial for crimes alleged against Paul, defendant was being tried for crimes alleged against Judy, but there was no direct proof of defendant's guilt and the district court ruled that the circumstantial evidence was insufficient for the government to have proved its case. Thus, with regard to no single child was there any legally sufficient proof that defendant had done any act which the law forbids. Only when all of the evidence concerning the nine other children and Paul is considered collectively is the conclusion impelled that the probability that some or all of the other deaths, cyanotic seizures, and respiratory deficiencies were accidental or attributable to natural causes was so remote, the truth must be that Paul and some or all of the other children died at the hands of the defendant. We think also that when the crime is one of infanticide or child abuse, evidence of repeated incidents is especially relevant because it may be the only evidence to prove the crime. . . .

B. Admissibility of Evidence Generally.

The government and the defendant agree that evidence of other crimes is not admissible to prove that an accused is a bad person and therefore likely to have committed the crime in question. . . . Defendant argues that while there are certain recognized exceptions to this rule, the instant case cannot be fitted into any of them, emphasizing that corpus delicti is not an exception. MCCORMICK ON EVIDENCE § 190 (Cleary Ed. 1972). The government, in meeting this approach, contends that the evidence was admissible on the theory that it tended to prove (a) the existence of a continuing plan, (b) the handiwork or signature exception,[36] (c) that the acts alleged in the indictment were not inadvertent, accidental, or unintentional, and (d) the defendant's identity as the perpetrator of the crime. We are inclined to agree with the defendant that the evidence was not admissible under the scheme or continuing plan exception because there was no evidence that defendant engaged in any scheme or plan, or, if so, the objective or motive. The evidence may have been admissible under the lack of accident exception, although ordinarily that exception is invoked only where an accused admits that he did the acts charged but denies the intent necessary to constitute a crime, or contends that he did the acts accidentally. . . .

---

[36] [8] *Rex v. George Joseph Smith*, [1914–15] All E.R. Rep. 262 ("Brides of Bath" case) permitted proof of unique methods of previous homicides to establish guilt of the accused.

The handiwork or signature exception is the one which appears most applicable, although defendant's argument that cyanosis among infants is too common to constitute an unusual and distinctive device unerringly pointing to guilt on her part would not be without force, were it not for the fact that so many children at defendant's mercy experienced this condition. In the defendant's case, the "commonness" of the condition is outweighed by its frequency under circumstances where only defendant could have been the precipitating factor. While we conclude that the evidence was admissible generally under the accident and signature exceptions, we prefer to place our decision upon a broader ground. Simply fitting evidence of this nature into an exception heretofore recognized is, to our minds, too mechanistic an approach.

McCormick, in listing the instances in which evidence of other crimes may be admissible, cautions "that the list is not complete, for the range of relevancy outside the ban is almost infinite. . . ." *Id.* 448. And then, McCormick states:

> [S]ome of the wiser opinions . . . recognize that the problem is not merely one of pigeonholing, but one of balancing, on the one side, the actual need for the other crimes evidence in the light of the issues and the other evidence available to the prosecution, the convincingness of the evidence that the other crimes were committed and that the accused was the actor, and the strength or weakness of the other crimes evidence in supporting the issue, and on the other, the degree to which the jury will probably be roused by the evidence to overmastering hostility. *Id.* 453.

This approach is one which finds support in . . . [numerous decisions]. These cases stand for the proposition that evidence of other offenses may be received, if relevant, for any purpose other than to show a mere propensity or disposition on the part of the defendant to commit the crime, provided that the trial judge may exclude the evidence if its probative value is outweighed by the risk that its admission will create a substantial danger of undue prejudice to the accused.   *} 403*

As we stated at the outset, we think that the evidence would prove that a crime had been committed because of the remoteness of the possibility that so many infants in the care and custody of defendant would suffer cyanotic episodes and respiratory difficulties if they were not induced by the defendant's wrong doing, and at the same time, would prove the identity of defendant as the wrongdoer. Indeed, the evidence is so persuasive and so necessary in case of infanticide or other child abuse by suffocation if the wrongdoer is to be apprehended, that we think that its relevance clearly outweighs its prejudicial effect on the jury. We reject defendant's argument that the proof was not so clear and convincing that its admissibility should not be sustained. As we stated at the outset, if the evidence with regard to each child is considered separately, it is true that some of the incidents are less conclusive than others; but we think the incidents must be considered collectively, and when they are, an unmistakable pattern emerges. That pattern overwhelmingly establishes defendant's guilt.

C. Admissibility of Evidence to Prove Corpus Delicti.

For the reasons stated, the sufficiency of the evidence of (a) what happened to the other children, (b) proof of the fact of Paul's death, and (c) the government's expert testimony of the probable cause of death, . . . to prove the corpus delicti was apparent. Defendant argues strenuously, however, that even if admissible for other purposes, the law does not permit evidence of prior acts to be employed to prove the corpus delicti. . . .

Counsel have not cited, nor have we found, any case which considers whether or not prior acts can be used to establish the corpus delicti of murder, but the law seems clear that prior acts can be proved to establish the corpus delicti of arson,[37] . . . . The rule in cases of arson would seem equally applicable incases of murder. . . . We therefore hold that in the instant case proof of the incidents involving other children was admissible to prove the corpus delicti of murder and other acts of child abuse.

Federal Rule of Evidence 404(b)
Character Evidence; Crimes or Other Acts

(b) Crimes, Wrongs, or Other Acts.

(1) Prohibited Uses. Evidence of a crime, wrong, or other act is not admissible to prove a person's character in order to show that on a particular occasion the person acted in accordance with the character.

(2) Permitted Uses; Notice in a Criminal Case. This evidence may be admissible for another purpose, such as proving motive, opportunity, intent, preparation, plan, knowledge, identity, absence of mistake, or lack of accident. On request by a defendant in a criminal case, the prosecutor must:

(A) provide reasonable notice of the general nature of any such evidence that the prosecutor intends to offer at trial; and

(B) do so before trial — or during trial if the court, for good cause, excuses lack of pretrial notice.

NOTES AND QUESTIONS

1.   How would *Woods* have been decided under Rule 404(b)? Should Rule 609 remoteness considerations be applicable? *Cf. United States v. Curtin*, 443 F.3d 1084 (9th Cir. 2006); *United States v. Lecroy*, 441 F.3d 914 (11th Cir. 2006), *United States v. Terry*, 702 F.2d 299 (2d Cir. 1983). May evidence of other crimes be admitted to prove intent or absence of accident when defendant does not dispute intent and has not raised a claim of accident? *See Estelle v. McGuire*, 502 U.S. 62 (1991); *United States v. Paulino*, 445 F.3d 211 (2d Cir. 2006). May a defendant avoid the impact of

---

[37] [13] *State v. Schleigh*, 210 Ore. 155, 310 P.2d 341, 348 (1957) (repeated fires by spontaneous combustion unlikely; eight fires along one country road immediately after defendant, his father and others drove by show "a deliberate plan to set them"); *State v. Smith*, 221 S.W.2d 158 (Mo. 1949) (proof of prior fire was admissible to show that fire charged in indictment was incendiary); *People v. Wolf*, 334 Ill. 218, 165 N.E. 619 (1929) (proof of separate fires admissible to prove corpus delicti). . . .

Rule 404(b) by offering to stipulate to the narrow point in issue? *See United States v. McLaughlin*, 164 Fed. Appx. 802, 2005 U.S. App. LEXIS 29139 (11th Cir. Dec. 30, 2005).

2.   Although Rule 404(b) admits evidence of other crimes under certain circumstance, it does not admit such evidence as an exception to the principle that evidence of bad character may not be used as a basis for inferring generally the defendant's guilt. *See* 2 WEINSTEIN'S EVIDENCE § 404[08] (1982). The other crimes evidence is still not admitted to prove bad character; rather, it's allowed solely to prove some narrow point other than the defendant's general character, and the court will instruct the jury that it may draw no inference about the defendant's character from such evidence. *See also People v Quinn*, 486 N.W.2d 139 (Mich. Ct. App. 1992) (chastising prosecution for arguing propensity based on evidence admitted under Rule 404(b)).

3.   A federal court asked to admit other bad acts under Fed. R. Evid. 404(b) need not make a preliminary finding that the defendant committed these acts. The court need only determine that there is sufficient evidence to support a finding by the jury that the defendant committed the act proffered under Rule 404(b). *Huddleston v. United States*, 485 U.S. 681 (1988).

4.   In *Dowling v. United States*, 493 U.S. 342 (1990), the Supreme Court ruled that the Double Jeopardy and Due Process Clauses of the Constitution do not bar "other crimes" evidence under Rule 404(b), despite the defendant's acquittal of criminal charges. The Supreme Court's analysis turned on the burden of proof, reasoning that the prosecution's failure to prove guilt beyond a reasonable doubt does not preclude its ability to provide sufficient evidence to support a finding (*i.e.*, a prima facie case) under Rule 404(b). *See also Huddleston v. United States*, 485 U.S. 681 (1988).

[handwritten margin note: What does acquittal really mean]

5.   May a criminal defendant use other crimes evidence affirmatively to prove that some third person committed the crime? *See United States v. Banky-Alli*, 2005 U.S. App. LEXIS 25427 (2d Cir. 2005); *United States v. Wilson*, 307 F.3d 596 (7th Cir. 2002). If allowed, is such evidence admissible to prove the third person's propensity to commit the crime at issue?

Rule 404(b) has generated a plethora of case law, thereby warranting treatment in a treatise devoted exclusively to these issues. *See* E. IMWINKELRIED, UNCHARGED MISCONDUCT EVIDENCE (1998).

UNITED STATES v. HEARST
563 F.2d 1331 (9th Cir. 1977)

PER CURIAM.

Appellant was tried under a two-count indictment charging her with armed robbery of a San Francisco bank. . . . The government introduced photographs and testimony descriptive of appellant's role in the robbery. Appellant raised the defense of duress, contending her co-participants compelled her to engage in the criminal activity. The jury found appellant guilty. . . .

*   *   *

I. Evidence of Subsequent Crimes

During its case-in-chief the government introduced evidence connecting appellant with criminal activity at a sporting goods store and with a kidnapping and theft. These incidents occurred in the Los Angeles area approximately one month after the San Francisco bank robbery. The evidence showed that appellant accompanied William and Emily Harris to Mel's Sporting Goods Store in Los Angeles, that the Harrises entered the store and left appellant outside in a truck, that a store clerk saw William Harris shoplifting and attempted to arrest him, and that appellant discharged an automatic rifle at the store, enabling Harris to escape. The evidence further showed that on the same day appellant and the Harrises stole a van and kidnapped its owner, Thomas Matthews. Matthews testified that during this incident the Harrises were outside the van and appellant had an opportunity to escape or give Matthews a message but did not do so. Appellant objects to admission of this evidence on three grounds. She asserts the evidence was irrelevant for any purpose except the improper one of convincing the jury that appellant acted in accordance with a criminal disposition. She argues that even if the evidence were relevant to the issue of intent, as the district court held, the incidents were so dissimilar to the bank robbery that its probative value was minimal and outweighed by its prejudicial effect. Finally, appellant contends the court erred in permitting the introduction of this evidence during the government's case-in-chief.

Evidence of other criminal acts may be persuasive that the accused is by propensity a probable perpetrator of the crime charged. Nonetheless, it is excluded when offered for this purpose because it may unduly influence the jury and deny the accused a fair opportunity to defend against the particular charge.

*   *   *

Evidence of other criminal acts may be admitted for purposes other than proving criminal predisposition, however. It may be received, for example, to prove knowledge, motive, and intent. Fed. R. Evid. 404(b). . . . The government contends that the evidence of appellant's criminal acts in Los Angeles a month after the bank robbery was relevant to the issue of appellant's intent when she participated in the San Francisco bank robbery, and to whether appellant was acting under duress.

Appellant raised the defense of duress at trial and offered substantial evidence to support it. To convict appellant, therefore, the government was required to show appellant was not acting under duress when she participated in the San Francisco robbery. The evidence of appellant's involvement in the Los Angeles activity was relevant to this issue because it tended to show appellant willingly engaged in other criminal activity with persons of the same group at a time not unduly remote.

Appellant correctly points out that though relevant, evidence of other criminal conduct by the accused should be excluded if its probative value is outweighed by its prejudicial impact upon the accused. Fed. R. Evid. 403. . . . This determination is largely a matter for the discretion of the district court. . . . Appellant challenges the discretionary determination made by the district court in this instance.

Appellant points out that the Los Angeles offenses were not similar to the San Francisco robbery with which she was charged. Because the events were so dissimilar, she contends, they offer little insight into her state of mind during the robbery. But to justify admission of evidence of other crimes, the crimes must be "similar" to the offense charged only if it is the similarity of the crimes that underlies the relevance of the evidence. . . . Here the relevance of the evidence did not depend on the similarity of the Los Angeles crimes to the bank robbery but on the circumstances surrounding the occurrence of the Los Angeles crimes, which indicated appellant had not acted under duress when she participated in the bank robbery. The tendency of the evidence regarding the Los Angeles crimes to prove appellant was not coerced when she participated in the San Francisco robbery is not diminished by the lack of similarity between the Los Angeles and San Francisco offenses.

Appellant also argues that the sequence of the San Francisco and Los Angeles events undermines the relevance of the latter to her state of mind during the San Francisco robbery. Absence of duress in the later Los Angeles incidents would not be probative of her state of mind during the San Francisco robbery, she contends, because the robbery itself made her an outlaw and a fugitive. This fact may have caused her to participate willingly in the Los Angeles events, she asserts, even if she were under duress during the earlier robbery. Appellant' s hypothesis does bear upon the probative value of the evidence, and it is an appropriate consideration in determining whether on balance the evidence should have been admitted. It is, however, only a hypothesis, and a highly speculative one. The mere assertion of this hypothesis does not so undermine the probative worth of the evidence of the Los Angeles incidents in establishing appellant's state of mind during the San Francisco robbery as to render admission of the evidence an abuse of discretion. The jury could well reject appellant's theory and conclude that if appellant had been forced to participate in the bank robbery against her will she would have refrained from criminal activity in Los Angeles or seized the opportunity to escape.

[handwritten marginalia: relevant]

The trial judge was called upon to balance the need for the evidence in the search for the truth against the possibility that the jury would be prejudiced against appellant because the evidence revealed she had participated in other conduct that was criminal. The district court acted well within its discretion in admitting the evidence. Appellant's state of mind during the San Francisco robbery was the central issue in the case. State of mind is usually difficult to prove, and the evidence on the issue was sharply divided. The timing and other circumstances of the Los Angeles incidents made evidence of them highly probative on this critical issue. Though criminal, the incidents were not of a kind likely to inflame the jury. The prejudice to appellant arose primarily from the light the evidence cast on appellant's state of mind during the San Francisco robbery and not from the incidental circumstance that it revealed appellant's involvement in other criminal acts.

[handwritten marginalia: went to the intent]

Appellant contends that even if evidence of the Los Angeles incidents were admissible, the district court erred in admitting it in the government's case-in-chief. The argument runs as follows. Bank robbery is a crime requiring a general rather than specific intent, . . . and the jury could infer the requisite intent from the commission of the act. . . . Since evidence of other criminal acts was not required to enable the government to carry its burden of proving intent, it should not have been admitted as part of the government's case-in-chief. . . . It was reversible error, appellant concludes, to admit to such prejudicial evidence when its only relevance was to rebut a defense of duress not yet raised.

*   *   *

Even before trial commenced it was appellant's announced intention to defend on the ground of duress. No other defense was available to her. If appellant defended at all, the evidence of the Los Angeles events would have been placed before the jury in the government's rebuttal. There is no basis for assuming appellant was prejudiced because the evidence was admitted in the government's case-in-chief rather than in rebuttal. The prejudice arose from the substance of the evidence, not from the timing of its introduction.

*   *   *

Affirmed.

Evidence of other crimes is usually proffered in criminal prosecutions. Rule 404(b), however, contains no such limitation, and potential civil applications occasionally arise. The following case addresses this point.

Evidentiary Foundation:
The Trial of Wayne Williams

[The background to this case is set forth *supra*. The admissibility of other crime evidence was a major issue at trial. In addressing this issue, the following colloquoy occurred.][38]

The Court:	. . . Mr. Drolet? We're now ready to proceed.
Mr. Drolet:	Thank you, Your Honor.

Your Honor, Pursuant to your pretrial order to set out the procedure for doing this, the State at this time is prepared to begin offering evidence in regard to other transactions which . . . there is evidence connecting the defendant. Now, this evidence is being offered for a limited purpose, the limited purpose being that it tends to prove plan, scheme, pattern, bent of mind, and identity.

* * *

What I'd like to do at this point, your Honor, is simply go through the offenses which we expect we will be presenting evidence on at this point. It's possible we may not present it on all of these, might not present all of these to the court.

The first case, Your Honor, is the case of Alfred Evans.

* * *

In this case, as in the two cases on trial, we are dealing with a victim who is black, a male victim. We're dealing with a victim who comes from a situation of poverty, as did the two victims in the case in chief.

---

[38] For this issue on appeal, see *Williams v. State*, 312 S.E.2d 40 (Ga. 1983).

This victim, like those victims, comes from a broken home, and like those victims, he is a street hustler, a street person, living the same basic lifestyle as our two victims.

As with the two victims that we're dealing with in this case, this young man had no vehicle. He was out on the street, very vulnerable to being picked up. As far as the crime itself, like the two offenses in question, the crime is where a person disappears with no apparent motive. There's no evidence of forced abduction. The person appears later dead.

* * *

As in the cases that we're dealing with, as in the case of Mr. Cater and Mr. Payne, there is a method of body disposal which is quite unusual. People apparently are killed and then dumped.

In this case, it is on land. Mr. Evans is not dumped in a river, but on land. But the method of dropping the person somewhere apparently after death is the same.

The place where the victim is dumped is, again, somewhat similar, off a major highway artery, easily accessible from the expressway is the location chosen, and that is where the body is found.

In the case of Mr. Evans, there is some clothing missing, the same as there are in the two cases that we're dealing with.

In the case of Mr. Evans, the cause of death is asphyxia by strangulation; again, similar to the case that we're dealing with.

Now, we have other evidence in this case, Your Honor, which not only increases the value or the number of similarities in the case, but is also evidence of identification. Fibers are found on Mr. Evans from the acetate of the bed-spread of the defendant. The Wellman carpet fibers are found. Dog hairs are found, and two other fibers are found. So a total of five fibers are found on this victim; again, similar to the ones in this case, unique in the combination, and very identifiable. In this case, as in the case of most of the others I will name, the defendant claims to have never been in contact with this person.

The next transaction is the case of Eric Middlebrooks. Again, we're dealing with a young black male, lives in a poor area, comes from a broken home. He is a street hustler. He has no vehicle.

Again, he disappears and is found dumped, laid out on his back. He, like Mr. Evans and the others, is found just off an expressway exit. As in the other case, the defendant claims no knowledge of this victim; yet, fibers, including the violet bedspread fiber, the dog hairs, and fibers from a vehicle the defendant is driving, are found on that victim.

The third—

The Court: How many fibers; Do you know?

Mr. Drolet:	Four different types of fibers, Your Honor.
The Court:	Proceed. I'm sorry.
Mr. Drolet:	The next case is the case of Charles Stephens. Again, young black male, very poor family situation, broken home, a street hustler. He has no vehicle.
	Again, as far as the crime itself, he is found, there's no apparent motive, he disappears overnight, there's no evidence of a forced abduction. Like the others, the body disposal system is the same—
The Court:	Excuse me. Back to Mr. Middlebrooks for one moment, the cause of death.
Mr. Drolet:	The cause of death in Mr. Middlebrooks is trauma to the back of the head, and he, also, has postmortem stab wounds on his body. I will comment on those later, your Honor.
The Court:	Go ahead.
Mr. Drolet:	Stephens, as I said, the characteristics of the victim are virtually identical. Again, he is killed and dumped along the side of the road a short distance from an expressway. Again, as in the case of the other victims, the cause of death here is asphyxia; he is strangled. Again, the same fibers appear.
The Court:	How many?
Mr. Drolet:	In this case, eight different fiber matches. Again, this is a case where the defendant claims no contact.
The Court:	Go ahead.
Mr. Drolet:	The next case is the case of Lubie Geter. Again, a young black male, a poor family. He's a street hustler. He's got no vehicle. He disappears, no apparent motive, no evidence of a forced abduction.
	The body, again, is disposed of after death. He's laid out on his back. Again, found close to a major expressway and artery going to that expressway. Again, the clothing is partially missing. Again, cause of death is asphyxia; he is strangled. In this case, there are four different carpet — fibers, including the carpet fiber, the bedspread fibers. And, again, the defendant claims having had no contact with this victim.
	We expect in that case there may also be a witness who can place the victim and the defendant together.
The Court:	Okay.
Mr. Drolet:	The next case, your Honor, is Terry Pue. Again, a young black male, poor. He's a street hustler. He has no vehicle. Disappears with no apparent motive. There's no evidence of a forced abduction here.
	He is found under the same circumstances, dumped, laid out on his back, just off I-20 in Rockdale County. The cause of death, again, is asphyxia. He is strangled.

Again, the defendant claims to have had no contact with this person; yet the similar fibers, five different fibers, appear on this victim.

The Court: That was five?

Mr. Drolet: That's correct, Your Honor.

The Court: Go ahead.

Mr. Drolet: The next victim is Patrick Baltazar. Again, we are dealing with a young black male, poor, from a broken home. He's a street person, a hustler like the others. He has no vehicle. He disappears with no apparent motive. There's no evidence of a forced abduction.

And then he appears, his body dumped. This is just off an expressway, again, off I-85. The cause of death the same, asphyxia, strangulation. The defendant claims no contact with this victim, yet eleven different fibers and hairs consistent with the defendant's environment are found.

The Court: Go ahead.

Mr. Drolet: The next victim is Jo Jo Bell. Again, we have a young black male, a poor home, a broken home. He is a street hustler. He has no vehicle. He disappears with no apparent motive, no evidence of forced abduction. His body, like the bodies of the two cases in the case in chief, is found dumped in a river. He is nude except for his shorts. Again, the place where he is found is easily accessible from I-20, just east of Atlanta.

The cause of death is asphyxia associated with a neck injury. Because of the effects of the river, only two fibers are found on Mr. Bell.

The Court: Go ahead.

Mr. Drolet: In this case, again, a witness will attempt to put these two people, the defendant and the victim, together.

The Court: Go ahead.

Mr. Drolet: Larry Rogers is the next victim. Again, we're dealing with a black male, very poor, comes from a broken home. He is a street hustler. He has no vehicle. There's no apparent motive. As with the others, he disappears. There's no evidence of a forced abduction.

Like many of the others, he is dumped, laid out on his back. He is nude except for shorts and a shirt stuffed down into those shorts. The cause of death, asphyxia by strangulation. And this victim is one of the older victims, 20 years old. This is where we again get into the adult victims.

The Court: How old was he, 20?

Mr. Drolet: 20 years old, though I would say, like Mr. Payne, he is a small, fairly small person, five feet three, in the range of a hundred and thirty pounds. Again, on Mr. Rogers, seven different fibers similar to the fibers found on the two present victims are found on Mr. Rogers. The defendant claims no contact. We anticipate the witness will put the defendant and Larry Rogers together.

The Court: Go ahead.

Mr. Drolet: The next victim is John Harold Porter. Mr. Porter is a 30-year-old black male. He's five foot ten and weighed a hundred and twenty-three pounds, very similar in stature to Mr. Cater, and age.

Like the others, he shares the same background as the victim, is very, very poor, comes from a broken home. He is a street hustler. He had no vehicle. He disappears with no apparent motive, no evidence of an abduction by force.

He is found dumped, laid out on his back, just off an expressway close to downtown. In his case, cause of death is different. It is stab wounds.

The Court: Go ahead.

Mr. Drolet: On this victim are found seven different types of fibers matching those from the Williams environment.

* * *

The final of the transactions is William Barrett. Mr. Barrett, like the others, is a black male, poor, comes from a broken home. He's a street hustler like the others, 17 years old, approximately the size as Mr. Payne, five feet four, a hundred twenty-five. He has no vehicle. He disappears with no apparent motive, no evidence of a forced abduction.

Like all the others, he is dumped out at the side of the road close to an expressway ramp. Some clothing is missing from this victim, and the cause of death on this victim is asphyxia, strangulation. And this victim also has stab wounds in the front portion of the body, as did Mr. Porter and Mr. Middlebrooks. As in the other cases, there are seven different fibers in which there is a match.

The defendant claims no contact with Mr. Barrett, and blood consistent with Mr. Barrett's is found in the 1970 Chevrolet Station Wagon. Those are the cases that we would anticipate offering or at least cases from among those. At this point I will reserve any rebuttal to objection which Mr. Binder may make to this evidence, inasmuch as I anticipate that the defense will object to the introduction of this evidence.

* * *

Mr. Binder: May it please the court, your Honor, in reply to the statements that were made by counsel regarding these cases and recalling my childhood which was one of abject poverty until I was about 18 or 19, I don't think I'll refer to these deceased as street hustlers.

The cases mentioned by the prosecution for the main seem to me to be young people, with the exception of a 30-year-old man and a 20-year-old male, almost adult.

When he talks about pattern, he talks about one thing they might have had in common is the fact that they were poor. But if you can get pattern legally in American because you're poor, the courts would be full of requests like this. That's not the criteria here.

If he would have stated that they were all children like the Atlanta murders were referred to consistently and constantly throughout the nation, I could understand that if he had picked that many cases concerning children. But he puts two grown males in there.

Now, he puts those two grown males in there because the two deceased in this case that this defendant has been indicted on are grown males. Why in the world why they ever picked those two to indict this defendant, I'll never know. But mine is not to question. We are defending against an indictment that alleges the death of two grown men.

Now, first, I'd like to call the court's attention to what is known as corpus delicti. Regardless of the fanfare, the problems, the community hysteria, the hurt of so many deaths, this is a murder case and I think it's my job in representing the defendant to always bring back to the realm of reality what the prosecution has to do in a murder case.

It is our position that in Georgia pattern is not admissible until you prove corpus delicti. That's number one.

Now, in this case, the independent evidence so far hasn't even established a homicidal death with regard to Payne. The Court only knows that these two victims are deceased because they say that these two victims are deceased because they say the death was caused by asphyxiation, and all that means is lack of oxygen, deprivation of oxygen, doesn't mean that a murder has been committed. These two bodies were found severely decomposed. Why, in one body, they didn't even take slides of the tissues.

You cannot speculate criminal agency in Georgia or any other state in this union, and we say to this present time he has not shown this court or the jury any criminal agency.

* * *

The Court: Mr. Binder, I want to make sure that I understand you. It's your contention that the state has not shown foul play in either the death of Cater or Payne; is that correct?

Mr. Binder: Yes, sir, and that they have not connected it. The second element of corpus delicti, if the court believes that they've shown foul play in Cater, then the second element of corpus delicti is not present yet so far. They're not through with their case, but they haven't shown corpus delicti yet. They haven't shown criminal connection between the defendant Williams.

For example, Your Honor, if you and I walked down the street today and you and I brushed each other and I got 14 fibers on my body and you were found dead tomorrow morning and no one saw me do one thing out of the way when you and I walked down the street today, then they certainly couldn't prove murder on me. That's my position.

Now, no independent evidence has been presented to your Honor during the trial to establish corpus delicti as of yet. Now, they may have it. They gave me a list of 600 some odd witnesses, and they may have the ability to do it. Lord knows I don't know what's going to happen, but I haven't seen it yet.

And we say that at this juncture of the trial that they can't use even the taint of a pattern to convict a defendant charged with crime because they can't prove corpus delicti. They've got to do the first one first. Now, on the issue of pattern, the general rule is that when the prosecutor prosecutes for a crime, any evidence which in any manner shows or tends to show that the accused has committed another crime wholly independent from that which he's on trial for, even though it be a crime of the same sort, is irrelevant and inadmissible. That's number one. That's the general rule.

Now, what they're talking about is an exception to the general rule, if the court please, and we say there are two conditions delineated by the courts of this state, the state of Georgia, similar to conditions in states that I'm familiar with, my home, that must be met before the trial court should allow an admission of an uncharged crime. And both of these conditions must be established, and the court may not proceed to the second step until the first step has been satisfied.

* * *

Condition one, the evidence must show that the defendant was the perpetrator of the independent crime. They must show that this defendant accomplished, perpetrated the independent crime, and in his statement today to you, he didn't tell you that he could prove that Wayne Williams killed these young men. Second, there must be sufficient similarity or connection between the independent crime and that charged so that proof of the former tends to prove the latter.

Now, this two-part test is essential before you can even consider whether some other crimes are pattern. I'm not talking at this juncture about argument as to whether these even ten deaths are even pattern at this point. And it says, first, the state must introduce all evidence regarding its case in chief as to the offenses which Mr. Williams is charged with, exclusive of evidence of independent crimes. And if the state is allowed to introduce evidence of these other crimes in the presence of the jury, we say that it would be a mistrial and the Supreme Court of Georgia will reverse your Honor.

Now, the Supreme Court of Georgia in Cawthon v. State, 119 Georgia 395, said that allowing those type crimes at the wrong state of the game without the two-pronged rule, I guess, is so prejudicial that no court could clear up the prejudice by a charge and that it would be naivete to believe that that type prejudice could be cured by instructions from the court.

* * *

There's been no testimony in this case by any one living human being that they saw Wayne Williams do anything in a criminal manner.

* * *

The Court: Let me ask you this, Mr. Binder. Is it your contention that circumstantial evidence cannot be used to identify the perpetrator of a crime?

Mr. Binder: No, sir; that's not my contention. My contention is that you have to have, first, the two essential elements of corpus delicti before pattern is admissible; second, that you have to have something more than a fiber to identify the perpetrator of a crime. And what I'm telling the court is that there is no witness that the state is going to call that I know of — now, they may have one — that will identify the defendant as the perpetrator of an independent act.

As Mr. Deadman said to you today, Your Honor, the evidence they've introduced so far is as cogent to the defendant's mother, father, visitor to the house or, quoting Mr. Deadman, anybody that had access to or drove that car as it is to this defendant.

Now, without any positive identification that Williams is, in fact, a perpetrator of an alleged independent crime, the evidence is not admissible, and we say it would be reversible error for this court to allow this evidence to go before the jury at this point.

The Court: You're saying that the state is a little premature?

Mr. Binder: I'm saying, Your Honor, with every breath in my body — I wouldn't try to mislead this court for anything in the world — yes, it is. To say these things in front of Your Honor without citing one case to you today, I can't help but think it was for the press because you weren't cited one case in that argument. You were told about ten people here, and two of them were apparently—

The Court: I think Mr. Drolet indicated that after you had made your presentation—

Mr. Binder: He's going to cite some, I'm sure, when I get through. But, you know, he brought this motion to you, not me. He brought the motion. Now, you've got two of these fellows with stab wounds. You've got several asphyxiated. They know that on, let's say, Baltazar that they have four suspects alive and well. They know one of the suspects is a known person to pick up little boys. On Terry Pue, he was blamed for a criminal act of his family shortly before his death.

On Lubie Geter, they know that there were two men in a white and black car, had nothing to do with a 1970 white station wagon, with witnesses alleged that they knew the killer other than and never heard of Wayne Williams. On Larry Rogers, they've got a composite down there. They have evidence that there was a green 1966 Chevrolet station wagon involved in that case; that on the day he disappeared, Larry Rogers, he got into that 1966 Chevrolet station wagon, green in color; that the composite was identified by someone other than the person that drew it.

On Jo Jo Bell, you've got a case fraught with family feud there, your honor. You've got homosexuality possibly in that case, and there has not been one witness in this trial to put his hand out to that young man and say that he was a homosexual, and you haven't heard any evidence to date. On Alfred Evans, they have many suspects, and a prime suspect. On Middlebrooks, they know that there are witnesses that threatened him. There was two suspects in Barrett, a burgundy van was involved and was involved in the carpet business, if the court please. A white male known to have picked up young people is involved in that case, and there's evidence to that effect.

On Charles Stephens, you were told about the fibers and hairs, but you weren't told that on Stephens, a caucasian head hair was found on him. And he was known to have sex with homosexuals, and there's no evidence in this case that my client is a homosexual. There's two white males involved in that one that were allegedly trying to kidnap that boy. And Mr. Porter met the grace of God by stab wounds. Now, if there's pattern in those cases, your honor, it's pattern as interpreted in the minds of those who indicted this defendant. But a careful examination of these cases does not reflect pattern, not the ones they've cited to you. I thank you.

6.   Special Rules for Cases Alleging Sexual Assaults

In sexual assault cases, defense counsel often attack the alleged victim's character. When this occurs, the inferential argument is that the woman was promiscuous and, therefore, consented to sexual intercourse. Because the introduction of such character evidence led to criticism that trial has become more of an ordeal for the victim than the defendant, Congress and some state jurisdictions have passed so-called rape shield laws. *See* Anderson, *From Chastity Requirement to Sexuality License: Sexual Consent and a New Rape Shield Law*, 70 GEO. WASH. L. REV. 51 (2002). Berger, *Man's Trial, Woman's Tribulation: Rape Cases in the Courtroom*, 77 COLUM. L. REV. 1 (1977). In this respect, consider to what extent, if any, Fed. R. Evid. 412, set forth immediately after the following article, affords victims extra protections. *See* Anderson, *supra*; Chris W. Sanchirico, *Character Evidence and the Object of Trial*, 101 COLUMB. L. REV. 1227 (2001); Comment, *Federal Rule of Evidence 412: Was the Change an*

Improvement?, 49 U. Cin. L. Rev. 244 (1980). In crafting a rape-shield law, constitutional factors required a balancing of interests as the following article explains.

J. Alexander Tanford & Anthony J. Bocchino, *Rape Victim Shield Laws and the Sixth Amendment*
128 U. Pa. L. Rev. 544, 546, 550 (1980)[39]

II. HISTORICAL PERSPECTIVES

At common law, the rules governing the use of a rape complainant's sexual history provided that such evidence was always admissible. Three elements combined to create the rule of admissibility. The first was the fear of false charges brought by vindictive women. Sir Matthew Hale, Lord Chief Justice of the King's Bench, stated that rape "is an accusation easily to be made . . . and harder to be defended by the party accused, tho never so innocent." Second was the concept that chastity was a character trait. If a woman could be shown to be unchaste by nature, then it could be inferred that she had consented to sex with the defendant. Third was the belief that premarital sex was immoral. Acts of previous illicit sexual relations, like other acts of moral turpitude, could thus be used to impeach the credibility of the complaining witness in a rape case. The fear expressed by Sir Matthew Hale, that it is difficult to defend against fabricated rape charges, pervaded the early writings justifying the need for sexual history evidence.

The unchaste (let us call it) mentality finds . . . expression in the narration of imaginary sex incidents of which the narrator is the heroine or the victim. On the surface the narration is straightforward and convincing. The real victim, however . . . is the innocent man; for the respect and sympathy naturally felt by any tribunal for a wronged female helps to give easy credit to such a plausible tale. To protect these innocent men, juries were usually instructed to scrutinize closely the testimony of a rape complainant: "Where the complaining witness and the defendant are the only witnesses, a charge of rape is one which, generally speaking, is easily made, and once made, difficult to disprove. Therefore, I charge you that the law requires that you examine the testimony of the prosecuting witness with caution." Dean Wigmore went so far as to urge that all women who brought rape charges undergo psychiatric examination before being allowed to testify in order to weed out charges stemming from sexual fantasy, rather than fact.

Whatever the situation may have been in times past, it is difficult to argue today that the danger of false charges is greater for rape than for any other kind of crime. If anything, the statistics show just the opposite. Rape is one of the most underreported crimes. In addition, rape allegations are carefully screened in most instances to assure that only legitimate cases go to trial. For no other category of crime is the scrutiny by the police and prosecutor closer. Most states today do not have a rule automatically allowing the use in rape trials of testimony about a woman's "character" for chastity. Not long ago, however, courts reasoned that most women were virtuous by nature and that an unchaste woman must therefore have

---

[39] Reprinted with permission.

an unusual character flaw. This character trait had caused her to consent in the past (when, obviously, a "normal" woman would never have consented) and made it likely that she would consent repeatedly. Because consent was a defense to rape, evidence that was thought to show a propensity towards sexual relations was always admissible to suggest consent in the particular instance. Courts and legislatures have adapted to the times and have realized that a woman who is unchaste — or in modern parlance, who has had extramarital sexual relationships — is no more likely to consent indiscriminately than is a chaste woman.

Another problem that led to dissatisfaction with viewing sexual history as evidence of character was the manner of proof. Character is usually proved by testimony about a person's reputation and less often by opinion testimony or by evidence of specific acts. Thus, in rape cases, the defendant was entitled to introduce testimony about the sexual reputation of the victim and could often have a witness testify to his opinion of the woman's chastity. Even if there is some probative value in showing that a rape victim is casual in her selection of sexual partners, the least accurate way of doing so is by evidence of her reputation or the opinion of one witness perhaps lacking any personal knowledge. Sensing the inherent weaknesses of relying on the character-evidence rationale for admitting sexual history evidence, some courts attempted to justify it on the ground that it impeached the complainant's credibility. This reasoning assumes that promiscuity is a form of dishonesty, and that, as in the case of other acts affecting honesty, promiscuity lessens the witness's credibility. This effort to justify admitting evidence of sexual history is seriously flawed. First, the cases offering this explanation limited the inference to women. Promiscuous men could not be similarly impeached. Second, only women who brought rape charges were open to this kind of impeachment. Female prosecuting witnesses who charged defendants with other types of crimes, such as robbery, could never be impeached by their prior sexual history.

In recent years, many law review articles and notes have attacked the old rule allowing evidence of the victim's previous sexual conduct in a rape trial. They argue that this system is manifestly unfair to women and a reflection of out-moded morality and an unenlightened male-dominated legal system. The growing awareness of the equality of women, and no doubt the published criticism, have caused most jurisdictions in this country to change the old laws and eliminate the automatic admissibility of this kind of evidence. Yet even as the old laws were premised on the myths of a male-dominated society, the vituperative attacks and much of the resulting legislation are themselves based on an emotional premise: that the rape victim is unfairly subject to a "second rape" by the criminal justice system. Uniformly, the cry for revision of the rape evidence laws calls for special protections for the rape victim not available to most prosecuting witnesses. Writers have gone so far as to advocate considering a rape victim as a "defendant," entitled to the same protections as defendants charged with crimes.

These authors are undoubtedly correct that the old laws that singled out rape cases for special evidentiary rules were unwarranted. This thesis, however, cuts both ways: just as testimony should not automatically be admissible in rape cases, it should not automatically be inadmissible solely because a trial involves rape instead of some other crime affecting the same people. A basic premise of evidentiary rules is that they focus on issues common to all trials and do not develop differently for each substantive crime and civil cause of action.

III. THE MODERN RESPONSE

The response of legislatures to criticism of rape evidence laws has been enormous. In recent years, forty-five states have rewritten their rules of evidence concerning the admissibility of testimony about a rape victim's prior sexual history. A majority of the new evidentiary laws tend to the opposite extreme of the old rule of automatic admissibility: presumptive inadmissibility. There is great variation from jurisdiction to jurisdiction in the extent to which sexual history evidence is allowed. Louisiana has barred all uses of prior sexual activity evidence, except evidence of a prior relationship with the defendant, while the Texas legislature has rewritten its law simply to allow judicial discretion overall uses of sexual history evidence. Other states cover the range between these two.

Rule 412 of the Federal Rules of Evidence, the most recent such enactment, states as a general rule that reputation or opinion evidence of the past sexual behavior of an alleged rape victim is never admissible, and that "evidence of a victim's past sexual behavior other than reputation or opinion evidence is also not admissible." The rule then follows the most common pattern, setting forth a few specific instances in which the defendant's obvious need to introduce such evidence is so great that preventing it would violate due process. Congress chose two situations in which to allow this evidence.

> (A) [P]ast sexual behavior with persons other than the accused, offered by the accused upon the issue of whether the accused was . . . the source of semen or injury; or
>
> (B) past sexual behavior with the accused and is offered by the accused upon the issue of whether the alleged victim consented. . . .

[handwritten margin note: exceptions]

Rule 412 is typical in a number of ways. First declaring a general rule that evidence of a rape victim's prior sexual activities is inadmissible, it creates a presumption that the defendant should not be allowed to introduce testimony on this point. The rule recognizes, however, that in certain limited situations the defendant may put such evidence before the jury; in some cases it would be manifestly unfair to prevent introduction of evidence with particular probative value. As with most similar statutes, rule 412 is restricted in its operation to criminal cases. It follows the majority in allowing evidence of specific sexual acts only in very limited situations, but it is more restrictive than most state rules by prohibiting reputation and opinion evidence altogether, no matter what the probative value.

Two instances of special admissibility appear most commonly in state statutes: (1) prior sexual relations with the defendant offered to show consent; and (2) a specific sexual act with another man to provide an alternative explanation for the physical indications of rape. The rape evidence laws universally allow the defendant who claims consent as a defense to show that he and the complainant had a prior consensual sexual relationship. Most statutes also permit the defendant to rebut evidence offered by the state to corroborate the sex act itself — presence of semen, resulting pregnancy or venereal disease, or the force inflicted — by showing that such evidence may have been the result of a sexual act with another man at about the same time. Less common exceptions allow such testimony to impeach the victim's credibility or to show a motive for fabrication. Finally, the sexual behavior of the prosecuting witness may be admissible if it indicates an unusual pattern of consensual sexual activity that is closely related to the defendant's version of the events leading to his claim of consent. There are a few other miscellaneous exceptions.

Much of the debate about rape victim shield laws has centered on the attempt to define precisely those situations in which fairness and due process demand that the defendant be allowed to introduce sexual history evidence. Professor Berger has written a comprehensive article defining seven particular types of evidence that, subject to judicial findings of relevance and fairness, the defendant ought to be allowed to introduce. Other writers have argued that a man accused of rape may delve into the victim's sexual history in far fewer instances. It is not the purpose of this Article to become involved in the debate over which of these various situations brings the due process clause into play and compels the admissibility of sexual behavior evidence. Such an approach rests on the assumption that the state has the constitutional authority to limit the defendant's introduction of evidence of the victim's sexual history. Berger, for example, states as an axiom that legislatures have the power to bar certain evidence as irrelevant and inadmissible in a trial and therefore can completely exclude evidence of sexual behavior by declaring it irrelevant. In marvelously circular reasoning, she cites the rape shield statutes themselves as the only support for this proposition. She, like most other authors, then discusses how this power of the state can be limited by the due process clause: in certain compelling situations a court must allow the defendant to present testimony excluded by statute.

The power of the state to legislate is limited, however, by more than due process concepts of fairness. Criminal defendants have been guaranteed numerous rights by the fourth, fifth, and sixth amendments, and states may not infringe upon them regardless of general legislative power. A state may decide in general that the statements of a party to a lawsuit are admissible, but, because of the protections of the fifth amendment, this determination cannot extend to statements coerced from a criminal defendant. Although the state may have the power to create a small claims court in which civil disputes are settled without attorneys, that court cannot try misdemeanor cases because of the sixth amendment guarantee of counsel. The power to determine the admissibility of evidence does not give the states the ability to permit introduction of evidence seized in warrantless searches in violation of the fourth amendment.

David J. Karp, *Evidence of Propensity and Probability in Sex Offense Cases and Other Cases*
70 CHI.-KENT. L. REV. 15 (1994)[40]

Public attention has been focused on this issue by the William Kennedy Smith case in Florida. As everyone knows, the case involved a sexual assault prosecution, in which the court excluded evidence that the defendant had engaged in sexual

---

[40] Reprinted by permission.

assaults against a number of other women.

However, the proposal for reform in this area pre-dates that particular case. It initially appeared in February of 1991 in bills introduced by Representative Susan Molinari and Senator Robert Dole. The bills proposed a general rule of admissibility in sexual assault and child molestation cases for evidence that the defendant has committed offenses of the same type on other occasions. The same proposal has subsequently been introduced in a number of other bills. These include the two violent crime bills that President Bush transmitted to 8131*16 the 102d Congress, and the proposed "Sexual Assault Prevention Act of 1992."

*   *   *

. . . I think it would be useful, as a kind of reality check, to describe two rape cases in which courts excluded evidence of this type under existing rules.

The first case is *People v. Sanza*, from New York state in 1986. The evidence in that case indicated that Sanza raped and murdered Theresa Cha when she came to meet her husband in the building where Sanza worked. Among other evidence, Sanza was in the building at the right time, and was seen wearing the victim's ring by his sister within a few hours of the crime. On the day after the killing, he ransacked the apartment where he was staying with his sister, took over $1,000 in jewelry and other items, and never returned. Another person also saw Sanza wearing the victim's ring, and observed scratches or a bruise on his arm, which Sanza explained away with a false story. Blood of the same type as the victim's was found on Sanza's boots, which he left at his sister's apartment.

The police subsequently found Sanza in Florida, where he had pleaded guilty to three other rapes. In the prosecution of Sanza for raping and murdering Theresa Cha, the government offered evidence of these other rapes. They involved some specific similarities to the charged offense, including the theft or attempted theft of jewelry in all instances. The trial court allowed the victims of Sanza's other rapes to testify concerning those crimes at the trial because the victim of the charged offense, having been murdered, was unavailable to identify her assailant.

The appellate court reversed Sanza's conviction for rape and murder because of the admission of this evidence. The court concluded that the evidence of the earlier offenses "demonstrated a propensity to commit rape" but "proved nothing about our case" because the similarities to the earlier offenses were " 'hardly "unique' or 'uncommon' in rape cases."

The second case is *People v. Key*, a California case from 1984. In that case, the evidence indicated that when the victim was driving home at 2:30 a.m., Key drove next to her and said one of her wheels was coming off. When she stopped, Key choked her and held a knife to her throat, pulled her into his car, and forced her to perform oral sex on him as he drove to his sister's apartment, where he raped her twice. Key claimed in his defense that the victim willingly came to his sister's apartment and had consensual sex with him there.

Key had prior convictions for assault with intent to commit rape, indecent assault, and assault with a deadly weapon, involving three separate victims. When Key raised his defense of consent, the victim of one of his earlier assaults was allowed to testify about Key's crime against her, which also involved a ruse, choking, threatening with a knife, and forced oral sex.

The appellate court reversed Key's conviction because of the admission of this evidence. The court stated: "The only effect of the prior act evidence in this case is to allow it to bolster the witness' credibility. While this would seem to be a socially acceptable purpose, it does not comport with the applicable statutory and decisional law."

To the average person, I think the results in these cases would appear strange, if not outrageous. The type of legislative reform I will be discussing would greatly reduce the likelihood of such cases in the future. . . .

The Proposed Rules

The legislative proposal would add three new rules to the Federal Rules of Evidence. The first of these, proposed Rule 413, would apply to sexual assault cases. The basic rule of admissibility, set out in subdivision (a) of the rule, reads as follows: "In a criminal case in which the defendant is accused of an offense of sexual assault, evidence of the defendant's commission of another offense or offenses of sexual assault is admissible, and may be considered for its bearing on any matter to which it is relevant."

Proposed Rule 414 states a parallel principle for criminal cases involving child molestation: Evidence that the defendant committed offenses of the same type on other occasions would be admissible. Proposed Rule 415 makes the same rules applicable in civil cases. Hence, for example, in a civil suit for damages by a rape victim, evidence of the defendant's commission of rapes on other occasions would be admissible.

All of the proposed rules include certain safeguards for the defendant. The prosecutor — or the plaintiff in a civil case — would be required to disclose the evidence of the uncharged offenses to the defendant, including statements of witnesses or a summary of the substance of any testimony that is expected to be offered. This prevents unfair surprise and ensures that the defendant will have an opportunity to prepare any response or rebuttal.

The following points should be noted concerning the interpretation and application of these rules:

> First, the proposed rules of admissibility mean what they say. Evidence admitted under the rules could be considered for its bearing on any matter to which it is relevant. This includes questions of the defendant's propensity or disposition to commit sex crimes. Evidence Rule 404(b)'s prohibition of "character" evidence would be superseded in this context.

> Second, these rules are rules of admissibility, and not mandatory rules of admission. The general standards of the rules of evidence would apply to evidence offered under these rules, including the limitations of hearsay evidence, and the authority of the court to exclude relevant evidence under Rule 403. However, the rules would eliminate in sex offense cases the special restrictions on evidence of uncharged acts, where the acts are

crimes of the same type as the charged offense. The analysis statement for the proposed Sexual Assault Prevention Act explained the effect of this change as follows:

Evidence admissible pursuant to these rules would remain subject to the normal authority of the court to exclude evidence pursuant to F.R.E. 403 if the evidence's probative value is "substantially outweighed by the danger of unfair prejudice" or other adverse effects noted in that rule.

It is not expected, however, that evidence admissible pursuant to proposed Rules 413–15 would often be excluded on the basis of Rule 403. Rather, the effect of the new rules is to put evidence of uncharged offenses in sexual assault and child molestation cases on the same footing as other types of evidence that are not subject to a special exclusionary rule. The presumption is in favor of admission. The underlying legislative judgment is that the sort of evidence that is admissible pursuant to proposed Rules 413–15 is typically relevant and probative, and that its probative value is normally not outweighed by any risk of prejudice or other adverse considerations.

Finally, the standard of proof with respect to uncharged offenses under the new rules would be governed by the Supreme Court's decision in Huddleston v. United States. In Huddleston, the Supreme Court held that information about uncharged offenses may be admitted conditionally, and that such offenses may properly be considered so long as a jury could reasonably conclude by a preponderance that the offenses occurred. While the case was directly concerned with admission under Rule 404(b), its reasoning on these points is also applicable to the proposed new rules for sex offense cases.

II. Arguments for the Proposed Rules

The proposal of these rules presupposes that they will be more effective than the current rules in promoting accurate fact-finding and achieving just results. What are the policy considerations supporting this view? Let's start with common sense.

One obvious ground is considerations of probability. The defense in a rape case will claim that the police or victim fingered the wrong man, or that the victim consented and then made up a false charge, or that the claim that a rape occurred is a complete fabrication. If the direct evidence of guilt is not conclusive, there may be no adequate basis for excluding these possibilities.

Evidence that the defendant has committed sexual assaults on other occasions, however, often puts an entirely different light on the matter. It would be quite a coincidence if a person who just happened to be a chronic rapist was falsely or mistakenly implicated in a later crime of the same type. In conjunction with the direct evidence of guilt, knowledge of the defendant's past behavior may foreclose reasonable doubt as to guilt in a case that would otherwise be inconclusive.

The second common sense ground for admitting and considering this type of evidence is the ground that the existing rules most strongly condemn — the inference concerning propensity or disposition. If we put aside preconceptions for the moment, however, the inference is certainly not an unreasonable one.

Ordinary people do not commit outrages against others because they have relatively little inclination to do so, and because any inclination in that direction is suppressed by moral inhibitions and fear of the practical risks associated with the commission of crimes. A person with a history of rape or child molestation stands on a different footing. His past conduct provides evidence that he has the combination of aggressive and sexual impulses that motivates the commission of such crimes, that he lacks effective inhibitions against acting on these impulses, and that the risks involved do not deter him. A charge of rape or child molestation has greater plausibility against a person with such a background.

In addition to these general grounds, the statements supporting the legislative proposal have pointed to the strength of the public interest in admitting all significant evidence of guilt in sex offense cases. This reflects in part the typically secretive nature of such crimes, and resulting lack of neutral witnesses in most cases; the difficulty of stopping rapists and child molesters because of the reluctance of many victims to report the crime or testify; and the gravity of the danger to the public if a rapist or child molester remains at large.

In cases involving adult victims, the issue of consent is a further reason. In violent crimes other than sexual assaults, there is rarely any colorable defense that the defendant's conduct was not criminal because of consent by the victim. The accused mugger does not claim that the victim freely handed over his wallet as a gift. In contrast, claims are regularly heard in rape cases that the victim engaged in consensual sex with the defendant and then falsely accused him. In such instances, knowledge that the defendant has committed rapes on other occasions is frequently critical in assessing the relative plausibility of these conflicting claims and accurately deciding cases that would otherwise become unresolvable swearing matches.

In child molestation cases, the importance of admitting similar crimes evidence is equally great, if not greater. Such cases regularly present the need to rely on the testimony of child victim-witnesses whose credibility can readily be attacked in the absence of substantial corroboration. In this context, the public interest in admitting all significant evidence that will illumine the credibility of the charge and any denial by the defense is truly compelling.

What can be said on the other side of the issue? Let me start by addressing the three standard justifications for restricting evidence of uncharged acts.

One ground is the need to provide fair notice to the defendant concerning the matters he will have to respond to at trial. The proposed rules meet this concern by requiring full disclosure to the defendant of the evidence that will be offered in support of the uncharged offenses. This is more than the defendant would be entitled to in connection with a formally charged offense.

The second standard rationale for limiting evidence of uncharged acts is the need to establish reasonable limits on the scope of the proceedings. The concern here is diffusing the focus of the proceedings and distracting the trier through prolonged explorations of the defendant's personal history.

The proposed rules also incorporate features which are responsive to this concern. They do not indiscriminately admit evidence of all the bad things the defendant may have done in the course of his life, but only admit evidence of criminal offenses of the same type as those with which he is formally charged. This limits the number of incidents for which evidence may be offered. In addition, the requirement of similarity in kind to the charged offense tends to ensure that the uncharged acts will have a high degree of probative value, and will not be mere distractions from the main issues.

In some instances, the operation of the proposed rules will complicate the proceedings. However, even if a large number of incidents are brought in, the complexity will not exceed that of a trial in which several counts are charged, or a large number of uncharged incidents are brought in under existing rules. For example, in the Atlanta child-murders case in 1982, the defendant Wayne Williams was formally charged with two murders, but evidence linking him to ten other killings was also presented. Similarly, if the defendant in a rape case has passed through life leaving a trail of women who say that he raped them, that fact is singular enough to justify the time required for presenting it to the jury.

The third standard rationale for the existing restriction is the concern over prejudice. The claim here, of course, is not just that admission of evidence of uncharged offenses increases the probability of conviction. That point is true, but admission of any other persuasive evidence of guilt has the same effect.

Rather, the "prejudice" rationale maintains that this type of evidence carries an unacceptable risk of convicting the innocent. This is premised on the view that jurors are likely to accord prior offenses more weight than they rationally merit as evidence of guilt, and are likely to return unwarranted convictions based on antagonism against the defendant that results from knowledge of his other offenses.

There is, however, no means of determining a priori whether particular categories of evidence are likely to be more prejudicial than probative. The lesson must be learned from experience, and in the context of sex offense prosecutions, the lesson of experience seems to point in the other direction. Courts in the United States have traditionally been inclined to admit evidence of other sex crimes by the defendant in sex offense prosecutions. In some states, this has involved the formal recognition of special case law rules of admissibility in sex offense cases.

Special rules of this sort have become less common in the past few decades, in part because of the widespread adoption of codified evidence rules that appear to leave no room for them. However, the same practical result is often achieved by stretching the existing rules. The contemporary edition of Wigmore's Evidence has described this tendency as follows:

There is a strong tendency in prosecutions for sex offenses to admit evidence of the accused's sexual proclivities. Do such decisions show that the general rule against the use of propensity evidence against an accused is not honored in sex offense prosecutions? We think so. . . . Some states and courts have . . . forthrightly and expressly recognized a "lustful disposition" or sexual proclivity exception to the general rule barring the use of character evidence against an accused. . . . Jurisdictions that do not expressly recognize a lustful disposition exception may effectively recognize such an exception by expansively interpreting in prosecutions for sex offenses various well-established exceptions to the character evidence rule.

Louis M. Natali, Jr & R. Stephen Stigall, *"Are You Going To Arraign His Whole Life?": How Sexual Propensity Evidence Violates the Due Process Clause*
28 Loy. U. Chi. L.J. 1 (1996)[41]

Rules 413–415 each state in mandatory language that evidence of other offenses of sexual assault or child molestation is admissible. Thus, the new rules require, in criminal and civil cases involving sexual assault and child molestation, admission of proffered evidence of the accused's or civil defendant's commission of other offenses of sexual assault or child molestation. Because of the mandatory nature of the rules, in sexual assault and child molestation cases, the Federal Rules' general prohibition on the admission of character evidence to show disposition to commit offenses does not apply.

Since the rules provide that propensity evidence may be considered for any matter to which it is relevant, it is clear that Rules 413–415 automatically invite introduction of prior offenses of sexual assault or child molestation. The federal prosecutor will proffer such evidence solely for the purpose of showing that, because the accused previously committed acts of sexual assault or child molestation, the accused is a person of dangerous and criminal character, a person likely to have sexually assaulted the victim or molested a child. Although character is relevant, as Justices Jackson and Cardozo noted, it has traditionally been excluded on policy grounds embedded in the fundamental notions of due process. . . .

. . . By requiring the admission of propensity evidence, the rules prevent a fundamentally fair trial, and thus violate due process, for several reasons. As the drafters of Rule 404 of the Federal Rules of Evidence recognized, the basic nature of propensity evidence prevents a constitutionally fair trial. If the federal prosecutor proffers evidence showing that the accused is by propensity more likely to have committed the sexual assault or act of child molestation in the case, jurors will likely credit the evidence with more weight than it deserves. Such evidence so over-persuades jurors that they will lose their impartiality and pre-judge the accused as one with a bad general character. Therefore, jurors exposed to propensity evidence more readily convict the accused. This denies the accused a "fair opportunity to defend against a particular charge." Moreover, "it is fundamental to American jurisprudence that "a defendant must be tried for what he did, not for who he is." '

The new rules also impair a fair trial because they overly burden the accused. The prosecutor, armed with the new rules as ammunition, will introduce evidence of prior offenses, thus forcing the accused to continuously mount defenses against such evidence. It should be remembered that the rules permit any type of evidence regarding sexual assault or child molestation. The propensity evidence does not have to be a prior conviction. Moreover, the rules do not restrict the evidence to a certain time frame. Thus, the rules permit a prosecutor to proffer testimony that

---

[41] Reprinted by permission

the defendant sexually assaulted or molested another person more than ten years in the past. The accused must counter the prosecutor's damning evidence seriatim, preventing him from mounting an adequate defense to the sexual assault or child molestation charge that is the subject of the trial. Further, not only is admission of propensity evidence overly burdensome, it also blurs the issues in the case. Rather than focusing on the sexual assault or child molestation at issue in the trial, the propensity evidence will redirect the jury's attention from the determination of the actual issue in the case.

In addition, the new rules prevent a fair trial by vitiating a district court's discretion to admit evidence regarding the commission of other offenses of sexual assault or child molestation. By mandating that prior acts evidence is admissible, the rules prohibit a district court from balancing the probativeness and prejudice of such evidence as permitted in Rule 403 of the Federal Rules of Evidence. Thus, the accused in cases involving sexual assault and child molestation does not receive potential fairness protections, because the rules are not subject to the district court's discretion to balance the potential prejudice and probativeness of the propensity evidence.

Regardless of whether the rules are subject to Rule 403 balancing, they needlessly and unduly prejudice the person accused in sexual assault and child molestation cases, in absolute contravention of Rule 404 of the Federal Rules of *Evidence.* Such evidence impresses upon the jurors the notion that the accused is a "wretch." Thus, there is a great risk that jurors will incorrectly decide a case because the jury will find the accused's prior acts repugnant. Propensity evidence tends to poison the jurors' minds, preventing them from being impartial triers of fact by generating hostility against the accused. This is especially true in sexual assault and child molestation cases. The Chicago Jury Project provided empirical confirmation of this observation. In that study, researchers discovered that jurors classified sex offenses as reprehensible, especially if the victim was a young child. Subsequent research has confirmed the Chicago Jury Project findings.

C.   OTHER EXAMPLES OF LEGAL RELEVANCE

1.   Habit and Custom

M.C. Slough, *Relevancy Unraveled, Part II*
5 U. KAN. L. REV. 404, 444–49 (1957)[42]

Habit and Custom.

If a collateral fact is to be considered relevant, it must tend to establish the fact in issue. It is enough that the inference to be drawn be a fairly possible one; and if it makes the material proposition more likely, it will appreciably advance the inquiry. Accepting this premise, one must agree that evidence of a well-constructed habit has probative value. Character evidence is panoramic and faces exclusion

---

[42] Reprinted with permission.

because is overemphasizes the importance of disposition and general traits; habit is specific and emphasizes regular practice. Habit "describes one's regular response to a repeated specific situation."

Loose language has mangled a simple concept. When habit evidence is excluded, so often one discovers the court speaking in terms of "habits of care" or "habits of carelessness," and in reality these so-called habits mirror little more than general disposition. There is no doubting that confusion will exist when decisions fail to draw elementary distinctions between habit and character.

Habit will be of probative value when it denotes a mechanical course of action. Proof of a course of action or dealing, carried out on a now-and-then basis, should be rejected, because evidential value is weak unless there is some indication of an invariable regularity. For example, in a negligence case, if evidence is offered showing that the deceased was a careful painstaking driver who had been awarded three certificates for safe driving, should it be received? The answer should be in the negative inasmuch as the proof offered points only to a general course of conduct; this is character, not habit. On the other hand, if proof were to indicate that the deceased had habitually approached a certain crossing in a careful manner, there would be reason to infer that the course of conduct was ingrained. This would be reliable habit evidence and should be received. Much will depend upon the circumstances of the individual case in determining whether or not sufficient regularity exists.

Since habit evidence is of far greater probative worth than character evidence, it is better able to withstand objections rooted in policy considerations. Of course the usual dangers are present, but the weighing of factors is a function that should remain in the discretion of the trial judge. If the habit is not sufficiently regular or uniform, and not tied specifically to the conduct involved in the individual case, then it may well be rejected as confusing and prejudicial. Although decisions are far from being in accord, the numerical weight of authority as of this date would admit reliable habit evidence, particularly in the absence of eyewitness testimony.

*   *   *

As was true in the case of receiving character evidence, courts are in dispute concerning the importance of eyewitness testimony. In a substantial number of jurisdictions habit evidence is excluded when eyewitnesses were present, and all too frequently this is a rule of thumb fashioned without reference to the competency and veracity of eyewitnesses available. In a very few jurisdictions, proof of habit has been received despite the presence of eyewitnesses, and undoubtedly a majority of text writers have concurred in this view. If eyewitnesses have had ample opportunity to observe the occurrence in question, and are able to give a relatively unbiased account of their observations, there is little or no need for admitting habit evidence. However, it seems preposterous to exclude strong habit evidence when witness' recollections are hazy or when these same recollections are shaped by bias and friendship for one of the litigants. How valid is eyewitness testimony, when the only testimony available is the prejudiced account of an employee? Furthermore, if one of the parties to the action is deceased, will his adversary be considered a competent eyewitness so as to bar use of habit evidence? The precedents of exclusion have never given adequate response to these questions, and more often than not, have avoided them altogether.

*   *   *

Custom also denotes human action, but it is the action of a group in accordance with an established routine or discipline. As an evidentiary factor, custom is superior to habit, because it is likely to be more stylized and regimented, thus more invariable than individual conduct. Furthermore it is the product of concerted planning, and is more often than not, the by-product of efficiency. It is no wonder then that courts are inclined to be lenient in receiving evidence of custom while relegating habit evidence to a plane of secondary importance.

NOTES AND QUESTIONS

1. Would evidence of "accident proneness" be admissible under Rule 406? Compare Anthony J. Sebok, *The Fall and Rise of Blame in American Tort Law*, 68 BROOKLYN L. REV. 1031 (2003) (discussing theory that most accidents are caused by people who are accident prone).

2. Assuming that habit evidence is admissible, how would you go about proving it? Could you rely upon proof of specific instances of conduct? *United States v. Serrata*, 425 F.3d 886, 906 (10th Cir. 2005); *Perrin v. Anderson*, 784 F.2d 1040 (10th Cir. 1986).

3. Is it possible to develop the habit of committing political murder? *See United States v. Sampol*, 636 F.2d 621, 656 n.21 (D.C. Cir. 1980).

4. For an excellent example of organizational habit, see *Martin v. Thrifty Rent A Car*, 1998 U.S. App. LEXIS 8259, 14–18 (6th Cir. Apr. 23, 1998); *In re Swine Flu Immunization Products Liability Litigation*, 533 F. Supp. 567 (D. Colo. 1980)

5. In a malpractice suit against a hospital alleging injuries incurred as a result of participation in a hospital research study, may the defense introduce evidence of its "routine practice" of obtaining consent from participants in the study? *See Wetherill v. University of Chicago*, 570 F. Supp. 1124 (N.D. Ill. 1983).

6. Oftentimes, evidence of alcohol consumption is proffered through this doctrine. *See Tommy's Elbow Room, Inc. v. Kavorkian*, 727 P.2d 1038 (Alaska 1986). For example, as probative of negligence, may evidence be introduced that a worker regularly stored a cooler of beer at his place of employment? *See Loughan v. Firestone Tire & Rubber Co.*, 749 F.2d 1519 (11th Cir. 1985). How about evidence that someone regularly drinks a six-pack of beer on weekends? *See Keltner v. Ford Motor Co.*, 748 F.2d 1265 (8th Cir. 1984).

7. In a civil rights action, should the court admit as proof of cover-up evidence of a police department's "code of silence" concerning the use of excessive force? *See Maynard v. Sayles*, 817 F.2d 50 (8th Cir. 1987).

2. Subsequent Remedial Measures

M.C. Slough, *Relevancy Unraveled, Part III*
5 U. KAN. L. REV. 675, 705–09 (1957)[43]

Subsequent Precautions and Remedial Measures

Following an accident a property owner is likely to repair or improve old defects and faults, or he may substitute a new mechanism for an old one. Realizing the inadequacy of former precautions he may install the latest safety device or institute a change in operating rules to meet the challenge of changing conditions. A manufacturer, guided by his will to compete and to offer a satisfactory product, may modify, or even radically alter original designs. Improving a condition may amount to an acknowledgement that the condition was capable of causing harm, but it is not an outright admission of lack of due care, hence the will to improve should not create an automatic inference of prior negligence. Baron Bram well was most emphatic when he stated his case against the admissibility of evidence of subsequent repair: "People do not furnish evidence against themselves simply by adopting a new plan in order to prevent there currence of an accident. I think that a proposition to the contrary would be barbarous. It would be . . . to hold that, because the world gets wiser as it gets older, therefore it was foolish before."

Since Bramwell's day an astounding majority of courts, both English and American, have rejected evidence of subsequent repair or improvement when offered to prove negligence or culpable conduct in connection with the event. . . . Grounds for exclusion are not always clearly stated in the many legal opinions touching the question, hence one is not always certain whether proof is rejected for lack of relevancy or for some other purpose. In many instances, evidence of subsequent precaution will be logically relevant, creating a fairly possible inference that the defendant had acted unreasonably. In others, the inference of negligence or admission to such, would be slight and equivocal, stressing hindsight rather than foresight. As ably put by Professor Trautman: "At best the question of logical relevancy is a variable depending upon the circumstances of each case."

* * *

Certainly the modern trend of judicial opinion justifies exclusion on grounds of policy, because admitting evidence of this nature would prove to be a deterrent against taking future precautions and would discourage the prudent implementation of safety measures. While recognizing the vulnerability of verbal admissions, a line must be drawn somewhere, and the law wisely chooses to encourage social betterment by blotting out reference to socially desirable conduct. . . .

The role of the rule of exclusion must not be oversimplified, or for that matter, overstated. It must be remembered that the rule operates only when evidence of subsequent precaution is offered to create an inference of negligence or the equivalent. The same evidence may be highly relevant upon another issue, in which

---

[43] Reprinted with permission.

case policy considerations may be relegated to a minor status. Where evidence of subsequent precautions is used otherwise than as an admission of negligence, the exclusionary rule is subject to exception and proof may be admitted accompanied by a proper qualifying instruction.

Evidence of subsequent repairs by a defendant is admissible to prove his dominion or control over the property or mechanism causing the injury. Ordinarily a landlord will not make repairs upon property which he does not control, nor will a manufacturer or business man promulgate regulations concerning an activity beyond his control. Therefore if one repairs a stairway or a sidewalk or a machine, it seems valid to infer the existence of control at the moment of injury or accident. Barring the fact that there may be ready proof of control based on other circumstances, there are few policy considerations which would deny use of evidence of subsequent precaution.

Evidence is similarly admissible by way of exception to show a duty on the part of the defendant to repair to protect against accidents. The rule of exclusion is relaxed to permit explanation of a photograph, particularly where the defendant has introduced a photograph of the scene of accident. Reference to subsequent repairs is permissible for purposes of identifying the defect in question, most notably when there is dispute as to the existence or location of the defect. If deemed necessary to establish the cause of accident or injury, evidence of later repair is relevant and admissible. Proof of change is sanctioned where an issue is presented as to the practicality of a precaution, especially where the defendant has asserted that an innovation is impractical.

The force of the rule of exclusion is weakened by a considerable body of authority which will allow evidence of change in conditions or proof of repair for the purpose of showing the condition of the premises or instrumentality prior to or at the time of injury. When the defendant disputes the existence of a claimed defect, the plaintiff by way of counterattack, may submit proof of repair as a circumstance indicating that the defect did in fact exist. Opportunities for circumventing the purpose of the rule are legion, and it is quite evident that admission or exclusion will be judged on the basis of subtle trial maneuvers. By the process of exaggeration and placing undue emphasis upon the importance of physical defects, the plaintiff may force the defendant to dispute his contentions, thus paving the way for admission of proof of subsequent repair. If issues pertaining to prior condition and defect are clearly and honestly in dispute, the trial judge may exercise his discretion in favor of admission, but resort to appellate precedent should never be accepted as a solution. Unless the trial judge can discern the motives of trial strategists and appreciate the psychological impact of testimony presented, there is little need for perpetuating a rule of exclusion. Enfeebling exceptions are known to point up the invalidity of a general rule.

FLAMINIO v. HONDA MOTOR CO.
733 F.2d 463 (7th Cir. 1984)

strict liability

POSNER, CIRCUIT JUDGE

    This appeal in a personal-injury diversity suit brings up a variety of interesting substantive and procedural questions. In 1978 a middle-aged man named Forrest Flaminio bought a "Gold Wing" motorcycle, a large and powerful touring motorcycle manufactured by the Honda Motor Company of Japan (Japanese Honda) and distributed in the United States by its wholly owned subsidiary, American Honda Motor Company (American Honda). The motorcycles are shipped from Japan partially assembled, but assembly is completed by the dealers to whom American Honda distributes the motorcycles rather than by American Honda itself. Three days after taking delivery, and shortly after a dinner at which he had one or two drinks, Flaminio was driving the motorcycle down a two-lane road at night when he came up behind a car traveling at about40 miles per hour. He passed it at a speed of somewhere between 50 and 70 m.p.h. (the speed limit was 50), and as he did so felt a vibration in the front end of the motorcycle. He tried to look at the front wheel to see what was wrong. This was an awkward maneuver because his feet were up on the motorcycle's "highway pegs" (supplied and installed by the motorcycle dealer rather than by either of the defendants), so that he was leaning backward. By his own admission the effort in this position to see the front wheel probably brought him up off the seat. In any event the motorcycle began to wobble uncontrollably and then it shot off the road and crashed, inflicting injuries that have left Flaminio a paraplegic.

    Joined by his wife, who is seeking to recover damages for loss of consortium, Flaminio sued Japanese Honda and American Honda, alleging that either the wobble was due to the defective design of the motorcycle, which should have been corrected, or the defendants should have warned users about the motorcycle's propensity to wobble.

*   *   *

    The issue with respect to the allegation of defective design is whether the district court erred in excluding evidence (consisting of two blueprints) that, the plaintiffs say, shows that after the accident Honda, in an effort to reduce wobble, made the struts ("front forks") that connect the Gold Wing's handlebars to its front wheel two millimeters thicker. Rule 407 of the Federal Rules of Evidence makes evidence of subsequent remedial measures "not admissible to prove negligence or culpable conduct in connection with the event," but adds:" This rule does not require the exclusion of evidence of subsequent measures when offered for another purpose, such as proving ownership, control, or feasibility of precautionary measures, if controverted, or impeachment." Flaminio argues that the blueprints were admissible under the exceptions for "proving . . . feasibility of precautionary measures, if controverted," and for impeaching the defendants' evidence. But the first of these exceptions is inapplicable because the defendants did not deny the feasibility of precautionary measures against wobble. Their argument was that there was a tradeoff between wobble and "weave," and that in designing the model on which

Flaminio was injured Japanese Honda had decided that weave was the greater danger because it occurs at high speeds and because the Gold Wing model — what motorcycle buffs call a "hog" — was designed for high speeds. The feasibility, as distinct from the net advantages, of reducing the danger of wobble was not in issue. As for the second exception, if the defendants had testified that they would never have thickened the struts on the Gold Wing the blueprints would have been impeaching. But the defendants offered no such testimony. Although any evidence of subsequent remedial measures might be thought to contradict and so in a sense impeach a defendant's testimony that he was using due care at the time of the accident, if this counted as "impeachment" the exception would swallow the rule.

Flaminio also argues that Rule 407 does not apply to strict liability cases. There is a conflict among circuits on the question. Most hold that it does.

*   *   *

. . . [W]e agree with the majority view that the rule does apply to strict liability cases. We are not persuaded by the purely semantic argument to the contrary that since "culpable conduct" is not the issue in such a case — the defendant is liable, at least prima facie, even if he is not blameworthy in the sense of being willful or negligent, provided that he caused the plaintiff's injury — the rule is inapplicable by its own terms. . . . A major purpose of Rule 407 is to promote safety by removing the disincentive to make repairs (or take other safety measures) after an accident that would exist if the accident victim could use those measures as evidence of the defendant's liability. One might think it not only immoral but reckless for an injurer, having been alerted by the accident to the existence of danger, not to take steps to correct the danger. But accidents are low-probability events. The probability of another accident may be much smaller than the probability that the victim of the accident that has already occurred will sue the injurer and, if permitted, will make devastating use at trial of any measures that the injurer may have taken since the accident to reduce the danger.

The analysis is not fundamentally affected by whether the basis of liability is the defendant's negligence or his product's defectiveness or inherent dangerousness. In either case, if evidence of subsequent remedial measures is admissible to prove liability, the incentive to take such measures will be reduced. It is true that when liability is strict the defendant may have no incentive to take subsequent remedial measures even if Rule 407 would be applicable if he did. The accident may have been unavoidable at reasonable cost by taking greater care, and if so the defendant would have no incentive to take greater care. But he would still be liable for having caused the accident — that is what strict liability means. *See* Shavell, *Strict Liability Versus Negligence*, 9 J. Legal Stud. 1(1980). The distinction is often stated in the following way: the focus of negligence is on the defendant's conduct, but the focus of strict liability is on the dangerousness of the product regardless of the defendant's conduct. That is why, when the standard is strict liability, a defendant may be held liable even though he was blameless, as in the case we put earlier where a component had a defect that the manufacturer of the final product — and defendant in the product liability suit — could not have discovered at reasonable cost. But this distinction does not justify a refusal to apply Rule 407 in product cases. In those cases where the defendant would have no incentive to take remedial measures anyway, because the accident was unavoidable, Rule 407 is academic; there will be, by assumption, no subsequent remedial measures. But in other cases, as should be apparent from our earlier remarks on the meaning of strict liability in products cases, the injurer would be held liable on a theory of strict liability even though the accident could have been avoided at reasonable cost by taking more care. Especially in a product case, the accident may have been readily avoidable either by eliminating some defect or by warning the consumer of some inherent danger, and in such a case the failure to apply Rule 407 might deter subsequent remedial measures just as much as in a negligence case. . . . This is more than conjecture; the premise of Flaminio's offer of proof was that the accident was caused by a defect that could be and was later eliminated by a minor change in the design of the motorcycle. The policy of Rule 407 is applicable.

NOTES AND QUESTIONS

1. In 1997, Congress amended Rule 407 to provide "that evidence of subsequent remedial measures may not be used to prove 'a defect in a product, a defect in a product's design, or a need for a warning or instruction.' Advisory Comm. Note to 1997 Amendment. This language codified the outcome in *Flaminio* applying Rule 407 to products liability cases.

2. *Flaminio* is also one of very few federal cases to discuss the interaction between the Federal Rules and the Erie doctrine. *See* 733 F.2d at 470–72.

3. Would Rule 407 apply to the following situation: Plaintiff buys a new truck. Shortly afterwards, the manufacturer incorporates a different gas tank design in its new model. Later, plaintiff is in an accident that he attributes to faulty gas-tank design. *See Chase v. General Motors Corp.*, 856 F.2d 17, 21–22 (4th Cir. 1988), *Arceneaux v. Texaco, Inc.*, 623 F.2d 924 (5th Cir. 1980), *cert. denied*, 450 U.S. 928 (1981).

4. Would Rule 407 apply to statements made in a post-accident memorandum describing improvements that might prevent future similar mishaps?

5. May evidence of subsequent repairs be offered by the defense as probative of plaintiff's contributory negligence? *See Public Service Co. v. Bath Iron Works Corp.*, 773 F.2d 783 (7th Cir. 1985). May the rule apply to actions taken by a nonparty to establish an alternative source of negligence? *See Koonce v. Quaker Safety Products*, 798 F.2d 700 (5th Cir. 1986).

3. Compromise Offers and Settlements

M.C. Slough, *Relevancy Unraveled, Part III*
5 U. Kan. L. Rev. 675, 718–20 (1957)[44]

Offers of Compromise or Settlement

This area of the law of evidence clearly delineates present day confusion over the significance of relevancy and policy considerations. The great majority of case authorities are in agreement that a compromise offered to furnish money or any other valuable thing is inadmissible to prove liability. Concomitant with this position, courts also agree that evidence of a person's accepting or promising to accept a sum of money or equivalent, shall be inadmissible. But at this juncture harmony splinters and disintegrates.

inadmissible

Wigmore tends to treat the question as one of relevancy, and there is no doubting that his advocacy has had tremendous effect upon the judicial strain. Some offers to buy peace will have little or no relevance in creating an inference of liability, and this is especially true when the offer is small in comparison with damages claimed. On the other hand, a generous offer to make good for eighty per cent of losses incurred will be tantamount to a confession of guilt. It appears absurd to argue that the latter offer is irrelevant when even a griffin would grasp the inference. In any event, acceptance of the relevancy theory spells a constant search for motivation, and who will determine the motivation behind the middle-sized offer?

A second theory is predicated upon contract. This theory rests upon the basis of contract, express or implied, that the negotiations are "without prejudice." It doubtless germinated in the practice of English business men and lawyers of inserting the words "without prejudice" in letters involving business and legal transactions. The precautionary device assured the writer that his letter would be excluded if offered as evidence and further prevented any reference to facts admitted during the course of negotiations. Too precise and too British for home consumption, the contract idea has found little in the way of heart-warming acceptance in American legal circles. As subtly phrased by an American jurist: "Aside from other objections to its perpetuation as a criterion it puts an entirely unwarranted premium on familiarity with a legal nicety not commonly encountered upon laymen."

A recognizable trend of judicial opinion points toward acceptance of a third theory of exclusion which rejects evidence of compromise on the basis of privilege, a rationale conceived in the social desirability of promoting amicable settlements of claims in dispute. Though not expressed in deliberate terms, this is the view championed . . . by an increasing tide of text authorities. Public policy is at the root of this concept, and logically the privilege rule should extend to all offers of compromise which would not be classed as outright admissions of liability. The privilege would also cover situations where defendant has made a settlement or compromise with third persons, not parties to the instant suit.

---

[44] Reprinted with permission.

4. Liability Insurance

M.C. Slough, *Relevancy Unraveled, Part III*
5 U. KAN. L. REV. 675, 710–18 (1957)[45]

Liability Insurance and the Personal Injury Action

As a matter of rule and general principle, evidence that the defendant was insured against liability is inadmissible as tending to prove negligence or other wrongdoing. Presumably, the fact that indemnity insurance is carried by one of the parties is clearly irrelevant, at least to the extent that it will inject collateral issues, prejudice and confuse the jury. There is slight danger that the feeling of security engendered by insurance "might tend to make the insured less careful, i.e., to evidence a motive for recklessness"; but it hardly seems rational to assume that one will relax standards of due care and court self-destruction because of an awareness of an insured property interest. In reality, experience denotes that the more responsible and trustworthy drivers are insured, whereas the irresponsible are known to peregrinate without benefit of company protection. Therefore it is highly unlikely that jurors will be impressed or "hood-winked" into believing that the insurance contract will give rise to reckless urges. Undoubtedly the chief reason for exclusion is a fear that the issue of insurance will motivate the jury to be reckless in awarding damages, thus to obscure the true basis for the verdict. If all jurors were born yesterday and were equipped with blank minds, the theoretical brilliance of this exclusionary rule would escape uncomely criticism. Fifty years ago when the principle was in the process of gestation very few motorists felt a need for insurance, and it is reasonable to assume that most jurors of that era were not given to thinking in terms of insurable interests. In these mid-century years it is safe to assume that seventy-five per cent of all motor vehicles registered in this nation are insured in one way or another, and it is also safe to assume that the average juror is aware of the role insurance plays in tort litigation.

Adherence to the rule as a fixed principle of law is in itself an admission that the courts do not choose to be aware of what everyone knows. It is conceivable that mention of the forbidden word will inject a so-called "collateral issue" into the case and consequent loss of time may be a measurable factor. Yet minutes consumed in portraying the insurance picture cannot be compared with hours and days lost arguing esoteric points of order respecting prejudice and good faith, not to mention the burdensome expense of new trials and crowded dockets. The law is fashioned to enhance justice, not to stifle it.

*   *   *

What figures as the greatest annoyance is the fact that counsel, from voir dire examination to closing argument, is never sure of the stand he should take. Even a most careful preparation of the case cannot guard against inadvertent references to insurance. And trial judges, wary of reversal, are inclined to be supersensitive to any mention of the word. Aiming to cure matters by instruction, they tend to

---

[45] Reprinted with permission.

accentuate the problem and only succeed in kindling curiosity. Subjecting the judicial system to psychological torment of this genre seems most unnecessary, particularly when one discerns that he is rendering fealty to an archaic legal principle. . . .

The impracticability of the rule of exclusion is best illustrated through the exceptions that rob its strength. It has [been] observed that evidence of insurance is made inadmissible only "as tending to prove negligence or wrongdoing." Consequently if relevancy can be justified on another basis, the exclusionary rule is discarded for lack of application. Facts tending to impeach a witness, pointing up bias or interest, may generally be established even though they disclose that the defendant is insured. However it will usually be necessary for the trial judge to instruct the jury to consider such testimony as bearing on the witness' credibility only. It may be shown that a civil engineer called by the defendant made his measurements at the scene of the accident at the direction of the insurance company. The interest of an attorney or claims adjuster testifying with relation to investigation of the claim may be brought to light. Questions aimed at clarifying the status of a medical expert witness are properly admitted for the purpose of disclosing bias.

When reference to insurance is an integral part of an otherwise admissible declaration, the whole is ordinarily admitted. Though courts very often rule that allusions to insurance must be omitted if such can be done without substantially impairing the natural force of the statement offered. Puzzling problems of admissibility are posed when the plaintiff offers statements allegedly made by the defendant as admissions of liability. The defendant may have said: "Don't worry about that, I'm covered"; or he may have uttered a conciliatory remark such as: "I'm sorry, I'll try to get my company to pay for this"; or he may simply have mentioned insurance without undue elaboration, scarcely accenting liability in a verbal sense. Obviously no pat solution is feasible as the quality of the admission will be determined by the state of mind of the individual declarant. Standing naked and alone, the verbal utterance tells little, and in the long run much will depend upon the wisdom of the trial judge. He must determine the worth of the statement in terms of the setting in which it was made, leaning upon his knowledge of the human will and instinct.

The fact of insurance may be relevant and admissible on an issue of dominion or control of the offending instrumentality. It may properly be introduced to prove a master-servant relationship where defendant denies that he was the master. In this latter situation evidence of insurance coverage may solve questions of disputed responsibility. Where insurance is compulsory, it is often held that it is not error for plaintiff's counsel to elicit the fact that the defendant is insured. Nor would the general rule of exclusion have application where the defendant or his counsel voluntarily introduces the matter to the attention of the jury.

When the rule of exclusion is clearly manifested counsel knows that he cannot enter upon the subject of insurance when examining witnesses or presenting argument to the jury, unless he acts with benefit of exception. Yet on voir dire examination the play of interests is less openly reached. Counsel understands that a principle of fairness allows him to determine by interrogation whether prospective jurors are given to any concealed prejudices rooted in insurance associations or interests. Questions concerning insurance cannot be suppressed absolutely as it is not only the right, but the duty of counsel, to court and client, to uncover the truth.

Most jurisdictions allow the plaintiff to pursue some form of inquiry on voir dire, provided the inquiry is conducted in "good faith." However, the process of gisting the meaning of "good faith" from a scattered collection of appellate precedents is more often than not a futile task. There is much talk about "good faith," but no one has offered or can supply a concrete definition of the term. Presumably in most cases, once it is established that the defendant is insured, courts are willing to permit some probing with regard to insurance connections; though even here, the trial judge will be faced with the problem of discerning the plaintiff's motivation. Declaration of mistrial is undoubtedly in order where a verdict is excessive and counsel has deliberately and willfully undertaken to inform the jury that the defendant enjoyed insurance protection.

EVIDENCE CHALLENGE: Challenge yourself to learn more about this topic. Enter the following address into your browser to access Evidence Challenge and apply these concepts to realistic problems set in a virtual courtroom.
http://www.EvidenceChallenge.com. Additional purchase required.

Chapter V

THE HEARSAY RULES

"We come here to the greatest and most distinctive contribution of Anglo-American law (next after jury trial) to trial procedure."

> — John Henry Wigmore[1]

"You must not tell us what the soldier, or any other man, said, sir," interposed the judge, "it's not evidence."

> — Charles Dickens[2]

A. THE RULE AGAINST HEARSAY

Federal Rule of Evidence 802
The Rule Against Hearsay

Hearsay is not admissible unless any of the following provides otherwise:

- a federal statute;
- these rules; or
- other rules prescribed by the Supreme Court.

NOTES

1. Rule 802 codifies a common law doctrine that dates back to the late 17th century. For an excellent review of the doctrine's historical roots, see 5 WIGMORE, EVIDENCE § 1364 (3d ed. 1940).

2. Although judges sometimes rule that "self-serving" statements are inadmissible hearsay, the law of evidence says no such thing. *See, e.g., Gibbs v. State Farm Mutual Ins. Co.*, 544 F.2d 423, 428 (9th Cir. 1976). All evidence is "self-serving" in the sense that its proponent offers it for that purpose. If the evidence is an out-of-court statement, it either is or is not hearsay. Whether the statement is hearsay depends on how courts in that jurisdiction define hearsay. If the statement meets the hearsay definition, it is inadmissible unless it falls within one of many exceptions to the rule.

3. Likewise, contrary to popular misconception, a statement is not automatically hearsay merely because it was made outside the presence of the party against whom it is being offered. Nor is a statement made in the party's presence

---

[1] JOHN H. WIGMORE, EVIDENCE § 8c, at 277 (3d ed. 1940).

[2] CHARLES DICKENS, THE PICKWICK PAPERS, 414 (Dodd Mead & Co. 1944).

automatically non-hearsay. In each instance, the statement's status as hearsay depends upon the jurisdiction's formal hearsay definition.

B. RATIONALE FOR THE RULE

Carl C. Wheaton, *What Is Hearsay?*
46 Iowa L. Rev. 210, 219–22 (1961)[3]

The history of this rule sheds little light on the reasons for the exclusion of hearsay evidence. Behind the hearsay rule may be the fear that admission of hearsay would permit the operation of too many sources of inaccuracy, mistake, fraud, and untrustworthiness.

It has been suggested that the hearsay rule had its origin in the distrust of the jury's capacity to evaluate evidence. Professor Morgan very logically sees little to support this view. It is true that the rule excluding hearsay has developed during the existence of the jury system. However, hearsay was freely admitted in jury trials for nearly a century after juries began to obtain evidence from witnesses in court, and for another century it was used as corroborative evidence. An even more potent argument against this opinion of the origin of the hearsay rule is that the rule applies to trials without juries. Dean Ladd has pointed out that the protection of the jury cannot be a strong reason for excluding hearsay evidence since the rule rejecting hearsay applies also in equity cases. Both Professor Morgan and Dean Ladd appear to believe that the real purpose of the hearsay rule is the protection of the party against whom hearsay is offered.

The fact that the declarant was not under oath has been advanced as another reason for the rejection of hearsay evidence. As a ceremonial and religious symbol, it has been thought that the oath induces a special obligation to speak the truth. Furthermore, it may impress upon the witness the danger of criminal punishment for perjury. Dean McCormick has suggested that this may be an important reason for the hearsay rule. Other writers, however, believe that the fact that the declarant is not under oath has had little to do with the development of the hearsay rule. Dean Wigmore has said that the requirement of an oath is incidental and merely the ordinary accompaniment of any testimony given on the witness stand. The oath, then, counts for nothing if there is no opportunity to cross-examine the sworn witness. It has been pointed out that an affidavit is not ordinarily admissible to prove the facts sworn to. A carefully written statement, though sworn to by one who perceived the facts referred to in the statement, is no more admissible than an oral statement casually made to another person. It has been held that a report of evidence given under oath in one case cannot be offered in another proceeding in which the parties are not the same. This makes clear the fact that the absence of an oath is not a valid basis for excluding hearsay.

It has also been said that the reason for the hearsay rule is the lack of opportunity to observe the demeanor of the out-of-court declarant when he speaks. This, in turn, results in the loss of one method of determining the credibility of the

---

declarant. This reason, however, fails to account for the exclusion of written hearsay. The danger of inaccurate reporting of oral declarations has been given as a ground for excluding hearsay. Dean McCormick gives considerable weight to this ground, but Professor Tracy has said this cannot be a valid ground since the hearsay rule applies to written as well as oral declarations. Further, Professor Morgan has pointed out that testimony concerning an oral out-of-court declaration which is an element of a cause or defense is admitted, yet it is subject to the same danger of inaccurate reporting as an oral hearsay statement.

Another suggested argument for the hearsay rule is that the party against whom the hearsay evidence is offered is not confronted by the declarant. This argument should be valid, if at all, only in criminal cases. Dean Ladd has pointed out that, although one is confronted by a declarant, the evidence may still be objectionable if there is no opportunity to cross-examine the declarant. This makes clear that cross-examination and not confrontation is the real basis for the hearsay rule. Accordingly, it has been said that the only purpose served by confrontation is that it provides an opportunity for cross-examination.

Most writers, both judicial and nonjudicial, feel that this lack of opportunity to cross-examine is the basic reason for rejecting hearsay. This was given as the reason as early as the seventeenth century and has been reiterated to the present time. It is only by the use of cross-examination that the various defects of testimony can be exposed. Thus, cross-examination may determine whether a declarant's observation is correct, whether his memory is accurate, and whether he has uttered a deliberate falsehood. Furthermore, the fear of exposure of falsehoods on cross-examination may incite truth-telling.

Edmund M. Morgan, *Hearsay Dangers and the Application of the Hearsay Concept*
62 HARV. L. REV. 177, 177–79 (1948)[4]

Hearsay must necessarily be discussed in the context of an investigation of the truth or falsity of a proposition of fact in which the investigator is asked to rely upon human testimony. The investigation may have been undertaken for the purpose of resolving a dispute between two interested parties. Assume such to be the case, and let the party asserting the proposition that event X occurred or condition X existed be called Proponent, the party denying it, Adversary, the person testifying, Witness, and the investigator, Trier. To establish the truth of his proposition, Proponent presents Witness to Trier, who, it may be supposed, uses and understands language in its generally accepted meaning. Witness utters a series of sounds by which he intends to express a proposition. What Proponent expects Trier to do, and what Trier must do if he is to make the desired finding, is consciously or unconsciously to draw from his hearing of these sounds the inference that Witness seems to be saying that he saw or heard or otherwise perceived X. Until Trier determines what Witness seems to have said, he has no basis for giving any value to it. If he concludes that Witness seems to have expressed the proposition that he perceived X, Trier must make the following additional inferences, each of which, after the first,

---

[4] Copyright © 1948 by the Harvard Law Review Association.

depends upon the one preceding it: (1) that Witness actually said what he seemed to have been saying; (2) that he intended thereby to express the proposition which Trier would have intended had Trier uttered the sounds; (3) that Witness then believed that he had perceived X, that is, that Witness believed the proposition to be true; (4) that this belief of Witness was due to an actual experience of Witness which at the time seemed to him to be the perception of X, that is, that Witness is remembering and is not reconstructing or attributing to himself the experience of another or otherwise unconsciously indulging his imagination; and (5) that what at the time seemed to Witness the experience of perceiving X was in fact the perception of X, that is, that the sense impressions of Witness corresponded with the objective fact. In determining what sounds Witness uttered, Trier must rely upon his own senses, principally that of hearing; in deciding what idea Witness intended to convey, Trier has to rely upon assumptions as to the use of language by Witness and upon his own power of translating language into ideas; and in reaching a conclusion as to the correspondence between the idea which Trier has decided that Witness intended to convey and the actual occurrence or existence of X, Trier must rely upon the sincerity, memory, and perception of Witness. Unless Trier understands that Witness intended to convey the idea that he perceived X, any further consideration of his vocal conduct is useless. If Trier concludes that Witness did not himself believe what he was saying, Trier will cast out his testimony. Even though Witness believed that he was uttering the truth, his statement will go for nought if Trier is convinced that his memory is worthless; and however deep his sincerity or trustworthy his memory, his words will not be persuasive unless Trier finds his perception to have been accurate.

If the investigation is a proceeding in an Anglo-American court, Trier will be a jury or a judge; and Witness will be required to speak under oath or under an equivalent sanction, liable to a penalty for perjury, usually present before Trier at a public hearing, and subject to cross-examination by Adversary. If Witness refuses to speak under these conditions, he will not be heard.

Now assume that the utterance of Witness, as understood by Trier, is, "Declarant told me that he had perceived X." Here the personal experience of which Witness speaks is not the perception of X, but the auditory perception of words uttered by Declarant. To determine from the utterance of Witness that Declarant spoke those words, Trier has to go through exactly the same mental processes as he used in the former situation in determining whether X existed or occurred; and when he has reached the conclusion that Declarant did speak those words, he has done nothing more than find that Declarant in the presence of Witness made a statement of a specified content. Declarant is not now speaking under oath, subject to a penalty for perjury, at a public hearing in the presence of Trier, and subject to cross-examination by Adversary. Furthermore, none of these conditions existed at the time when Declarant made the utterance. Yet Proponent is asking Trier to rely upon Declarant's use of language, his sincerity, his memory, and his perception; and if Trier is to find that X occurred or existed, he must treat Declarant in all respects as in the former situation he treated Witness. In short, for this purpose Witness is merely the means of getting to Trier the statement of Declarant, and Declarant is the real witness upon the issue of the occurrence or existence of X.

QUEEN v. HEPBURN
11 U.S. 290 (1813)

MARSHALL, CH. J., delivered the opinion of the court, as follows:

This was a suit instituted by the plaintiffs in the circuit court of the United States for the county of Washington, in which they claim freedom. On the trial of the issue, certain depositions were offered by the plaintiffs which were rejected by the court. . . . The verdict and judgment being rendered for the defendants, the plaintiffs have brought the cause into this court by writ of error, and the case depends on the correctness of the several opinions given by the circuit court.

The first opinion of the court to which exception was taken, was for the rejection of part of the deposition of Caleb Clarke, who deposed to a fact which he had heard his mother say she had frequently heard from her father.

The second exception is to the opinion overruling part of the deposition of Freeders Ryland, which stated what he had heard Mary, the ancestor of the plaintiffs, say respecting her own place of birth and residence.

*   *   *

The sixth exception is taken to an instruction given by the court to the jury on the motion of the counsel for the defendants. The plaintiffs had read the deposition of Richard Disney, who deposed that he had heard a great deal of talk about Mary Queen, the ancestor of the plaintiffs, and had heard divers persons say, that Captain Larkin brought her into this country, and that she had a great many fine clothes, and that old William Chapman took her on shore once, and that nobody would buy her some time, until at last James Caroll bought her.

Whereupon the defendant's counsel moved the court to instruct the jury that if they find the existence of this report and noise was not stated by the witness from his knowledge, but from what had been communicated to him, respecting the existence of such a report and noise, many years after her importation, without its appearing by whom, or in what manner, the same was communicated to him, then the evidence is incompetent to prove either the existence of such report and noise or the truth of it; which instruction the court gave.

The plaintiffs also read the deposition of Thomas Warfield, who deposed that John Jiams, an inspector of tobacco, told him that Mary, the ancestor of the plaintiffs, was free, and was brought into this country by Captain Larkin, and was sold for seven years. The court instructed the jury that if they should be satisfied upon the evidence that these declarations of John Jiams were not derived from his own knowledge, but were founded on hearsay or report communicated to him many years after the importation and sale of the said Mary, without its appearing by whom or in what manner such communication was made to him; then his said declarations are not competent evidence in this cause. To these instructions the counsel for the plaintiffs excepted.

These several opinions of the court depend on one general principle, the decision of which determines them all. It is this: That hearsay evidence is incompetent to establish any specific fact, which fact is in its nature susceptible of being proved by witnesses who speak from their own knowledge.

However the feelings of the individual may be interested on the part of a person claiming freedom, the court cannot perceive any legal distinction between the assertion of this and of any other right, which will justify the application of a rule of evidence to cases of this description which would be inapplicable to general cases in which a right to property may by asserted. The rule, then, which the court shall establish in this cause will not, in its application, be confined to cases of this particular description, but will be extended to others where rights may depend on facts which happened many years past.

It was very justly observed, by a great judge, that "all questions upon the rules of evidence are of vast importance to all orders and degrees of men; our lives, our liberty, and our property, are all concerned in the support of these rules, which have been matured by the wisdom of ages, and are now revered from their antiquity, and the good sense in which they are founded."

One of these rules is that "hearsay" evidence is in its own nature inadmissible. That this species of testimony supposes some better testimony which might be adduced in the particular case, is not the sole ground of its exclusion. Its intrinsic weakness, its incompetency to satisfy the mind of the existence of the fact, and the frauds which might be under its cover, combine to support the rule, that hearsay evidence is totally inadmissible.

To this rule there are some exceptions, which are said to be as old as the rule itself. These are cases of pedigree, of prescription, of custom, and in some cases, of boundary. There are also matters of general and public history, which may be received without that full proof which is necessary for the establishment of a private fact.

It will be necessary only to examine the principles on which these exceptions are founded, to satisfy the judgment that the same principles will not justify the admission of hearsay evidence to prove a specific fact, because the eye-witnesses to that fact are dead. But if other cases standing on similar principles should arise, it may well be doubted whether justice and the general policy of the law would warrant the creation of new exceptions. The danger of admitting hearsay evidence is sufficient to admonish courts of justice against lightly yielding to the introduction of fresh exceptions to an old and well-established rule; the value of which is felt and acknowledged by all.

If the circumstances that the eye-witnesses of any fact be dead, should justify the introduction of testimony to establish that fact from hearsay, no man could feel safe in any property, a claim to which might be supported by proof so easily obtained.

The general rule comprehends the case, and the case is not within any exception heretofore recognized. This court is not inclined to extend the exceptions further than they have already been carried.

*   *   *

There is no error in the proceedings of the circuit court, and the judgment is affirmed.

DUVALL, J. (dissenting)

The principal point in this case is upon the admissibility of hearsay evidence. The court below admitted hearsay evidence to prove the freedom of the ancestor from whom the petitioners claim, but refused to admit hearsay of hearsay. This court has decided that hearsay evidence is not admissible to prove that the ancestor from whom they claim was free. From this point I dissent.

In Maryland, the law has been for many years settled, that on a petition for freedom, where the petitioner claims from an ancestor who has been dead for a great length of time, the issue may be proved by hearsay evidence, if the fact is of such antiquity that living testimony cannot be procured. Such was the opinion of the judges of the General Court of Maryland, and their decision was affirmed by the unanimous opinion of the judges of the High Court of Appeals in the last resort, after full argument by the ablest counsel at the bar. I think the decision was correct. Hearsay evidence was admitted upon the same principle, upon which it is admitted to prove a custom, pedigree, and the boundaries of land; because, from the antiquity of the transactions to which these subjects may have reference, it is impossible to produce living testimony. To exclude hearsay in such cases, would leave the party interested without remedy. It was decided also that the issue could not be prejudiced by the neglect or omission of the ancestor. If the ancestor neglected to claim her right, the issue could not be bound by length of time, it being a natural inherent right. It appears to me that the reason for admitting hearsay evidence upon a question of freedom is much stronger than in cases of pedigree, or in controversies relative to the boundaries of land. It will be universally admitted that the right to freedom is more important than the right of property.

freedom v. property

And people of color, from their helpless condition under the uncontrolled authority of a master, are entitled to all reasonable protection. A decision that hearsay evidence in such cases shall not be admitted, cuts up by the roots all claims of the kind, and puts a final end to them, unless the claim should arise from a fact of recent date, and such a case will seldom, perhaps never, occur.

QUESTIONS

1. What is the "intrinsic weakness" of hearsay evidence which concerned Chief Justice Marshall?

2. Why didn't the fact that plaintiffs were offering sworn depositions into evidence take this case outside of the hearsay prohibition?

3. Given the "intrinsic weakness" of hearsay evidence, what is an appropriate analytical definition for hearsay?

Evidentiary Foundation:
The Trial of Harrison A. Williams, Jr.[5]

[The background to this case is set forth in § C.4.b.5 in Chapter III, *supra*. During the course of Melvin Weinberg's testimony, the witness referred to an out-of-court highly incriminating statement concerning co-defendant Alex Feinberg. This statement shows why, from a policy standpoint, hearsay is a statement that depends for its probative value on the credibility of a declarant who is not subject to cross-examination. (Note that the declarant, Angelo, Errichetti was notoriously corrupt.)]

Q.   Directing your attention to December of 1978, in connection with your undercover work, did you meet a man named Angelo Errichetti?

A.   That's correct.

Q.   Who did you learn Mr. Errichetti to be?

A.   The Mayor of Camden and the State Senator.

Q.   State Senator for the State of New Jersey?

A.   New Jersey, yes.

Q.   Did you and the undercover agent then have dealings with Mr. Errichetti in December of '78 and January '79?

A.   That's correct.

Q.   Now, I direct your attention to January 10, 1979. Did you have a conversation with Mr. Errichetti at the Holiday Inn, Atlantic City, New Jersey?

A.   That's correct.

Q.   Could you tell the jury what you recall about that conversation?

A.   The Mayor Errichetti said to me that he's bringing Alex Feinberg over at the Hyatt House in Cherry Hill, that Feinberg is a bag man from Senator Williams.

MR. KOELZER: Objection, for several reasons I ask that be striken. May I approach the sidebar.

THE COURT: All right, I sustain the objection and I instruct the jury to disregard the last part of the witness's answer.

---

[5] Excerpted from Trial Transcript, *supra*, at 719–20.

C. DEFINING HEARSAY — BASIC CONCEPTS

Carl C. Wheaton, *What Is Hearsay?*
46 Iowa L. Rev. 210, 210–11 (1961)[6]

None of the many attempts to define hearsay has produced a generally accepted definition. Scholars have usually been in closer agreement on what constitutes hearsay than have the courts. Dean Ladd has stated that hearsay consists of a statement or assertive conduct which was made or occurred out of court and is offered in court to prove the truth of the facts asserted. Dean McCormick has defined hearsay as testimony in court, or written evidence, of a statement made out of court, such evidence being offered as an assertion to show the truth of matters asserted therein, and which thus rests for its value upon the credibility of the out-of-court asserter. A definition fairly representing the position of Professor Morgan is that hearsay includes the evidence of any conduct of a person, verbal or nonverbal, which he intended to operate as an assertion, if it is used to prove that the assertion is true or that the asserter believes it is true, unless it is subject to cross-examination by the one against whom it is used at the trial at which it is offered. Morgan would also include as hearsay any conduct not intended as an assertion if it is offered to prove both the state of mind of such person and the external event or condition which caused him to have that state of mind. Wigmore has emphasized the importance of the lack of opportunity to cross-examine the declarant as the primary characteristic of hearsay.

While it has been contended that hearsay involves an intention to communicate, Professor Morgan has correctly pointed out that an utterance may be hearsay although there is no intent that it be a communication of thought. For example, when the writer of a letter files it away and the letter is found after the writer's death, the use of the letter to prove the truth of its contents would be an offer of hearsay evidence. Similarly, use of statements overheard from a soliloquy to prove the truth of those statements would involve hearsay.

Judicial definitions of hearsay have been many and varied, perhaps making up in variety for their apparently frequent lack of concision. The lack of consistency may be due to a tendency to define hearsay to meet the requirements of the case before the court. For example, it has been said that hearsay is evidence which derives its value, not solely from the credit to be given the witness upon the stand, but partly from the veracity and competency of some other person. Another court has held that the hearsay rule of exclusion applies only to extrajudicial utterances offered as evidence of the truth of the matter asserted. Further, one court has said that statements are called hearsay because they are not made in court under the sanctity of an oath.

From these and other definitions, there seems to be agreement that hearsay must be a statement or other communicative conduct offered to prove the truth of the matter asserted. This presupposes a lack of personal knowledge of the truth of the matter asserted on the part of the witness. To qualify as hearsay, the declaration must have been made out of court, at least in the sense that it was not made at the

---

[6] Copyright © 1961. Reprinted with permission.

hearing at which it is offered in evidence.

Roger C. Park,
McCormick on Evidence and the Concept of Hearsay: A Critical Analysis Followed by Suggestions to Law Teachers
65 MINN. L. REV. 423, 424 (1981)[7]

Definitions of hearsay are commonly either assertion-oriented or declarant-oriented. An assertion-oriented definition focuses on whether an out-of-court assertion will be used to prove the truth of what it asserts, while a declarant-oriented definition focuses on whether the use of the utterance will require reliance on the credibility of the out-of-court declarant.

NOTES AND QUESTIONS

1.   Which definitional orientation does the *Queen case emphasize*?

2.   Which definitional orientation do the Federal Rules of Evidence adopt?

3.   Professor McCormick, cited by Professor Wheaton, *supra*, seems to imply that the assertion-oriented and declarant-oriented definitions will always lead to the same result. Is that necessarily so? Consider this question as you evaluate the next two cases.

ANDERSON v. UNITED STATES
417 U.S. 211 (1974)

MR. JUSTICE MARSHALL delivered the opinion of the court.

Petitioners were convicted of violating 18 U.S.C. § 241, which, in pertinent part, makes it unlawful for two or more persons to "conspire to injure, oppress, threaten, or intimidate any citizen in the free exercise or enjoyment of any right or privilege secured to him by the Constitution or laws of the United States." . . . Specifically, the Government proved that petitioners engaged in a conspiracy to cast fictitious votes for candidates for federal, state, and local offices in a primary election in Logan County, West Virginia. At the trial, a question arose concerning the admissibility against all of the petitioners of certain out-of-court statements made by some of them. . . .

The underlying facts are not in dispute. On May 12, 1970, a primary election was held in West Virginia for the purpose of nominating candidates for the United States Senate, United States House of Representatives, and various state and local offices. One of the nominations most actively contested in Logan County was the Democratic nomination for County Commissioner, an office vested with a wide variety of legislative, executive, and judicial powers. Among the several candidates for the Democratic nomination for this office were the incumbent, Okey Hager, and his major opponent, Neal Scaggs.

---

[7] Reprinted with permission of Professor Roger C. Park and the University of Minnesota.

Petitioners are state or county officials, including the Clerk of the Logan County Court, the Clerk of the County Circuit Court, the Sheriff and Deputy Sheriff of the County, and a State Senator. The evidence at trial showed that by using the power of their office, the petitioners convinced three election officials in charge of the Mount Gay precinct in Logan County to cast false and fictitious votes on the voting machines and then to destroy poll slips so that the number of persons who had actually voted could not be determined except from the machine tally. While it is apparent from the record that the primary purpose behind the casting of false votes was to secure the nomination of Hager for the office of County Commissioner, it is equally clear that about 100 false votes were in fact cast not only for Hager, but also for Senator Robert Byrd and Representative Ken Hechler, who appeared on the ballot for renomination to their respective chambers of the United States Congress, as well as for other state and local candidates considered part of the Hager slate.

The conspiracy achieved its primary objective, the countywide vote totals showing Hager the winner by 21 votes, counting the Mount Gay precinct returns. About two weeks after the election, on May 27, 1970, the election results were certified. After that date Scaggs filed an election contest challenging certain returns. . . .

A hearing was held in the County Court on the election contest at which petitioners Earl Tomblin and John R. Browning gave sworn testimony. The prosecution . . . sought to prove that Tomblin and Browning perjured themselves at the election contest hearing in a continuing effort to have the fraudulent votes for Hager counted and certified. For example, one of the key issues in the election contest was whether sufficient voters had in fact turned out in Mount Gay precinct to justify the unusually high reported returns. Tomblin testified under oath at the election contest that he had visited Mount Gay precinct on election day and had observed one Garrett Sullins there as Sullins went in to vote. The prosecution . . . however, offered testimony from Sullins himself that he was in the hospital and never went to the Mount Gay precinct on election day.

At trial, the other defendants objected to the introduction of Tomblin's prior testimony on the ground that it was inadmissible against anyone but Tomblin. The District Court overruled the objection.

The obvious question that arises in the present case, then, is whether the out-of-court statements of Tomblin and Browning were hearsay. We think it plain they were not. Out-of-court statements constitute hearsay only when offered in evidence to prove the truth of the matter asserted. The election contest testimony of Tomblin and Browning, however, was not admitted into evidence to prove the truth of anything asserted therein. Quite the contrary, the point of the prosecutor's introducing those statements was simply to prove that the statements were made so as to establish a foundation for later showing, through other admissible evidence, that they were false. The rationale of the hearsay rule is inapplicable as well. The primary justification for the exclusion of hearsay is the lack of any opportunity for the adversary to cross-examine the absent declarant whose out-of-court statement is introduced into evidence. Here, since the prosecution was not contending that anything Tomblin or Browning said at the election contest was true, the other defendants had no interest in cross-examining them so as to put their credibility in issue.

QUESTIONS

1. The *Anderson* court suggests that the proffered statement was not hearsay under both the declarant and assertion-oriented definitions of hearsay. But didn't the statement's probative force depend on the credibility of a declarant not subject to cross-examination? As opposing counsel, wouldn't you have wanted to cross-examine the declarant? Perhaps the declarant made an honest mistake about Sullins having voted in the election. Admitting the statement as non-hearsay prevents opposing counsel from establishing this exculpatory possibility. Thus, although non-hearsay under the assertion-oriented definition, the statement was hearsay under the declarant oriented definition. In cases of such conflict, which definition prevails?

2. As you evaluate *Anderson*, consider under which definition the statement in the following hypothetical would constitute hearsay: "Suppose that *X* is charged with committing a crime in Boston. The police talk to *X*'s wife, who tells them that *X* was with her in Denver on the day in question." *Park, infra.* Assuming the statement to be "demonstrably false," may the prosecution "use it against *X* for the inference that *X*'s wife lied because she knew him to be guilty"? *Id.*

D.   THE APPLICATION OF BASIC CONCEPTS

Charles T. McCormick, *The Borderland of Hearsay*
39 YALE L.J. 488, 489 (1930)[8]

. . . It is familiar doctrine that the hearsay rule applies only to evidence of out-of-court statements offered for the purpose of proving that the facts are as asserted in the statement. Evidence of such statements made for any other purpose, *e.g.*, to prove the making of a declaration as evidence of the publication of a slander, or to show that the one who uttered or heard it had notice of the facts asserted, is, of course, not hearsay.

Carl C. Wheaton, *What Is Hearsay?*
46 IOWA L. REV. 210, 215–18 (1961)[9]

Since spoken or written words are hearsay only if they are offered in evidence to prove the truth of what was said, the hearsay rule is not involved when they are offered merely to prove that they were said. The ultimate fact is then within the personal knowledge of the witness, and his testimony is used to prove that the statement was made. For example, evidence offered in a slander action by one who heard the allegedly slanderous words to prove that the statement was made is

---

[8] Reprinted by permission of the Yale Law Journal Company and Fred B. Rothman & Company from the Yale Law Journal, Vol. 39, page 489.

[9] Copyright © 1961. Reprinted with permission.

certainly not hearsay. Similarly, in an action for libel, evidence of what was said, given by a witness who heard the statements in question, has been held not to be hearsay since what was said was in issue. When the issues turn on the terms of an oral contract, evidence of the words spoken to make the contract are not hearsay since these words are offered merely to prove that they were spoken.

*   *   *

Words which give notice have often been admitted to prove that a party had notice of a fact. Evidence of the making of a statement, oral or written, may be received to prove that the statement was made if the existence of the statement may tend to prove whether a party acted reasonably in light of the statement which was brought to his attention. Thus, in an action for damages caused by an automobile collision the plaintiff, who was the driver of one of the automobiles, was permitted to testify that her companion had told her that the intersection they were approaching was dangerous and that the plaintiff should be careful. The statement was not hearsay; it was offered, not to prove that the intersection was dangerous, but rather to suggest that the plaintiff, having been warned of the danger, would proceed with caution.

In another case in which damages were sought for injuries claimed to have been caused by an animal furnished to the plaintiff by defendant, evidence of what others said about the actions of the animal was admitted. The statements were admitted to show that the defendant's servant had noticed that the animal was not acting normally prior to the accident. This evidence was offered solely to show that the person in charge could have acted to avoid the injury to the plaintiff.

In an action for damages for non-delivery of goods the defendant alleged that a clause in the contract permitted refusal of delivery if, in the defendant's judgment, the buyer's credit had become impaired. It was held error to exclude evidence that the defendant had received a Bradstreet report indicating that the plaintiff was a poor credit risk. The decision was in effect a holding that such evidence was not hearsay. . . .

Utterances disclosing a state of mind are generally admitted as being without the limits of the hearsay rule. For example, utterances disclosing hatred, malice, fear or affection, when those states of mind are relevant, are admitted as circumstantial proof of those feelings. In *Hooper-Holmes Bureau, Inc. v. Bunn*, the plaintiff alleged that the defendant's conduct resulted in his loss of a position and his inability to get insurance. To support this claim he was per-mitted to prove malice on the part of the defendant by presenting evidence that the defendant, through an agent, had made unfavorable reports on the plaintiff when the latter applied for employment and insurance. Here again the evidence was used to show the defendant's feeling toward the plaintiff and was not offered to prove the truth or falsity of the statements contained in the report. A person accused of homicide has been permitted to give evidence of a threat against him to indicate his mental state at the time of the killing. . . .

Although some courts have admitted evidence of such a threat as part of the *res gestae*, Dean Ladd has pointed out that it is admissible because it is not hearsay at all. . . . This writer accepts that position and believes that evidence of the threat may be deemed evidence of reasonable fear on the part of the defendant.

Motive may be shown by evidence of an out-of-court statement without violating the hearsay rule. In a trial of police detectives for assault and battery a letter was allowed in evidence which charged the defendants with trying to extort money from the complaining witness. Since it was shown that the defendants had seen the letter prior to the assault, the letter was admitted to show that the defendants knew that the complaining witness had made accusations against them. From this fact the jury could infer a motive for retaliation, regardless of the truth or falsity of the accusations contained in the letter.

Proof of Mental State

Moreover, statements by a person may be evidence of his mental condition without reference to the truth of what he says.[10] Thus, in a will contest, evidence of delusions of the testator have been admitted to show lack of testamentary capacity. The same has been held in a proceeding to cancel a deed because of a lack of mental capacity of the grantor to make an effective deed. Similarly, in an action on an insurance policy where the recovery was based on the claim that the insured was suffering from dementia praecox, evidence of various hallucinations of the insured was held to be proper. In a proceeding to have a guardian appointed for a person claimed to be mentally defective, evidence has been admitted that the person had said that his wife was unfaithful, that he was not the father of some of his children, and that members of his family were trying to poison him. In contrast such evidence would be objectionable hearsay if offered to prove the fidelity of declarant's wife, the paternity of his children, or the fact that someone tried to poison him.

CREAGHE v. IOWA HOME MUTUAL CASUALTY CO.
323 F.2d 981 (10th Cir. 1963)

SETH, CIRCUIT JUDGE.

The plaintiff-appellant has an unsatisfied judgment against Muril J. Osborn obtained in a damage action which arose from a collision between the plaintiffs car and Osborn's truck. In the case at bar, appellant alleges that the appellee insurance company was the insurer of Osborn's truck at the time of the accident, and seeks to collect this judgment from it. The appellee admits that at one time it issued a liability policy to Osborn, but asserts that he canceled it shortly before the accident. . . . [T]he court found that there was no material fact for the jury and gave appellee a directed verdict. The plaintiff-appellant has taken this appeal.

*　　*　　*

When one of appellee's agents wrote the policy in appellee's company, only one-half of the premium was paid to the agent. The unpaid balances were on account between the agent and the insured, and did not involve appellee. The policy was thereafter changed from time to time as the coverage expanded, and the agent retained the policy in order to make the changes. As the coverage increased, so did the premium due. Osborn sent the agent a check for a part of the balance due after

---

[10] [Ed. — Note that, depending upon the form of such statements, they may technically be hearsay. Nevertheless, an exception exists for such occasions. *See* § I.2.d, *infra* this Chapter.]

the initial payment, but it was returned by the bank marked insufficient funds. The agent testified that he called Osborn about the check, and was told by Osborn that he was going to cancel the insurance and would come by to pick up the returned check. Osborn did come to the agent's office on October 19 and, in the presence of the agent and a secretary, stated he wanted the insurance canceled immediately.

* * *

Appellant challenges the action of the trial court in admitting the testimony of the agent of appellee and his employee as to what took place, and what was said by the insured, on the occasion when he came to the agent's office to receive back the check. The agent's testimony and that of his employee was, as mentioned, that the insured stated he wanted the policy canceled, also that his check for some of the premiums in addition to those initially made was then returned. Appellant asserts that this testimony was hearsay.

The hearsay rule does not exclude *relevant* testimony as to what the contracting parties said with respect to the making or the terms of an oral agreement. The presence or absence of such words and statements of themselves are part of the issues in the case. This use of such testimony does not require a reliance by the jury or the judge upon the competency of the person who originally made the statements for the truth of their content. Neither the truth of the statements nor their accuracy are then involved. In the case at bar we are not concerned with whether the insured was truthful or not when he told the agent he wanted the policy canceled and that he did not need it any more. It is enough for the issues here presented to determine only whether or not he made such statements to the agent. The fact that these statements were made was testified to by the agent, and his competency and truthfulness as to this testimony was subject to testing through cross-examination by counsel for appellant, and this was done at considerable length. The fact that the statements with which we are here concerned related to an oral termination of a written contract does not lead to a rule different from that prevailing for the formation of an oral agreement. The reasons for the rule permitting such testimony are the same in both instances.

* * *

. . . [T]he testimony with which we are here concerned is admissible since it is part of, or is the oral agreement to cancel the insurance policy. Oral agreements can only be established by testimony as to the conversation which was had between the parties. This testimony may be given by a witness to such conversation, as was the agent of the appellee in this instance.

* * *

Affirmed.

UNITED STATES v. JONES
663 F.2d 567 (5th Cir. 1981)

JAMES C. HILL, CIRCUIT JUDGE:

On May 4, 1979, appellant Lloyd Jones stood before the United States District Court, Northern District of Georgia, for sentencing in connection with his conviction for murder committed at the Atlanta Federal Penitentiary. Judge William C. O'Kelley addressed Jones, who appeared with counsel, to determine whether Jones wished to be heard on matters bearing upon his sentence. Jones responded:

> Yes, sir. I'd like to say that, I'd like to say that I don't think you passed sentence on me, you know, like, I think, during the process of the trial that I was totally insane, you know, which I also think that you should have looked over into the matter when I told you that them people *out* there was threatening me and stuff, which you said you would but you never have. But now today you bring me down here to pass sentence on me. It's nothing really too much I could do about it. When you can't beat them you join them. *So, Judge O'Kelley, U.S. Attorney, Mr. Bostic, I pass sentence on you, the sentence would be death, you and all your relatives.* Now you can pass your sentence. *It is death to you, you, and you, and all your relatives by gunshot wound.* Now do as you please. I don't give a fuck if you throw the whole Empire State building at me, the whole State of Georgia.

Record, Vol. I, at 98–99 (emphasis added). For threatening the lives of Judge O'Kelley and the prosecutor, Jones was indicted and convicted under 18 U.S.C. § 1503 (1976),[11] and sentenced to five years in prison. Jones has raised six points on appeal; they range from colorable to frivolous. None is persuasive. We affirm the conviction.

*   *   *

Defendant's fourth contention is that the district court erred by not admitting into evidence the entire transcript of the sentencing hearing before Judge O'Kelley. The district court permitted the transcript of the hearing, save certain prejudicial portions and a short final section, to be read to the jury. Only the language containing the actual threats . . . was admitted into evidence as an exhibit for the jury during its deliberation. . . . The statement at issue is paradigmatic nonhearsay; it was offered because it contains threats made against officers of the federal courts, *i.e.*, it contains the operative words of this criminal action. It was not "offered in evidence to prove the truth of the matter asserted," *id.* 801(c). . . .

Affirmed.

---

[11] [1] The statute, in pertinent part, punishes one who "by threats or force . . . endeavors to influence, intimidate or impede any . . . officer in or of any court of the United States . . . in the discharge of his duty . . . ."

UNITED STATES v. DeVINCENT
632 F.2d 147 (1st Cir. 1980)

Coffin, Chief Judge.

Appellant was convicted of making an extortionate extension of credit and of collection of an extension of credit by extortionate means in violation of 18 U.S.C. §§ 892 and 894. He assigns numerous errors on appeal, largely relating to the admission of evidence and instructions to the jury.

I.

The testimony at trial may be summarized as follows: The government's chief witness, Allan Klein, testified that he was the owner of a "bust-out" operation — that is, it would order merchandise from suppliers using fraudulent credit references and without any intention of paying for the goods, which were then sold for whatever they would bring.

In April of 1974, while delivering some "bust-out" merchandise, Klein, a heavy gambler, met appellant, who agreed to "take all the action that [Klein] wanted to bet with him" and to extend credit to Klein for the purpose of making bets. Klein won some $3,800 at first, but later in the week lost and failed to pay appellant on the day agreed to. Appellant, according to Klein, "started screaming and yelling and swearing" and ordered Klein to get the money even if he had to steal it. Appellant also threatened to shoot him "in the face" and "break both of [his] goddamn legs." Klein borrowed from another source and paid appellant.

Subsequently, Klein received a call from his cousin, Kenneth Weiner, who ran a "bust-out" operation similar to Klein's. Weiner told Klein that appellant was setting up a protection racket whereby he would get ten percent of the merchandise sold by the stores, and that he should comply because appellant "had just got out of jail for loan sharking and . . . he was a pretty bad guy." In August appellant came to Klein's store and accused him of "backdooring" merchandise — selling it to parties not approved by him. He then punched Klein in the face, knocking him off his chair, and left.

Klein subsequently incurred additional gambling debts, and in mid-August called one Visconti and asked to borrow $3,000. Visconti agreed. When Klein arrived at Vico Sales to pick up the money, appellant was there with Visconti. Visconti told Klein, "You know I don't lend money. Vinnie [appellant] is the guy that lends the money." Klein testified, "And at that time Vinnie handed me $3,000 in $100 bills and told me that Saturday was payday and he wanted $150 a week juice — and that would not come off the principal amount of the money until I could pay the whole money at one time, and I better be there every Saturday."

Klein testified that his understanding was that if he were dilatory in his payments, he would "either get beaten up or killed." He made interest payments for six to eight weeks and then paid the debt in full.

Klein's cousin, Kenneth Weiner, also testified for the government. His testimony was generally corroborative of Klein's, and covered, *inter alia*, conversations he had with Klein in which he told Klein of appellant's protection racket and warned him that appellant was "a vicious man," and in which Klein told him of his beating and threats at the hands of appellant.

Appellant produced no witnesses, and confined his case to attacking the credibility of the government's witnesses. The jury delivered a verdict of guilty.

*   *   *

III.

Appellant assigns as error the admission of Klein's testimony concerning the August beating and his conversations with Weiner in which the latter mentioned appellant's jail term and character, as well as Weiner's own testimony concerning his conversations with Klein. He asserts numerous grounds for exclusion, all of which we find without merit.

Appellant first characterizes this testimony as "reputation evidence" and argues that since there was direct evidence concerning the debtor's state of mind (*i.e.*, Klein's statement that he thought he would be beaten or killed if he did not pay), it should not have been admitted.

The only evidence in this case which could properly be labeled reputation evidence is Weiner's statement to Klein that appellant had been in jail for loan sharking and was "a pretty bad guy." This evidence, if it was indeed reputation evidence, was clearly admissible under section 892(b)(3)(B), which gives as an element of the prima facie case the debtor's reasonable belief that "the creditor had a reputation for the use of extortionate means to collect extensions of credit or to punish the nonrepayment thereof."

*   *   *

Appellant's characterization of this evidence as hearsay likewise must fail. Weiner's statement to Klein that appellant had been in jail for loan sharking and was "a pretty bad guy" falls within a familiar category of non-hearsay; statements offered, not for their truth, but for their effect on the hearer. *See* 6 WIGMORE, EVIDENCE § 1789 (Chadborn Re. 1976); McCORMICK, HANDBOOK OF THE LAW OF EVIDENCE § 249 at 589–90 (1972). The present statements were admissible for their probable effect on the debtor's understanding of the creditor's collection practices, an essential element of the extortionate extension of credit charge.

Finally, appellant's statement that evidence of a criminal record is never admissible except to show common scheme or purpose grossly overstates the case. Such evidence is not admissible to show character or propensity. Fed. R. Evid. 404(b). "However, if such evidence is relevant to another, legitimate purpose it may be admitted if its probative value is not substantially outweighed by the danger of unfair prejudice, confusion of issue or misleading the jury." *United States v. Barrett*, 539 F.2d 244, 248 (1st Cir. 1976) and cases cited; Fed. R. Evid. 403, 404(b). Its purpose here was not to show propensity, but to show its effect on the hearer; strictly speaking, the evidence was not that appellant had been in jail, but that Klein *thought* he had been.

* * *

Affirmed.

BETTS v. BETTS
473 P.2d 403 (Wash. Ct. App. 1970)

ARMSTRONG, CHIEF JUDGE.

Defendant Rita A. Betts, now Rita A. Caporale, appeals from a judgment modifying a California divorce decree which had awarded her custody of the children of the parties. In modifying the divorce decree the trial court awarded custody of the 5-year-old daughter, Tracy Lynn, now the sole child of the parties, to plaintiff Michael E. Betts.

* * *

The mother's next contention is that certain statements made by the daughter to her foster mother were inadmissible because they were hearsay statements.

The foster mother saw an item in the paper relative to the remarriage of the child's mother and with reference to it, testified as follows:

A.   So I told her that her mama and Mr. Ray Caporale had got married, and she started crying. She said — she ran and put her arms around me and her head in my lap and started crying real bad and hard and said, "He killed my brother and he'll kill my mommie too," — and she doesn't seem to ever get that out of her mind.

Q.   Does she say this often?

A.   Yes, she tells all her friends — explains why she is with us, and she goes into this tale, and I don't seem to be able to get her not to tell her problems to outsiders.

Q.   Did she ever make statements about this prior to the incident. . . .

A.   Yes, yes, she started telling about her little brother was in heaven and how he had gotten there and she always blamed him for it.

Q.   By "him," who do you mean?

A.   Mr. Caporale.

Q.   Has anyone in your presence tried to pull this information out of this child?

A.   No, because I didn't want to worry her. When she talks, we let her talk; but we don't try to change her mind, one way or the other, because we aren't there to do that — just give her a home.

The foster mother further stated, "She always mentioned, 'He's mean.' That is the word she uses 'He's mean.' "

We hold that use of this testimony does not violate the hearsay evidence rule.

The hearsay evidence rule prohibits the use of testimony in court, of a statement made by another person out of court, which is being offered to show the truth of the matter asserted therein. Such evidence derives its value, not solely from the credibility of the in-court witness himself, but also in part, from the veracity and competence of the person who made the out-of-court statement. . . .

The statements of the child were not admitted to prove the truth of the assertions she made, but merely to indirectly and inferentially show the mental state of the child at the time of the child custody proceedings.

In finding of fact 18, the trial court stated in part: "The fact that said statements had been made would tend to create a strained relationship between said Tracey Lynn Betts and her step-father, Raymond Don Caporale, and her mother, should she be awarded to her mother."

Professor Meisenholder had made the following pertinent remarks concerning the admissibility of such statements:

> Out-of-court statements are often circumstantial evidence of the declarant's state of mind when his state of mind is relevant in a case. Evidence of such statements is not hearsay under the classic definition of hearsay. The Washington cases contain many illustrations of this principle. . . .

It should be pointed out that there is a distinction between non-hearsay statements which circumstantially indicate a present state of mind *regardless of their truth*, and hearsay statements which indicate a state of mind *because of their truth*. The state of mind must be relevant in either instance. The distinction is based upon the question of whether the statement shows the mental state *regardless of the truth of the statement*. The distinction is usually disregarded in the cases because the statement will usually be admissible either under the exception to the hearsay rule or under the theory that it is not hearsay. . . .

An obvious example of an out-of-court non-hearsay statement which circumstantially indicates a state of mind regardless of the truth of the statement would be "I am Napoleon Bonaparte." This would be relevant in a sanity hearing.

The statements in question in this case are clearly non-hearsay statements which circumstantially indicate a state of mind regardless of their truth. Since they were relevant, they are admissible.

* * *

The judgment is affirmed.

NOTES AND QUESTIONS

1. *DeVincent* and *Betts* reflect different applications of the principle that a statement is not hearsay if it is not being offered for the truth of the matter asserted. In *DeVincent*, the Government introduced the statement to establish the listener victim's state of mind. By comparison, the statement in *Betts* established the declarant's state of mind.

2. Should the *Betts* court also have been concerned with whether the juvenile declarant could have qualified as a competent witness when she made her statement? *See State v. C.J.*, 63 P.3d 765 (Wash. 2003); *People v. Roberto V.*, 93 Cal. App. 4th 1350 (2001). Does the answer to this question depend on whether the statement was being offered for its truth?

Evidentiary Foundation:
The Trial of Westbrook Pegler[12]

[Quentin Reynolds, a journalist represented by famous trial attorney Louis Nizer, sued Westbrook Pegler for libel. The case arose out of one of Pegler's syndicated newspaper columns in which he attacked Reynolds, calling him everything from a coward to a nudist. During the trial Pegler gave the following testimony concerning a story he relied upon in claiming that Reynolds was a nudist:]

Pegler:	Mrs. Broun said she was in a rowboat on the Broun Lake at North Stamford and that Reynolds was standing in the water and he asked her to take him for a ride in the boat. She said she rowed over to where he was, and believing that he had on swimming trunks, invited him to get into the boat. She said he then got into the boat and she was shocked to discover that he was absolutely naked, and in her phrase, he didn't have on even a hair net.
Nizer:	I move to strike all this out.
Pegler:	My answer is not finished. Do I finish it, Mr. Counselor?
Court:	Finish your answer.
Pegler:	(continuing) She said she looked around at the trees and the sky, trying to avoid this spectacle but that he sat there with his lavaliere dangling.
Pegler's Attorney:	Did she use that exact phraseology?
Pegler:	That is Mrs. Connie Broun's phrase.
Nizer:	I move to strike all this out, your honor. . . .
Court:	The jury understands, as I have repeated so often, that this is not received as truth of the occurrence, but simply on the issue of mitigation of damages.

Evidentiary Foundation:
The Trial of Willie Riviello

[In 1984, Willie Riviello, a soldier in a New York organized crime family was prosecuted for extortion. The state alleged that Riviello, through the extortionate activity of two henchmen — Mistrulli and Blase — attempted to obtain control of a restaurant owned by one Vincent Cipolla. When Cipolla ultimately declined to

---

[12] Excerpted from L. NIZER, MY LIFE IN COURT 81 (Doubleday & Co., 1961).

surrender the restaurant, Riviello responded that "he would get back to Joe Pagano and whatever happens, happens." Joe Pagano was well known as the mob boss in the local area. The following colloquy occurred after the prosecution offered this statement into evidence:]

THE COURT: Ladies and gentlemen, a legal point has arose which must be handled outside the presence of the jury. We won't be leaving the courtroom. You must return to the jury room.

Do not discuss this case among yourselves or form or express any opinion as to the guilt or innocence of the defendant until the case is finally submitted to you.

(Whereupon, the following proceedings were had with Court and counsel and defendant present outside the presence of the jury at 10:55 a.m.)

MR. GOLDSMITH: I present to the Court a memorandum addressed to this issue.

Let me make an offer of proof at this time, if I may.

It is necessary for me at this time to get into Mr. Cipolla's connection with Mr. Pagano for a variety of reasons. Mr. Pagano enters into this case—

MR. RICHMAN: I have to make an objection and explain what my objection is.

THE COURT: This is the time for the offer of proof. Then you may make an objection. I've asked for an offer of proof at the side bar and this is why we sent the jury out.

MR. GOLDSMITH: Mr. Pagano is someone that Mr. Cipolla went to when he was having problems with Blase and Mistrulli. He went reluctantly, but he felt that some help might be rendered.

*   *   *

Shortly after their meeting occurred, there was a meeting in the Bronx. . . . [A]t that time there was a discussion about Mr. Riviello and his associates acquiring an interest in the restaurant.

The nature of the interest that was going to be acquired was basically that Mr. Cipolla was going to be out. He wasn't going to be receiving anything for it and Mr. Cipolla basically responded by saying to Mr. Riviello well, I'm interested in a deal if it's for [restaurant] stock in exchange for money. In other words, money in exchange for a share in the restaurant.

In response to that, Mr. Riviello says we don't buy restaurants. . . .

Then Mr. Cipolla responds by saying, well, in that case I'm not interested. Mr. Riviello then says, in substance, very well, I'll get back to Joe Pagano and whatever happens, happens.

Your Honor, that statement is the crux . . . of the People's case. That statement to Mr. Cipolla is a threat. Mr. Cipolla had a belief as to who Pagano was. That belief was obtained from reading the newspaper and what people said. Whether or not

Pagano is a boss in the County is not what is important. What is important is that Mr. Cipolla believed him to be.

Mr. Riviello by saying I'll get back to Pagano and whatever happens, happens, that is a threat, Your Honor, and it doesn't make any difference that Pagano is not involved in this case because it's that statement which puts fear into the heart of Mr. Cipolla.

This is an extortion case, and because of that fear, which is an element of the case, that needs to be established. If that statement isn't admissible, then the People are going to have great difficulty establishing the making of a threat and instilling of fear. . . .

By way of analogy, if I am attempting to extort someone and I say, Mr. X over there is a murderer and at the end of the conversation the victim of my extortion says he is not interested, I say well, I'll tell Mr. X and whatever happens, happens. It doesn't matter whether or not Mr. X is a murderer. The point is the victim believes him to be. . . . What is important here is that the statement is being offered not for its truth, but rather to establish the victim's state of mind.

* * *

And I point out to Your Honor that what is at issue here is not Mr. Riviello's reputation in the community, we're not talking about that. If that were the case, that would make the issue a lot closer. But this isn't prejudicial to Mr. Riviello. We're not making allegations as to him. This involves a third party not involved in the case and it is that third party who Mr. Riviello . . . used as the basis for his threat to the victim.

MR. RICHMAN: Your Honor, you know the argument that the People need it is not sufficient in and of itself to bring it into the case.

The People would, in this case, would like every bit of hearsay they can get to establish their case, and they're just not permitted to have it.

THE COURT: It's not hearsay. The conversation with Riviello is not hearsay.

NOTES

Riviello's statement was also admissible as an admission. *See* § H.2, *infra.*

UNITED STATES v. McLENNAN
563 F.2d 943 (9th Cir. 1977)

DUNIWAY, CIRCUIT JUDGE.

Defendants McLennan and Bender appeal from judgments convicting them of (1) making false statements in a matter within the jurisdiction of a department or agency of the United States, (2) making false statements for the purpose of influencing the action of the Department of Housing and Urban Development

(HUD), and (3) conspiring to make such false statements and to defraud the United States. . . .

From October, 1971, to April, 1975, the defendants received a total of $961,282 from HUD, which they repeatedly represented in loan applications, through owner-architect agreements, in fund requisitions and in final project costs decertifications, as being paid or payable to the project architect, Charles Dahlen. In reality, Dahlen was not an independent contractor as HUD was led to believe, but rather a salaried employee of the defendants. After paying Dahlen's salary and expenses, the defendants divided the remainder of the money received from HUD for architect's fees, roughly $600,000, between them. These criminal charges resulted from their false statements that this money was to pay or was paid to the architect. . . .

The defendants' former attorney, Burnett, testified about the advice which he had given them. The statement made by Burnett, which is now being challenged, was elicited in the following exchange on direct examination by the government.

Q.   Now, were you aware, in 1971, that funds were being paid from an account in the name of Charles Dahlen to Mr. Bender and Mr. McLennan?

A.   No.

Q.   Were you aware of that in 1972?

A.   No.

Q.   Did you become aware of that in 1973?

A.   In late 1973, yes.

                              *   *   *

Q.   When you did learn from Mr. Bender about these transfers, do you specifically recall what it was that you said to him?

A.   Yes.

Q.   And what was it?

A.   "For Christ's sake, I told you that was illegal." (Reporter's Transcript 407, 409.)

Defendants claimed that their good faith reliance upon the advice of counsel negated the fraudulent intent that was an essential element of the charge. Advice of counsel is no defense unless the defendant gave his attorney all of the facts, and unless counsel specifically advised the course of conduct taken by the defendant. . . .

Under these rules, the questions and answers about Burnett's awareness of the facts in 1971, 1972, and 1973 were clearly relevant. Moreover, because Burnett was speaking of what he knew, and when, his answers were not hearsay. Defendants do not disagree.

They concentrate their fire on the last answer quoted above. It was clearly relevant and damaging to their defense of good faith reliance upon their attorney's advice. The issue is whether it was admissible. Judge Skopil in his order denying the defendants' motion for a new trial concluded that the statement was not hearsay because it was offered to prove something other than the truth of what was said, Fed. R. Evid. 801(c), and therefore was admissible. He was right.

In late 1973, defendants' auditors raised questions about what defendants had done and were doing with the moneys that, according to defendants' certifications to HUD, were to go to the architect. One of the defendants thereupon called in Burnett, and the incident that is quoted resulted. At that time, moneys were still to be received from HUD, and thereafter the defendants again certified to HUD that a named percentage of the moneys claimed were to go to the architect. Two of the counts in the indictment, Counts VII and VIII, relate to those false certifications.

The exclamation was not a mere assertion by the attorney that he had told the defendants something in the past. In the circumstances in which it was made, the attorney having been called in for advice, and one of the defendants having just told him what they were really doing, the statement would clearly tell the defendants: "I'm telling you now that is illegal," or so a jury could find. The reference to the previous advice, and the attorney's obvious surprise and dismay strongly reinforce his opinion, making his statement even stronger than if he had merely said, "That is illegal." The statement was relevant as present notice; it was not merely an assertion of past notice to the defendants.

Moreover, the statement was not offered or admitted to prove the truth of what Burnett said — that defendants' actions were illegal or that in the past he had told them "That is illegal" — but simply to show that the statement concerning illegality had been made. When the defense is advice of counsel, the advice given, whether correct or not, and whether recitals in it are true or not, is always admissible. Usually the defense of advice of counsel is raised where the conduct involved is illegal. Thus, almost by definition the advice relied upon will have been erroneous but given and relied upon in good faith. The words spoken are the advice given. Advice is customarily given in words, and when advice is the question, the words which constitute the advice are classic examples of verbal acts, admissible because they were spoken, whether true or false. Such verbal acts are not hearsay. They come in to bring home notice to the defendant in a case like this. . . . Thus, if the attorney had added: "I told them that I had discussed this with several attorneys expert in these matters, and that they all agreed with me that that is illegal," that too would be admissible, whether or not the witness' statement of what he had done and what he had been told was true. It would still be a statement by the attorney of the advice he had given.

United States v. Freeman, 9 Cir., 1975, 519 F.2d 67, also supports this conclusion. In that case, Freeman was appealing her conviction for "bail jumping" which was based upon her failure to appear in district court on a specific date. A major issue in the district court was whether she knew that she had been ordered to appear on that date. Her attorney was asked, under oath, whether he had previously stated to the court that he had told his client when she was scheduled to appear. We said:

> Counsel was not asked whether he had advised appellant of the order that she appear on May 20th; instead, he was asked whether, on that date, he had stated to the court that he had done so. An affirmative response to the

former question, insofar as it constituted evidence of utterances and writings offered to show the effect on the hearer or reader, would not have been subject to attack as hearsay. *See, e.g.*, McCormick, Evidence § 249 (2d ed. 1972).

519 F.2d at 69.

In *Freeman*, the statement was not elicited to show its effect upon the court but rather to show that Freeman knew the date of the court appearance. The statement was relevant only if it showed that the attorney did tell Freeman, his client, when to appear. At issue was the very truth of the matter asserted. Here, the statement was offered to show its effect upon the defendants. Here, it is the fact that the statement was made, not its truth, that is relevant and material. That is precisely the distinction recognized by the court in *Freeman, supra*. Our case is like the case that would have been before the court in *Freeman* if in that case "[c]ounsel was . . . asked whether he had advised appellant of the order that she appear on May 20th. . . . An affirmative response to [that] question . . . would not have been subject to attack as hearsay."

Moreover, the fact that the statement was made was also compelling evidence that before November, 1973, Burnett was not aware that the defendants had been personally appropriating the architect's fees. It shows the attorney's lack of knowledge about the defendants' activities. From this the jury could conclude that the defendants had not fully informed their lawyer of all the material facts when they were soliciting his advice, thus undermining their defense of reliance on the advice of counsel. . . . Because Burnett's testimony was offered to show both defendants' and Burnett's knowledge, it was not hearsay, and its admission was proper.

*   *   *

Affirmed.

Choy, Circuit Judge, concurring specially:

I agree that the convictions of McLennan and Bender should be affirmed. I would reach that result, however, for reasons different from those advanced by Judge Duniway.

I am unpersuaded by Brother Duniway's attempt to distinguish the controlling precedent of *United States v. Freeman*, 519 F.2d 67 (9th Cir. 1975). Here, as there, the involved statements contained the words "I told" (or "stated" or "advised"), and thus at least that portion of the declarant-witness's out-of-court utterance cannot be said to have been offered merely for the nonhearsay purpose of proving notice, for previous notice in this context *is the very truth of the matter asserted:* that this statement was in fact previously uttered.[13] On the assumption that *Freeman* was

---

[13] [1] Judge Duniway's misreading of *Freeman* may stem from the focus of his attention in that opinion. He quotes the following language:

> Counsel was not asked whether he had advised appellant of the order that she appear on May 20th; instead, he was asked whether, on that date, he had stated to the court that he had done

correctly decided, therefore, Burnett's testimony in the instant case was hearsay. Even as such, however, I would hold that it is admissible under [an exception to the rule against hearsay].

NOTES AND QUESTIONS

1. In effect, Judge Choy's concurring opinion observes that the hearsay status of the statement "I told you that is illegal" depends on its probative purpose. When used to establish the defendant's notice concerning the illegality of a future course of action, the statement is non-hearsay. But when used to prove the matter which his statement describes — *i.e.*, that he previously told them that's illegal — the statement is hearsay under the assertion-oriented definition contained in Fed. R. Evid. 801(c). Thus, even in the same trial, a statement may be both hearsay and non-hearsay depending upon how it is used.

2. The *McLennan* Court gives three different reasons for concluding that the attorney's remarks are not hearsay. Each reflects a different application of the assertion-oriented hearsay definition. Identify these reasons and determine whether they accurately exemplify different applications of that definition.

3. Prior to 2000, when Federal Rule of Evidence 703 was amended by adding the last sentence designed to discourage the admission of the inadmissible data on which the expert relied in reaching her opinion, a large majority of federal courts admitted the inadmissible data either for its truth or with a limiting instruction. After the adoption of the 2000 amendment, federal courts continued to admit the "otherwise inadmissible data" though not necessarily for the truth in 50% of reported cases. Volek, *Federal Rule of Evidence 703: The Back Door and the Confrontation Clause, Ten Years Later*, 80 Fordham L. Rev. 959 (2011). Volek also points out that most federal courts find that because the "inadmissible data" is not offered for the truth of the matter asserted, its admission and disclosure to the jury does not violate the Confrontation Clause after *Crawford v. Washington. Id.* at 993. According to some federal appellate courts, though, where the government uses the expert's disclosure of otherwise inadmissible hearsay merely as a conduit or "transmitter" of hearsay as opposed to applying it to the expert's independent judgment, the Confrontation Clause is implicated and violated. *United States v. Lombardozzi*, 491 F.3d. 61 (2d Cir. 2007), *United States v. Mejia*, 545 F.3d 179 (2d Cir. 2008), *United States v. Johnson*, 587 F.3d 625 (4th Cir. 2009), *United States v. Ayala*, 601 F.3d 256 (4th Cir. 2010). (Cases collected at Volek, *supra*, at 995.)

---

so. An affirmative response to the former question, insofar as it constituted evidence of utterances and writings offered to show the effect on the hearer or reader, would not have been subject to attack as hearsay. *See, e.g.*, McCormick, Evidence § 249 (2d ed. 1972).

519 F.2d at 69. He overlooks, however, the very next sentence:

But an affirmative response to the latter inquiry — the response here given — was clearly evidence of out-of-court statements offered to prove the truth of the matters asserted therein.

Id. (footnote omitted).

PEOPLE v. BARNHART
66 Cal. App. 2d 714 (1944)

YORK, PRESIDING JUSTICE.

Following a trial upon . . . two counts charging that plaintiff on July 28, 1943, (1) kept and occupied a house at 1809 North Marengo Avenue, Pasadena, with paraphernalia used for the purpose of registering bets on horse races; and (2) recorded and registered bets on horse racing, in violation of . . . the Penal Code, plaintiff was found guilty as charged and sentenced to the County Jail for a term of thirty.

*   *   *

By stipulation, the cause was submitted to the trial court upon the transcript of the preliminary examination, which discloses that on July 28, 1943, around 12:10 p.m., Paul De Falla, a deputy sheriff of Los Angeles County, accompanied by another deputy sheriff, went to the premises in question, and, according to De Falla's testimony, he knocked at the back door and told appellant, who answered the summons, that he had come "to check some suspected gas leaks." Said premises consisted of a five room house where appellant and her husband resided, and a small house in the rear occupied by appellant's grandmother. Appellant was alone in the house, and as the officers walked through the front room and down a hall to a smaller room containing some bookmaking paraphernalia and two telephones, appellant preceded the officers at which time "One of the telephones was on its cradle and the other telephone was off its cradle. She (appellant) took one off while I was there. I saw her do it." At the instant trial, it was stipulated that "there were two phones in the rear house and one was connected with the telephone in her (appellant's) house."

*   *   *

When officers Hand and Hughes arrived at the scene the telephone receivers were replaced on the hooks and Mrs. Sherman, a clerk in the Pasadena Police Department, answered the telephones as they rang, to-wit: "There was one phone on a chair and the other was on the desk. And so I answered the one on the chair, and I said 'Go ahead', and a man's voice . . . answered and said 'Who is this' and I said 'Jane', not knowing the first name of Mrs. Barnhart. And he said, 'How are you' and I said, 'I am fine'; and then he said, 'Do you know who this is' and I said 'No'. I then said, 'Go ahead if you want to place any bets'. . . . And he said, 'What are you talking about' and I said, 'Go ahead'. Then he said, 'I just wanted to ask you for a date tonight', and I said 'What are you talking about'; I said 'you know I won't go out with you'. And he said, 'Well, never mind then', and hung up. In the meantime the other telephone was ringing and I answered that, and as soon as I answered that Officer De Falla asked Mrs. Barnhart her name and I overheard the conversation and she told him her name was Marjorie. So I answered the phone and I said 'Hello', and the voice on the other end of the line said 'Hello' and I said 'Hello', and he said 'Who is this' and I said 'This is Marjorie', and he said, 'No, it isn't'. He said, 'I know her voice'. Then I said, 'No, this isn't Marjorie, she is busy; can I help you' He said, 'Yes, in the 5th race at Saratoga', and I said 'which horse' and he said 'the same', and I said 'how much' and he said 5, 5 and 8. . . . Then the next time the phone rang I said 'Hello', and a voice said 'This is Charlie', and it then said, 'Hi, Marj.,' and he said, 'Give me one across on Diggie in the first race at New York'. I said 'Any others' and he said, 'One across on Number 17, the second at Washington'. Then the phone on the chair rang and I said 'Hello', and a voice said, 'Is this Marj.' and I said, 'Yes', I said 'This is Marj.' and a woman's voice said, 'What's the matter' and I said, 'Nothing', and then I said, 'Who is this' and she said, 'This is Erma, don't you recognize my voice' and I said, 'O, Hello, Erma, how are you' and she said 'Fine'. In the meantime the telephone on the desk rang and I said, 'Will you hold the phone as I want to take another call', and I answered that by saying 'Hello', and a voice said, . . . 'This is Ann and I want to place a bet for Katherine'. I said, 'Which race' and she said, 'In the third at Arlington', and she wanted two across on Bellmand and two across Buster and four across on Bitter End. Then she hung up and I returned to the telephone where Erma had been holding on and I said 'Okay', and she said 'I thought you were in trouble as it sure didn't sound like you at first', and so I coughed and said, 'I have a very bad cold'. I said, 'I am kind of rushed if you want to give me any wagers you better hurry with them', and she said 'Okay, give me the fifth at New York, number 1, two across, and number 10, one across'. Then the last bet I got, or the last party I talked to was a man named Dave, and that was also when I hung up after talking to Erma on the same phone. He said, 'This is Dave', and he started right out and said 'Give me the third at Suffolk, number 1, two across the board'. He then said, 'At Arlington Park, Margin in the 5th, two across, and Roiter in the sixth, two across, and Fortress in the second, two across', and then he said, 'Suffolk in the eighth, two across'."

*   *   *

Under the authority of *People v. Joffe*, 45 Cal. App. 2d 233, 235, 113 P.2d 901, and *People v. Reifenstuhl*, 37 Cal. App. 2d 402, 405, 99 P.2d 564, evidence of telephonic conversations between arresting officers and persons calling the establishment are properly admitted as tending to establish the fact that the premises were occupied for the purpose of bookmaking.

For the reasons stated, the judgment is affirmed.

DORAN, JUSTICE.

I concur in the judgment. But I know of no rule or principle of law that authorizes or justifies a relaxation of the hearsay rule for expediency. The evidence of the telephone conversations was pure hearsay. Evidence of the fact that a conversation was received would be admissible for the purpose of proving that the telephone was in order and functioning, but for no other purpose; the substance of the conversation is unnecessary for this purpose. The argument in *People v. Joffe*, 45 Cal. App. 2d 233, 235, 113 P.2d 901, 902, namely, that such evidence is admissible because "it tended to establish the fact that the premises were occupied for the purpose of recording wagers on horse races", clearly permits a consideration of hearsay for the purpose of proving the very offense charged. And the same inaccurate reasoning appears in *People v. Reifenstuhl*, 37 Cal. App. 2d 402, 405, 99 P.2d 564, 566, where the court declared, referring to such evidence, that "It was not subject to the hearsay rule. The conversation was not admitted for the purpose of proving its own contents (16

Cor. Jur. 624) but to prove the use to which the telephone was subjected by the public and to demonstrate the reaction of the defendant at the time. The use of the room occupied by defendant was in issue and the nature of the telephonic call was a circumstance to establish the truth. The uses to which a telephone is put reveal more truthfully the character of the establishment that houses the instrument than do the words of description attached to the listing."

It is futile to argue that such evidence is not hearsay. In my judgment the preservation of the hearsay rule is not only important but vital in the administration of justice. To relax the rule just to uphold the conviction of a book-maker, or for any other purpose, is nothing short of judicial stupidity.

QUESTIONS

1. Do the sheer volume of incoming calls in *Barnhart* make it a better case for admissibility than *Snow*? *See* Tribe, *Triangulating Hearsay*, 87 Harv. L. Rev. 957, 959 n.9 (1974).

2. Alternatively, is *Barnhart* a better case for admissibility because of the nonassertive nature of some of the statements involved? *See* § F, *infra*.

3. In *Snow*, the Court at least attempted to confront the hearsay issue analytically. The same, however, cannot be said for the majority opinions in *Felder* and *Barnhart* (regardless of how you come out on the merits). In other situations, courts have substituted certain magic words — such as *res gestae* — for analysis. This practice has been criticized. *See* § I.2.e, *infra*.

Evidentiary Foundation:
The Trial of Harrison A. Williams, Jr.[14]

[The background in this case is set forth § C.4.b.7 in Chapter III, *supra*. At one point in the trial, the judge allowed the following testimony to establish the context of an anticipated future meeting between FBI undercover agents and Senator Harrison Williams aide, defendant Alexander Feinberg.]

JOHN McCARTHY, called as a witness, having been first duly sworn by the Clerk of the Court, took the stand and testified as follows:

THE COURT: All right, Mr. Puccio, you may proceed.

MR. PUCCIO: Thank you.

DIRECT EXAMINATION BY MR. PUCCIO:

* * *

Q.   Did you have a conversation with Mr. Errichetti at the time concerning Mr. Feinberg, the defendant in this case, and Sandy Williams?[15]

---

[14] Excerpted from trial transcript, *supra*, p. 342.

[15] [Ed. — Sandy Williams is the nickname of Henry A. Williams, a personal friend and business

A.   Yes, sir, I did.

Q.   Now, tell us as best you can recall, what Mr. Errichetti said to you and what you said to Mr. Errichetti about Mr. Feinberg and Mr. Sandy Williams?

MR. BATCHELDER: Objection.

MR. KOELZER: Objection.

THE COURT: On what grounds?

MR. BATCHELDER: Irrelevant, your Honor. It is not background. He is not offering it for background. He's offering it for the truth . . .

MR. KOELZER: There are several questions. And I am mindful of your Honor's instructions.

THE COURT: Do you wish to be heard on the subject, Mr. Puccio, at side bar?

MR. PUCCIO: Yes, your Honor.

THE COURT: Side bar.

          (The following took place at the side bar.)

MR. PUCCIO: Judge, we seek to establish through the testimony of this witness that Mr. Errichetti in his conversation with Agent McCarthy set up a meeting for Feinberg and Sandy Williams to discuss the titanium mine proposal. And that meeting was held the next day on January 11th. I think that it's important that we be able to show that and how this whole thing got started because it was in fact, as the later evidence will show, Senator Williams who suggested that Mr. Errichetti get in touch with Mr. Feinberg and set up a meeting for Feinberg and Sandy Williams with the sheik's representatives. I think it was even alluded to during the opening statement. Mr. Koelzer said it was the Senator who had first spoken to Mr. Errichetti about this and that's how the ball got rolling.

THE COURT: What you are saying essentially is that you are offering it as background to put the next meeting into context?

MR. PUCCIO: Yes. . . .

MR. KOELZER: Is it a representation of Mr. Puccio that that is all that is going to be questioned about this meeting or — is that all that will be elicited?

MR. PUCCIO: The subject, yes.

*   *   *

---

associate of Senator Williams. The two are not relatives. Sandy Williams was an unindicted co-conspirator in this case.]

THE COURT: There may be a problem with the witness. And I suggest, Mr. Puccio, that you lead him a bit through the—

MR. PUCCIO: I already told him that I wasn't going to bring this up.

MR. KOELZER: Fine. That's all you had to say at the outset.

MR. BATCHELDER: I know you may have to lead him, but can we have a little bit less leading? I mean, I don't want to keep jumping up, but when the—

THE COURT: . . . This is largely preliminary. But he seems to be — the leading aspect, be careful of the way you phrase your questions, Mr. Puccio.

* * *

THE COURT: All right, Mr. Puccio, you may proceed.

MR. PUCCIO: Thank you, your Honor.

BY MR. PUCCIO:

Q.   Mr. McCarthy, tell us, please, what you said and what Mr. Errichetti said at this meeting on January 10th, 1979, at the Hyatt House?

A.   To the best of my recollection, Mr. Errichetti mentioned to me that he had an interesting financial deal which he would like to propose for my consideration. He mentioned to me that what he had were two individuals, an Alexander Feinberg and an individual by the name of Sandy Williams who had this financial proposal. He told me that he would try to — to the best of his ability, to have them meet with me at the Cherry Hill Hyatt House before I left the area the next day, which was January 11th. I agreed to meet them.

QUESTION

Did the court rule correctly? Does proof of context necessarily render the statement non-hearsay? Under a declarant-oriented definition of hearsay, doesn't the accuracy of the proffered context depend upon declarant Errichetti's truthfulness (that "Alexander Feinberg . . . had this financial proposal")? Alternatively, under an assertion oriented definition (as per Fed. R. Evid. 801(c)), doesn't the statement prove context only if the statement is being offered for the truth of the matter asserted (that "Alexander Feinberg . . . had this financial proposal.")?

E.   CONDUCT AND IMPLIED STATEMENTS

PARK v. HUFF
493 F.2d 923 (5th Cir. 1974)

Wisdom, Circuit Judge:

A.C. Park, the petitioner-appellant, was convicted in a Georgia court of murdering a local prosecuting attorney. The evidence against him consisted of hearsay statements introduced under Georgia's co-conspirator exception to the hearsay rule. After his conviction was affirmed by the Georgia Supreme Court, Park sought federal habeas corpus relief. . . .

I.

Between 7:00 and 7:30 in the morning on August 7, 1967, Floyd Hoard, the Solicitor General of the Piedmont Judicial Circuit in Georgia, was killed when dynamite wired to the ignition system of his car exploded. After a four-month investigation, a grand jury in Jackson County, Georgia, indicted five persons for the murder: Douglas Pinion, J. H. Blackwell, Loyd George Seay, George Ira Worley, and Park. The prosecution's theory was that the killing had been accomplished through a three-tiered conspiracy — Blackwell, Seay, and Worley had purchased the dynamite and wired it to the coil of Hoard's car; Pinion had paid the three $5,500 for the murder; and Park had been the prime mover of the project and had furnished at least $5,000 of the purchase price. As a motive for the killing, the State postulated Hoard's recent law-enforcement activities against Park, Pinion, and Seay, who were operating on a large scale the business of selling liquor in a dry county. . . .

Seay and Blackwell pleaded guilty to murder; Pinion and Worley were convicted of murder after trial. All were sentenced to life imprisonment. Park entered a plea of not guilty and was tried separately. He denied any knowledge of the murder and stated to the jury that he had not seen or talked with Seay for at least two years before Hoard's death.

Worley and Pinion did not testify at Park's trial. Blackwell and Seay testified for the State. Blackwell's testimony was largely corroborative; he had never seen nor talked with Park. But Seay's testimony was determinative. Indeed, the only evidence directly implicating Park in the slaying came from Seay's lips. Seay related several critical conversations he had had with other alleged members of the conspiracy. The testimony most damaging to Park were out-of-court declarations by Pinion. According to Seay, Pinion told him that "a man" wanted Hoard "done away with" and was willing to pay $5,000. Seay responded that he would "check around for him and see if anybody wanted to do it." Seay spoke to Worley who said he would murder Hoard, but he wanted $7,500 instead of $5,000. Seay then went back to Pinion and told him that he had found someone to do the job for $7,500. Pinion responded that he did not think "the man" would pay more than $5,000, but that he would inquire. Pinion left and was gone about forty-five minutes. When he returned he told Seay, "[T]he old man won't go up any more. I will put $500 on it. Make it

$5,500." It was established at trial that Park was generally known in the community as the "old man." The only other evidence directly implicating Park in the murder scheme was Seay's testimony that Worley had said that, if Seay did not go through with the killing, the "old man" would have "something done" to him or to his family. Seay testified that "other than what Doug Pinion told" him he knew nothing as to Park's "having any connection with" the money given him by Pinion, and other than that "he had no contact with Mr. Park at all with respect to any killing."

* * *

II.

"Hearsay" is defined as a "statement, other than one made by the declarant while testifying at the trial or hearing, offered in evidence to prove the truth of the matter asserted." Federal Rules of Evidence, Rule 801 (1972). Most definitions are substantially similar. . . . Taking these definitions literally, the statements of Pinion and Worley, recounted by Seay, were analogous to but not identical with typical hearsay in that they were not "offered to prove the truth of the matter asserted"; whether in fact the "old man" would raise the ante or would have "something done" to Seay's family if he did not cooperate was beside the point. The out-of-court statements of Pinion and Worley, however, clearly implied that Park was involved in the conspiracy to murder Solicitor General Hoard. As proof of Park's guilt the statements formed evidence just as damaging as direct declarations that Park was a leading member of the murder conspiracy. And the truth of the implication depended on the credibility, the trustworthiness, of the declarants who were not subject to cross-examination. . . . Twenty-five years ago, Professor Morgan analyzed the hearsay rule and identified its rationale as based on the untrustworthiness of hearsay statements: "[S]hould we not recognize that the rational basis for the hearsay classification is not the formula, 'assertions offered for the truth of the matter asserted,' but rather the presence of substantial risks of insincerity and faulty narration, memory, and perception?" Morgan, *Hearsay Dangers and the Application of the Hearsay Concept*, 62 Harv. L. Rev. 177, 218 (1948).

Implied assertions may in certain circumstances carry less danger of insincerity or untrustworthiness than direct assertions, . . . but not always. The danger of insincerity or untrustworthiness is decreased only where there is no possibility that the declarant intended to leave a particular impression. Finman, *Implied Assertions as Hearsay: Some Criticism of the Uniform Rules of Evidence*, 14 Stan. L. Rev. 682, 686 (1962); Rucker, *The Twilight Zone of Hearsay*, 9 Vand. L. Rev. 453, 478 (1956). Here we cannot exclude that possibility; Pinion's and Worley's statements carry the implication that they mentioned the "old man" to Seay with the intention of communicating to him, as a fact, Park's participation in the plot.

When the possibility is real that an out-of-court statement which implies the existence of the ultimate fact in issue was made with assertive intent, it is essential that the statement be treated as hearsay if a direct declaration of that fact would be so treated. Baron Parke made an observation to that effect more than a century ago in the famous case of *Wright v. Tatham*, 1837, 7 Adolphus & E. 313, 388–389, 112 Eng. Rep. 488, 516–17:

[P]roof of a particular fact, which is not of itself a matter in issue, but which is relevant only as implying a statement or opinion of a third person on the matter in issue, is inadmissible in all cases where such a statement or opinion not on oath would be of itself inadmissible.

Were the rule otherwise, the hearsay rule could easily be circumvented through clever questioning and coaching of witnesses, so that answers were framed as implied rather than as direct assertions. . . .

[Although the hearsay exception for co-conspirator's declarations, *infra* p. 572, was arguably available for this case, the Court reversed because Park had been denied his Sixth Amendment right to confront all witnesses against him. This aspect of the decision was reversed upon rehearing in 506 F.2d 849 (*en banc*), *cert. denied*, 423 U.S. 824 (1975). The Confrontation Clause and its relationship to the hearsay rule is discussed *infra* p. 749.]

NOTES AND QUESTIONS

1.   Although *Huff* pre-dates the effective date of the Federal Rules of Evidence (July 1, 1975), the Court purported to rely upon Fed. R. Evid. 801. Did the Court's analysis, however, fail to consider that Fed. R. Evid. 801, at least literally, does not treat implied assertions as hearsay? Although implied assertions contain potential hearsay dangers, other courts have declined to treat such remarks as hearsay. *See United States v. Ybarra*, 70 F.3d 362 (5th Cir. 1995).

2.   The Advisory Committee Notes to Fed. R. Evid. 801(a) recognize that sometimes "a preliminary demonstration will be required to determine whether an assertion is intended." The same Note states that in such cases "[t]he rule is so worded as to place the burden upon the party claiming that the intention existed; ambiguous and doubtful cases will be resolved against him and in favor of admissibility." Did the *Huff* Court apply this approach?

Evidentiary Foundation:
The Trial of Charles Manson[16]

[In the summer of 1970, Charles Manson and members of his so-called "Family" went on trial in Los Angeles for the notorious Tate-La Bianca murders of the preceding year. Linda Kasabian, a former member of Manson's "Family," was the state's star witness. In the following excerpt, Ms. Kasabian is asked about events that occurred on August 8, 1969, the day before the Tate murders. How should the Court have ruled on defense counsel Irving Kanarek's hearsay objection?]

"What happened on that day, August 8, 1969, after dinner?" inquired the prosecutor.

"On August 8, the family ate together after sundown. Dinner time," continued Mrs. Kasabian, "was fun time, fun hour." Then she added seriously, "Maybe an hour after dinner . . . people were sitting around on rocks outside. I was on the porch

---

[16]   Excerpted from W. Zamora, Trial by Your Peers 79 (1973). *See generally People v. Manson*, 61 Cal. App. 3d 102 (1976), *cert. denied*, 430 U.S. 986 (1977).

and Charlie came up and told me off . . . Then Charlie told me to get a change of clothes, a knife, and my driver's license."

Mr. Kanarek jumped up and objected, "Hearsay, and . . . may we approach the bench, Your Honor?"

*Not on final

SILVER v. NEW YORK CENTRAL R.R. CO.

105 N.E.2d 923 (Mass. 1952)

L⟶ before FRE

WILKINS, JUSTICE.

On January 14, 1948, Frances Silver became a passenger, bound from Boston to Cincinnati, on a train operated by the defendant railroad. The following morning the Pullman car in which she had a berth was detached at Cleveland and stood for nearly four hours in the yard to await connection with the next train to Cincinnati. She was suffering from a circulatory ailment known as Raynaud's disease. The temperature in the car became too cold for her, and she experienced ill effects. Mrs. Silver, who will be referred to as the plaintiff, brought this action against the defendant railroad and the Pullman Company. . . .

The judge found for the plaintiff against the railroad.

[Ed. — After finding that the judge applied an incorrect standard of negligence, the court turned to "questions that may arise" on retrial.]

*   *   *

The porter in the plaintiff's car was rightly allowed to testify as to the temperature conditions in that car. . . . He was giving at first hand his experience with the same conditions which confronted the plaintiff. . . . But he was not permitted to give evidence that eleven other passengers in that car made no complaint to him as to the temperature while at Cleveland. This is a somewhat different proposition, as it was sought to draw from the silence of those passengers a deduction that the car was not too cold, otherwise they would have spoken. In certain courts evidence of absence of complaints by customers has been excluded on the issue of defective quality of goods sold, and the hearsay rule has been relied upon or referred to. . . . In *Menard v. Cashman*, 94 N.H. 428, 433–434, 55 A.2d 156, which was an action of tort arising out of a fall on a defective stairway in a business block, it was held proper to exclude testimony of a tenant that none of her customers had ever complained of any defects, the court saying that the testimony had the characteristics of hearsay, and that if it was not hearsay, it was only evidence of inconclusive silence, which might be excluded in the discretion of the trial judge.

Evidence as to absence of complaints from customers other than the plaintiff has been admitted in four cases, all relating to breach of warranty in the sale of food, in this Commonwealth. In three of them the testimony was apparently received without objection. . . . In *Landfield v. Albiani Lunch Co.*, 268 Mass. 528, 168 N.E. 160, the plaintiff alleged that he had been made ill by eating beans purchased at the defendant's restaurant. Subject to his exception, evidence was admitted that on that day and on the day preceding no complaint as to the beans was made by any other customer. In upholding the ruling on evidence, it was said, 268 Mass. at page 530, 168 N.E. at page 160: "The fact that others than the plaintiff ate of the food complained of without ill effects is competent evidence that it was not unwholesome. . . . There is a reasonable inference based on common experience that one who ate and suffered as he believed in consequence would make complaint. There is a further reasonable inference, based on logic, that if no one complained no one suffered. Obviously, the latter conclusion is not convincing that the food was wholesome, unless one is satisfied that both plaintiff and others ate of it. Evidence of no complaint is too remote and should not be admitted unless, in addition to the fact that no complaints were made, there is evidence of circumstances indicating that others similarly situated ate and had opportunity for complaining."

It has often been said that where collateral issues may be opened, much must rest in the discretion of the trial judge. . . . In the case at bar, should the circumstances of the plaintiff and of the other passengers as to exposure to the cold be shown to be substantially the same, the negative evidence that none of the others spoke of it to the porter might properly be admitted. The evidence would not be equivocal, and would then be offered on the basis of a common condition which all in the car encountered. The porter's duties should be shown to include the receipt of that sort of complaints from those passengers. It should appear that he was present and available to be spoken to, and that it was not likely that complaints were made by those passengers to other employees of the railroad or the sleeping car company. This would not seem to be a situation where one might prefer to remain silent rather than to make any statement. Indeed, if the car was too cold, ordinary prudence might seem to require that one speak out. There would be no ambiguity of inference. There would be at least as strong a case for admissibility as in the food cases, and a far stronger one than those relating to the sale of allegedly defective goods in which little may be known in terms of sale to the noncomplaining buyers. Unlike the unknown users of a stairway in a business block, the uniform result of silence in the cases of a large number of passengers, here apparently eleven, would not be inconclusive. *See* Falknor, *Silence as Hearsay*, 89 U. Pa. L. Rev. 192.

Exceptions sustained.

QUESTION

Would the porter's testimony concerning the passenger's silence constitute a hearsay problem under the Federal Rules of Evidence?

F. DEFINING THE HEARSAY DECLARANT

PEOPLE v. CENTOLELLA
61 Misc. 2d 723 (N.Y. County Ct. 1969)

John J. Walsh, J.

During the course of this trial, a serious question of law has arisen which required a recess of this jury trial to permit its resolution before proceeding to hear any further testimony.

The prosecution has presented some 30 witnesses to establish its contention that the two defendants on trial and two co-defendants who have been granted severances for separate reasons, committed an armed robbery in the City of Rome, New York on April 19, 1968.

The testimony now sought to be introduced is that of State Trooper Suffolk. Through him, the prosecution seeks to establish the background, training and pedigree of two bloodhounds, "Colonel of Red Stone" and "Corporal of Red Stone." After a few preliminary questions as to the training and experience of the bloodhounds, defense counsel interposed an objection to such testimony upon the ground that it is completely inadmissible in evidence in a criminal action.

The weight of authority in this country, however, holds that evidence of trailing by bloodhounds is admissible in a criminal action provided a proper foundation is first laid. (*See* "Evidence of Trailing By Dogs In Criminal Cases" Ann. 19 ALR 3d 1221 *et seq.*)

. . . [I]t might be well to examine the argument made against the admission of such evidence:

1. That the actions of the bloodhounds are unreliable.

2. That such evidence constitutes hearsay.

3. That the defendant is deprived of his constitutional right to be confronted by the witnesses against him.

4. That the defendant should not be placed in jeopardy by the actions of an animal.

5. That a defendant cannot cross-examine the dogs.

6. That a jury might be awed by such testimony and give it much greater weight and importance than it warranted.

The theory upon which bloodhound evidence is offered is that the body of every human being constantly emanates microscopic particles of effluvia which possesses an odor characteristic of the particular individual, and the highly developed olfactory nerves of the bloodhound enable him to detect the peculiar odor of these particles, and thus to follow the trail by such scent. The term "bloodhound" has nothing to do with the traits, characteristics or disposition of the dog. It merely signifies that it is a blooded or thoroughbred hound. (*See* "The Bloodhound As a Witness" J.C. McWhorter, 54 AMER. L. REV. 109 [1920].) The dog's reliability must be established by means of testimony as to his pedigree, his training, his previous success or failure in following the trails of individuals, and all other circumstances from which a jury may make a finding of reliability before acting on such evidence.

Such evidence falls into the category of opinion evidence rather than hearsay. The animals are not witnesses against a defendant any more than a microscope or a spectograph.

These are not subject to cross-examination any more than the animal. It is the handler who is the witness and he is merely asked to testify to what the animal actually did, not his opinion as to the guilt or innocence of a person.

A person is no more placed in jeopardy by the action of an animal that he is by a breath analyzer or a blood test.

No convincing reason appears to warrant this court in rejecting the generally accepted rule that such evidence is admissible if a proper foundation is laid.

Charles T. McCormick, *The Turncoat Witness: Previous Statements as Substantive Evidence* 25 Tex. L. Rev. 573, 573–77 (1947)[17]

A frequent and dramatic incident in the trial of cases is the disclosure that a vital witness has on some previous occasion told a different story on a crucial point from his testimony on the stand. What effect shall be given to the evidence of the prior statement? Three recent cases will serve to illustrate.

A suit on a policy of insurance on the life of Julius B. Selden. Defense, suicide. At the trial it appeared that Selden was a healthy young man, about to be married to a girl to whom he was devoted. He was a private detective with a prosperous business in investigating the honesty of employees of large stores. One night at 2:00 A.M. his body was found in his office. Death was the result of a wound from a revolver, found nearby and ordinarily kept in the desk of another occupant of the office. The wound was through the right ear, with close-range powder burns. A witness, Berger, called by the insurance company, was evidently expected to testify that Selden had declared his intention to commit suicide. He failed to remember such declarations. Thereupon the insurance company produced as witnesses two detectives who testified that Berger had told them that Selden had said that he intended to commit suicide. Were the jury to be permitted to weigh this last evidence, along with the other circumstances, in answering the question of suicide or no?

Henry Carroll was tried for stealing four head of cattle from his brother Frank. His signed confession was placed in evidence by the State. Frank, on whose complaint the indictment was found, surprised the State by testifying that the stolen cattle belonged not to him, but to his wife. To impeach him, the State showed that this witness, in company with the sheriff, had identified these cattle as his, and had sworn out a complaint against his brother, the defendant, for theft of the cattle as belonging to the witness, and had testified to the same effect before the grand jury. Under the local law a confession does not support a conviction unless corroborated. Did this evidence of the previous complaint, identification, and testimony by Frank serve to corroborate the defendant's confession?

Deportation proceedings against Harry Bridges, an alien, on the ground that he had been a member of or affiliated with an organization advocating the overthrow of the Government of the United States, namely the Communist Party. One O'Neil, the editor of a labor paper and a former associate of Bridges, was called by the Government as a witness in the deportation hearing. Examined at great length, he denied knowledge of any connection of Bridges with the Communist Party and denied that he, the witness, had ever made any contrary statements. The Govern-

---

ment produced evidence that in the course of an interview with investigating officers, taken down by a stenographer, O'Neil had said that he himself had joined the Party in 1936; that he walked into Bridges's office one day in 1937 and saw Bridges pasting assessment stamps in a Communist Party book; and that Bridges reminded O'Neil that he had not been attending party meetings. The stenographer verified the making of this statement by O'Neil, and an officer testified that later O'Neil had repeated the statements to him and to other witnesses. The final administrative authority in deportation proceedings is the Attorney General. In making his decision to deport, was he entitled to rely on this evidence of O'Neil's previous statements in reaching his finding that Bridges was a member of the Communist Party?

In each of the three cases the court held that the prior statement of the witness could not be used as "substantive" evidence of the truth of the facts recited in the statement. Accordingly, in the insurance case the verdict of suicide was set aside, the conviction of the confessed cattle-theft was reversed, and the detention of Harry Bridges under the deportation order was held unlawful because the use of the statement as "substantive" evidence rendered the hearing unfair. This is orthodox doctrine, and on the faith of it cases are being disposed of in the trial and appellate courts every day.

Obviously this doctrine is highly inconvenient, not to say poisonous to the interests of a party who has had the misfortune of having his crucial witness persuaded, suborned, seduced, or intimidated into changing his story. The sinister influence may be suspected, but cannot always be proved. The doctrine is, on the other hand, highly benevolent and protective to the party who has been able to persuade the key witness that his former story was mistaken and to prevail on him to testify on the stand that the true facts are otherwise.

The reason for the orthodox view that a previous statement of the witness, though admissible to impeach, is not evidence of the facts stated, is clear and obvious. When used for that purpose, the statement is hearsay. Its value rests on the credit of the declarant, who was not under oath nor subject to cross-examination, when the statement was made.

Nevertheless, there are reasons for a contrary view, that the statements should be. received as "substantive" evidence of their truth. These reasons are not so obvious. They depend upon judgments as to the balancing of values, but the more maturely they are considered, the more impressive they seem.[18]

The two safeguards of the truth of testimony on the stand are the oath, with its accompanying liability to punishment for perjury, and the probe of cross-examination. It is only the former, the oath and its accompanying liability, that are lacking when the previous statement of a witness now on the stand or available in court is offered in proof of the facts stated. Probably most trial lawyers and most

---

[18] [7] Witness the conversion of our greatest scholar in this field, who after expressing the view that such statements should be received as substantive evidence adds: "The orthodox view was approved in the first edition of this Treatise. Further reflection, however, has shown the present writer that the natural and correct solution is the one set forth in the text above." 3 WIGMORE, EVIDENCE (3d ed. 1940) § 1018, n.2.

students in the field of evidence would now agree that the oath and the penalties of perjury, though of substantial value, are not the principal safeguard of the trustworthiness of testimony. In the common law tradition the affidavit, under oath as it is, does not gain admission as evidence at a plenary trial. Moreover, of all the fifteen or so instances when hearsay evidence is admitted exceptionally, only one exception requires that the hearsay to come in must have been under oath. That instance, namely prior testimony, can moreover probably best be understood as a situation where the policy of the hearsay rule has been satisfied rather than as an exception to its requirements.

It would doubtless be generally agreed among courts and lawyers, and among writers in the evidence field, that by all odds the major safeguard of the veracity of testimony and its main factor of superiority to out-of-court statements is its subjection to the test of cross-examination.

If the prior statement of the witness is contradictory of his present story on the stand, the opportunity for testing the veracity of the two stories by the two parties through cross-examination and re-examination is ideal. Too often the cross-examiner of a dubious witness is faced by a smooth, blank wall. The witness has been able throughout to present a narrative which may be false, yet is consistent with itself and offers no foothold for the climber who would look beyond. But the witness who has told one story aforetime and another today has opened the gates to all the vistas of truth which the common law practice of cross-examination and re-examination was invented to explore. It will go hard, but the two questioners will lay bare the sources of the change of face, in forgetfulness, carelessness, pity, terror or greed, and thus reveal which is the true story and which the false. It is hard to escape the view that evidence of a previous inconsistent statement, when the declarant is on the stand to explain it if he can, has in high degree the safeguards of examined testimony.

UNITED STATES v. DESISTO
329 F.2d 929 (2d Cir. 1964)

FRIENDLY, CIRCUIT JUDGE.

On a formal appeal, 289 F.2d 833 (2d Cir. 1961), we reversed DeSisto's conviction for hijacking a truck loaded with silk goods shipped from Japan, in violation of 18 U.S.C. § 1951, because of errors in the trial. After a new trial before Judge Mishler and a jury, DeSisto was again convicted. His appeal raises questions as to the sufficiency of the evidence in the light of a change in the identification testimony of the truck driver on cross-examination, as to the evidentiary status of the driver's prior identification, and as to charges and omissions to charge. We affirm.

In the early afternoon of September 1, 1959, a truck containing 31 cartons of imported Japanese silk goods was hijacked ten or fifteen minutes after leaving Pier 38 in Brooklyn, while turning from Carroll into Hicks Street. Its progress there was blocked by an Oldsmobile parked at a 45 degree angle. A man, whom Fine, the truck driver, later identified as DeSisto, walked over from the Oldsmobile, climbed on the running board of the truck on the driver's side, and, with his face about 18 inches away, told Fine, "Look straight ahead, Wimpy, and do what you are told. Pull over to the curb. Don't touch the key. Put the brake on. Do as you are told or I will kill you." Fine complied. Later, as ordered, he descended from the truck, and was herded into the Oldsmobile where taped glasses were placed over his eyes. Two other men who had assisted in this maneuver drove him off to a remote area where he was left handcuffed to a tree.

*   *   *

Assuming as we do that the Government was required to adduce evidence sufficient that a reasonable juror could be convinced of the guilt of the defendant beyond a reasonable doubt, . . . we think it plain that the evidence we have summarized — and there was more that we have not — amply passed that test if Fine's identification held. Not seriously challenging this, appellant argues that the identification was destroyed and that the Government's case fell with it.

In his direct testimony, Fine, after relating how he had seen the face of the hijacker, made a positive identification of DeSisto, as he had done at the first trial. But on cross-examination, after admitting that he had noticed the arms of the man on the occasion of the hijacking, he said he had seen no identifying marks and specifically no tattoo marks upon them. Defense counsel then had DeSisto remove his jacket to reveal large tattoo marks on the outside upper and lower portions of his arms, which he concededly bore in 1959. On further questioning Fine stated he could not say that DeSisto was the man who jumped on his truck.

The Government set about to repair the damage on redirect. Over objection Fine was allowed to testify that on September 1, 1959, he had told the FBI that his assailant was "A man approximately six feet tall, round face, heavy lips, one day or two days growth of stubble on his face, apparently Italian, heavy set, I think around 200 pounds, 180, 190, something to that effect, sir" — apparently a good description of DeSisto. He also was allowed to testify that on September 5, at FBI headquarters, he had picked DeSisto out of a line-up of four men; that he had identified a photograph of DeSisto's face before the grand jury on September 17; that he had again identified DeSisto at the first trial in November, 1959; and that he had identified a photograph of DeSisto's face in the United States Attorney's office shortly before the second trial. Further examination by both sides brought out that Fine had been told of the tattoo markings while he was being prepared to testify at the second trial and that when photographs of DeSisto's arms, taken at the lineup, were shown to him at his request, he had told the prosecutor that the man who jumped on the truck didn't have such marks and that he was now in doubt as to the identification — a doubt to which he adhered through a long examination. Two FBI agents who had attended the line-up testified, over objection, that DeSisto was then wearing a tee-shirt and that the tattoo marks were plainly visible.

We interrupt our discussion of the sufficiency of the evidence to consider appellant's objection to the receiving of Fine's prior identifications and the related testimony of the FBI agents. In the course of the Government's presentation of evidence of Fine's prior identifications, defense counsel sought an instruction to the effect that these could be considered only as bearing on Fine's present credibility[19] but not as substantive evidence. Receipt of this testimony without such a limitation is now claimed to have been error which was not cured when, several days later, the judge included in his charge a general instruction that an inconsistent statement by a witness "made prior to trial, not made under oath, is not to be considered as affirmative proof on the issue but only brought before you as impeaching testimony." Accepting that the charge would not correct the claimed error under the circumstances here presented, we are thus confronted with the issue as to the evidentiary status of prior statements. . . .

The rule limiting the use of prior statements by a witness subject to cross-examination to their effect on his credibility has been described by eminent scholars and judges as "pious fraud," "artificial," "basically misguided," "mere verbal ritual," and an anachronism "that still impede[s] our pursuit of the truth." . . . The sanctioned ritual seems peculiarly absurd when a witness who has given damaging testimony on his first appearance at a trial denies any relevant knowledge on his second; to tell a jury it may consider the prior testimony as reflecting on the veracity of the later denial of relevant knowledge but not as the substantive evidence that alone would be pertinent is a demand for mental gymnastics of which jurors are happily incapable. Beyond this the orthodox rule defies the dictate of common sense that "The fresher the memory, the fuller and more accurate it is. . . . Manifestly, this is not to say that when a witness changes his story, the first version is invariably true and the later is the product of distorted memory, corruption, false suggestion, intimidation, or appeal to sympathy [but] the greater the lapse of time between the event and the trial, the greater the chance of exposure of the witness to each of these influences." As against this, we are bound by the admonition, in *Bridges v. Wixon*, 326 U.S. 135, 153–154 (1945), against allowing "men to be convicted on unsworn testimony of witnesses — a practice which runs counter to the notions of fairness on which our legal system is founded."

Whether or not this ruling in *Bridges v. Wixon* will survive the attacks of scholars, we do not think the Supreme Court meant to require rigid adherence to the much criticized orthodox rule in the situation here presented where the prior statements were themselves testimony before a grand jury or at a former trial or were adopted by such testimony. The *Bridges* opinion emphasized that the statements there received as substantive evidence were simply a stenographer's notes of an investigative interview, whose accuracy the witness denied. "A written statement at the earlier interviews under oath and signed . . . would have afforded protection against mistakes in hearing, mistakes in memory, mistakes in transcription. Statements made under those conditions would have an important safeguard — the fear of prosecution for perjury." . . . These comments are inapplicable to testimony, transcribed by a court reporter, before a grand jury or at a former trial. Testimony at a former trial has already been once subjected "to the test of Cross-Examination" on which our law places primary reliance for the ascertainment of truth. Both such testimony and evidence before a grand jury have had the

---

[19] [3] The prior statements here at issue can be regarded either as inconsistent with and adversely affecting the credibility of Fine's partial recantation. or as consistent with and supporting the credibility of his identification on direct examination. . . .

sanction of what Wigmore calls the "prophylactic rules" relating to the oath and to perjury, influencing "the witness subjectively against conscious falsification, the one by reminding of ultimate punishment by a supernatural power, the other by reminding of speedy punishment by a temporal power." 6 EVIDENCE, §§ 1813, 1831 (3d ed. 1940) — with the oath administered not in any perfunctory fashion but in a setting calculated to impress the witness with the gravity of the responsibilities assumed. And in the case of identification testimony, we think the exception to the orthodox rule which seems to be permitted by the *Bridges* opinion may properly embrace not only testimony so given but the even more probative consistent earlier identifications for which the witness has later vouched under oath in the secrecy of the grand jury room or at a former trial.

The desirability of qualifying the orthodox rule to the extent indicated is illustrated by the circumstances of this case. The fact that Fine, only four days after the incident, had picked DeSisto out of a line-up with the latter's tattoos in full view, and had thereafter made a positive identification before the grand jury, at the first trial, and on other occasions, warranted a variety of inferences that would sustain his identification and discredit his doubts. It afforded a basis for the jury's thinking he had not in fact had an opportunity to observe these parts of DeSisto's arms during the hijacking; indeed Fine testified at the first trial that DeSisto had climbed onto the running board and with both hands had held onto the steel top frame of the cab — a position which would expose the insides, but not the tattooed outsides, of his arms to the driver. It could also be that with Fine's other preoccupations during the hijacking, the tattoo marks made no impression on him, or that though he had in fact recalled the marks at the line-up on September 5, 1959, he had forgotten them in the three and a half intervening years. It would be perfectly rational for the jury to decide that, for these reasons or for others not requiring mention, Fine's identification at the first trial and on direct examination at the second was more credible than the doubt he expressed about the tattoos. Consideration of such matters by a jury in a criminal case — the task which jurors are superbly equipped to perform — ought not be impeded by directing them to make a discrimination so elusive that it can scarcely be retained by a trained legal mind, let alone be applied by laymen in determining the guilt or innocence of an accused.

* * *

Affirmed.

NOTES AND QUESTIONS

1. Assuming that a witness' denial of a prior inconsistent statement is false, is that sufficient basis to conclude that his prior inconsistent statement is necessarily true? *See* Bein, *Prior Inconsistent Statements: The Hearsay Rule, 801(d)(1)(A) and 803(24)*, 26 UCLA L. REV. 967 (1979).

2. One might have read *DeSisto* as flatly recognizing the admissibility of a witness' extrajudicial statements to establish their truth. The Second Circuit itself, however, did not do so. *United States v. Nuccio*, 373 F.2d 168 (2d Cir.), *cert. denied*, 387 U.S. 906 (1967), made it clear that *DeSisto* was to be limited in some respect:

[T]he earlier testimony here in question, unlike that in *DeSisto*, was not given at a former trial in the same case where the witness' mind was focused on the identical fact at issue in the later one. Although testimony at the trial of another case can properly be used for impeachment subject to such explanation as the witness may make, where the prior testimony was given in a different case with different parties involving different issues, a trial judge may properly consider the dangers to be too great to warrant the admission of the testimony as affirmative evidence.

Id. at 173. But just one year before *Nuccio*, in *United States v. Armone*, 363 F.2d 385 (2d Cir. 1966), the court had held a witness' extrajudicial statement admissible under *DeSisto*, although the parties and issues were different. It follows that the limiting factor must be found outside the court's discussion in *Nuccio*. There are three possibilities:

(1) In *DeSisto*, the witness' extrajudicial statements had been spoken or adopted during the witness' testimony at an earlier trial, and, therefore, had been subjected to cross-examination. In *United States v. Insana*, 423 F.2d 1165 (2d Cir.), *cert. denied*, 400 U.S. at 841 (1970), however, extrajudicial statements not subjected to cross-examination were received under *DeSisto*, and *United States v. Mingoia*, 424 F.2d 710, (2d Cir. 1970), suggested *in dictum* that such cross-examination is not a prerequisite to admissibility.

(2) In *DeSisto*, the witness' extrajudicial statements concerned identification of the defendant as the guilty party. But in *Annona* and *Insana*, the statements admitted, on the authority of *DeSisto*, involved issues other than identification. Therefore, identification is not the limiting factor.

(3) In *DeSisto*, the witness' extrajudicial statements were made or repeated under oath. This circumstance is present in each Second Circuit case holding a witness' statement substantively admissible under *DeSisto*. Hence, notwithstanding *Nuccio*, it seems that the oath is the limiting factor.

3. To what extent, if any, are these *DeSisto* factors reflected in Federal Rule of Evidence 801?

4. Compare how the following codes treat this issue:

TOME v. UNITED STATES
513 U.S. 150 (1995)

JUSTICE KENNEDY delivered the opinion of the Court, except as to Part IIB [which is not provided].

Various federal Courts of Appeals are divided over the evidence question presented by this case. At issue is the interpretation of a provision in the Federal Rules of Evidence bearing upon the admissibility of statements, made by a declarant who testifies as a witness, that are consistent with the testimony and are offered to rebut a charge of a "recent fabrication or improper influence or motive."

Fed. Rule Evid. 801(d)(1)(B). The question is whether out-of-court consistent statements made after the alleged fabrication, or after the alleged improper influence or motive arose, are admissible under the Rule.

I

Petitioner Tome was charged in a one-count indictment with the felony of sexual abuse of a child, his own daughter, aged four at the time of the alleged crime. The case having arisen on the Navajo Indian Reservation, Tome was tried by a jury in the United States District Court for the District of New Mexico, where he was found guilty . . . .

Tome and the child's mother had been divorced in 1988. A tribal court awarded joint custody of the daughter, A.T., to both parents, but Tome had primary physical custody. In 1989 the mother was unsuccessful in petitioning the tribal court for primary custody of A.T., but was awarded custody for the summer of 1990 . . . . On August 27, 1990, the mother contacted Colorado authorities with allegations that Tome had committed sexual abuse against A.T.

The prosecution's theory was that Tome committed sexual assaults upon the child while she was in his custody and that the crime was disclosed when the child was spending vacation time with her mother. The defense argued that the allegations were concocted so the child would not be returned to her father. At trial A.T., then six and one half years old, was the Government's first witness. For the most part, her direct testimony consisted of one- and two-word answers to a series of leading questions. Cross-examination took place over two trial days. The defense asked A.T. 348 questions. On the first day A.T. answered all the questions posed to her on general, background subjects.

The next day there was no testimony, and the prosecutor met with A.T. When cross-examination of A.T. resumed, she was questioned about those conversations but was reluctant to discuss them. Defense counsel then began questioning her about the allegations of abuse, and it appears she was reluctant at many points to answer. As the trial judge noted, however, some of the defense questions were imprecise or unclear. The judge expressed his concerns with the examination of A.T., observing there were lapses of as much as 40–55 seconds between some questions and the answers and that on the second day of examination the witness seemed to be losing concentration. The trial judge stated, "We have a very difficult situation here."

After A.T. testified, the Government produced six witnesses who testified about a total of seven statements made by A.T. describing the alleged sexual assaults: A.T.'s babysitter recited A.T.'s statement to her on August 22, 1990, that she did not want to return to her father because he "gets drunk and he thinks I'm his wife"; the babysitter related further details given by A.T. on August 27, 1990, while A.T.'s mother stood outside the room and listened after the mother had been unsuccessful in questioning A.T. herself; the mother recounted what she had heard A.T. tell the babysitter; a social worker recounted details A.T. told her on August 29, 1990 about the assaults; and three pediatricians, Drs. Kuper, Reich and Spiegel, related A.T.'s statements to them describing how and where she had been touched by Tome. All but A.T.'s statement to Dr. Spiegel implicated Tome. (The physicians also testified that their clinical examinations of the child indicated that she had been subjected to vaginal penetrations. That part of the testimony is not at issue here.)

A.T.'s out-of-court statements, recounted by the six witnesses, were offered by the Government under Rule 801(d)(1)(B). The trial court admitted all of the statements over defense counsel's objection, accepting the Government's argument that they rebutted the implicit charge that A.T.'s testimony was motivated by a desire to live with her mother . . . . Following trial, Tome was convicted and sentenced to 12 years imprisonment.

On appeal, the Court of Appeals for the Tenth Circuit affirmed, adopting the Government's argument that all of A.T.'s out-of-court statements were admissible under Rule 801(d)(1)(B) even though they had been made after A.T.'s alleged motive to fabricate arose. The court reasoned that "the pre-motive requirement is a function of the relevancy rules, not the hearsay rules" and that as a "function of relevance, the pre-motive rule is clearly too broad . . . because it is simply not true that an individual with a motive to lie always will do so." 3 F.3d 342, 350 (10th Cir. 1993). "Rather, the relevance of the prior consistent statement is more accurately determined by evaluating the strength of the motive to lie, the circumstances in which the statement is made, and the declarant's demonstrated propensity to lie." *Ibid.* The court recognized that some Circuits require that the consistent statements, to be admissible under the Rule, must be made before the motive or influence arose, . . . but cited the Ninth Circuit's decision in *United States v. Miller*, 874 F.2d 1255, 1272 (9th Cir. 1989), in support of its balancing approach. Applying this balancing test to A.T.'s first statement to her babysitter, the Court of Appeals determined that although A.T. might have had "some motive to lie, we do not believe that it is a particularly strong one." . . . The court held that the district judge had not abused his discretion in admitting A.T.'s out-of-court statements. It did not analyze the probative quality of A.T.'s six other out-of-court statements, nor did it reach the admissibility of the statements under any other rule of evidence.

We granted *certiorari*, 510 U.S. 1109, 114 S. Ct. 1048, 127 L. Ed. 2d 370 (1994), and now reverse.

II

The prevailing common-law rule for more than a century before adoption of the Federal Rules of Evidence was that a prior consistent statement introduced to rebut a charge of recent fabrication or improper influence or motive was admissible if the statement had been made before the alleged fabrication, influence, or motive came into being, but it was inadmissible if made afterwards. As Justice Story explained: "[W]here the testimony is assailed as a fabrication of a recent date . . . in order to repel such imputation, proof of the *antecedent* declaration of the party may be admitted." *Ellicott v. Pearl*, 35 U.S. (10 Pet.) 412, 439, 9 L. Ed. 475 (1836) (emphasis supplied). . . .

McCormick and Wigmore stated the rule in a more categorical manner: "[T]he applicable principle is that the prior consistent statement has no relevancy to refute the charge unless the consistent statement was made before the source of the bias, interest, influence or incapacity originated." E. CLEARY, MCCORMICK ON EVIDENCE § 49, p. 105 (2d ed. 1972) (hereafter MCCORMICK). *See also* 4 J. WIGMORE, EVIDENCE § 1128, p. 268 (J. Chadbourn rev. 1972) (hereafter WIGMORE) ("A consistent statement, at a *time prior* to the existence of a fact said to indicate bias . . . will effectively explain away the force of the impeaching evidence") (emphasis in original)." The question is whether Rule 801(d)(1)(B) embodies this temporal requirement. We hold that it does.

A

Rule 801 provides:

(d) Statements which are not hearsay. — A statement is not hearsay if—

* * *

(1) Prior statement by witness. — The declarant testifies at the trial or hearing and is subject to cross-examination concerning the statement, and the statement is . . . .

* * *

(B) consistent with the declarant's testimony and is offered to rebut an express or implied charge against the declarant of recent fabrication or improper influence or motive.

Rule 801 defines prior consistent statements as nonhearsay only if they are offered to rebut a charge of "recent fabrication or improper influence or motive." Fed. Rule Evid. 801(d)(1)(B). Noting the "troublesome" logic of treating a witness's prior consistent statements as hearsay at all (because the declarant is present in court and subject to cross-examination), the Advisory Committee decided to treat those consistent statements, once the preconditions of the Rule were satisfied, as nonhearsay and admissible as substantive evidence, not just to rebut an attack on the witness's credibility. *See* Advisory Committee Notes on Fed. Rule Evid. 801(d)(1). . . . A consistent statement meeting the requirements of the Rule is thus placed in the same category as a declarant's inconsistent statement made under oath in another proceeding, or prior identification testimony, or admissions by a party opponent. *See* Fed. Rule Evid. 801.

The Rules do not accord this weighty, nonhearsay status to all prior consistent statements. To the contrary, admissibility under the Rules is confined to those statements offered to rebut a charge of "recent fabrication or improper influence or motive," the same phrase used by the Advisory Committee in its description of the "traditiona[l]" common law of evidence, which was the background against which the Rules were drafted. . . . Prior consistent statements may not be admitted to counter all forms of impeachment or to bolster the witness merely because she has been discredited. In the present context, the question is whether A.T.'s out-of-court statements rebutted the alleged link between her desire to be with her mother and her testimony, not whether they suggested that A.T.'s in-court testimony was true. The Rule speaks of a party rebutting an alleged motive, not bolstering the veracity of the story told.

This limitation is instructive, not only to establish the preconditions of admissibility but also to reinforce the significance of the requirement that the consistent statements must have been made before the alleged influence, or motive to fabricate arose. That is to say, the forms of impeachment within the Rule's coverage are the ones in which the temporal requirement makes the most sense. Impeachment by charging that the testimony is a recent fabrication or results from an improper influence or motive is, as a general matter, capable of direct and forceful refutation through introduction of out-of-court consistent statements that predate the alleged fabrication, influence or motive. A consistent statement that predates the motive is a square rebuttal of the charge that the testimony was contrived as a consequence of that motive. By contrast, prior consistent statements carry little rebuttal force when most other types of impeachment are involved. . . .

There may arise instances when out-of-court statements that postdate the alleged fabrication have some probative force in rebutting a charge of fabrication or improper influence or motive, but those statements refute the charged fabrication in a less direct and forceful way. Evidence that a witness made consistent statements after the alleged motive to fabricate arose may suggest in some degree that the in-court testimony is truthful, and thus suggest in some degree that that testimony did not result from some improper influence; but if the drafters of Rule 801(d)(1)(B) intended to countenance rebuttal along that indirect inferential chain, the purpose of confining the types of impeachment that open the door to rebuttal by introducing consistent statements becomes unclear. If consistent statements are admissible without reference to the time frame we find imbedded in the Rule, there appears no sound reason not to admit consistent statements to rebut other forms of impeachment as well. Whatever objections can be leveled against limiting the Rule to this designated form of impeachment and confining the rebuttal to those statements made before the fabrication or improper influence or motive arose, it is clear to us that the drafters of Rule 801(d)(1)(B) were relying upon the common-law temporal requirement.

The underlying theory of the Government's position is that an out-of-court consistent statement, whenever it was made, tends to bolster the testimony of a witness and so tends also to rebut an express or implied charge that the testimony has been the product of an improper influence. Congress could have adopted that rule with ease, providing, for instance, that "a witness's prior consistent statements are admissible whenever relevant to assess the witness's truthfulness or accuracy." The theory would be that, in a broad sense, any prior statement by a witness concerning the disputed issues at trial would have some relevance in assessing the accuracy or truthfulness of the witness's in-court testimony on the same subject. The narrow Rule enacted by Congress, however, cannot be understood to incorporate the Government's theory.

Our analysis is strengthened by the observation that the somewhat peculiar language of the Rule bears close similarity to the language used in many of the common law cases that describe the premotive requirement. "Rule 801(d)(1)(B) employs the precise language — 'rebut[ting] . . . charge[s] . . . of recent fabrication or improper influence or motive' — consistently used in the panoply of pre-1975 decisions." E.O. Ohlbaum, *The Hobgoblin of the Federal Rules of Evidence: An Analysis of Rule 801(d)(1)(B), Prior Consistent Statements and a New Proposal,*

1987 B<small>YU</small> L. R<small>EV</small>. 231, 245. *See, e.g., Ellicott v. Pearl*, 35 U.S. (10 Pet.) 412, 439, 9 L. Ed. 475 (1836); *Hanger v. United States*, 398 F.2d 91, 104 (8th Cir. 1968); *People v. Singer*, 300 N.Y. 120, 89 N.E.2d 710 (1949).

The language of the Rule, in its concentration on rebutting charges of recent fabrication, improper influence and motive to the exclusion of other forms of impeachment, as well as in its use of wording which follows the language of the common-law cases, suggests that it was intended to carry over the common-law pre-motive rule.

NOTES AND QUESTIONS

1.   Why doesn't Rule 801 require prior consistent statements or those involving identification to have been made at a legal proceeding or at least under oath?

2.   What is the potential scope of Rule 801(d)(1)(C)? Does it authorize admissibility even if the declarant cannot or will not confirm the prior identification at trial? *See United States v. Salameh*, 152 F.3d 88 (2d Cir. 1998). For example, Rule 801(d)(1) admits a witness's prior statements in limited situations based on the premise that opposing counsel will have an opportunity to cross examine the witness. Suppose, however, that the witness claims either no memory or no knowledge of the underlying event; is effective cross-examination possible under such circumstances? If not, why should the witness's prior statement be admitted for its truth? *See United States v. Owens*, 484 U.S. 554 (1988).

3.   If a statement does not qualify for admission as a prior consistent statement under Rule 801(d)(1)(B), might it still be admissible non-hearsay offered to rehabilitate a witness? *See United States v. Simonelli*, 237 F.3d 19 (1st Cir. 2001).

4.   Does Rule 801(d)(1)(C) require the statement of identification to have been made at a line-up or comparable pre-trial setting? Suppose a witness tells a responding police that he "saw the [defendant] at the crime scene" but never identifies him again? *See State v. Shaw*, 705 N.W.2d 620 (S.D. 2005) (collecting federal and state cases).

G.   NON-HEARSAY STATEMENTS ADMISSIBLE FOR THEIR TRUTH

1.   Introduction

The hearsay rule has never excluded all hearsay. Based upon principles of necessity and reliability, both the common law and Federal Rules of Evidence have recognized certain types of statements as exceptions to the hearsay rule. Other hearsay statements offered for their truth, though not necessarily reliable nor absolutely necessary, were treated as non-hearsay for other policy reasons. The following two articles identify the basis for recognizing exceptions to the hearsay rule. The remainder of this section addresses a category of statements that are labeled hearsay (rather than as hearsay exceptions) despite being admitted for their truth.

Judson F. Falknor, *The Hearsay Rule and Its Exceptions*
2 UCLA L. Rev. 43, 43–45 (1954)[20]

While Wigmore characterized the hearsay rule as "the greatest and most distinctive contribution of Anglo-American law (next after jury trial) to trial procedure," and asserted that cross-examination (the "fundamental test" which must be applied before a statement is entitled to testimonial consideration) "is beyond any doubt the greatest legal engine ever invented for the discovery of the truth," he, nevertheless, was firm in the conviction that "the inflexibility of [the] exceptions [to the rule]," "the rigidly technical construction of those exceptions by the Courts," and "the enforcement of the rule when its contravention would do no harm," result in "needless obstruction to investigation of truth." By all means, he said, "Keep [the rule] in its vital feature"; but "in its application to former testimony and depositions, liberalize its application"; also, "all the exceptions to the rule, now anywhere recognized, should be liberalized and enlarged"; and "in its application to extrajudicial assertions, adopt the Massachusetts statutory exception for admitting all statements made by persons now deceased." This last "is merely a logical extension of the spirit of the rule; for the rule aims to insist on testing all statements by cross-examination, *if they can be; i.e.*, if the person has passed beyond the power of the law to procure him, the test may be dispensed with." "No one," he continued, "could defend a rule which pronounced that all statements thus untested are *worthless;* for all historical truth is based on un-cross-examined assertions; and every day's experience of life gives denial to such an exaggeration. What the Hearsay Rule implies — and with profound verity — is that all testimonial assertions *ought to be* tested by cross-examination, as the best attainable measure; and it should not be burdened with the pedantic implication that they must be rejected as worthless if the test is unavailable."

Professor Charles T. McCormick believes that even the important "safeguarding" rules must be restated in more flexible terms.

> Chief of these, the great characteristic feature of the common law of evidence, is the group of rules requiring that testimony be limited to statements in court of witnesses who observed the facts at first hand, and are produced for cross-examination. This demand for the best, reduced to a rule, voices a high ideal, but manifestly one that in the every-day world must constantly be compromised. First-hand observers die and move away; their letters and declarations must be accepted as second-best. When will the second-best be good enough? It now seems strange that the courts should have attempted to answer this by defining in sharp categories the special situations when the secondary proof would be allowed. But the urge for certainty prevailed, and the particular situations where the second-hand evidence seemed most needed in the first half of the eighteen hundreds, as for example, dying declarations and book entries, were crystallized into exceptions to the hearsay rule. These now number from ten to twenty, depending on the minuteness of the classification. Of course, they were

---

[20] Originally published in 2 UCLA L. Rev. 43. Copyright © 1954, The Regents of the University of California. All Rights Reserved.

improvisations intended to be played by ear, but they fail of that purpose because the classes are grown so many and the boundaries so meandering that no one can carry any large part of this hearsay-exception-learning in his head. Moreover, the values of hearsay declarations or writings, and the need for them, in particular situations cannot with any degree of realism be thus minutely ticketed in advance. . . . Too much worthless evidence will fit the categories, too much that is vitally needed will be left out. A broader and more practical method will be developed. Massachusetts has made a beginning. . . .

Professor Edmund M. Morgan has observed that "there was a time under our system when no hearsay was excluded; there never has been a time when all hearsay has been excluded. . . . The early opinions reveal very little except that the judges were not doing much more than applying their own rough notions of psychology, and the generally accepted idea that litigants should produce the best available evidence. They point out, for example, that if the witness were alive, he could testify; since he is dead, his written hearsay is the next best evidence." "Had they applied this generally, hearsay would have been received whenever better evidence could not be obtained." But artificial restrictions were imposed and conflicting theories applied, with the result "that the law governing hearsay today is a conglomeration of inconsistencies. . . . Refinements and qualifications within the exceptions only add to its irrationality. The courts by multiplying exceptions reveal their conviction that relevant hearsay normally has real probative value, and is capable of valuation by a jury as well as by other triers of fact." In any case, "the number of cases tried before juries, as compared with the number tried before judges without juries and before administrative tribunals, is small indeed; and to make general rules based on a questionable distrust of the jury seems unwise." The hearsay rule "has long cried aloud for drastic revision."

Jack B. Weinstein, *The Probative Force of Hearsay*
46 IOWA L. REV. 331, 337–38 (1961)[21]

Wigmore's rationale for the hearsay exceptions expresses a compromise position between allowing all hearsay or no hearsay. Where, he argues, there is great necessity for a class of hearsay and there are general circumstantial grounds for concluding that a class of hearsay is reliable, an exception for the class may be created. This analysis, made possible by treating admissions and former testimony as not requiring the test of cross-examination and by applying variable standards of need and credibility to different classes, has satisfied the conscience of the bar[22] but not that of recent commentators. It should be emphasized that Wigmore's rationale

---

[21] Copyright © 1961. Reprinted with permission.

[22] [34] Morgan, The Future of the Law of Evidence, 29 TEXAS L. REV. 587, 593–94 (1951):

Too great praise of Wigmore's amazingly thorough consideration of hearsay would be impossible. . . . By classifying admissions, confessions, and admissible reported testimony as nonhearsay, he made the other exceptions appear to have a consistency and rationality which I believe non-existent. In each exception he found a necessity for the use of secondary evidence and a guaranty of trustworthiness in the admitted hearsay which is lacking in ordinary hearsay. In so doing he furnished ammunition for that large segment of the profession which asserts, and sometimes seems to believe, that the accepted rules represent the "crystallized

— as well as that of most of the cases — makes admissible a class of hearsay rather than particular hearsay for which, in the circumstances of the case, there is need and assurance of reliability. Nevertheless, Wigmore's analysis might have supported an exception based upon the individual case rather than upon a class — although it would have compounded his difficulty in synthesizing the cases for his treatise.

. . . [Another] factor underlying the hearsay rule referred to above — *i.e.*, that of trial convenience — might be used to support a class theory of exceptions. Since the classes of hearsay are defined in advance, the argument would go, lawyers cannot claim surprise when they are used. This rationale is not persuasive because, in the individual litigation, a lawyer may be surprised by his opponent's reliance on particular hearsay even though it falls within a class recognized as an exception. He may not, in fact, have time to investigate and obtain data to attack the extrajudicial declarant's credibility. Having *a priori* classes does, however, cut down the amount of hearsay that may be offered and thus offers him some protection. It also permits the judge to rule mechanically on admissibility without having to think of the particular circumstances of the case — and, as with many of our procedural rules, a judge may, in refusing to think, find satisfaction in the knowledge that this self-denial is required of him.

2.   Admissions

a.   Rationale

James L. Hetland, *Admissions in the Uniform Rules: Are They Necessary?*
46 Iowa L. Rev. 307, 308–10 (1961)[23]

* * *

For years the legal writers have waged an academic debate regarding the true nature and position of admissions as a hearsay exception. They all agree that admissions of a party are to be received into evidence but disagree as to the basis of admissibility and the effect to be given the admission. Greenleaf and Gifford asserted that admissions were substitutes for proof. Mr. Wigmore in his first edition stated admissions were received only for their impeaching effect. In later editions of his treatise, Wigmore advanced the theory that admissions were received because the hearsay rule was satisfied as a party could not object to his own lack of self-cross-examination or lack of personal oath. Morgan classified admissions as a hearsay exception justified on the adversary theory. Strayhorn advanced a circumstantial evidence theory as the proper basis for receiving admissions. McCormick adopted Morgan's theory for express admissions and Strayhorn's theory for admissions by conduct. Lev advanced an estoppel theory for vicarious admissions.

The reason for such diverse theory and rationalization is obvious. Admissions do

---

wisdom of the ages," and which, therefore, opposes changes that Wigmore would ardently champion.

[23] Copyright © 1961. Reprinted with permission.

not fit into the ordinary pattern of hearsay exceptions. Hearsay exceptions are based upon probability. (There can be no absolute assurance of truth for out-of-court statements any more than there can be for in-court statements.) Hearsay exceptions, other than admissions, can be said in varying degrees to have some rational basis for assuming a probability of truth. There is no rational basis for assuming a probability of truth for admissions.

The decision law clearly adopts the position that admissions are hearsay and are admissible as an exception to the hearsay rule for the substantive purpose of proving the truth of the matter stated therein. The basis upon which admissions are now received as a hearsay exception is of little concern to the courts. Perhaps the true basis for the decision law is, as Professor McCormick suggests, a popular feeling that a person should not be in a position to question the veracity of his own assertions regardless of the motive with which they were made. More likely a blind following of precedent is the better explanation, since historically admissions of a party antedated the general hearsay prohibition.

II. COMMON-LAW ADMISSIONS

The decisions and the legal writers agree that admissions to be received in evidence (a) must be made directly or indirectly by a party to the action and (b) must be contrary to that party's position at the time of the trial. No safeguard traditionally imposed on hearsay exceptions to warrant some probability of veracity is applied to admissions. Admissions are received even though the declarant would not be allowed to make the same statement from the witness stand. The declarant need not have testimonial capacity; for example, he may be an infant or intoxicated person. First-hand knowledge of the facts stated is not required. A party can make a statement based upon gross multiple hearsay or unreliable rumor, and if it turns out to be contrary to his position at the time of trial, that hearsay statement is admissible. The form of the statement need not be factual, but can be an opinion or a conclusion which the declarant in court would not be qualified to give. The circumstances under which the statement was made and the motive of the declarant for making the statement at the time it was made are not material to its admissibility. The party declarant need not be unavailable at the time of trial.

QUESTION

What policy consideration, if any, is served by categorizing admissions as nonhearsay rather than as hearsay exceptions? Alternatively, are admissions in some way analytically distinct from traditional hearsay exceptions?

STATE v. JOHNSON
245 N.W.2d 687 (Wis. 1976)

Connor T. Hansen, Justice.

Johnson was the incorporator of Midwestern Pacific Corporation, with offices in Appleton, Wisconsin. He served as president and director of the company from July of 1970, through September of 1972. He was charged with eleven counts of willfully failing to deposit with the State, certain withholding taxes as required by sec. 71.20(4), Stats., and contrary to sec. 71.11(41), Stats. . . .

EXCLUSION OF TESTIMONY AS HEARSAY

The prosecution called accountant, John Myron, as a witness. On direct examination, Myron testified extensively concerning accounting work which he had done for Johnson and Midwestern in 1971 and 1972. He stated that late in October, 1971, John Weber (of the Wisconsin Department of Revenue) assisted Johnson in filling out and filing new WT-6 forms (forms which reflected the total amount of income tax withheld from employees and due to the state) because the original WT-6 forms filled out by Myron had never been filed. In response to the question, "Did Mr. Johnson pay any amount at that time?" Myron answered, "Well, I know he didn't because later on he told me he hadn't." Defense counsel did not object to Myron's testimony.

On cross-examination, defense counsel asked Myron if he specifically remembered any conversations with Mr. Johnson about his financial condition. The prosecution objected that to the extent that Myron's answers would involve statements of the defendant, they would be hearsay. The trial court sustained the objection. Defense counsel acknowledged that the statements, if made by the defendant, would be self-serving and stated in his offer of proof:

> . . . Well, Your Honor, we would show that this man — that the statements were that he did instruct Mr. Johnson to pay these taxes and that Mr. Johnson indicated that he did not . . . and that he was very concerned about it . . . . But he indicated and expressed he did not control the funds. And he could not pay them and he was very disturbed about it.

*   *   *

The trial court subsequently ruled that there would be no valid objection if Myron testified that based on his observations of the defendant during discussions of the question of the tax liability, and in his opinion, the defendant was concerned about making payments; but that Myron could not testify as to what was said by the defendant in that such statements that were self-serving would be inadmissible.

Defendant contends that after a witness is called by the prosecution and testifies as to conversations with the defendant, the full substance of those conversations, as well as the substance of other conversations, elicited on cross-examination, between defendant and the witness which are favorable to defendant are not excludable as hearsay.

. . . Johnson makes two arguments: First that that testimony was not hearsay; and second, that since Johnson's admissions against interest were admitted, then he should have a correlative right to introduce beneficial admissions on cross-examination.

*   *   *

The testimony sought to be elicited by the defendant was clearly hearsay. As appears from the offer of proof, the questions at issue would have elicited testimony from Myron that Johnson had stated that he was concerned about his failure to pay the withholding taxes but that he did not control the funds from which such payment could be made. The testimony was hearsay and Johnson, neither here, nor at the trial, has argued any exception to the hearsay rule under which the testimony might be admitted.

Johnson argues that since admissions against interest were admitted, there should be a correlative right to introduce beneficial admissions on cross-examination. The Rules of Evidence do not allow for such symmetry in this case.

Both the prosecution and the defense misconceive the nature of evidence elicited from Myron on direct examination. The testimony of Myron that Johnson stated that he had not paid the withholding tax, did not constitute hearsay, nor could it be classified as an "admission against interest" as that term is used by the parties. It was specifically excluded from the definition of hearsay under the provisions of sec. 908.01(4)(b) 1, Stats., which states:

* * *

(4) Statements which are not hearsay. A statement is not hearsay if:

(a) . . .

(b) *Admission by party opponent.* The statement is offered against a party and is:

 (1) his own statement, in either his individual or a representative capacity. . . .

The testimony of Myron on direct examination constituted evidence of an "admission" of the defendant, a party to this action, which was offered against the defendant, and it was admissible on this basis, not on the basis of any exception to the hearsay rule.[24]

It appears that both the prosecution and the defense have confused "admission[s]" which are *excluded* from the definition of hearsay under sec. 908.01(4)(b), 1 Stats., with "STATEMENTS AGAINST INTEREST" which are hearsay, but which are *exceptions* to the hearsay rule, under the provisions of sec. 908.045(4).

In Wisconsin Rules of Evidence, . . . in the judicial council committee's notes, the observations by McCormick . . . point out the problems of confusing the two:

A type of evidence with which admissions may be confused is evidence of Declarations against Interest. Such declarations, coming in under a separate exception to the hearsay rule, to be admissible must have been against the declarant's interest when made. No such requirement applies to admissions. . . . Of course, most admissions are actually against interest when made, but there is no such requirement. Hence the common phrase in judicial opinions, "admissions against interest" is an invitation to confuse two separate exceptions to the hearsay rule. Other apparent distinctions

---

[24] [1] Prior to the adoption of the new Rules of Evidence, Wisconsin had considered admissions to be hearsay exceptions. . . .

are that admissions must be statements of a party to a lawsuit (or his predecessor or representative) and must be offered, not for, but against him, whereas the Declaration against Interest need not be and usually is not made by a party or his predecessor or representative, but by some third person. Finally the Declaration against Interest exception admits the declaration only when the declarant, by death or otherwise, has become unavailable as a witness, whereas obviously no such requirement is applied to admissions of a party.

In the same commentary . . . a rational basis for excluding such admissions from the definition of hearsay was set forth:

. . . The reasons for the hearsay rule are not applicable. There is no need for a party to cross-examine himself nor should he be heard to require that his own statements be under oath . . . .

The defendant's argument can have no merit when the Rules of Evidence state that one form of evidence, *i.e.*, admissions offered against a party, under sec. 908.01(4)(b), 1 Stats., shall not be hearsay, and another, *i.e.*, self-serving statements of a declarant offered through another witness to prove the truth of the matter asserted, shall be hearsay.

The testimony sought to be elicited from the witness Myron on cross-examination concerning self-serving statements made by the defendant was clearly hearsay and was properly excluded by the trial court.

* * *

Order Affirmed.

NOTES AND QUESTIONS

1.   What policy consideration is advanced by excluding a party's prior statements which presently favor his case? Can you conceive of any circumstance under which such statements enjoy limited admissibility?

2.   So-called declarations against interest are analytically distinct from admissions. Confusion, however, has developed because of the mistaken tendency to characterize all admissions as declarations against interest. This can be avoided by remembering that an admission is competent evidence even if it was not against the declarant's interest when it was made. Declarations against interest are analyzed *infra* p. 586).

3.   The rule for admissions allows a party's extra-judicial declarations to be admitted into evidence against him. At that point, the statement may be given whatever effect the fact-finder deems appropriate. In contrast, so-called judicial admissions — formal concessions made by a party or his counsel during the course of litigation proceedings — often have a conclusive impact. Specifically, they "have the effect of withdrawing a fact from issue and dispensing wholly with the need for proof of the fact." McCormick's Handbook of the Law of Evidence § 263, at 630 (2d ed. 1972); *see* Note, *Judicial Admissions*, 64 Colum. L. Rev. 1121 (1964). How might this principle impact upon a party who files alternative and possibly contradictory

pleadings? *See Garman v. Griffin,* 666 F.2d 1156 (8th Cir. 1981).

BILL v. FARM BUREAU LIFE INSURANCE CO.
119 N.W.2d 768 (Iowa 1963)

THOMPSON, JUSTICE.

The plaintiffs are beneficiaries in a policy of insurance issued by the defendant upon the life of their son, LeRoy Leo Bill, who died on January 12, 1961. Liability being denied by the insurer, this action was brought by the plaintiffs. The defendant alleged that the death of the insured was the result of suicide, which raises the only substantial question in the case. . . . The trial court held that the question of suicide was for the determination of the jury and submitted it accordingly. The jury returned its verdict for the plaintiffs, judgment was rendered on the verdict, and we have this appeal. The defendant contends it was entitled to a peremptory verdict; it raised the question in various ways, and also challenges certain rulings on evidence and instructions given the jury.

* * *

II.

Further error is assigned upon the refusal of the trial court to admit the testimony of the medical examiner, Dr. Willis K. Dankle, as to a conversation he had with the plaintiff Ernest Bill, in the presence of the other plaintiff, Norma Bill. Dr. Dankle testified that he had such a conversation at the Niedert farm on the evening after the death of LeRoy Bill. To the question "What was said at that time?" he answered "I asked him if there were any doubt in his mind that his son committed suicide." Then came a motion from plaintiffs' counsel to strike "as a conclusion and opinion on his part, in no way binding on this plaintiff, and certainly improper in a civil suit, what the man said at the time, what the doctor said." The court said: "Well, I think that originated with this witness and not with the plaintiffs. I think under the — ". Taking this as an expression of intent to sustain the motion to strike, defendant's counsel said "Your Honor, we would like to make an offer of proof in chambers." This was agreed to by the court, and later, in chambers, Dr. Dankle was interrogated in this way:

Q.   Doctor, did you have a conversation with Ernest Bill in the presence of Norma Bill at the Niedert farmhouse just before you left on the night of January 12th?

A.   Yes.

Q.   What did that conversation consist of in your part and on his?

A.   I said to Mr. Bill, "Is there any doubt in your mind that your son committed suicide?" and if I might describe the situation, he and his wife were sitting at the table, mourning and tearful, and he just shook his head.

Q.   In what direction, Doctor, if you will say it so that the record can
            pick it up?

A.   A lateral motion of the head.

Q.   That is commonly interpreted as a negative sign?

A.   Which I interpreted as a negative sign.

No objections were lodged by the plaintiff until all of the foregoing questions had
been asked and answered. Then counsel for plaintiffs said: "We object to the
proposed offer because there is no question that he died by his own hand. The issue
in the case is whether his death was intentional or unintentional." After some
discussion not material here, the court ruled:

> Well, I will tell you, I am going to follow my judgment on this. I think
> that if the plaintiff had volunteered that there wasn't any doubt in his mind
> the boy committed suicide that would be perfectly admissible but here we
> have got an entirely negative approach; somebody puts this subject of
> suicide out there in the form of a question; he doesn't make any audible
> answer to it at all. I think there is too much ground for conjecture there on
> the part of the jury as to the implications they can draw from that. If this
> goes into the record it surely would be argued to the jury that he admitted
> that it was suicide and I don't believe that is a fair inference to draw from
> this sort of thing. Now, if he had said, "No, there isn't any doubt in my mind
> but what the boy committed suicide, everything tends to show that," then I
> think you would have a different situation but here he doesn't say anything.
> He shakes his head; maybe it was a negative shake, but he was under stress
> and strain here. The record shows that there was some mourning; there
> was some crying going on there at the table where the husband and wife
> sat. I just don't believe that is enough that I dare let that go to the jury.

> My ruling is going to be that it is not going to be admitted.

It will be noted that no objections were made until all of the questions put to Dr.
Dankle had been asked and answered. There is no doubt that the matter inquired
into was a proper one, and the doctor should have been permitted to answer all of
the questions with the possible exception of the final one, which dealt with his
interpretation of the negative sign, the head shake. That the plaintiff Ernest Bill
had no doubt his son had committed suicide was an admission against interest; and
the error of the court in excluding it was further compounded by the fact that both
plaintiffs were permitted to testify, over objection, that they knew of no reason why
their son should have intentionally taken his life. The excluded testimony would not
only have shown an admission against interest, but would have tended to counter
and contradict the testimony last above referred to.

Neither the plaintiffs' motion to strike nor their objection made after all the
offered questions had been answered raised any real or substantial question as to
the validity of the testimony. Neither raised the point decided by the court, which
seems to have been that the lateral motion of the head made by Ernest Bill was too
uncertain in its meaning and so was so speculative the jury should not have been
permitted to pass upon it. With this we do not agree. A nod of the head is universally
understood to be an affirmative or "yes" answer; a shake of the head is equally well

understood to mean a negative or "no" reply. It is true the lateral motion might in some circumstances mean merely bewilderment or confusion, an "I don't know" answer. But this was an interpretation to be made by the jury.

* * *

The evidence was on an important point, and we cannot say it was not sufficiently prejudicial to require reversal. An admission by one of the plaintiffs, in the presence of the other who made no objection or comment that he had no doubt his son committed suicide if so interpreted by the jury would certainly have been an important matter for its consideration. Error appears at this point.

NOTE AND QUESTIONS

1.   How would *Bill* have been decided under Fed. R. Evid. 801?

2.   The court in *Bill* focused principally on Mr. Bill's purported admission. Did any other party arguably make an admission as well?

3.   Note that the court in *Bill* refers to Mr. Bill's lateral nodding of his head as an "admission against interest." Mr. Bill's expression constituted an admission but would not have qualifed as an admission (or statement) against interest. *Compare* Fed. R. Evid. 801(d)(2)(A) (admission by party-opponent) *with* Fed. R. Evid. 804(b)(3) (statement against interest). *See also State v. Johnson, supra*) (explaining distinction).

b.   Adoptive Admissions

Edmund M. Morgan, *Admissions*
12 Wash. L. Rev. 182, 186–87 (1937)[25]

A more limited but constantly expanding field is that of admissions by adoption, which tends to coincide on one border with the admissions by . . . conduct . . . and on the other with admissions by authorization. Of course, no objection could be made to treating as an admission a statement made by a third person if it is expressly adopted by a party. A certificate of a physician as to the cause of death of an assured is normally inadmissible against the beneficiary in an action on the policy, for it is pure hearsay. If in making proof of loss, however, the beneficiary, in answer to the question as to the cause of death, writes: "As stated in the attached certificate of Dr. X," it is exactly as if she had written the certificate herself. Under the generally accepted rule, the fact that the admission is in the form of opinion is immaterial. Suppose, however, that the party who is alleged to have adopted as an admission a statement made by another, has done nothing affirmatively to indicate his adoption. A third party makes an assertion in the presence of the defendant to which the defendant makes no response and upon which he takes no action. How can he be said to be in the same position as if he had uttered the same words? Obviously only if the circumstances are such that his silence or inaction can be reasonably interpreted as an assent. If he heard and understood the statement, if

---

[25] Reprinted with permission.

it was of such content that a reasonable man would deny it if untrue, and if he was in such a situation as to be free to deny it, it is reasonable to infer that he assented to it.

OLLERT v. ZIEBELL
114 A. 356 (N.J. 1921)

BERGEN, J.

This is an action by a husband, individually, and as administrator ad prosequendum of his wife, for injuries caused by defendant's negligence, which resulted in her death. The plaintiff recovered a judgment, from which the defendant has appealed. The basis of the judgment is that the defendant, a dentist, in treating the teeth of the deceased, did it so negligently as to injure the mouth of the deceased, from which tetanus set in, of which she died. . . .

There was evidence which, if competent, and credited by the jury, would justify them in finding that when deceased went to the defendant for treatment her mouth was not diseased, except that she was suffering from a toothache; that the teeth were treated by defendant with some disinfectant, and an appointment made for her return a few days later; that she did so, and although the defendant's arm was disabled so that he could not do the work he had provided another dentist to do it for him, and was present when the particular treatment complained of was performed; that the night after the treatment, which it is alleged caused the injury, the husband telephoned the defendant that his wife was suffering, and that her mouth was in bad condition; that the defendant and the operating dentist came to plaintiff's house, and defendant told him that he had brought a doctor from New York to see his wife; that the husband and the two dentists went to the bedroom of the wife, and the husband told her that the defendant had brought a doctor from New York, and the wife replied:

> He is not a doctor from New York. He is the man that worked at my mouth. He was drilling on my teeth, and I got an awful shock, and he left the drill in my mouth, walked across the room, turned off the electric current, and came back to me. When he took the drill out of my mouth he said, "My God, child, what have I done? I did not mean to do that. You must have suffered awful."

This statement was made to the defendant in response to his questions, and in the presence of the other dentist and her husband, and was not at the time denied by the defendant.

The first point made by the appellant is that this statement by the wife, not being under oath, was erroneously admitted, because it was a self-serving declaration, immaterial, and in violation of the hearsay rule. This objection is not sound. The statement was made by the wife in the presence of the defendant, at his request, of a matter which, if not true, was known by the defendant to be false and which he was then able to deny. The nondenial of a statement made in the presence of the party charged which tends to establish his liability may amount to an admission of its truth, if, as it appears in this case, the statement was heard and understood by the party, and he had knowledge of the facts stated, was not physically disabled from answering, had a motive for denying it, and would naturally do so if he does not intend to admit it, and was at liberty to make a reply. When the wife stated in defendant's presence, and in reply to his questions, that her injury resulted from the use by defendant of an instrument propelled by electricity, and he knew, as he testified, that such a statement was untrue, and did not at the time it was made deny it, his silence was admissible evidence from which an admission of its truth may be inferred, the inference to be drawn being left to the jury.

* * *

Finding no error in this record which justifies reversal, the judgment will be affirmed, with costs.

UNITED STATES v. FLECHA
539 F.2d 874 (2d Cir. 1976)

FRIENDLY, CIRCUIT JUDGE:

Appellant was tried before Judge Weinstein and a jury in the District Court for the Eastern District of New York in the spring of 1973 on a three count indictment, along with Jose Pineda-Marin, Hugo Suarez, Ernesto Santo Gonzalez and Moises Banguera. The indictment charged the importation of 287 pounds of marijuana, possession of this with intent to distribute it, and conspiracy to commit these two substantive offenses, in violation of 21 U.S.C. §§ 952(a), 841(a)(1), and 846 and 963. . . .

Not satisfied with this compelling case, the prosecutor elicited from Agent Cabrera that, as all five defendants were standing in line, he heard Gonzalez say in Spanish, apparently to Flecha: "Why so much excitement? If we are caught, we are caught."

The three lawyers who represented defendants Banguera, Suarez and Pineda-Marin immediately sought an instruction that this was "not binding" on their clients; the court said "Granted." Counsel for Flecha then joined in the application. Judge Weinstein asked Agent Cabrera how far away Flecha was from Gonzalez; Cabrera answered that Flecha was right next to Gonzalez, only six to twelve inches away. The judge then denied Flecha's application.

Although the judge did not articulate his reasons for granting the applications of Banguera, Suarez and Pineda-Marin but denying Flecha's, it is not difficult to reconstruct what his thought process must have been. . . . His allowing Gonzalez' statement to stand against Flecha although not against the three other objectors must thus have rested on a belief that as to Flecha the case fell within Rule 801(d)(2)(B), allowing receipt, as an admission of the party against whom it is offered, of "a statement of which he has manifested his adoption or belief in its truth."

The brief *voir dire* demonstrates that the judge fell into the error, against which Dean Wigmore so clearly warned, 4 WIGMORE, EVIDENCE § 1071, at 102 (Chadbourn rev. 1972), of jumping from the correct proposition that hearing the statement of a third person is a necessary condition for adoption by silence . . . to the incorrect conclusion that it is a sufficient one. After quoting the maxim "silence gives consent," Wigmore explains "that the inference of assent may safely be made only when no other explanation is equally consistent with silence; and there is always another possible explanation — namely, ignorance or dissent — *unless the circumstances are such that a dissent would in ordinary experience have been expressed if the communication had not been correct.*" (Emphasis supplied.) However, "the force of the brief maxim has always been such that in practice . . . a sort of working rule grew up that *whatever was said in a party's presence* was receivable against him as an admission, because presumably assented to. This working rule became so firmly entrenched in practice that frequent judicial deliverances became necessary in order to dislodge it; for in this simple and comprehensive form it ignored the inherent qualifications of the principle." (Emphasis in original.) Among the judicial deliverances quoted, it suffices to cite Chief Justice Shaw's statements in *Commonwealth v. Kenney*, 53 Mass. 235, 237 (1847), that before receiving an admission by silence the court must determine, *inter alia* "whether he [the party] is in such a situation that he is at liberty to make any reply" and "whether the statement is made under such circumstances, and by such persons, as naturally to call for a reply, if he did not intend to admit it"; and Lord Justice Bowen's more succinct statement in *Wiedemann v. Walpole*, 2 Q.B. 534, 539 (1891):

> Silence is not evidence of an admission, unless there are circumstances which render it more reasonably probable that a man would answer the charge made against him than that he would not.

We find nothing in the Advisory Committee's Note to Rule 801(d)(2)(B) to indicate any intention to depart from these sound principles. To the contrary the Committee noted that difficulties had been raised in criminal cases and that "the inference is a fairly weak one, to begin with."

We find it hard to think of a case where response would have been less expectable than this one. Flecha was under arrest, and although the Government emphasizes that he was not being questioned by the agents, and had not been given *Miranda* warnings, it is clear that many arrested persons know, without benefit of warnings, that silence is usually golden. Beyond that, what was Flecha to say? If the Spanish verb used by Gonzalez has the same vagueness as "caught," it would have been somewhat risible for Flecha, surrounded by customs agents, to have denied that he had been. Of course, Flecha could have said "Speak for yourself" or something like it, but it was far more natural to say nothing.

There is no force in the Government's argument that Gonzalez' statement "was not admitted for its truth, but rather for what it showed about Gonzalez' and Flecha's state of mind," and thus was not hearsay. Of course, it was not hearsay as to Gonzalez but in order to be relevant against Flecha, it would have to be at least a description by Gonzalez of Flecha's state of mind ("You know you are guilty") and that would be hearsay unless Flecha adopted it by silence. . . .

We have thought it desirable to write on this in order to prevent future reliance on the "working rule" so rightly condemned by Wigmore and other eminent jurists, rather than because of the effect of the ruling in this case. For we agree with the

Government that the error was harmless.

*   *   *

Affirmed.

UNITED STATES v. KILBOURNE
559 F.2d 1263 (4th Cir. 1977)

BUTZNER, CIRCUIT JUDGE:

Laurie Claudius Kilbourne, convicted of first degree murder, assigns the following errors: . . . (3) the trial court should have excluded evidence of an admission by silence, or at least conducted a hearing on this question in the absence of the jury.

Kilbourne had been having an affair with the decedent, a teen-age girl who was much younger than he. . . .

An hour and a half before the victim's body was found, and long before the police released news of the murder, Kilbourne told a friend that she was dead. More than a month later the same friend and Kilbourne had a conversation about which the friend testified as follows:

Q.   What did you say to him and what did he say to you?

A.   I said, "Laurie, if you killed that girl, you know, you have got to be inhuman because you act natural, nothing bothers you, you are the same way, you know."

He said to me, "Norman, you know I didn't do it."

I paused for a while, I said, "How did you know the girl died? How did you know about the girl's death?"

He said that a friend of his called him and told him about it about 8:00 o'clock.

I said to him, "But you called me before 8:00 o'clock," and the conversation was turned off right there. I didn't get any answer. No response from him. I bid him farewell.

At the trial Kilbourne objected to this testimony of admission by silence on the ground that the fifth amendment required its exclusion. He now claims as an additional error that the court failed to conduct a hearing to ascertain whether a sufficient foundation was laid for the testimony.

The district court properly permitted the witness to testify about Kilbourne's silence when he was confronted with his early, unexplained knowledge of the victim's death.

*   *   *

The judgment is affirmed.

NOTES AND QUESTIONS

1. Admissions by silence have, on occasion, been severely criticized. For example, consider the following judicial commentary:

> This rule, which has become known as the tacit admission rule, is too broad, wide-sweeping, and elusive for precise interpretation, particularly where a man's liberty and his good name are at stake. Who determines whether a statement is one which "naturally" calls for a denial? What is natural for one person may not be natural for another. There are persons possessed of such dignity and pride that they would treat with silent contempt a dishonest accusation. Are they to be punished for refusing to dignify with a denial what they regard as wholly false and reprehensible?[26]

Commonwealth v. Dravecz, 227 A.2d 904, 906 (Pa. 1967); *see* Gamble, *The Tacit Admission Rule: Unreliable and Unconstitutional — A Doctrine Ripe for Abandonment*, 14 GA. L. REV. 27 (1979).

2. Based upon *Flecha, Kilbourne*, and Rule 801(d)(2)(B), what foundation must be established as a prerequisite to admissibility under this theory? How is this determination made under Rule 104?

3. Which of the following situations, if any, qualify for admissibility as adoptive admissions?

a) Police secure a warrant authorizing the search of a single family dwelling. The warrant was based upon an affidavit alleging that one "Timmy" was selling drugs at that location. During the subsequent narcotics trial of William Morgan, the defense sought to introduce that affidavit as evidence that someone named "Timmy" actually lived at the designated location and was involved in selling drugs. *See United States v. Morgan*, 581 F.2d 933 (D.C. Cir. 1978).

b) Defendant Green's sister-in-law witnessed an argument between Green and his wife in which Green failed to respond to his wife's statement that "she wasn't scared of him just . . . because he had Frank [Moore] shot." At the time, that she made her accusatory statement she had a gun in her immediate possession. The prosecution now seeks to use the statement against Green in his trial for the murder of Moore. *See People v. Green*, 629 P.2d 1098 (Colo. Ct. App. 1981).

c) About an hour after allegedly having committed a bank robbery, defendants Sears, Werner, and Strozyk went to the home of Dolly and Jim Vorisek. "They proceeded to count the money, and Sears recounted the story of the robbery in detail without protest from either Strozyk or Werner." *United States v. Sears*, 663 F.2d 896, 899 (9th Cir. 1981), *cert. denied sub nom. Werner v. United States*, 455 U.S. 1027 (1982). *See also United States v. Ward*, 377 F.3d 671 (7th Cir. 2004).

---

[26] In his funeral oration on Roscoe Conkling, Robert G. Ingersoll said: "He was maligned, misrepresented and misunderstood, but he would not answer. He was as silent then as he is now — and his silence, better than any form of speech, refuted every charge." George Bernard Shaw said: "Silence is the most perfect expression of scorn." The immortal Abraham Lincoln summed up his philosophy on this subject in characteristic fashion: "If I should read much less answer, all the attacks made upon me this shop might as well be closed for any other business."

4. To what extent might constitutional considerations complicate the admissibility of a defendant's pre-arrest or post-arrest silence? *See Fletcher v. Weir*, 455 U.S. 603 (1982); *Jenkins v. Anderson*, 447 U.S. 231 (1980); *Doyle v. Ohio*, 426 U.S. 610 (1976).

5. Although personal knowledge is ordinarily not required for admissions to be competent, one judge has reasoned that logic compels such a showing when adoptions by silence are involved. *See White Industries, Inc. v. Cessna Aircraft Co.*, 611 F. Supp. 1049, 1062 (W.D. Mo. 1985).

6. How should a proferred adoptive admission be treated when the statement allegedly adopted is contained in a letter which the opposing party denies having received? This is another example of conditional relevance, *supra* (p. 99–104) and requires application of Rule 104(b).

c. Vicarious Admissions

Edmund M. Morgan, *The Rationale of Vicarious Admissions*
42 HARV. L. REV. 462, 463–64 (1929)[27]

It would be captious to refuse to apply to narrative utterances the ordinary principles of representation of the law of agency. If *B* authorizes *A* to speak for him, he can take no valid exception to the reception of *A's* statements against him which he could not take to the reception of his own. The test of the existence of such authority can be no other than that for determining authority to do other acts, verbal and non-verbal; it cannot depend upon the purpose for which the authority becomes material in the trial of a case. It is furnished by the substantive law. But the terms in which the doctrine of *respondeat superior is* expressed frequently lead to its erroneous application. The familiar phraseology puts it that if *A* makes an utterance within the scope of his authority or employment, as agent or servant of *B*, it is receivable against *B*. Thus where *B* employs *A* to investigate an event and report to him, it is said that *A's* report is made within the scope of his express authority and is therefore admissible against *B*. The slightest analysis of the situation reveals the fallacy of this reasoning. The doctrine of *respondeat superior* does not apply *inter sese* between principal and agent or between master and servant. It is only where the principal or master brings himself in contact with the outside world through his agent or servant that he becomes responsible for the latter's acts. If the agent or servant in gathering the data violates some right of a third party, the principal or master will have to answer for it. But where he merely transmits information to his superior, it is specious to say that it is as if the superior were speaking to himself. It is not so in fact; it is not so in substantive law; to hold it so for evidential purposes is to treat a limited generalization as a universal, and to apply a formula without discriminating examination of its basis. If such statements are to be received, their reception must be justified not on any ground of representation but because of the existence of some independent guaranty of trustworthiness.

Furthermore, it is important to distinguish between authority to do an act and

---

authority to talk about it. The mere fact that *B* has empowered *A* to do act *X* for him adds no whit of trustworthiness to *A's* narratives about *X;* nor does it furnish any grounds for depriving *B* of the usual protection against unexamined testimony.

MARTIN v. SAVAGE TRUCK LINE, INC.
121 F. Supp. 417 (D.D.C. 1954)

Morris, District Judge.

In this action the plaintiff sought to recover damages for the death of plaintiff's decedent, resulting from the alleged negligence in the operation of a truck owned by the defendant, and operated by one Allie F. Ray, an employee of the defendant, who has since died. The jury returned a verdict in favor of the plaintiff, and a motion has been filed on behalf of the defendant, seeking a judgment notwithstanding the verdict, or, in the alternative, a new trial.

There is only one ground urged which presents a substantial question of law and, therefore, requires a statement of the reasons which, in my view, compel the conclusion reached. During the course of the trial evidence was offered and received of a statement made by the driver of the truck to an investigating police officer at the scene of the collision, and almost immediately thereafter, before either of the vehicles concerned had been moved, to the effect that he was driving at the rate of thirty miles an hour, but that the green light was with him. The defendant objected to the admission of this evidence on the grounds that it was not part of the *res gestae*, and it was not admissible against the defendant as a statement against interest. The motion attacking the verdict urged that the admission of this statement was error on these grounds.

The authority heavily relied upon, and followed in a number of jurisdictions, is the case of *Vicksburg & M. R. Co. v. O'Brien*, 1886, 119 U.S. 99, where it was held by a divided Court of five to four that a statement made by the engineer of the train of the railroad company, shortly after the injury there involved, was not admissible against the said railroad company as a statement against interest. The dissenting members of the Court considered the statement admissible against interest on the ground that it was so close to the happening of the event that it could be considered part of the *res gestae*. Subsequent to this decision numerous cases considering similar questions have relaxed the rule greatly with respect to what constitutes *res gestae*, . . . but it seems to me that there is lamentable confusion in that a statement against interest is admissible independent of its constituting a part of the *res gestae*. The characteristic of truthfulness, which makes exception to the hearsay rule, attaches to a statement being made at the time of the occurrence, namely, as part of the *res gestae*, on the theory that it is the facts speaking through the speaker, while the characteristic of truthfulness as to a statement against interest is that it is a statement which would not have been made but for the fact that it was true. The primary objection urged to a statement such as is here involved is that, while it was a statement against the interest of the person making it, subjecting him, as it did, not only to civil liability, but possibly to criminal sanctions, it cannot be considered a statement against the interest of his principal, because he was the agent of the principal only for the purpose of operating the vehicle, and not for the purpose of making statements concerning its operation. Undoubtedly the decision of the United States Supreme Court would be binding upon the Court and compel a decision that the proffered statement was not admissible, unless very real and drastic changes have occurred since that decision which compel a different holding now. It is noteworthy that in more recent times decisions and text writers have held the results of the decision mentioned to be totally at variance with present-day reality. 2 WIGMORE ON EVIDENCE (2d Edition, 1923) Section 1078, 4 WIGMORE ON EVIDENCE (3d Edition, 1940) Section 1078.[28] . . . The question turns, as Dean Wigmore has put it, upon the principles of agency, as it is clearly admissible if the driver was acting in the course of his employment, and inadmissible if he was not.

Such changes in motor vehicular transportation have taken place since 1886 that, in this jurisdiction, and every other one of which I have any knowledge, it is a matter of public policy, expressed by legislative enactment and judicial decision, in the interest of safety, that the operation of such vehicles on streets and highways be rigidly controlled, and the operators and owners of such vehicles be held to strict accountability for improper operation. Drivers of such vehicles are required by law to report accidents resulting in injury in which their motor vehicles are involved. Police authorities have special units for the immediate investigation of the numerous injuries which are of daily occurrence. To say, in these circumstances, that the owner of a motor truck may constitute a person his agent for the purpose of the operation of such truck over public streets and highways, and to say at the same time that such operator is no longer the agent of such owner when an accident occurs, for the purpose of truthfully relating the facts concerning the occurrence (to an investigating police officer on the scene shortly thereafter) seems to me to erect an untenable fiction, neither contemplated by the parties nor sanctioned by public policy. It is almost like saying that a statement against interest in the instant case could only have been made had the truck been operated by an officer or the board of directors of the Corporation owning the truck; and trucks are not operated that way. To exclude the statement of the driver of the truck as to the speed of the truck at the time of the collision, which was not only clearly excessive in the circumstances, but even greater than the speed limit permitted on the highway between intersections, would be to deny an agency which I believe inherently exists regardless of whether the statement is made at the moment of the impact, or some minutes later to an investigating officer, or other authorized person. The motion will be denied.

NOTE

Martin concerned an extrajudicial statement which the Court characterized as "a statement against interest." Note that statements against interest do not necessarily qualify for admissibility as admissions. They do however constitute an independent hearsay exception, *see* § I.1.b, *infra*.

---

[28] [1] Note 2, page 121:

and yet it is absurd to hold that the superintendent has power to make the employer heavily liable by mismanaging the whole factory, but not to make statements about his mismanagement which can be even listened to in court; the pedantic unpracticalness of this rule as now universally administered makes a laughingstock of court methods.

MAHLANDT v. WILD CANID SURVIVAL
AND RESEARCH CENTER, INC.
588 F.2d 626 (8th Cir. 1978)

VAN SICKLE, DISTRICT JUDGE:

This is a civil action for damages arising out of an alleged attack by a wolf on a child. The sole issues on appeal are as to the correctness of three rulings which excluded conclusionary statements against interest. Two of them were made by a defendant, who was also an employee of the corporate defendant; and the third was in the form of a statement appearing in the records of a board meeting of the corporate defendant.

On March 23, 1973, Daniel Mahlandt, then 3 years, 10 months, and 8 days old, was sent by his mother to a neighbor's home on an adjoining street to get his older brother, Donald. Daniel's mother watched him cross the street, and then turned into the house to get her car keys. Daniel's path took him along a walkway adjacent to the Poos' residence. Next to the walkway was a five foot chain link fence to which Sophie had been chained with a six foot chain. In other words, Sophie was free to move in a half circle having a six foot radius on the side of the fence opposite from Daniel.

Sophie was a bitch wolf, 11 months and 28 days old, who had been born at the St. Louis Zoo, and kept there until she reached 6 months of age, at which time she was given to the Wild Canid Survival and Research Center, Inc. It was the policy of the Zoo to remove wolves from the Children's Zoo after they reached the age of 5 or 6 months. Sophie was supposed to be kept at the Tyson Research Center, but Kenneth Poos, as Director of Education for the Wild Canid Survival and Research Center, Inc., had been keeping her at his home because he was taking Sophie to schools and institutions where he showed films and gave programs with respect to the nature of wolves. Sophie was known as a very gentle wolf who had proved herself to be good natured and stable during her contacts with thousands of children, while she was in the St. Louis Children's Zoo.

Sophie was chained because the evening before she had jumped the fence and attacked a beagle who was running along the fence and yapping at her.

A neighbor who was ill in bed in the second floor of his home heard a child's screams and went to his window, where he saw a boy lying on his back within the enclosure, with a wolf straddling him. The wolf's face was near Daniel's face, but the distance was so great that he could not see what the wolf was doing, and did not see any biting. Within about 15 seconds the neighbor saw Clarke Poos, about seventeen, run around the house, get the wolf off the boy, and disappear with the child in his arms to the back of the house. Clarke took the boy in and laid him on the kitchen floor.

Clarke had been returning from his friend's home immediately west when he heard a child's cries and ran around to the enclosure. He found Daniel lying within the enclosure, about three feet from the fence, and Sophie standing back from the boy the length of her chain, and wailing. An expert in the behavior of wolves stated that when a wolf licks a child's face that it is a sign of care, and not a sign of attack; that a wolf's wail is a sign of compassion, and an effort to get attention, not a sign of attack. No witness saw or knew how Daniel was injured. Clarke and his sister ran over to get Daniel's mother. She says that Clarke told her, "a wolf got Danny and he is dying." Clarke denies that statement. The defendant, Mr. Poos, arrived home while Daniel and his mother were in the kitchen. After Daniel was taken in an ambulance, Mr. Poos talked to everyone present, including a neighbor who came in. Within an hour after he arrived home, Mr. Poos went to Washington University to inform Owen Sexton, President of Wild Canid Survival and Research Center, Inc., of the incident. Mr. Sexton was not in his office so Mr. Poos left the following note on his door:

> Owen, would call me at home, 727-5080? Sophie bit a child that came in our back yard. All has been taken care of. I need to convey what happened to you. . . .

Denial of admission of this note is one of the issues on appeal.

Later that day, Mr. Poos found Mr. Sexton at the Tyson Research Center and told him what had happened. Denial of plaintiff's offer to prove that Mr. Poos told Mr. Sexton that, "Sophie had bit a child that day," is the second issue on appeal.

A meeting of the Directors of the Wild Canid Survival and Research Center, Inc., was held on April 4, 1973. Mr. Poos was not present at that meeting. The minutes of that meeting reflect that there was a "great deal of discussion . . . about the legal aspects of the incident of Sophie biting the child." Plaintiff offered an abstract of the minutes containing that reference. Denial of the offer of that abstract is the third issue on appeal.

*   *   *

The trial judge's rationale for excluding the note, the statement, and the corporate minutes, was the same in each case. He reasoned that Mr. Poos did not have any personal knowledge of the facts, and accordingly, the first two admissions were based on hearsay; and the third admission contained in the minutes of the board meeting was subject to the same objection of hearsay, and unreliability because of lack of personal knowledge.

The Federal Rules of Evidence became effective in July 1975 (180 days after the passage of the Act). Thus, at this time, there is very little case law to rely upon for resolution of the problems of interpretation.

The relevant rule here is:

Rule 801. Definitions.

(d) (2) An Opposing Party's Statement. The statement is offered against an opposing party and:

(A) was made by the party in an individual or representative capacity;

(B) is one the party manifested that it adopted or believed to be true;

(C) was made by a person whom the party authorized to make a statement on the subject;

(D) was made by the party's agent or employee on a matter within the scope of that relationship and while it existed; or

(E) was made by the party's coconspirator during and in furtherance of the conspiracy.

The statement must be considered but does not by itself establish the declarant's authority under (C); the existence or scope of the relationship under (D); or the existence of the conspiracy or participation in it under (E).

So the statement in the note pinned on the door is not hearsay, and is admissible against Mr. Poos. It was his own statement, and as such was clearly different from the reported statement of another. . . . It was also a statement of which he had manifested his adoption or belief in its truth. And the same observations may be made of the statement made later in the day to Mr. Sexton that, "Sophie had bit a child. . . ."

Are these statements admissible against Wild Canid Survival and Research Center, Inc.? They were made by Mr. Poos when he was an agent or servant of the Wild Canid Survival and Research Center, Inc., and they concerned a matter within the scope of his agency, or employment, *i.e.*, his custody of Sophie, and were made during the existence of that relationship.

Defendant argues that Rule 801(d)(2) does not provide for the admission of "in house" statements; that is, it allows only admissions made to third parties.

The notes of the Advisory Committee on the Proposed Rules (28 U.S.C.A., Volume on Federal Rules of Evidence, Rule 801, p. 527 at p. 530), discuss the problem of "in house" admissions with reference to Rule 801(d)(2)(C) situations. This is not a (C) situation because Mr. Poos was not authorized or directed to make a statement on the matter by anyone. But the rationale developed in that comment does apply to this (D) situation. Mr. Poos had actual physical custody of Sophie. His conclusions, his opinions, were obviously accepted as a basis for action by his principal. . . . As the Advisory Committee points out in its note on (C) situations.

> communication to an outsider has not generally been thought to be an essential characteristic of an admission. Thus a party's books or records are usable against him, without regard to any intent to disclose to third persons. V WIGMORE ON EVIDENCE § 1557.

Weinstein's discussion of Rule 801(d)(2)(D) (WEINSTEIN's EVIDENCE § 801(d)(2)(D)(01), p. 801–137), states that:

> Rule 801(d)(2)(D) adopts the approach . . . which, as a general proposition, makes statements made by agents within the scope of their employment admissible. . . . Once agency, and the making of the statement while the relationship continues, are established, the statement is exempt from the hearsay rule so long as it relates to a matter within the scope of the agency.

After reciting a lengthy quotation which justifies the rule as necessary, and suggests that such admissions are trustworthy and reliable, Weinstein states categorically that although an express requirement of personal knowledge on the part of the declarant of the facts underlying his statement is not written into the rule, it should be. He feels that is mandated by Rules 805 and 403.

Rule 805 recites, in effect, that a statement containing hearsay within hearsay is admissible if each part of the statement falls within an exception to the hearsay rule. Rule 805, however, deals only with hearsay exceptions. A statement based on the personal knowledge of the declarant of facts underlying his statement is not the repetition of the statement of another, thus not hearsay. It is merely opinion testimony. Rule 805 cannot mandate the implied condition desired by Judge Weinstein.

Rule 403 provides for the exclusion of relevant evidence if its probative value is substantially outweighed by the danger of unfair prejudice, confusion of the issues, or misleading the jury, or by consideration of undue delay, waste of time, or needless presentation of cumulative evidence. Nor does Rule 403 mandate the implied condition desired by Judge Weinstein.

Thus, while both Rule 805 and Rule 403 provide additional bases for excluding otherwise acceptable evidence, neither rule mandates the introduction into Rule 801(d)(2)(D) of an implied requirement that the declarant have personal knowledge of the facts underlying his statement. So we conclude that the two statements made by Mr. Poos were admissible against Wild Canid Survival and Research Center, Inc.

As to the entry in the records of a corporate meeting, the directors as primary officers of the corporation had the authority to include their conclusions in the record of the meeting. So the evidence would fall within 801(d)(2)(C) as to Wild Canid Survival and Research Center, Inc., and be admissible. The "in house" aspect of this admission has already been discussed, Rule 801(d)(2)(D), *supra*.

But there was no servant, or agency, relationship which justified admitting the evidence of the board minutes as against Mr. Poos.

None of the conditions of 801(d)(2) cover the claim that minutes of a corporate board meeting can be used against a non-attending, non-participating employee of that corporation. The evidence was not admissible as against Mr. Poos.

There is left only the question of whether the trial court's rulings which excluded all three items of evidence are justified under Rule 403. He clearly found that the evidence was not reliable, pointing out that none of the statements were based on the personal knowledge of the declarant.

Again, that problem was faced by the Advisory Committee on Proposed Rules. In its discussion of 801(d)(2) exceptions to the hearsay rule, the Committee said:

> The freedom which admissions have enjoyed from technical demands of searching for an assurance of trustworthiness in some against-interest circumstances, and from the restrictive influences of the opinion rule and the rule requiring first hand knowledge, when taken with the apparently prevalent satisfaction with the results, calls for generous treatment of this avenue to admissibility. . . .

So here, remembering that relevant evidence is usually prejudicial to the cause of the side against which it is presented, and that the prejudice which concerns us is unreasonable prejudice; and applying the spirit of Rule 801(d)(2), we hold that Rule 403 does not warrant the exclusion of the evidence of Mr. Poos' statements as against himself or Wild Canid Survival and Research Center, Inc.

But the limited admissibility of the corporate minutes, coupled with the repetitive nature of the evidence and the low probative value of the minute record, all justify supporting the judgment of the trial court under Rule 403.

The judgment of the District Court is reversed and the matter remanded to the District Court for a new trial consistent with this opinion.

d. Co-Conspirator Declarations

Joseph H. Levie, *Hearsay and Conspiracy: A Reexamination of the Co-Conspirators' Exception to the Hearsay Rule*
52 MICH. L. REV. 1159, 1161, 1163–64 (1954)[29]

The co-conspirators' exception to the hearsay rule is soon stated: any act or declaration by one co-conspirator committed in furtherance of the conspiracy and during its pendency is admissible against each and every co-conspirator provided that a foundation for its reception is laid by independent proof of the conspiracy. Often the rule is stated in the negative: mere "narrative" declarations of the one co-conspirator cannot be admitted against co-conspirators. All three conditions of admissibility (furtherance, pendency, foundation) resemble principles of agency. Furtherance is "scope of employment" modified for conspiracy. Requiring the declaration to have been made during pendency follows logically for if the conspiracy does not exist acts cannot be within its scope. The independent foundation finds a parallel in the rule that agency cannot be proved by declarations of the agent alone.

The odd thing about this exception to the hearsay rule is its very existence. Why single out conspiracy for preferential treatment?

*   *   *

Once it was believed that admissions were not hearsay. Nobody today would adopt so naive a view. The usual reason given for the co-conspirators' exception is the classical agency rationale that conspirators are co-agents and, as such, liable for each other's declarations. Wigmore differs, claiming that such evidence is unusually trustworthy, like declarations against interest generally, and therefore is admitted although hearsay. It is submitted that neither view is really defensible, and that the true reason, aside from brute history, for admitting such evidence is the very great probative need for it.

. . . Learned Hand has said:

Such declarations are admitted upon no doctrine of the law of evidence, but of the substantive law of crime. When men enter into an agreement for an unlawful end, they become ad hoc agents for one another, and have made

---

[29] Reprinted with permission.

"a partnership in crime." What one does pursuant to their common purpose, all do, and as declarations may be such acts, they are competent against all.

UNITED STATES v. HALDEMAN
559 F.2d 31 (D.C. Cir. 1976)

PER CURIAM:

On March 1, 1974 a grand jury in Washington, D.C. returned a 13-count indictment against seven individuals. It charged what amounted to an unprecedented scandal at the highest levels of government, for most of the defendants had held major positions in the Nixon administration. Charged were John N. Mitchell, former Attorney General of the United States and later head of the Committee to Re-elect the President (CRP), President Nixon's campaign organization for the 1972 election; Harry R. Haldeman, former Assistant to the President, serving basically as chief of the White House staff; John D. Ehrlichman, once Assistant for Domestic Affairs to the President; Charles W. Colson, former Special Counsel to the President; Robert C. Mardian, earlier an Assistant Attorney General, then an official of CRP; Kenneth W. Parkinson, hired in June of 1972 as CRP's lawyer; and Gordon Strachan, once a staff assistant to Haldeman at the White House.[30] The counts of the indictment embraced conspiracy, 18 U.S.C. § 371 (1970), obstruction of justice, *id.* § 1503, and various instances of false statements made to the Federal Bureau of Investigation (FBI), *id.* § 1001, to the grand jury, *id.* § 1623, and to the Senate Select Committee on Presidential Campaign Activities, *id.* § 1621. . . .

Five defendants ultimately went to trial together before Judge Sirica . . . . The jury acquitted Parkinson, found Mardian guilty of conspiracy . . . and convicted Mitchell, Haldeman, and Ehrlichman of both conspiracy and obstruction of justice as well as all the individual perjury counts submitted . . . . We deal in the instant appeals only with the convictions of Haldeman, Ehrlichman, and Mitchell. We affirm.

Evidence at trial consisted of both direct testimony and actual tape recordings of key conversations of the co-conspirators. It established a wide-ranging conspiracy designed to impede a grand jury investigation into the break in at the Democratic National Committee (DNC) headquarters in the Watergate Office Building in Washington, D.C., and into other related matters.

*   *   *

---

[30] [2] The grand jury also authorized the Special Prosecutor to name 18 individuals as co-conspirators: Bernard L. Barker, William O. Bittman, John D. Caulfield, John W. Dean, III, Virgilio R. Gonzalez, Sally Harmony, Dorothy Hunt, E. Howard Hunt, Jr., Herbert W. Kalmbach, Fred C. LaRue, G. Gordon Liddy, Jeb S. Magruder, Eugenio R. Martinez, James W. McCord, Jr., Richard M. Nixon, Paul O'Brien, Frank L. Sturgis, and Anthony T. Ulasewicz. J.A. 483. Several of these individuals have been convicted in other cases of various offenses connected with the Watergate incident.

1. *Alleged Inadmissibility Under the Opinion and Firsthand Knowledge Rules*

Mitchell contends that a number of out-of-court declarations recorded on the tapes are inadmissible because they contain expressions of opinion or statements not based upon the declarants' firsthand knowledge.[31] The simple answer to this contention, as the Government notes in its brief, is that these rules are inapplicable to declarations admissible under the co-conspirator exception to the hearsay rule.
. . .

2. *Alleged Inadmissibility as Hearsay Falling Outside the Co-Conspirator Exception*

Mitchell next contends that numerous excerpts on the tape recordings constitute mere narratives of past events, rather than statements made in furtherance of the conspiracy, and hence fall outside the co-conspirator exception to the hearsay rule. We agree with the point that mere narratives of past events are not admissible hearsay statements. But as applied to the facts in this case, the argument is of limited value to Mitchell.

The conspiracy at issue required the coordination and control of a large number of individuals who had knowledge of the events that were being covered up. It also required the conspirators to make regular strategic decisions on how best to proceed to prevent the full story of "Watergate" from becoming known to the press, prosecutors, Congress, and the public. The tape recordings thus contain discussions of many aspects of Watergate strategy: what would happen if particular individuals were to talk, *e.g.*, Tape Tr. 195, how much knowledge those individuals possessed, *e.g.*, Tape Tr. 306, who was likely to volunteer or be compelled to talk, *e.g.*, Tape Tr. 213–214, 306, 310, what individuals could be dissociated from responsibility for reprehensible or illegal activity, *e.g.*, Tape Tr. 147, 265–267, 303, 458–459, whether certain officials should assert executive privilege, *e.g.*, Tape Tr. 193–194, whether public statements should be issued and what they might contain, *e.g.*, Tape Tr. 57, whether it was feasible to raise and distribute hush money, *e.g.*, Tape Tr. 131–132, 179, 189–191, whether promises of money or aid had been extended to particular persons, *e.g.*, Tape Tr. 325, and so forth, *see, e.g.*, Tape Tr. 64, 72, 82, 86, 89–91, 130, 135, 311.

As the threads of the cover-up began to unravel, it became increasingly important to review what had taken place in order to identify and shore up the loose ends. It became critical for the conspirators to try to ensure that any story they wished to present would not ring false and that any action they were considering would not backfire, a strategy whose success required total familiarity with the facts.[32]

In a conspiracy in which consideration of alternative strategies played so central

---

[31] [213] Because all of the challenged excerpts purport to be statements or observations of the declarants themselves, rather than repetition of other out-of-court declarations, the objection to the admission of these excerpts must be based on the firsthand knowledge and opinion rules, rather than on a claim that these hearsay declarations among co-conspirators contain a second layer of hearsay. *See* C. McCormick, Handbook of the Law of Evidence § 10, at 20–21 (Cleary ed. 1972).

[32] [216] Compare the old saw: "I don't lie because my memory isn't good enough."

a role,[33] statements which narrate past events are not necessarily "mere narratives" in the usual sense of that phrase. Rather, they can constitute activity that is plainly and importantly "in furtherance of" a conspiracy, and thereby be admissible under the co-conspirator exception to the hearsay rule. . . .

We have reviewed each of the excerpts to which Mitchell objects in context. Although most of the 39 excerpts contain statements of past facts, almost all of these statements are integral parts of the continual strategy sessions that took place in the White House concerning what to do *in the future* about Watergate. Only four of the excerpts strike us as possibly falling outside of the "in furtherance" requirement. But even were we to assume that it was error to admit these excerpts, the error is clearly harmless.[34]

The evidence of Mitchell's participation in the conspiracy was overwhelming. . . . Mitchell was involved in the conspiracy from its inception on June 17 and played a central role in virtually every stage. The Government is entirely correct when it states at page 37 of its brief that [t]here was no aspect of the obstruction in which

---

[33] [217] The following exchange, which directly followed a discussion on the subject of Watergate strategy, reflects the extent to which Ehrlichman and Haldeman and President Nixon — whose conversations constitute the great bulk of the tape recordings that were introduced into evidence — were involved in planning strategy on "Watergate":

   EHRLICHMAN: Oh, no. I was working on something I'll tell you about here.

   PRESIDENT: What did you do?

   EHRLICHMAN: Uh, well, not much last night.

   PRESIDENT: You mean another subject?

   EHRLICHMAN: Oh, no. No, this—

   HALDEMAN: There is no other subject. (Laughs)

   EHRLICHMAN: This week there's no other subject.

   PRESIDENT: Yeah.

Tape Tr. 348.

[34] [219] Mitchell also objects to the admission of hearsay declarations of co-conspirators on the theory that any conspiracy of which he was a member had ended by March of 1973, at which time Nixon, Ehrlichman, Haldeman, and Dean were considering a plan to make Mitchell the "fall guy." He alleges that this activity constituted a second conspiracy, of which he was not a member, and hence the excerpts pertaining to it could not be admitted against him under the co-conspirator exception to the hearsay rule. Although the only document in the Joint Appendix in which Mitchell objects to the admissibility of certain portions of the tapes does not mention this argument, J.A. 606-611, his counsel appears to have made this argument orally on at least one occasion, Tr. 3320. The District Judge, however, ruled the tapes admissible over this objection. We believe that there was no error in his finding sufficient evidence of a single and continuing conspiracy of which Mitchell was a member to permit the jury to listen to the excerpts in question. As the government argues, the abortive plan to have Mitchell step forward to take the blame was compatible with the conspiracy's central objective — to cover up any information that might embarrass the Nixon White House. When some information began to become public, it was logical and foreseeable that the conspirators would next try to limit the number of people whom that information might implicate, and having Mitchell assume the blame was one way to limit the vulnerability of others. But even then Mitchell was to be given veiled assurances of clemency if he agreed to go along with the plan. Perhaps most important, when this plan was not executed Mitchell remained a loyal member of the conspiracy in his later appearances before the grand jury and the Senate committee. Finally, there was no evidence that Mitchell made any attempt whatsoever to withdraw from the conspiracy. Thus there was ample evidence — independent of the tape recordings themselves — to support the existence of a single conspiracy to which Mitchell belonged and which extended into the summer of 1973.

[Mitchell] was not involved; the attempt to "spring" McCord; the false press release; the destruction of documents; the Magruder "cover story"; the attempted misuse of the CIA; the "hush money" payments; the veiled offers of clemency; and, finally, the false statements and perjurious testimony. And his complicity in these events was irrefutably established at trial through the testimony of Dean, Magruder, LaRue, and Kalmbach, as well as co-defendants Haldeman and Ehrlichman.

Finally, contained on the excerpts *that were* properly admitted were a large number of statements by Dean, Nixon, Ehrlichman, and Haldeman that fully implicated Mitchell in the crimes of which he was convicted. Any incriminating declarations on the four excerpts in question merely tracked the substance of a much larger number of declarations that were properly admitted. In light of this fact and the overwhelming evidence of Mitchell's guilt, any error that may exist is clearly harmless beyond any reasonable doubt.

NOTES AND QUESTIONS

1.   In *United States v. Nixon*, 418 U.S. 683 (1974), which rejected the President's claim of executive privilege as grounds for declining to produce President Nixon's now infamous Oval Office tape recordings, the Supreme Court recognized that these tapes were relevant to the grand jury's investigation because they potentially contained, *inter alia*, admissible declarations of co-conspirators. *Id.* at 701. The *Haldeman* case later substantiated the Supreme Court's earlier remarks.

2.   Suppose a defendant has been convicted on substantive counts, but acquitted of conspiracy. May he successfully argue on appeal that statements admitted under the co-conspirator exception should not have been admitted for jury consideration? *See United States v. Robinson*, 651 F.2d 1188, 1195–96 (6th Cir.), *cert. denied*, 454 U.S. 875 (1981); *United States v. Clark*, 613 F.2d 391 (2d Cir. 1979), *cert. denied*, 449 U.S. 820 (1980); *cf. United States v. Simmons*, 374 F.3d 313, 320–21 (5th Cir. 2004).

3.   Under the co-conspirator principle, the declarant need not be formally charged with conspiracy? *See United States v. Coe*, 718 F.2d 830 (7th Cir. 1983); *United States v. Brown*, 894 F. Supp. 1150–1155 (N.D. Ill. 1995). Why not?

4.   The co-conspirator rule also applies to civil litigation. *See Precision Piping & Instruments, Inc. v. E.I. Du Pont de Nemours & Co.*, 951 F.2d 613, 621 (4th Cir. 1991); *Paul F. Newton & Co. v. Texas Commerce Bank*, 630 F.2d 1111 (5th Cir. 1980); *Doe v. Lee*, 220 F. Supp. 2d 1307 (D. Ala. 2002). Why?

Evidentiary Foundation:
The Trial of Julius and Ethel Rosenberg[35]

[On March 6, 1951, Julius and Ethel Rosenberg went on trial for conspiring to commit espionage for the Soviet Union. The government charged that the Rosenbergs had agreed to give Soviet agents classified documents concerning the atomic bomb. They accomplished this objective in 1945 through the assistance of Ethel's brother, David Greenglass, who was a soldier stationed at the Los Alamos Scientific

---

[35] Excerpted from Vol. 1, Book 2, Transcript of the Record, at 438–41.

Laboratory where the bomb was being developed. The Rosenbergs were convicted, and despite numerous appeals and worldwide protest, were executed on June 19, 1954.

The first witness for the government was Max Elitcher, whom Julius Rosenberg had asked to participate in espionage affairs related to his employment for the Navy Department. Elitcher acknowledged having cooperated with Rosenberg in significant respects. At one point, the prosecution asked Elitcher about a conversation he had had with Morton Sobell, a co-defendant, concerning a proposed meeting with Julius Rosenberg.

When prosecution witness Max Elitcher testified about a conspiratorial conversation he had with Julius Rosenberg, co-defendant Sobell's counsel objected and the following colloquy occurred:]

Mr. Phillips: Just a minute. I object to any conversation about Sobell in the absence of Sobell.

The Court: Let us understand this right now; in a conspiracy after it has been established that the conspiracy exists, conversations by one conspirator are binding on the other conspirator even though not in his presence. Your objection is that no conspiracy has been shown?

Mr. Phillips: Precisely.

The Court: The Government can't prove its entire case in one hour.

Mr. Phillips: But they must first prove the thing they must prove first.

The Court: They can't prove their entire case in one hour. Your objection is overruled. It is taken subject to proof that a conspiracy exists.

Mr. Phillips: Exception.

BOURJAILY v. UNITED STATES
483 U.S. 171 (1987)

CHIEF JUSTICE REHNQUIST delivered the opinion of the Court.

Federal Rule of Evidence 801(d)(2)(E) provides: "A statement is not hearsay if . . . [t]he statement is offered against a party and is . . . a statement by a co-conspirator of a party during the course and in furtherance of the conspiracy." We granted *certiorari* to answer three questions regarding the admission of statements under Rule 801(d)(2)(E): (1) whether the court must determine by independent evidence that the conspiracy existed and that the defendant and the declarant were members of this conspiracy; (2) the quantum of proof on which such determinations must be based; and (3) whether a court must in each case examine the circumstances of such a statement to determine its reliability. 479 U.S. 881 (1986).

In May 1984, Clarence Greathouse, an informant working for the Federal Bureau of Investigation (FBI), arranged to sell a kilogram of cocaine to Angelo Lonardo. Lonardo agreed that he would find individuals to distribute the drug. When the sale became imminent, Lonardo stated in a tape-recorded telephone conversation that he had a "gentleman friend" who had some questions to ask about the cocaine. In a subsequent telephone call, Greathouse spoke to the "friend" about the quality of the drug and the price. Greathouse then spoke again with Lonardo, and the two arranged the details of the purchase. They agreed that the sale would take place in a designated hotel parking lot, and Lonardo would transfer the drug from Greathouse's car to the "friend," who would be waiting in the parking lot in his own car. Greathouse proceeded with the transaction as planned, and FBI agents arrested Lonardo and petitioner immediately after Lonardo placed a kilogram of cocaine into petitioner's car in the hotel parking lot. In petitioner's car, the agents found over $20,000 in cash.

Petitioner was charged with conspiring to distribute cocaine, in violation of 21 U.S.C. § 846, and possession of cocaine with intent to distribute, a violation of 21 U.S.C. § 841(a)(1). The Government introduced, over petitioner's objection, Angelo Lonardo's telephone statements regarding the participation of the "friend" in the transaction. The District Court found that, considering the events in the parking lot and Lonardo's statements over the telephone, the Government had established by a preponderance of the evidence that a conspiracy involving Lonardo and petitioner existed, and that Lonardo's statements over the telephone had been made in the course of and in furtherance of the conspiracy. App. 66–75. Accordingly, the trial court held that Lonardo's out-of-court statements satisfied Rule 801(d)(2)(E) and were not hearsay. Petitioner was convicted on both counts and sentenced to 15 years. The United States Court of Appeals for the Sixth Circuit affirmed. 781 F.2d 539 (1986). The Court of Appeals agreed with the District Court's analysis and conclusion that Lonardo's out-of-court statements were admissible under the Federal Rules of Evidence. The court also rejected petitioner's contention that because he could not cross-examine Lonardo, the admission of these statements violated his constitutional right to confront the witnesses against him. We affirm.

Before admitting a co-conspirator's statement over an objection that it does not qualify under Rule 801(d)(2)(E), a court must be satisfied that the statement actually falls within the definition of the Rule. There must be evidence that there was a conspiracy involving the declarant and the nonoffering party, and that the statement was made "during the course and in furtherance of the conspiracy." Federal Rule of Evidence 104(a) provides: "Preliminary questions concerning . . . the admissibility of evidence shall be determined by the court." Petitioner and the Government agree that the existence of a conspiracy and petitioner's involvement in it are preliminary questions of fact that, under Rule 104, must be resolved by the court. The Federal Rules, however, nowhere define the standard of proof the court must observe in resolving these questions.

We are therefore guided by our prior decisions regarding admissibility determinations that hinge on preliminary factual questions. We have traditionally required that these matters be established by a preponderance of proof. Evidence is placed before the jury when it satisfies the technical requirements of the evidentiary Rules, which embody certain legal and policy determinations. The inquiry made by a court concerned with these matters is not whether the proponent of the evidence wins or loses his case on the merits, but whether the evidentiary Rules have been satisfied. Thus, the evidentiary standard is unrelated to the burden of proof on the substantive issues, be it a criminal case, *see In re Winship*, 397 U.S. 358 (1970), or a civil case. *See generally Colorado v. Connelly*, 479 U.S. 157, 167–169 (1986). The preponderance standard ensures that before admitting evidence, the court will have found it more likely than not that the technical issues and policy concerns addressed by the Federal Rules of Evidence have been afforded due consideration. As in *Lego v. Twomey*, 404 U.S. 477 (1972), we find "nothing to suggest that admissibility rulings have been unreliable or otherwise wanting in quality because not based on some higher standard." We think that our previous decisions in this area resolve the matter. *See, e.g., Colorado v. Connelly, supra* (preliminary fact that custodial confessant waived rights must be proved by preponderance of the evidence); *Nix v. Williams*, 467 U.S. 431, 444, n.5 (1984) (inevitable discovery of illegally seized evidence must be shown to have been more likely than not); *United States v. Matlock*, 415 U.S. 164 (1974) (voluntariness of consent to search must be shown by preponderance of the evidence); *Lego v. Twomey, supra* (voluntariness of confession must be demonstrated by a preponderance of the evidence). Therefore, we hold that when the preliminary facts relevant to Rule 801(d)(2)(E) are disputed, the offering party must prove them by a preponderance of the evidence.[36]

*   *   *

We think that there is little doubt that a co-conspirator's statements could themselves be probative of the existence of a conspiracy and the participation of both the defendant and the declarant in the conspiracy. Petitioner's case presents a paradigm. The out-of-court statements of Lonardo indicated that Lonardo was involved in a conspiracy with a "friend." The statements indicated that the friend had agreed with Lonardo to buy a kilogram of cocaine and to distribute it. The statements also revealed that the friend would be at the hotel parking lot, in his car, and would accept the cocaine from Greathouse's car after Greathouse gave Lonardo the keys. Each one of Lonardo's statements may itself be unreliable, but taken as a whole, the entire conversation between Lonardo and Greathouse was corroborated by independent evidence. The friend, who turned out to be petitioner, showed up at the prearranged spot at the prearranged time. He picked up the cocaine, and a significant sum of money was found in his car. On these facts, the trial court concluded, in our view correctly, that the Government had established the existence of a conspiracy and peti-tioner's participation in it.

We need not decide in this case whether the courts below could have relied solely upon Lonardo's hearsay statements to determine that a conspiracy had been established by a preponderance of the evidence. To the extent that Glasser meant that courts could not look to the hearsay statements themselves for any purpose, it has clearly been superseded by Rule 104(a). It is sufficient for today to hold that a court, in making a preliminary factual determination under Rule 801(d)(2)(E), may examine the hearsay statements sought to be admitted. As we have held in other cases concerning admissibility determinations, "the judge should receive the

---

[36] [1] We intimate no view on the proper standard of proof for questions falling under Federal Rule of Evidence 104(b) (conditional relevancy). We also decline to address the circumstances in which the burden of coming forward to show that the proffered evidence is inadmissible is appropriately placed on the nonoffering party. *See* E. CLEARY, McCORMICK ON EVIDENCE § 53, p. 136, n.8 (3d ed. 1984). Finally, we do not express an opinion on the proper order of proof that trial courts should follow in concluding that the preponderance standard has been satisfied in an ongoing trial.

evidence and give it such weight as his judgment and experience counsel." *United States v. Matlock*, 415 U.S. at 175. The courts below properly considered the statements of Lonardo and the subsequent events in finding that the Government had established by a preponderance of the evidence that Lonardo was involved in a conspiracy with petitioner. We have no reason to believe that the District Court's factfinding of this point was clearly erroneous. We hold that Lonardo's out-of-court statements were properly admitted against petitioner.[37]

NOTES

1. After *Bourjaily*, Congress amended Rule 801(d)(2) to provide that "the contents of the statement shall be considered but are not alone sufficient to establish the declarant's authority under subdivision (C), the agency or employment relationship and the scope thereof under subdivision (D), or the existence of the conspiracy and the participation therein of the declarant and the party against whom the statement is offered under subdivision (E)."

2. As a result of this amendment, the proponent must provide corroboration beyond the statement itself to establish the foundation for admissibility. *See, e.g., United States v. Payne*, 437 F.3d 540 (6th Cir. 2006); *Mercado v. City of Orlando*, 407 F.3d 1152, 1161 (11th Cir. 2005).

Evidentiary Foundation:
The Trial of Harrison A. Williams, Jr.[38]

[The background to this case is set forth § C.4.b.7 in Chapter III, *supra*. During the course of Melvin Weinberg's testimony, the prosecution encountered difficulty establishing the foundation to admit certain statements as co-conspirator declarations.]

Q.   On the following morning, January 11th [1979], did you meet with Alex Feinberg, a man by the name of Sandy Williams, Mayor Errichetti and Jack McCloud, Jack McCarthy, at the Hyatt House in Cherry Hill, New Jersey?

A.   That's correct.

Q.   What were the circumstances in which you met?

A.   They brought up payments on a titanium mine in Virginia.

Q.   Who are you referring to by "they"?

A.   Alex Feinberg and Sandy Williams.

Q.   Did you have a conversation with them at that time?

A.   Yes.

Q.   What do you recall about that?

---

[37] [2] Given this disposition, we have no occasion to address the Government's argument, Brief for United States 21–25, that Lonardo's statements are admissible independent of Rule 801(d)(2)(E).

[38] Excerpted from Trial Transcript, *supra*, at 721–731.

A.   They spoke to us about the mine, down in Virginia there that had a mine on it and the plants that was there and they wanted us to invest in it and Alex Feinberg said to me on the side that whatever his share is he divided with Senator Williams.

MR. KOELZER: Objection. I move it be stricken. May I be heard on this, your Honor?

THE COURT: Do you wish to be heard at sidebar?

MR. KOELZER: If the Court wishes. We have discussed the legal aspects—

THE COURT: I understand your legal position at this stage of the events. Do you wish to be heard at sidebar, Mr. McDonald?

MR. MCDONALD: Yes, Your Honor.

(Sidebar discussion out of hearing of the jury as follows)

MR. KOELZER: Do you wish to hear from me first?

THE COURT: As I understand Mr. Koelzer's position, this is before any possible conspiracy could have been entered into, and therefore the conversations in no way affect Mr. Williams.

* * *

MR. MCDONALD: I beg to differ. . . . The conspiracy charges, the conspiracy charges that the conspiracy runs from the beginning of January, 1979, until February 2nd, 1980. One of the points of this conspiracy was to conceal Senator Williams' shares and his interest in this venture. The point of the conspiracy was not bribery at that point.

THE COURT: What was it?

MR. MCDONALD: To conceal Senator Williams' shares.

MR. KOELZER: That's not a crime.

* * *

MR. MCDONALD: Another point here, it's already been elicited that Senator Williams was the one who arranged for this meeting. He was the one who called Mayor Errichetti. He made statements to that effect on the tapes. I think what we have here is a decision where there was an agency relationship where Mr. Feinberg is representing Mr. Williams. That's the statement they're objecting to that he's representing Senator Williams on this venture. He's acting on behalf of the Senator.

MR. KOELZER: We're talking about January 11, 1979, there has been no discussion of government contracts, there have been no discussions of titanic metal. That doesn't arise until May of 1979. I don't think that is in dispute. Certainly that's the evidence on the times that have been made and shown to us.

Beyond that, in this—

THE COURT: Let me ask you a question: is it your position that if there was an arrangement among the group of people to engage in a legitimate business deal which, at a later time turned into an illegal activity, that the only time, the statements of one of this group could be used against another, under the co-conspirator rule, would be whether [sic] he illegitimately entered into the situation.

MR. KOELZER: May I say, the answer to that is "yes" for this reason: as I read 371, 18 United States section 371 you can't have a conspiracy for legal or legitimate or proper cause. One doesn't conspire within the framework of 371 to confederate together, for something that is legitimate. I think it's a non sequitur to suggest that. As of the point in time . . . that it becomes illegal that, it becomes a violation of the statute and agreement to violate a Federal statute, that is when the conspiracy begins.

THE COURT: How about a straight agency analysis as Mr. McDonald has urged.

MR. KOELZER: I don't follow the analogy—

THE COURT: An agent speaks for a principal.

MR. KOELZER: Do they prove the agent at the state of the record right now? All that has happened, as I said in my opening, I intend to prove it when we go on, Williams said to Feinberg there may be foreign capital available. That doesn't say you got to go and get it, you have to meet. That's not an agency as I understand the principal agency relationship . . .

MR. MCDONALD: The record indicates much more. It reveals that the Senator Williams says he's part of the venture at the time, that he meets with Mayor Errichetti and that as a result of the conversations with Mayor Errichetti, immediately comes up to Alex Feinberg and tells him to go over there to find out, "What the hell is going on," to use his words. The statement itself confirms the agency relationship. The testimony objected to is what confirms the agency relationship here. Whatever—

MR. KOELZER: I'm in a total loss to understand that last statement for this reason: so far as I know, there is no tape recording of the meeting in January between Errichetti and Senator Williams.

MR. MCDONALD: Only Senator Williams' statement.

MR. KOELZER: I—

THE COURT: I suggest that you gentlemen not fight each other today. We're not getting off at a very good note. I'll give the jury a limited instruction that this is not binding on Senator Williams. It's admissible certainly as to Mr. Fein-berg and other co-conspirators, but they're not on trial here, who were present at the time this statement was made. I don't know why there is a problem, about it, because what we heard on the tapes very much confirms what happened here. He was a part of something that was going on quite obviously, but I think the objection is hearsay, it's binding upon Feinberg because he's the one who makes the statement, at this stage certainly the jury couldn't find that it's binding on Senator Williams. I don't think there is much of a difference between a straight agency analysis and the co-conspirator exception that is required, with reference to the date to which some illegality may have crept into this mining venture in which the Senator apparently had an interest before he came before the cameras.

* * *

THE COURT: I'll give it limiting instructions.

MR. KOELZER: Thank you, your Honor.

* * *

(The following took place in open court in the presence of the jury.)

THE COURT: Ladies and gentlemen, with respect to conversations between this witness and Mr. Feinberg . . . you may weigh that evidence as to what took place in this conversation with respect to the defendant Feinberg since he was participating in the conversation. But you may not use it with respect to the defendant Williams.

H.   EXCEPTIONS TO THE RULE AGAINST HEARSAY

Reliability and necessity have been traditional justifications for virtually each hearsay exception that has been recognized. This conventional wisdom, however, has been called into question. *See* Note, *The Theoretical Foundation of the Hearsay Rule*, 93 Harv. L. Rev. 1786 (1980). Nevertheless, for each of the exceptions examined in this section, identify the extent to which reliability and necessity prongs are present.

1.   Exceptions Requiring Declarant Unavailability

a.   Introduction: The Concept of Unavailability

Comment, *Hearsay Under the Proposed Federal Rules: A Discretionary Approach*
15 Wayne L. Rev. 1077, 1101–05 (1969)[39]

The fourth and final definition in the hearsay section of the proposed Rules is of the term "unavailability." Under this definition, a witness is unavailable if any of four specified situations exist. This definition of unavailability is significant in that the hearsay exceptions are divided into two categories — one category of exceptions

---

[39] Reprinted with permission of The Wayne Law Review.

requiring that the declarant be unavailable, the other category having no such requirement. The theory behind the category of exceptions which does not require the declarant to be unavailable as a witness is that "the nature of the statement and the circumstances of its making justify the conclusion that no greater accuracy is likely to result from calling the declarant in person as a witness. . . ." The theory underlying the other category of exceptions, which requires the declarant to be unavailable as a witness, is that although it would be preferable to have the declarant testify as a witness, if he is unavailable there is sufficient circumstantial assurance of accuracy so that it is better to receive the statement in evidence than to do completely without it.

The definition of "unavailability" is unique in that its requirements are uniform for the entire class of exceptions requiring the declarant to be unavailable as a witness. This is a marked divergence from the common law where different unavailability requirements developed in connection with particular hearsay exceptions. Under the common law, the most liberal unavailability requirements are found in connection with the hearsay exception for former testimony. In addition to death, a witness is considered unavailable if unable to testify because of physical disability, mental incapacity, exercise of privilege, or if absent from the hearing and beyond the jurisdiction of the court. The common law exception to hearsay for dying declarations requires that the declarant be dead when the evidence is offered. Early cases dealing with the exception for declarations against interest also required that the declarant be dead. However, some jurisdictions have departed from this strict requirement of the early English courts by accepting other grounds of unavailability. Similarly, some courts require death of the declarant as a prerequisite to admissibility of statements of personal or family history, while others have liberalized the grounds of unavailability in regard to this exception. Thus, the question arises as to the advisability of having a uniform unavailability standard for an entire class of exceptions. The answer seems self-evident — whether a witness is deemed unavailable should not vary according to the specific exception involved. If the evidence is considered sufficiently reliable to qualify as a hearsay exception, the unavailability of the declarant should be determined by his actual ability to appear as a witness, something that is constant regardless of the exception involved.

The definition of unavailability specifies four instances where a declarant is unavailable. The first occurs if a witness is exempt, by ruling of the judge, from testifying concerning the subject matter of his statement because of a privilege. The exercise of a privilege has been recognized in the past as a ground for unavailability in connection with some exceptions. It should be a sufficient ground for any exception where unavailability is required.

The second ground for unavailability is the persistent refusal of a witness to testify despite an order by the judge. Although the common law did not recognize this as a ground for unavailability, it has been accepted by some jurisdictions. The better view is to consider continued refusal to testify as unavailability, since the true test should not be the unavailability of the witness but the unavailability of his testimony.

The third ground for unavailability recognized by the definition is death or physical or mental infirmity. Formerly, death was the only ground for unavailability common to all hearsay exceptions. Physical and mental infirmity also have been generally recognized as sufficient grounds, as they should be. If the disability is temporary, and the evidence is of substantial importance, the opponent would be sufficiently protected by his right to seek a postponement of the trial, if in the judge's discretion it is justified.

The final ground for unavailability is the absence of the declarant from the hearing and the jurisdiction of the court, with the failure of the proponent to procure his attendance through the exercise of reasonable diligence. Absence from the jurisdiction of the court has received recognition as a ground for unavailability. The requirement that the proponent exercise reasonable diligence to procure attendance of the witness is relatively new and is found in some recent evidence codes. Although the standard of reasonable diligence to procure attendance may be difficult to determine, this requirement reflects the preference of having the declarant testify if at all possible. Such a requirement at least acts as a deterrent to a party who knows of a witness' whereabouts but would rather use his prior statement. The deterrent effect would be the possibility of losing both the prior statement and the testimony of the witness because of a failure to show reasonable effort to procure his attendance. This requirement must be further considered in connection with the limitation that "[a] declarant is not unavailable as a witness if his exemption, refusal, inability, or absence is due to the procurement or wrongdoing of the proponent of his statement for the purpose of preventing the witness from attending or testifying." This latter limitation, which has found similar expression in other evidence codes, would appear to be necessary. The problem involved, however, is the difficulty of proving that the absence of the witness has been procured. The burden would be on the opponent of the hearsay statement to prove that the declarant's unavailability had been procured, an almost impossible task in most instances. The difficulty in proving that the absence of the declarant has been procured is probably the most substantial reason for requiring the proponent to make a reasonable effort to procure the declarant's attendance. This latter requirement places an affirmative duty on the proponent to show some effort at getting the declarant to testify, in addition to the burden of rebutting any charge that the absence of the declarant was procured. It is more difficult to conceal a procured absence when the party has to show a reasonable effort to procure attendance. Hopefully, this double-barreled protection will provide a reasonable degree of assurance that unavailability will be limited to situations where a witness is truly unable or unwilling to testify.

NOTES AND QUESTIONS

1.   Scholars often disagree over which hearsay exceptions should be conditioned upon declarant unavailability. *See* 4 WEINSTEIN'S EVIDENCE § 804(a)[01], at 223 (1982 Supp.). As you review each hearsay exception, consider whether it should be premised upon unavailability. Are the hearsay exceptions contained in Fed. R. Evid. 803, which do not require a showing of declarant unavailability, necessarily more reliable than those contained in Fed. R. Evid. 804 which require such a showing?

2.   To what extent, if any, does Fed. R. Evid. 804, as adopted, define unavailability more broadly than the proposed version discussed in the preceding

Comment?

b. Declarations Against Interest

Bernard S. Jefferson, *Declarations Against Interest: An Exception to the Hearsay Rule*
58 HARV. L. REV. 1, 1–2, 8, 39–40 (1944)[40]

One of the well-established exceptions to the hearsay rule admits statements of facts against interest. Numerous cases state that the admissibility of statements under this exception is to be tested by four requirements: (1) the declarant must be dead; (2) the declaration must be against the pecuniary or proprietary interest of the declarant; (3) the declaration must be of a fact or facts which were immediately cognizable by the declarant personally; and (4) the declarant must not have had a probable motive to falsify the fact declared. In many cases, the courts after reciting the four requisites decide with little or no discussion that proffered evidence satisfies the conditions for admissibility. With like ease, proffered statements are held lacking in some requisite and hence inadmissible. Such a mechanical approach invites a consideration of the place and scope of this exception in the law of evidence.

* * *

There are two general theories upon which the reliability and credibility of statements against interest may be predicated. One theory is that if a fact is against the pecuniary or proprietary interest of the declarant, it is unlikely that he will concede or admit its existence unless it is true. A second theory is that if the statement itself is contrary to the declarant's pecuniary or proprietary interest, it is improbable that he would consciously make such an unfavorable statement falsely. Both theories have their roots deep in human nature and experience. People are apt to speak freely and falsely in their own favor but are reluctant to speak falsely to their pecuniary or proprietary detriment.

* * *

On principle, the exception for declarations against interest would admit declarations contrary to any kind of interest of sufficient importance to a declarant to promote his telling the truth. Penal interest is certainly as important to a person as pecuniary and proprietary interest. The same may be said for social interest. One is not likely to concede the existence of facts which will subject him to criminal liability unless such facts are true. Nor is one likely to concede the existence of facts which would make him an object of social disapproval in the community unless the facts are true.

The rejection of the concept of penal interest for this exception in Anglo-American law is said to have been settled by the *Sussex Peerage* case, where the House of Lords stated that the exception for declarations against interest did not extend to declarations against penal interest. The American courts have overwhelmingly accepted the general principle of the *Sussex Peerage* case. It is hard to believe

---

that the real basis of rejection of the concept of penal interest is due to a notion that penal interest does not furnish a reliable probability of trustworthiness. If a declaration is contrary to both a penal and pecuniary interest, the courts have readily admitted it in a civil case. The presence of a penal interest does not destroy admissibility, but "would add to the weight of the testimony." Thus, a declaration by *X* that he has embezzled $5000 of his employer's money is admissible in a civil suit. A declarant's statement that he murdered *X* has been admitted in a civil suit on the theory that it destroyed the declarant's claim against the insurance company. In such cases it seems utterly illogical to argue that the guaranty of trustworthiness comes from the presence of pecuniary interest. The focal thought in the declarant's mind when he makes such a declaration must be the penal consequences, not the pecuniary effects. Although the courts have not stressed the nature of the suit but the nature of the declaration in these dual statements, it is doubtful whether such a declaration would be admitted in a criminal case, but the analysis which the courts make in these dual declarations would seem to require their admission in criminal cases unless a rule of policy intervenes to prevent a criminal defendant from offering in his behalf a declaration by a third person that he, and not the defendant, committed the crime.

QUESTIONS

1. How are declarations against interest distinguishable from admissions?

2. What exactly is it that must be against the declarant's interest — the statement or the underlying facts? Is there a difference? *Compare* Morgan, *Declarations Against Interest*, 5 VAND. L. REV. 451, 476 (1952), *with* Jefferson, *supra*, at 9–10.

3. Re-examine *United States v. Brown, supra* . To what extent, if any, did that case arguably involve declarations against interest on the part of taxpayers whom Agent Peacock interviewed? Why did the Court of Appeals not rely upon this hearsay exception to sustain the prosecution?

UNITED STATES v. MACDONALD
688 F.2d 224 (4th Cir. 1982)

ALBERT V. BRYAN, SENIOR CIRCUIT JUDGE:

[Ed. — Defendant MacDonald, formerly a physician in the Army Medical Corps, was charged with the brutal murder of his pregnant wife and two young daughters.]

In *United States v. MacDonald*, 102 S. Ct. 1497, 71 L. Ed. 2d 696 (1982), the Supreme Court reversed our holding that appellant's Sixth Amendment right to a speedy trial was abridged by the Government's delay in obtaining the indictment. On remand, we now speak to MacDonald's remaining advancements of error. . . . Since the Supreme Court's opinion scrupulously chronicles both the facts of record and the protracted history of the case, . . . we forego repetitious narration.

*   *   *

V. *The Stoeckley Witnesses*

Finally, appellant lays fault to the District Court's exercise of discretion in excluding the testimony of seven witnesses, all of whom would have testified to various inculpatory comments or statements assertedly made by Helena Stoeckley. The exclusion of this evidence, charges MacDonald, was error in that it abridged appellant's Fifth Amendment right to call witnesses in his own defense, [and] was admissible under Rule 804(b)(3). . . .

A

Since the commission of the crimes in February 1970, MacDonald has maintained that he and his family all were victims of a bizarre cult attack. He claims that the perpetrators included three men and a woman wearing a floppy hat, having blond hair, and wearing boots. The woman, he says, was Helena Stoeckley.

At trial, Stoeckley testified that although her hair was brown in color, she owned a blond wig at the time of the crimes. She further said that she owned a floppy hat and boots. Although her recollection of events on the evening of February 16 and during the early morning hours of February 17 was, at best, hazy, she recalls not wearing the blond wig. However, she admitted to burning the wig and discarding the boots two days later.

While Stoeckley offered this much evidence seeming to corroborate MacDonald's version of the killings, the remainder of her testimony either contradicted him or tended to undercut his narration of the events. For example, she testified that she had never seen MacDonald before trial, had never been in his Fayetteville apartment, and while she vaguely felt that she might have had some connection with the crimes, since she had no explanation of her whereabouts between midnight and 5:30 a.m., she insisted she was not present at their commission. In all, the evidence disclosed that Stoeckley's memory was exceedingly poor and that she was constantly under the influence of narcotic drugs.

Because of this faulty memory, appellant sought to introduce a series of inculpatory statements through other witnesses. In this proffer to the District Court, in the absence of the jury, it was shown that these witnesses would give evidence substantially as follows:

1) Robert A. Brisentine, an Army investigator assigned to the homicides, interviewed Stoeckley April 23 and 24, 1971, approximately 14 months after the crime. Stoeckley told him she was present during the murders, but did not think that she had taken part. She offered to divulge the participants and provide more details, but wanted immunity from prosecution. Subsequently, she said she had "said too much."

2) James Gaddis, an officer of the Nashville Police Department, revealed that Stoeckley had confessed her belief that she was involved in the crimes in the fall of 1970. She also said that she knew others who were involved.

3) P. E. Beasley, a former detective with the Fayetteville Police Department, explained that Stoeckley had been a reliable drug informant for several years prior to the murders. On the morning of February 18, 1970, a day after the fateful events,

reliability?

she told Beasley, in response to his accusation that she matched MacDonald's description of the female intruder, "[i]n my mind, it seems I saw this thing happen . . . . I was heavy on mescaline." Beasley also said that he observed funeral wreaths in the yard of Stoeckley's home. He added that she had told him she was mourning the MacDonalds.

4) Jane Zillioux, a Nashville neighbor of Stoeckley throughout the fall of 1970, said that Stoeckley had confided to her that she could not return to Fayetteville because she was involved in murders there. She further confessed that the victims were a woman and two small children and that she had disposed of the clothes she had been wearing to sever her connection with the crimes.

5) Charles Underhill, another Nashville acquaintance, testified that Stoeckley told him "they killed her and the two children."

6) William Posey, a neighbor of Stoeckley in Fayetteville, testified that Stoeckley told him a few days after the slayings that she didn't kill anyone herself, but did hold a light while the crime was in progress. She also confided to him that she was spotted by a policeman leaving the house.

7) Wendy Rouder, one of MacDonald's lawyers, testified that two days after Stoeckley had testified she could not remember anything about the night of the crime, she told Rouder "I still think I could have been there that night." Stoeckley also feared she would not be able to live with the guilt if MacDonald were convicted. Finally, she recalled standing by the couch in the MacDonald apartment holding a candle "only — you know — it wasn't dripping wax; it was dripping blood."

After all of these individuals had testified without the presence of the jury, the District Court excluded the evidence. It ruled the statements inadmissible hearsay because untrustworthy. In addition, the Court rejected MacDonald's attempt to use the statements as impeachment on the grounds that it was not impeachment, properly so called, and in any event, was excludible under Rule 403 as unduly confusing and prejudicial.

*   *   *

B

Relying on *Chambers v. Mississippi*, 410 U.S. 284 (1973), MacDonald complains that the exclusion of the testimony of these seven "Stoeckley witnesses" deprived him of due process. He also maintains that Fed. R. Evid. 804(b)(3) explicitly supplies an exception to the hearsay rule and authorized admission of the Stoeckley witnesses' testimony.

Chambers involved an appeal of a criminal conviction obtained after the refusal of the trial court to permit defendant to introduce the testimony of three witnesses who would have said that one Gable MacDonald admitted to each witness that he was guilty of the murder charged to Chambers. The Mississippi courts excluded the testimony on the ground that it was hearsay and not admissible under any exception recognized in that State. Particularly, Mississippi did not recognize statements against one's penal interest as an exception to the general hearsay prohibition.

The Supreme Court reasoned that enforcement of this hearsay rule denied Chambers' due process. In so concluding, it found sufficient indications of trustworthiness in the circumstances of MacDonald's admissions. . . . In circumstances "where constitutional rights directly affecting the ascertainment of guilt are implicated, the hearsay rule may not be applied mechanistically to defeat the ends of justice." *Id.* at 302.

This ruling, in large measure, is codified for Federal Courts in Fed. R. Evid. 804(b)(3). It conditions admissibility on the unavailability of the declarant, and provides that a statement of the declarant is admissible if at the time of its making [it was] so far contrary to the declarant's pecuniary or proprietary interest, or so far tended to subject him to civil or criminal liability, or to render invalid a claim by him against another, that a reasonable man in his position would not have made the statement unless he believed it to be true. A statement tending to expose the declarant to criminal liability and offered to exculpate the accused is not admissible unless corroborating circumstances clearly indicate the trustworthiness of the statement. Fed. R. Evid. 804(b)(3). Thus, as applied to criminal matters, three requisites must be met prior to reception of the hearsay testimony. First, the declarant must be unavailable. Second, from the perspective of the average, reasonable person, the statement must have been truly adverse to the declarant's penal interest, considering when it was made. . . . Finally, corroborating circumstances must clearly establish the trustworthiness of the statement. . . .

We have no difficulty in agreeing with appellant that declarant Stoeckley was unavailable[41] and that her statements, if true, clearly would be against her penal interest. The question remains, however, whether the "corroborating circumstances clearly indicate the trustworthiness of the statement[s]."

As corroborating circumstances, MacDonald adverts to the fact that Stoeckley owned and regularly wore boots, a blond wig, and a floppy hat, thus permitting her to fit the description of the female assailant described by defendant. In addition, defendant argues that Stoeckley had no motive to fabricate; that each admission was consistent with the others; that, for the most part, her declarations were spontaneous and to close associates; that at the time of their making, she was (and is) still subject to criminal liability, and in making these statements, she recognized this fact; that she cannot account for her whereabouts on the night of the crime; and that her mourning the deaths evinces a consciousness of guilt. The District Court, by contrast, concluded the declarations were untrustworthy because Stoeckley's pattern of remarks in admitting and denying complicity rendered her hopelessly unreliable, and because her pervasive involvement with narcotic drugs, and her admissions that she was under the virtually continual influence of the drugs when these statements were made further manifested unreliability.

As with other of these evidentiary objections, our role in reviewing decisions at *nisi prius* construing Rule 804(b)(3) is a limited one. We must uphold the trial court unless it has abused its discretion. . . . No such abuse is evident here.

---

[41] [14] Stoeckley actually testified at length at the trial. As to the subject matter of these statements, however, she claimed a loss of memory. Rule 804(a)(3) specifically includes asserted loss of memory as within the definition of "unavailability."

It is to be recalled that Rule 804(b)(3) places upon the proponent of a statement against interest a formidable burden. The declaration offered to exculpate the accused must be supported by corroborating circumstances that *"clearly* indicate the trustworthiness of the statement." (emphasis added). *Cf.* Fed. R. Evid. 804(b)(5) (residual exception only requires "equivalent circumstantial guarantee of trustworthiness"). As the Advisory Committee's Notes on this provision instruct, the risk of fabrication in this setting is significant. Consequently, rather than permitting only the jury to decide what weight to give the evidence, the initial responsibility is vested in the District Court. It is admonished that "[t]he requirement of corroboration should be construed in a manner [so] as to effectuate its purpose of circumventing fabrication." . . .

At bottom, the sticking point here, as recognized by the District Court, is the fundamental problem of trustworthiness. While MacDonald is able to point to a number of corroborating circumstances, he does not demonstrate, finally, that they make Stoeckley's alleged declaration trustworthy. Her apparent longstanding drug habits made her an inherently unreliable witness. Moreover, her vacillation about whether or not she remembered anything at all about the night of crime lends force to the view that everything she has said and done in this regard was a product of her drug addiction. Given the declarant's "pathetic" appearance, our conviction is that the District Court was not in error in adjudging that defendant failed to carry his burden under Rule 804(b)(3). Thus MacDonald's argued violation of the Due Process clause fails.

*   *   *

Affirmed.

MURNAGHAN, CIRCUIT JUDGE, concurring:

On the discretion of the district judge, the opinion of Judge Bryan rests. On the present state of the law as it applies to the particular case before us, I find myself, albeit not without substantial misgiving, obliged to concur.

Nevertheless, I perceive a useful purpose for future cases in addressing one troubling aspect. It is evident that a basis may be erected for finding the hearsay statements of Helena Stoeckley untrustworthy. Given the wide discretion vested in the trial judge, we should not fault Judge Dupree to the extent of reversing. Nevertheless, in view of the issues involved, and the virtually unique aspects of the surrounding circumstances, had I been the trial judge, I would have exercised the wide discretion conferred on him to allow the testimony to come in. My preference derives from my belief that, if the jury may be trusted with ultimate resolution of the factual issues, it should not be denied the opportunity of obtaining a rounded picture, necessary for resolution of the large questions, by the withholding of collateral testimony consistent with and basic to the defendant's principal exculpatory contention. If such evidence was not persuasive, which is what the government essentially contends in saying that it was untrustworthy, the jury, with very great probability, would not have been misled by it.

In deciding whether a statement against interest should be admitted under the exception to the hearsay rule, the court must determine whether the "corroborating circumstances clearly indicate the trustworthiness of the statement." Fed. R. Evid. 804(b)(3). The question is whether the statement is believable,[42] that is to say [sic] appears to have been clearly within the competence of the witness to observe, without a demonstrable intention or disposition to prevaricate. . . .

Credibility can be established in various ways. Considerations include the circumstances surrounding the statements, . . . and the absence of motivation on the part of the declarant to fabricate. . . . Another factor deserving recognition is that of the general societal frame of reference. The latter can provide increased support for the believability of statements such as the ones now at issue. The likelihood of the truth of a seemingly outrageous story grows when an appreciation of current events is applied to the known facts and circumstances of a given case.

The defense of a marauding, drug-crazed purposeless group of homicidal maniacs is one which, absent the events surrounding the behavior of Charles Manson and the excruciating horror of the indescribably base murder of Sharon Tate, would have been dismissed as so incredible as to merit no serious attention. All that changed with the advent of Manson. Thereafter the possibility of such an occurrence, while still macabre, was considerably enhanced. The evidence, in my humble judgment, tended to show an environment in the vicinity of the military base where MacDonald was stationed in which persons might indeed emulate Manson or independently behave in such a fashion. Helena Stoeckley was shown to be a person of no fixed regularity of life, roaming the streets nocturnally at or about the time of the crimes, dressing in a bizarre fashion, and capable of so short-circuiting her mental processes through an indiscriminate taking of drugs that (a) she could well accept her presence and, to some extent, her involvement in the MacDonald murders and (b) she could become so separated from reality that, on the fatal evening, she was ripe for persuasion to participate.

It should be emphasized that the condition on admissibility of corroborating circumstances indicating trustworthiness represents an accommodation between concern about third party confessions and their high potential for fabrication, on the one hand, and awareness of the enhancement of reliability flowing from the exposure to punishment for crime for the confessing declarant, on the other. Notes of the Advisory Committee on the Proposed Federal Rules of Evidence, Rule 804(b) *Exception* (3): "The requirement of corroboration should be construed in such a manner as to effectuate its purpose of circumventing fabrication." The reason prompting Congress to add the corroboration provision to Fed. R. Evid. 804(b)(3) derived from the "special dangers of a trumped-up confession by a professional criminal or some person with a strong motive to lie." 4 WEINSTEIN'S EVIDENCE ¶ 804(b)(3)[03], at 804-103.

The record in the case satisfies me that, among the possible motivations leading

---

[42] [2] Note that the test is not whether the district judge is satisfied that the statement is actually true as to the fact it is adduced to prove. Responsibility for that determination rests with the jury, as fact finder, not with the judge. The rule is not intended to allow the trial judge to admit only that evidence which satisfies him or conforms to his views as to what the disposition of the case should be. *Cf.* WEINSTEIN'S EVIDENCE ¶ 804(b)(3)[03] and the pungent comments relative to a trial judge's assessment of trustworthiness of the witness, rather than of the declarant: "The corroboration requirement should not be used as a means of usurping the jury's function."

to the statements of Helena Stoeckley, fabrication was not a likely one. The matter of what constitutes corroborating circumstances which clearly indicate the trust-worthiness of the statement was left for judicial (*i.e.* case-by-case) development. 11 MOORE'S FEDERAL PRACTICE § 804.06(3)[2], at VIII-281. "It is clear that the standard for corroboration must not be too high." *Id.* at VIII-283.

A factor of corroboration cited by Justice Holmes in his famous dissent in *Donnelly v. United States*, 228 U.S. 243, 277 (1913) was "that there be no connection between declarant and accused." 4 WEINSTEIN'S EVIDENCE ¶ 804-104, n.6. MacDonald and Stoeckley were not in any way acquainted.

Weinstein additionally has this to say:

> The court should only ask for sufficient corroboration to "clearly" permit a reasonable man to believe that the statement might have been made in good faith and that it could be true. If, for example, the proof is undisputed that the person confessing to a shooting could not have been at the scene of the crime because he was in prison, it will be excluded. But if there is evidence that he was near the scene and had some motive or background connecting him with the crime that should suffice.

Id. 804-104–05. . . .

For all those considerations, my view is that the testimony should have been admitted. But it would read out of the law the concept of trial court discretion were courts of appeals to label as "abuse of discretion" any action by a district court with which the appellate court disagrees. Accordingly, I do not regard it proper to dissent.

I conclude with the observation that the case provokes a strong uneasiness in me. The crimes were base and horrid, and whoever committed them richly deserves severe punishment. As Judge Bryan has pointed out, the evidence was sufficient to sustain the findings of guilt beyond a reasonable doubt. Still, the way in which a finding of guilt is reached is, in our enduring system of law, at least as important as the finding of guilt itself. I believe MacDonald would have had a fairer trial if the Stoeckley related testimony had been admitted. In the end, however, I am not prepared to find an abuse of discretion by the district court, and so concur.

NOTES AND QUESTIONS

1. What is the rationale for the rule requiring defendants seeking to use third party declarations against interest for exculpatory purposes to meet a higher standard than the prosecution must meet when it wants to use such statements for inculpatory purposes? Some jurisdictions have rejected such an approach. *See, e.g., People v. Edwards*, 242 N.W.2d 739 (Mich. 1976). Is the solution to eliminate the corroboration requirement or, instead, to impose it upon the prosecution as well? *See, e.g., United States v. Riley*, 657 F.2d 1377 (8th Cir. 1981). The issue is discussed in depth in Tague, *Perils of the Rulemaking Process: The Development, Application, and Unconstitutionality of Rule 804(b)(3)'s Penal Interest Exception*, 69 GEO. L.J. 851 (1981).

2. In applying the corroboration requirement should the court consider the credibility of the witness, or that of the out-of-court declarant, or both? *See United States v. Doyle*, 130 F.3d 523 (2d Cir. 1997); *United States v. Atkins*, 558 F.2d 133, 135–36 (3d Cir.), *cert. denied*, 434 U.S. 929 (1977).

UNITED STATES v. LANG
589 F.2d 92 (2d Cir. 1978)

MULLIGAN, CIRCUIT JUDGE:

On December 6, 1977, the defendant in this case, Nathan Lang, also known as "Cool Breeze," made the mistake of visiting Rikers Island, a New York City penal institution and the situs of a former incarceration. His hegira was prompted not by nostalgia but in order to retrieve some personal effects. Oddly enough he submitted to a routine search by a Corrections Officer. At his request Cool Breeze opened a black pouch he was carrying which contained a quarter-inch stack of brand new five dollar bills which were in four groups and each of which had identical serial numbers. When asked about the bills, Lang admitted that they Were "play money," a street term commonly employed to describe counterfeit bills. Cool Breeze, not surprisingly, was arrested, given *Miranda* warnings and was indicted on January 19, 1978. His trial lasted about two days. It took the jury about the same time to reach a verdict and then only after two *Allen* charges to the jury. . . .

reconsideration to get unanimous verdict

The principal characters in the transaction at issue include his girlfriend Donna Paola (spelled Payola in the transcript) also known as "Chicago." While there seems to be little doubt about the romantic relationship between Cool Breeze and Chicago, there is a serious question about their business relationship, a central issue on this appeal. Cool Breeze did not testify and Chicago, for reasons not made evident in the record, was an unavailable witness. The alleged supplier of the counterfeit bills was Ronson Carey, also known as "Raheem," who was also an unavailable witness for reasons we shall discuss in some detail. Finally, there was the inevitable undercover Secret Service Agent, Douglas James, to whom Raheem had sold counterfeit bills originating from the same plates as the bills found in the possession of Cool Breeze. There was no issue concerning the defendant's possession of the counterfeit bills and no constitutional infirmity suggested as to his search, arrest and the seizure of the bills. While some issue was raised as to whether he was knowingly in possession of counterfeit bills, his admission that it was "play money" undermined any real question on this point. The principal issue in the view of the trial judge and the one which may well have bothered the jury in its prolonged deliberations, was whether the Government had succeeded in establishing beyond a reasonable doubt that Lang possessed the money with the intent to defraud.

The trial judge's comments, made during several conferences with counsel which appear in the transcript, leave little doubt that the major source of the Government's proof and in fact its only proof that Lang intended to pass the money on for a profit consisted of a taped telephone conversation between Carey and the undercover agent James, which took place on December 9, 1977, three days after Lang's arrest. The admissibility of the taped conversation, which the trial judge characterized as "critical" to the Government's case, presents the dispositive issue on this appeal. It was admitted with considerable misgiving by the district judge, who on two occasions suggested that if he had erred, the Court of Appeals would provide guidance. We have considered the matter in detail and conclude that the taped conversation was inadmissible hearsay, not within the exceptions to the rule proposed to be applicable and further that the error cannot be characterized as harmless. Therefore, we reverse the conviction. . . .

Considerably bowdlerized, the taped conversation in issue here contained statements by Carey that Cool Breeze had gone to Rikers Island "all dust up and high" (according to expert testimony street jargon meaning under the influence of an hallucinogenic drug); that he had the counterfeit bills with him at that time; that he had been "busted" (arrested); that Carey had never met Cool Breeze but had been "juggling" (dealing) with him through his girl friend (Paola) who was his "contact" (middle person). The Government argued, and the trial court ultimately accepted into evidence, the tape recorded conversation. The conversation was held admissible as an exception to the hearsay rule, as either a statement against penal interest by an unavailable witness, Fed. R. Evid. 804(b)(3), or, alternatively as "a statement by a co-conspirator of a party during the course and in furtherance of the conspiracy," Fed. R. Evid. 801(d)(2)(E). Although their Runyonesque sobriquets are more colorful, we shall refer to the participants hereafter by their proper names.

I RULE 804(b)(3) — STATEMENT AGAINST PENAL INTEREST

a) *Unavailability as a Witness*

Before the hearsay exceptions under Rule 804 become applicable, subdivision (a) of the rule requires that the declarant whose statement is sought to be introduced be unavailable as a witness. Judge Conner properly found that Carey was unavailable as a witness under Rule 804(a)(1), which provides that a declarant is unavailable if he is exempted by ruling of the court on the ground of privilege from testifying concerning the subject matter of his statement. Carey appeared in court with his attorney pursuant to subpoena and on direct examination by the Government invoked the Fifth Amendment with respect to any questions concerning the sale in issue. In contesting the finding of unavailability, the appellant relies upon the last sentence of Rule 804(a) which provides that "a declarant is not unavailable as a witness if his exemption . . . is due to the procurement or wrongdoing of the proponent of his statement for the purpose of preventing the witness from attending or testifying." There is no suggestion that the Government in any way prevented Carey from testifying. He was represented by his own counsel and his refusal to testify was in his self-interest. Rather, the appellant proceeds on the theory that the Government acted wrongfully in not granting Carey immunity. However, the law appears to be well settled that the power of the Executive Branch to grant immunity to a witness is discretionary and no obligation exists on the part of the United States Attorney to seek such immunity.

b) *Statement Against Penal Interest*

Appellant also argues that Carey's statements were not against his penal interest and thus not within Rule 804(b)(3). This subsection of the Rule defines a statement against interest insofar as here relevant as one which "at the time of its making . . . so far tended to subject [the declarant] to . . . criminal liability . . . that a reasonable man in his position would not have made the statement unless he believed it to be true." That Carey's statement reveals his criminal conduct as a seller of counterfeit notes is not open to question. Appellant argues, however, that since Carey made the statement to a person to whom he had recently sold counterfeit bills and who he believed to be a confederate, he could not reasonably be aware that by making the statement he was subjecting himself to criminal liability. This position, in our view, is not tenable. The Rule does not require that the declarant be aware that the incriminating statement subjects him to immediate criminal prosecution. Rather, it simply requires that the incriminating statement sufficiently *"tended"* to subject the declarant to criminal liability "so that a reasonable man in his position would not have made the statement unless he believed it to be true." This is how Rule 804(b)(3) has been consistently interpreted. Thus, in *United States v. Barrett*, 539 F.2d 244, 249–51 (1st Cir. 1976), the court found that the reliability of an inculpatory hearsay statement made to an acquaintance during a card game was not impugned because the declarant "might not so readily have perceived the disserving character of what was said nor have expected his words to be repeated to the police." *Id.* at 251. We also note *United States v. Bagley*, 537 F.2d 162, 165 (5th Cir. 1976), *cert. denied*, 429 U.S. 1075 (1977), where the court held that an unavailable witness's statement to a cellmate that he knowingly possessed heroin was against his penal interest under Rule 804(b)(3).

We do not think that a reasonable man would falsely admit the commission of a serious crime to his cellmate, knowing that there was a chance, even if slight, that this admission could be used to convict him and subject him to such severe penalties. The fact that the statement was made to a friend and cellmate has no relevance to the determination whether the statement was against the declarant's penal interest. 537 F.2d at 165.

The Advisory Committee's Note to Rule 804 indicates that the determination of whether the statement is in fact against interest must be determined from the circumstances of each case. Thus, if Carey knew that James was a Government agent his statement implicating himself and Lang might well be motivated by a desire to curry favor with the authorities. As the Committee Note states, "[o]n the other hand, the same words spoken under different circumstances, *e.g.*, to an acquaintance, would have no difficulty in qualifying." We conclude that there was no motive here for Carey to lie to James. Moreover, the fact that the money sold to James was identical to that found on Lang supports an inference that the statement was not fabricated. We see no error in the district court's determination therefore that it was a declaration against penal interest within Rule 804(b)(3).

c) *The Personal Knowledge of the Witness*

Despite our holding that Carey was an unavailable witness and that his statement was against penal interest within Rule 804(b)(3), we nonetheless hold that the admission of the tape constituted error requiring a reversal of the conviction. Although that Rule does not expressly incorporate a requirement that the declarant have personal knowledge of the facts to which his statement relates, Fed. R. Evid. 602 states that "[a] witness may not testify to a matter unless evidence is introduced sufficient to support a finding that he has personal knowledge of the matter." The Advisory Committee Note to Rule 803 specifically provides:

> In a hearsay situation, the declarant is, of course, a witness, and neither this rule nor Rule 804 dispenses with the requirement of firsthand knowledge. It may appear from his statement or be inferable from circumstances. *See* Rule 602.

This requirement of firsthand knowledge has "always been inherent in the statement against interest exception . . . and is assured by Rule 602." . . .

The appellant contends that Carey could not possibly have had firsthand knowledge of Lang's presence and arrest on Rikers Island while under the influence of drugs. This particular information could have been harmful to the defense since Lang argues that he would not have submitted to a search of the pouch if he had been aware that the five dollar bills were in fact counterfeit. That argument would be somewhat defused if the jury accepted Carey's statement that Lang was in such a state of drug-induced euphoria that he was unconcerned about the discovery of the specious bills. The argument cuts both ways, however, because Lang's admission at Rikers Island that the bills were "play money," relied upon by the Government, could also be dismissed by the jury as unreliable if they believed Carey's statement. It is clear, however, that this part of the conversation should have been redacted since Carey was not on Rikers Island at the time of Lang's arrest and therefore lacked firsthand knowledge of that event. Moreover, this portion of Carey's statement was not contrary to his penal interest and for that reason should have been excluded. . . .

More crucial to the Government's case and Lang's defense was Carey's statement that the counterfeit money found in Lang's possession was supplied by Carey. Again, Carey did not personally know that he supplied counterfeit bills to Lang when Carey's statement itself admits that he dealt with Lang through Paola. More significantly, since intent to defraud was an essential element of the crime, Carey could not have had firsthand knowledge that Lang was the ultimate purchaser through Paola's agency when in the same conversation he admitted that he had never met Lang. Normally, one would expect that a dealer in counterfeit would have personal knowledge of the identity of his customers, thus satisfying the knowledge requirement implicit in Rule 804.

The trial court judge, keenly aware of the problem, suggested that Carey knew of Lang's participation as a purchaser of counterfeit money either directly from Lang or from his girl friend Paola. But in the conversation at issue here Carey denied ever having met Lang. In view of his other inculpatory admissions there is no reason to doubt the reliability of this disclaimer. Thus, we are left to speculate about the source of his knowledge. Whatever the speculation, we rule out firsthand knowledge and find no compliance with Rule 602.

The Government has argued in its supplemental memo that the likely source of Carey's belief that he was dealing with Lang was Paola. The Government then argues that even if Rule 804 is inapplicable, this multiple hearsay is admissible under Rule 805.

d) *Hearsay Within Hearsay*

Fed. R. Evid. 805 provides that "[h]earsay included within hearsay is not excluded under the hearsay rule if each part of the combined statements conforms with an exception to the hearsay rule provided in these rules." The Government argues that Carey's conversation with agent James was admissible as a statement against penal interest under Rule 804(b)(3). The Government contends that Carey's lack of firsthand knowledge is no longer a problem since his information was derived from Paola's statement to Carey that she was purchasing for Lang, and Paola's statement was itself admissible under Rule 801(d)(2)(E) as a statement by a co-conspirator of a party during the course and in furtherance of the conspiracy.[43] This bootstrapping argument finds support in the case of hospital or business records which are held admissible even where the entrant has no personal knowledge of the underlying event or transaction but bases his entry on information supplied by a third person and the statement of that person qualifies as a hearsay exception. . . . While somewhat ingenious, this argument must fail here. Unlike the cases cited, there is no proof at all that Carey's statement that he was dealing with Lang was based on a statement by Paola. As we have suggested, such a conclusion could only be based on the supposition that since Paola was Lang's girlfriend she was also his partner in crime. We have no evidence at all that the statement was made or, if it was made, under what circumstances or at what time. It is just as reasonable to suppose that if it was made by Paola, she was trying to minimize her role and to cast Lang in the role of principal culprit. There was evidence that Paola had attempted on her own to pass bills which were identical to those found in Lang's possession at Rikers Island. In sum, there is, on analysis, nothing here but sheer speculation with no indicia of reliability. We conclude that the Government's attempted proof of Lang's intent to defraud amounts to inadmissible hearsay and that in this case the requirement of Rule 602 is not saved by recourse to Rule 805.

---

[43] [2] It might well be argued that Rule 805 literally does not apply here at all since a statement by a co-conspirator of a party during the course and in furtherance of the conspiracy is classified by Rule 801(d) as a statement which is not hearsay. The statement is admissible not as an exception to the hearsay rule but rather as an admission by an agent of the party against whom it is to be used. Whether admissions are properly an exception to the hearsay rule is a subject which has long intrigued scholars in the field. *See* Morgan, *Admissions as an Exception to the Hearsay Rule*, 30 YALE L.J. 355 (1921); MCCORMICK, *supra*, at § 262; 4 WEINSTEIN'S EVIDENCE, *supra*, at 1801(d)(2)[01]; IV WIGMORE, *supra*, at § 1048. The admission by an absent agent would seem logically to constitute hearsay. Wigmore's argument that anything said by the party opponent may be used against him as an admission and satisfies the rule against hearsay since he is the only one to invoke that rule and he does not need to cross-examine himself, has no relevance when the statement is offered against him by an absent alleged agent. However, whatever logic supports Rule 805 would seemingly apply to the vicarious admission sought to be introduced here. Admissions rightly or wrongly are usually (although not in the Federal Rules of Evidence) regarded as an exception to the hearsay rule. MCCORMICK, *supra*, at § 262.

NOTES AND QUESTIONS

1. Did the *Lang* court persuasively treat the question of whether Carey's statement to a perceived confederate was truly against interest? Did the "reasonable person" standard contained in Fed. R. Evid. 804(b)(3) compel the court to reach the result it did? Suppose Carey made his statement to a close friend?

2. Would the co-conspirator doctrine have allowed the government in *Lang* to introduce Carey's conversation with the undercover agent? If so, wouldn't this have circumvented the personal knowledge requirement?

WILLIAMSON v. UNITED STATES
512 U.S. 594 (1994)

JUSTICE O'CONNOR delivered the opinion of the Court, except as to Part II-C.

In this case we clarify the scope of the hearsay exception for statements against penal interest. Fed. Rule Evid. 804(b)(3).

I

A deputy sheriff stopped the rental car driven by Reginald Harris for weaving on the highway. Harris consented to a search of the car, which revealed 19 kilograms of cocaine in two suitcases in the trunk. Harris was promptly arrested.

Shortly after Harris' arrest, Special Agent Donald Walton of the Drug Enforcement Administration (DEA) interviewed him by telephone. During that conversation, Harris said that he got the cocaine from an unidentified Cuban in Fort Lauderdale; that the cocaine belonged to petitioner Williamson; and that it was to be delivered that night to a particular dumpster. Williamson was also connected to Harris by physical evidence: The luggage bore the initials of Williamson's sister, Williamson was listed as an additional driver on the car rental agreement, and an envelope addressed to Williamson and a receipt with Williamson's girlfriend's address were found in the glove compartment.

Several hours later, Agent Walton spoke to Harris in person. During that interview, Harris said he had rented the car a few days earlier and had driven it to Fort Lauderdale to meet Williamson. According to Harris, he had gotten the cocaine from a Cuban who was Williamson's acquaintance, and the Cuban had put the cocaine in the car with a note telling Harris how to deliver the drugs. Harris repeated that he had been instructed to leave the drugs in a certain dumpster, to return to his car, and to leave without waiting for anyone to pick up the drugs.

Agent Walton then took steps to arrange a controlled delivery of the cocaine. But as Walton was preparing to leave the interview room, Harris "got out of [his] chair . . . and . . . took a half step toward [Walton] . . . and . . . said, . . . 'I can't let you do that'" threw his hands up and said "that's not true, I can't let you go up there for no reason." App. 40. Harris told Walton he had lied about the Cuban, the note, and the dumpster. The real story, Harris said, was that he was transporting the cocaine to Atlanta for Williamson, and that Williamson was traveling in front of him in another rental car. Harris added that after his car was stopped, Williamson turned around and drove past the location of the stop, where he could see Harris' car with its trunk open. *Ibid.* Because Williamson had apparently seen the police searching the car, Harris explained that it would be impossible to make a controlled delivery. *Id.* at 41.

Harris told Walton that he had lied about the source of the drugs because he was afraid of Williamson. *Id.* at 61, 68; *see also id.* at 30–31. Though Harris freely implicated himself, he did not want his story to be recorded, and he refused to sign a written version of the statement. *Id.* at 24–25. Walton testified that he had promised to report any cooperation by Harris to the Assistant United States Attorney. Walton said Harris was not promised any reward or other benefit for cooperating. *Id.* at 25–26.

Williamson was eventually convicted of possessing cocaine with intent to distribute, conspiring to possess cocaine with intent to distribute, and traveling interstate to promote the distribution of cocaine, 21 U.S.C. §§ 841(a)(1), 846; 18 U.S.C. § 1952. When called to testify at Williamson's trial, Harris refused, even though the prosecution gave him use immunity and the court ordered him to testify and eventually held him in contempt. The District Court then ruled that, under Rule 804(b)(3), Agent Walton could relate what Harris had said to him: "The ruling of the Court is that the statements . . . are admissible under [Rule 804(b)(3)], which deals with statements against interest. First, defendant Harris' statements clearly implicated himself, and therefore, are against his penal interest. "Second, defendant Harris, the declarant, is unavailable. And third, as I found yesterday, there are sufficient corroborating circumstances in this case to ensure the trustworthiness of his testimony. Therefore, under [*United States v. Harrell*, 788 F.2d 1524 (11th Cir. 1986)], these statements by defendant Harris implicating [Williamson] are admissible." App. 51–52.

Williamson appealed his conviction, claiming that the admission of Harris' statements violated Rule 804(b)(3) and the Confrontation Clause of the Sixth Amendment. The Court of Appeals for the Eleventh Circuit affirmed without opinion, judgt. order reported at 981 F.2d 1262 (1992), and we granted *certiorari.* 114 S. Ct. 681, 126 L. Ed. 2d 649 (1994).

II

A

The hearsay rule, Fed. Rule Evid. 802, is premised on the theory that out-of-court statements are subject to particular hazards. The declarant might be lying; he might have misperceived the events which he relates; he might have faulty memory; his words might be misunderstood or taken out of context by the listener. And the ways in which these dangers are minimized for in-court statements — the oath, the witness' awareness of the gravity of the proceedings, the jury's ability to observe the witness' demeanor, and, most importantly, the right of the opponent to cross-examine — are generally absent for things said out of court.

Nonetheless, the Federal Rules of Evidence also recognize that some kinds of out-of-court statements are less subject to these hearsay dangers, and therefore except them from the general rule that hearsay is inadmissible. One such category covers statements that are against the declarant's interest: "statement[s] which . . . at the time of [their] making . . . so far tended to subject the declarant to . . . criminal liability . . . that a reasonable person in the declarant's position would not have made the statement[s] unless believing [them] to be true." Fed. Rule Evid. 804(b)(3).

To decide whether Harris' confession is made admissible by Rule 804(b)(3), we must first determine what the Rule means by "statement," which Federal Rule of Evidence 801(a)(1) defines as "an oral or written assertion." One possible meaning, "a report or narrative," WEBSTER'S THIRD NEW INTERNATIONAL DICTIONARY 2229, defn. 2(a) (1961), connotes an extended declaration. Under this reading, Harris' entire confession — even if it contains both self-inculpatory and non-self-inculpatory parts — would be admissible so long as in the aggregate the confession sufficiently inculpates him. Another meaning of "statement," "a single declaration or remark," *ibid.* defn. 2(b), would make Rule 804(b)(3) cover only those declarations or remarks within the confession that are individually self-inculpatory. *See also id.* at 131 (defining "assertion" as a "declaration"); *id.* at 586 (defining "declaration" as a "statement").

Although the text of the Rule does not directly resolve the matter, the principle behind the Rule, so far as it is discernible from the text, points clearly to the narrower reading. Rule 804(b)(3) is founded on the commonsense notion that reasonable people, even reasonable people who are not especially honest, tend not to make self-inculpatory statements unless they believe them to be true.

This notion simply does not extend to the broader definition of "statement." The fact that a person is making a broadly self-inculpatory confession does not make more credible the confession's non-self-inculpatory parts. One of the most effective ways to lie is to mix falsehood with truth, especially truth that seems particularly persuasive because of its self-inculpatory nature.

In this respect, it is telling that the non-self-inculpatory things Harris said in his first statement actually proved to be false, as Harris himself admitted during the second interrogation. And when part of the confession is actually self-exculpatory, the generalization on which Rule 804(b)(3) is founded becomes even less applicable. Self-exculpatory statements are exactly the ones which people are most likely to make even when they are false; and mere proximity to other, self-inculpatory, statements does not increase the plausibility of the self-exculpatory statements.

* * *

C

In this case, however, we cannot conclude that all that Harris said was properly admitted. Some of Harris' confession would clearly have been admissible under Rule 804(b)(3); for instance, when he said he knew there was cocaine in the suitcase, he essentially forfeited his only possible defense to a charge of cocaine possession, lack of knowledge. But other parts of his confession, especially the parts that implicated Williamson, did little to subject Harris himself to criminal liability. A reasonable person in Harris' position might even think that implicating someone else would decrease his practical exposure to criminal liability, at least so far as sentencing goes. Small fish in a big conspiracy often get shorter sentences than people who are running the whole show, *see, e.g.*, UNITED STATES SENTENCING COMMISSION, GUIDELINES MANUAL § 3B1.2 (Nov. 1993), especially if the small fish are willing to help the authorities catch the big ones, *see, e.g., id.* at § 5K1.1.

Nothing in the record shows that the District Court or the court of Appeals inquired whether each of the statements in Harris' confession was truly self-inculpatory. As we explained above, this can be a fact-intensive inquiry, which would require careful examination of all the circumstances surrounding the criminal activity involved; we therefore remand to the Court of Appeals to conduct this inquiry in the first instance.

Needs to be cross examined

NOTE

The Supreme Court later relied upon *Williamson* in holding that an accomplice's statement shifting blame to the accused violated the Confrontation Clause of the Sixth Amendment.

c. Former Testimony

Note, *Affidavits, Depositions, and Prior Testimony*
46 IOWA L. REV. 356, 356–57 (1961)[44]

When a party desires to introduce into evidence an affidavit, deposition, or testimony given at another trial, the hearsay rule must be considered since the evidence is being offered in some form other than the personal testimony in open court of the one who perceived the facts reported. It should be initially noted that there is some disagreement as to whether depositions and prior testimony are hearsay at all. Most authorities state that they are hearsay but that they are, in certain circumstances, admissible as exceptions to the exclusionary rule. In order to meet the requirements of an exception, it is generally stated that (1) the testimony must have been given under oath and subject to an adequate opportunity for cross-examination, and (2) the witness must be unavailable to testify personally at the trial. Professor Wigmore, on the other hand, states that depositions and prior testimony are not hearsay if there was an adequate opportunity for cross-examination. Wigmore would, however, retain the requirement of unavailability as a prerequisite to admissibility. Thus, since the same requirements are present in either instance, it makes little difference whether depositions and former testimony are admitted because they are not hearsay or because they fall within an exception to the exclusionary rule. . . . All authorities agree that since affiants are not subject to cross-examination, affidavits are hearsay and inadmissible unless specifically made admissible by statute.

In addition, it should be recognized that affidavits, depositions, and prior testimony may be admitted without reference to the hearsay rule when they are

---

[44] Copyright © 1961. Reprinted with permission.

offered for some purpose other than to prove the truth of the facts asserted. For example in *State v. Wykert* [198 Iowa 1219, 199 N.W. 331 (1924)], where defendant was charged with subornation of perjury, the Iowa court allowed a court reporter to testify to testimony given by a third party at a previous trial to which defendant was not a party and in which she had no opportunity to cross-examine. The evidence was admitted, not to prove the truth of the prior testimony, but merely to prove that the testimony had been given. Similarly, affidavits, depositions, or prior testimony may be introduced to refresh recollection or to show inconsistent statements for the purpose of impeachment. If the testimony is offered to show the admissions of a party-opponent or under some other exception to the hearsay rule, only the requirements of the other exception need be satisfied.

UNITED STATES v. DINAPOLI
8 F.3d 909 (2d Cir. 1993) (en banc)

JON O. NEWMAN, CHIEF JUDGE:

On this criminal appeal, which is before our Court on remand from the Supreme Court, we have given *en banc* consideration to a fairly narrow issue of evidence that has potentially broad implications for the administration of criminal justice. The issue concerns Rule 804(b)(1) of the Federal Rules of Evidence, which provides that testimony given by a currently unavailable witness at a prior hearing is not excluded by the hearsay rule if "the party against whom the testimony is now offered . . . had an opportunity *and similar motive to develop* the testimony by direct, cross, or redirect examination." Fed. R. Evid. 804(b)(1) (emphasis added). Our precise issue is whether the prosecution had a "similar motive to develop" the testimony of two grand jury witnesses compared to its motive at a subsequent criminal trial at which the witnesses were unavailable. We hold that the "similar motive" requirement of Rule 804(b)(1) was not met and that the witnesses' grand jury testimony, offered by the defendants, was therefore properly excluded. . . .

Background

The facts concerning this case have been recounted in prior decisions of this Court, . . . and we therefore focus only on the details that concern the pending issue. Briefly, the case concerns conspiracy and substantive charges under the Racketeer Influenced and Corrupt Organizations Act ("RICO") against several defendants accused of participating in a bid-rigging scheme in the concrete construction industry in Manhattan. The trial evidence indicated the existence of a "Club" of six concrete construction companies that during 1980–1985 rigged the bids for concrete superstructure work on nearly every high-rise construction project in Manhattan involving more than $2 million of concrete work. Organized crime figures, notably members of the Genovese Family, orchestrated the scheme and enforced adherence to the bid allocations.

The grand jury investigating the matter returned its first indictment on March 20, 1986. That indictment alleged the essential aspects of the criminal activity and named all of the appellants as defendants. The grand jury continued its investigation in an effort to identify additional participants and additional construction projects that might have been victimized by the bid-rigging scheme. In this subsequent phase of the inquiry, the grand jury called Frederick DeMatteis and Pasquale Bruno as witnesses. They had been principals in Cedar Park Concrete Construction Corporation ("Cedar Park"), a company that other grand jury witnesses had testified had been briefly involved in the scheme. DeMatteis and Bruno, both testifying under grants of immunity, denied awareness of a bid-rigging scheme.

DeMatteis testified in the grand jury on three occasions in 1986 — June 3, June 12, and June 19. His first two appearances primarily concerned back-ground questioning about the construction industry and Cedar Park. At his third appearance, the prosecutor pointedly asked whether DeMatteis had been instructed not to bid on the Javits Convention Center project and whether he was aware of an arrangement whereby the successful bidder paid two percent of the bid price to organized crime figures. DeMatteis denied both the instruction not to bid and awareness of the two percent arrangement. The prosecutor, obviously skeptical of the denials, pressed DeMatteis with a few questions in the nature of cross-examination. However, in order not to reveal the identity of then undisclosed cooperating witnesses or the existence of then undisclosed wiretapped conversations that refuted DeMatteis's denials, the prosecutor refrained from confronting him with the substance of such evidence. Instead, the prosecutor called to DeMatteis's attention the substance of only the one relevant wiretapped conversation that had already become public — a tape played at a prior trial, *United States v. Persico*, 84 Cr. 809 (JFK) (S.D.N.Y. 1984).

Bruno testified at the grand jury on September 11, 1986. Much of the questioning concerned the operations of Cedar Park. Like DeMatteis, Bruno was asked about and denied knowledge of the "Club" and the two percent arrangement for successful bidders. And, like DeMatteis, he was briefly cross-examined and confronted with the contents of the publicly disclosed tape from the Persico trial but not with any of the information from undisclosed witnesses or wiretaps. After his denials and after giving an answer that sharply conflicted with an answer given by DeMatteis,[45] Bruno was briefly excused from the grand jury room. Upon his return, after the prosecutor had consulted with the grand jury, he was told by the prosecutor of the grand jury's "strong concern" that his testimony had "not been truthful." Four days later, Bruno's lawyer wrote the prosecutor stating that many of Bruno's answers had been inaccurate. The lawyer suggested that the prosecutor should resubmit his questions to Bruno in writing and that Bruno would respond by affidavit. The prosecutor declined the suggestion.

A thirteen-month trial on a superseding indictment, filed April 7, 1987, commenced April 6, 1987, against eleven defendants, and ended on May 4, 1988, with the convictions of nine defendants, including the six appellants, Vincent DiNapoli, Louis DiNapoli, Nicholas Auletta, Edward J. Halloran, Alvin O. Chattin, and Aniello

---

[45] [1] DeMatteis had testified that he had become partners with Paul Castellano's son-in-law, known as Joseph Conti, only after Bruno had interviewed Conti and assured DeMatteis of Conti's expertise. Bruno denied having interviewed Conti and claimed to have no idea of Conti's experience in the concrete industry.

Migliore.[46] During the trial, the defendants endeavored to call DeMatteis and Bruno as witnesses. Both invoked the privilege against self-incrimination. The defendants then offered the testimony DeMatteis and Bruno had given to the grand jury. After examining sealed affidavits presented by the prosecution, the District Court (Mary Johnson Lowe, Judge) refused to admit the grand jury testimony as prior testimony under Rule 804(b)(1). Judge Lowe appears not to have made specific findings with respect to the grand jury testimony. Instead, she ruled generally that the "motive of a prosecutor . . . in the investigatory stages of a case is far different from the motive of a prosecutor in conducting the trial" and hence the "similar motive" requirement of Rule 804(b)(1) was not satisfied.

On a prior consideration of the appeal, the panel reversed the convictions and ordered a new trial on the ground that it was error to exclude the witnesses' grand jury testimony. *United States v. Salerno*, 937 F.2d 797 (2d Cir. 1991). Though stating that "we agree that the government may have had no motive before the grand jury to impeach the allegedly false testimony of Bruno and DeMatteis," *id.* at 806, the panel ruled that the "similar motive" requirement of Rule 804(b)(1) need not be met because the witnesses were "available" to the prosecution at trial through a grant of immunity. *Id.* The panel subsequently denied rehearing after making a slight revision of its opinion, *United States v. Salerno*, 952 F.2d 623 (2d Cir. 1991), and rehearing *en banc* was denied by a divided vote, *United States v. Salerno*, 952 F.2d 624 (2d Cir. 1991).

Thereafter, the Supreme Court reversed the panel's reversal of the convictions. *United States v. Salerno*, 505 U.S. 317, 112 S. Ct. 2503, 120 L. Ed. 2d 255 (1992). The Supreme Court ruled that all of the requirements of Rule 804(b)(1) must be met, including the "similar motive" requirement. The Court declined to decide whether the "similar motive" requirement was satisfied in this case, believing it "prudent to remand the case for further consideration" of that issue. 112 S. Ct. at 2509. In dissent, Justice Stevens reached the "similar motive" issue and concluded that a similar motive was present in this case. [112 S. Ct.] at 2509–12.

Upon remand, the panel ruled that the "similar motive" requirement was satisfied. *United States v. Salerno*, 974 F.2d 231 (2d Cir. 1992). The panel considered the questioning of the witnesses conducted by an Assistant United States Attorney and concluded that what occurred "was the equivalent of what would have been done if the opportunity to examine them had been presented at trial." *Id.* at 241.

Discussion

Our initial task is to determine how similarity of motive at two proceedings will be determined for purposes of Rule 804(b)(1). In resolving this matter, we do not accept the position, apparently urged by the appellants, that the test of similar motive is simply whether at the two proceedings the questioner takes the same side of the same issue. The test must turn not only on whether the questioner is on the same side of the same issue at both proceedings, but also on whether the questioner

---

[46] [2] One of the convicted defendants, Anthony Salerno, died during the pendency of this appeal, and another subsequently pled guilty to an extortion conspiracy charge. *See United States v. Salerno*, 974 F.2d at 232.

had a substantially similar interest in asserting that side of the issue. If a fact is critical to a cause of action at a second proceeding but the same fact was only peripherally related to a different cause of action at a first proceeding, no one would claim that the questioner had a similar motive at both proceedings to show that the fact had been established (or disproved). This is the same principle that holds collateral estoppel inapplicable when a small amount is at stake in a first proceeding and a large amount is at stake in a second proceeding, even though a party took the same side of the same issue at both proceedings. This suggests that the questioner must not only be on the same side of the same issue at both proceedings but must also have a substantially similar degree of interest in prevailing on that issue.

Whether the degree of interest in prevailing on an issue is substantially similar at two proceedings will sometimes be affected by the nature of the proceedings. Where both proceedings are trials and the same matter is seriously disputed at both trials, it will normally be the case that the side opposing the version of a witness at the first trial had a motive to develop that witness's testimony similar to the motive at the second trial. The opponent, whether shouldering a burden of proof or only resisting the adversary's effort to sustain its burden of proof, usually cannot tell how much weight the witness's version will have with the fact-finder in the total mix of all the evidence. Lacking such knowledge, the opponent at the first trial normally has a motive to dispute the version so long as it can be said that disbelief of the witness's version is of some significance to the opponent's side of the case; the motive at the second trial is normally similar.

The situation is not necessarily the same where the two proceedings are different in significant respects, such as their purposes or the applicable burden of proof. The grand jury context, with which we are concerned in this case, well illustrates the point. If a prosecutor is using the grand jury to investigate possible crimes and identify possible criminals, it may be quite unrealistic to characterize the prosecutor as the "opponent" of a witness's version. At a preliminary stage of an investigation, the prosecutor is not trying to prove any side of any issue, but only to develop the facts to determine if an indictment is warranted. Even if the prosecutor displays some skepticism about particular testimony (not an uncommon response from any questioner interested in eliciting the truth), that does not mean the prosecutor has a motive to show the falsity of the testimony, similar to the motive that would exist at trial if an indictment is returned and the witness's testimony is presented by a defendant to rebut the prosecutor's evidence of guilt.

Even in cases like the pending one, where the grand jury proceeding has progressed far beyond the stage of a general inquiry, the motive to develop grand jury testimony that disputes a position already taken by the prosecutor is not necessarily the same as the motive the prosecutor would have if that same testimony was presented at trial. Once the prosecutor has decided to seek an indictment against identified suspects, that prosecutor may fairly be characterized as "opposed" to any testimony that tends to exonerate one of the suspects. But, because of the low burden of proof at the grand jury stage, even the prosecutor's status as an "opponent" of the testimony does not necessarily create a motive to challenge the testimony that is similar to the motive at trial. At the grand jury, the prosecutor need establish only probable cause to believe the suspect is guilty. By the time the exonerating testimony is given, such probable cause may already have been established to such an extent that there is no realistic likelihood that the grand jury will fail to indict. That circumstance alone will sometimes leave the prosecutor with slight if any motive to develop the exonerating testimony in order to persuade the grand jurors of its falsity.

Moreover, the grand jury context will sometimes present additional circumstances that render the prosecutor's motive to challenge the exonerating testimony markedly dissimilar to what the prosecutor's motive would be at trial. Frequently the grand jury inquiry will be conducted at a time when an investigation is ongoing. In such circumstances, there is an important public interest in not disclosing prematurely the existence of surveillance techniques such as wiretaps or undercover operations, or the identity of cooperating witnesses. The results of such techniques and the statements of such witnesses might be powerful ammunition to challenge the grand jury witness's exonerating testimony. By the time of trial, however, the public interest in not disclosing such ammunition will normally have dissipated, and the prosecutor will have a strong motive to confront the witness with all available contradictory evidence.

In recognizing these factors that distinguish the grand jury context from the trial context, we do not accept the position, urged by the Government upon the Supreme Court, that a prosecutor "generally will not have the same motive to develop testimony in grand jury proceedings as he does at trial." . . . Our point is simply that the inquiry as to similar motive must be fact specific, and the grand jury context will sometimes, but not invariably, present circumstances that demonstrate the prosecutor's lack of a similar motive. We accept neither the Government's view that the prosecutor's motives at the grand jury and at trial are almost always dissimilar, nor the opposing view, apparently held by the District of Columbia Circuit, that the prosecutor's motives in both proceedings are always similar. . . .

* * *

The proper approach, therefore, in assessing similarity of motive under Rule 804(b)(1) must consider whether the party resisting the offered testimony at a pending proceeding had at a prior proceeding an interest of substantially similar intensity to prove (or disprove) the same side of a substantially similar issue. The nature of the two proceedings — both what is at stake and the applicable burden of proof — and, to a lesser extent, the cross-examination at the prior proceeding — both what was undertaken and what was available but forgone — will be relevant though not conclusive on the ultimate issue of similarity of motive.

Having identified the proper approach to the determination of whether a similar motive existed, we might ordinarily remand to the District Court to apply the governing principles to the precise facts of this case. We decline to do so, however, both to avoid further delay in this already long-delayed matter and because this is the unusual case in which it can be shown beyond reasonable dispute that the prosecutor had no interest at the grand jury in proving the falsity of the witnesses' assertion that the "Club" did not exist. Two circumstances independently suffice. First, the defendants had already been indicted, and, as appellants' counsel conceded at argument, there existed no putative defendant as to whom probable cause was in issue. At most the Government had an interest in investigating further to see whether there might be additional defendants or additional projects within the criminal activity of the existing defendants. As to these matters, the prosecutor had no interest in showing that the denial of the Club's existence was false. The grand jury had already been persuaded, at least by the low standard of probable cause, to believe that the Club existed and that the defendants had participated in it to commit crimes. It is fanciful to think that the prosecutor would have had any substantial interest in showing the falsity of the witnesses' denial of the Club's existence just to persuade the grand jury to add one more project to the indictment.

Second, the grand jurors had indicated to the prosecutor that they did not believe the denial. The record is clear on this point. . . .

These two circumstances dispel similarity of motive, and the absence of similar motive is not rebutted by the limited cross-examination undertaken by the prosecutor at the grand jury. A prosecutor may have varied motives for asking a few challenging questions of a grand jury witness who the prosecutor thinks is lying. The prosecutor might want to afford the witness a chance to embellish the lie, thereby strengthening the case for a subsequent perjury prosecution. Or the prosecutor might want to provoke the witness into volunteering some critical new fact in the heat of an emphatic protestation of innocence. In this case, the cross-examination that occurred does not significantly show similarity of motive. Moreover, the strong inference of dissimilarity from the two factors already discussed is powerfully reinforced by the prosecutor's careful limitation of questioning to matters already publicly disclosed, the lack of questioning on the basis of undisclosed wiretaps and reports of cooperating witnesses, and the lack of any follow-up in response to Bruno's generous offer to correct inaccuracies in his testimony.

Since the grand jury as fact-finder had already resolved the issue of the Club's existence in the prosecutor's favor and had announced disbelief of the witnesses' contrary statements, dissimilarity of motive is beyond dispute. The District Court's exclusion of the witnesses' grand jury testimony was therefore entirely correct, and this ground for reversal of the convictions is rejected. We therefore vacate the panel's decision and return the appeal to the panel for further consideration of the appellants' remaining contentions.

QUESTIONS

1. Did the *DiNapoli* Court apply too strict a standard in determining similarity of motive? For example, did the Court, in effect, require identical motives to cross-examine at both proceedings? Note also that, even if the Grand Jury disbelieved the witness and had already decided to indict, prosecutors directing investigative grand juries often conduct extensive cross examinations for the sake of freezing a witness' testimony.

2. Is the following case consistent with *DiNapoli*?

UNITED STATES v. KOON
34 F.3d 1416 (9th Cir. 1994)

FLETCHER, CIRCUIT JUDGE:

Stacey Koon and Laurence Powell ("appellants") appeal their jury convictions for deprivation of rights under color of state law in violation of 18 U.S.C. § 242. The United States appeals Koon's and Powell's sentences under the Sentencing Guidelines. We affirm the convictions but remand for resentencing.

BACKGROUND

The arrest of Rodney King occurred in the early morning of March 3, 1991 in Los Angeles. After drinking malt liquor with two friends, King left a suburb of Los Angeles and began driving. At this time he was intoxicated. Officers Melanie Singer and Tim Singer, both California Highway Patrol ("CHP") officers, observed King's vehicle speeding on the 210 Freeway. The officers began to pursue the vehicle and called on the radio for help. Several Los Angeles Police Department ("LAPD") units joined in the pursuit. Among these units was one manned by Powell and his trainee, co-defendant Timothy Wind. The pursuit ended when King pulled his car over at an entrance to the Hansen Dam Recreation Area on Osborne St.

The officers ordered King and the other occupants of the vehicle to get out of the vehicle and assume a felony prone position (*i.e.* King was ordered to lie on his stomach with his arms behind his back, legs spread, heels turned toward the ground, and head turned away from the officers). King got out of the car but did not lie down. At this time Sergeant Koon arrived and took command. Police officers Ted Briseno and Roland Solano arrived soon after. The officers again ordered King to lie in a felony prone position.

King eventually got down on his hands and knees, but did not get into the felony prone position. Officers Powell, Wind, Briseno, and Solano attempted to place him in that position using a "team takedown" or "swarm." King became combative and the officers retreated. Koon then fired taser darts into King.

The events that occurred next were captured on videotape by George Holliday (the "Holliday videotape"). This videotape was the focus of much of the testimony at trial and is described in detail in the district court's sentencing opinion . . . . The following description of the events tracks the relevant time frames on the Holliday videotape.

As the videotape begins, it shows that King got to his feet in an attempt to escape. Powell and Wind began to strike King with their batons. At trial it was disputed whether Powell's first blow hit King in the head. The district court concluded that Powell struck King's head accidentally . . . . King fell to the ground and attempted to rise. At 18 seconds, Briseno put his hand on Powell's baton, which Powell had raised as he stood above King.

From 18 to 30 seconds, King attempted to get up, and was struck with batons by Powell and Wind. From the 35th second to the 51st second, Powell struck King repeatedly. At approximately 43 seconds, one or more of Powell's baton blows fractured King's right leg. At 55 seconds, Powell struck King on the chest or upper abdomen. After this blow, King rolled onto his stomach and lay prone. At this point the officers suspended the use of force and stepped back for about ten seconds. Powell began to reach for his handcuffs. The district court found this movement to be evidence that Powell perceived King no longer to be a threat. *Id.*

At 1:05, Briseno moved forward and used his left foot to stomp King in the upper back or neck. King's body writhed in response. At 1:07 on the videotape, Powell and Wind began to strike King again with their batons. At approximately 1:29, King put his hands behind his neck and subsequently was handcuffed.

After King was handcuffed, Powell radioed for an ambulance. Powell sent two messages over the Mobile Digital Terminal to other officers that said "ooops" and "I havent [sic] beaten anyone this bad in a long time." Koon sent a message to the police station that said "U[nit] just had a big time use of force. . . . Tased and beat the suspect of CHP pursuit big time."

King was taken to Pacifica Hospital, where he was treated for a fractured right leg, multiple facial fractures, and multiple bruises and contusions. At the hospital, Powell learned that King worked at Dodger stadium, and said to him, "We played a little ball tonight, didn't we Rodney?" King said, "I don't know." Powell said, "You know, we played a little ball, we played a little hardball tonight, we hit quite a few home runs." King responded, "Yeah I guess so." Powell said, "Yes, we played a little ball and you lost and we won."

Koon, Powell, Wind, and Briseno were tried in state court in Simi Valley, California on charges of assault with a deadly weapon and excessive use of force by a police officer. At the trial, Koon, Wind, and Powell's defense was that the force used during the arrest of King was justified and was not excessive. In contrast, Briseno testified that excessive force was used but that he had tried to prevent its use. The four officers were acquitted on all charges except for one count against Powell on which the jury hung.

On August 4, 1992, a federal grand jury indicted the four officers. Count 1 of the federal indictment charged Powell, Wind and Briseno with willfully depriving King of his constitutional rights in violation of 18 U.S.C. § 242 and with aiding and abetting each other in violation of 18 U.S.C. § 2. Count 2 charged Koon with willfully permitting the other officers to unlawfully strike King and willfully failing to prevent the assault of King by officers in his presence, in violation of 18 U.S.C. § 242.

The case was tried to a jury commencing February 25, 1993. The jury verdicts were handed down on April 17, 1993. Officers Briseno and Wind were acquitted; Officer Powell and Sergeant Koon were found guilty of violating § 242. Koon and Powell were sentenced on August 4, 1993 to thirty months imprisonment and two years of supervised release. *See Koon*, 833 F. Supp. at 792. Appellants timely appealed their convictions and the government timely appealed the sentences. We have jurisdiction.

DISCUSSION

A. Admission of Briseno's State Trial Testimony

Before trial, the government moved to admit a videotape recording of codefendant Briseno's testimony in the state court proceeding. The videotape, which was ultimately played as part of the government's rebuttal case, was the subject of many motions in the district court, and continues to be the subject of various claims on appeal.

Briseno's testimony was highly damaging to Koon and Powell. He testified, among other things, (1) that Powell's first blow hit King in the face — which was inconsistent with Powell's position at trial; (2) that Powell delivered a second series of much more forceful blows to King "from the shoulder up"; (3) that Briseno couldn't see or understand what justified the other officers' behavior; (4) that Briseno grabbed Powell's baton and told him to "get the hell off" King; (5) that Briseno yelled to Koon "what the fuck [is] going on out here," but Koon did not respond; (6) that the officers continued to strike King with the baton when he was neither aggressive nor combative; and (7) that Briseno went to the police station after the incident intending to report the use of force.

At the state trial, Briseno was cross-examined by all three of his co-defendants as well as the prosecutor, who spent part of his time trying to establish Briseno's own culpability. On both direct and cross-examination, Briseno stated repeatedly that he thought the other officers had acted wrongly. These statements of opinion were redacted from the videotape played at the federal trial.

On appeal, Koon and Powell contend that admission of the videotape violated their Confrontation Clause rights. They also argue that the videotape should not have been admitted as rebuttal evidence, and that it contained improper lay opinion evidence.

1. Confrontation Clause Challenge

"The Confrontation Clause promotes accuracy in the criminal process by ensuring that the trier of fact has a satisfactory basis for evaluating the truth of out-of-court statements." *Barker v. Morris*, 761 F.2d 1396, 1399 (9th Cir. 1985) (citations omitted). When a hearsay declarant is unavailable to testify at trial, his out-of-court statements may be admitted without violating the Confrontation Clause so long as those statements bear sufficient indicia of reliability. *Bourjaily v. United States*, 483 U.S. 171, 182–83 (1987).[47] "[N]o independent inquiry into reliability is required" under the Confrontation Clause, however, when the out-of-court statements "fall within a firmly rooted hearsay exception." *Id.* at 183. Since Rule 804(b)(1) is a firmly rooted exception to the hearsay rule, *Mattox v. United States*, 156 U.S. 237 (1895) (discussing history of the exception); *United States v. Kelly*, 892 F.2d 255, 262 (3d Cir. 1989) (collecting authorities), *cert. denied*, 497 U.S.

---

47 [Ed. — Note that the Supreme Court's subsequent ruling in *Crawford v. Washington*, dramatically altered the analytical framework for resolving the use of hearsay at a criminal trial.]

1006 (1990), our analysis focuses on whether the district court erred under Rule 804(b)(1) in admitting Briseno's former testimony.[48]

Under Rule 804(b)(1), testimony from another proceeding is not excluded by the hearsay rule if the declarant is unavailable,[49] and if "the party against whom the testimony is now offered . . . had an opportunity and similar motive to develop the testimony by direct, cross, or redirect examination."

Appellants argue that the Briseno videotape should not have been admitted because at the state trial they lacked sufficient opportunity to cross-examine Briseno. Appellants point out that in the state proceeding they did not have the benefit of various enhancements to the Holliday videotape which were available at the federal trial.[50]

We reject appellants' argument. Appellants had a full and fair opportunity to cross-examine Briseno in the state trial. Indeed, they do not argue that the state court in any way interfered with their ability to carry out an effective cross-examination. They instead claim that the absence of the enhancements to the videotape at the state trial amounts to a lack of opportunity. We disagree. The failure of a defendant to discover potentially useful evidence at the time of the former proceeding does not constitute a lack of opportunity to cross-examine. *See Thomas v. Cardwell*, 626 F.2d 1375, 1386 n.34 (9th Cir. 1980), *cert. denied*, 449 U.S. 1089 (1981). In *Thomas*, the prosecution introduced, at defendant's second trial, the testimony of a witness from defendant's first trial who had become unavailable. *Id.* at 1384. By the time of the second trial, the defendant claimed to have discovered evidence that this witness was schizophrenic. *Id.* at 1386 n.34. The *Thomas* court rejected the argument that the purported discovery of new evidence established defendant's lack of opportunity to cross-examine the witness at the first trial. After noting that there was no suggestion that the defendant's failure to discover the information was the prosecution's fault, the court explained that often information will surface after a trial which, if known to a defense attorney, would have made the cross-examination of a witness more thorough or even more advantageous to the defendant. Nevertheless, that lack of information does not make the opportunity for

---

[48] [1] The parties debate whether, given this collapse of the constitutional analysis into the Rule 804(b)(1) analysis, the abuse of discretion standard which governs admission of Rule 804(b)(1) evidence should apply, *see United States v. Lester*, 749 F.2d 1288, 1301 (9th Cir. 1984), or whether the court should review de novo those Rule 804(b)(1) cases in which a constitutional claim is raised. We need not decide the issued, however, because we conclude that appellants cannot prevail under either standard. *See United States v. Payne*, 944 F.2d 1458, 1468 n.9 (9th Cir. 1991).

[49] [2] Appellants do not dispute that Briseno, who chose not to testify in the federal trial, was "unavailable."

[50] [3] Three enhancements were used at the federal trial: (1) the "filtered audiotape," which filtered out helicopter noise and purportedly made audible certain commands by Koon as well as the sounds of a taser being activated just before King went down (prepared by the defense); and (2) the "zoom videotape," which blew up the frames showing Powell's first blow to King (prepared by the defense); and (3) the "registered videotape," which stabilized the video image (prepared by the government). In the district court, in addition to arguing that the lack of these enhancements hampered their ability to cross-examine Briseno during the state proceeding, appellants argued that their motive for cross-examination was different in the state than in the federal trial because in the federal trial the prosecution was required to show a higher level of intent. Appellants have not pursued this latter argument on appeal.

cross-examination ineffective even though the cross-examination itself is less than optimal for the defendant. *Id.*

Much the same applies here. Appellants did not lack the opportunity to cross-examine Briseno; they lacked only some of the tools which were later developed by the government or by appellants themselves, and which appellants argue would have allowed them to cross-examine Briseno to better effect. Appellants' failure to take full advantage of their opportunity to cross-examine in the first trial — by developing those tools earlier — cannot alter the fact that they had that opportunity. *See United States v. McClellan*, 868 F.2d 210, 215 (7th Cir. 1989) ("the emphasis in [the Rule 804(b)(1)] inquiry is upon the motive underlying the cross-examination rather than the actual exchange that took place"); *United States v. Salim*, 855 F.2d 944, 953–54 (2d Cir. 1988) (Under Rule 804(b)(1), defendant is entitled to "an opportunity for effective cross-examination, not cross-examination that is effective in whatever way, and to whatever extent, the defense might wish.") (quoting *Delaware v. Fensterer*, 474 U.S. 15, 20 (1985) (per curiam)).[51]

In addition to a full opportunity, Rule 804(b)(1) requires that appellants' motive in carrying out their state trial cross-examination of Briseno was similar to the motive they would have had in the later proceeding. We conclude easily that it was. The operative facts and legal issues in the state and federal trials were substantially similar, *see United States v. Salerno*, 112 S. Ct. 2503, 2509, 120 L. Ed. 2d 255 (1992) (Blackmun, J., concurring) ("'similar motive' does not mean 'identical motive'"), and appellants do not challenge the district court's finding to this effect. Appellants thus had every reason to develop Briseno's testimony in the state trial with an eye to undermining his credibility and casting into doubt his statements about their behavior. *See United States v. Poland*, 659 F.2d 884, 895–96 (9th Cir. 1981) (holding that defendant's motive for cross-examination at suppression hearing was similar under Rule 804(b)(1) to his motive for cross-examination at trial).

Appellants maintain that their position is supported by *People of the Territory of Guam v. Hayes*, 1993 WL 469357 (D. Guam 1993), in which a three-judge panel held that the trial court erred in admitting former testimony because the defendant had not had the same motive to cross-examine the witness about certain facts in the first trial as he had in the second trial. However, the Hayes court made clear that this difference in motive occurred because "different issues arose at the second trial which [defendant] could not possibly have anticipated at the first trial." *Id.* at *2.[52]

Here, by contrast, there is no suggestion that either the factual nature of the case

---

[51] [4] Appellants argue that the newly discovered information in *Thomas* pertained only to the credibility of the witness, whereas the newly developed enhancements here pertain to the crime itself. Appellants do not explain why this distinction matters, however, and nothing in *Thomas* reveals its significance either. At the state trial, appellants had the opportunity to cross-examine Briseno concerning both extrinsic facts about the charged crime, and circumstances in his own situation which might lessen his credibility. It is that opportunity, rather than the scope or efficacy of its employment, which is important under Rule 804(b)(1).

[52] [5] The victim in *Hayes*, "K.," testified at defendant's first trial, but then moved from Guam and was unavailable at the second trial. K's testimony from the first trial was introduced at the second trial. The prosecution also called as a witness Mrs. Muna, who testified about statements made by K. which were not disclosed at the first trial. The appellate court concluded that defendant's motive to cross-examine K. was different at the first than at the second trial, because at the first trial defendant did not have "the

against appellants or appellants' motive for cross-examining Briseno changed at all from the first to the second trial. All that changed was the technology that appellants might have used to enhanced the Holliday videotape as a basis for questions in the cross-examination. Because this change constitutes a deficiency in neither the opportunity to cross-examine nor the motive for doing so, appellants' argument under Rule 804(b)(1) must fail.

NOTES AND QUESTIONS

1.   Why condition the former testimony exception on declarant unavailability? Doesn't the presence of both an oath and a prior opportunity for cross-examination render this exception sufficiently reliable to warrant admissibility regardless of witness unavailability?

2.   For another example of a case in which the court found similarity of motive see *Shanklin v. Norfolk So. Ry. Co.*, 369 F.3d 978, 990–91 (6th Cir. 2004).

3.   Suppose a criminal defendant has an opportunity to cross-examine a witness at a preliminary hearing. Might there be tactical reasons for him to decline to do so? Alternatively, if he chooses to cross-examine, is the inquiry likely to be comparable to cross-examination at trial? *See generally Ohio v. Roberts*, 448 U.S. 56, 70 (1980); *United States v. Avants*, 367 F.3d 433, 443–44 (5th Cir. 2004); *People v. Fry*, 92 P.3d 970 (Colo. 2004). Similar problems could arise for defendants in the context of pre-trial suppression hearings. *See United States v. Zurosky*, 614 F.2d 779 (1st Cir. 1979), *cert. denied*, 446 U.S. 967 (1980).

4.   Assuming that evidence of former testimony is admissible, would the best evidence rule require the proponent to establish the former testimony by offering into evidence a transcript of the prior proceeding?

d. Statements Made in the Belief of Impending Death (Dying Declarations)

Charles W. Quick, *Some Reflections on Dying Declarations*
6 How. L.J. 109, 109–12 (1960)[53]

Go thou, and fill another room in hell

That hand shall burn in never-quenching fire,

That staggers thus my person. Exton, thy fierce hand Hath with thy king's blood stained the king's own land. Mount, mount, my soul! Thy seat is up on high, Whilst my gross flesh sinks downward, here to die.

SHAKESPEARE, RICHARD II, ACT V

One of the oldest exceptions to the hearsay rule is embalmed in the phrase "dying declaration." As a matter of fact, the admission of dying declarations

---

additional motivation . . . of proving that K. didn't make the statements attributed to her by Mrs. Muna." *Id.* at *2.

[53] Reprinted with permission.

preceded the development of the hearsay rule. Nevertheless, its doctrines and divergent admission procedures accentuate the conclusion that the law of evidence remains in chaotic confusion. The basic scope and conditions of its admission, though illogical, are fairly well established. Application, however, is neither so simple nor well understood. Unfortunately, attempts to reform the rules of evidence, still largely stymied, have bypassed the myriad problems attendant on the application of this exception. More thought should be given to a re-evaluation of the fictitious nature of its fundamental premise, and to some solution to the perplexity of many judges when asked to instruct as to the value or weight to be attributed to the dying declaration. It may still be helpful as a reminder, moreover, to note the differing ways courts handle the task of allocating the respective functions of judge and jury.

One important factor retarding clarification has been that many of the most persuasive legal scholars promoting evidence reform have generally ignored this exception by advocating instead the adoption of a broader hearsay exception providing that all declarations of deceased persons, or for that matter unavailable persons, who have perceived the event in issue be admissible in all civil and criminal cases. In this attempt to erect a new "evidential" structure the practical benefits of remodeling old legal doctrines have been minimized.

Deathbed statements have from ancient times enjoyed a general popular reputation for reliability. Literature abounds with dramatic stories of deathbed confessions, accusations, and exculpations. Once the hearsay rule had become established, however, a re-examination of the admission of such deathbed statements became necessary. This review seems to have been more implicit than explicit, however. Doubt still exists as to the reason for many of the proscriptions on the admission of such declarations. It is difficult, if not impossible, to take one example, to determine on what grounds accusatory and exculpatory declarations concerning the death of a declarant are admissible, while confessions or statements about the killing of, or harm to, one other than the declarant are denied admission.

*   *   *

All aspects of the "necessity" theory have been urged as justifications for the dying declaration exception. As so applied they are bottomed on the argument that homicide is generally a secret crime; dying declarations aid prosecutors in obtaining convictions; if they were not admitted many persons accused of homicide would go unpunished. This is obviously a makeshift reason. Certainly hearsay is not admitted merely on the ground that the proponent of the evidence will not otherwise be able to win his case, or the prosecutor gain a conviction. Nor do we admit hearsay evidence because the trier of fact would otherwise be deprived of the perception of a particular person. To do so in either case would be to make shambles of the hearsay rule. Necessity as a reason thus may be equated in soundness to the specious argument that dying declarations are let in because they have the same guaranty of sincerity as a statement under oath. Since affidavits have no higher standing than other extrajudicial statements, this, like the "necessity" argument, is an egregious non sequitur.

The principal argument for the exception hinges on the oft stated belief that the dying declarant, knowing that he is about to die would be unwilling to go to his maker with a lie on his lips. Thus his statements, at least of accusation or exculpation, are extremely likely to be truthful. It is thus assumed that knowledge of impending death will probably deter one from uttering falsehoods. Belief in the imminence of death, therefore, is considered an effective deterrent to conscious or unconscious falsification, and when supernaturalism had a more zealous following, this may have acted as a substantial barrier to falsification.

It is dubious, however, whether under modern conditions, with the breakdown of unquestioning belief in, and concern with, religious doctrines on the part of many, the inference is a valid one. Even in deeply religious communities it is very doubtful that the inference could be properly drawn. Certainly there is no longer universal acceptance even in such communities of doctrines of "hell fire" and "pie in the sky." This development deprives the doctrine of validity when applied to dying declarations in a civilized and sophisticated community. Moreover, no studies are available as to the psychological effect of the knowledge of immediately impending doom on perception, memory and ability to accurately communicate. Indeed, in many instances the declarant is either suffering from an appreciable amount of pain or anxiety which may itself cloud his perception and ability to communicate, or his perception and consciousness has been dulled by pain-depressant drugs. This is especially true in homicide cases. Under these circumstances, of course, the religious guaranty of sincerity may be merely a pious hope rather than a probable fact. Nevertheless, this basic premise remains, even today, the prime rationale given by the courts for the existence of this exception.

SHEPARD v. UNITED STATES
290 U.S. 96 (1933)

Mr. Justice Cardozo delivered the opinion of the Court.

The petitioner, Charles A. Shepard, a major in the medical corps of the United States army, has been convicted of the murder of his wife, Zenana Shepard, at Fort Riley, Kansas, a United States military reservation. . . .

The crime is charged to have been committed by poisoning the victim with bichloride of mercury. The defendant was in love with another woman, and wished to make her his wife. There is circumstantial evidence to sustain a finding by the jury that to win himself his freedom he turned to poison and murder. Even so, guilt was contested and conflicting inferences are possible. The defendant asks us to hold that by the acceptance of incompetent evidence the scales were weighted to his prejudice and in the end to his undoing.

The evidence complained of was offered by the Government in rebuttal when the trial was nearly over. On May 22, 1929, there was a conversation in the absence of the defendant between Mrs. Shepard, then ill in bed, and Clara Brown, her nurse. The patient asked the nurse to go to the closet in the defendant's room and bring a bottle of whisky that would be found upon a shelf. When the bottle was produced, she said that this was the liquor she had taken just before collapsing. She asked whether enough was left to make a test for the presence of poison, insisting that the smell and taste were strange. And then she added the words "Dr. Shepard has poisoned me."

The conversation was proved twice. After the first proof of it, the Government asked to strike it out, being doubtful of its competence, and this request was granted. A little later, however, the offer was renewed, the nurse having then testified to statements by Mrs. Shepard as to the prospect of recovery. "She said she was not going to get well; she was going to die." With the aid of this new evidence, the conversation already summarized was proved a second time. There was a timely challenge of the ruling.

She said, "Dr. Shepard has poisoned me." The admission of this declaration, if erroneous, was more than unsubstantial error. As to that the parties are agreed. The voice of the dead wife was heard in accusation of her husband, and the accusation was accepted as evidence of guilt. If the evidence was incompetent, the verdict may not stand.

1. Upon the hearing in this court the Government finds its main prop in the position that what was said by Mrs. Shepard was admissible as a dying declaration. This is manifestly the theory upon which it was offered and received. The prop, however, is a broken reed. To make out a dying declaration the declarant must have spoken without hope of recovery and in the shadow of impending death. The record furnishes no proof of that indispensable condition. . . .

We have said that the declarant was not shown to have spoken without hope of recovery and in the shadow of impending death. Her illness began on May 20. She was found in a state of collapse, delirious, in pain, the pupils of her eyes dilated, and the retina suffused with blood. The conversation with the nurse occurred two days later. At that time her mind had cleared up, and her speech was rational and orderly. There was as yet no thought by any of her physicians that she was dangerously ill, still less that her case was hopeless. To all seeming she had greatly improved, and was moving forward to recovery. There had been no diagnosis of poison as the cause of her distress. Not till about a week afterwards was there a relapse, accompanied by an infection of the mouth, renewed congestion of the eyes, and later hemorrhages of the bowels. Death followed on June 15.

Nothing in the condition of the patient on May 22 gives fair support to the conclusion that hope had then been lost. She may have thought she was going to die and have said so to her nurse, but this was consistent with hope, which could not have been put aside without more to quench it. Indeed, a fortnight later, she said to one of her physicians, though her condition was then grave, "You will get me well, won't you?" Fear or even belief that illness will end in death will not avail of itself to make a dying declaration. There must be "a settled hopeless expectation" . . . that death is near at hand, and what is said must have been spoken in the hush of its impending presence. . . . Despair of recovery may indeed be gathered from the circumstances if the facts support the inference. . . . There is no unyielding ritual of words to be spoken by the dying. Despair may even be gathered though the period of survival outruns the bounds of expectation. . . . What is decisive is the state of mind. Even so, the state of mind must be exhibited in the evidence, and not left to conjecture. The patient must have spoken with the consciousness of a swift and certain doom.

What was said by this patient was not spoken in that mood. There was no warning to her in the circumstances that her words would be repeated and accepted as those of a dying wife, charging murder to her husband, and charging it deliberately and solemnly as a fact within her knowledge. To the focus of that responsibility her mind was never brought. She spoke as one ill, giving voice to the beliefs and perhaps the conjectures of the moment. The liquor was to be tested, to see whether her beliefs were sound. She did not speak as one dying, announcing to the survivors a definitive conviction, a legacy of knowledge on which the world might act when she had gone.

The petitioner insists that the form of the declaration exhibits other defects that call for its exclusion, apart from the objection that death was not imminent and that hope was still alive. Homicide may not be imputed to a defendant on the basis of mere suspicions, though they are the suspicions of the dying. To let the declaration in, the inference must be permissible that there was knowledge or the opportunity for knowledge as to the acts that are declared . . . . The argument is pressed upon us that knowledge and opportunity are excluded when the declaration in question is read in the setting of the circumstances. . . . The form is not decisive, though it be that of a conclusion, a statement of the result with the antecedent steps omitted . . . . "He murdered me," does not cease to be competent as a dying declaration because in the statement of the act there is also an appraisal of the crime. . . . One does not hold the dying to the observance of all the niceties of speech to which conformity is exacted from a witness on the stand. What is decisive is something deeper and more fundamental than any difference of form. The declaration is kept out if the setting of the occasion satisfies the judge, or in reason ought to satisfy him, that the speaker is giving expression to suspicion or conjecture, and not to known facts. The difficulty is not so much in respect of the governing principle as in its application to varying and equivocal conditions. In this case, the ruling that there was a failure to make out the imminence of death and the abandonment of hope relieves us of the duty of determining whether it is a legitimate inference that there was the opportunity for knowledge. We leave that question open.

STATE v. ADAMSON
665 P.2d 972 (Ariz. 1983)

GORDON, VICE CHIEF JUSTICE:

On October 17, 1980, a jury found appellant guilty of first degree murder for the bombing death of newspaper reporter Donald Bolles. . . . The defendant was sentenced to death. Appellant now challenges the conviction on the basis of several allegations of error. . . .

Adamson was charged with the June 2, 1976, bombing murder of Donald Bolles. The evidence at trial showed that Bolles, an investigative reporter for the Arizona Republic newspaper, had arranged to meet the defendant at a Phoenix hotel in order to gather information for a potential news story. Two notes concerning the meeting were found after the bombing at Bolles' office. Bolles went to the hotel at the designated time and waited for Adamson in the lobby. While Bolles was waiting, he received a telephone call from an individual he later identified as the defendant.

Bolles later stated that Adamson wanted to change the place of the meeting and asked Bolles for directions to his office. Bolles then went to his car and began backing out of the parking space in route to the newly-arranged meeting. As he was backing out a bomb exploded sending pieces of Bolles' car throughout the parking lot and into a neighboring construction site. Witnesses testified that the force of the explosion shook neighboring buildings.

Several rescuers administered first aid to the victim who was still conscious although critically injured. Both of his legs and one arm were severely mutilated. Bolles made statements to the rescuers which implicated the defendant and asked one witness to call his wife. He mentioned the defendant's name several times and stated that "Adamson [set or sent] me." He also told the individuals rendering first aid, "You better hurry up, boys. I feel like I'm going."

The next day the victim responded to questions from the Phoenix Police by means of finger and hand signals. Bolles indicated that he had gone to the hotel the day before to meet Adamson and had received a call from him while waiting for his arrival. Bolles identified a driver's license photograph of the defendant and indicated that he was the man Bolles had met four days earlier while investigating the same story. After having both legs and one arm amputated, Bolles died June 13, 1976.

Intensive police investigations in the days immediately following the bombing revealed the structure of the bomb and that it was a radio-controlled device. The police also established that the defendant was involved in the incident and a warrant was issued to search his apartment. In searching Adamson's residence the police found materials similar to those used to construct the bomb which was attached by magnets to the underside of Bolles' automobile. Literature which contained information concerning the making of explosive devices was also seized. Further investigations revealed that Adamson had purchased remote control equipment two months earlier at a hobby shop in San Diego, California which could have been used to trigger the explosive device. Furthermore, in May, 1976, Adamson had gone to the Arizona Republic parking lot and asked the guard where "Don-So-and-so['s]" car was, saying he had some papers to drop off in the car. Adamson and his companion then went to an automobile dealership and inspected the underside of several cars similar to that owned by Bolles. In route to the dealership the defendant told the individual riding in his car that "he was going to blow up a car" and when asked why, Adamson responded because "this guy was giving people a lot of hard times and stepping on people's toes." At trial testimony was given to establish that Adamson was paid $10,000 to kill Donald Bolles.

*   *   *

Statements and Notes of Victim

A. Hospital Statements

The day after the bombing three detectives went to the hospital to question Bolles about the bombing. In response to their questions Bolles indicated that he had gone to the hotel to meet the defendant and that while at the hotel he received a call from Adamson. Bolles also identified a photograph of Adamson and indicated that the defendant was the person he had intended to meet on the morning of June 2nd. Appellant contends that the trial court erred in denying his motion to suppress the hospital statements on the grounds that they were inadmissible hearsay.

At the outset we set forth the standard for review: A trial court's denial of a motion to suppress will not be reversed in the absence of a clear abuse of discretion. . . . The trial court ruled that the statements were admissible as dying declarations under Ariz. R. Evid. 804(b)(2). That rule requires the following: (1) that the statements in this case are being used in a homicide prosecution; (2) the statements were made by a declarant while believing his death was imminent; and (3) that the statement concerned the cause of circumstances of what he believed to be his impending death. Defendant objects to the admission of the statements under this rule because there is no evidence that the victim believed death was imminent at the time the statements were made. We disagree. The law does not require that there be a direct assertion by the declarant that he is dying at the time the statements were made. . . . The party offering dying declarations may show that the victim was under a sense of impending death either by express language of the deceased or by the indubitable circumstances. . . . In this case the state has shown both. Witnesses who were at the scene of the bombing described Bolles' legs as having the consistency of hamburger. One witness testified that he had seen a piece of flesh the size of a softball on the pavement as he was rushing across the hotel parking lot toward Bolles' car. At the scene of the bombing the victim made the following statement to rescuers: "You better hurry up, boys, I feel like I'm going." Several hours after the bombing the victim's right leg was amputated. The hospital statements were made one day after the bombing. At the time of the statements Bolles was in grave condition in the intensive care unit. Under these conditions it is reasonable to conclude that when the statements were made Bolles was under a sense of impending death. There was no error in admitting the hospital statements.

B. Statements at the Scene

Immediately after the bombing Bolles made several statements to the individuals who were rendering emergency care. These statements indicated that in some manner the defendant was involved in the bombing. The victim further stated that a mafia-related organization could have played a role in the bombing. The trial court denied the defendant's motion to suppress these statements allowing them to come in as evidence by applying both the excited utterance and dying declaration exceptions to the hearsay rule. On appeal appellant contends that the statements should not have been admitted at trial since they were not based on the personal knowledge of the victim.

*   *   *

There is also a general requirement imposed on declarations coming in under all exceptions to the hearsay rule that the declarant, like witnesses, must have had an opportunity to observe or personal knowledge of the fact declared . . . Bolles, an investigative reporter, told rescuers that he was investigating "a mafia called Emprise . . ." and ". . . the mafia was responsible." The victim also stated that "Adamson did it . . ." and "Adamson [set or sent] me." We believe that Bolles' statements regarding the mafia and Emprise, as well as his statement that "Adamson did it . . . ," were not within his personal knowledge since they were mere suspicions. The statements were not "based on events perceived by [Bolles] through one of the physical senses." 3 WEINSTEIN EVIDENCE § 602[01] at 602-2. Therefore, the trial court erred in allowing these statements to be admitted.

Error does not require reversal if it can be said beyond a reasonable doubt that it had no influence on the verdict of the jury. . . . "The question is whether, without this evidence, the appellate court can say, beyond a reasonable doubt, that the jury would have found the defendant guilty." . . . In this case we believe that this question can be answered affirmatively.

*   *   *

[Dissenting opinion omitted.]

NOTES AND QUESTIONS

1. Police departments have adopted procedures to help officers meet the foundational requirements for the dying declaration exception. *See People v. Little*, 83 Misc. 2d 321 (N.Y. County Ct. 1975).

2. Some jurisdictions condition this exception upon the victim's actual death. *See e.g., People v. Greathouse*, 2004 Mich. App. LEXIS 914 (Mich. Ct. App. Apr. 13, 2004). How does Rule 804(b)(2) handle situations in which the declarant manages to survive?

3. If you are unable to meet the foundational requirements for this exception, be sure to consider other possibilities. Likely prospects are excited utterances and present sense impressions discussed *infra* in § I.2.c.

4. Suppose the dying declarant confesses to a murder he and an accomplice committed several years earlier. Would the dying declaration exception allow the prosecution to admit this statement in the accomplice's murder trial? If not, would the exception for statements against interest provide a way to admit this proof?

2. Exceptions Not Requiring Declarant Unavailability

a. Business Records

John E. Tracy, *The Introduction of Documentary Evidence*
24 IOWA L. REV. 436, 454–56 (1939)[54]

Under the rule which formerly excluded the testimony of interested parties, it was impossible for a tradesman doing business alone to prove even a simple case for goods sold and delivered. To remedy this situation, the courts developed the so-called "shop-book" rule, by which the tradesman's books of account were admissible in evidence to prove the facts stated therein, provided that the

---

[54] Reprinted with permission.

tradesman kept no clerk. At the same time this rule was being developed, the courts were confronted with other cases where the accounts of third parties and of tradesmen who did keep clerks were involved. In the first of these cases the tradesman was not ineligible as a witness, because he was not interested, and in the second class of cases the account could be proved by the clerks of the plaintiff, who also were not ineligible. In both classes of cases, however, the testimony of the person who knew about the transaction, whether proprietor or clerk, was often unobtainable because of death. In those cases the courts were able to work out a real exception to the hearsay rule, based on the necessity element arising from death. There thus grew up, side by side, two bodies of law, one for parties' books, where no clerks were employed, and the other as to the use of books of account in other cases. When the statutes were passed abolishing the disqualification of interest and making parties eligible to testify, the reasons for the shop-book rule vanished and the use of all book entries came to be governed by the same set of rules, except in a very few jurisdictions where legislation recognizing the shop-book rule has never been repealed.

As business practices and methods of accounting have become more complicated, the courts have found it necessary to broaden the whole theory of admissibility. Death of a witness is no longer a necessary condition to the introduction of the evidence and the disruption to business caused by calling clerks and accountants away from their work will now satisfy the necessity principle. The requirement that the book entries must be supported by the testimony of the person who conducted the transaction and gave the information to the book-keeper, once so rigorously enforced by the courts, has given way, in the realization by the courts that in a complicated modern business such a requirement can rarely be met, to the modern rule that it is sufficient if the books are verified on the witness stand by the supervising officer who knows them to be the books of regular entries kept in that establishment, and by such other persons as are readily available to show the correctness of the accounts. This broadened attitude of the courts has been adopted by many legislatures and by Congress, in enacting the so-called "model statutes," drafted by a committee of legal experts appointed under the Commonwealth Fund, which statute provides, in effect, that any writing or record made as a memorandum of any act shall be admissible in any judicial proceeding in proof of said act if it was made in the regular course of any business and if it was the regular course of such business to make such memorandum or record at the time of such act or within a reasonable time thereafter.

JOHNSON v. LUTZ
170 N.E. 517 (N.Y. 1930)

HUBBS, J.

This action is to recover damages for the wrongful death of the plaintiffs' intestate, who was killed when his motorcycle came into collision with the defendants' truck at a street intersection. There was a sharp conflict in the testimony in regard to the circumstances under which the collision took place. A policeman's report of the accident filed by him in the station house was offered in evidence by the defendants under section 374-a of the Civil Practice Act, and was excluded. The sole ground for reversal urged by the appellants is that said report was erroneously excluded. That section reads:

> Any writing or record, whether in the form of an entry in a book or otherwise, made as a memorandum or record of any act, transaction, occurrence or event, shall be admissible in evidence in proof of said act, transaction, occurrence or event, if the trial judge shall find that it was made in the regular course of any business, and that it was the regular course of such business to make such memorandum or record at the time of such act, transaction, occurrence of event, or within a reasonable time thereafter. All other circumstances of the making of such writing or record, including lack of personal knowledge by the entrant or maker, may be shown to affect its weight, but they shall not affect its admissibility. The term business shall include business, profession, occupation and calling of every kind.

FRE 803(6)

Prior to the decision in the well-known case of *Vosburgh v. Thayer*, 12 Johns. 461, decided in 1815, shopbooks could not be introduced in evidence to prove an account. The decision in that case established that they were admissible where preliminary proof could be made that there were regular dealings between the parties; that the plaintiff kept honest and fair books; that some of the articles charged had been delivered; and that the plaintiff kept no clerk. At that time it might not have been a hardship to require a shopkeeper who sued to recover an account to furnish the preliminary proof required by that decision. Business was transacted in a comparatively small way, with few, if any, clerks. Since the decision in that case, it has remained the substantial basis of all decisions upon the question in this jurisdiction prior to the enactment in 1928 of section 374-a, Civil Practice Act.

Under modern conditions, the limitations upon the right to use books of account, memoranda, or record, made in the regular course of business, often resulted in a denial of justice, and usually in annoyance, expense, and waste of time and energy. A rule of evidence that was practical a century ago had become obsolete. The situation was appreciated, and attention was called to it by the courts and text-writers. WOODS PRACTICE EVIDENCE (2d ed.) 377; 3 WIGMORE ON EVIDENCE (1923) § 1530.

The report of the Legal Research Committee of the Commonwealth Fund, published in 1927, by the Yale University Press, under the title, "The Law of Evidence — Some Proposals for Its Reform," dealt with the question in chapter 5, under the heading, "Proof of Business Transactions to Harmonize with Current Business Practice." That report, based upon extensive research, pointed out the confusion existing in decisions in different jurisdictions. It explained and illustrated the great need of a more practical, workable, and uniform rule, adapted to modern business conditions and practices. The chapter is devoted to a discussion of the pressing need of a rule of evidence which would "give evidential credit to the books upon which the mercantile and industrial world relies in the conduct of business." At the close of the chapter, the committee proposed a statute to be enacted in all jurisdictions. In compliance with such proposal, the Legislature enacted section 374-a of the Civil Practice Act in the very words used by the committee.

It is apparent that the Legislature enacted section 374-a to carry out the purpose announced in the report of the committee. That purpose was to secure the enactment of a statute which would afford a more workable rule of evidence in the proof of business transactions under existing business conditions.

In view of the history of section 374-a and the purpose for which it was enacted, it is apparent that it was never intended to apply to a situation like that in the case at bar. The memorandum in question was not made in the regular course of any business, profession, occupation, or calling. The policeman who made it was not present at the time of the accident. The memorandum was made from hearsay statements of third persons who happened to be present at the scene of the accident when he arrived. It does not appear whether they saw the accident and stated to him what they knew, or stated what some other persons had told them.

The purpose of the Legislature in enacting section 374-a was to permit a writing or record, made in the regular course of business, to be received in evidence without the necessity of calling as witnesses all of the persons who had any part in making it, provided the record was made as a part of the duty of the person making it, or on information imparted by persons who were under a duty to impart such information. The amendment permits the introduction of shop-books without the necessity of calling all clerks who may have sold different items of account. It was not intended to permit the receipt in evidence of entries based upon voluntary hearsay statements made by third parties not engaged in the business or under any duty in relation thereto. It was said, in *Mayor, etc., of New York City v. Second Ave. R. Co.*, 7 N.E. 905, 909:

> It is a proper qualification of the rule admitting such evidence that the account must have been made in the ordinary course of business, and that it should not be extended so as to admit a mere private memorandum, not made in pursuance of any duty owing by the person making it, or when made upon information derived from another who made the communication casually and voluntarily, and not under the sanction of duty or other obligation.

> An important consideration leading to the amendment was the fact that in the business world credit is given to records made in the course of business by persons who are engaged in the business upon information given by others engaged in the same business as part of their duty.

> Such entries are dealt with in that way in the most important undertakings of mercantile and industrial life. They are the ultimate basis of calculation, investment, and general confidence in every business enterprise. Nor does the practical impossibility of obtaining constantly and permanently the verification of every employee affect the trust that is given to such books. It would seem that expedients which the entire commercial world recognizes as safe could be sanctioned, and not discredited, by courts of justice. When it is a mere question of whether provisional confidence can be placed in a certain class of statements, there cannot profitably and sensibly be one rule for the business world and another for the court-room. The merchant and the manufacturer must not be turned away remediless because the methods in which the entire community places a just confi-

dence are a little difficult to reconcile with technical judicial scruples on the part of the same persons who as attorneys have already employed and relied upon the same methods. In short, courts must here cease to be pedantic and endeavor to be practical.

3 WIGMORE ON EVIDENCE (1923) § 1530, p. 278.

The Legislature has sought by the amendment to make the courts practical. It would be unfortunate not to give the amendment a construction which will enable it to cure the evil complained of and accomplish the purpose for which it was enacted. In construing it, we should not, however, permit it to be applied in a case for which it was never intended.

The judgment should be affirmed, with costs.

CARDOZO, C. J., and POUND, CRANE, LEHMAN, KELLOGG, and O'BRIEN, J.J., concur.

Judgment affirmed.

KELLY v. WASSERMAN
158 N.E.2d 241 (N.Y. 1959)

CONWAY, CHIEF JUDGE.

Plaintiff-appellant Alice M. Kelly, a 65-year-old woman, was, prior to June 4, 1950, in financial difficulties. She could not maintain the house she owned at 813 Greenwood Avenue in Brooklyn. She approached the defendant-respondent, a friend, and asked his assistance. There followed an agreement by which plaintiff was to convey her house to defendant in return for which he was to pay all of her debts and to allow her to continue to reside in her two rooms on the parlor floor of the premises, rent free. Plaintiff claims that she was to be given rent-free occupancy for her lifetime; defendant's version of the agreement is that she was to be permitted to live there only "as long as the Department of Housing and Building would not bother him because of her living there." That is the gist of the controversy. Plaintiff deeded the premises to defendant, who thereafter paid her debts. The agreement, whatever it was, was not put in writing.

Beginning on August 27, 1957, defendant had difficulties with the Department of Housing and Buildings. Three families, if plaintiff be considered one, occupied the house, making it a multiple dwelling unlawfully. Three families had occupied it at all times at and after its deeding to defendant, but it was claimed that it had become necessary for one of them to be evicted. Defendant chose plaintiff, the nonpaying occupant, and brought a summary proceeding to evict her, while plaintiff on her part brought an action to have the deed reformed to add "Subject to the life tenancy of Alice M. Kelly in two rooms on the second floor of said premises." After consolidation of the eviction proceeding and the reformation action, the latter was dismissed after trial and the plaintiff was ordered evicted. The Appellate Division has affirmed.

Plaintiff was and is a welfare beneficiary and, as such, the Department of Welfare maintains a file in her case. On several occasions department personnel have had contact with the defendant. Two of them are pertinent here. According to department records (held inadmissible below), its representative had a telephone conversation with the defendant on July 21, 1950, and made a personal visit to him on October 23, 1952. Memorandum of conversations had with him on each occasion were made by the person supervising plaintiff's welfare file and incorporated therein. In both of them defendant stated that he had agreed to allow plaintiff to occupy the premises rent free for life; in neither did he qualify his statement with the proviso that her occupancy could last only as long as the noninterference of the Housing Department. The two excluded entries read as follows:

7/21/50—

Phoned So. 8-8647 and spoke with Mr. Wasserman who advised as above-stated he had been advancing Miss K. a dollar or two daily for food needs but cannot continue this as he has his own family to support and his income will not warrant this added expenditure. If and when he acquires property, he will permit Miss K. to remain there rent free the remainder of her life — she will occupy the 2-room apartment that has no cooking facilities. She will eat all her meals in the restaurant (no cooking).

10/23/52—

Collateral to Mr. Wasserman.

We visited Mr. Paul Wasserman at his pharmacy at 1291 Prospect Avenue. Telephone [No.] So. 8-8904. He stated that he would permit Miss Kelly to live in her Apt. rent free for her lifetime. This includes electricity. He stated there was no cooking facilities since this would be a violation. He said that Applicant ate all of her meals out and that he loaned her the money to eat when she did not have any. He thought she woed [sic] him about $12 or $15 dollars.

Without the excluded entries, the record shows the plaintiff making contradictory statements while the defendant adheres to a consistent position. Were the entries admitted, the record would manifest inconsistencies on the part of both litigants. In view of the circumstances attending the transaction, a contrary result may well have ensued from such foundation. Thus if there was error in excluding the entries, it must be deemed prejudicial.

We are of opinion that their exclusion was error. It is not clear whether the ruling was grounded upon the supposition that the statements were hearsay, or upon the fact that they were sought in evidence as contradictory statements made by defendant out of court for the purpose of impeaching him. If the latter, the evidence was admissible to impeach defendant even though he was the plaintiff's witness. "When . . . it is said that one cannot impeach his own witness by contradictory statements made out of court, this statement must be limited to the case of a witness who is not the adverse party." . . .

However, it is more likely that the exclusion of the records was founded upon their being hearsay. When defendant stated, with reference to the questioned entries, that he was "going to object to anything that may be hearsay," the Referee said that he would not "pay any attention to anything that is hearsay."

But even if it be assumed that the matter offered was hearsay, still "The purpose of section 374-a of the Civil Practice Act was to *overcome* the objection of the hearsay rule" (*Matter of Coddington's Will*, 120 N.E.2d 777, 784 [emphasis supplied]).

One Frances Reynolds testified that she was a "social investigator" for the Welfare Department, and as such was "in charge of the welfare case of Miss Alice Kelly"; that the department kept records of telephone calls and visits made to plaintiff and those connected with her. It may be noted that the department is required by law to maintain such records. . . . It was also established that the disputed entries had been made by the department employee who first interviewed plaintiff. Section 374-a of the Civil Practice Act makes admissible in evidence "a memorandum or record of any act, transaction, occurrence or event . . . if . . . made in the regular course of any business as long as "it was the regular course of such business to make such memorandum or record at the time . . . or within a reasonable time thereafter." There can be no doubt but that the alleged statements of defendant, which are most germane to the question of plaintiff's shelter, were the Department of Welfare's business, and the practice (enjoined by law in this case) of maintaining records on those receiving welfare support qualified those records for admissibility under section 374-a.

It is true that the person who made the memoranda, since not testifying, could not be cross-examined. Nevertheless, in *Johnson v. Lutz*, . . . we said that, where the entrant has the duty of drawing the memorandum, section 374-a permits it "to be received in evidence without the necessity of calling as witnesses all of the persons who had any part in making it." It was also indicated that the proffered matter might be objectionable on the additional ground that there was "no evidence that she [the welfare worker] recognized the voice of the one with whom she spoke." But that is not basis for the exclusion of records; rather may it be taken into consideration only after their admission as affecting the weight to be given them. The statute is explicit thereon, providing, after the prerequisites above set forth have been met, that "All other circumstances of the making of such writing or record, including lack of personal knowledge by the entrant or maker, may be shown to affect its weight, but they shall not affect its admissibility." Moreover, whatever effect voice recognition might be given with regard to the telephone call of July 21, 1950, it has no bearing on the other excluded memorandum, which is a record of the in-person visit by the investigator to defendant on October 23, 1952.

The judgment of the Appellate Division should be reversed, and a new trial granted with costs to abide the event.

JUDGES DESMOND, DYE, FULD, FROESSEL, VAN VOORHIS and BURKE concur. Judgment reversed, etc.

NOTES AND QUESTIONS

1. Consider Professor Wigmore's criticism of *Johnson v. Lutz:* "[T]his decision shows how difficult it is to amend the law of procedure effectively even in the presence of an obvious and conceded need for it; the most explicit words of a statute do not always avail to change the cerebral operations of the judiciary." 5 WIGMORE, EVIDENCE § 1530(a) at 392, n.1 (3d ed. 1940). Did *Johnson v. Lutz* really ignore plain statutory language? Is it plausible that Professor Wigmore would have instead preferred to admit police reports containing bystander statements?

2.   *Johnson v. Lutz* and *Kelly v. Wasserman* cite the same statutory language yet reached different results. Can the two decisions be reconciled?

3.   To what extent, if any, is *Johnson v. Lutz* reflected in Fed. R. Evid. 803(6)?

4.   After *Johnson v. Lutz*, New York amended its business records exception to distinguish between statements made by persons with a business duty and third party informants. *See Lynn v. Bliden*, 2004 U.S. Dist. LEXIS 19312 (S.D.N.Y. Sept. 23, 2004) (analyzing N.Y. C.P.L.R. sec. 4518(a) and noting that police officer's statements within report were admissible; informant's statements within report were inadmissible). *See also United States v. Vigneau*, 187 F.3d 70 (1st Cir. 1999) (rejecting informant's statements under Fed. R. Evid. 803(6) because not made pursuant to business duty).

PALMER v. HOFFMAN
318 U.S. 109 (1943)

MR. JUSTICE DOUGLAS delivered the opinion of the Court:

This case arose out of a grade crossing accident which occurred in Massachusetts. Diversity of citizenship brought it to the federal District Court in New York. . . . On the question of negligence the trial court submitted three issues to the jury — failure to ring a bell, to blow a whistle, to have a light burning in the front of the train. The jury returned a verdict in favor of respondent individually for some $25,000 and in favor of respondent as administrator for $9,000. The District Court entered judgment on the verdict. The Circuit Court of Appeals affirmed one judge dissenting. . . . The case is here on a petition for a writ of *certiorari* which presents three points.

The accident occurred on the night of December 25, 1940. On December 27, 1940, the engineer of the train, who died before the trial, made a statement at a freight office of petitioners where he was interviewed by an assistant superintendent of the road and by a representative of the Massachusetts Public Utilities Commission. . . . This statement was offered in evidence by petitioners under the Act of June 20, 1936, 49 Stat. 1561, c. 640, 28 U.S.C.A. § 695. They offered to prove (in the language of the Act) that the statement was signed in the regular course of business, it being the regular course of such business to make such a statement. Respondent's objection to its introduction was sustained.

We agree with the majority view below that it was properly excluded.

We may assume that if the statement was made "in the regular course" of business, it would satisfy the other provisions of the Act. But we do not think that it was made "in the regular course" of business within the meaning of the Act. The business of the petitioners is the railroad business. That business like other enterprises entails the keeping of numerous books and records essential to its conduct or useful in its efficient operation. Though such books and records were considered reliable and trustworthy for major decisions in the industrial and business world, their use in litigation was greatly circumscribed or hedged about by the hearsay rule — restrictions which greatly increased the time and cost of making the proof where those who made the records were numerous.[55] 5 WIGMORE, EVIDENCE, 3d ed. 1940, § 1530. It was that problem which started the movement towards adoption of legislation embodying the principles of the present Act. *See* MORGAN ET AL., THE LAW OF EVIDENCE, SOME PROPOSALS FOR ITS REFORM (1927) c. V. And the legislative history of the Act indicates the same purpose.[56]

The engineer's statement which was held inadmissible in this case falls into quite a different category. It is not a record made for the systematic conduct of the business as a business. An accident report may affect that business in the sense that it affords information on which the management may act. It is not, however, typical of entries made systematically or as a matter of routine to record events or occurrences, to reflect transactions with others, or to provide internal controls. The conduct of a business commonly entails the payment of tort claims incurred by the negligence of its employees. But the fact that a company makes a business out of recording its employees' versions of their accidents does not put those statements in the class of records made "in the regular course" of the business within the meaning of the Act. If it did, then any law office in the land could follow the same course, since business as defined in the Act includes the professions. We would then have a real perversion of a rule designed to facilitate admission of records which experience has shown to be quite trustworthy. Any business by installing a regular system for recording and preserving its version of accidents for which it was potentially liable could qualify those reports under the Act. The result would be that the Act would cover any system of recording events or occurrences provided it was "regular" and though it had little or nothing to do with the management or operation of the business as such. Preparation of cases for trial by virtue of being

---

[55] [2] The problem was well stated by Judge Learned Hand in *Massachusetts Bonding & Ins. Co. v. Norwich Pharmacal Co.*, 18 F.2d 934, 937:

> The routine of modern affairs, mercantile, financial and industrial, is conducted with so extreme a division of labor that the transactions cannot be proved at first hand without the concurrence of persons, each of whom can contribute no more than a slight part, and that part not dependent on his memory of the event. Records, and records alone, are their adequate repository, and are in practice accepted as accurate upon the faith of the routine itself, and of the self-consistency of their contents. Unless they can be used in court without the task of calling those who at all stages had a part in the transactions recorded, nobody need ever pay a debt, if only his creditor does a large enough business.

[56] [3] Thus the report of the Senate Committee on the Judiciary incorporates the recommendation of the Attorney General who stated in support of the legislation,

> The old common-law rule requires that every book entry be identified by the person making it. This is exceedingly difficult, if not impossible, in the case of an institution employing a large bookkeeping staff, particularly when the entries are made by machine. In a recent criminal case the Government was prevented from making out a prima facie case by a ruling that entries in the books of a bank, made in the regular course of business, were not admissible in evidence unless the specific bookkeeper who made the entry could identify it. Since the bank employed 18 bookkeepers, and the entries were made by book-keeping machines, this was impossible.

S. Rep. No. 1965, 74th Cong. 2d Sess. pp. 1–2.

a "business" or incidental thereto would obtain the benefits of this liberalized version of the early shop book rule. The probability of trustworthiness of records because they were routine reflections of the day to day operations of a business would be forgotten as the basis of the rule. . . . Regularity of preparation would become the test rather than the character of the records and their earmarks of reliability . . . acquired from their source and origin and the nature of their compilation. We cannot so completely empty the words of the Act of their historic meaning. If the Act is to be extended to apply not only to a "regular course" of a business but also to any "regular course" of conduct which may have some relationship to business, Congress not this Court must extend it. Such a major change which opens wide the door to avoidance of cross-examination should not be left to implication. Nor is it any answer to say that Congress has provided in the Act that the various circumstances of the making of the record should affect its weight not its admissibility. That provision comes into play only in case the other requirements of the Act are met.

In short, it is manifest that in this case those reports are not for the systematic conduct of the enterprise as a railroad business. Unlike payrolls, accounts receivable, accounts payable, bills of lading and the like these reports are calculated for use essentially in the court, not in the business. Their primary utility is in litigating, not in railroading.

It is, of course, not for us to take these reports out of the Act if Congress has put them in. But there is nothing in the background of the law on which this Act was built or in its legislative history which suggests for a moment that the business of preparing cases for trial should be included. In this connection it should be noted that the Act of May 6, 1910, 36 Stat. 350, 45 U.S.C. § 38, 45 U.S.C.A. § 38, requires officers of common carriers by rail to make under oath monthly reports of railroad accidents to the Interstate Commerce Commission, setting forth the nature and causes of the accidents and the circumstances connected therewith. And the same Act, 45 U.S.C. § 40, 45 U.S.C.A. § 40, gives the Commission authority to investigate and to make reports upon such accidents. It is provided, however, that "Neither the report required by section 38 of this title nor any report of the investigation provided for in section 40 of this title nor any part thereof shall be admitted as evidence or used for any purpose in any suit or action for damages growing out of any matter mentioned in said report or investigation." . . . A similar provision, . . . bars the use in litigation of reports concerning accidents resulting from the failure of a locomotive boiler or its appurtenances. . . . That legislation reveals an explicit Congressional policy to rule out reports of accidents which certainly have as great a claim to objectivity as the statement sought to be admitted in the present case. We can hardly suppose that Congress modified or qualified by implication these long standing statutes when it permitted records made "in the regular course" of business to be introduced. Nor can we assume that Congress having expressly prohibited the use of the company's reports on its accidents impliedly altered that policy when it came to reports by its employees to their superiors. The inference is wholly the other way.

The several hundred years of history behind the Act (WIGMORE, *supra*, §§ 1517–1520) indicate the nature of the reforms which it was designed to effect. It should of course be liberally interpreted so as to do away with the anachronistic rules which gave rise to its need and at which it was aimed. But "regular course" of business must find its meaning in the inherent nature of the business in question and in the methods systematically employed for the conduct of the business as a business.

MELTON v. ST. LOUIS PUBLIC SERVICE CO.
251 S.W.2d 663 (Mo. 1952)

VAN OSDOL, COMMISSIONER.

In this action to recover damages in the sum of $45,000 for personal injuries, the jury returned a verdict for defendant, and plaintiff has appealed from the ensuing judgment. Plaintiff was injured when he, a pedestrian, and defendant's streetcar collided at the northwest corner of the intersection of defendant's Hodiamont streetcar tracks and Union Boulevard in St. Louis.

* * *

(3) Defendant introduced into evidence the record of the St. Louis City Hospital which record of July 24th disclosed an "Admission Note," in part as follows,

> This 52 year old white male (plaintiff) was admitted at about 11:00 P.M. this evening. Patient was conscious and rational. *He states that he walked into the front corner of a moving street car where the Hodiamont car line crosses Union Boulevard.* He was knocked to the ground and suffered an injury to his right leg and left thoracic region. X-ray examination reveals a fracture of the neck of the right femur. . . . (Our italics.)

And a further record of July 24th (or 25th) disclosed entries as follows,

> pain in right hip and left chest. *Patient was walking across the sidewalk at Union and Raymond, and either walked into street car or it struck him.* Patient was immediately knocked down and had immediate pain in right hip and left chest. *The patient was not knocked unconscious*, but was unable to get up and had pain and disability. . . ."(Our italics.)

Plaintiff-appellant objected on the ground that The Uniform Business Records as Evidence Law, Sections 490.660 to 490.690, RSMo 1949, V.A.M.S., does not apply to hospital records, and, furthermore, that the parts of the record which we have italicized were conclusions and hearsay.

The Missouri Act is in the precise language as the Model Act approved by the National Conference of Commissioners on Uniform State Laws in 1936. The Uniform Business Records as Evidence Law, hereinafter referred to as the Act, has the purpose of avoiding the many antiquated and technical rules of common law regarding the admissibility of business records as evidence. . . . Courts of other states where the Model Act has been adopted have considered the hospital business within the purview of the statute. . . . *Green v. City of Cleveland*, 83 N.E.2d 63, *affirming* Ohio App., 79 N.E.2d 676. . . . This is also our view. In this connection we note that the term "business" as used in the Act includes "every kind of business, profession, occupation, calling or operation of institutions, whether carried on for profit or not." Section 490.670.

*   *   *

Cases which we have examined are clear in ruling that the statutes making admissible records made in the regular course of business crystallize a rule which is an exception to the evidence-excluding hearsay rule. When the record entry is not of such a character as to give it the status of a *business* entry, the entry is relegated to the status of hearsay and is inadmissible under the hearsay rule. *Green v. City of Cleveland, supra.* "In general, the admissibility, under such statutes, of hospital records in accident cases depends upon whether they relate to acts, transactions, occurrences, or events incident to the hospital treatment." 144 A.L.R. 727, at page 731.

Consistently with the ruling of the *Green* case, a statement recorded by a railroad company of an employee's version of how an accident occurred, assuming the statement otherwise satisfied the provisions of the Act, was held inadmissible because such record was not one made in the regular course of the *railroad* business. *Palmer v. Hoffman*, 318 U.S. 109, *affirming* 2 Cir., 129 F.2d 976.

In *Green v. City of Cleveland, supra*, the plaintiff claimed defendant's streetcar was prematurely started and then suddenly stopped, causing plaintiff to fall to the street and to sustain injury. The reading into evidence of a hospital record containing the entry, "how happened: Fell off streetcar, caught heel," was held prejudicially erroneous. Paragraph One of the syllabus, concurred in by all members of the Supreme Court of Ohio, is as follows, "A hospital record, so far as it pertains to the cause of an accident resulting in injuries to a person causing his resort to a hospital, and not to the medical or surgical treatment of the patient in the hospital, is inadmissible in evidence as a business record within the purview of" the Ohio Act. The Court cited . . . *Palmer.* . . . The Court said it was the hospital's business to diagnose plaintiff's condition and treat her for her ailments, not to record a statement describing the cause of the accident in which she was injured.

We of course must agree with the view of the Supreme Court of Ohio that the entry in the hospital record in the Green case went to the "cause of the accident" and did not record "observable" facts or events incident to the treatment of the patient in the hospital. But we have the opinion that the record entries in our case, which we have italicized supra, reflect the result of an inquiry helpful to an understanding of the medical or surgical aspects of the patient's hospitalization. We do not think that the entries admissible under the Act are invariably limited to "observable" (in the sense of being visual) facts or events incident to the treatment of the patient in the hospital. In our case the italicized entries do indicate, in a way, the "cause of the accident"; but, in our opinion, the entries also indicate how *plaintiff was injured.* We believe the record of the statement made by the patient (plaintiff) in the instant case, in so far as the statement recorded was relevant, and helpful to or of aid in the diagnosis and treatment of the patient's injury, was admissible under the Act.

The hospital wanted to know how the patient got hurt. This was helpful to the hospital because it aided in determining the nature and extent and proper treatment of the plaintiff's injury. The patient stated how he got hurt; the statement was recorded for the apparent purpose of furthering the hospital's business of determining the nature and extent and proper treatment of the injury; and the record of the statement was apparently made by some one of the hospital staff who presumably, in the circumstances of the recording, had no occasion to falsify the record. The record was surely of something — an act, condition or event — in the regular course of the hospital's business.

* * *

The judgment should be affirmed.

WILLIAMS v. ALEXANDER
129 N.E.2d 417 (N.Y. 1955)

FULD, JUDGE.

Dessi Williams was struck by defendant's automobile as he was crossing a street in Brooklyn, with the traffic light in his favor. His right leg fractured, he was taken to Kings County Hospital for treatment. At the trial, the testimony of the parties as to the manner in which the accident occurred was sharply discrepant. According to plaintiff, defendant's automobile approached the intersection, at which he was crossing, without diminishing speed and ran into him. Defendant, on the other hand, insisting that he had brought his car to a complete stop at the light, maintained that another vehicle had struck it from the rear and propelled it forward and upon plaintiff.

In the early stages of the trial, plaintiff introduced so much of the Kings County Hospital record as bore upon his injuries and their treatment. Counsel for defendant thereupon offered the balance of the record and it was received in evidence over plaintiff's objection. Specifically challenged by plaintiff as inadmissible hearsay was an entry to the effect that he had stated to a physician at the hospital that "he was crossing the street and an automobile ran into another automobile that was at a standstill, causing this car (standstill) to run into him." Plaintiff denied making any such statement, and the doctor who recorded it was not called as a witness.

Upon this appeal — following a verdict in defendant's favor and an affirmance by a divided Appellate Division — we are called upon to decide whether the statement attributed to plaintiff, relating the manner in which the accident occurred, was properly admitted in evidence as a memorandum or record made "in the regular course of . . . business." Civil Practice Act, § 374-a. . . .

Section 374-a of the Civil Practice Act permits the introduction in evidence of "[a]ny writing or record . . . made as a memorandum or record of any act, transaction, occurrence or event," despite its hearsay character, "if the trial judge shall find that it was made in the regular course of any business, and that it was the regular course of such business to make such memorandum or record at the time of such act, transaction, occurrence or event, or within a reasonable time thereafter." The term "business" is broadly defined as including "business, profession, occupation and calling of every kind," and among the records within the section's ambit are those that a hospital keeps in diagnosing and treating the ills of its patients. . . .

The statute, similar to those in effect in most jurisdictions, is designed to harmonize the rules of evidence with modern business practice and give "evidential credit" to the memoranda or other writings upon which reliance is placed in the systematic conduct of business undertakings. *See Johnson v. Lutz.* . . . It rests upon the probability of trustworthiness which inheres in such records, by virtue of the fact, first, that they are the "routine reflections of the day to day operations of a business," *Palmer v. Hoffman,* . . . and, second, that it is the entrant's own obligation, and to his interest, to have them truthful and accurate, made and kept as they are with the knowledge, indeed, for the purpose, that they will be relied upon in the conduct of the enterprise. . . . It is this element of trustworthiness, serving in place of the safeguards ordinarily afforded by confrontation and cross-examination, which justifies admission of the writing or record without the necessity of calling all the persons who may have had a hand in preparing it. And it was to assure such accuracy and reliability that the legislature made explicit the condition that the memorandum may be received in evidence — and this is the heart of the provision — only if it was "made in the regular course of [the] business, and . . . it was the regular course of such business to make such memorandum."

As the statute makes plain, and we do not more than paraphrase it, entries in a hospital record may not qualify for admission in evidence unless made in the regular course of the "business" of the hospital, and for the purpose of assisting it in carrying on that "business." The business of a hospital, it is self-evident, is to diagnose and treat its patients' ailments. Consequently, the only memoranda that may be regarded as within the section's compass are those reflecting acts, occurrences or events that relate to diagnosis, prognosis or treatment or are otherwise "helpful to an understanding of the medical or surgical aspects of . . . [the particular patient's] hospitalization." *E.g., Green v. City of Cleveland.* . . .

It follows from this that a memorandum made in a hospital record of acts or occurrences leading to the patient's hospitalization — such as a narration of the accident causing the injury — not germane to diagnosis or treatment, is not admissible under section 374-a, and so it has been almost universally held under the identical or similar statutes of other jurisdictions. . . . In the words of the Ohio court in *Green v. City of Cleveland, supra,* . . . typical of those found in the other cases, "it was the business of the hospital to diagnose plaintiff's condition and to treat her for her ailments, not to record a statement describing the cause of the accident in which plaintiff's injuries were sustained."

In some instances, perhaps, the patient's explanation as to how he was hurt may be helpful to an understanding of the medical aspects of his case; it might, for instance, assist the doctors if they were to know that the injured man had been stuck by an automobile. . . . However, whether the patient was hit-by car A or car B, by car A under its own power or propelled forward by car B, or whether the injuries were caused by the negligence of the defendant or of another, cannot possibly bear on diagnosis or aid in determining treatment. That being so, entries of this sort, purporting to give particulars of the accident, which serve no medical purpose, may not be regarded as having been made in the regular course of the hospital's business. . . . Indeed, in discussing the matter, Wigmore observed that the essential "Guarantee of Trustworthiness" rests upon the fact that "the physicians and nurses . . . themselves rely upon the record" and that the record is designed to be "relied upon in affairs of life and death." . . . Such reasoning, however, will not support the use, or justify the receipt, of a statement detailing the circumstances of the accident where they are immaterial to, and were never intended to be relied upon in, the treatment of the patient. There is no need in that case for the physician to exercise care in obtaining and recording the information or to question the version, whatever it might be, that is given to him. The particulars may be a natural subject of the doctor's curiosity, but neither the inquiry nor the response properly belongs in a record designed to reflect the regular course of the hospital's business. . . .

In conclusion, then, that portion of the hospital record containing the statement assertedly made by plaintiff as to the manner in which the accident happened was erroneously admitted, and, since we cannot say that it did not influence the jury in arriving at its verdict for defendant, there must be a new trial.

The judgment of the Appellate Division and that of Trial Term should be reversed and a new trial granted, with costs to abide the event.

DESMOND, JUDGE (dissenting).

I see no error here, and no reason for retrying this simple question of fact.

Plaintiff, for his own convenience, chose to prove his injuries and the hospital treatment he received therefore, by putting a hospital record in evidence and without calling as a witness the physician who made the entries. In so doing, he of course vouched for the accuracy and regularity of that record. Defendant made no objection but in his turn offered in evidence so much of the same hospital record as showed a statement to the hospital physician by plaintiff that the accident had occurred in a manner quite different from that testified to at the trial by plaintiff. Plaintiff objected to any such "history" going into evidence. His alleged ground of objection was stated in the one word: "hearsay." That of course was meaningless in this context. An undoubted exception to the "hearsay" rule makes admissible extrajudicial declarations against interest. . . . Plaintiff's declaration to the hospital physician as to the way the accident happened was directly probative evidence of a main fact in issue. . . . It is, of course, conceivable (but unlikely) that by plaintiff's use of the word "hearsay" he referred to the failure of defendant to call as a witness the physician who had written up the notes. But plaintiff himself had put into evidence the (helpful to him) parts of that identical paper without calling the physician. Surely, plaintiff could not then demand that the other party prove the authenticity of the very record plaintiff had himself presented to the court. Since plaintiff had been allowed to prove by the record alone the diagnosis and treatment of his injuries, it would be absurd to forbid defendant using the same record, written in the same handwriting by the same physician at the same time, to prove an equally relevant, competent and material fact, that is, that plaintiff had stated to the physician that his injuries were caused in the manner asserted by defendant.

It follows from the above that section 374-a of the Civil Practice Act, our statutory rule as to admissibility of records made in the regular course of a business, has little or nothing to do with this case. What we have here is an admission against interest, proved not by the oral testimony of the person to whom it was made but by an authentic document already vouched for to the court by the opposing party himself.

But let us suppose that this is a section 374-a case. "Hospital records concededly are included within the records to which section 374-a of the Civil Practice Act is applicable." . . . The physician who made the entries need not be called as a witness. . . . True, as Judge Fuld points out, this court has not yet directly decided whether the section 374-a makes admissible that part of a hospital record which gives the history of the injury. But why should this court not adopt a practical and useful construction, rather than a narrow and unnecessarily restrictive one? And the statute itself seems to furnish the answer: "Any writing or record, whether in the form of an entry in a book or otherwise, made as a memorandum or record of any act, transaction, occurrence or event, shall be admissible in evidence in proof of said act, transaction, occurrence or event, if the trial judge shall find that it was made in the regular course of any business, and that it was the regular course of such business to make such memorandum or record at the time of such act, transaction, occurrence or event, or within a reasonable time thereafter." There is no reason why the "history" part of a hospital record, obtained not from unidentified persons but from the patient himself, should not be used in evidence against the patient. Of course, the writing must have been made in the regular course of the hospital's business and it must have been the regular course of the business of the hospital to make such entries. But in this case plaintiff did not object because of any failure to prove those requirements. . . . Indeed, he could not, after himself bringing the record to court, reasonably urge that it was not the regularly made record of this hospital. And he knew, as we all do, that an examining physician, especially in a hospital receiving department, always inquires as to the cause of a trauma. Certainly, in the absence of any suspicious circumstance, it is not up to the courts to decide just how thoroughly a qualified physician may delve into the cause of occasion of the injuries he is diagnosing and treating. Anyhow, all this is by the statute's own words committed to the trial judge's discretion. It is he who is charged with passing on the question of whether the entry was regularly made. Here, no one suggested that it was not so made or called for proof that it was. The trial justice, therefore, had no reason for excluding it, particularly since there was no suggestion that the physician or the hospital had any interest in the case or any possible reason for falsifying these records.

This was a routine trial of a simple issue of fact. Plaintiff said the accident happened one way, defendant said that it happened another way. A hospital book brought to court by plaintiff showed that he himself had described the occurrence in the way that defendant described it. Plaintiff denied that he had made such a statement at the hospital. The jury settled that dispute. It is most unfortunate, especially in these days of congested calendars, that such a case must now be retried.

The judgment should be affirmed, with costs.

Conway, C.J., and Froessel and Van Voorhis, J.J., concur with Fuld, J. Desmond J., dissents in an opinion in which Dye and Burke, J.J., concur. Judgments reversed, etc.

NOTES AND QUESTIONS

1. *Melton* and *Williams* reflect different judicial applications of the same principle (derived from the holdings in *Johnson v. Lutz* and *Palmer v. Hoffman*) which governs the business records exception: that all entries must be germane to the business at hand. *Melton* and *Williams*, however, demonstrate the difficulty courts have encountered in applying the germaneness requirement. Can these two cases be reconciled?

2. Can the germaneness requirement be fashioned in a manner that is capable of more predictable application? *See generally* Powell, *Admissibility of Hospital Records into Evidence*, 21 Md. L. Rev. 22 (1961); Hale, *Hospital Records as Evidence*, 14 S. Cal. L. Rev. 99 (1941).

3. Was Judge Desmond's dissent responsive to the germaneness issue? Did he fully consider the double-hearsay aspects of the case? For example, the treating physician could have testified about plaintiff's statements to him (*i.e.*, admissible as an admission), but neither side called the physician to testify. Instead, the defense proffered a hospital record (*i.e.*, the first hearsay link) that contained plaintiff's statement within (*i.e.*, the second hearsay link). But if plaintiff's statement did not bear upon his medical care (*i.e.*, if the statement was not germane), the treating physician lacked adequate incentive to record that statement accurately; as such, that portion of the entry concerning causation did not qualify as a true business record.

Evidentiary Foundation: The Trial of Alger Hiss[57]

[The background to this case is set forth in Chapter 4, § B.4, *supra*. In his defense, Alger Hiss presented testimony from Malcolm Cowley, a prominent writer, who had met Whittaker Chambers several years earlier. When Mr. Cowley sought to add detail to his testimony, the following colloquy occurred.]

MR. MURPHY: Wait a minute. What are you doing there? You keep looking at something.

Q. [by defense counsel] Did you make some notes that night when you returned to your home?

A. Yes, Mr. Cross.

Q. You may, if you care to, refer to those or any other memoranda which may refresh your memory in telling us what the conversation was that you had with Mr. Chambers.

---

[57] Excerpted from Transcript of the Record on Appeal, *supra*, at 1760–63.

MR. MURPHY: Your Honor, I think the direction should come from you as to what the witness can use and what he can't use. As I understand it the witness cannot refresh his recollection unless he says that his recollection is exhausted and he needs something to look at. But I see him here looking at a memorandum as he is testifying. Now I submit that the witness should be asked whether his memory is exhausted, and then if he says that it is, then I have no objection to his looking at it and refreshing his recollection, not reading from it.

THE COURT: He may not, of course, read from his memorandum unless he says he can't remember otherwise.

MR. CROSS: Well, I understand — I don't want by my silence to assent to Mr. Murphy's statement as to the law — I understand that a witness may at any time refer to a memorandum if it helps him refresh his memory.

THE COURT: You are too good a lawyer not to know the rule which is, I think you will agree, that a witness may not refer to a memorandum unless he states that without it he can't remember, and that by looking at the memorandum his memory is refreshed. I think that is the rule and you will agree with that. I think we are wasting some time.

Can you remember without looking at your memorandum?

THE WITNESS: Yes, your Honor.

Q.   Well have you given us all the conversation that you recall, Mr. Cowley?

A.   No, Mr. Cross.

* * *

Q.   Have you finished describing Mr. Chambers' appearance?

A.   Yes, Mr. Cross.

Q.   Have you the book in which you made your notations that night?

A.   I have, Mr. Cross.

Q.   May I see it?

A.   (Handing book to Mr. Cross.)

Q.   What is this book, Mr. Cowley?

A.   That is one of a series of notebooks which I have kept for years, this one dealing with the year 1940.

Q.   Was it your practice to keep notes in that book of matters that you wanted to keep a record of?

A.   It was my practice.

Q.   Is this a photostatic copy of what appears in the book itself?

A.   It is, Mr. Cross.

(Mr. Cross hands photostat to Mr. Murphy.)

MR. MURPHY: I have no doubt it is a photostat. I object to its being offered in evidence, if that is what you are going to do.

MR. CROSS: I understand that he had a practice of making these memorandum in his notebook, and it seemed to me that that would make it admissible, if your Honor please.

MR. MURPHY: Your Honor, I submit that the man —

THE COURT: It is not admissible.

Evidentiary Foundation:
The Trial of Julius and Ethel Rosenberg[58]

[The background to this case has been set forth earlier in this chapter. Part of the government's case against co-defendant Morton Sobell was based on his sudden flight to Mexico to avoid arrest. In this connection, the prosecution sought to introduce various records from the Immigration and Naturalization Service. This attempt provoked the following discussion:]

COLLOQUY BETWEEN COURT AND COUNSEL

Mr. Cohn: May this be marked for identification. (Marked Government's Exhibit 25 for identification.)

Mr. Cohn: Your Honor, the Government now offers in evidence a record from the Immigration and Naturalization Service of the Department of Justice of the United States, duly and properly authenticated concerning the circumstances of the departure of Sobell from Mexico to the United States.

I will show that to counsel (handing).

(Mr. Phillips and Mr. Kuntz examine proposed exhibit.)

Mr. Phillips: If your Honor please, that is merely a proof of the existence of a paper but not any proof of the fact, and there are numerous statements in this card —

The Court: Well, will you concede that if a representative of the Department of Naturalization and Immigration were called he would testify that that was an entry which was made in the regular course of business and that it was the regular course of business to make such an entry? The weight to be given to it, and so forth, under the statute, is another matter. That is a matter for the jury.

Mr. Phillips: No, I would have to have the man for the purpose of cross-examination.

The Court: There you are on a matter of concessions.

---

[58] Excerpted from the Transcript of the Record, *supra*, at 938–43.

Mr. Phillips:	I would have to find out how the record was made. I object to it. It is a self-serving declaration on the part of the Government and in fact contains statements here which we dispute.
The Court:	I thought that you were anxious to make concessions.
Mr. Phillips:	I beg your Honor's pardon?
The Court:	Here is your opportunity to make one. Now they have to call a representative of the Department of Justice.
Mr. Kuntz:	That is not the purpose of our objection, if your Honor please. I want both your Honor and the jury to understand the nature of our objection. Here is a record produced from the Immigration Department, which I think we can say is a self-serving declaration — it is an arm of the plaintiff in this action.
The Court:	That is not a good objection, I want you to know that.
Mr. Kuntz:	No, wait —
The Court:	Because most of these — this business of self-serving declarations — most of these entries are self-serving in that they are offered for the purpose of aiding the Government's case and doing some damage to the defendants' case. That is the purpose of it.
Mr. Kuntz:	But the point I am raising here, if your Honor please, is that contained in that card is a notation not about their records, their own records, which would be kept in the ordinary course of business — that I believe — but in regard to what somebody else did, and that if your Honor will only look at the card —
The Court:	Well, I assume that what you are saying is so but I want you again to know that there is a statute enacted by Congress that says, in substance, that the mere fact that there may be hearsay in the document is not enough to exclude it. That is something that may go to the weight of it but if it is an entry which is made in the regular course of business, that it is part of the regular course of business to make such entries, even though it might be hearsay, that the record in and of itself is admissible. The weight to be given to it is another question.
Mr. Kuntz:	Well, we cannot see our way clear, because of the statement in the record, to consent to its admission and we therefore object to it.
The Court:	Well—
Mr. Cohn:	Your Honor—
Mr. Phillips:	May I add, if your Honor please, in the paper and the card which are not, I think before you, there are statements not of something done by the person who made the record but of something done by others as to which he could not have personal knowledge.
The Court:	It is perfectly all right. You take the ordinary police blotter, that is a record that is made by what somebody else has told the policeman and he makes a record of it in the police blotter.

Mr. Phillips:	Even that is only admissible for certain purposes.
The Court:	Well, the point is this is only admissible for certain purposes.
Mr. Phillips:	This is purported to be a record which they are now submitting to be received in evidence for the contents as a fact.
The Court:	Well, so is the police blotter but the point is how much weight would be given to it. That is another question.
Mr. Phillips:	But if your Honor please—
The Court:	Let us not argue it any further.
Mr. Phillips:	I simply want it understood.
The Court:	I understand.
Mr. Phillips:	This is not a record made by the man who has made this record, but he is reporting something that somebody else told him as to which—
The Court:	I wish you would take a look at that statute. That is not a sound objection to a record made in the regular course of business. I get your point. It doesn't have to be a record made by the individual himself, on what he himself knows; it can be based on what somebody else told him.
Mr. Phillips:	Can we say someone in New York can make a record of something that happened in Europe as to which he knew nothing? Would that be admissible evidence?
The Court:	If it was part of the regular course of business of that individual to record those statements or those actions, and if it was part of his regular course to do so, then it would be admissible. Look at the statute. It is very clear.
Mr. Phillips:	If he said that somebody told him perhaps it would be that way, but when he states as a fact—
The Court:	Mr. Phillips, that is a matter which you can bring out by stipulation or by cross-examination. It is not based on his own knowledge but that doesn't affect the admissibility of it.
Mr. Phillips:	In the first place, the witness ought to be here so we can examine him.
The Court:	When they brought witnesses from Mexico you said it was silly to bring them.
Mr. Phillips:	There are differences in weight, are there not?
The Court:	Very well.
Mr. Cohn:	If I may be heard on this, your Honor:
	Under Section 1733, Title 28, when we produce a record property authenticated, under and by virtue of the law as provided by the statute, we are relieved from the requirement of producing the witness through whom the record is to be introduced. I think the

	mere presence of a seal and proper authentication makes the record admissible.
The Court:	There must be some testimony that the record itself that you are seeking to admit was made in the regular course of business.
Mr. Cohn:	I haven't examined that question.
The Court:	I think you ought to.
Mr. Cohn:	I will do that. In the meantime the card has been authenticated. Of course, it is a record kept in the regular course of business at a somewhat distant place. It means we will have to fly somebody up to show that this is a record kept in the regular course of business that was sent down here pursuant to subpoena.
The Court:	After recess today get some stipulation on it.

b. Public Records

Comment, *Hearsay Under the Proposed Federal Rules: A Discretionary Approach*
15 Wayne L. Rev. 1077, 1156–59 (1969)[59]

"Official written statements" or "public records and documents" represent a major exception to the hearsay rule. Recognized at common law, the exception has long been governed largely be statute, both state and federal. Premised primarily on the principle of necessity, the exception recognizes the inconvenience that would result from a requirement that the officer who made the report testify as to the authenticity of the official document. Since most trials involve to some degree the daily work of public officials, much of their time would be devoted to testifying rather than the business of government. The guarantee of trustworthiness is related to the presumption that public officials properly perform their duties. It is felt that the influence of an official duty to make accurate statements, coupled with the force of habit and routine, provide sufficient assurances of reliability. The courts agree that the requisite official duty may emanate from statute, regulation, or the custom and nature of the office. It is the existence and sanction of an official duty and the force of habit which operate to insure trustworthiness, not the source or the form of the duty imposed. Consequently, an official record is admissible only as evidence of those statements made pursuant to a duty concerning the specific subject matter of the record. Conversely, the scope of that duty includes all the facts of which the official must inform himself to make the record.

To come within the scope of official duty, the record must have been made upon the personal knowledge of the official. However, the sanction of duty and routine extends to the work of subordinates who are responsible to their superior. Consequently, a record based upon information furnished by a subordinate with personal knowledge of the facts satisfies the exception. Certain official duties, such as a notary's certificate of protest or acknowledgment of a deed, are not delegable,

---

[59] Reprinted with permission of The Wayne Law Review.

however, most official functions within this exception can be and are properly performable by subordinates.

Official statements are generally classified into three categories according to the form and custody of the particular document. An official register or record, the first classification, comprises in a single volume or file a series of homogeneous statements regularly recorded by entries and remains in official custody. Registers and records are largely required by statute which make them admissible as evidence. Registers of vital statistics, voters, real estate deeds, and automobile titles, plus records of the tax assessor, government land office, and judicial judgments present familiar examples.

The second class of official documents is an official's return or report of his activity, a single document made specifically for each occasion and kept by a public custodian. A return is distinguished from a report in that it involves something personally done or observed by the official. A report embodies the results of an investigation of a matter not originally within the official's personal knowledge. The common law only authorized the sheriffs and surveyor's return, but modern examples are multiple and generally are implied from the nature of the office. The weather bureau's records of rainfall, the pension office's records of the issuance of pensions, and treasury records of receipts and disbursements are a representative sample.

The "investigative" or "evaluative" report represents the controversial element of the official statement exception. In certain situations an official has a duty to investigate. At the scene of a fire, death, collision, or other accident, the official examines the premises and consults with possible eyewitnesses. Having made his findings, the official must incorporate the concrete fact discoveries, and often his conclusion as to the cause of the casualty, into a report. Under present law most evaluative reports would be admitted as evidence only of those facts based upon the official's personal knowledge and the rest excluded as hearsay or opinion. Police reports, fire reports, reports of special investigation boards, chemist's reports, autopsy reports, and coroner's reports are illustrative.

In order to be admitted into evidence, an official document must be authenticated. This function is performed by the third form of official statements — the certificate. A certificate is a written statement given to an applicant by a public official concerning something performed or observed by the official or his subordinates pursuant to an official duty. For purposes of authentication, the custodian of the public record certifies an exact copy of the record or, upon specific statutory authorization, issues a certificate paraphrasing the record's contents. The trial court then takes judicial notice of the certifier's official seal and signature. Other examples of certification include the birth certificate, marriage certificate, death certificate, certificates of protest, and certificates of service and discharge from the armed forces. Although the American common law probably does authorize certification of public documents, both Congress and the state legislatures have preempted the area by legislation.

BEECH AIRCRAFT CORPORATION v. RAINEY
488 U.S. 153 (1988)

JUSTICE BRENNAN delivered the opinion of the Court.

In this action we address a long-standing conflict among the Federal Courts of Appeals over whether Federal Rule of Evidence 803(8)(C), which provides an exception to the hearsay rule for public investigatory reports containing "factual findings," extends to conclusions and opinions contained in such reports. We also consider whether, on the facts of this litigation, the trial court abused its discretion in refusing to admit, on cross-examination, testimony intended to provide a more complete picture of a document about which the witness had testified on direct.

I

This litigation stems from the crash of a Navy training aircraft at Middleton Field, Alabama, on July 13, 1982, which took the lives of both pilots on board, Lieutenant Commander Barbara Ann Rainey and Ensign Donald Bruce Knowlton. The accident took place while Rainey, a Navy flight instructor, and Knowlton, her student, were flying "touch-and-go" exercises in a T-34C Turbo-Mentor aircraft, number 3E955. Their aircraft and several others flew in an oval pattern, each plane making successive landing/takeoff maneuvers on the runway. Following its fourth pass at the runway, 3E955 appeared to make a left turn prematurely, cutting out the aircraft ahead of it in the pattern and threatening a collision. After radio warnings from two other pilots, the plane banked sharply to the right in order to avoid the other aircraft. At that point it lost altitude rapidly, crashed, and burned.

Because of the damage to the plane and the lack of any survivors, the cause of the accident could not be determined with certainty. The two pilots' surviving spouses brought a product liability suit against petitioners Beech Aircraft Corporation, the plane's manufacturer, and Beech Aerospace Services, which serviced the plane under contract with the Navy.[60] The plaintiffs alleged that the crash had been caused by a loss of engine power, known as "rollback," due to some defect in the aircraft's fuel control system. The defendants, on the other hand, advanced the theory of pilot error, suggesting that the plane had stalled during the abrupt avoidance maneuver.

At trial, the only seriously disputed question was whether pilot error or equipment malfunction had caused the crash. Both sides relied primarily on expert testimony. One piece of evidence presented by the defense was an investigative report prepared by Lieutenant Commander William Morgan on order of the training squadron's commanding officer and pursuant to authority granted in the Manual of the Judge Advocate General. This "JAG Report," completed during the six weeks following the accident, was organized into sections labeled "finding of fact," "opinions," and "recommendations," and was supported by some attachments. The "finding of fact" included statements like the following:

---

[60] [1] The manufacturer of the plane's engine, Pratt & Whitney Canada, Ltd., was also a defendant, but it subsequently settled with respondents and is no longer a party to this action.

13. At approximately 1020, while turning crosswind without proper interval, 3E955 crashed, immediately caught fire and burned.

27. At the time of impact, the engine of 3E955 was operating but was operating at reduced power.

App. 10–12.

Among his "opinions" Lieutenant Commander Morgan stated, in paragraph 5, that due to the deaths of the two pilots and the destruction of the aircraft "it is almost impossible to determine exactly what happened to Navy 3E955 from the time it left the runway on its last touch and go until it impacted the ground." He nonetheless continued with a detailed reconstruction of a possible set of events, based on pilot error, that could have caused the accident.[61] The next two paragraphs stated a caveat and a conclusion:

6. Although the above sequence of events is the most likely to have occurred, it does not change the possibility that a "rollback" did occur.

7. The most probable cause of the accident was the pilots [sic] failure to maintain proper interval.

Id. at 15.

The trial judge initially determined, at a pretrial conference, that the JAG

---

[61] [2] Paragraph 5 reads in its entirety as follows:

Because both pilots were killed in the crash and because of the nearly total destruction of the aircraft by fire, it is almost impossible to determine exactly what happened to Navy 3E955 from the time it left the runway on its last touch and go until it impacted the ground. However, from evidence available and the information gained from eyewitnesses, a possible scenario can be constructed as follows:

a. 3E955 entered the Middleton pattern with ENS Knowlton at the controls attempting to make normal landings.

b. After two unsuccessful attempts, LCDR Rainey took the aircraft and demonstrated two landings "on the numbers." After getting the aircraft safely airborne from the touch and go, LCDR Rainey transferred control to ENS Knowlton.

c. Due to his physical strength, ENS Knowlton did not trim down elevator as the air craft accelerated toward 100 knots; in fact, due to his inexperience, he may have trimmed incorrectly, putting in more up elevator.

d. As ENS Knowlton was climbing to pattern altitude, he did not see the aircraft established on downwind so he began his crosswind turn. Due to ENS Knowlton's large size, LCDR Rainey was unable to see the conflicting traffic.

e. Hearing the first call, LCDR Rainey probably cautioned ENS Knowlton to check for traffic. Hearing the second call, she took immediate action and told ENS Knowlton she had the aircraft as she initiated a turn toward an upwind heading.

f. As the aircraft was rolling from a climbing left turn to a climbing right turn, ENS Knowlton released the stick letting the up elevator trim take effect causing the nose of the aircraft to pitch abruptly up.

g. The large angle of bank used trying to maneuver for aircraft separation coupled with the abrupt pitch up caused the aircraft to stall. As the aircraft stalled and went into a nose low attitude, LCDR Rainey reduced the PCL (power control lever) toward idle. As she was rolling toward wings level, she advanced the PCL to maximum to stop the loss of altitude but due to the 2 to 4 second lag in engine response, the aircraft impacted the ground before power was available.

App. 14–15.

Report was sufficiently trustworthy to be admissible, but that it "would be admissible only on its factual findings and would not be admissible insofar as any opinions or conclusions are concerned." *Id.* at 35. The day before trial, however, the court reversed itself and ruled, over the plaintiffs' objection, that certain of the conclusions would be admitted. *Id.* at 40–41. Accordingly, the court admitted most of the report's "opinions," including the first sentence of paragraph 5 about the impossibility of determining exactly what happened, and paragraph 7, which opined about failure to maintain proper interval as "[t]he most probable cause of the accident." *Id.* at 97. On the other hand, the remainder of paragraph 5 was barred as "nothing but a possible scenario," *id.* at 40, and paragraph 6, in which investigator Morgan refused to rule out rollback, was deleted as well.[62]

This action also concerns an evidentiary ruling as to a second document. Five or six months after the accident, plaintiff John Rainey, husband of the deceased pilot and himself a Navy flight instructor, sent a detailed letter to Lieutenant Commander Morgan. Based on Rainey's own investigation, the letter took issue with some of the JAG Report's findings and outlined Rainey's theory that "[t]he most probable primary cause factor of this aircraft mishap is a loss of useful power (or rollback) caused by some form of pneumatic sensing/fuel flow malfunction, probably in the fuel control unit." *Id.* at 104, 111.

At trial Rainey did not testify during his side's case in chief, but he was called by the defense as an adverse witness. On direct examination he was asked about two statements contained in his letter. The first was to the effect that his wife had unsuccessfully attempted to cancel the ill-fated training flight because of a variety of adverse factors including her student's fatigue. The second question concerned a portion of Rainey's hypothesized scenario of the accident:

> Didn't you say, sir, that after Mrs. Rainey's airplane rolled wings level, that Lieutenant Colonel Habermacher's plane came into view unexpectedly at its closest point of approach, although sufficient separation still existed between the aircraft. However, the unexpected proximitely [sic] of Colonel Habermacher's plane caused one of the air crew in Mrs. Rainey's plane to react instinctively and abruptly by initiating a hard right turn away from Colonel Habermacher's airplane?

Id. at 75.

Rainey admitted having made both statements. On cross-examination, Rainey's counsel asked the following question: "In the same letter to which Mr. Toothman made reference to in his questions, sir, did you also say that the most probably [sic] primary cause of this mishap was rollback?" *Id.* at 77. Before Rainey answered, the court sustained a defense objection on the ground that the question asked for Rainey's opinion. Further questioning along this line was cut off.

Following a 2-week trial, the jury returned a verdict for petitioners. A panel of the Eleventh Circuit reversed and remanded for a new trial. 784 F.2d 1523 (1986).

---

[62] [3] The record gives no indication why paragraph 6 was deleted. *See, e.g., id.* at 40 (striking most of paragraph 5, as well as paragraphs 8 and 9, but silent on paragraph 6). Neither at trial nor on appeal have respondents raised any objection to the deletion of paragraph 6.

Considering itself bound by the Fifth Circuit precedent of *Smith v. Ithaca Corp.*, 612 F.2d 215 (1980),[63] the panel agreed with Rainey's argument that Federal Rule of Evidence 803(8)(C), which excepts investigatory reports from the hearsay rule, did not encompass evaluative conclusions or opinions. Therefore, it held, the "conclusions" contained in the JAG Report should have been excluded. One member of the panel, concurring specially, urged however that the Circuit reconsider its interpretation of Rule 803(8)(C), suggesting that "*Smith* is an anomaly among the circuits." 784 F.2d at 1530 (opinion of Johnson, J.). The panel also held, citing Federal Rule of Evidence 106, that it was reversible error for the trial court to have prohibited cross-examination about additional portions of Rainey's letter which would have put in context the admissions elicited from him on direct.[64]

On rehearing *en banc*, the Court of Appeals divided evenly on the question of Rule 803(8)(C). 827 F.2d 1498 (11th Cir. 1987). It therefore held that *Smith* was controlling and consequently reinstated the panel judgment. On the Rule 106 question, the court unanimously reaffirmed the panel's decision that Rule 106 (or alternatively Rule 801(d)(1)(B)) required reversal. We granted *certiorari* to consider both issues. 485 U.S. 903 (1988).

II

Federal Rule of Evidence 803 provides that certain types of hearsay statements are not made excludable by the hearsay rule, whether or not the declarant is available to testify. Rule 803(8) defines the "public records and reports" which are not excludable, as follows:

> Records, reports, statements, or data compilations, in any form, of public offices or agencies, setting forth (A) the activities of the office or agency, or (B) matters observed pursuant to duty imposed by law as to which matters there was a duty to report, . . . or (C) in civil actions and proceedings and against the Government in criminal cases, factual findings resulting from an investigation made pursuant to authority granted by law, unless the sources of information or other circumstances indicate lack of trustworthiness.

Controversy over what "public records and reports" are made not excludable by Rule 803(8)(C) has divided the federal courts from the beginning. In the present litigation, the Court of Appeals followed the "narrow" interpretation of *Smith v. Ithaca Corp.*, *supra*, at 220–223, which held that the term "factual findings" did not encompass "opinions" or "conclusions." Courts of Appeals other than those of the Fifth and Eleventh Circuits, however, have generally adopted a broader interpretation. For example, the Court of Appeals for the Sixth Circuit, in *Baker v. Elcona Homes Corp.*, 588 F.2d 551, 557–558 (1978), *cert. denied*, 441 U.S. 933 (1979), held that "factual findings admissible under Rule 803(8)(C) may be those which are made by the preparer of the report from disputed evidence. . . ."[65] The other Courts of

---

[63] [4] In *Bonner v. Prichard*, 661 F.2d 1206 (1981), the newly created Eleventh Circuit adopted as binding precedent Fifth Circuit decisions rendered prior to October 1981.

[64] [5] In the alternative the court held that Rainey's testimony should have been admitted as a prior consistent statement under Rule 801(d)(1)(B).

[65] [6] *Baker* involved a police officer's report on an automobile accident. While there was no direct

Appeals that have squarely confronted the issue have also adopted the broader interpretation.[66] We agree and hold that factually based conclusions or opinions are not on that account excluded from the scope of Rule 803(8)(C).

Because the Federal Rules of Evidence are a legislative enactment, we turn to the "traditional tools of statutory construction," *INS v. Cardoza-Fonseca*, 480 U.S. 421, 446 (1987), in order to construe their provisions. We begin with the language of the Rule itself. Proponents of the narrow view have generally relied heavily on a perceived dichotomy between "fact" and "opinion" in arguing for the limited scope of the phrase "factual findings." *Smith v. Ithaca Corp.* contrasted the term "factual findings" in Rule 803(8)(C) with the language of Rule 803(6) (records of regularly conducted activity), which expressly refers to "opinions" and "diagnoses." "Factual findings," the court opined, must be something other than opinions. 612 F.2d at 221–222.[67]

For several reasons, we do not agree. In the first place, it is not apparent that the term "factual findings" should be read to mean simply "facts" (as opposed to "opinions" or "conclusions"). A common definition of "finding of fact" is, for example,

---

witness as to the color of the traffic lights at the moment of the accident, the court held admissible the officer's conclusion on the basis of his investigations at the accident scene and an interview with one of the drivers that "apparently unit #2 . . . entered the intersection against a red light." 588 F.2d at 555.

[66] [7] *See Melville v. American Home Assurance Co.*, 584 F.2d 1306, 1315–1316 (3d Cir. 1978); *Ellis v. International Playtex, Inc.*, 745 F.2d 292, 300–301 (4th Cir. 1984); *Kehm v. Procter & Gamble Mfg. Co.*, 724 F.2d 613, 618 (8th Cir. 1983); *Jenkins v. Whittaker Corp.*, 785 F.2d 720, 726 (9th Cir.), *cert. denied*, 479 U.S. 918 (1986); *Perrin v. Anderson*, 784 F.2d 1040, 1046–1047 (10th Cir. 1986).

Nor is the scope of Rule 803(8)(C) unexplored terrain among legal scholars. The leading evidence treatises are virtually unanimous in recommending the broad approach. *See* E. CLEARY, MCCORMICK ON EVIDENCE 890, n.7 (3d ed. 1984); M. GRAHAM, HANDBOOK OF FEDERAL EVIDENCE 886 (2d ed. 1986); R. LEMPERT & S. SALTZBURG, A MODERN APPROACH TO EVIDENCE 449–450 (2d ed. 1982); G. LILLY, AN INTRODUCTION TO THE LAW OF EVIDENCE 275–276 (2d ed. 1987); 4 D. LOUISELL & C. MUELLER, FEDERAL EVIDENCE § 455, pp. 740–741 (1980); 4 J. WEINSTEIN & M. BERGER, WEINSTEIN'S EVIDENCE para. 803(8)[03], pp. 803-250 to 803-252 (1987). *See generally* Grant, *The Trustworthiness Standard for the Public Records and Reports Hearsay Exception*, 12 WESTERN ST. U. L. REV. 53, 81–85 (1984) (favoring broad admissibility); Note, *The Scope of Federal Rule of Evidence 803(8)(C)*, 59 TEX. L. REV. 155 (1980) (advocating narrow interpretation); Comment, *The Public Documents Hearsay Exception for Evaluative Reports: Fact or Fiction?*, 63 TUL. L. REV. 121 (1988) (same).

[67] [8] The court in *Smith* found it significant that different language was used in Rules 803(6) and 803(8) (C): "Since these terms are used in similar context within the same Rule, it is logical to assume that Congress intended that the terms have different and distinct meanings." 612 F.2d at 222. The Advisory Committee Notes to Rule 803(6) make clear, however, that the Committee was motivated by a particular concern in drafting the language of that Rule. While opinions were rarely found in traditional "business records," the expansion of that category to encompass documents such as medical diagnoses and test results brought with it some uncertainty in earlier versions of the Rule as to whether diagnoses and the like were admissible. "In order to make clear its adherence to the [position favoring admissibility]," the Committee stated, "the rule specifically includes both diagnoses and opinions, in addition to acts, events, and conditions, as proper subjects of admissible entries." Advisory Committee's Notes on Fed. Rule Evid. 803(6), 28 U.S.C. App., p. 723. Since that specific concern was not present in the context of Rule 803(8)(C), the absence of identical language should not be accorded much significance. *See* 827 F.2d 1498, 1511–1512 (11th Cir. 1987) (*en banc*) (Tjoflat, J., concurring). What is more, the Committee's report on Rule 803(8)(C) strongly suggests that that Rule has the same scope of admissibility as does Rule 803(6): "Hence the rule, as in Exception [paragraph] (6), assumes admissibility in the first instance but with ample provision for escape if sufficient negative factors are present." Advisory Committee's Notes on Fed. Rule Evid. 803(8), 28 U.S.C. App., p. 725 (emphasis added).

"[a] conclusion by way of reasonable inference from the evidence." BLACK'S LAW
DICTIONARY 569 (5th ed. 1979). To say the least, the language of the Rule does not
compel us to reject the interpretation that "factual findings" includes conclusions or
opinions that flow from a factual investigation. Second, we note that, contrary to
what is often assumed, the language of the Rule does not state that "factual
findings" are admissible, but that "reports . . . setting forth . . . factual findings"
(emphasis added) are admissible. On this reading, the language of the Rule does not
create a distinction between "fact" and "opinion" contained in such reports.

Turning next to the legislative history of Rule 803(8)(C), we find no clear answer
to the question of how the Rule's language should be interpreted. Indeed, in this
litigation the legislative history may well be at the origin of the dispute. Rather than
the more usual situation where a court must attempt to glean meaning from
ambiguous comments of legislators who did not focus directly on the problem at
hand, here the Committees in both Houses of Congress clearly recognized and
expressed their opinions on the precise question at issue. Unfortunately, however,
they took diametrically opposite positions. Moreover, the two Houses made no
effort to reconcile their views, either through changes in the Rule's language or
through a statement in the Report of the Conference Committee.

The House Judiciary Committee, which dealt first with the proposed rules after
they had been transmitted to Congress by this Court, included in its Report but one
brief paragraph on Rule 803(8):

> The Committee approved Rule 803(8) without substantive change from the
> form in which it was submitted by the Court. The Committee intends that
> the phrase 'factual findings' be strictly construed and that evaluations or
> opinions contained in public reports shall not be admissible under this Rule.

H. R. Rep. No. 93-650, p. 14 (1973).

The Senate Committee responded at somewhat greater length, but equally
emphatically:

> The House Judiciary Committee report contained a statement of intent
> that "the phrase 'factual findings' in subdivision (c) be strictly construed
> and that evaluations or opinions contained in public reports shall not be
> admissible under this rule." The committee takes strong exception to this
> limiting understanding of the application of the rule. We do not think it
> reflects an understanding of the intended operation of the rule as explained
> in the Advisory Committee notes to this subsection. . . . We think the
> restrictive interpretation of the House overlooks the fact that while the
> Advisory Committee assumes admissibility in the first instance of evalua-
> tive reports, they are not admissible if, as the rule states, "the sources of
> information or other circumstances indicate lack of trustworthiness."
>
> The committee concludes that the language of the rule together with the
> explanation provided by the Advisory Committee furnish sufficient guid-
> ance on the admissibility of evaluative reports.

S. Rep. No. 93-1277, p. 18 (1974).

Clearly this legislative history reveals a difference of view between the Senate and the House that affords no definitive guide to the congressional understanding. It seems clear however that the Senate understanding is more in accord with the wording of the Rule and with the comments of the Advisory Committee.[68]

The Advisory Committee's comments are notable, first, in that they contain no mention of any dichotomy between statements of "fact" and "opinions" or "conclusions." What was on the Committee's mind was simply whether what it called "evaluative reports" should be admissible. Illustrating the previous division among the courts on this subject, the Committee cited numerous cases in which the admissibility of such reports had been both sustained and denied. It also took note of various federal statutes that made certain kinds of evaluative reports admissible in evidence. What is striking about all of these examples is that these were reports that stated conclusions. *E.g., Moran v. Pittsburgh-Des Moines Steel Co.*, 183 F.2d 467, 472–473 (3d Cir. 1950) (report of Bureau of Mines concerning the cause of a gas tank explosion admissible); *Franklin v. Skelly Oil Co.*, 141 F.2d 568, 571–572 (10th Cir. 1944) (report of state fire marshal on the cause of a gas explosion inadmissible); 42 U.S.C. § 269(b) (bill of health by appropriate official admissible as prima facie evidence of vessel's sanitary history and condition). The Committee's concern was clearly whether reports of this kind should be admissible. Nowhere in its comments is there the slightest indication that it even considered the solution of admitting only "factual" statements from such reports.[69] Rather, the Committee referred throughout to "reports," without any such differentiation regarding the statements they contained. What the Committee referred to in the Rule's language as "reports . . . setting forth . . . factual findings" is surely nothing more or less than what in its commentary it called "evaluative reports." Its solution as to their admissibility is clearly stated in the final paragraph of its report on this Rule. That solution consists of two principles: First, "the rule . . . assumes admissibility in the first instance. . . ." Second, it provides "ample provision for escape if sufficient negative factors are present."

That "provision for escape" is contained in the final clause of the Rule: evaluative reports are admissible "unless the sources of information or other circumstances indicate lack of trustworthiness." This trustworthiness inquiry — and not an arbitrary distinction between "fact" and "opinion" — was the Committee's primary safeguard against the admission of unreliable evidence, and it is important to note that it applies to all elements of the report. Thus, a trial judge has the discretion, and indeed the obligation, to exclude an entire report or portions thereof —

---

[68] [9] *See* Advisory Committee's Notes on Fed. Rule Evid. 803(8), 28 U.S.C. App., pp. 724–725. As Congress did not amend the Advisory Committee's draft in any way that touches on the question before us, the Committee's commentary is particularly relevant in determining the meaning of the document Congress enacted.

[69] [10] Our conclusion that the Committee was concerned only about the question of the admissibility vel non of "evaluative reports," without any distinction between statements of "fact" and "conclusions," draws support from the fact that this was the focus of scholarly debate on the official reports question prior to adoption of the Federal Rules. Indeed, the problem was often phrased as whether official reports could be admitted *in view of the fact that they contained the investigator's conclusions.* Thus Professor McCormick, in an influential article relied upon by the Committee, stated his position as follows: "[E]valuative reports of official investigators, though partly based upon statements of others, *and though embracing conclusions,* are admissible as evidence of the facts reported." McCormick, *Can the Courts Make Wider Use of Reports of Official Investigations?*, 42 Iowa L. Rev. 363, 365 (1957) (emphasis added).

whether narrow "factual" statements or broader "conclusions" — that she determines to be untrustworthy.[70] Moreover, safeguards built into other portions of the Federal Rules, such as those dealing with relevance and prejudice, provide the court with additional means of scrutinizing and, where appropriate, excluding evaluative reports or portions of them. And of course it goes without saying that the admission of a report containing "conclusions" is subject to the ultimate safeguard — the opponent's right to present evidence tending to contradict or diminish the weight of those conclusions.

Our conclusion that neither the language of the Rule nor the intent of its framers calls for a distinction between "fact" and "opinion" is strengthened by the analytical difficulty of drawing such a line. It has frequently been remarked that the distinction between statements of fact and opinion is, at best, one of degree:

> All statements in language are statements of opinion, *i.e.*, statements of mental processes or perceptions. So-called "statements of fact" are only more specific statements of opinion. What the judge means to say, when he asks the witness to state the facts, is: "The nature of this case requires that you be more specific, if you can, in your description of what you saw."

W. KING & D. PILLINGER, OPINION EVIDENCE IN ILLINOIS 4 (1942) (footnote omitted), *quoted in* 3 J. WEINSTEIN & M. BERGER, WEINSTEIN'S EVIDENCE para. 701[01], p. 701–6 (1988).

See also E. CLEARY, MCCORMICK ON EVIDENCE 27 (3d ed. 1984) ("There is no conceivable statement however specific, detailed and 'factual,' that is not in some measure the product of inference and reflection as well as observation and memory"); R. LEMPERT & S. SALTZBURG, A MODERN APPROACH TO EVIDENCE 449 (2d ed. 1982) ("A factual finding, unless it is a simple report of something observed, is an opinion as to what more basic facts imply"). Thus, the traditional requirement that lay witnesses give statements of fact rather than opinion may be considered, "[l]ike the hearsay and original documents rules . . . a 'best evidence' rule." McCormick, *Opinion Evidence in Iowa*, 19 DRAKE L. REV. 245, 246 (1970).

In the present action, the trial court had no difficulty in admitting as a factual finding the statement in the JAG Report that "[a]t the time of impact, the engine of 3E955 was operating but was operating at reduced power." Surely this "factual finding" could also be characterized as an opinion, which the investigator presumably arrived at on the basis of clues contained in the airplane wreckage. Rather than

---

[70] [11] The Advisory Committee proposed a non-exclusive list of four factors it thought would be helpful in passing on this question: (1) the timeliness of the investigation; (2) the investigator's skill or experience; (3) whether a hearing was held; and (4) possible bias when reports are prepared with a view to possible litigation (citing *Palmer v. Hoffman*, 318 U.S. 109 (1943)). Advisory Committee's Notes on Fed. Rule Evid. 803(8), 28 U.S.C. App., p. 725; *see* Note, *The Trustworthiness of Government Evaluative Reports under Federal Rule of Evidence 803(8)(C)*, 96 HARV. L. REV. 492 (1982).

In a case similar in many respects to these, the trial court applied the trustworthiness requirement to hold inadmissible a JAG Report on the causes of a Navy airplane accident; it found the report untrustworthy because it "was prepared by an inexperienced investigator in a highly complex field of investigation." *Fraley v. Rockwell Int'l Corp.*, 470 F. Supp. 1264, 1267 (S.D. Ohio 1979). In the present litigation, the District Court found the JAG Report to be trustworthy. App. 35. As no party has challenged that finding, we have no occasion to express an opinion on it.

requiring that we draw some inevitably arbitrary line between the various shades of fact/opinion that invariably will be present in investigatory reports, we believe the Rule instructs us — as its plain language states — to admit "reports . . . setting forth . . . factual findings." The Rule's limitations and safeguards lie elsewhere: First, the requirement that reports contain factual findings bars the admission of statements not based on factual investigation. Second, the trustworthiness provision requires the court to make a determination as to whether the report, or any portion thereof, is sufficiently trustworthy to be admitted.

A broad approach to admissibility under Rule 803(8)(C), as we have outlined it, is also consistent with the Federal Rules' general approach of relaxing the traditional barriers to "opinion" testimony. Rules 702–705 permit experts to testify in the form of an opinion, and without any exclusion of opinions on "ultimate issues." And Rule 701 permits even a lay witness to testify in the form of opinions or inferences drawn from her observations when testimony in that form will be helpful to the trier of fact. We see no reason to strain to reach an interpretation of Rule 803(8)(C) that is contrary to the liberal thrust of the Federal Rules.[71]

We hold, therefore, that portions of investigatory reports otherwise admissible under Rule 803(8)(C) are not inadmissible merely because they state a conclusion or opinion. As long as the conclusion is based on a factual investigation and satisfies the Rule's trustworthiness requirement, it should be admissible along with other portions of the report.[72] As the trial judge in this action determined that certain of the JAG Report's conclusions were trustworthy, he rightly allowed them to be admitted into evidence. We therefore reverse the judgment of the Court of Appeals in respect of the Rule 803(8)(C) issue.

NOTE

Given the limits Rule 803(8) places on the admissibility of public records in criminal cases, some prosecutors proffered these items instead as business records under Rule 803(6), which contains no comparable restrictions. Most courts, however, have rejected such efforts. As the Ninth Circuit observed:

> [D]istrict courts should admit . . . law-enforcement reports, if at all, only under the public-records exception contained in Federal Rule of Evidence 803(8). . . . see also *United States v. Sims*, 617 F.2d 1371, 1377 (9th Cir. 1980) (stating that "the plain language of Rule 803(8) makes it abundantly clear that it is the rule which covers reports made by law enforcement personnel") . . . .

---

[71] [12] The cited Rules refer, of course, to situations — unlike that at issue — where the opinion testimony is subject to cross-examination. But the determination that cross-examination was not indispensable in regard to official investigatory reports has already been made, and our point is merely that imposing a rigid distinction between fact and opinion would run against the Rules' tendency to de-emphasize that dichotomy.

[72] [13] We emphasize that the issue in this litigation is whether Rule 803(8)(C) recognizes any difference between statements of "fact" and "opinion." There is no question here of any distinction between "fact" and "law." We thus express no opinion on whether legal conclusions contained in an official report are admissible as "findings of fact" under Rule 803(8)(C).

Rule 803(8) allows the admission of public records "setting forth . . . matters observed pursuant to duty imposed by law as to which matters there was a duty to report, excluding, however, in criminal cases matters observed by police officers and other law enforcement personnel." Fed. R. Evid. 803(8)(B). . . . "[I]n excluding 'matters observed by . . . law enforcement personnel' from the coverage of the exception," . . . Congress "intended to [exclude] observations made by law enforcement officials at the scene of a crime or the apprehension of the accused and not 'records of routine, nonadversarial matters' made in a nonadversarial setting." . . . [s]ee also Fed. R. Evid. 803(8) advisory committee's note ("Ostensibly, the reason for this exclusion is that observations by police officers at the scene of the crime or the apprehension of the defendant are not as reliable as observations by public officials in other cases because of the adversarial nature of the confrontation between the police and the defendant in criminal cases.").

United States v. Pena-Gutierrez, 222 F.3d 1080, 1087 (9th Cir. 2000).

c. Excited Utterances and Present Sense Impressions

EDMUND M. MORGAN, BASIC PROBLEMS OF EVIDENCE
340–43 (1961)[73]

Contemporaneous or Spontaneous Statements. Rule 512 of the American Law Institute Model Code provides, "Evidence of a hearsay statement is admissible if the judge finds that the hearsay statement was made (a) while the declarant was perceiving the event or condition which the statement narrates or describes or explains, or immediately thereafter; or (b) while the declarant was under the stress of a nervous excitement caused by his perception of the event or condition which the statement narrates or describes or explains."

Rule 512(a) indicates the scope of the rule which James Bradley Thayer deduced from the numerous decisions dealing with declarations concerning an event or condition offered for the truth of the matter declared on the theory that they were part of the *res gestae.*[74] The reception of a declaration made in such circumstances, he explained, did not require the trier to rely solely upon the credibility of the unexamined declarant. If the witness were the declarant himself he could be fully examined as to the facts declared. If the witness were another, he could be cross-examined concerning his perception of the event or condition sufficiently to enable the trier to put a fair value upon the declarant's statement. Furthermore, the utterance must be substantially contemporaneous with the event or condition, and this would normally negative the probability of deliberate or conscious misrepresentation. The event or condition need not be exciting or such as to still the reflective faculties. It need not be the subject of an ultimate issue in the case; it may be an

---

[73] Copyright © 1961 by the American Law Institute. Reprinted with the permission of the American Law Institute-American Bar Association Committee on Continuing Professional Education.

[74] [273] Thayer, *Bedingfield's Case — Declarations as a Part of the Res Gestae*, 15 AM. LAW REV. 71, 83 (1881), LEGAL ESSAYS, 272 (1908).

item of circumstantial evidence. The insistence in the opinions that the utterance be substantially contemporaneous with the matter to which it related fully justified Thayer's theory; but in some instances the interpretation given to "contemporaneous" practically destroyed the possibility of the protection of cross-examination.

*   *   *

Rule 512(b) is in effect a statement of Wigmore's theory which requires (1) an event or condition the perception of which puts the declarant under a stress of nervous excitement, and (2) a statement concerning that event or condition made during that stress, so that it is spontaneous and unreflective. Spontaneity is the test: lapse of time between the event or condition and the utterance bears upon the likelihood of spontaneity but is not decisive. The subjective condition of the declarant which negatives the probability of his contriving anything to his advantage is a guaranty of his sincerity and makes the evidence worthy of consideration. The opportunity to cross-examine the witness is of secondary or no importance although it may be of great value when the declarant is the witness.

Theoretically the Wigmorean doctrine would require a finding of the exciting event based on evidence outside the declaration. There are, however, cases admitting declarations where such evidence was totally lacking or consisted solely of circumstances having very slight value of themselves.

There is little doubt that since Wigmore's great treatise became available to the profession his theory has been generally accepted and Thayer's theory neglected. Multitudes of cases can be explained on either theory; but only a few modern decisions expressly sanction Thayer's view. It is to be regretted that the acceptance of Wigmore has assumed rejection of Thayer, for both theories are needed, and certainly a declaration complying with the Thayer requisites, whether the event be exciting or not, carries greater safeguards for the adversary and at least as great protection of the trier in his effort to value it.

NAGER ELECTRIC CO. v. CHARLES BENJAMIN, INC.
317 F. Supp. 645 (E.D. Pa. 1970)

JOSEPH S. LORD, III, DISTRICT JUDGE.

These are five actions, consolidated for trial, to recover damages for the loss of plaintiffs' machinery resulting from a fire in defendants' warehouse. The verdict was for plaintiffs and defendants have moved for judgment or, in the alternative, for a new trial.

1. *The motion for a new trial*

a. *The admission of statements of defendants' employees*

Lt. P. W. Short, of the Philadelphia Fire Department, twice interviewed two of defendants' employees, Steinard and McElwee. Lt. Short first interviewed Wayne Steinard, who had been engaged in attempting to start a forklift truck by a battery jumper cable when the fire started. This interview was directly across the street from and in full view of the raging fire. Lt. Short's notes of that interview show:

— trying to start tow motor

— spilled gasoline on floor

— had jumper cables then gasoline ignited then cardboard cartons

Short also spoke to John McElwee at the same place a few minutes later. As to this interview, Short's testimony as to his notes was:

> Saw fire in adjoining bay. He was putting a rear in a truck, and I can't make out the next word, in bay area.

About 15–20 minutes after his first interview with Steinard, Short spoke to McElwee and Steinard together, in an office, out of sight of the fire and about a half block away. The following note resulted:

> Wayne took twelve-volt battery to jump forklift right next to the cartons. . . . next to the mechanic's bay in the second bay on the south side. Started the forklift. Told him to shut forklift. Float on carburetor stuck. Gasoline on concrete floor. Told to shut down. Spark from jumper on forklift ignited gasoline. Was in middle of fire. He got burned. Tried to fight fire. Used five or six extinguishers. Gasoline ignited the cartons. Three hundred cartons.

Short testified that his first conversation with Steinard occurred at about 2:30 p.m. During both interviews, Steinard and McElwee, according to Short, were "upset." Further, when defendant Sidney Benjamin spoke to the two men around 3:00 p.m., they were "upset, quite upset," "excited to a degree and quite nervous — I guess their hearts were pounding very bad." As to their ability to answer questions, Benjamin said "they answered more or less in a way that I imagine I would have been, I think, upset. . . ." Fire Marshal Connolly testified that

McElwee and Steinard willingly gave their statements as to how the fire started. He said: "We didn't have to coax them to tell us what happened, how the fire started. They came right out and spoke to us about it and told us."

Defendants now assert that we erred in admitting the statements as spontaneous utterances.[75] In defining the requirements for the admissibility of such statements, WIGMORE, Vol. IV, § 1750 (3d ed.) states:

> (a) *Nature of the occasion.* There must be some *occurrence, startling enough* to produce this nervous excitement and render the utterance spontaneous and unreflecting.

> (b) *Time of the utterance.* The utterance must have been *before there has been time to contrive and misrepresent, i.e.,* while the nervous excitement may be supposed still to dominate the reflective powers to be yet in abeyance. This limitation is in practice the subject of most of the rulings.

---

[75] [1] While the court and the parties referred to them at trial as "*res gestae* statements," we think the better nomenclature is "spontaneous utterances."

It is to be observed that the statements *need not be strictly contemporaneous* with the exciting cause; they may be subsequent to it, provided there has not been time for the exciting influence to lose its sway and to be dissipated. . . .

Furthermore, there can be *no definite and fixed limit* of time. Each case must depend upon its own circumstances. (Emphasis the author's.)

We think that the criteria for admissibility have been met in this case. The startling occurrence was a mammoth and devastating fire, one of the largest in the history of Philadelphia. From time to time it was punctuated by loud and violent explosions. The fire brought to its scene 28 engine companies, 2 fire boats, 6 ladder companies, 1 rescue squad, and between 200 and 300 firemen.

It must be recognized that an event such as this fire is not the momentary shock of the ordinary accident. It is an on-going terror, continuing until it is extinguished or brought under control. And the statements here involved were made at the height of the conflagration.

*   *   *

We have definite evidence of the condition of the declarants as being "upset," "very upset" and "excited." This coupled with the fact that the "progressive event," the fire, was still raging convinces us that the statements were properly admitted.

Evidentiary Foundation: The Trial of Mary Harris[76]

[In its day, the 1865 trial of Mary Harris was said to be "one of the most romantic of the celebrated jury trials in this country. . . ." J. DONOVAN, MODERN JURY TRIALS AND ADVOCATES 35 (1914). On trial for the murder of her ex-fiancé, the youthful defendant's apparent virtue and emotional despair won her the affection of the Washington, D.C. community in which the case was heard. Ms. Harris was acquitted based upon a defense of "emotional insanity." *Id.* at 30.]

[As part of its case in chief, the prosecution offered the following evidence to establish that Mary Harris killed her lover.]

Hugh McCullough, sworn — I saw Miss Harris in one of the rooms of the Treasury building, upon the floor where the body of Mr. Burroughs was lying. I think it is the first room on the left as you enter the eastern entrance. I think a police officer was in there at the time. It is possible he might have left the room, but my impression is that he remained all the time. He was certainly there most of the time. The conversation on the part of Miss Harris was chiefly exclamations. I put but few questions to her. I listened to her rather than carried on the conversation. I think the first question she put to me was, "Is he dead!" At that time, my impression is, that Mr. Borroughs was still breathing. I went out, and returned to her soon after with the information that he was dead. Miss Harris was much excited, and uttered such exclamations as — "Why did I do it? Why did I do it?"

---

[76] Excerpted from J. DONOVAN, MODERN JURY TRIALS AND ADVOCATES 60–61 (1914).

HOUSTON OXYGEN CO. v. DAVIS
161 S.W.2d 474 (Tex. 1942)

Taylor, Commissioner.

Pearl Davis, joined by her present husband, Johnie Davis, filed this suit against Houston Oxygen Company, Inc., and Oliver O. Stanbury, for damages for injuries sustained by Charles Appleby, Pearl's minor son, who, according to undisputed testimony, was by a former husband. . . . The jury returned a verdict for the mother for $4,000 and the $16,000 for the boy and judgment was rendered accordingly . . . . The Court of Civil Appeals affirmed . . . .

* * *

Defendants contend that the courts below erred in holding inadmissible a statement offered by them, made (according to their testimony) by Mrs. Sally Cooper shortly before the accident occurred. Mrs. Cooper testified that on the date of the accident a Plymouth car headed north on state highway No. 35 (in which the minor and several other colored passengers were riding) passed her about four or five miles from the scene of the accident; that she at the time was driving a car in the same direction on the highway and that Jack Sanders and M. C. Cooper, her brother-in-law, were passengers with her. Sanders testified the Plymouth passed them on a curve of the highway, rough and uneven at that point, traveling "sixty or sixty-five miles" an hour, about four miles from the scene of the accident, and that as it went out of sight it was "bouncing up and down in the back and zig zagging." When Sanders was asked if anyone in the car made any statement as the Plymouth went by, plaintiffs objected. Defendants' bill of exception discloses that the excluded statement of Mrs. Cooper, made just after the Plymouth passed by, was, as testified to by Sanders for inclusion in the bill, "they must have been drunk, that we would find them somewhere on the road wrecked if they kept that rate of speed up." The testimony of Earnest Cooper as to the speed of the passing car, and what was said by Mrs. Cooper, was substantially the same as Sanders', except that he (Cooper) said it was ten or fifteen minutes after the Plymouth passed them before they came to the scene of the collision, and that at the time it passed them he observed, besides the occupants of the car, a suitcase tied on behind. His testimony as well as Mrs. Cooper's as to what she said as the car passed by was substantially the same as that of Sanders.

* * *

We have concluded, though the question is not free from difficulty, that the statement of Mrs. Cooper was admissible; that the trial court erred in not admitting the proffered testimony of Cooper and Sanders that Mrs. Cooper made it, and in not permitting Mrs. Cooper herself to testify she made the statement; and that the Court of Civil Appeals erred in sustaining the trial court's ruling holding the statement was hearsay. . . . It is sufficiently spontaneous to save it from the suspicion of being manufactured evidence. There was not time for a calculated statement. McCormick & Ray in the section cited say: "In one class of cases the requirement of spontaneity is somewhat attenuated. If a person observes some situation or happening which is not at all startling or shocking in its nature, nor actually producing excitement in the observer, the observer may yet have occasion to comment on what he sees (or learns from other senses) at the very time that he is receiving the impression. Such a comment, as to a situation then before the declarant, does not have the safeguard of impulse, emotion, or excitement, but there are other safeguards. In the first place, the report at the moment of the thing then seen, heard, etc., is safe from any error from defect of memory of the declarant. Secondly, there is little or no time for calculated misstatement, and thirdly, the statement will usually be made to another (the witness who reports it) who would have equal opportunities to observe and hence to check a misstatement. Consequently, it is believed that such comments, strictly limited, to reports of present sense-impressions, have such exceptional reliability as to warrant their inclusion within the hearsay exception for spontaneous declarations."

UNITED STATES v. NARCISCO
446 F. Supp. 252 (E.D. Mich. 1977)

PHILIP PRATT, DISTRICT JUDGE.

° During the months of July and August, 1975, 35 patients at the Ann Arbor Veterans Administration Hospital suffered a total of 51 cardiopulmonary arrests. An intensive epidemiological and criminal investigation was begun to determine the cause of these unexpected events. In June, 1976 a grand Jury in this District returned an indictment charging the defendants with five counts of murder, ten counts of unlawfully mingling a poison in the food and medicine of certain patients, and conspiracy to commit those offenses. Before turning to the precise issues before the Court, it is appropriate to discuss some of the aspects of this case in general terms so that the rulings which follow may be put in proper perspective.

. . . The fact that the defendants were nurses at the Veterans Hospital at the time of these arrests has contributed to the intense public interest in the case.

MEMORANDUM OPINION AND ORDER
GRANTING DEFENDANTS'
MOTION IN LIMINE

The defendants have moved in advance of trial to exclude from evidence a note written by John McCrery — currently deceased but who is the alleged victim of Counts 1 (¶ 13) and 8 of the Superseding Indictment — which implicates the defendant Narciso. Relying on F. R. Cr. P. 12(a) and (b) and FRE 104(a) the defendants seek pretrial resolution of their claim that the note is inadmissible hearsay. The government concedes the note to be hearsay within the meaning on FRE 802, but denies that it is inadmissible. Since resolution of the dispute would be both time-consuming and potentially disruptive of the trial process, a hearing was scheduled to develop fully the factual circumstances surrounding the making of the note . . . .

The facts, in summary, as they appeared during the evidentiary hearings are: On August 15, 1975 at 4:30 p.m., while a patient in the Ann Arbor Veterans Hospital's cardiac care unit, McCrery suffered a respiratory arrest. Approximately 6:30 p.m.

that same day, in response to questions from his attending physician as to whether he had been given an injection and, if so, by whom, McCrery wrote the letters "PIA" on a Doctor's Progress Note form.[77]

* * *

I.

The government seeks to overcome the lack of trustworthiness the law traditionally ascribes to hearsay statements by claiming that the circumstances surrounding the making of the note in issue preclude defects in memory and the opportunity for calculated misstatements. It argues that both FRE 803(1) and (2) are applicable exceptions covering the note.

FRE 803(1) is the "present sense impression" exception. It provides:

> A statement describing or explaining an event or condition made while the declarant was perceiving the event or immediately thereafter is not excluded as hearsay.

"The underlying theory of Exception 803(1) is that the substantial contemporaneity of event and statement negative the likelihood of deliberate or conscious misrepresentation." Adv. Comm. Notes. These statements are found to be exceptionally trustworthy because the fact that they are *simultaneous* with the event eradicates possible memory deficiencies and fabrication. *Houston Oxygen Co. v. Davis*, 161 S.W.2d 474, 476–7 (Tex. 1942). Comment, *Hearsay Under the Proposed Federal Rules: A Discretionary Approach*, 15 WAYNE L. REV. 1077, 1116–7 (1969). The exception is thought to be most appropriate when the declaration in question is made before the declarant is aware that something startling would happen, so that the distortion brought on by excitement would be avoided. Weinstein and Berger, *Weinstein's Evidence*, 803–74 (1975); Slough, *Res Gestae*, 2 KAN. L. REV. 746, 766 (1954). Moreover, it should be a statement "describing" or "explaining" the event to come within the rule.

A similar exception to the hearsay rule is found in FRE 803(2) — the "excited utterance" exception. It provides that a hearsay statement will not be excluded if it is:

> A statement relating to a startling event or condition made while the declarant was under stress of excitement caused by the event or condition.

While exceptions (1) and (2) overlap somewhat, *see* Adv. Comm. Notes,

> The theory of Exception (2) is simply that circumstances may produce a condition of excitement which temporarily stills the capacity of reflection and precludes utterances free of conscious fabrication. 6 Wigmore § 1747, p. 135. Spontaneity is the key factor in each instance though arrived at by somewhat different routes. *Id.*

In order to come within the rule there must be a startling event or condition and

---

[77] [Ed. — Defendant Narcisco's nickname was "PI."]

a statement made by a person who was under the stress of excitement both while perceiving the event and when the statement was made. . . .

*   *   *

The case before the Court is surely a far cry from the classic situation of an excited utterance where a victim, lying bleeding immediately after a violent wound screams an accusation and a plea for help in the same breath. . . . The testimony of McCrery's attending physician, Dr. Lucy Goodenday, indicates that she noticed the onset of his arrest while attending to another patient in the Coronary Care Unit, at approximately 4:30 p.m. in the afternoon of August 15, 1975, and that at that time McCrery was alert but was not able to speak. His breathing became shallower and then stopped, at which time Dr. Goodenday commenced resuscitation procedures. An emergency medical team appeared in response to her call for help. McCrery was intubated[78] and then connected to a respirator. During the respiratory arrest McCrery also suffered a short period of heart arrhythmia and thereafter went into ventricular fibrillation for approximately 15 seconds. Electrical defibrillation (shock treatment) was employed to counteract that condition and within a few seconds McCrery's heart pattern returned to normal. After intubation was completed McCrery appeared, at least to Dr. Goodenday, to be "quite stable." Lidocine, atropine and neostigmine were subsequently administered. Throughout this procedure while McCrery was not moving, he gave Dr. Goodenday no reason to believe that he was not conscious. He later indicated to the doctor that he was conscious and awake throughout the entire resuscitation.

After intubation had been completed, McCrery's condition had stabilized and the above described drugs were administered to combat further heart rhythm disturbances, to enhance heart rate and vagal activity, Dr. Goodenday stayed for a period to observe McCrery. At that point he seemed to be conscious, and his eyes open and was attentive to his surroundings.

Dr. Goodenday then made rounds on the fifth floor of the hospital and approximately two hours later at about 6:30 p.m. returned to McCrery's room. At that time he appeared responsive, conscious, had a normal pulse and heart rate and appeared generally comfortable and normal. Dr. Goodenday began by explaining what had happened to him, "that he had stopped breathing for some reason and we had put a tube in his throat to make sure that he would be breathing all right."

Dr. Goodenday testified that McCrery understood what she was saying and appeared "somewhat concerned but not overly concerned when I prepped him and started to talk to him."

Dr. Goodenday stated that her motivation for talking to him was "to find out whether or not he had received any medications" as his chart did not indicate that any had been administered prior to the arrest. She first asked him whether he was aware of what had happened and he nodded "yes." She asked him whether he was awake during the entire resuscitation and he nodded "yes." She then asked him if he had received any medication before it all started and again he indicated he had.

---

[78] [2] Intubation is the insertion of a breathing tube through a patient's mouth into the lungs which renders speech impossible.

She asked him if it was given by mouth or through the vein and he indicated by hand gestures that it was administered through the intravenous tubing. Dr. Goodenday then asked who gave it to him, to which he signified a desire for pencil and paper and used them to make the note which is the subject of this inquiry.

Viewing the totality of the circumstances surrounding the making of this note by McCrery, it is clear to this Court that neither 803(1) or (2) are applicable exceptions to the hearsay rule; As stated in Weinstein and Berger, *supra*, at ¶ 803(1)[01],

> Underlying Rule 803(1) is the assumption that statements of perception substantially contemporaneous with an event are highly trustworthy because: (1) the statement being simultaneous with the event there is no memory problem; (2) there is little or no time for calculated misstatement; and (3) the statement is usually made to one who has equal opportunity to observe and check misstatements.

All of these requirements are lacking in the present case. The statement was not made while the event or condition was being perceived by the declarant or even "immediately thereafter" but rather some two hours later. As was correctly argued by the defendants, the applicability of this exception hinges on an absence of time for the declarant to reflect on what happened. The testimony adduced during the hearing indicates that not only was McCrery conscious for part of all of the resuscitation procedure (and certainly after the intubation) and thus had time to think about what was happening to him, before any questions were asked of him by Dr. Goodenday, but he was "prepped" or readied for her inquiries, by an explanation of what had happened to him. McCrery not only had time to reflect on what had transpired, he was intentionally encouraged to reflect on those events before answering. Finally, Dr. Goodenday could in no way corroborate the truth of what McCrery was indicating since she was not present before the inception of his arrest.

These same considerations (*i.e.*, lack of reflective capacity) are relevant to the exception of an excited utterance under 803(2) and preclude its application. That exception also requires that the utterance be made under the excitement and stress of the event provoking the statement and which the statement describes. In this case there was insufficient evidence to indicate that McCrery was excited or under particular nervous stress either when the event occurred or when he made his statement to Dr. Goodenday. The Court finds that McCrery did have the capacity to reflect on what had transpired, that this capacity was clearly manifested to Dr. Goodenday and that the presence of such reflection must negate the assumption of reliability of the statement made under 803(1) and (2).

NOTES AND QUESTIONS

1. To qualify as a present sense impression, the statement must have been made contemporaneously with the even it describes or immediately thereafter. Most courts have interpreted this to mean that the statement must have occurred within a few minutes or even a few seconds of the event. *See United States v. Mitchell*, 145 F.3d 572 (3d Cir. 1998) (40 minutes probably too long to qualify.); *Katona v. Federal Express*, 1998 U.S. Dist. LEXIS 3496 (S.D.N.Y. Mar. 18, 1998) (one hour too long); *United States v. Rosetta*, 1997 U.S. App. LEXIS 28862 (10th

Cir. Oct. 20, 1997) ("a delay of minutes or hours between an event and a statement bars resort to 803(1)").

2.   From a timing standpoint, the excited utterance offers the proponent more flexibility than the present sense impression? *See Christensen v. Economy Fire & Casualty*, 252 N.W.2d 81 (Wis. 1977). This occurs because, in contrast to the present sense impression, the excited utterance is governed by the declarant's emotional condition rather than by the temporal connection between the statement and the event it describes. *Cf. United States v. Carlisle*, 2006 U.S. App. LEXIS 7586, at *12 (11th Cir. Mar. 28, 2006) (the excited statement must normally be a matter of minutes after the event but recognizing that some situations are so stressful that the time may be prolonged — such as in this case where a declarant was shot by spouse); *United States v. Ledford*, 443 F.3d 702 (10th Cir. 2005) (35 minute lapse permissible so long as declarant still excited); *United States v. Baggett*, 251 F.3d 1087, 1090 n.1 (6th Cir. 2001) (statements qualified as excited utterances when offered several hours after the last of three separate spousal beatings over a three-day period). On this basis, courts have admitted statements that might not have qualified as present sense impressions.

3.   Should the excited utterance exception consider subjective qualities which both make the declarant more susceptible to stress and cause his reaction to persist for relatively long time periods? *See United States v. Hadley*, 431 F.3d 484, 504 (6th Cir. 2005); *State v. Edgar*, 317 N.W.2d 675 (Mich. Ct. App. 1982).

4.   Suppose the initial startling experience has passed, but an independent stimulus causes renewed excitement which, in turn, prompts the declarant.to make a statement about the original event. Is this statement admissible as an excited utterance? *See United States v. Lossiah*, 129 Fed. Appx. 434, 2005 U.S. App. LEXIS 7097 (10th Cir. Apr. 25, 2005); *Portillo v. United States*, 710 A.2d 883 (D.C. 1998); *United States v. Napier*, 518 F.2d 316 (9th Cir.), *cert. denied*, 423 U.S. 895 (1975).

[handwritten: one day after event]

5.   In determining whether an exciting event has occurred, may the judge consider the startled statement itself? *See* Slough, *Res Gestae*, 2 U. Kan. L. Rev. 246, 254 (1955); *United States v. Arnold*, 410 F.3d 895, 909–11 (6th Cir. 2005); *United States v. Brown*, 254 F.3d 454, 459–60 (3d Cir. 2001).

6.   May an excited utterance be admissible if the declarant would have been incompetent to testify? *Compare State v. Bouchard*, 639 P.2d 761 (Wash. Ct. App. 1982), *and* Annotation, *Declarant's Age as Affecting Admissibility as Res Gestae*, 83 A.L.R.2d 1368 (1962), *with United States v. Layton*, 549 F. Supp. 903 (N.D. Cal. 1982), *aff'd in part, rev'd in part on other grounds*, 720 F.2d 548 (9th Cir. 1983).

7.   A witness at a homicide trial testified that, during a telephone conversation shortly before her death, decedent made the following statements concerning the defendant: The first thing she [the decedent] said to me was, "It's a man." She went to the door and I could hear some conversation in the background, and she came back to the phone and she said, "It's Joan," and I said, "Did you let her in?" And she said, "Yes, I did." I said, "Well, just be careful." She said, "I will," and I said, "I'll talk to you later." And she hung up. *State v. Flesher*, 286 N.W.2d 215, 216 (Iowa 1979). This statement placed defendant at the scene of the crime. Was it admissible as a present sense impression?

8. As stated in *Houston Oxygen*, one of the justifications for the present sense impression exception is the likelihood that the declarant's statement will be corroborated by another eyewitness to the event. Is such corroboration a prerequisite to admissibility? What does *Narcisco* suggest about this? *See also United States v. Blakey*, 607 F.2d 779 (7th Cir. 1979); *United States v. Medico*, 557 F.2d 309 (2d Cir.), *cert. denied*, 434 U.S. 986 (1977). This issue is discussed in depth in Waltz, *The Present Sense Impression Exception to the Rule Against Hearsay: Origins and Attributes*, 66 Iowa L. Rev. 869 (1981).

9. Does the present sense impression threaten to swallow the rule against hearsay? For example, consider a business record that contains an entry reporting a statement. Assume a hearsay exception exists for the reported statement. Even so, the statement would ordinarily be inadmissible if the entry were not germane to the business at hand. If instead, however, the business entry were characterized as the entry maker's present sense impression of a statement that was made to him, each link of the double hearsay chain would arguably be met and admissibility should result. Does this analysis make sense?

d. Declarations of Physical Condition

Roy R. Ray, *Restrictions on Doctor's Testimony in Personal Injury Cases*
14 Sw. L.J. 133, 134–36 (1960)[79]

First to be considered is the admissibility of statements of the patient about his condition, made to a physician whom he is consulting for treatment. These may relate to present condition or to past symptoms. Whenever such declarations are used to prove the truth of the facts asserted they are within the prohibition of the hearsay rule and must qualify under some recognized exception to the hearsay rule in order to gain admission. For example, if the victim of an automobile collision says to the doctor, "my back aches," and the doctor testifies to this statement for the purpose of proving that the speaker actually did have a backache, this is clearly hearsay. However, it comes into evidence under the well-recognized exception to the hearsay rule for statements as to bodily condition. From such statements evidence of conduct other than statements, as well as statements which are not assertive, must be distinguished. Illustrations of these are inarticulate cries, screams, groans, facial contortions, and like indications of pain or bodily conditions. These are not hearsay at all, and come in simply as circumstantial evidence of the bodily states indicated, assuming, of course, that they are relevant. The same is true of any statement from which a bodily condition may be inferred (other than a direct assertion of its existence) as, for example, a request for aspirin, which would indicate a headache.

Today practically all courts receive statements as to present pain and bodily conditions made to a doctor consulted for the purpose of treatment. It should be noted, however, that language is to be found in some opinions which would restrict

---

[79] Copyright © 1960. Reprinted with permission from Roy R. Ray and the Southwestern Law Journal.

such statements to those made involuntarily in the sense that they were made without reflection and under pressure of pain. This is believed to be too restrictive, since in the very nature of things most of the statements are made with more or less reflection and in answer to questions asked by the physician. In these situations it is the prompting of the bodily condition, and not the excitement from any startling event, which is important. . . .

Statements of past symptoms, past pain and suffering, even though made to a physician consulted for treatment are rejected by most courts when offered as evidence of their truth. . . . It is believed that this position is unsound. The reason usually given is that these statements lack trustworthiness, since they are merely reflective of past occurrences and are not evoked by present pain. Where such statements are made to a physician upon whom the declarant is calling for treatment which he knows will be based in considerable degree upon the statements, there is a very practical motive for telling the truth, namely, the desire for correct treatment.

DEWITT v. JOHNSON
41 P.2d 476 (Okla. 1935)

Per Curiam.

Beulah B. Johnson, a minor, sued to recover damages for personal injuries on account of being struck and knocked down by an automobile owned and operated by the defendant, Ernest Dewitt. Damages were claimed for pain and suffering, impairment of strength, injuries to her leg and stomach, and permanent injuries. The jury awarded a verdict to the plaintiff in the sum of $2,000. From the judgment rendered, after motion for new trial was overruled, the defendant Dewitt appeals. The parties will be referred to as they appeared in the court below.

* * *

The defendant first contends that the trial court erred in permitting the mother of the plaintiff to testify concerning expressions of pain and suffering made to her by the plaintiff, some of them occurring long after the accident.

The plaintiff is a child of tender years, and there was no showing at the trial that these complaints were not spontaneous and natural, but the defendant urges that plaintiffs testimony concerning the same is hearsay and inadmissible. In support of this contention, defendant cites several cases from New York, one from Georgia and a federal court case from the Ninth Circuit, holding that unless made to a physician or as part of the *res gestae*, evidence of complaints of pain and suffering are not admissible.

The general rule is well stated in 64 A.L.R. 557:

> It is a well settled general rule that, where the bodily or mental feelings of a person are to be proved, the usual and natural expressions and exclamations of such person which are the spontaneous manifestations of pain and naturally flow from the pain being suffered by him at the time, are

competent and original evidence which may be testified to by any party in whose presence they are uttered.

. . . In the same annotation it is said:

The facts that expressions of present pain are made long after the injury is received will not render them inadmissible.

WIGMORE ON EVIDENCE (2nd ed.) vol. 3, pp. 684, 687, has the following to say concerning the admissibility of pain statements:

The general requirement (as the preceding quotations indicate) is merely that the statements shall be the spontaneous and natural expressions of the pain or suffering. This principle has in some cases been applied with extreme liberality. The main difficulty here has arisen over the question whether the rule is to be restricted to accounts of symptoms given by a patient in consultation with a physician for the cure of the illness. The origin of this supposed limitation seems to have been the language of Chief Justice Bigelow in a much cited Massachusetts opinion having some difficulties of interpretation. *Barber v. Merriam*, 11 All. 322. (Quoting therefrom.)

. . . Such has been the construction of the language in Massachusetts: and a general limitation to physicians is today not recognized in that state, nor in most jurisdictions, as having anything to do with ordinary present pain statements.

But in New York and a few other jurisdictions following the New York rulings, the doctrine has been established (apparently by a misconstruction of the widely quoted language in *Barber v. Merriam*) that all pain statements whatever are subject to the general limitation that they must have been made to a physician during consultation. . . .

The truth seems to be that the New York limitation is inconsistent alike with precedent, with principle, with good sense, and with itself. Unfortunately, however, its place as a local anomaly has not always been perceived, and courts in several other jurisdictions have accepted the physician-limitation of the modern New York cases as if they represented the orthodox rule. In a few other jurisdictions the limitation has been expressly or impliedly repudiated: in the remaining jurisdictions the orthodox rule, making no such limitation, would presumably be perpetuated.

* * *

Under the authorities cited in WIGMORE and 65 A.L.R. 557, *supra*, as well as the cases referred to in vol. 22 of CORPUS JURIS, at page 267, the general rule seems to be that evidence of complaints of pain and suffering if spontaneous and natural are admissible whether made to a physician or anyone else. We prefer to follow the general rule rather than the New York physician-limitation rule, and accordingly hold that the trial court did not err in admitting the testimony of the mother of plaintiff concerning the complaints made to her by the plaintiff tending to show pain.

* * *

The judgment of the trial court should be, and is, affirmed.

QUESTIONS

1. From which hearsay exception is the exception for statements of then-existing physical condition derived?

2. Presumably the reliability of such declarations stems from their contemporaneity with the condition that they describe, but is there also a necessity justification to this exception?

MEANEY v. UNITED STATES
112 F.2d 538 (2d Cir. 1940)

L. HAND, CIRCUIT JUDGE.

This is an appeal from a judgment entered upon the verdict of a jury, dismissing a petition in an action to recover upon a policy of war risk insurance. The insured was mustered out on December 31, 1918, and the policy lapsed on January 30, 1919; he died of pulmonary tuberculosis on July 6, 1922, and the question was whether he was permanently and totally disabled when the policy lapsed. He had consulted one physician at some time, not definitely fixed, in 1919, and another in December 1920, who found that he had contracted tuberculosis, and that it was already "moderately advanced." By April of 1921 the disease had so far developed that he had to go to a sanitarium, where he stayed till January, 1922, only six months before his death. The only error we need consider was a ruling, made during the examination of the physician who had first examined him in December, 1920. This witness said that he had taken care of the insured both at that time and after he came back from the sanitarium; and he was allowed to testify as to what he found on his several examinations, but the judge refused to let him say what the insured had told him of the "history of the case" . . . .

The first physician who had examined him was dead, and the insured's declarations as to the time of the onset of his disease and its immediate severity were quite likely to be determinative. If the testimony was competent, its exclusion probably affected "the substantial rights of the parties." Rule 61.

The insured's declarations seem to have been offered as a narrative of his past condition; so far as appears they were no part of the basis of the physician's opinion as to his condition; at least they were not offered as such. They were therefore hearsay, and moreover, they did not fall within the generally accepted exception in favor of spontaneous expressions of pain or the like. It is quite true that this exception includes narrative statements as well as mere ejaculations, and that it has been extended to a declaration of present symptoms told by a patient to a physician. . . . The utterances of a patient in the course of his examination, so far as they are spontaneous, may be merely ejaculatory — as when he emits a cry upon palpation — or they may be truly narrative; and it will often be impossible to distinguish rationally between the two; between an inarticulate cry, for example, and a statement such as: "That hurts." The warrant for the admission of both is the same; the lack of opportunity or motive for fabrication upon an unexpected occasion to which the declarant responds immediately, and without reflection. But most of what he tells will not ordinarily be of this kind at all; there may be, and there is in fact, good reason to receive it, but it is a very different reason. A man goes to his physician expecting to recount all that he feels, and often he has with some care searched his consciousness to be sure that he will leave out nothing. If his narrative of present symptoms is to be received as evidence of the facts, as distinguished from mere support for the physician's opinion, these parts of it can only rest upon his motive to disclose the truth because his treatment will in part depend upon what he says. That justification is not necessary in the case of his spontaneous declarations, even when they are narrative; but it is necessary for those we are now considering. This, as we understand it, is the doctrine of *Barber v. Merriam*, 11 Allen, Mass., 322.

The same reasoning applies with exactly the same force to a narrative of past symptoms, and so the Supreme Court of Massachusetts, declared obiter in *Roosa v. Boston Loan Co.*, 132 Mass. 439. A patient has an equal motive to speak the truth; what he has felt in the past is as apt to be important in his treatment as what he feels at the moment. Thus, in spite of the dicta . . . that only declarations of present symptoms are competent, several federal courts have seemed not to take the distinction between declarations of present and past symptoms, provided the patient is consulting the physician for treatment, and Professor Wigmore appears to assent. WIGMORE § 1722. . . . This situation is . . . obviously different from declarations of facts irrelevant to the declarant's treatment, such as what was the cause of his injury. It is true that this body of authority is not impressive as such, but it appears to us that if there is to be any consistency in doctrine, either declarations of all symptoms, present or past, should be competent, or only those which fall within the exception for spontaneous utterances. Nobody would choose the second, particularly as the substance of the declarations can usually be got before the jury as parts of the basis on which the physician's opinion was formed. It is indeed always possible that a patient may not really consult his physician for treatment; the consultation may be colorable. The judge has power to prevent an abuse in such cases, and here as elsewhere, when the competency of evidence depends upon a question of fact, his conclusion is final. He must decide before admitting the declarations whether the patient was consulting the physician for treatment and for that alone. Unless he is so satisfied, he must exclude them, though it is true that if he admits them, the defendant may still argue that they are untrustworthy. They will be evidence, but in estimating their truth the jury may have to decide for themselves the very issue on which the judge himself passed before he admitted them; the competency of evidence is always independent of its weight.

We hold that the insured's "history of the case" as narrated to the physician was competent and that its exclusion was error.

Judgment reversed; new trial ordered.

UNITED STATES v. TOME
61 F.3d 1446 (10th Cir. 1995)

Tacha, Circuit Judge.

I. BACKGROUND

A jury convicted defendant Matthew Wayne Tome of aggravated sexual abuse in violation of 18 U.S.C. 1153, 2241(c), and 2246(A) and (B). In his appeal to this court, defendant challenged the admissibility of the hearsay statements relayed by six witnesses. Each witness related out-of-court statements made by the child victim (A.T.). We concluded that the testimony of these witnesses was admissible because it was not hearsay under the Federal Rules of Evidence and affirmed defendant's conviction. *United States v. Tome*, 3 F.3d 342, 347 (10th Cir. 1993), rev'd, 115 S. Ct. 696 . . . (1995). We reasoned that the government offered the testimony of these six witnesses to rebut defendant's implied charge that the victim fabricated her allegations. *Id.* at 349. Consequently, we held that, even though A.T. made the statements after her alleged motive to fabricate had arisen, the statements were prior consistent statements admissible under Fed. R. Evid. 801(d)(1)(B). *Id.* at 351.

The United States Supreme Court reversed our decision. *Tome v. United States*, 115 S. Ct. 696, 705, 130 L. Ed. 2d 574 (1995). *Supra*, p. 538. Specifically, the Court held that Rule 801(d)(1)(B) "permits the introduction of a declarant's consistent out-of-court statements to rebut a charge of recent fabrication or improper influence or motive only when those statements were made before the charged recent fabrication or improper influence or motive." *Id.*

The case is now before us on remand. Pursuant to our order, the parties have submitted supplemental briefs addressing the remaining issues. On remand, we must first determine whether the challenged evidence could have been admitted under another rule of evidence. . . .

* * *

III. DISCUSSION

A. Testimony of Karen Kuper, Laura Reich, and Jean Spiegel

We first address the testimony of three pediatricians who examined A.T. In their testimony, the three doctors relayed statements made by A.T. either before or during the doctors' physical examinations of the child. At trial, the district court admitted the doctors' hearsay testimony under both Rules 801(d)(1)(B) and 803(4).

Although hearsay testimony is generally inadmissible, Fed. R. Evid. 802, the Federal Rules of Evidence contain a number of exceptions to the hearsay prohibition. *See* Fed. R. Evid. 803, 804. One of these exceptions, Rule 803(4), makes admissible "statements made for purposes of medical diagnosis or treatment and describing medical history, or past or present symptoms, pain, or sensations, or the inception or general character of the cause or external source thereof insofar as reasonably pertinent to diagnosis or treatment." Fed. R. Evid. 803(4). This exception is premised on the theory that a patient's statements to her physician are likely to be particularly reliable because the patient has a self-interested motive to be truthful: She knows that the efficacy of her medical treatment depends upon the accuracy of the information she provides to the doctor. *United States v. Joe*, 8 F.3d 1488, 1493 (10th Cir. 1993), *cert. denied*, 114 S. Ct. 1236, 127 L. Ed. 2d 579 (1994). Stated differently, "a statement made in the course of procuring medical services, where the declarant knows that a false statement may cause misdiagnosis or mistreatment, carries special guarantees of credibility." *White v. Illinois*, 502 U.S. 346, 356, 112 S. Ct. 736, 116 L. Ed. 2d 848 (1992).

A declarant's statement to a physician that identifies the person responsible for the declarant's injuries is ordinarily inadmissible under Rule 803(4) because the assailant's identity is usually unnecessary either for accurate diagnosis or effective treatment. *Joe*, 8 F.3d at 1494. This court held in Joe, however, that a hearsay statement revealing the identity of a sexual abuser who is a member of the victim's family or household "is admissible under Rule 803(4) where the abuser has such an intimate relationship with the victim that the abuser's identity becomes 'reasonably pertinent' to the victim's proper treatment. . . . In so holding, we reasoned that all victims of domestic sexual abuse suffer emotional and psychological injuries, the exact nature and extent of which depend on the identity of the abuser. The physician generally must know who the abuser was in order to render proper treatment because the physician's treatment will necessarily differ when the abuser is a member of the victim's family or household. In the domestic sexual abuse case, for example, the treating physician may recommend special therapy or counseling and instruct the victim to remove herself from the dangerous environment by leaving the home and seeking shelter elsewhere.

. . . Although the victim in *Joe* was an adult, we stated that "the identity of the abuser is reasonably pertinent in virtually every domestic sexual assault case," including those in which the victim is a child. . . . Thus, when a victim of domestic sexual abuse identifies her assailant to her physician, the physician's recounting of the identification is admissible under Rule 803(4) when it is "reasonably pertinent" to the victim's treatment or diagnosis. *Id.* at 1495; *see also* John W. Strong Et Al., 2 McCormick on Evidence 277, at 248 (4th ed. 1992) (hereinafter McCormick). After reviewing the testimony of each pediatrician, we conclude that A.T.'s statements to those doctors were reasonably pertinent to her diagnosis or treatment.

1. Testimony of Karen Kuper

Kae Ecklebarger of Child Protection Services referred A.T. to Dr. Karen Kuper, a board certified pediatrician, for a physical examination. Kuper testified that she examined A.T. on two occasions, in September and October 1990. Prior to the first examination, Kuper interviewed A.T. Kuper testified that the purpose of the interview was "to ascertain exactly what injuries had occurred." In response to Kuper's questions, A.T. told Kuper about the sexual abuse, at times pointing to the appropriate areas of dolls to answer Kuper's questions.

A.T. also identified defendant as her abuser. After the interview, Kuper performed a complete physical examination of A.T.

We find it clear that A.T.'s statement to Kuper was reasonably pertinent to Kuper's proper diagnosis and treatment of A.T. The information contained in the statement was important to Kuper's determination of A.T.'s condition. This statement was therefore admissible under Rule 803(4).

2. Testimony of Laura Reich

A.T. saw Dr. Laura Reich on September 21, 1990, for treatment of a skin rash in the vaginal area that was unrelated to any sexual abuse. At the time of Reich's examination of A.T., Reich was aware of the allegations of sexual abuse. Reich testified that, prior to conducting the physical examination, she asked A.T. several personal questions. One of these questions was whether "anybody had ever touched her in her private area." According to Reich's testimony, A.T. replied "that her father had put his thing in her." The remainder of Reich's testimony concerned her findings and conclusions from the physical examination.

Reich testified that the reason she had conducted a preexamination interview with A.T was "that the child needs to be comfortable with me before I examine her." Because the adequacy of Reich's examination in part depended on the child's comfort with her, we find that A.T.'s statement was reasonably pertinent to Reich's diagnosis or treatment. It consequently was admissible under Rule 803(4).

3. Testimony of Jean Spiegel

Dr. Jean Spiegel, an assistant professor of pediatrics at the University of New Mexico, testified that she examined A.T. for the purpose of offering a second opinion as to whether the child had been sexually abused. Spiegel had extensive training in the area of child sexual abuse, and teaches other doctors how to examine children to detect molestation. Most of Spiegel's testimony focused on the technical aspects of her examination of A.T. and her conclusion that A.T. had experienced chronic vaginal penetration.

On redirect examination, Spiegel testified that A.T. told her where on her body she had been touched during the abuse. Spiegel did not ask, nor did A.T. volunteer, who had touched her. Clearly, A.T.'s statement regarding where she had been touched was pertinent to Spiegel's diagnosis of A.T. The district court therefore properly admitted the statement under Rule 803(4).

B. Testimony of Kae Ecklebarger

Kae Ecklebarger, a caseworker for Colorado Springs Child Protection Services, interviewed A.T. on August 29, 1990. Ecklebarger testified that during the interview, A.T. gave Ecklebarger a detailed account of the alleged abuse, at times using anatomically correct dolls to demonstrate what had occurred. Ecklebarger also testified that A.T. claimed she had told her grandmother and aunt of the abuse. The government argues that Ecklebarger's testimony is admissible under . . . Rule 803(4). . . .

For a hearsay statement to be admissible under Rule 803(4), the declarant need not have necessarily made the statement to a physician. As the advisory committee's note to the rule explains, "statements to hospital attendants, ambulance drivers, or even members of the family might be included." Fed. R. Evid. 803(4) advisory committee's note. Accordingly, the government argues that

A.T.'s statement to Ecklebarger is admissible because the job of a Child Protection Services caseworker "was equivalent to that of a doctor under Fed. R. Evid. 803(4)," and because A.T. understood that Ecklebarger's role was to "help kids."

As stated previously, however, the test for admissibility under Rule 803(4) is "whether the subject matter of the statements is reasonably pertinent to diagnosis or treatment." McCormick 277, at 248. Ecklebarger neither diagnosed nor treated A.T. She described her role as "the initial short-term investigator." Ecklebarger spoke to A.T. two times, after which "the case was sent on to an ongoing protection worker." Clearly, Ecklebarger did not treat A.T. in any way.

Nor did Ecklebarger diagnose A.T. Indeed, Ecklebarger referred the child to Dr. Kuper for a medical opinion regarding the allegations of abuse. Moreover, Ecklebarger testified that she interviewed A.T. only to the extent necessary to make a decision whether a protective order was appropriate. Because Ecklebarger did not diagnose or treat A.T., the child's statement to Ecklebarger could not have been for the "purpose[] of medical diagnosis or treatment," and thus was not properly admitted under Rule 803(4).

* * *

IV. CONCLUSION

A.T.'s statements related by Kuper, Reich, and Spiegel were admissible hearsay pursuant to Rule 803(4). But the statements of A.T. included in the testimony of Ecklebarger . . . [and other witnesses] were inadmissible hearsay. Because the erroneous admission of this evidence was not harmless, the judgment of the district court is REVERSED, and the case is REMANDED for further proceedings consistent with this opinion.

HOLLOWAY, CIRCUIT JUDGE, concurring and dissenting:

I concur fully in the majority's well-reasoned analysis of the testimony of Kae Ecklebarger . . . .

However, I disagree with the majority's conclusion that A.T.'s out-of-court statements to Drs. Kuper, Reich, and Spiegel were admissible under Fed. R. Evid. 803(4). In *United States v. Joe*, 8 F.3d 1488, 1493 (10th Cir. 1993), *cert. denied*, 114 S. Ct. 1236, 127 L. Ed. 2d 579 (1994), we said "the Rule 803(4) exception to the hearsay rule is founded on a theory of reliability that emanates from the patient's own selfish motive — her understanding 'that the effectiveness of the treatment received will depend upon the accuracy of the information provided to the physician.' 2 McCormick on Evidence, 277, at 246–47 (John W. Strong ed., 4th ed. 1992)." (Emphasis added.) It is the patient's self-interest in furnishing accurate information which provides the guarantee of trustworthiness which justifies excepting these types of out-of-court statements from the general bar on the admission of hearsay. *See White v. Illinois*, 502 U.S. 346, 356, 112 S. Ct. 736, 116 L. Ed. 2d 848 (1992) ("a statement made in the course of procuring medical services, where the declarant knows that a false statement may cause misdiagnosis or mistreatment, carries special guarantees of credibility that a trier of fact may not think replicated by courtroom testimony." . . .). Thus, unless the declarant appreciates the fact that giving truthful information is necessary to ensure proper treatment or diagnosis, there is no guarantee of trustworthiness justifying the admission of the statement under Rule 803(4).

In *United States v. White*, 11 F.3d 1446 (8th Cir. 1993), the defendant was convicted of sexually abusing his wife's two grandsons, R.H. and L.H., who were nine and seven years old respectively at the time of defendant's trial. On appeal, the defendant argued that statements made by R.H. to a social worker were not admissible under 803(4). The court noted that in order for the statements to be admitted under 803(4) the government "must show that R.H. understood that he was speaking to a trained professional for the purposes of obtaining diagnosis of, or providing treatment for, emotional or psychological injuries." 11 F.3d at 1449. The court concluded "there is nothing in the record to suggest that R.H. appreciated that it was in his best interests to tell the truth and was therefore unlikely to lie." *Id.* at 1450. "How [the social worker] explained her role and purpose to R.H., how she asked him questions, and how and where she conducted the interview are matters that can provide evidence 'that the child understood the physician's [or therapist's] role in order to trigger the motivation to provide truthful information.' " *Id.*, quoting *United States v. Barrett*, 8 F.3d 1296, 1300 (8th Cir. 1993) . . . n.3.

Here the majority opinion correctly notes that the exception of Rule 803(4) "is premised on the theory that a patient's statements to her physician are likely to be particularly reliable because the patient has a self-interested motive to be truthful: She knows that the efficacy of her medical treatment depends upon the accuracy of the information provided to the doctor." Majority Opinion at 4, citing Joe. The majority thus appropriately recognizes the selfish treatment interest rationale supporting the exception. However, without proof that A.T. had such knowledge, the guarantee of trustworthiness disappears, and the statement then stands on no more reliable grounds than any other hearsay statement.

Turning to the trial record, there is no showing which demonstrates that A.T., who was four years old at the time of the alleged abuse, five at the time she saw Drs. Kuper and Reich, and six when she saw Dr. Spiegel, had the necessary understanding that "the efficacy of her medical treatment depended upon the accuracy of the information she provided to the doctor." . . . A.T.'s own testimony did not establish that she appreciated the importance of being truthful with the doctors. The government did not explore this area on direct examination. On cross-examination, defense counsel attempted to ask A.T. about the doctors she saw:

Q			What you talked with Tara [Neda, the prosecutor,] about Matthew, [the defendant,] that's what I'm asking you about, what you told Tara about Matthew, whatever it was, did you tell that to any doctor? And you can say yes or no or you don't remember.

A			(No audible response.)

Q			Do you remember, [A.T.]?

A   No.

Q   Do you know any doctors, [A.T.]?

A   (No audible response.)

Q   Do you know the names of any doctors that you went to see?

A   (No audible response.)

Q   Do you know the name of Dr. Kuper?

A   Yes.

Q   Is that doctor's job to help kids too?

A   Yes.

Q   Do you know the name of Dr. Spiegel?

A   No.

Q   How about Dr. Kuper, did she hurt you in any way?

A   No.

                          *   *   *

Q   . . . When you talked to Dr. Kuper, do you remember telling her the truth or not the truth, do you remember?

A   No.

VIIR. at 152, 154–56. On re-direct, the prosecutor asked

Q   Did you tell Dr. Kuper that Matthew did bad things to you, Dr. Kuper, the lady doctor?

A   (No audible response.)

Q   Do you remember?

A   (No audible response.) *Id.* at 159.

Thus, A.T.'s testimony is insufficient to establish that she knew the importance of telling the truth to Drs. Kuper, Reich, and Spiegel, and is therefore insufficient to satisfy the selfish interest rationale under Rule 803(4). Likewise, the testimony of the doctors themselves and of Beverly Padilla, A.T.'s mother, shows no such proof. Because the record does not show that A.T. appreciated the importance of telling the truth to the doctors, I must conclude that A.T.'s out-of-court statements to the doctors are not admissible under Rule 803(4). I therefore respectfully dissent from the majority's conclusion that those statements are admissible under Rule 803(4).

NOTES AND QUESTIONS

1. At least one circuit has taken a more restrictive approach to admissibility under Rule 803(4). The Eighth Circuit allows the victim's statements to a medical professional

> only when the prosecution is able to demonstrate that the victim's motive in making the statement was consistent with the purpose of promoting

treatment — that is, "where the physician makes clear to the victim that the inquiry into the identity of the abuser is important to diagnosis and treatment, and the victim manifests such an understanding."

Olesen v. Class, 164 F.3d 1096, 1098 (8th Cir. 1999). This approach, however, has been criticized as unduly rigid. *See Danaipour v. McLarey*, 386 F.3d 289, 297 n.1 (1st Cir. 2004). Suppose the victim makes the statement to a parent who then conveys it to a physician. Does this situation pose special risks in child custody disputes? *See Danaipour, supra.*

2. Suppose the patient visits the doctor to obtain a diagnosis for litigation purposes. Does Rule 803(4) apply? Does the rationale underlying this hearsay exception apply to such situations? If not, does the trial judge retain discretion to exclude a statement that seemingly fits within the parameters of the Rule?

e. Declarations of State of Mind

ADOPTION OF HARVEY
99 A.2d 276 (Pa. 1953)

HORACE STERN, CHIEF JUSTICE.

Proceedings for the adoption of a child must be carefully differentiated from those involving merely a question of its custody; they are of far greater import and involve more serious consequences. . . .

The facts are these: — Bonnie Sue Harvey, living in a small village in West Virginia, found herself pregnant, at the age of sixteen years and while still a pupil in high school, with an illegitimate child. She and her parents made arrangements with the Roselia Foundling and Maternity Hospital in Pittsburgh for her pre-natal care and confinement. After being there for two months her child, Sharon Ann, was born on April 29, 1951. Her father paid the Hospital for Bonnie Sue's board up to that time and also the charges for the delivery. Nine days thereafter she left in the company of her parents, returned to their home in West Virginia, and continued to reside with them until her marriage on August 18, 1951, to Kenneth Stanley; she then went to live with her husband in a small neighboring community. The child remained in the Roselia Hospital until September 27, 1951, when it was placed by the Hospital with Mr. and Mrs. Arthur J. Marhoefer of Meadville, Crawford County, for adoption; they have since had custody of it and have filed the present petition for its adoption. The mother, now Bonnie Sue Stanley, has filed a petition for a writ of habeas corpus to regain the custody of her child. The two petitions being heard together, the court made an order authorizing the Marhoefers to adopt the child and awarding them its custody. Bonnie Sue Stanley appeals.

The Act of April 4, 1925, P.L. 127, as amended by the Act of June 30, 1947, P.L. 1180, 1 P.S. § 2 provides that the consent (to the adoption) of a parent who has abandoned the child for a period of at least six months shall be unnecessary, provided such fact is proven to the satisfaction of the court or judge hearing the petition. The first question in the case, therefore, is whether Bonnie Sue abandoned her child for that length of time. . . .

Did Bonnie Sue abandon her child?

Abandonment has been defined in the authorities as importing "any conduct on the part of the parent which evidences a settled purpose to forego all parental duties and relinquishes all parental claim to the child. . . ."

For a mother to abandon her child means to give it up absolutely with the intent of never again claiming her right to it. Mere neglect does not necessarily constitute abandonment; ordinarily, to have that effect, it must be coupled with affirmative acts or declarations on her part indicating a positive intention to abandon. Abandonment may therefore be effected, sometimes by a mere formal legal instrument, sometimes by a course of conduct. *It is a matter of intention*, to be ascertained by what the parent says and does, viewed in the light of the particular circumstances of the case.

* * *

What, then, was the conduct of Bonnie Sue, apart from her signing the consent to the adoption, to justify the court's finding that she had abandoned her child? Her only acts of commission and omission in that regard, as testified to at the hearing, were (1) declarations made by her at the Hospital that she wanted her child adopted, and (2) that she did not seek to take it from the Hos-pital or pay for its support there, from the time of its birth, April 29, 1951, until December 29, 1951. As to her declarations made before and immediately after the child was born of her desire to have it placed for adoption, there must be balanced against them many other declarations made by her both before she went to the Hospital and after her return therefrom — declarations made to her father, to her mother, to her uncle, to her aunt, to her brother, to another patient in the Hospital — that she wanted to keep her baby, that she intended to leave it at the Hospital for a while but would fetch and bring it back to her parents' home, where she herself was living, as soon as possible; according to her mother's testimony, she wanted, on returning from the Hospital, to get a job as soon as she felt able to work; her brother testified that she said she was going to try to obtain the money necessary to pay for the child's board without calling on her father for its support. The court ruled out the testimony of these witnesses on the ground that such statements were self-serving declarations. This, in our opinion, was error extremely devastating to Bonnie Sue's case. Not only was it unfair, having admitted the testimony of her alleged declarations that she wanted to have the child placed for adoption, to reject her contrary declarations made to these other witnesses, but the rules of evidence do not require the holding of such declarations inadmissible on the ground that they are self-serving. Statements of design, intent, motive, feeling, etc. are always admissible where such design, intent, motive or feeling is the very fact to be proved, and, since such declarations are expressive of a condition of mind, the declarant's own statements as to the existence of that condition are admissible, the only limitations as to their use being that they reveal a then existing state of mind and that they be made in a natural manner and not under circumstances of suspicion: VI WIGMORE ON EVIDENCE, 3d ed., pp. 79, 80, § 1725.

QUESTIONS

1. What relationship, if any, does the state of mind exception have to the exception for present sense impressions?

2. Suppose that, several months after leaving the hospital, Bonnie Sue had told a friend, "I never intended to abandon my baby." Would this statement be admissible under the state of mind exception? Would your answer differ if Bonnie Sue had made this statement just a few days after leaving the hospital?

Evidentiary Foundation:
The Trial of Alger Hiss[80]

[The background to this case is set forth in Section [B][4] in Chapter IV. The defense called Clyde Eagleton, a professor of international law at New York University, both as a character witness and to establish that Hiss' viewpoints and actions had, on important issues such as Neutrality legislation, contradicted those of the Soviet Union. During the course of Eagleton's testimony, defense counsel offered into evidence a copy of *The Daily Worker*, a well-known communist newspaper to establish the Soviet Union's political viewpoint. The trial judge, however, ruled this evidence inadmissible. Did the court err in this regard? Should Eagleton's observations concerning Hiss' statement reflecting his attitude toward the Neutrality legislation likewise have been excluded? Did Hiss' statements about Communist doctrine represent "state of mind in issue" as characterized by Professor Slough and *Adoption of Harvey*? If not, how is such state of mind relevant?]

CLYDE EAGLETON, called as a witness on behalf of the defendant, being duly sworn, testified as follows:

* * *

Q.   Now will you tell us, Dr. Eagleton, just what was said?

A.   Well, I cannot remember details of the conversation, but I was at that time working for the — with the League of Nations Association and for collective security and against the isolationism which was represented by the Neutrality Legislation, and we were trying to get that Neutrality Legislation changed. And it was in connection with that effort that I talked to Mr. Hiss and was very much pleased I recall — this is the thing that I remember most about it — very much pleased to find someone in the State Department who took the viewpoint that the Neutrality Legislation was not the right course for us to follow and that we should take a stand so as to be able to aid England and France in the war — which was the forthcoming war; it was not a war yet.

Q.   What was the Neutrality Legislation to which you refer?

---

[80] Excerpted from Record of Appeals, *supra*, at 2415–19 (Vol. IV).

A.   Well, it was a law passed by Congress for the purpose of forbidding the United States to give aid to either side in the forthcoming conflict — for that reason called Neutrality Legislation. And what we were trying to do was to get help given to England and France, whereas the purpose of the Neutrality Legislation was to keep us out of war, to use the phrase that was used in those days.

Q.   What was the date of the Hitler-Stalin Compact, Dr. Eagleton?

A.   It was in August 1939.

Q.   August 1939?

A.   I do have an official document to show those dates, but as I recall it was around August 20th or 21st, somewhere in there, '39.

Q.   At that time, if you know, what was the attitude of the Communist Party in America with reference to this Neutrality Legislation?

MR. MURPHY: I object to that, if your Honor please.

THE COURT: If he knows he may answer it, but he must know of his own knowledge to answer that.

A.   Of my own knowledge I can only tell of my experiences with the student conferences in which the Communists were trying to get control. And I don't know whether that is a sufficient answer or not.

MR. CROSS: I will offer the photostatic copy from the Daily Worker, September 19, 1939.

MR. MURPHY: I object to it, if your Honor please. It is the rankest kind of hearsay.

THE COURT: The objection is sustained.

ZIPPO MANUFACTURING CO. v. ROGERS IMPORTS, INC.
216 F. Supp. 670 (S.D.N.Y. 1963)

FEINBERG, DISTRICT JUDGE.

This case involves the attempt of a manufacturer of a popular cigarette lighter to keep others from imitating the lighter's shape and appearance. Plaintiff Zippo Manufacturing Company ("Zippo"), a Pennsylvania corporation, alleges both trademark infringement and unfair competition on the part of defendant Rogers, Inc. ("Rogers"), a New York corporation, by reason of Rogers' sale of pocket lighters closely resembling Zippo's. . . .

I

Plaintiff Zippo has been primarily engaged in the manufacture of pocket lighters since 1932, and it has grown spectacularly over the years. Its annual national sales of these lighters grew from about 27,000 units in 1934 to over 3,180,000 in 1958, the year just prior to suit, and well over 4,000,000 in 1961. Today, Zippo produces more units than any other domestic lighter manufacturer. Its pocket lighters are made in two models, the "standard" and the "slim-lighter." The latter accounts for slightly less than twenty-five per cent of the number of pocket lighters sold by Zippo.

*   *   *

III

Plaintiff has relied heavily on a consumer study to prove the elements of its case. This study was prepared and conducted by the sampling and market research firm of W. R. Simmons & Associates Research, Inc. Mr. Simmons, the head of this firm, and Donald F. Bowdren, the project supervisor, appeared as witnesses; both are qualified experts in the field of consumer surveys. Mr. Bowdren testified that the purpose of the study was to determine whether the physical attributes of the Zippo standard and slim-lighters serve as indicators of the source of the lighters to potential customers and whether the similar physical attributes of the Rogers lighters cause public confusion. The study or project consisted of three separate surveys. In Survey A, the respondents, or intervie-wees, were shown a Zippo standard lighter which had all the Zippo identification markings removed and were asked, among other things what brand of lighter they thought it was and why. In Survey B, the same procedure was followed for the Zippo slim-lighter. In Survey C, respondents were shown a Rogers standard lighter that was being sold at the time of the survey, with all of its identifying markings, and they were asked, among other things what brand of lighter they thought it was and why.

Mr. Simmons' testimony and the project report made clear the principles and procedures by which the surveys were conceived and conducted. Testimony to this effect is important, because it is well settled that the weight to be given a survey, assuming it is admissible, depends on the procedures by which the survey was created and conducted.

Defendant objects to the admission of the surveys into evidence. It first contends that the surveys are hearsay. The weight of case authority, the consensus of legal writers, and reasoned policy considerations all indicate that the hearsay rule should not bar the admission of properly conducted public surveys. Although courts were at first reluctant to accept survey evidence or to give it weight, the more recent trend is clearly contrary. Surveys are now admitted over the hearsay objection on two technically distinct bases. Some cases hold that surveys are not hearsay at all; other cases hold that surveys are hearsay but are admissible because they are within the recognized exception to the hearsay rule for statements of present state of mind, attitude, or belief. Still other cases admit surveys without stating the ground on which they are admitted.

The cases holding that surveys are not hearsay do so on the basis that the surveys are not offered to prove the truth of what respondents said and, therefore, do not fall within the classic definition of hearsay. This approach has been criticized because, it is said, the answers to questions in a survey designed to prove the existence of a specific idea in the public mind are offered to prove the truth of the matter contained in these answers. Under this argument, when a respondent is asked to identify the brand of an unmarked lighter, the answer of each respondent who thinks the lighter is a Zippo is regarded as if he said, "I believe that this unmarked lighter is a Zippo." Since the matter to be proved in a secondary meaning case is respondent's belief that the lighter shown him is a Zippo lighter, a respondent's answer is hearsay in the classic sense. Others have criticized the non-hearsay characterization, regardless of whether surveys are offered to prove the truth of what respondents said, because the answers in a survey depend for their probative value on the sincerity of respondents. One of the purposes of the hearsay rule is to subject to cross-examination statements which depend on the declarant's narrative sincerity. *See* Morgan, *Hearsay Dangers and the Application of the Hearsay Concept*, 62 HARV. L. REV. 177 (1948). The answer of a respondent that he thinks an unmarked lighter is a Zippo is relevant to the issue of secondary meaning only if, in fact, the respondent really does believe that the unmarked lighter is a Zippo. Under this view, therefore, answers in a survey should be regarded as hearsay.

Regardless of whether the surveys in this case could be admitted under the non-hearsay approach, they are admissible because the answers of respondents are expressions of presently existing state of mind, attitude, or belief. There is a recognized exception to the hearsay rule for such statements, and under it the statements are admissible to prove the truth of the matter contained therein.

Even if the surveys did not fit within this exception, well-reasoned authority justifies their admission under the following approach: the determination that a statement is hearsay does not end the inquiry into admissibility; there must still be a further examination of the need for the statement at trial and the circumstantial guaranty of trustworthiness surrounding the making of the statement. This approach has been used to justify the admissibility of a survey.

Necessity in this context requires a comparison of the probative value of the survey with the evidence, if any, which as a practical matter could be used if the survey were excluded. If the survey is more valuable, the necessity exists for the survey, *i.e.*, it is the inability to get "evidence of the same value" which makes the hearsay statement necessary. When, as here, the state of mind of the smoking population (115,000,000 people) is the issue, a scientifically conducted survey is necessary because the practical alternatives do not produce equally probative evidence. With such a survey, the results are probably approximately the same as would be obtained if each of the 115,000,000 people were interviewed. The alternative of having 115,000,000 people testify in court is obviously impractical. The alternatives of having a much smaller section of the public testify (such as eighty witnesses) or using expert witnesses to testify to the state of the public mind are clearly not as valuable because the inferences which can be drawn from such testimony to the public state of mind are not as strong or as direct as the justifiable inferences from a scientific survey.

The second element involved in this approach is the guaranty of trustworthiness supplied by the circumstances under which the out-of-court statements were made. A logical step in this inquiry is to see which of the hearsay dangers are present. With regard to these surveys: there is no danger of faulty memory; the danger of faulty perception is negligible because respondents need only examine two or three cigarette lighters at most; the danger of faulty narration is equally negligible since the answers called for are simple. The only appreciable danger is that the respondent is insincere. But this danger is minimized by the circumstances of this or any public opinion poll in which scientific sampling is employed, because members of the public who are asked questions about things in which they have no interest have no reason to falsify their feelings. While the sampling procedure substantially guarantees trustworthiness insofar as the respondent's sincerity is concerned, other survey techniques substantially insure trustworthiness in other respects. If questions are unfairly worded to suggest answers favorable to the party sponsoring the survey, the element of trustworthiness in the poll would be lacking. The same result would follow if the interviewers asked fair questions in a leading manner. Thus, the methodology of the survey bears directly on trustworthiness, as it does on necessity. Since the two elements of necessity and trustworthiness are satisfied, I would admit these surveys under this approach to the hearsay rule, even apart from the state of mind exception.[81]

MUTUAL LIFE INSURANCE CO. v. HILLMON
145 U.S. 285 (1892)

[This case was brought by Sallie E. Hillmon as an action on four life insurance policies that had been issued to her husband, John W. Hillmon. At issue was whether a body found at a campsite in Crooked Creek, Kansas was that of the insured. The insurance companies maintained that the corpse was that of one Frederick Adolph Walters. In support of this defense, the insurance companies sought to introduce evidence of letters in which Walters had expressed his intention to travel with Hillmon to "Colorado or parts unknown to me." This evidence, however, was excluded at trial.]

MR. JUSTICE GRAY . . . delivered the opinion of the court.

* * *

There is, however, one question of evidence so important, so fully argued at the bar, and so likely to arise upon another trial, that it is proper to express an opinion upon it.

This question is of the admissibility of the letters written by Walters on the first days of March, 1879, which were offered in evidence by the defendants, and excluded by the court. In order to determine the competency of these letters, it is important to consider the state of the case when they were offered to be read.

---

[81] [104] *Irvin v. State*, 66 So.2d 288, 191–92 (Fla. 1953), *cert. denied*, 346 U.S. 927, 74 S. Ct. 316, 98 L. Ed. 419 (1954), raises a possible objection not stressed by defendant — "multiple hearsay." The multiple hearsay argument is as follows: when answers made by respondents to interviewers are admissible under a hearsay exception, the interviewers can testify to these answers; but when the interviewers themselves do not testify but instead "tell" these answers to another person in the market research organization who then testifies as to the answers, this testimony is inadmissible hearsay because the witness is relating what the interviewers told him rather than what respondents in the survey told him. I conclude that this argument should not preclude the admission of a properly conducted survey, possibly because the business entries exception to the hearsay rule covers the transmission of the answers from the interviewers to other people in the organization, at least where the organization involved is in the business of conducting and reporting on surveys, *see* 52 MICH. L. REV. 914 (1954).

The matter chiefly contested at the trial was the death of John W. Hillmon, the insured; and that depended upon the question whether the body found at Crooked Creek on the night of March 18, 1879, was his body, or the body of one Walters.

Much conflicting evidence had been introduced as to the identity of the body. The plaintiff had also introduced evidence that Hillmon and one Brown left Wichita in Kansas on or about March 5, 1879, and traveled together through Southern Kansas in search of a site for a cattle ranch, and that on the night of March 18, while they were in camp at Crooked Creek, Hillmon was accidentally killed, and that his body was taken thence and buried. The defendants had introduced evidence without objection, that Walters left his home and his betrothed in Iowa in March, 1878, and was afterwards in Kansas until March, 1879; that during that time he corresponded regularly with his family and his betrothed; that the last letters received from him were one received by his betrothed on March 3 and postmarked at Wichita March 2, and one received by his sister about March 4 or 5, and dated at Wichita a day or two before; and that he had not been heard from since.

The evidence that Walters was at Wichita on or before March 5, and had not been heard from since, together with the evidence to identify as his the body found at Crooked Creek on March 18, tended to show that he went from Wichita to Crooked Creek between those dates. Evidence that just before March 5 he had the intention of leaving Wichita with Hillmon would tend to corroborate the evidence already admitted, and to show that he went from Wichita to Crooked Creek with Hillmon. Letters from him to his family and his betrothed were the natural, if not the only attainable, evidence of his intention.

The position, taken at the bar, that the letters were competent evidence, within the rule stated in *Nicholls v. Webb*, 8 Wheat. 326, 337, as memoranda made in the ordinary course of business, cannot be maintained, for they were clearly not such.

But upon another ground [it is] suggested they should have been admitted. A man's state of mind or feeling can only be manifested to others by countenance, attitude or gesture, or by sounds or words, spoken or written. The nature of the fact to be proved is the same, and evidence of its proper tokens is equally competent to prove it, whether expressed by aspect or conduct, by voice or pen. . . . Whenever the intention is of itself a distinct and material fact in a chain or circumstances, it may be proved by contemporaneous oral or written declarations of the party.

The existence of a particular intention in a certain person at a certain time being a material fact to be proved, evidence that he expressed that intention at that time is as direct evidence of the fact, as his own testimony that he then had that intention would be. After his death there can hardly be any other way of proving it; and while he is still alive, his own memory of his state of mind at a former time is no more likely to be clear and true than a bystander's recollection of what he then said, and is less trustworthy than letters written by him at the very time and under circumstances precluding a suspicion of misrepresentation.

The letters in question were competent, not as narratives of facts communicated to the writer by others, nor yet as proof that he actually went away from Wichita, but as evidence that, shortly before the time when other evidence tended to show that he went away, he had the intention of going, and of going with Hillmon, which made it more probable both that he did go and that he went with Hillmon, than if there had been no proof of such intention. In view of the mass of conflicting testimony introduced on the question whether it was the body of Walters that was found in Hillmon's camp, this evidence might properly influence the jury in determining that question.

Upon principle and authority, therefore, we are of opinion that the two letters were competent evidence of the intention of Walters at the time of writing them, which was a material fact bearing upon the question in controversy; and that for the exclusion of these letters, as well as for the undue restriction of the defendants' challenges, the verdicts must be set aside, and a new trial had.

John M. Maguire, *The* Hillmon *Case — Thirty-Three Years After*
38 HARV. L. REV. 709 (1925)[82]

I

The *Hillmon* case has reached respectable middle age. More than forty-six years ago Frederick Adolph Walters, then at Wichita, Kansas, wrote letters to his sister and his sweetheart in Fort Madison, Iowa, declaring his intention to leave on an early date "with a certain Mr. Hillmon, a sheep-trader, for Colorado or parts unknown to me." The rest is silence. None of the persons who would naturally have heard from Walters if alive ever had any later communication of his existence or whereabouts. "Parts unknown" evidently included eternity.

Eternity, but not oblivion. About two weeks after Walters wrote his last letters a man was shot and killed at Crooked Creek, Kansas. Around the body raged a dispute as famous in its time as the fight over the body of Patroclus. For Hillmon had recently and heavily insured his life, and the dead man was said to be Hillmon. The insurance companies, resisting collection on the policies, and claiming that the deceased was not Hillmon at all but Walters, entered upon bitterly contested litigation. After two disagreements, the jury in the third trial found for the plaintiff. But on May 16, 1892, the Supreme Court of the United States reversed the resulting judgment and ordered a fourth trial. The Court took occasion to state that Walters' two letters were admissible in evidence and had been improperly excluded. This was because

(a) The declarations in the letters tended to prove Walters' "intention of going, and of going with Hillmon,"

(b) thus rendering it "more probable that he did go and that he went with Hillmon,"

(c) which increased probability in turn made possible the inference that Walters, an available victim, was murdered and that his corpse was used in the nefarious way asserted.

The controversy by virtue of its picturesque quality soon caught the public eye.

During twenty-three years of pendency it supplied many items for the newspapers. Realization, or at least expression, of its profound technical possibilities came more slowly. The editors of the Harvard Law Review saw only an evidential ruling stamped with practicality and common sense. The first edition of Wigmore's great work readily accepted this ruling. Dissent is not clearly voiced in Chamberlayne's ponderous volumes. Some jurisdictions, notably Illinois, refused to concur, but the dissentient opinions express no very noteworthy considerations. Not until twenty years after the Supreme Court decision was its significance really probed. Then came an acute article by Mr. Eustace Seligman, printed in the Harvard Law Review but sounding an entirely different chord from that of the earlier editorial comment. The author developed the disquieting proposition that if the state of mind which we call intention, proved in the standard manner by declarations of the person entertaining the intention, is considered material to an effort to prove the occurrence of the intended act, so likewise is the state of mind which we call memory, similarly proved, to be considered material to an effort to prove a past fact. This proposition is disquieting because it undermines our whole general doctrine of excluding hearsay evidence. That Mr. Seligman not only convinced himself but also affected the views of others is sufficiently indicated in an address by his former Evidence professor, the late Dean Thayer, before the Rhode Island Bar Association in 1914. Speaking of the doctrine in question, the Dean said:

> Yet even here more than one safety valve has automatically established itself. The use of declarations as evidence of a mental state, itself to be used in turn as circumstantial evidence of fact asserted, furnished attractive opportunities for extensions which if carried to their logical extreme would leave the hearsay rule scarcely discoverable.

It happened that the speaker had peculiar knowledge of his topic. For he was secretary to Mr. Justice Gray when that learned judge prepared the *Hillmon* opinion. Here is a striking passage from Dean Thayer's rough working notes on Evidence:

> That the doctrine of the *Hillmon* case is a new one no one knows better than I, as I remember how the opinion came to be written. In point of fact the point was miserably argued counsel putting it on practically no ground except course of business. The court voted to sustain the exceptions on general principles (N. B. Brown's comment as to "graveyard insurance") and Judge Gray was in dense darkness about the matter except as I fed him with matter obtained from J.B.T.[83] as he was writing the opinion. . . . [O]ne must remain in some doubt how generally and how fully it is to be accepted, but it seems that it has come to stay, and furthermore that it is sound and wise. The impossibility of drawing the line between voluntary and involuntary statements and the unsatisfactory nature of the *res gestae* limitations as applied to these cases leave the law in such a state that some broad and simple rule like this is really necessary.

From the foregoing description one is led to believe that luck rather than anything else prevented a more radical disturbance of the hearsay rule in the

---

[83] [12] Professor James Bradley Thayer.

Hillmon case itself. The Court was in no mood to dally with trifles, and might well have rendered an opinion to the effect that expressed memory is sometimes proper circumstantial evidence of past fact, if the state of the record had called for such a pronouncement. . . .

II

However, even though the extreme holding which later excited Mr. Seligman's apprehensions was at the moment avoided, the opinion under consideration can hardly be described as a gentle or tentative introduction of a new rule. It carries us past three or four possible stopping points.

1. Suppose a young man is negligently killed. At the time of his death he had not yet begun to contribute to the support of his parents. They bring suit for wrongful death under a statute conditioning either their right of action or the *quantum* of damages upon the reasonable anticipation of financial contributions from their son. They offer evidence of his frequent declarations that he would support them in their old age. Here intention has been frustrated. We can prove no more than the likelihood of an act. The natural, very likely the only, evidence of the parents' expectations lies in the son's declarations. Moreover, there is little risk that either court or jury will be misled into lending this evidence undue weight. The gap between expectation and realization is perfectly apparent. Evidence of intention might be allowed here without being allowed in any more advanced situation.

2. Take the next logical step. A controversy arises as to whether a certain deed was delivered to the grantee, or whether he stole it and wrongfully recorded it. Evidence is offered that the grantor asserted a present intention not to deliver the deed. It is always hard to prove a negative. Again it seems natural and in a sense necessary, although not quite so unobjectionable as in the preceding case, to make circumstantial use of our evidence of intention.

3. The third case is a prosecution for homicide. The defendant claims that the decedent killed himself, and offers evidence of his declarations indicating suicidal plan or design. Here is an ambiguous event to be explained, and we are told that a person having power to cause the event expressed his intention to cause it. We might accept this evidence, but refuse to carry the principle further.

4. The *Hillmon* situation resembles the one just put. There is a difference, however. The evidence offered bore less directly upon the ultimate question: "Was the dead man Hillmon or Walters?" It was intended to provide an inferential answer to the intermediate question: "When, with whom, and for what destination did Walters leave Wichita?" We must attach yet another inference to identify the deceased with Walters. This increases the remoteness of evidence at best none too close to the event. The jury may not perceive the additional logical jump, and may reason too directly and strongly from the probability that Walters left Wichita with Hillmon to the possibility that he was murdered to provide a corpse for an insurance fraud.

But the Supreme Court cleared all four hurdles in one vigorous leap, and seems likely to carry with it most of our other courts. Efforts to narrow the doctrine have not had much success. What of efforts to prevent its further extension?

The possibility of limitations in two directions is obvious. First, it may be urged that the evidential doctrine applies to the proof of nothing beyond the acts of the declarant. Second, it may be urged that the doctrine does not apply to the proof of past facts — that term being employed to designate both the acts of the declarant and events or matters in which he is only an observer . . .

SHEPARD v. UNITED STATES
290 U.S. 96 (1933)

[The facts of this case are set forth *supra*. JUSTICE CARDOZO's opinion continues as follows:]

2. We pass to the question whether the statements to the nurse, though incompetent as dying declarations, were admissible on other grounds.

The Circuit Court of Appeals determined that they were. Witnesses for the defendant had testified to declarations by Mrs. Shepard which suggested a mind bent upon suicide, or at any rate were thought by the defendant to carry that suggestion. More than once before her illness she had stated in the hearing of these witnesses that she had no wish to live, and had nothing to live for, and on one occasion she added that she expected some day to make an end to her life. This testimony opened the door, so it is argued, to declarations in rebuttal that she had been poisoned by her husband. They were admissible, in that view, not as evidence of the truth of what was said, but as betokening a state of mind inconsistent with the presence of suicidal intent.

(a) The testimony was neither offered nor received for the strained and narrow purpose now suggested as legitimate. It was offered and received as proof of a dying declaration. What was said by Mrs. Shepard lying ill upon her deathbed was to be weighed as if a like statement had been made upon the stand. The course of the trial makes this an inescapable conclusion. The Government withdrew the testimony when it was unaccompanied by proof that the declarant expected to die. Only when proof of her expectation had been supplied was the offer renewed and the testimony received again. For the reasons already considered, the proof was inadequate to show a consciousness of impending death and the abandonment of hope; but inadequate though it was, there can be no doubt of the purpose that it was understood to serve.

(b) Aside, however, from this objection, the accusatory declaration must have been rejected as evidence of a state of mind, though the purpose thus to limit it had been brought to light upon the trial. The defendant had tried to show by Mrs. Shepard's declarations to her friends that she had exhibited a weariness of life and a readiness to end it, the testimony giving plausibility to the hypothesis of suicide. . . . By proof of these declarations evincing an unhappy state of mind the defendant opened the door to the offer by the Government of declarations evincing a different state of mind, declarations consistent with the persistence of a will to live. The defendant would have no grievance if the testimony in rebuttal had been narrowed to that point. What the Government put in evidence, however, was something very different. It did not use the declarations by Mrs. Shepard to prove her present thoughts and feelings, or even her thoughts and feelings in times past. It used the declarations as proof of an act committed by someone else, as evidence that she was dying of poison given by her husband. This fact, if fact it was, the Government was free to prove, but not by hearsay declarations. It will not do to say that the jury might accept the declarations for any light that they cast upon the existence of a vital urge, and reject them to the extent that they charged the death to someone else. Discrimination so subtle is a feat beyond the compass of ordinary minds. The reverberating clang of those accusatory words would drown all weaker sounds. It is for ordinary minds, and not for psychoanalysts, that our rules of evidence are framed. They have their source very often in considerations of administrative convenience, of practical expediency, and not in rules of logic. When the risk of confusion is so great as to upset the balance of advantage, the evidence goes out. THAYER, PRELIMINARY TREATISE ON THE LAW OF EVIDENCE, 266, 516; WIGMORE, EVIDENCE §§ 1421, 1422, 1714.

These precepts of caution are a guide to judgment here. There are times when a state of mind, if relevant, may be proved by contemporaneous declarations of feeling or intent. *Mutual Life Ins. Co. v. Hillmon*, 145 U.S. 285, 295. . . .

So also in suits upon insurance policies, declarations by an insured that he intends to go upon a journey with another, may be evidence of a state of mind lending probability to the conclusion that the purpose was fulfilled. *Mutual Life Ins. Co. v. Hillmon, supra.* The ruling in that case marks the high water line beyond which courts have been unwilling to go. It has developed a substantial body of criticism and commentary.[84] Declarations of intention, casting light upon the future, have been sharply distinguished from declarations of memory, pointing backwards to the past. There would be an end, or nearly that, to the rule against hearsay if the distinction were ignored.

The testimony now questioned faced backward and not forward. This at least it did in its most obvious implications. What is even more important, it spoke to a past act, and more than that, to an act by someone not the speaker. Other tendency, if it had any, was a filament too fine to be disentangled by a jury.

The judgment should be reversed and the cause remanded to the District Court for further proceedings in accordance with this opinion.

Reversed.

NOTES AND QUESTIONS

1.   Why does retrospective use of state of mind declarations threaten to destroy the rule against hearsay?

2.   Hattie Smith is on trial for the murder of her husband. Her defense is self-defense. May she introduce into evidence the following statement attributed to her husband: "I'm going to kill that bitch"? *See State v. Smith*, 276 N.W.2d 104 (Neb. 1979).

3.   Does *Shepard* preclude admissibility of any state of mind declaration offered to prove a previous event or just those declarations offered for the purpose of

---

[84]   [*] Maguire, *The* Hillmon *Case*, 38 HARV. L. REV. 709, 721, 727; Seligman, *An Exception to the Hearsay Rule*, 26 HARV. L. REV. 146; Chafee, *Review of Wigmore's Treatise*, 37 HARV. L. REV. 513, 519.

establishing previous conduct by someone other than the declarant? When the proof is limited to previous declarant conduct, isn't a statement's retrospective inference often likely to be at least as reliable — if not more so — than the prospective inference which *Hillmon* appears to allow? For example, isn't the statement "I remember going to the movies yesterday" better proof of movie attendance than the statement "I intend to go to the movies next month"? *See* Payne, *The* Hillmon *Case — An Old Problem Revisited*, 41 Va. L. Rev. 1011, 1023–24 (1955).

4. Suppose Mrs. Shepard had simply said: "I'm afraid of Dr. Shepard." Would her statement be admissible in his murder prosecution? *Compare United States v. Brown*, 490 F.2d 758 (D.C. Cir. 1973), *and Shults v. State*, 616 P.2d 388 (Nev. 1980), *with United States ex rel. Jacques v. Hilton*, 423 F. Supp. 895 (D.N.J. 1976). Would your answer be different if she had said "Please do not let Dr. Shepard into my room"?

Evidentiary Foundation: The O.J. Simpson Civil Trial

During O.J. Simpson's civil trial for the wrongful death of his wife, *supra* p. 322, the plaintiffs wanted to call Mr. Wayne Hughes to testify that Simpson's wife, Nicole, told him that Mr. Simpson had struck her. Plaintiff argued that this statement qualified under the state of mind exception to the hearsay rule. Would this statement have been admissible under Rule 803(3)?

MR. BAKER: We have another issue, on the issue of Mr. Wayne Hughes. Mr. Wayne Hughes is apparently their first witness. Mr. Hughes, I think, at least in his statement to the District Attorney, indicated there was an incident that he may be asked about this morning, and that was an incident that occurred, he now has recollection, in 1979 and 1980, when Nicole Brown Simpson came to his house, saying that Mr. Simpson may have had physical contact with her. Mr. Hughes never discussed this matter with Mr. Simpson and will so testify. He has no knowledge of whether Nicole Brown Simpson's representations to him were accurate. He asked Nicole Brown Simpson — at least he'd be prepared to testify that if she wanted him to ever discuss this with O.J. Simpson, she said no. And based upon the hearsay nature of it . . . we move to exclude any reference to [it] . . . .

* * *

PETROCELLI: Your Honor, under People versus Zack and People versus Linkenauer, the relationship — the relationship between the defendant and the victim is relevant to the issue of motive and identity. And the Court specifically pointed out that acts of physical violence in that relationship are particularly relevant, in addition to evidence of quarrels and antagonism or enmity.

* * *

COURT: . . . You want to address the hearsay issue?

PETROCELLI: Yes, Your Honor. First of all, unlike the criminal case, the defense in this case has proffered Nicole's state of mind as . . . Nicole's state of mind is directly relevant to the issue of the relationship between Mr. Simpson and Nicole. So, . . . her state of mind furnishes an exception to get in this testimony. And secondly, in this particular case, as Mr. Hughes will testify, Mr. — Nicole came running to his house after being hit by Mr. Simpson, was extremely upset, and it would qualify, certainly, as a spontaneous statement. She also showed Mr. Hughes the mark on her body where Mr. Simpson had hit her. And again, I emphasize that in opening statement, Mr. Baker's spent quite a bit of time characterizing this relationship between the two and pointing out that there wasn't any violence or physical alterations, except on one occasion. And Mr. Simpson, at no time in his testimony, limited his answers. He said "never," categorically, did he ever touch Nicole, slap her, strike her, hit her, and so forth.

COURT: Okay. I'll permit Mr. Hughes to testify to the '89 incident, but not the '79 incidents.

PETROCELLI: Your Honor—

COURT: Let's get on with the trial.

PETROCELLI: Well, Your Honor, I object to this. I — just because he makes this argument — I mean, Mr. Simpson categorically testified that he never once hit Nicole and—

COURT: Mr. Petrocelli, I've heard your argument. I've made my ruling. Okay.

QUESTION

In 1977, Maryland Governor Marvin Mandel was prosecuted for mail fraud stemming from his efforts to provide improper assistance to a racetrack — Marlboro — which several of his close associates owned. *See* Chapter II, Section [D][5], *supra*. In his defense, Mandel offered the following testimony: Mrs. Rodgers [wife of a co-defendant and Mandel associate], would testify that she and her husband left Mr. Hollander's office in the company of Dale Hess [a co-defendant and a Mandel associate] and his wife. As they were walking to lunch, they continued to talk about the purchase of the racetrack and the secrecy of their act. In the course of the conversation, Mr. Hess, excited at the prospect of the new acquisition, exclaimed, in substance, that the Governor would be shocked if he were to learn that this group had purchased Marlboro. Mrs. Rodgers would also testify that, after lunch, while driving home, she participated in further discussion with her husband. Mrs. Rodgers would say that her husband instructed her that the acquisition of the racetrack was to remain a secret; that she was not to reveal it to anyone, including the Governor; and that the acquisition of interests in the track, by Mr. Hess and the Rodgers brothers was "none of the Governor's business." *United States v. Mandel*, 437 F. Supp. 262, 263 (D. Md. 1977), *aff'd*, 591 F.2d 1347 (4th Cir. 1979).

Should this testimony have been admitted?

UNITED STATES v. LAYTON

549 F. Supp. 903 (N.D. Cal. 1982), *aff'd in part, rev'd in part on other grounds*, 720 F.2d 548 (9th Cir. 1983)

PECKHAM, CHIEF JUDGE.

Laurence Layton has been indicted on four criminal counts arising from the events which occurred at the Port Kaituma airport in the nation of Guyana on November 18, 1978. Those events resulted in the death of Congressman Leo J. Ryan, then a member of the United States House of Representatives from the 11th Congressional District of California, and the wounding of Richard Dwyer, the Deputy Chief of Mission for the United States in the Republic of Guyana. Congressman Ryan had traveled to Guyana for the purpose of investigating certain allegations that had arisen concerning the Peoples Temple settlement in Jonestown. Mr. Layton had lived in Jonestown for the few months preceding the events in question here. The indictment charges Mr. Layton with (1) conspiracy to murder a Congressman, under 18 U.S.C. § 351(d); (2) aiding and abetting in the murder of a Congressman, under 18 U.S.C. § 351(a), 2; (3) conspiracy to murder an internationally protected person, under 18 U.S.C. § 1117; and (4) aiding and abetting in the attempted murder of an internationally protected person, under 18 U.S.C. § 1116(a), 2.

The jury trial on the foregoing charges commenced in this court on August 18, 1981. On September 26, 1981, after it had become clear that the jury would be unable to reach a verdict on any of the four counts, we declared a mistrial. The government has now indicated its intent to go forward with a retrial of the defendant.

The government has moved under Rule 12(d) of the Federal Rules of Criminal Procedure for an order allowing it to present at retrial certain statements that were ruled inadmissible during the first Layton trial. No new arguments have been advanced in support of the present motion. The government has instead called the court's attention to a number of materials already filed, and to relevant portions of the Layton transcript.

The items sought to be introduced are:

1. Statements of Jim Jones to the membership of the Peoples Temple prior to the arrival of Congressman Leo Ryan and his party.

*   *   *

3. Statement of Jim Jones to the members of the Peoples Temple shortly before and during the mass suicide at Jonestown, commonly known as the "Last Hour Tape."

B. Rulings on the Government's Motion

1. *Statements of Jim Jones to Peoples Temple members prior to the arrival of the Ryan party.* The tape sought to be introduced includes such statements by Jones as "If he [Congressman Ryan] stays long enough for tea, he's gonna regret it . . . . I want to shoot someone in the ass like him so bad . . . I'm not passing this opportunity up. Now if they come in . . . they come in on their own risk . . . . If they enter the property illegally, they will not leave it alive."

The government has sought to introduce this evidence on three theories: as a co-conspirator's statement, as falling within the state of mind exception to the hearsay rule, and as nonassertive conduct.

* * *

b. *State of mind.* Here, the theory is that Jones was indicating his then existing desire to kill members of the Ryan party, and that this indication should be taken at face value and admitted for the truth of the matter stated.

There are three requirements to the admissibility of statements under Rule 803(3) of the Federal Rules of Evidence, the state of mind exception to the hearsay rule. . . .

First, the statements must be contemporaneous with the later event sought to be proven — that is, Jones' statements must be shown to have been not too far distant in time from the shootings. That is true here. The statements appear to have been made within a day of the arrival of Congressman Ryan's party in Jonestown.

Second, it must be shown that the declarant had no chance to reflect — that is, no time to fabricate or to misrepresent his thoughts. It is less clear that this test can be met. At this early stage, it is not obvious that Jones did intend to kill Ryan. He said he did, but this may have just been done with the intent to stir up hostility against Leo Ryan. He may not have formed an intent to harm Ryan until later, despite his words. However, the distinction is not too significant here. Whether he intended to kill Ryan at that time or not, he made statements to the effect that that was his intent; and these statements were heard by his followers and were probably taken at face value by them. Considering the relevancy theory on which the statements are being offered, this showing of non-misrepresentativeness is adequate.

Third, the statements must be shown to be relevant to an issue in the case. Here, they are relevant to the question of conspiracy. The chain of logic is as follows: Jones indicated his desire to shoot Congressman Ryan, and to kill members of the Ryan party. Under the reasoning of *Mutual Life Ins. Co. v. Hillmon*, . . . the fact that Jones made these statements makes it somewhat more likely that, when the killings finally did occur, he had something to do with them. Since he was in a position of authority and was even an object of adulation at Jonestown, the fact that it is more likely he had something to do with the killings makes it somewhat more likely that a large number of his devoted followers were involved, too. Since it is more likely that a large number of his followers were involved, it makes it somewhat more likely that Layton was involved as well.

This is a very subtle chain of logic. Instead of thinking through each link in the chain, the jury is likely to assume that, in making the statements, Jones was acting as a mouthpiece for all of his followers, including Layton. The improper leap in the logic is quite dramatic: Jones said he wanted to shoot Ryan; therefore, Layton wanted Ryan to be shot, too.

The House Committee on the Judiciary has acknowledged that the state of mind exception to the hearsay rule is susceptible to such lapses in logic. Accordingly, it has recommended that a hearsay declaration of one person's state of mind be "admissible only to prove his future conduct, not the future conduct of another person." House Report No. 93-650, Note to Rule 803(3) of the Federal Rules of Evidence, 28 U.S.C.A. at 579.[85] While, strictly speaking, Jones' statements are not sought to be used to prove Layton's conduct, the danger that the jury will make a highly prejudicial leap is certainly present.

The most widely quoted language on this subject is Justice Cardozo's eloquent dictum in *Shepard v. United States*, 290 U.S. 96 (1933). . . .

The *Shepard* decision was . . . the basis for Justice Traynor's dissent in *People v. Alcalde*, 24 Cal. 2d 177, 148 P.2d 627 (1944). There, Frank Alcalde was charged with the murder of his friend, Bernice Curtis. The government sought to admit the victim's statement, prior to the killing, that she was going out with Frank. The California Supreme Court held the statement admissible for the limited purpose of showing that Bernice intended to be with Frank on that evening in question. In his vigorous dissent from the majority opinion, Justice Traynor argued that, while Bernice's statement was good evidence only that she intended to go out with Frank, the jury would inevitably and impermissibly accept the evidence as proof that Frank intended to go out with her. Justice Traynor thus objected to the admission of the statement, saying, "A declaration as to what one person intended to do . . . cannot safely be accepted as evidence of what another probably did."

*   *   *

The Ninth Circuit, too, has recognized the dangers of admitting statements under the state of mind exception to the hearsay rule. In *United States v. Pheaster*, 544 F.2d 353 (9th Cir. 1976), *cert. denied sub nom. Inciso v. United States*, 429 U.S. 1099 (1977), the trial judge had admitted hearsay testimony by two friends of a kidnapping victim, Larry, concerning statements made by Larry, on the day of his disappearance, to the effect that he planned to meet with one of the alleged

---

[85] [Ed. — The original Advisory Committee comments to Rule 803(3), however, did not purport to limit the scope of *Hillmon*:

> The exclusion of "statements of memory or belief to prove the fact remembered or believed" is necessary to avoid the virtual destruction of the hearsay rule which would otherwise result from allowing state of mind, provable by a hearsay statement, to serve as the basis for an inference of the happening of the event which produced the state of mind. *Shepard v. United States*, 290 U.S. 96 (1933); Maguire, *The* Hillmon *Case — Thirty-three Years After*, 38 HARV. L. REV. 709, 719–731 (1925); Hinton, *States of Mind and the Hearsay Rule*, 1 U. CHI. L. REV. 394, 421–423 (1934). The rule of *Mutual Life Ins. Co. v. Hillmon*, 145 U.S. 285 (1982), allowing evidence of intention as tending to prove the doing of the act intended, is of course, left undisturbed.

Note to paragraph (3), 28 U.S.C.A. at 586 (West 1973).]

kidnappers.[86] The Ninth Circuit carefully reviewed the law in the area. . . . Ultimately, the court concluded that it could not hold that the trial judge had erred in admitting the statements. However, the court did acknowledge "the force of the objection to the application of the *Hillmon* doctrine in the instant case." . . .

We recognize that in all of the cases which discuss the dangers of admitting statements indicating the declarant's state of mind and used to prove the declarant's future conduct, the defendant was actually mentioned by the declarant, so that there was great likelihood that the jury would misuse the evidence as proof of the defendant's conduct. In the present case, that factor is absent. Jones did not mention Layton by name in the course of the statements in question. However, after a careful review of the statements themselves and of the context in which they are offered as evidence, we conclude that the prudent course is to exclude Jones' statements under the reasoning articulated in the *Shepard* case. Given Jones' stature in the community of Jonestown, the risk that the jury will assume that, in expressing his desire to shoot Congressman Ryan, he was speaking for all his followers is particularly acute. The danger of confusion which would arise from the introduction of the statements is so great as to upset the balance and warrant their exclusion. Accordingly, we hold that the statements made by Jones prior to the arrival of the Ryan party cannot be admitted for the truth of the matter stated, not even for the limited purpose of showing Jones' state of mind.

3. *The Last Hour Tape.* The government has focused attention upon a number of statements on the Last Hour Tape. Some of them appear to have been made by Jones before word came back from the airstrip that the shootings had occurred; some of them to have been made after Jones had been notified of the shootings.

The former statements include the following: "One of the people on that plane is gonna . . . shoot the pilot. I know that . . . and down comes that plane in the jungle . . . . There's one man there who blames, and rightfully so, Debbie Blakey . . . for

---

[86] [Ed. — The *Pheaster* court characterized the problem in the following terms:

When hearsay evidence concerns the declarant's statement of his intention to do something with another person, the Hillmon doctrine requires that the trier of fact infer from the state of mind of the declarant the probability of a particular act not only by the declarant but also by the other person. Several objections can be raised against a doctrine that would allow such an inference to be made. One such objection is based on the unreliability of the inference but is not, in our view, compelling. A much more significant and troubling objection is based on the inconsistency of such an inference with the state of mind exception. This problem is more easily perceived when one divides what is really a compound statement into its component parts. In the instant case, the statement by Larry Adell, "I am going to meet Angelo in the parking lot to get a pound of grass," is really two statements. The first is the obvious statement of Larry's intention. The second is an implicit statement of Angelo's intention. Surely, if the meeting is to take place in a location which Angelo does not habitually frequent, one must assume that Angelo intended to meet Larry there if one is to make the inference that Angelo was in the parking lot and the meeting occurred. The important point is that the second, implicit statement has nothing to do with Larry's state of mind. For example, if Larry's friends had testified that Larry had said, "Angelo is going to be in the parking lot of Sambo's North tonight with a pound of grass," no state of mind exception or any other exception to the hearsay rule would be available. Yet, this is in effect at least half of what the testimony did attribute to Larry.

544 F.2d at 376-77.]

the murder of his mother and he'll sh-he'll stop that pilot by any means necessary. He'll do it. That plane will come out of the air. There's no way you can fly a plane without a pilot."

The statements which seem to have been made after word of the shootings reached Jones include the following: "The Congressman's dead, the Congressman lays dead, many of our traitors are dead, they're all laying out there dead . . . I didn't but, but my people did. My people did. They're my people . . . . I don't know who fired the shot, I don't know who killed the Congressman. But as far as I'm concerned, I killed him. He had no business coming. I told him not to come."

The government seeks to admit these statements on numerous theories.

*   *   *

b. *State of mind.* In order for the Last Hour Tape to qualify under the state of mind exception to the hearsay rule, it must pertain to Jones' own "intent, plan, motive, design, mental feeling, pain . . . [or] bodily health." Rule 803(3) of the Federal Rules of Evidence. The difficulty with applying this exception to Jones' statements is that the statements themselves largely concerned future or past acts of the persons at the airstrip. If admitted for the truth of the matter stated, they will enable the jury to accept as true: (1) Jones' statements as to what he believed other people were about to do; (2) Jones' statements as to what he believed other people had just done. Neither of these forms of hearsay falls within the state of mind exception. The statute specifies that the state of mind exception does not include "a statement of . . . belief to prove the fact . . . believed." . . . Thus, the portions of the statements just discussed are not admissible on the state of mind theory.

It is only the statements which truly reveal Jones' own state of mind that are susceptible to admission under Rule 803(3) — such as his statement "I don't know who fired the shot . . . . But as far as I'm concerned, I killed him. You understand what I'm saying? I killed him. He had no business coming. I told him not to come." If these statements are admitted under the state of mind exception, the jury will be permitted to accept these statements as a true indication that Jones intended to kill Congressman Ryan. . . . That result is objectionable because the statements . . . pose dangers of the sort identified in the Shepard case. Consequently, they are not admissible under Rule 803(3).

*   *   *

For the foregoing reasons, the government's motion under Rule 12(d) of the Federal Rules of Criminal Procedure is denied in its entirety.

SO ORDERED.

QUESTIONS

1. When courts admit a state of mind declaration to prove subsequent third party conduct, are they, in effect, violating *Shepard*? Under such circumstances, is the declaration really a *Shepard* in disguise?

2. In *United States v. Layton*, 767 F.2d 549 (9th Cir. 1985), *aff'd in part, rev'd in part on other grounds*, 720 F.2d 548 (9th Cir. 1983), most of the hearsay statements were ultimately admitted under the co-conspirator doctrine.

3. The Second Circuit has ruled that state of mind declarations "may . . . be admitted against a non-declarant when there is independent evidence which connects the declarant's statement with the non-declarant's activities." *United States v. Delvecchio*, 816 F.2d 859, 863 (2d Cir. 1986); *United States v. Best*, 219 F.3d 192 (2d Cir. 2000). Does Rule 803(3) support this interpretation or is this approach merely an attempt at compromise? *See also Coy v. Renico*, 414 F. Supp. 2d 744 (E.D. Mich. 2006) (detailed overview of post-*Hillmon* cases considering whether the declarant's statement of intent may be admitted to prove third party conduct).

3. The Residual Exception — Flexibility for the Future

Jack B. Weinstein, *The Probative Force of Hearsay*
46 Iowa L. Rev. 331, 344–46 (1961)[87]

Scholars have reached surprising agreement on the desirability of replacing our present hearsay rule with one based upon probative force in the particular case. In the last century Bentham in England and Appleton in this country recognized the ability of triers to assess probative force of hearsay and proposed that the best-evidence concept be applied to hearsay. More recently Thayer declared that "the attempt to make the group [of classes], in the form in which they finally chanced to settle, fit into a scheme having any measure of theoretical consistency is an undertaking so Procrustean as to defy even the brilliant ingenuity of Professor Wigmore"; the class system he denominated as "crude and primitive." Chamberlayne, in his important treatise, made a full scale and well-reasoned attack on the "archaic" hearsay rules as "an anomaly absolutely defying the established principles of a sound judicial administration," and referred to the exceptions as having developed in "the stone age of judicial evolution." McCormick has noted that "the values of hearsay declarations or writings, and the need for them, in particular situations cannot with any degree of realism be thus minutely ticketed in advance. . . . Too much worthless evidence will fit the categories, too much that is vitally needed will be left out." Morgan has repeatedly insisted that much of the hearsay excluded "raises the hearsay dangers to no greater extent than evidence now admitted under the hearsay exceptions." He has demonstrated by a series of devastating hypotheticals how much evidence of high probative force may be excluded and how much of low convincing power [is] admitted under our present rules. The notes to the Model Code of Evidence state that in many exceptions "the necessity resolves itself into mere convenience and the substitute for cross-examination is imperceptible." Summarizing their view of this pastiche in a manner probably considered derogatory when it was written a quarter of a century ago, Professor Maguire joined with Morgan to write: "[A] picture of the hearsay rule with its exceptions would resemble an old-fashioned crazy quilt made of patches cut from a group of paintings by cubists, futurists and surrealists." Davis has pointed

---

[87] Copyright © 1961. Reprinted with permission.

out that "technically incompetent evidence is often more reliable than technically competent evidence." The hearsay rules "more often serve to hinder than to promote justice" and "the distinction in probative value between statements admissible under the particular exceptions and statements that are not admissible is of the flimsiest description" was Tregarthen's evaluation. While Baker suggested a number of statutory modifications, he acknowledged that the long term trend was toward abolition of the rule. James concluded that our hearsay system failed to meet the tests of a rational system, and "largely archaic" was the recent judgment of Hart and McNaughten. Conrad, Falknor, Ladd, Loevinger, Peck, and Reed should also be listed with the critics.

Wigmore, whose masterly treatise has prevented our complex hearsay rule from collapsing of its own weight, judged it one "which may be esteemed, next to jury-trial, the greatest contribution of that eminently practical [Anglo-American] legal system to the world's jurisprudence of procedure." Nevertheless, he favored rules making a general exception "for *all statements of deceased persons*," giving the court discretion not to exclude hearsay where it would interrupt the narrative of the witness and allowing it to permit authenticated statements to be admitted. "What the times now demand," he declared, "is an attempt to simplify the use of the Hearsay rule."

NOTE

Judge Weinstein is a man who acts consistently with his principles. *See United States v. Barbati*, 284 F. Supp. 409 (E.D.N.Y. 1968).

Edmund M. Morgan,
Foreword to the Model Code of Evidence
38–47 (1942)[88]

In the early 1800s the courts were fond of saying that there were only two or three exceptional situations in which hearsay was received. Now at least eighteen different varieties may be found, each of which has some respectable authority to support it. In almost every one of these eighteen there are qualifications and limitations. Mr. Wigmore devotes 1145 pages to the hearsay rule and its exceptions, not including confessions and admissions, which require 304 additional pages — a total of 1449 pages. To make the subject appear to have some coherence he puts admissions, confessions and former testimony outside the realm of hearsay; this enables him to discover in each of the exceptions something which he calls a guaranty of trustworthiness — a something which amounts to nothing more than a situation in which the ordinary person in making the declaration would usually desire to tell the truth or would have no motive to falsify. It will be noted that this explanation goes at most to sincerity; it does not touch perception or memory.

A hypothetical case may demonstrate the existing judicial treatment of uncross-examined statements. Suppose that a car driven by Anderson with Blake as his guest collided with a car owned by defendant and driven by Carlson, a friend to

---

[88] Copyright © 1942 by The American Law Institute. Reprinted with permission.

whom defendant had loaned or rented the car for an afternoon. Suppose also that there is a statute making defendant responsible for Carlson's operation of the car. An investigation shows the following facts:

1. One Watson saw the accident as he was on his way to take a train. In great excitement he immediately called a policeman, and thereafter went to a notary public and dictated an account of what he saw. The notary reduced the matter to writing in the form of an affidavit; Watson executed the affidavit and mailed it to Anderson.

2. The policeman called by Watson came to the scene within a minute or two, and Watson immediately told him how the accident occurred.

3. Anderson was taken home and later told his wife how the accident occurred.

4. A few days later Anderson, realizing that he was about to die, made a full statement.

5. Blake likewise was fatally injured, and he made a dying declaration.

6. Carlson was indicted for the manslaughter of Anderson and in his trial testified that he had taken several drinks of whiskey before the accident.

7. Watson testified fully at Carlson's trial.

8. When Carlson was on his way to defendant's garage, he met one Wilson to whom he said that he was going to have defendant's car for the afternoon but first he was going to Zuber's saloon and get plenty of whiskey to put him in good spirits.

9. Carlson was convicted of manslaughter of Anderson.

10. At the criminal trial Carlson told Wilson privately that he knew he was liable to Anderson's widow and that he was going to sell his home and pay her. Carlson died in prison.

11. Defendant, who was out of the city at the time of the accident, called on the Andersons a week after the accident and told Mrs. Anderson that he was sorry about it, that Carlson was drunk at the time, that he wouldn't have let Carlson have the car if he had known that Carlson drank.

Anderson's administrator brought action against defendant for wrongful death under a statute like that in Massachusetts, which allowed recovery of not less than $500 nor more than $10,000 according to the degree of fault of the defendant, and in addition damages for the pain and suffering of the decedent. At the trial the following occurred:

1. Watson was called as a witness and testified fully on direct examination. He wanted to read the affidavit but the court would not permit it because he had a present recollection of the matter. There was a recess at the end of Watson's direct examination, and Watson was accidentally killed. Defendant moved to strike his direct examination. Motion granted.

2. Plaintiff thereupon offered in evidence Watson's affidavit. Rejected.

3. Plaintiff then offered in evidence, through the court reporter, the testimony given by Watson in the criminal prosecution of Carlson. Rejected.

4. Plaintiff then called the policeman who offered to testify to what Watson told him at the scene of the accident. Admitted.

Up to this point testimony given by Watson in open court at the present trial in the presence of the jury while confronting the defendant and expecting to be cross-examined by him has been rejected. His testimony given in the criminal trial while he was under oath, confronting Carlson against whom he was testifying and subject to cross-examination by Carlson has been rejected. A sworn statement in writing made by him a short time after the accident, but not on the scene nor while he was laboring under nervous excitement caused by the accident has been rejected. An unsworn oral statement, reported by the person who heard it, made by this same Watson whose sworn testimony and sworn statement has been rejected, has been received. Why? Watson's statements may carry strong guaranties of trustworthiness. There can be no question that his testimony in the criminal trial was given under conditions calculated to induce him to tell the truth and to enable a court and jury to put a fair value upon his statement. His direct examination at the present trial has the added merit of being given in the presence of the court and jury who are to consider it against this defendant. The affidavit is of less value but was given under sanction of an oath. In all three, however, there is the fatal lack of opportunity by defendant to cross-examine Watson. The adversary theory of litigation requires opportunity to cross-examine by the party against whom the evidence is offered. In these rejections, no deviation from that theory is permitted. In dealing with Watson's spontaneous statement, however, no consideration whatever is given to the adversary system. Attention is directed to Watson's mental condition. His statement is unreflective — made before he had a motive to contrive falsehood. To use the metaphor of some courts, the event speaks through Watson. (Some courts, indeed, let this metaphor run away with them, and hold that a deliberate statement inconsistent with the spontaneous statement is not admissible to impeach Watson; for it was not Watson but the event that was speaking and the event made no contradictory statement.) The short of it is that Watson spoke under such circumstances that he probably desired to tell the truth. The nervous excitement under which Watson was laboring may take the place of an oath as a guaranty of sincerity; but it can in no measure be a substitute for cross-examination as to observation and narration. Indeed, psychologists assure us that a person laboring under a nervous excitement is likely to observe and to narrate with more than normal inaccuracy.

[Now suppose for a moment that Watson had been cross-examined and that there had been a mistrial. At a second trial Watson has so far forgotten the relevant data as to be unable to testify from memory. He still has his affidavit, and the court reporter has a verbatim transcript of Watson's testimony at the first trial. The affidavit or its content is admissible as a record of past recollection, although any effective cross-examination of Watson is impossible. His former testimony is inadmissible although it contains a complete cross-examination. However, if Watson had died after the first trial, his former testimony would be admissible but his affidavit would be inadmissible. Resort to the adversary system will help explain these results, but can anything justify them?

A further supposition may be indulged, that after the Anderson action is over, Blake's administrator sues defendant for Blake's wrongful death, and at the trial offers in evidence Watson's testimony at the Anderson trial. By the orthodox view, it will be excluded, although it would be admitted at the second trial of the Anderson action. It is true that the issue is the same, and that defendant cross-examined Watson at the Anderson trial; but since Blake's administrator had no opportunity to cross-examine Watson, the evidence would be inadmissible against Blake's administrator; and if inadmissible against him, it is inadmissible in his favor. Why? Both adversaries must be treated alike; one shall have no handicap which the other does not bear. But what has this to do with an investigation of fact?]

Let us go on with the Anderson trial.

5. The plaintiff now offered both of Anderson's statements — that to his wife and his dying declaration. Rejected.

Incidentally, Anderson's dying declaration was offered and received in the criminal prosecution of Carlson for Anderson's death. Blake's dying declaration was there offered and rejected. In this civil action both of them are clearly inadmissible. Why? Certainly the adversary theory would cut them out in all three trials. The guaranty of the desire of the speaker to tell the truth is equally operative in all three. The awfulness of the situation, or a dying man's fear of going to his Maker with a lie on his lips, is as effective in one as in another; the circumstances in which the statement is made, not those of the litigation in which it is offered in evidence, control the motivation of the declarant. Consequently some other sort of consideration must be operating. Some judges have frankly said that the policy of facilitating the criminal prosecution of manslayers induces the courts to accept this evidence despite its frailties; hearsay is better than nothing, and it is needed because the chief witness in this class of case has always been put out of the way. But why should that policy operate against the reception of Blake's declaration in the prosecution for Anderson's death in the same accident? And why receive frail evidence against a man whose life or liberty is at stake and reject it when only his property is involved? The answer seems to be that the rule took on these qualifications at a time when the courts were rejecting all hearsay except that for the reception of which a precedent was found.

6. Plaintiff next offers evidence of Carlson's testimony at Carlson's trial in which he admitted that he had had several drinks of whiskey just before the accident. Rejected.

7. Then plaintiff offers through Wilson evidence of Carlson's statement that Carlson was going to get defendant's car but was first going to get plenty of whiskey, etc. Admitted.

Here the court rejects evidence of a sworn statement by Carlson which he must have known would be most damaging to him, which would tend to make the very jury in whose presence it was uttered more willing to find him guilty of a serious offense. The next instant the court receives evidence of an unsworn statement by this same Carlson. The fact to be proved by each item is the same, namely, that Carlson drank whiskey shortly before the accident. His sworn statement that he actually drank the whiskey is rejected, his unsworn statement of intention to drink it is received. Certainly Carlson's stimulus for telling the truth was greater as to the first than as to the second. To the first item, the court applies the adversary theory;

to the second, it seeks only for a so-called guaranty of trustworthiness.

8. Next plaintiff offers a duly authenticated copy of the judgment of conviction of Carlson for the manslaughter of Anderson and . . . Wilson's testimony that Carlson told him that he knew he was liable to Anderson's widow and would sell his home and pay her. The court rejects the former and admits the latter. The reason for the rejection is that the judgment is hearsay opinion, a mere conclusion of the jury based on hearsay, that is, on the testimony offered in the Carlson prosecution. To be sure the conclusion was reached as the result of a trial at which Carlson had every opportunity to present evidence and argument; it represented the considered judgment of twelve men, approved by the judge, that there was no reasonable doubt of Carlson's criminal negligence causing Anderson's death; but the adversary theory requires an opportunity to cross-examine, and defendant had no opportunity to cross-examine either the witnesses at Carlson's trial or the jury which rendered the verdict on which the judgment was entered. The reason for receiving Wilson's testimony is that Carlson's statement was of a fact against his pecuniary interest and Carlson was not likely to make such a statement unless he believed it to be true.

Finally, plaintiff offers evidence of defendant's statement to Mrs. Anderson that Carlson was drunk. If defendant were called to the stand and asked about Carlson's condition at the time of the accident, he would not be permitted to answer though under oath and subject to cross-examination, because he has no first-hand personal knowledge about Carlson's condition either at the time of the accident or at any other relevant time. Yet the offered evidence is admitted.

Anderson's statement to his wife is unadulterated hearsay and evidence of it, when offered for plaintiff, falls within no exception. But suppose that the statement had been favorable to defendant and he desired to offer it in evidence. If Mrs. Anderson, for whose benefit the administrator is prosecuting this action, had, in making proof of Anderson's death to a life insurance company, either attached Anderson's statement or repeated its content in answer to the question as to cause of death, this answer would have been admissible in evidence for defendant for its full value. But if she had not in some way adopted its content as an accurate account of the accident, it would not be admissible as tending to show the cause of Anderson's death upon the issue of plaintiff's right to recover the penalty, but would be admissible to show the cause of Anderson's death upon the issue of plaintiff's right to recover damages for Anderson's pain and suffering. Why these rulings? As to the statements of defendant and Mrs. Anderson, defendant cannot object that he had no opportunity to cross-examine himself, and Mrs. Anderson is treated as if she were the party to the action because she is the sole beneficiary. Every relevant item of conduct of one adversary may be given in evidence against him by the other. As to Anderson's statement, the administrator is in privity with Anderson as to the claim for Anderson's pain and suffering, but is not in privity with Anderson as to the claim for the penalty. The adversary theory of litigation here identifies the party with his predecessor in interest for procedural purposes because the party is claiming the identical substantive interest which the predecessor would have had. Obviously there is no greater guaranty of trustworthiness in the one instance than in the other; and just as obviously the party against whom the evidence is offered never had an opportunity to cross-examine the declarant. Why should he be prevented from objecting to lack of opportunity to cross-examine merely because he is the successor in interest of the declarant?

These examples of what might happen in an ordinary case are sufficient to indicate that the present law as to hearsay is a conglomeration of inconsistencies due to the application of competing theories haphazardly applied. Historical accidents play their part also. In the orthodox treatment of former testimony there is the most rigorous adherence to the adversary theory. Former testimony given under oath and subject to cross-examination by the very party against whom it is now offered is inadmissible merely because it would not be receivable if offered against the proponent. In admissions, personal or authorized, even the testimonial qualifications of the declarant are disregarded. In most of the other exceptions there is not a semblance of a substitute for cross-examination. To make such rulings as stated in the hypothetical case; to reject statements made with all the safeguards surrounding the giving of testimony in open court and to admit pedigree statements by a remote blood relative; to admit declarations against pecuniary interest and to exclude declarations against penal interest; to hamper the use of business entries by restrictions devised to care for entries by interested parties in their shop-books at a time when those parties were incompetent as witnesses; to receive a copy of a record of a deed as evidence that the purported grantor signed, sealed and delivered it and to reject a conviction in a criminal case as evidence that the defendant committed the offense of which he was found guilty beyond a reasonable doubt — all these make no sense to either laymen or lawyer; and no amount of discourse about the frailties of jurors or the virtues of cross-examination can give them the appearance of rationality.

QUESTIONS

1.   Apply the Federal Rules of Evidence to Professor Morgan's hypothetical. Do the results prove more satisfying?

2.   Does the next case in this section provide the answer to Professor Morgan's concerns? If not, is there a better way to resolve this matter?

DALLAS COUNTY v. COMMERCIAL UNION ASSURANCE CO.
286 F.2d 388 (5th Cir. 1961)

Wisdom, Circuit Judge.

This appeal presents a single question — the admissibility in evidence of a newspaper to show that the Dallas County Courthouse in Selma, Alabama, was damaged by fire in 1901. We hold that the newspaper was admissible, and affirm the judgment below.

On a bright, sunny morning, July 7, 1957, the clock tower of the Dallas County Courthouse at Selma, Alabama, commenced to lean, made loud cracking and popping noises, then fell, and telescoped into the courtroom. Fortunately, the collapse of the tower took place on a Sunday morning; no one was injured, but damage to the courthouse exceeded $100,000. An examination of the tower debris showed the presence of charcoal and charred timbers. The State Toxicologist, called in by Dallas County, reported the char was evidence that lightning struck the courthouse. Later, several residents of Selma reported that a bolt of lightning struck the courthouse July 2, 1957. On this information, Dallas County concluded that a lightning bolt had hit the building causing the collapse of the clock tower five days later. Dallas County carried insurance for loss to its courthouse caused by fire or lightning. The insurers' engineers and investigators found that the court-house collapsed of its own weight. They reported that the courthouse had not been struck by lightning; that lightning could not have caused the collapse of the tower; that the collapse of the tower was caused by structural weaknesses attributable to a faulty design, poor construction, gradual deterioration of the structure, and overloading brought about by remodeling and the recent installation of an air-conditioning system, part of which was constructed over the courtroom trusses. In their opinion, the char was the result of a fire in the courthouse tower and roof that must have occurred many, many years before July 2, 1957. The insurers denied liability.

The County sued its insurers in the Circuit Court of Dallas County. As many of the suits as could be removed, seven, were removed to the United States District Court for the Southern District of Alabama, and were consolidated for trial. The case went to the jury on one issue: did lightning cause the collapse of the clock tower?

The record contains ample evidence to support a jury verdict either way. . . . The jury chose to believe the insurers' witnesses and brought in a verdict for the defendants.

During the trial the defendants introduced a copy of the Morning Times of Selma for June 9, 1901. This issue carried an unsigned article describing a fire that occurred at two in the morning of June 9, 1901, while the courthouse was still under construction. The article stated, in part: "The unfinished dome of the County's new courthouse was in flames at the top, and . . . soon fell in. The fire was soon under control and the main building was saved. . . ." The insurers do not contend that the collapse of the tower resulted from unsound charred timbers used in the repair of the building after the fire; they offered the newspaper account to show there had been a fire long before 1957 that would account for charred timber in the clock tower.

As a predicate for introducing the newspaper in evidence, the defendants called to the stand the editor of the Selma Times-Journal who testified that his publishing company maintains archives of the published issues of the Times-Journal and of the Morning Times, its predecessor, and that the archives contain the issue of the Morning Times of Selma for June 9, 1901, offered in evidence. The plaintiff objected that the newspaper article was hearsay; that it was not a business record nor an ancient document, nor was it admissible under any recognized exception to the hearsay doctrine. The trial judge admitted the newspaper as part of the records of the Selma Times-Journal. The sole error Dallas County specifies on appeal is the admission of the newspaper in evidence.

In the Anglo-American adversary system of law, courts usually will not admit evidence unless its accuracy and trustworthiness may be tested by cross-examination. Here, therefore, the plaintiff argues that the newspaper should not be admitted: "You cannot cross-examine a newspaper."[89] Of course, a newspaper article is hearsay, and in almost all circumstances is inadmissible. However, the law governing hearsay is somewhat less than pellucid.[90] And, as with most rules, it is

---

89 [1] This argument, a familiar one, rests on a misunderstanding of the origin and the nature of the hearsay rule. The rule is not an ancient principle of English law recognized at Runnymede. And, gone is its odor of sanctity. Wigmore is often quoted for the statement that "cross-examination is beyond any doubt the greatest legal engine ever invented for the discovery of the truth." 5 WIGMORE § 1367 (3rd ed.). In over 1200 pages devoted to the hearsay rule, however, he makes it very clear that:

> [T]he rule aims to insist on testing all statements by cross-examination, if they can be. . . . No one could defend a rule which pronounced that all statements thus untested are worthless; for all historical truth is based on uncross-examined assertions; and every day's experience of life gives denial to such an exaggeration. What the Hearsay Rule implies — and with profound verity — is that all testimonial assertions ought to be tested by cross-examination as the best attainable measure; and it should not be burdened with the pedantic implication that they must be rejected as worthless if the test is unavailable.

1 WIGMORE § 8c. In this connection *see* Falknor, *The Hearsay Rule and Its Exceptions*, 2 UCLA L. REV. 43 (1954).

In The Introductory Note to Chapter VI, Hearsay Evidence, AMERICAN LAW INSTITUTE, MODEL CODE OF EVIDENCE (1942), Edmund M. Morgan, Reporter, it is pointed out that "the hearsay rule is the child of the adversary system." The Note continues:

> During the first centuries of the jury system, the jury based its decision upon what the jurors themselves knew of the matter in dispute and what they learned through the words of their fathers and through such words of these persons whom they are bound to trust as worthy. . . . Until the end of the sixteenth century hearsay was received without question. . . . The opportunity for cross-examination is not a necessary element of a jury system, while it is the very heart of the adversary system. . . . As the judges began their attempts to rationalize the results of the decisions dealing with evidence, they first relied upon the general notion that a party was obliged to produce the best evidence available, but no more. Had they applied this generally, hearsay would have been received whenever better evidence could not be obtained. Therefore the judges discovered a special sort of necessity in . . . exceptional cases . . . [making] the admissible hearsay less unreliable than hearsay in general. . . . [By 1840] it became the fashion to attribute the exclusion of hearsay to the incapacity of the jury to evaluate, and in the development of exceptions to the rule, courts have doubtless been influenced by this notion. . . . Modern text writers and judges have purported to find for each exception some sort of necessity for resort to hearsay and some condition attending the making of the excepted statement which will enable the jury to put a fair value upon it and will thus serve as a substitute for cross-examination. A careful examination of the eighteen or nineteen classes of utterances, each of which is now recognized as an exception to the hearsay rule by some respectable authority, will reveal that in many of them the necessity resolves itself into mere convenience and the substitute for cross-examination is imperceptible. . . . . . . In most of the exceptions, however, the adversary theory is disregarded. There is nothing in any of the situations to warrant depriving the adversary of an opportunity to cross-examine; but those rationalizing the results purport to find some substitute for cross-examination. In most instances one will look in vain for anything more than a situation in which an ordinary man making such a statement would positively desire to tell the truth; and in some the most that can be claimed is the absence of a motive to falsify.

For the history of the rule *see* 5 WIGMORE, EVIDENCE § 1364 (3rd ed.); 9 HOLDSWORTH'S HISTORY OF ENGLISH LAW, 214 (1926).

90 [3]

> The fact is, then, that the law governing hearsay today is a conglomeration of inconsistencies, developed as a result of conflicting theories. Refinements and qualifications within the exceptions only add to its irrationality. The courts by multiplying exceptions reveal their conviction that relevant hearsay evidence normally has real probative value, and is capable of

replete with exceptions.[91] Witnesses die, documents are lost, deeds are destroyed, memories fade. All too often, primary evidence is not available and courts and lawyers must rely on secondary evidence.

*   *   *

We turn now to a case, decided long before the Federal Rules were adopted, in which the court used an approach we consider appropriate for the solution of the problem before us. *G. & C. Merriam Co. v. Syndicate Pub. Co.*, 2 Cir., 1913, 207 F. 515, 518, concerned a controversy between dictionary publishers over the use of the title "Webster's Dictionary" when the defendant's dictionary allegedly was not based upon WEBSTER'S DICTIONARY at all. The bone of contention was whether a statement in the preface to the dictionary was admissible as evidence of the facts it recited. Ogilvie, the compiler of the dictionary, stated in his preface that he used WEBSTER'S DICTIONARY as the basis for his own publication. The dictionary, with its preface, was published in 1850, sixty-three years before the trial of the case. Ogilvie's published statement was challenged as hearsay. Judge Learned Hand, then a district judge, unable, as we are here, to find a case in point, for authority relied solely on WIGMORE ON EVIDENCE (then a recent publication), particularly on Wigmore's analysis that "the requisites of an exception to the hearsay rule are necessity and circumstantial guaranty of trustworthiness." WIGMORE ON EVIDENCE, §§ 1421, 1422, 1690 (1st ed. 1913). Applying these criteria, Judge Hand held that the statement was admissible as an exception to the hearsay rule:

> Ogilvie's preface is of course an unsworn statement and as such only hearsay testimony, which may be admitted only as an exception to the general rule. The question is whether there is such an exception. I have been unable to find any express authority in point and must decide the question upon principle. In the first place, I think it fair to insist that to reject such a statement is to refuse evidence about the truth of which no reasonable person should have any doubt whatever, because it fulfills both the requisites of an exception to the hearsay rule, necessity and circumstantial guaranty of trustworthiness. WIGMORE, §§ 1421, 1422, 1690. . . . Besides Ogilvie, everyone else is dead who ever knew anything about the matter and could intelligently tell us what the fact is. . . . As to the trustworthiness of the testimony, it has the guaranty of the occasion, at which there was no motive for fabrication.

---

valuation by a jury as well as by other triers of fact. This is further demonstrated by the majority view that inadmissible hearsay received without objection may be sufficient to sustain a verdict. Most statutes regulating procedure before administrative tribunals make hearsay admissible. And it is by no means clear that the administrative official ordinarily presiding at a hearing has more competence to value testimony than has a jury acting under the supervision of a judge. The number of cases tried before juries as compared with the number tried before judges without juries and before administrative tribunals, is small indeed.

ALI MODEL CODE OF EVIDENCE, p. 223 (1942).

[91] McCORMICK, LAW OF EVIDENCE, *Title 9: The Hearsay Rule and Its Exceptions* (especially Section 300, "Weaknesses of the Present Rules") (1954 ed.), Rucker, *The Twilight Zone of Hearsay*, 9 VAND. L. REV. 453 (1956); Morgan, *Hearsay and Non-Hearsay*, 48 HARV. L. REV. 1138 (1935); McCormick, *The Borderland of Hearsay*, 39 YALE L.J. 489 (1930).

207 F. 515, 518. The Court of Appeals adopted the district court's opinion in its entirety.

The first of the two requisites is necessity. As to necessity, Wigmore points out this requisite means that unless the hearsay statement is admitted, the facts it brings out may otherwise be lost, either because the person whose assertion is offered may be dead or unavailable, or because the assertion is of such a nature that one could not expect to obtain evidence of the same value from the same person or from other sources. WIGMORE, § 1421 (3rd ed.). "In effect, Wigmore says that, as the word necessity is here used, it is not to be interpreted as uniformly demanding a showing of total inaccessibility of firsthand evidence as a condition precedent to the acceptance of a particular piece of hearsay, but that necessity exists where otherwise great practical inconvenience would be experienced in making the desired proof. . . . If it were otherwise, the result would be that the exception created to the hearsay rule would thereby be mostly, if not completely, destroyed." . . .

The fire referred to in the newspaper account occurred fifty-eight years before the trial of this case. Any witness who saw that fire with sufficient understanding to observe it and describe it accurately, would have been older than a young child at the time of the fire. We may reasonably assume that at the time of the trial he was either dead or his faculties were dimmed by the passage of fifty-eight years. It would have been burdensome, but not impossible, for the defendant to have discovered the name of the author of the article (although it had no by-line) and, perhaps, to have found an eye-witness to the fire. But it is improbable — so it seems to us — that any witness could have been found whose recollection would have been accurate at the time of the trial of this case. And it seems impossible that the testimony of any witness would have been as accurate and as reliable as the statement of facts in the contemporary newspaper article.[92]

The rationale behind the "ancient documents" exception is applicable here; after a long lapse of time, ordinary evidence regarding signatures or hand-writing is virtually unavailable, and it is therefore permissible to resort to circumstantial evidence. Thus, in *Trustees of German Township, Montgomery County v. Farmers & Citizens Savings Bank Co.*, Ohio Com. Pl. 1953, 113 N.E.2d 409, 412, *affirmed*, Ohio App., 115 N.E.2d 690, the court admitted as ancient documents newspapers eighty years old containing notices of advertisements for bids relating to the town hall: "Such exhibits, by reason of age, alone, and unquestioned authenticity, qualify as ancient documents."[93] The ancient documents rule applies to documents a generation or more in age. Here, the Selma Times-Journal article is almost two generations old. The principle of necessity, not requiring absolute impossibility or

---

[92] [15] *Cf.* Rule 63(4) of the Uniform Rules of Evidence: "If the declarant is unavailable as a witness, a statement narrating, describing or explaining an event or condition which the judge finds was made by the declarant at a time when the matter had been recently perceived by him and while his recollection was clear, and was made in good faith prior to the commencement of the action [is admissible.]" *Cf. also* the Massachusetts Hearsay Act: "No declaration of a deceased person shall be excluded as evidence on the ground of its being hearsay if it appears to the satisfaction of the judge to have been made in good faith before the beginning of the suit and upon the personal knowledge of the declarant." Mass. Acts 1898, c. 535.

[93] [16] *See also* Wickes, *Ancient Documents and Hearsay*, 8 TEX. L. REV. 451 (1930); 7 WIGMORE, EVIDENCE, § 2137 (3rd ed.); MCCORMICK, EVIDENCE, §§ 190, 298 (1954 ed.).

total inaccessibility of first-hand knowledge, is satisfied by the practicalities of the situation before us.

The second requisite for admission of hearsay evidence is trustworthiness. According to Wigmore, there are three sets of circumstances when hearsay is trustworthy enough to serve as a practicable substitute for the ordinary test of cross-examination: "Where the circumstances are such that a sincere and accurate statement would naturally be uttered, and no plan of falsification be formed; where, even though a desire to falsify might present itself, other considerations, such as the danger of easy detection or the fear of punishment, would probably counteract its force; where the statement was made under such conditions of publicity that an error, if it had occurred, would probably have been detected and corrected." 5 WIGMORE, EVIDENCE, § 1422 (3rd ed.). These circumstances fit the instant case.

There is no procedural canon against the exercise of common sense in deciding the admissibility of hearsay evidence.[94] In 1901 Selma, Alabama, was a small town. Taking a common sense view of this case, it is inconceivable to us that a newspaper reporter in a small town would report there was a fire in the dome of the new courthouse — if there had been no fire. He is without motive to falsify, and a false report would have subjected the newspaper and him to embarrassment in the community. The usual dangers inherent in hearsay evidence, such as lack of memory, faulty narration, intent to influence the court proceedings, and plain lack of truthfulness are not present here. To our minds, the article published in the Selma Morning-Times on the day of the fire is more reliable, more trustworthy, more competent evidence than the testimony of a witness called to the stand fifty-eight years later.

We hold, that in matters of local interest, when the fact in question is of such a public nature it would be generally known throughout the community, and when the questioned fact occurred so long ago that the testimony of an eye-witness would probably be less trustworthy than a contemporary newspaper account, a federal court . . . may relax the exclusionary rules to the extent of admitting the newspaper article in evidence. We do not characterize this newspaper as a "business record," nor as an "ancient document," nor as any other readily identifiable and happily tagged species of hearsay exception. It is admissible because it is necessary and trustworthy, relevant and material, and its admission is within the trial judge's exercise of discretion in holding the hearing within reasonable bounds.

---

[94] [17] Judge Parker observed in *United States v. 25,406 Acres of Land, etc.*, 4 Cir., 1949, 172 F.2d 990, 995; "In cases of this sort, we must never forget that the common sense of the twelve men on the jury is a surer guaranty of justice than any attempt that might be made to give logical application to antiquated rules of evidence. If an honest and intelligent jury is given all the facts and is correctly instructed as to the law, it will come pretty near deciding a case correctly. Artificial rules of evidence which exclude from the consideration of the jurors matters which men consider in their everyday affairs hinder rather than help them at arriving at a just result." Judge Charles E. Clark, Chief Judge of the Second Circuit, the Reporter for the Advisory Committee on Rules for Civil Procedure, Supreme Court of the United States, has said: "I am convinced that judges generally have tended toward a pragmatic and common-sense attitude in the admission of evidence. They thus have already, with the exceptions noted, established the common-sense principle of Uniform Rule 7, which makes all evidence admissible unless otherwise expressly forbidden in the rules themselves." Clark, *Foreword to Symposium on the Uniform Rules of Evidence*, 10 RUTGERS L. REV. 479 (1956). . . .

Judgment is affirmed.

HUFF v. WHITE MOTOR CORP.
609 F.2d 286 (7th Cir. 1979)

Tone, Circuit Judge.

In the trial of this diversity action for wrongful death, the court excluded a statement of the plaintiff's decedent, made while he was hospitalized for treatment of the injuries from which he later died. We hold that unless the declarant was not mentally competent when he made the statement, it should have been admitted under the so-called residual exception to the hearsay rule established by Rules 803(24) and 804(b)(5) of the Federal Rules of Evidence. . . .

In a previous appeal in this case we held that under Indiana law a manufacturer has a duty to design a motor vehicle so that it will not be unreasonably dangerous if it is involved in a collision, and therefore we reversed a summary judgment for defendant based on a contrary view of Indiana law. *Huff v. White Motor Corp.*, 565 F.2d 104 (7th Cir. 1977). In the opinion in that case the essential facts were summarized as follows:

> On September 4, 1970, Jessee Huff was driving a truck-tractor manufactured by the defendant White Motor Corporation near Terre Haute, Indiana when it jack-knifed on the highway, sideswiped a guardrail, and collided with an overpass support. Aside from the structural damage to the tractor, the fuel tank ruptured and caught fire. The flames engulfed the cab area occupied by Huff. The severe burns he received in the fire caused his death nine days later. Helen L. Huff filed this action seeking damages for wrongful death of her husband based on the theory that the defective design of the fuel system caused the fire that took Huff's life.

Id. at 105.

At the trial on remand, the jury returned a verdict awarding plaintiff $700,000 in compensatory damages. Defendant appeals from the judgment on the verdict, arguing trial error. . . .

I.

Admissibility, of Decedent's Statement

Defendant offered and the trial court excluded the testimony of Melvin Myles, who was the husband of Mrs. Huff's cousin and a friend and neighbor of the Huffs for many years. Myles' testimony, presented out of the presence of the jury, was that, when he and one Richard King visited Huff in his hospital room two or three days after the accident, Huff gave the following description of how the accident occurred:

[H]e told us first more or less what happened and this U.S. 41 there has a bad curve there and he told us as he was approaching the curve or starting into it his pant leg was on fire and he was trying to put his pant leg out and lost control and hit the bridge abutment and then the truck was on fire. . . .

Tho district court excluded this testimony as hearsay, rejecting defendant's argument that Huff's statement was an admission under Rule 801(d)(2) or admissible under the residual exception, Rules 803(24) and 804(b)(5). On appeal, defendant argues that the evidence was admissible on both theories the district court rejected and also as a statement against interest under Rule 804(b)(3). We do not consider the latter argument, because Rule 804(b)(3) was not mentioned to the district court as a basis for admitting the evidence.

Defendant first argues that Huff's statement is admissible as an admission because privity exists between Huff and his widow, who brings this wrongful death action. At common law, privity-based admissions have been "generally accepted by the courts," according to McCormick, *Handbook of the Law of Evidence* 647 (2d ed. 1972). Plaintiff argues that privity is lacking here because under Indiana law . . . a wrongful death action is not derivative. We agree with McCormick that this should not be controlling, and that the exclusion by "some courts" of statements of the deceased in wrongful death cases because the action is not "derivative" is based on "a hypertechnical concept of privity." McCormick, *supra*, at 648 n.51.

The admissibility of privity-based admissions in the federal courts is now controlled, of course, by the Federal Rules of Evidence. A reading of Article VIII of those rules, the article on hearsay, leads us to conclude that privity-based admissions are to be tested for admissibility under the residual exception provided for in Rules 803(24) and 804(b)(5) rather than under the admissions provision, Rule 801(d)(2). Although neither the rules themselves nor the Advisory Committee Notes refer to privity-based admissions, and Congress added nothing on the subject in its consideration of the rules, the language of Rule 801(d)(2) and the general scheme of the hearsay article support our conclusion. Privity-based admissions are within the definition of hearsay, Rule 801(c), an extrajudicial statement offered "to prove the truth of the matter asserted," and are not among the specifically defined kinds of admissions that despite Rule 801(c) are declared not to be hearsay in Rule 801(d)(2). Nor are they covered by any of the specific exceptions to the hearsay rule listed in Rules 803 and 804. Thus privity-based admissions are not admissible as such, if the rules are to be read literally. Moreover, the very explicitness of Rule 801(d)(2) suggests that the draftsmen did not intend to authorize the courts to add new categories of admissions to those stated in the rule. No standards for judicial improvisation or discretion are provided in Rule 801(d)(2), as they are in Rules 803(24) and 804(b)(5).

The admissibility of Huff's statement depends, therefore, upon the residual exception, which is stated in Rules 803(24) and 804(b)(5):[95]

> A statement not specifically covered by any of the foregoing exceptions but having equivalent circumstantial guarantees of trustworthiness, if the court determines that (A) the statement is offered as evidence of a material fact;

---

[95] [4] The two provisions are identical, and Rule 804(b)(5) is therefore redundant, since 803(24) applies whether or not the declarant is a witness. *See* J. WALTZ, THE NEW FEDERAL RULES OF EVIDENCE 171 (2d ed. 1975).

(B) the statement is more probative on the point for which it is offered than any other evidence which the proponent can procure through reasonable efforts; and (C) the general purposes of these rules and the interests of justice will best be served by admission of the statement into evidence. However, a statement may not be admitted under this exception unless the proponent of it makes known to the adverse party sufficiently in advance of the trial or hearing to provide the adverse party with a fair opportunity to prepare to meet it, his intention to offer the statement and the particulars of it, including the name and address of the declarant.

We recognize at the outset that in applying this exception the district court has a considerable measure of discretion. . . . If, however, we arrive at "a definite and firm conviction that the court below committed a clear error of judgment in the conclusion it reached based upon a weighing of the relevant factors," . . . and that the error was prejudicial, we must reverse. We also recognize that Congress "intended that the residual hearsay exceptions will be used very rarely, and only in exceptional circumstances." Committee on the Judiciary, S. Rep. No. 93-1277, Note to Paragraph (24), 28 U.S.C.A. Fed. R. Evid. p. 583 (1975); *see also United States v. Kim*, 595 F.2d 755, 764–765 (D.C. Cir. 1979); *United States v. Bailey*, 581 F.2d 341, 346–347 (3d Cir. 1978). We think such circumstances are present here.

In reviewing a ruling made in the exercise of the trial court's discretion, we are greatly aided when the record contains a statement of the reasons for the ruling and any findings made under Rule 104(a) on preliminary questions of fact relevant to admissibility. Here nothing of this sort is available. Although the defendant relied on the residual exception, it was not mentioned in the court's explanation of its ruling excluding the evidence. Under these circumstances, we have little choice except to attempt to replicate the exercise of discretion that would be made by a trial judge in making the ruling.

Hearsay evidence must fulfill five requirements to be admissible under the residual exception. . . . We apply them to resolve the issue before us.

1. Trustworthiness

The circumstantial guarantees of trustworthiness on which the various specific exceptions to the hearsay rule are based are those that existed at the time the statement was made and do not include those that may be added by using hindsight. Evidence admissible under the residual exception must have *"equivalent* circumstantial guarantees of trustworthiness." Rules 803(24) and 804(b)(5) (emphasis added). Therefore, the guarantees to be considered in applying that exception are those that existed when the statement was made. In contrast, the probative value of an admission of a party-opponent, classified as non-hearsay by Rule 801(d)(2), is based on its inconsistency with the position asserted in court,[96] and that probative value does not depend on whether the party knew when making it that it would be

---

[96] [6] It is assumed in rationalizing admissibility that the admission may not possess circumstantial guarantees of trustworthiness. See Advisory Committee's Note to Rule 801(d)(2), 28 U.S.C.A. Fed. R. Evid. p. 530 (1975); McCormick, supra, at 629; Morgan, Basic Problems of Evidence 265 (1962).

against his interest in a later lawsuit.[97] Accordingly, in evaluating the circumstantial guarantees of trustworthiness with respect to Huff's statement, we may not consider its probative value as an admission of one who would be bringing the action if he had survived.

Turning to the circumstances we may properly consider for the present purpose, we note that Huff's statement was an unambiguous and explicit report of the events he had experienced two or three days earlier; it contained neither opinion nor speculation. He was not being interrogated, so there was no reason to give any explanation of how the accident happened unless he wanted to do so.[98] There was no reason for him to invent the story of the preexisting fire in the cab. The story was contrary to his pecuniary interest, *cf.* Rule 804(b)(3), whether or not he was aware of a possible claim against the manufacturer of the vehicle. A fire of unexplained cause on Huff's clothing would tend to indicate driver error and to fix the responsibility for the accident, with attendant adverse pecuniary consequences, on him. [Based on this reasoning, the Court concludes that the statement possesses circumstantial guarantees of trustworthiness so long as Huff was mentally competent to make a reasonable statement.]

Plaintiff also argues that it is unlikely that Huff made the statement, because Mrs. Huff testified that he was not physically able to carry on a conversation.

Even if we were to consider facts bearing on the reliability of Myles' reporting of the incident in determining its admissibility, we would not be persuaded that it should have been excluded for this reason. Mrs. Huff was an interested witness and, moreover, was assisted by her counsel's leading questions in giving the testimony relied on. No reason is suggested why Myles, a friend and relative by marriage, would have manufactured the story. Although the trial judge did not address the residual exception and made no credibility finding, it appears from his remarks that he credited Myles' testimony.

In our view, however, the reliability of the witness' testimony that the hearsay statement was in fact made is not a factor to be considered in deciding its admissibility. We recognize that the Third Circuit said otherwise in the *Bailey* case, 581 F.2d at 349. But, as we have already noted, the circumstantial guarantees of trustworthiness necessary under the residual exception are to be "equivalent" to the guarantees that justify the specific exceptions. Those guarantees relate solely to the trustworthiness of the hearsay statement itself. 5 WIGMORE, *supra*, §§ 1420,

---

[97] [7] See Strahorn A Reconsideration of the Hearsay Rule and Admissions, 85 U. PA. L. REV. 484, 564, 570, 573 (1937); 4 WIGMORE, EVIDENCE § 1048 (J. Chadbourn ed. 1972). Both authorities, which are cited in the Advisory Committee's Note to Rule 801(d)(2), 28 U.S.C.A. Fed. R. Evid. p. 530 (1975), agree that an admission has probative value because it is a prior assertion by the party "inconsistent with the validity of the contention" made by him in court. Strahorn at 573; WIGMORE § 1048. The admission need not, of course, be against interest to be admissible, although it usually is.

[98] [8] Huff appears to have wanted to tell Myles and King how the accident happened:

    Q. And was there a conversation in which [sic] you had with him and same that he had with you?

    A. [by Myles]. It was mostly us listening to Mr. Huff.

    Q. It was mostly what?

    A. We listened to what he had to say.

1422. The specific exceptions to the hearsay rule are not justified by any circumstantial guarantee that the witness who reports the statement will do so accurately and truthfully. That witness can be cross-examined and his credibility thus tested in the same way as that of any other witness. It is the hearsay declarant, not the witness who reported the hearsay, who cannot be cross-examined. Therefore, although we do not think Myles' testimony would fail a reliability test, that test is not to be applied by the court but by the jury, as with any other witness.

For the same reason, the probability that the statement is true, as shown by corroborative evidence, is not, we think, a consideration relevant to its admissibility under the residual exception to the hearsay rule. *But see Bailey*, 581 F.2d at 349. Because the presence or absence of corroborative evidence is irrelevant in the case of a specific exception, it is irrelevant here, where the guarantees of trustworthiness must be equivalent to those supporting specific exceptions. Accordingly, in reaching our decision we do not rely upon the evidence to which defendant has pointed as corroborating Huff's story of the fire in the cab.

*   *   *

We proceed now to a brief explanation of why we believe the other requirements of the residual exception to the hearsay rule have been met.

2. *Materiality*

Rules 803(24) and 804(b)(5) require that the statement be offered as evidence of a material fact, which we take to be a requirement of relevance. Defendant argues that the existence of a fire in the cab before the crash would be relevant to the issue of what caused the fuel to ignite after the crash, plaintiff having pleaded, offered proof, and argued that the location of the battery and battery mechanism as a result of a design error was a likely cause of ignition. Plaintiff responds that there were several possible sources of ignition. Assuming this to be true, the evidence was nevertheless relevant. The "fact that is of consequence" for purposes of the application of Rule 401 is that, as defendant contended, the fuel was ignited by a fire in the cab that was not due to a defect in the vehicle. If proved, that fact would be "of consequence to the determination of the action." The evidence in issue would tend "to make the existence of [that] fact . . . more probable or less probable than it would be without the evidence." Accordingly, the evidence is plainly relevant.

3. *Probative Importance of the Evidence*

To be admissible under the residual exception, the statement must be "more probative on the point for which it is offered than any other evidence . . . [the defendant] can procure through reasonable efforts." Huff's statement satisfies this requirement. The other evidence is expert opinion and Hicks' circumstantial testimony about what he saw when he arrived at the scene after the crash. Only Huff was in the cab immediately before the crash and knew whether there was a fire in the cab at that time. Unless the hearsay is admitted, there will be no direct evidence on that question. Moreover, the unique probative quality that would lie in Huff's admission if he had survived to bring this action, *see* note 7 *supra*, is not lost when the action is brought by his widow for his wrongful death.

4. *The Interests of Justice*

The hearsay statement is to be admitted only if doing so will best serve the general purposes of the Federal Rules of Evidence and the interests of justice. As we have already said, the circumstantial guarantees of trustworthiness and the probative value of the statement are strong. The need for the only available direct evidence on the issue of whether there was a fire in the cab, which, if it existed, would have been a likely source of ignition of the fuel, is obvious. There is no reason to believe the jury will not be equipped to evaluate the evidence. Admission of the evidence will best serve the interests of justice by increasing the likelihood that the jury will ascertain the truth about the cause of the accident.

5. *Notice*

Finally, the residual hearsay exception requires that the proponent of the hearsay statement notify his opponent of his intent to use the statement sufficiently in advance of the trial to give the opponent a fair opportunity to prepare to meet it. Plaintiff does not argue that defendant failed to comply with this notice provision, and the record reflects that defendant gave sufficient notice to plaintiff and the court.

[The case was then remanded for a determination of Huff's mental competency at the time of his declaration.]

UNITED STATES v. BAILEY
581 F.2d 341 (3d Cir. 1978)

JAMES HUNTER, III, CIRCUIT JUDGE:

In this case appellant Milton Bailey challenges his conviction for armed bank robbery. Although Bailey has raised several grounds on appeal, we find merit only in his contention that the introduction of certain evidence was error. We reverse and remand for a new trial.

I

On February 6, 1975, two men robbed a branch office of the Colony Federal Savings and Loan Association in Aliquippa, Pa. Five persons in the bank at the time of the robbery were ordered to lie down on the floor as the robbers rifled the tellers' cash drawers. The robbers fled the Bank and made their escape by car.

* * *

Palm prints removed from a teller's counter at the bank were identified as having been made by Johnny Bernard Stewart. Stewart was arrested, and after plea negotiations agreed to plead guilty. The terms of the agreement required Stewart to furnish a statement regarding the robbery, and to testify at any future proceedings concerning the robbery. In return, the government agreed to move for dismissal of one count of the two-count indictment brought against Stewart.

Prior to his sentencing, Stewart gave two oral statements to the FBI. The latter, made on April 29, 1976, was transcribed by an FBI agent. Stewart signed that statement, acknowledging that it was true. Both statements outlined Stewart's own involvement in the Colony Federal robbery and named Milton Bailey as the second bank robber. Stewart had counsel present at the time he made his agreement with the government and when both statements were made. One count of the indictment was dismissed pursuant to Stewart's agreement with the government, and he was sentenced several months prior to Bailey's trial.

Bailey was indicted on June 9, 1976. During his trial, the government learned that Stewart would refuse to testify concerning his earlier statements.

*   *   *

. . . [T]he government asked the court to rule on the admissibility of Stewart's written statement pursuant to Rules 804(b)(3) and 804(b)(5) of the Federal Rules of Evidence. Defendant's counsel objected, arguing that the rules did not permit admission of the statement. . . . The court made no ruling on the government's offer at that time but continued the proceedings temporarily so that counsel for both sides could research the questions raised and argue the matter the next morning.

After argument, the court ruled that the evidence was admissible under Rule 804(b)(5), but informed defense counsel that it would allow a three day continuance and any other time necessary. The court also informed counsel that it was willing to provide Stewart to the defense for cross-examination, or to notify the jury that Stewart was unwilling to testify. Bailey's counsel continued his objection to the introduction of the evidence. He declined the opportunity to bring Stewart to the stand for cross-examination after the confession was admitted, contending that if Stewart did answer questions at that time, Bailey's counsel might be placed in the position of proving the government's case against his client.

After the recess allowed by the trial judge, Bailey's lawyer informed the court that Stewart continued to refuse to testify and would not take the stand for defense cross-examination. The trial resumed and an FBI agent who was present when the statement was made by Stewart testified on the manner of taking the statement, as well as to the statement's contents. On cross-examination, Bailey's lawyer not only was allowed to question the agent about the circumstances surrounding the making of the statement, but also was permitted to impeach Stewart, through the agent, by eliciting prior convictions.

The jury found Bailey guilty, notwithstanding his alibi defense that he was working in his father's restaurant on the day of the robbery. Bailey then moved for a new trial, alleging, *inter alia*, that the introduction of the Stewart confession violated his right to confront witnesses against him and also did not meet the requirements of Rule 804(b)(5). The trial judge rejected these contentions, and Bailey has appealed to this court.

II.

A.

At trial, the government argued that the confession of Stewart was admissible as a declaration against penal interest, pursuant to Fed. R. Evid. 804(b)(8). The court determined that the requirements of that section had not been met, since the statement had been made by Stewart while he was in custody and after he had been offered a bargain involving dismissal of one count of the indictment against him. The government has not pressed its argument on this point here, and we do not disagree with the trial court.

B.

The trial court grounded the admissibility of the Stewart confession on rule 804(b)(5) of the Federal Rules of Evidence. That rule is one of two "residual" exceptions to the hearsay rule, providing for the admission of evidence even when the traditional requirements for the admission of hearsay are not met.

Prior to the adoption of the Federal Rules of Evidence, the out-of-court confession involved in this case could not have been used against Bailey.[99] Thus we must determine the extent to which the addition of the residual rule of 804(b)(5) has broadened the trial court's discretion in admitting evidence.

The trial court is vested with discretion in its determination whether hearsay evidence offered by a party meets the requirements of an exception set forth in the Federal Rules of Evidence. Our role, therefore, is to decide whether the trial court abused its discretion in determining that Stewart's confession met all requirements of rule 804(b)(5).

* * *

The history of Rule 804(b)(5) and its counterpart, Rule 803(24), indicates a congressional intention that the rules have a narrow focus. The initial "residual" rule for the introduction of hearsay not covered by one of the specific exceptions to the hearsay rule was phrased by the Advisory Committee as follows: A statement not specifically covered by any of the foregoing exceptions but having comparable circumstantial guarantees of trustworthiness. 56 F.R.D. 183, 322 (1972).

After the rules were submitted to Congress, the House Judiciary Committee removed from both Rules 803 and 804 the residual exceptions on the grounds that the rules added too much uncertainty to the law of evidence.[100] The Senate Judiciary Committee reinstated the deleted Advisory Committee residual excep-

---

[99] [6] In *Bruton v. United States*, 391 U.S. 123 (1968), the Court held inadmissible on confrontation grounds a confession made by defendant's accomplice implicating defendant in a joint trial when the accomplice had refused on fifth amendment grounds to be called as a witness. In upholding the confrontation claim, the Court noted that "We emphasize that the hearsay statement inculpating the petitioner was clearly inadmissible against him under traditional rules of evidence. . . ." 391 U.S. at 128 n.3.

[100] [7] The committee noted that some leeway was provided for the courts by Rule 102, which could

tions in a modified form. . . . The Senate Committee noted its fear that without residual rules of admissibility for hearsay in certain instances, the established exceptions would be tortured in order to allow reliable evidence to be introduced. Further, the new proposed residual rules were drafted to apply only when certain exceptional guarantees of trustworthiness exist and when high degrees of probativeness and necessity are present. The Senate Committee further stated that the residual exceptions were to be used only rarely, and in exceptional circumstances. The Senate Report cautioned that "[t]he residual exceptions are not meant to authorize major judicial revisions of the hearsay rules, including its present exceptions."

The House-Senate Conference Committee agreed to include the Senate residual rule with further modifications. . . . Representative Dennis, one of the floor managers of the Federal Rules of Evidence bill, stated in the House debate preceding passage of the bill, that the residual rules applied to situations "comparable to the ordinary hearsay exceptions." 120 Cong. Rec. 40894 (1974). In his view, the residual rule did not purport to accomplish much at all regarding expansion of traditional rules of evidence. Thus, in reviewing the admissibility of evidence under Rule 804(b)(5), we must keep in mind its limited scope as intended by Congress.

Defendant does not contest the trial judge's finding that Stewart was unavailable, or that the confession was evidence of a material fact — Bailey's identification as one of the bank robbers. Bailey contends, however, that other elements of Rule 804(b)(5) were not satisfied. Initially, he argues that the statement cannot be used against him since it was not until after trial had commenced that the government informed him that it would seek to have Stewart's statement introduced.

Before an out-of-court statement can be admitted pursuant to Rule 804(b)(5), the proponent of it must advise the adverse party [of] his intention to use the statement, as well as the "particulars of it, including the name and address of the declarant." The proponent must give notice "sufficiently before trial . . . to provide the adverse party with a fair opportunity to meet [the statement]. . . ."

Notice lacking.

The advance notice provision came into being during the House-Senate Conference on the proposed rules. . . .

The debates in Congress and the statements of Rep. William Hungate (Chairman of the House Judiciary Committee Subcommittee on Criminal Justice) indicate some understanding that the requirement of advance notice was to be strictly followed. . . . A number of courts of appeals have held that the purpose of the advance notice provision of the rule is satisfied even though notice is given after the trial begins, as long as there is sufficient opportunity provided for the adverse party

---

cover the anomalous situation calling for admission of hearsay not covered by an enumerated exception. Rule 102 states:

> These rules shall be construed to secure fairness in administration, elimination of unjustifiable expense and delay, and promotion of growth and development of the law of evidence to the end that the truth may be ascertained and proceedings justly determined.

The House Committee also stated that "if additional hearsay exceptions are to be created, they should be by amendments to the Rules, not on a case-by-case basis." H.R. Rep. No. 650, 93d Cong. 2d Sess. (1973), reprinted in [1974] U.S. Code Cong. & Admin. News, pp. 7051, 7079.

to prepare for and contest the admission of the evidence offered pursuant to the rule. . . .

Wo believe that the purpose of the rules and the requirement of fairness to an adversary contained in the advance notice requirement of Rule 803(24) and Rule 804(b)(5) are satisfied when, as here, the proponent of the evidence is without fault in failing to notify his adversary prior to trial and the trial judge has offered sufficient time, by means of granting a continuance, for the party against whom the evidence is to be offered to prepare to meet and contest its admission. Since the government was unable to notify Bailey's counsel prior to trial of Stewart's refusal to testify, and since the trial judge offered counsel time to conduct interviews as well as to research the evidentiary question, we feel that Bailey was not prejudiced by the lack of notice before trial. By examining the adequacy of the notice and the time allowed to prepare to meet a statement offered pursuant to these rules, a reviewing court may determine whether the adverse party has had "a fair opportunity to prepare to contest the use of the statement." . . .

Bailey also argues that Stewart's confession failed to meet the requirement that the evidence to be admitted pursuant to Rule 804(b)(5) must possess "guarantees of trustworthiness" equivalent to the other enumerated exceptions under Rule 804(b). We find this contention convincing.

The specific hearsay exceptions of Rule 804(b) include those for former testimony, dying declarations, statements against interest, and statements of family background or history. Each of these kinds of statements is admissible, though hearsay, because the circumstances in which the statements are made are indicative of a strong propensity for truthfulness (dying declarations), because there has been a previous opportunity for cross-examination (former testimony), or because the contents of the statements themselves are of such a nature that one reasonably would conclude that the speaker was telling the truth (statements against interest, statements of family history).[101]

The trial judge determined the reliability of the hearsay statement on the evidence that the bank robbers fled the crime in Bailey's girlfriend's car. Since the statement mentioned that Stewart and Bailey traveled to Aliquippa in the car, the trial judge held that Stewart's statement possessed sufficient indicia of reliability to justify its admission pursuant to 804(b)(5). We believe that the recitation of this single factor does not satisfy the requirement that the statement to be offered in evidence have "circumstantial guarantees of trustworthiness" equivalent to the other 804(b) exceptions. Indeed, if Stewart had borrowed the car from Bailey and had committed the robbery with another, the bargain he struck with the authorities provided him with the opportunity to sidetrack the investigation and protect his

---

[101] [12] As originally submitted to Congress, the proposed Federal Rules contained an additional exception for statements of recent perception. The House Committee, however, deleted this rule on the grounds that statements of the type encompassed within this exception did not bear "sufficient guarantees of trustworthiness to justify admissibility." H.R. Rep. No. 650, 93d Cong., 2d Sess., reprinted in [1974] U.S. Code Cong. & Admin. News at 7079–80. We think that an awareness of Congress' deletion of proposed Rule 804(b)(2) provides some guidance in determining whether a statement offered under Rule 804(b)(5) possesses guarantees of trustworthiness equivalent to those 804(b) exceptions included in the final version of the federal rules.

accomplice by naming Bailey, a plausible suspect, as his partner in the robbery.

We do not feel that the trustworthiness of a statement offered pursuant to the rule should be analyzed solely on the basis of the facts corroborating the authenticity of the statement. Since the rule is designed to come into play when there is a need for the evidence in order to ascertain the truth in a case, it would make little sense for a judge, in determining whether the hearsay is admissible, to examine only facts corroborating the substance of the declaration. Such an analysis in effect might increase the likelihood of admissibility when corroborating circumstances indicate a reduced need for the introduction of the hearsay statement. We do not believe that Congress intended that "trustworthiness" be analyzed in this manner. Rather, the trustworthiness of a statement should be analyzed by evaluating not only the facts corroborating the veracity of the statement, but also the circumstances in which the declarant made the statement and the incentive he had to speak truthfully or falsely. Further, consideration should be given to factors bearing on the reliability of the reporting of the hearsay by the witness.

In *United States v. Medico*, 557 F.2d 309 (2d Cir. 1977), the court held that circumstantial degrees of trustworthiness justified the admission of an unknown bystander's report of the license plate of a fleeing automobile used by escaping bank robbers. The bystander shouted the numbers out from the street to another bystander, who was stationed next to the locked door of the bank. The bystander near the door relayed the information into the bank to an employee who transcribed the description and tag number of the car. In assessing the reliability of the hearsay, the court looked to the opportunity of the declarants to observe, the amount of time for the information to be relayed to the bank employee, and the potential for misidentification or fabrication, determining that the situation in which the statements were offered provided a guarantee of trustworthiness on a par with the enumerated 804(b) exceptions.

*   *   *

In this case, the circumstances under which Stewart provided his statement implicating Bailey do not inspire confidence in its reliability. First, as we have discussed, the statement was made during negotiations for reduction of charges lodged against Stewart. Secondly, the statements were made in a face-to-face meeting with two FBI agents. Further, the statement was not made under oath and its veracity had not been tested, certainly not by cross-examination. Finally, the fact relied upon by the trial judge as corroborating Stewart's confession, the identification of the car, does not provide a sufficient degree of reliability to justify the statement's introduction. Thus we feel that the trial judge's determination as to the trustworthiness of the statement was an abuse of his discretion, since the assertions in the statement and the circumstances in which the statement was given do not provide guarantees of trustworthiness equivalent to the other Rule 804(b) exceptions that serve as benchmark for Rule 804(b)(5).

*   *   *

The judgment of the district court will be reversed and remanded for a new trial.

NOTES AND QUESTIONS

1. How do *Huff* and *Bailey* differ with respect to determining whether "equivalent circumstantial guarantees of trustworthiness" exist? *See Robinson v. Shapiro*, 646 F.2d 734, 743 n.7 (2d Cir. 1981).

2. *Bailey* suggests that courts should not apply the notice provision rigidly. For a contrary view, see *United States v. Mandel*, 591 F.2d 1347, 1369 (4th Cir. 1979), *cert. denied*, 445 U.S. 961 (1980); *United States v. Oates*, 560 F.2d 45, 72 n.30 (2d Cir. 1977).

3. After more than 30 years under the Federal Rules of Evidence, the residual exception is no longer as controversial as it was when the Rules first took effect. Although most courts still restrict the exception to rare or exceptional circumstances, judicial analysis has sometimes become somewhat cursory. *See, e.g., United States v. Dumeisi*, 424 F.3d 566 (7th Cir. 2005) (admitting into evidence so-called "Baghdad file" containing records of Sadam Huessein's Iraqi Intelligence Service). *See* § C.5 in Chapter II, *supra*.

4. Does the residual exception threaten to erode the hearsay rule? *See* Park, *Essay: Hearsay, Dead or Alive?*, 40 ARIZ. L. REV. 647 (1998); Fenner, *The Residual Exception to the Hearsay Rule: The Complete Treatment*, 33 CREIGHTON L. REV. 265 (2000).

5. The residual exception has also played a prominent role under state evidence codes. *See, e.g., Conn. v. Skakel*, 888 A.2d 985 (Conn. 2006) (murder prosecution of Kennedy family in-law).

David A. Sonenshein, *The Residual Exceptions to the Federal Hearsay Rule: Two Exceptions in Search of a Rule*
57 N.Y.U. L. REV. 867, 885–88 (1982)[102]

Near Misses

Another problem of interpreting the trustworthiness requirement of the residual exceptions is presented by the "near miss" situation. A near miss statement is an out-of-court statement that is in the realm of statements addressed by an enumerated exception to the hearsay rule but which just misses falling within the exception because it is lacking one or more of the factors which define the exception. For example, consider the situation in which the proponent offers a nineteen-year-old document, the authenticity of which is established, into evidence. The ancient document exception provides for the admissibility of "[s]tatements in a document in existence twenty years or more the authenticity of which is established." This proffer of a nineteen-year-old document could be said nearly to miss falling within an enumerated exception to the hearsay rule.

A number of courts have ruled that it is proper to admit hearsay that nearly misses meeting one of the enumerated exceptions under the residual hearsay

---

[102] Reprinted with permission.

exceptions. For example, in *United States v. Leslie*, the Fifth Circuit approved the admission under residual exception Rule 803(24) of an out-of-court, prior inconsistent statement made without oath as substantive evidence at a criminal trial despite the fact that Rule 801(d)(1)(A) permits the admission of such statements substantively only when made under oath at a court proceeding or in a deposition. Similarly, in *United States v. McPartlin*, the government offered the desk diaries of an unindicted co-conspirator in a bribery prosecution, which detailed the witness' bribery activities with the defendants. The Seventh Circuit found that even if the diaries had failed to meet the specific requirements of the business record exception, [w]here evidence complies with the spirit, if not the letter, of several exceptions, admissibility is appropriate under the residual exception.

Other courts have refused to admit hearsay in the near miss situation, holding that since the enumerated exceptions establish specific requirements that must be satisfied to render the hearsay trustworthy, the failure to satisfy all of those requirements precludes a finding of the requisite trustworthiness. For example, a document is inadmissible under the business record exception if it is not kept in the ordinary course of business. The "ordinary course of business" requirement is what makes the document trustworthy. If lacking, the rulemakers have determined that the statement contained in the document is not trustworthy enough to be admissible. Therefore, it must be inadmissible under the residual exceptions as well.

Perhaps the most convoluted rationale for rejecting at least some near miss hearsay is found in *Zenith Radio Corp. v. Matsushita Electric Industrial Co.* In *Zenith*, the court addressed the question whether courts should develop a per se rule to bar admission under the residual exceptions of near miss evidence, defined as generically of a type covered by another specific hearsay exception, but which fails to meet the precise requirements of that specific exception.

The court referred to the Report of the Advisory Committee which drafted the rules, explaining that the proposed residual exceptions were broader than the final congressional enactment, which were designed only for "new and presently unanticipated situations." In addition, the court quoted from the Senate Judiciary Committee report which commented that "an overly broad residual hearsay exception could emasculate the hearsay rule and the recognized exceptions or vitiate the rationale behind the codification of the rules." Recognizing the maxim of statutory construction that avoids the nullification of a specific statute by the overbroad application of a general one, the court concluded that "the residual exceptions cannot be invoked when there is a specific category which sets forth conditions governing the admissibility of a clearly defined category of hearsay evidence."

The court determined, however, that most of the enumerated exceptions to the hearsay rule fall outside the scope of this maxim, since most of them do not clearly define a category of hearsay. Though some of the hearsay exceptions, including former testimony, learned treatises, or judgment of previous conviction, exist only in one form, most of the hearsay exceptions "apply to a relatively amorphous category of evidence which is delimited solely by the requirements set forth in the rule itself." The court referred to business records, statements against interest, present sense impressions, and recorded recollections as examples of the less clearly defined exceptions. According to the *Zenith* court, to exclude, a priori, statements resembling this type of exception would sap the residual exceptions of their vigor.

The *Zenith* court's purported distinction between the two classes of enumerated exceptions is, however, a distinction without a difference. The court viewed the function of the residual rules as sanctioning the admission of hearsay statements presenting situations not anticipated by Congress when it announced the enumerated exceptions. On this reading of the rules, a near miss should be allowed under the rule only if, despite its close similarity to instances of hearsay that fall within an enumerated exception, it presents an unanticipated situation. To take just one example, to say that the admissibility of a record which falls short of the business records exception is an "unanticipated" situation is disingenuous. In formulating the business records exception, it cannot be gainsaid that the common law and Congress anticipated the existence of other records and determined that unless they possess the enumerated criteria, such records should not be admitted at trial. Hence, the *Zenith* court's proposal appears unhelpful.

This is not to deny that circumstantial factors other than those which define the enumerated exceptions can make near miss hearsay as reliable as hearsay within the enumerated exceptions. Courts admitting near miss hearsay should make it clear, however, that a near miss statement is to be admitted only when the court can articulate a circumstance in the making of the statement that substitutes for the missing enumerated elements and thus provides equivalent guarantees of trustworthiness. Otherwise, the enumerated exceptions could become dead letters because courts would be given the tools to create watered-down versions of the enumerated exceptions by judicial fiat.

David Sonenshein, *Impeaching the Hearsay Declarant*
74 TEMP. L. REV. 163 (2001)[103]

I. The Rationale for Rule 806

. . . So, why a Rule 806? The Advisory Committee Note to the Rule states the rationale simply: "The declarant of a hearsay statement which is admitted in evidence is in effect a witness. His credibility should in fairness be subject to impeachment and support as though he had in fact testified."[104]

A simple example will illuminate the Rule's rationale. Assume an automobile collision case in which the only eyewitness makes an excited utterance: "Oh my God, the Chevy ran the red light!" Since the Chevy belongs to the defendant in the lawsuit which arises from the accident, the plaintiff determines to offer evidence from the eyewitness. All things being equal, plaintiff's counsel would offer the eyewitness as a trial witness to recount her observations at the time of the collision with all of the evidentiary richness which a live witness can provide. Plaintiff could

---

[103] Copyright © 2001 Temple University of the Commonwealth System of Higher Education; David Sonenshein.

[104] [4] Fed. R. Evid. 806, Advisory Committee Note (1975).

then corroborate this testimony with the excited utterance pursuant to Rule 803(2)[105] reported by the eyewitness herself or by the live testimony of any other person who perceived or heard it.

Now suppose, however, that the investigation reveals that the vaunted eyewitness, on whose observations the case likely will turn, was on parole from convictions for welfare fraud, perjury, and filing a false accident report at the time of the collision. In the absence of Rule 806, plaintiff's counsel could wisely forego calling the eyewitness as a trial witness and simply call the hearer of the excited utterance, perhaps a highly-decorated police officer or a nun.

Thus, the jury would receive the reliable-sounding excited utterance, communicated by a highly credible reporter/messenger, never having any reason to suspect that the perceiver of the events recounted as evidence ought not to be believed. Further, in the absence of Rule 806, the Rules would discourage the calling of live witnesses only where the witness's presence is crucial, necessary, and desirable, and effectively mislead the jury by omission regarding the weight of the hearsay declarant's evidence. Rule 806 is a rule which levels the playing field between live witnesses and non-testifying hearsay declarants so that a party's failure to call a live witness where available will not result in a net gain for that party, and a net loss for the fact-finding process. . . .

I. CONFRONTATION AND HEARSAY

CRAWFORD v. WASHINGTON
541 U.S. 36 (2004)

SCALIA, J., delivered the opinion of the Court, in which STEVENS, KENNEDY, SOUTER, THOMAS, GINSBURG, and BREYER, JJ., joined. REHNQUIST, C. J., filed an opinion concurring in the judgment, in which O'CONNOR, J., joined.

Petitioner Michael Crawford stabbed a man who allegedly tried to rape his wife, Sylvia. At his trial, the State played for the jury Sylvia's tape-recorded statement to the police describing the stabbing, even though he had no opportunity for cross-examination. The Washington Supreme Court upheld petitioner's conviction after determining that Sylvia's statement was reliable. The question presented is whether this procedure complied with the Sixth Amendment's guarantee that, "[i]n all criminal prosecutions, the accused shall enjoy the right . . . to be confronted with the witnesses against him."

I

On August 5, 1999, Kenneth Lee was stabbed at his apartment. Police arrested petitioner later that night. . . . Petitioner eventually confessed that he and Sylvia had gone in search of Lee because he was upset over an earlier incident in which

---

[105] [5] Federal Rule of Evidence 803(2) provides for the admissibility of out-of-court statements for their truth where such statements relate to ". . . a startling event or condition made while the declarant was under the stress of excitement caused by the even or condition." Fed. R. Evid. 803(2).

Lee had tried to rape her. The two had found Lee at his apartment, and a fight ensued in which Lee was stabbed in the torso and petitioner's hand was cut. Petitioner gave the following account of the fight:

"Q.   Okay. Did you ever see anything in [Lee's] hands?

"A.   I coulda swore I seen him goin' for somethin' before, right before everything happened. He was like reachin', fiddlin' around down here and stuff . . . and I just . . . I don't know, I think, this is just a possibility, but I think, I think that he pulled somethin' out and I grabbed for it and that's how I got cut . . . ."

Sylvia generally corroborated petitioner's story about the events leading up to the fight, but her account of the fight itself was arguably different — particularly with respect to whether Lee had drawn a weapon before petitioner assaulted him:

"Q.   Did Kenny do anything to fight back from this assault?

"A.   (pausing) I know he reached into his pocket . . . or somethin' . . . I don't know what.

"Q.   Did you see anything in his hands at that point?

"A.   (pausing) um um (no)." *Id.*, at 137 (punctuation added).

The State charged petitioner with assault and attempted murder. At trial, he claimed self-defense. Sylvia did not testify because of the state marital privilege, which generally bars a spouse from testifying without the other spouse's consent. In Washington, this privilege does not extend to a spouse's out-of-court statements admissible under a hearsay exception, . . . so the State sought to introduce Sylvia's tape-recorded statements to the police as evidence that the stabbing was not in self-defense. Noting that Sylvia had admitted she led petitioner to Lee's apartment and thus had facilitated the assault, the State invoked the hearsay exception for statements against penal interest, Wash. Rule Evid. 804(b)(3) (2003).

Petitioner countered that, state law notwithstanding, admitting the evidence would violate his federal constitutional right to be "confronted with the witnesses against him." According to our description of that right in *Ohio v. Roberts*, 448 U.S. 56, (1980), it does not bar admission of an unavailable witness's statement against a criminal defendant if the statement bears "adequate 'indicia of reliability.' " . . . To meet that test, evidence must either fall within a "firmly rooted hearsay exception" or bear "particularized guarantees of trustworthiness." . . . The trial court here admitted the statement on the latter ground, offering several reasons why it was trustworthy. . . . The jury convicted petitioner of assault. . . .

*   *   *

We granted certiorari to determine whether the State's use of Sylvia's statement violated the Confrontation Clause. . . .

II

The Sixth Amendment's Confrontation Clause provides that, "[i]n all criminal prosecutions, the accused shall enjoy the right . . . to be confronted with the witnesses against him." We have held that this bedrock procedural guarantee applies to both federal and state prosecutions. . . . As noted above, *Roberts* says that an unavailable witness's out-of-court statement may be admitted so long as it has adequate indicia of reliability — *i.e.*, falls within a "firmly rooted hearsay exception" or bears "particularized guarantees of trustworthiness." . . . Petitioner argues that this test strays from the original meaning of the Confrontation Clause and urges us to reconsider it.

A

The Constitution's text does not alone resolve this case. One could plausibly read "witnesses against" a defendant to mean those who actually testify at trial, . . . , those whose statements are offered at trial, . . . or something in between. . . . We must therefore turn to the historical background of the Clause to understand its meaning.

The right to confront one's accusers is a concept that dates back to Roman times . . . The founding generation's immediate source of the concept, however, was the common law. English common law has long differed from continental civil law in regard to the manner in which witnesses give testimony in criminal trials. . . . The common-law tradition is one of live testimony in court subject to adversarial testing, while the civil law condones examination in private by judicial officers. . . .

Nonetheless, England at times adopted elements of the civil-law practice. Justices of the peace or other officials examined suspects and witnesses before trial. These examinations were sometimes read in court in lieu of live testimony, a practice that "occasioned frequent demands by the prisoner to have his 'accusers,' *i.e.* the witnesses against him, brought before him face to face." . . .

*　*　*

The most notorious instances of civil-law examination occurred in the great political trials of the 16th and 17th centuries. One such was the 1603 trial of Sir Walter Raleigh for treason. Lord Cobham, Raleigh's alleged accomplice, had implicated him in an examination before the Privy Council and in a letter. At Raleigh's trial, these were read to the jury. Raleigh argued that Cobham had lied to save himself: "Cobham is absolutely in the King's mercy; to excuse me cannot avail him; by accusing me he may hope for favour." . . . Suspecting that Cobham would recant, Raleigh demanded that the judges call him to appear, arguing that "[t]he Proof of the Common Law is by witness and jury: let Cobham be here, let him speak it. Call my accuser before my face. . . ." The judges refused, . . . , and, despite Raleigh's protestations that he was being tried "by the Spanish Inquisition," . . . the jury convicted, and Raleigh was sentenced to death.

One of Raleigh's trial judges later lamented that " 'the justice of England has never been so degraded and injured as by the condemnation of Sir Walter Raleigh.' " . . . Through a series of statutory and judicial reforms, English law developed a right of confrontation that limited these abuses. For example, treason statutes required witnesses to confront the accused "face to face" at his arraignment. . . . Courts, meanwhile, developed relatively strict rules of unavailability, admitting examinations only if the witness was demonstrably unable to testify in person. . . .

One recurring question was whether the admissibility of an unavailable witness's pretrial examination depended on whether the defendant had had an opportunity to cross-examine him. In 1696, the Court of King's Bench answered this question in the affirmative, in the widely reported misdemeanor libel case of *King v. Paine*, 5 Mod. 163, 87 Eng. Rep. 584. The court ruled that, even though a witness was dead, his examination was not admissible where "the defendant not being present when [it was] taken before the mayor . . . had lost the benefit of a cross-examination." . . .

[B]y 1791 (the year the Sixth Amendment was ratified), courts were applying the cross-examination rule . . . to examinations by justices of the peace in felony cases.

B

Controversial examination practices were also used in the Colonies. Early in the 18th century, for example, the Virginia Council protested against the Governor for having "privately issued several commissions to examine witnesses against particular men *ex parte*," complaining that "the person accused is not admitted to be confronted with, or defend himself against his defamers." . . . A decade before the Revolution, England gave jurisdiction over Stamp Act offenses to the admiralty courts, which followed civil-law rather than common-law procedures and thus routinely took testimony by deposition or private judicial examination. . . . John Adams, defending a merchant in a high-profile admiralty case, argued: "Examinations of witnesses upon Interrogatories, are only by the Civil Law. Interrogatories are unknown at common Law, and Englishmen and common Lawyers have an aversion to them if not an Abhorrence of them." . . .

Many declarations of rights adopted around the time of the Revolution guaranteed a right of confrontation. . . . The proposed Federal Constitution, however, did not. At the Massachusetts ratifying convention, Abraham Holmes objected to this omission precisely on the ground that it would lead to civil-law practices: "The mode of trial is altogether indetermined; . . . whether [the defendant] is to be allowed to confront the witnesses, and have the advantage of cross-examination, we are not yet told. . . . [W]e shall find Congress possessed of powers enabling them to institute judicatories little less inauspicious than a certain tribunal in Spain, . . . the *Inquisition.*" 2 DEBATES ON THE FEDERAL CONSTITUTION 110–111 (J. Elliot 2d ed. 1863). Similarly, a prominent Antifederalist writing under the pseudonym Federal Farmer criticized the use of "written evidence" . . . : "Nothing can be more essential than the cross examining [of] witnesses, and generally before the triers of the facts in question. . . . [W]ritten evidence . . . [is] almost useless; it must be frequently taken ex parte, and but very seldom leads to the proper discovery of truth." . . . The First Congress responded by including the Confrontation Clause in the proposal that became the Sixth Amendment.

Early state decisions shed light upon the original understanding of the common-law right. *State v. Webb*, 2 N. C. 103 (1794) *(per curiam)*, decided a mere three years after the adoption of the Sixth Amendment, held that depositions could be read against an accused only if they were taken in his presence. Rejecting a broader reading of the English authorities, the court held: "[I]t is a rule of the common law, founded on natural justice, that no man shall be prejudiced by evidence which he had not the liberty to cross examine." *Id.*

*   *   *

Many other decisions are to the same effect. . . .

III

This history supports two inferences about the meaning of the Sixth Amendment.

A

First, the principal evil at which the Confrontation Clause was directed was the civil-law mode of criminal procedure, and particularly its use of *ex parte* examinations as evidence against the accused. It was these practices that the Crown deployed in notorious treason cases like Raleigh's; . . . that English law's assertion of a right to confrontation was meant to prohibit; and that the founding-era rhetoric decried. The Sixth Amendment must be interpreted with this focus in mind.

Accordingly, we once again reject the view that condition the applies of its own force only to in-court testimony, and that its application to out-of-court statements introduced at trial depends upon "the law of Evidence for the time being." . . . Leaving the regulation of out-of-court statements to the law of evidence would render the Confrontation Clause powerless to prevent even the most flagrant inquisitorial practices. Raleigh was, after all, perfectly free to confront those who read Cobham's confession in court.

This focus also suggests that not all hearsay implicates the Sixth Amendment's core concerns. An off-hand, overheard remark might be unreliable evidence and thus a good candidate for exclusion under hearsay rules, but it bears little resemblance to the civil-law abuses the Confrontation Clause targeted. On the other hand, *ex parte* examinations might sometimes be admissible under modern hearsay rules, but the Framers certainly would not have condoned them.

The text of the Confrontation Clause reflects this focus. It applies to "witnesses" against the accused — in other words, those who "bear testimony." 1 N. Webster, An American Dictionary of the English Language (1828). "Testimony," in turn, is typically "[a] solemn declaration or affirmation made for the purpose of establishing or proving some fact." *Ibid.* An accuser who makes a formal statement to government officers bears testimony in a sense that a person who makes a casual remark to an acquaintance does not. The constitutional text, like the history underlying the common-law right of confrontation, thus reflects an especially acute concern with a specific type of out-of-court statement.

Various formulations of this core class of "testimonial" statements exist: "*ex parte* in-court testimony or its functional equivalent — that is, material such as affidavits, custodial examinations, prior testimony that the defendant was unable to cross-examine, or similar pretrial statements that declarants would reasonably expect to be used prosecutorially," . . . "extrajudicial statements . . . contained in formalized testimonial materials, such as affidavits, depositions, prior testimony, or confessions," *White v. Illinois*, 502 U.S. 346, 365, 112 S. Ct. 736, 116 L. Ed. 2d 848 (1992) (Thomas, J., joined by Scalia, J., concurring in part and concurring in judgment); "statements that were made under circumstances which would lead an objective witness reasonably to believe that the statement would be available for use at a later trial," Brief for National Association of Criminal Defense Lawyers et al. as Amici Curiae 3. These formulations all share a common nucleus and then define the Clause's coverage at various levels of abstraction around it. Regardless of the precise articulation, some statements qualify under any definition — for example, ex parte testimony at a preliminary hearing.

Statements taken by police officers in the course of interrogations are also testimonial under even a narrow standard. Police interrogations bear a striking resemblance to examinations by justices of the peace in England. The statements are not sworn testimony, but the absence of oath was not dispositive. Cobham's examination was unsworn, . . . , yet Raleigh's trial has long been thought a paradigmatic confrontation violation . . . .[106]

That interrogators are police officers rather than magistrates does not change the picture either. Justices of the peace conducting examinations [in England] . . . were not magistrates as we understand that office today, but had an essentially investigative and prosecutorial function. . . . England did not have a professional police force until the 19th century, . . . so it is not surprising that other government officers performed the investigative functions now associated primarily with the police. The involvement of government officers in the production of testimonial evidence presents the same risk, whether the officers are police or justices of the peace.

In sum, even if the Sixth Amendment is not solely concerned with testimonial hearsay, that is its primary object, and interrogations by law enforcement officers fall squarely within that class.[107]

---

[106] [3] These sources — especially Raleigh's trial — refute THE CHIEF JUSTICE's assertion, *post*, at 1375 (opinion concurring in judgment), that the right of confrontation was not particularly concerned with unsworn testimonial statements. But even if, as he claims, a general bar on unsworn hearsay made application of the Confrontation Clause to unsworn testimonial statements a moot point, that would merely change our focus from direct evidence of original meaning of the Sixth Amendment to reasonable inference. We find it implausible that a provision which concededly condemned trial by sworn *ex parte* affidavit through trial by *unsworn ex parte* affidavit perfectly OK. (The claim that unsworn testimony was self-regulating because jurors would disbelieve it, *cf. post*, at 1374, n. 1, is belied by the very existence of a general bar on unsworn testimony.) Any attempt to determine the application of a constitutional provision to a phenomenon that did not exist at the time of its adoption (here, allegedly, admissible unsworn testimony) involves some degree of estimation — what THE CHIEF JUSTICE calls use of a "proxy," *post*, at 1375 — but that is hardly a reason not to make the estimation as accurate as possible. Even if, as THE CHIEF JUSTICE mistakenly asserts, there were no direct evidence of how the Sixth Amendment originally applied to unsworn testimony, there is no doubt what its application would have been.

[107] [4] We use the term "interrogation" in its colloquial, rather than any technical legal, sense. *Cf. Rhode Island v. Innis*, 446 U.S. 291, 300–301, 100 St. Ct. 1682, 64 L. Ed. 2d 297 (1980). Just as various definitions of "testimonial" exist, one can imagine various definitions of "interrogation," and we need not select among them in this case. Sylvia's recorded statement, knowingly given in response to structured

B

The historical record also supports a second proposition: that the Framers would not have allowed admission of testimonial statements of a witness who did not appear at trial unless he was unavailable to testify, and the defendant had had a prior opportunity for cross-examination. The text of the Sixth Amendment does not suggest any open-ended exceptions from the confrontation requirement to be developed by the courts. Rather, the "right . . . to be confronted with the witnesses against him" . . . is most naturally read as a reference to the right of confrontation at common law, admitting only those exceptions established at the time of the founding. . . . As the English authorities . . . reveal, the common law in 1791 conditioned admissibility of an absent witness's examination on unavailability and a prior opportunity to cross-examine. The Sixth Amendment therefore incorporates those limitations. The numerous early state decisions applying the same test confirm that these principles were received as part of the common law in this country.

We do not read the historical sources to say that a prior opportunity to cross-examine was merely a sufficient, rather than a necessary, condition for admissibility of testimonial statements. They suggest that this requirement was dispositive and not merely one of several ways to establish reliability. This is not to deny, as the Chief Justice notes, that "[t]here were always exceptions to the general rule of exclusion" of hearsay evidence. . . . But there is scant evidence that exceptions were invoked to admit testimonial statements against the accused in a criminal case.[108] Most of the hearsay exceptions covered statements that by their nature were not testimonial — for example, business records or statements in furtherance of a conspiracy. We do not infer from these that the Framers thought exceptions would apply even to prior testimony. *Cf. Lilly v. Virginia*, 527 U.S. 116, 134, 119 S. Ct. 1887, 144 L. Ed. 2d 117 (1999) (plurality opinion) ("[A]ccomplices' confessions that inculpate a criminal defendant are not within a firmly rooted exception to the hearsay rule").[109]

---

police questioning, qualifies under any conceivable definition.

[108] [6] The one deviation we have found involves dying declarations. The existence of that exception as a general rule of criminal hearsay law cannot be disputed. *See, e.g., Mattox v. United States*, 156 U.S. 237, 243–244, 15 S. Ct. 337, 39 L. Ed. 409 (1895); *King v. Reason*, 16 How. St. Tr. 1, 24–38 (K.B.1722); 1 D. Jardine, Criminal Trials 435 (1832); Cooley, Constitutional Limitations, at *318; 1 G. Gilbert, Evidence 211 (C. Loft ed. 1791); see also F. Heller, The Sixth Amendment 105 (1951) (asserting that this was the *only* recognized criminal hearsay exception at common law). Although many dying declarations may not be testimonial, there is authority for admitting even those that clearly are. *See Woodcock, supra*, at 64; *cf. Radbourne, supra*, at 460–462, 168 Eng. Rep. at 332–333. We need not decide in this case whether the Sixth Amendment incorporates an exception for testimonial dying declarations. If this exception must be accepted on historical grounds, it is *sui generis*.

[109] [7] We cannot agree with The Chief Justice that the fact "[t]hat a statement might be testimonial does nothing to undermine the wisdom of one of these [hearsay] exceptions." *Post*, at 1377. Involvement of government officers in the production of testimony with an eye toward trial presents unique potential for prosecutorial abuse — a fact borne out time and time again throughout a history with which the Framers were keenly familiar. This consideration does not evaporate when testimony happens to fall within some broad, modern hearsay exception, even if that exception might be justifiable in other circumstances.

IV

Our case law has been largely consistent with these two principles. . . .

* * *

Testimonial statements of witnesses absent from trial have been admitted only where the declarant is unavailable, and only where the defendant has had a prior opportunity to cross-examine.

V

Although the results of our decisions have generally been faithful to the original meaning of the Confrontation Clause, the same cannot be said of our rationales. *Roberts* conditions the admissibility of all hearsay evidence on whether it falls under a "firmly rooted hearsay exception" or bears "particularized guarantees of trustworthiness." . . . This test departs from the historical principles identified above in two respects. First, it is too broad: It applies the same mode of analysis whether or not the hearsay consists of ex parte testimony. This often results in close constitutional scrutiny in cases that are far removed from the core concerns of the Clause. At the same time, however, the test is too narrow: It admits statements that do consist of ex parte testimony upon a mere finding of reliability. This malleable standard often fails to protect against paradigmatic confrontation violations.

Members of this Court and academics have suggested that we revise our doctrine to reflect more accurately the original understanding of the Clause. . . . They offer two proposals: First, that we apply the Confrontation Clause only to testimonial statements, leaving the remainder to regulation by hearsay law — thus eliminating the overbreadth referred to above. Second, that we impose an absolute bar to statements that are testimonial, absent a prior opportunity to cross-examine — thus eliminating the excessive narrowness referred to above.

In *White* [*v. Illinois*], we considered the first proposal and rejected it. . . . Although our analysis in this case casts doubt on that holding, we need not definitively resolve whether it survives our decision today, because Sylvia Crawford's statement is testimonial under any definition. This case does, however, squarely implicate the second proposal.

A

Where testimonial statements are involved, we do not think the Framers meant to leave the Sixth Amendment's protection to the vagaries of the rules of evidence, much less to amorphous notions of "reliability." . . . Admitting statements deemed reliable by a judge is fundamentally at odds with the right of confrontation. To be sure, the Clause's ultimate goal is to ensure reliability of evidence, but it is a procedural rather than a substantive guarantee. It commands, not that evidence be reliable, but that reliability be assessed in a particular manner: by testing in the crucible of cross-examination. The Clause thus reflects a judgment, not only about the desirability of reliable evidence . . . but about how reliability can best be determined. . . .

The *Roberts* test allows a jury to hear evidence, untested by the adversary process, based on a mere judicial determination of reliability. It thus replaces the constitutionally prescribed method of assessing reliability with a wholly foreign one. . . .

The *Raleigh* trial itself involved the very sorts of reliability determinations that *Roberts* authorizes. In the face of Raleigh's repeated demands for confrontation, the prosecution responded with many of the arguments a court applying *Roberts* might invoke today: that Cobham's statements were self-inculpatory, . . . that they were not made in the heat of passion, . . . and that they were not "extracted from [him] upon any hopes or promise of Pardon,". . . . It is not plausible that the Framers' only objection to the trial was that *Raleigh*'s judges did not properly weigh these factors before sentencing him to death. Rather, the problem was that the judges refused to allow Raleigh to confront Cobham in court, where he could cross-examine him and try to expose his accusation as a lie.

Dispensing with confrontation because testimony is obviously reliable is akin to dispensing with jury trial because a defendant is obviously guilty. This is not what the Sixth Amendment prescribes.

B

The legacy of *Roberts* in other courts vindicates the Framers' wisdom in rejecting a general reliability exception. The framework is so unpredictable that it fails to provide meaningful protection from even core confrontation violations.

Reliability is an amorphous, if not entirely subjective, concept. There are countless factors bearing on whether a statement is reliable. . . . Whether a statement is deemed reliable depends heavily on which factors the judge considers and how much weight he accords each of them. Some courts wind up attaching the same significance to opposite facts. For example, the Colorado Supreme Court held a statement more reliable because its inculpation of the defendant was "detailed," . . . while the Fourth Circuit found a statement more reliable because the portion implicating another was "fleeting." . . . The Virginia Court of Appeals found a statement more reliable because the witness was in custody and charged with a crime (thus making the statement more obviously against her penal interest) . . . while the Wisconsin Court of Appeals found a statement more reliable because the witness was not in custody and not a suspect. . . . Finally, the Colorado Supreme Court in one case found a statement more reliable because it was given "immediately after" the events at issue, . . . while that same court, in another case, found a statement more reliable because two years had elapsed. . . .

The unpardonable vice of the *Roberts* test, however, is not its unpredictability, but its demonstrated capacity to admit core testimonial statements that the Confrontation Clause plainly meant to exclude. . . . To add insult to injury, some of the courts that admit untested testimonial statements find reliability in the very factors that make the statements testimonial. As noted earlier, one court relied on the fact that the witness's statement was made to police while in custody on pending charges — the theory being that this made the statement more clearly against penal interest and thus more reliable. . . . Other courts routinely rely on the fact that a prior statement is given under oath in judicial proceedings. *E.g.,* . . . (plea allocution); . . . (grand jury testimony). That inculpating statements are given in a testimonial setting is not an antidote to the confrontation problem, but rather the trigger that makes the Clause's demands most urgent. It is not enough to point out that most of the usual safeguards of the adversary process attend the statement, when the single safeguard missing is the one the demands.

C

Roberts' failings were on full display in the proceedings below. Sylvia Crawford made her statement while in police custody, herself a potential suspect in the case. Indeed, she had been told that whether she would be released "depend[ed] on how the investigation continues." . . . In response to often leading questions from police detectives, she implicated her husband in Lee's stabbing and at least arguably undermined his self-defense claim. Despite all this, the trial court admitted her statement, listing several reasons why it was reliable. In its opinion reversing, the Court of Appeals listed several other reasons why the statement was not reliable. Finally, the State Supreme Court relied exclusively on the interlocking character of the statement and disregarded every other factor the lower courts had considered. The case is thus a self-contained demonstration of *Roberts'* unpredictable and inconsistent application.

Each of the courts also made assumptions that cross-examination might well have undermined. The trial court, for example, stated that Sylvia Crawford's statement was reliable because she was an eyewitness with direct knowledge of the events. But Sylvia at one point told the police that she had "shut [her] eyes and . . . didn't really watch" part of the fight, and that she was "in shock." . . . The trial court also buttressed its reliability finding by claiming that Sylvia was "being questioned by law enforcement, and, thus, the [questioner] is . . . neutral to her and not someone who would be inclined to advance her interests and shade her version of the truth unfavorably toward the defendant." . . . The Framers would be astounded to learn that ex parte testimony could be admitted against a criminal defendant because it was elicited by "neutral" government officers. But even if the court's assessment of the officer's motives was accurate, it says nothing about Sylvia's perception of her situation. Only cross-examination could reveal that.

* * *

We readily concede that we could resolve this case by simply reweighing the "reliability factors" under *Roberts* and finding that Sylvia Crawford's statement falls short. But we view this as one of those rare cases in which the result below is so improbable that it reveals a fundamental failure on our part to interpret the Constitution in a way that secures its intended constraint on judicial discretion. Moreover, to reverse the Washington Supreme Court's decision after conducting our own reliability analysis would perpetuate, not avoid, what the Sixth Amendment condemns. The Constitution prescribes a procedure for determining the reliability of testimony in criminal trials, and we, no less than the state courts, lack authority to replace it with one of our own devising.

We have no doubt that the courts below were acting in utmost good faith when they found reliability. The Framers, however, would not have been content to indulge this assumption. They knew that judges, like other government officers, could not always be trusted to safeguard the rights of the people; the likes of the dread Lord Jeffreys were not yet too distant a memory. They were loath to leave too much discretion in judicial hands. . . . By replacing categorical constitutional guarantees with open-ended balancing tests, we do violence to their design. Vague standards are manipulable, and, while that might be a small concern in run-of-the-mill assault prosecutions like this one, the Framers had an eye toward politically charged cases like *Raleigh*'s — great state trials where the impartiality of even those at the highest levels of the judiciary might not be so clear. It is difficult to imagine *Roberts'* providing any meaningful protection in those circumstances.

Where nontestimonial hearsay is at issue, it is wholly consistent with the Framers' design to afford the States flexibility in their development of hearsay law — as does *Roberts*, and as would an approach that exempted such statements from Confrontation Clause scrutiny altogether. Where testimonial evidence is at issue, however, the Sixth Amendment demands what the common law required: unavailability and a prior opportunity for cross-examination. We leave for another day any effort to spell out a comprehensive definition of "testimonial." Whatever else the term covers, it applies at a minimum to prior testimony at a preliminary hearing, before a grand jury, or at a former trial; and to police interrogations. . . .

In this case, the State admitted Sylvia's testimonial statement against petitioner, despite the fact that he had no opportunity to cross-examine her. That alone is sufficient to make out a violation of the Sixth Amendment. *Roberts* notwithstanding, we decline to mine the record in search of indicia of reliability. Where testimonial statements are at issue, the only indicium of reliability sufficient to satisfy constitutional demands is the one the Constitution actually prescribes: confrontation.

NOTES AND QUESTIONS

1.   Because *Crawford*, in effect, constitutionalized aspects of the hearsay rule in criminal cases, it had a cataclysmic impact. The availability of a hearsay exception no longer ordinarily guarantees admissibility in criminal cases.

2.   The Supreme Court's decision not to define testimonial hearsay made implementation of *Crawford* problematic — especially in domestic violence and child abuse cases in which victims are often unwilling or unable to testify. Some courts, in turn, attempted to avoid *Crawford* by finding the hearsay nontestimonial. *See* Lininger, *Prosecuting Batterers After* Crawford, 91 VA. L. REV. 102 (2005) (survey of cases showing one third found statements nontestimonial); *see also* Note, *Why the Sky Didn't Fall: Using Judicial Creativity to Circumvent* Crawford v. Washington, 38 LOY. L.A. L. REV. 1835 (2005).

MICHIGAN v. BRYANT
131 S. Ct. 1143 (2011)

I

Around 3:25 a.m. on April 29, 2001, Detroit, Michigan police officers responded to a radio dispatch indicating that a man had been shot. At the scene, they found the victim, Anthony Covington, lying on the ground next to his car in a gas station parking lot. Covington had a gunshot wound to his abdomen, appeared to be in great pain, and spoke with difficulty.

The police asked him "what had happened, who had shot him, and where the shooting had occurred." 483 Mich., at 143, 768 N.W.2d, at 71. Covington stated that "Rick" shot him at around 3 a.m. *Id.*, at 136, and n. 1, 768 N.W.2d, at 67, and n. 1. He also indicated that he had a conversation with Bryant, whom he recognized based on his voice, through the back door of Bryant's house. Covington explained that when he turned to leave, he was shot through the door and then drove to the gas station, where police found him.

Covington's conversation with the police ended within 5 to 10 minutes when emergency medical services arrived. Covington was transported to a hospital and died within hours. The police left the gas station after speaking with Covington, called for backup, and traveled to Bryant's house. They did not find Bryant there but did find blood and a bullet on the back porch and an apparent bullet hole in the back door. Police also found Covington's wallet and identification outside the house.

At trial, which occurred prior to our decisions in *Crawford*, 541 U.S. 36, and *Davis*, 547 U.S. 813, the police officers who spoke with Covington at the gas station testified about what Covington had told them. The jury returned a guilty verdict on charges of second-degree murder, being a felon in possession of a firearm, and possession of a firearm during the commission of a felony.

* * *

We granted certiorari to determine whether the Confrontation Clause barred admission of Covington's statements. 559 U.S. [970] (2010).

II

* * *

Crawford examined the common-law history of the confrontation right and explained that "the principal evil at which the Confrontation Clause was directed was the civil-law mode of criminal procedure, and particularly its use of *ex parte* examinations as evidence against the accused." 541 U.S., at 50. We noted that in England, pretrial examinations of suspects and witnesses by government officials "were sometimes read in court in lieu of live testimony." *Id.*, at 43. In light of this history, we emphasized the word "witnesses" in the Sixth Amendment, defining it as "those who 'bear testimony.'" *Id.*, at 51 quoting 2 N. WEBSTER, AN AMERICAN DICTIONARY OF THE ENGLISH LANGUAGE (1828)). We defined "testimony" as "'[a] solemn declaration or affirmation made for the purpose of establishing or proving some fact.' " 541 U.S., at 51 (quoting WEBSTER). We noted that "[a]n accuser who makes a formal statement to government officers bears testimony in a sense that a person who makes a casual remark to an acquaintance does not." *Ibid.* We therefore limited the Confrontation Clause's reach to testimonial statements and held that in order for testimonial evidence to be admissible, the Sixth Amendment "demands what the common law required: unavailability and a prior opportunity for cross-examination." *Id.*, at 68. Although "leav[ing] for another day any effort to spell out a comprehensive definition of 'testimonial,' " *Crawford* noted that "at a minimum" it includes "prior testimony at a preliminary hearing, before a grand jury, or at a former trial; and . . . police interrogations." *Ibid.* Under this reasoning, we held that Sylvia Crawford's statements in the course of police questioning were testimonial and that their admission when Michael Crawford "had no opportunity to cross-examine her" due to spousal privilege was "sufficient to make out a violation of the Sixth Amendment." *Ibid.*

In 2006, the Court in *Davis v. Washington* and *Hammon v. Indiana*, 547 U.S. 813, took a further step to "determine more precisely which police interrogations produce testimony" and therefore implicate a Confrontation Clause bar. *Id.*, at 822. We explained that when *Crawford* said that

> " 'interrogations by law enforcement officers fall squarely within [the] class' of testimonial hearsay, we had immediately in mind (for that was the case before us) interrogations solely directed at establishing the facts of a past crime, in order to identify (or provide evidence to convict) the perpetrator. The product of such interrogation, whether reduced to a writing signed by the declarant or embedded in the memory (and perhaps notes) of the interrogating officer, is testimonial." *Davis*, 547 U.S., at 826.

We thus made clear in *Davis* that not all those questioned by the police are witnesses and not all "interrogations by law enforcement officers," *Crawford*, 541 U.S., at 53, are subject to the Confrontation Clause.[110]

Davis and *Hammon* were both domestic violence cases. In *Davis*, Michelle McCottry made the statements at issue to a 911 operator during a domestic disturbance with Adrian Davis, her former boyfriend. McCottry told the operator, " 'He's here jumpin' on me again,' " and, " 'He's usin' his fists.' " 547 U.S., at 817. The operator then asked McCottry for Davis' first and last names and middle initial, and at that point in the conversation McCottry reported that Davis had fled in a car. *Id.*, at 818. McCottry did not appear at Davis' trial, and the State introduced the recording of her conversation with the 911 operator. *Id.*, at 819.

In *Hammon*, decided along with *Davis*, police responded to a domestic disturbance call at the home of Amy and Hershel Hammon, where they found Amy alone on the front porch. *Ibid.* She appeared " 'somewhat frightened,' " but told them "nothing was the matter.' " *Ibid.* (quoting *Hammon v. State*, 829 N.E.2d 444, 446–447 (Ind. 2005)). She gave the police permission to enter the house, where they

---

[110] [2] We noted in *Crawford* that "[w]e use the term 'interrogation' in its colloquial, rather than any technical legal, sense," and that "[j]ust as various definitions of 'testimonial' exist, one can imagine various definitions of 'interrogation,' and we need not select among them in this case." 541 U.S., at 53, n.4. *Davis* did not abandon those qualifications; nor do we do so here.

saw a gas heating unit with the glass front shattered on the floor. One officer remained in the kitchen with Hershel, while another officer talked to Amy in the living room about what had happened. Hershel tried several times to participate in Amy's conversation with the police and became angry when the police required him to stay separated from Amy. 547 U.S., at 819–820. The police asked Amy to fill out and sign a battery affidavit. She wrote: " 'Broke our Furnace & shoved me down on the floor into the broken glass. Hit me in the chest and threw me down. Broke our lamps & phone. Tore up my van where I couldn't leave the house. Attacked my daughter.' " *Id.*, at 820. Amy did not appear at Hershel's trial, so the police officers who spoke with her testified as to her statements and authenticated the affidavit. *Ibid.* The trial court admitted the affidavit as a present sense impression and admitted the oral statements as excited utterances under state hearsay rules. *Ibid.* The Indiana Supreme Court affirmed Hammon's conviction, holding that Amy's oral statements were not testimonial and that the admission of the affidavit, although erroneous because the affidavit was testimonial, was harmless. *Hammon v. State*, 829 N.E.2d, at 458–459.

To address the facts of both cases, we expanded upon the meaning of "testimonial" that we first employed in *Crawford* and discussed the concept of an ongoing emergency. We explained:

> "Statements are nontestimonial when made in the course of police interrogation under circumstances objectively indicating that the primary purpose of the interrogation is to enable police assistance to meet an ongoing emergency. They are testimonial when the circumstances objectively indicate that there is no such ongoing emergency, and that the primary purpose of the interrogation is to establish or prove past events potentially relevant to later criminal prosecution." *Davis*, 547 U.S., at 822.

Examining the *Davis* and *Hammon* statements in light of those definitions, we held that the statements at issue in *Davis* were nontestimonial and the statements in *Hammon* were testimonial. We distinguished the statements in *Davis* from the testimonial statements in *Crawford* on several grounds, including that the victim in *Davis* was "speaking about events *as they were actually happening*, rather than 'describ[ing] past events,' " that there was an ongoing emergency, that the "elicited statements were necessary to be able to *resolve* the present emergency," and that the statements were not formal. 547 U.S., at 827. In *Hammon*, on the other hand, we held that, "[i]t is entirely clear from the circumstances that the interrogation was part of an investigation into possibly criminal past conduct." *Id.*, at 829. There was "no emergency in progress." *Ibid.* The officer questioning Amy "was not seeking to determine. . . . 'what is happening,' but rather 'what happened.' " *Id.*, at 830. It was "formal enough" that the police interrogated Amy in a room separate from her husband where, "some time after the events described were over," she "deliberately recounted, in response to police questioning, how potentially criminal past events began and progressed." *Ibid.* Because her statements "were neither a cry for help nor the provision of information enabling officers immediately to end a threatening situation," *id.*, at 832, we held that they were testimonial.

Davis did not "attempt[t] to produce an exhaustive classification of all conceivable statements — or even all conceivable statements in response to police interrogation

— as either testimonial or nontestimonial." *Id.*, at 822.[111] The basic purpose of the Confrontation Clause was to "targe[t]" the sort of "abuses" exemplified at the notorious treason trial of Sir Walter Raleigh. *Crawford*, 541 U.S., at 51. Thus, the most important instances in which the Clause restricts the introduction of out-of-court statements are those in which state actors are involved in a formal, out-of-court interrogation of a witness to obtain evidence for trial.[112]

See *id.*, at 43–44. Even where such an interrogation is conducted with all good faith, introduction of the resulting statements at trial can be unfair to the accused if they are untested by cross-examination. Whether formal or informal, out-of-court statements can evade the basic objective of the Confrontation Clause, which is to prevent the accused from being deprived of the opportunity to cross-examine the declarant about statements taken for use at trial. When, as in *Davis*, the primary purpose of an interrogation is to respond to an "ongoing emergency," its purpose is not to create a record for trial and thus is not within the scope of the Clause. But there may be *other* circumstances, aside from ongoing emergencies, when a statement is not procured with a primary purpose of creating an out-of-court substitute for trial testimony. In making the primary purpose determination, standard rules of hearsay, designed to identify some statements as reliable, will be relevant. Where no such primary purpose exists, the admissibility of a statement is the concern of state and federal rules of evidence, not the Confrontation Clause.[113]

Deciding this case also requires further explanation of the "ongoing emergency" circumstance addressed in *Davis*. Because *Davis* and *Hammon* arose in the domestic violence context, that was the situation "we had immediately in mind (for that was the case before us)." 547 U.S., at 826. We now face a new context: a nondomestic dispute, involving a victim found in a public location, suffering from a fatal gunshot wound, and a perpetrator whose location was unknown at the time the

---

[111] [3] *Davis* explained that 911 operators "may at least be agents of law enforcement when they conduct interrogations of 911 callers," and therefore "consider[ed] their acts to be acts of the police" for purposes of the opinion. 547 U.S., at 823, n. 2. *Davis* explicitly reserved the question of "whether and when statements made to someone other than law enforcement personnel are 'testimonial.'" *Ibid.* We have no need to decide that question in this case either because Covington's statements were made to police officers. The dissent also claims to reserve this question, see *post*, n. 1 (opinion of SCALIA, J.), but supports one of its arguments by relying on *King v. Brasier*, 1 Leach 199, 200, 168 Eng. Rep. 202, 202–203 (K.B. 1779), which involved statements made by a child to her mother — a private citizen — just after the child had been sexually assaulted. *See also Crawford v. Washington*, 541 U.S. 36, 69–70 (2004) (REHNQUIST, C. J., concurring in judgment) (citing *King v. Brasier* for the different proposition that "out-of-court statements made by someone other than the accused and not taken under oath, unlike ex parte depositions or affidavits, were generally not considered substantive evidence upon which a conviction could be based").

[112] [4] Contrary to the dissent's excited suggestion, nothing in this opinion casts "favorable light," *post* (opinion of SCALIA, J.), on the conduct of Sir Walter Raleigh's trial or other 16th- and 17th-century English treason trials. The dissent is correct that such trials are "unquestionably infamous," *ibid.*, and our decision here confirms, rather than undermines, that assessment. See also n. 17, *infra*. For all of the reasons discussed in JUSTICE THOMAS' opinion concurring in the judgment, the situation presented in this case is nothing like the circumstances presented by Sir Walter Raleigh's trial. See *post*.

[113] [5] *See Davis v. Washington*, 547 U.S. 813, 823–824 (2006) (explaining the question before the Court as "whether the Confrontation Clause applies only to testimonial hearsay" and answering in the affirmative because "[a] limitation so clearly reflected in the text of the constitutional provision must fairly be said to mark out not merely its 'core,' but its perimeter"). *See also post* (SCALIA, J., dissenting).

police located the victim. Thus, we confront for the first time circumstances in which the "ongoing emergency" discussed in *Davis* extends beyond an initial victim to a potential threat to the responding police and the public at large. This new context requires us to provide additional clarification with regard to what *Davis* meant by "the primary purpose of the interrogation is to enable police assistance to meet an ongoing emergency." *Id.*, at 822.

III

To determine whether the "primary purpose" of an interrogation is "to enable police assistance to meet an ongoing emergency," *Davis*, 547 U.S., at 822, which would render the resulting statements nontestimonial, we objectively evaluate the circumstances in which the encounter occurs and the statements and actions of the parties.

A

* * *

An objective analysis of the circumstances of an encounter and the statements and actions of the parties to it provides the most accurate assessment of the "primary purpose of the interrogation." The circumstances in which an encounter occurs — *e.g.*, at or near the scene of the crime versus at a police station, during an ongoing emergency or afterwards — are clearly matters of objective fact. The statements and actions of the parties must also be objectively evaluated. That is, the relevant inquiry is not the subjective or actual purpose of the individuals involved in a particular encounter, but rather the purpose that reasonable participants would have had, as ascertained from the individuals' statements and actions and the circumstances in which the encounter occurred.[114]

B

As our recent Confrontation Clause cases have explained, the existence of an "ongoing emergency" at the time of an encounter between an individual and the police is among the most important circumstances informing the "primary purpose" of an interrogation. *See Davis*, 547 U.S., at 828–830; *Crawford*, 541 U.S., at 65. The existence of an ongoing emergency is relevant to determining the primary purpose of the interrogation because an emergency focuses the participants on something other than "prov[ing] past events potentially relevant to later criminal prosecution."[115] *Davis*, 547 U.S., at 822. Rather, it focuses them on "end[ing] a threatening

---

[114] [7] This approach is consistent with our rejection of subjective inquiries in other areas of criminal law. *See, e.g., Whren v. United States*, 517 U.S. 806, 813 (1996) (refusing to evaluate Fourth Amendment reasonableness subjectively in light of the officers' actual motivations); *New York v. Quarles*, 467 U.S. 649, 655–656, and n.6 (1984) (holding that an officer's subjective motivation is irrelevant to determining the applicability of the public safety exception to *Miranda v. Arizona*, 384 U.S. 436 (1966)); *Rhode Island v. Innis*, 446 U.S. 291, 301–302 (1980) (holding that a police officer's subjective intent to obtain incriminatory statements is not relevant to determining whether an interrogation has occurred).

[115] [8] The existence of an ongoing emergency must be objectively assessed from the perspective of

situation." *Id.*, at 832. Implicit in *Davis* is the idea that because the prospect of fabrication in statements given for the primary purpose of resolving that emergency is presumably significantly diminished, the Confrontation Clause does not require such statements to be subject to the crucible of cross-examination.

This logic is not unlike that justifying the excited utterance exception in hearsay law. Statements "relating to a startling event or condition made while the declarant was under the stress of excitement caused by the event or condition," Fed. Rule Evid. 803(2); see also Mich. Rule Evid. 803(2) (2010), are considered reliable because the declarant, in the excitement, presumably cannot form a falsehood. *See Idaho v. Wright*, 497 U.S. 805, 820 (1990) ("The basis for the 'excited utterance' exception . . . is that such statements are given under circumstances that eliminate the possibility of fabrication, coaching, or confabulation. . . ."); 5 J. WEINSTEIN & M. BERGER, WEINSTEIN'S FEDERAL EVIDENCE § 803.04[1] (J. McLaughlin ed., 2d ed. 2010) (same); Advisory Committee's Notes on Fed. Rule Evid. 803(2), 28 U.S.C. App., p. 371 (same). An ongoing emergency has a similar effect of focusing an individual's attention on responding to the emergency.[116]

*   *   *

IV

As we suggested in *Davis*, when a court must determine whether the Confrontation Clause bars the admission of a statement at trial, it should determine the "primary purpose of the interrogation" by objectively evaluating the statements and actions of the parties to the encounter, in light of the circumstances in which the interrogation occurs. The existence of an emergency or the parties' perception that an emergency is ongoing is among the most important circumstances that courts must take into account in determining whether an interrogation is testimonial because statements made to assist police in addressing an ongoing emergency

---

the parties to the interrogation at the time, not with the benefit of hindsight. If the information the parties knew at the time of the encounter would lead a reasonable person to believe that there was an emergency, even if that belief was later proved incorrect, that is sufficient for purposes of the Confrontation Clause. The emergency is relevant to the "primary purpose of the interrogation" because of the effect it has on the parties' purpose, not because of its actual existence.

[116] [9] Many other exceptions to the hearsay rules similarly rest on the belief that certain statements are, by their nature, made for a purpose other than use in a prosecution and therefore should not be barred by hearsay prohibitions. *See, e.g.*, Fed. Rule Evid. 801(d)(2)(E) (statement by a co-conspirator during and in furtherance of the conspiracy); 803(4) (Statements for Purposes of Medical Diagnosis or Treatment); 803(6) (Records of Regularly Conducted Activity); 803(8) (Public Records and Reports); 803(9) (Records of Vital Statistics); 803(11) (Records of Religious Organizations); 803(12) (Marriage, Baptismal, and Similar Certificates); 803(13) (Family Records); 804(b)(3) (Statement Against Interest); *see also Melendez-Diaz v. Massachusetts*, 557 U.S. 305, 129 S. Ct. 2527, 174 L. Ed. 2d 314, 329 (2009) ("Business and public records are generally admissible absent confrontation not because they qualify under an exception to the hearsay rules, but because — having been created for the administration of an entity's affairs and not for the purpose of establishing or proving some fact at trial — they are not testimonial"); *Giles v. California*, 554 U.S., at 376 (noting in the context of domestic violence that "[s]tatements to friends and neighbors about abuse and intimidation and statements to physicians in the course of receiving treatment would be excluded, if at all, only by hearsay rules"); *Crawford*, 541 U.S., at 56 ("Most of the hearsay exceptions covered statements that by their nature were not testimonial — for example, business records or statements in furtherance of a conspiracy").

presumably lack the testimonial purpose that would subject them to the requirement of confrontation.[117] As the context of this case brings into sharp relief, the existence and duration of an emergency depend on the type and scope of danger posed to the victim, the police, and the public.

Applying this analysis to the facts of this case is more difficult than in *Davis* because we do not have the luxury of reviewing a transcript of the conversation between the victim and the police officers. Further complicating our task is the fact that the trial in this case occurred before our decisions in *Crawford* and *Davis*. We therefore review a record that was not developed to ascertain the "primary purpose of the interrogation."

We first examine the circumstances in which the interrogation occurred. The parties disagree over whether there was an emergency when the police arrived at the gas station. Bryant argues, and the Michigan Supreme Court accepted, 483 Mich., at 147, 768 N.W.2d, at 73, that there was no ongoing emergency because "there . . . was no criminal conduct occurring. No shots were being fired, no one was seen in possession of a firearm, nor were any witnesses seen cowering in fear or running from the scene." Brief for Respondent 27. Bryant, while conceding that "a serious or life-threatening injury creates a medical emergency for a victim," *id.*, at 30, 768 N.W.2d 65, further argues that a declarant's medical emergency is not relevant to the ongoing emergency determination.

In contrast, Michigan and the Solicitor General explain that when the police responded to the call that a man had been shot and found Covington bleeding on the gas station parking lot, "they did not know who Covington was, whether the shooting had occurred at the gas station or at a different location, who the assailant was, or whether the assailant posed a continuing threat to Covington or others." Brief for United States as *Amicus Curiae* 15; Brief for Petitioner 16; see also *id.*, at 15, 768 N.W.2d 65 ("[W]hen an officer arrives on the scene and does not know where the perpetrator is, whether he is armed, whether he might have other targets, and whether the violence might continue at the scene or elsewhere, interrogation that has the primary purpose of establishing those facts to assess the situation is designed to meet the ongoing emergency and is nontestimonial").

The Michigan Supreme Court stated that the police asked Covington, "what had happened, who had shot him, and where the shooting had occurred." 483 Mich., at 143, 768 N.W.2d, at 71. The joint appendix contains the transcripts of the preliminary examination, suppression hearing, and trial testimony of five officers who responded to the scene and found Covington. The officers' testimony is essentially consistent but, at the same time, not specific. The officers basically agree

---

[117] [13] Of course the Confrontation Clause is not the only bar to admissibility of hearsay statements at trial. State and federal rules of evidence prohibit the introduction of hearsay, subject to exceptions. Consistent with those rules, the Due Process Clauses of the Fifth and Fourteenth Amendments may constitute a further bar to admission of, for example, unreliable evidence. See *Montana v. Egelhoff*, 518 U.S. 37, 53 (1996) (plurality opinion) ("[E]rroneous evidentiary rulings can, in combination, rise to the level of a due process violation"); *Dutton v. Evans*, 400 U.S. 74, 96–97 (1970) (Harlan, J., concurring in result) ("[T]he Fifth and Fourteenth Amendments' commands that federal and state trials, respectively, must be conducted in accordance with due process of law" is the "standard" by which to "test federal and state rules of evidence").

on what information they learned from Covington, but not on the order in which they learned it or on whether Covington's statements were in response to general or detailed questions. They all agree that the first question was "what happened?" The answer was either "I was shot" or "Rick shot me."[118]

As explained above, the scope of an emergency in terms of its threat to individuals other than the initial assailant and victim will often depend on the type of dispute involved. Nothing Covington said to the police indicated that the cause of the shooting was a purely private dispute or that the threat from the shooter had ended. The record reveals little about the motive for the shooting. The police officers who spoke with Covington at the gas station testified that Covington did not tell them what words Covington and Rick had exchanged prior to the shooting.[119] What Covington did tell the officers was that he fled Bryant's back porch, indicating that he perceived an ongoing threat.[120] The police did not know, and Covington did not tell them, whether the threat was limited to him. The potential scope of the dispute and therefore the emergency in this case thus stretches more broadly than those at issue in *Davis* and *Hammon* and encompasses a threat potentially to the police and the public.

This is also the first of our post-*Crawford* Confrontation Clause cases to involve a gun. The physical separation that was sufficient to end the emergency in *Hammon* was not necessarily sufficient to end the threat in this case; Covington was shot through the back door of Bryant's house. Bryant's argument that there was no ongoing emergency because "[n]o shots were being fired," Brief for Respondent 27, surely construes ongoing emergency too narrowly. An emergency does not last only for the time between when the assailant pulls the trigger and the bullet hits the victim. If an out-of-sight sniper pauses between shots, no one would say that the emergency ceases during the pause. That is an extreme example and not the situation here, but it serves to highlight the implausibility, at least as to certain weapons, of construing the emergency to last only precisely as long as the violent

---

[118] [14] *See* App. 76 (testimony of Officer McCallister); *id.*, at 101, 113–114 (testimony of Sgt. Wenturine); *id.*, at 127, 131–133 (testimony of Officer Stuglin). Covington told them that Rick had shot him through the back door of Rick's house, *id.*, at 127–128 (testimony of Officer Stuglin), located at the corner of Pennsylvania and Laura, *id.*, at 102 (testimony of Sgt. Wenturine), and that Covington recognized Rick by his voice, *id.*, at 128 (testimony of Officer Stuglin). Covington also gave them a physical description of Rick. *Id.*, at 84–85, 93–94 (testimony of Officer McAllister); *id.*, at 103, 115 (testimony of Sgt. Wenturine); *id.*, at 134 (testimony of Officer Stuglin).

[119] [15] *See id.*, at 114 ("Q Did he tell you what Rick said? A He said they were having a conversation. Q Did he tell you what Rick said? A He did not" (testimony of Sgt. Wenturine) (paragraph breaks omitted)); *see also id.*, at 79 (testimony of Officer McAllister); *id.*, at 128 (testimony of Officer Stuglin).

[120] [16] *See id.*, at 127–128 ("A He said he'd went up, he went up to the back door of a house; that a person he said he knew, and he was knocking and he was knocking on the door he said he'd talked to somebody through the door. He said he recognized the voice. Q Did he say who it was that he recognized the voice of? A That's when he told me it was, he said it was Rick a/k/a Buster. Q And did he say what the conversation was about at the door? A I don't, I don't believe so. Q All right. And did he say what happened there, whether or not they had a conversation or not, did he say what ended up happening? A He said what happened was that he heard a shot and then he started to turn to get off the porch and then another one and then that's when he was hit by a gunshot" (testimony of Officer Stuglin) (paragraph breaks omitted)). Unlike the dissent's apparent ability to read Covington's mind, *post* (opinion of SCALIA, J.), we rely on the available evidence, which suggests that Covington perceived an ongoing threat.

act itself, as some have construed our opinion in *Davis*. *See* Brief for Respondent 23–25.

At no point during the questioning did either Covington or the police know the location of the shooter. In fact, Bryant was not at home by the time the police searched his house at approximately 5:30 a.m. 483 Mich., at 136, 768 N.W.2d, at 67. At some point between 3 a.m. and 5:30 a.m., Bryant left his house. At bottom, there was an ongoing emergency here where an armed shooter, whose motive for and location after the shooting were unknown, had mortally wounded Covington within a few blocks and a few minutes of the location where the police found Covington.[121]

This is not to suggest that the emergency continued until Bryant was arrested in California a year after the shooting. *Id.*, at 137, 768 N.W.2d, at 67. We need not decide precisely when the emergency ended because Covington's encounter with the police and all of the statements he made during that interaction occurred within the first few minutes of the police officers' arrival and well before they secured the scene of the shooting — the shooter's last known location.

We reiterate, moreover, that the existence *vel non* of an ongoing emergency is not the touchstone of the testimonial inquiry; rather, the ultimate inquiry is whether the "primary purpose of the interrogation [was] to enable police assistance to meet [the] ongoing emergency." *Davis*, 547 U.S., at 822. We turn now to that inquiry, as informed by the circumstances of the ongoing emergency just described. The circumstances of the encounter provide important context for understanding Covington's statements to the police. When the police arrived at Covington's side, their first question to him was "What happened?"[122] Covington's response was either "Rick shot me" or "I was shot," followed very quickly by an identification of "Rick" as the shooter. App. 76. In response to further questions, Covington explained that the shooting occurred through the back door of Bryant's house and provided a physical description of the shooter. When he made the statements, Covington was lying in a gas station parking lot bleeding from a mortal gunshot wound to his abdomen. His answers to the police officers' questions were punctuated with questions about when emergency medical services would arrive. *Id.*, at 56–57 (suppression hearing testimony of Officer Brown). He was obviously in considerable pain and had difficulty breathing and talking. *Id.*, at 75, 83–84 (testimony of Officer McCallister); *id.*, at 101, 110–111 (testimony of Sgt. Wenturine); *id.*, at 126, 137 (testimony of Officer Stuglin). From this description of

---

[121] [17] It hardly bears mention that the emergency situation in this case is readily distinguishable from the "treasonous conspiracies of unknown scope, aimed at killing or overthrowing the king," *post*, about which *Justice Scalia*'s dissent is quite concerned.

[122] [18] Although the dissent claims otherwise, *post* (opinion of SCALIA, J.), at least one officer asked Covington something akin to "how was he doing." App. 131 (testimony of Officer Stuglin) ("A I approached the subject, the victim, Mr. Covington, on the ground and had asked something like what happened or are you okay, something to that line. . . . Q So you asked this man how are you, how are you doing? A Well, basically it's, you know, what's wrong, you know" (paragraph breaks omitted)). The officers also testified about their assessment of Covington's wounds. *See id.*, at 35 (suppression hearing testimony of Officer Brown) ("[H]e had blood . . . on the front of his body"); *id.*, at 75 (testimony of Officer McCallister) ("It appeared he had a stomach wound of a gunshot"); *id.*, at 132 (testimony of Officer Stuglin) ("Q Did you see the wound? A Yes, I did. Q You had to move some clothing to do that? A Yes" (paragraph breaks omitted)).

his condition and report of his statements, we cannot say that a person in Covington's situation would have had a "primary purpose" "to establish or prove past events potentially relevant to later criminal prosecution." *Davis*, 547 U.S., at 822.

For their part, the police responded to a call that a man had been shot. As discussed above, they did not know why, where, or when the shooting had occurred. Nor did they know the location of the shooter or anything else about the circumstances in which the crime occurred.[123] The questions they asked — "what had happened, who had shot him, and where the shooting occurred," 483 Mich., at 143, 768 N.W.2d, at 71 — were the exact type of questions necessary to allow the police to " 'assess the situation, the threat to their own safety, and possible danger to the potential victim' " and to the public, *Davis*, 547 U.S., at 832 (quoting *Hiibel v. Sixth Judicial Dist. Court of Nev., Humboldt Cty.*, 542 U.S. 177, 186 292 (2004)), including to allow them to ascertain "whether they would be encountering a violent felon,"[124] *Davis*, 547 U.S., at 827. In other words, they solicited the information necessary to enable them "to meet an ongoing emergency." *Id.*, at 822.

Nothing in Covington's responses indicated to the police that, contrary to their expectation upon responding to a call reporting a shooting, there was no emergency or that a prior emergency had ended. Covington did indicate that he had been shot at another location about 25 minutes earlier, but he did not know the location of the shooter at the time the police arrived and, as far as we can tell from the record, he gave no indication that the shooter, having shot at him twice, would be satisfied that Covington was only wounded. In fact, Covington did not indicate any possible motive for the shooting, and thereby gave no reason to think that the shooter would not shoot again if he arrived on the scene. As we noted in *Davis*, "initial inquiries" may "*often* . . . produce nontestimonial statements." *Id.*, at 832. The initial inquiries in this case resulted in the type of nontestimonial statements we contemplated in *Davis*.

Finally, we consider the informality of the situation and the interrogation. This situation is more similar, though not identical, to the informal, harried 911 call in *Davis* than to the structured, station-house interview in *Crawford*. As the officers'

---

[123] [19] Contrary to the dissent's suggestion, *post* (opinion of SCALIA, J.), and despite the fact that the record was developed prior to *Davis'* focus on the existence of an "ongoing emergency," the record contains some testimony to support the idea that the police officers were concerned about the location of the shooter when they arrived on the scene and thus to suggest that the purpose of the questioning of Covington was to determine the shooter's location. *See* App. 136 (testimony of Officer Stuglin) (stating that upon arrival officers questioned the gas station clerk about whether the shooting occurred in the gas station parking lot and about concern for safety); *see also ibid.* (testimony of Officer Stuglin) ("Q . . . So you have some concern, there may be a person with a gun or somebody, a shooter right there in the immediate area? A Sure, yes. Q And you want to see that area gets secured? A Correct. Q For your safety as well as everyone else? A Correct" (paragraph breaks omitted)); *id.*, at 82 (testimony of Officer McCallister). *But see id.*, at 83 (cross-examination of Officer McAllister) ("Q You didn't, you didn't look around and say, gee, there might be a shooter around here, I better keep an eye open? A I did not, no. That could have been my partner I don't know" (paragraph breaks omitted)).

[124] [20] *Hiibel*, like our post-*Crawford* Confrontation Clause cases, involved domestic violence, which explains the Court's focus on the security of the victim and the police: they were the only parties potentially threatened by the assailant. 542 U.S., at 186 (noting that the case involved a "domestic assault").

trial testimony reflects, the situation was fluid and somewhat confused: the officers arrived at different times; apparently each, upon arrival, asked Covington "what happened?"; and, contrary to the dissent's portrayal, *post,* at 1171–1172 (opinion of SCALIA, J.), they did not conduct a structured interrogation. App. 84 (testimony of Officer McCallister) (explaining duplicate questioning, especially as to "what happened?"); *id.,* at 101–102 (testimony of Sgt. Wenturine) (same); *id.,* at 126–127 (testimony of Officer Stuglin) (same). The informality suggests that the interrogators' primary purpose was simply to address what they perceived to be an ongoing emergency, and the circumstances lacked any formality that would have alerted Covington to or focused him on the possible future prosecutorial use of his statements.

Because the circumstances of the encounter as well as the statements and actions of Covington and the police objectively indicate that the "primary purpose of the interrogation" was "to enable police assistance to meet an ongoing emergency," *Davis,* 547 U.S., at 822, Covington's identification and description of the shooter and the location of the shooting were not testimonial hearsay. The Confrontation Clause did not bar their admission at Bryant's trial.

*   *   *

For the foregoing reasons, we hold that Covington's statements were not testimonial and that their admission at Bryant's trial did not violate the Confrontation Clause. We leave for the Michigan courts to decide on remand whether the statements' admission was otherwise permitted by state hearsay rules. The judgment of the Supreme Court of Michigan is vacated, and the case is remanded for further proceedings not inconsistent with this opinion.

It is so ordered.

 EVIDENCE CHALLENGE: Challenge yourself to learn more about this topic. Enter the following address into your browser to access Evidence Challenge and apply these concepts to realistic problems set in a virtual courtroom.
http://www.EvidenceChallenge.com. Additional purchase required.

Chapter VI

PRIVILEGES

A. INTRODUCTION

1. The Basis for Privileges

JOHN H. WIGMORE, 8 EVIDENCE § 2285
(3d ed. 1940)[1]

General principle of privileged communications. Looking back upon the principle of privilege, as an exception to the general liability of every person to give testimony upon all facts inquired of in a court of justice, and keeping in view that preponderance of extrinsic policy which alone can justify the recognition of any such exception . . . , four fundamental conditions are recognized as necessary to the establishment of a privilege against the disclosure of communications:

(1) The communications must originate in a confidence that they will not be disclosed.

(2) This element of confidentiality must be essential to the full and satisfactory maintenance of the relation between the parties.

(3) The relation must be one which in the opinion of the community ought to be sedulously fostered.

(4) The injury that would inure to the relation by the disclosure of the communications must be greater than the benefit thereby gained for the correct disposal of litigation.

Only if these four conditions are present should a privilege be recognized.

That they are present in more of the recognized privileges is plain enough; and the absence of one or more of them serves to explain why certain privileges have failed to obtain the recognition sometimes demanded for them. . . .

These four conditions must serve as the foundation of policy for determining all such privileges, whether claimed or established.

---

[1] Reprinted by permission of Little, Brown and Company, Boston, 1940.

2. The Federal Perspective

James W. Moore & Helen I. Bendex,
Congress, Evidence, and Rulemaking
84 YALE L.J. 9, 19–21 (1974)[2]

Article V — Privileges

The basic premise of the Advisory Committee in drafting Article V was that justice in the federal courts would be enhanced by reducing the number and scope of privileges. Accordingly, although the Committee broadened some of the rules set forth in its Preliminary Draft to meet demands for more protective privileges, the Article provides privileges only where most strongly justified by logic and experience: for the lawyer-client, psychotherapist-patient, husband-wife relationships, for communications to clergymen, for political votes, for trade secrets, for required reports, for secrets of state, and for informers. Privileges such as the general doctor-patient privilege and the privilege for accountants have been eliminated because of their unwarranted limitations on truth seeking. . . . This approach is also in line with the position of Wigmore and McCormick.

While hardly revolutionary, Article V as promulgated by the Court sets forth a more sensible approach to privileges than is found in the evidence law of many states. It rejects the unfortunate tendency toward the proliferation of privileges as professional status symbols.

After much testimony and controversy, the House rejected the Advisory committee's approach and amended Article V to provide for one general Rule 501:

> Except as otherwise required by the Constitution of the United States or provided by Act of Congress or in rules prescribed by the Supreme Court pursuant to statutory authority, the privilege of a witness, person, government, State, or political subdivision thereof shall be governed by the principles of the common law as they may be interpreted by the courts of the United States in the light of reason and experience. However, in civil actions and proceedings, with respect to an element of a claim or defense as to which State law supplies the rule of decision, the privilege of a witness, person, government, State, or political subdivision thereof shall be determined in accordance with State law.

Thus, as to federal issues, the House Rule has adopted a stopgap, incremental, common law development approach, to evidence law. This approach, like that of Criminal Rule 26,[3] relies too heavily on the evolution of privileges through case by

---

[2] Reprinted by permission of the Yale Law Journal Company and Fred B. Rothman & Company form the Yale Law Journal, Vol. 84, pages 19–21.

[3] [61] FED. R. CRIM. P. 26 provides:

> In all trials the testimony of witnesses shall be taken orally in open court, unless otherwise provided by an act of Congress or by these rules. The admissibility of evidence and the competency and privileges of witnesses shall be governed, except when an act of Congress or these rules otherwise provide, by the principles of the common law as they may be interpreted

case decisions. Judged by the experience under Criminal Rule 26, federal rules of privilege will emerge slowly. As the Court observed in *Michelson v. United States* (on a different evidence issue):

> [I]t is obvious that a court which can make only infrequent sallies into the field cannot recast the body of case law on this subject in many, many years, even if it were clear what the rules should be. . . .

> [T]o pull one misshapen stone out of the grotesque structure is more likely simply to upset its present balance between adverse interests than to establish a rational edifice.

* * *

Ironically, House deferral to future court decisions on federal issues may result in the adoption of most of the Court Rules on privileges. When, for example, a district judge is faced with a complex and confusing question of a privilege for state secrets, he may reasonably turn to the Court draft for guidance.

As to nonfederal issues, the House has constructed its amendment to the Court Rules on principles supposedly underlying *Erie Railroad Co. v. Tompkins*. It supported its position by these contentions: (1) Privileges are substantive for Erie purposes and there is no federal interest strong enough to justify departure from state policy; (2) a rule of privilege is outcome-determinative; (3) state policy should not be frustrated by the accident of diversity jurisdiction; (4) a contrary position would encourage forum shopping. This theory of the *Erie* doctrine is unfortunate.

It is now beyond question that the rulemaking power of the Supreme Court includes the power to make rules of evidence. This power includes the power to promulgate rules of privilege which supplant conflicting state rules of privilege, even in diversity or other cases involving enforcement of state created rights. Such rules do not violate the principles embodied in *Erie* or its progeny. Their adoption is both desirable and necessary, in diversity as in other cases, for the efficient and just determination of cases in the federal courts.

Without embarking on a detailed analysis of the meaning of "substance" and "procedure" in the context of the Rules of Evidence, it is clear that rules of privilege are subject to rational classification as procedural. The basic rule of evidence is relevancy. A privilege works to keep relevant and otherwise admissible evidence from the trier of facts. It alters the normal mode of proof in a trial by denying the trier information he would otherwise have before him in determining the facts. What is needed to establish a right and impose liability — a matter of substantive law — is naturally distinguishable from how those substantive requirements may be proved — a matter of procedure. Although a privilege may embody state social policies and may regulate persons' conduct outside of the courtroom, its effect in the courtroom is to alter the normal procedural functions of the system:

> The reality of the matter is that privilege is called into operation, not when the relation giving rise to the privilege is being litigated, but when the litigation involves something substantively devoid of relation to the privi-

---

by the Courts of the United States in the light of reason and experience.

lege. The appearance of privilege in the case is quite by accident, and its effect is to block off the tribunal from a source of information. Thus, its real impact is on the method of proof in the case, and in comparison any substantive aspect appears tenuous.

JAFFEE v. REDMOND
518 U.S. 1 (1996)

JUSTICE STEVENS delivered the opinion of the Court.

After a traumatic incident in which she shot and killed a man, a police officer received extensive counseling from a licensed clinical social worker. The question we address is whether statements the officer made to her therapist during the counseling sessions are protected from compelled disclosure in a federal civil action brought by the family of the deceased. Stated otherwise, the question is whether it is appropriate for federal courts to recognize a "psychotherapist privilege" under Rule 501 of the Federal Rules of Evidence.

I

Petitioner is the administrator of the estate of Ricky Allen. Respondents are Mary Lu Redmond, a former police officer, and the Village of Hoffman Estates, Illinois, her employer during the time that she served on the police force. Petitioner commenced this action against respondents after Redmond shot and killed Allen while on patrol duty.

On June 27, 1991, Redmond was the first officer to respond to a "fight in progress" call at an apartment complex. As she arrived at the scene, two of Allen's sisters ran toward her squad car, waving their arms and shouting that there had been a stabbing in one of the apartments. Redmond testified at trial that she relayed this information to her dispatcher and requested an ambulance. She then exited her car and walked toward the apartment building. Before Redmond reached the building, several men ran out, one waving a pipe. When the men ignored her order to get on the ground, Redmond drew her service revolver. Two other men then burst out of the building, one, Ricky Allen, chasing the other. According to Redmond, Allen was brandishing a butcher knife and disregarded her repeated commands to drop the weapon. Redmond shot Allen when she believed he was about to stab the man he was chasing. Allen died at the scene. Redmond testified that before other officers arrived to provide support, "people came pouring out of the buildings," App. 134, and a threatening confrontation between her and the crowd ensued.

Petitioner filed suit in Federal District Court alleging that Redmond had violated Allen's constitutional rights by using excessive force during the encounter at the apartment complex. The complaint sought damages under Rev. Stat. § 1979, 42 U.S.C. § 1983 and the Illinois wrongful death statute, Ill. Comp. Stat., ch. 740, § 180/1 et seq. (1994). At trial, petitioner presented testimony from members of Allen's family that conflicted with Redmond's version of the incident in several important respects. They testified, for example, that Redmond drew her gun before exiting her squad car and that Allen was unarmed when he emerged from the apartment building.

During pretrial discovery petitioner learned that after the shooting Redmond had participated in about 50 counseling sessions with Karen Beyer, a clinical social worker licensed by the State of Illinois and employed at that time by the Village of Hoffman Estates. Petitioner sought access to Beyer's notes concerning the sessions for use in cross-examining Redmond. Respondents vigorously resisted the discovery. They asserted that the contents of the conversations between Beyer and Redmond were protected against involuntary disclosure by a psychotherapist-patient privilege. The district judge rejected this argument. Neither Beyer nor Redmond, however, complied with his order to disclose the contents of Beyer's notes. At depositions and on the witness stand both either refused to answer certain questions or professed an inability to recall details of their conversations.

In his instructions at the end of the trial, the judge advised the jury that the refusal to turn over Beyer's notes had no "legal justification" and that the jury could therefore presume that the contents of the notes would have been unfavorable to respondents. The jury awarded petitioner $45,000 on the federal claim and $500,000 on her state-law claim.

The Court of Appeals for the Seventh Circuit reversed and remanded for a new trial. Addressing the issue for the first time, the court concluded that "reason and experience," the touchstones for acceptance of a privilege under Rule 501 of the Federal Rules of Evidence, compelled recognition of a psychotherapist-patient privilege.[4] 51 F.3d 1346, 1355 (1995). "Reason tells us that psychotherapists and patients share a unique relationship, in which the ability to communicate freely without the fear of public disclosure is the key to successful treatment." *Id.* at 1355–56. As to experience, the court observed that all 50 States have adopted some form of the psychotherapist-patient privilege. *Id.* at 1356. The court attached particular significance to the fact that Illinois law expressly extends such a privilege to social workers like Karen Beyer.[5] *Id.* at 1357. The court also noted that, with one exception, the federal decisions rejecting the privilege were more than five years old and that the "need and demand for counseling services has skyrocketed during the past several years." *Id.* at 1355–56.

The Court of Appeals qualified its recognition of the privilege by stating that it would not apply if "in the interests of justice, the evidentiary need for the disclosure of the contents of a patient's counseling sessions outweighs that patient's privacy

---

[4] [3] Rule 501 provides as follows:

Except as otherwise required by the Constitution of the United States or provided by Act of Congress, or in rules prescribed by the Supreme Court pursuant to statutory authority, the privilege of a witness, person, government, State, or political subdivision thereof shall be governed by the principles of the common law as they may be interpreted by the courts of the United States in the light of reason and experience. However, in civil actions and proceedings, with respect to an element of a claim or defense as to which State law supplies the rule of decision, the privilege of a witness, person, government, State or political subdivision thereof shall be determined in accordance with State law.

[5] [4] *See* Illinois Mental Health and Developmental Disabilities Confidentiality Act, Ill. Comp. Stat., ch. 740, §§ 110/1–110/17 (1994).

interests." *Id.* at 1357. Balancing those conflicting interests, the court observed, on the one hand, that the evidentiary need for the contents of the confidential conversations was diminished in this case because there were numerous eyewitnesses to the shooting, and, on the other hand, that Officer Redmond's privacy interests were substantial.[6] *Id.* at 1358. Based on this assessment, the court concluded that the trial court had erred by refusing to afford protection to the confidential communications between Redmond and Beyer.

The United States courts of appeals do not uniformly agree that the federal courts should recognize a psychotherapist privilege under Rule 501. *Compare In re Doe*, 964 F.2d 1325 (2d Cir. 1992) (recognizing privilege); *In re Zuniga*, 714 F.2d 632 (6th Cir.), *cert. denied*, 464 U.S. 983 (1983) (same), *with United States v. Burtrum*, 17 F.3d 1299 (10th Cir.), *cert. denied*, 513 U.S. 863 (1994) (declining to recognize privilege); *In re Grand Jury Proceedings*, 867 F.2d 562 (9th Cir.), *cert. denied sub nom. Doe v. United States*, 493 U.S. 906 (1989) (same); *United States v. Corona*, 849 F.2d 562 (11th Cir. 1988), *cert. denied*, 489 U.S. 1084 (1989) (same); *United States v. Meagher*, 531 F.2d 752 (5th Cir.), *cert. denied*, 429 U.S. 853 (1976) (same). Because of the conflict among the courts of appeals and the importance of the question, we granted *certiorari*. 516 U.S. [930], 116 S. Ct. 334, 133 L. Ed. 2d 234 (1995). We affirm.

II

* * *

Rule 501 of the Federal Rules of Evidence authorizes federal courts to define new privileges by interpreting "common law principles . . . in the light of reason and experience." The authors of the Rule borrowed this phrase from our opinion in *Wolfle v. United States*, 291 U.S. 7, 12 (1934),[7] which in turn referred to the oft-repeated observation that "the common law is not immutable but flexible, and by its own principles adapts itself to varying conditions." *Funk v. United States*, 290 U.S. 371, 383 (1933). *See also Hawkins v. United States*, 358 U.S. 74, 79 (1958) (changes in privileges may be "dictated by 'reason and experience' "). The Senate

---

[6] [5]

Her ability, through counseling, to work out the pain and anguish undoubtedly caused by Allen's death in all probability depended to a great deal upon her trust and confidence in her counselor, Karen Beyer. Officer Redmond, and all those placed in her most unfortunate circumstances, are entitled to be protected in their desire to seek counseling after mortally wounding another human being in the line of duty. An individual who is troubled as the result of her participation in a violent and tragic event, such as this, displays a most commendable respect for human life and is a person well-suited "to protect and to serve."

51 F.3d at 1358.

[7] [6]

[T]he rules governing the competence of witnesses in criminal trials in the federal courts are not necessarily restricted to those local rules in force at the time of the admission into the Union of the particular state where the trial takes place, but are governed by common law principles as interpreted and applied by the federal courts in the light of reason and experience. *Funk v. United States*, 290 U.S. 371.

Wolfle v. United States, 291 U.S. at 12–13.

Report accompanying the 1975 adoption of the Rules indicates that Rule 501 "should be understood as reflecting the view that the recognition of a privilege based on a confidential relationship . . . should be determined on a case-by-case basis." S. Rep. No. 93-1277, p. 13 (1974) U.S. Code Cong. & Admin. News 1974, pp. 7051, 7059.[8] The Rule thus did not freeze the law governing the privileges of witnesses in federal trials at a particular point in our history, but rather directed federal courts to "continue the evolutionary development of testimonial privileges." *Trammel v. United States*, 445 U.S. 40, 47 (1980); *see also University of Pennsylvania v. EEOC*, 493 U.S. 182, 189 (1990).

The common-law principles underlying the recognition of testimonial privileges can be stated simply. " 'For more than three centuries it has now been recognized as a fundamental maxim that the public . . . has a right to every man's evidence. When we come to examine the various claims of exemption, we start with the primary assumption that there is a general duty to give what testimony one is capable of giving, and that any exemptions which may exist are distinctly exceptional, being so many derogations from a positive general rule.' " *United States v. Bryan*, 339 U.S. 323, 331 (1950) (quoting 8 J. Wigmore, Evidence § 2192, p. 64 (3d ed. 1940)).[9] *See also United States v. Nixon*, 418 U.S. 683, 709 (1974). Exceptions from the general rule disfavoring testimonial privileges may be justified, however, by a " 'public good transcending the normally predominant principle of utilizing all rational means for ascertaining the truth.' " *Trammel*, 445 U.S. at 50, quoting *Elkins v. United States*, 364 U.S. 206, 234 (1960) (Frankfurter, J., dissenting).

Guided by these principles, the question we address today is whether a privilege protecting confidential communications between a psychotherapist and her patient "promotes sufficiently important interests to outweigh the need for probative evidence. . . ." 445 U.S. at 51. Both "reason and experience" persuade us that it does.

III

* * *

Like the spousal and attorney-client privileges, the psychotherapist-patient privilege is "rooted in the imperative need for confidence and trust." *Trammel*, 445 U.S. at 51. Treatment by a physician for physical ailments can often proceed

---

[8] [7] In 1972 the Chief Justice transmitted to Congress proposed Rules of Evidence for United States Courts and Magistrates. 56 F.R.D. 183 (hereinafter Proposed Rules). The rules had been formulated by the Judicial Conference Advisory Committee on Rules of Evidence and approved by the Judicial Conference of the United States and by this Court. *Trammel v. United States*, 445 U.S. 40, 47 (1980). The proposed rules defined nine specific testimonial privileges, including a psychotherapist-patient privilege, and indicated that these were to be the exclusive privileges absent constitutional mandate, Act of Congress, or revision of the Rules. Proposed Rules 501–513, 56 F.R.D., at 230–61. Congress rejected this recommendation in favor of Rule 501's general mandate. *Trammel*, 445 U.S. at 47.

[9] [8] The familiar expression "every man's evidence" was a well-known phrase as early as the mid-18th century. Both the Duke of Argyll and Lord Chancellor Hardwicke invoked the maxim during the May 25, 1742, debate in the House of Lords concerning a bill to grant immunity to witnesses who would give evidence against Sir Robert Walpole, first Earl of Orford. 12 T. Hansard, Parliamentary History of England 643, 675, 693, 697 (1812). The bill was defeated soundly. *Id.* at 711.

successfully on the basis of a physical examination, objective information supplied by the patient, and the results of diagnostic tests. Effective psychotherapy, by contrast, depends upon an atmosphere of confidence and trust in which the patient is willing to make a frank and complete disclosure of facts, emotions, memories, and fears. Because of the sensitive nature of the problems for which individuals consult psychotherapists, disclosure of confidential communications made during counseling sessions may cause embarrassment or disgrace. For this reason, the mere possibility of disclosure may impede development of the confidential relationship necessary for successful treatment.[10] As the Judicial Conference Advisory Committee observed in 1972 when it recommended that Congress recognize a psychotherapist privilege as part of the Proposed Federal Rules of Evidence, a psychiatrist's ability to help her patients

> "is completely dependent upon [the patients'] willingness and ability to talk freely. This makes it difficult if not impossible for [a psychiatrist] to function without being able to assure . . . patients of confidentiality and, indeed, privileged communication. Where there may be exceptions to this general rule . . . , there is wide agreement that confidentiality is a sine qua non for successful psychiatric treatment." Advisory Committee's Notes to Proposed Rules, 56 F.R.D. 183, 242 (1972) (quoting Group for Advancement of Psychiatry, Report No. 45, Confidentiality and Privileged Communication in the Practice of Psychiatry 92 (June 1960)).

By protecting confidential communications between a psychotherapist and her patient from involuntary disclosure, the proposed privilege thus serves important private interests.

Our cases make clear that an asserted privilege must also "serv[e] public ends." *Upjohn Co. v. United States*, 449 U.S. 383, 389 (1981). Thus, the purpose of the attorney-client privilege is to "encourage full and frank communication between attorneys and their clients and thereby promote broader public interests in the observance of law and administration of justice." *Ibid.* And the spousal privilege, as modified in *Trammel*, is justified because it "furthers the important public interest in marital harmony," 445 U.S. at 53. *See also United States v. Nixon*, 418 U.S. at 705; *Wolfle v. United States*, 291 U.S. at 14. The psychotherapist privilege serves the public interest by facilitating the provision of appropriate treatment for individuals suffering the effects of a mental or emotional problem. The mental health of our citizenry, no less than its physical health, is a public good of transcendent importance.[11]

In contrast to the significant public and private interests supporting recognition

---

[10] [9] *See* studies and authorities cited in the Brief for American Psychiatric Association et al. as *Amici Curiae* 14–17, and the Brief for American Psychological Association as *Amicus Curiae* 12–17.

[11] [10] This case amply demonstrates the importance of allowing individuals to receive confidential counseling. Police officers engaged in the dangerous and difficult tasks associated with protecting the safety of our communities not only confront the risk of physical harm but also face stressful circumstances that may give rise to anxiety, depression, fear, or anger. The entire community may suffer if police officers are not able to receive effective counseling and treatment after traumatic incidents, either because trained officers leave the profession prematurely or because those in need of treatment remain on the job.

of the privilege, the likely evidentiary benefit that would result from the denial of the privilege is modest. If the privilege were rejected, confidential conversations between psychotherapists and their patients would surely be chilled, particularly when it is obvious that the circumstances that give rise to the need for treatment will probably result in litigation. Without a privilege, much of the desirable evidence to which litigants such as petitioner seek access — for example, admissions against interest by a party — is unlikely to come into being. This unspoken "evidence" will therefore serve no greater truth-seeking function than if it had been spoken and privileged.

That it is appropriate for the federal courts to recognize a psychotherapist privilege under Rule 501 is confirmed by the fact that all 50 States and the District of Columbia have enacted into law some form of psychotherapist privilege. We have previously observed that the policy decisions of the States bear on the question whether federal courts should recognize a new privilege or amend the coverage of an existing one. *See Trammel*, 445 U.S. at 48–50; *United States v. Gillock*, 445 U.S. 360, 368, n.8 (1980). Because state legislatures are fully aware of the need to protect the integrity of the factfinding functions of their courts, the existence of a consensus among the States indicates that "reason and experience" support recognition of the privilege. In addition, given the importance of the patient's understanding that her communications with her therapist will not be publicly disclosed, any State's promise of confidentiality would have little value if the patient were aware that the privilege would not be honored in a federal court. Denial of the federal privilege therefore would frustrate the purposes of the state legislation that was enacted to foster these confidential communications.

*   *   *

IV

All agree that a psychotherapist privilege covers confidential communications made to licensed psychiatrists and psychologists. We have no hesitation in concluding in this case that the federal privilege should also extend to confidential communications made to licensed social workers in the course of psychotherapy. The reasons for recognizing a privilege for treatment by psychiatrists and psychologists apply with equal force to treatment by a clinical social worker such as Karen Beyer. Today, social workers provide a significant amount of mental health treatment. *See, e.g.*, U.S. Dept. of Health and Human Services, Center for Mental Health Services, Mental Health, United States, 1994 pp. 85–87, 107–114; Brief for National Association of Social Workers et al. as *Amici Curiae* 5–7 (citing authorities). Their clients often include the poor and those of modest means who could not afford the assistance of a psychiatrist or psychologist, *id.* at 6–7 (citing authorities), but whose counseling sessions serve the same public goals. Perhaps in recognition of these circumstances, the vast majority of States explicitly extend a testimonial privilege to licensed social workers. We therefore agree with the Court of Appeals that "[d]rawing a distinction between the counseling provided by costly psychotherapists and the counseling provided by more readily accessible social workers serves no discernible public purpose." 51 F.3d at 1358, n.19.

We part company with the Court of Appeals on a separate point. We reject the balancing component of the privilege implemented by that court and a small number of States. Making the promise of confidentiality contingent upon a trial judge's later evaluation of the relative importance of the patient's interest in privacy and the evidentiary need for disclosure would eviscerate the effectiveness of the privilege. As we explained in *Upjohn*, if the purpose of the privilege is to be served, the participants in the confidential conversation "must be able to predict with some degree of certainty whether particular discussions will be protected. An uncertain privilege, or one which purports to be certain but results in widely varying applications by the courts, is little better than no privilege at all." 449 U.S. at 393.

These considerations are all that is necessary for decision of this case. A rule that authorizes the recognition of new privileges on a case-by-case basis makes it appropriate to define the details of new privileges in a like manner. Because this is the first case in which we have recognized a psychotherapist privilege, it is neither necessary nor feasible to delineate its full contours in a way that would "govern all conceivable future questions in this area." *Id.* at 386.[12]

V

The conversations between Officer Redmond and Karen Beyer and the notes taken during their counseling sessions are protected from compelled disclosure under Rule 501 of the Federal Rules of Evidence. The judgment of the Court of Appeals is affirmed.

It is so ordered.

NOTES AND QUESTIONS

1. Do you agree that congressional action abrogating the Supreme Court's proposed Article V reflected an incorrect application of *Erie* principles?

2. Under Fed. R. Evid. 501, what is meant by the term "element" Is that term limited to formal substantive elements of a cause of action? *See* Rothstein, *The Proposed Amendments to the Federal Rules of Evidence*, 62 GEO. L.J. 125, 130 n.2 (1973).

3. How is Rule 501 to be applied in situations involving "mixed federal and state claims" *See* Comment, "In Light of Reason and Experience": Rule 501, 71 Nw. U. L. REV. 645, 650 (1976). Why does it make no sense in such instances simply to say that federal law applies to federal claims and state law to state claims? *See Samuelson v. Susen*, 576 F.2d 546, 551 (3d Cir. 1978). Moreover, assuming that state law governs, Judge Weinstein raises the following questions: "Should the court apply the privilege law 1) of the forum state, 2) of the state whose substantive law is being applied, 3) of the state where the privileged communication was made, or 4) of the state where a deposition was held at which a privilege was claimed?" 2

---

[12] [19] Although it would be premature to speculate about most future developments in the federal psychotherapist privilege, we do not doubt that there are situations in which the privilege must give way, for example, if a serious threat of harm to the patient or to others can be averted only by means of a disclosure by the therapist.

WEINSTEIN'S EVIDENCE § 501[02], at 501–22 (1982).

4.   Ultimately, Article V served both as the predicate for evidentiary privilege rules in several states, *see, e.g.*, Neb. Rev. Stat. § 27-503 (Supp. 1978), and as persuasive authority for federal courts in cases not involving state law. *See Diversified Industries, Inc. v. Meredith,* 572 F.2d 596, 605 n.1 (8th Cir. 1977) (en banc).

5.   Because the authors of the Federal Rules of Evidence could not agree on the enumeration of privileges and left it to the development of the common law and statute, absent the recognition of a privilege by the United States Supreme Court or Congress, the existence of particular privileges will vary from federal circuit to federal circuit. Does this mean that counsel forum shop in order to obtain the benefit of a particular privilege?

B.   THE EXECUTIVE PRIVILEGES

Archibald Cox, *Executive Privilege*
122 U. Pa. L. Rev. 1383, 1384–87 (1974)[13]

The Problem of Executive Privilege

The Constitution says nothing about the right of either the courts or the Congress to obtain documents, inter- or infra-departmental memoranda, or testimony about oral communications within the Executive Branch. Nor does the Constitution speak directly or indirectly about a privilege to withhold. The controversy over executive privilege arises from our constitutional separation of government into coordinate legislative, executive and judicial branches.

Consider first the Judicial Branch. Charged with adjudicating cases and controversies and with supervising grand jury investigations, the Judicial Branch has obvious need of evidence and therefore the implied authority to issue compulsory legal process for securing it. The need may occasionally extend to evidence in the possession of the President or his subordinates in the Executive Branch. The best opinion at Anglo-American law has always been that no man except the King is wholly free from the testimonial duty to give evidence required in the administration of justice. In the treason case against Aaron Burr, Chief Justice Marshall ruled that this obligation extends to the President. On this theory, the federal district court would seem to have had legal power to require President Nixon's testimony concerning relevant and unprivileged matters within his knowledge, although the Special Prosecutor chose not to press the issue. The public interest in a President's attention to other duties would doubtless make it appropriate to excuse him in instances in which his testimony was unessential and otherwise to take it by deposition. Various privileges to withhold evidence might or might not be applicable. The important point is that the powers vested in the Judicial Branch under article III of the Constitution logically extend to issuing orders for the production of material evidence by the President and other officers in the Executive Branch.

---

[13] Reprinted by permission.

The Legislative Branch — the Senate and the House of Representatives — also requires information, in order to enact laws and appropriate funds for the conduct of the government. Article I's grant of power to legislate is therefore held to carry implied authority to summon witnesses and to compel the production of evidence. Since much of the evidence must come from the Executive Branch, especially when its activities are under scrutiny, the implied power of Congress under article I logically extends to requiring the production of evidence by executive officials.

The Executive Branch, on the other hand, has an undeniably legitimate interest, at least under some circumstances, in preserving the confidentiality of internal communications in order to perform its duties under article II. Revealing specifications for, or locations of strategic military weapons could hazard national security. Disclosing diplomatic secrets might endanger negotiations vitally affecting national interests. Confidentiality also may be important to effective consultation. In 1955 President Eisenhower said:

> But when it comes to the conversations that take place between any responsible official and his advisers . . . expressing personal opinions on the most confidential basis, those are not subject to investigation by anybody; and if they are, will wreck the Government.

> There is no business that could be run if there would be exposed every single thought that an adviser might have, because in the process of reaching an agreed position, there are many, many conflicting opinions to be brought together. And if any commander is going to get the free, unprejudiced opinions of his subordinates, he had better protect what they have to say to him on a confidential basis.

The claim was made in very general terms applicable not only to presidential conversations and papers but also to papers and conversations throughout the Executive Branch. And from the need for confidentiality as an encouragement of candor it is argued that "[t]he same logic which holds that Congress has the power to investigate so that it may effectively exercise its legislative functions, supports the proposition that the President has the power to withhold information when the use of the power is necessary to exercise his Executive functions effectively. . . ."

Standing by itself each inference seems not only logical but necessary. The Judicial Branch, when it needs evidence, should have the power to obtain it. The Legislative Branch, when it needs information in order to perform its duties, should also have power to obtain it. Yet the Executive, when disclosure of information will impede the performance of its duties, should have power to withhold it. The third inference cuts across the first and second. In any given situation either the first or second, or the third, must yield. The questions are: (1) who, if anyone, shall decide which shall yield and when it shall yield; and (2) on what basis shall the decision, if any, be rendered.

UNITED STATES v. NIXON
418 U.S. 683 (1974)

MR. CHIEF JUSTICE BURGER delivered the opinion of the Court.

* * *

On March 1, 1974, a grand jury of the United States District Court for the District of Columbia returned an indictment charging seven named individuals with various offenses, including conspiracy to defraud the United States and to obstruct justice. Although he was not designated as such in the indictment, the grand jury named the President, among others, as an unindicted co-conspirator. On April 18, 1974, upon motion of the Special Prosecutor, . . . a subpoena duces tecum was issued pursuant to Rule 17(c) to the President by the United States District Court and made returnable on May 2, 1974. This subpoena required the production, in advance of the September 9 trial date, of certain tapes, memoranda, papers, transcripts, or other writings relating to certain precisely identified meetings between the President and others. The Special Prosecutor was able to fix the time, place, and persons present at these discussions because the White House daily logs and appointment records had been delivered to him. On April 30, the President publicly released edited transcripts of 43 conversations; portions of 20 conversations subject to subpoena in the present case were included. On May 1, 1974, the President's counsel filed a "special appearance" and a motion to quash the subpoena under Rule 17(c). This motion was accompanied by a formal claim of privilege. At a subsequent hearing,[14] further motions to expunge the grand jury's action naming the President as an unindicted co-conspirator and for protective orders against the disclosure of that information were filed or raised orally by counsel for the President.

On May 20, 1974, the District Court denied the motion to quash and the motions to expunge and for protective orders. 377 F. Supp. 1326. It further ordered "the President or any subordinate officer, official, or employee with custody or control of the documents or objects subpoenaed," *id.*, at 1331, to deliver to the District Court on or before May 31, 1974, the originals of all subpoenaed items, as well as an index and analysis of those items, together with tape copies of those portions of the subpoenaed recordings for which transcripts had been released to the public by the President on April 30. . . . [*Certiorari* was granted after this decision was affirmed by the Court of Appeals.]

* * *

---

[14] [6] At the joint suggestion of the Special Prosecutor and counsel for the President, and with the approval of counsel for the defendants, further proceedings in the District Court were held in camera.

IV

THE CLAIM OF PRIVILEGE

A

. . . [W]e turn to the claim that the subpoena should be quashed because it demands "confidential conversations between a President and his close advisors that it would be inconsistent with the public interest to produce." . . . The first contention is a broad claim that the separation of powers doctrine precludes judicial review of a President's claim of privilege. The second contention is that if he does not prevail on the claim of absolute privilege, the court should hold as a matter of constitutional law that the privilege prevails over the subpoena duces tecum.

In the performance of assigned constitutional duties each branch of the Government must initially interpret the Constitution, and the interpretation of its powers by any branch is due great respect from the others. The President's counsel, as we have noted, reads the Constitution as providing an absolute privilege of confidentiality for all Presidential communications. Many decisions of this Court, however, have unequivocally reaffirmed the holding of *Marbury v. Madison*, 1 Cranch 137 (1803), that "[i]t is emphatically the province and duty of the judicial department to say what the law is." *Id.* at 177. . . .

No holding of the Court has defined the scope of judicial power specifically relating to the enforcement of a subpoena for confidential Presidential communications for use in a criminal prosecution, but other exercises of power by the Executive Branch and the Legislative Branch have been found invalid as in conflict with the Constitution. . . . Since this Court has consistently exercised the power to construe and delineate claims arising under express powers, it must follow that the Court has authority to interpret claims with respect to powers alleged to derive from enumerated powers.

* * *

Notwithstanding the deference each branch must accord the others, the "judicial Power of the United States" vested in the federal courts by Art III, § 1, of the Constitution can no more be shared with the Executive Branch than the Chief Executive, for example, can share with the Judiciary the veto power, or the Congress share with the Judiciary the power to override a Presidential veto. Any other conclusion would be contrary to the basic concept of separation of powers and the checks and balances that flow from the scheme of a tripartite government. THE FEDERALIST, No. 47, p. 313 (S. Mittell ed. 1938). We therefore reaffirm that it is the province and duty of this Court "to say what the law is" with respect to the claim of privilege presented in this case. . . .

B

In support of his claim of absolute privilege, the President's counsel urges two grounds, one of which is common to all governments and one of which is peculiar to our system of separation of powers. The first ground is the valid need for protection of communications between high Government officials and those who advise and assist them in the performance of their manifold duties; the importance of this confidentiality is too plain to require further discussion. Human experience teaches that those who expect public dissemination of their remarks may well temper candor with a concern for appearances and for their own interests to the detriment of the decisionmaking process.[15] Whatever the nature of the privilege of confidentiality of Presidential communications in the exercise of Art. II powers, the privilege can be said to derive from the supremacy of each branch within its own assigned area of constitutional duties. Certain powers and privileges flow from the nature of enumerated powers;[16] the protection of the confidentiality of Presidential communications has similar constitutional underpinnings.

The second ground asserted by the President's counsel in support of the claim of absolute privilege rests on the doctrine of separation of powers. Here it is argued that the independence of the Executive Branch within its own sphere . . . insulates a President from a judicial subpoena in an ongoing criminal prosecution, and thereby protects confidential Presidential communications.

However, neither the doctrine of separation of powers, nor the need for confidentiality of high-level communications, without more, can sustain an absolute, unqualified Presidential privilege of immunity from judicial process under all circumstances. The President's need for complete candor and objectivity from advisers calls for great deference from the courts. However, when the privilege depends solely on the broad, undifferentiated claim of public interest in the confidentiality of such conversations, a confrontation with other values arises. Absent a claim of need to protect military, diplomatic, or sensitive national security secrets, we find it difficult to accept the argument that even the very important interest in confidentiality of Presidential communications is significantly diminished by production of such material for in camera inspection with all the protection that a district court will be obliged to provide.

The impediment that an absolute, unqualified privilege would place in the way of the primary constitutional duty of the Judicial Branch to do justice in criminal prosecutions would plainly conflict with the function of the courts under Art. III. In designing the structure of our Government and dividing and allocating the sovereign power among three co-equal branches, the Framers of the Constitution

---

[15] [15] There is nothing novel about governmental confidentiality. The meetings of the Constitutional Convention in 1787 were conducted in complete privacy. 1 M. FARRAND, THE RECORDS OF THE FEDERAL CONVENTION OF 1787, pp. xi–xxv (1911). Moreover, all records of those meetings were sealed for more than 30 years after the Convention. *See* 3 Stat. 475, 15th Cong., 1st Sess., Res. 8 (1818). Most of the Framers acknowledged that without secrecy no constitution of the kind that was developed could have been written. C. WARREN, THE MAKING OF THE CONSTITUTION 134–139 (1937).

[16] [16] The Special Prosecutor argues that there is no provision in the Constitution for a Presidential privilege as to the President's communications corresponding to the privilege of Members of Congress under the Speech or Debate Clause. But the silence of the Constitution on this score is not dispositive. "The rule of constitutional interpretation announced in *McCulloch v. Maryland*, 4 L. Ed. 579, 4 Wheat. 316, that that which was reasonably appropriate and relevant to the exercise of a granted power was to be considered as accompanying the grant, has been so universally applied that it suffices merely to state it." . . .

sought to provide a comprehensive system, but the separate powers were not intended to operate with absolute independence.

* * *

To read the Art. II powers of the President as providing an absolute privilege as against a subpoena essential to enforcement of criminal statutes on no more than a generalized claim of the public interest in confidentiality of nonmilitary and nondiplomatic discussions would upset the constitutional balance of "a workable government" and gravely impair the role of the courts under Art. III.

C

Since we conclude that the legitimate needs of the judicial process may outweigh Presidential privilege, it is necessary to resolve those competing interests in a manner that preserves the essential functions of each branch. The right and indeed the duty to resolve that question does not free the judiciary from according high respect to the representations made on behalf of the President. *United States v. Burr*, 25 F. Cas. 187, 190, 191–192 (No. 14,694) (C.C. Va. 1807).

The expectation of a President to the confidentiality of his conversations and correspondence, like the claim of confidentiality of judicial deliberations, for example, has all the values to which we accord deference for the privacy of all citizens and added to those values the necessity for protection of the public interest in candid, objective, and even blunt or harsh opinions in Presidential decision making. A President and those who assist him must be free to explore alternatives in the process of shaping policies and making decisions and to do so in a way many would be unwilling to express except privately. These are the considerations justifying a presumptive privilege for Presidential communications. The privilege is fundamental to the operation of government and inextricably rooted in the separation of powers under the Constitution. In *Nixon v. Sirica*, . . . 487 F.2d 700 (1973), the Court of Appeals held that such Presidential communications are "presumptively privileged," . . . 487 F.2d at 717, and this position is accepted by both parties in the present litigation. We agree with Mr. Chief Justice Marshall's observation, therefore, that "[i]n no case of this kind would a court be required to proceed against the President as against an ordinary individual." . . .

But this presumptive privilege must be considered in light of our historic commitment to the rule of law. This is nowhere more profoundly manifest than in our view that "the twofold aim [of criminal justice] is that guilt shall not escape or innocence suffer." . . . We have elected to employ an adversary system of criminal justice in which the parties contest all issues before a court of law. The need to develop all relevant facts in the adversary system is both fundamental and comprehensive. The ends of criminal justice would be defeated if judgments were to be founded on a partial or speculative presentation of the facts. The very integrity of the judicial system and public confidence in the system depend on full disclosure of all the facts, within the framework of the rules of evidence. To ensure that justice is done, it is imperative to the function of courts that compulsory process be available for the production of evidence needed either by the prosecution or by the defense.

Only recently the Court restated the ancient proposition of law, albeit in the context of a grand jury inquiry rather than a trial, "that 'the public . . . has a right to every man's evidence,' except for those persons protected by a constitutional, common-law, or statutory privilege. . . ."

The privileges referred to by the Court are designed to protect weighty and legitimate competing interests. Thus, the Fifth Amendment to the Constitution provides that no man "shall be compelled in any criminal case to be a witness against himself." And, generally, an attorney or a priest may not be required to disclose what has been revealed in professional confidence. These and other interests are recognized in law by privileges against forced disclosure, established in the Constitution, by statute, or at common-law. Whatever their origins, these exceptions to the demand for every man's evidence are not lightly created nor expansively construed, for they are in derogation of the search for truth.

In this case the President challenges a subpoena served on him as a third; party requiring the production of materials for use in a criminal prosecution; he does so on the claim that he has a privilege against disclosure of confidential communications. He does not place his claim of privilege on the ground they are military or diplomatic secrets. As to these areas of Art. II duties the courts have traditionally shown the utmost deference to Presidential responsibilities [citing Reynolds and other cases]. . . .

*   *   *

No case of the Court, however, has extended this high degree of deference to a President's generalized interest in confidentiality. Nowhere in the Constitution, as we have noted earlier, is there any explicit reference to a privilege of confidentiality, yet to the extent this interest relates to the effective discharge of a President's powers, it is constitutionally based.

The right to the production of all evidence at a criminal trial similarly has constitutional dimensions. The Sixth Amendment explicitly confers upon every defendant in a criminal trial the right "to be confronted with the witnesses against him" and "to have compulsory process for obtaining witnesses in his favor." Moreover, the Fifth Amendment also guarantees that no person shall be deprived of liberty without due process of law. It is the manifest duty of the courts to vindicate those guarantees, and to accomplish that it is essential that all relevant and admissible evidence be produced.

In this case we must weigh the importance of the general privilege of confidentiality of Presidential communications in performance of his responsibilities against the inroads of such a privilege on the fair administration of criminal justice.[17] The interest in preserving confidentiality is weighty indeed and entitled to great respect. However, we cannot conclude that advisers will be moved to temper the candor of their remarks by the infrequent occasions of disclosure because of the

---

[17] [19] We are not here concerned with the balance between the President's generalized interest in confidentiality and the need for relevant evidence in civil litigation, nor with that between the confidentiality interest and congressional demands for information, nor with the President's interest in preserving state secrets. We address only the conflict between the President's assertion of a generalized privilege of confidentiality and the constitutional need for relevant evidence in criminal trials.

possibility that such conversations will be called for in the context of a criminal prosecution.

On the other hand, the allowance of the privilege to withhold evidence that is demonstrably relevant in a criminal trial would cut deeply into the guarantee of due process of law and gravely impair the basic function of the courts. A President's acknowledged need for confidentiality in the communications of his office is general in nature, whereas the constitutional need for production of relevant evidence in a criminal proceeding is specific and central to the fair adjudication of a particular criminal case in the administration of justice. Without access to specific facts a criminal prosecution may be totally frustrated. The President's broad interest in confidentiality of communications will not be vitiated by disclosure of a limited number of conversations preliminarily shown to have some bearing on the pending criminal cases.

We conclude that when the ground for asserting privilege as to subpoenaed materials sought for use in a criminal trial is based only on the generalized interest in confidentiality, it cannot prevail over the fundamental demands of due process of law in the fair administration of criminal justice. The generalized assertion of privilege must yield to the demonstrated, specific need for evidence in a pending criminal trial.

D

We have earlier determined that the District Court did not err in authorizing the issuance of the subpoena. If a President concludes that compliance with a subpoena would be injurious to the public interest he may properly, as was done here, invoke a claim of privilege on the return of the subpoena. Upon receiving a claim of privilege from the Chief Executive, it became the further duty of the District Court to treat the subpoenaed material as presumptively privileged and to require the Special Prosecutor to demonstrate that the Presidential material was "essential to the justice of the [pending criminal] case." . . . Here the District Court treated the material as presumptively privileged, proceeded to find that the Special Prosecutor had made a sufficient showing to rebut the presumption, and ordered an in camera examination of the subpoenaed material. On the basis of our examination of the record we are unable to conclude that the District Court erred in ordering the inspection. Accordingly we affirm the order of the District Court that subpoenaed materials be transmitted to that court. We now turn to the important question of the District Court's responsibilities in conducting the in camera examination of Presidential materials or communications delivered under the compulsion of the subpoena duces tecum.

E

Enforcement of the subpoena duces tecum was stayed pending this Court's resolution of the issues raised by the petitions for *certiorari*. Those issues now having been disposed of, the matter of implementation will rest with the District Court. "[T]he guard, furnished to [the President] to protect him from being harassed by vexatious and unnecessary subpoenas, is to be looked for in the conduct of a [district] court after those subpoenas have issued; not in any circumstance which is to precede their being issued." . . . Statements that meet the test of admissibility and relevance must be isolated; all other material must be excised. At this stage the District Court is not limited to representations of the Special Prosecutor as to the evidence sought by the subpoena; the material will be available to the District Court. It is elementary that in camera inspection of evidence is always a procedure calling for scrupulous protection against any release or publication of material not found by the court, at that stage, probably admissible in evidence and relevant to the issues of the trial for which it is sought. That being true of an ordinary situation, it is obvious that the District Court has a very heavy responsibility to see to it that Presidential conversations, which are either not relevant or not admissible, are accorded that high degree of respect due the President of the United States. Mr. Chief Justice Marshall, sitting as a trial judge in the *Burr* case was extraordinarily careful to point out that "[i]n no case of this kind would a court be required to proceed against the president as against an ordinary individual." . . .

Marshall's statement cannot be read to mean in any sense that a President is above the law, but relates to the singularly unique role under Art. II of a President's communications and activities, related to the performance of duties under that Article. Moreover, a President's communications and activities encompass a vastly wider range of sensitive material than would be true of any "ordinary individual." It is therefore necessary[18] in the public interest to afford Presidential confidentiality the greatest protection consistent with the fair administration of justice. The need for confidentiality even as to idle conversations with associates in which casual reference might be made concerning political leaders within the country or foreign statesmen is too obvious to call for further treatment. We have no doubt that the District Judge will at all times accord to Presidential records that high degree of deference suggested in *United States v. Burr* . . . and will discharge his responsibility to see to it that until released to the Special Prosecutor no in camera material is revealed to anyone. This burden applies with even greater force to excised material; once the decision is made to excise, the material is restored to its privileged status and should be returned under seal to its lawful custodian.

Since this matter came before the Court during the pendency of a criminal prosecution, and on representations that time is of the essence, the mandate shall issue forthwith.

Affirmed.

---

[18] [21] When the subpoenaed material is delivered to the District Judge in camera questions may arise as to the excising of parts and it lies within the discretion of that court to seek the aid of the Special Prosecutor and the President's counsel for in camera consideration of the validity of particular excisions, whether the basis of excision is relevancy or admissibility or under such cases as . . . *United States v. Reynolds.* . . .

C. THE ATTORNEY-CLIENT PRIVILEGE

Geoffrey C. Hazard, Jr., *An Historical Perspective on the Attorney-Client Privilege*
66 CAL. L. REV. 1061, 1061–64, 1068–70 (1978)[19]

The attorney-client privilege may well be the pivotal element of the modern American lawyer's professional functions. It is considered indispensable to the lawyer's function as advocate on the theory that the advocate can adequately prepare a case only if the client is free to disclose everything, bad as well as good. The privilege is also considered necessary to the lawyer's function as confidential counselor in law on the similar theory that the legal counselor can properly advise the client what to do only if the client is free to make full disclosure.

There has always been some anxiety about the privilege, as there is about all privileges. As a matter of common sense it is unlikely that a client would wish to withhold from his lawyer information that puts him or his cause in a favorable light. Of course, it is possible that a particular client on a particular occasion may be concerned with the privilege as a matter of principle — wishing to avoid even the most flattering revelations of his affairs and his self. Yet assuming there are such instances, it seems fair to say they are greatly outnumbered by those in which the principle of privacy is invoked to conceal legally dubious or dirty business. And when dubious or dirty business has been done, most likely someone has suffered as a result. In the nature of things, then, the attorney-client privilege has its victims.

In the procedural contexts in which the attorney-client privilege is invoked, the identity of the victim is usually not difficult to discern. It is the party seeking disclosure of the confidence. Hence, the common sense estimate of situations involving the attorney-client privilege is that the lawyer, though an "officer of the court," is allowed to conceal wrong-doing by the client in the face of a specific demand for its disclosure by the very person suffering the wrong. There may be a sufficient justification for the privilege; indeed the verdict of our legal history is to that effect. But no argument of justification should ignore the fact that the attorney-client privilege, as far as it goes, is not only a principle of privacy, but also a device for cover-ups. That, of course, is what makes contemplation of it both interesting and troubling.

*   *   *

In present-day law, the issue concerning the attorney-client privilege is not whether it should exist, but precisely what its terms should be. There is no responsible opinion suggesting that the privilege be completely abolished. Total abolition would mean that an accused in a criminal case could not explain his version of the matter to his lawyer without its being transmitted to the prosecution. Defense counsel would become a medium of confession, a result that would substantially impair both the accused's right to counsel and the privilege against self-incrimination. Hence, it is common ground that the privilege ought to apply at

---

[19] Copyright © 1978 by The California Law Review, Inc. Reprinted from California Law Review Vol. 66, pp. 1061–64, 1068–70, by permission.

least to communications by an accused criminal to his counsel, in contemplation of defense of a pending or imminently threatened prosecution, concerning a completed crime. Beyond this there is controversy as to the proper scope of the privilege, although superficially the authorities are in substantial agreement.

One convenient statement of the rule of privilege appears in Rule 26 of the Uniform Rules of Evidence. In this formulation, the privilege attaches to "communications . . . between lawyer and his client in the course of that relationship and in professional confidence . . . unless the legal service was sought or obtained . . . to commit or plan to commit a crime or a tort. . . ." The rule applies to consultations concerning civil as well as criminal litigation, to plaintiffs as well as defendants, to consultations in which the client seeks advice only and not simply assistance in litigation, and to communications whose aim is assistance other than in litigation, such as drafting legal documents. And so the privilege is generally understood.

Yet upon closer reading, the scope of the rule is not so plain. This becomes evident when the rule is applied to situations (aside from the criminal defendant's communication to an attorney) where its exclusionary effect is really important. These are situations in which the client is doing or planning to do something that is very bad, such as committing a crime or destroying evidence, or where the client wants the lawyer to do something very bad, such as suborning perjury or aiding in fraud. In such circumstances, it is arguable that the privilege, by its own terms, is not applicable. That is, if the client has in mind anything but a "legitimate" purpose in consulting a lawyer, it might be said that communications between them are neither "in the course of" the attorney-client relationship nor in "professional" confidence. Furthermore, if the consultation is manifestly in aid of proposed conduct that would be a crime or a tort, it is excepted from the privilege by the express terms of the rule. And it may not be far-fetched to say that it is tortious to make any use of legal process for a purpose other than a "legitimate" one.

The scope of the attorney-client privilege in these borderline areas has never been well defined in the cases. . . .

Wigmore says of the privilege:

The history of this privilege goes back to the reign of Elizabeth, where the privilege already appears as unquestioned. . . . The policy of the privilege has been plainly grounded, since the latter part of the 1700s. . . . In order to promote freedom of consultations of legal advisors by clients, the apprehension of compelled disclosure by the legal advisors must be removed; and hence the law must prohibit such disclosure except on the client's consent.

There is something to this. Elizabethan cases do indeed refer to the privilege, and although some of the early cases express the idea that the privilege was that of the lawyer (a gentleman does not give away matters confided to him), as the rule developed the privilege became that of the client to have his secrets protected. It is also true that in order to prevent disclosure, the law must prohibit it, for otherwise the lawyer would be governed by the general rule that a witness must give evidence of facts within his knowledge.

But beyond this, the historical foundations of the privilege are not as firm as the tenor of Wigmore's language suggests. On the contrary, recognition of the privilege was slow and halting until after 1800. It was applied only with much hesitation, and exceptions concerning crime and wrong-doing by the client evolved simultaneously with the privilege itself. At least in the English cases, an exception to the rule was usually found if proof aliunde indicated that the client was indeed engaged in some malfeasance. Taken as a whole, the historical record is not authority for a broadly stated rule of privilege or confidence. It is, rather, an invitation for reconsideration.

IN RE BONANNO
344 F.2d 830 (2d Cir. 1965)

KAUFMAN, CIRCUIT JUDGE:

Contending that a privileged relationship justified his refusal to answer certain questions in the course of a grand jury inquiry and that the special proceedings rejecting the claim of privilege did not comport with due process requirements, Salvatore Bonanno appeals from a judgment of commitment for civil contempt. The contumacious conduct occurred when, despite the District Court's ruling that answers to the questions would not require disclosure of confidential attorney-client communications, Bonanno persisted in invoking the privilege both before the grand jury and the judge, despite his direction to answer the questions. Bonanno is presently committed to custody until he purges himself of contempt by answering the questions. We affirm, finding neither procedural nor substantive error in the District Court's determination that Bonanno failed to meet the burden of establishing the essential predicate to invocation of the privilege — existence of an attorney-client relationship.

On January 5, 1965, having been served with a material witness warrant in Tucson, Arizona, Bonanno appeared before the October 1964 Additional Grand Jury, sitting in the Southern District of New York, to testify concerning the sudden and dramatic disappearance of his father, Joseph Bonanno, during the grand jury's investigation. After he was granted immunity from prosecution, 47 U.S.C. § 409(1), thus effectively removing the cloak of the privilege against self-incrimination, Bonanno, on January 14, declined to answer two questions concerning telephone conversations between himself and William Power Maloney which took place on December 18 and 19, 1964. He claimed that Maloney, who concededly was his father's attorney, was his own counsel as well; if accepted, this claim would have insulated the allegedly confidential communications from grand jury scrutiny.

Following our direction in *United States v. Kovel*, . . . that proper practice in such instances requires a preliminary judicial inquiry, with the grand jury excused, into the existence of the privilege, a full hearing was held before Judge Tenney. The testimony, which we shall detail below, focused on the threshold but crucial question of the alleged attorney-client relationship between Maloney and Salvatore Bonanno. It was unnecessary to reach the further question whether the particular telephone conversations were themselves privileged communications between attorney and client because Judge Tenney, after giving "careful consideration" to the testimony before him, ruled that Bonanno had not "met or even approached" the burden of presenting evidence to support his claim that Maloney was his lawyer. Bonanno then was directed to answer the questions, but refused to do so when they were, once again, propounded before the Grand Jury and also after direction by the Judge in open court. His adjudication for civil contempt followed.

So that our assessment of the validity of the judgment may be understood, we have briefly summarized the testimony presented to Judge Tenney, which he characterized as "so filled with contradictions, improbabilities, and inconsistencies, as to render it unworthy of belief." The hearing before the Judge opened with Bonanno testifying that the attorney-client relationship arose when he and his father Joseph met with Maloney on an unspecified date in August 1964, after Joseph had returned to New York from Canada. He said he presented his own legal and tax problems to Maloney, feeling that they were closely related to similar problems of his father.

On cross-examination, Bonanno was confronted with his grand jury testimony, given just two weeks earlier, in which he denied ever having retained Maloney or any other attorney in New York, with the exception of his present counsel, retained in connection with the grand jury proceeding. Seeking to account for this glaring inconsistency, Bonanno explained that the earlier answers were limited to the specific grand jury proceedings in which he was then a witness, notwithstanding the fact that he had told the grand jury, "I know a few attorneys in New York, and I'm just trying to figure out if they've ever represented me in any matter."

Maloney also was a witness at the preliminary hearing. On direct examination, he said that in August 1964 Salvatore and Joseph Bonanno conferred with him and that Salvatore sought his advice as an attorney. But he, too, was unable to pinpoint either the date he was retained or corroborative details of the alleged retainer. And, although Salvatore testified that in August he paid Maloney a fee in cash, Maloney stated that the only sum he received was a payment of less than $500 for expenses in September, which he did not note in any office income or disbursement record.

The Government, on cross-examination, then confronted Maloney with his prior testimony before the grand jury in which he stated that he had been retained by Salvatore Bonanno during a telephone conversation on December 18, 1964. This testimony was not only inconsistent with the claim made by both parties in the hearing before Judge Tenney that their confidential relationship arose in August, but also contrary to Bonanno's denial that he discussed Maloney's representation during the December telephone conversation.

After the preliminary hearing had been closed, Bonanno alleged that he had acquired additional evidence to substantiate the claimed attorney-client relationship. Judge Tenney, in an effort to throw as much light as possible on the subject which up to this point consisted of a bundle of contradictions, granted the appellant's motion to reopen the hearing, over the Government's objection, and proceeded to take more testimony. This alleged "new evidence" consisted of a petition to the Tax Court which Bonanno claimed had been prepared in Maloney's office on August 10, 1964, the last day for answering a 90-day deficiency letter from the Internal Revenue Service. Maloney's secretary, Aileen Richmond, identified a photocopy of an incompletely executed copy of the original petition, which she testified was dictated jointly by Maloney and Lawrence P. D'Antonio, Salvatore Bonanno's Arizona counsel. Although she previously had told the grand jury she never overheard any conversations between Maloney and Bonanno, Mrs. Richmond now distinctly remembered that both men discussed the tax petition. But she was unable to produce any corroborative stenographic notes which recorded the alleged dictation taken from Maloney and D'Antonio.

The general tenor of Mrs. Richmond's testimony was echoed by both Bonanno and Maloney at this reopened hearing although, significantly, D'Antonio was never called by appellant to testify. On cross-examination, Maloney admitted that he had never consulted Bonanno in connection with tax matters before August 10, that this was the first and only occasion on which he participated in the preparation of any tax documents for Bonanno, that he could not recall ever representing any client at any time in the Tax Court, and, indeed, was not admitted to practice before that Court. Bonanno also admitted that the only time he sought tax advice from Maloney was on August 10 although other counsel had represented him at various conferences with the Internal Revenue Service concerning these tax deficiencies, and that he personally, rather than a member of Maloney's staff, registered the mailing of the petition and obtained the money order necessary to cover the filing fee.

I.

This brief review of the vague, confusing and what would appear to be contrived testimony before Judge Tenney, based on our independent reading of the record of the hearings, would alone furnish ample support for the conclusion that no attorney-client relationship ever existed between Salvatore Bonanno and Maloney.
. . .

We recognize that an attorney-client relationship arises when legal advice of any kind is sought from a professional legal adviser in his capacity as such. 8 WIGMORE, EVIDENCE (McNaughton Rev. 1961), § 2292.[20] Bonanno concedes, as he must, . . . that the burden of establishing the existence of the relationship rests on the claimant of the privilege against disclosure. That burden is not, of course, discharged by mere conclusory or *ipse dixit* assertions, for any such rule would foreclose meaningful inquiry into the existence of the relationship, and any spurious claims could never be exposed.

It is clear to us that the evidence presented to Judge Tenney consisted of little more than bare characterizations, both Bonanno and Maloney being unable, despite the passage of only five months, to recall the details — much less to furnish tangible evidence — of the events surrounding formation of the alleged relationship. The record is a veritable catalogue of inconsistencies concerning the date when Maloney was retained, whether that occurred in his office, at a restaurant, or over the telephone, and whether he was paid a fee in August or reimbursed for expenses in September. Moreover, we are not aware that Bonanno himself ever satisfactorily

---

[20] [Ed. — In pertinent part, this section of Professor Wigmore's treatise provides as follows:

(1) Where legal advice of any kind is sought (2) from a professional legal adviser in his capacity as such, (3) the communications relating to that purpose, (4) made in confidence (5) by the client, (6) are at this instance permanently protected (7) from disclosure by himself or by the legal adviser, (8) except the protection be waived.

Id. at 554 (footnote omitted).]

explained his testimony before the Grand Jury denying that he had ever retained Maloney "in connection with these proceedings or any other proceedings." And, as Judge Tenney noted, "whatever association Maloney had with [Bonanno] in August of 1964, it was not that of an attorney and client but merely an accommodation to [Bonanno's] lawyer, Mr. D'Antonio, in making Maloney's office and secretary available at the last moment for the purpose of preparing and mailing income tax papers." We see no basis, therefore, for upsetting or even questioning the conclusion, carefully arrived at by the Judge, that an attorney-client relationship "never existed."

Proposed Federal Rule of Evidence 503
Lawyer-Client Privilege
(not enacted)

(a) Definitions. As used in this rule:

(1) A "client" is a person, public officer, or corporation, association, or other organization or entity, either public or private, who is rendered professional legal services by a lawyer, or who consults a lawyer with a view to obtaining professional legal services from him.

(2) A "lawyer" is a person authorized, or reasonably believed by the client to be authorized, to practice law in any state or nation.

(3) A "representative of the lawyer" is one employed to assist the lawyer in the rendition of professional legal services.

(4) A communication is "confidential" if not intended to be disclosed to third persons other than those to whom disclosure is in furtherance of the rendition of professional legal services to the client or those reasonably necessary for the transmission of the communication.

(b) General rule of privilege. A client has a privilege to refuse to disclose and to prevent any other person from disclosing confidential communications made for the purpose of facilitating the rendition of professional legal services to the client, (1) between himself or his representative and his lawyer or his lawyer's representative, or (2) between his lawyer and the lawyer's representative, or (3) by him or his lawyer to a lawyer representing another in a matter of common interest, or (4) between representatives of the client or between the client and a representative of the client, or (5) between lawyers representing the client.

(c) Who may claim the privilege. The privilege may be claimed by the client, his guardian or conservator, the personal representative of a deceased client, or the successor, trustee, or similar representative of a corporation, association, or other organization, whether or not in existence. The person who was the lawyer at the time of the communication may claim the privilege but only on behalf of the client. His authority to do so is presumed in the absence of evidence to the contrary.

(d) Exceptions. There is no privilege under this rule:

(1) Furtherance of crime or fraud. If the services of the lawyer were sought or obtained to enable or aid anyone to commit or plan to commit what the client knew or reasonably should have known to be a crime or fraud; or

(2) *Claimants through same deceased client.* As to a communication relevant to an issue between parties who claim through the same deceased client, regardless of whether the claims are by testate or intestate succession or by inter vivos transaction; or

(3) *Breach of duty by lawyer or client.* As to a communication relevant to an issue of breach of duty by the lawyer to his client or by the client to his lawyer; or

(4) *Document attested by lawyer.* As to a communication relevant to an issue concerning an attested document to which the lawyer is an attesting witness; or

(5) *Joint clients.* As to a communication relevant to a matter of common interest between two or more clients if the communication was made by any of them to a lawyer retained or consulted in common, when offered in an action between any of the clients.

NOTES AND QUESTIONS

1. Under Proposed Fed. R. Evid. 503, who is the holder of the privilege? Who else may assert it? Absent a waiver, how long will the privilege last?

2. Suppose an attorney is merely providing business advice. Would the privilege apply? *See Colton v. United States,* 306 F.2d 633, 638 (2d Cir. 1962), *cert. denied,* 371 U.S. 951 (1963). What if counsel were acting in a dual capacity as one offering both business and legal advice? (This often occurs with respect to lawyers who serve as house counsel to a corporation or who also provide assistance as certified public accountants.) *See Diversified Industries, Inc. v. Meredith,* 572 F.2d 596 (8th Cir. 1978); Petersen, *Attorney-Client Privilege in Internal Revenue Service Investigations,* 54 MINN. L. REV. 67 (1969).

3. To what extent, if any, may the privilege protect against disclosure of the client's identity? *See Baird v. Koerner,* 279 F.2d 623 (9th Cir. 1960); *United States v. Pape,* 144 F.2d 778 (2d Cir.), *cert. denied,* 323 U.S. 752 (1944); *In re Kaplan,* 168 N.E.2d 660 (N.Y. 1960). Suppose that *W*, a grand jury witness, is the target of the grand jury's investigation. May *W*'s attorney be subpoenaed and questioned concerning other grand jury witnesses that *W* had hired him to represent? *See In re Grand Jury Proceedings in the Matter of Freeman,* 708 F.2d 1571 (11th Cir. 1983). *But see generally In re Grand Jury Proceedings in the Matter of Pavlick,* 680 F.2d 1026 (5th Cir. 1982). What if *W*'s attorney is just asked questions concerning his fee arrangement with *W*? *Compare In re Witnesses Before the Special March 1980 Grand Jury,* 729 F.2d 489 (7th Cir. 1984), *and In re Osterhoudt,* 722 F.2d 591 (9th Cir. 1983), *with United States v. Hodge & Zweig,* 548 F.2d 1347 (9th Cir. 1977). In a federal racketeering investigation, may an attorney be compelled to produce records establishing that an organized crime boss paid the legal fees of underlings who had been arrested? *See In re Grand Jury Subpoena (Slotnick),* 781 F.2d 238 (2d Cir. 1985) (*en banc*).

4. Are documents transferred to an attorney within the privilege's ambit? *See Fisher v. United States,* 425 U.S. 391 (1976); *United States v. Davis,* 636 F.2d 1028 (5th Cir.), *cert. denied,* 454 U.S. 862 (1981). Once so transferred, may counsel likewise assert any other defense or privilege potentially available to his client? *See id*; Note, *The Attorney and His Client's Privileges*, 74 YALE L.J. 539 (1965).

5. At common law, the privilege could only be waived by the client. Waiver, however, could occur either expressly or implicitly (the latter, for example, by a client who discloses the actual communication to a third party). *See generally* Note, *Evidence — Witness — Privileged Communications Between Attorney and Client — Waiver of Privilege*, 16 MINN. L. REV. 818 (1932).

6. At common law, an eavesdropper could testify to privileged conversations which he had overheard. This result reflected the belief that privileges should be strictly construed and that responsibility for ensuring the secrecy of private conversations devolves upon the holder of the privilege. Is this rationale still valid today? *See generally* Note, *Government Interceptions of Attorney-Client Communications*, 49 N.Y.U. L. REV. 87 (1974). How does Proposed Fed. R. Evid. 503 address this question? Alternatively, is this a matter of constitutional law? In this respect consider the following scenario by analogy: suppose the government plants an informant in the defense camp. Has the attorney-client privilege necessarily been violated? What about the Sixth Amendment right to effective assistance of counsel? *See Weatherford v. Bursey*, 429 U.S. 545 (1977).

7. The privilege does not extend to conversations in furtherance of crime. *See, e.g., United States v. King*, 536 F. Supp. 253 (C.D. Cal. 1982). What kind of showing should be required to establish that attorney-client communications are within the crime-fraud exception? *See In re Antitrust Grand Jury (Advance Publications)*, 805 F.2d 155 (6th Cir. 1986). *See generally* Sibert, *The Crime Fraud Exception to the Attorney-Client Privilege and Work-Product Doctrine, The Lawyer's Obligations of Disclosure, and the Lawyer's Response to Accusation of Wrongful Conduct*, 23 AM. CRIM. L. REV. 351 (1986).

8. During the course of determining whether a valid privilege exists, to what extent, if any, may the court mandate disclosure of privileged information? *See generally United States v. Kovel*, 296 F.2d 918, 924 (2d Cir. 1961).

UPJOHN v. UNITED STATES
449 U.S. 383 (1980)

JUSTICE REHNQUIST delivered the opinion of the Court.

We granted *certiorari* in this case to address important questions concerning the scope of the attorney-client privilege in the corporate context and the applicability of the work-product doctrine in proceedings to enforce tax summonses.

I.

Petitioner Upjohn manufactures and sells pharmaceuticals here and abroad. In January 1976 independent accountants conducting an audit of one of petitioner's foreign subsidiaries discovered that the subsidiary made payments to or for the benefit of foreign government officials in order to secure government business. The accountants so informed Mr. Gerard Thomas, petitioner's Vice President, Secretary, and General Counsel. Thomas is a member of the Michigan and New York Bars, and has been petitioner's General Counsel for 20 years. He consulted with outside counsel and R. T. Parfet, Jr., petitioner's Chairman of the Board. It was decided that the company would conduct an internal investigation of what were termed "questionable payments." As part of this investigation the attorneys prepared a letter containing a questionnaire which was sent to "All Foreign General and Area Managers" over the Chairman's signature. The letter began by noting recent disclosures that several American companies made "possibly illegal" payments to foreign government officials and emphasized that the management needed full information concerning any such payments made by Upjohn. The letter indicated that the Chairman had asked Thomas, identified as "the company's General Counsel," "to conduct an investigation for the purpose of determining the nature and magnitude of any payments made by the Upjohn Company or any of its subsidiaries to any employee or official of a foreign government." The questionnaire sought detailed information concerning such payments. Managers were instructed to treat the investigation as "highly confidential" and not to discuss it with anyone other than Upjohn employees who might be helpful in providing the requested information. Responses were to be sent directly to Thomas. Thomas and outside counsel also interviewed the recipients of the questionnaire and some 33 other Upjohn officers or employees as part of the investigation.

On March 26, 1976, the company voluntarily submitted a preliminary report to the Securities and Exchange Commission on Form 8-K disclosing certain questionable payments. A copy of the report was simultaneously submitted to the Internal Revenue Service, which immediately began an investigation to determine the tax consequences of the payments. . . . On November 23, 1976, the Service issued a summons pursuant to 26 USC § 7602 . . . demanding production of:

> All files relative to the investigation conducted under the supervision of Gerard Thomas to identify payments to employees of foreign governments and any political contributions made by the Upjohn Company or any of its affiliates since January 1, 1971 and to determine whether any funds of the Upjohn Company had been improperly accounted for on the corporate books during the same period.

> The records should include but not be limited to written questionnaires sent to managers of the Upjohn Company's foreign affiliates, and memorandums or notes of the interviews conducted in the United States and abroad with officers and employees of the Upjohn Company and its subsidiaries.

App 17a–8a.

The company declined to produce the documents specified in the second paragraph on the grounds that they were protected from disclosure by the attorney-client privilege and constituted the work-product of attorneys prepared in anticipation of litigation. On August 31, 1977, the United States filed a petition seeking enforcement of the summons. . . .

II.

Federal Rule of Evidence 501 provides that "the privilege of a witness . . . shall be governed by the principles of the common law as they may be interpreted by the courts of the United States in light of reason and experience." The attorney-client privilege is the oldest of the privileges for confidential communications known to the common law. 8 J. Wigmore, Evidence § 2290 (McNaughton rev. 1961). Its purpose is to encourage full and frank communication between attorneys and their clients and thereby promote broader public interests in the observance of law and administration of justice. The privilege recognizes that sound legal advice or advocacy serves public ends and that such advice or advocacy depends upon the lawyer being fully informed by the client. As we stated last Term in *Trammel v. United States,* . . . "[t]he lawyer-client privilege rests on the need for the advocate and counselor to know all that relates to the client's reasons for seeking representation if the professional mission is to be carried out." And in *Fisher v. United States,* . . . we recognized the purpose of the privilege to be "to encourage clients to make full disclosure to their attorneys." This rationale for the privilege has long been recognized by the Court. . . . Admittedly complications in the application of the privilege arise when the client is a corporation, which in theory is an artificial creature of the law, and not an individual; but this Court has assumed that the privilege applies when the client is a corporation, . . . and the Government does not contest the general proposition.

The Court of Appeals, however, considered the application of the privilege in the corporate context to present a "different problem," since the client was an inanimate entity and "only the senior management, guiding and integrating the several operations, . . . can be said to possess an identity analogous to the corporation as a whole." . . . The first case to articulate the so-called "control group test" adopted by the court below, *Philadelphia v. Westinghouse Electric Corp.,* 210 F. Supp. 483, 485 (E.D. Pa.), *petition for mandamus and prohibition denied sub. nom. General Electric Co. v. Kirkpatrick,* 312 F.2d. 742 (3d Cir. 1962), *cert. denied,* 372 U.S. 943 (1963), reflected a similar conceptual approach:

> Keeping in mind that the question is, Is it the corporation which is seeking the lawyer's advice when the asserted privileged communication is made?, the most satisfactory solution, I think, is that if the employee making the communication, of whatever rank he may be, is in a position to control or even to take a substantial part in a decision about any action which the corporation may take upon the advice of the attorney, . . . then in effect, he is (or personifies) the corporation when he makes his disclosure to the lawyer and the privilege would apply.

Such a view, we think, overlooks the fact that the privilege exists to protect not only the giving of professional advice to those who can act on it but also the giving of information to the lawyer to enable him to give sound and informed advice. . . . The first step in the resolution of any legal problem is ascertaining the factual background and sifting through the facts with an eye to the legally relevant. *See* ABA Code of Professional Responsibility, Ethical Consideration 4-1:

> A lawyer should be fully informed of all the facts of the matter he is handling in order for his client to obtain the full advantage of our legal

system. It is for the lawyer in the exercise of his independent professional judgment to separate the relevant and important from the irrelevant and unimportant. The observance of the ethical obligation of a lawyer to hold inviolate the confidences and secrets of his client not only facilitates the full development of facts essential to proper representation of the client but also encourages laymen to seek early legal assistance.

See also Hickman v. Taylor, 329 U.S. 495 (1947).

In the case of the individual client the provider of information and the person who acts on the lawyer's advice are one and the same. In the corporate context, however, it will frequently be employees beyond the control group as defined by the court below — "officers and agents . . . responsible for directing [the company's] actions in response to legal advice" — who will possess the information needed by the corporation's lawyers. Middle-level — and indeed lower level — employees can, by actions within the scope of their employment, embroil the corporation in serious legal difficulties, and it is only natural that these employees would have the relevant information needed by corporate counsel if he is adequately to advise the client with respect to such actual or potential difficulties. . . .

The control group test adopted by the court below thus frustrates the very purpose of the privilege by discouraging the communication of relevant information by employees of the client to attorneys seeking to render legal advice to the client corporation. The attorney's advice will also frequently be more significant to noncontrol group members than to those who officially sanction the advice, and the control group test makes it more difficult to convey full and frank legal advice to the employees who will put into effect the client corporation's policy. . . .

The narrow scope given the attorney-client privilege by the court below not only makes it difficult for corporate attorneys to formulate sound advice when their client is faced with a specific legal problem but also threatens to limit the valuable efforts of corporate counsel to ensure their client's compliance with the law. In light of the vast and complicated array of regulatory legislation confronting the modern corporation, corporations, unlike most individuals, "constantly go to lawyers to find out how to obey the law," Burnham, *The Attorney-Client Privilege in the Corporate Arena*, 24 Bus. Law. 901, 913 (1969), particularly since compliance with the law in this area is hardly an instinctive matter. . . . The test adopted by the court below is difficult to apply in practice, though no abstractly formulated and unvarying "test" will necessarily enable courts to decide questions such as this with mathematical precision. But if the purpose of the attorney-client privilege is to be served, the attorney and client must be able to predict with some degree of certainty whether particular discussions will be protected. An uncertain privilege, or one which purports to be certain but results in widely varying applications by the courts, is little better than no privilege at all. The very terms of the test adopted by the court below suggest the unpredictability of its application. The test restricts the availability of the privilege to those officers who play a "substantial role" in deciding and directing a corporation's legal response. Disparate decisions in cases applying this test illustrate its unpredictability. . . .

The communications at issue were made by Upjohn employees to counsel for Upjohn acting as such, at the direction of corporate superiors in order to secure legal advice from counsel. As the Magistrate found, "Mr. Thomas consulted with the Chairman of the Board and outside counsel and thereafter conducted a factual investigation to determine the nature and extent of the questionable payments and to be in a position to give legal advice to the company with respect to the payments." . . . Information, not available from upper-echelon management, was needed to supply a basis for legal advice concerning compliance with securities and tax laws, foreign laws, currency regulations, duties to shareholders, and potential litigation in each of these areas. The communications concerned matters within the scope of the employees' corporate duties, and the employees themselves were sufficiently aware that they were being questioned in order that the corporation could obtain legal advice. The questionnaire identified Thomas as "the company's General Counsel" and referred in its opening sentence to the possible illegality of payments such as the ones on which information was sought. App 40a. A statement of policy accompanying the questionnaire clearly indicated the legal implications of the investigation. The policy statement was issued "in order that there be no uncertainty in the future as to the policy with respect to the practices which are the subject of this investigation."

*   *   *

. . . This statement was issued to Upjohn employees worldwide, so that even those interviewees not receiving a questionnaire were aware of the legal implications of the interviews. Pursuant to explicit instructions from the Chairman of the Board, the communications were considered "highly confidential" when made, . . . and have been kept confidential by the company. Consistent with the underlying purposes of the attorney-client privilege, these communications must be protected against compelled disclosure.

The Court of Appeals declined to extend the attorney-client privilege beyond the limits of the control group test for fear that doing so would entail severe burdens on discovery and create a broad "zone of silence" over corporate affairs. Application of the attorney-client privilege to communications such as those involved here, however, puts the adversary in no worse position than if the communications had never taken place. The privilege only protects disclosure of communications; it does not protect disclosure of the underlying facts by those who communicated with the attorney:

> [T]he protection of the privilege extends only to communications and not to facts. A fact is one thing and a communication concerning that fact is an entirely different thing. The client cannot be compelled to answer the question, 'What did you say or write to the attorney' but may not refuse to disclose any relevant fact within his knowledge merely because he incorporated a statement of such fact into his communication to his attorney.

Philadelphia v. Westinghouse Electric Corp., 205 F. Supp. 830, 831 (E.D. Pa. 1962).

. . . *State ex rel. Dudek v. Circuit Court,* 150 N.W.2d 387, 399 (Wis. 1967) ("the courts have noted that a party cannot conceal a fact merely by revealing it to his lawyer"). Here the Government was free to question the employees who communicated with Thomas and outside counsel. Upjohn has provided the IRS with a list of such employees, and the IRS has already interviewed some 25 of them. While it would probably be more convenient for the Government to secure the results of petitioner's internal investigation by simply subpoenaing the questionnaires and notes taken by petitioner's attorneys, such considerations of convenience do not overcome the policies served by the attorney-client privilege. As Justice Jackson noted in his concurring opinion in *Hickman v. Taylor*, "Discovery was hardly intended to enable a learned profession to perform its functions . . . on wits borrowed from the adversary."

Needless to say, we decide only the case before us, and do not undertake to draft a set of rules which should govern challenges to investigatory subpoenas. Any such approach would violate the spirit of Federal Rule of Evidence 501. *See* S. Rep. No. 93-1277, p. 13 (1974) ("the recognition of a privilege based on a confidential relationship . . . should be determined on a case-by-case basis"). . . . While such a "case-by-case" basis may to some slight extent undermine desirable certainty in the boundaries of the attorney-client privilege, it obeys the spirit of the Rules. At the same time we conclude that the narrow "control group test" sanctioned by the Court of Appeals in this case cannot, consistent with "the principles of the common law as . . . interpreted . . . in the light of reason and experience," Fed. Rule Evid. 501, govern the development of the law in this area.

III.

Our decision that the communications by Upjohn employees to counsel are covered by the attorney-client privilege disposes of the case so far as the responses to the questionnaires and any notes reflecting responses to interview questions are concerned. The summons reaches further, however, and Thomas has testified that his notes and memoranda of interviews go beyond recording responses to his questions. . . . To the extent that the material subject to the summons is not protected by the attorney-client privilege as disclosing communications between an employee and counsel, we must reach the ruling by the Court of Appeals that the work-product doctrine does not apply to summonses issued under 26 U.S.C. § 7602. . . .

The Government concedes, wisely, that the Court of Appeals erred and that the work-product doctrine does apply to IRS summonses. . . . This doctrine was announced by the Court over 30 years ago in *Hickman v. Taylor*. . . . In that case the Court rejected "an attempt, without purported necessity or justification, to secure written statements, private memoranda and personal recollections prepared or formed by an adverse party's counsel in the course of his legal duties." . . . The Court noted that "it is essential that a lawyer work with a certain degree of privacy" and reasoned that if discovery of the material sought were permitted "much of what is now put down in writing would remain unwritten. An attorney's thoughts, heretofore inviolate, would not be his own. Inefficiency, unfairness and sharp practices would inevitably develop in the giving of legal advice and in the preparation of cases for trial. The effect on the legal profession would be demoralizing. And the interests of the clients and the cause of justice would be poorly served." . . . The "strong public policy" underlying the work-product doctrine was reaffirmed recently in *United States v. Nobles*, 422 U.S. 225, 236–240

(1975), and has been substantially incorporated in Federal Rule of Civil Procedure 26(b)(3).[21]

As we stated last Term, the obligation imposed by a tax summons remains "subject to the traditional privileges and limitations." . . . While conceding the applicability of the work-product doctrine, the Government asserts that it has made a sufficient showing of necessity to overcome its protections. The Magistrate apparently so found. . . . The Government relies on the following language in *Hickman*:

> We do not mean to say that all written materials obtained or prepared by an adversary's counsel with an eye toward litigation are necessarily free from discovery in all cases. Where relevant and non-privileged facts remain hidden in an attorney's file and where production of those facts is essential to the preparation of one's case, discovery may properly be had. . . . And production might be justified where the witnesses are no longer available or can be reached only with difficulty.

The Government stresses that interviewees are scattered across the globe and that Upjohn has forbidden its employees to answer questions it considers irrelevant. The above-quoted language from *Hickman*, however, did not apply to "oral statements made by witnesses . . . whether presently in the form of [the attorney's] mental impressions or memoranda." . . . As to such material the Court did "not believe that any showing of necessity can be made under the circumstances of this case so as to justify production. . . . If there should be a rare situation justifying production of these matters, petitioner's case is not of that type." . . . Forcing an attorney to disclose notes and memoranda of witnesses' oral statements is particularly disfavored because it tends to reveal the attorney's mental processes. . . .[22]

Rule 26 accords special protection to work-product revealing the attorney's mental processes. The Rule permits disclosure of documents and tangible things constituting attorney work-product upon a showing of substantial need and inability to obtain the equivalent without undue hardship. This was the standard applied by the Magistrate, 78-1 USTC ¶ 9277, p. 83, 604. Rule 26 goes on, however, to state that "[i]n ordering discovery of such materials when the required showing has been made, the court shall protect against disclosure of the mental impressions,

---

[21] [7] This provides, in pertinent part:

[A] party may obtain discovery of documents and tangible things otherwise discoverable under subdivision (b)(l) of this rule and prepared in anticipation of litigation or for trial by or for another party or by or for that other party's representative (including his attorney, consultant, surety, indemnitor, insurer, or agent) only upon a showing that the party seeking discovery has substantial need of the materials in the preparation of his case and that he is unable without undue hardship to obtain the substantial equivalent of the materials by other means. In ordering discovery of such materials when the required showing has been made, the court shall protect against disclosure of the mental impressions, conclusions, opinions, or legal theories of an attorney or other representative of a party concerning the litigation.

[22] [8] Thomas described his notes of the interviews as containing "what I considered to be the important questions, the substance of the responses to them, my beliefs as to the importance of these, my beliefs as to how they related to the inquiry, my thoughts as to how they related to other questions. In some instances they might even suggest other questions that I would have to ask or things that I needed to find elsewhere." . . .

conclusions, opinions or legal theories of an attorney or other representative of a party concerning the litigation." Although this language does not specifically refer to memoranda based on oral statements of witnesses, the *Hickman* court stressed the danger that compelled disclosure of such memoranda would reveal the attorney's mental processes. It is clear that this is the sort of material the draftsmen of the Rule had in mind as deserving special protection. *See* Notes of Advisory Committee on 1970 Amendment to Rules, 28 U.S.C. App., p. 442 ("The subdivision . . . goes on to protect against disclosure the mental impressions, conclusions, opinions, or legal theories . . . of an attorney or other representative of a party. The *Hickman* opinion drew special attention to the need for protecting an attorney against discovery of memoranda prepared from recollection of oral interviews. The courts have steadfastly safeguarded against disclosure of lawyers' mental impressions and legal theories . . .").

Based on the foregoing, some courts have concluded that no showing of necessity can overcome protection of work product which is based on oral statements from witnesses. . . . Those courts declining to adopt an absolute rule have nonetheless recognized that such material is entitled to special protection. *See, e.g., In re Grand Jury Investigation*, 599 F.2d 1224, 1231 (3d Cir. 1979) ("special considerations . . . must shape any ruling on the discoverability of interview memoranda . . . ; such documents will be discoverable only in a 'rare situation' "). . . .

We do not decide the issue at this time. It is clear that the Magistrate applied the wrong standard when he concluded that the Government had made a sufficient showing of necessity to overcome the protections of the work-product doctrine. The Magistrate applied the "substantial need" and "without undue hardship" standard articulated in the first part of Rule 26(b)(3). The notes and memoranda sought by the Government here, however, are work-product based on oral statements. If they reveal communications, they are, in this case, protected by the attorney-client privilege. To the extent they do not reveal communications, they reveal the attorneys' mental processes in evaluating the communications. As Rule 26 and *Hickman* make clear, such work-product cannot be disclosed simply on a showing of substantial need and inability to obtain the equivalent without undue hardship.

While we are not prepared at this juncture to say that such material is always protected by the work-product rule, we think a far stronger showing of necessity and unavailability by other means than was made by the Government or applied by the Magistrate in this case would be necessary to compel disclosure.

*   *   *

Accordingly, the judgment of the Court of Appeals is reversed, and the case remanded for further proceedings.

NOTES AND QUESTIONS

1.   Although *Upjohn* declined to embrace a definitive standard, the Court's analysis implicitly endorses the so-called "subject matter test" under which employee statements to counsel are privileged if the communication was both made at the direction of superior officials and concerned the subject matter of his

employment. *See Harper & Row Publishers, Inc. v. Decker*, 423 F.2d 487 (7th Cir. 1970), *aff'd by an equally divided court*, 400 U.S. 348 (1971).

2. How would a contrary decision in *Upjohn* have presented corporate counsel with a "Hobson's choice"?

3. Suppose that *Upjohn* had been willing to waive the privilege, but individual employees wanted to rely upon it. Would the employees have been entitled to do so? *See In re Grand Jury Proceedings*, 434 F. Supp. 648 (E.D. Mich. 1977), *aff'd*, 570 F.2d 562 (6th Cir. 1978). In this respect, consider the following commentary on *Upjohn*:

> Expressly left open by the Court's decision in *Upjohn* is the question of whether the attorney-client privilege applies to communications by former employees concerning activities during their period of employment. Numerous other questions remain, such as: can a parent corporation assert a privilege as to communications by employees of a subsidiary, who can waive the privilege, and to what extent can a privileged communication be circulated within the corporate entity without losing its privileged status? *Upjohn* also raises a host of ethical problems for the corporate lawyer. To what extent may he interview a corporate employee, whose interests may perhaps be somewhat antithetical to those of the corporation, without warning the employee that he does not represent the employee, and that the employee has a right not to talk to corporate counsel and to obtain separate counsel? Such warnings would, of course, undercut *Upjohn*'s rationale of enabling corporate attorneys to obtain as much information as possible in order to function most effectively. Furthermore, who would choose and pay for an employee's separate counsel? If the employee is not warned, the attorney may find himself in a conflict of interest situation where the corporation wishes to divulge the employee's communication, since the employee may reasonably have believed that he was speaking to his lawyer.
>
> Also left unresolved are the problems of reporting continuing crimes of an economic or environmental nature to various regulatory or law enforcement bodies or to third parties who may be adversely affected. These issues are the subject of intense debate in connection with proposed changes in ethical standards of the bar.

2 WEINSTEIN'S EVIDENCE § 503(b)[04], at 503–56 (1982).

4. May a corporation assert the privilege against minority stockholders who bring shareholder derivative suits? *See Garner v. Wolfinbarger*, 430 F.2d 1093 (5th Cir. 1970), *cert. denied*, 401 U.S. 974 (1971).

5. May a corporation's successor in interest, such as a bankruptcy trustee, waive the privilege? *See Commodity Futures Trading Comm. v. Weintraub*, 722 F.2d 338 (7th Cir. 1983).

6. Distinguish the attorney-client privilege from the work-product doctrine. To what extent do these principles operate independently of each other, and in what way, if any, do they overlap?

PEOPLE v. MEREDITH
631 P.2d 46 (Cal. 1981)

TOBRINER, JUSTICE.

Defendants Frank Earl Scott and Michael Meredith appeal from convictions for the first degree murder and first degree robbery of David Wade. Meredith's conviction rests on eyewitness testimony that he shot and killed Wade. Scott's conviction, however, depends on the theory that Scott conspired with Meredith and a third defendant, Jacqueline Otis, to bring about the killing and robbery. To support the theory of conspiracy the prosecution sought to show the place where the victim's wallet was found, and, in the course of the case this piece of evidence became crucial. The admissibility of that evidence comprises the principal issue on this appeal.

At trial the prosecution called Steven Frick, who testified that he observed the victim's partially burnt wallet in a trash can behind Scott's residence. Scott's trial counsel then adduced that Frick served as a defense investigator. Scott himself had told his former counsel that he had taken the victim's wallet, divided the money with Meredith, attempted to burn the wallet, and finally put it in the trash can. At counsel's request, Frick then retrieved the wallet from the trash can. Counsel examined the wallet and then turned it over to the police.

The defense acknowledges that the wallet itself was properly admitted into evidence. The prosecution in turn acknowledges that the attorney-client privilege protected the conversations between Scott, his former counsel, and counsel's investigator. Indeed the prosecution did not attempt to introduce those conversations at trial. The issue before us, consequently, focuses upon a narrow point: whether under the circumstances of this case Frick's observation of the location of the wallet, the product of a privileged communication, finds protection under the attorney-client privilege.

This issue, one of first impression in California, presents the court with competing policy considerations. On the one hand, to deny protection to observations arising from confidential communications might chill free and open communication between attorney and client and might also inhibit counsel's investigation of his client's case. On the other hand, we cannot extend the attorney-client privilege so far that it renders evidence immune from discovery and admission merely because the defense seizes it first.

* * *

We now recount the evidence relating to Wade's wallet, basing our account primarily on the testimony of James Schenk, Scott's first appointed attorney. Schenk visited Scott in jail more than a month after the crime occurred and solicited information about the murder, stressing that he had to be fully acquainted with the facts to avoid being "sandbagged" by the prosecution during the trial. In response, . . . Scott told Schenk . . . that [after the homicide] he had seen a wallet . . . on the ground near Wade. Scott said that he picked up the wallet, put it in the paper bag, and placed both behind a parking lot fence. He also said that he later . . . found

$100 in the wallet and divided it with Meredith, and then tried to burn the wallet in his kitchen sink. He took the partially burned wallet, Scott told Schenk, placed it in a plastic bag, and threw it in a burn barrel behind his house.

Schenk, without further consulting Scott, retained Investigator Stephen Frick and sent Frick to find the wallet. Frick found it in the location described by Scott and brought it to Schenk. After examining the wallet and determining that it contained credit cards with Wade's name, Schenk turned the wallet and its contents over to Detective Payne, investigating officer in the case. Schenk told Payne only that, to the best of his knowledge, the wallet had belonged to Wade.

The prosecution subpoenaed Attorney Schenk and Investigator Frick to testify at the preliminary hearing. When questioned at that hearing, Schenk said that he received the wallet from Frick but refused to answer further questions on the ground that he learned about the wallet through a privileged communication. Eventually, however, the magistrate threatened Schenk with contempt if he did not respond "yes" or "no" when asked whether his contact with his client led to disclosure of the wallet's location. Schenk then replied "yes," and revealed on further questioning that this contact was the sole source of his information as to the wallet's location.

At the preliminary hearing Frick, the investigator who found the wallet, was then questioned by the district attorney. Over objections by counsel, Frick testified that he found the wallet in a garbage can behind Scott's residence.

Prior to trial, a third attorney, Hamilton Hintz, was appointed for Scott. Hintz unsuccessfully sought an in limine ruling that the wallet of the murder victim was inadmissible and that the attorney-client privilege precluded the admission of testimony concerning the wallet by Schenk or Frick.

At trial Frick, called by the prosecution, identified the wallet and testified that he found it in a garbage can behind Scott's residence. On cross-examination by Hintz, Scott's counsel, Frick further testified that he was an investigator hired by Scott's first attorney, Schenk, and that he had searched the garbage can at Schenk's request. Hintz later called Schenk as a witness: Schenk testified that he told Frick to search for the wallet immediately after Schenk finished talking to Scott. Schenk also stated that Frick brought him the wallet on the following day; after examining its contents Schenk delivered the wallet to the police. Scott then took the stand and testified to the information about the wallet that he had disclosed to Schenk.

*   *   *

Defendant Scott concedes, and we agree, that the wallet itself was admissible in evidence. Scott maintains, however, that Evidence Code section 954 bars the testimony of the investigator concerning the location of the wallet. We consider, first, whether the California attorney-client privilege codified in that section extends to observations which are the product of privileged communications. We then discuss whether that privileged status is lost when defense conduct may have frustrated prosecution discovery.

Section 954 provides, "[T]he client . . . has a privilege to refuse to disclose, and to prevent another from disclosing, a confidential communication between client and lawyer. . . ." Under that section one who seeks to assert the privilege must establish that a confidential communication occurred during the course of the attorney-client relationship. . . .

Scott's statements to Schenk regarding the location of the wallet clearly fulfilled the statutory requirements. Moreover, the privilege did not dissolve when Schenk disclosed the substance of that communication to his investigator, Frick. Under Evidence Code section 912, subdivision (d), a disclosure which is "reasonably necessary" to accomplish the purpose for which the attorney has been consulted does not constitute a waiver of the privilege. If Frick was to perform the investigative services for which Schenk had retained him, it was "reasonably necessary," that Schenk transmit to Frick the information regarding the wallet.[23] Thus, Schenk's disclosure to Frick did not waive the statutory privilege.

The statutes codifying the attorney-client privilege do not, however, indicate whether that privilege protects facts viewed and observed as a direct result of confidential communication. To resolve that issue, we turn first to the policies which underlie the attorney-client privilege, and then to the cases which apply those policies to observations arising from a protected communication.

The fundamental purpose of the attorney-client privilege is, of course, to encourage full and open communication between client and attorney. "Adequate legal representation in the ascertainment and enforcement of rights or the prosecution or defense of litigation compels a full disclosure of the facts by the client to his attorney. . . . Given the privilege, a client may make such a disclosure without fear that his attorney may be forced to reveal the information confided to him." . . .

In the criminal context, as we have recently observed, these policies assume particular significance: " 'As a practical matter, if the client knows that damaging information could more readily be obtained from the attorney following disclosure than from himself in the absence of disclosure, the client would be reluctant to confide in his lawyer and it would be difficult to obtain fully informed legal advice.' . . . Thus, if an accused is to derive the full benefits of his right to counsel, he must have the assurance of confidentiality and privacy of communication with his attorney." . . .

Judicial decisions have recognized that the implementation of these important policies may require that the privilege extend not only to the initial communication between client and attorney but also to any information which the attorney or his investigator may subsequently acquire as a direct result of that communication. In a venerable decision involving facts analogous to those in the instant case, the Supreme Court of West Virginia held that the trial court erred in admitting an attorney's testimony as to the location of a pistol which he had discovered as the

---

[23] [3] Although prior cases do not consider whether section 912, subdivision (d) applies to an attorney's investigator, the language of that subdivision covers the circumstances of the instant case. An investigator is as "reasonably necessary" as a physician or psychiatrist . . . or a legal secretary, paralegal or receptionist. . . . Because the investigator, then, is a person encompassed by the privilege, he stands in the same position as the attorney for purposes of the analysis and operation of the privilege; the investigator cannot then disclose that which the attorney could not have disclosed. . . . Thus, the discussion in this opinion of the conduct of defense counsel, and of counsel's right to invoke the attorney-client privilege to avoid testifying, applies also to a defense investigator.

result of a privileged communication from his client. That the attorney had observed the pistol, the court pointed out, did not nullify the privilege: "All that the said attorney knew about this pistol, or where it was to be found, he knew only from the communications which had been made to him by his client confidentially and professionally, as counsel in this case. And it ought therefore, to have been entirely excluded from the jury. It may be, that in this particular case this evidence tended to the promotion of right and justice, but as was well said in *Pearce v. Pearce*, 11 Jar. 52, in page 55, and 2 De Gex & Smale 25–27: "Truth like all other good things may be loved unwisely, may be pursued too keenly, may cost too much." (*State of West Virginia v. Douglass* (1882) 20 W. Va. 770, 783.)

This unbearable cost, the *Douglass* court concluded, could not be entirely avoided by attempting to admit testimony regarding observations or discoveries made as the result of a privileged communication, while excluding the communication itself. Such a procedure, *Douglass* held, "was practically as mischievous in all its tendencies and consequences, as if it has required [the attorney] to state everything, which his client had confidentially told him about this pistol. It would be a slight safeguard indeed, to confidential communications made to counsel, if he was thus compelled substantially, to give them to a jury, although he was required not to state them in the words of his client." . . .

More recent decisions reach similar conclusions. In *State v. Olwell* (1964) 64 Wash. 2d 828, 394 P.2d 681, the court reviewed contempt charges against an attorney who refused to produce a knife he obtained from his client. The court first observed that "[t]o be protected as a privileged communication . . . the securing of the knife . . . must have been the *direct result of information* given to Mr. Olwell by his client." (P. 683) (Emphasis added). The court concluded that defense counsel, after examining the physical evidence, should deliver it to the prosecution, but should not reveal the source of the evidence; "[b]y thus allowing the prosecution to recover such evidence, the public interest is served; and by refusing the prosecution an opportunity to disclose the source of the evidence, the client's privilege is preserved and a balance reached between these conflicting interests." . . .

Finally, we note the decisions of the New York courts in *People v. Belge* (Sup. Ct. 1975) 83 Misc. 2d 186, 372 N.Y.S.2d 798, *affirmed in People v. Belge* (App. Div. 1975) 50 A.D.2d 1088, 376 N.Y.S.2d 771. Defendant, charged with one murder, revealed to counsel that he had committed three others. Counsel, following defendant's directions, located one of the bodies. Counsel did not reveal the location of the body until trial, 10 months later, when he exposed the other murders to support an insanity defense.

Counsel was then indicted for violating two sections of the New York Public Health Law for failing to report the existence of the body to proper authorities in order that they could give it a decent burial. The trial court dismissed the indictment; the appellate division affirmed, holding that the attorney-client privilege shielded counsel from prosecution for actions which would otherwise violate the Public Health Law.[24]

---

[24] [5] In each of the cases discussed in text, a crucial element in the court's analysis is that the attorney's observations were the direct product of information communicated to him by his client.

The foregoing decisions demonstrate that the attorney-client privilege is not strictly limited to communications, but extends to protect observations made as a consequence of protected communications. We turn therefore to the question whether that privilege encompasses a case in which the defense, by removing or altering evidence, interferes with the prosecution's opportunity to discover that evidence.[25]

* * *

When defense counsel alters or removes physical evidence, he necessarily deprives the prosecution of the opportunity to observe that evidence in its original condition or location. As the *amicus* Appellate Committee of the California District Attorneys Association points out, to bar admission of testimony concerning the original condition and location of the evidence in such a case permits the defense in effect to "destroy" critical information; it is as if, he explains, the wallet in this case bore a tag bearing the words "located in the trash can by Scott's residence," and the defense, by taking the wallet, destroyed this tag. To extend the attorney-client privilege to a case in which the defense removed evidence might encourage defense counsel to race the police to seize critical evidence. (*See In re Ryder* (E.D. Va. 1967)

[Ed. — The following observation by the *Belge* court might serve both to put the issue in perspective and to explain the ultimate disposition of the case:

Apparently, in the instant case, after analyzing all the evidence, and after hearing of the bizarre episodes in the life of their client, they [counsel] decided that the only possibility of salvation was in a defense of insanity. For the client to disclose not only everything about this particular crime but also everything about other crimes which might have a bearing upon his defense, requires the strictest confidence in, and on the part of, the attorney.

When the facts of the other homicides became public, as a result of the defendant's testimony to substantiate his claim of insanity, "Members of the public were shocked at the apparent callousness of these lawyers, whose conduct was seen as typifying the unhealthy lack of concern of most lawyers with the public interest and with simple decency." A hue and cry went up from the press and other news media suggesting that the attorneys should be found guilty of such crimes as obstruction of justice or becoming an accomplice after the fact. From a layman's standpoint, this certainly was a logical conclusion. However, the constitution of the United States of America attempts to preserve the dignity of the individual and to do that guarantees him the services of an attorney who will bring to the bar and to the bench every conceivable protection from the inroads of the state against such rights as are vested in the constitution for one accused of crime. Among those substantial constitutional rights is that a defendant does not have to incriminate himself. His attorneys were bound to uphold that concept and maintain what has been called a sacred trust of confidentiality.

372 N.Y.S.2d at 801–02.]

[25] [7] We agree with the parties' suggestion that an attorney in Schenk's position often may best fulfill conflicting obligations to preserve the confidentiality of client confidences, investigate his case, and act as an officer of the court if he does not remove evidence located as the result of a privileged communication. We must recognize, however, that in some cases an examination of evidence may reveal information critical to the defense of a client accused of crime. If the usefulness of the evidence cannot be gauged without taking possession of it, as, for example, when a ballistics or fingerprint test is required, the attorney may properly take it for a reasonable time before turning it over to the prosecution. . . . Similarly, in the present case the defense counsel could not be certain the burnt wallet belonged in fact to the victim: in taking the wallet to examine it for identification, he violated no ethical duty to his client or to the prosecution. (*See generally Legal Ethics and the Destruction of Evidence* (1979) 88 YALE L.J. 1665.)

263 F. Supp. 360, 369,[26] Comment, *The Right of a Criminal Defense Attorney to Withhold Physical Evidence Received From His Client* (1970) 38 U. CHI. L. REV. 211, 227–228.)

We therefore conclude that courts must craft an exception to the protection extended by the attorney-client privilege in cases in which counsel has removed or altered evidence. Indeed, at oral argument defense counsel acknowledged that such an exception might be necessary in a case in which the police would have inevitably discovered the evidence in its original location if counsel had not removed it. Counsel argued, however, that the attorney-client privilege should protect observations of evidence, despite subsequent defense removal, unless the prosecution could prove that the police probably would have eventually discovered the evidence in the original site.

We have seriously considered counsel's proposal, but have concluded that a test based upon the probability of eventual discovery is unworkably speculative. Evidence turns up not only because the police deliberately search for it, but also because it comes to the attention of policemen or bystanders engaged in other business. In the present case, for example, the wallet might have been found by the trash collector. Moreover, once physical evidence (the wallet) is turned over to the police, they will obviously stop looking for it; to ask where, how long, and how carefully they would have looked is obviously to compel speculation as to theoretical future conduct of the police.

We therefore conclude that whenever defense counsel removes or alters evidence, the statutory privilege does not bar revelation of the original location or condition of the evidence in question.[27] We thus view the defense decision to remove evidence as a tactical choice. If defense counsel leaves the evidence where he discovers it, his observations derived from privileged communications are insulated from revelation. If, however, counsel chooses to remove evidence to examine or test

---

[26] [Ed. — The pertinent facts of *In re Ryder* were said to be as follows:

The essential facts are not in dispute. In the course of his representation of an individual suspected of bank robbery, Ryder transferred from that person's safe deposit box to his own, stolen money and a sawed-off shotgun, in violation of state and federal law. At least one purpose, avowed by Ryder, was to conceal the articles and thereby avoid the presumption of guilt which would arise if the money and the weapon were found in the client's possession. Viewed in any light, the facts furnished no basis for the assertion of an attorney-client privilege. It is an abuse of a lawyer's professional responsibility knowingly to take possession of and secrete the fruits and instrumentalities of a crime. Ryder's acts bear no reasonable relation to the privilege and duty to refuse to divulge a client's confidential communication. Ryder made himself an active participant in a criminal act, ostensibly wearing the mantel of the loyal advocate, but in reality serving as accessory after the fact.

381 F.2d 713, 714 (4th Cir. 1967) (per curiam). There was, however, some evidence in the record suggesting that reputable community members, with whom Ryder had consulted, did not view his actions as unethical (though it appears that Ryder failed to follow every aspect of their advice). 263 F. Supp. at 362–64, 370.]

[27] [8] In offering the evidence, the prosecution should present the information in a manner which avoids revealing the content of attorney-client communications or the original source of the information. In the present case, for example, the prosecutor simply asked Frick where he found the wallet; he did not identify Frick as a defense investigator or trace the discovery of the wallet to an attorney-client communication.

it, the original location and condition of that evidence loses the protection of the privilege. Applying this analysis to the present case, we hold that the trial court did not err in admitting the investigator's testimony concerning the location of the wallet.

* * *

In other circumstances, when it is not possible to elicit such testimony without identifying the witness as the defendant's attorney or investigator, the defendant may be willing to enter a stipulation which will simply inform the jury as to the relevant location or condition of the evidence in question. When such a stipulation is proffered, the prosecution should not be permitted to reject the stipulation in the hope that by requiring defense counsel personally to testify to such facts, the jury might infer that counsel learned those facts from defendant.

NOTES AND QUESTIONS

1. Had counsel's investigator simply left the wallet where it was originally found, wouldn't the prosecution have been left in a materially worse position? Would the court's ruling have been any different if counsel had returned the wallet to its original site?

2. Are *Ryder* and *Belge*, cited in *Meredith*, distinguishable from one another? Suppose that a client tells his counsel the following: "I have just committed a crime and am in fear of criminal prosecution. What should I do with the proceeds (*e.g.*, the cash) to maximize my defense at trial?" How should counsel respond? Not surprisingly, both *Ryder* and *Belge* have generated considerable discussion. *See, e.g.*, Annotation, *Fabrication or Suppression of Evidence as Ground of Disciplinary Action Against Attorney*, 40 A.L.R.3d 169 (1971); Edwards, *Hard Answers for Hard Questions: Dissenting in Part from Dean Freedman's Views on the Attorney-Client Privilege*, 11 CRIM. L. BULL. 478 (1975); Freedman, *Where the Bodies Are Buried: The Adversary System and the Obligation of Confidentiality*, 10 CRIM. L. BULL. 979 (1974). *See also People v. Nash*, 341 N.W.2d 439 (Mich. 1983); *People v. Swearingen*, 649 P.2d 1102 (Colo. 1982); Note, *Ethics, Law, and Loyalty: The Attorney's Duty to Turn over Incriminating Physical Evidence*, 32 STAN. L. REV. 977 (1980).

3. To what extent, if any, does the privilege shield from disclosure observations made by counsel independently of actual client communications? *See United States v. Kendrick*, 331 F.2d 110 (4th Cir. 1964).

Evidentiary Foundation:
The Trial of Harrison A. Williams, Jr.[28]

[The background to this case is set forth in § C.4.b.5 in Chapter III, *supra*. A key government witness concerning the events of the alleged conspiracy was Henry A. Williams. Witness Williams was a personal friend and business associate of the Senator. The two, however, were not related. During cross-examination, the

---

[28] Excerpted from Trial Transcript, *supra*, at 1043–55.

prosecution suggested that defense counsel's line of inquiry was impinging upon the witness' attorney-client privilege. The matter was resolved in the following manner:]

Q.   Were you told in September and October of 1980 that you could not be given a job unless the matter in which you were involved here with the government was cleared up; yes or no.

A.   I don't even remember that conversation.

Q.   Did you ever tell your lawyer that, that you had to clear up this matter so that you could get a job in public relations with a television station; yes or no.

A.   Oh—

Q.   Tell me yes or no.

A.   I did tell my lawyer that, yes, yes, I did.

Q.   The answer is yes?

A.   The answer is yes.

Q.   And that was in October 1980?

A.   Yes, that's correct.

Q.   Is that correct?

A.   Yes.

MR. MCDONALD: I object to the repeating, that is correct. Is he making statements or asking questions? I object.

MR. KOELZER: Notice the witness was using the statement. I am just trying to move it along.

THE COURT: It doesn't move it along by repeating.

MR. KOELZER: Probably correct. But the reporter is probably happy. He is making money.

MR. PUCCIO: Could we have a side bar for a moment, your Honor?

THE COURT: Side bar.

(The following occurred at side bar.)

THE COURT: What is the problem, Mr. Puccio?

MR. PUCCIO: Judge, based upon our discussions with this witness we have been told that after the investigation became public in this case he was brought to Mr. Koelzer — or brought to Mr. Koelzer's office and interviewed extensively by Mr. Koelzer and assistants to Mr. Koelzer.

And we were told through Mr. Koelzer that arrangements were made for him to get counsel.

And I believe the man's name is Horowitz.

Now questions are being asked about conversations that he had with his lawyer.

MR. KOELZER: I am not referring to Mr. Horowitz, if that is what you are talking about. I am not referring to Mr. Horowitz.

MR. PUCCIO: I am concerned about conversations which are privileged are being questioned about.

         I would like to have a proffer.

MR. KOELZER: Let me clear something else up first, because I don't want any record floating around with the accusation the government is making here.

Unknown to me because the Monday Abscam broke I was finishing up a six-day deposition at the offices of Kerlin & Keating at 120 Broadway of a Russian ship captain, believe it or not and from there went to a pretrial conference in federal court in New Jersey and returned to my Jersey office seven o'clock at night. And sitting there was Sandy Williams,[29] whom I had never met, laid eyes on and whom I never heard of before the day before in my life with his son. He wanted to speak to me. Although the grand jury testimony says I did, it is false. I had two of my partners there, Mr. Osborne with an E and a Mr. Nimmo. And I told him quite frankly I would not talk to him alone because of what I read in the paper, he might be a target of an investigation and that I could not represent him. There are numerous copious notes to this effect.

Slipping along because the details become very important at the end, he said, what do I do? Do I need a lawyer? And I would be a fool if I said otherwise. All you have to do is read the New York Times. And I said of course you do.

And he said, do you know anyone, and I gave him three names and I would be glad to give the names. Two are in Manhattan, one is in New Jersey. The one in New Jersey is a former United States attorney. He said to me he knew Mr. Horowitz because they had grown up together in Paterson, which was totally new to me. And he therefore said he would go to Mr. Horowitz. That is the sum total of my involvement in what Mr. Puccio says here. I didn't arrange it. . . .

I gave him a list of three names and he picked from that.

The record should not reflect that I picked his lawyer or had anything to do with that or anything else.

It is simply false.

THE COURT: I have difficulty seeing how that bears on everything [sic].

MR. KOELZER: I agree with you, but let me get to the gist of the problem.

THE COURT: You asked this witness about a conversation with his attorney.

MR. KOELZER: And I am referring to Tamar Benamy.

THE COURT: That raises questions of attorney-client privilege. And I have been told that his attorney is sitting in the audience.

MR. KOELZER: That's right.

---

[29] [Ed. — The witness' nickname was Sandy.]

THE COURT: I suppose for the purpose of protecting his rights?

MR. KOELZER: Yes. She is sitting here. The person I am referring to is sitting in this very courtroom.

MR. PUCCIO: I also saw Mr. Horowitz' name on the question of proposed witnesses, and it struck me that the question was being asked as — as to an attorney — your Honor, I withdraw any objection.

I wanted if I could to have a proffer as to what attack Mr. Koelzer was taking in asking questions about an attorney.

MR. KOELZER: The woman here in court is whom I am referring to. And I can't see anything improper about it at all.

THE COURT: Well, is your purpose to get him to claim a privilege?

MR. KOELZER: No.

THE COURT: How do you know then what his conversation with the attorney was?

MR. KOELZER: Do I have to disclose that, your Honor?

THE COURT: It sounds to me like it is privileged information.

MR. KOELZER: Not if someone chooses to disclose it.

THE COURT: Not if the party or the attorney chooses to disclose it.

MR. KOELZER: I wasn't there and I think your Honor can appreciate me working long and hard running down a number of things. Obviously I am correct. And obviously one of the two disclosed it, otherwise I would not be here shooting in the dark.

THE COURT: The office could have been bugged.

MR. KOELZER: Your Honor, please, I beg your pardon.

THE COURT: When you say things are obvious they are not always obvious.

MR. KOELZER: I beg your pardon. Our investigation led us to that, your Honor, and a great deal more I wish to go into.

THE COURT: More along that line?

MR. KOELZER: About certain things he said to his attorney.

THE COURT: I better advise him of his rights as a witness.

MR. KOELZER: Your Honor, because they have proceeded to disclose it to third parties. And once that happens it is no longer privileged.

If somebody says something to him as an attorney I am bound and I can't disclose it. But if the person discloses it to me decides to tell everybody in the world, including the Times and whatever, then it is no longer privileged.

THE COURT: That may be a correct statement of the law, but it is not — it does not necessarily determine the fact that it was disclosed to third parties.

MR. KOELZER: If I represent to you that it was, your Honor — I don't want to sit here and give up my file to the prosecution any more than they wanted to show me the files this morning in your chambers.

THE COURT: I don't know if the witness wishes to claim his attorney-client privilege or whether there is any basis for claiming it under the circumstances. But I have an obligation as to alert a witness that there may be a problem here.

MR. PUCCIO: If you do advise him of that I would request you do it out of the presence of the jury, rather than putting a layman on the spot as to whether or not he should refuse to answer any questions.

This way he can have an opportunity to think about it and consult with his attorney.

* * *

I think what I'll do is take a recess at this point and I'll tell Mr. Williams that he may wish to consult his attorney on this point, and we will resume after the short recess.

We'll take a short recess, ladies and gentlemen. Don't discuss the case during the recess.

(At 3:20 P.M., the jury withdrew from the courtroom) (The following occurred out of hearing of the jury:)

THE COURT: May I have it quiet, please.

Mr. Williams, one of the more recent questions put to you, asked you about something you may have talked to your attorney about, I suggest during the recess you reflect on the fact that you, whether you are aware of it or not, communications between you and your attorney are privileged, they're matters you don't have to answer questions about unless you choose to, unless there are circumstances that would indicate in some light that privilege had been waived. I wanted you to be aware of the fact that there is such a thing as an attorney-client privilege. It may apply under circumstances here. I'm told by Mr. Koelzer he may be asking you some other questions about communications between you and your attorney. There is some suggestion to me that the privilege may have been waived and that I wouldn't know unless I knew more of the circumstances and I'm not even going to inquire over the circumstances unless you assert your privilege. But I want you to know you have it. You may assert it and if you do, I'll determine whether or not you are to answer questions, you can waive the privilege.

THE WITNESS: I would like to assert it. I really would.

THE COURT: The witness said he would like to assert his privilege, attorney-client privilege.

MR. KOELZER: At an appropriate point in the cross examination I'd like to get to it, I know I will not be done with this witness this afternoon and at an appropriate time I would like to go into the point of waiver and whether or not he has waived it and whether he has attempted to conceal it.

THE COURT: You may wish to consult with your attorney on this point during the recess as well. Whenever there is a question put to you that asks you to reveal a communication, either by your attorney, confidential communication by your attorney to you, or by you to your attorney, if that is a question which you wish to assert your privilege with respect to, it's a bad sentence, but I think you understand me, you'll indicate it at that time and then later we'll determine whether or not there has been a waiver and we'll have to go into it.

THE WITNESS: Thank you very much.

IN RE BRUCE R. LINDSEY (GRAND JURY TESTIMONY)
148 F.3d 1100 (D.C. Cir. 1998)

On January 30, 1998, the grand jury issued a subpoena to Bruce R. Lindsey, an attorney admitted to practice in Arkansas. Lindsey currently holds two positions: Deputy White House Counsel and Assistant to the President. On February 18, February 19, and March 12, 1998, Lindsey appeared before the grand jury and declined to answer certain questions on the ground that the questions represented information protected from disclosure by a government attorney-client privilege applicable to Lindsey's communications with the President as Deputy White House Counsel. . . .

On March 6, 1998, the Independent Counsel moved to compel Lindsey's testimony. The district court granted that motion on May 4, 1998. . . . It rejected Lindsey's government attorney-client privilege claim on similar grounds, ruling that the President possesses an attorney-client privilege when consulting in his official capacity with White House Counsel, but that the privilege is qualified in the grand jury context and may be overcome upon a sufficient showing of need for the subpoenaed communications and unavailability from other sources. . . .

II.

The attorney-client privilege protects confidential communications made between clients and their attorneys when the communications are for the purpose of securing legal advice or services. *See In re Sealed Case*, 737 F.2d 94, 98–99 (D.C. Cir. 1984). It "is one of the oldest recognized privileges for confidential communications." *Swidler & Berlin v. United States*, 118 S. Ct. 2081, 2084, 141 L. Ed. 2d 379 (1998).

The Office of the President contends that Lindsey's communications with the President and others in the White House should fall within this privilege both because the President, like any private person, needs to communicate fully and frankly with his legal advisors, and because the current grand jury investigation may lead to impeachment proceedings, which would require a defense of the

President's official position as head of the executive branch of government, presumably with the assistance of White House Counsel. The Independent Counsel contends that an absolute government attorney-client privilege would be inconsistent with the proper role of the government lawyer and that the President should rely only on his private lawyers for fully confidential counsel. . . .

Fed. R. Evid. 501. Although Rule 501 manifests a congressional desire to provide the courts with the flexibility to develop rules of privilege on a case-by-case basis, see *Trammel v. United States*, 445 U.S. 40, 47, 100 S. Ct. 906, 63 L. Ed.2d 186 (1980), the Supreme Court has been "disinclined to exercise this authority expansively," *University of Pa. v. EEOC*, 493 U.S. 182, 189, 110 S. Ct. 577, 107 L. Ed. 2d 571 (1990). "[T]hese exceptions to the demand for every man's evidence are not lightly created nor expansively construed, for they are in derogation of the search for truth." *Nixon*, 418 U.S. at 710, 94 S. Ct. 3090; see also *Trammel*, 445 U.S. at 50, 100 S. Ct. 906. Consequently, federal courts do not recognize evidentiary privileges unless doing so "promotes sufficiently important interests to outweigh the need for probative evidence." *Id.* at 51, 100 S. Ct. 906. . . .

A.

Courts, commentators, and government lawyers have long recognized a government attorney-client privilege in several contexts. Much of the law on this subject has developed in litigation about exemption five of the Freedom of Information Act ("FOIA"). *See* 5 U.S.C. § 552(b)(5) (1994). Under that exemption, "intra-agency memorandums or letters which would not be available by law to a party other than an agency in litigation with the agency" are excused from mandatory disclosure to the public. *Id.; see also* S. Rep. No. 89-813, at 2 (1965) (including within exemption five "documents which would come within the attorney-client privilege if applied to private parties"). We have recognized that "Exemption 5 protects, as a general rule, materials which would be protected under the attorney-client privilege." *Coastal States Gas Corp. v. Department of Energy*, 617 F.2d 854, 862 (D.C. Cir. 1980). "In the governmental context, the 'client' may be the agency and the attorney may be an agency lawyer." *Tax Analysts v. IRS*, 117 F.3d 607, 618 (D.C. Cir. 1997); see also *Brinton v. Department of State*, 636 F.2d 600, 603–04 (D.C. Cir. 1980). In Lindsey's case, his client-to the extent he provided legal services-would be the Office of the President. . . .

Thus, when "the Government is dealing with its attorneys as would any private party seeking advice to protect personal interests, and needs the same assurance of confidentiality so it will not be deterred from full and frank communications with its counselors," exemption five applies. *Coastal States*, 617 F.2d at 863.

Furthermore, the proposed (but never enacted) Federal Rules of Evidence concerning privileges, to which courts have turned as evidence of common law practices, *see, e.g., United States v. Gillock*, 445 U.S. 360, 367–68, 100 S. Ct. 1185, 63 L. Ed. 2d 454 (1980); *In re Bieter Co.*, 16 F.3d 929, 935 (8th Cir. 1994); *Linde Thomson Langworthy Kohn & Van Dyke v. Resolution Trust Corp.*, 5 F.3d 1508, 1514 (D.C. Cir. 1993); *United States v. (Under Seal)*, 748 F.2d 871, 874 n. 5 (4th Cir. 1984); *United States v. Mackey*, 405 F. Supp. 854, 858 (E.D.N.Y. 1975), recognized a place for a government attorney-client privilege. Proposed Rule 503 defined "client" for the purposes of the attorney-client privilege to include "a person, public officer, or corporation, association, or other organization or entity, either public or private." Proposed Fed. R. Evid. 503(a)(1), *reprinted in* 56 F.R.D. 183, 235 (1972). The commentary to the proposed rule explained that "[t]he definition of 'client' includes governmental bodies." *Id.* advisory committee's note. The Restatement also extends attorney-client privilege to government entities. *See* Restatement (Third) of the Law Governing Lawyers § 124 (Proposed Final Draft No. 1, 1996) [hereinafter Restatement].

The practice of attorneys in the executive branch reflects the common understanding that a government attorney-client privilege functions in at least some contexts. The Office of Legal Counsel in the Department of Justice concluded in 1982 that

> [a]lthough the attorney-client privilege traditionally has been recognized in the context of private attorney-client relationships, the privilege also functions to protect communications between government attorneys and client agencies or departments, as evidenced by its inclusion in the FOIA, much as it operates to protect attorney-client communications in the private sector. . . .

We therefore turn to the question whether an attorney-client privilege permits a government lawyer to withhold from a grand jury information relating to the commission of possible crimes by government officials and others. Although the cases decided under FOIA recognize a government attorney-client privilege that is rather absolute in civil litigation, those cases do not necessarily control the application of the privilege here. The grand jury, a constitutional body established in the Bill of Rights, "belongs to no branch of the institutional Government, serving as a kind of buffer or referee between the Government and the people," *United States v. Williams*, 504 U.S. 36, 47, 112 S. Ct. 1735, 118 L. Ed. 2d 352 (1992), while the Independent Counsel is by statute an officer of the executive branch representing the United States. For matters within his jurisdiction, the Independent Counsel acts in the role of the Attorney General as the country's chief law enforcement officer. *See* 28 U.S.C. § 594(a) (1994). Thus, although the traditional privilege between attorneys and clients shields private relationships from inquiry in either civil litigation or criminal prosecution, competing values arise when the Office of the President resists demands for information from a federal grand jury and the nation's chief law enforcement officer. As the drafters of the Restatement recognized, "More particularized rules may be necessary where one agency of government claims the privilege in resisting a demand for information by another. Such rules should take account of the complex considerations of governmental structure, tradition, and regulation that are involved." restatement § 124 cmt. b. For these reasons, others have agreed that such "considerations" counsel against "expansion of the privilege to all governmental entities" in all cases. 24 CHARLES ALAN WRIGHT & KENNETH W. GRAHAM, JR., FEDERAL PRACTICE AND PROCEDURE § 5475, at 125 (1986). . . .

Because the "attorney-client privilege must be 'strictly confined within the narrowest possible limits consistent with the logic of its principle,' " *In re Sealed Case*, 676 F.2d 793, 807 n. 44 (D.C. Cir. 1982) (quoting *In re Grand Jury*

Investigation, 599 F.2d 1224, 1235 (3d Cir. 1979)); *accord Trammel*, 445 U.S. at 50, 100 S. Ct. 906, and because the government attorney-client privilege is not recognized in the same way as the personal attorney-client privilege addressed in *Swidler & Berlin*, we believe this case poses the question whether, in the first instance, the privilege extends as far as the Office of the President would like. In other words, pursuant to our authority and duty under Rule 501 of the Federal Rules of Evidence to interpret privileges "in light of reason and experience," Fed. R. Evid. 501, we view our exercise as one in defining the particular contours of the government attorney-client privilege.

When an executive branch attorney is called before a federal grand jury to give evidence about alleged crimes within the executive branch, reason and experience, duty, and tradition dictate that the attorney shall provide that evidence. With respect to investigations of federal criminal offenses, and especially offenses committed by those in government, government attorneys stand in a far different position from members of the private bar. Their duty is not to defend clients against criminal charges and it is not to protect wrongdoers from public exposure. The constitutional responsibility of the President, and all members of the Executive Branch, is to "take Care that the Laws be faithfully executed." U.S. Const. art. II, § 3. Investigation and prosecution of federal crimes is one of the most important and essential functions within that constitutional responsibility. Each of our Presidents has, in the words of the Constitution, sworn that he "will faithfully execute the Office of President of the United States, and will to the best of [his] Ability, preserve, protect and defend the Constitution of the United States." *Id.* art. II, § 1, cl. 8. And for more than two hundred years each officer of the Executive Branch has been bound by oath or affirmation to do the same. *See id.* art. VI, cl. 3; *see also* 28 U.S.C. § 544 (1994). This is a solemn undertaking, a binding of the person to the cause of constitutional government, an expression of the individual's allegiance to the principles embodied in that document. Unlike a private practitioner, the loyalties of a government lawyer therefore cannot and must not lie solely with his or her client agency. . . .

In sum, it would be contrary to tradition, common understanding, and our governmental system for the attorney-client privilege to attach to White House Counsel in the same manner as private counsel. When government attorneys learn, through communications with their clients, of information related to criminal misconduct, they may not rely on the government attorney-client privilege to shield such information from disclosure to a grand jury. . . .

NOTE

In *In re Grand Jury Investigation*, 399 F.3d 527 (2d Cir. 2005), the Second Circuit disagreed with the D.C. Circuit opinion in *Lindsey*, holding that the government attorney-client privilege is as sacrosanct as the individual attorney-client privilege and that the government lawyer cannot be compelled to disclose such protected information to a grand jury investigating government criminal activity. The Second Circuit found that the consistent application of the privilege's benefits of confidentiality promotes a broader public interest than the need of the grand jury to investigate governmental criminal activity.

D.   THE PRIVILEGE FOR MARITAL COMMUNICATIONS

Comment, *The Husband-Wife Privilege of Testimonial Non-Disclosure*
56 Nw. U. L. Rev. 208, 216–19 (1961)[30]

The . . . most widely accepted privilege, is that for confidential communications. . . . Succinctly, the privilege for confidential communications prohibits testimony by a spouse concerning intra-spousal, confidential communications made during marriage. Surprisingly, its common law origins are obscure, and though there is evidence of its having existed as early as 1600, it was not clearly distinguished from other privileges until 1853. One might question the necessity for a co-existing incompetency and communications privilege at common law, or the statutory co-existence of a privilege for ante-marital facts and a communications privilege. This seeming redundancy is probably explained by a combination of two or more of the following factors: As the incompetency of interested parties began to disappear and writers like Jeremy Bentham inveighed against the privilege, legislatures and courts willing to expunge prior "privileges" or anticipating their eventual destruction, turned to the communications privilege, having the attorney-client privilege as a precursor. Further, the communications privilege transcends both death and divorce, but the privilege for ante-marital facts does not. Finally, the courts which opposed privilege in the interest of revealing truth might have found it too harsh to force a spouse to reveal both what she knew of her own knowledge, and that which she acquired as a result of the intimate confidence of marriage. The adoption of a communications privilege would permit a spouse to testify as to matters independently known, but would preserve intact the privacy of marital communication.

Perhaps the most basic policy justification for this privilege is found in the fact that, though marriage is perhaps not the sacrosanct institution it once was, the body of law surrounding marriage and the volume of literature devoted thereto compels the conclusion that marriage is a vital and respected institution in our society, and few will dispute the necessity of confidence and freedom of communication between the spouses if the marriage is to be maintained. In the interests of protecting communication from public disclosure in court, and pre-venting the natural repugnance experienced by society upon seeing one partner to a marriage forced to testify against the other by disclosing marital communications, the privilege was drawn and is widely accepted.

TRAMMEL v. UNITED STATES
445 U.S. 40 (1980)

Mr. Chief Justice Burger delivered the opinion of the Court.

We granted *certiorari* to consider whether an accused may invoke the privilege against adverse spousal testimony so as to exclude the voluntary testimony of his

---

[30] Reprinted with permission.

wife. . . . This calls for a re-examination of *Hawkins v. United States*, 358 U.S. 74 (1958).

I

On March 10, 1976, petitioner Otis Trammel was indicted with two others, Edwin Lee Roberts and Joseph Freeman, for importing heroin into the United States from Thailand and the Philippine Islands and for conspiracy to import heroin. . . . The indictment also named six unindicted co-conspirators, including petitioner's wife Elizabeth Ann Trammel.

According to the indictment, petitioner and his wife flew from the Philippines to California in August 1975, carrying with them a quantity of heroin. . . . Elizabeth Trammel then travelled to Thailand where she purchased another supply of the drug. On November 3, 1975, with four ounces of heroin on her person, she boarded a plane for the United States. During a routine customs search in Hawaii, she was searched, the heroin was discovered, and she was arrested. After discussions with Drug Enforcement Administration agents, she agreed to cooperate with the Government.

* * *

Prior to trial . . . [petitioner] advised the court that the Government intended to call his wife as an adverse witness and asserted his claim to a privilege to prevent her from testifying against him. At a hearing on the motion, Mrs. Trammel was called as a Government witness under a grant of use immunity. She testified that she and petitioner were married in May 1975 and that they remained married.[31] She explained that her cooperation with the Government was based on assurances that she would be given lenient treatment. She then described, in considerable detail, her role and that of her husband in the heroin distribution conspiracy.

After hearing this testimony, the District Court ruled that Mrs. Trammel could testify in support of the Government's case to any act she observed during the marriage and to any communication "made in the presence of a third person"; however, confidential communications between petitioner and his wife were held to be privileged and inadmissible. . . .

At trial, Elizabeth Trammel testified within the limits of the court's pretrial ruling; her testimony, as the Government concedes, constituted virtually its entire case against petitioner. He was found guilty on both the substantive and conspiracy charges. . . .

II

The privilege claimed by petitioner has ancient roots. Writing in 1628, Lord Coke observed that "it hath beene resolved by the Justices that a wife cannot be produced either against or for her husband." 1 E. COKE, A COMMENTARIE UPON LITTLETON 6b

---

[31] [1] In response to the question whether divorce was contemplated, Mrs. Trammel testified that her husband had said that "I would go my way and he would go his." App 27.

(1628). *See generally* 8 J. WIGMORE, EVIDENCE § 2227 (McNaughton rev. 1961). This spousal disqualification sprang from two cannons of medieval jurisprudence: first, the rule that an accused was not permitted to testify in his own behalf because of his interest in the proceeding; second, the concept that husband and wife were one, and that since the woman had no recognized separate legal existence, the husband was that one. From those two now long-abandoned doctrines, it followed that what was inadmissible from the lips of the defendant-husband was also inadmissible from his wife.

Despite its medieval origins, this rule of spousal disqualification remained intact in most common-law jurisdictions well into the 19th century. . . . Indeed, it was not until 1933, in *Funk v. United States*, 290 U.S. 371 . . . that this Court abolished the testimonial disqualification in the federal courts, so as to permit the spouse of a defendant to testify in the defendant's behalf. Funk, however, left undisturbed the rule that either spouse could prevent the other from giving adverse testimony. . . . The rule thus evolved into one of privilege rather than one of absolute disqualification. *See* J. MAGUIRE, EVIDENCE, COMMON SENSE AND COMMON LAW 78–92 (1947).

The modern justification for this privilege against adverse spousal testimony is its perceived role in fostering the harmony and sanctity of the marriage relationship. Notwithstanding this benign purpose, the rule was sharply criticized. Professor Wigmore termed it "the merest anachronism in legal theory and an indefensible obstruction to truth in practice." 8 WIGMORE § 2228, at 221. The Committee on Improvements in the Law of Evidence of the American Bar Association called for its abolition. 63 American Bar Association Reports 594–595 (1938). In its place, Wigmore and others suggested a privilege protecting only private marital communications, modeled on the privilege between priest and penitent, attorney and client, and physician and patient. *See* 8 WIGMORE § 2332 *et seq.*[32]

These criticisms influenced the American Law Institute, which, in its 1942 Model Code of Evidence, advocated a privilege for marital confidences, but expressly rejected a rule vesting in the defendant the right to exclude all adverse testimony of his spouse. *See* American Law Institute, Model Code of Evidence, Rule 215 (1942). In 1953 the Uniform Rules of Evidence, drafted by the National Conference of Commissioners on Uniform State Laws, followed a similar course; it limited the privilege to confidential communications and "abolishe[d] the rule, still existing in some states, and largely a sentimental relic, of not requiring one spouse to testify against the other in a criminal action." . . .

In *Hawkins v. United States*, . . . this Court considered the continued vitality of the privilege against adverse spousal testimony in the federal courts. There the District Court had permitted petitioner's wife, over his objection, to testify against him. With one questioning concurring opinion, the Court held the wife's testimony inadmissible; it took note of the critical comments that the common-law rule had engendered, . . . but chose not to abandon it. Also rejected was the Government's

---

[32] [5] This Court recognized just such a confidential marital communications privilege in *Wolfle v. United States*, 291 U.S. 7 (1934), and in *Blau v. United States*, 340 U.S. 332 (1951). In neither case, however, did the Court adopt the Wigmore view that the communications privilege be substituted in place of the privilege against adverse spousal testimony. The privilege as to confidential marital communications is not at issue in the instant case; accordingly, our holding today does not disturb *Wolfle* and *Blau*.

suggestion that the Court modify the privilege by vesting it in the witness spouse, with freedom to testify or not independent of the defendant's control. The Court viewed this proposed modification as antithetical to the widespread belief, evidenced in the rules then in effect in a majority of the States and in England "that the law should not force or encourage testimony which might alienate husband and wife, or further inflame existing domestic differences." . . .

FRE 501

Hawkins, then, left the federal privilege for adverse spousal testimony where it found it, continuing "a rule which bars the testimony of one spouse against the other unless both consent." . . .[33] However, in so doing, the Court made clear that its decision was not meant to "foreclose whatever changes in the rule may eventually be dictated by 'reason and experience.' "

*   *   *

III

The Federal Rules of Evidence acknowledge the authority of the federal courts to continue the evolutionary development of testimonial privileges in federal criminal trials "governed by the principles of the common law as they may be interpreted . . . in the light of reason and experience." Fed. Rule Evid. 501. . . . The general mandate of Rule 501 was substituted by the Congress for a set of privilege rules drafted by the Judicial Conference Advisory Committee on Rules of Evidence and approved by the Judicial Conference of the United States and by this Court. That proposal defined nine specific privileges, including a husband-wife privilege which would have codified the *Hawkins* rule and eliminated the privilege for confidential marital communications. *See* proposed Fed. Rule Evid. 505. In rejecting the proposed Rules and enacting Rule 501, Congress manifested an affirmative intention not to freeze the law of privilege. Its purpose rather was to "provide the courts with the flexibility to develop rules of privilege on a case-by-case basis," 120 Cong. Rec. 40891 (1974) (statement of Rep. Hungate), and to leave the door open to change. . . .

Although Rule 501 confirms the authority of the federal courts to reconsider the continued validity of the *Hawkins* rule, the long history of the privilege suggests that it ought not to be casually cast aside. That the privilege is one affecting marriage, home, and family relationships — already subject to much erosion in our day — also counsels caution. At the same time, we cannot escape the reality that the law on occasion adheres to doctrinal concepts long after the reasons which gave them birth have disappeared and after experience suggests the need for change. . . .

---

[33] [7] We have recognized an exception to *Hawkins* for cases in which one spouse commits a crime against the other. . . . This exception, placed on the ground of necessity, was a longstanding one at common law. *See Lord Audley's Case*, 123 Eng. Rep. 1140 (1631); 8 Wigmore § 2239. It has been expanded since then to include crimes against the spouse's property, . . . and in recent years crimes against children of either spouse. . . . Similar exceptions have been found to the confidential marital communications privilege. *See* 8 Wigmore § 2338.

B

Since 1958, when *Hawkins* was decided, support for the privilege against adverse spousal testimony has been eroded further. Thirty-one jurisdictions, including Alaska and Hawaii, then allowed an accused a privilege to prevent adverse spousal testimony. . . . The number has now declined to 24. . . . The trend in state law toward divesting the accused of the privilege to bar adverse spousal testimony has special relevance because the law of marriage and domestic relations are concerns traditionally reserved to the states. . . . Scholarly criticism of the *Hawkins* rule has also continued unabated.

C

Testimonial exclusionary rules and privileges contravene the fundamental principle that "the public . . . has a right to every man's evidence." . . . As such, they must be strictly construed and accepted "only to the very limited extent that permitting a refusal to testify or excluding relevant evidence has a public good transcending the normally predominant principle of utilizing all rational means for ascertaining truth." . . . Here we must decide whether the privilege against adverse spousal testimony promotes sufficiently important interests to outweigh the need for probative evidence in the administration of criminal justice.

It is essential to remember that the *Hawkins* privilege is not needed to protect information privately disclosed between husband and wife in the confidence of the marital relationship — once described by this Court as "the best solace of human existence." . . . Those confidences are privileged under the independent rule protecting confidential marital communications. . . . The *Hawkins* privilege is invoked, not to exclude private marital communications, but rather to exclude evidence of criminal acts and of communications made in the presence of third persons.

No other testimonial privilege sweeps so broadly. The privileges between priest and penitent, attorney and client, and physician and patient limit protection to private communications. These privileges are rooted in the imperative need for confidence and trust. The priest-penitent privilege recognizes the human need to disclose to a spiritual counselor, in total and absolute confidence, what are believed to be flawed acts or thoughts and to receive priestly consolation and guidance in return. The lawyer-client privilege rests on the need for the advocate and counselor to know all that relates to the client's reasons for seeking representation if the professional mission is to be carried out. Similarly, the physician must know all that a patient can articulate in order to identify and to treat disease; barriers to full disclosure would impair diagnosis and treatment.

The *Hawkins* rule stands in marked contrast to these three privileges. Its protection is not limited to confidential communications, rather it permits an accused to exclude all adverse spousal testimony. As Jeremy Bentham observed more than a century and a half ago, such a privilege goes far beyond making "every man's house his castle," and permits a person to convert his house into "a den of thieves." 5 Rationale Of Judicial Evidence 340 (1827). It "secures, to every man, one safe and unquestionable and ever ready accomplice for every imaginable crime." *Id.* at 338.

The ancient foundations for so sweeping a privilege have long since disappeared. Nowhere in the common-law world — indeed in any modern society — is a woman regarded as chattel or demeaned by denial of a separate legal identity and the dignity associated with recognition as a whole human being. Chip by chip, over the years those archaic notions have been cast aside so that "[n]o longer is the female destined solely for the home and the rearing of the family, and only the male for the marketplace and the world of ideas." . . .

The contemporary justification for affording an accused such a privilege is also unpersuasive. When one spouse is willing to testify against the other in a criminal proceeding — whatever the motivation — their relationship is almost certainly in disrepair; there is probably little in the way of marital harmony for the privilege to preserve. In these circumstances, a rule of evidence that permits an accused to prevent adverse spousal testimony seems far more likely to frustrate justice than to foster family peace.[34] Indeed, there is reason to believe that vesting the privilege in the accused could actually undermine the marital relationship. For example, in a case such as this, the Government is unlikely to offer a wife immunity and lenient treatment if it knows that her husband can prevent her from giving adverse testimony. If the Government is dissuaded from making such an offer, the privilege can have the untoward effect of permitting one spouse to escape justice at the expense of the other. It hardly seems conducive to the preservation of the marital relation to place a wife in jeopardy solely by virtue of her husband's control over her testimony.

IV

Our consideration of the foundations for the privilege and its history satisfy us that "reason and experience" no longer justify so sweeping a rule as that found acceptable by the Court in *Hawkins*. Accordingly, we conclude that the existing rule should be modified so that the witness spouse alone has a privilege to refuse to testify adversely; the witness may be neither compelled to testify nor foreclosed from testifying. This modification — vesting the privilege in the witness spouse — furthers the important public interest in marital harmony without unduly burdening legitimate law enforcement needs.

*   *   *

Mr. Justice Stewart, concurring in the judgment.

Although agreeing with much of what the Court has to say, I cannot join an opinion that implies that "reason and experience" have worked a vast change since the *Hawkins* case was decided in 1958. In that case the Court upheld the privilege

---

[34] [12] It is argued that abolishing the privilege will permit the Government to come between husband and wife, pitting one against the other. That, too, misses the mark. Neither *Hawkins*, nor any other privilege, prevents the Government from enlisting one spouse to give information concerning the other or to aid in the other's apprehension. It is only the spouse's testimony in the courtroom that is prohibited.

of a defendant in a criminal case to prevent adverse spousal testimony, in an all-but-unanimous opinion by Mr. Justice Black. Today the Court, in another all-but-unanimous opinion, obliterates that privilege because of the purported change in perception that "reason and experience" have wrought.

The fact of the matter is that the Court in this case simply accepts the very same arguments that the Court rejected when the Government first made them in the *Hawkins* case in 1958. I thought those arguments were valid then, and I think so now.

The Court is correct when it says that "[t]he ancient foundations for so sweeping a privilege have long since disappeared." . . . But those foundations had disappeared well before 1958; their disappearance certainly did not occur in the few years that have elapsed between the *Hawkins* decision and this one. To paraphrase what Mr. Justice Jackson once said in another context, there is reason to believe that today's opinion of the Court will be of greater interest to students of human psychology than to students of law.

NOTES AND QUESTIONS

1. Is the Supreme Court's analysis in *Trammel* inconsistent with the language of Proposed Rule 505, which had been promulgated by the Court only eight years earlier?

2. Under Proposed Rule 505, the privilege for marital communications would have been totally abrogated. Underlying this approach was the belief that the communications privilege has little, if any, impact since most couples are unaware of its existence. *See* Advisory Comm. Note, Proposed Rule of Evidence 505. Is this a valid rationale? Even if it is, does it warrant total abrogation of the marital communications privilege? *See* Black, *The Marital and Physician Privilege — A Reprint of a Letter to a Congressman*, 1975 DUKE L.J. 45.

3. Most common law jurisdictions declined to extend the privilege's protection to conversations overheard by eavesdroppers. What would be the basis for this restriction? Would the same rationale be applicable if the eavesdropping was arranged through the cooperation of a betraying spouse? *See United States v. Neal*, 532 F. Supp. 942 (D. Colo. 1982).

4. At common law, the marital communications privilege was not applied to spousal conversations involving joint criminal activity. Would it make sense to apply a similar exception to the broader privilege against adverse spousal testimony? *See Appeal of Malfitano*, 633 F.2d 276 (3d Cir. 1980).

5. Suppose that a defendant declines to call his wife as a witness in his behalf. May the prosecution comment upon this failure during closing argument? *See George v. State*, 644 P.2d 510 (Nev. 1982).

E. THE PHYSICIAN-PATIENT PRIVILEGE

UNITED STATES EX REL. EDNEY v. SMITH
425 F. Supp. 1038 (E.D.N.Y. 1976)

WEINSTEIN, DISTRICT JUDGE.

Petitioner seeks a writ of habeas corpus. . . . He was found guilty in a New York State court of the kidnapping and killing of the eight-year-old daughter of his former girlfriend. . . . His claim now is that the State violated his federal constitutional rights by calling a psychiatrist who had interviewed petitioner before trial at his counsel's request. While the rules of privilege relied upon by petitioner are preferred, they are not constitutionally mandated. For the reasons detailed below the petitioner must be denied.

FACTS

At the trial the only significant issue was sanity. A defense psychiatrist testified that defendant, as a result of mental illness, was unaware of the nature and quality of his acts and did not know that his acts were wrong. In rebuttal, the prosecution called Dr. Daniel Schwartz, a psychiatrist, who had examined defendant at the request of defendant's attorney. The attorney had not been present during the examination. The defense objected on the grounds of the attorney-client and physician-patient privileges. Dr. Schwartz found no evidence of an underlying disease or defect. It was his opinion that at the time of the murder defendant knew and appreciated the nature of his conduct and knew that his conduct was wrong. . . .

The jury found the petitioner guilty and he was sentenced to 25 years to life. He appealed, chiefly on the ground that the admission of Dr. Schwartz's testimony over objection was reversible error. The Appellate Division unanimously affirmed. . . . Its order was in turn affirmed by the Court of Appeals. . . .

The State's highest court, in a full opinion, with one judge dissenting, discussed the privilege issue. It held that where the defense of insanity was asserted and the defendant offered evidence to establish the claim, a waiver of privileges was effected. Under such circumstances, it concluded, the prosecution could call a psychiatric expert who had examined the defendant at his attorney's request.

The sole issue before this court in this habeas corpus proceeding is whether the admission of Dr. Schwartz's testimony violated petitioner's federal constitutional rights. Petitioner anchors his constitutional claim primarily to the Sixth Amendment guarantee of effective assistance of counsel. He argues that unless the communications of a defendant to a psychiatrist are protected by either the physician-patient or attorney-client privilege an accused, fearing revelation of these communications to the State will not be candid with the psychiatrist. This will, in turn, impede the lawyer's ability to present the effective defense guaranteed by the Constitution. Thus, his argument goes, by necessary implication, either the attorney-client or physician-patient privilege is, to the extent indicated by the facts of this case, embodied in the Sixth Amendment.

PHYSICIAN-PATIENT PRIVILEGE

The physician-patient relationship, unlike that of attorney-client, did not give rise to a testimonial privilege at common law; a physician called as a witness had a duty to disclose all information obtained from a patient. *See generally* 8 WIGMORE, EVIDENCE §§ 2380–2391 (McNaughton rev. 1961). In 1828 New York became the first jurisdiction to alter the common-law rule by establishing a statutory privilege. . . . Since that time approximately three-quarters of the states have followed New York's lead and enacted similar statutory provisions.

* * *

Legal scholars have been virtually unanimous in their condemnation of these legislative attempts to foster the doctor-patient relationship by rules of exclusion. *See, e.g.,* 8 WIGMORE, EVIDENCE § 2380a at 831–32 (McNaughton rev. 1961); Morgan, *Suggested Remedy for Obstructions to Expert Testimony by Rules of Evidence*, 10 U. CHI. L. REV. 285, 290–92 (1943); SLOVENKO, PSYCHOTHERAPY, CONFIDENTIALITY, AND PRIVILEGED COMMUNICATION 20–24 (1966). They repeatedly argue that while the adverse impact of the privilege on the fact-finding function of the courts is immediate and unquestionable, empirical evidence of the alleged benefits of the privilege is speculative at best and more realistically non-existent. Professor Chafee's well-known criticism is typical:

> The reasons usually advanced for extending the privilege of silence to the medical profession are not wholly satisfactory. First, it is said that if the patient knows that his confidences may be divulged in future litigation he will hesitate in many cases to get needed medical aid. But although the man who consults a lawyer usually has litigation in mind, men very rarely go to a doctor with any such thought. And even if they did, medical treatment is so valuable that few would lose it to prevent facts from coming to light in court. Indeed, it may be doubted whether, except for a small range of disgraceful or peculiarly private matters, patients worry much about having a doctor keep their private affairs concealed from the world. This whole argument that the privilege is necessary to induce persons to see a doctor sounds like a philosopher's speculation on how men may logically be expected to behave rather than the result of observation of the way men actually behave. Not a single New England state allows the doctor to keep silent on the witness stand. Is there evidence that any ill or injured person in New England has ever stayed from a doctor's office on that account?

> The same *a priori* quality vitiates a second argument concerning the evils of compelling medical testimony, namely, that a strong sense of professional honor will prompt perversion or concealment of the truth. Has any member of the numerous medical societies in New England observed such a tendency among New England doctors to commit perjury for the sake of "professional honor"

Chafee, *Privileged Communications: Is Justice Served or Obstructed by Closing the Doctor's Mouth on the Witness Stand?*, 52 YALE L.J. 607, 609–10 (1943).

Legal practice in the states which have adopted a general medical privilege confirms the criticism of the commentators. Although no state has repealed the privilege once it has been adopted, recognition of its undesirable effects has led to judicial and legislative whittling away so that its scope has been considerably reduced. Numerous nonuniform exceptions have evolved which have rendered the privilege "substantially impotent," Comment, *Federal Rules of Evidence and the Law of Privileges*, 15 WAYNE L. REV. 1286, 1324 (1969), and difficult to administer.

In the federal sphere awareness of these difficulties led the Advisory Committee on the Federal Rules of Evidence to omit any provision for a general physician-patient privilege. It noted that:

> [w]hile many states have by statute created the privilege, the exceptions which have been found necessary in order to obtain information required by the public interest or to avoid fraud are so numerous as to leave little if any basis for the privilege.

*   *   *

Advisory Committee's Note to Proposed Rule 504, 36 F.R.D. 183, 241–242 (1972).

These extensive criticisms bear strongly on whether the states and federal government are subject to constitutional pressures to afford protection to physician-patient communications. It is implausible that a privilege that has almost uniformly been found to be practically undesirable and burdensome should nonetheless be constitutionally compelled. Nonetheless, it has been suggested that the doctor-patient relationship, even absent statutorily privileged status, is entitled to constitutional protection. Thus, in criticizing the absence of a general doctor-patient privilege in the proposed Federal Rules of Evidence, Professor Charles L. Black, relying on the right to privacy, eloquently declared:

> There is something very important at stake in these Rules of Evidence. At several points they give major aid and comfort to that diminishment of human privacy which is one of the greater evils of our time, thus raising not only prime questions of value, but also questions of constitutional law which could never have been dismissed as trivial, but which are even more plainly substantial in the light of such recent decisions as *Griswold v. Connecticut*, 381 U.S. 479 (1965). . . . The question here is not only whether people might be discouraged from making full communication to physicians, though it seems flatly impossible that this would not sometimes happen — a consideration which would in itself be enough to make incomprehensible the absolute subordination of this privacy interest to any trivial interest arising in litigation. But evaluation of a rule like this entails not only a guess as to what conduct it will motivate, but also an estimate of its intrinsic decency. All of us would consider it indecent for a doctor, in the course, say, of a television interview, or even in a textbook, to tell all he knows, naming names, about patients who have been treated by him. Why does this judgment of decency altogether vanish from sight, sink to absolute zero, as soon as somebody files any kind of a non-demurrable complaint in a federal court? Here, again, can a rule be a good one when the ethical doctor must violate it, or hedge, or evade?

In *Rochin v. California*, 342 U.S. 165 (1952), the late Mr. Justice Frankfurter, for the Court, condemned as utterly indecent the forced pumping of a man's stomach to get criminal evidence. Does not the forced revealing of every medical and personal fact, stomach contents and all, learned by the doctor of a person not even suspected of anything, just to serve the convenience of any litigant, partake at least a little of the same indecency? Do not these and many other considerations lead to the discernment of constitutional as well as policy issues here? If so, then the same remarks as those made above apply to the posture in which those constitutional issues are put by the promulgation of these Rules.

Hearings on Proposed Rules of Evidence Before the Special Subcommittee on Reform of Federal Criminal Laws of the House Comm. on the Judiciary, 93d Cong., 1st Sess., Ser. 2 at 241–42 (1973).

* * *

Whatever merit these privacy arguments have in favor of a general patient-physician privilege their persuasiveness is increased where the medical relationship implicated is that between psychotherapist and patient. First, the pragmatic, empirical objections to the rationale of the general physician-patient privilege are not applicable to this specialized relationship. The practical need for and efficacy of a privilege covering this unique relationship is clear.

> Among physicians, the psychiatrist has a special need to maintain confidentiality. His capacity to help his patients is completely dependent upon their willingness and ability to talk freely. This makes it difficult if not impossible for him to function without being able to assure his patients of confidentiality and, indeed, privileged communication. Where there may be exceptions to this general rule . . . , there is wide agreement that confidentiality is a sine qua non for successful psychiatric treatment. The relationship may well be likened to that of the priest-penitent or the lawyer-client. Psychiatrists not only explore the very depths of their patients' conscious, but their unconscious feelings and attitudes as well. Therapeutic effectiveness necessitates going beyond a patient's awareness and, in order to do this, it must be possible to communicate freely. A threat to secrecy blocks successful treatment.

Advisory Committee Notes to Proposed Rule 504, Federal Rules of Evidence, 56 F.R.D. 183, 242 (1972), quoting Report No. 45, Group for the Advancement of Psychiatry 92 (1960).

Second, and perhaps more significant for the purpose of determining the validity of a constitutional claim grounded in a right to privacy, is the depth and extraordinarily intimate nature of the patient's revelations.

> The psychiatric patient confides more utterly than anyone else in the world. He exposes to the therapist not only what his words directly express; he lays bare his entire self, his dreams, his fantasies, his sins, and his shame. Most patients who undergo psychotherapy know that this is what will be expected of them, and that they cannot get help except on that condition. . . . It would be too much to expect them to do so if they knew that all they

say — and all that the psychiatrist learns from what they say — may be revealed to the whole world from a witness stand.

Taylor v. United States, 222 F.2d 398, 401 (1955), quoting from GUTTMACHER AND WEIHOFEN, PSYCHIATRY AND THE LAW 272 (1952).

In consideration of this deep-rooted and justifiable expectation of confidentiality harbored by most individuals seeking psychiatric therapy the California Supreme Court has said, in dictum, that

> a patient's interest in keeping such confidential revelations from public purview, in retaining this substantial privacy, has deeper roots than the California [statutory rules of evidence] and draws sustenance from our constitutional heritage. In *Griswold v. Connecticut, supra,* 381 U.S. 479, 484, 85 S. Ct. 1678, 1681, 14 L. Ed. 2d 510, the United States Supreme Court declared that "Various guarantees [of the Bill of Rights] create zones of privacy," and we believe that the confidentiality of the psychotherapeutic session falls within one such zone.

In re Lifschutz, 2 Cal.3d 415, 431 (1970). This strong subjective desire and pragmatic need for privacy in the psychotherapist-patient relationship is certain to give birth to intricate, far-reaching questions of constitutional law. But we need not consider the validity of any such broad contentions in our disposition of this petition.

To the extent that the desirability or constitutionality of the psychiatrist-patient privilege is grounded in its tendency to promote that relationship for purposes of diagnosis and treatment and to increase the likelihood of the ultimate success of such consultations, the privilege cannot be supported on the facts of the instant case. The record indicates that petitioner's examination by Dr. Schwartz was for the purpose of litigation — to enable Edney's attorney to more effectively explore the defenses available to his client. Petitioner and his attorney sought neither treatment nor diagnosis for medical purposes, but rather expert advice for legal purposes. The relationship actually implicated by the facts of this case is that of attorney-client, for it was the petitioner's interest in effective legal advice, rather than in effective psychotherapeutic counseling, that was sought to be furthered by the consultation with Dr. Schwartz.

A significant number of state courts have recognized and relied on this distinction in interpreting and determining the non-applicability of their own statutory physician-patient privileges to analogous fact-patterns. . . . The inapplicability of a physician-patient analysis to a situation similar to that now before us was also recognized by the one published federal opinion discussing this precise issue. *See United States v. Alvarez,* 519 F.2d 1036, 1046 n.13 (3d Cir. 1975).

The reasoning in these cases seems to us to be irrefutable. But even were we to assume that the physician-patient privilege is somehow remotely involved here, we simply could not find a constitutional flaw in the New York rule that when the issue as to which the physician has knowledge is placed in question by the party relying on the privilege — typically in negligence cases, but in criminal proceedings as well — the privilege is deemed waived. The New York Court of Appeals put its reasons persuasively in stating the rule and its waiver rationale in this case:

[handwritten margin note: —How/why would the atty seeking psych consult for seeing if the defense is viable? ↓ If doesn't work, then D is screwed]

where insanity is asserted as a defense and . . . the defendant offers evidence tending to show his insanity in support of this plea, a complete waiver is effected, and the prosecution is then permitted to call psychiatric experts to testify regarding his sanity even though they may have treated the defendant. When the patient first fully discloses the evidence of his affliction, it is he who has given the public the full details of his case, thereby disclosing the secrets which the statute was designed to protect, thus creating a waiver removing it from the operation of the statute; and once the privilege is thus waived, there is nothing left to protect against for once the revelation is made by the patient there is nothing further to disclose "for when a secret is out it is out for all time and cannot be caught again like a bird, and put back in its cage. . . . The legislature did not intend to continue the privilege when there was no reason for its continuance and it would simply be an obstruction to public justice."

People v. Edney, 350 N.E.2d 400, 402 (N.Y. 1976) (quoting from *People v. AlKanani*, 307 N.E.2d 43 (N.Y. 1973) (citations omitted).

*   *   *

Even those commentators who vigorously advocate a general broadening of the psychotherapist privilege acknowledge the justifiability of compelling the disclosure of relevant psychotherapeutic communications when the patient has himself raised an issue concerning his mental condition. Two "model" psychotherapist-patient privilege acts, drafted by such proponents, have included a provision recognizing a patient-litigant exception. Note, *A State Statute to Provide A Psychotherapist-Patient Privilege*, 4 HARV. J. LEGIS. 307, 322 (1968); Fisher, *The Psychotherapeutic Professions and the Law of Privileged Communication*, 10 WAYNE L. REV. 609, 644 (1964).

Uniform Rule of Evidence 504 adopted by the Commissioners on Uniform State Laws in 1974, while creating a psychotherapist-patient privilege, also provides for its waiver:

as to communications relevant to an issue of the mental or emotional condition of the patient in any proceeding in which he relies upon the condition as an element of his claim or defense. . . .

Uniform Rule 504(d)(3). The substance of the Uniform Rule and its waiver provision have been enacted in all seven states following the 1974 Uniform Rules of Evidence. . . .

In embracing this strong legislative, judicial and scholarly trend New York has, like its sister states, neither chosen to enshroud "the patient's communication to the psychotherapist in the black veil of absolute privilege" nor to expose "it to the white glare of absolute publicity." . . . Given this background, it is difficult to say that the states have grossly and unconstitutionally discounted the acknowledged need of confidentiality in the psychiatrist-patient relationship against the pressing societal need for the ascertainment of truth in litigation.

Our opinion is strongly buttressed by consideration of Rule 504 of the Federal Rules of Evidence as promulgated by the Supreme Court. . . . As noted earlier, the

Rules contained no provision for a general physician-patient privilege. They did incorporate a psychotherapist-patient privilege.

* * *

Even under that Rule, however, placing the patient's condition in issue would have constituted a waiver. . . .

Although the rules of privilege embodied in Rule 504 as promulgated by the Supreme Court were not adopted by Congress, the Supreme Court has, in effect, rendered an advisory opinion on their constitutionality. . . . In light of this fact and the other considerations previously adduced, the aspect of petitioner's claim based on a physician-patient relationship must fail. We turn now to consider the attorney-client privilege.

* * *

[The Court proceeded to hold that, under New York law, petitioner's insanity defense had also effected a waiver of his attorney-client privilege insofar as Dr. Schwartz' testimony was concerned. While acknowledging that a waiver rule may be undesirable, no constitutional principle was found to have been violated.]

NOTES AND QUESTIONS

1. Putting aside petitioner *Smith*'s waiver problem, on what basis could it plausibly be said that his communications with Dr. Schwartz fit within the attorney-client privilege?

2. For a detailed analysis of the interface between the attorney-client and psychotherapist-client privileges, see Saltzburg, *Privileges and Professionals: Lawyers and Psychiatrists*, 66 VA. L. REV. 597 (1980).

3. Proposed Rule 504 purports to be a psychotherapist-patient privilege. To what extent, however, might communications to a general practitioner (or other medical doctor) fall within the ambit of this rule?

4. Under what circumstances, if any, might statements to a social worker be covered by Proposed Rule 504? Are such communications deserving of independent protection under a separate privilege? *See generally* Note, *The Social Worker-Client Relationship and Privileged Communications*, 1965 WASH. U. L. Q. 362.

5. How would Proposed Rule 504 handle statements made to a psychiatrist during group therapy (*e.g.*, therapy involving the participation of convicted sex offenders)?

6. In the course of investigating a psychiatrist for fraudulent billing of his patients' insurance companies, a grand jury subpoenas his records identifying his patient's names, the period of treatment, and their billings. Is there a privilege the psychiatrist may successfully assert to avoid compliance? *See In re Zuniga*, 714 F.2d 632 (6th Cir. 1983).

7. May a psychotherapist face civil or criminal liability for failing to warn law enforcement authorities about potential dangers posed by a client? *See Tarasoff v.*

Regents of University of California, 551 P.2d 334 (Cal. 1976).

F. THE PRIEST-PENITENT PRIVILEGE

Donna Oneta Reese, *Confidential Communications to the Clergy*
24 Ohio St. L.J. 55, 60–61 (1963)[35]

It is not always easy to determine the rationale behind the enactment of the priest-penitent statutes. Perhaps some legislators may have thought that the privilege was closely related to freedom of religion where the confession is required as a matter of the discipline of a particular church. Or, it may be that some thought of it more as the individual communicating with his God through an emissary. Some may have regarded it as a necessary therapeutic process whereby the penitent could obtain psychological and physical relief from fear, tension and anxiety. Or, maybe it was considered as being in the general realm of the right to privacy. Whatever the rationale was, the priest-penitent privilege is deeply embedded in American jurisprudence.

Who and what are affected by the statutes?

1. The individual clergyman is benefited because he knows that he can proceed with the complete assurance that confidences are protected by public policy.

2. The confessant is benefited by having a feeling of security in confiding in a priest without inhibitions when he is in need of spiritual aid and comfort. This security does not only apply to particular confessions that have been, or may be, revealed, but also to the member's general attitude toward the church as a protected institution.

3. The church, as an institution, is benefited. Public sanction through legislative enactments to protect the doctrines and practices of an institution is indicative of the prestige it enjoys in our society.

4. The judiciary of the trial courts benefits from the privilege. In a jurisdiction where there is no privilege statute, a trial judge is placed in a very uncomfortable situation when a clergyman is called to testify about matters revealed in a confession or other communication which he is under obligation to keep secret. The trial judge has no common-law authority by which he can declare the communication privileged. Yet, to attempt to make the clergyman testify will only end in refusal and possible imprisonment for contempt. He also would be aware of the fact that public opinion in all probability would be with the clergyman. . . .

There are many aspects of the privilege and many variations in the statutes of the forty-four states.[36] Therefore, the following questions need to be answered:

1. What do the statutes provide?

---

[35] Reprinted with permission from Donna Oneta Reese and the Ohio State Law Journal.

[36] [Ed. — For an update on state legislation concerning this issue, *see* Comment, *Catholic Sisters, Irregularly Ordained Women, and the Clergy-Penitent Privilege*, 9 U.C.D. L. Rev. 523, 526–27 (1976).]

2. What qualifications must a "priest" or "clergyman" have to receive confidential communications under the statutes? Must he be ordained? Could a deacon exercise the privilege? Could members of a church board?

3. In addition to sacramental penance required by the discipline of the church, does the privilege apply (a) where the church has only voluntary confession of a formal nature (*e.g.*, the Episcopal Church), and also (b) where there is in fact no discipline requiring or permitting a formal confession? Could "discipline" apply to the obligation of the profession of the clergy? Must the penitent be a member of the clergyman's church? How informal can the confidential communication be?

4. In what kind of legal proceedings may the privilege be used? Criminal? Civil? Legislative committee? Administrative agency?

5. How is the determination made as to whether the privilege will be granted?

6. Is the privilege an absolute prohibition to testify or may it be waived? And, if so, by whom? And how?

7. What are the sanctions that may be imposed upon a clergyman who violates a statute?

8. What problems of public policy are involved and what are the dangers, pro and con?

9. Are the statutes constitutional?

G.   THE NEWSGATHER'S PRIVILEGE

UNITED STATES v. CRIDEN
633 F.2d 346 (3d Cir. 1980)

ALDISERT, CIRCUIT JUDGE.

In *United States v. Cuthbertson*, 630 F.2d 139, (3d Cir. 1980), we held that CBS had a qualified privilege, partially overridden in that case, not to disclose unpublished information in its possession in criminal cases. Earlier, in *Riley v. City of Chester*, 612 F.2d 708 (3d Cir. 1979), a civil case, we emphasized that special circumstances exist in a criminal case that must be considered in evaluating a witness' claim of journalists' privilege. Specifically, the trial court must consider whether the reporter is alleged to possess evidence relevant to the criminal proceeding and the effect of disclosure on two important constitutionally based concerns: the journalist's privilege not to disclose confidential sources and the constitutional right of a criminal defendant to every reasonable opportunity to develop and uncover exculpatory information. . . .

This appeal requires us to decide if a journalist, summoned as a defense witness in a criminal proceeding, may refuse to affirm or deny that she had a conversation with a particular individual who has already publicly testified that the conversation occurred and that certain matters arguably relevant to the judicial inquiry were discussed. Unlike *Cuthbertson*, this case implicates published information from a self-avowed source; unlike *Riley*, it is a criminal proceeding. We emphasize at the outset that the ultimate judicial inquiry with which this appeal is concerned seeks not the source of the reporter's information, but the motivation and the credibility of a single self-avowed source.

I.

The case comes to us on an appeal by Jan Schaffer, a reporter for the *Philadelphia Inquirer*, from an order of the district court holding her in civil contempt for refusing to answer a question during a hearing on defendants' motions to dismiss their indictments. On May 22, 1980, defendants Howard L. Criden, an attorney practicing in Philadelphia, and Philadelphia City Councilmen Harry P. Jannotti, Louis C. Johanson, and George X. Schwartz were indicted by a federal grand jury in the Eastern District of Pennsylvania and charged with violations of federal laws exposed during a government undercover operation known as AB-SCAM.[37] The indictment charges defendants with violating the Anti-Racketeering Act, 18 U.S.C. § 1962, and the Hobbs Act, 18 U.S.C. § 1951, by receiving bribes from government undercover agents posing as Arab sheiks.

Among the grounds presented for dismissing the indictment are allegations of prosecutorial misconduct and massive prejudicial pre-indictment and pretrial publicity. The charge of prosecutorial misconduct consists of an allegation that representatives of the Department of Justice and the United States Attorney's Office of the Eastern District of Pennsylvania released sensational and prejudicial information to the news media with intent to create an atmosphere inimical to the rights of the defendants. The parties concede that the ABSCAM investigation has received widespread publicity and the government has stipulated that the source of the disclosures to the press was one or more persons employed by the Department of Justice, the Federal Bureau of Investigation, and the United States Attorney's Office.

FBI officials have described ABSCAM as an operation of major proportions, apparently beginning in 1978 or earlier but not focusing on public officials until the fall of 1979. Thomas P. Puccio, chief of the Justice Department's Organized Crime Strike Force in Brooklyn, New York, was the chief prosecutor and head of the operation from its inception. Around December 12, 1979, Mr. Puccio transmitted a detailed memorandum to Phillip Heyman, Assistant Attorney General in charge of the Criminal Division of the Department of Justice, summarizing developments and analyzing applicable federal statutes. This memorandum was disseminated to top officials of the Department of Justice in Washington as well as to Robert Del Tufo, United States Attorney for the District of New Jersey, and to William Webster, Director of the FBI. The memorandum does not mention defendants.

Early in 1980, the U.S. Attorney's Office for the Eastern District of Pennsylvania became actively involved in the operation. On January 29, 1980, Peter F. Vaira, U.S. Attorney for the Eastern District of Pennsylvania, met with Brian Ross of the

---

[37] [1] "ABSCAM" is a code name for an operation by the Federal Bureau of Investigation called Abdul Enterprises, Inc., in which Federal undercover agents posing as representatives of Middle Eastern businessmen sought help from public officials for various enterprises.

National Broadcasting Company. Vaira testified during the dismissal hearing that Ross was aware of certain details of the operation but that, as of the date of the meeting, he was unaware that the defendants had been implicated.

On Saturday, February 2, government agents invited Criden to New York and revealed the true nature of the ABSCAM operation to him. As part of a plan to continue the operation, Vaira and others tried to convince Criden to cooperate with them in continuing undercover operations. On that date, Ross released the ABSCAM story during an evening news broadcast on Channel 4 in New York. The news story contained films of government agents visiting the homes of certain public officials. Shortly thereafter, the *New York Times*, in a story written by Leslie Maitland, carried a detailed account of the operation. Neither the NBC broadcast nor the *Times* story contained information concerning the defendants here. Puccio and Vaira testified that the *New York Times* story contained much of the information found in the earlier memorandum from Puccio to Heyman and that Maitland probably had gained access to the memorandum. Government officials acknowledged in testimony before the district court that leaks to the press came from within the government. Both Puccio and Vaira denied that they were the original source of the leaks.

II.

The testimony relevant to this appeal is Vaira's statement at the indictment dismissal hearing that he learned on February 2, 1980, that the ABSCAM operation was about to be exposed in the national media. As a favor to Schaffer, and while still negotiating with Criden, he telephoned Schaffer from Strike Force headquarters in New York, told her that the story was breaking in the national news, and advised her to "catch up" on the story. . . . Vaira was asked on direct examination if he was the source of information that appeared in Schaffer's article published by the *Inquirer* on Monday, February 4. He denied that he was . . . Vaira then said that he had at least one other telephone conversation with Schaffer:

> I recall that she returned a phone call and said, "I understand that there are Philadelphia city councilmen involved" and she had . . . two correct names and one incorrect. I don't recall who it was.

> At that point it looked to me she had some bad information.

> *   *   *

> I just said, "You are incorrect." At that time I realized she had picked up the story from Philadelphia which I thought was not a part of this bigger story, not a part of the *New York Times* work. . . .

> [S]he called me about two times or three times up in New York[.] [T]he third time she called me she had . . . the correct names.

Q.   Did you then say she was correct?

A.   Yes . . . I said, "That is all I'm going to say." In the meantime she had got some incorrect and it looked like she was going to include some incorrect names.

. . . During questioning by counsel for Criden, Vaira revealed that he first telephoned Schaffer "late in the afternoon, February 2, at sometime after an NBC-TV newscast aired at 6 or 6:30 p.m." He said that during his third conversation with Schaffer, sometime between 7:30 and 8:30 p.m. Saturday evening, he realized that she "had the full story" but that he did not confirm it. . . .

Schaffer was subpoenaed as a defense witness. Prior to her testimony, the court emphasized that it would not require her to reveal the sources of her information. . . . Schaffer's attorney objected to the court's order requiring Schaffer to testify, arguing that the government's concession that its employees were responsible for the releases obviated Schaffer's testimony. The court rejected this argument, however, reasoning that the need to preserve confidentiality of sources evaporates when the source himself has admitted his disclosure. In addition, the court stated that issues of Vaira's motivation and credibility remained unresolved. . . .

When Schaffer's attorney continued to press the motion to quash the subpoena, the court denied the motion in a ruling that is critical to this appeal. It indicated that questions regarding the balance between the journalist's privilege and the defendant's right to a fair trial must "be made on the question by question basis." Following a sidebar conference counsel for defendant Schwartz continued the direct examination. Schaffer disclosed her occupation and her acquaintance with Vaira before the colloquy at issue occurred:

Q.   On February 2, 1980, did you have a conversation with Mr. Vaira concerning ABSCAM?

MR. KOHN: That's objected to your Honor.

THE COURT: Objection overruled.

MR. SPRAGUE: Would you answer that question?

MISS SCHAFFER: May I confer with counsel? . . . Your Honor, I am going to respectfully decline —

THE COURT: You are directed to answer the question yes or no . . .

> [T]he court has ordered you now to answer the question either yes or no.

> You're not being asked anything more [than] whether you had a conversation with him. Now, do you answer the question or do you refuse to answer the question?

THE WITNESS: I continue to decline to answer the question.

THE COURT: All right, you're held in contempt and it's civil contempt.

> You may purge yourself of contempt by answering the question and the contempt is that you be remanded to the custody of the marshal until you answer the question. If you haven't answered it within six months, you'll be turned loose.

. . . The trial court remanded Schaffer into the custody of her attorney pending disposition of this appeal.

In her brief, Schaffer has described her refusal to answer the one question as a "constitutional crisis." . . . Relying on Riley, she argues that she has a privilege to refuse to answer the question. She predicates her defense on an assertion that an answer would have revealed, directly or indirectly, a source of news; that the defendants have failed to show that the information sought is crucial to their defense; that they have failed to show that the information sought is unavailable from other sources; and that the compelled disclosure of sources was premature.

* * *

V.

We must emphasize at the outset that this case does not implicate only the first amendment. Rather, it highlights a tension between the first amendment and the fifth and sixth amendments. The first amendment states: "Congress shall make no law . . . abridging the freedom of speech, or of the press." The sixth amendment requires that in all criminal prosecutions, the accused shall have compulsory process for obtaining witnesses, and the fifth amendment guarantees that he shall not be deprived of life, liberty, or property without due process of law. The tension has been described as a balance between the "freedom of the press and the obligation of all citizens to give relevant testimony with respect to criminal conduct." *Branzburg v. Hayes*, 408 U.S. 665, 710 (1972) (Powell, J., concurring). . . .

A.

We are guided by previous interpretations of the constitutional text by both the Supreme Court and this court. The first amendment "was fashioned to assure unfettered interchange of ideas for the bringing about of political and social changes desired by the people," . . . and bottomed on "a profound national commitment to the principle that debate on public issues should be uninhibited, robust, and wide-open. . . ." This national commitment to an unfettered exchange of ideas has been described most recently as a bulwark against "arbitrary interference with access to important information. . . ." This characterization is justified not because of the journalist's role as a private citizen employed by a private enterprise, but because reporters are viewed "as surrogates for the public." . . . This court has held flatly that journalists have a federal common law privilege, albeit qualified, to refuse to disclose their confidential sources. *Riley v. City of Chester*, 612 F.2d 708, 715 (3d Cir. 1979).

But we believe that very pragmatic reasons as well as these more abstract concerns underlie our national commitment. The courts have made a value judgment that it is far better for there to be immediate, unshackled distribution of news, at the risk of some factual error, . . . than a restraint of the flow of public information that more likely than not would result if confidential news sources had to be identified. This judgment is based on a candid recognition of private human experience, completely outside the media world, in which it is commonplace for a private individual, when conveying news, information, or plain gossip to a friend, to preface the disclosure with "Please don't tell anyone that I told you, but. . . ." More often than not, unless the declarant has faith that the recipient will preserve the confidence, he will not bestow it; also more often than not, when the recipient of the information conveys it to a third person, he respects the confidence of the original source.

Moreover, there is a general expectation in certain sectors of society that information flows more freely from anonymous sources. . . . The rule protecting a journalist's source therefore does not depart significantly from daily experience in informal dissemination of information.

The reporters' privilege also attempts to protect the source from retribution. If a practice in private industry is exposed by a person in a given employment hierarchy, he risks retribution at the hands of his superiors and his peers if he is identified as the source. Similar retribution is not unknown in government services. The danger of retaliation against a private citizen who reports criminal activities is obvious.

Our national commitment to the free exchange of information also embodies a recognition that the major sources of news are public figures, and that in addition to being newsmakers, these sources fashion public policy for government at all levels and in all branches. New ideas must be tested in the crucible of public opinion if our representatives are to receive guidance in deciding whether a suggested policy will receive public endorsement or opposition. It is extremely important therefore that varying concepts of public policy be defined and redefined, tested and retested, by wide public dissemination. In this respect, the communications media not only serve as the vehicle that widely disperses information but also constitute an important instrument of democracy that assists our officials in fashioning public policy. Without the protection of the source, the cutting edge of this valuable societal instrument would be severely dulled and public participation in decisionmaking severely restricted. The brute fact of human experience is that public officials are far more willing to test new ideas under the public microscope through anonymous disclosure than when they are required to be identified as the sources.

These extremely impressive pragmatic reasons, as well as conceptually abstract a priori principles, underlie the precept that a journalist does in fact possess a privilege that is deeply rooted in the first amendment. When no countervailing constitutional concerns are at stake, it can be said that the privilege is absolute; when constitutional precepts collide, the absolute gives way to the qualified and a balancing process comes into play to determine its limits. Thus, there are sound reasons for safeguarding the qualified privilege within the limits dictated by the purposes it serves. The rule follows where its reason leads; where the reason stops, there stops the rule. . . .[38]

B.

The journalists' privilege therefore must be considered in the context of Supreme Court teachings that there is no absolute right for a newsman to refuse to answer relevant and material questions asked during a criminal proceeding. *Branzburg v. Hayes.* . . . Although briefs filed in support of *Schaffer* exaggerate both the scope

---

[38] [6] The source of this sentence is, of course, K. LLEWELLYN, THE BRAMBLE BUSH 157–58 (1960).

of the privilege and the gravity of this particular appeal,[39] this court has taken a more reasonable view of the balance between the privilege and a criminal defendant's rights. We have previously adopted the formulation in the concurring opinion of Justice Powell in *Branzburg*:

> The asserted claim to privilege should be judged on its facts by striking a proper balance between freedom of the press and the obligation of all citizens to give relevant testimony with respect to criminal conduct. The balance of these vital constitutional and societal interests on a case-by-case basis accords with the tried and traditional way of adjudicating such questions.

Riley v. City of Chester, 612 F.2d at 716 (quoting *Branzburg v. Hayes*, 408 U.S. at 710 (Powell, J., concurring)). . . . We therefore reject any implication by appellant or *amici* that the first amendment necessarily must override other important values whenever a conflict arises. . . .

The appellant seeks to strike even the threshold question of whether Vaira had a conversation with her. The Supreme Court teaches us, however, that "[e]videntiary privileges in litigation are not favored, and even those rooted in the Constitution must give way in proper circumstances" . . . and that, " '[w]hatever their origins, these exceptions to the demand for every man's evidence are not lightly created nor expansively construed, for they are in derogation of the search for truth.' " *Id.* (quoting *United States v. Nixon*). The Court has placed particular emphasis on the production of evidence in criminal trials. It has grounded this need for evidence on both the confrontation and compulsory process clauses of the sixth amendment and on the due process clause of the fifth amendment. To protect these constitutionally-founded rights, courts must assure that all relevant and admissible evidence is produced. . . . Courts must tread carefully on the hallowed ground where these basic concerns, the free flow of information and the fair administration of criminal justice, conflict. . . .

Notwithstanding the agonizing difficulty that attends an accommodation of

---

[39] [7] For example, the Bulletin Company's brief states that "[i]t is difficult to put a more disturbing example of arbitrariness destroying a constitutionally protected right. Unless corrected, the error below exposes every reporter to the same kind of constitutionally indefensible treatment whenever an allegedly admitted source testifies." Brief for Bulletin Company, *Amicus Curiae*, at 19. The New York Times Company states:

> Unless the decision below is reversed, reporters will be called routinely and repeatedly to testify — without preliminary findings that their testimony is crucial or unobtainable from other sources — with respect to matters that go to the very core of the newsgathering process. The deterrent effect on these reporters and on reporters covering other sensitive stories, as well as on their sources, would be inevitable.

Brief for New York Times Company, *Amicus Curiae*, at 3. Perhaps more incredible is the statement by the Reporters Committee for Freedom of the Press:

> The Justice Department is cooperating in this hunt for news sources by failing to aggressively, oppose these subpoenas, as it has done in previous cases. It is helping the defendants to undermine its own indictment because it believes, apparently, that by sacrificing this news reporter, the government will be able to purge itself before the Congress and the public of its conceded role in leaking news of the ABSCAM investigation.

Brief for Reporters Committee for Freedom of the Press, *Amicus Curiae*, at i–ii.

conflicting interests in a clash of constitutional principles, this court has neverthe-less fashioned a formula in a related context that may serve as a compass in this case: "In striking the delicate balance between the assertion of the privilege on the one hand and the interest of either criminal or civil litigants seeking the information the materiality, relevance and necessity of the information sought must be shown." *Riley v. City of Chester.* . . . Moreover, we have declared that the requisite balance cannot be reached unless the moving party shows that he has attempted to obtain the information from other sources . . .

C.

We make clear that the *Riley* test is utilized to determine under what circumstances a journalist no longer possesses the qualified privilege to refuse to name a source. We make equally clear that this case does not require disclosure of sources. Instead, it presents the explicit question whether this reporter is required to affirm or deny that she had a conversation with Vaira, a self-avowed source. It also presents an implicit question: whether she is required to reveal the substance of Vaira's conversation with her, omitting portions that explicitly identify other sources.

Under the circumstances of this case it is not necessary to fashion a test other than *Riley* to decide these questions. Even under the more stringent test developed to determine when a reporter may be compelled to divulge a source, the defendants have established a record sufficient to demonstrate their entitlement to the limited information sought. We need not develop a precise test for the peculiar circum-stances presented here, although we will venture the view that the defendants probably should be required to prove less to obtain the reporter's version of a conversation already voluntarily disclosed by the self-confessed source than to obtain the identity of the source itself.

Riley isolated three criteria that must be met before a reporter can be compelled to disclose a confidential source. . . . First, the movant must demonstrate that he has made an effort to obtain the information from other sources. Second, he must demonstrate that the only access to the information sought is through the journalist and her sources. Finally, the movant must persuade the court that the information sought is crucial to the claim. Although this case does not require a source disclosure, we conclude that defendants have met their burden under the stringent Riley test for source disclosure.

Defendants have attempted to obtain information relevant to their motion elsewhere, and therefore meet the first criterion under *Riley*. They called Vaira to testify regarding his knowledge of disclosures from his office. They also sought disclosure of "The Blumenthal Report," a Department of Justice investigation into the source of the ABSCAM leaks. . . . The district court denied their motion for release of the Blumenthal Report by order of July 31, 1980. . . . More importantly, however, Schaffer is the most logical source of information about the conversation with Vaira because she was the other participant in it. Having called Vaira, and having noted the unresolved questions regarding his testimony, defendants' next step was to call Schaffer.

The same analysis applies to the second criterion under *Riley*. The district court stated that the purpose of Schaffer's testimony was to shed light on Vaira's motivations in disclosing certain information to her and on his credibility. Only Schaffer will be able to testify to Vaira's credibility with respect to the conversation. Her recollection of Vaira's remarks in the context of the conversation is also a valuable source of information about his motives for disclosing, and particularly for initiating the dialogue with her. Defendants quite clearly have no other source from which they can acquire this insight.

The final criterion under *Riley*, relevance and importance to the particular proceeding, follows from the preceding discussion. To compile a complete record for purposes of the motion to dismiss for prosecutorial misconduct, the motivations and credibility of Vaira must be examined. We realize that defendants may fail in their attempt to prove outrageous conduct sufficient to warrant dismissal, but even though we cannot intimate the standards for granting their motions we can at least assume that motivation and credibility would be important to a court entertaining such a motion. We conclude, therefore, that defendants have met the test under *Riley* and, because no source disclosure is currently requested, that they have justified the court's order for Schaffer to answer the question put to her.

Appellant argues that if she testifies that Vaira did not speak to her, the subsequent line of questions may lead to disclosure of sources. This argument gets appellant nowhere. First, the district court has declared that it is going to rule on a question-by-question basis and that its intention is to have no additional sources revealed. Second, even though the court imposed strict limitations on the inquiry, we must not forget that *Riley* indicates the circumstances in which the reporter may not assert her qualified privilege. Satisfaction of the *Riley* test means that countervailing constitutional rights override the reporter's privilege to protect her sources. In view of the district court's announced limitations, and our assumption that future disputes will be resolved under the framework constructed in *Riley*, we do not reach the source disclosure issue here. We hold only that the district court did not err in ordering Schaffer to answer a question unrelated to source disclosure, and that her refusal to do so was grounds for civil contempt.

D.

Appellant also cannot bottom her claim on the abstract statement in *United States v. Cuthbertson*, 630 F.2d 139, 147 (3d Cir. 1980): "Nor does the fact that the government has obtained waivers from its witnesses waive the privilege. The privilege belongs to CBS, not the potential witnesses, and it may be waived only by its holder." As we have noted previously, Vaira admitted that he was a source. In the view we take; this is not a case of waiving any privilege. . . .

VI.

Accordingly, the order of the district court declaring appellant to be in civil contempt of the district court will be affirmed.

NOTES

1. For a detailed discussion of this privilege, *see* Edelstein & Lobue, *Journalist's Privilege and the Criminal Defendant*, 47 FORDHAM L. REV. 913 (1979); Goodale, Branzburg v. Hayes *and the Developing Qualified Privilege for Newsmen*, 26 HASTINGS L.J. 709 (1975); Muraski, *The Journalist's Privilege: Branzburg and Its Aftermath*, 52 TEX. L. REV. 829 (1974).

2. State laws vary in the protection they afford newsmen against process compelling the disclosure of sources. A comprehensive list of existing state legislation is set forth in Note, *Journalist's Privilege:* In re Farber *and the New Jersey Shield Law*, 32 RUTGERS L. REV. 545 (1979). Currently, there is no federal provision concerning this issue.

3. May an academic researcher be entitled to a privilege protecting his confidential sources and methods? *See In re Grand Jury Subpoena*, 583 F. Supp. 991 (E.D.N.Y. 1984).

4. How should the term "journalist" be defined? Suppose someone begins to gather research materials for personal reasons and later decides to publish a book when the materials become newsworthy. Is such a person a journalist? *See Von Bulow v. Von Bulow*, 811 F.2d 136 (2d Cir. 1987). *See generally* Note, *A Press Privilege for the Worst of Times*, 75 GEO. L.J. 361 (1986).

 EVIDENCE CHALLENGE: Challenge yourself to learn more about this topic. Enter the following address into your browser to access Evidence Challenge and apply these concepts to realistic problems set in a virtual courtroom.
http://www.EvidenceChallenge.com. Additional purchase required.

Chapter VII

BURDENS AND PRESUMPTIONS

Fleming James, *Burdens of Proof*
47 Va. L. Rev. 51, 51–58 (1961)[1]

The term "burden of proof" is used in our law to refer to two separate and quite different concepts. The distinction was not clearly perceived until it was pointed out by James Bradley Thayer in 1898. . . . The two distinct concepts may be referred to as (1) the risk of non-persuasion, or the burden of persuasion or simply persuasion burden; (2) the duty of producing evidence, the burden of going forward with the evidence, or simply the production burden or the burden of evidence.

RISK OF NON-PERSUASION OR PERSUASION BURDEN

Burden of proof often means what Wigmore has called the risk of non-persuasion. Wherever in human affairs a question of the existence or nonexistence of a fact is to be decided by somebody, there is the possibility that the decider, or trier of the fact, may at the end of his deliberations be in doubt on the question submitted to him. On all the material before him, he may, for example, regard the existence or non-existence of the fact as equally likely — a matter in equipoise. If, now, the trier is operating under a system which requires him to decide the question one way or the other, then to avoid caprice that system must furnish him with a rule for deciding the question when he finds his mind in this kind of doubt or equipoise. Where the parties to a civil action are in dispute over a material issue of fact, then that party who will lose if the trier's mind is in equipoise may be said to bear the risk that the trier will not be affirmatively persuaded or the risk of non-persuasion upon that issue.

* * *

Many civil cases are tried by a court without a jury; in them the judge acts as trier of fact as well as law. As trier of fact he may be faced with the problem of doubt or equipoise upon one or more issues. Where that is the case the judge must meet and resolve the problem and he does so under our system by applying the same guides or tests as would be laid down for a jury if it were deciding the issue.

Where an issue of fact is tried to a jury, it is the members of the jury whose minds may be in doubt or equipoise and the judge is not directly concerned in solving the

---

[1] Reprinted with permission.

problem. Under our system, however, the court does not leave this problem entirely to the jury, but attempts to formulate guides or tests for them in its charge. Moreover courts have devised different tests or measures of persuasion to be applied to different types of cases or issues. All this has meant:

(1) The court *allocates* the persuasion burden on each issue and thereby "decides each issue of fact which the jury is unable to decide"; that is he tells them what to do in case they cannot decide it.

(2) The court has tried to retain a measure of control over the jury's mental processes by describing for them the required measure of persuasion.

(3) To do so courts have had to formulate expressly these measures and tests and this had led to refinements — often over-refinements — of language, and to many reversals that might have been avoided had the court, as trier, applied the test without the need for making it articulate.

The usual formulation of the test in civil cases is that there must be a *preponderance of evidence* in favor of the party having the persuasion burden (the proponent) before he is entitled to a verdict. An alternative phrase often used is *greater weight* of the evidence. The general statement (in either form or both, coupled in the alternative as "preponderance or greater weight of the evidence") is usually explained as referring not to the number of witnesses or quantity of evidence but to the convincing force of the evidence.

$$* \quad * \quad *$$

All would agree that what counts is the jury's belief in the existence (or non-existence) of the disputed fact, and the extent to which the evidence actually produces that belief; surely we are not seeking the jury's estimate of the weight of evidence in the abstract, apart from its power actually to convince or persuade them. Moreover it is doubtful whether such abstract weighing can be done (except quantitatively as by counting noses). For these reasons a more meaningful and accurate statement would require the jury to believe that the existence of a fact is more probable than its nonexistence before they may find in favor of the party who has the burden to persuade the trier of the fact's existence. Some courts accept this formulation of the test; others have balked at it.

Most if not all courts accept the usual formulation of the test, and it is probably unlikely in fact to mislead a jury into making the difficult and abstract evaluations which the language literally invites. Indeed that meaning of the words used in describing the preponderance of evidence test would probably never occur to the average juryman, whose tendency will always be to interpret the charge in a personal and subjective way — in terms of his own feelings and experiences.

Another quite different question is whether the preponderance of evidence test (however phrased) is to be applied to all types of civil actions and to all issues in them. A much stronger degree of conviction or belief is, of course, required in criminal cases. There the burden is to show the guilt of the accused beyond a reasonable doubt. Such a test is scarcely ever applied to issues in civil actions. Yet courts have devised an intermediate test which is occasionally applied in civil controversies. This calls for "clear and convincing evidence" or evidence which is

"clear, precise and indubitable," before the proponent's persuasion burden is met.
. . .

BURDEN OF PRODUCING EVIDENCE

The second meaning which is commonly given to the term burden of proof refers to the burden of going forward with, or of producing evidence. This is sometimes called the burden of evidence or the production burden. Here again, as with the persuasion burden, a more accurate term might be the risk of nonproduction, but this expression is not in general use.

* * *

The production burden first comes into play at the very beginning of the trial. We have seen that the judge and jury do not have the responsibility of investigating cases or furnishing the evidence upon which they are to be decided. Our system leaves it to the parties to do those things. If, now, neither party offers any evidence at the trial, what will happen? The answer is that one party loses. He may, therefore, be said to bear the risk of this consequence of non-production of evidence. Or, as we more often say, he bears the burden of producing at least some evidence.

The next question is: how much evidence need the original proponent produce to lift this burden? The answer may be divided into two parts: (a) The proponent must introduce sufficient evidence to justify a verdict in his favor, (b) on each of the propositions of fact which he must establish as part of his case. This answer does not get us very far; it simply invites further inquiry and refers us to the concept of sufficiency of the evidence and the test for determining what propositions of fact constitute essential elements of the proponent's case rather than the case of his adversary — that is the test for allocating the production burden on each issue of fact in the case. . . .

We have seen that the consequence of failure to produce evidence — or sufficient evidence — is loss of the case. This loss is brought about by means of the procedural device of nonsuit, directed verdict, or dismissal. Each of these is an order made by the court either on motion of a party or on its own motion after the proponent has rested his case, *i.e.* has indicated that he has put in all the evidence upon the issue which he intends to — which may of course be no evidence at all.

Since it is the judge who passes upon such motions, it is the judge who determines questions of the sufficiency of evidence and who allocates the production burden on each issue. Thus these concepts may be viewed as part of the apparatus for controlling the jury. The court screens all cases initially to see whether they will even go to the jury.

We may next consider the consequences of the proponent's meeting, or lifting, the production burden. In the first place the proponent thereby escapes a non-suit, directed verdict, or dismissal when he rests his case. But is he entitled to more, for example, a directed verdict in his favor? He will not be, of course, if the opponent puts in controverting evidence as he usually does. But what if the opponent also rests his case at this point without putting in any evidence? Even then the proponent is not generally entitled to a directed verdict; the opponent is entitled to have the jury pass on the proponent's evidence. Testimony, even if uncontradicted, usually raises questions of credibility (*i.e.*, honesty, bias, accuracy of observation, memory, expression and the like). Circumstantial evidence usually permits more than one possible inference. Admitted conduct may often be evaluated differently (as reasonable, negligent, or the like) by different persons. All of these matters are properly for the jury.

* * *

So much for the usual case. It will sometimes happen, however, that the proponent's evidence leaves open no question of credibility, of evaluation of conduct, or of choice among competing inferences, about which reasonable minds might differ. In such a case the court will direct the verdict in favor of the proponent *unless* the opponent offers evidence to controvert or avoid the effect of the proponent's evidence. At this point the production burden rests on the party who was originally the opponent. The original opponent then may meet this burden by offering evidence which either (a) presents a question for the jury, so that the production burden rests on neither party, or (b) is of such compelling force as to shift the production burden back again to the party who bore it at the outset — the original proponent.

From the above, the following appears:

(1) The concept of the production burden is addressed to the court's function, not the jury's. It is simply a device whereby the court determines whether, if the trial were stopped at any given point, it would send the case to the jury. If not, the court decides the case and the jury has no role to play. If the case is sent to the jury, the production burden drops out of the case and has no role to play. The jury will be concerned only with the persuasion burden.

(2) The question of allocation of the production burden arises at the very beginning of the trial and at various points thereafter. And while this burden rests on one party at the beginning, it may shift to his opponent, and then shift back again.

(3) The concept has primarily a procedural consequence when evidence is available to both parties on the issue in question; it simply determines the order in which they shall put it in. Where, however, no evidence is available to a party on an issue, then the allocation to him of the production burden will mean that he loses upon that issue, and often upon the whole case. Thus in an action for wrongful death caused by negligence where there is no evidence, direct or circumstantial, of the decedent's own conduct leading up to his death, plaintiff cannot recover under a system which allocates to him the production burden on the issue of contributory negligence.

(4) The concept of a production burden will be fully applicable in cases tried to a judge without a jury, although the jury trial has probably pointed up and dramatized its importance. Under a system in which the tribunal itself or some other agency of society had the responsibility for acquiring the materials for decision on its own initiative, however, there would be no need to allocate the production burden to one of the parties.

California Law Revision Commission, A Study Relating to the Uniform Rules of Evidence — Burden of Producing Evidence, Burden of Proof, and Presumptions
6 Reports, Recommendations and Studies 1049, 1116–18 (1964)

Factors Determining the Allocation of Burdens

Thayer denied that we have a "right to look to the law of evidence for a solution of such questions" of allocation. On the whole, however, it is only in the writings on evidence law that any guidance is offered. The authors agree that there is no single guide. It is clear, also, that neither logic nor grammar will provide the answer. Thus, the writers are substantially in accord as to three general considerations that seem to determine the allocation of burdens: (1) policy, (2) fairness and convenience, and (3) probabilities. Each of these merits detailed discussion.

Policy. As an example of the influence of policy considerations on the allocation of burdens, Professor Cleary points out that freedom of a plaintiff from contributory negligence is an "essential element" of the plaintiff's right to recover under the common law rule. Whether or not it is a "defense" which is allocated to the defendant for the purposes of pleading, producing evidence, and persuading depends on how the court views it. Modern courts are not friendly to the rule of complete bar to recovery because of contributory negligence, however slight; as a consequence, they have allotted the burdens of pleading, proving, and persuading to the defendant. In other words, unless affirmatively persuaded that contributory negligence exists, the courts prefer to act as though it did not because the consequences of its existence are so drastic.

Fairness and Convenience. In many cases, superior access to proof is also a reason for assigning the initial burden to the defendant. An example Cleary uses is the payment of a debt sued upon. . . . California law is somewhat divided upon this issue at the pleading stage, some cases indicating that the plaintiff must plead nonpayment to state a cause of action. However, it is clear enough that the burden of producing evidence and the burden of persuasion rest upon the defendant and that he must plead payment to produce such evidence.

Another example, also discussed by Professor Cleary, is a bailee's liability for nonreturn of bailed goods. *George v. Bekins Van & Storage Co.* finally resolved for California a question which had been much discussed in California and elsewhere. Goods of the plaintiff in the possession of the defendant were destroyed by fire. It was at least as probable as not that the fire was caused by the negligence of defendant's employees; the evidence would have supported either finding. The question thus turned on which party had the burden of proof. With the aid of the Warehouse Receipts Act, the court held that the burden of proof of freedom from negligence was upon defendant Bekins as bailee. It is significant that the court held that "the burden of proving that the goods were not lost because of negligence is on the defendant, *whether plaintiff frames his complaint on a negligence or a breach of contract theory.*"

Analogous to the allocation of burden of proof because of greater access to evidence is one of the reasons underlying the doctrine of res ipsa loquitur. It functions more as a presumption, however . . . .

Much of the precedent on the burdens of pleading, of producing evidence, and of persuasion was crystallized before the inauguration of free discovery. Now that pretrial examination of witnesses and parties is permitted, and interrogatories to parties and opportunity to inspect are readily available, the question of access to evidence may be less significant than it previously was. . . .

Probability. One reason for determining which party should have the respective burdens is that one result is, generally speaking, more likely than another. Thus, Cleary suggests that one reason for having the defendant plead, prove, and persuade that a debt sued upon has been paid is that people are not prone to sue upon paid debts. Absent any evidence on the point of payment, the probabilities are that the debt, if one was owed, has not been paid. This justifies placing the burden of producing evidence on the defendant. Even when evidence is produced, it is best to resolve the issue against the defendant unless the trier of fact is persuaded that payment was made.

This is a purely statistical evaluation of the problem. Thus, if one assumes that 80 out of every 100 debts sued upon have not been paid, then the best overall justice will be achieved by acting as if none have been paid. All plaintiffs will prevail on the issue where there is no evidence or where the trier of fact is not persuaded by the evidence. However, it is better to have 100 win, although only 80 should have won, than to have 100 lose, where only 20 should have lost.

Again, the analogy to *res ipsa loquitur* should be noted. Flour barrels usually, although not always, do not roll out of lofts unless the person in possession has been negligent.

An aspect of probability which Professor Cleary does not mention is procedural economy. If, using the hypothesis above, 80 percent of all debts sued upon have not been paid, it is wasteful to the parties and to the courts to require all plaintiffs to prove nonpayment when in only 20 percent of the cases is there any question about the matter. One method of avoiding the waste is to put the burden of pleading payment upon the defendant. This helps identify those cases in which there is an issue about payment. It does not necessarily follow that the burden of producing evidence and the burden of persuasion should also be placed upon the defendant; this point is illustrated by the practice of requiring the defendant to specify that conditions precedent have not been performed before the plaintiff, suing on a contract, is required to produce evidence on the subject.

NOTES

1.   For another classic study on burden of proof concepts, *see* Cleary, *Presuming and Pleading: An Essay on Juristic Immaturity*, 12 Stan. L. Rev. 5 (1959).

2.   The distinctions between various burdens of persuasion are ably discussed in *United States v. Fatico*, 458 F. Supp. 388 (E.D.N.Y. 1978), *aff'd*, 603 F.2d 1053 (2d Cir. 1979), *cert. denied*, 444 U.S. 1073 (1980).

David W. Louisell, *Construing Rule 301: Instructing the Jury on Presumptions in Civil Actions and Proceedings*
63 Va. L. Rev. 281, 289–92 (1977)[2]

PROBLEMS OF DEFINITION: PRESUMPTIONS, INFERENCES, PRIMA FACIE CASE, RES IPSA LOQUITUR

Neither rule 301 nor any of the other Federal Rules of Evidence defines, lists, or illustrates presumptions. Rule 301 simply assumes the existence of presumptions and prescribes their function. Therefore, a mastery of rule 301 requires an understanding of the definitional problems that have plagued presumptions. While some of the earlier confusion in terminology has been overcome, the use of different words for the same idea or of the same word for different ideas continues to threaten to distort the application of rule 301.[3]

* * *

Rule 301 is concerned with true presumptions, otherwise known as rebuttable presumptions. Such presumptions require the assumption of one fact upon proof of another fact in the absence of adequate evidence contradicting the assumed fact.

Regardless of the terminology used to express such rules, so-called "conclusive presumptions" — if truly conclusive — are rules of law that no amount of proof will dislodge. For example, if proof that a child was born during wedlock creates a "conclusive presumption" of legitimacy, then proof of such a birth precludes evidence of illegitimacy as a matter of controlling substantive law.[4] Similarly, it is often said that a child proved to be under seven years of age is "conclusively presumed" not to have been able to commit a felony. This is only an indirect way of saying that the substantive law renders a child under seven incapable of committing a felony. Therefore, the so-called "conclusive presumption" is an awkward synonym for an absolute legal rule. Rule 301 governs only true, or rebuttable, presumptions.

The expressions "mandatory presumption" and "permissive presumption" sometimes appear in the cases, especially the older ones. By definition, a presumption is a required conclusion in the absence of adequate countervailing evidence. Therefore the term "mandatory presumption" is redundant; the precise term is simply "presumption." "Permissive presumption" when intended to mean that the fact finder may draw the conclusion, but is not *compelled* to do so, in the absence of sufficient countervailing evidence is a synonym for inference. The preferred term is

---

[2] Reprinted with permission.

[3] [20] Jury instructions should not include the words "presumption," "presume," "inference," or "infer." These words, so often misunderstood and confused by lawyers, will almost certainly be misunderstood and confused by jurors. Better practice is to avoid them altogether when instructing the jury.

[4] [22] California statutes create a "conclusive" presumption of legitimacy and a rebuttable presumption of paternity. Compare Cal. Evid. Code § 621 (West Supp. 1977) ("Notwithstanding any other provision of law, the issue of a wife cohabiting with her husband who is not impotent or sterile, is conclusively presumed to be . . . a child of the marriage . . . .") with Cal. Civ. Code § 7004 (West Supp. 1976) (rebuttable presumption that a man is the natural father of a child if the man was married to the natural mother within 300 days preceding the birth).

"inference," because it is clearly distinct from "presumption," as set forth in more detail below.

* * *

An inference is a deduction, warranted by human reason and experience, that the trier of fact may make on the basis of established facts — a process of reasoning from premise to conclusion without the directive force of a rule of law, which characterizes a presumption. The expressions "mandatory" or "compulsory inference" and "permissive inference" are confusing. If an inference is truly mandatory, it amounts to a presumption. "Permissive inference" is redundant. Perhaps on occasion the use of "compulsory inference" is justified to indicate an inference so strong as to be arguably obligatory for reasonable minds, although not amounting to a recognized presumption.

"Prima facie case" is an ambiguous expression. When used to mean evidence so cogent as to require a particular conclusion in the absence of explanation, prima facie case has the probative effect of a presumption. When used to mean evidence only cogent enough to permit the suggested conclusion, it has the effect of an inference.

A final definitional word should be added about the doctrine of *res ipsa loquitur*, called by Dean Prosser "a simple matter of circumstantial evidence." Under the majority view, *res ipsa loquitur* amounts only to an inference of negligence. Some courts, however, have given the doctrine the significance of a true presumption, under its aegis even shifting to the defendant the burden of proof (which may be sound where the facts imply great rational force for the doctrine's application). The California Evidence Code has an elaborate section on *res ipsa loquitur* that centers around a provision that the doctrine is a presumption affecting the burden of production. Neither rule 301 nor any of the other Federal Rules of Evidence helps to classify *res ipsa loquitur* as either a presumption or an inference.

**CALIFORNIA LAW REVISION COMMISSION,
A STUDY RELATING TO THE UNIFORM RULES OF
EVIDENCE —BURDEN OF PRODUCING EVIDENCE,
BURDEN OF PROOF, AND PRESUMPTIONS**
6 Reports, Recommendations and Studies 1049, 1051–57 (1964)

The URE Presumptions Article

Rules 13 through 16, constituting Article III of the Uniform Rules of Evidence, provide as follows:

RULE 13. *Definitions.* A presumption is an assumption of fact resulting from a rule of law which requires such fact to be assumed from another fact or group of facts found or otherwise established in the action.

RULE 14. *Effect of Presumptions.* Subject to Rule 16, and except for presumptions which are conclusive or irrefutable under the rules of law from which they arise, (a) if the facts from which the presumption is derived have any probative value as evidence of the existence of the presumed fact, the presumption continues to exist and the burden of establishing the non-existence of the presumed fact is upon the party against whom the presumption operates, (b) if the facts from which the presumption arises have no probative value as evidence of the presumed fact, the presumption does not exist when evidence is introduced which would support a finding of the non-existence of the presumed fact, and the fact which would otherwise be presumed shall be determined from the evidence exactly as if no presumption was or had ever been involved.

RULE 15. *Inconsistent Presumptions.* If two presumptions arise which are conflicting with each other the judge shall apply the presumption which is founded on the weightier considerations of policy and logic. If there is no such preponderance both presumptions shall be disregarded.

RULE 16. *Burden of Proof Not Relaxed as to Some Presumptions.* A presumption, which by a rule of law may be overcome only by proof beyond a reasonable doubt, or by clear and convincing evidence, shall not be affected by Rules 14 or 15 and the burden of proof to overcome it continues on the party against whom the presumption operates.

The Thayer View Versus the Morgan View

For a better understanding of Uniform Rules 13–16, their background should be surveyed. This requires taking note of various theories[5] respecting the nature of presumptions. The two major theories will be referred to frequently throughout this

---

[5] [2] Professor Morgan has discovered and stated a total of eight divergent theories which he summarizes as follows:

1. The presumption has no effect whenever there is evidence in the case from which a jury could reasonably find the non-existence of the presumed fact. It is immaterial that neither judge nor jury believes the testimony. If the evidence is introduced before the basic fact is established, there is no compelled assumption; if after the basic fact is established, the compulsion ceases. The issue as to the existence or non-existence of the presumed fact is to be determined exactly as if no such presumption were known to the law. In short, the presumption fixes only the risk of non-production of evidence sufficient to justify a finding of non-existence of the presumed fact. This view is approved by Thayer, Wigmore, and the American Law Institute and is found stated in numerous judicial opinions.

2. Where there is such evidence in the case, the presumption is operative only if the jury positively disbelieves the evidence.

3. Where there is such evidence in the case, the presumption is operative unless and until the jury believes the evidence.

In these two situations what conclusion as to the non-existence of the presumed fact the jury would draw from the evidence is immaterial. Only a very few opinions exhibit either of these views, and other decisions by the same courts clearly indicate disapproval of them.

4. The effect which the first view gives to the presence in the case of evidence sufficient to justify a finding of the non-existence of the presumed fact occurs only where the evidence is "substantial." The cases expressing this doctrine do not define "substantial," but they do make it clear that the evidence must be of greater persuasive effect than the minimum which would carry the issue to the jury. At times they point out that the rule is not satisfied by testimony from interested witnesses, and in some instances seem to require evidence that would almost, if not quite, call for a directed verdict.

5. The compelled assumption persists until the jury is convinced that the non-existence of the

study. At the outset, therefore, they should be considered rather extensively.

The "Thayer Doctrine"

Writing in 1898, in his learned *Preliminary Treatise*, James Bradley Thayer of Harvard described as follows the nature and office of a presumption: "[F]ixing the duty of going forward with proof . . . *and this alone*, appears to be characteristic and essential work of the presumption." [Emphasis added.]

Thayer thus gave birth to what has since become known as the "Thayerian Doctrine." Under this doctrine, any evidence which would warrant a finding of the nonexistence of the presumed fact causes the presumption to disappear. When such evidence is introduced, the existence or nonexistence of the presumed fact is to be determined precisely as if no presumption had ever been operative in the case. It follows that the judge — and the judge alone — is to determine whether a presumption has been rebutted. If he decides that the evidence would *not* warrant a finding of nonexistence, he directs the jury to find the presumed fact. The presumption is undispelled and, therefore, requires a finding of the presumed fact. If he finds that the evidence would warrant a finding of nonexistence, he submits the issue to the jury, saying nothing of the presumption — for that has disappeared — and charging the jury as if no presumption had ever been operative. Put another way, a presumption exerts its force by requiring the opponent of the presumption to produce enough evidence to avoid an adverse directed verdict. But this is all a presumption does; when the opponent has satisfied this requirement, the force of the presumption is spent and the presumption disappears. It follows that the presumption should not be the subject of any charge to the jury. As Judge Learned Hand has said: "If the trial is properly conducted, the presumption will not be mentioned at all."

Beginning with his first edition in 1904, Wigmore adopted Thayer's view and adhered to it in the subsequent editions of his monumental work. Wigmore's early and continuous endorsement has naturally caused Thayer's view to gain wide

---

presumed fact is as likely or as probable as its existence. This seems to be the result of decisions in Ohio and California.

6. The establishment of the basic fact fixes the burden of persuasion as well as the burden of producing evidence upon the party relying upon the non-existence of the presumed fact. This was once believed to be accepted doctrine in Pennsylvania; and it is the rule applied with reference to some presumptions in other states.

7. Where the presumption is created because the opponent has peculiar knowledge or peculiar access to the evidence of facts from which the existence or non-existence of the presumed fact may be deduced, the presumption fixes the burden of persuasion as to those facts upon the opponent, but does not affect that burden as to the presumed fact itself. This view was advocated by Professor Bohlen as to the presumption of negligence of a railroad company in an action by a passenger for injuries received in a wreck of the train, and has been applied in cases of statutory presumptions as to the responsibility of the owner of an automobile for the conduct of its driver.

8. Though the compelled assumption ceases to operate under the conditions prescribed by the first, fourth or fifth views mentioned above, it is to be given the effect of evidence tending to prove the existence of the presumed fact. [MORGAN, BASIC PROBLEMS OF EVIDENCE 33–35 (1954). . . .]

The major theories are numbers one and six.

acceptance — so much so that today it is appropriate to call this view "orthodox." The Supreme Court of Oregon has given the following colorful summary of this classic view:

> [W]hen evidence is introduced to rebut the presumption — however weak the evidence may be — the presumption is overcome and destroyed. Some text writers, law professors, and judges who have espoused the Wigmore doctrine have vied with one another in an effort to show how flimsy and unsubstantial a presumption of law really is. This "phantom of the law" has been likened to "bats flitting about in the twilight and then disappearing in the sunshine of actual facts," and to a house of cards that topples over when rebutted by evidence. It remained for Professor Bohlen to head the class when he said a presumption of law was like Maeterlinck's male bee which, after functioning, disappeared.

If a jurisdiction which does not presently adhere to the Thayer doctrine wished to adopt it by legislation, the appropriate text for a statute to accomplish this objective might be formulated as follows:

> A presumption does not continue to exist when evidence is introduced which would support a finding of the nonexistence of the presumed fact, and the fact which would otherwise be presumed shall be determined from the evidence exactly as if no presumption had ever been involved.

The following example illustrates how this statute would operate. Suppose plaintiff, having the burden of proof to show the death of X, proves that X has been absent for a period of seven years and that no tidings have been received from X. This, of course, gives rise to a presumption (the so-called "Enoch Arden presumption") that X is dead. Defendant, conceding the seven years' absence and want of tidings, has X's brother, Y, testify that Y saw "X" recently at an airport in a distant city; that "X" was boarding a plane and Y got only a fleeting glimpse of him; that Y was unable to attract "X's" attention and received no sign of recognition from him. Now, defendant's evidence, "would support a finding of the nonexistence of the presumed fact" (that is, if the jury found on the basis of this evidence that X is alive and if the trial judge refused a new trial for insufficiency of the evidence to support the verdict, the appellate court would not reverse the judgment). This being so, the presumption disappears. However, the facts which once raised the now-vanished presumption (X's absence and want of tidings) remain in the case as circumstantial evidence of sufficient force to require the submission of the case to the jury. That is, these facts have logical value as the foundation for a permissible deduction of death which the jury may or may not infer. Summarizing the situation in terms of labels, the *presumption* of death is dispelled; the *inference* of death remains; the inference is adequate to make *a prima facie* case. This is, therefore, a case to be submitted to the jury, and the issue is to be determined from the evidence — *i.e.*, plaintiff's evidence of disappearance and defendant's evidence of his recognition witness — "exactly as if no presumption had ever been involved." In charging the jury, therefore, the judge must omit all references to the presumption; he must charge the jury of plaintiff's burden of proof; and he may, if the law of his jurisdiction permits, make such reasonable comment on the weight of the evidence as his discretion suggests.

The "Morgan Theory"

Dissent from Thayerian orthodoxy began with an article published by Professor Bohlen in 1920. Since that time, other respected writers — notably Morgan and McCormick — have likewise become dissident, and the second major theory of presumptions, which may appropriately be called the "Morgan Theory," has emerged.

Morgan attacks the Thayer doctrine on the following grounds: A presumption, as conceived by Thayer, is a paradox — so strong that it controls absent countervailing evidence, yet so weak that it vanishes in the face of merely enough evidence to forestall a directed verdict. (The word "merely" is used because even evidence of very questionable credibility may preclude a directed verdict.) As Morgan expresses this in his own words: "It seems absurd to say that considerations of sufficient worth to cause a court or a legislature to create a presumption upon the establishment of a basic fact having logical significance can be utterly destroyed by the mere introduction of evidence which has no persuasive effect upon the judge or jury, or which, indeed, neither judge nor jury believes." Thus, he contends, a presumption should "have enough vitality to survive the introduction of opposing evidence which the trier of fact deems worthless or of slight value." However, a presumption, if it is to be an efficient legal tool, must (1) be left in the hands of the judge to administer and not be submitted to a jury for a decision as to when it shall cease to have compelling force, (2) be so administered that the jury never hear the word, presumption, used, since it carries unpredictable connotations to different minds. The rule, Morgan holds, which best meets these tests is "a rule which gives a presumption the effect of fixing the burden of persuasion," for:

> A party with that burden cannot discharge it by the introduction of evidence which has no convincing power with the trier of fact. His evidence must be credited and must have persuasive force. If a presumption have any appreciable effect other than merely fixing the burden of producing evidence, it can have no less effect than would be given to an item of evidence of sufficient weight to tip mental scales which are in equilibrium. This is not to say that the presumption is evidence or is to be treated as evidence. It is to say merely that a presumption is a procedural device for securing a decision of a disputed question of fact when the mind of the trier is in equilibrium, that is, when the trier thinks that the existence and non-existence of the fact are equally probable.

> Surely it is reasonable to give to a presumption the perfectly definite effect of (1) fixing the risk of non-production of evidence sufficient to justify a finding of the non-existence of the presumed fact and (2) determining the result where without it the mind of the trier is in equilibrium as to the existence or non-existence of the fact. For it must be remembered that the reasons which cause the creation of presumptions are very similar to those which cause the fixing of the burden of persuasion. Such a rule is easy of application. The judge need never mention the word, presumption, to the jury.

McCormick's analysis differs somewhat from Morgan's, albeit he reaches substantially the same conclusion. McCormick's approach may be summarized as follows: Thayer's doctrine that the judge shall not charge the jury respecting presumptions works an injustice when taken in connection with the rule (presently in force in most states) which forbids the judge to comment upon the weight of evidence or the credibility of the witnesses. Thus, suppose P, possessing the burden of proof of an issue, relies wholly on a presumption; that is, P establishes the basic facts necessary to invoke the presumption and rests. D testifies, admitting P's basic facts but directly contradicting the presumed fact. Now, according to Thayer, P's presumption has vanished; P's only remaining stake is the logical inference, if any, which may be derived from P's basic facts — the facts that previously raised the now spent presumption. Although these facts may constitute cogent circumstantial evidence, this is most difficult for the jury to understand. Juries are notoriously suspicious of inferential, circumstantial evidence and overly credulous of direct evidence. In the case under consideration, therefore, there is the danger that the jury will think that P's evidence could not possibly be "a preponderance" sufficient to satisfy P's burden. Despite all this, the judge is helpless to advise the jury respecting P's situation. Under Thayer's doctrine, he can say nothing of a presumption; under the no-comment rule, he can say nothing of the weight of P's evidence. Being thus tongue-tied, he can do no more than tell the jury of P's burden of proof. McCormick suggests that this is unjust to P. He maintains that the best solution is to (1) give the presumption the effect of shifting the burden of proof, and (2) advise the jury of the presumption, telling them that the presumption means D has the burden of proof. This unloads the dice as far as P is concerned, does not operate unfairly upon D, and calls for a charge to the jury in terms they can readily understand. In other words:

> [T]he presumption is a "working" hypothesis which works by shifting the burden to the party against whom it operates of satisfying the jury that the presumed inference is untrue. This often gives a more satisfactory apportionment of the burden of persuasion on a particular issue than can be given by the general rule that the pleader has the burden. One looks rather to the ultimate goal, the case or defense as a whole, the other to a particular fact-problem within the case. Moreover, an instruction that the presumption stands until the jury are persuaded to the contrary, has the advantage that it seems to make sense, and so far as we may judge by the other forms thus far invented of instructions on presumptions by that name, I think we can say that it is almost the only one that does.

Uniform Rule of Evidence 301(a) & (b) (1974)

Rule 301. [Presumptions in General in Civil Actions and Proceedings]

(a) Effect. In all actions and proceedings not otherwise provided for by statute or by these rules, a presumption imposes on the party against whom it is directed the burden of proving that the nonexistence of the presumed fact is more probable than its existence.

(b) Inconsistent Presumptions. If presumptions are inconsistent, the presumption applies that is founded upon weightier considerations of policy. If considerations of policy are of equal weight neither presumption applies.

Model Code of Evidence 704(1) & (2) (1942)

Rule 704. Effect of Presumptions.

(1) Subject to Rule 703, when the basic fact of a presumption has been established in an action, the existence of the presumed fact must be assumed unless and until evidence has been introduced which would support a finding of its non-existence or the basic fact of an inconsistent presumption has been established.

(2) Subject to Rule 703, when the basic fact of a presumption has been established in an action and evidence has been introduced which would support a finding of the non-existence of the presumed fact or the basic fact of an inconsistent presumption has been established, the existence or non-existence of the presumed fact is to be determined exactly as if no presumption had ever been applicable in the action.

NOTES AND QUESTIONS

1. Which theory of presumptions was ultimately adopted by the Federal Rules of Evidence?

2. How does Uniform Rule of Evidence 301 differ from an earlier version of the Uniform Rules as set forth *supra*? What policy reasons underlie the change in perspective? *See* Gausewitz, *Presumptions in a One-Rule World*, 5 Vand. L. Rev. 324 (1952).

3. What quantum of evidence should be required to rebut a Thayerian presumption? *See In re Emerald Oil Co.*, 695 F.2d 833 (5th Cir. 1983).

4. For an interesting criticism of Morgan's burden shifting presumptions, see Lansing, *Enough Is Enough: A Critique of the Morgan View of Rebuttable Presumptions in Civil Cases*, 62 Or. L. Rev. 485 (1983).

5. What alternatives to the Thayer and Morgan approaches are available? For example, once rebutted, would it be plausible (and appropriate) to treat the presumption as either evidence or as a permissive inference? *See* McCormick's Handbook of the Law of Evidence § 345, at 825 (2d ed. 1972); Morgan, *Instructing the Jury upon Presumptions and Burdens of Proof*, 47 Harv. L. Rev. 59 (1933). Might another possibility be to raise the standard of evidence necessary to rebut a presumption? *See* Morgan's divergent theories in footnote 2 in the second California Law Revision Commission, *supra*.

ESTATE OF McGOWAN
250 N.W.2d 234 (Neb. 1977)

McCown, Justice.

This is an action to contest the admission of a will to probate on the grounds of lack of testamentary capacity and undue influence. The county court of Douglas County admitted the will to probate and the contestants appealed to the District Court. The case was tried to a jury in the District Court and the jury found in favor of the proponent and against the contestants on both grounds. The District Court entered judgment admitting the will to probate and the contestants have appealed.

Joseph L. McGowan died at Omaha, Nebraska, on April 14, 1973, leaving a last will and testament. He was 80 years old and a bachelor. His nearest relatives and only heirs-at-law were two nieces and three nephews, the children of his deceased brother. The proponent, who was the principal beneficiary and executor under the will, was Thomas F. McGowan, a second cousin and a godson of the testator.

The estate consisted exclusively of personal property, principally stocks, bonds, and cash, with a value of approximately $770,000. Approximately $40,000 of that amount was in the stock of Uncle Sam Breakfast Food Company, a closely held family corporation.

The will, after several minor bequests, left all the Uncle Sam Breakfast Food Company stock in equal shares to the five nieces and nephews or the survivors of them. The remainder of the estate was left to the First National Bank of Omaha in trust for the benefit of Thomas F. McGowan during his lifetime. Upon his death, or when the younger of his two named sons became 25 years of age, whichever was later, the trust was to terminate and be distributed to the two sons or their children by right of representation.

*　　*　　*

The contentions of the contestants on this appeal rest on the assertion that the instructions to the jury erroneously placed the burden on the contestants to prove undue influence. The argument is grounded on the assumption that the evidence was sufficient to establish a presumption of undue influence, and that under the provisions of section 27-301, R.R.S. 1943, the establishment of the presumption shifted the burden of proof from the contestants to the proponent and the instructions were therefore erroneous. The critical issues involve the effect of section 27-301, R.R.S. 1943, and whether it applies to a "presumption" of undue influence in the making and execution of a will.

Section 27-301, R.R.S. 1943, is a part of the Nebraska Evidence Rules adopted by the Legislature in 1975, and is effective as to all trials commenced after December 31, 1975. That section provides: "In all cases not otherwise provided for by statute or by these rules a presumption imposes on the party against whom it is directed the burden of proving that the nonexistence of the presumed fact is more probable than its existence."

Prior to the effective date of section 27-301, R.R.S. 1943, the effect of a presumption in Nebraska was only to shift the burden of going forward with the evidence, and the burden of proof or persuasion did not shift. When evidence was introduced to rebut the presumption, the presumption disappeared. The presumption was not evidence itself but only sustained the burden of proof until evidence rebutting the presumption was introduced. . . .

The Nebraska Evidence Rules, including section 27-301, R.R.S. 1943, were essentially the same as the then proposed Federal Rules of Evidence, but were adopted by the Nebraska Legislature prior to the final adoption of the federal rules by Congress. When Congress finally adopted the federal rules later in the same year, Rule 301 was completely changed. Instead of the language of section 27-301,

R.R.S. 1943, Rule 301 of Public Law 93-595 reads: "In all civil actions and proceedings not otherwise provided for by Act of Congress or by these rules, a presumption imposes on the party against whom it is directed the burden of going forward with evidence to rebut or meet the presumption, but does not shift to such party the burden of proof in the sense of the risk of non-persuasion, which remains throughout the trial upon the party on whom it was originally cast." In essence, the new federal rule is the former Nebraska rule. Although the Nebraska Legislature adopted the proposed version of federal Rule 301, it did not adopt the special section on the procedural effect of that rule. Neither the Nebraska rules nor the federal rules define or prescribe what constitutes a presumption within the meaning of Rule 301.

A presumption is a standardized practice under which certain facts are held to call for uniform treatment with respect to their effect as proof of other facts. McCormick on Evidence (2d ed.), § 342, p. 802. The same authority suggests that "presumption" is the slipperiest member of the family of legal terms, except its first cousin, "burden of proof." Reasons for the creation of presumptions are numerous and the treatment of presumptions also differs widely. There are at least eight senses in which the term has been used by courts. The former Nebraska approach to presumptions is ordinarily referred to as the "bursting bubble" theory. Under that approach when evidence was introduced to rebut the presumption, the presumption disappeared and the burden of proof or persuasion did not shift. Under such a rule whether a particular set of basic facts gave rise to the dignity of a presumption was ordinarily not critical in the matter of instructing a jury after trial. What was many times referred to as a "presumption" was often merely a permissible or probable inference, or was a method of indicating that the evidence was sufficient to withstand a motion for a directed verdict or to constitute a prima facie case. In terms of instructions to the jury the new rule poses far greater problems. An additional problem is posed in a case such as this because the presumed fact of undue influence is also the ultimate fact to be determined by the jury.

Ordinarily the basic facts which give rise to a true presumption are specific and definite. They can be readily determined and uniformly applied. That is not the case with the so-called presumption of undue influence in Nebraska. An analysis of the Nebraska cases demonstrates that the basic facts which have been held to give rise to a presumption of undue influence in the making of a will have not been specific nor definite nor uniform. Instead the basic facts have themselves varied, and have been formulated from the facts and circumstances of each particular case. Almost without exception we have used the term "presumption" in connection with undue influence to mean that the evidence was sufficient to constitute a prima facie case or to withstand a motion for a directed verdict. In most instances the term "presumption" seems to have been intended to mean a permissible or probable inference when used in undue influence cases.

The Report of the Committee on Practice and Procedure in connection with the proposed Nebraska Rules of Evidence confirms the conclusion that this court can place the burden of proof in the first place, or hold that a particular set of basic facts does not rise to the dignity of a presumption under the rule. It is also obvious that situations which have previously been referred to as presumptions when only permissible or probable inference was meant, or those where the term "presumption" was used to indicate that the basic facts were sufficient to constitute a prima facie case or to withstand a motion for directed verdict, are cases which may be excluded from the operation of the rule. *See* Proposed Nebraska Rules of Evidence, Article III, Presumptions, p. 35 (1973).

We therefore hold that under Nebraska law a so-called "presumption of undue influence" is not a presumption within the ambit and meaning of section 27-301, R.R.S. 1943.

The policy considerations which support the right of a competent testator to dispose of his property at death by a duly executed will also demand that the burden of proof on the issue of undue influence be placed upon the party contesting the will. We therefore hold that in a will contest the burden of proof or the risk of non-persuasion on the issue of undue influence is on the contestant and remains there throughout the trial.

In the case at bar it is clear that the factual issues of undue influence were for the jury, and that the instructions placed the burden of proof on the contestants, and the jury brought in its verdict for the proponent. If the instructions properly placed the burden of proof, the verdict and judgment must be affirmed. In view of the determinations made, the burden of proof was properly placed and the judgment is affirmed.

AFFIRMED.

TEXAS DEPARTMENT OF COMMUNITY AFFAIRS v. BURDINE
450 US. 248 (1981)

JUSTICE POWELL delivered the opinion of the Court.

This case requires us to address again the nature of the evidentiary burden placed upon the defendant in an employment discrimination suit brought under Title VII of the Civil Rights Act of 1964, 42 U.S.C. § 2000e *et seq*. The narrow question presented is whether, after the plaintiff has proved a prima facie case of discriminatory treatment, the burden shifts to the defendant to persuade the court by a preponderance of the evidence that legitimate, nondiscriminatory reasons for the challenged employment action existed.

I

Petitioner, the Texas Department of Community Affairs (TDCA), hired respondent, a female, in January 1972, for the position of accounting clerk in the Public Service Careers Division (PSC). PSC provided training and employment opportunities in the public sector for unskilled workers. When hired, respondent possessed several years' experience in employment training. She was promoted to Field Services Coordinator in July 1972. Her supervisor resigned in November of that year, and respondent was assigned additional duties. Although she applied for the supervisor's position of Project Director, the position remained vacant for six months

PSC was funded completely by the United States Department of Labor. The Department was seriously concerned about inefficiencies at PSC. In February 1973, the Department notified the Executive Director of TDCA, B.R. Fuller, that it would terminate PSC the following month. TDCA officials, assisted by respondent, persuaded the Department to continue funding the program conditioned upon PSC's reforming its operations. Among the agreed conditions were the appointment of a permanent Project Director and a complete reorganization of the PSC staff.

After consulting with personnel within TDCA, Fuller hired a male from another division of the agency as Project Director. In reducing the PSC staff, he fired respondent along with two other employees, and retained another male, Walz, as the only professional employee in the division. Respondent soon was rehired by TDCA and assigned to another division of the agency. She received the exact salary paid to the Project Director at PSC, and the subsequent promotions she has received have kept her salary and responsibilities commensurate with what she would have received had she been appointed Project Director.

Respondent alleged that the failure to promote and the subsequent decision to terminate her had been predicated on gender discrimination in violation of Title VII. After a bench trial, the District Court held that neither decision was based on gender discrimination. The court relied on the testimony of Fuller that the employment decisions necessitated by the commands of the Department of Labor were based on consultation among trusted advisors and nondiscriminatory evaluation of the relative qualifications of the individuals involved. He testified that the three individuals terminated did not work well together, and that TDCA thought that eliminating this problem would improve PSC's efficiency. The court accepted this explanation as rational and, in effect, found no evidence that the decisions not to promote and to terminate respondent were prompted by gender discrimination.

The [Fifth Circuit] Court of Appeals held that the District Court's "implicit evidentiary finding" that the male hired as Project Director was better qualified for that position than respondent was not clearly erroneous. Accordingly, the court affirmed the District Court's finding that respondent was not discriminated against when she was not *promoted*. The Court of Appeals, however, reversed the District Court's finding that Fuller's testimony sufficiently had rebutted respondent's prima facie case of gender discrimination in the decision to *terminate* her employment at PSC. The court reaffirmed its previously announced views that the defendant in a Title VII case bears the burden of proving by a preponderance of the evidence the existence of legitimate nondiscriminatory reasons for the employment action and that the defendant also must prove by objective evidence that those hired or promoted were better qualified than the plaintiff. The court found that Fuller's testimony did not carry either of these evidentiary burdens. It, therefore, reversed the judgment of the District Court and remanded the case for computation of backpay. Because the decision of the Court of Appeals as to the burden of proof borne by the defendant conflicts with interpretations of our precedents adopted by other Courts of Appeals, we granted certiorari. We now vacate the Fifth Circuit's decision and remand for application of the correct standard.

II

In *McDonnell Douglas Corp. v. Green*, 411 U.S. 792 (1973), we set forth the basic allocation of burdens and order of presentation of proof in a Title VII case alleging discriminatory treatment. First, the plaintiff has the burden of proving by the preponderance of the evidence a prima facie case of discrimination. Second, if the plaintiff succeeds in proving the prima facie case, the burden shifts to the defendant "to articulate some legitimate, nondiscriminatory reason for the employee's rejection." *Id.*, at 802. Third, should the defendant carry this burden, the plaintiff must then have an opportunity to prove by a preponderance of the evidence that the legitimate reasons offered by the defendant were not its true reasons, but were a pretext for discrimination; *Id.*, at 804.

The nature of the burden that shifts to the defendant should he understood in light of the plaintiff's ultimate and intermediate burdens. The ultimate burden of persuading the trier of fact that the defendant intentionally discriminated against the plaintiff remains at all times with the plaintiff. *See generally* 9 J. WIGMORE, EVIDENCE § 2489 (3d ed. 1940) (the burden of persuasion "never shifts").

The burden of establishing a prima facie case of disparate treatment is not onerous. The plaintiff must prove by a preponderance of the evidence that she applied for an available position for which she was qualified, but was rejected under circumstances which give rise to an inference of unlawful discrimination.[6] The prima facie ease serves an important function in the litigation: it eliminates the most common nondiscriminatory reasons for the plaintiff's rejection. As this Court explained in *Furnco Construction Corp. v. Waters*, 438 U.S. 567, 577 (1978), the prima facie case "raises an inference of discrimination only because we presume these acts, if otherwise unexplained, are more likely than not based on the consideration of impermissible factors." Establishment of the prima facie case in effect creates a presumption that the employer unlawfully discriminated against the employee. If the trier of fact believes the. Plaintiff's evidence, and if the employer is silent in the lace of the presumption, the court must enter judgment for the plaintiff because no issue of fact remains in the case.[7] [Have we seen cases skipping the "belief" requirement? — Ed.]

---

[6] In McDonnell Douglas, supra, we described an appropriate model for a prima facie case of racial discrimination. The plaintiff must show:

> (i) that he belongs to a racial minority; (ii) that he applied and was qualified for a job for which the employer was seeking applicants; (iii) that, despite his qualifications he was rejected; and (iv) that, after his rejection, the position remained open and the employer continued to seek applicants from persons of complainant's qualifications.

411 U.S. at 802.

In the instant case, it is not seriously contested that respondent has proved a prima facie case. She showed that she was a qualified woman who sought an available position, but the position was left open for several months before she finally was rejected in favor of a male, Walz, who had been under her supervision.

[7] The phrase "prima facie case" may denote not only the establishment of a legally mandatory, rebuttable presumption, but also may be used by courts to describe the plaintiff's burden of producing enough evidence to permit the trier of fact to infer the fact at issue. 9 J WIGMORE, EVIDENCE § 2494 (3d ed. 1940). McDonnell Douglas should have made it apparent that in the Title VII context we use "prima facie case" in the former sense.

The burden that shifts to the defendant, therefore, is to rebut the presumption of discrimination by producing evidence that the plaintiff was rejected, or someone else was preferred, for a legitimate, nondiscriminatory reason. The defendant need not persuade the court that it was actually motivated by the proffered reasons. It is sufficient if the defendant's evidence raises a genuine issue of fact as to whether it discriminated against the plaintiff.[8] To accomplish this, the defendant must clearly set forth, through the introduction of admissible evidence, the reasons for the plaintiff's rejection.[9] The explanation provided must be legally sufficient to justify a judgment for the defendant. If the defendant carries this burden of production, the presumption raised by the prima facie case is rebutted,[10] and the factual inquiry proceeds to a new level of specificity. Placing this burden of production on the defendant thus serves simultaneously to meet the plaintiff's prima facie case by presenting a legitimate reason for the action and to frame the factual issue with sufficient clarity so that the plaintiff will have a full and fair opportunity to demonstrate pretext. The sufficiency of the defendant's evidence should be evaluated by the extent to which it fulfills these functions.

The plaintiff retains the burden of persuasion. She now must have the opportunity to demonstrate that the proffered reason was not the true reason for the employment decision. This burden now merges with the ultimate burden of persuading the court that she has been the victim of intentional discrimination. She may succeed in this either directly by persuading the court that a discriminatory reason more likely motivated the employer or indirectly by showing that the employer's proffered explanation is unworthy of credence.

III

In reversing the judgment of the District Court that the discharge of respondent from PSC was unrelated to her sex, the Court of Appeals adhered to two rules it had

---

8 [8] This evidentiary relationship between the presumption created by a prima facie case and the consequential burden of production placed on the defendant is a traditional feature of the common law. "The word 'presumption' properly used refers only to a device for allocating the production burden." F. JAMES & G. HAZARD, CIVIL PROCEDURE § 7.9, p. 255 (2d ed. 1977) (footnote omitted). See Fed. Rule Evid. 301. See generally 9 J. WIGMORE, EVIDENCE § 2491 (3d ed. 1940). Cf. J. MAGUIRE, EVIDENCE, COMMON SENSE AND COMMON LAW 185–186 (1947). Usually, assessing the burden of production helps the judge determine whether the litigants have created an issue of fact to be decided by the jury. In a Title VII case, the allocation of burdens and the creation of a presumption by the establishment of a prima facie case is intended progressively to sharpen the inquiry into the elusive factual question of intentional discrimination.

9 [9] An articulation not admitted into evidence will not suffice. Thus, the defendant cannot meet its burden merely through an answer to the complaint or by argument of counsel.

10 [10] See generally J. THAYER, PRELIMINARY TREATISE ON EVIDENCE 346 (1898). In saying that the presumption drops from the case, we do not imply that the trier of fact no longer may consider evidence previously introduced by the plaintiff to establish a prima facie case. A satisfactory explanation by the defendant destroys the legally mandatory inference of discrimination arising from the plaintiff's initial evidence. Nonetheless, this evidence and inferences properly drawn there from may be considered by the trier of fact on the issue of whether the defendant's explanation is pretextual. Indeed, there may be some cases where the plaintiff's initial evidence, combined with effective cross-examination of the defendant, will suffice to discredit the defendant's explanation. [Is the effect the court gives the defendant's rebutting evidence the effect F.R.E. 301 necessarily prescribes? Is the court interpreting F.R.E. 301? If not, why? — Ed.]

developed to elaborate the defendant's burden of proof. First, the defendant must prove by a preponderance of the evidence that legitimate, nondiscriminatory reasons for the discharge existed. Second, to satisfy this burden, the defendant "must prove that those he hired . . . were somehow *better* qualified than was plaintiff; in other words, comparative evidence is needed." 608 F.2d at 567 (*emphasis in original*). *See East v. Romine, Inc.*, 518 F.2d 332, 339, 340 (CAS 1975).

A

The Court of Appeals has misconstrued the nature of tile burden *McDonnell Douglas* and its progeny place on the defendant. We stated *Sweeney* that "the employer's burden is satisfied if he simply 'explains what has done' or 'produc[es] evidence of legitimate nondiscriminatory reasons.' 439 U.S., at n. 2 quoting *id* at 28, 29 (Stevens, J. dissenting) It is plain the Court of Appeals required much more: it placed on the defendant burden of persuading the court that it had convincing, objective reasons preferring the chosen applicant above the plaintiff.[11]

We have stated consistently that the employee's prima facie case of discrimination will be rebutted if the employer articulates lawful reasons for action, that is, to satisfy this intermediate burden, the employer need produce admissible evidence which would allow the trier of fact rationally conclude that the employment decision had not been motivated/by discriminatory animus. The Court of Appeals would require the defendant to introduce evidence which, in the absence of any evidence of pretext, would *persuade* the trier of fact that the employment action was lawful. This exceeds what properly can be demanded to satisfy a burden of production.

The court placed the burden of persuasion on the defendant apparently because it feared that "[i]f an employer need only *articulate* — not prove — a legitimate, nondiscriminatory reason for his action, he may compose fictitious, but legitimate, reasons for his actions." We do not believe, however, limiting the defendant's evidentiary obligation to a burden of production unduly hinder the plaintiff. First, as noted above, the defendant's explanation of its legitimate reasons must be clear and reasonably specific. This obligation arises both from the necessity of rebutting the inference of discrimination arising from the prima facie case and from the requirement that the plaintiff be afforded "a full and fair opportunity" to demonstrate pretext. Second, although the defendant does not bear a formal burden of persuasion, the defendant nevertheless retains an incentive to persuade the trier of fact that the employment decision was lawful.

---

[11] [11] The court reviewed the defendant's evidence and explained its deficiency:

"Defendant failed to introduce comparative factual data concerning Burdine and Walz. Fuller merely testified that he discharged and retained personnel in the spring shakeup at TDCA primarily on the recommendations of subordinates and that he considered Walz qualified for the position he was retained to do. Fuller failed to specify any objective criteria on which he based the decision to discharge Burdine and retain Walz. He stated only that the action was in the best interest of the program and that there had been some friction within the department that might be alleviated by Burdine's discharge. Nothing in the record indicates whether he examined Walz' ability to work well with others. This court in *East* found such unsubstantiated assertions of 'qualification' and 'prior work record' insufficient absent data that will allow a true *comparison* of the individuals hired and rejected."

Thus, the defendant normally will attempt to prove the factual basis for its explanation. Third, the liberal discovery rules applicable to any civil suit in federal court are supplemented in a Title VII suit by the plaintiff's access to the Equal Employment Opportunity Commission's investigatory files concerning her complaint. Given these factors, we are unpersuaded that the plaintiff will find it particularly difficult to prove that a proffered explanation lacking a factual basis is a pretext.

B

The Court of Appeals also erred in requiring the defendant to prove by objective evidence that the person hired or promoted was more qualified than the plaintiff. *McDonnell Douglas* teaches that it is the plaintiff's task to demonstrate that similarly situated employees were not treated equally. The Court of Appeals' rule would require the employer to show that the plaintiff's objective qualifications were inferior to those of the person selected. If it cannot, a court would, in effect, conclude that it has discriminated.

The views of the Court of Appeals can be read, we think, as requiring the employer to hire the minority or female applicant whenever that person's objective qualifications were equal to those of a white male applicant. But Title VII does not obligate an employer to accord this preference. Rather, the employer has discretion to choose among equally qualified candidates, provided the decision is not based upon unlawful criteria.

The judgment of the Court of Appeals is vacated, and the case is remanded for further proceedings consistent with this opinion.

NOTES AND QUESTIONS

1. Professor Allen has stated that "[p]resumptions have been used to accomplish four distinct ends. They have been used to construct rules of decision to avoid factual impasse at trial; to allocate burdens of persuasion; to instruct the jury on the relationship between facts; and to allocate burdens of production." Allen, *Presumptions in Civil Cases Reconsidered*, 66 IOWA L. REV. 843, 845 (1981). Which of these distinct ends, if any, were arguably being served by the presumption at issue in *McGowan*?

2. The Supreme Court has indicated that, even in civil cases, there must be some "rational connection" between the proven fact and the presumed fact. *See Western & A. R.R. v. Henderson*, 279 U.S. 639 (1929); *Mobile, J. & K.C. R. Co. v. Turnipseed*, 219 U.S. 35 (1910). Should the rational connection standard be equally applicable to permissive inferences? To what extent should the required qualitative connection between proven and presumed fact reflect the "distinct end" that the presumption is seeking to achieve?

Ronald J. Allen, *Structuring Jury Decisionmaking in Criminal Cases: A Unified Constitutional Approach to Evidentiary Devices*
94 HARV. L. REV. 321, 321–24 (1980)[12]

The manner in which facts are established at trial in a criminal case is often very complex. The process begins with assigning to the defendant and the state burdens of production and persuasion on the various factual issues, and on occasion includes the creation of affirmative defenses that shift to the defendant the burden of proving exculpatory facts. But beyond the problem of structuring the parties' formal presentation of evidence lies the complexity of the jury's inferential process when it assesses the evidence to determine guilt or innocence. Legislatures and judges have sought to guide this inferential process toward a rational result through the creation of statutory presumptions and inferences and by judicial comment on the evidence.

These devices attempt to resolve difficulties for the jury by clarifying the relationship among facts and legal conclusions, but they have been seen to pose constitutional questions, as has the creation of affirmative defenses. When a judge instructs a jury that it may presume the existence of certain unproved incriminating facts from the proof at trial of other less incriminating facts, or suggests by comment that the jury may draw various reasonable inferences, the effect is to increase the weight of the evidence presented by the prosecution. As a result, the constitutional requirement of proof beyond a reasonable doubt may be circumvented. Similarly, the creation of an affirmative defense relieves the state from establishing beyond reasonable doubt at least one factual element relevant to culpability. Accordingly, the courts have been forced to address the question of when these evidentiary devices are constitutionally permissible. Unfortunately, no consistent resolution has as yet been achieved.

* * *

. . . [C]onceptual disarray is primarily attributable to two factors. The first is the very complexity of the process of proof and the myriad manifestations of constitutional questions that it engenders. The second is the lack of satisfactory guidance from the Supreme Court on these issues. By developing a separate constitutional analysis for each evidentiary device, the Court has significantly increased the complexity of these issues.

The Court's approach has been to estimate the likely effect of each evidentiary device on the defendant's interests and then to adopt a standard of review commensurate with the anticipated effect — the greater the likely effect on the defendant's interests, the more stringent the standard of review. As a result, much of the Court's current constitutional analysis turns on how a device is classified within the Court's hierarchy. For example, "permissive inferences," which allow but do not require a jury to infer one fact from another, are considered to have relatively limited impact, and therefore the constitutional inquiry is limited to whether the inferred fact is "more likely than not" to flow from the proved fact. "Mandatory presumptions," on the other hand, are viewed as a direct shift of the burden of persuasion because they conclusively establish some inference and are therefore generally unconstitutional. At the same time, affirmative defenses are distinguished from mandatory presumptions and held constitutional, but only when they do not shift the burden of persuasion on an "element" of the offense. Shifts of burdens of production, by contrast, are governed by rules that are apparently quite different from the rules regulating shifts of burdens of persuasion, although the extent of the differences remains ambiguous. Finally, judicial comment has been permitted so long as it does not invade the province of the jury, but the distinction between legitimate guidance and illegitimate influence is unclear, and the relationship of judicial comment to these other evidentiary devices has not been satisfactorily explained.

FARRELL v. CZARNETZKY
566 F.2d 381 (2d Cir. 1977)

PER CURIAM:

After the argument of the instant consolidated appeals, the Supreme Court heard and decided *Patterson v. New York*, 432 U.S. 197 (1977). We hold that *Patterson* controls our decision here.

*   *   *

Under attack on the instant appeals is New York's first degree robbery statute, N.Y. PENAL LAW § 160.15(4) (McKinney 1975), which permits a defendant who, in the course of a robbery, "[d]isplays what appears to be a pistol, revolver, rifle, shotgun, machine gun or other firearm" to raise as "an affirmative defense that such pistol, revolver, rifle, shotgun, machine gun or other firearm was not a loaded weapon from which a shot, readily capable of producing death or other serious physical injury, could be discharged." If he does not sustain his burden of proving the affirmative defense by a preponderance of the evidence, the defendant can be convicted of first degree robbery. If he does sustain the burden, he will be convicted of second degree robbery. N.Y. PENAL LAW § 160.10(2)(b) (McKinney 1975). By placing the burden of proving the affirmative defense on a defendant, New York was said, prior to the Supreme Court's decision in Patterson, to have contravened the due process clause of the Fourteenth Amendment as interpreted in *Mullaney v. Wilbur*, 421 U.S. 684 (1975).

The Supreme Court in *Patterson*, however, restricted *Mullaney* by holding that a state, without violating the Constitution, may place on a defendant the burden of proving by a preponderance of the evidence a matter not defined by the legislature as a necessary ingredient of the crime but which mitigates the degree of the offense. Under the New York first degree robbery statute, possession of a weapon actually capable of causing death is not a necessary ingredient of the offense, since the prosecutor is not required to prove the presence of such a factor in order for a defendant to be convicted of first degree robbery. Moreover, proof that the gun was not capable of causing death does not entirely exonerate the defendant of criminal liability.

We hold that under *Patterson* the New York first degree robbery statute is constitutional.

OAKES, CIRCUIT JUDGE (concurring):

I join in the judgment of the court, but for somewhat different reasons.

In *Mullaney v. Wilbur*, 421 U.S. 684 . . . (1975), the Supreme Court held unconstitutional Maine's allocation of the persuasion burden to murder defendants on the mitigating circumstance of action "in the heat of passion on sudden provocation." . . . In *Patterson v. State of New York*, 432 U.S. 197 (1977), the Court upheld New York's allocation of the persuasion burden to murder defendants on the mitigating circumstance of action "under the influence of extreme emotional disturbance." . . . Mr. Justice Powell, who wrote *Mullaney*, dissented in Patterson. He criticized the purported distinction between the two cases as purely "formalistic." . . . Unlike the Maine statute,[13] the New York legislature denoted the mitigating factor as an affirmative defense without mentioning either the presence or absence of the factor in the core definition of the crime.[14]

Farrell and Reidout question the constitutionality of New York's robbery statute to the extent that it requires a defendant to prove that his firearm was unloaded. If he can prove that it was, then his crime is mitigated from first to second degree robbery.[15] With all due respect, the *Patterson* decision, and its failure to overrule *Mullaney*, . . . raises as many questions as it answers.

First, it could be argued that the statute effects a shift of the persuasion burden on an element of the crime. Because a defendant may be convicted of first degree robbery when, inter alia, he "[d]isplays what appears to be a pistol, revolver, rifle, shotgun, machine gun or other firearm," N.Y. PENAL LAW § 160.15(4) (McKinney

---

[13] [1] Maine law defined murder as the unlawful killing of a human being "with malice aforethought," Me. Rev. Stat. Ann., Tit. 17, § 2651 (1964), and manslaughter as an unlawful killing "in the heat of passion, on sudden provocation, without express or implied malice aforethought." *Id.* § 2551. The effect of the Maine statute, as interpreted by the Maine Supreme Judicial Court, was to shift the burden of persuasion to the defendant to disprove malice aforethought for the purpose of mitigating his crime. *Mullaney* found this shift of the burden to violate the due process standards of *In re Winship*, 397 U.S. 358 (1970). . . .

[14] [2] The *Patterson* majority's definitional compartmentalization of elements of the crime from mitigating factors was thought to be formalistic by Mr. Justice Powell, because as he pointed out the Maine Supreme Judicial Court had held that malice was not an independent element of the crime of murder in Maine. . . . The state had so held even though the language of malice appeared in the definition of crime.

[15] [3] N.Y. PENAL LAW § 160.15(4). The statute states in pertinent part:

A person is guilty of robbery in the first degree when he forcibly steals property and when, in the course of the commission of the crime or of immediate flight therefrom, he or another participant in the crime:

Displays what appears to be a pistol, revolver, rifle, shotgun, machine gun or other firearm; except that in any prosecution under this subdivision, it is an affirmative defense that such pistol, revolver, rifle, shotgun machine gun or other firearm was not a loaded weapon from which a shot, readily capable of producing death or other serious physical injury, could be discharged. Nothing contained in this subdivision shall constitute a defense to a prosecution for, or preclude a conviction of, robbery in the second degree, robbery in the third degree or any other crime.

1975), the core definition of the crime does not require that the weapon be loaded. It need only "appear" to be such. The operative effect of the statute, however, is to create a presumption that the weapon is loaded. The defendant must rebut that presumption or stand convicted of first degree robbery. If the defendant's rebuttal fails, he stands convicted of a crime under the statute which, even though drafted not to require that the weapon be loaded, in fact so operates. Otherwise, it would make no sense to differentiate first from second degree robbery on the basis of whether a weapon is loaded. Because the defendant must prove the negative of the first degree robbery statute's operative effect, this case arguably resembles that aspect of *Mullaney* which condemned the shift of the persuasion burden on the factor of heat of passion on sudden provocation.[16]

Patterson might also be viewed as suggesting that the only factors significant enough to require the prosecution to shoulder the burden of proving are those which are part of the core definition of the crime and which are therefore determinative of guilt. Thus, if the negative of one such factor were required to be proved by the defendant, presumably even under *Patterson*'s strictures, a due process violation could be found. Under that view, this case could be disposed of as merely presenting a difference between degrees of crime and not between guilt or innocence.[17] That is what the majority opinion here suggests, I presume, when it concludes that "proof that the gun was not capable of causing death does not entirely exonerate the defendant of criminal liability." . . . Of course, proof of acting in the heat of passion in *Mullaney* did not entirely exonerate the defendant there of criminal liability; it only reduced his crime from murder to manslaughter.

Ultimately, it may be that the *Patterson* Court opted for a highly "formalistic" approach, as the dissenting opinion suggests, . . . thereby leaving lower court judges without "a conceptual framework," . . . for distinguishing *Mullaney* shifts from *Patterson* shifts. In any event, *Mullaney*, while not expressly overruled, has been drained "of much of its vitality," . . . and for present purposes perhaps all.

I come then to the same result as my brethren, only in a somewhat less inexorable, slightly more perplexed way. I suppose that I am left with the proposition after *Patterson* that if a legislature includes in the definition of a crime a significant factor whose negative may be proved by the defendant as an affirmative defense, and the affirmative defense has been one of historical significance "in the Anglo-American legal tradition," . . . and the crime is historically and conceptually separate in kind, as opposed to degree, from the crime if the affirmative defense were proven, there may still be a due process violation where the burden of proof

---

[16] [4] This is not to suggest that [petitioners] have fully satisfied what were thought to be the due process requirements of *Mullaney*. Mr. Justice Powell's *Patterson* dissent pointed out that the mitigating defense here involved was a "[n]ew ameliorative affirmative defense" which "need not [have been] disturbed" even if *Patterson* had followed *Mullaney* more enthusiastically. . . . The very statute here at issue was his first example of such a "[n]ew ameliorative affirmative defense." . . . Thus, this case would not satisfy the *Mullaney* test, not because it met *Patterson*'s formalistic requirements, but because the distinguishing feature of first from second degree robbery — whether the gun was loaded — does not have the same historical significance in the common law definition of robbery as had the "malice aforethought" language at issue in *Mullaney*. . . .

[17] [5] *Mullaney* would then have to be looked at as involving two separate crimes, murder and manslaughter, rather than degrees of homicide. . . .

has shifted to the defendant. Under this proposition, however, appellant . . . lose[s].

I therefore concur in the judgment.

NOTES AND QUESTIONS

1. Why is the distinction between presumptions and permissive inferences of particular importance in criminal rather than civil cases? *See United States v. Martin Linen Supply Co.*, 430 U.S. 564 (1977); Note, *The Unconstitutionality of Statutory Criminal Presumptions*, 22 Stan. L. Rev. 341 (1970); Note, *The Constitutionality of Rebuttable Statutory Presumptions*, 55 Colum. L. Rev. 527 (1955).

2. Can the different outcomes in *Mullaney* and *Patterson* be reconciled simply by recognizing that *Mullaney* arguably involved a rebuttable presumption that shifted the burden of persuasion as to an element of the crime while *Patterson* was concerned with an affirmative defense that did not affect any element of the crime? *See* Allen, *The Restoration of* In re Winship: *A Comment on Burdens of Persuasion After* Patterson v. New York, 76 Mich. L. Rev. 30 (1977); Jeffries & Stephan, *Defenses, Presumptions, and Burdens of Proof in the Criminal Law*, 88 Yale L.J. 1325 (1979).

3. May the burden of persuasion for self-defense ever be placed on the defendant? *Compare Holloway v. McElroy*, 632 F.2d 605 (4th Cir. 1980), *cert. denied*, 451 U.S. 1028 (1981), *with Williams v. Mohn*, 462 F. Supp. 756 (N.D. W. Va. 1978), *modified*, 605 F.2d 1208 (4th Cir. 1979), *and Porter v. Leeke*, 457 F. Supp. 253 (D.S.C. 1978).

ULSTER COUNTY COURT v. ALLEN
442 U.S. 140 (1979)

Mr. Justice Stevens delivered the opinion of the Court.

A New York statute provides that, with certain exceptions, the presence of a firearm in an automobile is presumptive evidence of its illegal possession by all persons then occupying the vehicle.[18]

The United States Court of Appeals for the Second Circuit held that respondents may challenge the constitutionality of this statute in a federal habeas corpus

---

[18] [1] New York Penal Law § 265.15(3)(McKinney 1967):

The presence in an automobile, other than a stolen one or a public omnibus, of any firearm defaced firearm, firearm silencer, bomb, bombshell, gravity knife, switchblade knife, dagger, dirk, stiletto, billy, blackjack, metal knuckles, sandbag, sandclub or sling-shot is presumptive evidence of its possession by all persons occupying such automobile at the time such weapon, instrument or appliance is found, except under the following circumstances:

(a) if such weapon, instrument or appliance is found upon the person of one of the occupants therein; (b) if such weapon, instrument or appliance is found in an automobile which is being operated for hire by a duly licensed driver in the due, lawful and proper pursuit of his trade, then such presumption shall not apply to the driver; or (c) if the weapon so found is a pistol or revolver and one of the occupants, not present under duress, has in his possession a valid license to have and carry concealed the same.

proceeding *and* that the statute is "unconstitutional on its face." . . .

Four persons, three adult males (respondents) and a 16-year-old girl (Jane Doe, who is not a respondent here), were jointly tried on charges that they possessed two loaded handguns, a loaded machinegun, and over a pound of heroin found in a Chevrolet in which they were riding when it was stopped for speeding on the New York Thruway shortly after noon on March 28, 1973. The two large-caliber handguns, which together with their ammunition weighed approximately six pounds, were seen through the window of the car by the investigating police officer. They were positioned crosswise in an open handbag on either the front floor or the front seat of the car on the passenger side where Jane Doe was sitting. Jane Doe admitted that the handbag was hers. The machinegun and the heroin were discovered in the trunk after the police pried it open. The car had been borrowed from the driver's brother earlier that day; the key to the trunk could not be found in the car or on the person of any of its occupants, although there was testimony that two of the occupants had placed something in the trunk before embarking in the borrowed car. The jury convicted all four of possession of the handguns and acquitted them of possession of the contents of the trunk.

Counsel for all four defendants objected to the introduction into evidence of the two handguns, the machinegun, and the drugs, arguing that the State had not adequately demonstrated a connection between their clients and the contraband. The trial court overruled the objection, relying on the presumption of possession created by the New York statute. . . . Because that presumption does not apply if a weapon is found "upon the person" of one of the occupants of the car, *see* n.1. *supra*, the three male defendants also moved to dismiss the charges relating to the handguns on the ground that the guns were found on the person of Jane Doe. Respondents made this motion both at the close of the prosecution's case and at the close of all evidence. The trial judge twice denied it, concluding that the applicability of the "upon the person" exception was a question of fact for the jury. . . .

At the close of the trial, the judge instructed the jurors that they were entitled to infer possession from the defendants' presence in the car. He did not make any reference to the "upon the person" exception in his explanation of the statutory presumption, nor did any of the defendants object to this omission or request alternative or additional instructions on the subject.

Defendants filed a post-trial motion in which they challenged the constitutionality of the New York statute as applied in this case. The challenge was made in support of their argument that the evidence, apart from the presumption, was insufficient to sustain the convictions. The motion was denied, . . . and the convictions were affirmed by the Appellate Division without opinion. . . .

The New York Court of Appeals also affirmed. . . .

*   *   *

Respondents filed a petition for a writ of habeas corpus in the United States District Court for the Southern District of New York contending that they were denied due process of law by the application of the statutory presumption of possession. The District Court issued the writ, holding that . . . the mere presence of two guns in a woman's handbag in a car could not reasonably give rise to the inference that they were in the possession of three other persons in the car. . . .

The Court of Appeals for the Second Circuit affirmed, but for different reasons. . . . [T]he majority of the court, without deciding whether the presumption was constitutional as applied in this case, concluded that the statute is unconstitutional on its face because the "presumption obviously sweeps within its compass (1) many occupants who may not know they are riding with a gun (which may be out of their sight), and (2) many who may be aware of the presence of the gun but not permitted access to it." Concurring separately, Judge Timbers agreed with the District Court that the statute was unconstitutional as applied but considered it improper to reach the issue of the statute's facial constitutionality. . . .

* * *

In this case, the Court of Appeals undertook the task of deciding the constitutionality of the New York statute "on its face." Its conclusion that the statutory presumption was arbitrary rested entirely on its view of the fairness of applying the presumption in hypothetical situations — situations, indeed, in which it is improbable that a jury would return a conviction,[19] or that a prosecution would ever be instituted.[20] We must accordingly inquire whether these respondents had standing to advance the arguments that the Court of Appeals considered decisive. An analysis of our prior cases indicates that the answer to this inquiry depends on the type of presumption that is involved in the case.

Inferences and presumptions are a staple of our adversary system of factfinding. It is often necessary for the trier of fact to determine the existence of an element of the crime — that is, an "ultimate" or "elemental" fact — from the existence of one or more "evidentiary" or "basic" facts. . . . The value of these evidentiary devices, and their validity under the Due Process Clause, vary from case to case, however, depending on the strength of the connection between the particular basic and elemental facts involved and on the degree to which the device curtails the factfinder's freedom to assess the evidence independently. Nonetheless, in criminal cases, the ultimate test of any device's constitutional validity in a given case remains constant: the device must not undermine the factfinder's responsibility at trial,

---

[19] [14] Indeed, in this very case the permissive presumptions in § 265.15(3) and its companion drug statute, N.Y. PENAL LAW § 220.25(1) (McKinney Supp. 1978), were insufficient to persuade the jury to convict the defendants of possession of the loaded machinegun and heroin in the trunk of the car notwithstanding the supporting testimony that at least two of them had been seen transferring something into the trunk that morning. . . .

The hypothetical, even implausible, nature of the situations relied upon by the Court of Appeals is illustrated by the fact that there are no reported cases in which the presumption led to convictions in circumstances even remotely similar to the posited situations. In those occasional cases in which a jury has reached a guilty verdict on the basis of evidence insufficient to justify an inference of possession from presence, the New York appellate courts have not hesitated to reverse. . . .

In light of the improbable character of the situations hypothesized by the Court of Appeals, its facial analysis would still be unconvincing even were that type of analysis appropriate. This Court has never required that a presumption be accurate in every imaginable case. . . .

[20] [15] . . . Thus, the assumption that it would be unconstitutional to apply the statutory presumption to a hitchhiker in a car containing a concealed weapon does not necessarily advance the constitutional claim of the driver of a car in which a gun was found on the front seat, or of other defendants in entirely different situations.

based on evidence adduced by the State, to find the ultimate facts beyond a reasonable doubt. . . .

The most common evidentiary device is the entirely permissive inference or presumption, which allows — but does not require — the trier of fact to infer the elemental fact from proof by the prosecutor of the basic one and which places no burden of any kind on the defendant. . . . In that situation the basic fact may constitute prima facie evidence of the elemental fact. . . . When reviewing this type of device, the Court has required the party challenging it to demonstrate its invalidity as applied to him. . . . Because this permissive presumption leaves the trier of fact free to credit or reject the inference and does not shift the burden of proof, it affects the application of the "beyond a reasonable doubt" standard only if, under the facts of the case, there is no rational way the trier could make the connection permitted by the inference. For only in that situation is there any risk that an explanation of the permissible inference to a jury, or its use by a jury, has caused the presumptively rational factfinder to make an erroneous factual determination.

A mandatory presumption is a far more troublesome evidentiary device. For it may affect not only the strength of the "no reasonable doubt" burden but also the placement of that burden; it tells the trier that he or they must find the elemental fact upon proof of the basic fact, at least unless the defendant has come forward with some evidence to rebut the presumed connection between the two facts.[21] . . .

---

[21] [16] This class of more or less mandatory presumptions can be subdivided into two parts: presumptions that merely shift the burden of production to the defendant, following the satisfaction of which the ultimate burden of persuasion returns to the prosecution; and presumptions that entirely shift the burden of proof to the defendant. The mandatory presumptions examined by our cases have almost uniformly fit into the former subclass, in that they never totally removed the ultimate burden of proof beyond a reasonable doubt from the prosecution. . . .

To the extent that a presumption imposes an extremely low burden of production — e.g., being satisfied by "any" evidence — it may well be that its impact is no greater than that of a permissive inference, and it may be proper to analyze it as such. . . .

In deciding what type of inference or presumption is involved in a case, the jury instructions will generally be controlling, although their interpretation may require recourse to the statute involved and the cases decided under it. . . .

The importance of focusing attention on the precise presentation of the presumption to the jury and the scope of that presumption is illustrated by a comparison of *United States v. Gainey*, 380 U.S. 63 . . . with *United States v. Romano* [382 U.S. 136 (1965)]. Both cases involved statutory presumptions based on proof that the defendant was present at the site of an illegal still. In *Gainey* the Court sustained a conviction "for carrying on" the business of the distillery in violation of 26 U.S.C. § 5601(a)(4), whereas in *Romano*, the Court set aside a conviction for being in "possession, or custody, or . . . control" of such a distillery in violation of § 560(a)(1). The difference in outcome was attributable to two important differences between the cases. Because the statute involved in *Gainey* was a sweeping prohibition of almost any activity associated with the still, whereas the *Romano* statute involved only one narrow aspect of the total undertaking, there was a much higher probability that mere presence could support an inference of guilt in the former case than in the latter.

Of perhaps greater importance, however, was the difference between the trial judge's instructions to the jury in the two cases. In *Gainey*, the judge had explained that the presumption was permissive; it did not require the jury to convict the defendant even if it was convinced that he was present at the site. On the contrary, the instructions made it clear that presence was only "a circumstance to be considered along with all the other circumstances in the case." As we emphasized, the "jury was thus specifically told that the statutory inference was not conclusive." . . . In *Romano*, the trial judge told the jury that the

In this situation, the Court has generally examined the presumption on its face to determine the extent to which the basic and elemental facts coincide. . . . To the extent that the trier of fact is forced to abide by the presumption, and may not reject it based on an independent evaluation of the particular facts presented by the State, the analysis of the presumption's constitutional validity is logically divorced from those facts and based on the presumption's accuracy in the run of cases.[22] It is for this reason that the Court has held it irrelevant in analyzing a mandatory presumption, but not in analyzing a purely permissive one, that there is ample evidence in the record other than the presumption to support a conviction. . . .

Without determining whether the presumption in this case was mandatory, the Court of Appeals analyzed it on its face as if it were. In fact, it was not, as the New York Court of Appeals had earlier pointed out. . . .

The trial judge's instructions make it clear that the presumption was merely a part of the prosecution's case,[23] that it gave rise to a permissive inference available

---

defendant's presence at the still "shall be deemed sufficient evidence to authorize conviction." . . . Although there was other evidence of guilt, that instruction authorized conviction even if the jury disbelieved all of the testimony except the proof of presence at the site. This Court's holding that the statutory presumption could not support the Romano conviction was thus dependent, in part, on the specific instructions given by the trial judge. Under those instructions it was necessary to decide whether, regardless of the specific circumstances of the particular case, the statutory presumption adequately supported the guilty verdict.

[22] [17] In addition to the discussion of *Romano* in n. 16, *supra*, this point is illustrated by *Leary v. United States*, 395 [U.S. 6 (1969)]. In that case, Dr. Timothy Leary, a professor at Harvard University, was stopped by customs inspectors in Laredo, Tex., as he was returning from the Mexican side of the international border. Marihuana seeds and a silver snuffbox filled with semirefined marihuana and three partially smoked marihuana cigarettes were discovered in his car. He was convicted of having knowingly transported marihuana which he knew had been illegally imported into this country in violation of 21 U.S.C. § 176a (1964 ed.). That statute included a mandatory presumption: "possession shall be deemed sufficient evidence to authorize conviction [for importation] unless the defendant explains his possession to the satisfaction of the jury." Leary admitted possession of the marijuana and claimed that he had carried it from New York to Mexico and then back.

Mr. Justice Harlan for the Court noted that under one theory of the case, the jury could have found direct proof of all of the necessary elements of the offense without recourse to the presumption. But he deemed that insufficient reason to affirm the conviction because under another theory the jury might have found knowledge of importation on the basis of either direct evidence or the presumption, and there was accordingly no certainty that the jury had not relied on the presumption. . . . The Court therefore found it necessary to test the presumption against the Due Process Clause. Its analysis was facial. Despite the fact that the defendant was well educated and had recently traveled to a country that is a major exporter of marihuana to this country, the Court found the presumption of knowledge of importation from possession irrational. It did so, not because Dr. Leary was unlikely to know the source of the marihuana, but instead because "a majority of possessors" were unlikely to have such knowledge. . . . Because the jury had been instructed to rely on the presumption even if it did not believe the Government's direct evidence of knowledge of importation (unless, of course, the defendant met his burden of "satisfying" the jury to the contrary), the Court reversed the conviction.

[23] [19] It is your duty to consider all the testimony in this case, to weigh it carefully and to test the credit to be given to a witness by his apparent intention to speak the truth and by the accuracy of his memory, to reconcile, if possible, conflicting statements as to material facts and in such ways to try and get at the truth and to reach a verdict upon the evidence. . . .

To establish the unlawful possession of the weapons, again the People relied upon the presumption and, in addition thereto, the testimony of Anderson and Lemmons who testified in their case in chief. . . .

Accordingly, you would be warranted in returning a verdict of guilt against the defendants or

only in certain circumstances, rather than a mandatory conclusion of possession, and that it could be ignored by the jury even if there was no affirmative proof offered by defendants in rebuttal.[24] The judge explained that possession could be actual or constructive, but that constructive possession could not exist without the intent and ability to exercise control or dominion over the weapons. He also carefully instructed the jury that there is a mandatory presumption of innocence in favor of the defendants that controls unless it, as the exclusive trier of fact, is satisfied beyond a reasonable doubt that the defendants possessed the handguns in the manner described by the judge. In short, the instructions plainly directed the jury to consider all the circumstances tending to support or contradict the inference that all four occupants of the car had possession of the two loaded handguns and to decide the matter for itself without regard to how much evidence the defendants introduced.[25]

Our cases considering the validity of permissive statutory presumptions such as the one involved here have rested on an evaluation of the presumption as applied to the record before the Court. None suggests that a court should pass on the constitutionality of this kind of statute "on its face." It was error for the Court of Appeals to make such a determination in this case.

*   *   *

As applied to the facts of this case, the presumption of possession is entirely rational. Notwithstanding the Court of Appeals' analysis, respondents were not "hitchhikers or other casual passengers," and the guns were neither "a few inches in length" nor "out of [respondents'] sight." . . . The argument against possession by any of the respondents was predicated solely on the fact that the guns were in Jane Doe's pocketbook. But several circumstances — which, not surprisingly, her counsel repeatedly emphasized in his questions and his argument, . . . made it highly improbable that she was the sole custodian of those weapons.

Even if it was reasonable to conclude that she had placed the guns in her purse

---

defendant if you find the defendants or defendant was in possession of a machine gun and the other weapons and that the fact of possession was proven to you by the People beyond a reasonable doubt, and an element of such proof is the reasonable presumption of illegal possession of a machine gun or the presumption of illegal possession of firearms, as I have just before explained to you. . . .

[24] [20] Our Penal Law also provides that the presence in an automobile of any machine gun or of any handgun or firearm which is loaded is presumptive evidence of their unlawful possession. In other words, these presumptions or this latter presumption upon proof of the presence of the machine gun and the hand weapons, you may infer and draw a conclusion that such prohibited weapon was possessed by each of the defendants who occupied the automobile at the time when such instruments were found. The presumption or presumptions is effective only so long as there is no substantial evidence contradicting the conclusion flowing from the presumption, and the presumption is said to disappear when such contradictory evidence is adduced. . . .

The presumption or presumptions which I discussed with the jury relative to the drugs or weapons in this case need not be rebutted by affirmative proof or affirmative evidence but may be rebutted by any evidence or lack of evidence in the case.

[25] [23] The verdict announced by the jury clearly indicates that it understood its duty to evaluate the presumption independently and to reject it if it was not supported in the record. Despite receiving almost identical instructions on the applicability of the presumption of possession to the contraband found in the front seat and in the trunk, the jury convicted all four defendants of possession of the former but acquitted all of them of possession of the latter. . . .

before the car was stopped by police, the facts strongly suggest that Jane Doe was not the only person able to exercise dominion over them. The two guns were too large to be concealed in her handbag.[26] The bag was consequently open, and part of one of the guns was in plain view, within easy access of the driver of the car and even, perhaps, of the other two respondents who were riding in the rear seat.

Moreover, it is highly improbable that the loaded guns belonged to Jane Doe or that she was solely responsible for their being in her purse. As a 16-year-old girl in the company of three adult men she was the least likely of the four to be carrying one, let alone two, heavy handguns. It is far more probable that she relied on the pocketknife found in her brassiere for any necessary self-protection. Under these circumstances, it was not unreasonable for her counsel to argue and for the jury to infer that when the car was halted for speeding, the other passengers in the car anticipated the risk of a search and attempted to conceal their weapons in a pocketbook in the front seat. The inference is surely more likely than the notion that these weapons were the sole property of the 16-year-old girl.

Under these circumstances, the jury would have been entirely reasonable in rejecting the suggestion — which, incidentally, defense counsel did not even advance in their closing arguments to the jury[27] — that the handguns were in the sole possession of Jane Doe. Assuming that the jury did reject it, the case is tantamount to one in which the guns were lying on the floor or the seat of the car in the plain view of the three other occupants of the automobile. In such a case, it is surely rational to infer that each of the respondents was fully aware of the presence of the guns and had both the ability and the intent to exercise dominion and control over the weapons. The application of the statutory presumption in this case therefore comports with the standard laid down in *Tot v. United States*, . . . and restated in *Leary v. United States*. . . . For there is a "rational connection" between the basic facts that the prosecution proved and the ultimate fact presumed, and the latter is "more likely than not to flow from" the former.[28]

---

[26] [24] Jane Doe's counsel referred to the .45-caliber automatic pistol as a "cannon."

[27] [26] Indeed, counsel for two of the respondents virtually invited the jury to find to the contrary:

> One more thing. You know, different people live in different cultures and different societies. You may think that the way [respondent] Hardrick has his hair done up is unusual; it may seem strange to you. People live differently. . . . For example, if you were living under their times and conditions and you traveled from a big city, Detroit, to a bigger city, New York City, *it is not unusual for people to carry guns, small arms to protect themselves, is it?* There are places in New York City policemen fear to go. But you have got to understand; you are sitting here as jurors. These are people, live flesh and blood, the same as you, different motives, different objectives.

Id. at 653–654 (emphasis added). *See also id.* at 634.

It is also important in this regard that respondents passed up the opportunity to have the jury instructed not to apply the presumption if it determined that the handguns were "upon the person" of Jane Doe.

[28] [27] The New York Court of Appeals first upheld the constitutionality of the presumption involved in this case in *People v. Russo*, 303 N.Y. 673, 102 N.E.2d 834 (1951). That decision relied upon the earlier case of *People v. Terra*, 303 N.Y. 332, 102 N.E.2d 576 (1951), which upheld the constitutionality of another New York statute that allowed a jury to presume that the occupants of a room in which a firearm was located possessed the weapon. The analysis in *Terra*, which this Court dismissed for want of a substantial federal question . . . is persuasive:

Respondents argue, however, that the validity of the New York presumption must be judged by a "reasonable doubt" test rather than the "more likely than not" standard employed in *Leary*.[29] Under the more stringent test, it is argued that a statutory presumption must be rejected unless the evidence necessary to invoke the inference is sufficient for a rational jury to find the inferred fact beyond a reasonable doubt. . . . Respondents' argument again overlooks the distinction between a permissive presumption on which the prosecution is entitled to rely as one not necessarily sufficient part of its proof and a mandatory presumption which the jury must accept even if it is the sole evidence of an element of the offense.

In the latter situation, since the prosecution bears the burden of establishing guilt, it may not rest its case entirely on a presumption unless the fact proved is sufficient to support the inference of guilt beyond a reasonable doubt. But in the former situation, the prosecution may rely on all of the evidence in the record to meet the reasonable-doubt standard. There is no more reason to require a permissive statutory presumption to meet a reasonable-doubt standard before it may be permitted to play any part in a trial than there is to require that degree of probative force for other relevant evidence before it may be admitted. As long as it is clear that the presumption is not the sole and sufficient basis for a finding of guilt, it need only satisfy the test described in *Leary*.

*　　*　　*

[T]here can be no doubt about the "sinister significance' " of proof of a machine gun in a room occupied by an accused or about the reasonableness of the connection between its illegal possession and occupancy of the room where it is kept. Persons who occupy a room, who either reside in it or use it in the conduct and operation of a business or other venture — and that is what in its present context the statutory term "occupying" signifies . . . — normally know what is in it; and, certainly, when the object is as large and uncommon as a machine gun, it is neither unreasonable nor unfair to presume that the room's occupants are aware of its presence. That being so, the legislature may not be considered arbitrary if it acts upon the presumption and erects it into evidence of a possession that is "conscious" and "knowing." . . .

See also Interim Report of Temporary State Commission to Evaluate the Drug Laws, N.Y. Leg. Doc. No. 10, p. 69 (1972), in which the drafters of the analogous automobile/narcotics presumption in N.Y. PENAL LAW § 220.25 (McKinney Supp. 1978), explained the basis for that presumption:

We believe, and find, that it is rational and logical to presume that all occupants of a vehicle are aware of, and culpably involved in, possession of dangerous drugs found abandoned or secreted in a vehicle when the quantity of the drug is such that it would be extremely unlikely for an occupant to be unaware of its presence. . . .

We do not believe that persons transporting dealership quantities of contraband are likely to go driving about with innocent friends or that they are likely to pick up strangers. We do not doubt that this can and does in fact occasionally happen, but because we find it more reasonable to believe that the bare presence in the vehicle is culpable, we think it reasonable to presume culpability in the direction which the proven facts already point. Since the presumption is an evidentiary one, it may be offset by any evidence, including the testimony of the defendant, which would negate the defendant's culpable involvement.

Legislative judgments such as this one deserve respect in assessing the constitutionality of evidentiary presumptions. . . .

29 [28] "The upshot of *Tot, Gainey,* and *Romano* is, we think that a criminal statutory presumption must be regarded as 'irrational' or 'arbitrary,' and hence unconstitutional, unless it can at least be said with substantial assurance that the presumed fact is more likely than not to flow from the proved fact on which it is made to depend." . . .

The judgment is reversed. So ordered.

MR. JUSTICE POWELL, with whom MR. JUSTICE BRENNAN, MR. JUSTICE STEWART and MR. JUSTICE MARSHALL join, dissenting.

I agree with the Court that there is no procedural bar to our considering the underlying constitutional question presented by this case. I am not in agreement, however, with the Court's conclusion that the presumption as charged to the jury in this case meets the constitutional requirements of due process as set forth in our prior decisions. On the contrary, an individual's mere presence in an automobile where there is a handgun does not even make it "more likely than not" that the individual possesses the weapon.

I

In the criminal law, presumptions are used to encourage the jury to find certain facts, with respect to which no direct evidence is presented, solely because other facts have been proved. . . . The purpose of such presumptions is plain: Like certain other jury instructions, they provide guidance for jurors' thinking in considering the evidence laid before them. Once in the juryroom, jurors necessarily draw inferences from the evidence — both direct and circumstantial. Through the use of presumptions, certain inferences are commended to the attention of jurors by legislatures or courts.

Legitimate guidance of a jury's deliberations is an indispensible part of our criminal justice system. Nonetheless, the use of presumptions in criminal cases poses at least two distinct perils for defendants' constitutional rights. The Court accurately identifies the first of these as being the danger of interference with "the factfinder's responsibility at trial, based on evidence adduced by the State, to find the ultimate facts beyond a reasonable doubt." . . . If the jury is instructed that it must infer some ultimate fact (that is, some element of the offense) from proof of other facts unless the defendant disproves the ultimate fact by a preponderance of the evidence, then the presumption shifts the burden of proof to the defendant concerning the element thus inferred.[30]

But I do not agree with the Court's conclusion that the only constitutional difficulty with presumptions lies in the danger of lessening the burden of proof the prosecution must bear. As the Court notes, the presumptions thus far reviewed by the Court have not shifted the burden of persuasion; . . . instead, they either have required only that the defendant produce some evidence to rebut the inference suggested by the prosecution's evidence . . . or merely have been suggestions to the

---

[30] [2] The Court suggests that presumptions that shift the burden of persuasion to the defendant in this way can be upheld provided that "the fact proved is sufficient to support the inference of guilt beyond a reasonable doubt." As the present case involves no shifting of the burden of persuasion, the constitutional restrictions on such presumptions are not before us, and I express no views on them.

It may well be that even those presumptions that do not shift the burden of persuasion cannot be used to prove an element of the offense, if the facts proved would not permit a reasonable mind to find the presumed fact beyond a reasonable doubt. My conclusion in Part II, *infra*, makes it unnecessary for me to address this concern here.

jury that it would be sensible to draw certain conclusions on the basis of the evidence presented.[31] . . . Evolving from our decisions, therefore, is a second standard for judging the constitutionality of criminal presumptions which is based — not on the constitutional requirement that the State be put to its proof — but rather on the due process rule that when the jury is encouraged to make factual inferences, those inferences must reflect some valid general observation about the natural connection between events as they occur in our society.

This due process rule was first articulated by the Court in *Tot v. United States,* *supra,* in which the Court reviewed the constitutionality of § 2(f) of the Federal Firearms Act. That statute provided in part that "possession of a firearm or ammunition by any . . . person [who has been convicted of a crime of violence] shall be presumptive evidence that such firearm or ammunition was shipped or transported [in interstate or foreign commerce]." As the Court interpreted the presumption, it placed upon a defendant only the obligation of presenting some exculpatory evidence concerning the origins of a firearm or ammunition, once the Government proved that the defendant had possessed the weapon and had been convicted of a crime of violence. Noting that juries must be permitted to infer from one fact the existence of another essential to guilt, "if reason and experience support the inference," . . . the Court concluded that under some circumstances juries may be guided in making these inferences by legislative or common-law presumptions, even though they may be based "upon a view of relation broader than that a jury might take in a specific case." . . . To provide due process, however, there must be at least a "rational connection between the fact proved and the ultimate fact presumed" — a connection grounded in "common experience." . . . In *Tot,* the Court found that connection to be lacking.

Subsequently, in *Leary v. United States,* . . . the Court reaffirmed and refined the due process requirement of *Tot* that inferences specifically commended to the attention of jurors must reflect generally accepted connections between related events. At issue in *Leary* was the constitutionality of a federal statute making it a crime to receive, conceal, buy or sell marihuana illegally brought into the United States, knowing it to have been illegally imported. The statute provided that mere possession of marihuana "shall be deemed sufficient evidence to authorize conviction unless the defendant explains his possession to the satisfaction of the jury." After reviewing the Court's decisions in *Tot v. United States,* supra, and other criminal presumption cases, Mr. Justice Harlan, writing for the Court, concluded "that a criminal statutory presumption must be regarded as 'irrational' or 'arbitrary,' and hence unconstitutional, unless it can at least be said with substantial assurance that the presumed fact is more likely than not to flow from the proved fact on which it is made to depend." . . . The Court invalidated the statute, finding there to be insufficient basis in fact for the conclusion that those who possess

---

[31] [3] The Court suggests as the touchstone for its analysis a distinction between "mandatory" and "permissive" presumptions. . . . For general discussions of the various forms of presumptions, *see* Jeffries & Stephan, *Defenses, Presumptions, and Burden of Proof in the Criminal Law,* 88 YALE L.J. 1325 (1979); F. JAMES, CIVIL PROCEDURE § 7.9 (1965). I have found no recognition in the Court's prior decisions that this distinction is important in analyzing presumptions used in criminal cases. *Cf. ibid* (distinguishing true "presumptions" from "permissible inferences").

marihuana are more likely than not to know that it was imported illegally.[32]

Most recently, in *Barnes v. United States*, we considered the constitutionality of a quite different sort of presumption — one that suggested to the jury that "[p]ossession of recently stolen property, if not satisfactorily explained, is ordinarily a circumstance from which you may reasonably draw the inference . . . that the person in possession knew the property had been stolen." . . . After reviewing the various formulations used by the Court to articulate the constitutionally required basis for a criminal presumption, we once again found it unnecessary to choose among them. As for the presumption suggested to the jury in Barnes, we found that it was well founded in history, common sense, and experience, and therefore upheld it as being "clearly sufficient to enable the jury to find beyond a reasonable doubt" that those in the unexplained possession of recently stolen property know it to have been stolen. . . .

In sum, our decisions uniformly have recognized that due process requires more than merely that the prosecution be put to its proof. In addition, the Constitution restricts the court in its charge to the jury by requiring that, when particular factual inferences are recommended to the jury, those factual inferences be accurate reflections of what history, common sense, and experience tell us about the relations between events in our society. Generally, this due process rule has been articulated as requiring that the truth of the inferred fact be more likely than not whenever the premise for the inference is true. Thus, to be constitutional a presumption must be at least more likely than not true.

II.

Undeniably, the presumption charged in this case encouraged the jury to draw a particular factual inference regardless of any other evidence presented: to infer that respondents possessed the weapons found in the automobile "upon proof of the presence of the machine gun and the hand weapon" and proof that respondents "occupied the automobile at the time such instruments were found." I believe that the presumption thus charged was unconstitutional because it did not fairly reflect what common sense and experience tell us about passengers in automobiles and the possession of handguns. People present in automobiles where there are weapons simply are not "more likely than not" the possessors of those weapons.

. . . As the Court of Appeals noted, there are countless situations in which individuals are invited as guests into vehicles the contents of which they know nothing about, much less have control over.

*   *   *

As I understand it, the Court today does not contend that in general those who are present in automobiles are more likely than not to possess any gun contained

---

[32] [5] Because the statute in *Leary v. United States* was found to be unconstitutional under the "more likely than not" standard, the Court explicitly declined to consider whether criminal presumptions also must follow "beyond a reasonable doubt" from their premises, if an essential element of the crime depends upon the presumption's use. . . . The Court similarly avoided this question in *Turner v. United States*, 396 U.S. 398, 416 . . . (1970).

within their vehicles. It argues, however, that the nature of the presumption here involved requires that we look, not only to the immediate facts upon which the jury was encouraged to base its inference, but to the other facts "proved" by the prosecution as well. The Court suggests that this is the proper approach when reviewing what it calls "permissive" presumptions because the jury was urged "to consider all the circumstances tending to support or contradict the inference." . . .

It seems to me that the Court mischaracterizes the function of the presumption charged in this case. As it acknowledges was the case in *Romano, supra,* the "instruction authorized conviction even if the jury disbelieved all of the testimony except the proof of presence" in the automobile. . . . The Court nevertheless relies on all of the evidence introduced by the prosecution and argues that the "permissive" presumption could not have prejudiced defendants. The possibility that the jury disbelieved all of this evidence, and relied on the presumption, is simply ignored.

I agree that the circumstances relied upon by the Court in determining the plausibility of the presumption charged in this case would have made it resortable for the jury to "infer that each of the respondents was fully aware of the presence of the guns and had both the ability and the intent to exercise dominion and control over the weapons." But the jury was told that it could conclude that respondents possessed the weapons found therein from proof of the mere fact of respondents' presence in the automobile. For all we know, the jury rejected all of the prosecution's evidence concerning the location and origin of the guns, and based its conclusion that respondents possessed the weapons solely upon its belief that respondents had been present in the automobile.[33] For purposes of reviewing the constitutionality of the presumption at issue here, we must assume that this was the case. . . .

The Court's novel approach in this case appears to contradict prior decisions of this Court reviewing such presumptions. Under the Court's analysis, whenever it is determined that an inference is "permissive," the only question is whether, in light of all of the evidence adduced at trial, the inference recommended to the jury is a reasonable one. The Court has never suggested that the inquiry into the rational basis of a permissible inference may be circumvented in this manner. Quite the contrary, the Court has required that the "evidence necessary to invoke the inference [be] sufficient for a rational juror to find the inferred fact. . . ." Under the presumption charged in this case, the only evidence necessary to invoke the inference was the presence of the weapons in the automobile with respondents — an inference that is plainly irrational.

---

[33] [8] The Court is therefore mistaken in its conclusion that, because "respondents were not 'hitchhikers or other casual passengers,' and the guns were neither 'a few inches in length' nor 'out of [respondents'] sight,' " reference to these possibilities is inappropriate in considering the constitutionality of the presumption as charged in this case. . . . To be sure, respondents' challenge is to the presumption as charged to the jury in this case. But in assessing its application here, we are not free, as the Court apparently believes, to disregard the possibility that the jury may have disbelieved all other evidence supporting an inference of possession. The jury may have concluded that respondents — like hitchhikers — had only an incidental relationship to the auto in which they were traveling, or that, contrary to some of the testimony at trial, the weapons were indeed out of respondents' sight.

In sum, it seems to me that the Court today ignores the teaching of our prior decisions. By speculating about what the jury may have done with the factual inference thrust upon it, the Court in effect assumes away the inference altogether, constructing a rule that permits the use of any inference — no matter how irrational in itself — provided that otherwise there is sufficient evidence in the record to support a finding of guilt. Applying this novel analysis to the present case, the Court upholds the use of a presumption that it makes no effort to defend in isolation. In substance, the Court — applying an unarticulated harmless-error standard — simply finds that the respondents were guilty as charged. They may well have been but rather than acknowledging this rationale, the Court seems to have made new law with respect to presumptions that could seriously jeopardize a defendant's right to a fair trial. Accordingly, I dissent.

Proposed Federal Rule of Evidence 303
Presumptions in Criminal Cases
(not enacted)

(a) Scope. Except as otherwise provided by Act of Congress, in criminal cases, presumptions against an accused, recognized at common law or created by statute, including statutory provisions that certain facts are prima facie evidence of other facts or of guilt, are governed by this rule.

(b) Submission to Jury. The judge is not authorized to direct the jury to find a presumed fact against the accused. When the presumed fact establishes guilt or is an element of the offense or negatives a defense, the judge may submit the question of guilt or of the existence of the presumed fact to the jury, if, but only if, a reasonable juror on the evidence as a whole, including the evidence of the basic facts, could find the guilt or the presumed fact beyond a reasonable doubt. When the presumed fact has a lesser effect, its existence may be submitted to the jury if the basic facts are supported by substantial evidence, or are otherwise established, unless the evidence as a whole negatives the existence of the presumed fact.

(c) Instructing the Jury. Whenever the existence of a presumed fact against the accused is submitted to the jury, the judge shall give an instruction that the law declares that the jury may regard the basic facts as sufficient evidence of the presumed fact but does not require it to do so. In addition, if the presumed fact establishes guilt or is an element of the offense or negatives a defense, the judge shall instruct the jury that its existence must, on all the evidence, be proved beyond a reasonable doubt.

NOTES AND QUESTIONS

1. Under *Ulster*, may mandatory presumptions be permissible in criminal cases?

2. Two weeks after *Ulster*, the Supreme Court in *Sandstrom v. Montana*, 442 U.S. 510 (1979), struck down an instruction in a homicide case on the following basis:

> The prosecution requested the trial judge to instruct the jury that "[t]he law presumes that a person intends the ordinary consequences of his voluntary acts." Petitioner's counsel objected, arguing that "the instruction

has the effect of shifting the burden of proof on the issue of" purpose or knowledge to the defense, and that "that is impermissible under the Federal Constitution, due process of law." *Id.* at 34. He offered to provide a number of federal decisions in support of the objection, including this Court's holding in *Mullaney v. Wilbur*, . . . but was told by the judge. "You can give those to the Supreme Court. The objection is overruled." . . . The instruction was delivered, the jury found petitioner guilty of deliberate homicide, . . . and petitioner was sentenced to 100 years in prison.

The threshold inquiry in ascertaining the constitutional analysis applicable to this kind of jury instruction is to determine the nature of the presumption it describes. *See Ulster County Court v. Allen.* . . . That determination requires careful attention to the words actually spoken to the jury, . . . for whether a defendant has been accorded his constitutional rights depends upon the way in which a reasonable juror could have interpreted the instruction.

Respondent argues, first, that the instruction merely described a permissive inference — that is, it allowed but did not require the jury to draw conclusions about defendant's intent from his actions — and that such inferences are constitutional. . . . These arguments need not detain us long, for even respondent admits that "it's possible" that the jury believed they were required to apply the presumption. . . . Sandstrom's jurors were told that "[t]he law presumes that a person intends the ordinary consequences of his voluntary acts." They were not told that they had a choice, or that they might infer that conclusion; they were told only that the law presumed it. It is clear that a reasonable juror could easily have viewed such an instruction as mandatory. . . .

In the alternative, respondent urges that, even if viewed as a mandatory presumption rather than as a permissive inference, the presumption did not conclusively establish intent but rather could be rebutted. On this view, the instruction required the jury, if satisfied as to the facts which trigger the presumption, to find intent unless the defendant offered evidence to the contrary. Moreover, according to the State, all the defendant had to do to rebut the presumption was produce "some" contrary evidence; he did not have to "prove" that he lacked the required mental state. Thus, "[a]t most, it placed a burden of production on the petitioner," but "did not shift to petitioner the burden of persuasion with respect to any element of the offense. . . ." Brief for Respondent

Again, respondent contends that presumptions with this limited effect pass constitutional muster.

We need not review respondent's constitutional argument on this point either, however, for we reject this characterization of the presumption as well. Respondent concedes there is a "risk" that the jury, once having found petitioner's act voluntary, would interpret the instruction as automatically directing a finding of intent. . . . Nonetheless, the State contends that the only authoritative reading of the effect of the presumption resides in the Supreme Court of Montana. And the State argues that by holding that "[d]efendant's sole burden . . . was to produce some evidence that he did not intend the ordinary consequences of his voluntary acts, not to disprove that he acted 'purposely' or 'knowingly,' " the Montana Supreme Court decisively established that the presumption at most affected only the burden of going forward with evidence of intent — that is, the burden of production.

The Supreme Court of Montana is, of course, the final authority on the legal weight to be given a presumption under Montana law, but it is not the final authority on the interpretation which a jury could have given the instruction. If Montana intended its presumption to have only the effect described by its Supreme Court, then we are convinced that a reasonable juror could well have been misled by the instruction given, and could have believed that the presumption was not limited to requiring the defendant to satisfy only a burden of production. Petitioner's jury was told that "[t]he law presumes that a person intends the ordinary consequences of his voluntary acts." They were not told that the presumption could be rebutted, as the Montana Supreme Court held, by the defendant's simple presentation of "some" evidence; nor even that it could be rebutted at all. Given the common definition of "presume" as "to suppose to be true without proof," WEBSTER'S NEW COLLEGIATE DICTIONARY 911 (1974), and given the lack of qualifying instructions as to the legal effect of the presumption, we cannot discount the possibility that the jury may have interpreted the instruction in either of two more stringent ways.

First, a reasonable jury could well have interpreted the presumption as "conclusive," that is, not technically as a presumption at all, but rather as an irrebuttable direction by the court to find intent once convinced of the facts triggering the presumption. Alternatively, the jury may have interpreted the instruction as a direction to find intent upon proof of the defendant's voluntary actions (and their "ordinary" consequences), unless the defendant proved the contrary by some quantum of proof which may well have been considerably greater than "some" evidence — thus effectively shifting the burden of persuasion on the element of intent. Numerous federal and state courts have warned that instructions of the type given here can be interpreted in just these ways.

* * *

We do not reject the possibility that some jurors may have interpreted the challenged instruction as permissive, or, if mandatory, as requiring only that the defendant come forward with "some" evidence in rebuttal. However, the fact that a reasonable juror could have given the presumption conclusive or persuasion-shifting effect means that we cannot discount the possibility that Sandstrom's jurors actually did proceed upon one or the other of these latter interpretations. And that means that unless these kinds of presumptions are constitutional, the instruction cannot be adjudged valid. . . .

Id. at 513–18. To what extent, if any, did the instructions used in *Ulster* carry the same potential for jury misinterpretation? *See* Lushing, *Faces Without Features:*

The Surface Validity' of Criminal Inferences, 72 J. Crim. L. & Criminology 82 (1981). May a Sandstrom instruction ever be treated as a harmless error? *See Petition of Hamilton*, 721 F.2d 1189 (9th Cir. 1983).

3. How would Ulster have been decided under Proposed Rule 303?

4. Consider the presumption of sanity in criminal cases. Once a defendant has introduced evidence of insanity, may a prosecutor rely exclusively upon this presumption to avoid a directed verdict? May conviction be predicated exclusively upon this presumption? *See United States v. Hendrix*, 542 F.2d 879 (2d Cir. 1976), *cert. denied*, 430 U.S. 959 (1977); *People v. Silver*, 310 N.E.2d 520 (N.Y. 1974). How would this matter be decided under Proposed Rule 303?

5. Proposed Rule 303 was not enacted because Congress wanted to give the matter of criminal presumptions further consideration in connection with the proposed revision of the overall federal criminal code. The provision, however, has been adopted by several states. In such jurisdictions, how should presumptions that operate against the government in criminal cases be handled?

TABLE OF CASES

[References are to pages]

[References are to pages]

[References are to pages]

[References are to pages]

N

O

[References are to pages]

[References are to pages]

[References are to pages]

TABLE OF STATUTES

[References are to pages]

[References are to pages]

INDEX

[References are to sections.]

[References are to sections.]

[References are to sections.]